Fundamentals of Psychology

THE BRAIN, THE PERSON, THE WORLD

Stephen M. Kosslyn
Harvard University

Robin S. Rosenberg
ADJUNCT FACULTY
Lesley University

Boston   New York   San Francisco
Mexico City   Montreal   Toronto   London   Madrid   Munich   Paris
Hong Kong   Singapore   Tokyo   Cape Town   Sydney

Executive Editor, Psychology: Rebecca Pascal
Development Editor: Lisa McLellan
Series Editorial Assistant: Kate Edwards
Senior Marketing Manager: Wendy Gordon
Editorial Production Administrator: Beth Houston
Editorial Production Service: Andrea Cava
Composition and Prepress Buyer: Linda Cox
Manufacturing Buyer: Megan Cochran
Cover Administrator: Linda Knowles
Interior Design: Gladys Rosa-Mendoza, rosa+wesley
Photo Research: Sarah Evertson, ImageQuest
Electronic Composition: Omegatype Typography, Inc.

Library of Congress Cataloging-in-Publication Data

Kosslyn, Stephen Michael, 1948–
    Fundamentals of psychology : the brain, the person, the world / Stephen M. Kosslyn,
Robin S. Rosenberg.
      p. cm.
    Includes bibliographical references and indexes.
    ISBN 0-205-35480-7 (alk. paper)
    1. Psychology.   I. Rosenberg, Robin S.   II. Title.

    BF121 .K585 2002
    150—dc21   2001056629

Printed in the United States of America

10 9 8 7 6 5 4 3 2 1 VHP 06 05 04 03 02

*To our parents
—Bunny, Rhoda,
Duke, and Stanley—
for all of life's lessons
that you taught us*

Brief Contents

Contents

2 The Brain
THE PSYCHOLOGICAL ORGAN
42

3 Sensation and Perception
HOW THE WORLD ENTERS THE MIND

4 Learning   120

5 Memory
LIVING WITH YESTERDAY
156

Contents   **xi**

7 Emotion and Motivation
FEELING AND STRIVING
238

8 Personality
VIVE LA DIFFERENCE! 274

9 Psychology Over the Life Span
GROWING UP, GROWING OLDER, GROWING WISER   308

12 Treatment 430

13 Social Psychology
MEETING OF THE MINDS

464

Preface

Many brief psychology textbooks are available—would ours contribute anything new? This is what we, as coauthors, asked each other as we started to consider writing this book. One of us is a cognitive neuroscientist and the other a clinical psychologist. In working together, we began to see how our different areas of psychology dovetailed. We had both come to view psychology in terms of events that occur at different levels of analysis: the brain (biological factors), the person (beliefs, desires, and feelings), the group (social, cultural, and environmental factors), and their interactions. This view of psychology is exciting because it can be applied to all psychological phenomena and can offer a way to organize a diverse range of theories and discoveries. We realized that this was an important way of teaching psychology. Different fields of psychology are interconnected, although they are not often presented this way in textbooks. We wanted to be able to show these interconnections to all students, those using comprehensive texts like *Psychology: The Brain, the Person, the World,* as well as those using briefer textbooks.

We also wanted to show students that applying the results of psychological research can make learning and remembering easier—not just for this course, but for any course, from economics to art history, and for the demands of life in general. We wanted to do more than just tell students how psychology can help them to be better learners—we wanted to apply these principles in this book, and teach students how to use these principles for themselves. A detailed explanation of this idea is found in the introduction, "Using Psychology to Learn Psychology," on pages 1–5.

Organization of This Textbook

Our goal was to write a textbook that would better integrate the field of psychology and engage students. We felt we could do this by exploring both how psychology can be viewed from various levels of analysis and how psychological principles can be applied to enhance learning. Both of these themes are reflected in the overall organization of the text and its individual chapters.

Most brief psychology textbooks have anywhere from 14 to 16 chapters; ours has 13. When using brief textbooks with more chapters, introductory psychology instructors often end up skipping chapters or parts of chapters in the interest of time, or requiring students to read multiple chapters per week. Neither option is ideal; both are likely to result in only a superficial grasp of the field as a whole. Because introductory psychology is intended to be a survey of the entire field, we believed that a more compact book would allow students to sample all the areas of psychology. We have carefully chosen both core and cutting-edge concepts, theories, and findings, to give students a deeper understanding of the field.

To achieve a more compact book, we have combined several topics that we think are best covered in a more integrated manner. For example, Chapter 1 includes both an introduction to the field of psychology and an overview of the methods used in psychological research. To understand any science, students need to learn about the kinds of questions that are asked and the methods for answering them. By considering the methods, students get a concrete sense of the shape of the science as it stands today. Appendix A (Statistics) and Appendix B (How to Read, Critically Evaluate, and Write Research Papers) further enhance this coverage and can be assigned at any time in the course.

Chapter 3 covers both sensation and perception. These two topics are strongly related, and recent brain research suggests that the same brain systems underlie both types of phenomena. Combining the two topics in one chapter makes it easier for students to see how sensation and perception work to achieve the same ends—specifically, the identification of stimuli and the representation of spatial relations.

The topics of language, thinking, and intelligence are combined into a single chapter (Chapter 6) so that the student can clearly see the connections among these topics. In fact, "intelligence" is not "one thing," but rather draws on language and thinking—among other abilities.

Similarly, Chapter 7 discusses the essentials of emotion and motivation in one chapter. The reason for including the two topics in one chapter is straightforward: Emotion is a major factor that motivates us. Unlike most other textbooks, ours introduces emotion first. By beginning the chapter with emotion, we are able to show how dramatic breakthroughs in the study of emotion (which have occurred, in part, because of discoveries about the brain) can illuminate aspects of human motivation.

To make a compact and manageable textbook for courses needing a brief text, we integrated the topic of sleep into the health, stress, and coping chapter (Chapter 10), focusing on how stress can affect sleep and how sleep deprivation can affect health and coping. In addition, the coverage of drugs and alcohol has been integrated into the same chapter, as the use of such substances is often related to a maladaptive coping strategy.

We include a single chapter on social psychology, Chapter 13. This chapter is further divided into two sections: social cognition and social behavior, the traditional domains of the field. Again, by including both topics in a single chapter, we are better able to show how they are related. Students learn how cognition about other people's beliefs, desires, and feelings plays a key role in our social interactions.

In addition to providing more detailed information about research methods used in psychology, Appendix B walks students through the American Psychological Association (APA) format for research articles. This appendix helps students understand not only the APA format for a research paper, but also how a research study is designed to answer a particular question (or questions) of interest, and whether the data support a particular answer to the question. Appendix B also helps students to organize their own research papers and to know what should be included in each section. Finally, this appendix also helps students think critically about psychological studies that they may read or learn about through television, print, and online resources.

Pedagogical Features

The introduction, "Using Psychology to Learn Psychology," is a roadmap devoted exclusively to the pedagogical features of this book; we ask students to read this introduction before they turn to Chapter 1. It will not only explain how to make the most of their time and effort in reading this text, but it will also teach them general principles that they can apply to their other courses. Each chapter of the text follows the format described in the introduction, which is based, in part, on psychological findings about how people best learn and remember information.

Chapter Story

Each chapter begins with a different story about a person or set of people. The story is then elaborated on throughout the chapter, providing a framework for the chapter's discussion of relevant psychological theories and research. These stories serve several purposes. They allow students to see how the psychological material covered in the chapter might apply to people outside of a psychological laboratory. This also makes the material more interesting and applicable to their lives, thus facilitating learning and remembering. In addition, the story integrates the various topics contained within a chapter, creating a coherent, thematic whole. Finally, the story itself provides retrieval cues to help students remember the material. For instance, Chapter 4, the chapter on learning principles, portrays a couple, Maria and Chris. As readers learn more about Maria's and Chris's relationship over the course of the chapter, they also learn more about learning principles and their applications. Because readers are likely to remember the couple's relationship, they will also remember a lot about learning principles.

The chapter story is continued at the beginning of each section. This fosters integration with the rest of the chapter and introduces each section's topic in an applied context.

Learning Objectives

At the beginning of each section, after the continuation of the story, we provide learning objective questions that highlight the most important points to be discussed, learned, and remembered. These questions are then answered at the end of the section (see *Consolidate!* below).

Looking at Levels

Near the end of each section, we take some aspect of its content—a theory, a research study, the application of a psychological phenomenon—and consider it from three levels of analysis: the brain, the person, and the group, as well as interactions among events at each level. For instance, the section on eating disorders (Chapter 11) examines binge eating from the point of view of the brain (what happens at the biological level), the person (viewing eating as "bad" and restricting food intake as "good," and how this perspective affects the person's beliefs, desires, and feelings), and the group (how it affects interactions with others). We then show how events at the three levels affect one another. The events in the brain, for instance, clearly affect the urge to binge, which in turns affects how the person feels about herself and her interactions with others (eating disorders primarily affect women).

The information in the "Looking at Levels" feature serves to integrate knowledge about the brain; personal beliefs, desires, and feelings; and group interactions within each chapter, rather than relegating such information to only one or two chapters. This feature also provides an opportunity to integrate information across chapters, leading to more effective learning and remembering.

Consolidate!

At the end of each section are answers to the learning objective questions posed at the beginning. These answers also review the most important aspects of the material. All of this will help *consolidate* learning (hence the name of the feature).

Minidemonstrations

Most chapters have what we call *minidemonstrations*: demonstrations of psychological phenomena for students to try alone or with others. Trying out these brief exercises will (1) provide another modality of learning about the phenomenon—experiencing, not merely reading about it; (2) make the material more vivid, thereby enhancing attention and memory; and (3) bring psychological principles to life for students through their participation. The minidemonstrations include:

Introspection (p. 13)	False memory (pp. 176, 178)
Simulated participation in a research study (pp. 32–33)	Discovering syntax (pp. 193–194)
Measuring neural conduction time (p. 47)	Mental imagery (pp. 199–200)
	The hiking monk problem (p. 205)
The Stroop effect (p. 86)	The candle problem (p. 206)
Pop-out (p. 88)	Wason and Johnson-Laird's card task (p. 209)
Finding your blind spot (p. 93)	Representativeness (p. 210)
Seeing afterimages (p. 94)	Smile demonstration (p. 245)
Motion cues (p. 98)	"Fake" personality reading (p. 277)
Recognition and identification (pp. 102–103)	Myths about suicide (p. 410)
Modality-specific memory (pp. 162–163)	Progressive muscle relaxation (pp. 439–440)
Lincoln's head on a penny (p. 168)	

A Deeper Level: Recap and Thought Questions

Several features at the end of the chapter help students further consolidate what they have learned and provide an opportunity for additional learning by applying the material to new situations.

Summary At the close of each chapter is a section-by-section review of the material. These summaries highlight the key points that students should know after a thorough reading of the material. This feature helps consolidate the core material even further in memory.

Story Questions and Answers This feature poses questions about the characters in the chapter story, followed by answers. The questions and answers show students how to apply each section's psychological principles and research to life outside the psychology laboratory, using the chapter story as an extended example.

Think It Through Additional critical thinking questions called "Think It Through" are also provided for each section of the chapter. These questions ask students to apply the material to real-world settings and require them to think deeply about the material. Such active processing enhances memory.

End-of-Chapter Review Tests There are 15 multiple-choice practice test questions at the end of each chapter, with answers provided at the end of the test. We ask both factual and conceptual questions to help student assess their knowledge of the chapter material, identify topics that may need additional study, and further consolidate the material in memory.

Illustration Program: Showing and Telling

Many of the most important studies are not only described in the text, but are also visually demonstrated in step-by-step illustrations. These multimodal presentations enhance learning in several ways. First, the panel illustrations walk through each study, allowing the reader to understand its details more fully. Second, the clear, uncomplicated illustrations use perceptual principles to convey information effectively. Third, this dual-mode format allows for both visual and verbal learning; students can recall either the words in the text *or* the illustrations when remembering the study. Finally, working through these displays leads to active processing—and better remembering. Examples include a study on alcohol and sexual aggression (p. 380),

Watson's famous experiment with Little Albert (p. 126), Garcia's taste aversion conditioning (p. 132), the training of dolphins at Sea World (p. 143), Bandura's Bobo doll experiment (p. 151), Kosslyn's imagery scanning experiment (p. 200), the Schacter-Singer experiment (p. 246), and systematic desensitization (p. 441).

Like the illustrations, the evocative chapter opening photographs may serve the function of "priming" readers with ideas and expectations about what will come in the chapter.

First-Person Accounts of Psychological Disorders

Chapter 11, Psychological Disorders, provides an opportunity to understand the major disorders not only from the psychologist's perspective, but also from the point of view of people experiencing those disorders. Discussion of each of the major disorders includes first-person accounts from individuals who have struggled with a disorder and who describe the ways it affected their lives. These accounts, entitled " . . . From the Inside," allow students to see beneath the clinical description—to understand how psychological disorders affect real people.

Instructor and Student Supplements

Instructor Resources

Instructor's Resource Manual Written by Gary Piggrem at the Devry Institute of Technology, Columbus, this helpful teaching aid includes for each chapter: chapter-at-a-glance table, chapter overview, chapter outline, list of teaching objectives, list of key terms with page references, discussion questions, classroom demonstrations, student activities, list of media and Internet resources, and Web activities.

Test Bank Prepared by Majorie Hardy at Eckerd College, in conjunction with Robin Rosenberg and Stephen Hoyer, this resource includes 125–140 questions per chapter in multiple-choice and essay formats. Each question is rated for difficulty and categorized as factual, conceptual, or applied. Page references to the text are provided for each question.

Allyn and Bacon Test Manager—Computerized Test Bank (Available for Windows, CD-ROM and disk, and Macintosh disk; DOS disk available upon request.) Allyn and Bacon Test Manager is an integrated suite of testing and assessment tools for Windows and Macintosh. You can use Test Manager to create professional-looking exams in just minutes by building tests from the existing database of questions, editing questions, or adding your own. Course management features include a class roster, gradebook, and item analysis. Test Manager also has everything you need to create and administer online tests. For first-time users, there is a guided tour of the entire Test Manager system and screen wizards to walk you through each area.

Call-In and Fax Testing One toll-free call to our testing center will have a finished, ready-to-duplicate test on its way to you within 48 hours, via mail or fax.

Allyn and Bacon Transparencies for Introductory Psychology, 2001 A full set of color acetate transparencies is available to enhance classroom lectures and discussions. These images include those from the Kosslyn and Rosenberg text and other sources, to support and extend teaching and learning.

Kosslyn and Rosenberg PowerPoint Presentation CD-ROM This book-specific presentation provides detailed outlines of key points for each chapter, supported by charts, graphs, diagrams, and other visuals from the textbook. Resources from the Kosslyn and Rosenberg companion Web site are also integrated for easy access to this Web site from your classroom. This material is also available in a Web format accessible at www.ablongman.com/ppt.

Allyn and Bacon Digital Media Archive CD-ROM for Psychology, Version 3.0 Allyn and Bacon provides an array of media products to help liven up your classroom presentations. The Digital Media Archive provides charts, graphs, tables, and figures electronically on one cross-platform CD-ROM. The Digital Media Archive also provides video and audio clips along with the electronic images that can be easily integrated into your lectures. This helpful resource extends the coverage found on the Kosslyn and Rosenberg PowerPoint Presentation CD-ROM.

Allyn and Bacon Mind Matters CD-ROM Faculty Guide This helpful instructor resource offers detailed overviews of each unit of the Mind Matters CD-ROM (described below), supplemented by additional test questions and chapter-by-chapter references correlating content from the CD-ROM with the Kosslyn and Rosenberg textbook. This in-depth guide makes it easy to integrate the Allyn and Bacon Mind Matters CD-ROM into your syllabus. Visit the Allyn and Bacon Mind Matters Web site at www.ablongman.com/mindmatters to download samples of this helpful resource.

Allyn and Bacon Interactive Video and Video Package *Fundamentals of Psychology: The Brain, the Person, the World* is supported by a unique interactive video containing brief video clips based on content in each chapter of the text. Each video clip contains contextualizing information and critical thinking questions, further relating the video content to that in the textbook chapter. A wide variety of other videos are also available upon adoption of the Kosslyn and Rosenberg textbook. Please contact your local Allyn and Bacon publisher's representative for more information.

Course Management Systems Course Management Systems combine Allyn and Bacon's premium online content with enhanced class management tools such as syllabus building, quizzing and grading, and results reporting. To find out which systems are available with the Kosslyn and Rosenberg text, visit the Kosslyn and Rosenberg Web site at http://www.ablongman.com/kosslyn for more information.

Student Resources

Grade Aid Student Study Guide With Practice Tests This study guide, written by Marjorie Hardy of Eckerd College, contains a wide variety of helpful study tools including, for each chapter: "Before You Read" preview sections with chapter summaries; "As You Read" self-tests; "A Deeper Level" thought questions that focus on critical thinking; glossary term identification exercises; "After You Read" multiple-choice post-tests; and Web resources. Marjorie Hardy is also the author of the text-specific Kosslyn and Rosenberg Web site content, ensuring consistency in practice and review across the Study Guide and Web resources.

Allyn and Bacon Mind Matters CD-ROM This student CD-ROM features in-depth units on the history of psychology, research methodology, biopsychology, learning, memory, sensation, and perception. Each unit includes self-contained modules that cover core psychological concepts through a combination of text, graphics, humor, activities, and extensive assessment. This resource is available packaged with new copies of the Kosslyn and Rosenberg textbook and is supported by an in-depth faculty guide (see above).

iSearch 2003 Updated to reflect the most current URLs related to the study of psychology, this easy-to-read guide helps point you and your students in the right direction when looking at the tremendous array of information related to psychology on the Internet. Available free packaged with new copies of the Kosslyn and Rosenberg textbook (value package option only).

Companion Web Site The Companion Web site for *Fundamentals of Psychology: The Brain, the Person, the World,* which can be accessed at www.ablongman.com/kosslyn, offers a wealth of information to enhance and supplement learning. This site contains a wide range of resources for both students and instructors, including learning objectives, practice tests, and links to Web destinations.

Additional Resources

How to Think Straight About Psychology, 6th Edition This well-known critical thinking manual by Keith Stanovich helps students become educated consumers of psychological information, particularly those topics they may encounter in the media or self-help literature.

Diversity Activities for Psychology This student manual, developed by Valerie Whittlesey, offers a wide variety of hands-on activities to help incorporate issues of diversity into your classroom. Activities are correlated with all major areas of psychological research, making it easy to assign this supplement with the Kosslyn and Rosenberg textbook.

Ask Dr. Mike: Frequently Asked Questions About Psychology Developed by Mike Atkinson, author of the popular "Ask Dr. Mike" column on the Psychology Place™ Web site, this manual contains a collection of commonly asked student questions with in-depth answers, organized by major topics in the introductory psychology course.

Evaluating Psychological Information: Sharpening Your Critical Thinking Skills, 3rd Edition Developed by James Bell, this workbook focuses on helping students to evaluate psychological research systematically and to improve their critical thinking skills.

How to Write Psychology Papers, 2nd Edition Les Parrot provides a brief overview for writing APA-style psychology papers, including information on overcoming paper panic, using the Internet, preparing a working reference list, avoiding plagarism, and using inclusive language. This book extends and elaborates on the material in Appendix B.

Acknowledgments

We want to give a heartfelt thanks to the reviewers who have contributed helpful comments on this new textbook:

Sally Bing
University of Maryland,
Eastern Shore

Joseph Davis
San Diego State
University

Mike Garza
Brookhaven
Community College

Harvey Ginsburg
Southwest Texas State
University

Stephen Hoyer
Pittsburgh State
University

Beth Post
University of California,
Davis

Celia Reaves
Monroe Community
College

We also thank the many reviewers of *Psychology*, from which this textbook was derived; the book is far better for their efforts:

Sharon Akimoto
Carleton College

Jeff Anastasi
Francis Marion
University

Joe Bean
Shorter College

James Benedict
James Madison
University

James F. Calhoun
University of Georgia

Brad Carothers
Evergreen Valley College

James Carroll
Central Michigan
University

M. B. Casey
St. Mary's College of
Maryland

Dave Christian
University of Idaho

George A. Cicala
University of Delaware

Gerald S. Clack
Loyola University of
New Orleans

Verne C. Cox
University of Texas,
Arlington

Nancy Dickson
Tennessee Technical
College

William O. Dwyer
University of Memphis

Valeri Farmer-Dougan
Illinois State University

William Ford
Bucks County
Community College

Mary Gauvain
University of California,
Riverside

Dan Gilbert
Harvard University

Peter Graf
University of British
Columbia

Peter Gram
Pensacola Junior College

Karl Haberlandt
Trinity College

Richard Hackman
Harvard University

Richard Haier
University of California,
Irvine

Marjorie Hardy
Eckerd College

Bruce Henderson
Western Carolina
University

James Hilton
University of Michigan

Rick Ingram
San Diego State
University

John H. Krantz
Hanover College

Richard Lippa
California State
University, Fresno

Walter J. Lonner
Western Washington
University

Michael Markham
Florida International
University

Pam McAuslan
University of Michigan,
Dearborn

David G. McDonald
University of Missouri

Rafael Mendez
Bronx Community
College

Sarah Murray
Kwantlen University
College

Paul Ngo
Saint Norbert College

Thomas R. Oswald
Northern Iowa Area
Community College

Carol Pandey
Los Angeles Pierce
College

Robert J. Pellegrini
San Jose State University

Dorothy C. Piontkowski
San Francisco State
University

Brad Redburn
Johnson County
Community College

Cheryl Rickabaugh
University of Redlands

Alan Salo
University of Maine,
Presque Isle

Jim Schirillo
Wake Forest University

Michael Scoles
University of Central
Arkansas

Michael Shaughnessy
Eastern New Mexico
University

Nancy Simpson
Trident Technical
College

Linda J. Skinner
Middle Tennessee State
University

Michael Spiegler
Providence College

Don Stanley
North Harris College

Bruce B. Svare
State University of New
York at Albany

Thomas Thielan
College of St. Catherine

Paul E. Turner
Lipscomb University

Lori Van Wallendael
University of North
Carolina, Charlotte

Frank J. Vattano
Colorado State
University

Rich Velayo
Pace University

Rick Wesp
East Stroudsburg
University

We also profited enormously from conversations with our friends and colleagues, particularly Nalini Ambady, Mark Baxter, Alain Berthoz, John Cacioppo, David Caplan, Alfonso Caramazza, Patrick Cavanagh, Verne Caviness, Christopher Chabris, Jonathan Cohen, Suzanne Corkin, Francis Crick, Richard Davidson, Susan Edbril, Jeffrey Epstein, Michael Friedman, Al Galaburda, Giorgio Ganis, Jeremy Gray, Anne Harrington, Marc Hauser, Kenneth Hugdahl, Steven Hyman, Jerome Kagan, Denis Le Bihan, Fred Mast, Richard McNally, Merrill Mead-Fox, Ken Nakayama, Kevin O'Regan, Alvaro Pascual-Leone, Steven Pinker, Scott Rauch, Melissa Robbins, Robert Rose, Steven Rosenberg, Daniel Schacter, Jeanne Serafin, Lisa Shin, Dan Simons, Edward E. Smith, Elizabeth Spelke, David Spiegel, Larry Squire, Eve vanCauter, and Laura Weisberg. We thank Maya and Alain Berthoz, Maryvonne Caraftan, Tom Cohen, Michel Denis, Elizabeth Hickling, Christian and Denis Le Bihan, Josette and Jacques Lautrey, Bernard Mazoyer, and Nathalie Tzurio for their hospitality during our year in France, which made it possible and enjoyable to work productively there. We also thank the staff at the Collège de France for their help, in too many ways to list. And to our parents (Bunny, Stanley, Rhoda, and Duke) and our children (Nathaniel, David, and Justin), a huge thanks for your patience with our work-filled weekends and evenings, and for your love, support, and good humor. You have sustained us.

Other people have been instrumental in making this book a reality. These include Andrea Volfova (for her good-humored assistance and incisive comments), Jennifer Shephard, Bill Thompson, David Hurvitz, Steve Stose, Cinthia Guzman, Nicole Rosenberg, and Deborah Bell for their patience and willingness to help us dig out references and check facts, especially via long-distance communication during the year we were in France. The idea for the book developed over years of working with the Sophomore Tutors and Assistant to the Head Tutor, Shawn Harriman, at Harvard University, and we want to thank them all; helping them grapple with the concept of levels of analysis led us to make this book clearer. We are particularly indebted to two of them, Laurie Santos and Jason Mitchell, who read an early draft of the book and offered copious and wise comments.

The professionals at Allyn and Bacon have been instrumental in bringing this book to you. Rebecca Pascal, Bill Barke, Sandi Kirshner, Joyce Nilsen, Nancy Forsyth, and Marcia Mealia have supported our vision of the textbook. Moreover, we are indebted to our Development Editor, Lisa McLellan, for her assistance, unflagging support, and open-mindedness in bringing this project to fruition, and to Carolyn Merrill for her help in the final hours. Beth Houston, Editorial Production Administrator, transformed electrons in our computers into a book you can hold in your hands. Andrea Cava's careful attention to the artwork and manuscript has enhanced the book's clarity, as have the thoughtful and probing comments of Jill Hobbs. Wendy Gordon, Brad Parkins, and Deidre Jacobson were very creative in their marketing and advertising; without them, this book may not have been able to come to your attention. We also want to thank Kate Edwards, Editorial Assistant, for her help in selecting the test questions. Many thanks to those involved in the creation of the original textbook, *Psychology: The Brain, the Person, the World,* from which this text is mostly derived: Sean Wakely, Sue Gleason, Nancy Brooks, Kathy Fields, Susan McIntyre, Elaine Ober, Hannah Rubenstein, and Kathryn Daniel.

And finally, to you the reader, thank you for taking the time and effort to read this preface to its conclusion. We hope that this book helps you learn about psychology, about yourselves, and about the world.

Interest in gender and cultural diversity issues remains an important theme in modern psychology. These topics are treated throughout the text in an integrated fashion.

Integrated Coverage of Gender Issues

Integrated Coverage of Cross-Cultural Issues

About the Authors

Stephen M. Kosslyn

Stephen Kosslyn is John Lindsley Professor of Psychology at Harvard University and Associate Psychologist in the Department of Neurology at Massachusetts General Hospital. He received his B.A. from UCLA and his Ph.D. from Stanford University, both in psychology. His first academic position was at Johns Hopkins University, where he was appointed Assistant Professor. He joined the Harvard faculty in 1977 as Associate Professor, and left in 1980 to take a Research Career Development Award. After a brief stay at Brandeis and a visit to Johns Hopkins in 1983, Kosslyn returned to Harvard as a Full Professor. His research has focused primarily on the nature of visual mental imagery and visual communication, and he has published 5 books and over 200 papers on these topics. Kosslyn has received numerous honors, including the National Academy of Sciences Initiatives in Research Award, the Prix Jean-Louis Signoret, and election to the American Academy of Arts and Sciences and the Society of Experimental Psychologists. He is currently "head tutor," supervising graduate students who teach a year-long introductory psychology course using levels of analysis, and chairs the Committee on Undergraduate Instruction in the Department of Psychology at Harvard. He is currently on the editorial boards of many professional journals; is a Fellow of the American Psychological Association, American Psychological Society, and American Association for the Advancement of Science; and has served on several National Research Council committees to advise the government on new technologies. Kosslyn has been a guest on local National Public Radio stations, CBS radio, CNN news, and *Nova*, and has been quoted in many newspapers and magazines.

Robin S. Rosenberg

Robin Rosenberg is a clinical psychologist in private practice and has taught introductory psychology at Lesley University. She is certified in clinical hypnosis and is a member of the Academy for Eating Disorders. She received her B.A. in psychology from New York University, and her M.A. and Ph.D. in clinical psychology from the University of Maryland, College Park. She did her clinical internship at Massachusetts Mental Health Center and had a postdoctoral fellowship at Harvard Community Health Plan before joining the staff at Newton-Wellesley Hospital's Outpatient Services, where she worked for a number of years before leaving to expand her private practice. She specializes in treating people with eating disorders, depression, and anxiety and is interested in the integration of different therapy approaches. She was the founder and coordinator of the New England Society for Psychotherapy Integration and has given numerous professional talks on various topics related to the treatment of people with eating disorders, as well as popular talks on relapse prevention and on developing a healthy relationship with food, and with one's body.

Fundamentals of Psychology

Using Psychology to Learn Psychology

Scientific psychology has made massive leaps and bounds in recent decades. Its impressive progress has given us a window into ourselves that could scarcely have been imagined in earlier years, and the view from that window provides insights into the ways we learn and remember. The structure of this book reflects those insights. In fact, its organization is built on specific psychological principles that will help you to make the material your own, yours to remember and build on.

Organization, Organization, Organization

It seems only common sense that the more you know about something, the easier it is to learn even more about it. But wait a minute: If you're filling your head with stuff—facts, relationships, ideas—won't you have *less* room available for new material?

This is what researchers who study memory call the "paradox of the expert." They have learned that instead of filling up, our memory storage capacity seems to *increase* as more material is stored. How can this be? Part of becoming an expert in an area is developing an efficient way to organize information about it; and the better the organization, the easier it is to learn new things in that area.

When you first start learning psychology, you face what seems like a random collection of theories and facts. But as you learn more and more, you begin to see how the facts interconnect—perhaps because you learn, for instance, that the same parts of the brain are activated during different behaviors. As you read on, facts begin to "fall into place," and each new fact becomes easier to learn and remember than the previous ones.

The organization of this book gives you the framework you need to begin categorizing and learning more quickly. Each chapter deals with a particular area of psychological discovery and begins with a story, which serves multiple purposes in learning. First, the story helps you see how events in the "real world," which may be much like events in your life or in the lives of those around you, arise from the working of psychological principles. Thus new facts are fitted with the facts of your own experiences, making it easier for you to organize the new material and thus to learn it. Second, the opening story runs like a thread through the chapter, as an illustration of the various topics discussed and as a connection to a real-world situation. Third, because each chapter has its own story, each story becomes a reminder that will help you remember the material in that chapter.

Each major section within a chapter begins with an aspect of a story and learning objectives questions, targeting the general ideas to be explored in that section. At the end of each section is a *Consolidate!* summary that answers those learning objective questions. At the end of the chapter is a summary called *A Deeper Level: Recap and Thought Questions* that revisits the major themes of the chapter, helping you to see the overall picture that was painted in each section. Here, too, you will find questions and answers that link back to the chapter story, as well as *Think It Through* questions, hypothetical situations that invite you to think about the broader implications of what you have learned—and thereby to understand the material better. Each chapter ends with a *Review Test* that assesses your understanding of the material and further consolidates learning.

Connections Across Topics

In these pages we will consider a wide range of human mental processes and behavior. Our explorations—and thus the chapters of this book—are tied together by a specific and fruitful kind of analysis we apply to all of them. In every chapter, in every area of psychological activity, we consider the contributions of events in the *brain,* of *personal beliefs, desires, and feelings,* and of *group interactions.* A direct example: Events in the brain might be the chemicals produced by fatigue or excitement, which affect your ability to understand what you read in this book; your personal goals and interests may motivate you to undertake the study of psychology; and interactions among your group of friends can further spark your interest and help you study effectively.

French philosopher René Descartes's famous observation, "I think, therefore I am," can be appropriately paraphrased for us as "I think, therefore I have a brain." In other words, we cannot fully consider how and why we behave as we do without knowing how the brain works (and, sometimes, doesn't work). The way the brain operates is a facet of all psychological phenomena, and we ignore it at the peril of missing key insights into why we think, feel, and behave as we do. In every chapter, for every topic, you will see how events in the brain, along with personal beliefs, desires, and feelings, and group interactions, are relevant to our understanding of ourselves. Looking at events at these three "levels" helps you to organize and integrate the material *within* each chapter and *across* all the chapters. At the end of each major section within a chapter is *Looking at Levels,* which presents a high-interest issue and examines it by considering events at all three levels, illustrating how they constantly interact.

Learning Without Straining

One of the most interesting findings about memory is that you don't have to *try* to store something in memory; you merely have to "process" the material thoroughly. For instance, if—without a conscious attempt to memorize—you talk about the possible reasons why people who have more genes in common have more similar IQs, the simple act of considering these factors will probably cause you to learn them. A key aim of this book is to lead you to process the material thoroughly. This is accomplished in various ways: through the figures, the minidemonstrations and exercises described in the text, the *Consolidate!* and *Think It Through* sections, and the headings that include memorable phrases to help you integrate the material with what you already know.

Illustrations: Showing and Telling

In a review of 46 experiments comparing the effectiveness of learning from text alone and learning from text with pictures, Levie and Lentz (1982) found that 45 of them showed that pictures do help. In some situations, an effective picture can literally double your chances of remembering the information. Moreover, Alan Paivio (1971) showed that when people can store both verbal and pictorial information, they can later remember the material far better than when they can store only verbal information. For example, if you are learning vocabulary in a foreign language, having a picture that illustrates the meaning along with the definition will boost your memory. Thus, many of the important studies described in this book are presented in multipanel displays, with the events in each panel explained in detail. This device gives you a double-barreled shot of learning—with the combined effectiveness of both verbal and pictorial modalities.

But not just any picture will do. Levie and Lentz also found that if the illustrations are not relevant, they don't help; a later survey (Levin et al., 1987) found that pictures that are purely decorative actually get in the way of learning. The figures in this book take this finding to heart. Illustrations are particularly effective when they teach according to the principle "seeing is believing."

A major difficulty with many visual displays is information overload. The point is illustrated in the left panel of Figure 1. We cannot take in too much information at a time (that's why telephone numbers and most license plates traditionally have had only 7 or 8 digits or characters). A method we use to avoid

For better or worse (given what can be done with computers these days), seeing is often believing.

this problem is designing displays in accordance with the principles of perceptual organization. You are overloaded not by the number of elements that are present, but by the number of *perceptual units* they form. For example, you can take in two flocks of geese heading south for the winter as easily as two individual geese flying solo—but if the flocks disband, and 80 birds fly randomly through the sky, your ability to track them would be overwhelmed.

Psychological research has also shown that an effective visual display doesn't require you to search and memorize any more than is absolutely necessary to understand the message. A well-designed VCR has the "power" and "play" buttons in obvious locations and prominent enough so you can spot them immediately. If a display is too complex, you won't bother to try to unravel it; and

Figure ① Avoiding Information Overload

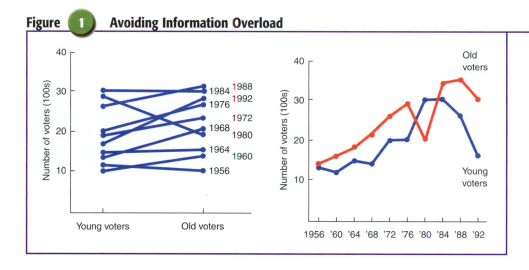

Which graph is easiest to figure out? These graphs represent the same data, but only one is arranged in a way that your visual system can organize easily. (From Kosslyn, 1994a.)

Because your visual system draws your attention to aspects of the world that are different from their surroundings, you are immediately drawn to the person in black. This would be appropriate only if the discussion focused on the clergy member. The same principles are at work when you look at the world and when you look at an illustration. (Adapted from Holmes, 1984. Data from National Opinion Research Center, 1994.)

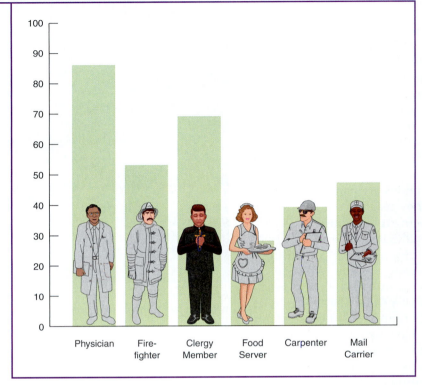

why should you? The illustrations in this book have been designed to guide your eye through them systematically. It is known, for example, that sharp changes along a visual dimension, such as the use of a strong color, reflexively grab the viewer's attention. Properties such as this (look at Figure 2) are used appropriately throughout this text to define the more important parts of displays.

In this way, we accomplish two aims. First, the material in the illustrations aids learning, instead of getting in its way. Second, the helpfulness of the design is itself an example of the utility of psychological findings, providing a practical demonstration. These illustrations both show and tell.

In Sum . . .

Table 1 summarizes the many tools built into the structure of this book to smooth the occasionally rough path of learning. The most important learning tools of all, of course, are the excitement inherent in the ideas and the connections you will make with your own experience. What you learn here can be applied to all learning, not just psychology or literature or physics, but also on the job and in life in general. We hope you will find yourself thinking about these ideas at odd moments away from class, away from this book. If you do, the book has been a success.

TABLE 1 Summary of Learning Tools

Chapter Outline
- Provides an overall framework for learning.
- Headings include memorable phrases to help you integrate the material with what you already know.

Chapter Story
- Relevance to real world allows new information to be integrated with prior knowledge.
- Integrates topics throughout the chapter.
- Provides retrieval cues.

Chapter Sections
- Learning objective questions provide a structure for each section, highlighting the most important points to be discussed.
- Expansion of the opening story at the outset of each section relates back to the story, thereby fostering integration and introducing specific topics.
- Sections "chunk" material into easily learned units.

Glossary
- Key terms are defined in the margin, highlighting essential information.
- Related terms are often grouped together, promoting conceptual links.

Consolidate!
- Reinforces the main points of each section.
- Connects back to the section learning objective questions, providing answers.

A Deeper Level
- Shows connections among the material discussed in the chapter sections, thereby providing an overall organization for the chapter's main messages.
- Questions about the opening story are posed and answered, providing a connection to real-world contexts.
- *Think It Through* exercises require thinking deeply about the material, thereby enhancing memory.

End-of-Chapter Review Test
- Assesses knowledge of the chapter material.
- Identifies topics that may need additional study.
- Provides an opportunity for further consolidation of the material in memory.

Levels of Analysis
- Integrates information about the brain; personal beliefs, desires, and feelings; and group interactions within chapters.
- Integrates information across chapters.
- *Looking at Levels* sections reinforce integration of the different types of events (the brain, the person, the group).

Minidemonstrations
- Active learning increases comprehension by integrating information with common experience.
- Active learning increases memory by leading you to think more deeply about the material.

Illustrations: Showing and Telling
- Multipanel displays encourage both visual and verbal learning.
- Clear, uncomplicated illustrations use psychological principles of effective communication.

1

The Science

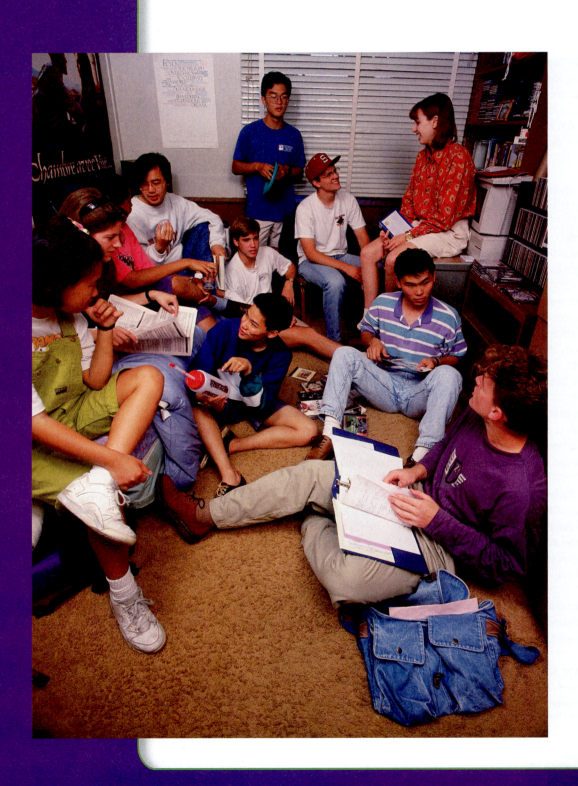

# of Psychology

YESTERDAY AND TODAY

On a balmy April day in 2001, a young man was playing golf. Nothing unusual about that. But when this young man sank his final putt, the watching crowd let out a roar. The golfer looked for his parents and soon embraced them, fighting back tears. The occasion was The Masters, and the young man was Tiger Woods.

Think of the magnitude of this victory: At age 25, Woods became the only golfer in history to hold all four major championship titles at the same time. And golf's reigning champion—in a sport that has long been effectively closed to all but whites—is of Asian, black, white, and Native American ancestry. If you could discern and explain the events that led up to this dramatic moment, you would be a very insightful psychologist.

But where would you begin? You could look at Tiger Woods's hand–eye coordination, his concentration and focus, his ability to judge distances and calculate factors of wind, temperature, and humidity.

You could look at his personality—his reaction to racist hate mail (as a college student at Stanford University, he even kept one particularly vile letter taped to his wall), his religious beliefs (he was raised in his mother's faith, Buddhism), his demeanor during play, his discipline in training.

You could look at his relationships with the social world around him—his family, his competitors, his fans.

Is this psychology? Indeed it is. Psychology asks and, in scientific ways, attempts to answer questions about why and how people think, feel, and behave as they do. Because we are all human and so have much in common, sometimes the answers are universal. But we are also, like snowflakes, all different, and psychology helps to explain our uniqueness. In this chapter we show you how to look at and answer such questions by methods used in current research and (because the inquiry into what makes us tick has a history) how psychologists over the past century have approached them.

Psychology is about mental processes and behavior, both exceptional and ordinary.

Psychological Science: Getting to Know You

Virtually everything any of us does, thinks, or feels falls within the sphere of psychology. You may observe psychology in action when you watch people interacting in a classroom or at a party, or notice that a friend is in a really terrible mood. Psychology is at work when you daydream as you watch the clouds drift by, when you have trouble recalling someone's name, even when you're asleep.

1 Psychology can illuminate all aspects of a person's life, but what is psychology?

2 What is the concept of "levels of analysis," and how can you use it to understand psychology?

What Is Psychology?

Although it may seem complex and wide-ranging, the field you are studying in this textbook can be defined in one simple sentence: ***Psychology*** *is the science of mental processes and behavior.* Let's look at the key words in this definition.

First, *science*. From the Latin *scire*, "to know," science avoids mere opinions, intuitions, and guesses, and strives to nail down facts—to *know* them—by using objective evidence to answer questions such as, What makes the sun shine? Why does garlic make your breath smell strong? How is Tiger Woods able to direct his swings so superbly? Science uses logic to reason about the possible causes of a phenomenon and then tests the resulting ideas by collecting additional facts, which will either support the ideas or refute them, and thus nudge the scientist farther along the road to the answer.

Second, *mental processes*. **Mental processes** are what your brain is doing not only when you engage in "thinking" activities such as storing memories, recognizing objects, and using language, but also when you feel depressed, jump for joy, or savor the experience of being in love. How can we find objective facts about mental processes, which are hidden and internal? One way, which has a long his-

Psychology: The science of mental processes and behavior.

Mental processes: What the brain does when a person stores, recalls, or uses information, or has specific feelings.

tory in psychology, is to work backward, observing what people do and inferring from outward signs what is going on "inside." Another, as new as the latest technological advances in neuroscience, is to use brain-scanning techniques to take pictures of the living brain that show its physical changes as it works.

Third, *behavior.* By **behavior** we mean the outwardly observable acts of a person, either alone or in a group. Behavior consists of physical movements, voluntary or involuntary, of the limbs, facial muscles, or other parts of the body. A particular behavior is often preceded by mental processes such as a perception of the current situation (how far the golf ball must travel) and a decision about what to do next (how forcefully to swing the club). A behavior may also be governed by the relationship between the individual and a group. Tiger Woods might not have performed the way he did in 2001 had he been playing in 1920, when many in the crowd would not have wanted a nonwhite person to win. So there are layers upon layers: An individual's mental processes affect his or her behavior, and these processes are affected by the surrounding group (the members of which, in turn, have their own individual mental processes and behaviors).

The goals of psychology are not simply to *describe* and *explain* mental processes and behavior, but also to *predict* and *control* them. As an individual, you'd probably like to be able to predict what kind of person would make a good spouse for you, or which politician would make sound decisions in crisis situations. As a society, we all would greatly benefit by knowing how people learn most effectively, how to control addictive and destructive behaviors, and how to cure mental illness.

Levels of Analysis: The Complete Psychology

The areas you might explore to answer questions about Tiger Woods's success—his coordination and focus, his beliefs and attitudes, his relationships with his parents and his audience—occur at three levels of scale, each of which provides a field for analysis. First, at the level of the *brain,* we can ask questions about his visualization techniques, hand–eye coordination, and concentration. Second, at the level of the whole *person,* we can ask how his beliefs and goals may have motivated him. And third, at the level of the *group,* we can investigate the roles of his parents and the reactions of crowds. At any moment in Tiger Woods's day, or yours, events are happening at all three levels: brain, person, and group. Of course, a person is not just a larger-scale brain, and a group is not a larger-scale person. But looking at the individual at a microlevel (the brain) and a macrolevel (in relation to a group) reveals much that would be hidden were we to look at only one level. The concept of levels of analysis has long held a central role in science in general (Anderson, 1998; Nagel, 1979; Schaffner, 1967) and in the field of psychology in particular (Fodor, 1968, 1983; Kosslyn & Koenig, 1995; Looren de Jong, 1996; Marr, 1982; Putnam, 1973).

Events Large and Small

Imagine that it's the first day of class. You are standing at the front of the room, gazing over the lecture hall full of students (see Figure 1.1 on page 10). Focus on a single student sitting near the middle of the room. Like a camera lens, zoom in so that the student's head fills your field of view. Zoom in even closer, to a small spot on the forehead, and shift an inch forward and zoom closer yet, to visualize the inside of the brain. As you continue to zoom in, magnification increases, and groups of brain cells appear. Finally, you home in on a single brain cell (which you will examine close up in the next chapter).

Now, reverse the journey: Zoom back until you see the entire person, whose psychology you would describe in terms of his or her beliefs, desires, and feelings, not just as a container of brain cells. Continue zooming back, to the point where you can take in the entire view, the full lecture hall. Now you see the world surrounding that particular student—the 20 or 30 other students, the color of the

Behavior: The outwardly observable acts of an individual, alone or in a group.

Figure **1.1** **Levels of Analysis**

Levels of analysis differ in the size of the events being considered, ranging from very large to very small.

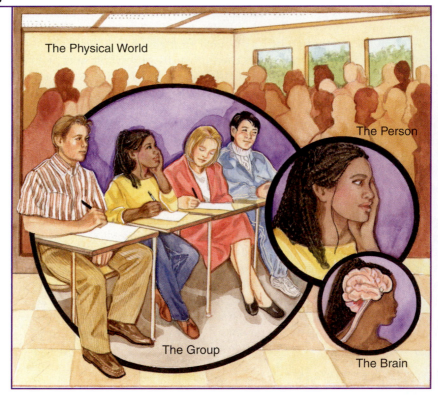

walls, the height and width of the room, the arrangement of chairs into rows, the sunlight streaming in.

At the **level of the brain**, psychologists focus on very small things. At this level we consider not only the activity of the brain but also the structure and properties of the organ itself—brain cells and their connections, the chemical soup in which they exist (including the hormones that alter the way the brain operates), and the genes that give rise to them. At the level of the brain, you are able to hear and understand a lecture because the appropriate cells are firing and making various connections. At the level of the brain, a psychologist might want to design an experiment that would test the effectiveness of Tiger Woods's techniques for focusing his attention on his swing.

The brain is only part of the story, though. As we've said, brains are not people. People have beliefs (such as ideas, knowledge, expectations), desires (such as hopes, goals, needs), and feelings (such as fears, guilts, attractions). The brain is in many ways a canvas on which life's experiences are painted. To talk about the picture itself, we must shift to another level of analysis. At the **level of the person**, psychologists focus on a larger unit, the person as a whole and his or her beliefs, desires, and feelings. At this level we consider the *content* of mental processes, not just their internal mechanics. At the level of the person, you are in a psychology class because you hope it will be interesting, because you want to learn about people, and perhaps because you know that the course is a graduation requirement. At the level of the person, a psychologist might want to investigate the factors— among them, possibly, Tiger Woods's Buddhist faith—behind the strong sense of inner calm he displays under pressure.

"No man is an island," the poet John Donne wrote. We all live in *social environments* that vary over time and space and that are populated by our friends and professors, our parents, the other viewers in a movie theater, the other drivers on a busy highway. Our lives are intertwined with other people's lives, and from birth to old age, we take our cues from other people around us. The relationships that arise within groups make them more than simply a collection of individuals. Mental

Level of the brain: Events that involve the structure and properties of the organ itself—brain cells and their connections, the chemical soup in which they exist, and the genes.

Level of the person: Events that involve the nature of beliefs, desires, and feelings—the *content* of the mind, not just its internal mechanics.

processes and behavior characterize groups as well as individuals. Street gangs and reading clubs both have distinct identities based on shared beliefs and practices that are passed on to succeeding generations of members as *culture,* which has been defined as the "language, beliefs, values, norms, behaviors, and even material objects that are passed from one generation to the next" (Henslin, 1999). Thus, at the **level of the group**, psychologists focus on units even larger than the brain or the person, looking at the ways collections of people (as few as one other person, as many as a society) shape individual mental processes and behavior. As you shift in your seat in the lecture hall, you are not alone: Other students' reactions, their questions, their irritating habits or encouraging comments, affect the way you experience the course. At the level of the group, a psychologist might want to examine the role of a supportive and enthusiastic audience in helping Tiger Woods birdie instead of bogey.

Events that occur at every level of analysis—brain, person, and group—are intimately tied to conditions in the physical world. All our mental processes and behaviors take place within, and are influenced by, a specific *physical environment.* A windy day at the golf course changes the way Tiger Woods plays a shot; if the classroom is too hot, you may have trouble focusing on the lecture. The group is only part of the world; to understand the events at each level of analysis, we must always relate them to the physical world that surrounds us.

All Together Now

Events at the different levels not only occur at the same time, but are constantly interacting. As you sit in the lecture hall, the signals among your brain cells that enable you to understand the lecture, and the new connections among your brain cells that enable you to remember it, are happening because your desire to pass the course has put you in the room: That is, events at the level of the person are affecting events at the level of the brain. But as you listen to the lecture, your neighbor's knuckle cracking is really getting to you, and you're finding it hard to concentrate: Events at the level of the group are affecting events at the level of the brain. Because you really want to hear this stuff, you're wondering how to get your neighbor to cut it out, and you decide to shoot a few dirty looks his way: Events at the level of the person are affecting events at the level of the group (which, as we've seen, affect events at the level of the brain). And all of this is going on within the physical environment of the room, where the sunlight that had seemed warm and welcoming is now pretty hot, and you're getting drowsy, and you're *really* irritated, and you finally change your seat. . . . And round and round. Events at the three levels of analysis, in a specific physical context, are constantly changing and influencing one another. To understand fully what's going on in life situations, you need to look at all three.

Level of the group: Events that involve relationships between people (e.g., love, competition, cooperation), relationships among groups, and culture. Events at the level of the group are one aspect of the environment; the other aspect is the physical environment itself (the time, temperature, and other physical stimuli).

LOOKING AT LEVELS

Drought Among the Maasai

The Maasai, a native people of Kenya and Tanzania, keep herds of cattle, following them as they graze across the plains of East Africa. Rather than feeding their infants on a fixed schedule, Maasai mothers feed them whenever they cry or otherwise make their needs known. At the height of a 10-year drought in the early 1970s, many cattle died; some families lost 98% of their herd. With cow's milk scarce, the infants were more dependent on their mothers' milk. Psychiatrist Marten deVries (1984), who was studying the Maasai children when the drought began, had been following the development of a group of 48 infants. He had focused on 20 of them, characterizing

Interactions among events at the different levels of analysis can explain why, during a drought, "easy" babies died but "difficult" babies survived.

half as "easy" and half as "difficult"; easy babies were calm and cooperative, difficult ones testy and demanding. As the drought intensified, deVries tried to track down these 20 babies, now 6 to 8 months old. He expected that the "difficult" babies would stress their caregivers even more than usual and hence these babies would suffer behavioral impairments and ill health. To his surprise, he found the opposite: More of the easy babies had died (five of the seven he could find, compared to only one of the six diffi-cult babies). Despite the small number of cases, the results were highly suggestive. Apparently the difficult babies demanded to be fed more often, boosting their mothers' milk supply (frequent breast-feeding stimulates milk pro-duction), even though the mothers were malnourished. The less demanding, easy babies died when their mothers' milk supplies dwindled.

The deaths of the easy babies illustrate the crucial role played by events at each of the three levels of analysis and their interactions within a physical context. Temperament is at least in part biologically determined, a topic we explore in Chapters 8 and 9. The child's temperament (*level of the brain*) regulated the mother's behavior; her behavior, based on her belief that she should feed her child only when it fussed (*level of the person*), in turn affected how her body functioned. Finally, in the Maasai culture (*level of the group*), babies are cared for by an extended family, and thus the stress presented by difficult babies does not fall on the mother only, as is common in our society. Thus, a difficult baby was not as stressful as he or she would be for a single caretaker. Moreover, because the Maasai are nomads (*level of the group*), they were dependent on the naturally available supplies of water (they didn't farm or irrigate). As a result, the physical envi-ronment—that is, the drought—was disastrous for them.

Note that we cannot understand what happened to the babies by considering only the physical environment. Although the drought set the stage for the psychological drama that followed, it did not determine the outcome. Nor can we understand what happened if we consider events only at a single level. To understand fully why more difficult babies than easy babies survived the drought, we must consider how events at all three levels interacted. Only by investigating the interactions among the babies' temperaments, the mothers' beliefs about feeding, and the Maasai's culture can we understand the psychological factors that led to the deaths of the easy children.

CONSOLIDATE!

 1 *Psychology can illuminate all aspects of a per-son's life, but what is psychology?* Psychology is the science of mental processes and behavior. Sci-ence is a way of answering questions that relies on, first, using logic to reason about the possible causes of a phenomenon and, then, collecting new facts to test the resulting ideas. Psychology focuses on both the internal events that underlie our thoughts, feelings, and behavior and the behavior itself.

2 *What is the concept of "levels of analysis," and how can you use it to understand psychology?* Any psychological phenomenon can best be under-stood by considering events at three levels of analy-sis: the brain (its functioning and its structure), the person (his or her beliefs, desires, and feelings), and the group (social interactions and cultural influ-ences). All these events occur in the context of the physical world. Events at the different levels are constantly interacting, and thus it is impossible to explain mental processes or behavior adequately in terms of only a single level of analysis.

Psychology Then and Now

How do you think psychologists 50 or 100 years ago might have interpreted Tiger Woods's performance? Would they have focused on the same things as psychologists do today? One hallmark of the sciences is that rather than casting aside earlier findings, researchers use them as stepping stones to the next set of discoveries. Reviewing how psychology has developed over time will help us understand where we are today. In the century or so during which psychology has taken shape as a formal discipline, the issues under investigation have changed, the focus has shifted from one level of analysis to another, and events at each level have often been viewed as operating separately or occurring in isolation.

 1 How has psychology evolved over time?

 2 What are the different types of psychology, and what do different types of psychologists do?

The Evolution of a Science

In one form or another, psychology has probably always been with us. People have apparently always been curious about why they and others think, feel, and behave the way they do. In contrast, the history of psychology as a scientific field is relatively brief, spanning little more than a century. The roots of psychology lie in philosophy (the use of logic and speculation to understand the nature of reality, experience, and values) on the one hand and physiology (the study of the biological workings of the body, including the brain) on the other hand. From philosophy, psychology borrowed theories of the nature of mental processes and behavior (for example, the idea that thinking relies on a series of mental images). From physiology, psychologists learned to recognize the role of the brain in giving rise to mental processes and behavior and acquired tools to investigate these processes. These twin influences of philosophy and physiology remain in force today, shaped and sharpened by developments over time.

Early Days: Structuralist, Functionalist, and Gestalt Psychology

The earliest scientific psychologists were not much interested in why we behave as we do. Instead, these pioneers focused their efforts on understanding the operation of perception (the ways in which we sense the world), memory, and problem solving—events at what we now think of as the level of the brain. Wilhelm Wundt (1832–1920), usually considered the founder of scientific psychology, set up the first psychology laboratory in 1879 in Leipzig, Germany. The work of Wundt and his colleagues led to **structuralism**, the first formal movement in psychology. The structuralists sought to identify the "building blocks" of consciousness. Part of Wundt's research led him to characterize two types of elements of consciousness. The first comprised sensations, which arise from the eyes, ears, and other sense organs; the second consisted of feelings, such as fear, anger, and love. The goal of this school of psychology was to describe the rules that determine how particular sensations or feelings may occur at the same time or in sequence, combining in various ways into mental *structures*. Edward Titchener (1867–1927), an American student of Wundt, broadened the structuralist approach to apply it to the nature of concepts and thinking in general.

The structuralists developed and tested their theories partly with objective techniques, such as measures of the time it takes to respond to different sensations. Their primary research tool, however, was **introspection**, which means literally "looking within." Here is an example of introspection: Try to recall how many windows and doors are in your room. Are you aware of "seeing" the room in a mental image, of scanning along the walls and counting the windows and doors? Introspection is the technique of noticing your mental processes as, or immediately after, they occur.

Had the structuralists been asked to analyze Tiger Woods's golf success—how, for example, he perceives distances, fairway terrain, and wind direction—they probably would have trained him to use introspection to describe his mental processes. Let's say that although you are able to use introspection as a tool to recall the numbers of windows and doors in your room, your best friend doesn't seem to be able to do the same. How could you prove that mental images actually exist and objects can indeed be visualized? For the early psychologists, this was the core of the problem. Barring the ability to read minds, there was no way to resolve disagreements about the nature of introspection.

Rather than trying to chart the elements of mental processes, the adherents of **functionalism** sought to understand how our minds help us to adapt to the world around us—in short, how to *function* in it. As psychology historian Edwin G. Boring (1950) put it, the structuralists were interested in "the psychology of the *Is*," whereas the functionalists were interested in the "*Is-for*." Whereas the structuralists

Structuralism: The school of psychology that sought to identify the basic elements of experience and to describe the rules and circumstances under which these elements combine to form mental *structures*.

Introspection: The process of "looking within."

Functionalism: The school of psychology that sought to understand the ways that the mind helps individuals *function*, or adapt to the world.

asked *what* are mental processes and *how* do they operate, the functionalists wanted to know *why* humans think, feel, and behave as we do. The functionalists, many of whom were Americans, shared the urge to gather knowledge that could be put to immediate use. Sitting in a room introspecting simply didn't seem worthwhile to them. The functionalists' interest lay in the methods by which people learn and in how goals and beliefs are shaped by environment. As such, their interests spanned the levels of the person and the group.

The functionalists were strongly influenced by Charles Darwin (1809–1882), whose theory of natural selection in evolution stressed that some individual organisms in every species, from ants to oaks, possess characteristics that enable them to survive and reproduce more fruitfully than others. The phrase "survival of the fittest," often quoted in relation to natural selection, doesn't quite capture the key idea. (For one thing, these days "the fittest" implies the muscle-bound star of the health club rather than its older meaning of something "fit for" or "suited to" its situation.) The idea of natural selection is that certain inborn characteristics make particular individuals more fit for their environments, enabling them to have more offspring that survive, and they in turn have more offspring, and so on, until the characteristics that led them to flourish are spread through the whole population. Darwin called the inborn characteristics that help an organism survive and produce many offspring *adaptations*. (Chapter 2 covers Darwin's theory more fully.)

The functionalists applied Darwin's theory to mental characteristics. For example, William James (1842–1910), who set up the first psychology laboratory in the United States at Harvard University, studied the ways in which consciousness helps an individual survive and adapt to an environment. The functionalists likely would have tried to discover how Tiger Woods's goals and beliefs enable him to press on in the face of adversity such as losing an important match or receiving hate mail.

The functionalists made several enduring contributions to psychology. Their emphasis on Darwin's theory of natural selection and its link between human and nonhuman animals led them to theorize that human psychology is related to the psychology of animals. This insight meant that the observation of animals could provide clues to human behavior. The functionalist focus on issues of society, such as improving methods of education, also spawned research that continues today.

Although their work began in earnest nearly 50 years later, the Gestalt psychologists, like the structuralists, were interested in consciousness, particularly as it arises during perception (and thus also focused on events at the level of the brain). But instead of trying to dissect the elements of experience, **Gestalt psychology**—taking its name from the German word *Gestalt,* which means "whole"— emphasized the overall patterns of thoughts or experience. Based in Germany, scientists such as Max Wertheimer (1880–1943) and his colleagues noted that much of the content of our thoughts comes from what we perceive and, further, from inborn tendencies to structure what we see in certain ways.

Have you ever glanced up to see a flight of birds heading south for the winter? If so, you probably didn't pay attention to each individual bird but instead focused on the flock. In Gestalt terms, the flock was a *perceptual unit,* a whole formed from individual parts. The Gestalt psychologists developed over 100 perceptual laws, or principles, that describe how our eyes and brains organize the world. Most of these principles illustrate the dictum that "the whole is more than the sum of its parts." When you see the birds in flight, the flock has a size and shape that cannot be predicted from the size and shape of the birds viewed one at a time. To Gestalt psychologists, just as the flock is an entity that is more than a collection of individual birds, our patterns of thought are more than the simple sum of individual images or ideas. Gestaltists would want to know how Tiger Woods can take in the overall layout of each hole, or even 18-hole course, and plan his strategy accordingly.

Gestalt psychology: An approach to understanding mental processes that focuses on the idea that the whole is more than the sum of its parts.

Today the study of perception has grown beyond the province of Gestalt psychology alone and is now a central focus of psychology, as well it should be. Perception is, after all, our gateway to the world; if our perceptions are not accurate, our corresponding thoughts and feelings will be based on a distorted view of reality.

Psychodynamic Theory: More Than Meets the Eye

Sigmund Freud (1856–1939), a Viennese physician specializing in neurology (the study and treatment of diseases of the brain and nervous system), developed detailed and subtle theories of how thoughts and feelings affect our actions. These theories address mental processes and behavior less at the level of the brain and more at the level of the person (and, to some extent, the level of the group). We consider Freud and theorists who followed in his footsteps in Chapter 8; here we touch briefly on key points of his theory.

Freud stressed the notion that many mental processes are **unconscious**—that is, they are outside our conscious awareness and beyond our ability to bring to awareness at will. Freud believed that we have many unconscious sexual, and sometimes aggressive, urges. Even young infants, Freud wrote, are highly sexual beings, a notion that disturbed many of his contemporaries, and disturbs many of us. On a conscious level, Freud argued, we find these urges unacceptable and so banish them to the unconscious. According to Freud, unconscious thoughts and feelings build up until, eventually and inevitably, they demand release as thoughts, feelings, or actions.

Freud developed what has since been called a **psychodynamic theory.** From the Greek words *psyche,* or "mind," and *dynamo,* meaning "power," the term refers to the continual push-and-pull interaction among conscious and unconscious forces. Freud believed that it was these interactions that produced abnormal behaviors, such as obsessively washing one's hands until they crack and bleed. According to Freud, such hand-washing might be traced to unacceptable unconscious sexual or aggressive impulses bubbling up to consciousness (the "dirt" perceived on the hands) and that washing symbolically serves to remove the "dirt." Freud interpreted many statements and events symbolically, often assigning a sexual meaning to them. For example, he believed that long, thin objects often represented the penis and that objects with holes in them symbolized the vagina. What would followers of psychodynamic theory say about Tiger Woods? The long skinny club that he wields so effectively might be considered a symbol for a penis, and a Freudian would probably ask Woods about his earliest memories and experiences and try with him to analyze the sexual or aggressive urges that led to his intense interest in golf.

Rather than deriving from objective scientific studies, the guiding principles of psychodynamic theories rest on subjective interpretations of what patients say and do. As such, critics charge, there is no objective way to verify whether a given interpretation is correct: as Freud (a cigar smoker) himself remarked, "Sometimes a cigar is only a cigar." Psychodynamic theory can usually explain any given observation or research result as easily as its opposite, and thus it becomes impossible to evaluate the theory, obviously a serious drawback. Nevertheless, the key idea of psychodynamic theory, that behavior is driven by mental processes that are often hidden from conscious awareness, has proven invaluable; also invaluable is its focus on the level of the person. In addition, psychodynamic theories led to entirely new approaches to treating psychological problems, which have since been modified and refined (see Chapter 12).

Behaviorism: The Power of the Environment

By the early part of the twentieth century, a new generation of psychologists calling themselves behaviorists began to question a key assumption shared by their predecessors, that psychologists should study hidden mental processes. Because they found the theories of mental processes so difficult to pin down, American

Unconscious: Outside conscious awareness and not able to be brought to consciousness at will.

Psychodynamic theory: A theory of how thoughts and feelings affect behavior; refers to the continual push-and-pull interaction among conscious and unconscious forces.

© 1988 FarWorks, Inc

8-28   Larson

"Stimulus, response! Stimulus, response!
Don't you ever *think?*"

psychologists such as Edward Lee Thorndike (1874–1949), John B. Watson (1878–1958), and Clark L. Hull (1884–1952) rejected the idea that psychology should focus on these unseen phenomena. Instead, these followers of **behaviorism** concluded that psychology should concentrate on understanding directly observable behavior.

B. F. Skinner and his followers went so far as to argue that there is no such thing as mental processes, that people don't really have "thoughts." For instance, rather than saying that someone treats dogs well because she "likes" them ("liking" being an unobservable mental process), these behaviorists would say that she approaches dogs, protects them from harm, pets them, and otherwise treats them well because such responses have come to be associated with the stimulus of perceiving a dog. Behaviorists thus cut out the middleman of mental processes: The behaviors that are generally regarded as reflections of the internal state of "liking" can instead be viewed as direct responses to particular stimuli. Because of their concern with the content of the stimulus–response associations, the behaviorists focused on events at the level of the person.

The behaviorists pointed out that responses usually produce consequences, either negative or positive, which in turn affect how the organism responds the next time it encounters the same stimulus. Say you put money in a vending machine (a response to the stimulus of seeing the machine) and the machine dispenses a tasty candy bar; chances are good that you will repeat the behavior in the future. If, on the other hand, the machine serves up a stale candy bar with a torn wrapper, you will be less inclined to use this or another machine like it again (see Chapter 4 for a detailed discussion of how consequences affect learning).

How might the behaviorists explain Tiger Woods's success? A key idea in behaviorism is *reinforcement,* the strengthening or supporting consequences that result from a given behavior. A reward, such as payment for a job, is a common type of reinforcement. If the consequences of a behavior are reinforcing, we are likely to repeat the behavior. Conversely, if a behavior produces an undesirable outcome ("punishment"), we are less likely to do it again. From his earliest days, Tiger Woods received an extraordinary amount of reinforcement for playing well, at first from his father and then from an increasingly larger affirming public. It was this reinforcement, the behaviorists would argue, that spurred him to repeat those acts that brought desirable consequences, while shunning behaviors (including ineffective golfing techniques) that did not help him play well.

The behaviorists developed many principles that describe the conditions in which specific stimuli lead to specific responses, many of which have stood up well in later investigations (as you will see in Chapter 4). On the other hand, as you will see, many of the behaviorists' objections to the study of mental processes have since been refuted by subsequent research.

Behaviorism: The school of psychology that focuses on how a specific stimulus (object, person, or event) evokes a specific response (behavior in reaction to the stimulus).

Humanistic psychology: The school of psychology that assumes people have positive values, free will, and deep inner creativity, the combination of which leads them to choose life-fulfilling paths to personal growth.

Humanistic Psychology

Partly as a reaction to the mechanistic theories of the Freudians and behaviorists, which viewed people as driven either by the content of their mental processes or by external stimuli, in the late 1950s and early 1960s a new psychology emerged. According to **humanistic psychology**, people have positive values, free will, and a deep inner creativity, which in combination allow us to choose life-fulfilling paths to personal growth. The humanistic approach (focused on the level of the person) rests on the ideas that the "client" (no longer the "patient") must be respected as equal to the therapist and that each person has dignity and self-worth.

Psychologists such as Carl Rogers (1902–1987) and Abraham Maslow (1908–1970) developed therapies based on these theories. Rogers's *client-centered therapy* incorporated Maslow's theory that people have an urge to *self-actualize*— that is, to develop to their fullest potentials—and that given the right environment this development will in time occur. How might humanistic psychologists explain Tiger Woods's psychology? No doubt they would point to him as someone who is striving to reach his full potential. They might question, however, whether in the long run his intense focus on golf will prove entirely satisfying, especially if he ignores other aspects of life.

Humanistic psychology continues to attract followers today, but it is no longer a major force in the field. Nevertheless, many of the therapies now in use reflect the influence of humanistic thinking (as we discuss in Chapter 12).

The Cognitive Revolution

The tension between psychological approaches—on the one hand, structuralism, functionalism, and psychoanalytic psychology, which studied unobservable mental processes, and on the other hand, behaviorism, which addressed only directly observable behavior—was resolved by an unlikely source: the computer. The computer led to the *cognitive revolution* of the late 1950s and early 1960s; its proponents looked to the computer as a model for the way human mental processes work. This movement came into full flower in the mid-1970s, led by, among others, psychologist/computer scientists Herbert A. Simon and Alan Newell (Simon went on to win a Nobel Prize, in part for this work) and linguist Noam Chomsky. (Gardner [1985] provides a detailed history of the cognitive revolution.)

The cognitive revolution produced a new way to conceive of mental events, giving birth to **cognitive psychology**, which attempts to characterize the nature of human *information processing*—that is, the way information is stored and operated on internally (Neisser, 1967). In this view, mental processes are like computer software (programs), and the brain is like the hardware (the machine itself). Computers showed, once and for all, why it is important that there be a science of the unobservable events that take place in the head, not just a science of directly observable behavior. Consider, for example, how you might react if your word-processing program produced *italics* whenever you entered the command for **bold-face**. Noticing the software's "behavior" is only the first step in fixing this error: You need to dig deeper to find out where the program has gone wrong. This would involve seeing what internal events are triggered by the command and how those events affect what the program does. So, too, for people. If somebody is acting oddly, we must go beyond the essential step of noticing the unusual behavior; we also need to think about what is happening inside and consider what is causing the problem. Indeed, the cognitive revolution led to new ways of conceptualizing and treating mental disorders, such as depression.

The theories and research methods developed by cognitive psychologists have also proved crucial in the recent development of **cognitive neuroscience**, which blends cognitive psychology and neuroscience (the study of the brain). Cognitive neuroscientists argue that "the mind is what the brain does" (Kosslyn & Koenig, 1995) and hope to discover the nature, organization, and operation of mental processes by studying the brain. This is one of the most exciting areas of psychology today, in part because new brain-scanning technologies have allowed us, for the first time in history, to observe human brains at work.

The cognitive neuroscience approach considers events at the three levels of analysis, but with a primary focus on the brain. Cognitive neuroscientists seeking to explain Tiger Woods's golfing achievements would likely investigate how different parts of his brain function while he plays golf, looking to discover the way his brain processes information. For example, how does the visual input he receives standing at the tee allow him to judge distance to the pin? They would also compare Woods's brain function with that of less accomplished golfers and would even program computers to mimic the way his brain works during play.

Cognitive psychology: The approach in psychology that attempts to characterize how information is stored and operated on internally.

Cognitive neuroscience: A blending of cognitive psychology and neuroscience (the study of the brain) that aims to specify how the brain stores and processes information.

Probably the best source of evidence for theories in evolutionary psychology is cultural universality, instances of the same practice occurring in all cultures. People in all cultures have been found to share certain concepts and practices, including playing music, dancing, lying, telling stories, gossiping, expressing emotions with facial expressions, fearing snakes, giving gifts, and making medicines (Brown, 1991).

Evolutionary psychology: The approach in psychology that assumes that certain cognitive strategies and goals are so important that natural selection has built them into our brains.

Evolutionary Psychology

One of the most recent developments in the field, **evolutionary psychology**, first made its appearance in the late 1980s. This school of thought has a heritage—with a twist—in the work of the functionalists and their emphasis on Darwin's theory of natural selection. Central to the approach is the idea that certain cognitive strategies and goals are so important that natural selection has built them into our brains. But instead of proposing that evolution has selected specific behaviors per se (as earlier evolutionary theorists, including Charles Darwin himself, believed), these theorists believe that general cognitive strategies (such as using deception to achieve one's goals) and certain goals (such as finding attractive mates) are inborn. This approach is currently being developed by researchers such as Lida Cosmides and John Tooby (1996), David Buss (1994, 1999), and Steven Pinker (1994, 1997; see also Barkow et al., 1992; Plotkin, 1994, 1997). For example, these theorists claim that we have the ability to lie because our ancestors who could lie had an advantage: They could trick their naïve companions into giving up resources. These more devious ancestors had more children who survived than their nonlying contemporaries, and their lying children had more children, and so on, until the ability to lie was inborn in all members of our species. Notice that lying is not a specific behavior; it is a strategy that can be expressed by many behaviors, all of them deceitful.

Evolutionary psychologists compare human abilities with those of animals, particularly nonhuman primates (Hauser, 1996). For example, by studying the way animals communicate, researchers try to infer which abilities formed the basis of human language. By studying animals, researchers hope to discover the abilities of our common ancestors and, from those data, develop theories about the way they may have been refined over the course of evolution. When asked about what might underlie Tiger Woods's achievements, an evolutionary psychologist might note that although our species did not evolve to play golf, the abilities that arose via natural selection for hunting game and avoiding predators could also be used in other ways, including sports.

But evidence of universality or shared abilities in nonhuman animals and humans does not tell us *why* those characteristics are present. Are they really adaptations? Evolutionary theories are notoriously difficult to test because we don't know what our ancestors were like and how they evolved. Just because we are born with certain tendencies and characteristics does not mean that these are evolutionarily selected adaptations. As Stephen Jay Gould and Richard Lewontin (1979) point out, at least some of our modern characteristics are simply by-products of other characteristics that were in fact selected. Your nose evolved to warm air and direct scents; and once you have a nose, you can use it to hold up your eyeglasses. But just as nobody would claim that the nose evolved to hold up glasses, nobody should claim that all the current functions of the brain resulted from natural selection. The various schools of psychological thought are summarized in Table 1.1.

TABLE 1.1   Schools of Psychological Thought

Dates based on Boring (1950).

NAME	LANDMARK EVENTS	KEY IDEAS
Structuralism	Wundt founds first psychology laboratory, 1879	Use introspection to discover the elements of mental processes and rules for combining them.
Functionalism	James's *Principles of Psychology* published, 1890	Study why thoughts, feelings, and behavior occur, how they are adaptive.
Gestalt psychology	Wertheimer's paper on perceived movement, 1912	Focus on overall patterns of thoughts or experience; "the whole is more than the sum of its parts."
Psychodynamic theory	Freud publishes *The Ego and the Id,* 1927	Conflicts among conscious and unconscious forces underlie many thoughts, feelings, and behaviors.
Behaviorism	Watson's paper *Psychology as the Behaviorist Views It,* 1913; Skinner's *The Behavior of Organisms,* 1938	Behavior is the appropriate focus of psychology, and it can be understood by studying stimuli, responses, and the consequences of responses.
Humanistic psychology	Maslow publishes *Motivation and Personality,* 1954	Nonscientific approach; belief that people have positive values, free will, and deep inner creativity.
Cognitive psychology	Neisser's book *Cognitive Psychology* gives the "school" its name, 1967	Mental processes are like information processing in a computer.
Cognitive neuroscience	First issue of the *Journal of Cognitive Neuroscience* appears, 1989	"The mind is what the brain does."
Evolutionary psychology	Barko, Cosmides, and Tooby edit *The Adapted Mind,* 1992	Mental strategies and goals are often inborn, the result of natural selection.

The Psychological Way:
What Today's Psychologists Do

As the field of psychology developed, different schools of thought focused on different aspects of mental processes and behavior, and their varying influences are felt in what today's psychologists do. And just what is that?

There are many types of psychologists and many ways to apply psychology in practice. Here we consider three major types of psychologists: those who help people deal with personal problems or stress, those who study mental processes and behavior scientifically, and those who seek to solve specific practical problems, such as helping athletes perform better.

Clinical and Counseling Psychology: A Healing Profession

Andrea is a **clinical psychologist** who specializes in treating people with eating disorders. Many of Andrea's clients have a disorder called *anorexia nervosa,* characterized by refusal to maintain a healthy weight. Others, who have a disorder called *bulimia nervosa,* eat and then force themselves to vomit or take laxatives immediately afterward. Andrea sees each patient once or twice a week, for 50 minutes per session. During these sessions, Andrea's job is usually to discover why behaviors that are so destructive in the long run seem so desirable to the patient in the short run. She then helps her patients phase out the destructive behaviors and replace them with more adaptive behaviors—for instance, responding to anxiety after eating by taking a quick walk around the block instead of vomiting. Depending on the setting in which Andrea works (probably a private office, clinic, or hospital), she will spend varying portions of her day with patients; meeting with other psychologists to discuss how to be more helpful to patients; supervising psychotherapists in training; going out into the community, perhaps lecturing about eating disorders at high school assemblies; and doing paperwork, including writing notes on each patient, submitting forms to insurance companies for payment, and reading professional publications to keep up with new findings and techniques.

Clinical psychologist: The type of psychologist who provides psychotherapy and is trained to administer and interpret psychological tests.

There are many kinds of psychotherapy, and different training prepares therapists in different ways. Psychiatrists, for example, typically would not treat families, but clinical psychologists and social workers—as well as other mental health professionals—might.

Psychotherapy: Talking and listening to patients about their problems and helping them to see the causes and—more important—to find solutions.

Counseling psychologist: The type of psychologist who is trained to help people with issues that naturally arise during the course of life.

Psychiatrist: A physician who focuses on mental disorders; unlike psychologists, psychiatrists can prescribe drugs, but they are not trained to administer and interpret psychological tests, nor are they trained to interpret and understand psychological research.

Social worker: A mental health professional who helps families (and individuals) with psychotherapy and helps clients use the social service systems in their communities.

Psychiatric nurse: A nurse who holds a master's degree in nursing as well as a certificate of clinical specialization in psychiatric nursing (M.S.N., C.S.), and who provides psychotherapy and works with medical doctors to monitor and administer medications.

Andrea has been trained to provide **psychotherapy**, which involves listening and talking to patients and helping them discover the causes of, and solutions to, their difficulties; she also administers and interprets psychological tests, which can help in diagnosis and planning the appropriate treatment. *Clinical neuropsychologists* are clinical psychologists who work specifically with tests designed to diagnose the effects of brain damage on thoughts, feelings, and behavior and to indicate which parts of the brain are impaired following trauma. Other clinical psychologists work with organizations such as corporations to help company groups function more effectively; for example, a psychologist might advise a company about reducing stress among workers in a particular unit, or teach relaxation techniques to all employees. Some clinical psychologists have a Ph.D. (doctor of philosophy) degree, awarded by a university psychology department; these graduate programs teach students not only how to do psychotherapy and psychological testing, but also how to conduct and interpret psychological research. A clinical psychologist may also have a Psy.D. (doctor of psychology), a graduate degree from a program with less emphasis on research.

If Andrea had been trained as a **counseling psychologist**, she would have learned to help people deal with issues we all face, such as choosing a career, marrying, raising a family, and performing at work. Counseling psychologists often provide career counseling and vocational testing to help people decide which occupations best suit their interests and abilities. They sometimes provide psychotherapy, but these professionals may have a more limited knowledge of therapeutic techniques than clinical psychologists. They may have a Ph.D. (often from a program that specifically trains them in this area) or often an Ed.D. (doctor of education) degree granted by a school of education.

Andrea could also have become a **psychiatrist.** If she had gone this route, her training and competence would have differed from that of the other mental health professionals. First, as a physician with an M.D. (doctor of medicine) degree, a psychiatrist has extensive medical training and can prescribe drugs, whereas in general psychologists cannot (some psychologists in understaffed rural areas have had intensive training about medications for mental illnesses and have been given limited prescribing privileges). Second, a medical doctor, unlike a clinical psychologist, has typically not been trained to interpret and understand psychological research or psychological testing.

There are two other types of clinical mental health practitioners who are not psychologists, and her interest in clinical work might have led Andrea to choose either of those professions: social work or psychiatric nursing. If she had earned an M.S.W. (master of social work) degree, as a **social worker** she would typically focus on helping families and individuals by psychotherapy, and she also would teach clients how to use the social service system in their community. A **psychiatric nurse** holds a master's degree in nursing (M.S.N, master of science in nursing) as well as a certificate of clinical specialization (C.S.) in psychiatric nursing. A psychiatric nurse provides psychotherapy, usually in a hospital or clinic, or in private practice, and works closely with medical doctors to monitor and administer medications; in some cases, a psychiatric nurse can prescribe medications.

Academic Psychology: Teaching and Research

James is a professor of psychology at a large state university. Most mornings he prepares lectures, which he delivers three times a week. He also has morning office hours, when students can come by to ask questions about their program of courses in the department or their progress in one of James's classes. Once a week at noon he has a committee meeting; this week the committee on computer technology is discussing how best to structure the department computer network. His afternoons are taken up mostly with research. (If he worked at a smaller college, he might spend more time teaching and less time on research; alternatively, if he worked at a hospital, he might spend the lion's share of his time doing research and very little time teaching.) James's specialty is *developmental psychology,* the study of how thinking, feeling, and behaving develop with age and experience. Today his research work takes place at a laboratory preschool at the university, where he and his assistants are testing the ways children become attached to objects such as dolls and blankets. James also must find time to write papers for publication in professional journals, and he regularly writes grant proposals requesting funding for his research, so that he can pay students to help him test the children in his studies. He also writes letters of recommendation, grades papers and tests, and reads journal articles to keep up with current research in his and related fields. James tries to eat lunch with colleagues at least twice a week to keep up-to-date on departmental events and the work going on at the university in other areas of psychology.

Developmental psychologists often take special care to prevent their presence from affecting the child's behavior in any way.

Although the activities of most **academic psychologists** are similar in that they all teach and conduct research, the kinds of research vary widely. Different types of psychologists focus on different types of questions. For example, if James had become a *cognitive psychologist* (one who studies thinking, memory, and related topics), he might ask, "How was Tiger Woods able to hit the ball with the appropriate force in the correct direction?" but not "What was the role of the audience, and would it have been different if the tournament had been held 50 years ago?" If he had become a *social psychologist* (one who studies how people think and feel about themselves and other people, and how groups function), he might ask the second question, but not the first. And in neither case would he ask, "What aspects of Tiger Woods's character help him deal with the extreme stress he faces?" That question would interest a *personality psychologist* (one who studies individual differences in preferences and inclinations).

Because psychology is a science, it rests on objective tests of its theories and ideas. It is through research that we learn how to diagnose people's problems and how to cure them; it is through research that we determine what kind of career will make good use of a particular person's talents; it is through research that we understand how to present material so that students can understand and remember it most effectively. Theories about such issues can come from anywhere, but there is no way to know whether an idea is right or wrong except by testing it scientifically, through research.

There are at least as many different types of academic psychologists as there are separate sections in this book. In fact, this book represents a harvest of their research. Thousands of researchers are working on the topics covered in each chapter, and it is through their efforts that we have learned enough that a book like this can be written.

Applied Psychology: Better Living Through Psychology

Maria is an applied psychologist, who spends her day working to improve software so that it is more intuitive and useful. **Applied psychologists** use the principles and theories of psychology in practical areas such as education, industry, and marketing. An applied psychologist may hold a Ph.D. or, sometimes, only a master's degree in an area of psychology (in North America a master's degree typically requires two years of postgraduate study instead of the four to six for a Ph.D.).

Academic psychologist: The type of psychologist who focuses on conducting research and teaching.

Applied psychologist: The type of psychologist who studies how to improve products and procedures and conducts research to help solve specific practical problems.

Applied psychologists have many roles, one of which is to help attorneys decide which potential jurors are likely to be sympathetic or hostile to the defendant.

Applied psychologists not only work on improving products and procedures but also—like Maria—conduct research aimed at solving specific practical problems. Working in applied psychology, a *developmental psychologist* may be employed by or consult with the product development department of a toy company. Using her knowledge of children, she can help design toys that would be appropriate for particular age levels; she would then bring children to a playroom at the company to see how they play with new toys. A *physiological psychologist* studies the brain and brain–body interactions and may work at a company that makes drugs or brain-scanning machines. A *social psychologist* may help lawyers decide which possible jurors should be rejected. A *personality psychologist* may design a new test to help select suitable personnel for a job. An *industrial/organizational (I/O) psychologist* focuses on using psychology in the workplace; he or she might help an employer create a more comfortable and effective work environment so as to increase worker productivity or might redesign work spaces to promote more effective employee communication. A *sport psychologist* works with athletes to help them improve their performances, by helping them learn to concentrate better, deal with stress, and practice more efficiently (Tiger Woods works with a sport psychologist). An *educational* or *school psychologist* works with educators (and sometimes families), devising ways to improve the cognitive, emotional, and social development of children at school.

The occupations of the various types of psychologists are summarized in Table 1.2.

TABLE 1.2 What Psychologists Do

Clinical psychologist	Administers and interprets psychological tests; provides psychotherapy.
Clinical neuropsychologist	Diagnoses effects of brain damage on thoughts, feelings, and behavior, and diagnoses the locus of damage.
Counseling psychologist	Helps people with issues that arise during everyday life (career, marriage, family, work).
Developmental psychologist	Researches and teaches the development of mental processes and behavior with age and experience.
Cognitive psychologist	Researches and teaches the nature of thinking, memory, and related aspects of mental processes.
Social psychologist	Researches and teaches how people think and feel about themselves and other people and how groups function.
Personality psychologist	Researches and teaches individual differences in preferences and inclinations.
Physiological psychologist	Researches and teaches the nature of the brain and brain–body interactions.
Industrial/organizational psychologist	Applies psychology in the workplace.
Sport psychologist	Applies psychology to improve athletic performance.
Educational or school psychologist	Applies psychology to improve cognitive, emotional, and social development of schoolchildren.

LOOKING AT LEVELS

A Science of the Obvious?

Science is an attempt to cajole Mother Nature into giving up her secrets. Over the years, the science of psychology has made many such attempts at unveiling the secrets of mental processes and behavior by means of the various approaches just reviewed. In the process, research psychologists of various persuasions are sometimes accused of merely demonstrating the obvious.

For example, the old saw that familiarity breeds contempt states the obvious—or does it? Let's see how a social psychologist would approach testing the obvious in this case. Robert Zajonc (1968, 1970) was interested in the factors that lead us to like something or someone. He found, repeatedly, that people like previously seen things *better* than unfamiliar ones; research shows that familiarity breeds not contempt but affinity (Bornstein, 1989). This is called the *mere-exposure effect.* At the level of the brain, the repeated presentation of a picture allows it to be taken in with less effort, which at the level of the person leads to positive feelings and preferences (Bornstein & D'Agostino, 1994). These effects can in turn alter behavior, including behavior toward other people (the level of the group).

In another study, Leone and Galley (Bornstein, 1987) demonstrated that the mere-exposure effect is not just a laboratory curiosity. They showed participants photographs of one of two faces, flashing them so briefly that the faces could not be identified. Following this, the participant met with the person in the photograph and a third person, ostensibly to decide whether the author of some poems was a man or a woman. As arranged beforehand, the two other people disagreed, and the participant had to be the tie-breaker. The participants tended to side with the person whose face they had seen in the photograph, even though they were unaware they had seen it. The mere-exposure effect was at work here across levels, an event in the brain affecting a preference (level of the person) that in turn affected a social interaction (level of the group).

So, not all results from psychological research are obvious, and in fact you will see many such examples of discoveries that are not obvious as you continue in this book. The following section explores in more detail just how studies can be conducted to discover new and sometimes surprising facts about mental processes and behavior.

CONSOLIDATE!

1 **How has psychology evolved over time?** Wundt, Titchener, and the other structuralists aimed to understand the elements of mental processes and how they are organized; this approach relied largely on introspection ("looking within"), which turned out to be not very reliable and not always valid—people often have no idea how their mental processes work, at least not in ways they can easily report. The functionalists rejected this approach as disconnected from real-world concerns and focused instead on how mental processes adapt to help us survive in the natural world; their pragmatic concerns led them to apply psychology to education and other social activities. In contrast, the Gestalt psychologists, who reacted to the attempt to dissect mental processes into isolated elements, studied the way the brain organizes material into overarching patterns. Freud and his colleagues shifted attention primarily to the level of the person; their psychodynamic theories were concerned largely with the operation of unconscious mental processes and primitive impulses (often related to sex) in dictating what people think, feel, and do. The behaviorists denounced the assumption, shared by all their predecessors, that mental processes should be the focus of psychology; they urged us to stick with what we could see—stimuli, responses, and the consequences of responses. But this view turned out to be too limiting. The humanists, in part reacting against the scientific approach, developed psychotherapies that relied on respect for individuals and their potentials. Elements of the various strands came together in the cognitive revolution, and many researchers who study cognition today conceive of mental processes as "what the brain does." Evolutionary psychology treats many goals and cognitive strategies as adaptive results of natural selection.

2 **What are the different types of psychology, and what do different types of psychologists do?** Clinical and counseling psychologists administer diagnostic tests and help people with their problems; academic psychologists teach and do research; and applied psychologists trained in various areas of psychology seek to solve specific practical problems, such as making better products and improving procedures in the workplace.

The Science of Psychology: Designed to Be Valid

You could probably speculate for hours about how Tiger Woods came to be such a superb golfer. Let's say, however, that you really want to *know* why some people are able to perform at high levels in spite of extraordinary pressure. How could you find out for sure?

1. What is the scientific method?

2. What research tools can psychologists use to study mental processes and behavior scientifically?

3. What should you look for when deciding whether to accept a study's conclusions?

4. What are proper ethics in research with humans and animals?

5. What are proper ethics in clinical practice?

The Scientific Method

The **scientific method** is a way to gather facts that will lead to the formulation and validation of a theory. It involves *specifying a problem; systematically observing events; forming a hypothesis of the relation between variables; collecting new observations to test the hypothesis; using such evidence to formulate and support a theory; and, finally, testing the theory.*

Let's take a closer look at the scientific method, one step at a time. First, what do we mean by "specifying a problem"? Science tries to answer questions, any one of which may be rephrased as a "problem." Despite the way the word is often used in ordinary conversation, a problem is not necessarily bad: It is simply a question you want to answer, or a puzzle you want to solve. A scientist might notice what seems to be a consistent pattern, for example, and wonder whether it reflects a connection or a coincidence. For example, a scientist might notice that many cultures have an afternoon siesta or "tea time" and wonder whether humans have a biological rhythm that makes us sluggish at that time of day. Speaking metaphorically, a scientist might notice a nail sticking above the boards and ask why it is different from other nails. Even as a child, Tiger Woods's abilities and discipline made him stand out from other children. Why? Was there something different about his brain or the way he was being raised?

Second, consider the idea of "systematically observing events." Scientists are not content to rely on impressions or interpretations. They want to know the facts, as free from any particular notions of their significance as possible. Facts are established by collecting **data**, which are careful observations or numerical measurements of a phenomenon. Properly collected data can be **replicated**—that is, found again by the original investigator or someone else. Scientists often prefer quantitative data (numerical measurements), such as how many seconds it takes a rat to run a maze, how many people gather at the scene of an accident, or how many times in a row Tiger Woods can sink a 10-foot putt. In addition to numerical data, scientists rely on systematic observations, which simply document that a certain event occurs—for example, that brain damage can cause someone to fail to name fruits and vegetables while still being able to name other objects (Hart et al., 1985). But unless numbers are involved, it is often difficult to sort the observation from the interpretation. Thus scientists prefer to have careful observation produce numbers (for example, the number of fruits and vegetables that could be named out of a possible 100).

Third, what do we mean by "events"? An event in the scientific sense is the occurrence of a particular phenomenon. Scientists study two kinds of events: those that are themselves directly observable (such as how many times in an hour a mother strokes her infant) and those that, like thoughts or emotions, can only be inferred. For example, when people smile without really meaning it, the muscles used are not the same ones that produce a sincere smile (Ekman, 1985). It is possible to observe directly which set of muscles is in use, and the recorded data would distinguish between the two kinds of contractions. But the researcher's interest goes beyond the directly observable contractions to the link with inner (and invisible)

Scientific method: A method that involves specifying a problem; systematically observing events; forming a hypothesis of the relation between variables; collecting new observations to test the hypothesis; using such evidence to formulate and support a theory; and, finally, testing the theory.

Data: Careful observations or numerical measurements.

Replicate: To repeat a study and obtain the same results as were found previously.

thoughts and feelings. By studying what's observable (the muscles), researchers can learn about the unobservable (the mental state of the smiler).

Fourth, what about "forming a hypothesis of the relation between variables"? A **hypothesis** is a tentative idea that might explain a set of observations. Say you are inspired by Tiger Woods's example and decide to take golf lessons. On the course, you notice a particularly good player and ask her for tips. She says that when she's off the course, she often practices her swings mentally, imagining herself whacking the ball straight down the fairway or out of the sand trap; she assures you that the mental practice has improved her game. Well, maybe there's a connection between two **variables**—aspects of the situation that are liable to change, that can vary. Here the variables are the time spent visualizing giving the ball a good whack and the golf score. The idea appeals to you, in part because it means that you can practice even at night, or whenever you are bored, or when the course is covered with snow. But it's a hypothesis only. Before you go to the trouble of imagining yourself playing, over and over and over, you ought to test the hypothesis to find out whether it's correct.

Thus, you must go about "collecting new observations to test the hypothesis." Are there reliable studies that bear on the expert golfer's testimony? In fact, much research has been conducted on mental practice, and many studies have documented that it actually does improve performance. In a typical study, people are divided into two groups, and the performance of both groups is assessed. One group then uses mental practice for a specified period, while the other makes no preparation. Then the performance of both groups is assessed again. Usually, the people who engage in mental practice show greater improvement (Doheny, 1993; Driskell et al., 1994; Druckman & Swets, 1988; White & Hardy, 1995; Yagueez et al., 1998).

Now consider "using such evidence to formulate and support a theory." A **theory** consists of a set of principles that are supposed to explain a set of observations; in other words, the theory is an answer to the question being asked. In our example, the idea that mental practice leads to better performance is a hypothesis, not a theory. A theory might explain that mental practice works because the brain activity that allows you to perform an action is also induced when you practice mentally, and thus after mental practice, the appropriate processes are more efficient when you later engage in the actual behavior. Hypotheses and theories both produce **predictions**, expectations about specific events that should occur in particular circumstances if the hypothesis or theory is correct.

Finally, what do we mean by "testing the theory"? A theory is only a tentative answer; it must be tested. The theory of mental practice predicts that the parts of the brain used to produce a behavior—in our example, swinging a golf club—are activated by merely imagining the behavior. This prediction has also been tested by using new brain-scanning techniques to observe what happens in the brain when an individual imagines moving. And, in fact, parts of the brain used in controlling actual movements have been found to be activated when the movements are only imagined (Jeannerod, 1994, 1995; Kosslyn et al., 1998; Parsons, 1987, 1994; Parsons & Fox, 1998). Each time a theory makes a correct prediction, the theory is supported, and each time it fails to make a correct prediction, the theory is weakened. If enough of its predictions are unsupported, the theory must be rejected and the data explained in some other way. A good theory is *falsifiable;* that is, it makes predictions it cannot "squirm out of." A falsifiable theory can be rejected if the predictions are not confirmed.

Having examined all the steps of the scientific method, you can now use it to evaluate a claim. Say you've heard that putting a crystal under your bed will focus cosmic energies and improve your athletic ability. Should you believe this? First, you specify the problem, phrasing it as a question: Can crystals under beds improve performance? Second, you systematically observe events: Perhaps you notice that on days after the members of a golf team place crystals under their beds, they do perform better. Third, from those data you form a hypothesis: Something about the crystals themselves, not the beliefs of the players who use them or any other

Hypothesis: A tentative idea that might explain a set of observations.

Variable: An aspect of a situation that can vary, or change.

Theory: A statement of a set of underlying principles that are supposed to explain a set of observations.

Prediction: An expectation about specific events that should occur in particular circumstances if a theory or hypothesis is correct.

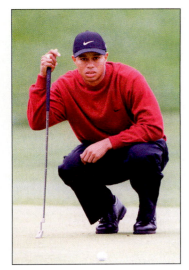

Would putting a crystal ball under his bed make him play better?

factors, is responsible for the improvement. Fourth, you test the hypothesis: Before some of Tiger Woods's games, you sneak a crystal under his bed, making sure he never knows when it is there and when it isn't; then you observe whether he plays better on post-crystal days. Fifth, if the hypothesis is supported and Woods *does* play a better game on days after a crystal was under his bed, you would need a theory to explain how the crystal works (for example, you might hypothesize that it somehow alters the magnetic field of the earth). Finally, you would test the theory: You might put the crystal in a magnetically shielded box and see whether the crystal still raises Tiger's level of play.

The Psychologist's Toolbox: Techniques of Scientific Research

Although all sound investigations rely on the scientific method, the different areas of psychology often pose and answer questions differently. Psychologists use a variety of research tools, each with its own advantages and disadvantages.

Experimental Design

Independent variable: The aspect of the experimental situation that is intentionally varied.

Dependent variable: The aspect of the experimental situation that is measured as an independent variable is changed; the value of the dependent variable *depends on* the value of the independent variable.

Much psychological research relies on conducting experiments, controlled situations in which variables are manipulated. The variables in a situation—for example, "time spent in mental practice" and "change in golf score"—are the aspects of a situation that can vary. The experimenter deliberately alters one aspect of a situation, which is called the **independent variable**, and measures another, called the **dependent variable.** In other words, the value of the dependent variable *depends on* the value of the independent variable (see Figure 1.2). In our mental practice/golf improvement example, the amount of time participants in the experiment spent in mental practice was the independent variable (it was deliberately varied), and the golf score was the dependent variable (it was measured). By examining the link between independent and dependent variables, a researcher hopes

Figure 1.2   Relationship Between Independent and Dependent Variables

The independent variable is the aspect of the situation that is intentionally varied, such as whether a person engages in mental practice (*top left*) or not (*bottom left*); the dependent variable is the aspect of the situation that is measured, such as subsequent performance on the golf course.

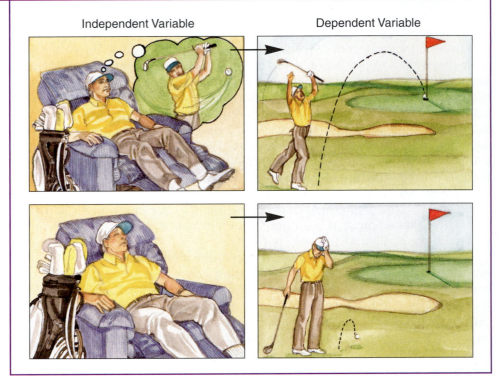

Independent Variable   Dependent Variable

to discover exactly which factor is causing an **effect**, the difference in the dependent variable that results from a change in the independent variable. In our golf example, the effect is the degree of improvement from the first assessment of performance (before mental practice) to the second assessment (after mental practice).

Once researchers have found a relation between two variables, they need to test that relation to rule out other possible explanations for it. Say we had tested only one group, the one that used mental practice. The fact that these players improved would not necessarily show that mental practice works. Why? Perhaps simply practicing during the first test session (before the mental practice) is enough to cause an improvement by the second test session. Or perhaps people are simply more relaxed at the time of the second test session, and that is why they perform better. **Confounds**, or **confounding variables**, are other possible aspects of the situation that have become entangled with the aspects that you have chosen to vary. Confounds thus lead to results that are ambiguous, that do not have a clear-cut interpretation.

One way to disentangle confounds is to use a **control group**. A control group is a second group that is treated identically in the course of the experiment *except* with regard to the one variable you want to study. A good control group holds constant—or controls—all the variables in the experimental group except the one of interest. In the mental practice experiments, the experimental group does mental practice; the control group does not. If the kinds of people assigned to the two groups differ markedly, say, in age, gender, or previous athletic experience (or all three), those factors could be confounds that would mask a clear reading of the experiment's results, because any difference in the group's golf play could have been caused by those elements. In a properly conducted experiment, therefore, participants are assigned *randomly*—that is, by chance—to the experimental and the control groups, so that no biases can sneak into the composition of the groups.

Similarly, you can use a **control condition**, either for a single person or for a group of people. Instead of testing a separate control group, you test the same group another time, keeping everything the same as in the experimental condition except for the single independent variable of interest. You are using a control condition when on some nights you *don't* put a crystal under Tiger Woods's bed. To avoid confounding the order of testing with the condition (experimental versus control), you would test half the people in the control condition first and half in the experimental condition first, or would carefully balance the order of conditions for a single person.

A particularly dramatic example of a confounding variable in everyday life was present during the Victorian age. At this time in history, some women were considered frail and delicate creatures, at least partly because they seemed prone to fainting spells. Did they faint because of their "inner natures" or for some other reason? Consider the fact that many of these women wore extremely tight corsets to give them tiny waists. In fact, the corsets were so tight that women could only take shallow breaths—if they took a deep breath, they ran the risk of being stabbed by the whale bone "stays" in the corset. These stays were thin and very sharp, and not only could cause a bloody wound, but also could puncture a lung! One consequence of continued shallow breathing is dizziness—hence the fainting spells common among stylish Victorian women. These fainting spells were viewed as evidence of a weak nature and frail constitution. How could you design an experiment to show conclusively that the corsets were to blame? How do you think views of women would have been different if men had worn tight corsets too?

Quasi-Experimental Design

One element of a true experiment is that the assignment of participants to the different groups is random. But in the real world, it is not always possible to achieve randomness, and so sometimes designs must be *quasi-experimental* (*quasi* means "as

Effect: The difference in the dependent variable that is due to changes in the independent variable.

Confound (or confounding variable): An independent variable that varies along with the one of interest and could affect what is measured.

Control group: A group that is treated exactly the same way as the experimental group, except for the one aspect of the situation under study—the independent variable—and so holds constant, or controls, all of the other variables.

Control condition: Like a control group, but administered to the same participants who receive the experimental condition.

During Victorian times, some women were considered frail and delicate. However, there were confounding variables, such as the fact that their corsets were so tight, they couldn't take a deep breath.

Correlation: An index of how closely interrelated two measured variables are; the higher the correlation, the better the values of one variable predict the values of the other.

if" in Latin). Say you want to discover whether the effects of mental practice are different for people of different ages, so you decide to test four groups of people: teenagers, college students, middle-aged people, and the elderly. Obviously you cannot assign people to the different age groups randomly. You should control for as many variables (such as health and education level) as you can to make the groups as similar as possible; however, the real world does not always cooperate, and it may be necessary to use special statistical techniques after you have established the groups to remove the effects of potential confounds. Similarly, if you want to track changes over time (for example, the happiness of single mothers as their children grow older), it is not possible to assign people randomly to the groups as time goes by because you are taking measurements only from people you have measured before. In all these examples, participants are not assigned randomly to groups, and such quasi-experiments rely on comparing multiple groups or multiple sets of measurements taken over time, attempting to eliminate potential confounds as much as possible.

Correlational Research

Experiments and quasi-experiments allow researchers to zero in on exactly what variables cause what effects. But sometimes it is not possible to do an experiment or even a quasi-experiment, particularly if you are interested in studying large groups or if it is difficult (or unethical) to manipulate the variables. Let's say you want to answer this question: Does intelligence increase with body size? Not only is there a problem in assigning randomly to groups people who have different levels of intelligence, but it is also unethical to manipulate a person's body size. For a question like this, not even a quasi-experiment can be performed.

In such situations, researchers use another method to study the relations among variables, a method that relies on the idea of **correlation**. Correlation is a relationship in which changes in the measurements of one variable are matched by changes in the measurements of another variable. Thus, a correlation is an index of how closely related two measured variables are. Figure 1.3 illustrates three predicted correlations between variables. The more tightly the numbers cluster around the line, the higher the correlation. A *positive correlation* means that the

Figure 1.3   Strength of Correlation

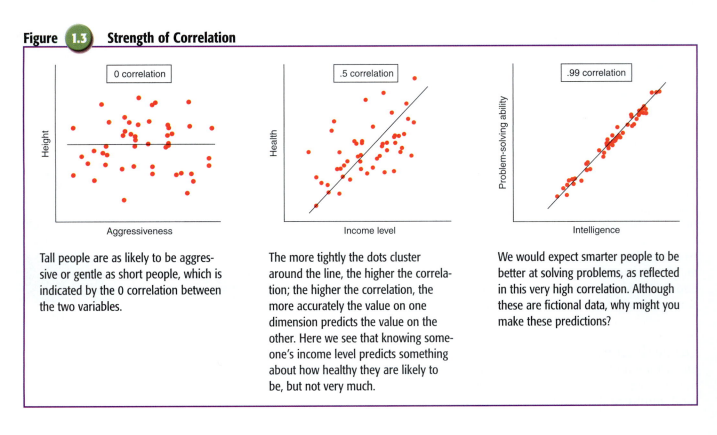

Tall people are as likely to be aggressive or gentle as short people, which is indicated by the 0 correlation between the two variables.

The more tightly the dots cluster around the line, the higher the correlation; the higher the correlation, the more accurately the value on one dimension predicts the value on the other. Here we see that knowing someone's income level predicts something about how healthy they are likely to be, but not very much.

We would expect smarter people to be better at solving problems, as reflected in this very high correlation. Although these are fictional data, why might you make these predictions?

values of one variable increase as the values of another variable increase. Conversely, a *negative correlation* means that the values of one variable increase as the values of another decrease. If we had plotted "sickness" instead of "health" in the middle panel, the line would have gone down—and the correlation we plotted would have been −.4 instead of +.4.

Correlational research involves measuring at least two things about each of a set of individuals or groups (or measuring the same individuals or groups at a number of different times), and looking at the way one set of measurements goes up or down in tandem with another set of measurements; correlations always compare one pair of measures at a time. For example, researchers have found that the lower the level of a chemical called monoamine oxidase (MAO) in the blood, the more the person will tend to seek thrills (such as sky diving and bungee jumping) (Zuckerman, 1995). Thus there is a negative correlation between the two measures: as MAO levels go down, thrill seeking goes up.

The main advantage of correlational research is that it allows researchers to compare variables that cannot be manipulated directly. The main disadvantage is that correlations indicate only that two variables tend to vary together, not that one causes the other. Does the correlation between MAO levels and thrill seeking mean that a low level of MAO *causes* the behavior? No. We don't know whether MAO level causes the behavior or vice versa—or if some other chemical, personality trait, or social factor causes the levels of both MAO and thrill seeking to vary. Remember: *Correlation does not equal causation*. Nevertheless, the existence of correlations does allow us to make predictions.

Naturalistic Observation

Essential to the scientific method is careful observation, and some researchers specialize in collecting data from real-world settings. As we noted earlier, observation—usually—precedes the formulation of a testable hypothesis; in fact, a set of careful observations often suggests a hypothesis. Some comparative psychologists use this method to study animal behavior in the wild and, say, consider to what degree it resembles human behavior; developmental psychologists use observation to study children interacting with caregivers; social psychologists use it to study people in shopping malls. This work is not simply the collecting of impressions, but of specific documented observations that can be repeated by others. For example, researchers observing caregivers found that they change their language and speech patterns when talking to young children, using short sentences and speaking in a high pitch. This speech modification, originally dubbed "motherese," is now often called *child-directed speech* (Morgan & Demuth, 1996; Snow, 1991, 1999).

Although naturalistic observation is an essential part of science, it does not provide explanations. You cannot control for confounded variables, and you cannot change the variables to see what the critical factor in a particular mental process or behavior might be. The discovery of child-directed speech does not tell us whether caregivers use it to help children understand them, or to entertain them, or simply to imitate other caregivers they have heard. In science, observing an event is only the first step.

Case Studies

Sometimes nature performs unique experiments that change an independent variable in a novel way. For example, accidents can cause damage to specific parts of the brain that affects the victim's thoughts, feelings, or behavior; depending on which part of the brain has been damaged, different abnormalities occur. A **case study** focuses on a single instance of a situation, examining it in detail. Many neuropsychologists study individual brain-damaged patients in depth to discover which abilities are "knocked out" following certain types of damage (in Chapter 2 you will read about a young soldier who, after suffering brain injury, had bizarre visual impairments). A psychologist who studies abnormal behavior might study

Case study: A scientific study that examines a single instance of a situation in detail.

a reported case of multiple personalities to discover whether there's anything to the idea (books such as *Sybil* and *The Three Faces of Eve* describe such cases in great detail), and a cognitive psychologist may investigate how an unusually gifted memory expert is able to retain huge amounts of information almost perfectly.

Unlike naturalistic observation, case studies permit experimentation (such as testing the ability of the memory expert to recall lists of familiar versus unfamiliar things, or to remember words versus pictures) and can help us understand the particular situation in detail. Nevertheless, as with other forms of research, we must always be cautious about *generalizing* from the one case; that is, we must be careful in assuming that the findings in the case study extend to all other similar cases. Any particular person may be unusual for many reasons and so may not be at all representative of people in general.

Surveys

A **survey** is a search for information, usually in the form of a set of questions put to the participants about their beliefs, attitudes, preferences, or activities. Surveys are a relatively inexpensive way to collect a lot of data fairly quickly, and they are popular among psychologists who study personality and social interactions. Surveys provide data that can be used to formulate or test a hypothesis. However, as with introspection, the value of surveys is limited by what people are capable of reporting accurately. You would not use a survey to ask people how their brains work, or to report subtle behaviors, such as body language, that they may engage in unconsciously. Moreover, even if they are capable of answering, people may not always respond honestly; as we note in Chapter 7, this is especially a problem when the survey touches on sensitive personal issues, such as sex. And even if people do respond honestly, what they say does not always reflect what they do. We cite a classic example in Chapter 13 in which restaurant managers were asked whether they would serve Chinese people; although most said they would not, when Chinese people had actually come to their restaurants, virtually all served them without question (La Piere, 1934). Finally, not everyone who is asked to respond does in fact fill in the survey. Because a particular factor (such as income or age) may incline some people, but not others, to respond, it is difficult to know if you are justified in generalizing from the respondents to the rest of the group of interest.

Survey questions have to be carefully worded so that they don't lead the respondent to answer in a certain way and yet still get at the data of interest. In the survey mentioned earlier in which the respondents had to decide which was worse, a mate having sex with or becoming emotionally involved with someone else, people who disliked both possibilities equally had no way to say so, and the forced choice would not reflect their true position.

In short, when you see the results of a survey in the news, ask yourself whether people are capable of reporting what they think about the topic, whether they would be likely to report honestly, whether their opinions are likely to predict their behavior, whether the sample was representative of the group of interest, and whether the wording invited particular responses—if so, none of the other variables matters.

Meta-Analysis

Science is a community effort. Usually many people are conducting studies on the same problem, each one painting additional strokes onto an emerging picture. **Meta-analysis** is a technique that allows researchers to combine results from different studies. This is particularly useful when results have been mixed, with some studies showing an effect and some not. Meta-analysis can determine whether a relationship exists among variables that transcends any one study, a strand that cuts across the entire set of findings.

Sometimes results that are not evident in any individual study become obvious in a meta-analysis. Why? Studies almost always involve observing or testing a

Survey: A set of questions, typically about beliefs, attitudes, preferences, or activities.

Meta-analysis: A technique that combines the results from different studies to discover patterns in the data.

sample from the **population;** the sample is the group that is measured or observed, and the population is the entire set of relevant people or animals (perhaps defined in terms of age, gender, or race). The crucial fact is that there is always variation in the population. Just as people vary in height and weight, they also vary in their behavioral tendencies, cognitive abilities, and personality characteristics. Thus, samples taken from the population will vary, and if a sample is relatively small, the luck of the draw could obscure an overall difference that actually exists in the population. For example, if you stopped the first two males and first two females you saw in a shopping mall and measured their heights, the females might actually be taller than the males. The problem of variation in samples is particularly severe when the difference of interest—the effect—is not great. If men averaged 8 feet tall and women 4 feet tall, small samples would not be a problem; you would quickly figure out the usual height difference between men and women. But if men averaged 5 feet 10 inches and women averaged 5 feet 9 inches, you would need to measure many men and women before you were assured of finding the difference. Meta-analysis is a way of combining the samples from many studies, giving you the ability to detect even subtle differences or relations among variables (Rosenthal, 1991). Table 1.3 summarizes the major methods used by psychologists.

TABLE 1.3 **Summary of Research Methods**

Experimental design	Participants are assigned randomly to groups, and the effects of manipulating one or more independent variables on a dependent variable are studied.
Quasi-experimental design	Experiments in which participants are not assigned to groups randomly.
Correlational research	Relations among different variables are documented, but causation cannot be inferred.
Naturalistic observation	Observed events are carefully documented.
Case study	A single instance of a situation is analyzed in depth.
Survey	Investigation requires participants to answer specific questions.
Meta-analysis	The results of many studies are combined in a single overall analysis to discover underlying general patterns in the data.

Be a Critical Consumer of Psychology

No technique is always used perfectly, so you must be a critical consumer of all science, including the science of psychology. Metaphorically speaking, there are no good psychologists on salt-free diets—we take everything with at least a grain of salt! Whenever you read a report of a psychological finding in a newspaper, a journal article, or a book (including this one), look for aspects of the study that could lead to alternative explanations. You already know about the possibility of confounds; here are a few other issues that can cloud the interpretation of experiments.

Reliability: Count on It!

Not all data are created equal; some are better than others. One way to evaluate data is in terms of **reliability.** Reliability means consistency. A reliable car is one you can count on to behave consistently in the same way, starting even on cold mornings and not dropping random parts on the highway. A reliable study is one that can be replicated—that is, repeated with the same results. When you read a result, find out if it has been replicated; if it has, then you can have greater confidence that the findings are reliable.

Sample: The group from which a researcher obtains measures or observations.

Population: The entire set of relevant people or animals.

Reliability: A study is reliable if it yields the same results when repeated.

Validity: What Does It Really Mean?

Something is said to be *valid* if it is well grounded in the facts, if its claims are justifiable. A study may be reliable but not valid. **Validity** means that a study provides a true measure of what it is *meant* to measure.

To understand the concept of validity, it is useful to see what it is like to be a participant in a study. This is one of many mini-demonstrations built into this text to help you apply what you learn as you read. Before reading further, try this exercise. Table 1.4 contains a list of words. Decide whether the first word names a living object or a nonliving one (circle the word "living" at the right if it is living; otherwise move to the next word); then decide whether the second word begins with the letter *t* (circle the words "begins with *t*" if it does; otherwise move to the next word); then decide whether the third word names a living or a nonliving object, whether the fourth word begins with the letter *t*, and so on, alternating judgments as you go down the list. Please do this now.

TABLE 1.4 What's in a Word?

Circle the word or words on the right if the word on the left has the named property; otherwise, move on to the next word. After you finish the list, read on.

salmon	living	trout	living
tortoise	begins with *t*	donkey	begins with *t*
airplane	living	teapot	living
toad	begins with *t*	house	begins with *t*
guitar	living	table	living
goat	begins with *t*	terrain	begins with *t*
timber	living	tiger	living
automobile	begins with *t*	rosebush	begins with *t*
snake	living	bacteria	living
tent	begins with *t*	carpet	begins with *t*
toast	living	staple	living
television	begins with *t*	tricycle	begins with *t*

When you have finished marking the list, take out a piece of paper and (without looking!) write down as many of the words as you can. How many words from the list were you able to remember?

The standard result from this kind of study is that people will remember more words after making a living/nonliving judgment than after making a *t*/non-*t* judgment (for example, see Craik & Tulving, 1975). This result is usually interpreted to mean that the more we think about (or "process") the material, as we must to make the living/nonliving decision, the better we remember it; for the *t* words, we only need to look at the first, not think about the named object at all. In fact, if we are forced to think about something in detail but don't consciously try to learn it, we end up remembering it about as well as if we *did* try to learn it (we discuss this curiosity more in Chapter 5).

Does this demonstration of differences in memory following differences in judgment really bear out this interpretation? What if you remembered the words you judged as living/nonliving better because you had to read the whole word to make the required judgment, but you only looked at the first letter of the other words to decide whether they began with *t*? If this were the case, your better memory of words in the living/nonliving category would have nothing to do with

Validity: A measure is valid if it does in fact measure what it is supposed to measure.

"thinking about it more." Therefore, the experiment would not be valid—it would not be measuring what the investigator designed it to measure.

When you read a result, always try to think of as many interpretations for it as you can; you may be surprised at how easy this can be. And if you can think of an alternative interpretation, see whether you can think of a control group or condition that would allow you to tell who was right, you or the author of the study.

Bias: Playing With Loaded Dice

Sometimes beliefs, expectations, or habits alter how participants in a study respond or affect how a researcher sets up or conducts a study, thus influencing its outcome. This leaning toward a particular result, whether conscious or unconscious, is called **bias**, and it can take many forms. One form of bias is **response bias**, in which people have a tendency to respond in a particular way regardless of their actual knowledge or beliefs. For example, many people tend to say yes more than no, particularly in some Asian cultures (such as Japanese). This sort of bias toward responding in "acceptable" ways is a devilish problem for survey research. Another form of bias is **sampling bias**, which occurs when the participants or items are not chosen at random but instead are selected so that an attribute is over- or underrepresented. Back to the shopping mall: What if you measured the males outside a toy store (and so were likely to be measuring little boys), but measured the women outside a fashion outlet for tall people (and so were likely to find especially tall women)? Or, what if the words in the living/nonliving group in Table 1.4 were interesting words such as *centipede* and *boomerang* and the words in the *t*/non-*t* group were bland words such as *toe* and *broom*? Or, perhaps the living/nonliving words were more emotionally charged than the *t*/non-*t* words, or were more familiar. What if only language majors were tested, or only people who read a lot and have terrific vocabularies? Could we assume that all people would respond the same way? Take another look at Table 1.4; can you spot any potential confounds?

A dramatic example of sampling bias occurred in the state of Florida on election night, November 7, 2000. Based on surveys of voters exiting their polling places, the TV commentators predicted that Al Gore would win the presidential election, not George W. Bush. The news organizations that conducted the surveys, however, did not factor in how absentee voters would cast their ballots. The absentee voters included many members of the armed services, who tend to vote Republican. In such a close election, sampling only from those who voted on election day produced a biased view of how the entire population voted.

Experimenter Expectancy Effects: "Making It Happen"

Clever Hans, a horse that lived in Germany in the early 1890s, apparently could add (Rosenthal, 1976). When a questioner (one of several) called out two numbers to add, say, "6 plus 4," Hans would tap out the correct answer with his hoof. Was Hans a genius horse? Was he psychic? No. Despite appearances, Hans wasn't really adding. He *seemed* to be able to add, and even to spell out words (with one additional tap for each letter in the alphabet), but he responded only if his questioner stood in his line of sight and knew the answer. The questioner, who *expected* Hans to begin tapping, always looked at Hans's feet right after asking the question—thereby cuing Hans to start tapping. When Hans had tapped out the right number, the questioner always looked up—cuing Hans to stop tapping. Although in fact Hans could neither add nor spell, he was a pretty bright horse: He was not trained to do this; he "figured it out" on his own.

The cues offered by Hans's questioners were completely unintentional; they had no wish to mislead (and in fact some of them were probably doubters). But unintentional cues such as these lead to **experimenter expectancy effects**, which occur when an investigator's expectations lead him or her (consciously or unconsciously) to treat participants in a way that encourages them to produce the expected results.

A good experiment uses a **double blind design.** Not only is the participant "blind" to (unaware of) the predictions of the study and so unable consciously or

Bias: Occurs when previous beliefs, expectations, or habits alter the participants' responses or affect the design or conduct of a study.

Response bias: A tendency to respond in a particular way regardless of knowledge or beliefs relevant to performing the task correctly.

Sampling bias: Occurs when the participants or items are not chosen at random, so that an attribute is over- or underrepresented.

Experimenter expectancy effects: Occur when an investigator's expectations lead him or her (consciously or unconsciously) to treat participants in a way that induces the expected results.

Double blind design: An experimental procedure in which the participant is "blind" to (unaware of) the predictions of the study (and so cannot try, consciously or unconsciously, to produce the predicted results), and the experimenter is "blind" to the condition assigned to the participant (and so cannot induce the predicted results).

unconsciously to serve up the expected results, but also the experimenter is "blind" to the condition assigned to the participant and thus unable to induce the expected results. What would have happened if a questioner of Clever Hans had not known the answer to the question?

Psychology and Pseudopsychology: What's Flaky and What Isn't?

Are you a fire sign? Do you believe your Zodiac sign matters? So many people apparently do that the opening page for the Yahoo! search engine on the World Wide Web will provide your horoscope every day. But astrology, along with palm reading and tea-leaf reading and all their relatives, is not a branch of psychology; it is **pseudopsychology**. Pseudopsychology is not just "bad psychology," which rests on poorly documented observations or badly designed studies and thus has questionable foundations. Pseudopsychology is not psychology at all. It may look and sound like psychology, but it is superstition or unsupported opinion pretending to be science.

Some people claim to have supernormal "psychic" powers, such as the ability to read minds. These claims can be treated as hypotheses, but until they are supported by clear-cut research results, they cannot be regarded as psychology.

But appearances can be misleading. Consider extrasensory perception (ESP). Is this pseudopsychology? ESP refers to a collection of mental abilities that do not rely on the ordinary senses or abilities. Telepathy, for instance, is the ability to read minds. This sounds not only wonderful but magical. No wonder people are fascinated by the possibility that they, too, may have latent, untapped, extraordinary abilities. The evidence that such abilities really exist is shaky, as discussed in Chapter 3. But the mere fact that many experiments on ESP have come up empty does not mean that the experiments themselves are bad or "unscientific." One can conduct a perfectly good experiment, guarding against confounds, bias, and expectancy effects, even on ESP. Such research is not pseudopsychology.

Let's say you want to study telepathy. You might arrange to test pairs of participants, with one member of each pair acting as "sender" and the other as "receiver." The sender and receiver both would look at hands of playing cards that contained the same four cards. The sender would focus on one card (say, an ace), and would "send" the receiver a mental image of the chosen card. The receiver's job would be to guess which card the sender is seeing. By chance alone, with only four cards to choose from, the receiver would guess right about 25% of the time. So the question is, can the receiver do *better* than mere guesswork? In this study, you would measure the percentage of times the receiver picks the right card, and compare this to what you would expect from guessing alone.

But wait! What if the sender, like the questioners of Clever Hans, provided visible cues (accidentally or on purpose) which have nothing to do with ESP, perhaps smiling when "sending" an ace, grimacing when "sending" a two. A better experiment would have sender and receiver in different rooms, thus controlling for such possible confounds. Furthermore, what if people have an unconscious bias to prefer red over black cards, which leads both sender and receiver to select them more often than would be dictated by chance? This difficulty can be countered by including a control condition, in which a receiver guesses cards when the sender is not actually sending. Such guesses will reveal response biases (such as a preference for red cards), which exist independently of messages sent via ESP.

Whether ESP can be considered a valid, reliable phenomenon will depend on the results of such studies. If they conclusively show that there is nothing to it, then people who claim to have ESP or to understand it will be trying to sell a bill of goods—and engaging in pseudopsychology. But as long as proper studies are under way, we cannot dismiss it as pseudopsychology.

Pseudopsychology: Theories or statements that look like psychology but are in fact superstition or unsupported opinion pretending to be science.

Ethics: Doing It Right

Let's say that Tiger Woods wants to learn how to overcome pain so that he can practice hard even when he is hurt, but that practicing when injured might cause long-term damage to his body. Would it be ethical for a sport psychologist to teach Tiger—or anyone else—techniques for continuing to work out through damaging pain? Or, what if Tiger developed a "block" that impaired his playing. Would it be ethical for a therapist to treat him with new, unproven techniques?

Ethics in Research

Following World War II, people were horrified to learn that the Nazis had performed ghastly experiments on human beings. The war trials in Nuremberg led directly to the first set of rules, subscribed to by many nations, outlawing these sorts of experiments.

Sometimes the actions of psychologists also call for a set of rules, especially when participants' rights conflict with a research method or clinical treatment. Certain methods are obviously unethical; everybody knows not to cause people in experiments to become addicted to drugs to see how easily they can overcome the addiction, and not to beat people to help them overcome a psychological problem. But most situations are not so clear-cut.

Research With People: Human Guinea Pigs? In 1996 some New York psychiatrists were tapping the spines of severely depressed teenagers at regular intervals to see whether the presence of certain chemicals in the spinal fluid could predict whether particular teens would attempt suicide. As required by law, the youths' parents had given permission for the researchers to draw the fluids. However, this study was one of at least ten that a court in New York brought to a screeching halt on December 5, 1996 (*New York Times*, page A1). The New York State Appeals Court found that the existing rules for the treatment of children and the mentally ill were unconstitutional because they did not properly protect these participants from abuse by researchers. However, the researchers claimed that without these studies they would never be able to develop the most effective drugs for treating serious impairments, some of which might lead to suicide. Do the potential benefits of such studies outweigh the pain they cause?

New York was more lax in its policies than many other states. California, Connecticut, Massachusetts, and Illinois do not allow researchers to conduct experiments in which the gain is not outweighed by the pain, or that have risks but do not benefit a participant directly, unless the participants themselves (not someone else for them) provide **informed consent.** Informed consent means that before agreeing to take part, potential participants in a study must be told what they will be asked to do and must be advised of the possible risks and benefits of the procedure. They are also told that they can withdraw from the study at any time without being penalized. Only after an individual clearly understands this information and gives consent by signature can he or she take part in a study.

Any study that uses funds from the U.S. government or from most private funding sources must be approved by an Institutional Review Board (IRB) at the university, hospital, or other institution that sponsors or hosts the study. The IRB monitors all research projects at that institution, not just those of psychologists. An IRB usually includes not only scientists but also physicians, clergy, and representatives from the local community. The IRB considers the potential risks and benefits of each research proposal and decides whether the study can be performed. In many universities and hospitals, researchers are asked to discuss their projects with the board, to explain in more detail what they are doing and why.

Concerns about the ethical treatment of human participants lead most IRBs to insist that participants be **debriefed**—that is, interviewed after the study about their experience. The purpose of debriefing is to ensure that they are having no negative reactions as a result of their participation and that they have understood the purposes of the study. Deceiving participants with false or misleading information is frowned on and approved only when the participants will not be harmed and the knowledge gained clearly outweighs the use of dishonesty.

Informed consent: The requirement that a potential participant in a study be told what he or she will be asked to do and possible risks and benefits of the study before agreeing to take part.

Debriefing: An interview after a study to ensure that the participant has no negative reactions as a result of participation and understands why the study was conducted.

In large parts of India, animals are not eaten (some are even considered sacred). Many in that culture may believe that animal research is not appropriate.

Research With Animals. Animals are studied in some types of psychological research, particularly studies that focus on understanding the brain. Animals, of course, can't give informed consent, don't volunteer, and can't decide to withdraw from the study if they get nervous or uncomfortable. But this doesn't mean animals are not protected. Animal studies, like human ones, must have the stamp of approval of an IRB. The IRB makes sure the animals are housed properly (in cages that are large enough and cleaned often enough) and that they are not mistreated. Researchers are not allowed to cause animals pain unless that is explicitly what is being studied—and even then, they must justify in detail the potential benefits to humans (and possibly to animals, by advancing veterinary medicine) of inflicting pain.

Is it ethical to test animals at all? This is not an easy question to answer. Researchers who study animals argue that their research is ethical. They point out that although there are substitutes for eating meat and wearing leather, there is no substitute for the use of animals in certain kinds of research. So if the culture allows the use of animals for food and clothing, it is not clear why animals should not be studied in laboratories if the animals do not suffer and the findings produce important knowledge. This is not a cut-and-dried issue, however, and thoughtful people disagree. As the new brain-scanning technologies improve (see Chapter 2), the need for some types of animal studies may diminish.

Ethics in Clinical Practice

Imagine a Dr. Smith who has developed a new type of therapy that she claims is particularly effective for patients who are afraid of some social situations, such as public speaking or meeting strangers. You are a therapist who has a patient struggling with such difficulties and not responding to conventional therapy. You haven't been trained in Smith therapy, but you want to help your patient. Should you try Smith therapy? According to the American Psychological Association guidelines (see Table 1.5), the answer is clear: No. If you have not been trained appropriately or are not learning the therapy under supervision, you have no business delivering it.

This sort of ethical decision is relatively straightforward. But the process of psychotherapy sometimes requires careful stepping through emotional and ethical minefields. Psychologists are bound by their states' laws of confidentiality and may not communicate about a patient without specific permission from the patient, except in certain extreme cases, as when a life or (in some states) property is at stake. Therapists have gone to jail rather than reveal personal information about their patients. Indeed, difficult cases sometimes cause new laws to be written. A patient at the University of California told a psychologist at the student health center that he wanted to kill someone and named the person. The campus police were told; they interviewed the patient and let him go. The patient then killed his target. The dead woman's parents sued the university for "failure to warn." The case eventually wound its way to California's highest court. One issue was whether the therapist had the right to divulge confidential information from therapy sessions. The court ruled that a therapist is obligated to use reasonable care to protect a potential victim. More specifically, in California (and in most other states now), if a patient has told his or her psychologist that he or she plans to harm a specific other person, and the psychologist has reason to believe the patient can and will follow through with that plan, the psychologist must take steps to protect the target person from harm, even though doing so may violate the patient's confidentiality. Similar guidelines apply to cases of potential suicide.

Further, a therapist cannot engage in sexual relations with a patient or mistreat a patient physically or emotionally. The American Psychological Association has developed many detailed ethical guidelines based on the principles listed in Table 1.5.

Source: From APA (1992), with portions abridged and adapted; for a complete description, see http://www.apa.org/ethics/code.html.

Principle A: Competence

Psychologists provide only those services and use only those techniques for which they are qualified by education, training, or experience.

Principle B: Integrity

Psychologists are honest, fair, and respectful of others in the science, teaching, and practice of psychology. In describing or reporting their qualifications, services, products, fees, research, or teaching, they do not make statements that are false, misleading, or deceptive. Psychologists avoid improper and potentially harmful dual relationships (e.g., improper friendships or sexual relationships).

Principle C: Professional and Scientific Responsibility

Psychologists uphold professional standards of conduct, clarify their professional roles and obligations, accept appropriate responsibility for their behavior, and adapt their methods to the needs of different populations.

Principle D: Respect for People's Rights and Dignity

Psychologists accord appropriate respect to the fundamental rights, dignity, and worth of all people. They respect the rights of individuals to privacy, confidentiality, self-determination, and autonomy; psychologists do not knowingly participate in or condone unfair discriminatory practices.

Principle E: Concern for Others' Welfare

Psychologists seek to contribute to the welfare of those with whom they interact professionally. In their professional actions, psychologists weigh the welfare and rights of their patients or clients, students, supervisees, human research participants, and other affected persons, and the welfare of animal subjects of research.

Principle F: Social Responsibility

Psychologists are aware of their professional and scientific responsibilities to the community and the society in which they work and live. They apply and make public their knowledge of psychology to contribute to human welfare.

LOOKING AT LEVELS

Gambling With a Mind

Schizophrenia is a devastating brain disease that often cripples a person's ability to function in the world. Research has found that its victims benefit greatly if medicated as soon as possible after the onset of the disease (DeQuardo, 1998; Johnstone, 1998; Wyatt et al., 1998). Given this finding, we have an ethical dilemma: When new treatments are created, how can we justify trying them when we know that delaying the treatments already *known* to be effective will cause long-term negative effects for the patient?

You've seen earlier how the levels approach helps us to understand psychological events, and now you can see that it also guides us in asking appropriate questions. Focusing on the level of the brain, you would consider how likely it is that a new drug or treatment will be better than available treatments. If a well-supported theory of

brain functioning leads you to be confident that a new drug will be better than the available ones, it would be easier to justify trying it. At the level of the person, you must consider whether delaying effective treatment will change how the person can function in everyday life. If the possible changes would be drastic (for example, leading the person to lose a job), a strong note of caution should temper your deliberations. At the level of the group, you might ask how the new drug might affect the person's family. Would it make him or her more irritable? less responsive? And of course, you must think about how events at the different levels could interact: If the treatment makes the patient more irritable, how will the reactions of the family affect the sufferer? Considering such concerns, what is *your* view on this dilemma?

CONSOLIDATE!

1 *What is the scientific method?* The scientific method is a way to gain objective knowledge that involves specifying a problem; systematically observing events; forming a hypothesis of the relation between variables; collecting new observations to test the hypothesis; using such evidence to formulate and support a theory; and, finally, testing the theory.

2 *What research tools can psychologists use to study mental processes and behavior scientifically?* Psychologists use experimental designs, assigning participants randomly to groups and studying the effects of one or more independent variables on a dependent variable; quasi-experimental designs, which are similar to experimental designs except that participants are not randomly assigned to groups; correlational research, in which the relations among variables are documented but causation cannot be inferred; naturalistic observation, involving careful documentation of events; case studies, which are detailed analyses of a single instance of a situation; surveys, in which participants are asked sets of specific questions; and meta-analysis, in which the results of many studies are considered in a single overall analysis.

3 *What should you look for when deciding whether to accept a study's conclusions?* The measures taken must be reliable (repeatable), valid (assess what they are supposed to assess), unbi-

ased, free of experimenter expectancy effects (leading participants to respond in specific ways), well designed (eliminating confounds and having appropriate controls), and properly interpreted (alternative accounts are ruled out).

4 *What are proper ethics in research with humans and animals?* For humans, informed consent is necessary before a person can participate in a study (informed consent requires that the person appreciate the potential risks and benefits); in the vast majority of cases, studies must be approved in advance by an Institutional Review Board (IRB); and participants must be debriefed after the study, to ensure that they have no negative reactions and to confirm their understanding of the purpose of the study. Animals must be treated humanely; animal studies must be approved in advance by the IRB; and animals cannot be caused pain or discomfort unless that is what is being studied (even then, researchers must justify the potential benefits to humans or animals).

5 *What are proper ethics in clinical practice?* Although guidelines vary across states, in general strict confidentiality is observed unless a specific person may be harmed, suicide appears to be a real possibility, or (in some states) another's property may be damaged. Therapists must not take advantage of their special relationships with patients in any way.

A DEEPER LEVEL

Recap and Thought Questions

Psychological Science: Getting to Know You

Psychology is the science of mental processes and behavior. The goals of psychology are to describe, explain, predict, and control mental processes and behavior. Psychology can best be understood by studying events at different levels of analysis: (1) The level of the brain, where we examine the activity of certain brain systems, structural differences in people's brains, and effects of various chemicals (such as hormones) on mental processes and behavior. (2) The level of the person, where we study the contents of mental processes, not just the machine that gives rise to them. The contents of our memories, beliefs, goals, feelings, and the like are part and parcel of who we are. (3) The level of the group—both our previous and our

present social interactions. Events at the different levels are interdependent and are always interacting.

How can we think about what makes Tiger Woods special and what his exceptional abilities tell us about people in general? The best approach would consider events at the different levels of analysis. For example, at the level of the brain, we would ask if there were something special about the parts of Tiger Woods's brain that control movement. At the level of the person, we would note that he was raised to have certain goals and beliefs, and we could consider how they contributed to his current success. At the level of the group, it is clear that his relationships, particularly with his parents, were crucial factors in shaping his development. These factors affect us all.

Psychology Then and Now

Psychology began as the study of mental processes, such as those that underlie perception, memory, and reasoning. The structuralists tried to understand such processes; their goal was to identify the elements of consciousness and the rules by which these elements are combined into mental structures. One of their primary methods, introspection ("looking within"), turned out to be unreliable and not always valid. The functionalists rejected the goal of identifying mental processes and how they operated in favor of seeking explanations for thoughts, feelings, and behavior. The functionalists were interested in how mental processes adapt to help people survive in the natural world. In contrast, the Gestalt psychologists also reacted against the structuralists, but they were more disturbed by the emphasis on breaking mental processes into distinct elements. The Gestaltists studied the way the brain organizes material into overall patterns, both in perception and in thinking. All of these approaches focused primarily on events at the level of the brain. Freud and his colleagues shifted focus to events at the level of the person (and, to some extent, the level of the group). Their psychodynamic theories of the mind were concerned largely with the operation of unconscious mental processes and primitive impulses (often related to sex) in dictating what we think, feel, and do. The behaviorists rejected the assumption that psychology should focus on mental processes; they urged us to stick with what we could see—stimuli, responses, and the consequences of responses. The humanists, in part reacting against the scientific approach, were interested in developing treatments of psychological problems that relied on respect for individuals and their potentials. Elements of the various strands came together in the cognitive revolution, which began by thinking of the mind by analogy to a computer program; in this view, mental processing is information processing. Today, cognitive neuroscientists study the relation between events at all three levels of analysis, with an emphasis on how the brain gives rise to thoughts, feelings, and behavior. Evolutionary psychol-

ogy treats many goals and cognitive strategies as adaptations that are the results of natural selection.

The three types of psychologists are distinguished by their training, work settings, and types of work. Clinical and counseling psychologists administer and interpret psychological tests, provide psychotherapy, offer career and vocational counseling, and help people with specific psychological problems. Academic psychologists teach and do research, in addition to helping to run their universities, colleges, or institutions. Applied psychologists use the findings and theories of psychology to solve practical problems.

If Tiger Woods were being studied by adherents of a single psychological "school," which would be least likely to produce useful insights? Most likely? When asked to account for his remarkable skill, Tiger Woods professes to have no conscious knowledge about how he plays so well. Thus, introspection would not be a useful tool for studying his abilities, and it is similarly unlikely that a structuralist approach would yield much of interest. In contrast, both behavioral (studying his responses to particular stimuli, social and physical) and cognitive (studying the way his brain processes information) approaches would be more likely to be fruitful. The quality of the results, however, would be only as good as the quality of the research designs.

The Science of Psychology: Designed to Be Valid

The science of psychology relies on the scientific method, which involves specifying a problem; systematically observing events; forming a hypothesis of the relation between variables; collecting new observations to test the hypothesis; using such data to formulate and support a theory; and, finally, testing the theory. Psychologists test hypotheses and look for relations among variables using a variety of tools, including (1) experiments, in which the effect of manipulating one or more independent variables on the value of a dependent variable is measured, and participants are assigned randomly to groups; (2) quasi-experiments, in which participants are not assigned to groups randomly; (3) correlational studies, in which the relation between pairs of variables is assessed, but shifts in one variable cannot be assumed to cause shifts in the other; (4) naturalistic observation, which involves careful observation and documentation of events; (5) case studies, which are detailed investigations of a single instance of a situation (the detailed exploration of Tiger Woods's story would be a case study); (6) surveys, in which participants answer sets of specific questions; and (7) meta-analyses, which combine the results of many studies in an attempt to discover common threads.

When reading reports of studies, you should be alert to the following: evidence that the data are reliable, which means that they can be obtained again; evidence that the data are valid, which means that they measure what they are supposed to measure; possible contamination from confounds, which are other independent variables that change along with the one of interest; biases, including a general tendency to respond in a particular way (response bias) and the nonrandom selection of participants or experimental materials (sampling bias); and experimenter expectancy effects, which are factors that convey the investigator's expectations to the participants, leading them to respond in the desired ways. In addition, the results should be appropriately interpreted—no leap of logic should be required to get from the data to the investigator's conclusions. Pseudopsychology differs from psychology not necessarily in its content, but in how it is supported by data.

Research with humans or nonhuman animals at universities, hospitals, and most industrial settings requires approval from an Institutional Review Board (IRB). For research with humans, the IRB will insist that the study include informed consent, which is information in advance about the possible risks and benefits of participation; debriefing, which is an interview after the study; and lack of deception, unless the deception is harmless and absolutely necessary. For research with animals, the IRB requires that the animals be treated well (for example, housed in clean cages) and that pain be inflicted only if that is what is studied and is justified by the benefits from the research. In clinical practice, psychotherapists have clear ethical guidelines to follow, which include maintaining confidentiality unless a specific other person (or, in some states, property) is clearly in danger or suicide is a genuine concern. In addition, therapists cannot use techniques that they have not been trained to use or engage in inappropriate personal behavior with patients.

What methods would be most appropriate for studying Tiger Woods? A case study is clearly appropriate, as we have presented the story of Woods that way, but many other methods could be used within that context. We could not only ask him questions about his beliefs and goals, but also compare his performance on attention and motor tasks to that of a matched control group. We could also correlate his feelings and other characteristics, such as the amount of sleep he had, or the amount of food or liquids he ingested on a given day, with his performance.

> **Think It Through.** Say that you read a report by Dr. Sales, an applied psychologist, that watching television commercials with the sound muted actually makes people remember the commercials better. What questions would you want to ask about the study before you would accept the results? Suppose this were a correlational study: The more people used their mute buttons during commercials, the better their memories. What possible confounding factors might account for this result? (Hint: Do you think people who mute the sound a lot watch the same amount of TV as people who tolerate the sound?) If you were going to write to an advertising firm and offer to design a better study (for a hefty fee, of course), what would you do to improve it?

REVIEW TEST

For each of the following items, choose the single correct or best answer. The correct answers appear at the end.

 1 Which of the following is not likely to happen?
   a. Events at the level of the person affect events at the level of the brain.
   b. Events at the level of the group affect events at the level of the brain.
   c. Events at the level of the person affect events at the level of the group.
   d. All are likely to happen.

 2 Which of the following statements is most likely to have been said by Freud?
   a. "The past is less important than the future in determining behavior."
   b. "The whole is greater than the sum of its parts."
   c. "The unconscious plays a powerful role in determining our behaviors."
   d. "Humans are fully aware of and responsible for their behaviors."

3 According to behaviorists, individuals will respond most vigorously when ____.
   a. they unconsciously wish to be successful
   b. they are punished intermittently
   c. they are punished for every response
   d. they are reinforced for every response

4 A ____ psychologist is likely to study how groups behave.
   a. humanistic   c. social
   b. clinical   d. personality

5 A good theory is ____.
   a. falsifiable   c. hard to find
   b. a definitive answer d. provable

6 Dr. Seever is interested in studying the effects of heroin on the motivation of lab rats to explore a maze. In this study, the independent variable is ____ and the dependent variable ____.
   a. heroin; motivation   c. motivation; heroin
   b. heroin; the rats   d. the rats; heroin

7 Dr. Charles is investigating the effectiveness of a new antipsychotic medication in reducing the hallucinations experienced by people with schizophrenia. He randomly assigns patients to three groups, two of which receive different amounts of the drug and one of which receives an inactive substance. The patients in this second group constitute the ____ condition.
   a. confounding   c. independent
   b. replication   d. control

8 A negative correlation reflects a relationship between two variables that is ____.
   a. directly proportional   c. nonexistent
   b. inversely proportional   d. causal

9 What is the main disadvantage of correlational research?
   a. The findings do not generalize to populations outside of the study.
   b. The researcher is limited to studying animals.

c. The researcher must make field observations.
   d. Causal relationships cannot be established.

10 Which of the following research techniques would offer the least control?
   a. naturalistic observation
   b. a case study
   c. a quasi-experiment
   d. an experiment

11 If there have been mixed results across many studies investigating the same phenomenon, a researcher may want to conduct a(n) ____ to combine the results of the different studies to see whether there is any finding that is consistent across them all.
   a. mixed sampling study
   b. correlational study
   c. meta-analysis
   d. observational study

12 A reliable study is one that can be ____.
   a. observed   c. validated
   b. meta-analyzed   d. replicated

13 A valid study is one that ____.
   a. makes common sense
   b. accurately assesses what it purports to assess
   c. has statistics
   d. has been replicated many times

14 An experimenter may want to have someone else code her data, someone who is not aware of her hypotheses, to avoid ____.
   a. pseudopsychology
   b. negative correlational findings
   c. sampling bias
   d. expectancy effects

15 When may a psychologist breach confidentiality?
   a. In the case of threatened homicide or suicide
   b. When his/her client threatens another individual
   c. Never
   d. When his/her client threatens suicide

ANSWERS: 1.d 2.c 3.b 4.c 5.a 6.a 7.d 8.b 9.d 10.a 11.d 12.c 13.b 14.d 15.a

2 The Brain

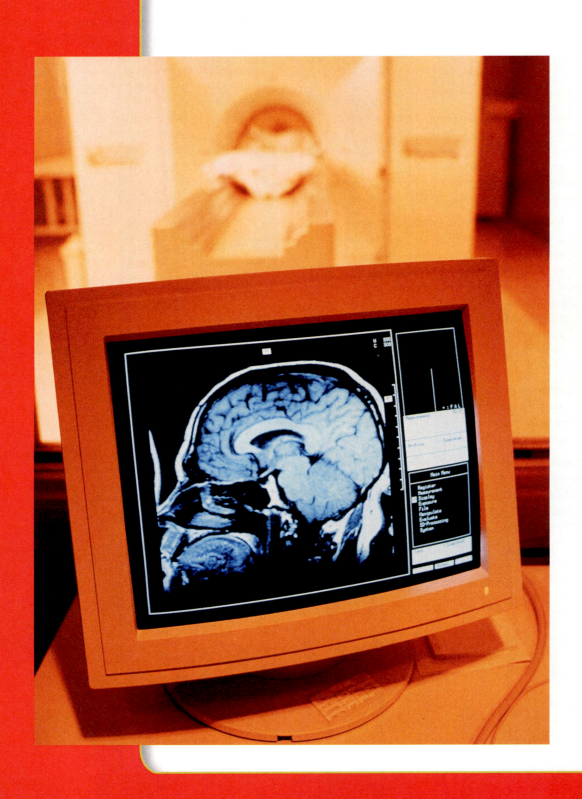

THE PSYCHOLOGICAL ORGAN

As the hard jets of water massaged the 25-year-old soldier while he showered, colorless and odorless fumes of carbon monoxide, which are known to cause brain damage, slowly seeped into the stall. Unaware that he was gradually being poisoned, the soldier continued his routine until he eventually passed out.

After the soldier was discovered and revived, doctors examined him. The young man could get around with ease, but he presented a host of bizarre symptoms. He was unable to name objects by sight, but as soon as he touched them, he could say what they were. He could identify things by smell and sound, he could name colors or identify them by pointing to a color named by someone else, and he had no difficulty recognizing familiar people when they spoke. But he couldn't identify these same people by sight alone. In fact, when he looked at his own face in the mirror, he thought he was looking at his doctor. When he was shown a rubber eraser, he identified it as "a small ball"; when shown a safety pin, he said it was "like a watch or nail clipper." When the doctors asked the soldier to inspect a picture of a nude woman and show where her eyes were, he pointed to her breasts (Benson & Greenberg, 1969).

Clearly, something was wrong with the young soldier's vision, but the problem had nothing to do with his eyes; it had to do with his brain. He couldn't get knowledge by way of his sense of sight. Why? Though he retained some aspects of his vision, he had lost others—he seemed unable to recognize what he clearly could see. The fumes the soldier had inhaled had affected his brain, but how? What, exactly, had gone wrong? To consider these questions, you need to understand how the brain works.

As you have seen, events at the level of the brain can influence many aspects of behavior, in ways not immediately apparent. If you should break your hand, you will have trouble holding a pencil: The effect of the accident is direct and mechanical. If you were in any doubt before your mishap about the role of muscle and bone in grasping and holding, you will be in no doubt now, when those abilities are distinctly impaired because muscles are torn and bones fractured. But although it is a physical organ like muscle and bone, the brain is unique: It is also a *psychological* organ, ultimately responsible for our moods of despair and elation, our sense of well-being and our sense that something's wrong, our perception of the outside world and our awareness of its meaning. The effects of an accident in the brain are no less real than a broken hand, but the path to them is less obvious (and, indeed, until recently was invisible). It is this path, through a thicket of sometimes difficult names and processes, that we must trace if we are to gain a meaningful understanding of who we are and why we behave as we do.

So, how does it work, this mysterious brain? What is it made up of; what are its building blocks? Can we ever see the brain at work? How could we find out exactly which parts of the soldier's brain were damaged? Do all our brains respond the same way to the same environmental influences? Or do different people, with different genetic makeups and life experiences, respond differently? Let's start finding out.

Brain Circuits: Making Connections

The carbon monoxide fumes that the soldier breathed interfered with his brain's ability to use oxygen, causing him to pass out. Unfortunately, he inhaled enough of these fumes that some brain cells probably died; ordinarily, brain cells begin to succumb after a few minutes without oxygen. But just saying that brain cells "died" isn't much of an explanation—that would be a little like saying that a building fell down because its molecules were rearranged. Why did the death of these cells have the effects it did?

 How do neurons work? What could cause neurons to die?

 How do chemicals allow neurons to communicate? What happens if healthy neurons can no longer communicate?

The Neuron: A Powerful Computer

All brain activity hinges on the workings of brain cells, or **neurons**. There are three types of neurons. Some, the **sensory neurons**, respond to input from the senses; others, the **motor neurons**, send signals to muscles to control movement; finally, **interneurons** stand between the neurons that register what's out there and those

Neuron: A cell that receives signals from other neurons or sense organs, processes these signals, and sends the signals to other neurons, muscles, or bodily organs; the basic unit of the nervous system.

Sensory neuron: A neuron that responds to input from sense organs.

Motor neuron: A neuron that sends signals to muscles to control movement.

Interneuron: A neuron that is connected to other neurons, not to sense organs or muscles.

Figure 2.1 **Examples of Types of Neurons**

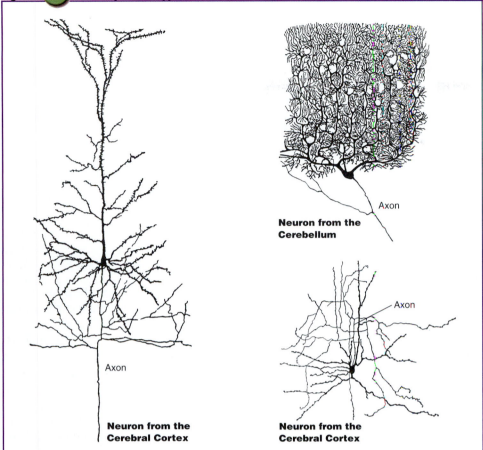

Neurons come in many shapes and sizes. Researchers are still discovering the ways in which the differences among cells affect their functioning. (From Dowling, 1992.)

Axon

Neuron from the Cerebellum

Axon

Axon

Neuron from the Cerebral Cortex

Neuron from the Cerebral Cortex

that control movement (or, they stand between other interneurons). Most of the neurons in the brain are interneurons.

Neurons differ in their size, shape, and function. Some typically excite other neurons to send signals; others typically inhibit them. Some major types of neurons are shown in Figure 2.1. Just as you can use stone to build either a hut or a palace, the same neural building blocks can build very different brains. For example, most mammals, from horses to humans, largely share the same types of neurons. But as you will see, what made Secretariat a horse and you a human is the number of neurons and how they are arranged and connected.

The average human brain contains about 100 billion neurons, plus ten times as many **glial cells** (the name comes from the Greek word for "glue"), which fill the gaps between neurons. Glial cells facilitate the communication between neurons, clean up the remains of dead neurons, and generally help in the care and feeding of neurons.

Neurons would not be much good if they did not affect other neurons or the rest of the body—how useful would your home telephone be if nobody else had one? **Brain circuits** are sets of neurons that affect one another. When one neuron in a circuit is triggered by another neuron, it in turn triggers others, and so on, causing a chain reaction. Neurons often receive and put together many inputs at the same time. The result can be the awareness that a sumptuous dessert is on the table, a command to the muscles to turn up the volume of a stereo, a sudden memory of an assignment due yesterday, a flash of feeling for an attractive classmate—anything we perceive, think, feel, or do.

Glial cell: A cell that fills the gaps between neurons, influences the communication among them, and generally helps in the care and feeding of neurons.

Brain circuit: A set of neurons that affect one another.

Figure **2.2**   **Major Parts of a Neuron**

A neuron has many parts. The
major ones are labeled here,
but much of the action occurs
internally where a complex dance
of chemicals occurs.

Structure of a Neuron: The Ins and Outs

To understand psychological events, you need to know a few facts about the structure of the neuron. As you can see in Figure 2.2, each neuron has a receiving end,
a sending end, and a part in the middle.

The part in the middle is called the **cell body.** Like all cells, it has a nucleus,
which regulates the cell's functions, and a **cell membrane,** which is the skin of
the cell. The membrane has very small holes, or pores, called **channels.** The channels open and close: When they are open, different chemicals in the surrounding
fluid flow into the cell, and substances inside the cell flow out.

The sending end of the neuron is the **axon,** the long, cablelike structure
extending from the cell body, along which signals travel to other neurons, muscles, or bodily organs. Most axons divide into many branches so that a neuron can
send a message to more than one place at a time. At the end of the axon are
terminal buttons, little knoblike structures that release chemicals into the space
between neurons when the neuron has been triggered. Most neurons communicate this way, releasing chemicals that affect other neurons, usually at their receiving end. (A few neurons, such as some of those in the eye, communicate via
electrical impulses, but this electrical communication is rare.)

Each neuron has only one sending end—that is, only one axon—but a neuron may have many receiving ends. These are the **dendrites;** their name is derived
from the Greek word *dendron,* meaning "tree," which makes sense when you look
at their shape, in Figure 2.2. The dendrites receive messages from the axons of
other neurons. Although sometimes axons connect directly to the cell body of
another neuron, the connection is usually made from axon to dendrite.

Neural Impulses: The Brain in Action

When a neuron receives enough stimulation from other neurons, some of the channels in the cell membrane open, allowing a complex exchange of **ions** (atoms that
are positively or negatively charged). This exchange works its way down to the end
of the axon, finally causing the terminal buttons to open, releasing chemicals that
will affect other neurons. The shifting change in charge that moves down the axon
is known as an **action potential.** This process, the basis of the neural communication that permits us to live in the world and respond to it, is illustrated in Figure 2.3.

Notice that the action potential obeys an **all-or-none law.** If enough stimulation reaches the neuron, it fires. In other words, the sequence of shifting charges
sends the action potential all the way down the axon, releasing chemicals from
the terminal buttons. Either the action potential occurs or it doesn't. Many neurons can fire hundreds of times a second because chemical reactions reset the neuron so it can fire again if it receives adequate stimulation.

Cell body: The middle part of a cell,
which contains the nucleus.

Cell membrane: The skin of a cell.

Channel: A small hole in the skin of cells
that can open and close.

Axon: The sending end of the neuron, or
the long cable extending from the cell
body.

Terminal button: A structure at the end
of axons that, when the neuron is triggered, releases chemicals into the space
between neurons.

Dendrite: The twiggy part of a neuron
that receives messages from the axons of
other neurons.

Ion: An atom that has a positive or negative charge.

Action potential: A shifting change in
charge that moves down the axon to the
end, causing the terminal buttons to
release a chemical signal.

All-or-none law: States that if the neuron is sufficiently stimulated, it fires, sending the action potential all the way down
the axon and releasing chemicals from the
terminal buttons; either the action potential occurs or it doesn't.

Na$^+$ channels open after the neuron is stimulated, and Na$^+$ ions rush into the cell. The inside of the cell then becomes positively charged.

The Na$^+$ channels close and the K$^+$ channels briefly open. K$^+$ goes outside the cell. (K$^+$ is pushed out because of the addition of the positively charged Na ions.)

"Na pumps" actively push Na$^+$ back outside, and K$^+$ is drawn inside, until the inside/outside concentrations are returned to baseline levels.

When you feel like stretching, does it seem as if no sooner has the thought occurred to you than your limbs are in motion—as if the physical response to the idea is instantaneous? Many people have this sense, and it comes as a surprise to realize just how slow our neurons actually are. In fact, in the fastest neurons, impulses travel only about 120 meters per second, compared with 300,000,000 meters per second for the speed of light. Even compared with the impulses traveling in a computer, our neurons are extremely slow. To convince yourself that neurons require a measurable amount of time to work, try the simple exercise described in Figure 2.4 with some friends (developed by Rozin & Jonides, 1977).

Figure **Measuring Neural Conduction Time**

Sit in a row with some friends, with each person using his or her left arm to grasp the ankle of the person on his or her left. The person at the head of the line, the leader, says "Go" and starts a stopwatch at the same time he or she squeezes the ankle of the person to his or her left; as soon as that person feels the squeeze, he or she squeezes the ankle of the next person to the left; and so on. When the last person feels the squeeze, he or she says "Done." The leader records the time.

Now repeat the exercise, but each of you should grasp not the ankle but the shoulder of the person to your left. Less time is required for the squeezes to make their way down the row when shoulders are squeezed than when ankles are squeezed. Why? Because the impulses have farther to travel when the ankle is squeezed. By subtracting the difference in times and estimating the average distance from ankle to shoulder for each person, you can actually estimate neural transmission time! This exercise should be done several times, first ankle, then shoulder, then shoulder, and then ankle; this procedure helps to control for the effects of practice in general.

Neurons would operate even more slowly were it not for the fact that most axons are covered with **myelin,** a fatty substance that helps impulses travel down the axon more efficiently. Multiple sclerosis (MS) is one of several disorders that illustrates the importance of myelin. MS causes myelin to deteriorate, which makes impulses stumble as they move down the axon. People with MS experience impaired sensation in their limbs, loss of vision, and paralysis. Could myelin loss have caused the young soldier's problem? Probably not: His visual problem was selective, whereas myelin loss creates overall problems in seeing.

Neurotransmitters and Neuromodulators: Bridging the Gap

When just one neuron in your brain fires, it might be sending a chemical message to thousands of other neurons. Each neuron is typically connected to about 10,000 others (and some neurons are connected to up to 100,000 others; Shepherd, 1999). The number of possible connections among neurons is shockingly large. In fact, Thompson (1993) has estimated that the number of possible connections in your brain is greater than the number of atoms in the universe! There are about 100,000,000,000 neurons in the brain, and if each could be connected to an average of even 10,000 others (varying which ones are connected in all combinations), the numbers of ways your brain can be "connected up" becomes . . . well, astronomical!

How do neurons actually communicate? What are the connections between them like? The site where communication between neurons occurs is the **synapse,** where an axon of one neuron sends a signal to the membrane of another neuron. In most cases, the sending and receiving neurons are not hooked up physically but are separated by a gap called the **synaptic cleft,** shown in Figure 2.5.

Figure **2.5   The Synapse**

Impulses cross between neurons at the synapse. Chemicals released at the terminal buttons cross the synaptic cleft, where they bind to receptors and trigger events in the receiving neuron.

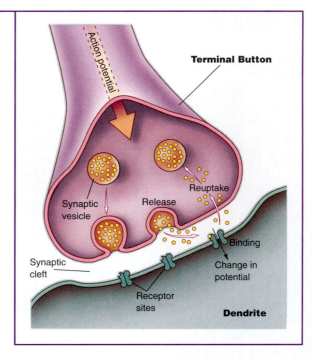

Myelin: A fatty substance that helps impulses travel down the axon more efficiently.

Synapse: The place where an axon of one neuron meets the membrane (on a dendrite or cell body) of another neuron.

Synaptic cleft: The gap between the axon of one neuron and the membrane of another, across which communication occurs.

Neurotransmitter: A chemical that sends signals from the terminal buttons on one neuron to the dendrites or cell body of another.

Neuromodulator: A chemical that alters the effects of neurotransmitters.

Chemical Messages: Signals and Modulators

As their name suggests, the chemicals that send signals, crossing from the terminal buttons across the synaptic clefts, are the **neurotransmitters.** The **neuromodulators** are chemicals that modulate, or alter, the effects of the neurotransmitters.

Imagine that you are using a pair of tin cans with a string between them as a walkie-talkie. When you speak into one can and your friend holds the other up to her ear, sound waves transmit the message. The gap from your mouth to one of the cans, and from the other can to her ear, is crossed by these waves, which carry the message. Neurotransmitters play the same role as the sound waves, allowing the message to cross the gap.

In contrast to the neurotransmitters, neuromodulators would produce the effect of tightening or loosening the string connecting the cans. When the string is drawn tight, the message is transmitted more effectively from one can to the other; when it is slackened, the sound must be louder to be heard. Other substances (which are not, strictly speaking, called neuromodulators) can affect what happens at the gap itself, for example, by affecting how quickly the neurotransmitters are removed from the synaptic cleft. Imagine that the room holding the linked tin cans has very thin air, with fewer molecules to vibrate. In this case, a louder sound would be needed to cause the bottoms of the tin cans to vibrate. On the other hand, if the air pressure were greater, a softer sound could convey the signal.

Glial cells, the cells that fill the gaps between neurons, also influence what goes on at the synaptic cleft. These cells control the amount of neurotransmitters that can reach a neuron. Some of them apparently produce substances that increase or decrease a neuron's sensitivity to inputs from other neurons (Newman & Zahs, 1998).

Receptors: On the Receiving End

What do the neurotransmitters do once they cross the gap? That depends. Each neuron has **receptors,** specialized sites on the dendrites or cell bodies that respond to specific neurotransmitters or neuromodulators. The receptor sites are the places where "messenger molecules" of the released chemicals—neurotransmitters or neuromodulators—attach themselves. A good analogy here is an ordinary lock set: The lock is the receptor, which is opened by the keylike action of a particular neurotransmitter or neuromodulator.

When neurotransmitters or neuromodulators become attached to receptors, they are said to *bind.* After binding, they can have one of two general types of effects. They can be *excitatory,* making the receiving neuron more likely to fire an action potential. Or they can be *inhibitory,* making the receiving neuron less easily triggered. Because the typical axon divides into many branches and each neuron has many dendrites, there are many binding sites, so the neuron can receive thousands of different inputs from different sending neurons at the same time. The exciting and inhibiting inputs to each receiving neuron add up or cancel one another out, and their sum determines whether and when the neuron fires an action potential down its axon.

The same neurotransmitter can have opposite effects on a neuron depending on which type of receptor accepts it, and the same chemical that can act as a neurotransmitter (sending a signal) in one context can act as a neuromodulator (altering a signal) in another (Dowling, 1992).

Not all of a given neurotransmitter released by the terminal buttons is taken up by receptors; some of it remains in the gap. Special chemical reactions are required to reabsorb—or **reuptake**—the excess neurotransmitter back into the *vesicles* (which store a neurotransmitter) of the sending neuron.

Unbalanced Brain: Coping With Bad Chemicals

By piecing together the story of how neurons communicate, scientists are not only developing a clear picture of how the brain works but also learning how its functioning can go awry and how they can use drugs to repair it. Drugs that affect the way the brain works either increase or decrease the effectiveness of neural activity. Some of these drugs are **agonists,** which mimic the effects of a neurotransmitter or neuromodulator by activating a particular type of receptor. Other drugs may actually increase the amount of a neurotransmitter, sometimes by slowing down its

Receptor: A site on the dendrite or cell body where a messenger molecule attaches itself; like a lock that is opened by one key, a receptor receives only one type of neurotransmitter or neuromodulator.

Reuptake: The process by which surplus neurotransmitter is reabsorbed back into the sending neuron so that the neuron can effectively fire again.

Agonist: A chemical that mimics the effects of a neurotransmitter (sometimes by preventing reuptake).

reuptake. Depression, for example, is currently treated by several types of drugs that affect neurotransmitters and neuromodulators, including **selective serotonin-reuptake inhibitors (SSRIs)**, which block the reuptake of the neurotransmitter serotonin. (Prozac, Zoloft, and Paxil are all SSRIs.) Still other drugs interfere with the effect of a neurotransmitter or neuromodulator. Some of these drugs are **antagonists**, which block a particular receptor. (As a memory aid, think of an "antagonist" at a party who is "blocking you" from meeting a charmer across the room.)

Could the young soldier whose vision was so strangely disrupted have had malfunctioning neurotransmitters or neuromodulators? Could such a disturbance have produced the highly selective impairments he experienced after inhaling the carbon monoxide fumes? It's possible, if just the right combinations of chemicals were disrupted. However, this scenario is unlikely. Because most neurotransmitters and neuromodulators are used widely throughout the brain, not solely in the parts of the brain involved in visual perception, we would expect their disruption to create more widespread difficulties, such as in hearing, understanding language, walking, and other functions.

We have every reason to think, however, that the soldier's difficulty with visual recognition had something to do with the operations of neurons. To understand why only some neurons were disrupted but not others, we need to look further and consider the structure of the brain. Now that you know the essentials of how neurons work, and how they affect each other via neurotransmitters and neuromodulators, you are ready to examine how neurons work within different brain structures and how their functioning can break down. First, however, let's pause to review how the effects of neurotransmitter and neuromodulator activity can ripple outward from the brain and body to profoundly change a person's life.

LOOKING AT LEVELS

Parkinson's Disease

The connection between brain and behavior is seen in the devastating effects of *Parkinson's disease,* a classic brain disorder. Named after the British physician James Parkinson, who first described the disorder in 1817, Parkinson's afflicts about half a million Americans, from every slice of life—from celebrity Michael J. Fox to the lady next door. The hands of people with Parkinson's disease shake; they may move sluggishly, with a stooped posture and shuffling walk; their limbs often seem frozen in position and resist attempts to bend them.

A piano tuner named John had to stop working because he developed Parkinson's disease. He had difficulty controlling his movements, and his behavior changed as well. He became so listless that he rarely left his house. He missed meals. And he started to contract various minor illnesses, which worsened his other symptoms.

All these changes, physical and behavioral, were caused directly or indirectly by the death of particular neurons in John's brain. In the brains of people with Parkinson's disease, cells that produce the neurotransmitter *dopamine* have died. Dopamine plays a key role in the areas of the brain that are involved in planning movements. When patients take a drug that helps produce dopamine, L-Dopa, symptoms decrease, often for a long period of time.

When John's neurons no longer produced enough dopamine, the working of his brain was affected and his muscle control impaired. Events at the level of the brain interacted with events at the level of the person: Shaky hands made it almost impossible for him to tune pianos, so John had to retire. After he gave up the work he loved, he became depressed. He began to think of himself as diseased, and he began interpreting all his behaviors in terms of his disease and predicting his future behaviors in that light. As a consequence, he lost interest in going out. Now events at the level of the person affected events at the level of the group: He stopped seeing many people, who in turn stopped seeing, and helping, him. The events in his brain influenced his feelings about himself and his relationships with other people.

Events at the different levels interact in both directions: The brain-based symptoms of shaking hands and shuffling gait became worse when John was ill from other causes, which occurred more often than before because he stopped taking care of himself; and the lack of social interactions led to his physical health deteriorating even further, making him more depressed and less likely to seek out the company of others. If John had been a member of a close-knit family, he might have had more support and suffered less loneliness and depression.

1 *How do neurons work? What could cause neurons to die?* Neurons receive input from other neurons (which themselves may be connected to a sense organ), on either their dendrites or their cell bodies. If the sum of all the inputs is strong enough, the neuron fires, sending a rapid exchange of ions across the cell membrane. This exchange works its way down the axon, until the terminal buttons release a neurotransmitter (which sends a signal) or a neuromodulator (which alters the effect of a signal). This chemical crosses the synaptic cleft to the dendrites or cell bodies of other neurons.

2 *How do chemicals allow neurons to communicate? What happens if healthy neurons can no longer communicate?* Neurons have receptors, which are like locks that can be opened by certain keys; the keys are the neurotransmitters and the neuromodulators. Depending on the properties of the particular receptors, these chemicals can excite the neuron to fire or inhibit it from firing. Agonists mimic the action of neurotransmitters or neuromodulators, whereas antagonists block their effects.

The Nervous System: An Orchestra With Many Members

Consider some additional problems experienced by the young soldier who was poisoned while taking a shower. When researchers showed him a blue page on which white letters were printed, he thought he was looking at a "beach scene"—the blue was water and the white letters were "people seen on the beach from an airplane." He could visually pick out similar objects when they were placed in front of him, but only if they were of a similar color and size. His doctors found that he could be trained to name a few everyday objects by sight as children are taught to recognize sight words on *Sesame Street* without actually reading them, but this training broke down when the color or size of the objects changed. The young man learned to name a red toothbrush as "toothbrush," but he couldn't properly name a green toothbrush, and when he was shown a red pencil, he called it "my toothbrush."

The results of the entire series of tests made it clear that the soldier could see and understand color and size, but not shape. He had *some* sense of shape, though; he didn't call the pencil a "shoe" or a "basketball" but a "toothbrush." To understand what had gone wrong in the soldier's brain, you need to know what the different parts of the nervous system do.

1 What are the major parts of the nervous system that can sustain damage?

2 What is the cerebral cortex? What are the major cortical and subcortical systems, and what do they do?

3 How do the functions of the two sides of the brain differ?

4 What parts of the brain lie under the cerebral cortex? What do these subcortical structures do?

Overview

A brain living in a vat wouldn't be of much use to anyone—it would be like a computer with no keyboard or monitor. To do its job, the brain needs both to receive

Spinal cord: The flexible rope of nerves that runs inside the backbone, or spinal column.

Central nervous system (CNS): The spinal cord and the brain.

input from the body and the outside world and to be able to act on these inputs. To understand the brain's job, then, you must see what it receives and what it sends out.

The Cranial Nerves: Cables to Command Central

The brain sends and receives information from the 12 cranial nerves, so named because they connect to the brain through holes in the cranium, the part of the skull that encloses the brain. These nerves control specific muscles, such as those responsible for eye movements; glands, such as the salivary glands; and internal organs, such as the heart and stomach. The cranial nerves also receive information from sense organs, such as the eyes, ears, nose, and those in the skin. Damage to a cranial nerve can cut off key inputs or outputs from the brain. If you weren't wearing a seat belt in an automobile accident, for example, your head might slam into the steering wheel. This could cause your brain to slosh forward and scrape along the underside of your skull. The scraping could disrupt the functioning of your olfactory nerves, and thus impair your ability to smell. This may not sound like a severe problem, but as you will see in the following chapter, smell plays a major role in taste—and food would never taste the same again.

The Central Nervous System: Reflex and Reflection

The largest conduit for information going to and from the brain is the **spinal cord**, the flexible rope of nerves that runs inside the backbone, or *spinal column*. In fact, so intimately connected is the spinal cord to the brain that the two together are called the **central nervous system (CNS)**. At each of 31 places, spinal nerves emerge from the spinal cord in pairs, one on the left and one on the right, as Figure 2.6 shows. Through these nerves the spinal cord plays a key role in sending the brain's commands to the body and in turn allowing the brain to register infor-

Figure 2.6   The Spinal Cord

Thirty-one pairs of nerves come out of the spinal cord. The nerves at the front (the ventral position) carry commands from the brain to the body, and the nerves at the back (the dorsal position) send information from the body (the internal organs and skin) to the brain.

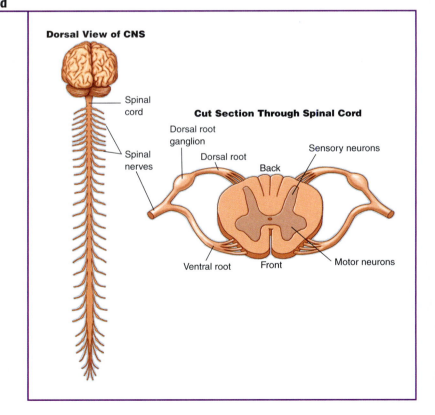

mation about the state of the body. The spinal cord also allows us, through our sense of touch, to gain information about the world.

The spinal cord isn't simply a set of cables that relays commands and information between brain and body. The spinal cord itself can initiate some aspects of our behavior, such as reflexes. A **reflex** is an automatic response to an event, an action that does not require thought. Even a simple reflex requires hundreds of neurons. How do reflexes work? When sensory neurons in the skin detect a sharp thorn, for example, they send signals that stimulate sensory neurons in the spinal cord. These neurons in turn are connected to interneurons in the spinal cord. When you jerk away from something that pricks you, interneurons have sent signals to motor neurons, which then cause the muscles to jerk, pulling your finger away from the source of pain. This arrangement allows you to respond immediately, bypassing the brain—it wouldn't pay to be lost in thought every time a threat appeared.

The Peripheral Nervous System: A Moving Story

As shown in Figure 2.7, the CNS (which consists of the brain and the spinal cord) hooks into the **peripheral nervous system (PNS)**. The PNS links the central nervous system to the organs of the body. The PNS has two parts: the autonomic nervous system and the skeletal (or somatic) system. The **autonomic nervous system (ANS)** controls the smooth muscles in the body and some glandular functions. Smooth muscles, so called because they look smooth under a microscope, are found in the heart, blood vessels, stomach lining, and intestines. Many of the activities that the ANS controls, such as digestion and circulation, are self-regulating and are usually not under conscious control. In contrast, the **skeletal system** consists of nerves that are attached to voluntary muscles; these muscles are also known as striated muscles because under a microscope they appear "striated," or striped. If you clench your fist and "make a muscle," you are using this system.

The ANS itself has two major divisions. The **sympathetic nervous system** readies an animal (including you and the authors) to cope with an emergency.

Reflex: An automatic response to an event.

Peripheral nervous system (PNS): The autonomic nervous system and the skeletal system.

Autonomic nervous system (ANS): Controls the smooth muscles in the body, some glandular functions, and many of the body's "self-regulating" activities such as digestion and circulation.

Skeletal system: Consists of nerves that are attached to striated muscles and bones.

Sympathetic nervous system: Part of the ANS that readies an animal to fight or to flee by speeding up the heart, increasing breathing rate to deliver more oxygen, dilating the pupils, producing sweat, increasing salivation, inhibiting activity in the stomach, and relaxing the bladder.

Figure 2.7 **Major Parts of the Nervous System**

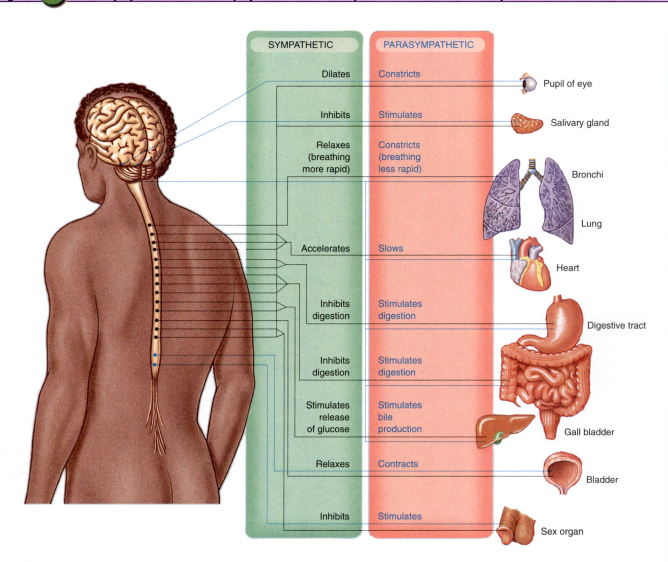

The two major branches of the ANS are the sympathetic and parasympathetic nervous systems. In general the sympathetic nervous system prepares the body to fight or flee, and the parasympathetic dampens down the sympathetic nervous system.

This system usually comes into play in response to a threat in the environment, perhaps a near-accident when you are driving in heavy traffic. As Figure 2.8 shows, the sympathetic system speeds up the heart, increases the breathing rate to provide more oxygen, dilates the pupils for greater light sensitivity and thus sharper vision, produces sweat slightly (giving your hand a better grip), slightly increases salivation, inhibits stomach activity, and relaxes the bladder. If your heart is pounding and your palms are sweaty, it's a good bet that your sympathetic system has kicked in. The overall effect of these changes is to prepare your body to react—to fight or to flee. More oxygen flows into your muscles, your vision is improved, and the rest of your body is ready to support physical exertion. The visual difficulties that plagued the young soldier also threatened the smooth operation of his sympathetic nervous system, a vital system for soldiers. Even if his sympathetic nervous system were to remain perfectly intact after carbon monoxide poisoning, because he no longer accurately recognizes objects and people, he cannot react appropriately to danger.

Fight-or-flight situations are not the only conditions that activate the sympathetic nervous system. This system also operates in circumstances that may be less extreme but nonetheless threatening, such as getting ready to give an important speech, having a conversation with a touchy authority figure, or rushing to avoid being late for an important meeting. People prone to excessive amounts of anxiety tend to have sympathetic nervous systems that overshoot the mark and get the body too revved up. They might hyperventilate (that is, breathe in too much oxygen), sweat profusely, or experience a pounding heart when there is no apparent threat. These and other unpleasant physical symptoms of anxiety occur whenever the sympathetic nervous system responds too strongly. Sweat makes your skin conduct electricity more readily, and researchers take advantage of this fact by measuring skin conductance to study arousal.

The **parasympathetic nervous system** lies, figuratively, "next to" the sympathetic system (*para* is Greek for "next to" or "alongside") and tends to counteract its effects (see Figure 2.8). The sympathetic system speeds things up, and the parasympathetic system slows them down. Heart rate slows, pupils contract, salivation increases massively, digestion is stimulated, the bladder contracts. Whereas the sympathetic system tends to affect all the organs at the same time and can be thought of as increasing arousal in general, the parasympathetic system tends to affect organs one at a time or in small groups.

The sympathetic and parasympathetic systems don't exactly have a push-and-pull relationship; they don't always work against each other. For example, an erection is caused by the parasympathetic system, but the sympathetic system controls ejaculation. If a man is too tense about sex, the sympathetic system will override the parasympathetic system, and (metaphorically speaking) desire will remain solely in the young man's heart.

The Visible Brain: Lobes and Landmarks

You've worked your way down through the spinal cord and have seen its marvelous abilities to control some behaviors. But these behaviors are very limited when viewed in light of all we can do. To understand the range of human abilities, you need to turn to the other part of the central nervous system, the brain itself.

Imagine that you could see through someone's hair and scalp, even through the skull itself. The first thing you would see under the skull are the **meninges**, three layered protective membranes that cover the brain (*meningitis* is an infection of these membranes). Under this lies a network of blood vessels on the surface of the brain itself. Viewing the brain from above—looking down through the top of the head—you can see that the brain is divided into two halves, left and right, separated by a deep fissure down the middle. Each half-brain is called a **cerebral hemisphere** (*cerebrum* is Latin for "brain") because each is shaped roughly like half a sphere. Curiously, each hemisphere receives information from, and controls the muscles of, the opposite side of the body. For example, if you are right-handed, your left hemisphere controls your hand as you write.

Each hemisphere is divided into four major parts, or **lobes:** the occipital lobe, at the back of the brain; the temporal lobe, which lies below the temples, in front of the ears, where sideburns begin to grow down; the parietal lobe, in the upper middle/rear of the brain, above the occipital lobe; and the frontal lobe, behind the forehead (see Figure 2.9 on page 56). The two halves of the brain are connected by the **corpus callosum**, which contains somewhere between 250 million and 300 million nerve fibers (some other smaller connections exist between the two halves of the brain, but they are less important).

Now, peer deeper. Immediately under the network of blood vessels on the surface of the brain is the convoluted, pinkish-gray surface of the brain itself: This is the **cerebral cortex** (*cortex* means "rind" or "shell" in Latin). This is where most

Parasympathetic nervous system: Part of the ANS that is "next to" the sympathetic system and that tends to counteract its effects.

Meninges: The covering of the brain.

Cerebral hemisphere: A left or right half-brain, roughly half a sphere.

Lobes: The four major parts of each cerebral hemisphere—occipital, temporal, parietal, and frontal.

Corpus callosum: The huge band of nerve fibers that connects the two halves of the brain.

Cerebral cortex: The convoluted pinkish-gray surface of the brain, where most mental processes take place.

Most of your brain is water; the average brain weighs about 3 pounds, but if the water were removed, it would weigh only 10 ounces; this extra material (which includes proteins and fats, as well as various types of ions) includes the neurons, glial cells, and everything else that gives the brain a structure.

Figure 2.9 The Lobes of the Brain

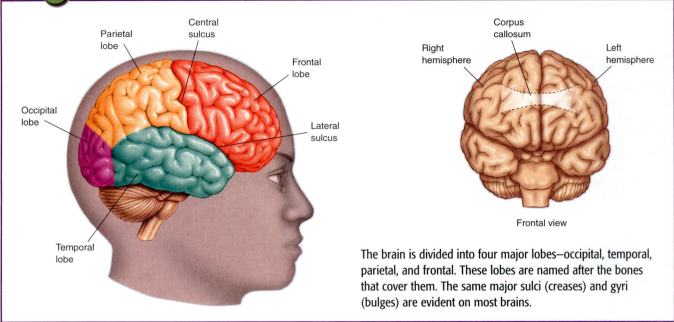

The brain is divided into four major lobes—occipital, temporal, parietal, and frontal. These lobes are named after the bones that cover them. The same major sulci (creases) and gyri (bulges) are evident on most brains.

of the brain's mental processes take place. Although the cerebral cortex is only about 2 millimeters thick, it is brimming with the cell bodies of neurons, giving the cortex its characteristic color and its nickname, "gray matter." Looking directly at the surface of the brain, you can see that the cortex has many creases and bulges, as shown in Figure 2.9. The creases are called **sulci** (the singular is sulcus), and the areas that bulge up between the sulci are the **gyri** (singular, gyrus). The cortex, so vital to our functioning, is crumpled up this way so that more of it can be stuffed into the skull.

Let's focus more closely on some of these regions of the human brain.

The Cerebral Cortex: The Seat of the Mind

Most of the neurons in the brain are located in the lobes of the cerebral cortex, and it is here that most thinking takes place. These different areas of the cortex, the lobes of each cerebral hemisphere, have different functions, and we discuss them one at a time. But always remember that the lobes do not function in isolation; they usually work in concert with one another.

Occipital Lobes: Looking Good

The **occipital lobes** are concerned entirely with different aspects of vision, and most of the fibers from the eyes lead to these lobes. If somebody were to hit you in the back of the head with a brick (an experiment we do not recommend), the "stars" you are likely to see appear because of the impact on this area. The occipital lobes contain many separate areas that work together to specify visual properties such as shape, color, and motion. Damage to these lobes results in partial or complete blindness.

Because of the way the major arteries feed blood to the back of the brain, poisoning by carbon monoxide (which displaces oxygen) often leads to scattered cell death in the occipital lobe. Our young soldier probably suffered damage to the occipital lobes, perhaps in addition to injury to other parts of the brain. Such damage often affects visual perception, making the entire world seem fuzzy and making it difficult to organize information. Still, this probably does not sufficiently

Sulcus: A fold in the cerebral cortex.

Gyrus: A bulge between sulci in the cerebral cortex that forms a crease.

Occipital lobe: The brain lobe at the back of the head; concerned entirely with different aspects of vision.

explain all of the soldier's vision problems; if this were all there was to it, why would he confuse white letters with sunbathers on the beach?

Temporal Lobes: Up to Their Ears in Work

The **temporal lobes**, which lie in front of the ears and roughly where sideburns start, play a key role in many functions, including processing sound, storing new memories, and comprehending language. Sounds are processed in the top part of the temporal lobes; visual memories of shapes are stored in the bottom. Animals that have had their temporal lobes removed are not blind (we know this because they don't bump into things), but they can no longer recognize objects by sight; their visual memories are gone. They are said to be "mindblind," a phenomenon Sigmund Freud termed *agnosia*. The soldier may have had damage in either one or both temporal lobes or in the connections from an occipital lobe to one or both temporal lobes. If the connections were damaged, only a small amount of information might now reach the part of the temporal lobes where visual memories of shapes are stored, and he might be able to take in only fragments of what he sees. This diagnosis would go a long way toward explaining his problem. For example, to see a letter, he would have to look at one segment at a time (a vertical line, then a curved line, and so on), which isn't good enough to recognize the shape of a letter as whole. The world might look to the soldier like the images in Figure 2.10.

Figure 2.10   Shattered Vision

a.

b.

c.

d.

a. Scissors handle; b. table leg;
c. telephone receiver; d. baseball hat

Some forms of brain damage may lead the victims to see only small fragments of objects at a time, as shown here. Note how hard it is to recognize these common objects based on the parts in isolation.

Parietal Lobes: Inner Space

When you recall where you left your keys, how to drive to a friend's house, or what's over your left shoulder, your **parietal lobes** (see Figure 2.9) are at work. Right now, your parietal lobes are playing a role in allowing you to define the distance between your face and the book and to shift attention to each of these words; they are even helping control your eye movements. The parietal lobes are also involved when you do arithmetic and when you think about the relationships among objects in space.

Part of each parietal lobe, right behind the central sulcus (which runs across the brain, roughly at right angles to the fissure between the hemispheres; see Figure 2.11 on page 58), is the **somatosensory strip**. This area registers sensation on your body. In fact, sensations from each part of your body are registered in a specific section of this strip of cortex. Tickling your toes, for example, activates neurons in the cortex next to the area devoted to stimulation from your ankle, as you

Temporal lobe: The brain lobe under the temples, in front of the ears, where sideburns begin to grow down; among its many functions are visual memory and hearing.

Parietal lobe: The brain lobe at the top, center/rear of the head, involved in registering spatial location, attention, and motor control.

Somatosensory strip: The gyrus, located immediately behind the central sulcus, that registers sensation on the body and is organized by body part.

Figure 2.11   **The "Homunculus" of the Somatosensory Strip**

The somatosensory strip is organized so that different parts of the body are registered by adjacent portions of cortex; the size of the picture indicates the amount of tissue dedicated to that part of the body.

can see in Figure 2.11. Larger areas of the cortex correspond to areas of the body that are more sensitive (notice the amount of space devoted to lips and hands).

Frontal Lobes: Leaders of the Pack

Probably the most dramatic difference between the appearance of a human brain and a monkey brain is how much the human brain bulges out in front of the central sulcus. The size and development of the **frontal lobes** are one of the features that make us uniquely human. The frontal lobes are critically involved in speech, the search for specific memories, reasoning (including the use of memory in reasoning), and emotions. These crucial lobes also contain the **motor strip** (also called the *primary motor cortex*), which is located in the gyrus immediately in front of the central sulcus. The motor strip controls fine movements and, as with the somatosensory strip, is organized in terms of parts of the body. Relatively large areas of this strip of cortex are dedicated to those parts of the body that we control with precision, such as the hands and mouth.

Hints about the functions of the frontal lobes, like other parts of the brain, have emerged from studies of patients with brain damage. Phineas Gage, the foreman of a gang of workers building a railroad in Vermont late in the nineteenth century, is perhaps the most famous case of a patient with damage to the frontal lobes. Gage's unfortunate loss was psychology's gain, as researchers were able to observe the consequences of damage to this vital area of the brain. The story began when Gage became distracted as he was packing blasting powder into a hole in rock. When the metal bar he was using to pack in the powder accidentally hit the rock, it created a spark, which set off the powder. The metal bar, like a spear shot from a cannon, went right through the front part of his head, flew high in the air, and landed about 30 meters behind him. Miraculously, Gage lived, but he was a changed man. Previously, he had been responsible and organized; he now led a disorderly life. He couldn't stick to any decision, had little self-control, and his formerly decent language was now laced with profanity (Macmillan, 1986, 1992). Like Phineas Gage, people with damage to the frontal regions of the brain have difficulty reasoning.

A computer-reconstructed picture of the path taken by the metal bar as it passed through Phineas Gage's skull.

Frontal lobe: The brain lobe located behind the forehead; the seat of planning, memory search, motor control, and reasoning, as well as numerous other functions.

Motor strip: The gyrus, located immediately in front of the central sulcus, that controls fine movements and is organized by body part; also called the *primary motor cortex.*

The Dual Brain: Thinking With Both Barrels

Researchers have long suspected that the cortex of the two cerebral hemispheres, left and right, play distinct roles in cognition. This idea has even made it into the popular culture; Saab, for example, once advertised that its cars satisfied both the left and right brains (implying that other cars were seriously lacking, by half). What do the hemispheres do differently?

Split-Brain Research: A Deep Disconnect

The most compelling evidence to date that the two half-brains perform distinct functions has come from looking at the effects of severing the connection between the two hemispheres. When this is done, neuronal impulses no longer pass from one hemisphere to the other. Patients who have undergone this surgery are called **split-brain patients.** Why would such drastic surgery be performed? This procedure has been used to help patients with severe, otherwise untreatable epilepsy. *Epilepsy* is a disease that causes parts of the brain to go into spasm, leading to bodily convulsions; in severe form, it prevents sufferers from leading a normal life. Cutting the corpus callosum prevents the spasm that originates in one hemisphere from reaching the other hemisphere, and thus the whole brain does not become involved in the convulsions and their severity is thereby lessened. Ida McKinley, the wife of President William McKinley, apparently experienced such seizures. During these spells, she lost consciousness but nevertheless remained upright in her chair. When others were present, President McKinley would put a handkerchief over her face and continue his conversation (Seuling, 1978).

Although it is easy to see how cutting the corpus callosum would decrease the severity of epileptic convulsion, the full effects of this procedure on mental processes cannot be understood without discussing vision. As shown in Figure 2.12, the left half of each eye is connected directly to the left hemisphere, but not to the right hemisphere; similarly, the right half of each eye is connected directly, and only, to the right hemisphere. (Note that it's not that the left eye is connected only to the left hemisphere, and the right only to the right.) Thus, if you stare straight ahead, objects to the left are seen first by the right brain, and those to the right are seen first by the left brain. If the corpus callosum is cut, the input stays

Figure 2.12   The Eyes, Optic Chiasm, and Cerebral Hemispheres

Eye

Optic
nerve

Optic
chiasm

Lateral
geniculate
nucleus

Visual
cortex

The backs of the eyes are actually parts of the brain pushed forward during development; the left half of each eye is connected only to the left cerebral hemisphere, whereas the right half of each eye is connected only to the right cerebral hemisphere.

Split-brain patient: A person whose corpus callosum has been severed for medical reasons, so that neuronal impulses no longer pass from one hemisphere to the other.

Figure **2.13** **Gazzaniga and LeDoux Experiment**

The right hemisphere of split-brain patients is capable of understanding and responding to simple stimuli, but not speaking about them. Thus, the left hemisphere will sometimes make up stories to explain actions that are based on the right hemisphere.

in the hemisphere that receives the information; in normal people, it also crosses over to the other side.

What are the practical effects of this division? One way to find out is to present pictures or words to the left or right side (fast enough so that the participant can't move his or her eyes to look directly at them). In a classic study of a split-brain patient, illustrated in Figure 2.13, Gazzaniga and LeDoux (1978) presented a picture of a snow scene to the right hemisphere (which controls the left hand) and, at the same time, a picture of a chicken's claw to the left hemisphere (which controls the right hand and, usually, speech). The patient was then shown several other pictures and asked to choose which of them was implied by the stimulus. The patient used his right hand (controlled by the left hemisphere) to select a picture of a chicken, and his left hand (controlled by the right hemisphere) to select a picture of a shovel. The investigators then asked the patient what he had seen. "I saw a claw and I picked a chicken," he replied. Because the left hemisphere controls almost all of speech, it described what the left hemisphere saw. The patient continued: "And you have to clean out the chicken shed with a shovel." The left hemisphere did not actually know what the right hemisphere had seen, so it made up a story. The left hemisphere, in right-handed people (and most left-handed people), not only controls most aspects of language but also plays a crucial role in interpreting the world, in making up stories, and in many forms of reasoning (Gazzaniga, 1995; LeDoux et al., 1977).

Hemispheric Specialization: Not Just for the Deeply Disconnected

Perhaps you've wondered whether you are a "left-brain person" or a "right-brain person." It's often said that the left brain is analytical and verbal, whereas the right brain is intuitive and perceptual. In fact, these generalizations must be made with caution. For example, the left brain is actually better than the right at some types of perception (such as determining whether one object is above or below another; Hellige & Michimata, 1989; Kosslyn et al., 1989), and the right brain is better than the left at some aspects of language (such as making the pitch of the voice rise at the end of a question or understanding humor; Bihrle et al., 1986; Brownell et al., 1984; Ellis & Young, 1987). Moreover, the abilities of the two hemispheres often differ only in degree, not in kind. A major exception to this generalization is language; many aspects of language are carried out by a single hemisphere, usually the left.

Although researchers have not yet been able to pinpoint precisely all of the ways in which the two hemispheres differ, they do know that in normal people the two hemispheres work together. The hemispheres appear to have adopted the strategy of division of labor, with both operating at the same time to carry out different aspects of a task. For example, in perception, the left hemisphere captures the details of a shape while the right captures the overall shape (Delis et al., 1986; Robertson & Delis, 1986; Robertson et al., 1988); in language comprehension, the left hemisphere registers the literal meaning of a message while the right extracts metaphors and allusions (Brownell et al., 1984).

Could it be that the young soldier with difficulties in visual recognition had suffered a functional deficit in his right hemisphere that prevented him from being able to see the overall shapes of objects? The right temporal lobe in particular appears to play a key role in recognizing overall shapes (Ivry & Robertson, 1998). After such damage, he would have had to rely on his left hemisphere, which tends to register details only, not overall shape.

Beneath the Cortex: The Inner Brain

Some parts of the brain lie deep beneath the cortex and so are called *subcortical*. These parts are often similar to the corresponding parts of other animals' brains, which leads some people to think that subcortical areas are somehow simpler than the more recently evolved parts of the brain. Not so. These areas often carry out extraordinarily complex tasks. Moreover, the inner brain is intimately connected with the cortex. Although the examiners of the young soldier did not mention this, it is likely that the soldier became lethargic after his accident—as is typical of people who have suffered brain damage. But why would brain damage cause someone to be less vigorous? The answer lies in the connections between the cortex and inner parts of the brain that are concerned with motivation and emotion. The most important of these subcortical areas are illustrated in Figure 2.14 on page 62. Together with the cortex, most of these structures are considered to be part of the **forebrain** (so called because in a four-legged, horizontal animal such as a rat, these areas are at the front); but given their great variety of function, this traditional category is not very useful.

Thalamus: Crossroads of the Brain

The **thalamus** is often compared with a switching center but could also be likened to an airline hub where planes converge and then take off for far-flung destinations. The sensory systems, such as vision and hearing, and the motor systems that control muscles send fibers to the thalamus, which routes their signals to other parts of the brain. The intricate connections of the thalamus appear to explain a puzzling phenomenon reported by patients who have had a limb amputated. These people sometimes have the sensation that the limb is still there; they feel a *phantom limb*. Davis and her colleagues (1998) studied the thalamus in such patients and found that mild electrical stimulation of the thalamus produced sensations that seemed to come from the missing limb. Moreover, phantom limb sensations can be painful, and mild electrical stimulation of the thalamus has been found to relieve the pain.

The thalamus is also involved in attention; as a matter of fact, at this very second your thalamus is allowing you to fix your attention on each word you read. The thalamus is also involved in sleep control. The thalamus plays such a critical

Forebrain: The cortex, thalamus, limbic system, and basal ganglia.

Thalamus: A subcortical region that receives inputs from sensory and motor systems and plays a crucial role in attention; often thought of as a switching center.

Figure **2.14** **Key Subcortical Brain Areas**

Many of the parts of the brain needed for day-to-day living are located beneath the cortex, such as those illustrated here.

Hypothalamus: A brain structure that sits under the thalamus and plays a central role in controlling eating and drinking, and in regulating the body's temperature, blood pressure, and heart rate.

role in daily life that if it is badly damaged, the patient will die, even if the cortex remains untouched.

Hypothalamus: Thermostat and More

The **hypothalamus** sits under the thalamus, as illustrated in Figure 2.15. The small size of this structure shouldn't fool you: It is absolutely critical for controlling many bodily functions, such as eating and drinking; keeping body temperature, blood pressure, and heart rate within the proper limits; and governing sexual behavior. The hypothalamus also regulates hormones, such as those that prepare an animal to fight or to flee when confronted by danger. Again, if visual recognition is impaired, as in the case of our young soldier, this organ would not receive the information it needs to function properly. If confronted by an enemy in the field, the soldier would not be able to register the information required to cause the right chemicals to flow into his bloodstream to marshal the body's resources for fight or flight.

Figure **2.15** **The Limbic System**

These are the key structures that make up the "limbic system," which plays a role in emotions and other psychological events.

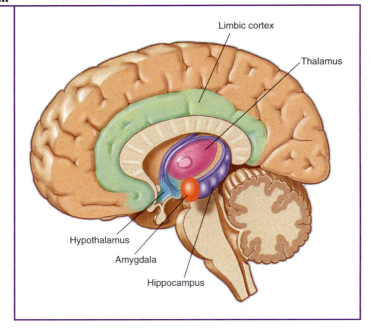

Hippocampus: Remember It

The **hippocampus** is a structure that looks something like a seahorse (at least to some people), which explains its name, from the Greek *hippokampos*, a mythological "seahorse" monster. This structure plays a key role in allowing us to store new information in the brain's memory banks. The role of the hippocampus was vividly illustrated by the case of patient H.M., who had his hippocampus (and nearby structures) removed in an effort to control his epilepsy. After the operation, his doctors noticed something unexpected: H.M. could no longer learn new things (Milner et al., 1968). His memory for events that occurred a year or so before the operation seemed normal, but he was stuck at that stage of his life. Each day began truly anew, with no memory of what had occurred earlier—in fact, he could not even remember what had happened a few minutes ago, let alone hours or days. Later, more careful study revealed that, in fact, he also could not remember events that had occurred in the year or so before the operation (Squire, 1987). H.M. does not seem particularly aware of his deficit, and when one of us interviewed him years after the operation, he was in good spirits and remarkably comfortable with himself. When asked about the meanings of words that were coined after his operation, he gamely offered definitions, suggesting, for example, that a jacuzzi is a "new kind of dance." He didn't seem to notice what was missing in his life. (Perhaps this is a case of the left hemisphere telling stories to fill in gaps, as Gazzaniga and LeDoux noted in their study of a split-brain patient.)

Patients such as H.M. led researchers eventually to discover that the hippocampus plays a key role in storing new information in memory. If the young soldier had damage to the occipital or temporal systems that register visual input, these areas would not feed the proper information to the hippocampus—and thus he would not be able to store in memory the stimuli he saw.

Amygdala: Inner Feelings

The **amygdala** is an almond-shaped structure (its name means "almond" in ancient Greek) near the hippocampus. The amygdala plays a special role in emotions such as fear and anger. Ralph Adolphs and his colleagues (1996) described a patient who had a rare disorder that destroyed both of her amygdalae (there is one in each hemisphere); this patient not only had difficulty expressing emotion but also had lost the ability to read fear in the facial expressions of other people. The young soldier probably couldn't register emotions very well either—he couldn't even tell when he was seeing a face. Adolphs's patient could recognize faces, but not the emotions on them.

The hypothalamus and amygdala play crucial roles as bridges between the CNS and the PNS. Indeed, both are key components of the **limbic system**, shown in Figure 2.15. The limbic system has long been thought of as being involved in the basics of emotion and motivation: fighting, fleeing, feeding, and sex. But each of the structures in this "system" is now known to have distinct roles that do not involve these functions (for example, the hippocampus is crucially important in storing new memories); further, other brain structures, outside this set, also play a role in emotion. For these reasons, some researchers regard the very concept of a "limbic system" as out of date (LeDoux, 1996).

Basal Ganglia: Getting in the Habit

The **basal ganglia**, positioned to the outer sides of the thalami, are involved in planning and producing movement. These structures have rich connections with parts of the frontal lobes that are also involved in controlling movement. Neurons in part of the basal ganglia have been found to fire right before an animal makes an intentional movement (Iansek & Porter, 1980). Moreover, people with Parkinson's disease, which produces trembling and impairs movement, often have abnormal basal ganglia; the functioning of this structure depends crucially on dopamine.

Hippocampus: A subcortical structure that plays a key role in allowing new information to be stored in the brain's memory banks.

Amygdala: A subcortical structure that plays a special role in fear and is involved in other sorts of emotions, such as anger.

Limbic system: A set of brain areas, including the hippocampus, amygdala, and other areas, that has long been thought of as being involved in fighting, fleeing, feeding, and sex.

Basal ganglia: Subcortical structures that play a role in planning and producing movement.

The basal ganglia also play a critical role in a particular type of learning: forming a habit. When you learn to put your foot on the brake automatically at a red light, the basal ganglia are busy connecting the stimulus (the light) with your response (moving your foot). As discussed in Chapters 4 and 5, this system is distinct from the one used to learn facts (the one, that, presumably, is at work right now, as you read this page).

Brainstem: The Brain's Wakeup Call

As illustrated in Figure 2.14, at the base of the brain are structures that feed into, and receive information from, the spinal cord. These structures are often collectively called the **brainstem**. The **medulla**, at the lowest part of the lower brainstem (see Figure 2.14), is important in the automatic control of breathing, swallowing, and blood circulation. The brainstem also contains a number of small structures together called the **reticular formation**, which has two main parts. The "ascending" part, the *reticular activating system (RAS)*, plays a key role in keeping you awake and making you perk up when something interesting happens. The RAS produces neuromodulators (as do several other specialized structures deep in the brain) that affect the operation of many other parts of the brain. Neurons of the RAS have long axons that reach up to other parts of the brain and alter the functioning of distant neurons. Some of these structures play a critical role in sleep, arousal, and attention; when the connections from these structures to the cerebral cortex are disrupted, the cortex may receive less activating input from these subcortical structures. It is this kind of disruption in particular that would have caused the soldier to be sluggish following the damage to his brain. The "descending" part of the reticular formation receives input from the hypothalamus and is important in producing autonomic nervous system reactions. It is also involved in connecting impulses from muscles not under voluntary control to those under voluntary control (such as those used in swallowing and speech).

The **pons** is a bridge (*pons* is Latin for "bridge") connecting the brainstem and the cerebellum; it is involved with a variety of functions, ranging from sleep to control of muscles used to form facial expressions.

Cerebellum: Walking Tall

The **cerebellum** is concerned in part with physical coordination. If your cerebellum were damaged, you might walk oddly and have trouble standing normally and keeping an upright posture. In addition, damage to some parts of the cerebellum might disrupt your ability to estimate time or to pay attention properly. The surface area of the cerebellum is nearly the same as that of the entire cerebral cortex, and hence it will not be surprising if this structure turns out to be involved in many cognitive functions. The medulla, pons, and cerebellum are often grouped together as the **hindbrain**, so named because they lie at the rear end of the brain of a horizontal animal such as a rat; the other brainstem structures form the **midbrain**, which lies between the hindbrain and forebrain.

The Neuroendocrine System: It's Hormonal

You now know that the central nervous system can affect the body not only by moving muscles voluntarily, but also by moving muscles automatically and by influencing the autonomic nervous system. In addition, some structures in the brain affect the body by producing (or causing to be produced) certain chemicals. For example, something happens during puberty that changes a child's body into an adult's and changes the child's behavior as well. Charming boys and sweet girls can become sullen and rebellious, moody and impulsive. That "something" is hormones. **Hormones** are chemicals that are produced by glands and can act as neuromodula-

Brainstem: The set of neural structures at the base of the brain, including the medulla and pons.

Medulla: The lowest part of the lower brainstem, which plays a central role in automatic control of breathing, swallowing, and blood circulation.

Reticular formation: A two-part structure in the brainstem; the "ascending" part plays a key role in keeping a person awake and alert; the "descending" part is important in producing autonomic nervous system reactions.

Pons: A bridge between the brainstem and the cerebellum that plays a role in functions ranging from sleep to control of facial muscles.

Cerebellum: A large structure at the base of the brain that is concerned in part with physical coordination, estimating time, and paying attention.

Hindbrain: The medulla, pons, and cerebellum.

Midbrain: Brainstem structures that connect the forebrain and hindbrain, including the reticular formation.

Hormone: A chemical produced by glands that can act as a neuromodulator.

Figure **2.16** **The Major Endocrine Glands**

The locations of major glands in the body.

tors. The CNS hooks into the **neuroendocrine system,** which makes hormones that affect many bodily functions. The CNS not only regulates this system, but also receives information from it—which in turn alters the way the CNS operates.

Figure 2.16 shows the locations of the major *endocrine glands;* endocrine glands secrete substances into the bloodstream, as opposed to other glands, such as sweat glands, that excrete substances outside the body. Some hormones affect sexual development and functioning. Among these, **testosterone** causes boys to develop facial hair and other external sexual characteristics, as well as to build up muscle, and **estrogen** causes girls to develop breasts and is involved in the menstrual cycle. Some hormones affect the levels of salt and sugar in the blood, and others help the body cope with stressful situations. The outer layer of the adrenal glands produces **cortisol,** which helps the body cope with the extra energy demands of stress by breaking down protein and fat and converting them to sugar; the sugar provides energy to the body, increases blood flow, and allows you to respond more vigorously and for a longer period of time.

A part of the brain called the **pituitary gland** is particularly interesting because its hormones actually control the other glands; for this reason it has sometimes been called the "master gland." But master or not, this gland is still controlled by the brain, primarily via connections from the hypothalamus. If information from the world isn't interpreted properly by the young soldier's cortex, it won't have the normal effect on the hypothalamus, which in turn will not produce the normal hormonal response.

The Neuroimmune System: A Healthy Brain in a Healthy Body

Finally, the brain plays a major role in regulating the **immune system,** which protects the body from disease by producing chemicals and specific types of cells to fight invasions by foreign organisms. A field called *psychoneuroimmunology* has emerged

Neuroendocrine system: The system regulated by the CNS, that makes hormones that affect many bodily functions; also provides the CNS with information.

Testosterone: The hormone that causes males to develop facial hair and other sex characteristics and to build up muscle volume.

Estrogen: The hormone that causes breasts to develop and is involved in the menstrual cycle.

Cortisol: A hormone produced by the outer layer of the adrenal glands that helps the body cope with the extra energy demands of stress by breaking down and converting protein and fat to sugar.

Pituitary gland: The "master gland" that regulates other glands but is itself controlled by the brain, primarily via connections from the hypothalamus.

Immune system: The system that protects the body from disease by developing chemicals and specific types of cells to fight against foreign organisms.

to focus on the ways in which mental and emotional states affect the immune system. For example, researchers have found that elderly traditional Chinese people are more likely to die right after the Chinese New Year than just before it, whereas orthodox Jews show no difference in mortality rates during this period. However, the pattern is exactly reversed around the High Holy Days, the most important days in the Jewish year; it is now the Jews who hold on until the holidays are over and Chinese people who are unaffected (Phillips & Smith, 1990; Phillips et al., 1992). What does this have to do with the neuroimmune system? People probably live longer because their bodies are fighting off whatever ailment is killing them. In fact, Spiegel and his colleagues (Spiegel, 1994, 1997) have found that women with breast cancer who take part in groups that offer emotional support live longer than those who do not—and this effect may occur because these same people have more of a type of blood cell (part of the immune system) that removes foreign bodies (Spiegel et al., 1998). As you will see in Chapter 10, there is no question about it: The brain affects the immune system. Researchers know that the hypothalamus has something to do with this, but the details of how are just now being discovered.

LOOKING AT LEVELS

Brain Damage and Divorce

At this point, it should be clear that damage to various parts of the brain can have wide-ranging effects on the victim's life. Damage to the left side of the brain can disrupt the ability to produce and understand language. Damage to the right side can disrupt speech patterns, making the voice flat and robotic. The lore in neurology wards (which to our knowledge has never been studied directly) is that more patients with right-hemisphere damage than left-hemisphere damage end up divorced. The reason? It seems that even though the left-hemisphere damage may disrupt language (sometimes leaving the patient able to mutter little more than a few words), this is less troublesome to an intimate relationship than losing the ability to express emotional nuance.

Think about this possibility from the perspective of the three levels of analysis. A damaged brain can leave some aspects of thinking, feeling, and behavior impaired. This disruption can alter basic aspects of personality—of the self. Emotional expressiveness, for example, is an aspect of personality so important that it may have crucial roles at the level of the group: People respond differently if emotional expressiveness is lacking than if other aspects of behavior have been altered by brain damage. Such considerations lead us to predict that right-hemisphere damage will in fact impede intimate relationships. However, note that even if intimate relationships are harmed or even destroyed by the absence of expressed emotion, in other relationships, such as in business, this particular deficit may be less catastrophic than losing one's memory, perception, or language abilities. The likely consequences of brain damage on someone's life depend on the kind of damage, the sort of person he or she was prior to the injury, and the kinds of relationships at the center of his or her life.

CONSOLIDATE!

1. **What are the major parts of the nervous system that can sustain damage?** All parts of our nervous systems are vulnerable, from the cranial nerves, to the spinal cord, to the brain itself or the peripheral nervous system.

2. **What is the cerebral cortex? What are the major cortical systems, and what do they do?** The cortex is a thin (about 2 mm) layer of neurons on the surface of the brain. Most cognitive functions depend crucially on the cortex. The major cortical systems are organized into the functions of the four major lobes. The occipital lobe is the first part of the cortex to process visual input in detail. The temporal lobe receives inputs from the occipital lobe and is the seat of visual memories. It is also involved in language comprehension and hearing, storing new memories, and some aspects of consciousness. The parietal lobe registers three-dimensionality and location in space. This lobe, which is also involved in arithmetic, attention, and motor control, includes the somatosensory strip, which registers sensation from parts of the body. Different regions of the

somatosensory strip register input from different parts of the body, with larger areas being devoted to more sensitive parts of the body. The frontal lobes are involved in producing speech, searching for memories, reasoning, and making decisions. The frontal lobes contain the motor strip, which controls fine motor movements. The motor strip is organized so that larger areas are devoted to parts of the body that we can control more precisely.

3 *How do the functions of the two sides of the brain differ?* The left hemisphere plays a larger role in language, and the right hemisphere plays a larger role in spatial attention and nonverbal functions. The left brain appears to play a critical role in inventing stories to make sense of the world. However, these differences are usually matters of degree, and both hemispheres often can perform all functions to some extent. A major exception to this generalization is that most aspects of language are restricted to a single hemisphere (typically the left).

4 *What parts of the brain lie under the cerebral cortex? What do these subcortical structures do?*

The thalamus is often thought of as a switching center; its many separate parts handle connections to and from distinct parts of the brain. Attention depends on portions of the thalamus. The hypothalamus controls many bodily functions, such as eating, drinking, and sex. It is also critically involved in regulating hormones. The hippocampus plays a key role in storing new memories in the brain, and the amygdala is involved in fear and other emotions. The hippocampus, amygdala, and other structures make up the limbic system, which is essential for fighting, fleeing, feeding, and sex. The basal ganglia are important in planning and producing movements, as well as in learning new habits. The brainstem contains a number of structures, many of which are crucial for alertness, sleep, and arousal; damage to these structures would cause sluggishness. The cerebellum is noteworthy because its cortex is about as large as the cortex covering the outer brain (the cerebral cortex) and thus may prove to have important roles in cognitive processes. This structure is involved in motor control, timing, and attention.

Probing the Brain

Having toured the major parts of the brain and noted their major functions, you can make a pretty good guess about what areas of the brain were damaged when the soldier suffered carbon monoxide poisoning. We cannot know for sure, given the limitations of the tests available at the time of his accident, in 1966. Today, however, doctors can obtain impressive high-quality images of a living brain. These images can show damage to particular brain structures and record brain activity, or the disruption of it, in specific areas.

1 What can researchers learn about the brain's function by studying behavior following brain damage?

2 What techniques allow us to record the activity of neurons in the brain as they function?

3 How can different parts of the brain be stimulated to see whether they are working properly?

4 What is neuroimaging?

The Damaged Brain: What's Missing?

The first evidence that different parts of the brain do different things came from *natural experiments*, accidents in which people suffered damage to the brain. Such damage typically produces a region of impaired tissue, called a **lesion**. The most frequent source of damage is a **stroke**, which occurs when blood, with its life-sustaining nutrients and oxygen, fails to reach part of the brain (usually because a clot clogs up a crucial blood vessel), causing neurons in the affected area to die.

Lesion: A region of impaired tissue.

Stroke: A result of the failure of blood (with its life-giving nutrients and oxygen) to reach part of the brain, causing neurons in that area to die.

In such cases, researchers study the patients in two ways: First, they are interested in the way function breaks down: which abilities tend to be impaired together and which tend to be impaired separately. Such data provide clues about the way information is stored (for example, by category, such as fruits versus vegetables) (Hart et al., 1985) and how it is processed (for example, reading by converting text to sounds versus recognizing the written word directly) (Shallice & Warrington, 1980). Second, researchers try to relate the *location* of the damage to subsequent behavioral problems. Say, for example, that the young soldier had a lesion in the right temporal lobe and thereafter was unable to perceive overall shapes. The link between the two events offers a hint about one function of this area of the brain.

Strokes are acts of nature. To test specific theories, researchers sometimes remove specific parts of animal brains. If the theory specifies that an area has a particular function, then damage to that area should disrupt all tasks that require that function. However, lesioning studies do not provide a complete picture of brain function, and thus this technique has been supplemented by other methods.

Recording Techniques:
The Music of the Cells

Rather than having to rely on the indirect evidence supplied by damaged brains, researchers can now make use of several methods to record the activity of normal brains.

To some extent, brain activity can be measured by making an electromagnetic recording. In one version of this technique, an **electroencephalograph (EEG)** machine records electrical current produced by the brain, as shown in Figure 2.17. When neurons fire, they produce electrical fields. Researchers can record electrical activity in response to a particular stimulus or can record the activity over time; the result is a tracing of these "brain waves" of electrical fluctuation called an **electroencephalogram** (see Figure 2.17). It is through EEGs, for example, that psychologists learned that people go through distinct stages of sleep marked by different types of brain activity (see Chapter 10 for a detailed discussion of these stages).

Figure 2.17   The Electroencephalograph

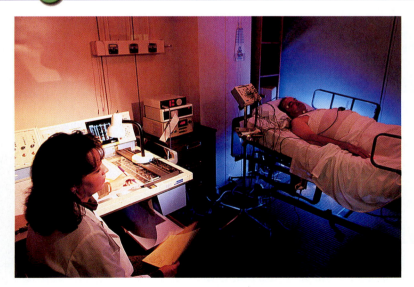

Relaxed/rest

Task performance

The top image shows an EEG during relaxed rest, whereas the bottom image shows an EEG during performance of a task; clearly, the brain is more active when an individual is performing a task than when he or she is relaxed.

This equipment allows researchers to record electrical activity on the scalp, which reflects electrical activity in the brain.

In addition, in *single-cell recording,* tiny probes called **microelectrodes** can be placed in individual cells in the brain; these record the firing rates of neurons. A typical microelectrode is at most only 1/10 as wide as a human hair (and some are only 1/100 as wide!). Microelectrodes are sometimes put in human brains before brain surgery to find out what a part of the brain does before it is cut. Studies with microelectrodes have yielded some fascinating results. For example, when people look at words, some neurons respond to specific words but not others (Heit et al., 1988).

Stimulation: Tickling the Neurons

To come closer to detecting just what neurons do, researchers can also stimulate them and observe the results. Three kinds of stimulation studies have been used to find out what parts of the human brain do.

In one technique, mild electricity is delivered to parts of the participant's brain, and the person is then asked to report what he or she experiences. Wilder Penfield and his colleagues (Penfield & Perot, 1963; Penfield & Rasmussen, 1950) pioneered this method with patients who were about to undergo brain operations. Penfield reported that people experience different images, memories, and feelings depending on the area in the brain that is stimulated. A problem with this method, however, is that researchers cannot be sure whether actual memories are activated or whether the participants are making up stories.

In a second, recently developed method, **transcranial magnetic stimulation (TMS),** researchers stimulate the brain by putting a wire coil on a person's head and discharging a large current through the coil, thus creating a magnetic field. This magnetic field is so strong that it causes a cluster of neurons under it to fire. Using this technique, for example, researchers can make a person's fingers move by shifting the coil over the parts of the brain that control the fingers (in the motor strip) and producing on/off magnetic pulses (Pascual-Leone et al., 1997; Pascual-Leone et al., 1998).

In the third type of stimulation study, electrodes are placed on the surface of a human brain or inside it (in preparation for brain surgery), and researchers observe which activities are disrupted when current is applied (Ojemann, 1983; Ojemann et al., 1989). Like TMS, this method is limited because stimulating particular neurons can lead to the activation of remote neurons, and these other neurons could produce the observed effects.

Neuroimaging: Picturing the Living Brain

Today if you had an emergency like the young soldier's, you would probably be rushed to a hospital and immediately have your brain scanned. Your doctors would order the procedure to determine both the structural damage (which areas were physically affected) and the functional deficits (which areas were performing below par). Because they yield an actual picture of neuronal structure and function, scanning techniques are referred to as **neuroimaging.** It is fair to say that neuroimaging techniques have transformed psychology, allowing researchers to answer questions that were hopelessly out of reach before the mid-1980s (Cabeza & Nyberg, 2000; Posner & Raichle, 1994).

Visualizing Brain Structure

The oldest neuroimaging techniques involve taking pictures of brain structures using X rays. The invention of the

Microelectrode: A tiny probe inserted into the brain to record electrical activity.

Transcranial magnetic stimulation (TMS): A procedure that involves stimulation of the brain from the outside, by putting a wire coil on a person's head and delivering a magnetic pulse. The magnetic fields are so strong that they make neurons under the coil fire.

Neuroimaging: Brain scanning techniques that produce a picture of the structure or functioning of neurons.

On the left, a computer-assisted tomography (CT) scan, and on the right, a magnetic resonance imaging (MRI) scan. The invention of MRI has provided much higher-resolution images of structures of the brain.

A positron emission tomography (PET) machine.

Brighter colors indicate regions of greater blood flow in the brain while the participant performed a particular task (from Posner & Raichle, 1994).

Computer-assisted tomography (CT, formerly **CAT):** A neuroimaging technique that produces a three-dimensional image of brain structure using X rays.

Magnetic resonance imaging (MRI): A technique that uses magnetic properties of atoms to take sharp pictures of the structure of the brain.

Positron emission tomography (PET): A neuroimaging technique that uses small amounts of radiation to track blood or energy consumption in the brain.

Functional magnetic resonance imaging (fMRI): A type of MRI that usually detects the amount of oxygen being brought to a particular place in the brain.

computer allowed scientists to construct machines for **computer-assisted tomography (CT,** formerly **CAT).** In this technique, a series of X rays builds up a three-dimensional image, slice by slice (*tomography* comes from a Greek word meaning "section"). More recently, **magnetic resonance imaging (MRI)** makes use of the magnetic properties of different atoms to take even sharper pictures of the structure of the brain.

Visualizing Brain Function

CT scans and MRIs give amazing views of the physical structure of the living brain; but for images that reflect the brain in action, researchers need other types of brain scans, ones that track the amount of blood, oxygen, or nutrients moving to particular parts of the brain. When you take a shower or wash a load of laundry, water is drawn into the plumbing pipes from the water main. Similarly, when a part of the brain is working, it draws more blood.

One of the most important techniques for measuring blood flow or energy consumption in the brain is **positron emission tomography (PET).** Small amounts of radiation are introduced into the blood, which is then taken up into different brain areas in proportion to how hard the neurons are working. The amount of radiation emitted at different parts of the head is recorded, and a computer uses this information to build three-dimensional images of the brain.

Probably the most popular type of neuroimaging today is **functional magnetic resonance imaging (fMRI).** The most common sort of fMRI reveals function by detecting the amount of oxygen that is being brought to a particular place in the brain.

LOOKING AT LEVELS

The Musical Brain

Because even medium-size hospitals have MRI machines for medical diagnosis, many researchers have been able to use these machines to explore all manner of human abilities. Part of the motor strip in the right half of the brain controls the fingers of the left hand. MRI has shown that this part of the brain is larger in orchestra members who play string instruments than in nonmusicians (Elber et al., 1995; Schlaug et al., 1995). Apparently brain areas that are used a lot actually grow larger, probably because of the formation of additional connections among neurons. Consider this finding from the levels perspective: the size of brain areas—the physical structure of your brain—depends in part on what you do! If you have musical talent and interest (characteristics at the level of the person) and have the opportunity to develop musical ability, your brain can be altered by the experience. If your playing is smiled upon by others (the level of the group), you will be even more motivated to continue practicing—and chang-ing your brain. And once your brain is altered, your playing improves—leading to more praise from others. Even the structure of your brain can be fully understood only from the levels perspective. These findings do not apply only to musicians: Consider the fact that taxi drivers have been found to have unusually large hippocampi (used to store spatial memories)—and the longer a driver has worked, the larger they are (Maguire et al., 2000).

CONSOLIDATE!

1 *What can researchers learn about the brain's function by studying behavior following brain damage?* By looking at altered performance after brain damage, researchers can gain hints about how information is stored and processed and about what functions are carried out by particular parts of the brain. They can also test a theory of the specific functions carried out by a particular part of the brain—if the theory is correct, then all patients with damage to that part should have specific deficits.

2 *What techniques allow us to record the activity of neurons in the brain as they function?* Electroencephalography (EEG) records "brain waves"—fluctuations of electrical fields from the brain. This technique relies on electrodes placed on the skull and can record, for example, electrical variations immediately after someone has received a stimulus or made a decision. Researchers can also use microelectrodes to record neural activity directly, in both humans and animals.

3 *How can different parts of the brain be stimulated to see whether they are working properly?* Transcranial magnetic stimulation (TMS) can be used to stimulate clusters of neurons by pulsing magnetic fields into the brain. More precise stimulation can be achieved by placing electrodes on the surface of the brain, or actually into specific neurons, and applying small amounts of electric current.

4 *What is neuroimaging?* Neuroimaging techniques allow researchers to visualize the structure and function of the brain. At present, four major techniques are used: computer-assisted tomography (CT), which uses X rays to obtain images of the structure of the brain; magnetic resonance imaging (MRI), which uses the effects of different magnetic fields to produce sharp pictures of the brain; positron emission tomography (PET), which relies on small amounts of radioactivity to track neural activity; and functional magnetic resonance imaging (fMRI), which tracks the movement of oxygen-bearing red blood cells in the brain as a task is performed.

Genes, Brain, and Environment: The Brain in the World

Why was the brain of the young soldier vulnerable to such damage from carbon monoxide fumes? Could he have done anything in advance to prepare his brain to survive such an event? Could he have done anything after the accident to speed his recovery? Let's consider the factors of environment and heredity that shape our brains so that they operate in particular ways and not in others, and the degree to which parts of the brain can change their functions if need be.

1 Can "bad genes" make you more vulnerable to the environment? How do genes and the environment interact as the brain develops and functions?

2 What does *heritability* mean?

3 How has evolution shaped the functions of the brain?

Genes as Blueprints: Born to Be Wild?

Figure 2.18 illustrates the **deoxyribonucleic acid (DNA)** molecule that contains our genes. A **gene** is a stretch of DNA that produces a specific protein (including enzymes), which in turn forms building blocks of our bodies (including our brains) or drives the processes that allow us to live. Genes affect us from the instant of conception and are in turn affected by the environment surrounding us at every phase of our lives.

Genetic Programs: The Genes Matter

Genes affect not only obvious traits—such as eye color, height, and other physical features—but also behavior. Consider a startling result reported in late 1996 by Ryner and her colleagues. These researchers identified a single gene that can change the sexual behavior of fruit flies. Usually, fruit flies engage in a "courtship dance" before they mate. The male follows the female, uses his forelegs to tap her body, produces a "song" by vibrating his wings, then licks her genitals, curls his abdomen, and tries to mate with her (Ferveur et al., 1995; Hall, 1994 [as cited in Ryner et al., 1996]). By altering one gene, scientists produced male fruit flies that performed this courtship dance for other males. In fact, when a group of males with this gene were together, they lined up in a long chain, each male both being courted by and courting other males. The gene that produced this behavior affects only about 500 of the 100,000 neurons in the insect's head. A small genetic change, affecting a relatively small num-

Figure **2.18** **The Secret of DNA**

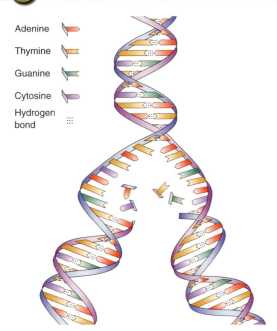

Adenine
Thymine
Guanine
Cytosine
Hydrogen bond

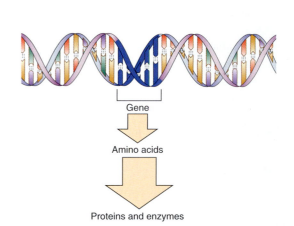

Gene

Amino acids

Proteins and enzymes

What, exactly, is a gene? Let's begin with a chromosome, which is a long, twisted molecule of deoxyribonucleic acid, or DNA, contained in the nucleus of all cells. Every cell of the human body (except for sex cells) has 23 pairs of chromosomes. The two strands in the DNA molecule are separated by pairs of four types of bases. The base adenine (A) always hooks up with thymine (T), and guanine (G) always hooks up with cytosine (C). Thus, if the helix is unzipped down the middle, the extra bases floating about will hook up correctly to form two complete copies of the original molecule. This is how this amazing molecule is able to reproduce itself.

The particular ordering of pairs of bases codes genes; a gene is a segment along the strand of DNA that produces amino acids, which in turn are converted into proteins and enzymes. Everything else in our bodies (including our brains) is built of these molecules.

ber of neurons, had a big effect. The affected neurons apparently coordinate many other neurons, which in turn produce the behavior. The far-reaching power of relatively small genetic changes can be seen dramatically by comparing chimpanzees with humans: About 99% of the genetic material in both species is identical.

Tuning Genetic Programs: The Environment Matters

There can be no question that genes play a major role in shaping our abilities. But it is critical to point out that genes *cannot* program the structure of the brain entirely in advance. Your brain contained far more connections at birth than it does now. As you interacted with the environment, certain neural connections were used over and over again, while others were used hardly at all. Connections between neurons in parts of the brain that are used frequently survive, while others, which are not used frequently, are pruned away (Huttenlocher, in press). **Pruning** is a process whereby certain neural connections are eliminated (Cowan et al., 1984; Huttenlocher, in press): As the saying goes, "Use it or lose it." In short, the genes define the possibilities for brain circuits, but interactions with the environment lead some connections to persist and others to disappear.

Pruning is only one of the ways in which your brain changes as you experience the world. Connections are also added. In fact, researchers have found that if rats are raised in enriched environments, with lots of toys and things to do, their brains actually become heavier than those of rats raised in average environments. The additional weight comes about in large part because more blood flows to the cortex (Jones & Greenough, 1996), and in part because new connections are formed (Black et al., 1998; Comery et al., 1995; Diamond et al., 1972; Greenough & Chang, 1985; Greenough et al., 1987; Nelson, 1999; Turner & Greenough, 1985). The environment not only helps to select among connections established by the genes, but can also cause new connections to form.

In fact, even adult brains are capable of dramatic reorganization. If a finger is lost or immobilized, the part of the brain that used to register its input is soon taken over by inputs from other fingers (Merzenich, Kaas, Wall, Nelson, Sur, 1983; additional evidence is provided by Ramachandran, 1993; Ramachandran et al., 1992; Xerri et al., 1999). We also now know that adult brains can create new neurons, at least in some regions (Gould et al., 1999). Thus, genes are not destiny; they don't fix our characteristics forevermore. Interactions with the environment can alter both the structure and the function of the brain.

Genes and Environment: A Single System

How do interactions with the environment alter the brain? Some people think of genes as blueprints for the body, providing the instructions on how to build organs, but this notion captures only part of the gene story. For one thing, rather than being filed away in a dusty drawer once their instructions have been followed, many genes keep working throughout your life. They are the reason some people go bald, others develop high cholesterol, still others get varicose veins. Even more important, genes are not simply time bombs that are set at birth and ready to explode at the proper hour. Many genes change their operation constantly, sometimes producing proteins and sometimes not. Genes work by coding the production of proteins that affect the workings of the cells in your body, including those in your brain; a gene that issues an "instruction" to produce a protein is said to be *expressed*. Psychiatrist Steven Hyman suggested to one of us the following illuminating example: Say you want bigger biceps, so you go to the gym and start lifting weights. After the first week, all you have to show for your time and sweat is aching arms. But after a few weeks, the muscles begin to firm up and soon may even begin to bulge. What has happened? When you first lifted weights, you actually damaged the muscles, and the damage caused the release of certain chemicals. Those chemicals then—and this is the important part—*turned on* genes in the muscle cells. By "turn on" we mean that the proteins coded by the genes were produced. These proteins

Pruning: A process whereby certain connections among neurons are eliminated.

Some songbirds learn the songs of their particular species only by hearing other birds sing them. Mello and colleagues (1992) showed that the process of learning a song begins when certain genes are turned on when the bird first hears the song, which in turn regulates the effects of other genes that actually produce the learning.

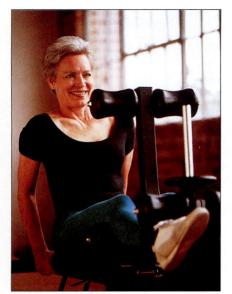

Exercise does more than build muscles; it also turns on genes in the brain that build better neurons. Neeper and colleagues (1995, 1996) showed that exercise turns on genes that produce a chemical called brain-derived neurotrophic factor (BDNF). BDNF protects neurons and helps them continue to function properly.

were used to build up the damaged muscles. If the damage stops, so do the chemicals that signal the genes to turn on, and the genes will no longer produce those extra proteins. So, you need to lift increasingly heavier weights to keep building more muscle. No pain, no gain.

The important point to remember is that many genes are constantly being turned on and off, as needed, to produce new substances. As you read this, for example, terminal buttons are releasing neurotransmitters that enable you to understand the printed words. Genes are turned on to replenish the buttons' supply of neurotransmitter. Similarly, genes regulate the flow of neuromodulators, and it is the genes that lead to new connections among cells during learning of new material.

The efficiency of a neuron depends on the way its genes are operating. Just as interacting with the environment (such as lifting weights) can lead to bulging muscles, interacting with the environment can set your brain to operate more or less efficiently. And depending on how your brain is working, you behave differently. By regulating the brain, genes affect behavior.

It is commonplace today for scientists to stress that both genes and environment are important. This is true, but simply stated, it misses the mark. Genes and environment cannot really be considered as separate factors; they are instead *different aspects of a single system*. In much the same way as you can focus separately on the brushstrokes, texture, composition, and color of a painting, you can discuss genes and the environment as discrete entities. But, as with a painting, to appreciate the "whole picture," you must consider genes and environment together (Gottlieb, 1998).

Environment and Genes: A Two-Way Street

Genes can affect the environment, and the environment can regulate the genes. Remember, we are talking about a single system here. Plomin and colleagues (1997), Scarr and McCartney (1983), and others distinguish three ways that the genes and environment interact. First, **passive interaction** occurs when the parents' or sibling's genetically shaped tendencies produce an environment that is passively received by the child. An example: Parents with higher intelligence tend to read more and thus have more books in the house. Given that parents with higher intelligence tend to have children with higher intelligence, this means that children with higher intelligence will tend to be born into environments with more books (see Plomin, 1995). Second, **evocative** (or **reactive**) **interaction** occurs when our genetically influenced characteristics draw out behaviors from other people. We might call this the "blondes have more fun" effect. As it happens, responses to this stereotype vary, at least in U.S. culture. Some people react to blondes more positively than to brunettes. Others, however, may think blondes are less substantial people than are brunettes. Third, genes and environment interact when people deliberately choose to put themselves in specific situations and aggressively avoid others. Such **active interaction** involves constructing situations or shaping and modifying existing ones in ways that are comfortable for existing genetic tendencies. A timid child, for instance, may avoid loud parties and amusement parks, instead seeking out peaceful settings and quiet pastimes.

Behavioral Genetics

Researchers in the field of **behavioral genetics** try to determine how much of the differences among people's abilities are due to their different genetic makeups and how much to differences in their environments. The environment varies at different times and places, so this is a difficult question indeed. Throughout this book, we talk about the relative contributions of genes and the environment to differences in mental processes or behavior. Here we need to stress a crucial point: Any conclusions about the relative contributions of genes and environment can apply only

Passive interaction: Occurs when the parents' or sibling's genetically shaped tendencies produce an environment that is passively received by the child.

Evocative (or reactive) interaction: Occurs when genetically influenced characteristics draw out behaviors from other people.

Active interaction: Occurs when people choose, partly based on genetic tendencies, to put themselves in specific situations and to avoid others.

Behavioral genetics: The field in which researchers attempt to determine how much of the differences among people are due to their genes and how much to the environment.

to the specific circumstances in which they were measured. To see why, let's say you have two types of apple trees, one bred to produce large apples and one bred to produce small ones. If you plant the seeds with "big apple genes" in the shade, in rocky soil, and scrimp on water, they will probably produce apples even smaller than those produced by seeds with "small apple genes" planted in better circumstances. The point of this example is simple, and vitally important: The effects of the genes vary in different environments. Genes cannot be described in isolation; they can be characterized only in relation to the specific environments in which they operate. Statements about relative contributions of genes and environments therefore apply only to the situation at hand and have no bearing on different circumstances.

Heritability, Not Inheritability

Researchers in behavioral genetics focus on estimating the "heritability" of various characteristics, ranging from intelligence to personality, as they occur in specific environments. **Heritability** is perhaps an unfortunate term. It does not indicate the amount of a characteristic or trait that is inherited, but rather how much of the variability in that characteristic in a population is due to genetics. Height in Western countries is about 90% heritable. This statement means that 90% of the *variability* among the heights of these people is genetically determined, not that *your* height was determined 90% by your genes and 10% by your environment. In fact, the possible differences in height owing to diet may actually be greater than the differences owing to genes; but *in a specific environment* (for example, one in which diet is constant), heritability indicates the contribution of the genes to variations. If the environment were different, the heritability might be different too.

Twin Studies: Only Shared Genes?

Twin studies compare the two types of twins, identical and fraternal. Identical twins start life when a single egg (which later divides) is fertilized by a single sperm; these twins are **monozygotic** (like many scientific terms, this comes from Greek: *monos,* meaning "single," and *zygotos,* meaning "yoked," as occurs when a sperm and egg are joined). Monozygotic twins have identical genes. In contrast, fraternal twins grow from two separate eggs that are fertilized by two different sperm; these twins are **dizygotic.** Fraternal twins share only as many genes as any other pair of brothers or sisters—on average, half. By comparing identical twins and fraternal twins, we get an idea of the contribution of the genes, if we assume that the environment is the same for members of both sets of twins.

An even better way to gather evidence for the relative contributions of genes and environment is to study either related children who were separated at birth and raised in different households or unrelated children who were raised in the same versus different households. Called an **adoption study,** this type of investigation is particularly powerful when twins who have been separated at birth, or shortly thereafter, grow up in different environments. Even in these cases, however, it is difficult to separate genetic from environmental influences. If the twins are cute, for instance, caregivers in both households will treat them differently than if they look like little trolls; if they are smart and curious, both sets of parents may be inclined to buy books and read to them. So findings from studies of twins separated at birth are fascinating, but even they don't allow us to separate genes from environment with confidence. The best we can say is that genes contribute a certain amount to differences among people in particular environments, and that environments contribute a certain amount to such differences when people have particular genes.

Evolution and the Brain:
The Best of All Possible Brains?

The loss of consciousness and brain damage suffered by the young soldier occurred because he breathed toxic fumes and was deprived of oxygen. Not all species would

Heritability: The degree to which variability in a characteristic is due to genetics.

Twin study: A study that compares identical and fraternal twins to determine the relative contribution of genes to variability in a behavior or characteristic.

Monozygotic: From the same egg and having identical genes.

Dizygotic: From different eggs and sharing only as many genes as any pair of brothers or sisters—on average, half.

Adoption study: A study in which characteristics of children adopted at birth are compared to those of their adoptive parents or siblings versus their biological parents or siblings (often twins). These studies often focus on comparisons of twins who were raised in the same versus different households.

react the way this member of our human species did, though, if faced with this situation. Sperm whales, for instance, do just fine if they take a breath every 75 minutes or so. Why don't our brains give us this extra protection? This question leads to thoughts about **evolution**, the gene-based changes in the characteristics of members of a species over successive generations.

Natural Selection: Reproduction of the Fittest

A major driving force of evolution is **natural selection,** which was first described in detail in 1858 by Charles Darwin and, independently, Alfred Russel Wallace. Inherited characteristics that contribute to survival in an environment are the ones that will come to be widespread in a population because the individuals with those characteristics are the ones that live long enough to have many offspring. In turn, those offspring, equipped with the favorable characteristics inherited from their parents, will survive to have more offspring. In this way, the "selection" of the survivors is made by "nature." An inherited characteristic that contributes to such selection is called an **adaptation.** The term "survival of the fittest," coined by Darwin, is perhaps unfortunate; the key point is that some characteristics lead some organisms to have more offspring, who in turn have more offspring, and so on—until their inheritable characteristics are spread throughout the population. Plomin and colleagues (1997) point out that the principle might better have been termed "reproduction of the fittest."

Darwin saw this pattern in a brilliant insight; but where are the genes in the story? Nowhere. Genes were not discovered until the early part of the twentieth century, and not discovered to correspond to DNA until 1953. Darwin never knew that the mechanism for the transmission of traits from one generation to the next is the gene. Today, we would say that natural selection depends on the fact that there is variation in the genes carried by members of a population, and if a gene allows an organism to have more offspring that survive (and they have more offspring, and so on), eventually more of that particular gene will be present in the population.

Evolution via natural selection tends to mold the characteristics of a group of organisms to the requirements of its environment. If a certain animal lives at the North Pole, those individuals with warm fur will tend to have more babies that survive, and those individuals that are white (and thus harder for predators to spot in the snow) will tend to have more babies that survive. If these characteristics are useful enough in that environment, eventually the species as a whole will have warm white fur.

Here's a contemporary analogy of the way natural selection works. There were two Chinese brothers; one settled in Louisiana and the other in Ohio. They both opened Chinese restaurants and began with identical menus. After the first month, the brother in Louisiana noticed that his blander dishes were not selling well, so he dropped them from the menu; in Ohio, they were doing fine, so they remained. In Louisiana, the chef one day accidentally knocked a jar of chili powder into a pot of chicken he was simmering. He found he liked the taste, so this new dish became the special of the day. It sold so well that it became a standard on the menu. Hearing the tale, the brother up north in Ohio tried the chili dish, but it didn't sell well. This chef bought a lot of corn, which was on sale. He tried adding it to a traditional dish and called it the special of the day. The Ohio chef wasn't trying to achieve a particular taste, he was just experimenting. That corn dish did not sell well, and so was dropped. But when he added corn to another recipe, the result was an instant hit. Both chefs continued with new elements in their cooking, with varying degrees of success on different occasions. After two years, the brothers' menus had little in common.

Two important principles of evolution are illustrated here. First, the "environment"—the hungry restaurant patrons—"selected" different aspects of the menus: The southerners, for example, apparently liked spicy food better than did the patrons in Ohio. Second, variation is at the heart of the process. Without the accidents and substitutions, the process would not have worked—the menus

Evolution: Gene-based changes in the characteristics of members of a species over successive generations.

Natural selection: Changes in the frequency of genes in a population that arise because genes allow an organism to have more offspring that survive.

Adaptation: A characteristic that increases "fitness" for an environment.

Menus of Chinese restaurants in different locales undergo evolution. Even if they start the same, the chefs will vary their menus from time to time. Depending on the diners' tastes, "natural selection" will eventually produce different menus in the different locales.

would not have evolved over time. Natural selection in the evolution of the two menus depended on random variation, which provided the "options" that proved more or less adaptive.

The same is true in the evolution of species, but in this case the "menu" is the set of genes different organisms possess. Genes that lead an organism to have offspring who have still more offspring stay on the menu, and ones that do not lead to this result eventually get dropped.

So, back to the question of the sperm whale and breathing. If our ancestors had had to go for long periods without breathing in order to survive, then only those who could do so would have survived and had offspring—and we lucky descendants would have inherited this ability. And the story of our young soldier might have had a happier ending.

Not Just Natural Selection: Accidents Do Happen

A word of warning: Always exercise caution when trying to use the idea of natural selection to explain our present-day characteristics. Just because a characteristic exists doesn't mean that it is an adaptation to the environment or that it is the result of natural selection. Natural selection may or may not be the reason, for example, why some people are more prone than others to alcoholism; it may or may not explain certain students' violent rampages in high schools or the frequency of heart disease in certain groups. For one thing, as human brains and bodies evolved, the environment also changed: People created not only furniture, houses, and cities but also automobiles, guns, computers, and candy. Our brains may not be ideally suited for what they are doing now.

Furthermore, natural selection is not the only way that evolution works. Accidents, sometimes very happy ones, occur. Sometimes characteristics piggyback on other characteristics. For example, sickle-cell anemia, a blood problem that is common among African Americans, is an unfortunate side effect of protection from malaria. (The gene that causes the anemia codes for a protein that destroys cells infected with the malaria-causing parasite, which is useful in the parts of Africa where malaria is common.) And sometimes characteristics appear because the original adaptation can be put to good use in a new role that has nothing to do with the original adaptation (Gould & Lewontin, 1979). For example, once we have the brain machinery to see lines and edges, abilities that probably helped our ancestors to discern prey, the brain can allow us to learn to read.

In short, some of our abilities, personality types, social styles, and so forth may have arisen from natural selection because they are useful, and others may have been accidental. It is not easy to sort out which is which, and we should not assume that there is a sound evolutionary reason for everything people do.

Alcoholism, Muslims, and Mormons

As we've seen from our discussion of the interaction between genes and the environment, only rarely do genes determine completely whether you will have a specific characteristic. For example, men with a particular gene (for which they can be tested) are likely to become alcoholics if they drink at all (Goedde & Agarwal, 1987). Having this gene presents no downside, however, for men who obey the norms of a strict Muslim or Mormon culture, in which alcohol is forbidden. And why do people adhere to certain rules and norms? At least in part, because of their beliefs. Thus, the adherence to group norms leads to behavior that regulates the genes. If a man knows he has this gene, this knowledge might even serve to support his beliefs and his group affiliation. Genes are merely one element in a larger system, which necessarily includes interactions among events at the different levels of analysis.

1 *Can "bad genes" make you more vulnerable to the environment? How do genes and the environment interact as the brain develops and functions?* When the brain is developing, there are more neurons and neural connections than are later used; the process of pruning eliminates connections that are not useful or effective. In addition, neurons grow more connections with use. The genes govern not only how neurons grow, but also how they function internally. Many genes are constantly being turned on and off, and the brain functions more or less efficiently depending on which genes are turned on and hence which proteins are produced.

2 *What does* **heritability** *mean?* Heritability refers to how much of the *variability* in a characteristic in a population is due to genetics. Even if there is virtually no variability—and hence virtually zero heritability—in a characteristic, it can still be heavily under genetic influence (as is true not only for the number of arms, but also for the components of the nervous system).

3 *How has evolution shaped the functions of the brain?* Evolution has shaped the functions of the brain both through the process of natural selection (of characteristics that are adaptive) and accidents (including when one characteristic piggybacks on another).

Recap and Thought Questions

Brain Circuits: Making Connections

The key building block of the brain is the neuron. The cell body receives inputs from the dendrites (or, sometimes, directly from axons of other neurons) and sends output via its axon. The axon is covered with myelin, a fatty insulating material that makes neural transmission more efficient. The terminal buttons at the end of the axon contain chemical substances that are released by an action potential. These substances are either neurotransmitters or neuromodulators. Neurotransmitters cross the synaptic cleft (the gap between the end of the sending axon and the receiving neuron) to affect another neuron. Both neurotransmitters and neuromodulators affect receptors, which are like locks that are opened by the right key. Once opened, the receptor sets off a chain of events inside the neuron. Glial cells not only support neurons but also help to regulate neurotransmitters and can affect neurons directly. When the total input to a neuron is sufficiently excitatory, the neuron "fires"—that is, chemical reactions work their way down the axon. After a neuron has fired, surplus neurotransmitter is reabsorbed into the cells. Some drugs block this reuptake mechanism, so that enough neurotransmitter becomes available to affect other neurons.

How did the fumes the soldier inhaled affect his brain? We can narrow our explanation for his problems to the following three aspects of brain function: First, many—but not all—neurons in the occipital lobes died because of a lack of oxygen. This damage caused his fuzzy vision. Second, the parietal lobes, thalamus, or some other area that is used in attention was also damaged, so that he had a narrow range of attention and thus could not perceive the context in which shapes appeared. Hence, he saw only small details. Third, he saw small details because of damage to the temporal lobe in his right hemisphere, an area that typically registers overall shapes, or, possibly, the connections to the right temporal lobe from the occipital lobes were damaged. But his left hemisphere, particularly his left frontal lobe, apparently was intact enough to allow him to make up a story based on what he saw, allowing him to try to make sense of the stimulus. Thus, the soldier saw details in isolation and tried to guess what they might be.

Think It Through. Say you are a health-care provider who specializes in helping patients who have suffered brain damage. What would you try to do to help the young soldier? Are there any special strategies you could teach him that might help him? What jobs might he be trained to do in spite of the damage?

Imagine that you have invented a new drug that protects one particular cognitive ability from being disrupted by brain damage. If you could choose, which ability would your drug protect? Why?

The Nervous System: An Orchestra With Many Members

The nervous system has two major parts, the central nervous system (CNS) and the peripheral nervous system (PNS).

The central nervous system consists of the spinal cord and the brain itself. In addition to sending commands from the brain to the body and passing along sensory input to the brain, the spinal cord underlies some reflexes. Reflexes depend on the action of interneurons, neurons that hook up to other neurons. The brain itself is organized into lobes and is covered by the cortex, a thin layer of neurons. The cortex contains many bulges (gyri) and creases (sulci), allowing a lot of cortex to be crammed into a relatively small space. The four major lobes in each hemisphere are the occipital, temporal, parietal, and frontal lobes. The occipital lobe processes visual input; the temporal lobe is the seat of visual memories and is also involved in language comprehension,

hearing, storing new memories, and arithmetic. The parietal lobe registers size, three-dimensionality, and location in space, and is also involved in attention and motor control; it includes the somatosensory strip, which registers sensation from parts of the body. The frontal lobe is involved in speech production, searching for memories, reasoning (and using memory to help in reasoning), fine motor control (governed by the motor strip), and making decisions. Each lobe is duplicated, one on the left and one on the right. The left hemisphere plays a larger role in language, and the right hemisphere plays a larger role in spatial attention and nonverbal functions. One apparent function of the left brain, particularly the frontal lobe, is to invent stories to make sense of the world.

Under the cortex, many subcortical areas are crucial to the brain's mission. The thalamus manages connections to and from distinct parts of the brain; the hypothalamus regulates hormones, which is important as it operates to control bodily functions such as eating, drinking, and sex; the hippocampus is involved in the storage of new memories; and the amygdala plays a role in fear and other emotions. The basal ganglia are used in planning and producing movements, as well as in learning new habits. The brainstem contains structures involved in alertness, sleep, and arousal; and the cerebellum is involved in motor control, timing, and attention.

The peripheral nervous system, which is engaged in part via the amygdala and hypothalamus, consists of two parts: the autonomic nervous system (ANS) and the skeletal system. The ANS is in turn divided into the sympathetic and parasympathetic nervous systems, which are critically involved in the "fight or flight" response. The neuroendocrine system produces hormones, which affect not only the body but also the brain itself (as in, for example, altering moods). Finally, the immune system is also affected by the brain.

How would his brain damage have affected the young man's ability to be a soldier? The brain damage disrupted his ability to recognize and identify objects. Thus, not only would he have difficulty distinguishing friend from foe, he would also have trouble identifying his weapons, places of shelter, vehicles, and everything else used by the army. In addition, because recognition is the first step to reaction, he would not have the appropriate "fight or flight" emotional response. Indeed, he probably did not have the physical energy or stamina to perform on the parade field, let alone on the battlefield. In short, his damage would have devastating effects on the young man's ability to be a soldier.

Think It Through. Clearly, the organization of the brain has a lot to do with why brain damage produces one disorder and not another. It is possible that some parts of the brain receive information that is not available to the parts that control language. If so, can you think of types of behaviors that might reveal that the information was "in there"?

Can you think of a way to find out whether the soldier had a problem with attention, or whether his paying attention to a small area was just a strategy? That is, perhaps he believed that by focusing on details he would see better, and did so even though he was in fact able to pay attention to overall shapes. What difference, if any, would it make whether his problem stemmed from a faulty strategy or a problem beyond his control?

More careful examination of the soldier might have suggested that his problem was not confined to visual processing. What would you think if it could be shown that his personality was particularly unemotional? What if he had shown little interest in eating or sex?

Probing the Brain

The earliest method used to discover what the various parts of the brain do was to observe the effects of brain damage on behavior. Such so-called natural experiments led scientists to investigate the effects of lesioning, or damaging, parts of animal brains. Scientists can record electrical activity produced by neural firings while people and animals perform specific tasks, either from the scalp or from tiny electrodes placed in neurons; they find more vigorous activity in brain areas involved in the task than in those that are not being used. In addition, neurons can be electrically or magnetically stimulated to fire and the effects on behavior observed. Neuroimaging techniques include the following: computer-assisted tomography (CT), which uses X rays to obtain images of the structure of the brain; magnetic resonance imaging (MRI), which makes use of magnetic fields to produce very sharp pictures of the brain; positron emission tomography (PET), which relies on small amounts of radioactivity to track blood flow or energy consumption in the brain; and functional magnetic resonance imaging (fMRI), which uses changes in the magnetic properties of blood when oxygen is bound to red blood cells to track blood in different brain areas.

Which techniques would be most useful for diagnosing the effects of the soldier's accident? If the soldier had his accident today, he would first receive either a CT or an MRI scan (depending on the facilities available at the local hospital) to discover the location and extent of the injury. To discover the functional consequences of the injury, he would receive either a PET or an fMRI scan. In addition, he would be given behavioral tests (like those described at the beginning of this chapter) to dis-

cover whether he had deficits in his vision, memory, reasoning, and other cognitive abilities.

Think It Through. Dr. Scannering has invented a new form of brain scan, which shines very-low-power lasers safely through the head and projects an image of brain activity as it is happening. This machine will be sold for less than the price of a personal computer. What uses can you think of for such a machine? What sort of education would you need to make the best use of this technological breakthrough?

Genes, Brain, and Environment: The Brain in the World

The genes lay down the basic structure of the brain, but the environment molds both its structure and its function. During brain development, the environment affects brain structure and function by pruning connections that are not working well or frequently, and causes the brain to form new connections in response to increased activity. The genes place limits on what is possible, however (for example, people can't grow wings), and even small genetic changes can significantly affect cognition and behavior. Many of your genes are under the control of the environment and are turned on and off depending on what you are doing; specific genes can cause the manufacture of new neurotransmitters or neuromodulators at the terminal buttons, and can even cause neurons to hook up in new ways.

Behavioral genetics attempts to discover how much of the variability in a trait or ability is due to the genes versus the environment, but such estimates apply only to the environments in which the trait or ability is measured. We have our present sets of genes because of evolution, which is partly a consequence of natural selection and partly of accidents.

How did the soldier's genes make him vulnerable to the fumes? Two ways: First, as a member of our species, he inherited a brain that requires certain amounts of oxygen. Thus, like any of us, his brain suffered when not enough oxygen reached it. Second, every one of us is unique, partly because of variations in our genes and partly because of effects those variations have had in response to our individual environments. Thus, depending on his genes and environment, the soldier could have been a bit more or a bit less vulnerable than the average person.

Think It Through. Did natural selection design the brain so that it is vulnerable to damage such as the soldier's brain sustained? Is there reason to think that natural selection formed the brain so that vision is carried out by separate areas from hearing and language? Which parts of the human brain would you expect to be shared by other animals, and why?

Can you think of any human abilities that you would bet are "adaptations"? How about ones that could be accidents? How could you tell whether a characteristic has prevailed because of natural selection?

REVIEW TEST

For each of the following items, choose the single correct or best answer. The correct answers appear at the end.

1. The cells that act as housekeepers of the brain, cleaning up debris and helping in the care and feeding of other cells, are called ____.
   a. brain circuits
   b. neurons
   c. interneurons
   d. glial cells

2. The direction of the nervous impulse is ____.
   a. axon→cell body→dendrites→terminal buttons
   b. dendrites→axon→cell body→terminal buttons
   c. cell body→dendrites→axon→terminal buttons
   d. dendrites→cell body→axon→terminal buttons

3. Action potentials move quickly because of ____, which insulate(s) the axon and speeds up neural transmission.
   a. negative ions
   b. potassium
   c. glial cells
   d. myelin

4. Communication between neurons takes place primarily at the ____.
   a. dendrites
   b. synapse
   c. axon
   d. cell body

5. The two divisions of the peripheral nervous system are ____.
   a. the autonomic nervous system and the skeletal system
   b. the central nervous system and the autonomic nervous system
   c. the skeletal system and the central nervous system
   d. the sympathetic nervous system and the parasympathetic nervous system

6. Which system could you blame if you wet your pants when scared?
   a. central nervous system
   b. skeletal nervous system
   c. sympathetic nervous system
   d. parasympathetic nervous system

7. A patient with his corpus callosum cut is flashed a picture of a car to his right visual field. When asked, what is he likely to say he saw?
   a. "Vrooom Vrooom"
   b. "A car"
   c. "I don't know"
   d. "A cat"

8. The ____ controls body temperature, blood pressure, and heart rate.
   a. corpus callosum
   b. thalamus
   c. amygdala
   d. hypothalamus

9. Damage to the hippocampus would result in ____.
   a. an inability to pay attention
   b. excessive thirst and hunger
   c. difficulty storing new memories
   d. a flattening of affect

10. Which of the following is *not* considered a part of the brainstem?
    a. medulla
    b. reticular formation
    c. hypothalamus
    d. pons

11. Hormones can act as ____.
    a. neurotransmitters
    b. glial cells
    c. blood clotters
    d. neuromodulators

12. A three-dimensional X ray of the brain, which displays structure but not function, is called a(n) ____.
    a. CT scan
    b. EEG
    c. MRI
    d. PET scan

13. Genes produce ____, which in turn form(s) the building blocks of our bodies.
    a. proteins
    b. fats
    c. sugars
    d. DNA

14. Difficult babies tend to elicit punitive reactions from their caregivers, in an example of ____ interaction.
    a. passive
    b. active
    c. evocative
    d. sensitive

15. Saying that intelligence is 50% heritable means ____.
    a. in a specific environment, 50% of people are intelligent and 50% are not
    b. you get 50% of your intelligence from your parents, and 50% from the environment
    c. in a specific environment, 50% of the variability in intelligence among people is due to genetics
    d. you get 50% of your intelligence from your mom, and 50% from your dad

ANSWERS: 1.d 2.d 3.d 4.b 5.a 6.c 7.b 8.d 9.c 10.c 11.d 12.a 13.a 14.c 15.c.

3 Sensation and

Perception

HOW THE WORLD
ENTERS THE MIND

Sue hated going to art museums. To her, some paintings just looked like scribblings or drips of paint, something a three-year-old would make. Others looked like bad photographs taken through a lens left out in the rain. The sculptures were even worse: Some of them looked to Sue like huge cardboard boxes that had been through a giant food processor operating at slow speed. But Sue's friend Tai liked to look at things like this and wanted Sue to come along while she did. It puzzled Sue, who was bored and annoyed in a museum or a sculpture garden, that Tai didn't feel the same way. And Tai couldn't understand why Sue took no pleasure in art, or why she didn't come away feeling refreshed and invigorated, as Tai did, after an afternoon at the museum.

Curiously, the friends had exactly opposite reactions when they went together to a rock concert. (They had agreed on "equal time" for their favorite adventures.) Sue would become completely absorbed, moving her body with the music, while Tai would become almost physically uncomfortable. Sue couldn't understand why Tai wasn't energized. Tai's reaction was that the groups were primitive and crude; she didn't understand how Sue could enjoy such loud and violent music.

At first glance, these reactions might seem mere "personality differences" between the two friends. But from the levels perspective, so-called personality differences can arise from differences in how our brains work, in what we believe and desire, in how we respond to the surrounding group.

How, when faced with the same stimuli—the same painting, the same music—can people's reactions be so different? Do Sue's and Tai's different perceptions reflect differences in their abilities to register different kinds of sensations? Or are they the products of differing degrees of exposure and learning? Or both? Could it be that the eyes and ears of the two friends, the visual and auditory parts of their brains, are different, and thus produce different responses?

Despite their disagreement—the possible reasons for which we explore in this chapter—Sue and Tai share the fundamental ability to register and process (that is, to receive and interpret) the dizzying array of colors, shapes, sounds, and other sensations that whirl around them. How do our brains register that something is "out there"? And what of the other senses through which we register this amazing world—how do we smell, and hear, and taste; how are we able to be aware of our bodies? And is there a perception beyond these—a perception that is literally "extrasensory"—that some, if not all, of us possess? To a psychologist, the investigation of these questions provides fruitful clues in our discovery of ourselves.

Sensing and Selecting: Opening Up to the World

Electric guitars grated on Tai's ears and made her feel edgy, but they made Sue feel alive. Color and form delighted Tai and made her thirst for more; the same color and form gave Sue a headache. The act of sensing and perceiving stimuli of any kind, whether a song, a color-soaked canvas, or a soft caress, encompasses a remarkable series of events at the levels of the brain, the person, and the social group, all happening within the context of the physical world. The processes of sensation and perception lie at the root of our experience of being alive, serving as the foundation for most of what we know and do. If we cannot sense the world, then for all practical purposes it does not exist for us; if we sense it incorrectly, our world will be bent and distorted. To understand mental processes and behavior, then, we must understand how our senses allow us to make contact with the world.

1 What is "sensation," and how does it differ from "perception"?

2 People may vary in how they direct their attention; just what is "attention"?

Sensation and Perception: Being in the World

The Greek philosopher Plato, who some 2,500 years ago theorized about many aspects of existence, psychological and otherwise, offered an interesting explanation of how humans see. Plato believed that the eyes produce rays that illuminate objects and that these rays are the basis of sight. Recent surveys of college students reveal that a surprisingly high proportion of them—fully one third—believe the same thing! The percentage of students accepting this explanation actually doubled (to 67%) when participants were shown a computer-graphic illustration of the concept (Winer et al., 1996; see Winer & Cottrell, 1996). Furthermore, two thirds of the college students who believe in such rays also believe that a person whose rays fail will go blind (Winer et al., 1996).

To set the record straight, there are no rays that shine from your eyes; in fact, essentially the process works the other way. Rather than producing rays, the eye registers light that is reflected from, or is produced by, objects in the line of sight. Similarly, the ear registers vibrations of air, and the skin responds to an object when pressure from it stimulates nerves. Psychologists define **sensation** as the immediate experience of basic properties of an object or event that occurs when a type of receptor (such as those at the back of the eye, in the ear, on the skin) is stimulated. When enough physical energy strikes a receptor, the cell sends neural impulses to the brain. As discussed in Chapter 2, receptors in general are like locks, which are opened by the appropriate key; for these sensory receptors, the appropriate physical energy serves as the key. The entire cell that responds to physical stimulation is called a receptor, not just the key parts that register the input. It is the signals sent by these receptors that cause us to become aware of the outside world.

Psychologists call the registering of sensation when a physical event excites the appropriate receptors *early processing,* but this is not yet **perception,** which occurs when you organize and interpret the sensory input as signaling a particular object or event. Perception includes two major phases. In the first phase, called *intermediate processing,* the input is organized into coherent units. In vision, for example, you don't see isolated blobs and lines, you see surfaces and objects. In the second phase, termed *late processing,* your perceptual system interprets the meaning of these units. When Tai and Sue stand before the same abstract painting, Tai may discern a distinct pattern, whereas Sue perceives only a jumble of random markings. This is because Tai's visual system has had previous exposure to such paintings and has learned how to see them. But this window on the world is not permanently closed to Sue: She, like the rest of us, can learn to perceive things in new ways, and to enjoy the art she previously found unpleasant.

As with a painting or a piece of music, in which form and color, harmony and rhythm, are at work simultaneously, so too with processing. "Early," "intermediate," and "late" seem to indicate a simple sequential process, but more is happening. Processing may be **bottom up**, initiated by the stimulus, or **top down**, guided by knowledge, expectation, or belief. And the two sorts of processes may be in play at the same time (Humphreys et al., 1997; Kosslyn & Koenig, 1995). Here's how it works.

If you turn on the TV to a random channel, you will be able to understand what appears on the screen even if it's a complete surprise: the processing is bottom up, from the stimulus alone, unaided by any expectation you might have. Your eyes and ears register what's there, and your brain processes the resulting signals. Bottom-up processing operates like a row of standing dominoes: When the neural equivalent of the first domino is tripped by the light impulses reaching your eye and the sound vibrations reaching your ear, other neural signals are successively tripped, like falling dominoes, until you've understood what you're seeing and hearing.

Figure 3.1 on page 86 illustrates a classic example of bottom-up processing. Bottom-up processes lead you to read the meaning of the word. Such processes also lead you to see the color the word is written in—and if the meaning of the word is different from the color of the ink, you experience interference when you try to name the color of the ink.

Back to the couch, watching TV. After the first few moments of watching this randomly selected channel, even if you are the very picture of a vegetating couch potato, you are in fact actively anticipating what will appear next and using this information to help you see. Now you are engaging in top-down processing, which occurs when you use your knowledge of what to expect to help you look for specific characteristics and fill in missing parts of the stimulus. You can watch top-down processing at work if the TV image is really blurry and you use the sound track to provide clues to what's in the picture. For example, if the sound track

Sensation: The immediate experience of basic properties of an object or event that occurs when a receptor is stimulated.

Perception: The act of organizing and interpreting sensory input as signaling a particular object or event.

Bottom-up processing: Processing that is initiated by stimulus input.

Top-down processing: Processing that is initiated by knowledge, expectation, or belief.

Figure 3.1   The Stroop Effect

In 1935, John Ridley Stroop published a classic paper describing what is now known as the Stroop effect. Name the color of the ink used to print each word in the left column (not the color named by the word); then do the same for the words in the right column. Which is easier? You cannot help both seeing the color and reading the word, and when the meaning of the word is different from the color of the ink, you experience interference.

GREEN	RED
RED	BLUE
BLUE	GREEN
BLACK	BLACK
BLUE	GREEN
RED	BLUE
GREEN	BLACK
BLACK	RED
RED	BLUE
BLUE	GREEN

makes it clear that two people are about to kiss, you will be able to make out the outlines of the faces more easily.

Psychophysics: A World of Experience

You may think that you have direct contact with the world—but you don't. You know the world only as it is filtered through your senses, and your senses are not always accurate. Your senses are your windows on the world, but sometimes the glass is not entirely transparent. The examples in Figure 3.2 show how far off base your perception can be.

Well over a hundred years ago, scientists began trying to discover the relation between the properties of events in the world and people's sensations and perceptions of them. German scientist Gustav Theodor Fechner (1801–1887) founded the field of **psychophysics**, which studies the relation between physical events and the corresponding experience of those events. Researchers in psychophysics made a series of discoveries, which apply to all the senses.

Thresholds: "Over the Top"

Much as you cross a doorway when going from one room to the next, you cross a **threshold** when a physical event becomes strong enough to be noticed. For example, sometimes Tai feels that there is not quite enough light for her to appreciate a painting and wishes she could ask the museum guard to brighten the lighting. She knows that the guard can't change the lighting and, even if he could, how much should he turn it up? Just a tiny bit, just until Tai can tell that the lighting is in fact brighter? This sort of fine-tuning would result in a **just-noticeable difference (JND)**, which is the size of the difference in a stimulus property (such as the brightness of light) needed for the observer to notice a difference. A JND is a kind of threshold. The change in light level might be so slight that sometimes you notice it, and sometimes you don't. This change would be defined as a **difference threshold** if you noticed the difference half the time.

The size of a difference threshold depends on the overall magnitude of the stimulus. If you are a thin person, a weight gain of 5 pounds is often noticeable at a glance, but if you are on the hefty side, a 5-pound gain might not be detected by anyone but you. Similarly, turning up the light the same amount is much more noticeable when the dimmer starts at a low setting than when it starts at a high setting. Why is this? Psychophysicists have an answer. **Weber's law** (named after another German researcher, Ernst Weber) states that a constant percentage of a magnitude change is necessary to detect a difference. So, the greater the magnitude of the light (or the thickness of the waist, or the volume of the sound), the greater the extra amount must be to be noticed. Weber's law is remarkably accurate except for very large or very small magnitudes of stimuli.

Psychophysics: The study of the relation between physical events and the corresponding experience of those events.

Threshold: The point at which stimulation is strong enough to be noticed.

Just-noticeable difference (JND): The size of the difference in a stimulus property needed for the observer to notice that a change has occurred.

Difference threshold: The difference needed to notice a stimulus change half the time.

Weber's law: The rule that a constant percentage of a magnitude change is necessary to detect a difference.

Figure **3.2** **Visual Illusions**

Visual systems are not like cameras that accurately capture the world, as illustrated by these visual illusions. In these examples, the two lines with the arrow heads are in fact the same length; the diagonal line that cuts across the vertical path is straight, not jagged; and the circles in the center of the two displays are in fact the same size.

Have you ever wondered how far away something can be and still be seen, or how low you can turn down the sound before it becomes inaudible? An **absolute threshold** is the smallest amount of a stimulus needed to notice that the stimulus is present at all. But in spite of its label, there is nothing "absolute" about an absolute threshold. Like the difference threshold, the absolute threshold is defined as the magnitude of the stimulus needed to make it noticeable to the observer half the time. In establishing absolute thresholds, you are distinguishing between the background and the stimulus, and the stimulus must have enough of its defining quality that you are in fact able to notice it. If a warning light isn't bright enough, you won't notice that it's on—which could be a serious deficiency if the light is meant to indicate that your car's radiator is about to boil over.

Detecting Signals: Noticing Needles in Haystacks

Acting on the "equal time" principle, Sue and Tai are at a rock concert. Because of a bomb scare the previous day, the audience was warned at the outset to listen for a fire alarm that would be a signal to evacuate the arena. For Tai, who isn't enjoying the concert, the possibility that an alarm might call a halt to the event is almost appealing. Sue, on the other hand, devoutly hopes the concert will continue without interruption. Which of the friends do you think is more likely to hear a fire alarm? Tai might even "hear" an alarm bell that does not exist. This sort of error proved very important in World War II, when radar operators sometimes "saw" airplanes that did not exist and sometimes missed airplanes that did.

The simple fact that people make these kinds of errors led to a new way of thinking about thresholds. **Signal detection theory** seeks to explain why people detect signals in some situations but miss them in others. The key idea is that signals are always embedded in noise, and thus the challenge is to distinguish signal from noise. Noise, in this case, refers to other events that could be mistaken for the stimulus. Two key concepts explain how signals are detected or missed: sensitivity and bias. Greater **sensitivity** means a lower threshold for distinguishing between a stimulus (the "signal") and the background (the "noise"). For example, on a radar screen, the signal dots indicating enemy aircraft would not need to be very large or bright compared with the noise composed of random-appearing

Absolute threshold: The smallest amount of a stimulus needed to detect that the stimulus is present.

Signal detection theory: A theory explaining why people detect signals, which are always embedded in noise, in some situations but not in others.

Sensitivity: In signal detection theory, the threshold level for distinguishing between a stimulus and noise; the lower the threshold, the greater the sensitivity.

Bias: In signal detection theory, a person's willingness to report noticing a stimulus.

Attention: The act of focusing on particular information, which allows it to be processed more fully than what is not attended to.

Selective attention: The process of picking out a particular quality, object, or event for relatively detailed analysis.

Pop-out: Occurs when a stimulus is sufficiently different from the ones around it that it is immediately evident.

specks. **Bias** is the willingness to report noticing a stimulus (such as the willingness of a radar operator to risk identifying random specks as aircraft). At the concert, Tai and Sue have different biases to hear the alarm because Tai would be happy to leave and Sue longs to stay. And so Tai is continually nudging Sue to confirm whether an alarm really has sounded. Sensitivity and bias can be assessed by comparing the occasions when people *say* a stimulus is or is not present with the occasions when the stimulus is *in fact* present or not (Green & Swets, 1966; McNicol, 1972).

Attention: The Gateway to Awareness

Do you think you would be more sensitive to a slight change in lighting conditions if you were on the lookout for such a change? Research has shown that paying attention increases sensitivity to the attended events (Nakayama & Mackeben, 1989; Yeshurun & Carrasco, 1998, 1999). **Attention** is the act of focusing on particular information, which allows that information to be processed more fully than information that is not attended to. **Selective attention** allows you to pick out a particular object or event. Another form of attention, *vigilance,* occurs when you are anticipating and waiting for a particular event, for example, waiting to see whether a softball is going to be whacked your way when you are standing in the outfield. We are aware only of what we pay attention to. Attention operates in virtually all domains of human thought and feeling, not only in perception. We can pay attention to a nuance of a word, a feeling, a taste, a particular place, or a characteristic sound.

Certain qualities or features of displays, such as advertisements, automatically leap out—a phenomenon psychologists refer to as **pop-out.** For example, look at the left panel of Figure 3.3. Is a red dot present? The red dot appears to pop out; it is immediately evident without your having to search for it. Attention is immediately drawn to this "odd man out." In general, pop-out occurs when objects differ in their fundamental qualities, such as size or frequency (you immediately hear a high-pitched flute in a band if all the other instruments are playing low notes). Conversely, when you try to find an object that is not distinct from the others around it, you aren't automatically drawn to it but must search for it, looking at each possible candidate one at a time. Treisman and her colleagues (Treisman & Gormican, 1988; Treisman & Souther, 1985) demonstrated how this works in an experiment like the one illustrated in Figure 3.3.

Figure 3.3 Pop-Out Versus Search

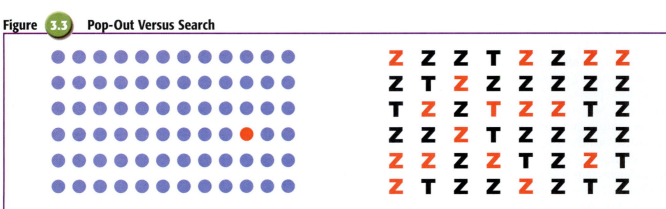

As shown in the left panel, basic features, such as color, are registered without the need for an item-by-item search. Is there a red T in the right panel? To find a conjunction, such as the arrangements of segments or a shape with a particular color, you must search the items one at a time.

Romantic Interludes

The pupils of the eye expand, admitting more light when you are paying attention to something; this is a function of the sympathetic nervous system. So one way you can tell if someone is paying attention to you is to watch his or her pupils. Indeed, Hess (1975) showed that people judge faces with larger pupils as more attractive, which may reflect the knowledge (perhaps unconscious) that larger pupils indicate interest. During the Middle Ages, women used the juice of the poisonous plant belladonna to dilate their pupils and, they believed, make themselves more attractive. And they were right—about the effect, if not the safety, of the practice.

The pupils also enlarge in dim light. Say you are in a romantic situation, the lights are low, and you want to make use of some psychological principles by using pupil size as a cue that your companion is fascinated by what you are saying. To distinguish between pupil expansion due to dim light and pupil expansion due to rapt attention, you need both increased perceptual sensitivity (to notice a small difference in pupil expansion) and an absence of bias (either hoping for the best or fearing the worst). Fortunately, research has shown that the ability to distinguish one fea-

ture from another actually increases in situations in which discrimination is difficult. For example, Spitzer and colleagues (1988) located neurons in part of a monkey's brain that fired more vigorously when a closer discrimination had to be made (this study measured discrimination among colors or tilts). This increase in firing rate is important because it allows the animals to perform the discriminations more accurately. These findings show that, as expected, selective attention causes more brain activity in the relevant perceptual areas of the human brain (Corbetta et al., 1990, 1991, 1993; Gauthier et al., 1997; Wojciulik et al., 1998).

Thus, you can see how a social event—one person's trying to assess another's interest—can be understood in part by analysis at the level of the brain. Not only do events in the brain make the pupils larger, but other events in the brain allow you to notice when someone else's pupils are in fact larger than they otherwise would be. And, of course, the desire to monitor a particular person's pupils in the first place depends on your beliefs and previous social interactions. Moreover, depending on what you think you see, you may respond differently, and that response will in turn have social consequences.

Which version of the picture do you find more attractive? If you are male, you probably find the one with the larger pupils (left) "more feminine," "soft," or "pretty," whereas the one with the small pupils (right) may appear "hard," "selfish," or "cold" (Hess, 1975).

CONSOLIDATE!

1 ***What is "sensation," and how does it differ from "perception"?*** Sensations occur when a physical event in the world stimulates receptors (such as those at the back of the eye, in the ear,

and on the skin), which then send signals to the brain. We detect events that are over threshold (a difference threshold to notice them against a background; an absolute threshold to see that they are present at all), but our sensitivity to stimuli must be distinguished from our bias to classify input as signal versus noise. Perception occurs when input is organized and interpreted as indicating that a particular object or event is present. Bottom-up processing is initiated by the stimulus, whereas top-down processing is guided by knowledge, expectation, or belief.

2 *People may vary in how they direct their attention; just what is "attention"?* Attention is the act of focusing on particular information, which allows it to be processed more fully than information to which you are not attending. Selective attention leads us to pick out a particular object or event, and we are aware only of what is captured by our attention. Some types of basic stimulus qualities pop out when they differ from surrounding ones, but other qualities must be searched for one at a time.

Vision

As Sue and Tai stood in front of a painting that seemed to Sue to be no more than blurry, smudged, and indistinct shapes, Tai spoke admiringly of the way the impressionists tried to present the changing effects of light and color in nature.

Monet painted haystacks at different times of day in order to appreciate how people actually see.

Rather than competing with the realism of the camera, they sought to evoke the visual sensations leading to perception. To accomplish this, the artists used qualities inherent in color itself and took advantage of the way the human visual system works. The 19th century French impressionist Claude Monet produced a series of paintings of haystacks in a field as day wore on to evening, and from season to season. The shadows he painted on the stacks were in colors complementary to the haystacks themselves; his large green fields were accented with small strokes of complementary red. His brush strokes were broken, so there are no sharp edges in the forms he depicted. By this use of color, and the merging of subject (the "figure") and background (the "ground"), the impressionists—as their name suggests—tried to paint in a way that would replicate the process by which people actually see.

Visual perception is not accomplished in one fell swoop but, like other sensory processes, occurs in the three broad phases noted earlier (Marr, 1982; Nakayama et al., 1995): early, intermediate, and late. The registering of visual sensation relies on *early visual processes*. These occur in the eye and in the first parts of the brain to register visual input. An example of early visual processing is registering the colors in a painting. Patches of color are then, in *intermediate visual processing*, organized into coherent units, which usually correspond to objects, such as the haystacks in a Monet painting. These intermediate processes can operate on the initial input even if you don't know in advance "the whole picture" of what you will be seeing. They are a bridge between the early processes and *late visual processes*, which involve stored information. It is only in late visual processing that what you see becomes meaningful, that you realize you are seeing a haystack and not a honeycomb.

1 What is the nature of light, and how do we see color, shape, and motion?

2 How are we able to separate figure from ground and see the world as a stable collection of objects?

3 How do we make sense of what we see?

Early Vision: It's Sensational!

Early visual processing is the crucial first step of our ability to see the world around us. Without early vision, we could have no bottom-up processing—no visual stimulus could reach us—and our only visual experience would be hallucinations.

Let There Be Light

You know, as Plato did not, that rays don't come from your eyes; rather, to see, you need light that either bounces off an object or is produced by the object. Light is a form of electromagnetic radiation. All of us swim in a sea of electromagnetic radiation. This sea has waves: some large, some small, some that come in rapid succession, some spaced far apart. The height of a wave is its **amplitude**, and the rate at which the wave peaks move past a given point is its **frequency**. With higher frequency, the peaks of the waves arrive more often—and thus the length of time between peaks is shorter. When the length of time between arrivals of the peaks is shorter, the light is said to have a shorter **wavelength**. In the electromagnetic spectrum, which ranges from the terrifically long radio waves and alternating currents to the very short X rays and gamma rays, there is a narrow band of radiation perceived as visible light. An almost uncountable number of colors are conveyed in this light; the traditional seven we readily distinguish are red, orange, yellow, green, blue, indigo, and violet. The lower frequencies (and longer wavelengths) are toward the red end of the spectrum; the higher frequencies (and shorter wavelengths) are toward the violet end, as illustrated in Figure 3.4.

Figure 3.4 **The Range of Electromagnetic Radiation**

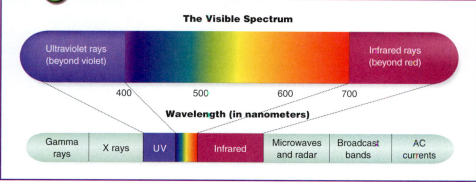

The Brain's Eye: More Than a Camera

The eye converts the electromagnetic energy that is light into nerve impulses; this conversion process is called **transduction**. As illustrated in Figure 3.5 on page 92, light enters the eye through an opening called the **pupil**. Surrounding the pupil is a circular muscle called the **iris**. The iris changes the size of the pupil to let in more or less light. The light is focused partly by the **cornea**, the transparent covering over the eye, and then focused even more by the **lens**. Unlike a camera lens, the lens in a human eye flexes. In fact, muscles can adjust the lens into a more or less round shape to focus light from objects that are different distances away. **Accommodation**, the automatic adjustment of the eye for seeing at different distances, occurs when muscles change the shape of the lens so that it focuses light on the retina from near and faraway objects. The world appears sharp and clear because we are constantly moving our eyes, and what we choose to look at can quickly be moved into focus. With age, the lens thickens and becomes less flexible (Fatt & Weissman, 1992), often causing older people to have trouble seeing nearer objects—for example, reading material.

Amplitude: The height of the peaks in a light wave.

Frequency: The rate at which light waves move past a given point.

Wavelength: The time between the arrival of peaks of a light wave; shorter wavelengths correspond to higher frequencies.

Notice that only a small portion of the range gives rise to visible light. Also notice that the hue depends on the particular wavelength.

Transduction: The process whereby physical energy is converted by a sensory neuron into neural impulses.

Pupil: The opening in the eye through which light passes.

Iris: The circular muscle that adjusts the size of the pupil.

Cornea: The transparent covering over the eye, which serves partly to focus the light onto the back of the eye.

Lens: The flexible disk under the cornea that focuses light onto the back of the eye.

Accommodation: Occurs when muscles adjust the shape of the lens so that it focuses light on the retina from objects at different distances.

Figure 3.5   Anatomy of the Eye

The many parts of the eye either focus an image on the retina or convert light into neural impulses that are sent to the brain.

Cornea
Pupil
Iris
Lens
Retina
Fovea
Optic nerve
Blood vessels

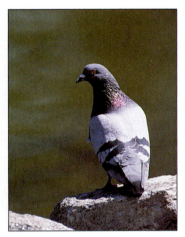

When it comes to foveas, some animals have it all over us humans; some types of birds, for example, have two foveas. Next time you are annoyed at a noisy pigeon, appreciate the fact that it can focus to the side and ahead at the same time.

Retina: A sheet of tissue at the back of the eye containing cells that convert light to neural impulses.

Fovea: The small, central region of the retina with the highest density of cones and the highest resolution.

Rods: Retinal cells that are very sensitive to light but register only shades of gray.

Cones: Retinal cells that respond most strongly to one of three wavelengths and that play a key role in producing color vision.

The critical step in the transduction process occurs at the **retina**, a sheet of tissue at the back of the eye that is about as thick as a piece of paper. The central part of the retina contains densely packed cells that transform light to nerve impulses, and this region—called the **fovea**—gives us the sharpest images. We are not usually aware of how fuzzy our world looks. Most of the time we pay attention only to the images that strike the fovea, which are sharp and clear, but much of what we see is in fact not very sharply focused. Take a moment to look up and focus on a single spot on the other side of the room; notice how blurry things look even a short distance to the side of that spot.

Two kinds of cells in the retina convert light to nerve impulses: rods and cones (see Figure 3.6). **Rods** (which actually look like little rods) are extraordinarily sensitive to light, but they register only shades of gray. Each eye contains between 100 million and 120 million rods. The **cones** (which look like, yes, cones) are not as sensitive to light as are the rods, but they respond most vigorously to particular wavelengths of light, allowing us to see color. Each eye contains between 5 million and 6 million cones (Beatty, 1995; Dowling, 1992). The cones are densest near the fovea, and the rods are everywhere within the retina except in the fovea. At night, there isn't enough light for the less-light-sensitive cones to work, so night vision is based on the firing of the rods alone. That is why an apple looks black and an orange cat looks gray under a moonlit night sky.

When you first enter a darkened theater, you can't see a thing. You may have noticed, though, that the risk of tripping or bumping into someone is a lot less if you wait even a brief time because you soon can see much better. In fact, after about 30 minutes in the dark, you are about 100,000 times more sensitive to light than you are during full daylight. In ideal conditions, the rods can respond when they receive a single photon, the smallest unit of light. This process of acclimatization is called **dark adaptation**. Part of the increased sensitivity to what light there is arises because your pupil enlarges when you are in darkness; in fact, it can expand to let in about 16 times as much light as enters in full daylight. In addition, the rods actually become more sensitive as your eyes remain in the dark because your genes cause the production of a crucial chemical, called *rhodopsin,* that responds to light. Here's a hint: Because of the way the rods are arranged on the retina, if you want to see best at night, look slightly to the side of what you want to examine.

The axons from retinal cells in each eye are gathered into a single large cord called the **optic nerve**, which is about as thick as your little finger. There are no rods or cones at the place where the optic nerve exits the retina, which causes a "blind spot" in what you can see laid out in front of you. Because the brain completes patterns that fall across this blind spot, you are not aware of it as you look

Figure **3.6** **Rods and Cones**

Two types of cells in the retina convert light into neural responses. The rods allow us to see with less light, but not in color; the cones allow us to see in color but are not as light-sensitive as the rods.

Cones

Rods

Light

Back of eyeball

Nerve impulses to higher brain pathways

around every day. Look at Figure 3.7, though, and you can "see" where your blind spot is.

Researchers have known about rods and cones for well over 100 years, but only recently have they discovered evidence for a third kind of receptor in the eye that also registers light. Freedman and her colleagues (1999) observed that even mice whose eyes had no rods or cones still shifted their "circadian" behavior when light was shined on them. Circadian behavior is behavior that follows the daily pattern of light, such as waking and sleeping; in this case, the behavior was running, which in these mice varies depending on the time of day. But when the eyes were removed, the mice no longer made the adjustment in their "running schedule." Thus, the third kind of light-sensitive receptor must be in the eyes. In another study, Lucas and his colleagues (1999) investigated the decrease in production of a hormone called melatonin in the presence of light (melatonin is the hormone that some people use to overcome jet lag). Even mice without rods or cones showed a normal decrease in melatonin production when placed in light. Clearly, light affects the brain even when there are no rod or cone sensory cells. This work opens an exciting new frontier in the investigation of how we see.

Dark adaptation: The process whereby exposure to darkness causes the eyes to become more sensitive, allowing for better vision in the dark.

Optic nerve: The large bundle of nerve fibers carrying impulses from the retina into the brain.

Figure **3.7** **Finding Your Blind Spot**

X

Cover your left eye and stare at the X with the other. Now slowly bring the book closer to you, continuing to focus on the X. When the picture on the right disappears, you have found your right eye's blind spot.

Trichromatic theory of color vision:
The theory that color vision arises from the combinations of neural impulses from three different kinds of sensors, each of which responds maximally to a different wavelength.

Opponent process theory of color vision: The theory that if a color is present, it causes cells that register it to inhibit the perception of the complementary color (such as red versus green).

Color Vision: Mixing and Matching

How can you tell whether an apple is ripe? One way is to look at its color. Color also plays a key role in our appreciation of beauty in art, nature, and people. One of the remarkable aspects of human vision, which makes painting and appreciation of painting such rich experiences, is the huge range of colors that people can use and see.

At one point in the study of color vision, there was a debate about how humans can see such a large range of colors. One camp took its lead from observations reported by Thomas Young and Hermann von Helmholz in the 19th century. This approach focused on phenomena such as the mixing of colors to produce new colors (as mixing yellow and blue paint produces green). These researchers, arguing by analogy, believed that the brain registers color by combining responses to separate wavelengths. In particular, they argued that the eye contains three kinds of color sensors, each most sensitive to a particular range of wavelength: long, medium, and short. This view was therefore called the **trichromatic theory.**

The other camp followed the lead of German physician Ewald Hering, who worked at the end of the 19th century and the beginning of the 20th century. Hering noticed that some colors cannot be mixed—you can't make reddish-green or yellowish-blue. (As any preschooler would be happy to demonstrate, you can of course mix the colors—but yellow and blue produce green, not yellowish blue, and red and green produce the color of mud.) This and similar observations led him to develop the **opponent process theory,** which states that the presence of one color of a pair (red/green, yellow/blue, and black/white) inhibits the perception of the other color.

Happily, it turns out that *both* theories are correct, but they describe processing at different places in the eye and brain. Consistent with trichromatic theory, our perception of colors arises because we possess three different types of cones. One type of cone is most responsive to light in the wavelength seen as yellow, another to light in the wavelength seen as green, and another in the wavelength seen as violet (Reid, 1999). The trick is that at least two of the three types of cones usually respond to *any* wavelength of visible light, but to different degrees (De Valois & De Valois, 1975, 1993). And here's the important part: The *mixture* of the three types of response signals is different for each of a huge range of wavelengths, and it is this mixture that is the crucial signal to the brain. The brain responds to the mixture, not the outputs from individual cones. Color television operates on this principle. Stare very closely at a color TV screen, and you will see little bubbles of three colors (red, green, and blue). Stand back, and a wide range of colors appears. Why? Because your eyes and your brain respond differently, depending on the mixture of wavelengths produced by clusters of these bubbles.

The mixtures of responses of the cones is not the whole story of color vision. If this were all there were to it, we should be able to see all mixtures of colors—but, as Hering originally observed, we can't. As the opponent process theory predicts, there's another factor, too, which will become apparent when you take a look at the strange colored flag in Figure 3.8. Stare at the flag, and then look at

Figure **3.8   Seeing Afterimages**

Does this flag look strange to you? Stare at the dot in the center for about 60 seconds in a bright light, and then look at the blank space. You should see a brilliant afterimage of Old Glory, with red and white stripes and a blue field.

the space to its right; you should see an **afterimage**, an image left behind by a previous perception. Furthermore, the flag should look normal in the afterimage, not strangely colored as it is actually printed. Why are the colors of afterimages different from those of the object? You need to understand more about color vision to answer that question. A key fact is that the cones feed into special types of cells in the retina and the lateral geniculate nucleus of the brain (part of the thalamus): red/green, yellow/blue, and black/white **opponent cells**. These cells are set up to pit the colors in each pair against each other, with exactly the effect Hering predicted. For example, when wavelengths that produce blue are registered by these cells, they inhibit the perception of wavelengths that produce yellow, and vice versa (Hurvich & Jameson, 1957). This process helps you to distinguish among colors that have similar wavelengths, such as green and yellow (Reid, 1999, discusses the role of the cortex in such processing, as do Livingstone & Hubel, 1984). This is why you can't see greenish red or yellowish blue: Seeing one member of a pair inhibits seeing the other. It also explains why you see afterimages like the one illustrated by staring at Figure 3.8. An afterimage occurs when one member of a pair of opponent cells inhibits the other (for example, green inhibits red), and then releases it. In the process, the previously inhibited one (red) temporarily overshoots the mark, creating an afterimage.

Color is thus the result of a complicated process that mixes and inhibits. And making matters more complex is the fact that colors vary in three separate ways. First, different wavelengths of light produce the sensation of different colors. This aspect of color—whether it looks red, blue, and so on—is called *hue*. Second, the purity of the input (the amount of white that's mixed in with the color) produces the perception of *saturation*—that is, how deep the color appears. Third, the amplitude of the light waves produces the perception of *lightness* or *brightness* (if the object, such as a television screen, produces light)—how sharp the color appears. An area of the brain called visual area 4 (or V4) in monkeys plays a major role in processing color (Zeki, 1993); a corresponding area lights up in human brains when color is perceived. If this area is damaged, the ability to see hue is lost. This acquired color blindness is called *acquired achromotopsia* (Damasio, 1985). In Oliver Sacks's book *An Anthropologist on Mars* (1995), a color-blind artist describes how hard it is for him to eat food, particularly red food (such as apples and tomatoes), which appears to him to be a repulsive deep black.

People who have **color blindness** are either unable to distinguish one hue from another or, in more serious cases, are unable to see hue at all. Most color blindness is present from birth. Depending on the specific group, as many as 8% of European men but less than 0.5% of European women are born color-blind (Reid, 1999). Rather than being completely insensitive to hue, most color-blind people are unable to distinguish red from green. Researchers have found that people with the most common type of color blindness possess genes that produce similar pigments in

Afterimage: The image left behind by a previous perception.

Opponent cells: Cells that pit the colors in a pair, notably blue/yellow or red/green, against each other.

Color blindness: An inability, either acquired (by brain damage) or inherited, to perceive hue.

People with normal color vision would see the crayons as shown on the left. People with the most common form of color blindness—inability to distinguish red from green—would see the crayons as shown on the right. Before traffic lights were arranged with red always on the top, not being able to see colors made driving hazardous for people with red/green color blindness. In what other ways would such a disorder affect your life?

their cones (Neitz et al., 1996), and thus the cones do not respond to wavelengths as they should. A small number of people (roughly 2% of males, and a very small number of females) are actually missing a type of cone. Even more severe deficits occur when more than one type of cone is affected (Reid, 1999).

Intermediate Vision: Organizing the World

Can you see which animals are present? The coloring of the horses blends nicely with the background. Why might animals look like their surroundings?

Although it seems that we perceive what we see in, literally, the blink of an eye, a large number of mental steps actually occur between the moment a pattern of light strikes our eyes and the time we become aware of seeing an object. At each step, different areas of the brain are crucial (Grill-Spector et al., 1998). The second, intermediate phase of vision is necessary before the input can become meaningful. The intermediate processes organize the input into shapes that correspond to surfaces and objects (Marr, 1982; Nakayama et al., 1995). Key features of intermediate-level vision include organizing the input into units that correspond to objects and registering the basic properties of objects, such as their actual sizes and shapes.

Perceptual Organization: Seeing the Forest For the Trees

On its own, the eye cannot organize visual input into shapes that correspond to objects: It is the brain that does this. To recognize the **figure** (the object of interest), the viewer must first distinguish it from the **ground** (the background). When figure and ground are similar, the figure is said to be *camouflaged*. Armies the world over have long taken advantage of this property of the perceptual system.

Separating figure from ground involves organizing regions into shapes that are likely to correspond to objects or their parts. A critical part of this process is finding edges. Visual areas in the occipital lobe of the brain are *topographically orga-*

Figure: In perception, a set of characteristics (such as shape, color, texture) that corresponds to an object.

Ground: In perception, the background, which must be distinguished to pick out figures.

Tootell and colleagues (1982) produced this remarkable illustration of retinotopic mapping in the monkey brain. The animal looked at the figure on the left while radioactive sugar was being ingested by the brain cells. The dark lines on the right show which brain cells in the primary visual cortex were working hardest when the animal viewed the figure. The spatial structure of the figure is evident on the surface of the brain.

nized—that is, the pattern falling on the retina is spatially laid out on the cortex. This arrangement helps the brain to delineate the edges of objects. Because of the way intermediate visual processes operate, however, people do not see isolated lines, dots, and so on, but rather overall patterns. Gestalt psychologists, who were introduced briefly in Chapter 1, discovered a set of laws that describe how the brain organizes the input from the eyes (Koffka, 1935; Wertheimer, 1923). The most important of these **Gestalt laws of organization** follow:

Proximity: Marks that are near one another tend to be grouped together. So, for example, we see **XXX XXX** as two groups, and **XX XX XX** as three groups, even though they have the same total number of **X** marks.

Continuity (also called "good continuation"): Marks that tend to fall along a smooth curve or a straight line tend to be grouped together. So, for example, we see _ _ _ _ as a single line, not four separate dashes; and we see – – – – _ _ _ _ as two separate lines because all eight of the dashes do not fall on the same plane.

Similarity: Marks that look alike tend to be grouped together. So, for example, we see **XXXxxx** as two groups. Whether the elements are the same or different colors also affects similarity, another reason color vision is so important.

Closure: We tend to close any gaps in a figure, so a circle with a small section missing will still be seen as a circle.

Good Form: Marks that form a single shape tend to be grouped together. So, for example, we see [ ] as a single shape, but not [_.

Additional laws have been added since the time of the Gestalt psychologists (who began work in 1912). For example, Palmer (1992b) has shown that marks occurring in a common region tend to be grouped together. The details of how the brain actually works to organize the world in these ways are just now being discovered (Grossberg et al., 1997; Kovacs, 1996; Kovacs & Julesz, 1993; von der Heydt & Peterhans, 1989; von der Heydt et al., 1984).

Sometimes a figure can be organized and perceived in more than one way. Figure 3.9 shows some of the classic *ambiguous figure-ground relationships*.

You can see the middle part of this picture as a set of birds or a set of fish, which illustrates how the figure can serve as the ground, and vice versa. Such artwork demonstrates the roles of figure and ground, and your participation in interpreting which is which.

Gestalt laws of organization: A set of rules describing the circumstances under which marks will be grouped into perceptual units, such as proximity, continuity, similarity, closure, and good form.

Figure 3.9 Ambiguous Figures

In the left panel, you can see either two silhouetted faces or a vase, depending on what you pay attention to as the figure; in the right panel, you can see an old or a young woman, again depending on how you organize the figure.

Magic Eye® drawings like this produce the experience of depth after you stare at them for a while because there are two versions of the same object, slightly displaced. If you focus your gaze just right, your brain will figure out the distance the object would be to produce this disparity. And voilà! You'll see depth! (© 2000 Magic Eye Inc., www.magiceye.com)

Binocular cues: Cues to the distance of an object that arise from both eyes working together.

Retinal disparity: The difference between the images striking the retinas of the two eyes; also called *binocular disparity.*

Stereopsis: The process that registers depth on the basis of retinal disparity.

Motion cues: Information that specifies the distance of an object on the basis of its movement.

Knowing the Distance

Intermediate-level visual processing also specifies the layout of surfaces. Because the world is three-dimensional, we need to register distances (for example, to be able to reach and navigate properly). This poses an interesting problem: Our eyes project images onto the two-dimensional surface of our retinas, but we need to see objects in three dimensions. Given that our eyes capture images in only two dimensions, how is it that we see in three? Once again, the answer lies with the brain, which uses different types of cues to derive three dimensions from the two-dimensional images on the retinas of the eyes.

Binocular cues, those that arise from both eyes working together, help you assess how far away an object is. Your brain uses slight differences in the images striking your eyes to assess the distance of an object. Because your eyes are separated, you need to cross them to focus on an object (so that the same image appears on the central, high-resolution fovea in each eye). When you do this, however, the images of *other* objects—ones in front of or behind the one you are focused on—appear slightly differently on the retinas of the two eyes. This difference between the images on the two eyes is called **retinal disparity** (also called binocular disparity), and the brain uses the amount of binocular disparity to determine which objects are in front of and which are behind others (Pinker, 1997, pp. 220–233). The process of figuring out depth from binocular disparity is called **stereopsis** (Anderson & Nakayama, 1994). Some neurons in the visual areas of the brain have been found to respond best with relatively little binocular disparity, whereas others fire more vigorously when lots of binocular disparity is present (Ohzawa et al., 1990; Patterson & Martin, 1992). Thus, neurons register the information the brain needs to figure out distance from the objects in view.

Stereopsis works only for objects up to about 10 feet away—at distances greater than that, the eyes don't need to cross in order to focus, and thus there is no binocular disparity. **Motion cues**, on the other hand, can operate at any distance, and they are effective even with one eye. In fact, these cues work so well that Wesley Walker, blind in one eye from birth, could catch a football well enough to be the star wide receiver for the New York Jets football team (in fact, he played for them for 13 years). To notice a motion cue, try this: Hold up this book and move your head back and forth as you look at it. Note how the images of objects behind the book seem to shift. As you shift your head to the left, the distant objects seem to move to the left; as you shift to the right, they shift to the right. Now focus on the background, still holding the book, and move your head back and forth; note how the image of the book seems to shift. This time the object you aren't focusing on, the book, seems to shift in the opposite direction to the way you move your head! Objects closer than the one you are fixated on seem to move in the opposite direction to your movements, whereas ones farther away than the fixation point seem to move in the same direction. And depending on the distance, the objects will seem to shift at different speeds. This difference in shifting provides information about relative distance, a cue called *motion parallax.*

You use several types of cues to perceive motion. For example, if you are moving directly toward an object, it seems to expand symmetrically around its center and thus loom closer. Likewise, if you are moving toward its right side, that side will loom closer than the other. When silent movies were first shown to the public, the movement of an on-screen train rushing toward viewers was so startling that many moviegoers panicked and fled the theaters (Seuling, 1976). Only after they had experienced watching moving objects on a screen could they distinguish between the usual motion cues and the bogus ones in films (which are a kind of illusion), and relax and enjoy the show. Such learning was necessary because these cues are ordinarily so important. In fact, neuroimaging research with humans has revealed that special areas in the brain detect this kind of motion (Tootell et al., 1997; Zeki, 1978, 1993). Also, studies of brain-damaged patients have documented the role of particular brain areas for processing motion. For example, one patient could not pour tea into a cup; she would see the tea suddenly appear, not continuously flow. Instead of motion, she saw a series of static images (Zihl et al., 1983).

Not all cues for distance involve motion. **Monocular static cues** for distance can be picked up with one eye even without movement. Such monocular ("one-eyed") and static ("unmoving") cues are used effectively by artists to create the illusion of distance. One of these is the **texture gradient**, a progressive change in the texture of an object. Gibson (1966) described the way texture gradients signal distance. Look at the brick street in the photograph (or, for that matter, in life). The bricks that are closer to you, the observer, are larger in the photograph and appear so in life; you use this cue to determine distance.

In drawing pictures, artists also use *linear perspective*, or *foreshortening*, making the parts of objects that are farther away from the viewer actually smaller on the page. You also infer distance if one object partially covers another, indicating that the obscured object is behind the other and thus farther away; this relation is called an *occlusion cue*. And if the base of an object appears higher on the horizon than the base of another object, you take that as a cue that the higher one is farther away. Figure 3.10 provides good examples of the power of these monocular cues, and Figure 3.11 on page 100 summarizes monocular and binocular depth cues.

Notice the relative sizes and spacing of the bricks in this example of a texture gradient, one cue that the street is receding into the distance.

Figure 3.10 A Monocular Depth Cue

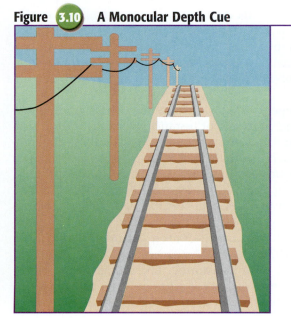

Even though you know that the two white bars on the rails are in fact the same size, the one that appears farther away also appears larger. Because you see the top one as farther away, the fact that it is the same size on the page signals that it is larger. Painters use depth cues like these to fool the eye.

Perceptual Constancies: Stabilizing the World

Information about distance is important for more than separating figure from ground; it also helps to specify the three-dimensional shape of an object seen from different vantage points. Imagine strapping a camera onto your head and making a videotape as you walk. What do you think the pictures would look like? The images striking your eyes change wildly depending on your viewpoint, but

Monocular static cues: Information that specifies the distance of an object that can be picked up with one eye without movement of the object or eye.

Texture gradients: Progressive changes in texture that signal distance.

Figure 3.11 Depth Cues

Depth perception depends on both monocular cues and binocular cues.

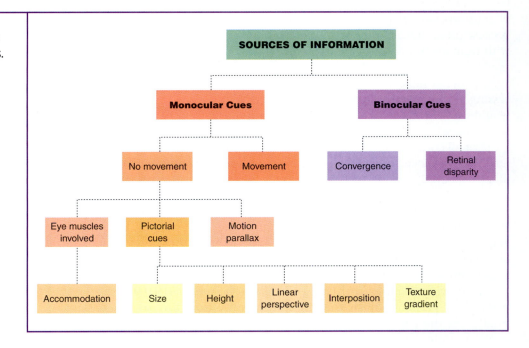

the objective world you relate to seems stable. Objects in the world appear to keep their shapes, their sizes, their colors, and so on, even when you view them in very different positions or circumstances. **Perceptual constancy** is the perception of the characteristics of objects (such as their shapes and colors) as the same even though the sensory information striking the eyes changes. For example, **size constancy** occurs when you see an object (such as a car) as the same size even when it is at different distances, so that its image (as in a photograph) is at different sizes. **Shape constancy** occurs when you see an object as the same shape, even when you view it from different angles (again, so that its image in a photograph would be different). This stabilization occurs not in the eyes, but in the brain, and is fundamental to the ability to recognize objects and know how to interact with them.

The cues we use to preserve shape constancy are also used in drawings. Interestingly, such cues are not used in all cultures. For instance, in some rural parts of Africa, children's books are very rare. Thus, it is not surprising that these children have difficulty understanding the depth, shading, and perspective cues in drawings (Liddell, 1997). Cross-cultural studies have shown that people must learn how to interpret these cues in drawings (for example, Duncan et al., 1973). On the other hand, Western children appear to master these cues at earlier ages today than they did a century ago, possibly because children's books are more widely available (Peeck, 1987). In all cases, learning plays an important role in understanding how pictures portray depth (Leibowitz, 1971).

Finally, consider **brightness and color constancy**. Take a page from a notebook and look at it on a table indoors. Now take it outdoors on a day when the sun is out. It probably appears roughly as bright in the two conditions, but in fact there is much more light bouncing off the page when it is outside. Most researchers now believe that the key to understanding this phenomenon is that we do not see brightness as an absolute quality, but rather see *ratios* of brightness. We see the brightest thing as "bright" (regardless of the actual amount of light) and the brightness of everything else as proportional to it (Arend, 1994; Jacobsen & Gilchrist, 1988a, 1988b). Similarly, our ability to see colors as constant (green as green, red as red, and so on) even when the lighting changes (for example, in sunlight or in shadow) may arise because we see the lightest thing in a scene as white and everything else relative to that color (Land, 1959, 1977, 1983).

Perceptual constancy: The perception of characteristics that occurs when an object or quality (such as shape or color) looks the same even though the sensory information striking the eyes changes.

Size constancy: Seeing an object as being the same size when viewed at different distances and visual angles.

Shape constancy: Seeing objects as having the same shape even when the image on the retina changes.

Brightness and color constancy: Seeing objects as having the same lightness, brightness, or color in different viewing situations.

Late Vision: Recognition and Identification

Vision is more than organizing the world into shapes, of course. If that were all, how would you know if something was good to approach (such as a useful tool or a tasty sweet) or necessary to avoid (such as a dangerous animal or an angry boss). Late visual processes accomplish two major goals: They allow you to assign meaning to the shapes you see, and they allow you to map space so that you can guide your movements according to your goals (Goodale & Milner, 1992; Kosslyn, 1994b; Milner & Goodale, 1995; Ullman, 1996). These tasks are handled by separate mechanisms in the brain. From the results of experiments conducted with monkeys, Ungerleider and Mishkin (1982) described two major neural pathways, which they dubbed the *"what"* and *"where" pathways*. Further evidence for the existence of these distinct mechanisms comes from studies of humans who have had strokes. A stroke that affects the bottom parts of the temporal lobes impairs the patient's ability to recognize objects by sight, and a stroke that affects the back parts of the parietal lobes impairs the patient's ability to register locations (Levine, 1982). Moreover, these separate brain areas have been found to be activated during brain-scanning studies in which normal people are asked to distinguish shapes or locations (Bly & Kosslyn, 1997; Haxby et al., 1991, 1994; Kohler et al., 1995; Ungerleider & Haxby, 1994). The two pathways come together in the frontal lobes, where information about an object's identity and location is used to make decisions (Rao et al., 1997). Before reading on, take a moment to pick a card from Figure 3.12 on page 102; we will return to these cards shortly.

Look at these faces, and then turn the book and look at them right-side up. One explanation for the peculiar lapse in noticing the parts is that when you view the entire face, you are attending to a single pattern, and to see the parts in detail, you need to attend to the output from processes that register smaller things. Notice that if you focus on each part, you can see that some are upside down. But when you focus on the entire face, you see the overall pattern, not a collection of parts.

Knowing More Than You Can See

When you see an apple, intermediate visual processes indicate a red, shiny object of a certain shape and size that is at a certain distance. But nothing in this information tells you that inside this object are seeds and, maybe, a worm. For you to know these things, the visual input somehow must activate information from your prior experience, which you have stored in your memory. To interpret what you see, you need to compare the input to stored information. If the input matches something you've stored, the information stored in memory can be applied to the present case (and that's how you know that an apple *may* have a worm inside, even if you can't see one *this time*). If the object is *recognized*, it seems familiar; if it is *identified*, you know additional facts about it.

Objects are sometimes recognized as collections of parts. Irving Biederman and his colleagues (Biederman, 1987; Hummel & Biederman, 1992) have suggested

Figure 3.12   **Pick a Card, Any Card**

Before beginning, put your right hand over Figure 3.13, the set of cards on the page to the right. After you do that, look at this display and pick out a card. Then cover this display with your left hand, lift up your right hand from the display to the right, and read that caption.

that objects are represented in the brain as collections of simple shapes, with each shape representing a part of the object, such as the head, neck, body, and legs of a dog. It is clear that we can see parts of objects individually (Hoffman & Richards, 1984). But take a look at the two photographs of Ms. Spears, and then turn the book around so you can see the figure rightside up. It should also be clear that we do not always recognize or identify objects in terms of their individual parts. If that were the case, we wouldn't need to turn the book over to see how weird one of the versions is. Rather, we usually attend to overall views of shapes, and look for details only if we need them (Cave & Kosslyn, 1993). When we do look at individual features, however, we need to pay attention to ensure that they are properly combined, as demonstrated in Figures 3.12 and 3.13.

Informed Perception: The Active Viewer

Top-down processing can alter the mechanisms used in bottom-up processing (Humphreys et al., 1997; Kosslyn, 1994b). In a study by Delk and Fillenbaum (1965), for example, participants were shown stimuli that were all cut from the same orangish-red cardboard, including objects that are normally red (an apple and a valentine heart) and objects that are not normally red (a mushroom and a bell). The participants were to adjust the color of a display until they thought it matched the color of the cutouts. Apparently, the knowledge of the usual color of the objects affected how participants saw the actual color; when asked to match the color of the normally red objects, they consistently selected a redder color than the one they chose to match the color of the mushroom and the bell.

Depending on your beliefs and expectations, you will expect to see certain objects in certain contexts. When you walk into a restaurant, you will be surprised if there are no chairs (you may have had this experience the first time you visited an authentic Ethiopian or Japanese restaurant). People often use the context to form such *perceptual expectancies,* perceptions dependent on their previous experience. Loftus and his colleagues (1972) have shown that people require more time to identify an object when it is in an unusual context. When asked if an octopus is present in a picture display, for instance, people require more time to answer if the setting is unlikely—a barnyard, say—than if the setting is an underwater scene (Palmer, 1992a, reports similar findings).

Seeing Without Awareness

Some people who suffer strokes that leave them blind can nevertheless report accurately when spots of light are presented, and even know where they are. These people have no awareness of seeing the dots but rather simply "know" when they are present. Similarly, animals with damage to the visual cortex in the occipital lobe may appear to be blind at all other times, but when they are lowered onto a surface, they stick out their legs to support themselves at just the right point; some of these animals can avoid obstacles when walking, even though the primary

Figure 3.13 Is Only Your Card Missing?

Look at this display only after you picked out a card in the display on the page on the left. After you picked out a card, look for it here. Did we remove the card you were thinking of? At first glance, it probably appears that we have removed only that card and left the others alone. Magic? No. Your brain coded the suits and values of the cards separately, and so you only see them combined properly when you pay attention to them (Arguin et al., 1994; Treisman & Schmidt, 1982). Thus, if you only paid attention to one particular card, you will notice its absence. As for the other cards, you will notice only the values and suits, not their combinations.

visual cortex has been removed (Cowey & Stoerig, 1995). Such behavior has been called *blindsight* (Weiskrantz, 1986). Multiple pathways from the eye lead to many places in the brain (Felleman & Van Essen, 1991; Zeki, 1978, 1993). As noted, some of these pathways allow the brain to register movement, location, and other qualities—and some of these can function even though they do not pass through brain areas that give rise to conscious experience. Thus, even when the areas crucial for consciousness, or connections from these areas, are damaged, some visual function nevertheless persists. However, people are remarkably bad at noticing even large changes in stimuli if they are not paying attention to the relevant parts (O'Regan, 1992; Simons, 1999; Simons & Levin, 1997).

A bird in the hand is worth two in the the bush. Did you notice anything odd about the sentence you just read? Many people miss the repeated the, and in fact this is said to be the hardest error for a proofreader to catch. Kanwisher (1987, 1991) has dubbed this effect **repetition blindness** and has shown that people will fail to see a second example of an object if it occurs soon after the first instance. A related phenomenon is the **attentional blink,** in which attention is lost for a certain time immediately following a stimulus to which attention was paid. In contrast to repetition blindness, the attentional blink can occur for a different

Repetition blindness: The inability to see the second occurrence of a stimulus that appears twice in succession.

Attentional blink: A rebound period in which a person cannot pay attention to one thing after having just paid attention to another.

The two versions of these scenes were alternated every 640 milliseconds. In the pair of photos on the left, the railing changes, which is not of central interest. People had a difficult time noticing this change, requiring 16.2 alternations on average to spot it. In the pair of photos on the right, the location of the helicopter changes, which is of central interest. People noticed this change after only 4.0 alternations, on average (from Rensink et al., 1997).

stimulus, not necessarily a second instance of the same or a closely related one, and the effect may actually be larger for stimuli that occur a few items after the one attended to (Arnell & Jolicoeur, 1999; Chun, 1997; Jolicoeur, 1998; Luck et al., 1996; Raymond et al., 1992). Proofreaders and copyeditors experience this unfortunate phenomenon all the time, missing obvious errors that happen to fall in the wake of a large error or string of errors. Repetition blindness appears to result because the stimuli are not registered as individual events, but simply as a "type" of event (Kanwisher, 1987), whereas the attentional blink may occur because the act of registering information in detail may "lock up" the system for a brief period, during which attention cannot easily be reengaged.

The Importance of Body Parts in Physical Beauty

Vision is used for more than identifying objects and registering their locations, as Tai surely knows from the pleasure she takes in looking at art. Through the visual system we also perceive what we call "beauty," including physical attractiveness. David Perrett and his collaborators (1998) asked Asian people (Japanese in Japan) and Caucasians (Scots in Scotland) to choose the most attractive faces from a set of photographs, some of which had been altered to emphasize features that reflect high levels of male or female hormones. The researchers found that both national groups preferred women's faces with a female "hormone enhanced" look to average faces. However, the effect was larger for faces within each participant's own

population, a finding that was interpreted as indicating that this is a learned preference. In addition, both groups also found *male* faces more attractive if they showed effects of *female* hormones. Faces that showed effects of high levels of male hormones were rated as having high "perceived dominance," as being older, and as having less warmth, emotionality, honesty, and cooperativeness (as well as other attributes). Apparently, the effects of female hormones not only made faces look younger but also softened these negative perceptions.

However, when it comes to bodies, the story is not so consistent. For example, Ford and Beach (1951) considered what people in over 200 cultures looked at when

Facial images of Caucasian and Japanese females and males were "feminized" and "masculinized" 50% in shape. Which face do you prefer? In general, faces that reveal effects of female sex hormones are seen as more attractive.

| Caucasian female, feminized | Caucasian female, masculinized | Caucasian male, feminized | Caucasian male, masculinized |

| Japanese female, feminized | Japanese female, masculinized | Japanese male, feminized | Japanese male, masculinized |

evaluating attractiveness and found that different cultures focused on different parts and characteristics of the body (such as the size of the pelvis, pudginess, and height). How can there be such differences in what is thought of as "beautiful" if everyone has the same visual equipment? Several reasons become apparent when we use the levels of analysis approach. First, at the level of the group, values and tastes develop and are taught, either explicitly (via instruction) or implicitly (via example) to the individual members of the group. These standards may evolve for different reasons. For example, before the spread of AIDS, gay men were often very thin; after AIDS, having a little extra weight was perceived as a sign of health and thus became attractive. Second, at the level of the person, these standards produce values and beliefs. These values and beliefs in turn affect top-down processing, leading people to look for certain body parts or attributes. And of course, at the level of the brain, the mechanisms of attention are at work when people fixate on a salient part, registering it in detail. Once you evaluate someone as beautiful, various expectations and beliefs come to mind. Just as you know that once you've identified an object as an apple, you know it has seeds inside, you also believe that an attractive person is likely to be kind, nurturing, and sensitive, and to have other positive attributes to boot (Dion et al., 1972).

CONSOLIDATE!

1 *What is the nature of light, and how do we see color, shape, and motion?* Light is made up of electromagnetic waves. These waves enter the pupil of the eye, and the lens focuses the light on the retina. Special receptors and sensory cells in the retina transduce the light waves into neural signals, which continue along the optic nerve to the brain. There are two kinds of receptors in the retina: rods and cones. Rods are very sensitive to light but register only shades of gray. Cones are not as sensitive and respond to particular wavelengths of light, which is essential for color vision. There are three different types of cones, each most responsive to a particular color: yellow, green, and violet. Opponent cells, on the other hand, work in pairs— blue/yellow, red/green, and black/white. The activation of one color in the opponent cell pair inhibits the other. By changing the hue, saturation, and brightness of colors, artists can lead the viewer to have an almost infinite range of color experiences. Special parts of the brain register motion.

2 *How are we able to separate figure from ground and see the world as a stable collection of objects?* We perceive figures as distinct from ground by using organizational principles, such as those described by the Gestalt laws of organization; these principles include proximity, similarity, continuity, closure, and good form. Various cues, from both eyes or only one, from static images or moving images, help establish the perceptual constancies. Critical constancies include size constancy (objects appear the same size in spite of differences in the images that are projected on the retina), shape constancy (objects seem to have the same shape in spite of differences in the shape of their images on the retina), brightness constancy (the brightest object in a scene appears the same brightness in spite of large differences in the light reflected, and the brightness of other objects is seen relative to the brightest one), and color constancy (colors appear the same in different lighting conditions).

3 *How do we make sense of what we see?* If we have seen an object before, information about it is stored in memory; when we see it again, we can match the input to the stored information and apply the information stored previously to the current example. We identify an object when associated information stored in memory is applied to the current stimulus. Once we have identified an object, information in memory can fill in information missing from the stimulus itself. In at least some situations, we can identify objects that we are not even aware of seeing, but in most situations attention is necessary to identify objects.

Hearing

Tai knew that loud noises could destroy her hearing, and this knowledge made blaring rock concerts even less appealing to her. When she went to a concert with Sue, she wore earplugs and took aspirin to ward off the inevitable headache she would otherwise suffer. But Sue reveled in the loud chords and jangling harmonies. How could the two friends have such different responses to the same music?

1. How do ears normally register sound?

2. What auditory cues allow us to organize sounds into coherent units and locate their sources?

3. How do we make meaning out of sound?

Early Audition: If a Tree Falls But Nobody Hears It, Is There a Sound?

We know that rays don't emanate from our eyes when we see. Now for a trick question: Do you think that sound waves emanate from our ears when we hear? In 1978, researchers found that when a click is presented to someone, the ear soon produces an echo (Kemp, 1978). Not long after this discovery, researchers (Kemp, 1979; Zurek, 1981, 1985; Zwicker & Schloth, 1984) found that even when a person isn't hearing a particular stimulus, the ear sometimes actually makes a sound. In fact, about 40% of normal people emit a detectable soft humming sound from their ears, of which they are unaware. In some cases, the humming is loud enough that other people can hear it. These sounds are not like the natural sonar used by whales, sound waves bouncing off objects and returning to the ear. These sounds play no role in hearing. They are probably caused by feedback from the brain to the ear; feedback (not the sounds produced by it) helps us hear slight differences in sounds (Pickles, 1988; Zurek, 1985). As in vision, there are many feedback connections between areas of the brain that process sound, and between these areas and the ear (Felleman & Van Essen, 1991). This is not the only similarity between hearing and seeing, as you will soon discover.

Sound Waves: Being Pressured

Like visual perception, auditory processing occurs in three phases: early, intermediate, and late. Early auditory processing begins with the sensation of sound. Sound usually arises when something vibrates, creating waves of moving air that enter our ears. Sound can arise when any type of molecules—gas, liquid, or solid—move and create pressure waves. Thus we can hear when we are surrounded by either air or water or when we put an ear to the ground, to a wall, or to another solid object. An old (but true) cliché of Western movies is listening with an ear pressed to a rail to hear whether a train is approaching. But movies sometimes get it wrong. In outer space—where there are no molecules to be moved—we could not hear anything; the loud explosion of the demolished Death Star in the original *Star Wars* movie would in fact have been silent as the grave.

Back to pressure waves: They go up, and then down, repeatedly. Each complete up-and-down movement is called a *cycle*. As with light waves for vision, sound waves have both frequency and amplitude. We usually hear variations in frequency as differences in **pitch**—how high or low the sound seems—and we hear variations in amplitude as differences in **volume.** (It probably is no coincidence that people are most sensitive to the frequencies of a baby's cry, around 2,000–5,000 Hertz; a Hertz, or Hz, is the number of cycles per second.) The same psychophysical concepts that apply to vision, such as thresholds, JNDs, and so on, also apply to hearing and are measured in comparable ways.

A question often asked in beginning philosophy classes is this: If a tree falls in the forest but nobody hears it, is there a sound? The answer is now clear: No. Sound is *caused* by waves of molecules (a physical event), but the waves themselves are not sound. Sound is a psychological event and hence depends on a nervous

Pitch: How high or low a sound seems; higher frequencies of pressure waves produce the experience of higher pitches.

Volume: The strength of a sound; pressure waves with greater amplitude produce the experience of louder sound.

system to transduce the physical energy of the vibrations to nerve energy. Without a brain to register the physical energy, there can be no sound. The situation is exactly analogous to the relationships of wavelength to hue and of amplitude to lightness. Physical properties *lead to* psychological events, but they are not the events themselves. The discipline of psychophysics charts the relationship between physical events and our experience of them.

The Brain's Ear: More Than a Microphone

The anatomy of the ear is illustrated in Figure 3.14. The ear has three parts: the outer ear, middle ear, and inner ear. The eardrum (the *tympanic membrane*) stretches across the inside end of the auditory canal, and everything between the eardrum and the auditory nerve is designed to convert movements of the eardrum to nerve impulses that are sent to the brain. Specifically, waves move the eardrum, which in turn moves three bones in the middle ear (incidentally, these are the smallest bones in the human body). If you hear a loud sound, the muscles in the ear reflexively tighten, which protects against damage (Borg & Counter, 1989). These muscles also contract when you talk, which protects you from hurting your own ears. Such protection is necessary because the ear is amazingly sensitive: We can hear a sound when the eardrum is moved less than one-billionth of an inch (Green, 1976). The three bones of the middle ear not only transfer but also amplify the vibration and cause the *basilar membrane* (which is inside the cochlea, as shown in Figure 3.14) to vibrate. The basilar membrane is where different frequencies of sound are coded into different nerve impulses. Hairs sticking up from cells lining the basilar membrane in turn trigger nerve impulses, which are then sent to the brain. These **hair cells** function in hearing the same way rods and cones do in vision; they produce the initial nerve impulses.

There are two main theories about the way the basilar membrane converts pressure waves to perceived sound. **Frequency theory** holds that higher frequencies produce greater neural firing. This theory cannot explain the full extent of our ability to hear: Neurons can fire only about 1,000 times a second at most, so how is it that we can hear sounds produced by much higher frequencies (Gelfand, 1981)? According to **place theory**, different frequencies activate different places

Hair cells: The cells with stiff hairs along the basilar membrane of the inner ear that, when moved, produce nerve impulses that are sent to the brain; these cells are the auditory equivalent of rods and cones.

Frequency theory: The theory that higher frequencies produce higher rates of neural firing.

Place theory: The theory that different frequencies activate different places along the basilar membrane.

Figure 3.14 Anatomy of the Ear

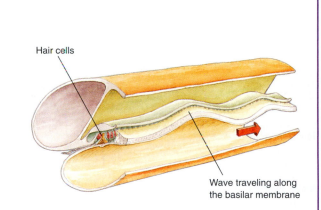

The major parts of the outer ear, middle ear, and inner ear. The semicircular canals have no role in hearing; they help us keep our balance.

If you unwound the cochlea and looked into it, you would see the basilar membrane with its hair cells.

Figure 3.15 **Place Coding of Sound Frequency**

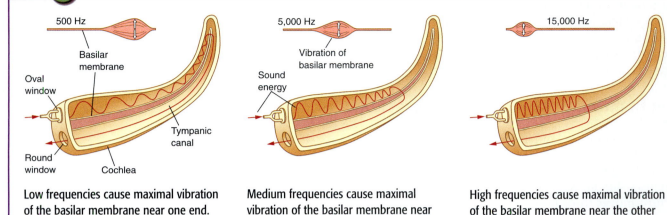

Low frequencies cause maximal vibration of the basilar membrane near one end.

Medium frequencies cause maximal vibration of the basilar membrane near the middle.

High frequencies cause maximal vibration of the basilar membrane near the other end.

along the basilar membrane, as shown in Figure 3.15. This theory appears to be correct, at least for most frequencies; it is possible, however, that the rate of vibration does help us hear relatively low tones.

As in vision, a number of brain areas working together allow us to sense sound. The first part of the cortex to receive auditory information, the *primary auditory cortex,* is spatially organized. Researchers have shown that the lower the pitch, the farther activity shifts along this structure. Again, just as in vision, in which the pattern of activation on the eye is in turn laid out on the brain (see p. 97), the spatial arrangement of vibration on the basilar membrane is mimicked in the brain. This sort of spatial arrangement is called **tonotopic organization** (Clarey et al., 1992; Romani et al., 1982).

Given the complexity of hearing, you won't be surprised to learn that deafness can occur for many reasons. For example, one of the most serious is **nerve deafness,** which typically occurs when the hair cells are destroyed by loud sounds. A rock band heard at close range can produce sounds loud enough to cause this sort of damage; indeed, one study found that of a group of college students who went regularly to a dance club featuring loud music, almost a third exhibited permanent hearing loss for high-frequency sounds (Hartman, 1982). Nerve deafness may affect only certain frequencies; in those instances, a hearing aid can amplify the remaining frequencies, and hearing can be improved. Many researchers believe that surgery will soon allow doctors to make an end run around a damaged ear and allow auditory input to stimulate the auditory cortex directly (Ubell, 1995). Sue may have suffered some nerve deafness from the many concerts she attended and so wasn't bothered by the loud music that Tai experienced as painful. In addition, **conduction deafness** can result from any accident or other cause that impairs the functioning of the external ear or middle ear. A broken eardrum, for example, can cause conduction deafness.

Tonotopic organization: The use of distance along a strip of cortex to represent differences in pitch.

Nerve deafness: A type of deafness that typically occurs when the hair cells are destroyed by loud sounds.

Conduction deafness: A type of deafness caused by a physical impairment of the external or middle ear.

Intermediate Hearing: Organizing the Auditory World

Watch people crossing a two-way street; how many of them look both ways before stepping off the curb? Many people apparently rely in part on their hearing when crossing a street, stepping forward before looking carefully. Intermediate auditory processing allows us to organize sounds as coming from distinct objects and to locate the sources of sounds.

Sorting Out Sounds: From One, Many

In daily life, a single complex jumble of many sounds usually assaults our ears, not individual sounds one at a time. To make sense of what we hear, we first need to sort out individual sounds. As in vision, we need to distinguish figure from ground. Bregman (1990, 1993) calls this process *auditory scene analysis,* which relies on organization very much like what occurs in vision. Indeed, the Gestalt laws help us here, too. For example, people organize sounds partly based on similarity (for example, grouping sounds with the same pitch) and good continuation (grouping the same pitch continued over time). Recognizing and identifying speech is a good example of auditory scene analysis because the actual stimulus is continuous, with no indication of breaks to delineate the beginnings and ends of words, and yet to communicate, people must identify individual words. This problem is the **speech segmentation problem.** By analogy, *thisproblemisliketheoneyouarenowsolving* in vision.

In vision, we see continuous variations in the frequency of light not as continuous variations in hue, but rather as a set of distinct colors. Similarly, we hear speech sounds as distinct categories. This **categorical perception** produces categories with remarkably sharp boundaries. For example, if a computer is programmed to vary the time between the start of a syllable (the consonant being pronounced, such as *b*) and the "voiced" part of the syllable (the sound of the vowel being pronounced, such as *a*), we will hear "ba" if the voice starts from 0 to around 25 thousandths of a second after the consonant starts; but if the voice starts after a longer interval, we will hear "pa." There is very little intermediate ground; we hear one or the other (Eimas & Corbit, 1973). Monkeys, chinchillas, and various other animals also show categorical perception (Kuhl, 1989; Moody et al., 1990), which suggests that the perceptual system itself does this work—not the language systems of our various cultures. Indeed, the common ancestor of monkeys and humans may have evolved many of the "building blocks" that were later incorporated into speech.

Locating Sounds: Why Two Ears Are Better Than One

In vision, our brains use slight differences in the images striking the two eyes to assess the distance of an object. Similarly, hearing makes use of differences in the stimuli reaching the two ears to assess the distance of a sound source (Yost & Dye, 1991). For example, a difference in volume at the two ears is used as a cue. In addition to all their other functions, our heads are useful because they block sound, and thus the amplitude of sound waves is smaller when it reaches the ear on the side of the head away from the sound source.

As in vision, we use many different cues to assess where an object is. Some cues depend on only one ear, not two. For example, by moving our heads and bodies, we can compare the relative volume of a sound from different vantage points, which helps us locate its source.

Bats and barn owls are adept at using sound to localize objects (Konishi, 1993; Suga, 1990). The structure of the barn owl's face has developed to direct sound to its ears to maximize location cues. And bats produce sounds, and then listen for the echoes coming back. The echoes are precise enough for the bat to discern the shapes of even small objects (Simmons & Chen, 1989).

Late Audition: Recognition and Identification

We use sound in many ways. In addition to interpreting speech and music, we recognize that the snap of a green bean indicates freshness, that a knock on a door means someone wants to come in, that a cat's mewing may mean she wants to be fed. As in vision, sounds become meaningful when they are matched to information already stored in memory, which is the job of late auditory processing.

More Than Meets the Ear

Just as in vision, top-down processing leads what you expect to hear to influence what you actually hear. If Tai tries to talk to Sue at the rock concert, Sue may be

Speech segmentation problem: The problem of organizing a continuous stream of speech into separate parts that correspond to individual words.

Categorical perception: Identifying sounds as belonging to distinct categories that correspond to the basic units of speech.

Cocktail party phenomenon: The effect of not being aware of other people's conversations until your name is mentioned, and then suddenly hearing it.

able to hear her friend, but a large part of what she hears is probably being supplied by her brain. A demonstration of such an effect was reported by Warren and Warren (1970), who asked people to listen to a tape-recorded sentence after part of a word had been replaced with the sound of a cough. Although part of the word was actually missing, all the participants claimed that they actually heard the entire word and denied that the cough covered part of it. In fact, the listeners were not exactly sure at what point the cough occurred. This effect, more obvious for words in sentences than for words standing alone, is called the *phonemic restoration effect* (a phoneme is the smallest segment of spoken speech, such as "ba" or "da"). This filling-in effect occurs not only with speech sounds but also with musical instruments. In fact, if you see someone bowing the strings of a cello at the same time you hear the strings being plucked, the sight is enough to distort the sound you hear (Saldana & Rosenblum, 1993).

Hearing Without Awareness

As happens in vision, we pick up some auditory information without being aware of it. Perhaps the most common experience of perception without awareness is the **cocktail party phenomenon.** At an event like a party, you may not be aware of other people's conversation until someone mentions your name—which you hear immediately (Cherry, 1953). But to become aware of the sound of your name, you must have been tracking the conversation all along (using bottom-up processing); you simply were not aware of the conversation until that important word was spoken. In experiments she performed as an undergraduate, Treisman (1964a, 1964b) showed that when people listen to stimuli presented separately to the two ears (through headphones) and are instructed to listen to only one ear, they still register some information—such as whether the voice is male or female—from the ignored ear.

This discovery spawned an industry that proclaimed people can learn in their sleep, simply by playing tapes (purchased at low, low discount prices). Unfortunately, it turns out that unless a person is paying attention, not much gets through. And even when information does get through, it is retained very briefly; when tested hours later, people remember virtually none of the information presented outside awareness (Greenwald et al., 1991).

LOOKING AT LEVELS
Beethoven, the Deaf Composer

Beethoven was stone deaf when he wrote much of his greatest music. How is this possible? The levels of analysis approach will help us understand his remarkable achievement. First, at the level of the brain, auditory mental imagery allowed him to hear music with his "mind's ear" as he was composing it. Auditory imagery arises when brain areas that are used in hearing are activated from stored memories (Halpern, 1988; Zatorre & Halpern, 1993). Right now, decide whether the first three notes of "Three Blind Mice" go up or down; to do this, you probably "heard" the tune in your head—you evoked auditory imagery. Imagery can occur even when the sense organs are damaged (for example, if the hair cells in the ear die). What Beethoven heard in his mind's ear would probably have been very similar to what he would have heard carried by sound waves had he not been deaf. Second, consider the level of the person. We can only speculate, but being forced to practice by his tyrannical father may have had at least two consequences for the young composer. Not only did he become a superb pianist and music theorist, but he also may have come to use his music as a refuge from his father (Freud would have called this reaction "sublimation," as you will see in Chapter 8). Third, at the level of the group, his playing may have been a way to appease his father and win his approval. Also, Beethoven lived in a society that appreciated music, and thus he was able to raise financial support for his work, despite the fact that he was deaf. (Beethoven was the first composer to "freelance" for a living.) Finally, music itself is a cultural invention, as are the various detailed systems of notation that different human societies use to write it down.

1 *How do ears normally register sound?* Normally, pressure waves move the eardrum, which in turn causes the bones of the middle ear to move, creating movement of the hair cells of the basilar membrane, which transduce the waves into neural impulses. The frequency of the waves determines the pitch of the sound, and the amplitude determines its volume. Frequency theory may explain the conversion of pressure waves to sound at low frequencies, and place theory explains it at most frequencies, especially high ones. Nerve deafness occurs when the hair cells do not function properly; conduction deafness occurs when the external or middle ear is impaired.

2 *What auditory cues allow us to organize sounds into coherent units and locate their sources?* We use similarity of sounds and other Gestalt principles to organize sounds into units. In addition, categorical perception allows us to hear some types of sounds—particularly those from speech—as distinct units, not as continuous variations. We use a variety of cues to localize the sources of sounds, some of which hinge on differences in the way sound is registered by the two ears.

3 *How do we make meaning out of sound?* As in vision, sounds become meaningful when they are matched to information already stored in memory. Both bottom-up and top-down processes are at work in audition. Top-down processes, which produce phenomena such as the phonemic restoration effect, can fill in fragmentary information. Some auditory recognition and identification takes place outside awareness and can guide attention.

Sensing in Other Ways

One of the reasons why Tai hates rock concerts is that they are so crowded, and Tai is particularly sensitive to body odor. She also dislikes the food that is available at the concession stands, which she finds greasy and unhealthy. Neither of these circumstances seem to bother Sue. On the other hand, unlike Tai, Sue finds that she sometimes becomes literally dizzy when she looks at art. Dizziness is not a novel feeling for her; she gets dizzy easily. Although she enjoys the sensation in other contexts, such as dancing spins, the dizziness makes her queasy in a gallery. Despite their differences, both friends agree strongly that they share another kind of sense. They believe they can sense other people's thoughts and are sometimes aware of future events.

1 How does the sense of smell work?

2 How does the sense of taste work?

3 How do we sense our bodies?

4 Does extrasensory perception (ESP) exist?

Smell: A Nose for News?

Smell and taste are often grouped together as the **chemical senses** because both, unlike the other senses, rely on registering the presence of specific chemicals. People differ widely in their sense of smell, or *olfaction*. Some people are 20 times more sensitive to odors than are other people (Rabin & Cain, 1986), a finding that might explain Tai's discomfort in a crowd. However, most people are remarkably poor at identifying odors, even though they often think they are good at it (de Wijk et al., 1995). Cain (1979) found that people could correctly identify only about half of 80 common scents; although we may know that an odor is familiar—that is, we recognize it—we may be unable to identify it. In general, women are better than men at detecting many types of odors (Cain, 1982), and younger adults are better than either children (up to 14 years old) or middle-aged adults (between 40 and

Chemical senses: Taste and smell, which rely on sensing the presence of specific chemicals.

50 years old) (Cain & Gent, 1991; de Wijk & Cain, 1994; Murphy, 1986). So much the worse for Tai, who was probably at the peak of her olfactory sensitivity.

Distinguishing Odors: Lock and Key

The best theory of odor detection can be described using the lock and key metaphor. Molecules have different shapes, and the olfactory receptors are built so that only molecules with particular shapes will fit in particular places. The molecules are like keys, and the receptors like locks. When the right-shaped molecule arrives at a particular receptor, it sends a signal to the brain and we sense the odor. Just as there is not a single type of cone for each color we can see, there is not a single receptor for each odor we can smell (see Figure 3.16); rather, the overall pattern of activity signals a particular odor (Freeman, 1991).

Two major neural tracks leave the olfactory bulb. One, passing through the thalamus, is particularly involved in memory; the other, connected to the limbic system, is particularly involved in emotions. These connections explain why odors often tap emotionally charged memories—remember the way you felt when you unexpectedly smelled an old girlfriend's perfume or boyfriend's aftershave?

Olfaction Gone Awry: Is It Safe to Cook Without Smell?

Have you ever wished you could not smell? Maybe that would be a relief once in a while, but losing your sense of smell completely is not a good idea. Smell serves to signal the presence of noxious substances; our brains are wired so that odors can quickly activate the "fight-or-flight" system. It would not be wise to ask a friend who has no sense of smell to cook dinner on a regular basis: Smell is often the only signal that meat or other food is spoiled. Relatively few people have no olfactory sense, a deficit that can arise from brain damage or a virus (Doty et al., 1991).

Figure 3.16   The Olfactory System

Depending on which olfactory receptor cells are stimulated, different messages are sent to the olfactory bulb, the first part of the brain to process such signals.

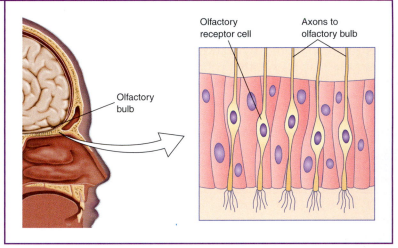

Taste: The Mouth Has It

When scientists discuss taste, they are talking about sensing via receptors located solely in the mouth. **Taste buds** (see Figure 3.17) are microscopic structures mounted on the sides of the little bumps you can see on your tongue in a mirror. You have taste buds in other places in your mouth as well, such as the back of the throat and cheeks (Smith & Frank, 1993). Your taste buds die and are replaced, on average, every 10 days (McLaughlin & Margolskee, 1994). Humans have more taste buds than some species, such as chickens, but fewer than others; some fish have taste buds spread all over their skin (Pfaffmann, 1978). Children have more sensitive taste buds than

Taste buds: Microscopic structures on the bumps on the tongue surface, at the back of the throat, and inside the cheeks; the four types of taste buds are sensitive to sweet, sour, salty, and bitter tastes.

Figure 3.17   Taste Buds on the Tongue

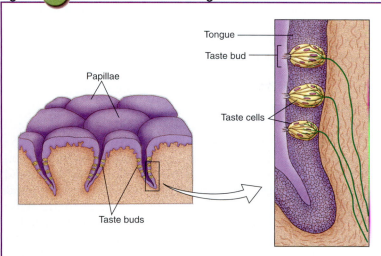

Papillae

Tongue

Taste bud

Taste cells

Taste buds

The taste buds on the tongue line the *papillae,* the visible bumps.

adults, so flavors are presumably stronger for them than for adults—which may account for children's notoriously strong likes and dislikes of foods.

Sweet, Sour, Salty, Bitter

You've seen how a wide range of colors arises from three types of cones, and how patterns of odors arise from the combinations of receptors being activated. The brain uses this same mixing-and-matching trick for taste. The tastes of all foods are made up of combinations of four tastes: sweet, sour, salty, and bitter (Bartoshuk & Beauchamp, 1994; Scott & Plata-Salaman, 1991). In addition, free nerve endings in the mouth appear to be irritated by spicy foods (Lawless, 1984). These provide another source of information about taste, one that is not directly related to the taste buds. Different parts of the mouth and tongue are more or less sensitive to different tastes; you can detect bitter flavors best in the back of your mouth (Shallenberger, 1993). However, these different sensitivities are a matter of degree: All kinds of taste buds are found in most locations on the tongue. Curiously, there is a "taste hole" in the middle of the tongue, an area where there are no taste buds at all. Moreover, you cannot taste something unless it can be at least partially dissolved by your saliva (Seuling, 1986); that is why you can't taste a marble.

Taste and Smell

Most people think that the flavor of food arises from its taste (Rozin, 1982), but in fact much of what we think of as taste is actually smell, or a combination of smell and taste. In rats the two types of information converge on a region of the frontal lobes that is critical for the perception of flavor (Schul et al., 1996). Next time you have a stuffy nose, notice the flavor of your food, or lack thereof—particularly when you close your eyes and eliminate top-down processing to fill in your perception of the flavor. Researchers have found that people have a much harder time detecting most flavors when smell is blocked (Hyman et al., 1979). Tai might like the idea of not being able to smell the press of sweaty bodies, but not smelling at all would ruin the taste of everything from hot chocolate to pepperoni.

Somasthetic Senses: Not Just Skin Deep

The traditional five senses—sight, hearing, smell, taste, and touch—were listed and described by Aristotle more than 2,000 years ago. It would be a sad commentary on the value of science if we couldn't do better after all this time. Today, we are able to argue that there are nine senses, perhaps ten: sight, hearing, smell, taste, and then a collection of five senses that together are called **somasthetic senses.** These senses all have to do with perceiving the body and its position in space: kinesthetic (sense of where the limbs are and how they move), vestibular (sense of balance), touch, temperature sensitivity, and pain. There may be a sixth somasthetic sense, magnetic sense. And, finally, there is possibly one more sense: extrasensory perception, or ESP (also sometimes called *psi*).

Kinesthetic Sense: A Moving Sense

Read this, and then close your eyes and hold out your left arm in an odd position. Now, keeping your left arm in place, touch your left hand with your right hand. You shouldn't have any trouble doing this because you know where your hands are without having to see them. You know because of your **kinesthetic sense,** which registers the movement and position of the limbs. Two types of specialized cells sense this information: One type is in the tendons (the material that connects muscles to bones) and is triggered by tension; the other is in the muscles themselves and is triggered by the length of the muscle (Pinel, 1993).

Vestibular Sense: Being Oriented

The inner ear is used not only for hearing, but also for balance. The **vestibular sense,** which provides information about how you are oriented relative to gravity, relies on an organ in the inner ear that contains three *semicircular canals* (illustrated in Figure 3.14). If these structures are disrupted, say by infection or injury (or spending too much time in weightlessness in outer space, as happens to astronauts), people have a difficult time keeping their balance.

In general, women are more sensitive to touch than are men (Weinstein, 1968). Moreover, women are especially sensitive (relative to men) on some parts of their bodies, such as their backs and stomachs.

Touch: Feeling Well

Here's another trick question: What's your body's largest organ? The lungs? the intestines? The answer is the skin. As well as protecting our bodies from the environment (such as dirt, germs, flying objects, changes in temperature), making crucial vitamins, and triggering the release of various hormones, the skin is a massive sensory organ. Millions of receptors in the skin produce impulses when stimulated in specific ways. Moreover, using the same mechanism as other senses, it is the particular combination of receptors being stimulated that produces a particular sensation. The mix-and-match principle is at work here, too: We can feel many more types of sensations than we have types of receptors. Receptors in the skin in different parts of the body send impulses to different parts of the somatosensory cortex (see Chapter 2); and in general the more cortex devoted to a particular area of the skin, the more sensitive we are there (Weinstein, 1968).

Temperature

The skin has separate systems for registering hot and cold; indeed, there are distinct spots on your skin that register *only* hot or *only* cold. These spots are about 1 mm across (Hensel, 1982). If a cold spot is stimulated, you will feel a sensation of cold even if the stimulus is something hot. This phenomenon is called **paradoxical cold.** People are not very good at telling exactly where a hot or cold stimulus is located, particularly if it is near the skin but not touching it (Cain, 1973).

Pain

Despite the discomfort, even the agony, pain brings, the inability to feel pain is even worse in the long run than the inability to smell odors. Sternbach (1978) described children who could not feel pain normally and who picked off the end of their noses and bit off their fingers because they didn't notice what they were doing. Pain serves to warn us of impending danger, and it is crucial to survival.

The sensation of pain arises when three different kinds of nerves are stimulated. These nerves differ in size and in the speed with which they transmit impulses. Thus, we can feel **double pain:** the first phase, of sharp pain, occurs at the time of the injury; it is followed by a dull pain. The two kinds of pain arise from different fibers sending their messages at different speeds (Rollman, 1991).

One of the ways we deal with pain is by producing substances in our brains, called **endorphins,** that have painkilling effects. Some drugs, such as morphine, bind to the same receptors that accept endorphins, which explains how those drugs can act as painkillers (Cailliet, 1993). However, pain involves more than simple bottom-up processing. Top-down processing can directly inhibit the interneurons that regulate the input of pain signals to the brain (Melzack & Wall, 1982). This **gate control** mechanism may explain how hypnosis can control pain (Kihlstrom, 1985); indeed, hypnosis can selectively alter our experience of the unpleasantness of pain without affecting how intense it feels. Hypnosis thus may alter processing in only some of the brain areas that register pain (Rainville et al., 1997). Inhibitory impulses from the brain to neurons that send signals from the body may also occur when pain is reduced by a *counter-irritant*—a painful stimulus elsewhere in the body (Willer et al., 1990). Such effects may explain how acupuncture, the placing of small needles to treat pain, works (Chapman & Nakamura, 1999).

People differ widely in the amount of pain they can stand; Rollman and Harris (1987) found that some people could put up with as much as eight times as much pain as others. However, women at certain phases of the menstrual cycle have a lower threshold for pain (Hapidou & De Catanzaro, 1988). MacGregor and colleagues (1997) found that the threshold for pressure-based pain was highly correlated among twins, but this correlation was equally high for both identical and fraternal twins. Because identical twins share all their genes, but fraternal twins share only half their genes, the finding of the same correlation suggests that there is no substantial genetic component to pain thresholds. Instead, this common correlation is more likely a result of common family environment.

Other Senses?

Two additional senses are more controversial; one—magnetic sense—may not exist in humans, and the other—extrasensory perception—may not exist at all.

Magnetic Sense: Only for the Birds?

Many birds migrate long distances each year, guided in part by the magnetic field of the earth. Tiny bits of iron found in crucial neurons of these birds apparently play a role in this sense. There is some evidence that humans have a weak form of this sense (Baker, 1980), and magnetic fields have been shown to disrupt spatial learning in mice, at least for brief periods of time (Levine & Bluni, 1994). However, the evidence is still not strong enough for you to worry about having an MRI scan.

Extrasensory Perception (ESP)

The ability to perceive and know things without using the ordinary senses is described as **extrasensory perception (ESP).** Many forms of ESP have been asserted, including *telepathy,* the ability to send and transmit thoughts directly, mind to mind; *clairvoyance,* the ability to know about events directly, without using the ordinary senses or reading someone else's mind; and *precognition,* the ability to foretell future events. In addition, *psychokinesis (PK),* the ability to move objects directly, not by manipulating them physically, has also been reported (this ability does not derive from ESP proper, since it does not involve perception or knowing). Many experiments have been conducted in an effort to demonstrate

Double pain: The sensation that occurs when an injury first causes a sharp pain, and later a dull pain; the two kinds of pain arise from different fibers sending their messages at different speeds.

Endorphins: Painkilling chemicals produced naturally in the brain.

Gate control of pain: The top-down inhibition of interneurons that regulate the input of pain signals to the brain.

Extrasensory perception (ESP): The ability to perceive and know things without using the ordinary senses.

the existence of the different forms of ESP (for example, Bem & Honorton, 1994; Haraldsson & Houtkooper, 1992). Most psychologists are skeptical about ESP and PK, for at least three reasons (Alcock, 1987, provides additional ones). First, the effects are difficult to repeat (Milton and Wiseman, 1999a, 1999b). To be fair, some ESP researchers have argued that such failures to replicate occur because the phenomena depend on personality, details of the setting, and other variables (Brugger et al., 1990; Honorton, 1997; Watt & Morris, 1995). But as more such qualifications are added, the harder it becomes to disprove the claims, and the field is thus nudged farther away from science. Second, it is not known how the brain could possibly produce or pick up ESP signals or produce PK signals. Third, it is not known what form these signals might take.

LOOKING AT LEVELS

Is Body Odor a Problem?

Can culture affect senses as basic as smell? It can, and it does. Norwegians are less compulsive about eliminating all trace of natural human odors than are Americans (who, according to the *Los Angeles Times,* spent about $6 billion in 1997 on products to eliminate or mask body odor). Hence, the garments of Norwegians often retain more body odor than ours typically do. A young child, when his or her mother is gone, is sometimes given one of the mother's blouses to smell and is said to be comforted by this smell. To our knowledge, no rigorous studies of this phenomenon have been done, but observation alone is sufficient to make our point—that the interpretation of smell is in large part determined by cultural norms. In a pinch, one could probably hand the child a blouse from the mother's sister; Porter (1991) showed that people who share more genes also have more similar body odors. Chemicals (specifically, steroids) are produced by the sweat glands, and the genes

determine the composition of these chemicals. Bacteria, which digest the chemicals, then produce the odor. Bartoshuk and Beauchamp (1994) have identified the genes that produce the distinguishing characteristics of body odor. Perhaps fortunately, simply living with someone will not make your body odor similar to his or hers, and vice versa (Porter et al., 1985).

So, consider the problem of body odor: It is only a problem if the culture defines it as such. If a person believes it is a problem, he or she will act accordingly—by buying deodorants (or feeling embarrassment). Consider the interactions among events at the different levels: If you feel threatened, the sympathetic branch of your autonomic nervous system is activated, producing sweat. The sweat contains chemicals that feed the ever-present bacteria, which produce more odor. The smell, at least in the United States, may then make others turn away from you.

CONSOLIDATE!

1 *How does the sense of smell work?* We are able to smell when molecules are the right shape to fit into specific olfactory receptors, which in turn send impulses to the brain. As in vision, the range of possible smells arises from the combinations of outputs from different receptors; we do not have a different receptor for every possible odor we can distinguish.

2 *How does the sense of taste work?* Taste arises from four types of taste buds (which produce the sensation of sweet, sour, salty, and bitter tastes) and from nerves that respond to irritation; combinations of outputs from these receptors produce taste. However, what we commonly think of as taste in fact relies in part on our sense of smell working in combination with taste.

3 *How do we sense our bodies?* We sense the positioning of our bodies via the vestibular and kines-

thetic senses. An impairment of the vestibular sense can cause the perception of imbalance and dizziness. The kinesthetic sense lets you know the positions of your limbs and identify whether your body has actually moved. We are also aware of our bodies if stimuli trigger receptors on the skin, which can produce the sensations of pressure, temperature, or pain. It is also possible that we are aware of our location in part by sensing changes in the magnetic field of the earth, but this has yet to be solidly established.

4 *Does extrasensory perception (ESP) exist?* Although there is some evidence for some forms of ESP, these findings are difficult to replicate. It is not clear how the brain would register ESP signals or how ESP signal transmission would work. Thus, at this point, there is no convincing evidence for the existence of ESP, but the issue is still open.

Recap and Thought Questions

Sensing and Selecting: Opening Up to the World

The brain relies on sensory organs that have particular kinds of receptors. When these receptors are stimulated appropriately (for example, by light for the rods and cones, vibration for the hair cells, and pressure for some receptors in the skin), these neurons transduce this physical energy into neural signals. These neural signals are sent into the brain and initiate the processes of sensation and perception. Sensation is the immediate experience of basic properties of an object or event, such as its color or volume, whereas perception is the organization and interpretation of the sensory input as signaling a particular object or event.

We detect signals when they cross a threshold, but the level of that threshold depends in part on how hard we try to detect the signals. In addition, we can adjust our criteria so that we are more or less willing to guess.

We can shift the focus of our attention, which usually allows us to detect signals more easily. For most types of stimuli, whatever is attended to is in focus and more easily detected than what is not attended. However, when simple features are embedded in other simple features (like a red light in a sea of green lights), the stimulus "pops out" and attention is not necessary for easy detection. Perception relies on a combination of bottom-up processes, which are initiated by stimulus properties striking receptors, and top-down processes, which are guided by knowledge, expectation, or belief.

Could Sue's and Tai's abilities to register sensations differ in basic ways, which might explain why they have such different reactions to the sensory delights of an art museum versus a rock concert? Yes, people vary in their abilities to register basic sensations. In addition, because of perceptual learning, in which previous exposure teaches us to perceive things in particular ways, Tai may have been "tuned" to be more sensitive than Sue to noises during rock concerts, just as she is more aware of what to look for at art museums. This could explain the friends' differing sensitivities for registering certain kinds of stimuli.

Think It Through. Do you think "boosted" or enhanced sensory sensitivities would be an advantage or a disadvantage? (Say you could hear a pin drop 50 feet away, or you could see the dirt in the pores on a friend's face across the room.) In what ways would such superabilities be a benefit? A drawback? What about being able to adjust your "sensitivity" and "bias" at will? In what kinds of situations would this power be desirable?

Vision

Visual perception can be divided into three main phases. The first, early visual processing, begins with light, which consists of physical energy of certain wavelengths. The retina, a thin sheet of tissue at the back of the eye, contains two known types of cells that convert light to nerve impulses. Rods are sensitive to light but do not register color, whereas cones register color but are not as sensitive to light. The operation of the three kinds of cones (each tuned to be most sensitive to a different wavelength of light), in combination with the color-opponent cells, underlies our ability to see color. Attention can be guided both by stimulus properties and by personal knowledge and expectations.

The second phase, intermediate visual processing, takes the outputs from early visual processing and organizes them into sets of perceptual units. These sets are figures, which are likely to correspond to objects (or sometimes to parts of objects). The Gestalt laws of organization (such as similarity, proximity, continuity, good form, and closure) describe how the visual system organizes lines, dots, and other elements into units. The distance, size, and shape of figures are also specified in ways that do not vary when the object is seen from different viewpoints. Some of these processes are built in; some are learned.

Finally, late visual processing involves making the input meaningful. This is accomplished by matching the input to information already stored in memory, which allows you to know more about the stimulus than you can see at the time.

We do not simply wait for input, nor do we process only what is in the stimulus. Rather, the brain, guided by past learning (both personal and cultural), sends feedback via top-down processing to supplement the input. Finally, some information can be identified outside awareness.

Could Sue's and Tai's eyes, or visual parts of their brain, differ? Tai clearly sees more in a work of art than Sue does. It is possible that Tai's genetic makeup makes the cones in her eyes more sensitive to color differences. Beyond that, Sue is not color-blind and has no trouble seeing the paintings, but portions of her brain involved in interpreting what she sees may not be as well developed as Tai's, due to differences in the young women's exposure and experience.

Think It Through. What do you think would happen if you had been born blind and suddenly had vision at age 50? Such cases have been studied in depth (see Gregory, 1974; Sacks, 1995). Even though light was being properly transduced in the eyes, these persons failed to realize they were viewing a human face (that of the person who took off their bandages) until the person spoke. Why? If you had to help such as person adjust after the sight-giving operation, what would you do? Why might part of your training involve attention?

Do you think that the way a musician looks or behaves when he or she is performing could influence the way the music sounds? How could this occur?

Hearing

Like vision, hearing can be understood in terms of three broad phases. Early auditory processing involves registering sound waves, pressure waves that move molecules. Sounds differ in pitch (which reflects variations in frequency) and volume (which reflects variations in amplitude). For most frequencies, the ear uses the position of maximal activity on the basilar membrane to specify the frequency, but for low frequencies the rate of vibration of the basilar membrane may also indicate frequency. Hair cells along the basilar membrane, when stimulated, produce nerve impulses, which are sent to the brain. Hair cells that respond to specific frequencies can be impaired by exposure to loud sounds. The primary auditory area (the first cortical area to receive auditory input) is laid out as a strip, and the location of activation in this area depends on the frequency of the sound.

Intermediate auditory processing involves organizing sound into units and specifying the locations of those units in space. Sounds are organized using Gestalt principles (such as similarity in pitch) and are localized using a combination of different cues.

Late auditory processing involves using stored information to make sounds meaningful. Such processing can actually fill in missing sounds, as occurs in the phonemic restoration effect. Not only can we understand speech sounds by accessing the appropriate stored memories, but we can also understand other sorts of sounds.

Might Sue's and Tai's ears, or auditory cortex, differ in how they register auditory sensations? It is possible that Sue is deaf to certain frequencies (which is likely if she has been listening frequently to loud music) and thus is not bothered by loud sounds. The role of experience, however, should not be underestimated. As is evident in cultural differences in music, you learn to interpret what you hear. The friends also might differ in how they have learned to organize sound, in what they have learned to pay attention to, and in how they interpret what they hear. Moreover, depending on associations they have made to music, the music may give rise to different feelings. For Sue, rock music may remind her of the fun of a concert; for Tai, it may remind her of packed bodies and bad smells.

Think It Through. Will wearing a motorcycle helmet affect your ability to recognize sounds and localize them to the same extent? Why or why not? If one side of the helmet were made of thicker plastic than the other, which cues would be most affected?

Sensing in Other Ways

The senses of smell and taste are considered the "chemical senses" because they detect the presence of particular chemicals. Both involve a lock-and-key arrangement in which the right molecule triggers a specific receptor, which in turn sends neural signals to the brain. And both smell and taste rely on combinations of receptors being activated.

Instead of the traditional five senses, we have at least nine and possibly up to eleven: In addition to sight, hearing, smell, taste, and touch, we have a kinesthetic sense, vestibular sense, temperature sensitivity, pain sense, and possibly a magnetic sense. These additional senses all inform us about the state of our bodies (where limbs are located, how we are positioned or located, what is touching us or otherwise affecting our skin). Each part of the skin is mapped out on the somatosensory cortex, with the amount of brain surface reflecting our relative sensitivity in that region. Pain is registered by two different systems, which can produce the feeling of double pain. Top-down processing can affect interneurons involved in pain, allowing your beliefs and desires to affect the degree to which you feel pain.

Finally, some researchers have argued for extrasensory perception (ESP). However, the evidence for ESP is shaky, and there has yet to be a reliable demonstration that any form of ESP actually exists.

In what other ways could Sue and Tai differ when they are registering the world? Is it possible that Sue is better able to smell or taste things than Tai, but Tai has better extrasensory perception? Tai certainly seems to be more sensitive to odors and tastes than Sue is—just one more example of the wide range of individual differences in the most basic sensations. Her perception of odors and tastes as repugnant, however, probably involves previous experiences with unfamiliar foods and with strangers in crowded areas. Because the neural structures underlying various sensory systems are largely distinct, the two friends (and anyone else, for that matter) can vary in unique ways.

Think It Through. Say your uncle is a food fanatic, loving every morsel and seeking out only the best. Should you recommend that he blow his nose before each meal and not waste his money going to fancy restaurants when he has a bad cold? Why?

Should researchers spend time studying ESP instead of learning, perception, or other more ordinary senses? What are the potential pros and cons of studying ESP rather than abilities that clearly are used by everyone every day?

REVIEW TEST

For each of the following items, choose the single correct or best answer. The correct answers appear at the end.

1 Sensation is ____ processing and perception is ____ processing.
- **a.** early; intermediate and late
- **b.** intermediate; early and late
- **c.** early and intermediate; late
- **d.** early and late; intermediate

2 Your willingness to say that you have heard your mother call you to dinner reflects ____.
- **a.** accommodation
- **b.** sensitivity
- **c.** signal detection
- **d.** bias

3 Accommodation occurs when muscles change the shape of the ____ so that it focuses light on the retina from objects at different distances.
- **a.** fovea
- **b.** cornea
- **c.** pupil
- **d.** lens

4 There are no ____ at the point where the optic nerve leaves the retina.
- **a.** rods
- **b.** cones
- **c.** both a and b
- **d.** cells

5 People who are color-blind are unable to distinguish one ____ from another.
- **a.** hue
- **b.** saturation
- **c.** amplitude
- **d.** brightness

6 Being able to register distances is at a(n) ____ level of visual processing.
- **a.** very late
- **b.** intermediate
- **c.** late
- **d.** early

7 A texture gradient is a ____ cue for distance.
- **a.** monocular
- **b.** binocular
- **c.** Gestalt
- **d.** stereoptic

8 An artist uses ____ to achieve the effect of depth in his or her paintings.
- **a.** monocular static cues
- **b.** stereopsis
- **c.** motion parallax
- **d.** binocular disparity cues

9 The "what" and "where" pathways that help us to identify objects by sight and to locate where the objects are in space come together to help us make decisions in the ____ lobes of the brain.
- **a.** frontal
- **b.** parietal
- **c.** occipital
- **d.** temporal

10 Rods and cones are to vision what the ____ is (are) to hearing.
- **a.** hair cells
- **b.** cochlea
- **c.** ossicles
- **d.** basilar membrane

11 Which of the following indicates the pathway that a sound wave takes in the ear?
- **a.** cochlea→basilar membrane→eardrum→ossicles
- **b.** ossicles→eardrum→cochlea→auditory nerve
- **c.** eardrum→basilar membrane→ossicles→auditory nerve
- **d.** eardrum→ossicles→basilar membrane→auditory nerve

12 Which of the following are considered chemical senses?
- **a.** touch and smell
- **b.** smell and taste
- **c.** sound and smell
- **d.** sight and sound

13 Neural tracks leaving the olfactory bulb pass through the ____, evoking memories, and through the ____, evoking emotions.
- **a.** temporal lobe; occipital lobe
- **b.** limbic system; thalamus
- **c.** occipital lobe; temporal lobe
- **d.** thalamus; limbic system

14 Which of the following statements about taste buds is false?
- **a.** Humans have more taste buds than any other species.
- **b.** Children have more sensitive taste buds than adults
- **c.** Taste buds die and are replaced every ten days on average.
- **d.** Taste buds are located not only on the tongue, but in the back of the throat and cheeks.

15 The ____ sense keeps one from falling over because of dizziness.
- **a.** somasthetic
- **b.** vestibular
- **c.** kinesthetic
- **d.** magnetic

ANSWERS: 1.a 2.d 3.d 4.c 5.a 6.b 7.a 8.a 9.a 10.a 11.d 12.b 13.d 14.a 15.b

4 Learning

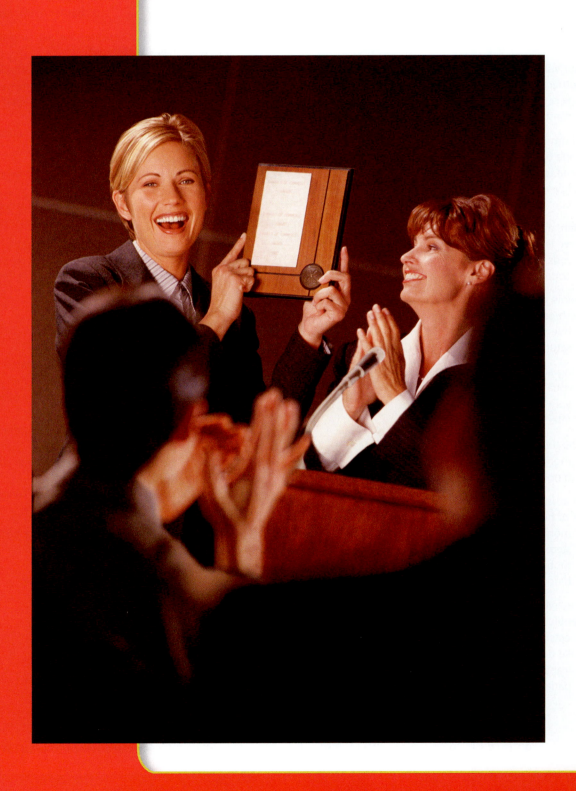

1 t's a Friday night, and two couples in their late twenties are having dinner together at a restaurant. Each couple has been together for a few years. Isabel and Tony have a solid relationship and plan to marry; Paula and Chris's relationship has been more up and down, and although they are still together, they have no plans to marry. Isabel and Tony treat each other courteously, even when one of them privately thinks the other is being a little thick, and each tries to listen to what the other is saying. In contrast, Paula and Chris have been snapping at each other and not getting along too well recently, although they were both very happy the first year they were together. Now they fight a great deal, often over trivial matters.

Over coffee and dessert, the conversation turns to plans for the weekend. "Why don't we go to the beach?" asks Paula.

"Paula!" Chris responds in a tone of voice Paula has heard before and now dreads. "I already told you I don't want to go to the beach. I'm really tired, and I'm not up for all that driving and hassle with sand in my car. How can you be so selfish? Don't you listen when I talk to you?" Paula sits mute. Chris goes on, "You never listen to me. . . . What's the point?"

Now Paula reacts angrily. "Wait just a minute, Chris, don't lay all this on me! It's not just the beach—you never want to go anywhere fun. And you always call me selfish if I don't do exactly what you want! Well, I'm not going to play that game this time." In the silence that follows, Paula and Chris see that Isabel and Tony are looking at them, dumbstruck. Only then do they realize how much their relationship has deteriorated and how quick they've become to berate and hurt each other.

Sadly, scenes like this are far from uncommon, although not necessarily in public. Conflict—and specifically the question of how to resolve it—is one of the many situations in life that spur our interest in learning. To learn is to discover, and the need to discover compels us from birth to the end of our days. Learning helps us both to survive and to realize our deepest dreams. It underlies virtually all our behavior: what we eat and the way we eat it, the way we dress ourselves, how we acquire the knowledge contained in books like this one, how we live in a society with other people. And not all learning is positive in its results: As Paula and Chris demonstrate, learning is a double-edged sword. We can learn to do things that hurt as well as help.

Whereas many fields focus on the content of what people learn (historians add to their knowledge by finding out more facts about history), psychologists interested in the field of learning focus on the *process* of learning: How does learning occur? To discover this, researchers have investigated both humans and animals, and in this chapter we look at some of the principles their research has uncovered. How did Paula "learn" to be alarmed when Chris spoke her name in a certain way? How did they learn to accept rude behavior from each other? Could Paula and Chris learn to behave differently toward each other by watching Isabel and Tony?

Psychologists define **learning** as a relatively long-term change in behavior that results from experience. When, for example, you have mastered tying your shoelaces, you will likely be able to secure your shoes properly for the rest of your life. This durability is true of all learned behavior, in virtually every domain of life, from riding a bicycle to participating in a conversation.

But what about this case: Suppose you watch someone write your name in Japanese characters. Having seen it done, can you claim that you have *learned* how to do it? What if you are able to duplicate the characters successfully? Can you legitimately say that you have learned to write your name in Japanese?

In the first instance, unless you have a photographic memory and excellent drawing ability, the answer is probably no. Merely watching someone do something complex and unfamiliar on a single occasion is usually not enough to allow you to learn it. In the second instance, even if you copy the characters correctly, the answer is still likely to be no. Just performing an action once is not enough; unless you can do it repeatedly and without assistance, you cannot claim that you have really learned to do it. You may have learned some elements of the task, but not the entire pattern, and so you cannot claim to have mastered it.

Learning can take place in a variety of ways. We often learn by association—relating one object or event with another object or event. This general phenomenon is what psychologists call *associative learning*. For instance, most people associate going to the dentist with pain. Specifically, with *classical conditioning*, learning occurs when a stimulus becomes associated with a reflexive behavior. At the dentist's office, this might occur when your palms get sweaty on seeing the dentist's drill. Learning also occurs when we link acts to their consequences; this process is known as *operant conditioning*. Operant conditioning is at work when children make the connection between asking for something politely and the increased likelihood of getting it. Another kind of learning occurs by watching other people, a process called *observational learning*. And, finally, we also learn by mentally storing material to be used at some later time; this is called *cognitive learning*. Regardless of which mode is in effect, the criterion for learning—that we demonstrate a relatively long-term change brought about by experience—remains the same.

Let's begin by exploring the model of associative learning investigated not quite a hundred years ago: classical conditioning.

Learning: A relatively permanent change in behavior that results from experience.

Classical Conditioning

When Chris said "Paula!" in a certain tone of voice, her reaction—fear—was an automatic response. Chris had never done anything to Paula to make her physically afraid; he had never been violent or even threatened violence. But they had been verbally abusive to each other in the past. Paula developed a fear response to Chris's tone of voice because early in their relationship, he had used this tone whenever he had wanted to make the painful point that he thought their relationship wasn't going to work.

Paula's emotional response to the tone of Chris's voice is a complex example of classical conditioning. In its simplest form, **classical conditioning** is a type of learning in which a neutral stimulus becomes associated, or paired, with a stimulus that causes a reflexive behavior and, in time, becomes sufficient to produce that behavior. In this case, the tone of Chris's voice is the stimulus, which is paired with an unhappy memory that elicits the physiological response of fear in Paula.

The simplest example of the way classical conditioning works is found in the famous experiments that established the principle: the work of Pavlov and his dogs.

1 What is classical conditioning? How was it discovered?

2 How are conditioned responses eliminated?

3 What are common examples of classical conditioning in daily life?

Pavlov's Experiments

Classical conditioning is also sometimes called Pavlovian conditioning because it was discovered, accidentally, by Ivan Pavlov (1849–1936), a Russian physiologist. As part of his work on the digestive processes, which won him a Nobel Prize, Pavlov studied salivation in dogs. To measure the amount of saliva that dogs produced when given meat powder (food for the dog), Pavlov collected the saliva in tubes attached to the dogs' salivary glands (see Figure 4.1). Pavlov and his colleagues

Figure 4.1   Pavlov's Apparatus for Measuring Salivation

Ivan Pavlov started out measuring saliva production in dogs as part of his research on the digestive system. He went on to use this same saliva collection technique with his investigations into classical conditioning.

Classical conditioning: A type of learning that occurs when a neutral stimulus becomes paired (associated) with a stimulus that causes a reflexive behavior and, in time, is sufficient to produce that behavior.

Unconditioned stimulus (UCS): A stimulus that elicits an automatic response (UCR), without requiring prior learning.

Unconditioned response (UCR): The reflexive response elicited by a particular stimulus.

noticed that even though salivation usually occurs *while* rather than *before* eating, his dogs were salivating *before* they were fed: They would salivate simply on seeing their food bowls or hearing the feeder's footsteps.

Intrigued, Pavlov pursued the issue with more experiments. His basic method is still in use today (see Figure 4.2). Pavlov would sound a tone on a tuning fork just before the food was brought into the dogs' room. After several times of pairing the tone with the food, the dogs would salivate on hearing the tone alone. Because food by itself elicits salivation, Pavlov considered the food the **unconditioned stimulus (UCS)**—that is, a stimulus that elicits an automatic response and is not conditional on prior learning. The dogs' salivation is termed the **unconditioned response (UCR)**, the reflexive or automatic response elicited by a UCS. The UCR does not require learning, but it does depend on certain circumstances. For

Figure **The Three Phases of Classical Conditioning**

Before conditioning occurs, the CS does not lead to a conditioned response, but the UCS does. Then the CS is paired with the UCS—here, the tone is sounded and then the food is presented. Classical conditioning is complete when the CS elicits the conditioned response—here, the dog salivates after hearing the tone.

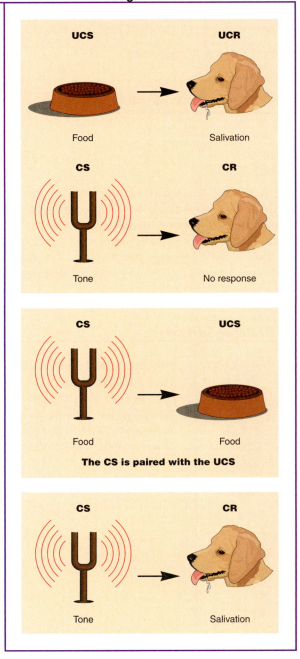

example, if an animal has just eaten and is full, it will not salivate when presented with food. In Pavlov's experiment, the tone is the **conditioned stimulus (CS)**—that is, an originally neutral stimulus that acquires significance through the "conditioning" of repeated pairings with a UCS. After hearing the tuning fork a number of times before they were fed, the dogs began to associate the tone with food. Now, whenever the dogs heard the tone, even when presented by itself, they salivated. From these observations, Pavlov theorized that when a CS (in this case, the tone) is paired with a UCS (in this case, food), it will, on its own, elicit the same or similar response as would the UCS alone (in this case, salivation). Salivation in response to the tone alone is thus a **conditioned response (CR)**, a response that depends (is conditional) on pairings of the CS with a UCS (Pavlov, 1927). Not surprisingly, psychologists call the initial learning of the conditioned response **acquisition**.

Classical Conditioning: How It Works

Researchers studying classical conditioning have discovered a good deal about how organisms (human or otherwise) respond to this form of learning. Some conditioned responses remain with us all our lives; others fade and even disappear altogether.

In an attempt to see what factors might affect the process of conditioning, Pavlov and researchers after him altered the variables involved in creating a conditioned response. Initially, researchers thought that to create a conditioned response, the UCS (the food) must immediately follow the CS (the tone). Now they wanted to see whether varying the timing of the presentations could still lead to a conditioned response. Pavlov tried the reverse order: He fed the dogs first and presented the tone 10, 5, or 1 second later. He found no conditioning; the dogs did not salivate when hearing the tone after eating the food. Even presenting the UCS and CS simultaneously did not lead to a conditioned response (Hall, 1984). Generally, for conditioning to occur, the UCS (food) should follow the CS (tone) immediately; however, there are exceptions, as is the case with certain food aversions, in which there may be a longer interval between the presentation of conditioned and unconditioned stimuli.

Another Russian researcher, Vladimir Bechterev (1857–1927), also conducted conditioning experiments. Here the UCS was a shock, and the UCR was the dog's withdrawal of its foot. When a neutral stimulus such as a bell (CS) was paired with the shock, the dog learned to withdraw its foot (CR) after the bell but before the shock, thus successfully learning to avoid pain. Bechterev's findings were an important expansion of Pavlov's work in that he extended the conditioned response to motor reflexes. Bechterev also established the basis for **avoidance learning** (Viney, 1993)—classical conditioning with a CS and an unpleasant UCS that leads the organism to try to avoid the CS. Does avoidance learning explain why some people put off going to the dentist for many years?

Conditioned Emotions: Getting a Gut Response

Paula came to dread hearing Chris speak to her in a certain tone of voice, even though this tone was not particularly offensive in itself and did not alarm her when she first heard it. But in one of their first fights, Chris had sounded this way when he said that their relationship was doomed from the start. This created a specific type of conditioned response called a **conditioned emotional response (CER)**—an emotionally charged conditioned response elicited by a previously neutral stimulus. Only after Chris made the painful remark did Paula pair his tone of voice with his dismal pronouncement, and the association produced a conditioned emotional response.

A landmark study by John B. Watson, the founder of behaviorism (see Chapter 1), and his assistant Rosalie Raynor (Watson & Raynor, 1920) illustrates how

Conditioned stimulus (CS): An originally neutral stimulus that acquires significance through the "conditioning" of repeated pairings with an unconditioned stimulus (UCS).

Conditioned response (CR): A response that depends, or is conditional, on pairings of the conditioned stimulus with an unconditioned stimulus; the conditioned response occurs in response to the CS alone.

Acquisition: The technical name given to the initial learning of the conditioned response (CR).

Avoidance learning: In classical conditioning, learning that occurs when a CS is paired with an unpleasant UCS that leads the organism to try to avoid the CS.

Conditioned emotional response (CER): An emotional response elicited by a previously neutral stimulus.

Initially, Little Albert did not show a fear of animals, but he did exhibit fear if a loud noise was made behind his back (a hammer striking a steel bar).

Then the researchers presented a white rat (CS) and made the loud noise (UCS).

After five presentations of the CS and UCS, Albert developed a phobia of rats—he began whimpering and withdrawing (the conditioned emotional response) and trying to avoid the rat. After two more presentations of CS and UCS, he immediately began crying on seeing the rat. "He . . . fell over on his left side, raised himself . . . and began to crawl away so rapidly that he was caught with difficulty before reaching the edge of the table" (Watson and Raynor, 1920, p. 5).

classical conditioning can produce a straightforward conditioned emotional response of fear, and how fear can lead to a **phobia**, an irrational fear of a specific object or situation. Watson and Raynor classically conditioned fear and then a phobia in an 11-month-old infant—Albert B.—whom they called "Little Albert" (see Figure 4.3). Through the use of classical conditioning, Watson and Raynor created in Albert a fear of rats; on seeing a white rat, Albert would cry and exhibit signs of fearfulness. This study could not be done today because of the rigorous ethical principles that govern psychological research (see Chapter 1), which did not exist at the time the study was undertaken. Although Watson and Raynor did have some concerns about the nature of the experiment and the possible effect on the child, their rationale was that this type of conditioning occurs not infrequently in life, and studying it experimentally would help people understand this phenomenon (Viney, 1993). Neither Watson nor Raynor ever mentioned what became of Albert after the study, and they did nothing to help the child overcome the fear of white furry objects that they had induced (Benjafield, 1996).

Although it was initially thought that any response could be conditioned by any stimulus (Kimble, 1981), this supposition is not entirely true. Organisms seem to have a **biological preparedness**, a built-in readiness for certain conditioned stimuli to elicit particular conditioned responses, so that less learning is necessary to produce such conditioning. Research has shown that it is easier to condition a fear response to some objects than to others. Ohman and colleagues (1976) used pictures as the CS and shock as the UCS. They found that the fear-related response

Phobia: An irrational fear of a specific object or situation.

Biological preparedness: A built-in readiness for certain conditioned stimuli to elicit certain conditioned responses so that less learning is necessary to produce conditioning.

of sweaty hands is more easily conditioned, and less easily lost, if the CS is a picture of a snake or spider than if it shows flowers or mushrooms. Snakes, rats, and the dark are typical objects of a phobia. Some have argued that this makes sense from an evolutionary perspective—sensitivity to the presence of such possibly dangerous elements could help an organism survive (Seligman, 1971).

Contrapreparedness is a built-in disinclination (or even an inability) for certain conditioned stimuli to elicit particular conditioned responses. For example, Marks (1969) described a patient he was treating as an adult. When this woman was 10 years old, she was on a car trip and had to go to the bathroom. Her father pulled off the road so she could go in a ditch. As she stepped out of the car, she saw a snake in the ditch—and at that moment her brother accidentally slammed the door on her hand. At 43, she was still deathly afraid of snakes, but she was not afraid of car doors, which had actually done the damage. Similarly, Bregman (1934) failed—with 15 different infants—to replicate Watson and Raynor's experiment when, instead of a rat as the CS, she used various inanimate objects, such as wooden blocks and pieces of cloth. There was no evidence of conditioning when the UCS was a loud noise and the CS was an inanimate object. These two examples highlight the point that certain stimuli, such as a car door and a wooden block, do not make successful conditioned stimuli.

Extinction and Spontaneous Recovery in Classical Conditioning: Gone Today, Here Tomorrow

It is indeed tragic that Watson never followed the history of Little Albert because even after a conditioned response (such as Albert's fear of white rats) is acquired, it is possible to stop the response from occurring in the presence of the CS. This process is called **extinction** because the CR is gradually eliminated, or "extinguished," by repeated presentations of the CS without the UCS. How would this work with Pavlov's dogs? If the tone continues to be presented, but is not followed by the presentation of food, after a while the dogs will no longer salivate at the tone: The CR will be extinguished. This process is graphed in Figure 4.4.

However, when a conditioned response has been extinguished, the organism allowed to rest, and the CS presented again after the rest period, the CS will again elicit the CR, although sometimes not as strongly as before extinction. This event is called **spontaneous recovery** (see Figure 4.4). Look again at the case of the dogs: After the tone has been presented several times without any food forthcoming, the dogs' salivation response will extinguish, and they will stop salivating to the

Figure 4.4   Extinction and Spontaneous Recovery in Classical Conditioning

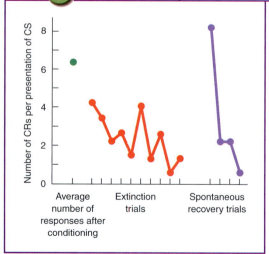

Using a tone (CS) and food pellets (UCS), rats were initially conditioned to respond to the tone alone (left), the response was extinguished (center), and then, after a rest period of 6 days, the rats exhibited spontaneous recovery (right).

Contrapreparedness: A built-in disinclination (or even an inability) for certain conditioned stimuli to elicit particular conditioned responses.

Extinction: In classical conditioning, the process by which a CR comes to be eliminated through repeated presentations of the CS without the presence of the UCS.

Spontaneous recovery: In classical conditioning, the process by which the CS will again elicit the CR after extinction has occurred.

tone alone. However, if the tone is not presented for a period of time and then is presented, the previously learned conditioned response of salivation on hearing the tone alone will return. The dogs have spontaneous recovery of the response, but they may not salivate as much as they did when they were first classically conditioned to the tone.

Once classical conditioning has occurred, the stimulus–response connection apparently never completely vanishes. Once extinction occurs and the organism is then retrained so that the CS again elicits the conditioned response, learning takes place more quickly than it did during the original training period. It is much easier to condition again, after extinction, than it was in the first place.

In his work on extinction and spontaneous recovery, Bouton (1993, 1994) showed that what occurs during extinction is not the forgetting of old learning, but rather the overlayering of old learning by new learning. The new learning that occurs during extinction is that the CS (say, the tone) does *not* signal that the UCS (say, the food) will occur. This new learning interferes with the previous classically conditioned response. Thus, according to Bouton's work, if Little Albert's fear of rats had been extinguished (that is, if the rat had been presented without the loud noise), it is not that Albert's association between the rat and the noise would have disappeared, but rather that new learning would have occurred "on top of" his previous learning.

Generalization and Discrimination in Classical Conditioning: Seen One, Seen 'em All?

Watson and Raynor wrote that, five days after the conditioning of Little Albert, a rabbit, a dog, a fur coat, cotton, and a Santa Claus mask all elicited the conditioned response of fear. This is an example of **stimulus generalization**, a tendency for the conditioned response to be elicited by neutral stimuli that are like, but not identical to, the conditioned stimulus; in other words, the response *generalizes* to similar stimuli. Moreover, because of a *generalization gradient*, the more closely the new stimulus resembles the original CS, the stronger the response. Stimulus generalization can be helpful for survival because often a dangerous stimulus may not occur in exactly the same form the next time. Without stimulus generalization, we might not know to be afraid of lions as well as tigers.

In addition to stimulus generalization, organisms are able to distinguish, or discriminate, among stimuli similar to the CS and to respond only to actual conditioned stimuli; this ability is called **stimulus discrimination**. Stimulus discrimination can be extremely helpful for survival; consider that one type of mushroom may be poisonous, but another type is food. Should Albert have been shown a pile of cotton balls without a loud noise occurring (but continued to be presented with a rat paired with the loud noise), only the rat would elicit fear. Albert would have been able to discriminate between the two similar stimuli.

Cognition and the Conditioned Stimulus

Although strict behaviorists might not agree that thoughts play a role in classical conditioning, research suggests otherwise (see Chapter 1 for an explanation of behaviorism). The context in which classical conditioning occurs and the expectations that arise following classical conditioning influence the learning (Hollis, 1997). For example, Rescorla (1967) presented rats with a tone (CS) immediately before delivering a shock (UCS); these rats quickly learned a fear response to the tone. However, another group of rats heard the tone and were shocked, but sometimes the tone was presented *after* the shock. As Pavlov had found years before, presenting the CS after the UCS does not produce conditioning: This group did not come to fear the tone. Apparently, the CS provides information by signaling the upcoming UCS (and therefore UCR), and conditioning occurs because the animal is learning that relationship: The CS is a signal that the UCS will occur.

Stimulus generalization: A tendency for the CR to be elicited by neutral stimuli that are like, but not identical to, the CS; in other words, the response *generalizes* to similar stimuli.

Stimulus discrimination: The ability to distinguish among similar conditioned stimuli and to respond only to actual conditioned stimuli.

Kamin (1969) provided more evidence that mental processes lie between stimulus and response during conditioning. He conditioned rats by pairing a tone with a brief shock; the rats developed a conditioned fear response to the tone. But when he added a second CS by turning on a light with the tone, the rats did not develop a conditioned fear response to the light alone. Kamin hypothesized that the original pairing of tone and shock was blocking new learning. The light did not add new information and was therefore of no consequence and not worth their attention. The tone was enough of a signal, and the rats didn't seem to view the light as a signal. Thus, Kamin concluded that classical conditioning takes place only if the pairing of CS and UCS provides useful information about the likelihood of occurrence of the UCS.

In addition, a mental image of an object—what you see in your "mind's eye" when you imagine something—can play a role in classical conditioning, either as a CS or a UCS. For instance, imagining food can lead to salivation in humans (see Dadds et al., 1997 for a review).

Dissecting Conditioning: Brain Mechanisms

Classical conditioning has at least three distinct components; we know this because it has been shown that three different brain processes are involved. LeDoux (1995, 1996; also Beggs et al., 1999) and his colleagues have studied conditioned fear in detail and established that registration of the stimulus, the production of the response, and the connection between the two rely on distinct parts of the brain. Consider the case of a driver who has been honked at by a huge truck as it roars by and has barely missed being crushed; the driver experienced fear. When later hearing the sound of a horn and seeing a truck drive by, the images and sounds are registered in the visual and the auditory cortex. A specific part of the amygdala (see Figure 4.5) registers the sound and sight that triggers the conditioned fear. In experimental studies with animals, it has been shown that if this particular structure is removed, animals cannot learn that a shock will soon follow a tone.

Another part of the amygdala, the central nucleus, leads to the behaviors that express conditioned fear—for example, wincing when an eighteen-wheeler blasts

Figure 4.5   The Role of the Amygdala in Fear Conditioning

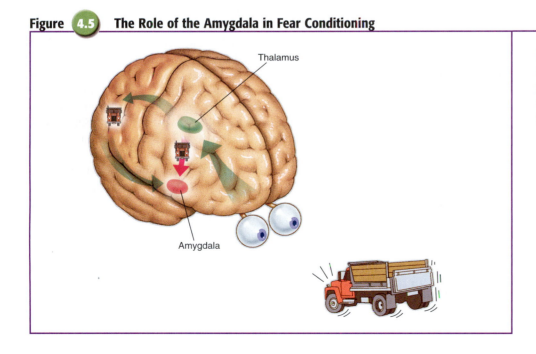

When the eyes see a stimulus (speeding truck), the thalamus first processes the stimulus and then quickly sends the information to the amygdala.

its horn. When this part of the amygdala is removed, the movements, autonomic responses, and other signs of fear are not produced.

Conditioning causes brain cells that register the stimulus (in the case of the honking truck, cells in the auditory cortex in the temporal lobe) to fire in tandem with cells in the amygdala that produce the fear response. Activity in the two sets of neurons becomes hooked together, so that whenever the stimulus occurs, the response is automatic. A crucial finding is that this linked activity never disappears entirely: Even after conditioning has been extinguished, linked activity remains, making it very easy for an animal to relearn a conditioned response. Indeed, extinction depends on the active suppression of the response, which is accomplished in part by the frontal lobe's inhibition of the amygdala (LeDoux, 1995, 1996).

Classical Conditioning Applied

If the investigation of classical conditioning had ended with the study of dogs' salivation, the great psychological importance of this kind of learning might not have been recognized. But classical conditioning showed that emotional responses, such as the fear response, can be conditioned, and emotional responses exert a powerful effect on people's lives. If a friend slaps you hard on the back every time you meet him, you are likely to wince even as he lifts his arm to begin his greeting, and in time classical conditioning affects how you feel about him. Classical conditioning can play a role in the effectiveness of medicines, affect your immune system, and influence other aspects of health and illness (as you will see in Chapter 10). Even without our awareness, it contributes to our feelings about events and objects (Bunce et al., 1999), even our sexual interests (Lalumiere & Quinsey, 1998).

Classical conditioning plays a role in deaths caused by drug overdoses. A user who generally takes a drug in a particular setting—the bathroom, say—develops a conditioned response to that place (Siegel, 1988). Here's what happens. Because of classical conditioning, as soon as the user walks into the bathroom, his or her body begins to compensate for the influx of drug that is soon to come. This conditioned response is the body's attempt to counteract, or dampen, the effect of the drug. When the user takes the drug in a new setting, perhaps a friend's living room, this conditioned response does not occur. Because there is no conditioned response to the new setting, the user's body does not try to counteract the effect of the drug. The net result is a higher effective dose of the drug than the user can tolerate, leading to an overdose. Similarly, classical conditioning also helps explain why people addicted to cocaine get drug cravings merely from handling money (Hamilton et al., 1998). Part of the experience of using cocaine is buying it, often just before using it. Thus, handling money becomes a CS. In the same way, among cigarette smokers certain environmental stimuli can elicit a desire for a cigarette (Lazev et al., 1999). So, classical conditioning explains why some smokers automatically reach for a cigarette when they get a phone call or have a cup of coffee, often without realizing what is happening.

Classical conditioning also serves as the basis for a number of therapy techniques based on learning principles, including *systematic desensitization,* which has been used to treat phobias (this therapeutic technique and others are discussed in more detail in Chapter 12). Systematic desensitization is the structured and repeated presentation of a feared conditioned stimulus in circumstances designed to reduce anxiety. Systematic desensitization works to extinguish this response by teaching people to be relaxed in the presence of the feared object or situation, such as an elevator for those with an elevator phobia. With systematic desensitization, the CS no longer elicits the CR of fear; extinction has occurred.

Watson formalized the use of behavioral principles when he took a job in advertising. The use of "sex appeal" to sell products stems from Watson's ideas.

Figure **4.6** **Classically Conditioned Animal Training**

Dogs learn not to go beyond the boundary of an "invisible fence" because the fence delivers a mild shock through their collars. The boundary marker (shown to them by their owners) is the CS, the shock (when they attempt to cross the boundary) is the UCS, and fear is the conditioned emotional response.

Sex isn't the only unconditioned stimulus that can work to produce a desired response; Razran (1940) did a study showing that political slogans (CS) paired with the eating of food (UCS) led people to view those slogans favorably. Classical conditioning continues to be used in advertising to promote consumers' positive attitudes about a product (Grossman & Till, 1998; Kim et al., 1998; Till & Priluck, 2000). And, as shown in Figure 4.6, classical conditioning can be used to train animals. Two special cases of the application of classical conditioning are taste aversion and the conditioning of the immune system.

Taste Aversion

When animals or people find a particular food or taste extremely unpleasant (and try to avoid it), they may have a **food** or **taste aversion.** This type of classical conditioning usually involves learning after only a single experience of the CS–UCS pairing. The UCS is the nausea- or vomiting-inducing agent, and the CS is a previously neutral stimulus that was paired with it, such as the sight or smell of food. The UCR is nausea or vomiting, and so is the CR.

If you have ever had food poisoning, you may have developed a classically conditioned food aversion. A likely scenario is that the food that made you sick had some unhealthy and unwanted ingredient, such as *Salmonella* bacteria. The bacteria are the UCS, and the ensuing nausea and vomiting are the UCR. If the *Salmonella* was in your dinner of broiled trout, trout might become a CS for you; whenever you eat it (or perhaps another fish similarly prepared), you become nauseated (the CR). Rather than put yourself through this experience, you are likely to avoid eating broiled trout, and a food aversion is born.

Garcia and Koelling (1966) accidentally discovered the occurrence of taste aversion when looking at the effects of radiation on rats. The rats were exposed to high enough doses of radiation that they became sick. The researchers noticed that the rats drank less water from the plastic water bottle in the radiation chamber than from the glass water bottle in their "home" cage. Although this preference could have been due to many factors, it turned out that the water in the

Food aversion (taste aversion): A classically conditioned avoidance of a certain food or taste.

plastic bottle had a slightly different taste, thanks to the plastic, than the water in the glass bottle.

After uncovering this first finding, the researchers shifted their focus to discover *why* the rats drank less from the plastic than the glass bottle. Was it because the taste of the water in the plastic bottle had become associated, and thus conditioned, to the radiation that made the rats sick? If so, then the radiation was the UCS, the taste of the water from the plastic bottle the CS, and getting sick both the UCR and the CR. They tested this hypothesis and found that it was correct: The taste of water in the plastic bottle was a CS, causing the CR of the rats getting sick (see Figure 4.7). But this wasn't the surprise. The surprise was that the rats avoided the water even if the nausea didn't occur until several hours after the plastic-tainted water was presented. Garcia's research showed that, at least in this case, the UCS doesn't need to come immediately after the CS.

The Garcia research uncovered another important fact. Previously, researchers believed that conditioning could be created using just about any stimulus. As it happened, however, while the rats became sickened by different flavors of water that were presented in subsequent trials, they did not get sick from repeated pair-

Figure **4.7** **Taste Aversion Conditioning**

Garcia and Koelling (1966) had inadvertently created a classically conditioned taste aversion. The UCS was the radiation, the CS was the taste of water in the plastic bottle, and the UCR and CR were the rats getting sick.

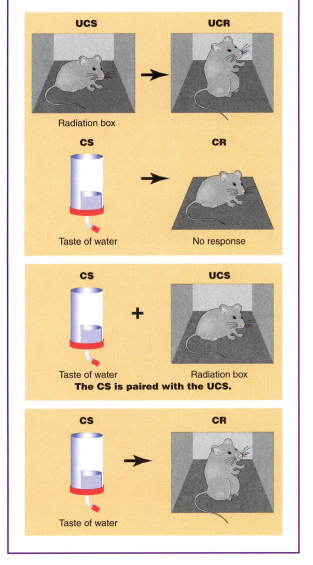

ings of other types of stimuli, such as lights, buzzers, or shocks, with the radiation (or sickness-inducing drugs). No matter how the researchers manipulated these visual and auditory stimuli, they could not elicit a conditioned response of nausea. Thus, not all stimuli can be conditioned to elicit a given response.

Garcia's findings stirred considerable controversy because they described exceptions to the "rules" of classical conditioning. Taste aversion can lead to a more generalized response; just the sight of the food can elicit a conditioned response. President Ulysses S. Grant, a soldier who had seen the carnage of the Civil War, became nauseated at just the sight of rare meat (Seuling, 1978). Classically conditioned taste aversion is the mechanism behind the use of Antabuse to treat alcoholism. Antabuse is a medicine that causes violent nausea and vomiting when mixed with alcohol. If an alcoholic took Antabuse and then drank, he or she would throw up and, if the drug was successful in its larger purpose, develop a taste aversion to alcohol. Unfortunately, Antabuse has not been as successful as was originally hoped; those who were having difficulty refraining from drinking tended to stop taking their Antabuse so that they could drink without getting sick. If Antabuse is used consistently, it does decrease how often alcoholics drink, but it does not increase the likelihood of total abstinence (Fuller et al., 1986; Sereny et al., 1986). It is the rare person who is willing to take Antabuse as recommended (Brubaker et al., 1987); married alcoholics whose spouses help ensure that Antabuse is taken at regular intervals have the best success with it (Azrin et al., 1982).

Classical conditioning is adaptive, whether it involves an animal's (including a human's) ability to learn which foods are poisonous, or which animals or objects in the environment (such as predators or guns) to fear and avoid. The more readily an organism learns these associations, the more likely that organism (or that species) will survive. Learned food aversions based on one exposure can be particularly adaptive: Animals who readily learn what not to eat will probably live longer and have more young.

Conditioning the Immune System

Let's suppose you once worked day and night for a week, hardly taking the time to sleep or eat, and so severely weakened your immune system that you became very sick. During that exhausting work-filled week, you spent all your waking hours with a laptop computer on your bed, which has a bright red bedspread. Do you think that, after your recovery, simply sitting on the bedspread could cause your immune system to weaken? Ader and his colleagues (Ader, 1976; Ader & Cohen, 1975) have shown that this kind of conditioning does in fact happen in rats. Ader and Cohen paired saccharin-flavored water with injections of cyclophosphamide, a drug given to organ transplant donors that suppresses the immune system and has a side effect of nausea. Ader had intended to use this drug not for its immune-suppressing qualities, but as a way to induce nausea in a study of taste aversion. He wanted to see how long the taste aversion would last once injections of cyclophosphamide stopped. But a few rats died on day 45 of the experiment, and more died over the next several days. Ader was confused; he had done similar experiments before with a different nausea-inducing drug and none of his animals had died. He eventually showed that the taste of the sweetened water was triggering not just the nausea, but a suppression of the immune system (as the actual drug would do), causing the eventual death of the rodents. Each time the rats drank the sweetened water, their immune systems were weakened—even without the immune-suppressing drug! The taste of the saccharine-sweetened water was acting as a CS and was in essence a **placebo**, a medically inert substance that nevertheless seems to have medicinal effects. The rats' bodies responded to the CS as if it were cyclophosphamide.

Ader's accidental discovery and his follow-up studies were noteworthy for two reasons: First, they showed that the placebo effect could be induced in animals, not just humans; second, they showed that the organism doesn't have to believe that the placebo has medicinal properties to produce a placebo response. Although

Placebo: A medically inert substance that nevertheless seems to have medicinal effects.

Ader and Cohen could not ask the rats what they believed would happen when drinking sweet water, we have no reason to think that they "believed" it would impair their immune systems (Dienstfrey, 1991). Ader and Cohen have reported a number of follow-up studies, all trying to rule out other explanations of their results, and their hypothesis about the conditioning of the immune system has stood up well. Indeed, another study with rats showed that the immune response could actually be boosted by conditioning (Gorcynski, cited in Dienstfrey, 1991). There is evidence that the placebo response may be a conditioned immune response that occurs in humans (Voudouris et al., 1985).

LOOKING AT LEVELS

Sick at the Thought of Chemotherapy

Like most psychological phenomena, classical conditioning provides an opportunity to understand how many events at the different levels of analysis affect one another in various organisms, including Pavlov's dogs and Ader's rats. The interplay of events at the levels of the brain, person, and group are easy to understand even in humans.

Cancer patients undergoing chemotherapy often experience intense nausea and vomiting as side effects of the treatment. But some patients develop anticipatory nausea, a classically conditioned response to chemotherapy triggered by a previously neutral CS (Burish & Carey, 1986; Carey & Burish, 1988; Davey, 1992). Such a stimulus might be as innocuous as a florist's shop seen en route to the hospital. For others undergoing chemotherapy, just thinking about the hospital where the treatment is received can produce nausea (Redd et al., 1993).

What is happening? At the level of the brain, the activity of neurons that feed into the patient's immune and autonomic nervous systems, stimulated by the UCS of the chemotherapeutic drugs that induce the UCR and CR of nausea, becomes paired with the activity of neurons that register certain sights and sounds—for example, the CS of the florist shop. After enough such pairings, the two groups of neurons become functionally connected, and activity in one group triggers activity in the other.

In addition, some patients are more likely than others to develop anticipatory nausea. Some people are generally more autonomically reactive than others; that is, they have a tendency toward a stronger autonomic response to given levels of stimulation. Such autonomically reactive people are more likely to develop anticipatory nausea (Kvale & Hugdahl, 1994). At the level of the person, such adverse effects can lead to a sense of helplessness and can cause some chemotherapy patients to stop the treatment altogether (Siegel & Longo, 1981). Fortunately, behavioral interventions such as relaxation training can be helpful in controlling anticipatory nausea, as can newer antinausea medications (Vasterling et al., 1993).

At the level of the group, chemotherapy involves a social component. It is administered by medical staff, in the social setting of a hospital or clinic, and the patient may be escorted to treatment by a friend or family member. Those involved in the chemotherapy treatment can become the CS, leading a patient to become nauseated at the sight of a particular nurse who always administers the treatment (Montgomery & Bovbjerg, 1997). Events at these levels interact. Autonomic reactivity influences the likelihood of developing anticipatory nausea, which can create yet another challenge for chemotherapy patients, affecting how they see the illness and their ability to fight it, and how they deal with medical staff, family, and friends. Moreover, the social interaction of being taught behavioral interventions for the anticipatory nausea (such as relaxation techniques) can influence events at the level of the brain and the person by giving the patient some sense of control over the nausea.

CONSOLIDATE!

 What is classical conditioning? How was it discovered? Ivan Pavlov discovered classical conditioning through his studies of dogs' salivation. This phenomenon involves the pairing of a conditioned stimulus (CS, such as a tone) with an unconditioned stimulus (UCS, such as food). The UCS reflexively elicits an unconditioned response (UCR,

such as salivation), and with repeated UCS–CS pairings, the CS will come to elicit a conditioned response (CR, salivation).

How are conditioned responses eliminated? Extinction, the "unpairing" of the CS and UCS, is achieved by repeatedly presenting the CS without the UCS. If extinction is followed by a rest period, the CS may again elicit the classically conditioned response; this is known as spontaneous recovery. In stimulus generalization, a similar but nonidentical stimulus elicits the CR. In stimulus discrimination, the organism learns to distinguish among similar stimuli so that only a particular stimulus will elicit the CR.

 3 *What are common examples of classical conditioning in daily life?* Classical conditioning is used in advertising, behavior therapy, and animal training, and is the mechanism underlying food and taste aversion and conditioned immune responses (such as can occur with a placebo effect).

Operant Conditioning

Paula came to have an emotionally painful response to Chris's tone of voice through the effects of classical conditioning. However, the destructive pattern of interaction between these two people doesn't end there. Paula becomes tense and angry. She yells; he yells. But they want to improve their relationship, so Chris agrees to try not to use that tone of voice or to yell at her, and Paula also agrees to try not to yell. This sounds great in theory, but the reality is not that easy. Yelling is a habit Paula and Chris have learned, and changing habits is hard. If they are not to yell at each other when they are angry or annoyed, they must learn new behaviors, new ways of communicating with each other.

In contrast to Paula and Chris's explosive style, Isabel and Tony's interactions with each other are calmer and more constructive. When they are angry or annoyed, they try to verbalize their anger constructively, talking it through until they reach some understanding or compromise. While they hash out a disagreement, each tries not to say something rash or critical that might be hurtful or regretted later. How can Paula and Chris learn to interact more as Isabel and Tony do? The answer might lie with another kind of learning, **operant conditioning**, the process whereby a behavior becomes associated with its consequences.

1 What is operant conditioning? How does it occur?

2 What is the difference between reinforcement and punishment?

3 How are complex behaviors learned? How are these new behaviors maintained?

4 What changes occur in the brain during operant conditioning?

The Roots of Operant Conditioning: Its Discovery and How It Works

If your behavior is followed by a positive consequence, you are more likely to repeat the act in the future; if it is followed by a negative consequence, you are less likely to repeat it. This observation underlies the mechanism of operant conditioning. Unlike classical conditioning, in which the organism is largely passive, operant conditioning requires the organism to "operate" in the world, to *do* something. Whereas classical conditioning usually involves involuntary reflexes, operant conditioning usually involves voluntary, nonreflexive behavior.

Isabel and Tony have apparently learned to talk about their differences relatively calmly and without anger, rather than yelling at each other at the first sign of tension. They learned this more peaceful behavior because when they calmly talked about their disagreements, the conversations had satisfying conclusions: no

Operant conditioning: The process by which a behavior becomes associated with its consequences.

fights, no tears, no sulks. Because of this positive outcome, they are more likely to express their concerns calmly when they disagree.

Thorndike's Puzzle Box

At about the same time that Pavlov was working with his dogs, American psychologist Edward L. Thorndike (1874–1949) was investigating a different kind of learning with cats. Thorndike created a puzzle box, a cage with a latched door that a cat could open by pressing on a pedal inside the cage (see Figure 4.8); food was placed outside the cage door. Although the cat took a while to get around to pressing the pedal, once it did (and the door opened), the cat was quicker to press the pedal in its subsequent sessions in the box: It had learned that pressing the pedal opened the door and enabled it to get the food (see Figure 4.9). Thorndike called this type of learning "trial-and-error learning." His finding led to his famous formulation of the **Law of Effect** (Thorndike, 1927), which lies at the heart of operant conditioning: Actions that subsequently lead to a "satisfying state of affairs" are more likely to be repeated (1933/1949, p. 14).

Figure **4.8** **Thorndike's Puzzle Box**

Thorndike placed a hungry cat inside the box and a piece of fish just outside the door in the cat's sight. The cat tried to get out of the box to the fish by emitting many behaviors, but only pressing the pedal would open the door. Eventually the cat pressed the pedal and the door opened. When the cat was put back inside the box, it pressed the pedal more quickly, improving each time.

Figure **4.9** **The Phases of Operant Conditioning**

Unlike classical conditioning, operant conditioning requires the organism to emit the desired behavior (the response). That behavior is then followed by positive or negative consequences.

Stimulus	Response	Consequence
Pedal	Pushing pedal	Food

The Skinner Box

B. F. Skinner (1904–1990), the twentieth century's foremost proponent of behaviorism, is important in the history of psychology not only because he most fully developed the concept of operant conditioning, but also because he showed how conditioning could explain much of our daily behavior. Working mostly with pigeons, he developed an apparatus to minimize his handling of the birds, which

Law of Effect: Actions that subsequently lead to a "satisfying state of affairs" are more likely to be repeated.

Figure 4.10 **Skinner Box and Cumulative Recorder**

In a Skinner box, a hungry rat presses a lever (or pigeons peck a key). As with Thorndike's cat, the rat will emit random behaviors, eventually pressing the lever, causing a food pellet (reinforcement) to come down the chute into the food dish, increasing the likelihood of the response in the future. It presses the lever again, and another food pellet appears. It presses the lever (and eats) more frequently—it has learned that pressing the lever will be followed by the appearance of a food pellet. On the outside of the box is a device that records each lever press and the time interval between presses.

is now often referred to as a Skinner box. The box (see Figure 4.10) could both feed the animals and record the frequency of their responses, making it easy to quantify the responses (this enormously helpful feature was in fact an unintended bonus of the box's design; Skinner, 1956). If a rat is put in a Skinner box, it learns to associate pressing the lever or bar with the likelihood of a food pellet's appearing. Here, the lever is the stimulus, pressing the lever is the response, or behavior, and receiving the food pellet is the consequence.

Principles of Operant Conditioning

Operant conditioning involves an association between a stimulus, the response to the stimulus (a behavior), and its consequence. (In classical conditioning, the association is between a neutral stimulus and a reflexive behavior.) With the rat, the bar or lever is the stimulus, pressing the bar is the behavior (or response to the stimulus), and the delivery of the food pellet is the consequence. Operant conditioning relies on **reinforcement**, the process by which consequences lead to an increase in the likelihood that the response will occur again. To be most effective, the reinforcement should be contingent on a desired response. Not surprisingly, this relationship between the response and the consequence is called **response contingency**; it occurs when a consequence is dependent on the organism's emitting the desired behavior.

A **reinforcer** is any object or event that comes after the desired response and strengthens the likelihood of its recurrence. In Thorndike's puzzle box and in the Skinner box, the reinforcer, or consequence, is food. Which reinforcer works best? The answer to this question is tricky: What one person considers a "reward" might leave another person cold. Reinforcement therefore is in the eyes of the recipient. For instance, for one person, a night at the ballet might be a wonderful reinforcer for doing well on a test. To another, a night at the ballet might seem like punishment. Parents who give stickers to their child for good behavior might conclude that behavioral programs don't work if that child makes no effort to win them. They'd be wrong: The problem is that their child doesn't view stickers as a reward. The parents simply need to find a reinforcer that *will* work for their child. For instance, when we were toilet training our children, we used reinforcers whenever they tried to use the potty. We had asked each child to name a reinforcer, and one of our children requested black olives. This is a reminder that the proof is in the pudding—the degree to which an object or event is a reinforcer is determined by

Reinforcement: The process by which consequences lead to an increase in the likelihood that the response will occur again.

Response contingency: The relationship that occurs when a consequence is dependent on the organism's emitting the desired behavior.

Reinforcer: Any object or event that follows the desired response and changes the likelihood of the recurrence of that response.

its effect on the individual organism. Just calling something a reinforcer doesn't make it so.

What's the connection with Paula and Chris? Each responded to the other's negative behavior with negative behavior of his or her own, as can happen in couples (Weiss & Heyman, 1990). Learning to communicate without yelling will take some work, but if they reinforce each other for calmer, lowered voices, they will increase the likelihood of success. Of course, this assumes that the "reward" each of them receives is in fact a reinforcer. Paula may or may not want to ask Chris what reinforcement he wants. If she tries to guess, she might use affection as a reinforcer, perhaps smiling warmly, giving him a kiss, or saying something like, "Thanks, Chris, for not speaking to me in that tone of voice I dislike. I appreciate that you're making the effort, and it makes it much easier for me to hear what you're trying to say." However, she shouldn't assume that she is using the right reinforcer for him—Chris might find such a speech patronizing. To find out, she will need to see whether the desired behavior increases.

Reinforcement: Getting Your Just Desserts

There are two types of reinforcement, positive and negative. In **positive reinforcement**, a desired reinforcer is presented after a response, thereby increasing the likelihood of a recurrence of that response. The food for Thorndike's cat and black olives for our toddler are examples of positive reinforcement. Food is the usual positive reinforcer for animals; for humans, toys, money, and intangibles such as praise and attention can also be positive reinforcers. Sometimes even "bad attention," such as a scolding, can be a positive reinforcer if the only time a child receives any attention at all is when he or she misbehaves. Again, reinforcement is particular to the individual.

In contrast, **negative reinforcement** is the *removal* of an unpleasant event or circumstance following a desired behavior, thereby increasing the probability of the behavior's occurring again. If a rat is being mildly shocked in its cage, and the shocks stop when it presses a bar, then bar pressing is negatively reinforced. A teacher who gives a "time out" to a continually disruptive child may inadvertently be negatively reinforcing the disruptive behavior if the child views the time out as relief from having to sit at a desk and do schoolwork (Piazza et al., 1998). Imagine this common scenario: A child whines to get his way, his father gives in to the whining, the child stops whining. What has happened? The aversive stimulus—the whining—has been removed, and so the father has been negatively reinforced for his behavior of giving in to the child. Dad is then more likely to give in the next time his child whines. This principle is at work when people use substances, such as alcohol, to decrease their anxiety (Hohlstein et al., 1998; Samoluk & Stewart, 1998). Both positive and negative reinforcement are described as reinforcing because they *increase* the likelihood of a behavior's recurring.

On a very hot day, going to an air-conditioned restaurant for lunch is negative reinforcement: You escape the heat by going to that restaurant and are thus reinforced for doing so. After this experience, you will be more likely to go to an air-conditioned restaurant again on another very hot day.

Punishment

A **punishment** is an unpleasant event that occurs as a consequence of a behavior. Punishment *decreases* the probability of the recurrence of a behavior, in contrast to reinforcement (both positive and negative), which *increases* the likelihood of recurrence. Although punishment is commonly confused with negative reinforcement, they are not the same; whereas punishment decreases the probability of a recurrence of a behavior, negative reinforcement increases the probability by removing an unpleasant consequence of the behavior (see Table 4.1).

TABLE 4.1   The Effects of Reinforcement and Punishment

Operant conditioning can be implemented with positive reinforcement, negative reinforcement, and punishment. In the examples below, the targeted behavior is Ben's playing the computer game *Spelling Blizzard*. Notice the effect that both types of reinforcement and punishment are likely to have on his game playing.

CONSEQUENCE	DEFINITION	EXAMPLE
Positive Reinforcement	The presentation of a desired reinforcer after a response, *increasing* the likelihood of a recurrence of that response.	After Ben plays the computer game Spelling *Blizzard*, his mother gives him something that he likes (such as praise or a treat). This increases the probability that Ben will play *Spelling Blizzard* again.
Negative Reinforcement	The removal of an unpleasant event after a response, *increasing* the likelihood of a recurrence of that response.	Ben's mother nags him to play *Spelling Blizzard* until he actually does so, at which point she stops nagging. This increases the probability that Ben will play *Spelling Blizzard* again.
Punishment	The occurrence of an unpleasant event as a consequence of a response, *decreasing* the likelihood of a recurrence of that response. The disagreeable consequence can be either the addition of something noxious or the removal of something pleasant.	After Ben refuses to play *Spelling Blizzard*, his mother punishes him by either doing something unpleasant (such as making him clean the bathroom) or taking away something he likes (such as denying TV privileges). Both of her actions decrease the probability that Ben will refuse again.

Punishment is most effective if it has three characteristics. First, punishment should be swift, occurring immediately after the undesired behavior. The old threat "Wait till you get home!" undermines the effectiveness of the punishment. Second, punishment must be consistent. The undesired behavior must be punished each and every time it occurs. If the behavior is punished only sporadically, the person or animal doesn't effectively learn that the behavior will be followed by punishment, and so doesn't decrease frequency of the behavior as consistently. Finally, the punishment should be sufficiently aversive without being overly aversive. If a child doesn't mind being alone in her room, then being sent there for pushing her brother won't be a very effective punishment; as with reinforcement, punishment is in the eye of the receiver.

We must make several cautionary points about the use of punishment. First, although punishment may decrease the frequency of a behavior, it doesn't eliminate the capacity to engage in that behavior. Your little sister may learn not to push you because your mother will punish her, but she may continue to push her classmates at school because the behavior has not been punished in that context. She has learned not to push when she will be punished for it. Moreover, sometimes people are able to avoid punishment, but continue to exhibit the response. Suppose your little sister figured out that if she hit you, but then apologized, she would not get punished. This kind of learning is called **avoidance learning;** an organism learns to avoid an unpleasant consequence by emitting a particular response—in this case, apologizing. Whereas classically conditioned avoidance learning is based on previous experience with an unpleasant stimulus (US), operantly conditioned avoidance learning is based on previous experience with an unpleasant consequence.

Second, physical punishment, such as a spanking, may actually increase aggressive behavior in the person on the receiving end. Although punishment provides an opportunity for operant learning, seeing others use physical violence also creates an opportunity for learning by watching the behavior of others. Such learning would account for the finding that abusive parents (and physically aggressive juvenile delinquents) tend to come from abusive families (Straus & Gelles, 1980; Straus & McCord, 1998).

Avoidance learning: In operant conditioning, the process by which an organism learns to avoid an unpleasant consequence by emitting a particular response.

Simply punishing someone does not provide that person with appropriate alternative behaviors. This mother clearly stated an appropriate alternative to biting someone when angry—using words to express the feeling.

A third problem created by punishment is that, through classical conditioning, the one being punished may come to fear the one doing the punishing. This may happen even if the punishment is infrequent. If the punishment is severe, a single instance may be enough for the person being punished to learn to live in fear of the punisher. Constantly living in fear can make people and animals chronically stressed, lead to depression, and contribute to the development of other mental and physical disorders.

Punishment alone hasn't been found to be as effective as punishment used in combination with reinforcement. This is because punishment doesn't convey information about what behavior should be exhibited in place of the undesired, punished behavior. Consider a preschool-age boy who draws on the wall. You don't want him to ruin the wallpaper so you punish him, and he learns not draw on the wall. But now when he's feeling creative, he draws on the floor or the door instead. However, if you punish him for wall- or floor-drawing *and then* provide him with paper and reinforce him for drawing on the paper, he is more likely to be artistically creative without inviting punishment. Because of the disadvantages of punishment, many training programs for parents emphasize positive reinforcement for good behavior; if children don't feel their parents are noticing and appreciating their efforts at good behavior, the incentive to keep it up may diminish.

Primary and Secondary Reinforcers

There are different levels of reinforcers: **Primary reinforcers** are events or objects that are inherently reinforcing (such as food, water, or relief from pain). **Secondary reinforcers,** such as attention, praise, money, good grades, or a promotion, are learned reinforcers and do not inherently satisfy a physical need. The theme park Sea World uses food as a primary reinforcer for its dolphins. It also uses secondary reinforcers such as touching and squirting the dolphins' faces with water. Secondary reinforcers are generally not instinctually satisfying.

Behavior modification is a technique that brings about therapeutic change in behavior through the use of secondary reinforcers. Programs involving mentally retarded children and adults, psychiatric patients, and prisoners have made use of secondary reinforcement. Participants in such programs earn tokens that can be traded for candy or for privileges such as going out for a walk or watching a particular television show. Behavior modification techniques using secondary reinforcement have also been used in the workplace; when employees received bonus vouchers for arriving at work on time, management found a significant reduction in tardiness (Hermann et al., 1973).

An unusual use of behavior modification with secondary reinforcers was undertaken by researchers in the rural Philippines who wanted to improve nutrition among poor children (Guthrie et al., 1982). The study was designed to discover whether reinforcement would be more beneficial than simply providing mothers with information about health and nutritional care for children. All the mothers were given appropriate information. Then the health clinic provided reinforcement in various forms for increases in the children's heights and weights. Three different villages participated in the study. In one, the reinforcement was a ticket in a clinic lottery in which the prize was food; the reinforcer used in the second village was a photograph of the child. The third village was a control group, and these people received no reinforcement for height or weight gains. One year later, children in the two villages that received reinforcement had more growth

Primary reinforcer: An event or object that is inherently reinforcing, such as food, water, or relief from pain.

Secondary reinforcer: An event or object that is reinforcing but that does not inherently satisfy a physical need, such as attention, praise, money, good grades, or a promotion.

Behavior modification: A technique that brings about therapeutic change in behavior through the use of secondary reinforcers.

and less malnutrition than those in the third village; no differences were observed between the first and second village.

Immediate Versus Delayed Reinforcement

The interval of time between behavior and its consequence can affect operant conditioning. In the Skinner box, for instance, if the rat receives a food pellet immediately after pressing the bar, it is receiving **immediate reinforcement**, reinforcement given immediately after the desired behavior. If the food pellet doesn't appear immediately but comes, say, 30 seconds later, the rat is receiving **delayed reinforcement**. With delayed reinforcement, the rat has some difficulty learning that bar pressing is followed by food. After pressing the bar but before receiving reinforcement, the rat may have sniffed some other section of the cage, scratched its ear, or done any number of things. It would be hard for the rat to "figure out" which behavior had produced the pellet.

One of the ways humans are different from rats is that we can learn effectively even if we receive delayed reinforcement. We work hard to get a promotion or raise, we practice kicking the soccer ball into the goal so that we'll be able to score at the next game, we study hard in college to get into graduate school or land a good job. Walter Mischel and his colleagues (1989) found that among the four-year-olds they studied, those who would forgo a small reward now for a big one tomorrow became more socially competent and were more likely to be high achievers during adolescence.

Beyond Basic Reinforcement

Operant conditioning can play a powerful role in people's lives. To see how, let's look at ways in which conditioning can be more than simply learning to respond when reinforcement is likely to result.

Generalization and Discrimination in Operant Conditioning

Just as in classical conditioning, the abilities to generalize and discriminate occur during operant conditioning, but in relation to responses as well as stimuli. Thus, in operant conditioning, **generalization** is the ability to generalize from the desired response to a similar response. When a child has a runny nose, most parents teach her to wipe her nose on a tissue. She may then generalize the response of wiping her nose and begin to wipe it on any available soft surface—her sleeve, her parent's shirt, her pillow. Similarly, if Paula or Chris begin to speak calmly to each other all the time, they will have generalized the response of speaking calmly (or at least not yelling) when angry to speaking calmly in all situations.

Discrimination is the ability to distinguish between the desired response (wiping a runny nose on a tissue or handkerchief) and a similar but undesirable one (wiping a runny nose on a shirt sleeve). The child's parents could help her make this discrimination by reinforcing her every time she wipes her nose with tissues or handkerchiefs (making sure they are readily available), and not reinforcing her when she wipes her nose on her sleeve or theirs.

Discrimination depends on the ability to distinguish among the different situations in which a stimulus may occur. Animals can be trained to press a bar to get food only if a tone is sounding, or only if they hear a high tone (not a low or medium tone). A **discriminative stimulus** is the cue that tells the organism whether a specific response will lead to the expected reinforcement. Experienced drivers react to a red light without thinking, automatically putting a foot on the brake pedal. In this situation, the red light is the stimulus, stopping the car is the response, and the reinforcement (negative, in this case) is escaping a dangerous situation. But drivers don't stomp their right feet down if they encounter a red

Immediate reinforcement: Reinforcement given immediately after the desired behavior is exhibited.

Delayed reinforcement: Reinforcement given some period of time after the desired behavior is exhibited.

Generalization: The ability to generalize both to similar stimuli and from the desired response to a similar response.

Discrimination: The ability to distinguish between the desired response and a similar but undesirable one.

Discriminative stimulus: The cue that tells the organism whether a specific response will lead to the expected reinforcement.

light while walking on the sidewalk. Driving a car is the discriminative stimulus that cues the response to stomp the right foot.

Extinction and Spontaneous Recovery in Operant Conditioning: Gone Today, Back Tomorrow

Have you ever lost money in a vending machine? If so, does this sequence of behaviors sound familiar? You deposit coins in the machine and press the button for your selection because you have learned that the reinforcement (the food) will come down the chute. When you press the button and no food appears, you press the button again. You then have a burst of pressing the button several times (and maybe a few other buttons for good measure), and only after these responses fail to make the machine deliver the goods do you give up. As this example shows, when someone has learned a behavior through operant conditioning (putting money in a vending machine), and the reinforcement stops (the food doesn't appear), initially there is an increase in responding. After this initial burst of behavior, the response fades. This is how **extinction** works in operant conditioning.

As with classical conditioning, the original response isn't lost through extinction; what happens is that new, opposing learning takes place. In the vending machine example, the opposing learning is that dropping coins in the slot does *not* lead to the appearance of food. As with classical conditioning, **spontaneous recovery** occurs: If a break follows extinction, the old behavior will reappear. So if you don't use that vending machine for a month, you might very well put money in it again, expecting it to dispense your bag of chips.

Building Complicated Behaviors: Shaping Up

Many complex behaviors are not learned all at one time, but rather are acquired gradually. Moreover, complex behaviors may often be built on previously learned behaviors. How do the animal trainers at Sea World train the dolphins to do a high jump? The dolphins don't naturally do it, so they can't be reinforced for that behavior. Similarly, the tone of voice that Paula finds so upsetting in Chris might be so automatic for him that he isn't even aware of using it. **Shaping** is the gradual process of reinforcing an organism for behavior that gets closer and closer to the behavior you ultimately wish to condition. It is the method that helps train dolphins to do high jumps (see Figure 4.11), and it could also train Chris to speak quietly to Paula even when he's angry. It is used when the desired response is not one that the organism would emit in the normal course of events. Shaping must be done in phases, nudging the organism closer and closer to the desired response. In shaping, the final behavior is considered as a series of smaller behaviors, which become increasingly similar to the desired behavior; these smaller behaviors are called **successive approximations.**

If Paula were to use shaping to help Chris change his tone of voice, she might start out reinforcing Chris for apologizing when he does use "that tone." With time and effort, Chris will probably catch himself whenever he uses the disturbing tone of voice and repeat Paula's name in a more pleasant way. Paula would then shift the response that she reinforces from his apology after the fact to his catching himself as he's doing it. Finally, she reinforces him only for using her name in the new, calmer way. To shape this new behavior, they might have "practice sessions" in which Chris pretends to be angry. Thus, the two of them would begin shaping the desired behavior—a more pleasant tone of voice—in successive approximations, with each approximation more closely resembling the desired behavior.

Reinforcement Schedules: An Hourly or a Piece-Rate Wage?

A critical element that can change the frequency of an organism's response is the schedule on which the reinforcement is delivered. Reinforcement can be given every time a desired response occurs, or it can be given less frequently. When an

Extinction: In operant conditioning, the fading out of a response following an initial burst of a behavior after the withdrawal of reinforcement.

Spontaneous recovery: In operant conditioning, the process by which an old response reappears if there is a break after extinction.

Shaping: The gradual process of reinforcing an organism for behavior that gets closer to the desired behavior.

Successive approximations: The series of smaller behaviors involved in shaping a complex behavior.

Figure 4.11 Shaping Dolphins at Sea World

Training dolphins at Sea World to jump requires a number of phases, each getting closer to the final goal.

First the dolphin receives reinforcement (a food treat) after touching a target on the surface of the water.

The target is raised slightly out of the water. When the dolphin touches the target, it receives food.

The target continues to be raised until eventually the dolphin's body must come out of the water for it to touch the target. The dolphin receives a treat for doing so.

organism is reinforced for each desired response, it is receiving **continuous reinforcement.** When reinforcement does not occur after every response, but only intermittently, the organism is receiving **partial reinforcement.** Initial learning is slower with partial reinforcement than with continuous reinforcement. For this reason, when trying to shape a new behavior, continuous reinforcement is the best method until the desired behavior is stable. Thus, Sea World trainers reward a dolphin every time it touches the target on the surface of the water. An advantage of a partial reinforcement schedule, however, is that it is more resistant to extinction: The organism learns that it won't receive reinforcement after each response so it doesn't stop doing the behavior right away when no reinforcement is forthcoming. Some partial reinforcement schedules, called **interval schedules,** are based on time; reinforcement is given for responses after a specified interval of time. Other schedules, called **ratio schedules,** are based on a specified number of the desired responses; reinforcement is given after that number of responses is emitted.

On a **fixed interval schedule,** the organism receives reinforcement for a response emitted after a fixed interval of time. In a Skinner box, a rat on a fixed interval schedule of 10 minutes would receive reinforcement for the first bar press that occurs 10 minutes after the previous reinforcement was given, but not during that 10 minutes, regardless of how many times it pressed the bar. The same applies for the next 10-minute interval: The rat would receive a food pellet only for the first bar press after 10 minutes since the last reinforcement. A study break after every hour of studying is reinforcement on a fixed interval schedule. So is a weekly paycheck: No matter how hard you work, you will not get an additional paycheck that week. With animals on a fixed interval schedule, the frequency of desired behavior tends to slow down right after reinforcement and pick up again right before reinforcement. As shown in Figure 4.12 on page 144, this pattern has a scallop shape on the graph of cumulative responses.

In **variable interval schedules,** the interval is an average over time. If a rat were reinforced for its first response after 8 minutes, then after 12 minutes, then

Continuous reinforcement: Reinforcement given for each desired response.

Partial reinforcement: Reinforcement given only intermittently.

Interval schedule: Partial reinforcement schedule based on time.

Ratio schedule: Partial reinforcement schedule based on a specified number of emitted responses.

Fixed interval schedule: Reinforcement schedule in which reinforcement is given for a response emitted after a fixed interval of time.

Variable interval schedule: Reinforcement schedule in which reinforcement is given for a response emitted after a variable interval of time.

Figure 4.12 Schedules of Reinforcement

Research findings are mixed with regard to how well rodents' and humans' cumulative frequencies on four schedules of reinforcement correspond. Some studies with humans have found similar patterns of responding (Higgens and Morris, 1984); others have not (Lowe, 1979; Matthews et al., 1977). For both humans and rodents, however, variable reinforcement schedules induce a more consistent rate of responding than their fixed reinforcement schedule counterparts.

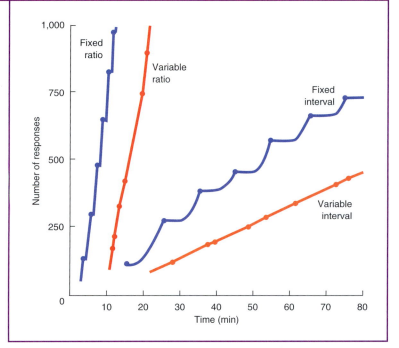

13 minutes, then 7 minutes, it would be on a variable interval schedule of 10 minutes. If you took a study break after approximately an hour of studying, but sometimes after 45 minutes, sometimes after an hour and 15 minutes, sometimes after half an hour, sometimes after an hour and a half, the average would be every hour, and so you would be on a variable interval 60-minute schedule. In animals, this schedule creates consistent although somewhat slow responding (see Figure 4.12).

Fixed ratio schedules provide reinforcement after a fixed number of responses. If a rat is on a "fixed ratio 10," it receives a food pellet after its tenth bar press, then again after another 10, and so on. Factory piecework is paid on a fixed ratio schedule; for example, in the garment industry, workers may be paid a certain amount for every 10 completed articles of clothing. When responses on this schedule are graphed, they assume a steplike pattern (see Figure 4.12): a high rate of response until reinforcement is delivered, then a lull, followed by a high rate of response until the next reinforcement, and so on. This schedule has a high rate of responding when compared with fixed interval responding. For this reason, piecework can be exhausting, whether the work is inputting data (being paid for every 100 lines of data entered), sewing garments, or assembling machinery. On this schedule, workers have a good reason not to take breaks (they will not be paid for that time), but as people work long hours without breaks, efficiency and accuracy decline (Proctor & Van Zandt, 1994).

Variable ratio schedules present reinforcement at a variable rate. If reinforcement occurs on average after every tenth response, reinforcement could be presented after 5, 18, 4, and 13 responses, or it could presented after 24, 1, 10, and 5 responses. You never really know when the reinforcement will come. This is often called the "gambling reinforcement schedule" because most gambling relies on this type of unpredictable reinforcement. Slot machines hit the jackpot on a variable ratio reinforcement schedule. If you play long enough (and spend enough money), eventually you will win; unfortunately, you might spend years, and tens of thousands of dollars, trying to hit the jackpot. The variable ratio schedule is the most resistant to extinction (which is part of the reason why some people get hooked

Fixed ratio schedule: Reinforcement schedule in which reinforcement is given after a fixed ratio of responses.

Variable ratio schedule: Reinforcement schedule in which reinforcement is given after a variable ratio of responses.

on gambling). Because you don't know exactly when you will be reinforced (but expect that eventually reinforcement will come), you keep responding. Animals on this schedule tend to respond frequently, consistently, and without long pauses, and this schedule tends to get the highest response rate; for example, Skinner (1953) found that when he shifted to reinforcing a pigeon on a variable, infrequent schedule, the pigeon continued to peck at a disk 150,000 times without reinforcement, as if still expecting reinforcement! Commission sales jobs are based on the same principle: The hope of an eventual sale (and therefore reinforcement in the form of an eventual commission) keeps salespeople pushing their wares. Returning to our couple, Paula and Chris each held their ground during a disagreement because each had been occasionally reinforced (by "winning" an argument) for doing so. Each had been reinforced on a variable ratio schedule, except that neither knew what the ratio was! This partly explains why their behavior had become so entrenched. In trying to change it, they should probably start out on a continuous reinforcement schedule, then switch to some type of partial reinforcement schedule; realistically, they could probably manage only a variable interval or variable ratio schedule. Of course, a variable ratio schedule would make their new behaviors the most resistant to extinction.

The variable ratio reinforcement schedule, often referred to as the gambling reinforcement schedule, is the most resistant to extinction. If you were playing a slot machine and didn't hit the jackpot, how long would you need to play before you might think there was a problem with the machine?

The Learning Brain

Until recently, learning theorists ignored the role of the brain in learning, focusing instead on overt behaviors. We now know, however, that an understanding of how the brain works can shed considerable light on this fundamental process (as shown by Beggs et al., 1999, among others). Recent research suggests, for example, that two neurotransmitters, acetylcholine and dopamine, play critical roles in several different aspects of learning.

Different Parts for Different Jobs

Learning isn't a single process. As discussed earlier, when you walk down a street you don't stomp your right foot every time you see a red light. From this we can infer that learning involves at least two major phases. First, we learn to discriminate the proper situation in which to make a response. Here the hippocampus plays an important role. The neurotransmitter acetylcholine (ACh) is key to the functioning of the hippocampus, and scopolamine is an antagonist for this chemical—in other words, it blocks it. Animals that are given scopolamine can't learn which stimuli should be grouped together as a signal for an appropriate response (Mishkin & Appenzeller, 1987).

Second, we learn the stimulus–response association itself. The key to operant conditioning is that specific consequences follow a response. Various parts of the brain produce the neurotransmitter dopamine, but one part—the nucleus accumbens, located behind the amygdala—appears particularly important for reward to be effective. When researchers block dopamine receptors, animals fail to respond to reinforcement, either positive (Spyraki et al., 1982) or negative (Beninger et al., 1980). Studies show, for example, that animals trained to press a lever to get a squirt of a dopamine agonist (which causes the production of dopamine) into their veins will work hard to obtain such reinforcement (Koob & Bloom, 1988). Similarly, amphetamines and cocaine, as well as nicotine and caffeine, are dopamine agonists; addicts will work hard to acquire these substances.

Thus, at the level of the brain, the fact that different neurotransmitters are crucial for different aspects of learning again shows us that learning is not a single activity.

TABLE 4.2 — Classical and Operant Conditioning Compared

	CLASSICAL CONDITIONING	OPERANT CONDITIONING
Similarities	• Learning is based on an association between stimulus and response.	• Learning is based on an association between response and reinforcement.
	• Avoidance learning.	• Avoidance learning.
	• Extinction.	• Extinction.
	• Spontaneous recovery.	• Spontaneous recovery.
	• Stimulus generalization.	• Generalization.
	• Stimulus discrimination.	• Discrimination.
	• External factors can affect learning.	• External factors can affect learning.
Differences	• The organism is passive.	• The organism is active, "operating" on the world.
	• Responses are reflexes (limited number of possible responses).	• Responses are voluntary behaviors (limitless possible responses).
	• Responses are elicited.	• Responses are emitted.
	• Responses are not followed by a reinforcer.	• Responses are followed by a reinforcer.

Classical Versus Operant Conditioning: Are They Really Different?

Table 4.2 presents a comparison of classical and operant conditioning. Both types of conditioning depend on an association, either between a stimulus and response or between a response and reinforcement. Both classical and operant conditioning involve extinction and spontaneous recovery, generalization, and discrimination. Both types of learning are subject to moderating factors that affect response acquisition, such as time (in classical conditioning, the length of time between CS and UCS; in operant conditioning, immediate versus delayed reinforcement), and for both types of learning biological factors influence what can be learned easily.

Noting these similarities, some researchers have debated whether these two types of conditioning are really so distinct after all. Perhaps they are just different procedures toward a similar end. Indeed, the differences are not so clear cut. Some studies, for example, show that voluntary movements can be shaped via classical conditioning (Brown & Jenkins, 1968). Similarly, involuntary responses, such as learning to control tense jaw muscles to decrease facial pain, can be operantly conditioned (Dohrmann & Laskin, 1978). However, the fact that the same ends can be reached with either type of conditioning does not imply that the means to those ends are the same. After all, bats, birds, and helicopters fly, but they do so in different ways.

Perhaps the best evidence that the two kinds of conditioning are truly different is that different neural systems are used in each. Although the debate over making neat distinctions between classical and operant conditioning continues, recent research on the brain appears to discount the position that they are variations of the same process. Not only do classical and operant conditioning clearly draw on different mechanisms, but different forms of classical conditioning also rely on different brain structures, depending on the response to be conditioned. For example, whereas classical conditioning of fear draws on the amygdala (LeDoux, 1996), classical conditioning of eye blinks relies heavily on the cerebellum (Thompson & Krupa, 1994). In contrast, operant conditioning involves neither structure, using instead the dopamine-based "reward system" centered in the nucleus accumbens (Robbins & Everitt, 1998). By providing evidence that different neural systems are used in the different types of learning, studies of the brain establish that the two types of conditioning are essentially different.

Cornering the Professor

When one of the authors was an undergraduate, the teaching assistant in a course on learning coached the class to alter the behavior of the professor. As instructed, the class looked down and shuffled papers whenever the professor was in the center of the stage. But as soon as he moved, even a little, toward the back left corner of the stage, we students looked up attentively. After a while, we went back to shuffling, and then looked up only when the professor had moved a bit farther toward the corner. As the period wore on, we found that we actually were able to maneuver the professor into the corner! We had apparently shaped the professor's behavior, using our attention as the reinforcer, a powerful reinforcer for most teachers.

Consider this scenario from the levels perspective. Based on what we know about reward systems in the brain, it is reasonable to suppose that the way we oriented ourselves toward the professor (a social variable) literally manipulated his brain. When he drifted toward the corner, our bright and eager faces probably caused dopamine to squirt in his brain, making this behavior more likely in the future. Our professor later claimed that he didn't notice what was going on. If he had been more observant (level of the person), he might have seen what we were up to and been able to extinguish the response or not find attentive students reinforcing. Our ability to maneuver the professor depended on events at all three levels of analysis: The brain allowed his behavior to be shaped; his personality led him to be susceptible to this process; and the group provided the reinforcement. If we hadn't liked him as much as we did, and felt that he liked us, we might not have dared to try this experiment, and thus aspects of his personality affected the social reinforcement, which in turn affected his brain. And of course we were delighted as he gradually began to hang around in the corner (courtesy, ultimately, of brain mechanisms), so we were all the more engaged in the process and willing to play our group role as social reinforcer.

CONSOLIDATE!

1 *What is operant conditioning? How does it occur?* Operant conditioning is a process whereby a behavior becomes associated with the consequences of performing that behavior; in contrast to classical conditioning, these behaviors are usually voluntary. Thorndike's work with cats in a puzzle box led him to develop the Law of Effect. Skinner's work with pigeons (and later, with rats) in a Skinner box showed that operant conditioning could explain much of everyday human behavior.

2 *What is the difference between reinforcement and punishment?* Reinforcement *increases* the likelihood that a behavior will recur; punishment *decreases* that likelihood. Positive reinforcement is the *presentation* of a desired reinforcer after a particular response; negative reinforcement is the *removal* of an unpleasant stimuli after a particular response. Punishment by itself is not particularly effective. Reinforcement can be given via primary or secondary reinforcers (examples of the latter are money, praise, good grades); behavior modification programs make use of secondary reinforcers.

3 *How are complex behaviors learned? How are these new behaviors maintained?* Complex behaviors are learned through shaping, which involves reinforcing behaviors that are successive approximations toward the desired, complex behavior. Generalization, discrimination, extinction, and spontaneous recovery all occur with operant conditioning. Reinforcement schedules help maintain learned behaviors, with the variable ratio schedule producing behaviors most resistant to extinction.

4 *What changes occur in the brain during operant conditioning?* Learning has different aspects, each with its own brain changes. We learn to discriminate the proper situation in which to make a response; the hippocampus, through the functioning of the neurotransmitter acetylcholine, is involved in this phase. In addition, we learn the stimulus–response association itself. The neurotransmitter dopamine is involved here, as is the nucleus accumbens, a structure behind the amygdala. Research shows that although operant and classical conditioning share some similarities, they are also distinct from each other, relying on different brain systems.

Cognitive and Social Learning

At a friend's suggestion, Paula and Chris took a couples' communication class, which met once a week for 6 weeks. Two coleaders (one male, one female) led the group. Each class began with the leaders role-playing a couple who were unsuccessful in resolving their differences. They then repeated the role play, this time incorporating techniques the couple might use to resolve their differences. Afterward, the leaders asked volunteers to act out the same scene, this time attempting to come to a resolution.

As part of the class, each couple received a manual and video on conflict resolution to read and view at home. The video included additional problem scenarios and demonstrated both maladaptive and adaptive ways that couples can react to such situations. In essence, both the manual and the video encouraged users to find new ways of interacting with their partners, and of thinking about conflict and its resolution in general. These aids relied on **cognitive learning**, the acquisition of information that is often not immediately acted on but is stored for later use.

1. What is cognitive learning? How does it differ from classical and operant conditioning?

2. What is insight learning?

3. How can watching others help people learn?

4. What makes some models better than others?

Cognitive Learning

The learning we have discussed so far focuses on behavior. In classical conditioning, the learned behavior is the conditioned response (CR); in operant conditioning, the learned behavior is the reinforced response. But even these types of learning involve the storing of new information, which guides the behavior. Information acquired through cognitive learning, on the other hand, may be used in planning, evaluating, and other forms of thinking, without producing any behavior—only, perhaps, more information to be stored. Learning how to add is an example of cognitive learning, as is learning the names of the 50 states or the meaning of a new word. You are engaged in cognitive learning right now.

Illustrating the fact that cognitive learning is more than simply associations between stimuli and responses, Tolman and Honzik (1930b, 1930c) conducted a series of classic studies of learning with rats. One group of rats was put in a maze that led to a food box, thus receiving a food reward for completing the maze (Figure 4.13, left panel). The other group was also put in the maze but received no reinforcement; the rats were simply removed from the maze after a certain amount of time. Sometimes routes were blocked, and the rats had to find a different way to the end. The first group of rats, those that were rewarded with food, quickly increased their speed in the maze and decreased the number of mistakes; the speed and accuracy of the unrewarded second group did not particularly improve. This finding was consistent with what behaviorists would predict. However, when rats in the second group received a food reward on the 11th day, their speed increased and their errors decreased, both dramatically (Figure 4.13, right panel). It appears that these rats had learned how to run the maze quickly and correctly before the 11th day, but had no reason to do so. Such learning that occurs without behavioral signs is called **latent learning**. Tolman reasoned that the unreinforced rats, in their wanderings around the maze, had developed a *cognitive map* of the maze, storing information about its spatial layout. However, they did not use the map until they were motivated to do so by the reinforcement. This study, and the con-

Cognitive learning: The acquisition of information that often is not immediately acted on but is stored for later use.

Latent learning: Learning that occurs without behavioral signs.

Figure **4.13**   **Tolman and Honzik's Discovery of Latent Learning**

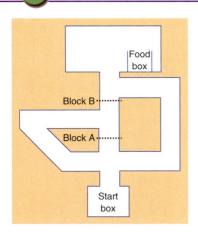

Three routes of differing lengths wind from start to finish. If two points along the most direct route are blocked, it is still possible to get to the end.

Rats that were rewarded for getting to the end of the maze made fewer "navigation" errors than rats that were not rewarded. Once rewarded (on day 11), the previously unrewarded rats made fewer mistakes than regularly reinforced rats, illustrating that the unrewarded rats had learned the spatial arrangement of the maze but did not apply that knowledge until reinforced.

cept of latent learning, also reminds us of the important distinction between learning something and performing it. Piaget (1962) described a situation in which one of his daughters watched another child have a dramatic temper tantrum, complete with writhing on the floor and howling. His daughter also saw the other child's parents react with concern. Days later, his daughter tried out this behavior, presumably to see whether she would be given the attention she thought a tantrum deserved. She did not have to engage in the behavior at the time to learn it. Researchers now know that latent learning depends on the hippocampus (Myers et al., 2000), which is generally used when new facts are stored (Schacter, 1996).

The study of learning focuses on the *acquisition* of information; in contrast, the study of memory focuses on the *retention* of information. By its very nature, cognitive learning relies crucially on how information is stored in memory, and most of the recent research on this topic (explored in the next chapter) focuses on the way information is stored in memory.

Insight Learning: Seeing the Connection

Insight learning consists of suddenly grasping what something means and incorporating that new knowledge into old knowledge. It is based on the phenomenon known as the "aha experience," the triumphal moment when an idea becomes crystal clear. By its very nature, insight learning, unlike other types of learning, is accompanied by a sudden flash of awareness that one has learned.

The most famous psychological experiments regarding insight learning were done by Wolfgang Köhler (1887–1967), a German Gestalt psychologist. Köhler (1925) put a chimpanzee named Sultan in a cage; outside the cage, and out of reach, Köhler put fruit. Also outside the cage and out of reach, but closer than the fruit, he placed a long stick. Inside the cage, Köhler put a short stick. Initially, Sultan showed signs of frustration as he tried to reach the food. Then he stopped. He seemed suddenly to have an insight into how to snag the fruit: He used the short stick to get the long one, and then capture the fruit. In another study, Köhler put

Insight learning: Learning that occurs when a person or animal suddenly grasps what something means and incorporates that new knowledge into old knowledge.

In another instance of opportunity for insight learning, Sultan is faced with a variant of the two-stick solution to help him retrieve food that is out of reach. Here, there are four sticks.

bananas in the cage but high, out of Sultan's reach. Also in the cage were stacks of boxes. At first, Sultan tried to jump up to grab the bananas. Eventually, he looked around at the objects in the cage and again appeared to have a flash of insight; he saw that stacking the boxes and climbing on them would enable him to reach the bananas.

Observational Learning: To See Is to Know

Everyone, like Piaget's daughter, has had the experience of watching someone else's behavior and then being able to reproduce it. The behavior is probably voluntary (and thus not the result of classical conditioning) and may not have been reinforced (and thus not the result of operant conditioning), but it was learned nonetheless. A group of psychologists, led by Albert Bandura, developed *social learning theory*, which emphasizes the fact that much learning occurs in a social context. This kind of learning, which results simply from watching others and does not depend on reinforcement, is called **observational learning.** Observational learning helps people learn how to behave in their families (Thorn & Gilbert, 1998) and in their cultures: By watching others, we learn how to greet people, eat, laugh, tell jokes. Observational learning has helped you figure out how to behave in your class and on campus. Do you remember your first few days at college? By watching others, you learned how people talked to each other, what clothes were "fashionable," and how to interact with instructors.

Observational learning influenced Paula and Chris's behavior: Chris learned to yell by watching his father yell at his mother. In fact, most people in his family yelled at one another, and he grew up thinking that all families acted that way. In contrast, Paula's parents didn't yell very often, and when they did, the episode was over quickly and everyone apologized. Thus, through observational learning, Paula and Chris had learned dramatically different ways of resolving disagreements and expressing anger.

Bandura focused much of his work on *modeling,* a process in which someone learns new behaviors through observing other people. These other people function as models, presenting a behavior to be imitated. With modeling, you observe others' behaviors, and then none, some, or all of these behaviors may be learned and repeated, or modified. In one of Bandura's famous studies involving a Bobo doll, an inflated vinyl doll that pops back up when punched (Figure 4.14; Bandura et al., 1961), children were divided into three groups: One group watched an adult beating up a Bobo doll, one group watched an adult ignoring the Bobo doll, and the third didn't see an adult at all. After being mildly frustrated by being placed in a room with toys, but not being allowed to play with some of them, all the children were then placed in another room with many toys, including a Bobo doll. Children who had observed the adult behaving aggressively with Bobo were themselves more aggressive. Similar studies have found similar results, including the observation that watching aggression by a live person has more of an impact than watching a video of a person exhibiting the same behaviors. In turn, a realistic video has more of an impact than a cartoon version of the same behaviors (Bandura et al., 1963).

Observational learning: Learning that occurs through watching others, not through reinforcement.

Figure **4.14   Bandura's Study on Observational Learning**

Three groups of children were tested; the groups differed only in the first part of the study. Children in one group watched an adult abuse a Bobo doll, for example, by slamming it with a mallet, kicking it, and yelling at it.

Children in a second group watched adults play with Tinkertoys and ignore the Bobo doll.

Children in a third group never saw a model (an adult) in the playroom.

In the second part of the study, all the children played in a room with a variety of toys, including Bobo. Children in the first group tended to imitate what they had seen, mistreating the doll (and inventing new ways to abuse it) and being more aggressive with the other toys in the room.

Children who observed the adult ignoring the Bobo doll were even less aggressive toward it than the control group!

When Paula and Chris observed the leaders and group members role-play more adaptive ways of interacting, they were presented with an opportunity to learn by observation. These sorts of opportunities occur frequently in everyday life. An apprentice spends large amounts of time observing a master before ever doing anything more than handing over a tool. How-to videos ranging from cooking to home repair may be more effective than how-to books because they allow the viewer to see the desired behavior. Observational learning is the way we learn first languages, form standards of judgment, and even discover how to solve many types of problems (Bandura, 1986).

Learning From Models

Learning from models has many advantages over other sorts of learning. By learning from models, you can avoid going through all the steps that learning usually requires and go directly to the end product.

We learn from models by seeing which of their responses are reinforced and which are punished. We are then able to make predictions about the reactions that our behaviors will provoke. This pattern of learning is one of the reasons why parents and others have become increasingly concerned about the amount and type of violence, foul language, and sexuality portrayed on television. Many television shows geared toward children contain violence, which is often imitated by viewers. Moreover, television violence often shows no harm to the victim and no negative consequences for the perpetrator.

Observational learning can produce both desired and undesired learning. Models may say one thing and do another, and the observer learns both, saying what the model said and doing what the model did (Rice & Grusec, 1975; Rushton, 1975). If you are surrounded by positive models, you have the opportunity to learn a lot of positive behaviors; but if you don't have that opportunity, you may find it difficult to learn certain "skills." If adults in a family have trouble holding jobs, become explosively angry, exhibit little patience, and treat others rudely, it can be harder for the children to learn the skills involved in maintaining a job, effectively controlling anger, managing impatience and frustration, and treating others kindly. On a more positive note, Bandura and colleagues (1967) did a study in which preschool children who were afraid of dogs observed another child who had no fear of dogs. Over eight sessions, as prearranged, the model on each occasion played more closely with a dog and for a longer time. Fearful children who watched the other child with the dog had significantly more "approach" behaviors (those oriented toward a dog) than a control group of fearful children who did not observe the model.

Both modeling and operant conditioning are involved in learning about culture and gender. You may learn how to behave by observing others, but whether you'll actually perform those behaviors depends, in part, on the consequences that occur when you try. Imagine the following family interaction in a culture that has different expectations of what constitutes appropriate play for girls and boys. A boy observes his older sister asking her parents for a new doll and sees that they buy it for her. He then asks his parents for a doll for himself and is severely punished. His request was prompted by modeling; but because it resulted in punishment, he is unlikely to make that request again. Similarly, ninth and tenth graders were more likely to get involved in community activity if their parents were involved, or if parents reinforced them for minor involvement (Fletcher et al., 2000).

Researchers have discovered that several characteristics of models can make learning through observation more effective (Bandura, 1977a, 1986). Not surprisingly, the more you pay attention to the model, the more you learn. You are more likely to pay attention if the model is an expert, is good looking, has high status, or is socially powerful (Brewer & Wann, 1998). Perhaps intuitively realizing the importance of models for children's learning through observation, and recognizing the high-status position of his office, cigar enthusiast President William McKinley refused to be photographed with a cigar (Seuling, 1978). We know that children learn by observing others, and powerful, high-status models such as presidents, athletes, or celebrities are likely to be more influential.

LOOKING AT LEVELS

Mom and Dad on Drugs

In the 1980s, a long-running TV public service advertisement showed a father confronting his son with what is obviously the boy's drug paraphernalia. The father asks his son incredulously, "Where did you learn to do this?" The son, half in tears, replies, "From you, okay? I learned it from watching you!" Observational learning clearly appears to be a factor in an adolescent's willingness to experiment with drugs and alcohol. Andrews and her colleagues (1997) found that adolescents' relationships with

their parents influence whether they will model the substance use patterns of the parents. Specifically, they found that adolescents who had a positive relationship with their mothers modeled her use (or nonuse) of cigarettes, and those who had a close relationship with their fathers modeled the father's marijuana use (or nonuse). Similarly, those who had a negative relationship with their parents were less likely to model their parents' use of drugs or alcohol. Although some of the more complex results of this study depended on the age and sex of the adolescent, the general findings can be understood by thinking about them from the three levels of analysis and their interactions.

At the level of the brain, observing someone engage in a behavior causes you to store new memories, which involves the hippocampus and related brain systems. These memories later can guide behavior, as they do in all types of imitation. At the level of the person, if you are motivated to observe someone, you are likely to be paying more attention to them (and therefore increasing the likelihood of your learning from them and remembering what you learn). At the level of the group, you are more likely to be captivated by models who have certain attractive char-

acteristics. In this case, adolescents who had a positive relationship with their parents were more likely to do what their parents did; if their parents didn't smoke, the adolescents were less likely to do so. The events at these levels interact: Children who enjoy a positive relationship with their parents may accord their parents higher status than children who have a negative relationship with their parents. Thus, the former group of children probably increase the amount of attention they give to their parents' behavior. And, as you will see in the following chapter, paying attention engages the frontal lobes and other brain areas that are crucial for storing new information effectively.

CONSOLIDATE!

1 *What is cognitive learning? How does it differ from classical and operant conditioning?* Cognitive learning is the acquisition of information that often is not acted on immediately, but rather is stored for later use. This process contrasts with classical and operant conditioning, which focus on learning behaviors. Latent learning (such as creating a cognitive map) is an example of cognitive learning.

2 *What is insight learning?* Learning can occur following an insight, by suddenly grasping what something means and incorporating that new knowledge into old knowledge. Insight learning is based on the "aha experience" and is marked by a cognitive "leap."

3 *How can watching others help people learn?* Observational learning allows you to acquire knowledge "second hand," without having to perform a behavior yourself. This sort of learning helps explain how children (and adults) learn their family's and their culture's rules, and the different rules that sometimes exist for men and women, boys and girls.

4 *What makes some models better than others?* Modeling is the process of learning a new behavior through observing others, and the more attention paid to the model, the more effective the learning will be. You are more likely to pay attention to a model who is an expert, is good looking, or has high status.

A DEEPER LEVEL

Recap and Thought Questions

Classical Conditioning

Classical conditioning, which was discovered by Ivan Pavlov, has four basic elements:

1. The unconditioned stimulus (UCS), such as food, reflexively elicits an unconditioned response.
2. The unconditioned response (UCR), such as salivation, is automatically elicited by a UCS.
3. The pairing of a conditioned stimulus (CS), such as a tone, with a UCS, such as food, elicits a conditioned response (CR), such as salivation. (Note that saliva-

tion can be either a conditioned or an unconditioned response, depending on the stimulus that elicits it.)
4. The presentation of the CS alone then elicits the UCR (the tone presented alone elicits the response of salivation now as a CR).

A conditioned emotional response is involved in the development of phobias, as shown by Watson and Raynor in the case of Little Albert. Extinction is the unpairing of the CS and UCS; spontaneous recovery is the return of a classically conditioned response after a rest period following extinction. In stimulus generalization, a similar, but not identical, stimulus elicits the CR; in stimulus discrimination, the organism learns to distinguish among similar stimuli so that only a particular stimulus elicits the CR.

Why was Paula initially fearful when Chris said her name in a certain tone of voice? She was fearful because she had developed a conditioned emotional response to it: That tone of voice (CS) had become paired with his telling her he had doubts about the relationship (UCS), causing a fear response in Paula (UCR and CR).

Think It Through. Dog obedience classes suggest that the following procedure will train a dog to stop barking. When the dog starts to bark, squirt water (from a water bottle) in its face. Right before you squirt, say, "Don't bark!" The dog startles because of the water and stops barking. Is this classical conditioning? If so, identify the UCS, CS, UCR, and CR. What would be happening if the dog stops barking as soon as you say, "Don't bark"? What learning process has occurred if the dog stops barking only when you give the command in a particular tone of voice?

Operant Conditioning

Operant conditioning is the process whereby a behavior (usually a voluntary one) becomes associated with the consequences of performing that behavior. Operant conditioning has three basic elements:

1. The stimulus, such as a pedal
2. The response, such as pressing the pedal
3. The consequence, such as a cage door opening

Shaping makes it possible to learn, by successive approximations, behaviors that would otherwise not be emitted. Both negative and positive reinforcement *increase* the behavior that precedes it; punishment *decreases* the behavior that precedes it. Extinction, spontaneous recovery, generalization, and discrimination all occur in operant conditioning. Reinforcers can be primary or secondary; the latter can be tokens that are exchanged for a primary reinforcer. Reinforcement schedules can be continuous or partial; if partial, reinforcement may be given for responses after an interval of time (interval schedule), or after a set number of responses (ratio schedule).

How did Paula and Chris learn to behave disrespectfully to each other? Paula and Chris would keep yelling at each other and saying hurtful things in an effort to "win" a fight. Sometimes one would win, sometimes the other, in the fashion of a variable reinforcement schedule. These hollow victories reinforced hurtful behavior and persistent arguing, making this harmful interaction pattern difficult to extinguish.

Think It Through. You are babysitting, and the child's parents have explicitly instructed you not to give her any more food. She whines for dessert, you say no, and she has a temper tantrum. What can you conclude about how her parents have handled her requests for snacks in the past? If you want her to stop carrying on, what would be two different types of operant conditioning you could use to increase the likelihood of changing her behavior? (Physical or emotional violence, threats of cruelty, and yelling are not options.) Which technique do you think will be the most effective? Why?

Cognitive and Social Learning

Cognitive learning involves the acquisition of information that may be used in planning, evaluating, and other forms of thinking, but is not necessarily acted on immediately; latent learning and insight learning are examples. Observational learning is learning by watching the behavior of others. The more you pay attention to the model, the more you are likely to learn. Through observational learning, children may learn to behave aggressively from watching violent television shows.

Could Paula and Chris learn to behave differently toward each other by reading a manual and watching other couples? Reading a manual about conflict resolution for couples could help Paula and Chris to acquire new ways of resolving conflict, although they might not use those new methods immediately. Rather, such methods would likely be stored for later use. Watching other couples engage in more positive methods of conflict resolution would provide them with an opportunity for observational learning. Both modes of learning could help them behave differently with each other.

Think It Through. Curare is a drug that so totally paralyzes an animal, a heart–lung machine is necessary to keep it alive. Although the animal can't move, it can perceive and remember normally. Imagine showing a person in that situation how to open a simple combination lock on a box to obtain the $1,000 inside. When the effect of the curare has worn off and the person is able to move normally, will he know how to open the lock to get the reward? Why or why not?

REVIEW TEST

For each of the following items, choose the single correct or best answer. The correct answers appear at the end.

1. Generally, for acquisition to occur in classical conditioning, the ____ should be immediately followed by the ____.
   a. UCS; CS
   b. CR; UCR
   c. CS; UCS
   d. UCR; CR

2. Watson and Raynor's famous study of Little Albert demonstrated how it was possible to classically condition ____.
   a. anger
   b. surprise
   c. disgust
   d. fear

3. Freddie was bitten by a German shepherd when he was a child, and now he is frightened of shepherds, labradors, and Rottweilers, an occurrence that can be attributed to ____.
   a. similarity phenomenon
   b. spontaneous recovery
   c. stimulus generalization
   d. contrapreparedness

4. The best reinforcer is ____.
   a. money
   b. praise
   c. determined by its effect on the target behavior.
   d. food

5. To avoid being punished, Jimmy has learned to hit his little brother only when his mother is not around, demonstrating the principle of ____.
   a. avoidance learning
   b. classical conditioning
   c. negative reinforcement
   d. latent learning

6. Which of the following is not a secondary reinforcer?
   a. food
   b. praise
   c. attention
   d. money

7. Sherry raises her hand in algebra class because she knows the teacher will call on her, but she doesn't raise her hand in social studies, because the teacher in that class never calls on her when she does. For Sherry, the teachers have become ____.
   a. primary reinforcers
   b. subjective stimuli
   c. secondary reinforcers
   d. discriminative stimuli

8. Continuous reinforcement is a quicker way to achieve ____, but partial reinforcement better protects against ____.
   a. generalization; discrimination
   b. acquisition; extinction

   c. extinction; spontaneous recovery
   d. success; failure

9. Weekly paychecks are an example of a ____ schedule of reinforcement.
   a. variable ratio
   b. fixed ratio
   c. variable interval
   d. fixed interval

10. The ____ schedule is the one most resistant to extinction.
    a. variable interval
    b. variable ratio
    c. fixed ratio
    d. fixed interval

11. Recent research suggests that ____ and ____ play a crucial role in learning.
    a. acetylcholine; serotonin
    b. acetylcholine; dopamine
    c. serotonin; norepinephrine
    d. dopamine; adrenaline

12. Classical and operant conditioning differ from one another in that ____.
    a. classical conditioning involves extinction; operant conditioning does not
    b. they draw on different neural mechanisms in the brain
    c. classical conditioning involves generalization; operant conditioning does not
    d. only classical conditioning can control involuntary responses

13. The acquisition of information that is often not immediately acted upon but is stored for later use is called ____.
    a. classical conditioning
    b. social learning
    c. operant conditioning
    d. cognitive learning

14. A child observes a model, imitates his behavior, and is then punished for the behavior by his parent. What is the child likely to do?
    a. become angry at the model
    b. not repeat the behavior
    c. become angry at the parent
    d. repeat the behavior anyway

15. Judy Andrews and her colleagues found that adolescents were more likely to imitate their parents' illicit drug use if ____.
    a. their parents were close in age to them
    b. their parents tried to hide their drug use from their children
    c. they had low grades in school and few friends
    d. they had a positive relationship with their parents

ANSWERS: 1.c 2.d 3.c 4.c 5.a 6.a 7.d 8.b 9.d 10.b 11.b 12.b 13.d 14.b 15.d

5 Memory

LIVING WITH YESTERDAY

Juan and Fiona would never have met under ordinary circumstances. Juan works as a paralegal, spending much of his time sorting through papers and tracking down obscure references to laws and cases. Fiona is a high school basketball coach who spends most of her waking hours working with young would-be stars or thinking about sports. But, by coincidence, both happened to be on the corner of Elm and River Streets one day at about 5:00 in the afternoon when an accident took place. A young man, late to meet his fiancée at the airport, sped through the intersection, not seeing a bicycle in his path. He ran straight into it, knocking bike and rider high into the air. The rider's head struck the pavement with a sickening thud. He lay flat on his stomach, his bike twisted like a pretzel nearby.

Afterward, Juan told the police that the driver had ignored the stop sign at the intersection and ran right into the bike. Fiona, however, claimed that the driver had stopped, but very briefly, before racing ahead. Both agreed that the driver had been going too fast. Juan and Fiona also agreed that, after a single whole-body twitch, the downed rider lay ominously still. The driver, they both said, had pulled over immediately, rushed to the victim's side, and then gently cradled the bike rider's head.

Fortunately, the cyclist soon started to mumble softly and then to move about. Fiona, who knew first aid from her coaching duties, ran over and cautioned the driver not to move the injured rider. Looking up, Fiona saw Juan standing a few feet away and asked him to call an ambulance. The driver glanced at his watch and let out a groan of despair. He dashed off a note, handed it to Fiona, and rushed to his car. It was later discovered that the driver had written his phone number incorrectly on the note.

The ambulance arrived; the police weren't far behind. They interviewed everyone on the scene. The cyclist regained consciousness, but he had no memory at all of what had happened; in fact, he couldn't remember anything about the last day or so. Fiona said that the car's license plate number was similar to the score of a game she had just coached and claimed to have no trouble recalling it. Juan recalled that the driver had spoken with a slight Southern accent and seemed to be well educated. He also was confident that he had remembered the license plate number, but the number he recalled was different from Fiona's version. Juan didn't remember exactly when the driver had left the scene, or what had been happening then.

As eyewitnesses to the same occurrence but with different stories to report, Juan and Fiona illustrate the complicated nature of memory, a multifaceted and fascinating psychological terrain. One theme we will revisit throughout this chapter is that memory is not a single ability and that, as Juan and Fiona demonstrate, people differ in their abilities to use certain types of memory. Another theme is that memory is constructive; that is, we assemble memories from bits and pieces that we've stored, and sometimes we fill in what's missing on the basis of our beliefs and expectations. We will also consider the subjective nature of memory: We remember what we experience, not necessarily what actually occurred. The levels perspective lends particular insight into the nature of memory because so much is now known about how memories are stored in the brain, and how events at the levels of the person and group affect them.

Memory:
A Many-Splendored Thing

Because she could usually remember complicated game plays very well, Fiona believed that she had an excellent memory, but in fact she had a hard time remembering names. And Juan, equally confident of his memory, couldn't remember dance moves to save his life, although he could recall facts flawlessly.

Both Juan and Fiona assumed that people have either "good" memories or "poor" ones—that memory is a single ability that either works well or doesn't. In fact, several kinds of memory operate within us simultaneously; we know this in part because different brain systems underlie these different forms. Even in the time it takes you to read this page, several kinds of memory are at work. Thus, rather than having a good memory or a poor one, people have different abilities to remember different kinds of information.

1. What is a memory store? How do memory stores differ?

2. How are different types of information stored over a long period of time?

3. What role do genes play in memory?

Storing Information: Time and Space Are of the Essence

Until someone asks for your address, chances are you aren't consciously aware of it—or even that you have one. But once you are asked, the information is at your mental fingertips. This difference, between memories we are aware of holding and those we are not, is one sign that different types of "memory stores" are at work. A **memory store** is a set of neurons that serves to retain information over time.

Three Types of Memory Stores

Although to Fiona it seems that her "hands remember" how to shoot baskets and that her "fingers remember" how to play the guitar, all memories are stored in the brain. We can distinguish among three types of memory stores, which differ in the time span over which they operate and in the amount of information they can hold. These three are known as sensory, short-term, and long-term memory stores.

Have you ever looked at scenery rushing past the window of a moving car and noticed that although you see literally miles and miles of landscape slipping by, you need to make an effort to remember more than fleeting images, which last about as long as the instant it takes for the image to flash by? **Sensory memory (SM)** holds a large amount of perceptual input for a very brief time, typically less than one second. Sensory memory happens automatically, without effort (via bottom-up processes; see Chapter 3); sensory memory arises because the activation of perceptual areas of your brain by the stimulus persists for a few brief moments. George Sperling (1960) reported an experiment, presented in Figure 5.1 and now regarded as a classic, that demonstrated this lingering sensory memory in vision (the visual form of sensory memory is called *iconic memory*). When shown sets of many letters or digits very briefly, people can report only a handful afterward. However, they claim that they can remember all the items for an instant or two, but then the memory fades too quickly to "read off" all of them during recall. Sperling was able to demonstrate that this claim was in fact correct. He briefly

Figure 5.1   The Sperling Study

Participants saw sets of letters, arranged in three rows. When the letters were flashed very quickly (for less than 0.25 second), people were able to report around seven letters even though they recalled seeing more.

In another part of the study, a high, medium, or low tone was presented immediately after the rows of letters were flashed. Participants reported the top row if the tone was high, the middle row if it was medium, and the bottom row if it was low. They could report the appropriate row almost perfectly, showing that they had briefly stored more than they could report aloud.

Memory store: A set of neurons that serves to retain information over time.

Sensory memory (SM): The "lowest" level of memory, which holds a large amount of perceptual input for a very brief time, typically less than one second.

In iconic memory, sensory input lingers only briefly.

showed participants displays of items, more than they could report, and then presented a tone that cued which row to report. The participants were able to report the cued row virtually perfectly. Because the cue was presented *after* the display was removed, the participants had to have retained some memory of all of the rows in order to perform so well. This finding shows that iconic memory stores a large amount of information but that it fades very quickly. The sense of a fleeting memory after the stimulus has ceased holds true for hearing as well. You can continue to hear the sound of a voice after it finishes speaking for the brief time it is still in auditory SM (Cherry, 1953; the auditory form of sensory memory is called *echoic memory*).

Whereas sensory memory retains information for the briefest of time, **short-term memory (STM)** holds information for several seconds, perhaps as long as 30. Also in contrast to SM, which can hold a large amount of information, STM holds only a handful of separate pieces of information. You are conscious only of the information you have currently stored in STM. The very fact that you are aware of information, such as a telephone number you've just looked up and are rushing to the telephone to dial, is a sure sign that the information is in STM. Information in SM can enter STM and thus you are aware of it; when it fades from SM, it also usually fades from STM and thus you lose awareness of it.

How much remembered information can we be aware of at one time—in other words, how much information can STM hold? Miller (1956) argued that STM can hold only about seven "chunks" at once, but more recent research suggests that the number is more like four (Cowan, 2001). A **chunk** is a unit of information, such as a digit, letter, or word. The definition of a chunk is not precise, however, and research has shown that the amount of information STM can hold depends on the type of materials and the individual's experience with them (see, for example, Baddeley, 1992; Broadbent, 1971; Mandler, 1967). For instance, a word is usually treated as a chunk, but you can store more one-syllable words than five-syllable ones. Generally speaking, STM can handle somewhere between five and nine items; this is why most telephone and license plate numbers are fairly easy to remember. Can you intentionally retain information such as telephone numbers in STM? Yes indeed. When you see something you want to remember (such as the numbers on a license plate of a car involved in an accident), you can hold this information in STM by **rehearsal**, repeating the information over and over. When you dash from telephone book to telephone, repeating like a mantra the number you've just looked up, you are rehearsing.

Rehearsal is important in part because it provides us with an opportunity to move information into a third type of memory store, **long-term memory (LTM)**. LTM holds a huge amount of information for a long time, from hours to years. You are not directly aware of the information in LTM—it has to move into STM before you are conscious of it. As an analogy, think of the difference between storing a file on your hard drive versus having it only in RAM, or random-access memory, the active memory in a computer. Once information is saved on the hard drive, it can be stored indefinitely; it cannot be disrupted if the power fails. If information faded rapidly from RAM (instead of being lost instantly when you close without "saving"), the difference between storing words simply by typing them into RAM and saving them on the hard drive would be much like the difference between memories stored in STM versus LTM.

LTM stores the information that underlies the meanings of pictures, words, and objects, as well as your memories of everything you've ever done or learned. Unlike the single general-purpose hard drive on a computer, LTM is divided into specialized parts, as if (to continue the analogy) it had different drives for different sensory modalities (such as vision and audition), verbal information, and motor memories. The storage capability of LTM is so large that some researchers

Short-term memory (STM): A memory store that holds relatively little information (typically 5 to 9 items) for a few seconds (but perhaps as long as 30 seconds); people are conscious only of the current contents of STM.

Chunk: A unit of information, such as a digit, letter, or word.

Rehearsal: The process of repeating information over and over to retain it in STM.

Long-term memory (LTM): A memory store that holds a huge amount of information for a long time (from hours to years).

question whether it has a limit. Shepard (1967), for example, investigated the capacity of LTM by showing people more than 600 pictures (photographs, colored prints, illustrations), mostly from magazines, and then testing for recognition. Pairing pictures seen in the first round with new, previously unseen ones, Shepard asked his participants to pick out the ones they had been shown in the first part of the study. He found that the participants could recognize over 99% of the images correctly two hours after seeing them, and 87% a week later. This remarkable degree of retention was found even though the participants had spent an average of only 5.9 seconds looking at each picture.

Is STM Really Different From LTM?

The distinction between STM and LTM matters in everyday life, sometimes a great deal. If you see the license number of a car that has just hit a cyclist but lose that information from STM, it is gone forever unless it has moved into LTM. But if the information has been stored in LTM, you should be able to retrieve it.

Evidence for distinct short-term and long-term memory stores has been shown in many studies. The earliest of these took place over 100 years ago, when German philosopher and pioneering memory researcher Hermann Ebbinghaus (1850–1909) undertook a series of experiments to discover the factors that affect memory. To see how well he could memorize letters, digits, and nonsense syllables (such as *cac, rit,* and the like, which are not words but can be pronounced), Ebbinghaus (1885) wrote out a set of these stimuli, each on its own card; he then studied them, one at a time, seeing how many he later could recall. Ebbinghaus found—as many researchers have since confirmed—that the first and last ones studied were more easily remembered than the ones in the middle. Figure 5.2 illustrates this *memory curve.* The increased memory for the first few stimuli is called the **primacy effect**, which reflects the storage of information in LTM; the increased memory for the last few stimuli is the **recency effect**, which reflects the storage of information in STM.

Figure 5.2   The Memory Curve

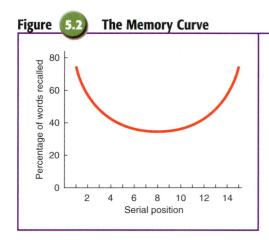

Memory is typically better for the first few and last few items in a set, producing the "memory curve" shown here. Memory is better for the last few items because they are still in short-term memory, and it is better for the first few items because they have a greater chance of having been entered into long-term memory.

Working Memory: The Thinking Person's Memory

When Fiona was asked how fast the motorist was driving, she thought about the amount of time it took him to move across the intersection. What kind of memory was she using? She was doing more than retrieving items from STM or LTM; she was *using* that information to draw inferences. Whenever you reason something out, whether determining the best route to a destination, buying a comforter that matches your sheets, or deciding which candidate to vote for, you remember relevant facts and use them to help you evaluate the options. In these kinds of situations, you have moved specific information into STM because you are using it or preparing to use it in some way.

Primacy effect: Increased memory for the first few stimuli in a set.

Recency effect: Increased memory for the last few stimuli in a set.

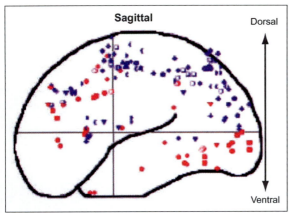

Sagittal

Dorsal

Ventral

During working memory tasks, both the frontal lobes and perceptual areas of the brain are often activated. Working memory involves a system of areas operating together, not a single area. Depending on the nature of the task (for example, tasks that require holding locations in mind, indicated by blue, versus tasks that require holding shapes in mind, indicated by red), different portions of the frontal lobes and other brain regions are used (Smith, 2000).

Using information relies on yet another form of memory. **Working memory (WM)** comprises the components of the whole system that includes STM and the processes that interpret and transform information in STM as required by a given task (Baddeley, 1986, 1992). In some ways, the concept of working memory is an updated view of STM; instead of regarding STM as a passive receptacle, we think of it as part of a system that uses information retained "on line" for brief periods of time (Cohen et al., 1997; D'Esposito et al., 1995; Smith, 2000; Smith & Jonides, 1999).

The idea of working memory extends the original view of STM in two ways, as illustrated in Figure 5.3. First, we now know that there is more than one type of STM and that these types differ in the kinds of information stored. Second, there is a **central executive** function that operates on information in one or another of these STMs to plan, reason, or solve a problem. Baddeley (1986, 1992) distinguishes between a STM that holds verbally produced sounds, which he calls the *articulatory loop,* and another STM that holds visual and spatial information, which he calls the *visuospatial sketchpad.* The articulatory loop is like a continuous-play loop on a tape recorder, on which the sound impulses fade when the tape isn't being played; you need to rehearse repeatedly to continue to store sounds. In contrast, the visuospatial sketchpad is like a pad with patterns drawn in fading ink, which briefly retains mental images of the locations of objects (Logie, 1986; Logie & Baddeley, 1990; Logie & Marchetti, 1991; Quinn, 1991).

Figure **5.3**   **Working Memory**

Working memory is a system that involves a central executive and different types of short-term memory (STM). The two forms of STM most often studied are one that holds pronounceable sounds (the articulatory loop) and one that holds visual-spatial patterns (visuospatial sketchpad).

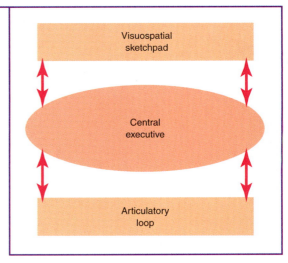

Types of Long-Term Memories: The Multimedia Brain

The fact that memory is not a single capacity becomes especially clear when we look closely at how different kinds of information are stored in LTM. Unlike computers, the brain has multiple "hard drives," if you will.

Modality-Specific Memories

Which is the darker green, a pine tree or a frozen pea? Or, as we asked in Chapter 3, do the first three notes of "Three Blind Mice" go up or down? When answering

Working memory (WM): The system that includes specialized STMs and the "central executive" processes that operate on them.

Central executive: The set of processes that operates on information in one or another STM; part of working memory.

such questions, most people report recalling visual or auditory memories, "seeing" a tree and a pea, "hearing" the nursery song. Fiona was apparently very good at this type of memory. As we saw in the discussion of perception in Chapter 3, our brains store visual memories so that we may recognize previously seen objects, auditory memories to recognize environmental sounds and melodies, olfactory memories to recognize previously encountered smells, and so on. These **modality-specific memory stores** retain input from a single sense or processing system. In addition to visual, auditory, and olfactory memory stores, we have separate memory stores for touch, movement, and language. Interestingly, nearly everyone finds visual memories easier to recall than verbal memories. If you have a vivid mental image of an event, your chances of accurately remembering the event increase (Brewer, 1988; Dewhurst & Conway, 1994). Thus, Fiona's excellent visual recall suggests that we can be more confident of the accuracy of her memory for the accident.

Many of the brain structures that register input during perception also store that input (Fuster, 1997; Karni & Sagi, 1993; Squire, 1987; Ungerleider, 1995). Damage to particular parts of the brain can disrupt each of these types of LTM (visual, auditory, and so forth) separately while leaving the others intact, which indicates that the information is stored separately (Gardner, 1975; Schacter, 1996; Squire, 1987). Furthermore, researchers have found that when people recall visual versus auditory information into STM (as you did when you answered the questions about the tree and the pea and the tune), different perceptual areas are activated (Halpern & Zatorre, 1999; Mellet, Petit et al., 1998; Thompson & Kosslyn, 2000). The fact that different brain areas are used for the different memories is solid evidence that distinct memory stores are at work.

Semantic Versus Episodic Memory

In each modality-specific LTM store, you can retain two types of information. **Semantic memories** are memories of the meanings of words (a pine is an evergreen tree with long needles), concepts (heat moves from a warmer object to a cooler one), and general facts about the world (the original 13 colonies were established by the British). For the most part, you don't remember when, where, or how you learned this kind of information. In contrast, **episodic memories** are memories of events that are associated with a particular time, place, and circumstance (when, where, and how); in other words, episodic memories provide a *context*. The meaning of the word *memory* is no doubt firmly implanted in your semantic memory, whereas the time and place you first began to read this book are probably in your episodic memory. At first, a new word may be entered in both ways, but after you use it for a while you probably don't remember when, where, or how you learned its meaning. But even though the episodic memory may be gone, the word's meaning is nevertheless retained in semantic memory. Episodic memory for events of your own life are called *autobiographical memories* (Conway & Rubin, 1993).

Brain-scanning studies have provided evidence that semantic and episodic memories are distinct. The frontal lobe, for instance, plays a key role in looking up stored information. However, when we recall semantic memories, the left frontal lobe tends to be activated more than the right, but the reverse is true when we recall episodic memories. If the two types of memories were the same, the same parts of the brain would access both (Cabeza & Nyberg, 1997; Nyberg et al., 1996; Shallice et al., 1994).

Implicit Memories: Not Just the Facts, Ma'am

When you consciously think about a previous experience, you are recalling an **explicit** also called a **declarative) memory**. Explicit memories can be "looked up" at will and represented in STM; verbal and visual memories are explicit if you can call them to mind in words or images (as you did with the pine tree and the pea). Episodic and semantic memories are explicit memories. Explicit memories are what

Modality-specific memory stores: The memory stores that retain input from a single sense, such as vision or audition, or from a specific processing system, such as language.

Semantic memories: The memories of the meanings of words, concepts, and general facts about the world.

Episodic memories: The memories of events that are associated with a particular context—a time, place, and circumstance.

Explicit (or declarative) memories: The memories that can be retrieved at will and represented in STM; verbal and visual memories are explicit if the words or images can be called to mind.

is stored after cognitive learning occurs (see Chapter 4). When explicit memories are activated, they can be operated on in working memory: You can think about the recalled information in different ways and for different purposes, and build on them with new ideas.

But think of how exhausting it would be if every time you met a friend, you had to try consciously to recall everything you knew about him or her before you could have a conversation. The reason you don't have to go through such a tedious process is that you are guided through the world by **implicit memories**, memories you are unaware of having that nonetheless predispose you to behave in certain ways in the presence of specific stimuli or that make it easier to repeat an action you performed previously (Roediger & McDermott, 1993; Schacter, 1987, 1996). Unlike explicit memories, implicit memories cannot be voluntarily called to mind—that is, brought into STM and thus into awareness.

The first hint that memory can be either explicit or implicit arose from a dreadful accident. H.M., whom you met in Chapter 2, suffered from such a severe case of epilepsy that nothing could control his body-wracking convulsions. Finally, in 1953, at age 27, he underwent surgery to remove his hippocampus (and related parts of the brain in the front, inside part of the temporal lobe). His doctors, whom H.M. had met many times, were pleased that the operation lessened his epileptic symptoms, but they were bewildered when he seemed not to recognize them. He could not remember ever having met them, and every time he saw them, he introduced himself and shook hands. To discover just how thorough this memory loss was, one day one of the doctors concealed a pin in his hand and gave H.M. a jab at the handshake. The next day, H.M. again behaved as if he had never seen the doctor before, but as he reached out to shake hands, he hesitated and pulled his hand back. Even though he had no conscious memory of the doctor, his actions indicated that he had learned something about him. He had acquired a type of implicit memory (Hugdahl, 1995a).

Implicit memories are of three major types. The first type is classically conditioned responses of the sort H.M. developed after the pin prick (see Chapter 4; Hugdahl, 1995b). The second type of implicit memory is habits. A **habit,** as the term is defined by memory researchers, is a well-learned response that is carried out automatically (without conscious thought) when the appropriate stimulus is present. Habits include the entire gamut of automatic behaviors we engage in every day. When you see a red light, you automatically lift your foot from the accelerator, shift it left, and press it on the brake (we hope!); if you think something is automatic, that's a give-away that the action is being guided by implicit memory. Most of Fiona's memories about how to shoot baskets, for example, are stored as implicit memories. Some of H.M.'s implicit memory was revealed by the working of habit. When one of us examined him some years ago, H.M. was using a walker because he had injured himself slipping on ice. The walker was made of aluminum tubes, and several operations were needed to fold it properly for storage. H.M. did not remember falling on the ice (which would have been an explicit memory), but he could fold and unfold the walker more quickly than the examiner could—thanks to the habit learned through using the device. He clearly had acquired a new implicit memory, even though he had no idea how he had come to need the walker in the first place. The intact ability to learn new habits, but not new episodic memories, demonstrates the difference between implicit and explicit memory.

We know that habits are stored differently from explicit memories because different brain systems underlie the two types of memory. First, consider the neural bases of explicit memories. Explicit memories cannot form unless the hippocampus and the nearby areas that feed into the hippocampus and receive information from it are functional. The removal of the hippocampus disrupts memory for facts (Mishkin, 1982; Squire, 1987, 1992), and brain-scanning studies have shown that the hippocampus and nearby parts of the cortex are activated when people learn and remember information (Dolan & Fletcher, 1997; Schacter, 1996; Schacter & Wagner, 1999; Squire et al., 1992). Differences in how effectively these brain areas

Implicit memories: Memories that cannot be voluntarily called to mind, but nevertheless influence behavior or thinking in certain ways.

Habit: A well-learned response that is carried out automatically (without conscious thought) when the appropriate stimulus is present.

operate could in part explain Juan's and Fiona's different memories of the accident: Nyberg and colleagues (1996) found that people who had more active hippocampi when they studied words later recognized more of the words (Brewer et al., 1998, and Wagner et al., 1998, report similar findings). Second, in contrast to explicit memories, habits can be acquired by animals and humans (remember H.M.) even when the hippocampus and nearby cortex are not functional (Squire, 1987, 1992). In fact, another circuit that bypasses the hippocampus allows us to learn habits (Mishkin & Appenzeller, 1987).

The third major type of implicit memory is **priming**, the result of having just performed a task that makes it easier to perform the same or an associated task more easily in the future (Schacter, 1987, 1996). If you just saw an ant on the floor, you would be primed to see other ants, and thus primed you would now notice them in places where you might previously have missed them (such as on dark surfaces). Priming occurs when a preexisting memory or combination of memories is activated and the activation lingers. Priming that makes the *same* information more easily accessed in the future is called **repetition priming** (this is the kind of priming that enables you to see more ants). Many studies have shown that you can recognize a word or picture more quickly if you have seen it before than if it is novel. Such priming can be very long-lasting; for example, Cave (1997) found that people could name previously seen pictures faster when shown them again 48 weeks after the initial, single viewing. Your first exposure to the stimulus "greases the wheels" for your later reaction to it; in fact, after priming with a familiar object, the brain areas that perform the task work less hard when repeating it than they did initially (Gabrieli et al., 1995, 1996; Henson et al., 2000; Squire et al., 1992). Priming that makes *related* information more easily accessed in the future is called **associative priming**. After discussing the condition of the apples and pears at the local market, you might be more inclined than usual to refer to something weird as "fruity." As with other implicit memories, we are not aware of this sort of priming. The major different types of memory are summarized in Figure 5.4.

Figure 5.4 Types of Memories

Not only are there many types of memories, as shown here, but also each type can occur in multiple stimulus modalities (visual, auditory, and so on).

Genetic Foundations of Memory

The next time someone complains that they have a bad memory, you now know to wonder, What sort of memory? Short-term or long-term? Which modalities? Explicit or implicit? In most cases, the different types of memory operate surprisingly independently of one another. Evidence is emerging that different genes underlie different types of memory, serving to demonstrate further that the different types of memory are in fact distinct.

Priming: The result of having just performed a task that facilitates repeating the same or an associated task.

Repetition priming: Priming that makes the same information more easily accessed in the future.

Associative priming: Priming that makes related information more easily accessed in the future.

How could we tell whether different genes affect different aspects of memory? One answer comes from the study of *knock-out mice,* so named because a particular gene has been "knocked out." Genes are knocked out when a part of the genetic code has been snipped away, deleting all (or crucial parts) of the gene so that it is disabled. The basic idea is that if a gene is used in a particular function, then knocking out the gene should create a deficit in that function. But tracing that connection is easier said than done. For example, early investigators thought they had found that knocking out particular genes disrupted a mouse's ability to remember the location of a concealed platform in a pool of water (the mice wanted to swim to the platform so that they could rest and hence were motivated to remember where it was; Morris, 1984). However, in one such study, Heurta and colleagues (1996) observed that the mice without the "remembering" gene weren't lost; they just didn't swim. When the researchers tickled the mice's hind feet, the animals swam and learned where the platform was located as quickly as normal mice. Their inability to find the platform wasn't caused by poor memory but by a lessened motivation to swim. (We have to wonder whether the researchers may have stumbled on a laziness gene!) One moral of this story is that removing a given gene can have multiple effects, which can cause the animal to do poorly on a test for a number of reasons (Gerlai, 1996).

In spite of these confounded results in early experiments, recent research with knock-out mice has revealed that certain genes do influence memory, but their effects are limited to specific types of memory. Working together, groups led by Susumu Tonegawa of MIT and Eric Kandel of Columbia University were able to modify a certain gene that is necessary for the receptors used in memory (McHugh et al., 1996; Tsien et al., 1996). In these studies, a *control sequence,* which turns specific genes on and off, was inserted into the DNA. This control sequence turned off the gene of interest only after the mouse had grown up, and thus the gene would stop working in an otherwise normal adult mouse. Researchers were able to eliminate the functioning of a gene that affects a single part of the hippocampus. Therefore, these animals did not show general problems, such as a lack of enthusiasm for swimming, but they did exhibit difficulty remembering locations. However, the knock-out mice were not totally clueless in memory tasks. They did retain some information, and hence this part of the hippocampus alone cannot be responsible for all memory. Again we see evidence that memory is not a single ability.

Finally, strong evidence for the role of genes in memory has come from researchers who succeeded in altering genes of mice so that processing is *enhanced* in the hippocampus and other areas of the brain used in memory. The mutation made the adult mice's neurons respond more like the neurons of young mice, who generally learn better than older ones. These mutated mice could remember more effectively than normal mice. For example, the mutated mice learned to find the concealed platform in a pool of water more quickly than normal mice (Tang et al., 1999; see also Manabe et al., 1998). No question about it: Genes affect the neural machinery of memory, and thereby affect different aspects of memory in different ways.

LOOKING AT LEVELS

Stressed Memories

When you are stressed, your brain sends signals to your body to prepare it for a fight-or-flight response. One of these signals increases the production of the hormone cortisol (see Chapter 2), which converts protein and fat into sugar, readying the body for rapid action. However, cortisol is a two-edged sword. Sapolsky and his colleagues have shown that in rats and monkeys long-term exposure to cortisol actually kills neurons in the hippocam-

pus (McEwen, 1997; Sapolsky, 1992). And the loss of hippocampal neurons disrupts memory.

Sapolsky studied a troop of monkeys in Africa. The monkeys had a well-defined social order, with some members of the troop being "on top" (getting the first choice of food, mates, and shelter), and others "on the bottom." The monkeys on the bottom were found to have higher levels of cortisol in their blood; their social circumstances put them in a state of near-constant stress. When Sapolsky examined the brains of some of the monkeys who died, he found that those near the bottom of the social order had smaller hippocampi than those who were not continually stressed.

Think about this situation from the levels perspective: The social situation caused the monkeys to be stressed; the stress caused them to produce high levels of cortisol; the cortisol degraded their hippocampi; the impaired hippocampi caused them to have poorer memories. Now shift to the monkeys' evolutionary cousins—ourselves. MRI studies of the brains of people who have undergone prolonged stress during combat have shown that they have smaller hippocampi than people who were spared these experiences (Bremner et al., 1993). These and similar findings suggest that the results from monkeys may apply to humans. People may become irritated with others who forget tasks, putting stress on the forgetful person. The irritation and implied or stated criticism would probably affect the forgetter's view of him- or herself, and that lowered self-esteem would likely affect whether the forgetter could rise in the social order. So social circumstances (the level of the group) cause stress, which triggers events in the brain that disrupt memory; bad memory can lead to more stress and lowered self-esteem and beliefs about abilities (the level of the person)—which in turn affect behavior in social settings (the level of the group). Fortunately, in humans the effects of stress on the hippocampus may be reversed if the environment changes (McEwen, 1997), a circumstance that introduces yet another set of possible interactions among events at the different levels of analysis.

CONSOLIDATE!

1 *What is a memory store? How do memory stores differ?* A memory store is a set of neurons that serves to retain information. Three types of memory stores have been identified: sensory memory (SM), which briefly stores a large amount of perceptual information; short-term memory (STM), which stores relatively little information for a few seconds (but for perhaps as long as 30 seconds); and long-term memory (LTM), which stores a large amount of information for a long time (hours to years). Only information in STM is in immediate awareness, and such information can be recalled faster than information only in LTM. Working memory is a system that includes specialized STM stores plus a central executive that operates on information stored in STM.

2 *How are different types of information stored over a long period of time?* Each sensory modality (such as vision, audition, and touch) has a separate LTM store; separate memories also exist for motor and verbal information. In addition, each of these types of LTM can be divided into semantic memory—which is memory for meaning, concepts, and facts about the world—and episodic memory—which is memory for events that occur in the context of a specific time, place, and circumstance. Finally, in addition to explicit memories, which can be voluntarily brought to mind, implicit memories in each modality are evident only in a single context and guide our actions outside our awareness.

3 *What role do genes play in memory?* Some genes affect the functioning of specific parts of the brain, which can affect particular aspects of memory.

Encoding and Retrieving Information From Memory

The statements Juan and Fiona each gave to the police after witnessing the accident presented certain difficulties. For one thing, they reported seeing different license plate numbers. To make matters worse, Juan was absolutely positive that the driver was of medium height and had dark brown hair, while Fiona insisted that he was rather small and had mousy brown hair. Both witnesses might have stored accurate information in memory but later had trouble digging it out. As you will see, some ways of retrieving information from memory are more effective than others.

1 What factors affect whether we retain information in memory?

2 How are memories reconstructed?

Figure **5.5** **Which Coin Is Correct?**

Nickerson and Adams (1979) found that people perform remarkably poorly when asked to choose the correct coin. Because we need only to identify pennies versus other coins, not to notice which way Abe faces, we do not encode the profile information very well.

Making Memories

Encoding is the process of organizing and transforming incoming information so that it can be entered into memory, either to be stored or to be compared with previously stored information. Look at Figure 5.5; do you remember which way Abraham Lincoln faces on a penny? Most people don't. Unless you've had reason to pay attention to this feature and encode it, you probably didn't store this information explicitly. In this section we will examine what it means to "store" information in memory and then look at several factors that determine whether this storage will occur.

Information not only goes into STM and then LTM, but often moves in the other direction, from LTM to STM. Indeed, for a stimulus to be meaningful, information in LTM must have been activated because this is where meaning is stored. And most information in STM is *meaningful:* that is, you don't see the squiggle "6" as a curved line but as a recognizable number that conveys meaning; similarly, without conscious thought you see the letter pattern WORD as a recognizable word. (Remember the Stroop effect, described in Chapter 3: You can't ignore the meaning of color words when you try to report the color of the ink used to print them.) So when you look up a telephone number, you must first access LTM to know how to pronounce the numbers and then keep them in STM as you prepare to make the call. Nevertheless, STM is important in storing information in LTM because working memory relies on STM, and working memory plays a crucial role in helping you organize information in a memorable way.

Coding: Packaged to Store

How convenient it would be if every time you scanned a picture into a computer, the computer automatically named it and stored a brief description. With such a feature, you could easily search for the picture (and its characteristics). As it happens, humans have this capacity and then some. In fact, we often register information using more than one memory system. Paivio and his collaborators (Paivio, 1971) have made a convincing case that the reason pictures are remembered better than words is because pictures can be stored using *dual codes*. A **code** is a mental representation, an internal "re-presentation" of a stimulus or event. Just as you can print letters, draw pictures, or write the dots and dashes of Morse code on a blackboard (all these forms are different representations), your brain can use many types of representations. Pictures can be stored with both a visual and a verbal code; that is, you can describe what you see in words as well as store it visually, so you can later recall it in your mind's eye. Research shows that illustrations improve memory for text (Levie & Lentz, 1982; Levin et al., 1987), particularly if the picture appears before the text (which is why in this book we have tried to place the pictures as close to the relevant text as possible).

As part of the encoding process, you can create new codes for storing material. For example, you can verbally describe visually perceived objects, creating a

Encoding: The process of organizing and transforming incoming information so that it can be entered into memory, to be either stored or compared to previously stored information.

Code: A mental representation; an internal "re-presentation" of a stimulus or event.

verbal code, or you can visualize verbally described information, creating a visual code. By creating and storing a verbal code when you perceive information, you don't need to use visual parts of the brain when later recalling the information. Thus, when people were asked to name from memory the colors of objects shown to them in black and white drawings, such as fire trucks and tractors, the "color areas" of the brain were not activated (Chao & Martin, 1999). In this study, participants claimed not to use visual mental imagery; the associations apparently were stored verbally, and thus it was not necessary to access modality-specific memories themselves, which would be stored in the perceptual areas that originally registered the information.

Portions of the frontal lobes are often active when people encode new information, an indication that organizational processing is at work (Buckner et al., 1999; Kelley et al., 1998). Indeed, the degree of activation of the frontal lobes when information is studied predicts how well it will be remembered later (Brewer et al., 1998; Wagner et al., 1998).

Consolidation

If you were ever in a play, you probably found that although you knew your lines well for the performances, a week or two later you had almost forgotten them. What happened? Consider the following metaphor: Say you want to remember a path you are supposed to take in a few days. Someone shows it to you on a lawn, and to remember it you walk the path over and over, repeatedly tracing its shape. This is a metaphor for *dynamic memory;* if it is not continually active, it is lost. But if you stick with your chosen route long enough, the path you're tracing becomes worn, and grass no longer covers it; this kind of memory is called *structural memory,* and like the path, it no longer depends on continuing activity. When memories are stored in a dynamic form, they depend on continuing neural activity; when they are stored in a structural form, they no longer require ongoing activity to be maintained. The process of wearing a dirt path, of storing the memory as a new structure, is called **consolidation.** One goal of our *Consolidate!* sections is to help you accomplish just this process.

Many studies have shown that memories are initially stored in LTM in a dynamic form and are consolidated only after considerable amounts of time. For example, patients receiving electroshock therapy—powerful jolts of electricity to the head (see Chapter 12)—experience disruption of memory for recent events, even those that are no longer in STM, but memory for older information is unaffected (McGaugh & Herz, 1972). For some kinds of information, such as memories of current events, politics, and television shows, consolidation occurs after a couple of years; but consolidation of memories about your own life may take much longer (Nadel & Moscovitch, 1997).

Depth and Breadth of Processing

If you want to remember the material in each of the sections of this book, we recommend you do the *Think It Through* exercises at the end of each chapter. We have designed these exercises to take advantage of a fundamental fact about memory: The more you think through information, the better you will remember its meaning. Craik and Lockhart (1972) account for this effect in terms of **depth of processing,** the number and complexity of the operations used when you process information. They argue that the greater the depth of processing, the greater the likelihood of remembering what you have processed. Craik and Tulving (1975) reported a particularly effective demonstration of this effect. They asked participants to read a list of 60 words, telling them that the experiment was a study of perception and "speed of reaction."

Consolidation: The process of converting information stored dynamically in long-term memory into a structural change in the brain.

Depth of processing: The number and complexity of the operations involved in processing information, expressed in a continuum from shallow to deep.

This man is likely to remember later whatever he's thinking about so intently.

Cramming is a good way to learn material for an exam, right? Wrong. Research has shown that people remember material much better if they rely on distributed practice, *which takes place over a period of time, than if they rely on* massed practice, *which is crammed into one or two intensive sessions.*

On seeing each word, the participants were asked a question about it. Three types of questions were posed (but only one for any particular word, randomly interspersed): One question required participants simply to look at the appearance of the word (to decide whether it was printed in capital letters), which did not require accessing detailed information stored in memory; the second led them to access stored information about the sound (for example, to decide whether it rhymes with *train*), requiring a bit more processing; and the third, to access complex semantic information (for example, to decide whether the word would fit into the sentence "The girl placed the _____ on the table"), requiring the most processing. Following this exercise, the participants were unexpectedly asked to recognize as many words from the list as they could in a new list of 180 words (containing the 60 original words and 120 new words). Craik and Tulving found that the greater the depth of processing required to answer the question, the more likely participants were to recognize the word.

What you pay attention to plays a key role in what is encoded into memory. However, the effect is not simply one of "depth," of a matter of degree: If you are shown words and asked which ones rhyme with *train* (which forces you to pay attention to the sounds of the words), you later will recall the *sounds* of the words better than if you were initially asked to decide which words name living versus nonliving objects. But the reverse effect occurs if you are shown words and asked later to recall their meanings; in this case, you will later recall better if you initially judge whether the words named living versus nonliving objects than if you initially evaluated their sounds. The most effective processing is tailored to the reasons the material is being learned (Fisher & Craik, 1977; Morris et al., 1977; Moscovitch & Craik, 1976). Practice on one task will help you perform another to the extent that the two tasks require similar processing; this is the principle of **transfer appropriate processing** (Morris et al., 1977).

If your goal is to understand the material presented in this book, you would do best to think of examples that demonstrate statements made in the text (or, conversely, to think of examples that seem to refute these statements). As to success on tests, you should try to find out what kind of test the instructor will give: If it is an essay test, you would be better off figuring out the connections between the various facts you have read and asking yourself "why" questions about them (Pressley et al., 1995); this sort of studying will be much more helpful than simple memorization, both for success on the test and for lasting understanding. For a multiple-choice or true–false test, however, simple memorization might do as well as more complicated strategies designed to integrate and organize the material, but even here you probably will retain more of the relevant information if you understand the material better.

Information is encoded more effectively if it is *organized* and *integrated* into what you already know, thus engaging greater **breadth of processing**. Encoding that involves breadth of processing is called **elaborative encoding** (Bradshaw & Anderson, 1982; Craik & Tulving, 1975). Perhaps the most dramatic demonstration of the benefits of elaborative encoding involved an undergraduate, S.F., who after a few months' practice could repeat lists of over 80 random digits (Chase & Ericsson, 1981). This is many, many more digits than can be held in STM, so how could he do it? S.F. was on the track team and was familiar with the times for various segments of races; thus, he was able to convert the numbers on the list into times, data with which he had associations. The digits 2145, for example, might be the times (with two digits each) needed to run two segments of a particular course. But in spite of his spectacular memory for numbers, S.F. was no better than

Transfer appropriate processing: Processing that transfers to a task that requires similar processing.

Breadth of processing: Processing that organizes and integrates information into previously stored information, often by making associations.

Elaborative encoding: Encoding that involves breadth of processing.

average with letters. His memory in general had not improved over the months of practice with lists of numbers, only his tricks for organizing and integrating information about numbers.

One of the most remarkable discoveries in the study of memory is that it barely matters how much or how hard you *try* to learn something; what matters is how well you integrate and organize the material. Bower (1972) describes experiments in which participants were asked to form a mental image connecting each pair of words in a list (for example, pairing *car* and *desk,* perhaps by imagining a desk strapped to the roof of a car). In one part of the study, the participants were told to use the image to memorize the pairs of words; this kind of learning, in which you *try* to learn something, is called **intentional learning.** In another part, the participants were told simply to rate the vividness of the image and did not try to learn the pairs of words; learning that occurs without intention is called **incidental learning.** The interesting finding was that participants in the incidental learning part did as well as those who were told to memorize the words. The effort that went into organizing the objects into an image appears to have helped the participants learn, even without a specific instruction. This effect has been found repeatedly, with different kinds of learning tasks (Anderson, 2000; Hyde & Jenkins, 1973).

Emotionally Charged Memories

Because Juan had previously lost a close relative in a car crash, the accident he witnessed with Fiona was an especially emotional event for him. This is an important factor in memory: People store emotionally charged information better in episodic memory than they do neutral information. Bradley and colleagues (1992) showed people slides with positive, negative, and neutral images—for example, an attractive nude young man hugging an attractive nude young woman, a burned body, a table lamp. The participants later remembered the arousing stimuli, both positive and negative, better than the neutral ones.

Why does emotion boost memory? Cahill, McGaugh, and colleagues (1994) have begun to answer this question in detail. They showed people pictures that illustrated a story. For some participants, the pictures were all described in a neutral way ("While walking along, the boy sees some wrecked cars in a junk yard, which he finds interesting."); for others, the pictures at the beginning and end were described in a neutral way, but the ones in the middle were described as depicting a bloody accident ("While crossing the road, the boy is caught in a terrible accident which critically injures him."). An hour before seeing the slides, half of each set of participants was given a medically inactive sugar pill; the other half was given a drug that interferes with noradrenaline, a neurotransmitter essential for the operation of the hippocampus (which, in turn, plays a crucial role in encoding new information into memory). A week later, all the participants were given surprise memory tests. As expected, the group that received the sugar pill showed better memory for the pictures that had an emotional context, but the group that received the noradrenaline blocker failed to show this memory boost for emotional material.

But why does emotion result in more noradrenaline's being produced, which in turn causes enhanced memory encoding? Cahill and McGaugh thought that the boost in memory for emotional material reflects the activity of the amygdala, which is known to play a key role in emotion. To test this idea, Cahill and his colleagues (1996) used PET scanning to examine the relation between activity in the amygdala and the degree to which people could recall emotionally arousing or neutral film clips. The amount of activity in the right amygdala when the participants had seen the clips later predicted remarkably well how many clips they could recall. Thus, the enhanced memory for emotional material relies on the activation of the amygdala, which in turn influences the hippocampus.

A special case of emotionally charged memory is **flashbulb memory,** an unusually vivid and accurate memory of a dramatic event. It is as if a flashbulb in the mind goes off at key moments, creating instant records of the events. Perhaps

Intentional learning: Learning that occurs as a result of trying to learn.

Incidental learning: Learning that occurs without intention.

Flashbulb memory: An unusually vivid and accurate memory of a dramatic event.

Many people remember where they were and what they were doing when they first heard about the events of September 11, 2001. Do you?

you have such a memory for the moment you heard about the death of Princess Diana in 1997, or the collapse of the World Trade Center towers on September 11, 2001. Brown and Kulik (1977) coined the term "flashbulb memory" and conducted the first studies of the phenomenon. They polled people about a number of events, counting the recollections as flashbulb memories if respondents claimed to remember details about where they were when they learned of the event, from whom they heard about it, and how they or others felt at the time. Most of the people they polled at the time had flashbulb memories of President John F. Kennedy's assassination. In contrast, although three-quarters of the African Americans interviewed had flashbulb memories for the assassination of Martin Luther King, fewer than one-third of the whites had such memories. Brown and Kulik suggested that only events that have important consequences for a person are stored as flashbulb memories. Neisser and Harsch (1992) studied college students' memory of the *Challenger* disaster, interviewing them within a day of the accident and again two and a half years later. They found that although people may be very confident of their flashbulb memories, these memories often become distorted over time. Moreover, this distortion becomes progressively worse with the passage of time (Schmolck et al., 2000). Nevertheless, in general, flashbulb memories are more accurate than other types of memories (Schacter, 1996, pp. 197–201), perhaps because of their emotional content.

The Act of Remembering: Reconstructing Buried Cities

It is tempting to think of memory as a collection of file drawers that contain assorted documents, books, tapes, and disks, and that to recall something we simply open a drawer and fetch the sought contents, all neat and complete in labeled folders. But memory doesn't work this way. When we open that file drawer, we don't find, say, a book, but instead a bunch of partially torn pages that are not necessarily in order. Remembering is in many ways similar to the work archaeologists do when they find fragments of buildings, walls, furniture, and pottery, and reconstruct from them a long-buried city; they fit the pieces together in a way that makes sense and fill in the missing parts (Neisser, 1967). We store in episodic memory only bits and pieces of a given event and use information from episodic memories of similar situations and from semantic memories of general facts about the world to fit the pieces together and fill in the gaps.

The most famous demonstration that memory involves reconstruction was reported by British psychologist Frederic C. Bartlett in 1932. Bartlett had college students read a version of a Native American legend, previously unfamiliar to them, called *The War of the Ghosts* (these Cambridge University students knew little about Native American culture). According to the legend, a young Indian was hunting seals when he was recruited into a war party. He was wounded during a battle and thought he was being taken home by ghosts, but in fact he was rescued by others in his war party. Although he did not feel himself to be injured, he soon died; then something black came out of his mouth.

At different intervals after their first readings, the students were asked to recall the story. Bartlett found that as time went on, the students' memories of the story changed. Sometimes they added new events; for example, one student misremembered hearing that someone cried out that the enemies were ghosts. Sometimes they reorganized the events in the story, scrambling the order. Bartlett concluded that we store key facts and later use them to reconstruct a memory by filling in the missing information. This conclusion has been borne out by many subsequent studies (Alba & Hasher, 1983).

Recognition Versus Recall

All remembering involves tapping into the right fragments of information stored in long-term memory. We remember information in two ways. **Recall** is the intentional bringing to mind of explicit information or, put more technically, the transfer of explicit information from LTM to STM. Once information is in STM, you are aware of it and can communicate it. **Recognition** is the matching of an encoded input to a stored representation, which allows you to know that it is familiar and that it occurred in a particular context, such as on a list (as used by memory researchers, the term *recognition* also implies identification; see Chapter 3). Essay tests demand recall; the essay writer must retrieve facts from memory. Multiple-choice tests call for recognition; the test-taker must recognize the correct answer among the options.

All else being equal, tests that require you to recognize information are easier than tests that demand recall. But recognition can become difficult if you must discriminate between similar choices, as shown in Figure 5.6. The more similar the choices, the harder it is to recognize the correct one. Similar objects or concepts have more characteristics in common than do dissimilar ones. If the choices are dissimilar, you can pick out the correct one on the basis of just a few stored features. But if the choices are similar, you must have encoded the object or concept in great detail to recognize the correct answer. Professors who want to make devilishly hard multiple-choice tests put this principle to work. If the alternative answers on the test have very similar meanings, the test-taker must know more details than if the choices are very different. In general, the more distinctive properties of a stimulus you have stored in memory, the better you can recognize it.

Of course, you do not always know in advance which details you will need to remember. Suppose Juan and Fiona are asked to pick the driver who hit the cyclist

Recall: The act of intentionally bringing explicit information to awareness, which requires transferring the information from LTM to STM.

Recognition: The act of encoding an input and matching it to a stored representation.

Figure 5.6 Discriminating Among Choices

In which lineup would it be easier to pick out the culprit? In which lineup would you be more likely to identify the wrong person?

from a police lineup. In the lineup both the driver and another man in the group of six are tall, a bit overweight, and brown haired. The major difference between them is that the driver has a scar on his left cheek. If neither Fiona nor Juan noticed the driver's cheek, they will be hard pressed to identify him. Both recognition and recall rely on activating collections of fragments stored in LTM. If the appropriate fragments are not present, you cannot distinguish among similar alternatives and will have difficulty recalling information.

The Role of Cues: Hints on Where to Dig

How does an archaeologist know where to dig to find the right bits of pottery to reconstruct a water jug? A logical place to start might be in the ruins of a kitchen. The archaeologist digs, finds bits of a typical kitchen floor from the period, and then is encouraged to continue digging in the same area. Similarly, a good cue directs you to key stored fragments, which then allow you to remember. **Cues** are stimuli that help you remember; they are reminders of an event.

Imagine running into an acquaintance in a bookstore and trying to remember his name. You might recall that when you met him, he reminded you of someone else with the same name who had a similar hairline. Here the hairline is a cue, reminding you of your friend Sam and allowing you to greet this new Sam by name. Would it help Fiona and Juan to remember details if they later saw a photograph of the crumpled bike and the injured cyclist at the scene of the accident? What makes something a good cue? A helpful cue matches fragments of information stored in LTM.

Godden and Baddeley (1975) dramatically illustrated the role of cues in an ingenious experiment. They asked scuba divers to learn a list of words either when they were underwater or when they were on land. They then tested half the divers in the same setting where they learned the list, and the other half in the other setting. The results showed that the participants remembered more words if they were tested in the environment in which they had originally learned the words. The significance of this finding is that when we learn, we are learning not only the material, but also the general setting and other incidental events that occur at the same time; these events can later help cue us to recall the information (Flexser & Tulving, 1978; Koutstaal & Schacter, 1997; Parker & Gellatly, 1997). So, if at all possible, study as much as you can in circumstances similar to those of the testing room—if there won't be music playing during the test, don't study while listening to music.

If you have seen both the original Frankenstein *movie and the 1974 Mel Brooks film* Young Frankenstein, *you may have noticed how "authentic" Dr. Frankenstein's laboratory looked in the newer movie. This authenticity is not accidental; Brooks bought the original laboratory set from the 1931 Boris Karloff version of* Frankenstein *and used it in his movie (Seuling, 1976). This set and its furnishings were retrieval cues, which Brooks hoped would help you experience the movie in the way he intended.*

Supplying Your Own Cues

Some cues are internally generated. We remember information better if we are in the same mood or psychological state (such as being hungry or sleepy) when we try to remember it as when we first learned it. If you were hungry when you studied material, you will remember it better if you are hungry at the time of recall than if you are stuffed. This can be a sobering thought if you are preparing for an exam: If you drink alcohol while studying, you will recall the information better if you are drinking later when you try to remember it. This effect is called **state-dependent retrieval** (Eich, 1989): Information is better remembered if recall is attempted in the same psychological state as when the information was first encoded. A closely related effect occurs with mood: If you are in a happy mood at the time you learn something, you later may remember it better when you are feeling happy than when you are feeling sad (Bower, 1981, 1992). The effects of mood are not always very strong, however, and they can be overshadowed by other factors, such as how well the information is organized (Eich, 1995). Neither your psychological state nor your mood appears to be a very powerful retrieval cue.

As shown in Godden and Baddeley's study of divers, the properties of the environment in which you learn something become associated with that information in memory and can also serve as retrieval cues. If you are not in the original environment when you want to remember particular information, try to "supply the environment yourself" by visualizing it; memory is improved when you can mentally supply cues from the original setting in which the material was learned (Smith, 1988). If you lose your keys or wallet, retrace your steps in your mind's eye, if not in reality. This retracing puts you in the same environment as when you last saw the missing item, so that you are more likely to remember where you left it.

LOOKING AT LEVELS

Memory in Tribal Africa

Michael Cole and his colleagues (Cole et al., 1971, p. 120) tested members of the Kpelle tribe in rural western Africa by giving them names of objects in different categories and then asking them to recall these words. What would you do if you were asked to remember the words *shirt, apple, pear, sock, pants, banana, grapes,* and *hat.* Westerners tend to organize the words into categories (in this case, clothing and fruit). But the tribal members did not. They could use this strategy when it was pointed out to them, but they did not do so on their own. Why not? Their culture stresses the importance of each object, animal, and person as an individual being. Organizing according to categories is not important in their society and in fact might impede them in going about their daily lives.

At the level of the group, learning the words was affected by the fact that categorization is not important to this culture. At the level of the person, the culture led tribe members to hold beliefs about the worth and uniqueness of each object and event in the world. At the level of the brain, it is known that parts of the frontal lobes are critically involved in categorization. Indeed, patients with brain damage to these regions often fail to group objects normally when recalling them (Gershberg & Shimamura, 1995; Stuss et al., 1994).

Think about how events at these levels interact: The training that the members of the tribe receive when growing up, during which time they absorb their culture's worldview, affects how their brains work. At the level of the person, according to their values categorizing is not particularly useful, and categorizing words is not useful at all. It was also clear that when asked by the investigators to categorize (which is a social interaction), the members of the tribe could perform the task—which is another example of the influence of events at the level of the group on the operation of the brain. All normal adults can categorize; whether they choose to do so is another question.

CONSOLIDATE!

1 **What factors affect whether we retain information in memory?** One key to storing memories effectively is to organize the information well. In addition, using two codes, verbal and visual, is more effective than using only a single code. Material must be consolidated, that is, stored structurally, which can take years to complete. In general, thinking deeply about material, which requires retrieving information from memory at the time, results in more effective storage, as does breadth of encoding, that is, thinking about how the new material relates to previously stored material. However, the effectiveness of encoding depends on its purposes; for example, encoding sound ("superficial" encoding) at the time of study is more effective than encoding the meaning of a word ("deep" encoding) if the memory test

requires recalling sound. Finally, emotionally charged material is generally stored more effectively than emotionally neutral material.

2 **How are memories reconstructed?** Recognition is the determination that presented information is familiar or that it occurred in a particular context; recall is the retrieval of required information from long-term memory. Both recognition and recall rely on activating collections of fragments stored in LTM. If the appropriate fragments are not present, you cannot distinguish among similar alternatives and will have difficulty recalling information. Cues, or reminders, are effective to the extent that they match material stored in LTM. To aid memory, you can supply your own cues by thinking about the context in which the information was encoded, such as the time of day or the physical environment.

Fact, Fiction, and Forgetting:
When Memory Goes Wrong

Afew months after the accident, Fiona was still convinced that her memory was accurate, even though it was now conclusively proved that the car did not stop at the stop sign. Moreover, both Juan and Fiona had forgotten what they had said was the car's license plate number. They could, however, still remember other things they'd noticed about the accident. But the injured bike rider could not remember anything he had seen or done for many hours before the accident, or the accident itself. What causes losses and failures of memory such as these?

1 How can actual memories be distinguished from false ones?

2 Is a forgotten memory necessarily gone forever, or is it still stored but difficult to retrieve?

3 What is amnesia?

4 Are memories ever repressed?

False Memories

Not everything we remember actually happened. **False memories** are memories of events or situations that did not in fact occur.

Figure 5.7 **False Memory**

Please read this list of words. Now go to Figure 5.8 on page 178.

candy	caramel
soda pop	chocolate
honey	cake
pie	icing
fudge	cookie
cotton candy	

Implanting Memories

Deese (1959) and Roediger and McDermott (1995) showed that people regularly make errors of the sort illustrated by Figures 5.7 and 5.8. (If you weren't fooled, read the list of words to a friend and wait 5 minutes before testing; this will increase the likelihood of an error.) We associate the idea of "sweet" with all the words, so its representation in LTM becomes activated and associated with the context of the list, and we misremember having seen it. Here is the critical point: In general, we do not necessarily remember what actually happened but rather what we *experience* as having happened.

Lest you think that misremembering only occurs when associated material is stored, consider this disturbing study reported by psychologist Elizabeth Loftus (1993). She asked one member of a pair of siblings to tell his younger, 14-year-old brother about the time the younger brother had been lost in a shopping mall when he was five years old. This story was told as if it were fact, but it was entirely fiction. No special effort was made to encourage the younger brother to remem-

False memory: Memory for an event that did not actually occur.

ber the story. However, after merely hearing about being lost, the youngster later gave every indication of having genuine memories of the event, adding rich detail to the story he had been told. For example, the boy claimed to remember the flannel shirt worn by the old man who found him, his feelings at the time, and the scolding he later received from his mother. When this study was repeated with many participants, about one-quarter of them fell victim to the implanting of such false memories (Loftus & Pickrell, 1995). Moreover, these participants clung steadfastly to their false memories, refusing even on debriefing to believe that they had been artificially created. Similar results have been reported by Hyman and his collaborators (Hyman & Billings, 1998; Hyman & Pentland, 1996).

However, some false memories are easier to create than others. Pezdek and colleagues (1997) found that whereas some participants did acquire false memories of being lost in a shopping mall, none acquired false memories of having been given a rectal enema during childhood. People may have an intuitive grasp of the role of emotion in memory, which leads us to know that we would be sure to remember such an incident if it had actually happened. (The ethics of carrying out such studies might be an interesting topic for discussion.)

These kinds of memory errors have direct practical—and often quite serious—implications. After a crime is committed, for instance, witnesses are interviewed by the police, read newspaper stories about the crime, perhaps see television reports. All this information can interfere with actual memories. Moreover, during a trial, the way a question is asked can influence a witness's faith in his or her recollection, or even change the testimony altogether.

Distinguishing Fact From Fiction

Does any aspect of false memories distinguish them from real memories? Daniel Schacter and his colleagues (1996) performed the "sweet" experiment, using similar key terms, while the participants' brains were being scanned. The participants were then asked which words were on the list and which words were merely implied by the listed ones. The hippocampus, which plays a key role in encoding new information into memory, was activated both when participants recognized actual words listed *and* when they identified associated words not on the original list. Crucially, when words actually on the list were correctly recognized, brain areas in the temporal and parietal lobes that register the sound and meaning of spoken words also were activated. In contrast, these areas were *not* active when people encountered words not on the list. Apparently, the construction of memory activates the representations of the perceptual qualities of stored words. Because the false words were not actually heard when the original list was read, this information was not activated. This cue of a "missing perception" may not be used all the time, but it is clearly operative in many situations (Johnson et al., 1997).

The same principle applies to remembering a real versus an imagined event. Johnson and her colleagues (Johnson & Raye, 1981; Johnson et al., 1993) found that people often confuse actually having seen something with merely having imagined seeing it (which may be the basis of some false memories; Garry & Polaschek, 2000). Indeed, Dobson and Markham (1993) found that people who experience vivid mental images are more likely to confuse having read a description of an event with having seen it. **Reality monitoring** is the ongoing awareness of the perceptual and other properties that distinguish real from imagined stimuli. Reality monitoring can be improved greatly if people are led to pay attention to the context in which stimuli occur (Lindsay & Johnson, 1989). Mather and colleagues (1997) and Norman and Schacter (1997) found that when people are asked to pay attention to the amount of perceptual detail in their memories (as would occur if they tried to notice the texture of objects, other nearby objects, and shadows), they are better able to distinguish actual memories from false memories. However, there is a limit to how well people can use such cues to distinguish real from false memories; false

Reality monitoring: An ongoing awareness of perceptual and other properties that distinguish real from imagined stimuli.

Figure 5.8 True or False?

Did the words *candy, chocolate,* or *sweet* appear on the list you read on page 176? Are you sure? In fact, the word *sweet* does not appear. If you think it did, you are not alone; most people do. This exercise is an example of a false memory that was easily implanted in your head.

candy	chocolate
soda pop	cake
honey	sweet
pie	icing
fudge	cookie
cotton candy	

memories produced in the "sweet" task, for example, are remarkably persistent even when people are warned in advance about the possibility of such memories (McDermott & Roediger, 1998).

Forgetting: Many Ways to Lose It

It was unfortunate that the police took as long as they did to arrive at the scene of the accident. As first shown in 1885 by Hermann Ebbinghaus, people recall recent events better than more distant ones, and most forgetting occurs soon after learning. However, as time goes on, people lose less and less additional information from memory (Wixted & Ebbesen, 1991, 1997). Ebbinghaus discovered the **forgetting curve**, illustrated in Figure 5.9, which shows the rate at which information is forgotten over time.

Why do people lose information from memory? Sometimes the information was not well encoded in the first place. But even if information is properly encoded, it can be lost later. Why? For many years memory researchers hotly debated the fate of information that was once stored but then forgotten. One camp argued that once memories are gone, they are gone forever. The memory decays and disappears, just as invisible ink fades until nothing is left. The other camp claimed that the memories themselves are intact but cannot be "found." The ink hasn't faded, but the message has been misfiled. Both camps were partly right.

Figure 5.9 Ebbinghaus's Forgetting Curve

The forgetting curve shows that information becomes harder to recall over time but that most forgetting occurs relatively soon after learning.

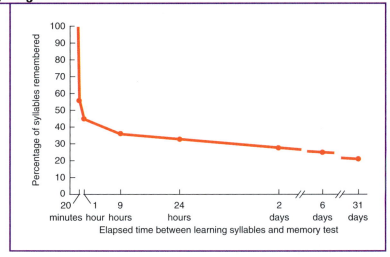

Decay: Fade Away

The invisible ink theory proposes that memories **decay**; that is, they degrade with time. The relevant connections between neurons are lost. What evidence supports this theory? In the sea slug *Aplysia*, which has a relatively simple nervous system, it has been possible to document that the strength of the connections between neurons established by learning fades away over time (Baily & Chen, 1989). If human neurons are similar, as seems likely, memories may in fact decay over time. Indeed, researchers have produced evidence not only that certain genes promote stronger connections among neurons, but also that other genes prevent such connections and hence block memory (Abel et al., 1998). When these "memory suppressor genes" are turned on, they could cause the decay of connections that store memories.

Evidence refuting the decay theory seemed to come from dramatic findings described by Penfield (1955). Before performing brain surgery, neurosurgeons such as Penfield sometimes put small electrodes on the exposed cortex of awake patients and stimulated neurons electrically. A few patients reported vivid images and memories of long-forgotten events. For example, on having a particular area of the brain stimulated, one patient said, "Yes, sir, I think I heard a mother calling her little boy somewhere. It seemed something that happened years ago." However, at least some of these reports may not have been memories but images created on the spot (Squire, 1987). There is no strong evidence that all memories stay stored forever. In fact, these oft-cited results occurred for only a minority of patients, and later work failed to reveal compelling evidence that memories are stored forever.

Interference: Tangled Up in Memory

The view that a mix-up in memory often explains forgetting has long been supported by strong direct evidence. If every summer you work with a group of kids as a camp counselor, you will find that learning the names of the current crop impairs your memory of the names of last year's campers. This is an example of interference. **Interference** is the disruption of the ability to remember one piece of information by the presence of other information. Two types of interference can plague your memories: retroactive and proactive.

Retroactive interference is interference that disrupts memory for something learned earlier. Learning the names of the new campers can interfere with your memory of the names of the previous group. **Proactive interference** is interference by something already learned that makes it difficult to learn something new. Your having learned the names of previous groups of kids may interfere with your learning the names on this summer's roster, particularly if some of the new names are similar to old ones.

Why does interference occur? The capacity of LTM is not the problem. You are not overloading a "memory-for-people" box in your brain; some politicians, after all, can remember the names of thousands of people with little or no difficulty. Interference probably occurs because the retrieval cues for various memories are similar, and thus a given cue may call up the wrong memory. The more similar the already-known and to-be-remembered information, the more interference you get (Adams, 1967).

The first president of Stanford University, David Starr Jordan, apparently worried that he might eventually fill up his memory if he learned too much. (He was wrong, of course; remember the paradox of the expert discussed in *Using Psychology to Learn Psychology*.) President Jordan was an ichthyologist, an expert on fish who knew the names and habits of thousands of underwater species. At the beginning of each year he met the new students and politely smiled as they were introduced, but ignored their names. One bold student asked President Jordan if he had heard his name clearly, and repeated it. Jordan listened and realized he had now learned the student's name. He slapped himself on the forehead and exclaimed, "Drat, there goes another fish!"

Decay: The fading away of memories with time because the relevant connections between neurons are lost.

Interference: The disruption of the ability to remember one piece of information by the presence of other information.

Retroactive interference: Interference that occurs when new learning impairs memory for something learned earlier.

Proactive interference: Interference that occurs when previous knowledge makes it difficult to learn something new.

Amnesia: Not Just Forgetting to Remember

When the bike rider regained consciousness, he could not recall anything that had happened to him since the previous evening. Why? Neither normal decay nor interference accounts for such unusual losses of memory. Instead, the cyclist's memory failure is an example of **amnesia**, a loss of memory over an entire time span, typically resulting from brain damage caused by accident, infection, or stroke. Amnesia is not like normal forgetting, which affects only some of the material learned during a given period.

Amnesia produced by brain damage usually affects episodic memories while leaving semantic memories intact (Warrington & McCarthy, 1988). Most people who have an accident such as the cyclist's have no idea what they were doing immediately before the accident, but they can remember semantic information such as their names and birth dates. Sometimes, however, amnesia impairs only semantic memory. For example, De Renzi and colleagues (1987) report a patient who forgot the meanings of words and most characteristics of common objects. Nevertheless, she remembered details about key events in her life, such as her wedding and her father's illness.

Amnesia may be retrograde or anterograde (Mayes & Downes, 1997; Parkin, 1987). **Retrograde amnesia** disrupts previous memories. This is the sort of amnesia often popularized in soap operas and movies. In the movie *Regarding Henry,* the title character played by Harrison Ford is shot during a convenience store robbery and loses his memories about his family, his job, and other aspects of his life history. But he can still speak fluently and seems to know everyday facts about the world and even facts about the nature of his job as a lawyer. Most of us suffer from a special form of retrograde amnesia called *infantile amnesia* or *childhood amnesia* (Newcombe et al., 2000): We don't remember our early childhood experiences. **Anterograde amnesia** leaves already consolidated memories intact but prevents the learning of new facts. It affects all explicit memories—that is, memories of facts that can be brought to consciousness voluntarily—and produces massive encoding failure. H.M. had a form of anterograde amnesia. Its manifestation is well presented in an old joke. A man runs into a doctor's office, screaming, "Doc! I've lost my memory!" The doctor asks him, "When did this happen?" The man looks at him, puzzled, and says, "When did what happen?" It is no joke for people with anterograde amnesia, who live as if frozen in the present moment of time.

What happens in the brain to produce amnesia? Often, as in the case of H.M., the cause involves damage to the hippocampus or its connections to or from other parts of the brain. Indeed, Zola-Morgan and colleagues (1986) studied the brain of an unfortunate man who suffered a bizarre fencing injury in which a long narrow foil slipped up his nostril and damaged part of his brain. This accident produced anterograde amnesia. The researchers studied his brain after his death and found only a tiny amount of damage to one part of the hippocampus. This seemingly slight damage, in just the wrong spot, had a major impact on the fencer's memory, and thus on his life.

Sometimes amnesia can result when areas of the cortex that serve as memory stores become degraded. As noted earlier, all memories are a result of changes in the interactions of individual neurons, and most neurons involved in memory are in the cortex. *Alzheimer's disease,* for example, typically begins with small memory deficits, which become progressively worse. In the later stages of the disease, people with Alzheimer's cannot remember who they are, where they are, who their family and friends are. Alzheimer's disease not only affects the hippocampus, but also degrades other parts of the brain that serve as memory stores. Depending on which other parts of the brain are affected, these

A gunshot wound to the head, as happened to Harrison Ford's character in the movie Regarding Henry, *is only one way that amnesia can occur.*

patients can have greater amnesia for one form of information or another; for example, some patients have worse spatial memory than verbal memory, and vice versa for others (Albert et al., 1990).

Repressed Memories: Real or Imagined?

Recent years have witnessed many dramatic reports of suddenly recollected memories. Some people claim to have suddenly remembered that they were sexually molested by their parents decades before, when they were no more than 3 years old. One person claimed that as a child he had been strapped to the back of a dolphin as part of a bizarre devil worship ritual. Are these false memories, or are they **repressed memories,** real memories that have been pushed out of consciousness because they are emotionally threatening, as Freud believed? Whether repressed memories exist is perhaps the most controversial issue in memory research today (Benedict & Donaldson, 1996; Golding et al., 1996; Knapp & VandeCreek, 1996; Melchert, 1996; Pope, 1996; Rubin, 1996).

Evidence for repressed memories comes from studies reported by Williams (1994). She interviewed 129 women 17 years after each had been admitted to a hospital emergency room for treatment of sexual abuse in childhood. Thirty-eight percent of the women had no memory of an event of sexual abuse; in fact, 12% claimed that they had never been abused. These results suggest that some people may forget traumatic memories. Could this finding simply reflect infantile amnesia, the forgetting of events that occurred in early childhood? Not likely, for two reasons: First, whereas 55% of the women who had been 3 years old or younger at the time of abuse had no recall, fully 62% of those who were between 4 and 6 years old at the time had no recall; if forgetting were simply a reflection of age, the women abused at a younger age should have had poorer memory. Second, more of the women who were abused by someone they knew, as was determined from independent evidence, claimed to have forgotten the incident than women who were abused by a stranger. Again, this difference should not have occurred if the forgetting simply reflected infantile amnesia. Indeed, a review of 28 studies of memory for childhood sexual abuse found robust evidence that such memories can be forgotten and later recalled (Scheflin & Brown, 1996). In some cases, people who suddenly remembered being abused as children then proceeded to track down the evidence for the event (Schacter, 1996).

There is a mystery here. As noted earlier, highly charged, emotional information is typically remembered *better* than neutral information. So why should this particular kind of emotionally charged information be recalled poorly, or forgotten for decades? Schacter (1996) suggests that, in these cases of forgetting, the person has not really unconsciously pushed the memories out of awareness. Instead, it is as if the individual were "someone else" during the abuse and thus has few retrieval cues later for accessing the memories. Nevertheless, the memories may be stored and may under some circumstances, with appropriate cues, filter into awareness. If so, then people sometimes would seem to forget emotionally charged events, but after long periods of time could come to remember them. Clancy, McNally, and Schacter (1999) have found that people who experience recovered memories of childhood abuse are more likely to mistakenly remember words such as "sweet" when asked to remember a previously presented list of sweet things in experiments along the lines of the Deese-Roediger-McDermott technique discussed earlier. This finding might suggest that these people are unusually sensitive to stored fragments of information. Leavitt (1997) has shown that people who recover memories are not especially prone to making up information when given suggestions, which indicates that they are not simply prone to forming false memories. That said, not all claims of recovered memories can be taken at face value; you've already seen how false memories (perhaps including being strapped to the back of a dolphin) can be implanted.

Repressed memories: Real memories that have been pushed out of consciousness because they are emotionally threatening.

False Truths

Social psychologist Daniel Gilbert (1991) reports experiments in which people are given statements about nonsense objects, such as "A bilicar is a spear." For each statement, participants are told that it is true or false. Later, memory for the truth of the statements is tested. When people forget whether a statement was true or false, they are biased to say it was true. Thus the participants end up with unwarranted beliefs about objects. The same principle probably operates regarding facts about people. For example, if you hear that a beloved high school teacher does not seduce students, you may later misremember that he does seduce them. It's fascinating, but disturbing, that a person's reputation could easily be ruined because of a simple psychological principle.

According to Gilbert, it requires extra effort to realize that a statement is false than to accept it as true; to determine that it is false, you must search for stored information that is inconsistent with the statement, which requires using working memory. Thus, because of properties of the brain, specifically the increased processing in the frontal lobes to look up and process stored information, events at the level of the person are affected: The person's beliefs are distorted. And the influences work the other way, too: Depending on your beliefs, you will be inclined to work more or less hard to search memory to verify a statement. If you are not strongly motivated to put in the extra work, you will be more inclined to fall prey to the bias to believe an assertion is true. This distortion in turn affects social interactions. And of course, social interactions lead us to hear about characteristics of people, "So-and-so is this or that," statements that may lead to false beliefs.

CONSOLIDATE!

1 *How can actual memories be distinguished from false ones?* At least under some circumstances, real memories include perceptual information from the modality in which a fact was learned—perhaps by seeing it, hearing it, reading it—whereas false memories do not include this sort of information. In many circumstances, however, it is difficult to distinguish between actual and false memories.

2 *Is a forgotten memory necessarily gone forever, or is it still stored but difficult to retrieve?* Memories may be lost by decay, probably because the relevant connections between neurons are lost. However, many "forgotten" memories are in fact still present, just difficult to retrieve. Memories become difficult to retrieve because of retroactive interference, in which current learning disrupts previously acquired knowledge, or because of proactive interference, in which earlier learning impairs the ability to learn something new.

3 *What is amnesia?* Amnesia is a loss of explicit memory, typically (but not always) only episodic memory. Retrograde amnesia disrupts previous memories; anterograde amnesia disrupts the ability to acquire new memories. These sorts of amnesia usually involve damage to the hippocampus or related brain structures or damage to the areas of the cortex that store particular types of LTM. Infantile amnesia, the forgetting of early childhood events, is very common.

4 *Are memories ever repressed?* Memories have been thought to be repressed as a defense against trauma—threatening information is forced into the unconscious. But little evidence backs the existence of such a mechanism. Nevertheless, at least in some situations, encoding failure or a failure to encode information that can later be used as retrieval cues could result in poorer memory for traumatic events. In general, however, strong emotion enhances, not reduces, memory.

Improving Memory: Tricks and Tools

If, like Juan's and Fiona's, your memory is not as good in some areas as in others and you want to improve the accuracy of your memory overall, what should you do? In many bookstores you can find at least a dozen books on the topic, all containing similar messages. Ways of improving your odds of retaining information in memory include linking visual images with text (dual coding); thinking through information (depth and breadth of processing); and studying in small chunks while trying to integrate and organize material (distributed practice). Let's now look at techniques that take advantage of such principles to improve memory.

Mnemonic devices: Strategies that improve memory, typically by using effective organization and integration.

1 How should you try to organize and integrate new information to remember it?

2 What tricks will help you dig out information you want to retrieve?

You can improve the accuracy of your memory at both ends: when information goes in and when it is taken out. The fact that memory is so dependent on the strategies people use explains why it has among the lowest heritabilities (see Chapter 2) of all specific cognitive abilities. Even if a number of people in your family are extremely good at memorization, their gifts won't help you a bit. Memory ability is made, not inherited (Nichols, 1978). For memory, the crucial differences between "good" and "bad" memories appear to be the strategies and tricks used when storing and retrieving information.

Storing Information Effectively: A Bag of Mnemonic Tricks

Tricks for improving memory typically require elaborative encoding and often involve either visualizing objects interacting with other objects or forming organized units where none previously existed. The essential element is that you *organize* the material so that you *integrate* it, making connections between what you want to remember and what you already know. Here are some **mnemonic devices**, or strategies that improve memory (*mnemonic* is derived from the Greek word for "memory"). Such memory tricks rely on organization and integration. Mnemonics can easily double your recall and are well worth the effort of learning and using. Using mnemonic devices not only helps you learn something in the first place, but should you forget it, you will be able to relearn it more effectively.

Probably the single most effective mnemonic device is the use of *interactive images*. As discussed earlier, forming images of objects interacting will improve memory even without any effort to learn the material (Bower, 1972; Paivio, 1971). For example, if you want to learn someone's first name, visualize someone else you already know who has the same name, and imagine that person interacting with your new acquaintance in some way. You might envision them hugging, or fighting, or shaking hands. Later, when you see the new person, you can recall this image, and thus the name.

A related method was discovered by an ancient Greek orator named Simonides. He was attending a banquet one evening when he was called out of the room to receive a message. Shortly after he left, the ceiling collapsed, mangling the guests' bodies so badly that they were difficult to identify. When asked who had been at the feast, Simonides realized that he could remember easily if he visualized each person sitting at the table. This led him to develop a technique now called the *method of loci* (*loci*, the plural of *locus*, means "places" in Latin). To use this method, first memorize a set of locations. For example, you could walk through your house and memorize 12 distinct places, such as the front door, the computer desk, the potted plant, and so on. Later, when you want to memorize a list of objects, such as those on a shopping list, you can imagine walking along this path and placing an image of one object in each location. For instance, you might visualize a lightbulb leaning against the front door, a box of tissues on the computer desk, a can of coffee beside

To use the method of loci, pick out a set of locations in your house and visualize each to-be-remembered object in a different location as you mentally walk through the house. To recall, later repeat this mental walk and "see" what's in each location.

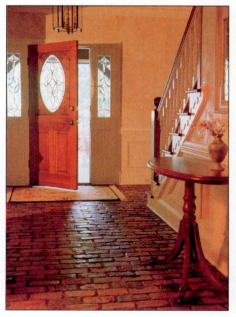

the plant, and so on. When you want to recall the list, all you need to do is visualize the scene and walk through it, "looking" to see what object is at each place.

The *pegword system* is similar to the method of loci, except that instead of places, you first memorize a set of objects in order. For example, you might memorize a list of rhymes, such as "One is a bun, two is a shoe, three is a tree, four is a door," and so on. Then you can treat the memorized objects (bun, shoe, tree, door) in the same way as the locations in the method of loci. You could associate the first item on your grocery list, for example, with a bun, the second with a shoe, and so on. In this case, when you want to remember the list, you remember each of the pegwords (such as bun and shoe) in order and "see" what is associated with it.

When Henry Roediger (1980) asked people to use different mnemonic devices to remember sets of words, he found that these three methods—interactive imagery, the method of loci, and the pegword system—were the most effective. However, as you know, there are many types of memory, and people differ in how well they can use various techniques. You might find these other mnemonic devices more useful:

Rhyming words provide a simple method for keeping concepts straight. For example, learning the rhyme "rhyming priming rhyming" might help you remember that priming makes the same processing (like the same word repeated) easier to repeat in the future.

Hierarchical organization can improve learning and memory. You might memorize the errands you need to do by organizing your tasks in the same way you organize your trip: Break the trip down into separate segments, and organize the events in each of those separately. Think about which tasks need to be done at one end of town, or in one part of the store, which need to be done at another specific location, and so on. The key is to think of ways to organize the material hierarchically, so that the big task breaks down into smaller ones, which themselves may break down into yet smaller ones; the goal is to group together relatively small sets of material.

Acronyms are pronounceable words made from the first letters of the important words in a phrase, such as NOW for National Organization for Women; *initialisms* are simply the initial letters, pronounceable or not, such as DNA for deoxyribonucleic acid. Initialisms may be easier to make up for most situations; the idea in both cases is to create a single unit that can be unpacked as a set of cues for something more complicated.

In short, the key to mnemonics is figuring out a way to organize information so that you can link something new with something you already know. For example,

MNEMONIC. A memory aid. Think of trying to remember something by putting a name on it: putting a NEM-ON-IC.

You can use mnemonics throughout this book, setting up mental connections or associations from one thing to another, perhaps with the use of imagery. For example, to remember that the word *suppression* means "voluntarily forcing unwanted thoughts back into the unconscious," you might visualize SUPerman PRESSing down demons that are bursting out of someone's head, shoving them back inside. When you form the image, you need to remember that the first part of Superman's name and what he's doing (pressing) are critical, so make sure the S on his cape is very vivid and visible, and that he is clearly pressing with his hands. Showing you a drawing of the scene would work almost as well; challenging you to make up your own image, however, has the added advantage of forcing you to "process" the information more thoroughly, which in and of itself improves memory.

In addition, you can remember information by stringing it into a story. For example, if you wanted to remember that Freud came before the cognitivists, you can make up a story in which Freud wishes he had a computer to help him bill his patients but gets depressed when he realizes it hasn't been invented yet. Making the story a bit silly or whimsical may actually help memory (McDaniel & Einstein, 1986; McDaniel et al., 1995)—and certainly makes it more fun to think about!

One of the fundamental facts about learning is that you will learn better if you are actively involved. Instead of just reading, try to find connections across areas and try to think of your own mnemonics. You won't go wrong if you simply form a visual image, make up an association, or invent a rhyme or joke.

Improving Memory Retrieval

As Juan and Fiona discovered when asked to give statements to the police, sometimes you need to remember things that you didn't expect to need or didn't have the opportunity to store effectively. Police officers are regularly faced with the effect of this unexpected demand on witnesses' memories. The need for accurate witness statements has been one impetus for developing methods to help people remember after the fact. Fisher and colleagues (1989) used the results of laboratory studies to develop a method to help witnesses and victims of crimes recall what actually happened (see also Fisher & Geiselman, 1992). Detectives trained with their methods were able to lead witnesses to recall 63% more information than was obtained with the standard police interview then in use. Their methods made use of the following memory principles and techniques:

1. Recall is better when you mentally reinstate the environment in which information was learned. If you want to remember something, try to think of where you were when you learned it, what the weather was like, how you felt at the time, and so on.

2. Focus. Searching for information in LTM requires effort and is easily disrupted by other stimuli. To remember well, focus on the task, shutting out distractions.

3. Keep trying. The more times you try to remember something, the more likely you are eventually to retrieve it (Roediger & Thorpe, 1978).

4. If you cannot recall something immediately, try to think of characteristics of the information sought. Fisher and colleagues, in their 1989 study, advised detectives that if a witness could not remember a criminal's name, they should try to remember its length, first syllable, ethnic origin, and so on. This information can serve as retrieval cues.

5. For certain kinds of memory retrieval, you can arrange the world in such a way that you are reminded what to remember. In other words, use *external cues* as mnemonic devices. If you are prone to forgetting your backpack, leave it by the door; if you forget to check the weather forecast before you leave home in the morning, put an umbrella on the door handle. A clever use of external cues was developed by historian Alistair Cooke, who hit on a novel way to remember where he shelved his books. He had a large number of books on the United States and its regions, but he couldn't always recall the author of a particular book. Arranging the books alphabetically by state didn't work because he couldn't decide where to put books about regions, such as the Rocky Mountains. The system that finally worked was simple: He arranged the books about western regions on the left, eastern regions at the right, northern regions at the

Arranging your world properly can aid memory. In this case, the pill holder makes it easy to recall whether you've taken your medication each day.

top, and southern regions at the bottom. The location in the bookcase mirrored the location in the country, and his problem was solved—all he had to do was look in the right place on his bookcase "map" (Morris, 1979).

If you can find a method that is fun and easy, and that works for you, you are more likely to use it and benefit by it. As in the case of mnemonic devices, our advice is to try each of the methods we have noted and see which suit you.

LOOKING AT LEVELS

Hypnosis and Memory

Would hypnotizing Juan and Fiona help the police clear up the disparities between their memories of the accident? Possibly; hypnosis sometimes improves memory of prior events. In 1976 in Chowchilla, California, a school bus was hijacked, and all of the children within kidnapped. The bus and all those inside were buried and held for ransom. When freed, the bus driver remembered the car driven by his assailants but no other details. In a hypnotic trance, he was able to recall the car's license plate, which ultimately led to the arrest of the kidnappers.

In many cases, however, hypnosis increases people's confidence in their recollections but not their accuracy (Sheehan, 1988; Worthington, 1979). Indeed, studies have found no overall differences in accuracy of memory between witnesses who were hypnotized and those who were interviewed using techniques based on cognitive strategies such as those summarized above (Geiselman et al., 1985). In addition, hypnosis may actually lead people to believe that suggested events happened, rather than simply help them to recall actual events (e.g., Barber, 1997; Bryant & Barnier, 1999; Green et al., 1998). Thus, after hypnosis Fiona and Juan might still have different memories, but each would be even more convinced that he or she was right.

Hypnosis affects the brain, in part by focusing attention. But attention can be focused on material suggested by an interviewer (a social interaction), and such suggestions can change the interviewee's beliefs. Thus, the social interaction between the hypnotist and the person hypnotized need not alter the ability to access memories, but instead can implant false memories. And false memories, if taken at face value, can have a devastating impact on how other people are treated.

CONSOLIDATE!

1 *How should you try to organize and integrate new information to remember it?* Tricks for improving memory typically require elaborative encoding: they often involve either visualizing the objects interacting with other objects or forming organized units where none previously existed. How can you decide which methods are best for you? The imagery-based techniques have been shown to be generally the most successful, and given Fiona's strong visual memory, we would definitely recommend them for her. Juan is more verbally oriented, and rhyming or a similar technique may be better for him. For you, the best course of action is to try the different techniques and see which ones are most effective.

2 *What tricks will help you dig out information you want to retrieve?* Mentally recreating the situation in which learning occurred, focusing attention on retrieving the information, repeatedly trying to recall, generating new cues based on partial recall, and paying attention to the source of remembered information are all techniques that can improve retrieval. It is also possible to arrange the world—your immediate circumstances—in such a way that you are reminded of what to do.

Recap and Thought Questions

Memory: A Many-Splendored Thing

The three types of memory stores—sensory memory (SM), short-term memory (STM), and long-term memory (LTM)—differ in the amount of information they can retain and how long they can retain it. Working memory (WM) is the use of STM to reason or to solve problems; working memory involves not only specialized STMs (such as the articulatory loop and visuospatial sketchpad) but also a central executive, which is a set of processes that manipulates information in these temporary storage structures. In addition, we store information in different sensory modalities, such as the visual and auditory. Some of the information stored in LTM is episodic, pertaining to events that occurred at a specific time, place, and circumstance, and some is semantic, pertaining to meaning, concepts, and facts about the world. Some memories in LTM are explicit (stored so information can voluntarily be retrieved) and others are implicit (stored as tendencies to process information in specific ways). Implicit memories in LTM include classical conditioning, habits (automatic responses to appropriate stimuli), and priming; repetition priming makes it easier to repeat a process in the future. The process of storing new memories depends on the actions of specific genes.

Might Fiona and Juan differ in what sorts of memories they can store effectively? Because different systems are used for different types of memories, people can be good at one type of memory but poor at another. Fiona stores habits well in memory, but she may not generally store explicit memories exceptionally well; the opposite situation applies to Juan—he stores explicit memories well, but not habits.

Think It Through. If you were Fiona or Juan, how could you try to discover which aspects of your memory are good and which are not? Would it help to test yourself on a set of tasks that assess the different forms of memory? In what ways could you use the results of such testing?

Encoding and Retrieving Information From Memory

Encoding is the act of organizing and transforming incoming information so that it can be entered into memory. The effectiveness of encoding depends in part on what is perceived to be important. Memory is improved as more time is spent thinking about the material to be stored and how it relates to your current knowledge, and memory is most effective if the learner focuses on the properties that will be relevant later.

Depth of processing involves thinking about the more complex properties of objects; elaborative encoding involves thinking of relations and associations of material to be stored. In addition, the information already in LTM makes it more or less easy to encode new information. It takes time to consolidate information to be stored, converting it from a dynamic form to a structural form.

Memory retrieval depends on a constructive process—you must retrieve the right pottery fragments to build the right jug. Recognition is often easier than recall, but the ease of recognition depends on the choices you must distinguish among; the more attributes the choices have in common, the harder it is to distinguish among them. Effective retrieval depends on having cues, or reminders, that match part of what is in memory, allowing you to reconstruct the rest.

What factors could lead Juan and Fiona to have different memories of the accident? If Juan and Fiona thought about different aspects of the accident, their resulting memories would be different because of differences in elaborative encoding. In addition, as a sports coach, Fiona may be familiar with different postural cues and body positions, making it easier for her to remember that kind of information. It is also possible that if Fiona has a better visual memory than Juan, she is better able to take advantage of dual coding. On the other hand, if Juan was more emotionally aroused by the accident because of his previous association with a car crash, he may have encoded it better. In addition, Juan and Fiona's memories might differ because of the retrieval cues they use—which lead them to summon up different information.

Think It Through. Would you study the same way for a multiple-choice test and an essay exam? What would be different about your methods?

If you were setting up a new business to teach executives how to improve their memories, what would you need to know about your clients' daily activities? What would you include in your curriculum?

If you were advising detectives, how could you help them determine which witness was remembering more accurately? What new retrieval cues could you produce that might be effective?

Fact, Fiction, and Forgetting: When Memory Goes Wrong

False memories occur when a person stores information about an event that did not happen, or that did not happen in the way that is "remembered." False memories may not include information about the perceptual features of the stimuli, and thus it may be possible to distinguish them from actual memories. Reality monitoring can be used to check for such features in memory.

Forgetting occurs in various ways. Decay results when neural connections are weakened to the point where they are no longer functional, whereas interference (either retroactive or proactive) prevents the digging out of stored information. In contrast to ordinary forgetting, amnesia wipes out explicit memory for a span of time, not just isolated aspects of memories. Finally, strong emotion seems to amplify memory, not diminish it. However, memories may be difficult to recall because the stored information may not match later retrieval cues, and thus the information is difficult to summon up from memory.

What factors could have led Juan and Fiona to forget key features of the accident? Fiona's and Juan's memories could have suffered from either decay or interference (from movies, books, or similar experiences in the past). In addition, they may have failed to remember key facts because of encoding failure, which prevents information from being entered into LTM in the first place. However, it is unlikely that either had amnesia, or that Fiona or Juan experienced repressed memories that were unconsciously pushed out of awareness.

Think It Through. If methods for implanting false memories effectively are demonstrated conclusively, should they be outlawed? In general, or only in certain circumstances (such as their being used by advertisers who want you to "remember" how much you like their products)? Can you think of any circumstances under which implanting a false memory might be a good idea? Explain.

From a practical point of view, what difference does it make whether Fiona had experienced decay, encoding failure, or interference? What would you do differently in each case? In what circumstances would her forgetting some information actually improve her memory for other information? In what circumstances would such forgetting be a good idea? Why?

Passionate controversy surrounds the topic of repressed memories. Why do you think it is so important to some people to believe in them, and so important to others to debunk them?

Improving Memory: Tricks and Tools

Many methods are proven memory boosters. Some techniques help you store information effectively by organizing it and integrating it into other information in memory. These include interactive images, including the method of loci; the pegword system; rhyming words; hierarchical organization; and acronyms and initialisms. Mental imagery is generally the most effective of these techniques when it is used to organize information in a meaningful way.

Other techniques have also been shown to help dig out information previously stored in long-term memory. One trick is to provide effective retrieval cues by thinking about where you were and how you felt at the time. Another major factor is effort: Focus and keep trying, and if you cannot recall the information, then try to recall its characteristics or associated information (which in turn can serve as retrieval cues). Finally, sometimes just arranging for external cues to remind you can be enormously helpful.

What could Fiona and Juan do to help improve their memories of the accident? After the fact, they can only try to enhance retrieval. They could try visualizing the scene of the accident, and keep trying to "see" different aspects of the situation in their images. Better yet, they could return to the scene of the accident. In any case, they should keep trying to recall key features of the situation that could serve as retrieval cues.

Think It Through. In his work as a paralegal, Juan had learned to describe and organize hundreds of situations that led to judicial rulings, which helped him memorize abstract material. Fiona, in contrast, rarely had to consider abstract material in her work, and so had little practice in such processing. In what ways do you think this difference may have affected their memories of the accident?

Can you think of additional ways to improve memory, either at the time of learning or at the time of recall? If a technique works for you, can you think of a way to remind yourself to use it? It isn't enough simply to be able to use a technique effectively—you must *remember* to use it!

REVIEW TEST

For each of the following items, choose the single correct or best answer. The correct answers appear at the end.

1 A set of neurons that serves to retain information over time is called a(n) ____.
a. sensory store
b. memory store
c. neural shunt
d. automatic network

2 The visual form of sensory memory is called ____ memory.
a. iconic
b. short-term
c. imagery
d. echoic

3 Carl forgot to bring the written list of grocery items to the store, and when he arrived home, he found that he had remembered the first five items, but few others, demonstrating the ____ effect.
a. recency
b. primacy
c. reversal
d. Ebbinghaus

4 ____ memories are associated with a particular time, place, and circumstance.
a. Implicit
b. Explicit
c. Modality-specific
d. Episodic

5 Explicit memories are also known as ____ memories.
a. declarative
b. implicit
c. primacy
d. potentiated

6 Memories that are consolidated are ____.
a. dynamic
b. easily lost
c. stored in a structural form
d. visual and verbal

7 Learning without intention is called ____ learning.
a. inherent
b. incidental
c. imaginal
d. intentional

8 Multiple-choice tests require ____ rather than ____.
a. recall; recognition
b. explicit memory; incidental memory
c. recognition; recall
d. implicit memory; incidental memory

9 When recalling false memories of having heard something (that you actually did not hear), the ____ will probably not become activated.
a. temporal lobe
b. frontal lobe
c. hippocampus
d. all of the above

10 James couldn't remember his new phone number because the numbers were similar to his old phone number, demonstrating ____.
a. retroactive interference
b. decay
c. amnesia
d. proactive interference

11 Typically, amnesia produced by brain damage affects ____ memories.
a. implicit
b. semantic
c. false
d. episodic

12 ____ amnesia disrupts previous memories but doesn't prevent the learning of new facts.
a. Semantic
b. Anterograde
c. Retrograde
d. Episodic

13 Probably the single most effective mnemonic device is the use of ____.
a. rhyming
b. interactive images
c. acronyms
d. chunking

14 Which of the following mnemonic devices was *not* one that Henry Roediger (1980) found to be most effective?
a. pegword system
b. method of loci
c. interactive imagery
d. rhyming

15 Hypnosis ____.
a. usually enhances confidence in recollections but not actual memories
b. almost always enhances memory and confidence in recollections
c. enhances neither memory nor confidence in recollections
d. usually enhances memory but not confidence in recollections

ANSWERS: 1.b 2.a 3.b 4.d 5.a 6.c 7.b 8.c 9.a 10.d 11.d 12.c 13.b 14.d 15.a

6 Language,

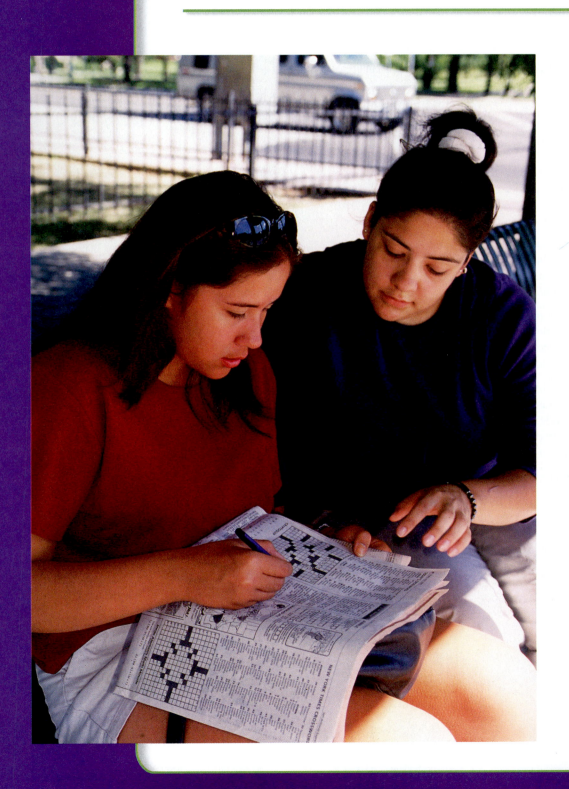

Thinking, and Intelligence

I n the year 2180, a cop's best friend was his android, or droid for short. Droids had been perfected some 30 years before, and now it was hard to imagine a time when they didn't exist. Frank was thinking about this as he and his droid partner, Hans, cruised a few feet above the ancient road surfaces of New York City. Droids were decent companions, but they were sometimes a little peculiar. Just today Frank had joked with Hans about a weird hat he'd seen a woman wearing, a hat that looked like a cross between an umbrella and a water lily. He'd said to Hans, "Boy, is that supposed to be the latest fashion from Mars?" He knew perfectly well that Mars had neither rain nor exposure to the sun, but thought it wasn't a bad joke. Hans's response was dry and literal: The hat, he said, was "not fully functional for that planet in the solar system."

Frank realized that he could have felt threatened by Hans's machine-like accuracy, but he didn't: Even though Hans was more advanced than humans in many ways, in others he fell woefully short. For one thing, although Hans spoke perfect English (as well as 13 other languages), never making an error in pronunciation or grammar, he almost never got a joke. And Frank's fluent and frequent use of metaphor and slang was beyond him; Hans could neither make word play nor understand it, unless he'd heard and stored the meaning of a particular expression before. And although Hans could read very obvious nonverbal cues, recognizing that a smile reflects pleasure and a frown displeasure, he often missed nonverbal subtleties—an ironic glance or a subtle shrug was lost on him.

But overall, Hans's mind was sharp as a laser scalpel, making him a valuable companion to a policeman. When faced with a difficult problem, Hans could start from the known facts and make deductions that would have put Sherlock Holmes to shame; his logic was flawless. Nevertheless, unlike Frank, he was utterly incapable of making leaps of intuition or of approaching a problem from a different angle. This wasn't a drawback when the partners were dealing with cases in which the facts were firmly established and the solution was in sight if not yet achieved, but Hans's literal-mindedness could be an obstacle in cases that were not so clear-cut.

These differences between the human Frank and and his droid partner Hans reflect differences in language, cognition, and intelligence—the subjects of this chapter. At first glance, you might think that Hans is very—perhaps even "super"—intelligent. But what does it mean to say that someone is "very intelligent"? In this chapter we'll discuss in what ways Hans should be considered intelligent. We'll also see what Hans is missing cognitively—that is, what keeps him from being able to think as we understand thinking. As for Frank, how does his human brain enable him to use language and to think in ways that would be a mystery to Hans (if Hans could conceive of them at all)? On the other hand, what limitations in solving problems and reasoning does Frank face simply because he is a human?

We begin by considering first the nature of language and then its role in thought. Next, we look at other forms of thought and at the various ways in which people can solve problems and use reasoning. Finally, we see where this path leads us when we ask whether there is more than one way to be smart, and we consider the role of "nature" and "nurture" in intelligence.

Language: More Than Meets the Ear

When Frank first began to work with Hans, he was startled when Hans failed to understand, for instance, that being a "rigid thinker" had nothing to do with the solidity of one's gray matter. After a while, Frank learned that Hans could hear an expression and store it for future use, but only in an identical context. Even though he looked like an adult, Hans was only about 5 years old, and some aspects of language cannot be preprogrammed. For example, slang and expressions are constantly changing and thus can be acquired only by encountering them.

1 What are the essential characteristics of all languages?

2 Are first and second languages used in different ways?

The Essentials: What Makes Language Language?

Language is a two-pronged process of sending and receiving. **Language production** is our ability to speak or otherwise use language to *send* information. Perhaps the most remarkable thing about language production is that it is *generative*. We create, or "generate," new sentences all the time; we don't simply retrieve and repeat stored sentences. The number of new sentences we can produce is astounding. Psychologist Steven Pinker (1994, p. 86) estimates that we would need at least 100 trillion years to memorize all the sentences any one of us can possibly produce. **Language comprehension** is the ability to understand language. Unlike the droid Hans, who

Language production: The ability to speak or otherwise use language to send information.

Language comprehension: The ability to understand language.

can be programmed to decode literal references but not much more, we humans are endowed with the extraordinary ability to comprehend even fragments of speech, "mizprunounced" or "speech badly with grammar." We can understand the speech of the very young, speech flavored with foreign or regional accents, and lisping speech, even though in each case the actual sounds made are very different. To put things in perspective, even today's most sophisticated speech recognition devices can decode only a fraction of what a competent 5-year-old can do effortlessly.

So, if language is a process of sending and receiving information, what about a dog that whines when it is hungry, barks to go for a walk, and sits when told to? This pet is sending and receiving all right, but is it using language? The intuitive answer is no, and the intuitive answer is right—there's more to language than that. Language units are built from simple building blocks that can be combined in many ways, but only according to specific rules. Four types of units, and the rules for combining them, distinguish language from other communicative sounds such as whines. These units and rules are described by the phonology, syntax, semantics, and pragmatics of a language. Let's look at each of these aspects of language in turn.

Phonology: Some Say "Tomato"

Phonology is the structure of the sounds that can be used to produce words in a language. Linguists Roman Jakobson and Morris Halle (1956) provided evidence that the sounds of any language are built up from sets of **phonemes**, which are the basic building blocks of speech sounds (Halle, 1990). The difference between *boy* and *toy* is one phoneme.

Humans can produce about 100 phonemes, but no single language uses all 100; English, for instance, uses about 45. Back-of-the-throat, soft French *r*'s do not exist in the world of hard American *r*'s, and Japanese has no *r*'s at all. One of the reasons why French is difficult for people who learned English as their native tongue, in fact, is that the two languages use different phonemes (such as those for *r* and *u*).

In English, some sounds in each word are accented, given extra emphasis. Some say *toMAYto* and some say *toMAHto*, but in both cases the second syllable is stressed. Some other languages do not usually stress one of the syllables in a word. In French, for example, each sound typically is given equal emphasis. Linguist Lisa Selkirk (personal communication) suggests that this difference explains why French rock and roll often sounds bland: French rock artists can't synchronize the "beats" in the language with the rhythm of the music.

Curiously, the left cerebral hemisphere is primarily activated when males process phonemes, but both hemispheres are strongly activated when females process phonemes (Shaywitz et al., 1995); perhaps this is one reason females tend to be better with language than males (Halpern, 1997).

Syntax: Are the Rules of the Road Learned or Innate?

Every language has building blocks of sound and rules for cementing them together into words. Similarly, all languages include rules for how words can be organized into sentences. Sentences in any language contain an internal structure, an acceptable arrangement of words called **syntax**. The syntax of a sentence is determined by the **grammar** of a language, a set of rules for combining different categories of words, such as nouns, verbs, and adjectives. For example, in English you cannot say, "Kicked girl ball the blue." The basic units of a grammar are parts of speech, not the individual words that fall into each category. A sentence in English needs a noun phrase (which must at a minimum have a noun—a word that names a person, place, or thing) and a verb phrase (at a minimum a single verb—a word that describes an action or a state of being). Thus, the shortest possible sentence in English has only three letters: "I am."

Ask a friend to help you perform this experiment. Turn on the lights and shut all the blinds in your room at night. Read aloud from any book. Ask your friend to turn off the lights at some random point. You should find that you can keep

Phonology: The structure of the sounds that can be used to produce words in a language.

Phoneme: The basic building block of speech sounds.

Syntax: The internal grammatical structure of a sentence, determined by how words that belong to different parts of speech are organized into acceptable arrangements.

Grammar: The rules that determine how words that belong to different parts of speech can be organized into acceptable sentences.

saying the words leading up to the next major syntactic boundary (usually indicated by a verb, a conjunction, or a comma, period, or other punctuation). Fluent readers take in entire parts of the syntactic structure, one part at a time.

As a philosophy, **empiricism** takes the view that all knowledge derives from experience, and the behaviorist B. F. Skinner believed that language is entirely the result of learning. In contrast, **nativism** centers on the idea that the crucial aspects of language are innate (inborn). Linguist Noam Chomsky (1972) championed this view, theorizing that we are all born with an internal **language acquisition device (LAD)**, which contains a set of grammatical rules common to all languages. According to Chomsky, we don't actually learn the grammar of a language. Rather, we *discover* which particular human language is being spoken around us, and our LAD "tunes" our built-in set of rules so that we can speak that language. Others, including Elman, Bates, and their colleagues (Elman et al., 1996), have argued that language emerges from more general cognitive abilities, such as ones used in motor control and perception; but even these theorists assume that at least some of these abilities are built in, part of our genetic heritage. The fact that virtually all normal humans come to speak a language, even without formal instruction, is evidence that there is something special about the way our brains are constructed to acquire and use language. In fact, different parts of the brain have been found to contribute to different aspects of language (see Figure 6.1).

Figure **Major Language Areas of the Brain**

Traditionally, Broca's area has been identified with speech production and Wernicke's area with speech comprehension, but we now know that Broca's area is also involved in the use of grammar to understand sentences (Stromswald et al., 1996).

Broca's area   Wernicke's area

Semantics: The Meaning Is the Message

Language is, of course, more than sounds and sentence structures. To do its job, language must convey meaning. The **semantics** of a word or sentence is its meaning. Just as the sounds of words are represented by smaller elements (phonemes) and the syntactic aspects of a sentence are represented by grammatical elements (parts of speech), semantics is represented by **morphemes**, the smallest units of *meaning* in a language. The word *wet* includes but a single morpheme, but the meanings of many words are determined by more than one morpheme. Prefixes and suffixes are obvious examples of such morphemes used in combination with other morphemes. For example, adding the morpheme *-ing* to a verb, as in *walking, talking, flirting*, creates a word expressing a continuing state, whereas adding the morpheme *-ed* indicates a completed state. Just as the other elements of language are combined according to rules, so, too, with morphemes. We cannot add *-ing* at the front of a word, or *mis-* (another morpheme) to the end. Different sets of morphemes underlie the different meanings of ambiguous words, words with more than one meaning; thus *park* as in "park the car" has different morphemes than *park* as in "place with benches and pigeons."

Meanings are often assigned arbitrarily to different sounds or written words; the sound *dog* could easily have been assigned to refer to that feline we keep as a pet, and *cat* to the animal that likes to gnaw on bones and slippers. Specific events

Empiricism (approach to language): The approach that views language as entirely the result of learning.

Nativism (approach to language): The approach that views crucial aspects of language as innate.

Language acquisition device (LAD): An innate mechanism, hypothesized by Chomsky, that contains the grammatical rules common to all languages and allows language acquisition.

Semantics: The meaning of a word or sentence.

Morpheme: The smallest unit of meaning in a language.

in the past have a lot to do with how particular words have come to have their meanings. For example, early medieval Scandinavian warriors wore bearskin shirts, for which the Old Norwegian word is *berserkr;* from the ferocity of the Vikings' frenzied attacks in battle we inherit the expression "going berserk." Of more recent vintage is the word *bedlam,* which since the 16th century has meant "chaos and confusion"; its origins are in the name of the Hospital of St. Mary of Bethlehem in London, where "lunatics" were confined. Sometimes the meanings of words seem to reveal deeper aspects of a culture: The Chinese character for *crisis* is composed of two other characters, one signifying "risk" and the other "opportunity."

The meaning of a sentence and its syntax are to a large extent distinct. For example, Chomsky (1957) pointed out that the sentence "Colorless green ideas sleep furiously" is grammatically correct—it has an acceptable English syntax— but entirely meaningless. On the other hand, "Fastly dinner eat, ballgame soon start" has the opposite properties: It is grammatically incorrect but completely understandable. The wise alien Yoda of the *Star Wars* movies often uttered grammatically incorrect but comprehensible sentences, probably in part to remind the audience that he was not an ordinary person.

Pragmatics: Being Indirect

The droid Hans was perfectly able to understand the semantics of words (he understood morphemes and how they are combined into words) and sentences (he understood how the meanings of words are combined into phrases and sentences), but he often failed at a third aspect of meaning. Utterances have not only a literal meaning but also an *implied* meaning. The **pragmatics** of a language are concerned with the way language implies meaning. Have you ever asked a 13-year-old, "Do you know where the restroom is?" and got back the response "Yes"? This question can be interpreted literally as an inquiry about your knowledge of, say, the layout of a large building or indirectly as a request for directions. In some contexts, such as kids being addressed by a parent who is dropping them off at an auditorium by themselves, the question might really be meant literally. But in most instances you would understand that the questioner has a need for the facilities. This understanding depends on your grasp of pragmatics, which often involves knowledge of the world as well as of language and its specific conventions about how to communicate (Grice, 1975).

Although some aspects of pragmatics depend on being able to understand the meaning of rising or falling pitch in a sentence, as in spoken questions, pragmatics are pervasive in linguistic communication—even in reading (Kintsch, 1998). Pragmatics depend critically on our ability to draw correct inferences. The fact that we humans can draw the correct inferences quickly and seemingly without effort obscures how difficult these processes really are. Indeed, the use of pragmatics has stymied attempts to create computer programs that can truly understand language, which is one of the reasons why droids probably won't be on patrol for a couple of hundred years. And when they do arrive, they may often seem a bit dense, even denser than Hans.

Pragmatics play a key role in understanding metaphor, a direct comparison of two things in which one is described as being the other. "The road snaked down the mountain" cannot be understood literally; one must understand that *snaked* implies "following a long, twisted path." The fact that pragmatics involve different mechanisms than the rest of language is attested to by the role of the right cerebral hemisphere. Other language abilities depend primarily (in right-handed people) on the left hemisphere, but pragmatics as well as the ability to understand humor, depend crucially on the brain's right hemisphere. Patients who have suffered damage to the right hemisphere might understand a metaphorical statement such as "Can you lend me a hand" as asking literally for a hand on a platter. Indeed, in normal people, the right hemisphere is particularly active (as measured in PET) when they are interpreting metaphors (Bottini et al., 1994).

Pragmatics: The way that language conveys meaning indirectly, by implying rather than asserting.

Bilingualism: A Window of Opportunity?

All normal people learn a language, but only some learn a second language at some point in life. Is learning a second language the same as learning a first one? Using functional magnetic resonance imaging (fMRI), Kim and his colleagues (1997) scanned the brains of two groups of bilingual people while they thought about what they had done the previous day, using each of their two languages in turn. One group had learned their second languages as young children, the other as adults. Wernicke's area, involved in comprehension, was activated the same way in both languages and in both groups. But Broca's area told a different story: If the participants had learned the second language as young children, the same part of Broca's area displayed activity for both the first and the second languages. If they learned the second language after childhood, however, activity for that language appeared in a different part of the left frontal lobe—in a part used in working memory.

In spite of the fact that languages learned as an adult are not as well learned as those acquired during childhood, it is remarkably easy to learn some aspects of second languages. Dupuy and Krashen (1993) asked third-semester college students who were taking French to read five scenes from a script from a French movie, after having seen the first five scenes to get the story line. The scenes that were read contained many highly colloquial words that the students were unlikely to have seen or heard before. A surprise vocabulary test after reading showed that participants were learning almost five words per hour, without trying! This rate is remarkably close to the learning rates of children who are reading in their native languages.

Unfortunately, it is not so easy to learn the grammar of a second language as an adult. In addition, it is not easy to learn the sound pattern of a second language after childhood. Indeed, the vast majority of people who learn a second language after puberty will make grammatical errors and speak with an accent. But even for these difficult tasks, some people can learn to pronounce words in another language almost flawlessly (Snow, in press). People differ greatly (perhaps even genetically?) in their abilities to acquire second languages.

LOOKING AT LEVELS

Aping Language?

In evolutionary terms, chimpanzees are very close to humans: We have at least 98% of our genes in common. Does this similarity mean that chimps or other nonhuman primates should be able to talk? To answer this question, the meaning of language clearly must be understood at the different levels of analysis.

At the level of the group, we learn language from others. Some heroic researchers have gone so far as to raise a chimp alongside their own child, but even then the animal did not learn to speak (Kellogg & Kellogg, 1933). More recent studies have told much the same story (Terrace et al., 1976; Terrace, 1979).

At the level of the brain, however, we need to ask not simply whether the brain can use language, but also whether it can control the parts of the body needed to *express* language. Because part of the problem seems to be that the animal's throat cannot make the sounds of speech, some researchers have tried to teach chimps to use sign language (Gardner & Gardner, 1969; Terrace, 1979) or arbitrary symbols such as cut-out plastic shapes or computer icons to communicate (Greenfield & Savage-Rumbaugh, 1990; Savage-Rumbaugh et al., 1986). With both sign language and arbitrary shapes, animals can be taught to string symbols together to make "sentences." Terrace (1979), however, found that the chimps were usually imitating sequences that they had previously seen and could not learn rules for reordering the signs to produce novel sentences.

Nevertheless, members of one species of chimp, the pygmy chimpanzee, have spontaneously created new statements using symbols (Greenfield & Savage-Rumbaugh, 1990), and at least some researchers believe that certain nonhuman primates are capable of using true language (Fouts & Mills, 1997). Nevertheless, at the level of the person, we must note that only humans spontaneously invent language (Pinker, 1994). Even if other animals have the potential to use language, only humans are driven to do so.

Thus, we see how events at the different levels interact: We need others to teach us language (your language is different if you are raised in China or Chile), but we can acquire and use language only if our brains have the

Some nonhuman primates can be trained to understand the meaning of symbols, such as these pieces of plastic, and to arrange them to form simple sentences. But is this true language?

appropriate capacities (including capacities to control key parts of our bodies); even if we have the right social input and brains, however, we must be motivated to pay attention and use language. Even the most fundamental human characteristics—and language surely qualifies—can be fully understood only by considering events at the different levels and the ways in which they interact.

1 *What are the essential characteristics of all languages?* All languages have four key characteristics. First, they have phonology. Phonemes are the basic units of speech, and they are arranged in sequences to form words. Second, languages have grammar. Grammar is a set of rules for combining words that is based on the relationships among parts of speech. Every sentence has a syntax, which is its grammatical organization. We use grammar for both producing and understanding language. Third, languages have semantics, which specify meaning. The semantics of a word arises from its morphemes, small elements of meaning. Fourth, languages have pragmatics, the indirect or implied aspects of meaning. Pragmatics play a key role in understanding whether a question is actu-

ally a request, and whether a statement ending with a rising pitch is actually a question. Pragmatics are also involved in understanding metaphor.

2 *Are first and second languages used in different ways?* Depending on your age when you learn it, a second language functions in the brain either in the same way as the first language or in a different way. Using a language learned later in life appears to rely, at least in part, on working memory (whereas using a language learned at an early age does not require working memory to the same degree). At least for people of college age, acquiring vocabulary in a second language is remarkably easy. However, mastering the grammar and sound patterns (phonology) of a second language learned after puberty is extraordinarily difficult.

Foundations of Thought

One day it hit Frank that some of his difficulties in communicating with his droid might stem from the fact that Hans didn't think the same way he did—if Hans thought at all. Frank gently tried to find out just how Hans "thought." Frank usually thought in words, but he supposed that someone could also think in pictures. So he asked Hans if he often pictured things in his mind's eye. Hans's first response was, "How should I know?" This stumped Frank. Then he asked Hans if he talked to himself. This query merely earned him a cold stare. Hans did offer that he was not experiencing any mental instabilities, if that was the point, and how was Frank feeling today?

Thinking involves manipulating information in your head. Sometimes it involves solving problems; sometimes it involves simply determining what is implied by or associated with information at hand. Frank wasn't alone in assuming that we reason and solve problems partly by using language, but this isn't always the case. As you will see, language is a tool that may be used in thinking, but it is not the sole basis of thought.

1 Does language mold our thoughts?

2 Can we think with mental images? How might the brain give rise to these images?

3 What is a concept?

4 What methods can we use to solve problems?

We are usually aware of what we are thinking about, but our awareness appears to be limited to language and mental images. Inner speech—talking to ourselves—and images are manipulated in working memory, and thus they play a key role in thinking; as discussed in Chapter 5, working memory operates on stored information to allow us to perform a task. Language and images help us to think but cannot themselves be the only means by which we think. To see why, let's consider each in turn, and then look at another way in which information is specified in the mind.

Words: Inner Speech and Spoken Thoughts

Many people, if asked, would say they think with words. And at first glance, that seems plausible: After all, to communicate with someone we usually have to express ourselves in words, so why not use words when thinking?

Putting Thoughts Into Words

There are at least three problems with the idea that thinking is just talking to yourself, as was claimed by the founder of behaviorism, John B. Watson (1913). First, if this were true, why would you ever have trouble "putting a thought into words"? If thoughts were already formed in language, expressing them in language should be child's play. Second, words are often ambiguous, but thoughts are not. If you are thinking about "the port," you don't wonder whether you are thinking about a wine or a harbor. Third, anyone who has owned a dog or cat probably has sensed that at least some animals can think, and yet they don't use language. In fact, there is ample evidence that many animals can not only think but also can solve problems—remember Kohler's work with the chimpanzee Sultan, discussed in Chapter 4.

Does Language Shape Thought?

Even if thought is not the silent equivalent of talking to yourself, many people have been fascinated by the possibility that our perceptions and thoughts are shaped by the particular language we speak. This idea, known as the **linguistic relativity hypothesis**, was championed by Benjamin Lee Whorf (1956). For example, some have suggested that because the Inuit of northern Canada have many words for the different types of snow they recognize, they can see and think about subtle differences in snow better than speakers of English can with their paltry single word for the white stuff. If this idea is correct, then people who speak languages with lots of color words should be able to perceive more distinctions among colors than people who speak languages with few such words. Rosch (1973, 1975) tested this idea by studying the Dani, a remote tribe living in Papua New Guinea. The Dani use only two words for color, corresponding to *light* and *dark*. However, they perceive variations in color and are able to learn shades of color as readily as people who speak languages with words that label many colors.

Nevertheless, even if language does not entirely determine how we can think, it does influence some aspects of thought and memory. In some cases, we do

Linguistic relativity hypothesis: The idea that perceptions and thoughts are shaped by language, and thus people who speak different languages think differently.

appear to use words as a crutch to help us think, particularly when working memory is involved. In such circumstances, we often perform relatively slow, step-by-step reasoning—for example, memorizing a series of directions and recalling them one at a time, holding them in working memory long enough to turn the right way and continue to the next landmark. In addition, language can enhance memory. For example, if you look at clouds, you can remember their shapes better if you come up with a distinctive characterization for each (such as "a rabbit sticking out of a tube" or "a face without a chin") than if you use a single label for them all (Ellis, 1973). If the label really does help to identify the object, then remembering both the label and the visual form of the cloud gives you two ways to recall it later (see Chapter 5). However, this relationship between language and perception is not the same thing as language's actually shaping the nature of our thoughts.

Even though the Dani have only two words for color, light *and* dark, *they can perceive and learn shades of color as easily as people who speak languages with many terms for color.*

Mental Imagery: Perception Without Sensation

If language is not the basis of thinking, what might be? Virtually all the great thinkers who applied themselves to this question in the past, including Plato and Aristotle, and later John Locke and other British philosophers, identified thought with a stream of mental images (Kosslyn, 1980). **Mental images** are representations like those that arise during perception, but they arise from stored information rather than from immediate sensory input. Visual mental images give rise to the experience of "seeing with the mind's eye," an experience you probably will have if someone asks you, for example, whether the Statue of Liberty holds the torch in her left or right hand. Auditory mental images give rise to the experience of "hearing with the mind's ear," as likely happened when you were deciding whether the first three notes of "Three Blind Mice" rise or fall in pitch. Because visual imagery is the most common form of imagery (Kosslyn et al., 1990; McKellar, 1965), we will focus on it here.

Mental Space

There are many types of mental images (Kosslyn, 1994b); the most common seems to occur in a kind of "mental space." This space has three properties: spatial extent, limited size, and grain (grain is the equivalent of resolution on a television screen or computer monitor). Let's investigate these properties in turn.

First, visualize your living room, and count the number of windows. Does it feel as if you are scanning the walls? As illustrated in Figure 6.2 on page 200, the greater the extent of your scan, the longer it takes to do the job; these results show that when you visualize something, its mental representation has a definite *spatial extent* (Denis & Kosslyn, 1999).

Second, how large can an object in a mental image be? When you mentally counted the windows in your living room, you scanned across each wall one by one because you couldn't "see" the whole extent at once; you have only a limited field of view in a mental image. Now imagine you are walking toward an elephant, mentally staring at the center of its body. Imagine walking closer and closer to it,

Mental images: Internal representations like those that arise during perception, but based on stored information rather than immediate sensory input.

Figure 6.2 **Scanning Visual Mental Images**

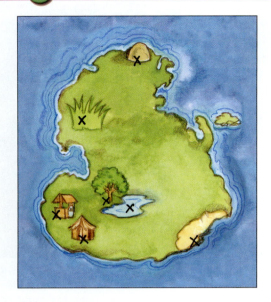

Participants memorized a map like this one, paying special attention to the locations of the seven objects.

Later, the participants were asked to close their eyes and focus on one location (such as the hut) and then to scan to another named location if it was on the map; they were to press one button if they found the second object and another if they could not (and the time was recorded). Participants scanned between every possible pair of objects.

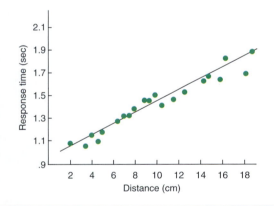

Even though their eyes were closed, the farther the participants had to scan from the first object to the second, the longer it took.

keeping your mental gaze fixed on its center. Most people doing this exercise report that when they are at a certain distance from the elephant, its edges seem to blur, to "overflow" their field of vision—that is, their mental space. Note the distance at which the edges of the elephant seem to blur. Now try the same exercise with a rabbit. Fixate on its center, and imagine seeing it loom up as you get closer and closer to it. When you imagine walking toward the rabbit, can you get closer to it than you could to the elephant before the edges seem to blur? When this study was done carefully, the larger the object, the farther away it seemed to be in the mental image when it began to overflow (Kosslyn, 1978). This result is as expected if mental space has a *limited size:* Bigger objects must be "seen" from farther away to fit within it.

Third, try this: Imagine stretching out your arm and looking at a butterfly perched on your fingertip. Can you see the color of its head? Many people find that they have to "zoom in" mentally to answer that question. Now move the butterfly to your palm and gently bring it to within 10 inches from your eyes; this time, zooming probably isn't necessary to "see" its head. Studies have shown that people require more time to "see" properties of objects that are visualized at small sizes than large ones (Kosslyn, 1975, 1976). It is as if the imagery space has a *grain*. If you look at a television screen close up, you will see that the picture is made up of lots of small dots. The dots are the grain of the screen; if an object is too small, there will not be enough dots to define the details, and thus the details will be blurred.

In short, objects in images have many of the properties of actual objects, and thus images can "stand in" for objects. You can think about an object in its absence by visualizing it.

The Visualizing Brain

Visual images rely on many—about two-thirds—of the same parts of the brain that are used in visual perception (Kosslyn et al., 1997). This overlap may explain some of the key facts about imagery.

First, *spatial extent.* Many of the areas of the brain that process visual input are organized so that images on the retina are laid out on the cortex in what are called "topographically organized areas" (from the Greek *topos*, "place"). As shown in Chapter 3, there are literally "pictures in the brain" in these areas. Many researchers have found that when people visualize with their eyes closed, these areas are active (Chen et al., 1998; Kosslyn et al., 1993; 1995; 1996; 1999; LeBihan et al., 1993). Moreover, if these areas are temporarily impaired by the effect of strong magnetic pulses, visual mental imagery is disrupted (Kosslyn et al., 1999).

Second, *limits* on spatial extent. The brain needed to evolve only to process input from the eyes, and we don't see behind our heads. Objects in images overflow at about the same size that actual objects seem to become blurred in perception (Kosslyn, 1978). Like screens, topographically organized areas have definite boundaries, and images cannot extend beyond them. Of course, these areas are not literally screens, functioning like movie or television screens: No hidden observer in the brain looks at them—rather, the areas organize and process signals, which are sent to other areas in the brain.

Third, *grain.* Topographically organized visual areas of the brain have a property called *spatial summation:* If a neuron is excited by a point of light in a particular place in space, another point of light close to it typically will add to the effects of the first. In contrast, if the spots are far enough apart, they are registered by different neurons. Spatial summation produces a kind of grain: If objects are small enough, points on their surfaces are too close together to be discriminated, and hence details are lost.

In short, we can understand the properties of this sort of mental imagery, which clearly depicts the surfaces of objects, because images arise in brain areas used in vision. Other types of images, such as the sense you have of where things are around you at any given moment, do not depict surfaces but rather specify locations; such spatial images, which even blind people can have, do not activate topographically organized areas (Mellet, Petit et al., 1998; Thompson & Kosslyn, 2000). In addition, in at least some tasks for some people, it is possible that images arise on the basis of memories formed by topographically organized areas, but may no longer rely on such memories (Behrmann, 2000).

But images take us only so far. Their limitations prevent them from being the only tools of the mind, even in combination with words. For one thing, images cannot represent abstract concepts. Take justice, for example. How would you represent "justice" with an image? You might choose a blindfolded woman holding a pair of scales. But how would you know if that image represented the familiar statue or was supposed to stand for the abstract concept of justice? Another problem is that images are often ambiguous. An image of a box seen from the side could just as easily be an image of that side alone, detached from the box. Furthermore, not everybody can produce good images; perhaps 2% of the population have poor visual imagery (McKellar, 1965). Yet another problem is, how do you "decide" which images to form? Some other process must pick out which images will be useful. Like language, imagery can contribute to our thought processes, and like language, it cannot be the only means by which we think.

Concepts: Neither Images nor Words

A **concept** is a grouping of a set of objects (which may include living things) or events (which can specify relations between things, such as "falling" or "on"). A concept is an unambiguous internal representation that may be abstract (such as the concept of truth or justice). Concepts may be *expressed* by images and words, but they are not the same as either (Kosslyn, 1980; Pinker, 1994). Thought arises from the manipulation of concepts, but words and images are used to express thoughts and further expand on them in working memory. Words and images play much the same role that a notepad does when you are planning a shopping trip; they not only help you work through and organize your thoughts, but also provide a way to store them.

The oldest idea of the nature of concepts was proposed by Aristotle in the fourth century B.C. According to this view, a concept corresponds to a set of features. For example, for the concept "bird" the features might be "wings, feathers, a beak, and the ability to fly." The features not only describe perceivable characteristics (such as wings and beak), but also specify appropriate activities (such as flight). The morphemes that underlie the meaning of the word *bird* would capture each of these properties. Some concepts are captured by the meanings of words, but others require a phrase or two to be fully expressed. Like the meanings of words, concepts are unambiguous.

Prototypes: An Ostrich Is a Bad Bird

According to Aristotle, the features of a concept must be both necessary and sufficient. A *necessary* feature is one that all members of the group must have; a *sufficient* condition is one that is enough—that "suffices"—to put an entity into a given category (so feathers would be a sufficient condition for "birdness"; if it has feathers, it's a bird). But Aristotle's formula doesn't always work: Although "the ability to fly" is a feature of birds, it is also a feature of insects and bats, but they're not birds; so flying is not a sufficient condition for birds. And an ostrich is a bird, but it can't fly, so flying is not a necessary condition for birds.

In addition, Aristotle's notion leads us to make wrong predictions. For example, according to his theory of how concepts are specified, if an object has the required properties, it is a member of the concept, period; all members of concepts have equally good standing. But Rosch (1978) showed that some objects are actually "better" members of their concept category than others. How good an example of its category an object is depends on its **typicality**—that is, how representative it is of that type of thing. As illustrated in Figure 6.3, people name objects that are typical members of a concept category faster than objects that are not typical members. If asked whether the headgear Frank saw (the one that looked like a cross between an umbrella and a water lily) was a hat, most people might say yes but take a long time to make the decision and still be a little uncertain. The droid's thought processes apparently did not operate the same way as the human's; for a droid, a hat is a hat if it's worn on the head, and that's all there is to it. Typicality affects not only the time it takes you to identify an object, but also your confidence in naming the object as an example of a specific concept (Smith & Medin, 1981).

Most such effects can be explained if a concept corresponds to a set of features that describe the **prototype** of the category—that is, its most typical member—but only a *percentage* of those features need to be present in any particular member. In this case, the more features that apply, the faster you can name the object—and more prototypical members of a concept have more such distinguishing features (Rips et al., 1973). Thus, people take longer to name ostriches as

Concept: An unambiguous, sometimes abstract, internal representation that defines a grouping of a set of objects (including living things) or events (including relationships).

Typicality: The degree to which an entity is representative of its category.

Prototype: A representation of the most typical example of a category.

Figure 6.3 Name These Animals

Research has shown that you will name the center one most readily, and in fact the mutt is most typical for the category "dog."

birds because fewer bird features apply to them (they cannot fly; they are not the size of the standard bird); on the other hand, robins are named faster because more of the features of birds in general apply to them.

However, some researchers have argued that at least some concepts may be stored as prototypes that are not collections of features, such as the prototype of an odd number between 1 and 10 (Armstrong et al., 1983). Quick, think of an odd number between 1 and 10. Most people select 3, and on that basis 3 can be considered as the most typical member of this category. But such concepts are unusual in that, by definition, they require selecting a single example, so these special cases may be represented by a single example stored individually. Other researchers have made the case that not all concepts are stored as prototypes, but rather some concepts rely on storing sets of examples of the category (Medin & Schaffer, 1978; Smith & Medin, 1981). For example, your concept of a chair might correspond to representations of a collection of chairs (rocking, desk, easy chair, and so on), not a single prototype. At least some concepts may be stored in multiple ways, and the different representations are used in different situations (Medin et al., 2000; Smith et al., 1998).

How Are Concepts Organized?

Many concepts can be applied to any given object. We can name an object with words that correspond to concepts at different levels of specificity: "Granny Smith apple" is very specific, "apple" is more general, and "fruit" more general still. How are different concepts organized?

Look at the objects in Figure 6.4 on page 204 and name them as fast as you can. We bet that you named them "apple," "tree," and "dog." We strongly suspect that you didn't name the apple a "fruit" or a "Granny Smith," or call the tree an "oak" or the dog a "mammal" or an "animal." People consistently name objects at what Rosch and her colleagues (1976) have called the **basic level.** The basic level is like the middle rung of a ladder, with more general concepts above it and more specific concepts below it. So "apple" is the basic level; "fruit" is on a rung above it, and "Granny Smith" on a rung below. Each more general concept includes a number of more specific concepts; for example, "apple" includes "Granny Smith," "Delicious," "McIntosh," and many more.

At each level there are prototypes for the concept. For example, apple might be the prototypical fruit, and McIntosh might be the prototypical apple. The basic level indicates the level of specificity with which we are likely to apply a concept to an object. Rosch offered several ways to identify the basic level. For example, one way is based on shape: At the most specific level, if we compare individual Delicious apples with other Delicious apples, their shapes are pretty similar. Moving up a rung of generality, if we compare Delicious apples with McIntosh

Basic level: A level of specificity, which is usually the most likely to be applied to an object.

Figure **6.4** **Basic-Level Names**

Name these objects as fast as you can. It is remarkable that most people choose the same three names, a feat no computer vision system can match.

apples, Cortland apples, and so on, their shapes are pretty similar. But, moving up another rung, if we compare apples with other fruits, such as bananas, watermelons, or grapes, their shapes are not similar at all. The basic-level category is the one that is as general as possible while still limited to objects having similar shapes.

Some researchers theorize that sets of concepts are organized not only according to levels that vary in specificity, but also into schemas (Rumelhart, 1975; Schank & Abelson, 1977). If the basic level is like a rung on a ladder that organizes concepts in terms of specificity, a schema is like a basket that contains things that usually go together. A **schema** is a collection of concepts that specify necessary and "optional" aspects of a particular situation. For example, the schema for "room" indicates that it must have walls, a floor, a ceiling, and at least one door. In addition, this schema indicates that a room can have windows, carpeting, and various types of furniture. If you know that something is a room, the "room" schema is activated, the necessary concepts apply to this case, and the schema guides you to look to see which other, optional features also apply.

Concepts in the Brain

Studies of how concepts are stored in the brain have shown that they are organized not only in terms of specificity and their interrelations in schemas, but also according to how they are used. For example, brain damage can cause impairment to the ability to name living things but not manufactured objects (Warrington & Shallice, 1984), or vice versa (Warrington & McCarthy, 1987). This finding suggests that the brain organizes concepts according to these two general classes. In addition, Martin and colleagues (1996) found that when the participants in their study named tools, one of the areas of the brain that was activated (as measured by PET) is used to direct movements. In contrast, this area was not activated when the participants named animals, although in this case visual areas were activated. Characteristic actions are important for specifying the concept "tool," whereas visual properties are particularly important for specifying the concept "animal."

How to Solve Problems:
More Than Inspiration

Forming concepts is only a small part of what we do while thinking. Once we form concepts, we use them in various ways, such as in solving problems. Hans was particularly good at solving problems that were clearly stated. One day an old woman's life savings, stored in bags under her bed, were stolen. The perpetrator had pried open a window and crawled through into the bedroom. Using his enhanced eyes

Schema: A collection of concepts that specify necessary and optional aspects of a particular situation.

and perfect memory, Hans was able to see microscopic threads on the window sill and to identify them immediately as a type of Australian wool used in only one brand of coat. Hans then spotted a long blond hair on the floor of the bedroom. Searching his infallible memory, he came up with three suspects. Their photographs were printed, and one of them was immediately identified by the saleswoman at the one store in town that carried those coats. In 2 hours, the case was closed.

Clearly, many different skills feed into our ability to solve problems. You can use language, images, or word–image combinations to specify the problem, but first you must conceptualize it—otherwise you won't know which words and images to use. Once you set up a problem in a particular way, you can manipulate your verbal descriptions and mental images to try to solve it.

A **problem** is an obstacle that must be overcome to reach a goal. Problems come in many types and can often be solved in many ways. In this section, we consider the tools at your disposal for solving a diverse range of puzzles and predicaments.

Solving the Representation Problem: It's All in How You Look at It

The first step to solving any problem is figuring out how to look at it. This fundamental challenge is called the **representation problem.** If you hit on the right way to represent a specific problem, the solution can be amazingly simple. Consider the example of the hiking monk in Figure 6.5 (based on Duncker, 1945). You have to decide whether at any one time of day the monk would be at precisely the same spot on the path going up and coming down. At first glance, this problem may seem difficult. If the precise specifications of departure times, speed, and so on lure you into trying to use algebra, you may work on it for hours. But if you hit on the right representation, it's easy: Imagine a mountain with a monk leaving from the top at the same time that another monk leaves from the bottom. It is clear that the two monks must pass each other at a particular point on the path, so the answer is simply yes.

Finding the right representation for a problem can be tricky because once you think of a problem in a certain way, you may find it hard to drop this view and

Figure 6.5   The Hiking Monk Problem

A monk leaves the bottom of a mountain every Monday at 5:00 A.M. and walks up a twisty path, climbing at a rate of 1.5 miles an hour, until he reaches the top at 4:00 P.M., having taken off a half-hour for lunch. He meditates on the mountain until sundown. At 5:00 the next morning he departs and walks down the path, going 3.5 miles an hour, until he reaches the bottom. Is there any point in the two journeys when he is at precisely the same location at precisely the same time of day? You don't need to say what that time is, just whether there would be such a time.

Problem: An obstacle that must be overcome to reach a goal.

Representation problem: The challenge of how best to formulate the nature of a problem.

Figure 6.6 **The Candle Problem**

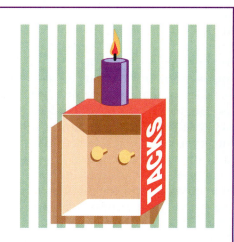

Participants are asked to use the materials provided to mount the candle on the wall so that it can be lit. Some participants are given the materials as shown in the left panel; others, as shown in the center panel. Participants given the materials as shown in the center panel are more likely to solve the problem. When the box is presented as a container, functional fixedness prevents people from imagining the box as a shelf.

try out others (Smith & Blankenship, 1989, 1991). For example, consider the problem in Figure 6.6 (adapted from Duncker, 1945). At first, you probably thought of the box simply as a container, and not as a potential part of the solution. Becoming stuck on one interpretation of an object or aspect of the situation is called **functional fixedness**.

Algorithms and Heuristics: Getting From Here to There

To solve a problem, you need a **strategy**, an approach to solving a problem determined by the type of representation used and the processing steps to be tried. There are two types of strategies: algorithms and heuristics. Let's say you heard about a fantastic price being offered on a hit alternative music CD by an independent record store, but you don't know the name of the store. You could try to find it by calling every relevant listing in the yellow pages. This process involves using an **algorithm**, a set of steps that if followed methodically will guarantee the right answer. But you may not have time to call every store. Instead, you might guess that the record store is in a part of town where many students live. In this case, having reduced the list of candidates to those located near the campus, you might find the store after calling only a few. This process reflects use of a **heuristic**, a rule of thumb that does not guarantee the correct answer but offers a likely shortcut to it. One common heuristic is to divide a big problem into parts and solve them one at a time.

Solving Problems by Analogy: Comparing Features

Another way to solve problems requires you to compare the features of two situations (Hummel & Holyoak, 1997). Let's begin with the following problem (based on Duncker, 1945): A surgeon has to remove a cancerous tumor from deep within a patient's brain. The use of a scalpel would cause permanent brain damage. An alternative is to use a beam of X rays to demolish the cancerous cells. However, the beam will also kill healthy cells in its path. Is there a way to reach only the cancerous cells and spare the healthy ones?

The solution is to split the beam into several minibeams, each aimed from a different angle. Each minibeam is so weak that it will not hurt the healthy tissue, but their combined impact will destroy the tumor. Gick and Holyoak (1980, 1983) found that most people do not realize this solution. However, if they are first pre-

Functional fixedness: When solving a problem, getting stuck on one interpretation of an object or one part of the situation.

Strategy: An approach to solving a problem, determined by the type of representation used and the processing steps to be tried.

Algorithm: A set of steps that, if followed methodically, will guarantee the solution to a problem.

Heuristic: A rule of thumb that does not guarantee the correct answer to a problem but offers a likely shortcut to it.

sented with an analogous problem and are told to think about how it relates to the second problem, success rates skyrocket. In this case, they first read about a problem faced by a general who wants to attack a fortress. If he advances all of his troops along a single road, mines would blow them to pieces. But smaller groups could travel on various approach roads without exploding the mines. The solution is to divide the army into smaller parties and have each take a separate road to the fortress. Once people see this solution and know it is relevant, the solution to the tumor problem becomes much easier (in fact, close to 80% get the problem right). If the participants are not told that the army problem is relevant to the tumor one, however, thinking about it does not help them much. At first glance, the two problems are unrelated. One involves soldiers and a fortress; the other, beams of radiation and a tumor. But beneath these surface differences, the problems have the same structure: Something too big is broken into parts, the parts are delivered separately, and then they are recombined. To see how a previous experience can be applied to a present case, you must recognize the similarities in the structure of the problems.

Insight: A new way to look at a problem that implies the solution.

Sudden Solutions

People do not always have to work consciously through a problem, step by step. In some cases, they can "see" the solution right away; in others, the solution dawns on them after they have set the problem aside for a while.

Many researchers have suggested that people sometimes can see a solution to a problem in a flash, full-blown and complete (Guilford, 1979; Olton, 1979; Torrance, 1980). This phenomenon results from an **insight**, a new way to look at a problem that implies the solution. Insights can arise following a trial-and-error exploration in which the problem is represented in different ways. Once the problem is represented in the right way, the answer is obvious. A good example of insight is the *Wheel of Fortune* experience; once you solve the word puzzle yourself, the solution becomes so obvious that you can't imagine how the stumped television contestants can be so dense.

LOOKING AT LEVELS

Prototypes That Lead to Heavy Drinking

Prototypes not only play a key role in thinking, but also affect how we behave. Gibbons and Gerrard (1995) theorized that whether someone will engage in a health-risk behavior, such as excessive drinking of alcohol, depends on how similar they think they are to a prototype of the typical person who engages in that behavior. Blanton and colleagues (1997) tested this theory by studying 463 adolescents (roughly half male, half female) who lived in rural Iowa. To assess prototypes for drinking, the participants were told, "We would like you to think for a minute about the type of person your age who drinks (alcohol) frequently." They stressed that they were not interested in anyone in particular, just "the typical teenage drinker." Following this introduction, the participants were given a set of adjectives and rated the degree to which those adjectives described their prototype. On the basis of these ratings, Blanton and colleagues inferred the degree to which the typical teenage drinker was generally viewed by the participant as "self-assured–together (such as self-confident and independent), unattractive (unattractive and

dull), or immature (immature and careless)." To the extent that an individual participant rated people who drink high on the first factor and low on the other two, he or she was said to have a "positive prototype" of drinkers.

Three results are of particular interest. First, participants who had more positive prototypes of drinkers reported drinking more. This finding was exactly as predicted, if feeling that you are similar to the prototype shapes your behavior. Second, the positive prototype itself was apparently a consequence of the participant's peer group; the more their peers tended to drink, the more the participants tended to drink. Third, adolescents who had poor relationships with their parents were more likely to associate with a drinking peer group. Thus the parents had an indirect influence on drinking by affecting the choice of peer group, which in turn affected the prototype.

Consider these findings from the levels perspective: The brain is set up to store representations of prototypes. In this case, the prototypes arose from social experience, particularly with the peer group. In addition, social interactions with the parents led teens to favor particular peer groups, which in turn helped mold a positive prototype for drinking. And the prototype in turn affects behavior. The events interact: By becoming a heavier drinker, a person will tend to spend more time with a peer group of drinkers, which will further mold his or her prototypes.

CONSOLIDATE!

1 *Does language mold our thoughts?* Although some researchers have claimed that language shapes thought, the evidence does not support this view. Thinking cannot rely entirely on words; for example, words are ambiguous, but thoughts are not, and people sometimes have difficulty putting thoughts into words. Nevertheless, some thought does make use of language, and it is clear that being able to name something makes that object or idea easier to remember.

2 *Can we think with mental images? How might the brain give rise to these images?* Objects in images can "stand in" for the actual objects, as evidenced by the facts that they have spatial extent, occur in a mental space with a limited extent, and have grain. Many studies have found that the visual parts of the brain in the occipital lobe are activated when people visualize shapes, and the properties of these areas may explain the characteristics of images. Nevertheless, thinking cannot rely entirely on mental images; such images are difficult to use to represent abstract ideas and, like words, can be ambiguous.

3 *What is a concept?* A concept is a grouping of a set of objects or events (including relations, such as the concept of one object's being "on" another object). This grouping often can be accomplished by sets of unambiguous features that specify key characteristics of the concept, but only a percentage of the features must apply in any given instance. Members of concepts that have more of the key features are "better" (more typical) examples of the concept. A member that possesses the most specifying features is a prototype. Some concepts may be specified by prototypes that are not collections of features; others may be specified by sets of examples of the concept. Concepts are organized according to levels of specificity as well as according to their relevance to particular situations (schemas). Although words and images are not themselves concepts, they can be used to express concepts.

4 *What methods can we use to solve problems?* The first step is to discover how best to specify the problem, how to represent it to yourself. If you find the proper representation, the solution is sometimes obvious. To solve a problem, you can use an algorithm or heuristic. One common heuristic is to divide a problem into a set of smaller problems and then tackle those subproblems one at a time. In addition, you can search for correspondences with other situations and use analogical thinking to solve a problem.

Logic, Reasoning, and Decision Making

Frank was proud to be a human being instead of a machine—even a machine with superhuman sensory abilities and a flawless memory. Frank firmly believed that he had something no machine would ever have: intuition. When Frank spoke of acting on a hunch, or using his intuition, the droid Hans had no idea what Frank was talking about. Hans made decisions not on the basis of some vague feeling, but rather on the firm foundation of the laws of logic.

1 Do people reason logically?

2 Why do we commit reasoning errors?

Are People Logical?

Not all thinking consists of figuring out how to overcome obstacles; sometimes thinking is considering what follows from what, evaluating alternatives, and deciding what to do next. Decision making requires us to evaluate possible outcomes and choose one over the other. **Logic** is the process of applying the principles of correct reasoning to reach a decision or evaluate the truth of a claim. "Hector is a man; all men are human; therefore Hector is a human" is correct logic. But note that "Hector is a man; all men are Martians; therefore Hector is a Martian" is *also* correct logic. The first two statements in each case are the *premises,* and the only question in logic is whether the final statement, the *conclusion,* follows from the premises. The *content*—the actual meaning of the premises—is irrelevant to logic; only the *form,* the sequence of what-implies-what, counts in logic. If you accept the premises, logic dictates the conclusions you must also accept. In this process of **deductive reasoning**—that is, reasoning from the general to the particular— the rules of logic are applied to a set of assumptions stated as premises to discover what conclusions inevitably follow from those assumptions.

Much research has shown that, unlike the Vulcan Mr. Spock and the droid Hans, humans are not entirely logical. For example, people often make the error of **affirming the consequent;** that is, we assume that a specific cause is present because a particular result has occurred. Here is a cause–effect relation: "If it is sunny out, Hector wears a hat." Does it follow that this statement is true: "Hector is wearing a hat; therefore, it is sunny out"? Not necessarily. Maybe Hector's on his way to a ballgame and has put on a hat with his team's logo. Maybe after checking The Weather Channel, he has put on a rain hat. Maybe he simply thinks a particular hat looks good with his outfit. Maybe—well, there might be any number of reasons, including that it is in fact sunny out. Affirming the consequent occurs because we incorrectly work backward, from result to cause.

Wason and Johnson-Laird (1972) devised a task that laid bare more of our reasoning frailties. Look at Figure 6.7: What would you do? The answer is that both *A* and *7* must be flipped. People tend to flip *A,* to see whether an even number is on the other side; if not, the rule would be wrong. If there is an even number on the reverse of *A,* most people assume the rule is confirmed. Very few think to turn over the *7:* If there is a vowel on the other side, then the rule is wrong no matter what's on the reverse of *A.* Most people do not think about what it would take to *disconfirm* the rule. A **confirmation bias** occurs when people seek information that will confirm a rule but do not seek information that might refute it.

Figure 6.7 Wason and Johnson-Laird's Card Task

Here is a rule: If a card has a vowel on one side, then it will have an even number on the other side. How many and which of these cards must be flipped over to decide whether this rule is true?

Reasoning can be inductive as well as deductive. The opposite of deductive reasoning, **inductive reasoning** works toward a conclusion by moving from the particular case to a generalization. Induction uses individual examples to figure out a rule that governs them. If you ate two green apples and each was sour, you might induce that green apples in general are sour. However, your conclusion would be faulty: You ignored the evidence of Granny Smiths (which are sweet). Here's another example. What number comes next: 2, 4, 6, _? You probably said 8, but what if the underlying rule were simply "larger numbers"? Then 21, or 101, would also work. Or the rule might be "even numbers," and 2 would satisfy the condition, or "one-digit numbers," in which case 7 would work, and so on. The point is that every one of these additional generalizations is just as consistent with the set 2, 4, 6 as is the number 8 (Goodman, 1983). That inductive reasoning works at all is something of a miracle—nevertheless, it often does (Prasada, 2000),

Logic: The process of applying the principles of correct reasoning to reach a decision or evaluate the truth of a claim.

Deductive reasoning: Reasoning that applies the rules of logic to a set of assumptions (stated as premises) to discover whether certain conclusions follow from those assumptions; deduction goes from the general to the particular.

Affirming the consequent: A reasoning error that occurs because of the assumption that if a result is present, a specific cause must also be present.

Confirmation bias: A tendency to seek information that will confirm a rule, and not to seek information that is inconsistent with the rule.

Inductive reasoning: Reasoning that uses examples to figure out a rule; induction goes from the particular (examples) to the general (a rule).

Star Trek's Mr. Spock and the droid Hans agree: Emotion clouds reason and distorts our ability to be objective. Doesn't it? Well, not exactly. Researchers have found that emotion can sometimes help reasoning. Bechara and colleagues (1997) found that people played a gambling game better once they had "hunches," even though they were not aware of the basis of the hunch. Patients who had suffered damage to the ventral medial frontal lobes of the brain never experienced such hunches and did poorly on the task; this part of the brain is known to play a crucial role in using emotional information to guide behavior (Damasio, 1996). But Mr. Spock and Hans weren't all wrong: It is true that negative emotion can sometimes disrupt reasoning (Gray, 1999).

Representativeness heuristic: The heuristic that the more similar something is to a prototype stored in memory, the more likely it is to belong to the prototype's category.

Base-rate rule: The rule stating that if something is sampled at random, the chances of obtaining a particular type are directly proportional to its percentage in the set from which the sample is taken.

Availability heuristic: The heuristic that the easier events or objects are to bring to mind, the more likely, common, or frequent they are judged to be.

and much of scientific discovery relies on just this kind of reasoning. To remember the difference between deductive and inductive reasoning, try these mnemonics: To DEduce is to move DOWN FROM something larger; to INduce is to move INTO something larger.

Heuristics and Biases: Cognitive Illusions?

If the laws of logic lead to inescapable conclusions, why do people make errors in reasoning? The answer is implied in the question: because people do not always use the laws of logic, but rely instead on sets of heuristics. While often useful, these heuristics, or rule-of-thumb strategies, sometimes steer us to the wrong conclusions.

Representativeness

The **representativeness heuristic** assumes that the more similar something is to a prototype stored in memory, the more likely the entity belongs to the category of the prototype. Tversky and Kahneman (1974) asked participants to read this passage:

Jack is a 45-year-old man. He is married and has four children. He is generally conservative, careful, and ambitious. He shows no interest in political and social issues and spends most of his free time on his many hobbies, including home carpentry, sailing, and mathematical puzzles.

The participants were told that Jack was selected at random from a group of 100 people, all of whom were either lawyers or engineers. Here's the trick: Half the participants were told that 70 members of the group were lawyers and 30 were engineers; the other participants were told that 30 members of the group were lawyers and 70 engineers. Pause for a moment and imagine that there are 100 balls in a jug, 70 red and 30 black, randomly mixed up. Imagine shutting your eyes and drawing out one ball. Do you think you would be more likely to pluck out a red one than a black one? Sure. Now reverse the colors, so that 70 are black and 30 red. Now you would be more likely to pull out a black one. When asked to decide whether Jack, who was selected at random from the group, was a lawyer or an engineer, the great majority of all participants, no matter what they had been told about the constitution of the group, said he was an engineer. The description of Jack, especially his interest in mathematical puzzles, fit the participants' ideas about the characteristics of engineers better than it fit their ideas about lawyers, and thus they labeled Jack "engineer" because he matched the prototype. The participants used their knowledge—or assumptions—about typical properties of people in different professions to make their decision, ignoring the **base-rate rule.** This rule states that if something is sampled at random, the chances of obtaining a particular type are directly proportional to its percentage in the set from which the sample is taken. Our failure to appreciate the working of this rule can be thought of as a *cognitive illusion.*

Availability

Another shortcut is the **availability heuristic,** which states that we tend to judge objects or events as more likely or frequent if they are easier to bring to mind. For example, Tversky and Kahneman (1974) asked people to judge the relative proportions of words that begin with the letter *k* and words with *k* in the third position. What do you think? Most of the participants in the study thought that *k* occurred more often as a first letter than a third letter, but in fact almost three times as many words have *k* in the third position as in the first one. Why this error? Because it is much easier to bring to mind words starting with *k* than words that have *k* in the third position. The availability heuristic may also explain why people tend to think that infrequent but highly memorable events, such as murders

If you have ever budgeted time to work on a paper, and then run out of hours far too soon, you may have fallen victim to the planning fallacy, the tendency to underestimate the time it takes to accomplish a task. This error may arise because the completion of similar tasks is more available in your memory than is their duration. The good news is that you can reduce the planning fallacy by thinking carefully about how long past projects actually took to complete (Buehler et al., 1994).

and plane crashes, are more common than they really are, and that more frequent but mundane killers, such as stomach cancer and stroke, are less common.

LOOKING AT LEVELS

Reasoning Rhythms

Are you more clear-headed in the morning or the evening? There is good evidence that people differ in this regard, a finding that has obvious implications for timing your major decisions. Bodenhausen (1990) asked people to fill in a questionnaire that assessed whether they were "morning people" or "evening people." Both groups were tested in the morning and in the evening with two stories and asked to make judgments about them. For example, participants were asked whether the woman in one story was more likely to be a feminist, a bank teller, or a feminist bank teller. Logically, the combination should always be less likely than either feature alone, but if someone is described as a prototype of the category of "feminist bank teller," people will say that the combined categories are more likely than either alone (Tversky & Kahneman, 1974). The morning people made fewer errors when tested in the morning than in the evening, and vice versa for evening people.

Mental effort is required to avoid making such errors in reasoning, and people don't expend this energy when their circadian rhythms (which produce fluctuations in blood pressure, pulse rate, body temperature, blood sugar level, and metabolism) are at a low point. Bodenhausen's findings show that to understand a person's reasoning ability, we need to know about events in the brain, such as individual circadian rhythm fluctuations. In addition, we expect events at the group and brain levels to be modulated by events at the level of the person. For example, perhaps if someone believed that it was really crucial to reason properly in a given situation (for instance, to support a good friend), the strength of the motivation could overcome the effects of being at a low point in the daily cycle. To our knowledge, this possibility has yet to be investigated. The levels perspective not only allows us to see how events at the different levels interact, but also directs our attention to novel questions—which clearly can be answered by new studies.

CONSOLIDATE!

1 *Do people reason logically?* In deductive reasoning, logic involves following rules to determine what specific conclusions must follow from a set of general premises. People often make errors in this kind of reasoning, for example, by affirming the consequent and by having a confirmation bias. Inductive reasoning goes in the other direction, from particulars to a generalization. Inductive reasoning is also prone to errors because it is not always obvious what general principle is suggested by a set of examples.

2 *Why do we commit reasoning errors?* We often use heuristics in reasoning, which can lead to specific types of errors. The representativeness heuristic, for example, can lead us to ignore the base-rate rule. The availability heuristic can lead to the planning fallacy, which arises because different aspects of an event are more or less easy to recall.

Is There More Than One Way to Be Smart?

Frank realized that Hans could do many things better than he could, but didn't give up on the idea that in some ways humans are smarter than machines. Frank felt uncomfortable pitting his IQ against Hans's, but he still felt that he was smart. What does it mean to be "smart"? Psychologists have offered many definitions of intelligence, and considerable disagreement exists about what intelligence is and whether it can be measured accurately (Gardner et al., 1996; Sternberg, 1986b, 1990; Sternberg & Detterman, 1986). What most researchers mean by **intelligence** is fairly close to the standard dictionary definition: the ability to solve problems well and to understand and learn complex material. Does IQ really measure intelligence? Could Frank be smarter than Hans in some specific ways but not in others?

 What is IQ?

 Is intelligence a single characteristic or a complex set of characteristics?

What Is IQ?

Let's look at exactly what "IQ" is.

What Is an IQ Test?

IQ is short for **intelligence quotient**, a test score used in Western countries as a general measure of intelligence. To understand the IQ test, and the meaning of IQ scores, it will be helpful to see how this test has evolved over time. The original test from which modern IQ tests derive had a more specific and different purpose than the modern test. Responding to a call from the French government, which had recently enacted universal elementary education, a French physician named Alfred Binet (1857–1911) and his collaborator, Theodore Simon (1873–1961), devised the first intelligence test between 1904 and 1911 (Matarazzo, 1972). Their aim was to develop an objective way to identify children in the public schools who needed extra classroom help. They started with the idea that intelligence shows itself in a wide variety of things people do, a perspective that led them to construct a test consisting of many sorts of tasks. Among other things, children were asked to copy a drawing, repeat a string of digits, recognize coins and make change, and explain why a particular statement did not make sense. Binet and Simon assumed that the children's performance on the tests reflected educational experience, and thus that special classes could help those who did poorly.

To assess performance, Binet and Simon first gave the test to a group of normal children of various ages. They noted which problems were solved by most of the 6-year-olds, most of the 10-year-olds, and so forth; then they compared the performance of other children of the same age with those "normal" scores. So if a child could solve all the problems solved by most 9-year-olds, but failed those passed by most 10-year-olds, the child's *mental age (MA)* was said to be 9. Children with a mental age lower than their *chronological age (CA)* were considered relatively slow.

Binet and Simon's test was quickly adopted and adapted to suit new purposes. In 1916 Lewis Terman and his colleagues at Stanford University developed the Stanford-Binet Revision of the Binet-Simon test, which is still used to test people ages 2 to adult. David Wechsler (1958) developed another set of intelligence tests, the **Wechsler Adult Intelligence Scale (WAIS)** and the *Wechsler Intelligence Scale for Children (WISC)*. Today, the WAIS-III and the WISC-III ("III" denoting the third major version) are the most widely used IQ tests in the United States.

Intelligence: The ability to solve problems well and to understand and learn complex material.

Intelligence quotient (IQ): A score on an intelligence test, originally based on comparing mental age to chronological age but later based on norms.

Wechsler Adult Intelligence Scale (WAIS): The most widely used intelligence test; consists of both verbal and performance subtests.

Believing that Binet's test relied too much on verbal skills, Wechsler divided his test into two major parts, summarized in Table 6.1. The *verbal subtests* assess the test-taker's ability to understand and use language by assessing vocabulary, comprehension, and other aspects of verbal ability. The *performance subtests* consist of nonverbal tasks such as arranging pictures in an order that tells a story and spotting the missing element in a picture. Because the performance subtests do not focus on the ability to use and manipulate words, they probably rely less heavily than do the verbal subtests on the test-taker's education or cultural experiences.

Scoring IQ Tests: Measuring the Mind

Modern IQ tests have been modified from earlier versions both in the nature of the tasks and in the way they are scored. Binet and Simon were satisfied with simply knowing whether a child was below or at par for his or her age, but later researchers wanted a more precise measure of the degree of intelligence. Early in the 20th century, William Stern, a German psychologist, developed the idea of an *intelligence quotient,* computed by dividing mental age (MA) by chronological age (CA) and multiplying by 100 to avoid fractional scores. Thus, a score of 100 meant that a child's mental age exactly matched the child's actual age. Computing IQ scores using the MA/CA ratio presents a major disadvantage, however: Because mental age does not keep developing forever, whereas chronological age marches on, older test-takers cannot help but appear to become less intelligent with age. For example, if your mental age is 25 and you are 25 years old, you would be average; but if your mental age is the same in 5 years, your IQ would drop from 100 to 83, even though you are just as smart at 30 as you were at 25. And at 40, your IQ would be about 62. But people do not automatically become stupider with age.

The WISC-III is administered to children individually by a trained examiner.

TABLE 6.1   **WAIS-III Subtests With "Simulated" Examples of Questions**

Actual test items cannot be published; part of this table was adapted from Gardner et al., 1996, pp. 80–81. This version is intended for people aged 16 to 89. Three additional tests are included as "spares," to be used if there are problems in administering the basic set summarized here.

I. VERBAL SUBTESTS	II. PERFORMANCE SUBTESTS
• *Vocabulary:* Written and spoken words, which must be defined; the words are ordered in terms of increasing difficulty. *Example:* "What does 'trek' mean?"	• *Picture Completion:* Drawings of common objects or scenes, each of which is missing a feature. The test-taker must point out what's missing. *Example:* A beach umbrella that isn't casting a shadow, even though the sun is high in a cloudless sky.
• *Similarities:* Questions that require explaining how the concepts named by two words are similar. *Example:* "How are an airplane and a car alike?"	• *Digit Symbol-Coding:* The test-taker learns a symbol for each of the numbers 1–9 and then sees numbers and must write their appropriate symbols; the test is timed. *Example:* The digit 1 is paired with +, 2 with X, and so forth.
• *Arithmetic:* Problems, all but one presented orally (one involves using blocks); the test is timed. *Example:* "If two men need four days to paint a house, how long would four men need?"	• *Block Design:* Problems that require the test-taker to arrange blocks colored on each side—white, red, or half white and half red—to reproduce a white-and-red pattern in a fixed amount of time. *Example:* A white arrow on a red background.
• *Digit Span:* Lists of digits, 2–9 numbers long, are presented. The test-taker repeats the digits, either in the same or reverse order. *Example:* "6, 1, 7, 5, 3."	• *Matrix Reasoning:* Items that require the test-taker to study a progression of stimuli in a sequence from which a section is missing. The test-taker must choose which of five given possibilities completes the sequence.
• *Information:* Questions that draw on literature, history, general science, and common knowledge. *Example:* "Who was Martin Luther King, Jr.?"	• *Picture Arrangement:* Sets of cards that must be arranged to tell a story. *Example:* Pictures of a bird sitting on the ground, a bird taking off from the ground, a cat sitting licking its lips.
• *Comprehension:* Questions that require understanding of social mores and conventions. *Example:* "Why are there taxes?"	

Therefore, today's IQ tests are scored not by the MA/CA ratio but by specifying how a test-taker stands relative to the performance of other people of the same age. A score of 100 is set as the average score.

Although the average IQ score is set as 100, most people do not achieve this precise score. How can we interpret the meaning of scores above or below this benchmark? IQ test scores are based on a large **standardized sample**, a random selection of people from the appropriate population. In this sense, a **population** is defined as a group of people who share certain characteristics such as age, sex, or any other relevant variables. Almost always, scores are spread along a **normal curve**, illustrated in Figure 6.8. When the distribution of scores follows a normal curve, most scores fall near the middle, with gradually fewer scores toward either extreme (see Appendix A for a further discussion of normal curves).

After the test has been given to a standardized sample, the developers "norm" the test to make it easy to interpret the meaning of any one test-taker's score relative to the others in the standardized sample. **Norming** a test involves setting two measures: The first is the mean, or average; the mean of an IQ test is set at 100. The second is the **standard deviation**, which indicates the degree to which the individual scores deviate from the mean. The greater the number of standard deviations from the mean, the farther above or below the score is from the mean (see Appendix A for details). If the scores fall into a normal distribution, a certain percentage of them occur at each standard deviation from the mean, as shown in Figure 6.8 (each marked unit on the bottom corresponds to one standard deviation).

For the WAIS-III IQ test, scores are adjusted so that a standard deviation is 15 points. As shown in Figure 6.8, about two-thirds of all people have IQs from 85 to 115 points (that is, within one standard deviation above or below the mean), but only a bit more than a quarter have IQs between 70 and 85 and between 115 and 130 (within the second standard deviation above or below the mean). Only 4.54% are above or below those scores.

For IQ scores to be meaningful or useful, the test must be *reliable*. A reliable test produces consistent results; that is, if you test the same group of people on two occasions, the two scores will be highly positively correlated. The WAIS-III has been shown to be highly reliable. In addition, a useful test must be *valid*. A valid test measures what it is supposed to measure. Do IQ tests really measure intelligence—that is, the ability to solve problems well and to understand and learn complex material? One way to find out whether IQ tests in fact measure intelligence is to see whether scores on these tests are related to measures of performance in other tasks that seem to require intelligence, an investigation we will pursue in the next section.

Figure 6.8 The Normal Curve and WAIS-III IQ Scores

Because of its shape, the normal curve is also known as the bell curve. In nature most characteristics clump around the midpoint, and progressively fewer have very high or very low measures. This diagram indicates the percentage of people who have scores on the WAIS-III IQ test that fall within different regions of the distribution.

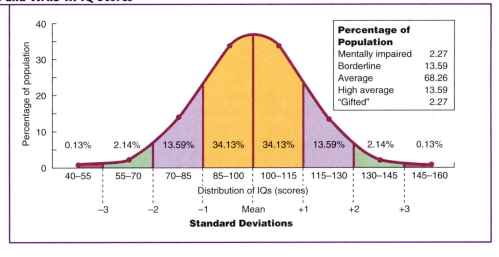

Percentage of Population	
Mentally impaired	2.27
Borderline	13.59
Average	68.26
High average	13.59
"Gifted"	2.27

The issue of validity has become more complex recently with the realization that more than one type of intelligence may exist. Many of today's tests, such as the WAIS-III, provide both an overall score and scores for various subtests, such as those that measure arithmetic and vocabulary. Thus "intelligence" is broken down into abilities of different types, and we can ask whether each measure is valid for a particular type of intelligence. This is a crucial idea, to which we will return repeatedly: The single-number "IQ score" can signify very different things depending on the relative scores on the subtests that contribute to it.

Intelligence: One Ability or Many?

In the United States a high IQ score predicts, to some degree, success in school and in life (Cronbach, 1990; Herrnstein & Murray, 1994; Jensen, 1980, 1998; Wagner, 1997). To interpret these findings, we need to know more about what, precisely, IQ tests measure. Is there some general ability, some basic intelligence, that determines IQ score? And do IQ tests tap everything meant by "intelligence"? There are different ways to solve problems, and so it seems reasonable that there should be different forms of intelligence. There is ample evidence that this is true.

IQ, *g*, and Specialized Abilities

How do researchers determine whether IQ scores reflect some basic, overall type of intelligence or a collection of various cognitive abilities such as the ability to solve puzzles or identify patterns? Psychologists who have investigated this question have used correlations and other statistical measures as key tools in their attempts to find an answer. As discussed, IQ tests include a variety of subtests, such as the picture completion, vocabulary, block design, and arithmetic subtests included in the WAIS-III. It turns out that people who do well on one subtest tend to do well on others; that is, scores on different types of tests are positively correlated.

This finding has led researchers to infer that there is a single form of intelligence that cuts across the different subtests. Early in this century, British psychologist Charles Spearman (1927) argued that the positive correlations among scores on different types of mental tests indicate the existence of a single underlying intellectual capacity, which he labeled *g*, for "general factor." But if intelligence is simply *g*, then all of the scores from the different subtests should be correlated to the same degree. This is not the case: Spearman also noted a wide variation in the sizes of the correlations, which he took to reflect the influence of "specific factors," or *s*. When you perform a task, according to Spearman, you are drawing on *g* as well as on a particular type of ability, *s*, specific to that task. For example, spelling draws on a specialized ability, which is largely independent of other abilities. The very first First Lady of the United States, Martha Washington, is a case in point: She was generally very intelligent (that is, she probably had a high *g*) but was such a poor speller, misspelling words such as *cat* with two *t*s, that her husband, George, frequently wrote her letters for her (Seuling, 1978). Some tasks, such as being able to analyze Shakespeare, rely more on *g* than on *s*; others, such as discriminating musical tones, rely more on a particular *s* than on *g*. But in Spearman's view, IQ scores depend mostly on *g*; how smart you are overall depends on how much of this general intellectual capacity you have.

A second perspective on what IQ scores reflect comes from Louis L. Thurstone (1938). Thurstone devised a battery of 56 tests and then analyzed the correlations of scores on these tests using a method, worked out by Spearman, called factor analysis. **Factor analysis** is a statistical method that uncovers the particular attributes ("factors") that make scores more or less similar. A factor analysis of the correlations among different measures of performance would show, for example, that speed of processing is one important factor in many tasks, and the amount of information that can be held in short-term memory is another.

g: "General factor," a single intelligence that underlies the positive correlations among different tests of intelligence.

s: "Specific factors," or aspects of performance that are particular to a given kind of processing—and distinct from *g*.

Factor analysis: A statistical method that uncovers the particular attributes (factors) that make scores more or less similar; the more similar the scores, the more attributes they should have in common.

When Thurstone analyzed his test results, he found that how well you can do arithmetic has little if anything to do with how well you can notice whether a scene has changed or how well you can figure out the best way to get home when traffic is heavy (Thurstone & Thurstone, 1941). Instead of believing in a single general capacity, such as *g*, Thurstone found evidence that intelligence consists of seven separate **primary mental abilities**, fundamental abilities that are the components of intelligence and that are not outgrowths of other abilities. Verbal comprehension and spatial visualization are two of Thurstone's primary mental abilities; the others are listed in Table 6.2. According to this view, Frank could well be superior to Hans in specific ways, even if Hans has a higher total IQ score.

In the decades since Thurstone proposed his list of primary abilities, other researchers seeking to discover the facets of intelligence have analyzed and reanalyzed similar data with varying results. Carroll (1993) infers over 70 separate abilities, and some (such as J. P. Guilford, 1967) have reported finding more than a hundred distinct factors that underlie intelligence. One especially influential alternative, however, was proposed by Raymond B. Cattell (1971), and then developed further by his student and collaborator John Horn (1985, 1986, 1989, 1994; Horn & Cattell, 1966). These researchers suggested that instead of possessing one general capacity, *g*, people possess two types of intelligence: crystallized and fluid. **Crystallized intelligence** relies on knowing facts and having the ability to use and combine them. This is the sort of intelligence that develops as you become an expert in an area. If you make good use of your college experience, you should boost your crystallized intelligence. In contrast, **fluid intelligence** is the more free-form ability to figure out novel solutions, such as how to catch fish without a hook. As we grow older, crystallized intelligence does not suffer much, if at all; we are still able to maintain our expertise in areas of strength. But the ability to shift gears quickly to solve new problems tends to decrease (Horn, 1985, 1986, 1994; Horn & Noll, 1994; Salthouse, 1996). That age affects the two types of intelligence differently is evidence that they are in fact different; if there were only a single form of intelligence, aging should have the same effects on it. After the discovery of crystallized and fluid intelligence, Cattell and Horn provided evidence for a number of other "broad" factors (to use Jensen's term [Jensen, 1998]), as listed in Table 6.2.

Table 6.2 summarizes five prominent views about the makeup of intelligence. Today, psychologists generally agree with Spearman's theory that people have a collection of special mental abilities (*s*), and most agree that something like *g* exists. However, there is considerable disagreement over exactly what *g* is. Researchers have found that the higher people score on IQ tests overall, the more often there are sharp disparities in the scores on different subtests: In other words, the relative strengths and weaknesses of people with high IQs are likely to differ greatly from individual to individual (Deary & Pagliari, 1991; Detterman & Daniel, 1989; Hunt, 1995; Spearman, 1927). For example, some high scorers may be particularly good at vocabulary and digit span; others at digit span, matrix reasoning, and block design; and still others at yet additional combinations of abilities. In contrast, people who score low on IQ tests tend to perform consistently and generally poorly on all of the tasks. As Hunt (1995) observed, "It appears that general intelligence may not be an accurate statement, but general lack of intelligence is!" (p. 362).

Multiple Intelligences: More Than One Way to Shine

Howard Gardner (1993b, 1995, 1999) developed a very influential view of intelligence, the **theory of multiple intelligences**, which holds that there are eight basic forms of intelligence:

1. *Linguistic intelligence.* The ability to use language well, as relied on by journalists and lawyers.
2. *Spatial intelligence.* The ability to reason well about spatial relations, as relied on by architects and surgeons.

Primary mental abilities: According to Thurstone, seven fundamental abilities that are not outgrowths of other abilities.

Crystallized intelligence: According to Cattell and Horn, the kind of intelligence that relies on knowing facts and having the ability to use and combine them.

Fluid intelligence: According to Cattell and Horn, the kind of intelligence that underlies the creation of novel solutions to problems.

Theory of multiple intelligences: Gardner's theory of eight distinct types of intelligence, which can vary separately for a given individual.

TABLE 6.2 — The Nature of Intelligence: Seven Views

Spearman (1927)	• *g* (generalized ability) • *s* (specialized abilities) • IQ mostly reflects *g*
Thurstone and Thurstone (1941)	7 primary mental abilities: • Verbal comprehension • Word fluency (how well one can produce words) • Number facility (how well one can do arithmetic) • Associative memory • Perceptual speed (for recognizing stimuli) • Reasoning • Spatial visualization
Carroll (1993)	• *g* plus 8 special abilities similar to those identified by Thurstone • Special abilities broken down into even more specialized aspects of intelligence • More than 70 separate abilities
Guilford (1967)	150 distinct abilities underlie intelligence, each with three facets: • Contents (such as visual, auditory, or semantic) • Products (such as some type of unit or transformation) • Operations (such as memory or evaluation)
Cattell (1971) and Horn (1985, 1986, 1989)	Cattell's original theory: • Crystallized intelligence • Fluid intelligence Later versions added: • Speed of inspecting visualized patterns • Visual-spatial reasoning • Auditory thinking • Quantitative reasoning • Fluency of recall (for example, how quickly one can recall names of common objects) • No *g*
Gardner (1993b, 1999)	• Linguistic • Spatial • Musical • Logical-mathematical • Bodily-kinesthetic • Intrapersonal • Interpersonal • Naturalistic
Sternberg (1985, 1988b)	• Analytic • Practical • Creative

Linguistic intelligence is the ability to use language well, as relied on by journalists and lawyers.

Spatial intelligence is the ability to reason well about spatial relations, as relied on by architects and surgeons.

3. *Musical intelligence.* The ability to compose and understand music, as relied on by audio engineers and musicians.
4. *Logical-mathematical intelligence.* The ability to manipulate abstract symbols, as used by scientists and computer programmers.
5. *Bodily-kinesthetic intelligence.* The ability to plan and understand sequences of movements, as drawn on by dancers and athletes.
6. *Intrapersonal intelligence.* The ability to understand oneself, as used by clergy.
7. *Interpersonal intelligence.* The ability to understand other people and social interactions, as used by politicians and teachers.
8. *Naturalist intelligence.* The ability to observe carefully, as used by forest rangers. (Gardner, 1995)

Musical intelligence is the ability to compose and understand music, relied on by audio engineers and musicians.

In more recent formulations of the theory, Gardner (1999) has tentatively suggested a ninth form of intelligence: *existential intelligence,* which is the ability to address "the big questions" about existence. Gardner's classifications are not isolated "special abilities" that allow a person to become skilled at a narrow range of particular tasks. Rather, these are separate *types* of intelligence, which involve a collection of abilities working together. Each type of intelligence allows you to solve a range of problems well and to understand and learn complex material of the appropriate type.

We have shown repeatedly that different parts of the brain perform different functions; the brain is like an orchestra with separate sections playing different parts of the improvisational symphony of thinking, feeling, and behaving. Gardner's theory is unique in that it grew not out of correlations among test scores, but rather from a variety of distinct types of neurological and behavioral observations. Gardner worked for many years at the Boston Veterans Administration Medical Center, where he studied people who had suffered brain damage. He noticed that brain damage often resulted in the loss of a certain ability while leaving others relatively intact. For example, language would be disrupted but patients could still sing, and vice versa; mathematical ability would be disrupted but patients could still speak, and vice versa; social skills would be disrupted while ordinary reasoning was unimpaired, and vice versa. In developing his theory, Gardner also considered other kinds of data. He noted, for example, that although everybody learns their first language in a few years, very few people master complex mathematics so easily. If two abilities develop at different rates during childhood, he reasoned, they must rely on different underlying processes. In addition, he observed that some abilities, such as music and mathematics, can be extraordinarily well developed in child prodigies, whereas these same children perform at average levels in other areas. This coexistence of the extraordinary and the ordinary, Gardner believes, suggests that some capacities, such as those related to music and mathematics, may be psychologically distinct from other capacities.

According to Gardner, most professions require combinations of different types of intelligence; to be a good novelist, for example, you need linguistic, intrapersonal, and interpersonal intelligence. Each person can be characterized by a *profile of intelligences,* with some types of intelligence being relatively strong and others relatively weak (Walters & Gardner, 1985). Part of being successful in life is matching your particular profile to your career goals. President Richard Nixon is reported to have said, "I never made the [football] team. . . . I was not heavy enough to play the line, not fast enough to play halfback, and not smart enough to be a quarterback" (Collier, 2000). What do you think he meant by "smart" when he lamented his inadequacy?

As appealing as Gardner's theory of multiple intelligences is to many, it has not been embraced by all researchers. One problem is that the theory is difficult to test rigorously because some of the types of intelligence (such as bodily-kinesthetic, intrapersonal, and interpersonal) are difficult to measure reliably. Another problem is more fundamental: Some question whether the word *intelligence* should be applied so liberally; many of the abilities Gardner identifies, they say, have more to do with talents and skills than with intelligence per se.

Robert Sternberg (1985, 1988b) has also developed a theory of multiple intelligences, but he proposes only three types: analytic, practical, and creative. *Analytic intelligence,* the ability to learn to write clearly, do math, and understand literature, is critical for academic performance. *Practical intelligence* involves knowing how to do such things as fix a car or sew on a button, and sometimes relies on implicit memories, the unconscious biases and tendencies that guide our actions (see Chapter 5); "street smarts" are a form of practical intelligence. *Creative intelligence,* which seems closely related to fluid intelligence, is the ability to formulate novel solutions to problems.

How do these three types of intelligence relate to IQ? Analytic intelligence is what IQ tests measure. According to Sternberg and his colleagues (Sternberg & Wagner, 1993; Sternberg et al., 1993), however, measures of practical intelligence are better predictors of how well someone will do on the job than are standard measures of IQ, and practical intelligence is largely distinct from analytic intelligence. One study found that some Brazilians who as children failed math in school nevertheless could do the math required in their business lives (Carraher et al., 1985). Creative intelligence is also distinct from IQ, but people do need a certain level of IQ to be able to find creative solutions to problems or create novel products that have specific uses (Guilford, 1967; Runco & Albert, 1986; Sternberg, 1985).

People unquestionably differ in their relative strengths and weaknesses of various aspects of intelligence. Sternberg and his colleagues (summarized in Sternberg, 1997) found that if you are taught in a way that is compatible with your strongest type of intelligence, you will learn better. Thus, if you tend toward the practical, you would more easily learn how to construct something by observing a hands-on demonstration than by reading a set of directions. This is exciting research, which may eventually allow the detailed characterization of learning styles, permitting the development of teaching methods that play to the strengths of different students.

Children learn more easily if the teaching technique is compatible with their particular cognitive strengths.

Emotional Intelligence: Knowing Feelings

In everyday life, whether you act intelligently often depends in large part on how well you understand both your own emotions and how your actions will affect others. Have you ever seen someone you *know* is smart do something incredibly dumb—for instance, unintentionally or uncontrollably make a remark that infuriates a spouse or boss? Salovey and Mayer (1990) refer to the ability to understand and regulate emotions effectively as **emotional intelligence (EI).**

Emotional intelligence comprises five key abilities (Goleman, 1995; Mayer & Salovey, 1997, p. 5):

1. *Knowing your emotions,* which involves the ability to recognize emotions as they occur. For example, if you have high EI, you notice when you are becoming angry or depressed; by recognizing emotions as they arise, you are in a position to manage them rather than be managed by them.
2. *Managing your feelings,* which is essential for controlling impulses and bouncing back from failures. For example, when you feel yourself getting angry, you know that you should take a deep breath, count to 10, and bite back the reflexive nasty response on the tip of your tongue. Similarly, if you have high EI, you can put your disappointment at not reaching a goal in perspective and not let that emotion cloud your judgment.
3. *Self-motivation,* which is essential for persistence and self-control. For example, if you have high EI, you are able to decide that you want a good grade in a particular course (perhaps this one?) and be disciplined enough to study hard in spite of the tempting social distractions of college life.
4. *Recognizing others' emotions,* which is crucial for empathy. If you have high EI, you are able to infer how someone else feels, and to respond to them accordingly. People with high EI can easily learn to become good negotiators.
5. *Handling relationships,* which involves knowing how others will react emotionally to you. If you have high EI, you not only can recognize and understand your own emotions and those of others, but you also can anticipate what emotions your actions will trigger in others.

Emotional intelligence would seem to underlie at least part of what Sternberg means by practical intelligence, but it extends beyond that (Fox & Spector, 2000). Emotional intelligence can help you reason analytically by not allowing emotion to distract you or cloud your judgment; it can also inspire creative acts. Emotional intelligence can play a role in each of Gardner's multiple intelligences. Clearly, there is more than one type of intelligence, and IQ tests assess only some of them.

LOOKING AT LEVELS

A Threat in the Air

Taking IQ tests isn't simply a matter of flexing your intellectual muscles. As you no doubt know from experience, test-taking of any kind, whether an achievement test such as the SAT, or an IQ test, can be anxiety provoking. Test stress may manifest itself in distinct physical symptoms, such as a speeded-up heart rate and sweaty palms. And as you feel literally "put to the test," your thinking may become clouded by a variety of distracting thoughts. Thus, factors unrelated to intelligence may affect IQ scores and other test scores.

Researchers Steele and Aronson (1995) conducted a study to investigate the possible effects of negative racial stereotypes on the test-taking performance of African

Americans. They asked African American and white college students to take a test that included the most difficult items from the verbal portion of the Graduate Record Examination (GRE), an SAT-like test for graduate school. Some students, both African Americans and whites, were told that the test assessed intellectual ability; another mixed group was told that it was a study conducted by the laboratory. African Americans and whites did equally well when they were told that the test was simply a laboratory experiment, but African American students did much worse than whites when they thought the test measured intelligence. In another study, Steele and Aronson (1995) asked half the participants of each race to list their race immediately before taking the test. The test was always described as a laboratory study, not a test of intelligence. African Americans and whites performed the same when they did not list their races, but the simple act of being asked to list race drastically reduced the African American students' scores (such effects have since been reported by others, such as Croizet & Claire, 1998).

These studies dramatically illustrate the interactions of events at the levels of the brain, the person, and the group. According to Steele (1997), asking African Americans about race activates information in long-term memory about negative stereotypes, such as that African Americans are not smart. If you believe that a negative stereotype addresses issues that are important to you, then the mere possibility that others will see you as conforming to the image is threatening, even if you do not believe that you have the properties of the stereotype. Steele terms this phenomenon *stereotype threat*. When you are threatened, the autonomic nervous system is aroused (see Chapter 2) and leads you to become highly focused. In this case, the African American students may have focused on the threat presented by the stereotype. If so, then they would not focus as well on the task at hand. Gray (1999) has shown that reasoning is disrupted when a person has just witnessed an upsetting event, and a similar mechanism may be at work here.

Thus, a social invention—stereotypes about groups—can become part of an individual's knowledge (level of the person). And that knowledge in turn can be activated by social situations. When activated, the knowledge produces events in the brain (as well as in the body—pounding heart, sweaty palms, and so on; see Chapter 10 for a discussion of the stress response), which in turn disrupt performance. And the disrupted performance can then reinforce the stereotypes.

CONSOLIDATE!

1 **What is IQ?** IQ (intelligence quotient) is a score on an intelligence test. IQ originally was a comparison of mental age to chronological age, but now IQ scores relate performance to a norm. The most common tests, the Wechsler Adult Intelligence Scale (WAIS) and the Wechsler Intelligence Scale for Children (WISC), consist of two main parts, one that assesses verbal performance and one that assesses nonverbal performance. The scores are normed so that 100 is the mean, and each standard deviation is 15 points.

2 **Is intelligence a single characteristic, or a complex set of characteristics?** Intelligence has many facets. Although intelligence probably involves, as Charles Spearman theorized, a single general intellectual ability (symbolized as *g*), virtually all theorists agree that it also includes many specialized abilities. These abilities may be strong or weak, independently of *g*. Thurstone, for example, proposed that intelligence consists of seven primary mental abilities. Cattell and Horn initially theorized that instead of one general capacity, *g*, people possess two types of intelligence—crystallized and fluid—and then later expanded this list to include abilities like those identified by Thurstone. Gardner, in his theory of multiple intelligences, suggests eight basic forms of intelligence ranging from linguistic, to logical, to interpersonal. According to Sternberg, the different types of intelligence boil down to three: analytic, practical, and creative. Finally, emotional intelligence may affect the operation of all other types.

What Makes Us Smart? Nature and Nurture

Frank couldn't help but be envious of Hans's wonderful memory. Frank firmly believed that he would have possessed a much better memory if his parents had quizzed him frequently when he was a child. He knew that Hans's abilities were "hard-wired," courtesy of the droid's manufacturer, but felt that his own abilities were of a different sort. Was he right? How did the circumstances of Frank's life mold his intellectual strengths and weaknesses? It's difficult to know, in part because the vast majority of research on intellectual development has focused solely on IQ. Nevertheless, psychologists have learned a great deal about the forces that shape those aspects of intelligence that are indexed by IQ scores.

1 How do environment and genetics contribute to intelligence?

2 How can we interpret group differences in IQ?

3 What are the extremes of intelligence, high and low?

Smart Genes, Smart Environment: A Single System

Frank clearly had his strengths and weaknesses—as did Hans. Hans's weaknesses resulted from the way in which his "brain" was designed. Could the same be true, at least in part, for Frank? Could he be bright in some ways and less bright in others because of the genetic deck of cards he was dealt by his parents?

To understand the genetic contributions to intelligence, we first need to discover a bit more about genes themselves. In 1866 Gregor Mendel, an Augustinian monk living in what is now the Czech Republic, wrote one of the most fundamental papers in all of science. In it he formulated the core ideas of what is now known as **Mendelian inheritance**, the transmission of characteristics by individual elements of inheritance, each acting separately. Two ideas are key: (1) for each trait, an offspring inherits an "element" from each parent; and (2) in some cases, one of the elements dominates the other, and that is the one whose effect is apparent. If an element is not *dominant,* it is *recessive:* The effect of a recessive element is evident only when the offspring receives two copies of it, one from each parent. Mendel, through careful experimentation and record-keeping, traced these patterns of inheritance for a number of organisms (such as pea plants), but he never knew their mechanism. That great biochemical discovery, that the mysterious "elements" are genes, was not made until the early part of the 20th century.

In his pea plants, Mendel studied *traits,* such as skin texture and color; each trait, he observed, could appear in different "flavors," such as smooth or wrinkled, yellow or green. Thus a gene for a trait can have different forms, called *alleles,* one for each flavor. To inherit attached ear lobes or flat feet, for example, you need to receive the appropriate recessive allele from each of your parents. The sum total of your particular set of genes is your *genotype.*

Many genes express their effects only in combination with other genes. When this occurs, we see *quantitative* variations in characteristics, such as differences in height, size, or intelligence, not *qualitative* variations such as attached versus unattached ear lobes. In general, when a characteristic varies continuously, it reflects **complex inheritance**, the joint action of combinations of genes working together, rather than Mendelian inheritance, which describes the effects of individual elements of inheritance (Plomin & DeFries, 1998).

The genetic basis of intelligence is so complex that researchers initially had trouble identifying genes that are related to general intelligence as measured by IQ (Ball et al., 1998; Hill et al., 1999; Petrill et al., 1997a, 1997b; Skuder et al., 1995), and it took years to locate genes involved with intelligence (Chorney et al., 1998; Fisher et al., 1999; Miller, 1997). However, because intelligence is not unitary, we would not expect it to be determined by a single gene, or even a small number of genes. Studies have shown that multiple genes contribute to intelligence (for instance, Fisher et al., 1999), and it is now possible to use genetic data to help identify the different types of intelligence. For example, a portion of DNA has been found to be associated with one type of spatial ability (Berman & Noble, 1995) and not with general cognitive ability (Petrill et al., 1997b). These genes affect the brain, but in some yet-to-be-discovered ways.

Albert Einstein's name has become nearly synonymous with genius. Could his genes have given him a souped-up brain? Researchers found that his brain had unusually large numbers of neurons in both parietal lobes (Witelson et al., 1999) and large numbers of glial cells (which help to support neurons; Chapter 2) in the bottom portions of the left parietal lobe (Gardner et al., 1996); this part of the brain is involved in mathematical thinking (Dehaene, 1997) and spatial visualization (Kosslyn, 1994b). Other areas of Einstein's brain were relatively small, making the overall size of his brain only average.

How Important Are Genes for Intelligence?

Since genes contribute to intelligence in complex ways, how can we begin to sort out the relative contributions to intelligence of the genetic component and of other factors? How strong is the genetic influence?

The most common method of assessing the contribution of genes to a characteristic is to observe correlations among relatives who share different proportions of their genes versus unrelated people (see Chapter 2). Virtually all the research on the genetics of intelligence has focused on IQ scores, and this research is worth considering; however, we must always keep in mind the limited implications of such scores.

One way that researchers have tried to sort out the effects of genes versus environment is through *adoption studies*. In these studies the scores of adopted children are compared to those of their adopted versus biological relatives. In some of these studies, tests are given to twins who were separated soon after birth and adopted into different families (for example, Bouchard et al., 1990). Because these twins were reared in different homes, any similarities between them are thought to reflect their common genetics. What do adoption studies find? The correlations of IQs of adult identical twins who were raised apart is higher than that both for fraternal twins and for nontwin siblings raised together (Bouchard & McGue, 1981; Bouchard et al., 1990; Plomin, 1990). In addition, an adopted child's IQ correlates higher with the biological mother's IQ than with the adopted mother's IQ. Moreover, although the IQs of an adopted child and the biological children in a family are positively correlated, by the time the children grow up, virtually no correlation remains (Plomin, 1990; Scarr & Weinberg, 1983). These findings provide clear evidence that genes affect IQ.

Other studies have tried to find out exactly how large a role genes play in determining IQ by comparing IQs of people with different numbers of genes in common. The results clearly show that the more genes in common, the higher the correlations (Figure 6.9). The usual estimate is that the heritability of IQ is around .50, which means that about half the variation in IQ can be attributed to inherited characteristics (Chipuer et al., 1990; Loehlin, 1989). (Heritability scores indicate what proportion of observed variability in a characteristic is caused by inherited factors [Bell, 1977; Lush, 1937]; see Chapter 2 for a further discussion of

Figure 6.9 Genetic Relatedness and IQ

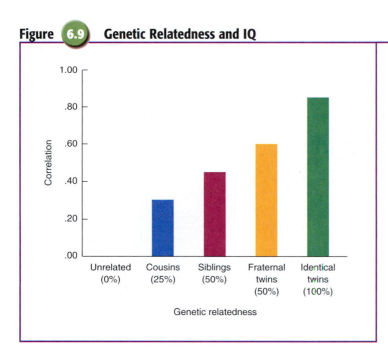

The correlations between people who are unrelated, cousins, siblings (nontwin brothers and sisters), and twins are graphed, along with their shared amounts of genes (in parentheses).

heritability.) Keep in mind that heritability estimates have no bearing on how much of *your* personal intelligence is the result of your genes versus environmental factors. The number that denotes heritability refers to the proportion of causes of variation within a population, not to the proportion of the characteristic that is inherited; and because it is an average, it does not apply to individuals.

Effects of the Environment: More Real Than Apparent?

Take another look at Figure 6.9, and compare the correlations between fraternal twins and those between other siblings. These pairs have the identical amount of common genes, 50%, and thus their IQ scores should be the same if intelligence is wholly determined by genes. But as you can see in the figure, the IQs of non-twin siblings are less correlated than those of fraternal twins (.45 versus .60), even though they have the same percentage of genes in common. What can account for this difference? Researchers assume that if scores are not related to genes, they must reflect effects of the environment.

It is clear that the environment affects intelligence as assessed by IQ. The observed relationship between IQ and achievement, noted earlier, can also run in the opposite direction: People who achieve more can develop higher scores (for example, see Kohn & Schooler, 1973; Neisser et al., 1996). Perhaps the best evidence for this comes from studies of the effects of formal schooling. For example, when poor black children moved from the rural South to Philadelphia in the 1940s, their IQs increased by a bit more than half a point for each year they spent in their new schools (Cahan & Cohen, 1989; Ceci, 1991; Ceci & Williams, 1997; Lee, 1951).

The correlations on which heritability scores are based may overestimate the role of genes and underestimate the role of the environment, even when the correlations are drawn from adoption studies. Consider some factors that make it difficult to interpret heritability scores based on studies of twins and relatives.

First, twins share much the same environment in the womb before birth and are subject to most of the same pluses and minuses of that residence. The fetus suffers when the mother has a bad diet, takes drugs or alcohol, smokes, or experiences a great deal of stress; the fetus profits when the mother eats well, takes vitamins, and doesn't drink, smoke, or take drugs. In addition, about two thirds of identical twins even share the same placenta and amniotic sac in the uterus (see Figure 6.10),

Figure **Fraternal and Identical Twins**

Twins can have separate placentas and separate amniotic sacs or share a single placenta and sac; sharing results in greater similarity prior to birth. Virtually all fraternal twins are in separate sacs (left), whereas about two thirds of identical twins are in the same sac (right).

which increases the similarity of the prenatal environment compared with that of fraternal twins, who are almost always in separate sacs (Phelps et al., 1997). Twins in the same sac share blood, which contains chemicals that affect brain development. Aspects of this common environment affect later IQ (Devlin et al., 1997) and are shared even by twins separated at birth and raised apart (Phelps et al., 1997). Thus, the high correlations between identical twins separated at birth may reflect their early shared environment as well as their shared genes.

Second, after birth, it is not clear just how different the environmental influences on twins raised in different homes really are. Families that seek to adopt a child share many characteristics, and these similarities are further enhanced by the fact that adoption agencies frown on placing children in deprived conditions. The households in which twins are placed often are more similar than not. When Stoolmiller (1999) mathematically corrected for the small variations among adopting families, he estimated the effects of environment on IQ to be 57%. It is not clear, however, whether this estimate applies only to this special situation of twins raised apart or can be taken as a general estimate.

Third, aspects of the genes can help shape the environment itself. The **microenvironment** is the environment you create by your very presence. For one thing, identical twins may have more aspects of their environments in common than fraternal twins because much of our environment is social, and people respond to us in part because of the way we look and behave. So if both twins are physically appealing, they will be treated very differently than if both are homely; ditto for twins who are sluggish and overweight or are athletic and trim. Also, to the extent that children have similar inborn tendencies, their behavior may shape their environments in similar ways. For example, children who enjoy being read to will reinforce adults for this activity, leading the adults to buy or borrow more books and thus providing more opportunity for stimulating interactions. In addition, depending on their personalities, people select aspects of the environment that appeal to them (perhaps, initially, for genetic reasons), and thus what appear to be different environments may in fact function as very much the same environment for two people with similar inclinations. For example, two homes may differ in the number of books they contain, but a child who likes to read may seize on whatever is available and end up reading as much in a home with few books as a child who lives in a home with many books. In short, identical twins share many characteristics that define the microenvironment, and so they live in more similar microenvironments than do other siblings. Even twins separated at birth may create similar microenvironments, and so it is not clear exactly how different the environmental influences on the twins are in the different homes.

Finally, researchers have typically observed that only about a quarter or a third of the variability in *g* can be explained by shared environment, aspects of the family setting that are present for all siblings in a household, such as the number of books in the house (Plomin et al., 1997, p. 142). If genes account for about half the variability, and shared environment for less than half of what remains, what accounts for the rest? Some aspects of the environment don't have the same effect on all children growing up in the household; the same event can be a very different experience for different people. Watching television can be the mindless pastime of a couch potato, or it can be a stimulating experience. Even if the environment of two children appears to be identical, its influence depends in part on each child's predispositions and inclinations, which may be partly innate (Kagan, 1994a; Turkheimer & Waldron, 2000). A shy child, for example, will be pleased to be left alone to find solitary amusements; the same treatment would be a punishment for an outgoing, gregarious child. The *perceived* environment, not the objective environment, is the important one.

In general, any effects of a shared family environment on children's IQs, which produce positive correlations among the scores of all children who grow up in the same house, wear off by adulthood, and genetic influences become increasingly

Microenvironment: The environment created by a person's own presence, which depends partly on appearance and behavior.

evident with age (McCartney et al., 1990; McGue et al., 1993; Plomin, 1990). Why? One theory is that, as people age, they are increasingly able to select their environments, and genetically determined properties, such as temperament, lead people to select some environments over others. For example, if you are temperamentally shy, you will not take a job in sales; if you are outgoing, you might enjoy managing a hotel. Thus, as you grow older and have more choices about how to live, the effects of your early environment are increasingly dependent on the effects of genes (Neisser et al., 1996). This does not mean, however, that the environment is not playing a crucial role in helping you function well.

These two men may have similar genes for height, but if so these genes have exerted different effects. The reaction range *(Scarr, 1976; Scarr & McCartney, 1983; Weinberg, 1989) is the set of possible reactions to environmental events that is established by the genes. Where you fall within this range depends on environmental factors (such as nutrition). In general, the narrower the reaction range, the more deterministic the effects of the genes. For some genes, such as those associated with Huntington's disease (De Marchi & Mennella, 2000; Gontkovsky, 1998), simply having the gene is enough to produce an effect. Most genes that affect our psychologies, however, are regulated by our interactions with the environment.*

Group Differences in Intelligence

How would you feel if you were told that you are a member of a group that is genetically stupid? Many groups have faced such charges, often with far-reaching consequences. The Immigration Act of 1924 aimed to minimize immigration to the United States of "biologically weak stocks," a term that was defined to include Italians and Jews of southern and eastern Europe. During congressional testimony, supporters of the bill pointed to the results of intelligence tests, on which recent immigrants scored less well than established Americans with northern European roots. There is debate about the extent to which this testimony mattered (Snyderman & Herrnstein, 1983), but no debate over the catastrophic effects of this bill less than 20 years later, during World War II, when Jews attempting to escape Nazi Germany were severely restricted from immigrating to the United States.

Contemporary studies comparing IQ scores find that some groups score lower than others on IQ tests; for example, Jews of European descent in Israel score about 15 points higher than Jews of North African descent. What do such findings mean?

Within-Group Versus Between-Group Differences

If, as most experts have concluded, about 50% of the differences in IQ can be accounted for by differences in genes, is it reasonable to say that differences in IQs between groups are largely genetic? Absolutely not. The genetic contribution to intelligence *within* a given group cannot say anything about possible genetic differences *between* groups (Block, 1995; Lewontin, 1976a, 1976b; Plomin, 1988). To see why not, imagine that you have two orchards with the same kind of apple trees. You make sure that each orchard receives exactly the same amounts of sunlight, fertilizer, water, and so on. If you succeed in making the environments identical, then any differences in the sizes of apples from the two orchards should reflect genetic differences among the trees. However, say the two orchards have overall different conditions, that one gets more sunshine and water than the other. *Within* each orchard, differences in the sizes of the apples would reflect genetic differences. But those differences say nothing about the differences *between* the orchards. The disadvantaged environment puts the trees in one orchard in a generally lower part of the reaction range than those benefiting from the advantaged environment. It is even possible that the differences within the "advantaged" orchard reflect the operation of one set of genes, whereas the differences within the "disadvantaged" orchard reflect the operation of another set that allows the trees to make the most of skimpy amounts of sunshine or water. No question about it: Differences within one group cannot be used to explain differences between groups or within another group.

When you see an apple, all you have to go on is its present size; you have no way of knowing the range of possible sizes. Similarly, when you meet Frank, you have no way of knowing the range of his possible intelligence. Further, heritability tells you only about the effects of a *certain environment* on the genes; it says nothing about the possible effects of *other environments* (Hirsch, 1971, 1997). There is no way to know how tall, or smart, Frank would have been if he (or his mother, while pregnant) had had a different diet, experienced less stress at certain periods of their lives, and so on.

Test bias: Test design features that lead a particular group to perform well or poorly and that thus invalidate the test.

Race Differences: Bias in Testing?

Asian Americans tend to score higher on IQ tests than white Americans, who in turn tend to score higher than African Americans (Neisser et al., 1996; Rushton, 1995; Suzuki & Valencia, 1997); Hispanics tend to score between whites and African Americans. For decades, the relatively low IQ scores of African Americans have attracted attention, and controversy has flared over arguments that their scores, and their poorer achievement, are rooted in their genes. A firestorm of debate raged when Richard Herrnstein and Charles Murray (1994) published *The Bell Curve,* in which they argued that IQ not only predicts many aspects of life and performance, but also that differences in IQ are largely genetic. However, as discussed earlier, it's not easy to disentangle effects of the environment (particularly the microenvironment) and genes. Although we focus on whites and African Americans in the following discussion, as has most of the research literature, keep in mind that the same issues also apply to all groups that generally score relatively poorly on IQ tests.

What do we make of the finding that white Americans have an average IQ that is 10 to 15 points higher than the average among African Americans? Block (1995) and Nisbett (1996), among others, discuss this issue at length. The following observations are worth some thought.

First, some have argued that the disparity in test scores simply reflects the fact that the tests were designed for a white middle-class culture and thus are biased against African Americans, who have a different set of common experiences. This sort of **test bias** is relevant for the verbal and general information parts of the IQ test, but what about the performance parts? The race difference in IQ is present even here. So a simple "biased testing" explanation is probably not correct (Neisser et al., 1996). However, it is possible that people with different backgrounds are more or less comfortable taking these sorts of tests at all. Indeed, Serpell (1979) found that Zambian children could reproduce patterns better using wire models (which they often used to make their own toys) than using pencil and paper, but vice versa for English children from the same social class (who were used to paper and pencil but not wire models).

Second, others have argued that the IQ difference is caused by environmental differences. The people who are best off in U.S. society tend to score higher on IQ tests, and so do their children. (Some children from better-off families even receive expensive tutoring in how to take SAT tests, which are in many ways similar to IQ tests; Schwartz, 1999.) African Americans typically make less money than do whites, and this factor could cause environmental differences that lead them to score lower than whites. Some orchards get less sun and water than others, and thus the trees tend to bear smaller fruit. If this is the crucial cause of the IQ difference, then we would expect IQ to rise among African Americans as their economic circumstances improve. And in fact researchers have noted that recently the gap between African American and white IQ scores is shrinking. For older children the difference between the IQs of African Americans and whites is now only two-thirds of what it had been (Thorndike et al., 1986); some researchers have found even smaller differences (Vincent, 1991; see also Flynn, 1999c). Flynn (1999b) points out that IQ differences between whites and African Americans can be accounted for if "the average environment for African Americans of 1995 matches the quality of the average environment for whites in 1945" (p. 15).

African children who are accustomed to making their own playthings, like this toy car made of wire, are more adept at using wire models in pattern reproduction tests.

The increased scores may reflect more than the rising economy. Grissmer and colleagues (1994) report that the education level of the parents of African American children has risen faster than that of other groups, and this factor appears to affect the children's achievement. In addition, children from smaller families tend to have higher IQ scores, and African Americans showed the largest shift of any racial or ethnic group toward smaller family sizes in the years 1970 to 1990. The fact that such environmental factors can contribute to changing IQ scores suggests that these factors may have had something to do with the scores in the first place. However, these data are only correlations, which cannot tell us about causes and effects.

Third, some have argued that the microenvironment plays a key role in race differences. African American people have darker skin, which is part of their microenvironment; in the United States, this cue may elicit certain negative treatment from the white majority. What would happen in a society in which the majority did not respond this way? Consider this example: Eyferth (1961) studied the IQs of German children who were fathered by white or African American U.S. servicemen right after World War II. If the African American fathers had lower IQs than the white fathers, which is not known but is likely given the group averages, then the notion that genes are responsible for this difference would lead us to expect that their children should also have had lower IQs. But they didn't. Both groups of children had the same average IQs. At that time, there were very few African Americans in Germany and the majority whites may not have had negative stereotypes about them. Thus, the children may not have experienced negative environmental influences because of their racial background.

Finally, it is crucial to realize that the distributions in IQ between races overlap; plenty of African Americans have higher IQs than plenty of whites. Group differences do not necessarily apply to any particular individual.

Sex Differences

Group differences in intelligence are often cast as race differences, but consider another possible group difference that would affect fully half the population. Are there sex differences in IQ scores? Although some findings may suggest very small sex differences in IQ (Dai & Lynn, 1994; Held et al., 1993), these effects are not always found (Aluja-Fabregat et al., 2000; Jensen, 1998). Instead, researchers typically find that males are better at some tasks than are females, and vice versa. In general, males tend to be better than females at tasks that require spatial reasoning, whereas females tend to be better than males at tasks that require verbal reasoning. Such differences have been found in at least 30 countries (Beller & Gafni, 1996; Halpern, 1992; Vogel, 1996).

Some theorists have tried to explain sex differences in spatial ability by pointing to the role differences of our primitive ancestors (D. Buss, 1995; Eals & Silverman, 1994; Geary, 1996a). The men, in this view, were out hunting, which required the ability to navigate and recall where the home cave was, whereas the women stayed home, picking berries, weaving baskets, and tending children. But we really don't know much about what our male and female ancestors actually did, and even in this scenario it isn't clear that women engaged in fewer spatial tasks. Gathering food requires remembering where the food is likely to grow and remembering how to return home, and weaving baskets and cloth certainly requires spatial processing (Halpern, 1997).

At least some of the sex differences arise from the effects of sex hormones (Kimura, 1994). One study examined women who were about to have sex-change operations to become men. As part of the procedure, the women received massive doses of male hormones, specifically testosterone. Within three months of treatment, spatial abilities increased and verbal abilities decreased (Van Goozen et al., 1995). Researchers have even found that a woman's spatial abilities shift during the course of her monthly cycle, as the balance of hormones changes (Hampson, 1990; Hampson & Kimura, 1988). By the same token, the level of male hormones shifts during the course of the day and over the seasons, and researchers have found that American males are worse at spatial abilities in the fall, when their levels of male hormones are highest, than in the spring. The effects of these hormones are not more-is-better, but rather are like an upside-down U: Too little or too much is worse than intermediate amounts (Kimura, 1994). Elderly men have low levels of male hormones, and thus it is interesting that testosterone supplements boost their scores on spatial tests (Janowsky et al., 1994).

Researchers are also now discovering differences in the structure and function of the brains of men and women. For example, it has long been known that the cerebral hemispheres are not as sharply specialized in women as in men (Jancke & Steinmetz, 1994; Springer & Deutsch, 1998), and such anatomical differences may underlie some functional differences (Gur et al., 1999; Mansour et al., 1996; Shaywitz et al., 1995).

In addition, at least part of the sex differences may arise from how boys and girls are treated in our society. Boys and girls are encouraged to take part in "sex appropriate" activities (Lytton & Romney, 1991). This is important in part because if you do not perform spatial activities, spatial abilities do not develop (Baenninger & Newcombe, 1989). Traditionally, girls have not been encouraged to participate in as many spatial activities, such as climbing trees and playing ball, as boys. In terms of genes, it's analogous to your muscles getting bigger only if you lift heavy things, causing genes to turn on to produce more proteins. Lack of participation in spatial activities means that the neural systems that underlie spatial activities are not exercised. Subrahmanyam and Greenfield (1994) showed that spatial abilities could be improved by having children play certain video games, and that boys and girls in their studies improved the same amount. However, sex differences can be measured even in early childhood, and so are unlikely to be totally the result of learning (Reinisch & Sanders, 1992; Robinson et al., 1996).

Finally, keep in mind that many females are better at spatial reasoning than many males, and many males are better at verbal abilities than many females. Here, too, differences in the means of groups say nothing about differences among particular individuals.

Researchers have discovered that people living today are generally smarter than their ancestors! This change was documented by James R. Flynn (1984, 1999a, 1999b, 1999c) and is now called the Flynn effect. In the Western world, IQ scores have generally risen about three points every 10 years. There is even evidence that the Flynn effect is accelerating: Between 1972 and 1982, IQ increased by an average of 8 points. Why? Perhaps because life today is more challenging, we have better nutrition, or technology (such as TV and computers) has taught us how to think in ways that are required to do well on IQ tests (Flynn, 1999a; Lynn, 1990; Neisser et al., 1996; Williams, 1998).

Diversity in Intelligence

Hans was the 501st "Enforcer Droid" produced by the factory, each of which was absolutely identical in appearance and abilities. As a biological species, humans have variety. Frank thought of himself as basically average, but when it came to solving problems creatively he was in some ways gifted. Other humans have not been so lucky and are mentally impaired. In this section, we consider the extreme forms of intelligence, high and low. Moreover, we examine the bases of perhaps the highest form of thought (that which most clearly puts Hans's merely mechanical mind to shame), creativity.

Mental Retardation: People With Special Needs

For want of a better definition, people with an IQ score of 70 or lower (that is, who fall more than two standard deviations below the mean) are traditionally considered to be **mentally retarded.** The American Association for Mental Retardation (1992) specifies two additional criteria: "significant limitations" in two or

Mentally retarded: People who have an IQ of 70 or less and significant limitations in at least two aspects of everyday life since childhood.

more everyday abilities, such as communication, self-care, and self-direction; and the presence of the condition since childhood.

About 7 million Americans are considered mentally retarded (Fryers, 1993). Mental retardation affects about 100 times more people than does total blindness (Batshaw & Perret, 1992). One out of every 10 families in the United States is directly affected by mental retardation (American Association for Mental Retardation, 1992).

Retardation does not imply an inability to learn. Mildly retarded people can learn to function well as adults, and behavioral techniques that involve explicit shaping and reinforcement (see Chapter 4) can allow even severely retarded people to master many tasks.

Mental retardation results when the brain fails to develop properly, which can happen in the womb or during childhood. Although hundreds of causes have now been identified, the causes of about one-third of all cases are still mysteries. However, it is clear that both genetic and environmental factors can lead to retardation (see Table 6.3).

The most common type of mental retardation (occurring in about 1 in 1,000 births) is known as **Down syndrome**, first described by British physician J. Langdon Down in 1866. Down children have an average IQ of 55, and as teenagers they have the linguistic abilities of 3-year-olds. The most common form of Down syndrome is not inherited, but it is caused by a genetic problem—the creation of

TABLE 6.3 **Causes of Retardation: Common Examples**

Source: From http://thearc.org/faqs/mrqa.html

Genetic conditions
- Down syndrome
- Fragile X syndrome
- Phenylketonuria (PKU)

Problems during pregnancy
- Use of alcohol or drugs
- Malnutrition
- Rubella
- Glandular disorders and diabetes
- Illnesses of the mother during pregnancy
- Physical malformations of the brain and HIV infection in the fetus

Problems at birth
- Prematurity
- Low birth weight

Problems after birth
- Childhood diseases such as whooping cough, chicken pox, and measles, which may lead to meningitis and encephalitis, which can in turn damage the brain
- Accidents such as a blow to the head or near drowning
- Lead and mercury poisoning

Poverty and cultural deprivation
- Malnutrition
- Disease-producing conditions
- Inadequate medical care
- Environmental health hazards

Down syndrome: A type of retardation that results from the creation of an extra chromosome during conception; it is genetic but not inherited.

Fetal alcohol syndrome: A type of retardation caused by excessive drinking of alcohol by the mother during pregnancy.

Gifted: People who have IQs of at least 135, but more commonly between 150 and 180.

Prodigies: People who early in life demonstrate immense talent in a particular domain, such as music or mathematics, but who are normal in other domains.

Creativity: The ability to produce something original of high quality or to devise effective new ways of solving a problem.

an extra chromosome (number 21) during conception. This problem is more likely to occur in older mothers, whose eggs have been dormant for many years.

Drinking and driving don't mix; neither do drinking and pregnancy. If the mother drinks heavily during pregnancy, her child can be born with **fetal alcohol syndrome.** Part of this syndrome is mental retardation (Streissguth et al., 1989, 1999). Indeed, many environmental factors can lead to mental retardation. If the pregnant mother experiences malnutrition, rubella, diabetes, HIV infection, high doses of X rays, or any of a number of infections, her child may be born with mental retardation. Streissguth and colleagues (1989) found that taking antibiotics and even aspirin during pregnancy also can adversely affect the developing baby's brain. Because in these cases the condition is environmentally induced, people whose retardation is due to such circumstances tend not to have retarded children themselves.

Mental retardation can also arise if the birth is unusually difficult and the infant's brain is injured. Premature birth and low birth weight put the child at risk for retardation. In addition, some childhood diseases, such as chicken pox and measles, can sometimes cause brain damage, as can ingesting lead, mercury, or poisons. Vaccines and other treatments have greatly reduced the incidence of mental retardation over the past several decades (Alexander, 1991).

If a mother drinks alcohol heavily during pregnancy, her child can be born with fetal alcohol syndrome—one aspect of which is mental retardation.

The Gifted

There is no hard and fast way to determine whether a person is **gifted;** the term is sometimes used to refer to people who have IQs of at least 135, but more commonly *gifted* denotes the 150–180 range (Winner, 1997). Much of the research on the gifted has focused on people with very high IQs, greater than 150, and that is the criterion we will adopt here. It is not known how genes and the environment, including the environment in the womb, contribute to the condition.

As expected from the idea of multiple intelligences, children can be gifted in some domains while not being gifted in others. **Prodigies,** children with immense talent in a particular area, may be perfectly normal in other domains; for example, mathematically gifted children often are not gifted in other domains (Benbow & Minor, 1990). Achter and colleagues (1996) found that over 95% of the gifted children they tested had sharply differing mathematical and verbal abilities.

According to some researchers (such as Jackson & Butterfield, 1986), gifted children do the same kinds of processing as average children but simply do it more effectively. As Winner (1997) notes, however, some children "as young as three or four years of age have induced rules of algebra on their own (Winner, 1996), have memorized almost instantly entire musical scores (Feldman & Goldsmith, 1991), and have figured out on their own how to identify all prime numbers (Winner, 1996)" (p. 1071). Such intellectual feats suggest that the cognition of gifted children may be qualitatively different from that of the rest of us. Specifically, Winner suggests that gifted children may be exceptionally able to intuit solutions to problems and may be driven by an extraordinary passion to master tasks.

The gifts are sometimes bestowed with a price. Gifted children are often socially awkward and are sometimes treated as "geeks" and "nerds" (Silverman, 1993a, 1993b; Winner, 2000). In addition, they are often solitary and introverted (Silverman, 1993b). They have twice the rate of emotional and social problems as nongifted children (Winner, 1997).

If you aren't gifted as a child, does this mean you have no hope of becoming a gifted adult? Not at all. Many distinguished adults—Charles Darwin, for example—showed no signs of being gifted as children (Simonton, 1994); conversely, most gifted children grow up to be rather ordinary adults (Richert, 1997; Winner, 2000).

Creative Smarts

Creativity is the ability to produce something original of high quality or to devise effective new ways of solving problems. Some people are undoubtedly more creative than others. Why?

Creativity often involves an interplay between two types of thinking, convergent *and* divergent *(Guilford, 1967). With convergent thinking, you stay focused on one particular approach to a problem and work through a series of steps to arrive at a solution. With divergent thinking, you approach a problem from a variety of angles, exploring many possible solution strategies before settling on one (Mednick, 1962). For example, divergent thinking might lead you to consider bricks as doorstops, supports for bookshelves, or as bookends. Convergent thinking also has an important role in creativity—in setting up a problem in the first place, or in cutting back the lush jungle of ideas created by divergent thinking.*

Amabile (1983, 1998) found that creative people keep options open, do not make snap decisions about the likely outcome of an effort, and are good at seeing a problem from a new vantage point. Similarly, when Guilford used factor analysis to discover which underlying abilities are tapped by various tests of creativity, he found that flexibility and the ability to reorganize information were key (similar conclusions were drawn by Aguilar-Alonso, 1996, and Eysenck, 1995). In addition, creative people are often highly motivated and persistent, driven to create (Sulloway, 1996).

Are creative people born that way? Unlike IQ, differences in creativity are not strongly related to genetic differences, if at all. Moreover, and also in contrast to IQ, shared aspects of the home (such as exposure to cultural resources, home libraries, or parents' mechanical or artistic hobbies) strongly affect creativity (Canter, 1973; Nichols, 1978; Simonton, 1988).

Other researchers have looked for the roots of creativity by examining the lives of creative people. Simonton (1984, 1988, 1990) found that in spite of romantic images of the moody Russian composer, the drunken Irish poet, and the poor Southerner beaten as a child, the amount of stress people experience is not related to how creative they are, and social recognition of a person's accomplishments neither increases nor decreases creativity. In addition, the most creative people had intermediate amounts of formal education; either too much or too little formal education apparently stifles creativity (Simonton, 1988).

Are highly creative people mentally unstable? It has long been believed that certain mental disorders promote creativity (Kraepelin, 1921). Manic-depressive (bipolar) mental illness can result in shifts between very "high" energetic moods and very "low" depressed ones. Kay Redfield Jamison and her collaborators (Goodwin & Jamison, 1990; Jamison, 1989; Jamison et al., 1980; see also Hershman & Lieb, 1988, 1998) have argued that a "loosening" of thought that occurs during the manic phase enhances creativity. If so, the manic phase may spur creativity by increasing the number of possible solutions a person can formulate during the creative process. Isaac Newton, Charles Dickens, and Kurt Cobain apparently suffered from this disorder, and Andreasen (1987) found that almost half the visiting faculty in the University of Iowa Writers' Workshop, an intensive course for creative writers, had experienced it. Jamison (1989) reports similar findings, particularly for poets.

Others have claimed, however, that mental illness is independent of creativity; these claims are consistent with analyses of Dennis (1966) and Simonton (1984, 1997), who showed that the quality of a creative person's work tends to be constant over their productive years; in years when a large number of particularly good works are produced, a correspondingly large number of inferior works are also produced.

In short, many different factors underlie creativity. Although creative people may share certain general strategies, they have little else in common.

In some ways creativity is like pitching in baseball. Cy Young was the pitcher with the greatest number of wins in baseball history. The pitcher with the most losses? Cy Young. People who produce increased numbers of creative works are also likely to produce increased numbers of mundane works.

LOOKING AT LEVELS

Creative Freedom?

Many people believe that true creative thought requires freedom; others have argued that creativity thrives in the presence of a great deal of structure. According to the latter view, the more precisely a problem is specified, and the clearer the approach, the easier it is to be creative.

A particularly powerful demonstration of this idea was provided by Goldenberg and colleagues (1999), who programmed a computer to engage in the most extreme form of structured thinking: following an algorithm, a step-by-step set of rules. The researchers first studied effective advertisements and noticed that they seemed to rely on a few simple ideas (which are involved in creativity in general; Boden, 2000). For instance, many involved replacing the properties of one thing with the properties of another thing. An ad for Bally shoes, for example, suggested that their shoes gave wearers a sense of freedom by showing clouds or an inviting island in the shape of a shoe; the sense of freedom conveyed by clouds and the island was intended to transfer to the shoes. After being armed with such rules, the computer was asked to describe ads for specific products that conveyed certain messages; its suggestions were then compared to those from humans (who were not in the ad business). Here are some examples of what the computer and humans produced (as reported by Angier, 1999):

Goal: Convey that Apple computers are user-friendly.
Computer idea: An Apple computer offers flowers.
Human idea: An Apple computer next to a PC, with the claim: "This is the friendliest computer."

Goal: Convey that Jeeps have very quiet engines.
Computer idea: Two Jeeps communicating in sign language.
Human idea: A car alone in the country.

Goal: Convey that an airline has on-time performance.
Computer idea: A cuckoo in the shape of a jumbo jet popping out of a cuckoo clock.
Human idea: A family running to an airplane, with one of the parents screaming, "Let's run, I know this airline's planes are always right on time."

Which ideas do you like better? When the ads were judged by both advertising professionals and others, the computer's ideas came out on top: The judges rated its suggestions as more creative and original than those of the humans. In fact, the computer's suggestions were often judged virtually as good as actual award-winning ads.

But don't give up on the power of human creativity. When humans were taught the rules programmed into the computer (which involved events at the level of the group, which in turn altered processing in the brain), they did as well as, and sometimes better than, the computer. Although such training remains highly limited to a particular type of problem, such as writing advertisements, it is important to recognize that structure—in both the social and physical world and the rules we learn—can help creativity rather than hinder it. Why should people be motivated to learn the rules and work within structure? Because they learn (from events at the level of the group) that following this road can make them perform better, and thus they change their beliefs and motivations (at the level of the person).

CONSOLIDATE!

1 *How do environment and genetics contribute to intelligence?* In general, approximately 50% of the variability in IQ scores can be attributed to variations in genes. At least some of these effects may, in fact, reflect the way that the environment is regulating the genes or the way that genes in turn affect the environment (including by influencing appearance and temperament, which affect the microenvironment). Genes define a range of possibilities, and the environment places each individual within that range.

2 *How can we interpret group differences in IQ?* Although group differences definitely exist, it is impossible to sort out the relative contributions made by genes and the environment in creating such differences. Findings about the genetic contribution to within-group differences do not apply to between-group differences. In addition, all distributions of abilities within any group overlap those of other groups; for this reason, group differences cannot be applied to particular individuals.

3 *What are the extremes of intelligence, high and low?* Mental retardation is usually defined as having since childhood an IQ that is more than two standard deviations below the mean IQ and having significant limitations in two or more everyday abilities. Researchers have identified hundreds of causes of mental retardation. Some types are caused by genetic abnormalities; others are caused by environmental events, such as childhood infections. Gifted people are defined as those having high IQs, typically more than two standard deviations above the mean, and often three or more standard deviations above the mean. It is not clear how the genes and environment interact to produce such high IQs. Finally, creative people are not born that way, but rather have learned certain cognitive strategies. Although creative people are typically highly motivated and driven to create, their creativity is not a by-product of mental instability.

Recap and Thought Questions

Language: More Than Meets the Ear

Language relies on phonology (proper speech sounds), syntax (sentences that are formed according to the rules of grammar), semantics (words, phrases, and sentences that convey meaning), and pragmatics (indirect or implied meaning). Some aspects of language may be learned well only during childhood, particularly phonology and grammar.

Could Hans really use language? Hans has perfect phonology, syntax, and semantics, but his pragmatics are faulty. He is unamused by humor and befuddled by novel metaphors. He would probably understand metaphors better if he memorized more of them, but the droid might always be humor-challenged. The fact that Hans hadn't mastered pragmatics perfectly does not mean that he fails to have language; in fact, he has the ability to use all four of the key characteristics—just not perfectly. Similarly, someone who speaks a language with an accent still speaks it, but not perfectly.

Think It Through. If it had been your job to teach English to Hans, where would you have started? Is one aspect of language—phonology, syntax, semantics, or pragmatics—more important than the others? Which aspect, if partially lacking, would be least missed? Hans apparently has difficulty using the pragmatic aspects of language. How would this shortcoming affect him socially?

When George Washington became the first president of the United States, the question of a title and form of address suitable for the leader of this new nation arose. John Adams proposed "His Highness, the President." For a time, Washington's own favorite was "His Mightiness, the President" (Seuling, 1978). Do you think the title would make any difference in how people thought of or treated the President?

Foundations of Thought

Thought cannot rely solely on words or images: For one thing, both types of representations are ambiguous, and thoughts are not. Thoughts arise from manipulations of concepts, which specify groupings of objects or events; the representations of concepts are unambiguous and can be concrete (such as the concept of a bird) or abstract (such as the concept of justice). We use words and images in thinking as a way of keeping track of our thoughts and storing them effectively, much as we might make notations on a pad of paper while devising a plan. Both images and words can play important roles in helping you keep track of where you are in a problem and in

providing insights about how best to proceed. A great deal of thinking involves solving problems. If a problem is not specified appropriately from the outset, it will be difficult to solve. People can solve problems by using heuristics (rules of thumb) and algorithms (sets of steps that are guaranteed to produce the answer).

Could Hans have been built to use only language when thinking? No "natural language" (such as English or Spanish) could be used as the sole means of thought. If Hans is to work effectively with Frank and other humans, he needs to speak English or another natural language—and such languages cannot be the sole vehicle of thought.

Think It Through. Is it better to use words or images when thinking? In general or for certain purposes? If only for certain purposes, which kinds of thinking would best be accomplished with words? With images?

Some forms of representation play critical roles in pragmatics. Consider this joke: A man showed up at his job one day with a huge bandage over each ear. A coworker asked him what happened. He replied, "I was ironing and was lost in thought. The phone rang, and without thinking I lifted my hand to answer it." The coworker was aghast, but then asked, "But what about the other ear?" "Oh," the man replied, "then I had to call the doctor." This is a visual joke, and people who do not form mental images well don't seem to get it. Can you think of other such jokes? If Hans lacked the ability to use mental imagery, such jokes would be lost on him. What other sorts of things would you avoid asking him? How would such a limitation affect his social life?

Logic, Reasoning, and Decision Making

Reasoning involves seeing what follows from a given set of circumstances and making decisions at pivotal points. Decisions require you to evaluate possible outcomes and choose one while discarding the others. We often rely on heuristics, such as availability, when reaching decisions. These shortcuts often lead us to draw the correct conclusion faster than we could with a step-by-step algorithm; however, they may also lead to errors.

In what ways is Frank's reasoning superior to Hans's? Hans is literally a logic machine, but Frank's heuristic shortcuts often enable him to draw the correct conclusion faster than Hans does, despite Hans's superfast circuits.

Is There More Than One Way to Be Smart?

Frank is average at most things, but unusually good at creative problem solving. The most common measure of intelligence is the score on an intelligence test, IQ. This measure is a composite of many different underlying abilities, and the same IQ score can arise from different mixtures of relative strengths and weaknesses. Today, scores are based on norms, which are updated periodically so that the mean score on the WAIS and the WISC is always 100 and the standard deviation is 15. To be smart in a particular way means to be able to solve difficult problems of particular types and to understand and learn particular types of information more effectively than those who are intellectually slower. You can be smart in some ways, but not so smart in others.

Is Frank smart? This question has built into it an unwarranted assumption—namely, that anyone could be described simply as "smart" in general. Frank has only a middling memory ability, but his verbal fluency and creative abilities are above average. Frank is neither "smart" nor "stupid"; like the rest of us, he has an intelligence profile, which includes areas of relative strength and weakness.

What Makes Us Smart: Nature and Nurture

How can we explain differences in intelligence among individuals? These variations probably reflect an intimate dance between the genes and environment. Genes set the possible limits of an individual's different aspects of intelligence; the environment positions an individual within this range. Although about 50% of the variability

in scores on IQ tests can be explained in terms of inheritance, this number is an average and does not apply to individuals.

Group differences in IQ have been well documented, but the interpretation of such variations remains unclear. Group differences on some abilities, such as sex differences for spatial abilities, may reflect biological differences—for example, in hormone levels. Other group differences—in IQ, for example—may arise in part from the ways in which the environment affects individuals and the ways your characteristics, which create your microenvironment, influence the reactions of others to you. Environmental effects can also occur at the time one is actually taking an IQ test; when this happens, test scores are not valid indicators of ability.

Are Frank's intellectual weaknesses genetic? All we have to go on is Frank's present intelligence profile. Thus, it is impossible to know the range of possibilities that were inherent in his genes. His present levels of intelligences arose from a combination of his genes and the way they interacted with his environment.

Diversity in Intelligence

Intelligence varies according to a normal curve, so there are as many people at the top end as there are at the bottom end. Retardation is traditionally defined on the basis of overall IQ score and significant difficulty with everyday tasks, with both conditions having existed since childhood. By this definition, someone who is retarded cannot be gifted; giftedness is defined by a very high IQ score. Mental retardation can arise for many reasons, some genetic and some environmental. Some genetic reasons reflect accidents during conception or environmental damage to the genes.

Creativity leads to the production of something original or new ways of effectively solving a problem. True creativity involves producing something of value, not just something novel. This ability is not influenced strongly by genetic factors, but instead appears to reflect specific strategies that people have developed. Creative people are not any more likely than anyone else to be mentally ill or unstable.

Could Hans be considered gifted? Yes, by standard definitions of the term he could be considered gifted. This classification, however, does not imply that he can perform all kinds of tasks at superior levels.

Think It Through. The eugenics movement seeks to improve the human species by encouraging those with extremely low IQs not to have children. Do you think this is a good idea? What counts as "smart" depends on the problems that need to be solved. Can you think of ways in which the problems that need to be solved in everyday life have changed since prehistoric times, since the Middle Ages, since the 19th century, or even since the 1920s? Has what counts as "being smart" changed as well? Can we predict what kinds of abilities "being smart" will require in the future?

Do you think it is useful to define people as mentally retarded or gifted? Why or why not?

Is creativity always a good idea? What would the world be like if everyone were supercreative, always trying to change things? In what circumstances might creativity be more of a problem than a benefit?

REVIEW TEST

For each of the following items, choose the single correct or best answer. The correct answers appear at the end.

1 The structure of the sounds that can be used to produce words in a language is called ____.
a. syntax
b. phonology
c. semantics
d. pragmatics

2 The word "walking" has ____ morphemes.
a. 4
b. 1
c. 3
d. 2

3 When 5-year-old Julie answered the phone, the caller asked her, "Is your mommy there?" Julie answered, "Yes," and then waited for the caller to respond. Clearly, Julie didn't understand the ____ of the question.
a. syntax
b. morphology
c. semantics
d. pragmatics

4 Which of the following is *not* a property of mental space?
a. meaning
b. limited size
c. spatial extent
d. grain

5 A schema specifies both ____ and ____ features of a concept.
a. necessary; prototypical
b. necessary; optional
c. necessary; sufficient
d. sufficient; optional

6 Kimberly couldn't find the rice, but started in aisle 3 first, because she thought it might be with the pasta. Then she tried aisle 10, because she thought it might be with the international foods. Kimberly used a(n) ____ to find the rice.
a. representational analysis
b. pattern analysis
c. algorithm
d. heuristic

7 When someone assumes a cause was present because a particular result has occurred, he or she has made the error of ____.
a. deductive reasoning
b. inductive reasoning
c. affirming the consequent
d. confirming the antecedent

8 Using William Stern's calculation of intelligence quotient, a 20-year-old adult with a mental age of 10 would have an IQ of ____.
a. 10
b. 100
c. 50
d. 20

9 According to studies by Sternberg and colleagues, ____ intelligence is the best predictor of job success.
a. intrapersonal
b. creative
c. practical
d. analytic

10 Mendelian inheritance best describes variations in ____.
a. intelligence
b. height
c. weight
d. hair curl

11 In general, the greater the reaction range, _____.
  a. the more evident the effects of the environment
  b. the more intelligent the individual
  c. the more evident the effects of genetics
  d. the less important genetics and environment are

12 Differences in intelligence *between* groups of people are due to _____.
  a. unknown reasons
  b. primarily environment
  c. primarily genetics
  d. only the microenvironment

13 Females tend to be better than males at tasks requiring _____.
  a. fluid intelligence
  b. crystallized intelligence
  c. verbal reasoning
  d. spatial reasoning

14 Which of the following is *not* a criterion for mental retardation?
  a. significantly subaverage IQ
  b. inability to learn
  c. significant limitations in two or more everyday abilities
  d. condition present since childhood

15 Which of the following is *not* a characteristic of creative individuals?
  a. High levels of stress
  b. Intermediate amounts of formal education
  c. Flexibility and the ability to reorganize information
  d. Specific knowledge skills and general abilities

7

Emotion

and Motivation

F E E L I N G A N D S T R I V I N G

John had been looking forward all day to his evening's date. Dinner with his girlfriend, Barbara, would mark the first anniversary of their meeting. But he had become absorbed working on his computer. With a start he noticed the time and realized that he might be late. Agitated at the thought of beginning a romantic evening on the wrong foot, he dashed out of the building and rushed down the street. He decided to take a shortcut down an alley. In the last of the daylight, the narrow alley was in deep shadow, but he could see the other end and felt sure he could get through quickly. There was so little light between the old warehouses that he had to look carefully to avoid bumping into trash cans and dumpsters. As he hurried along, he thought he heard a noise behind him, and he became edgy. He walked faster. The noise seemed to be coming closer. He walked even faster. He tried to convince himself that what he heard was only a cat, but in his heart he knew better.

Suddenly he felt a strong hand grab his shoulder and then an arm snake around his neck, while something sharp dug into his ribs. His entire body froze; he felt literally paralyzed by fear. He handed over his wallet as he was told, although his heart was pounding so hard that he could barely hear the mugger's demand. Without another word, the mugger ran away, leaving John shaken but not really hurt. John ran ahead and gasped with relief when he emerged into the main street.

John hurried on to the restaurant, now far more interested in the comfort of talking to Barbara than in his romantic fantasies. Although he had been hungry when he left work, he was no longer thinking about food. He just wanted to be away from that alley, safe in his girlfriend's company.

In that harrowing experience John was driven by emotion and motivation. What these two forces have in common is their power to "move" us. (The root of both these English words comes from the Latin *movere*, "to move.") Our motivations and emotions are intimately interwoven: We are often motivated to do something because we are feeling an emotion, as happens when love leads us to hug someone; or we are motivated because we look forward to changing our emotions, as happens when we work on a project in the expectation of replacing guilt with pride. Our emotions and motivations are not always obvious; they may confuse us, or compel us to do things that surprise us. In this chapter we consider first the nature of emotion and how it affects our behavior. This leads us to consider motivation—what makes us act. Finally, we focus on two of the most important motivations: hunger and sex.

Emotion: 1 Feel, Therefore 1 Am

John felt an odd mixture of emotions as he continued to the restaurant after his encounter with the mugger. He had no thought of what might happen later in the evening; his romantic after-dinner plans were no longer on his mind. Instead, he was trembling with fear. Now he felt nervous when he passed an alley, even though the mugger who had assaulted him was surely far away. Also, he was surprised at the strength of his feelings both when he was grabbed by the mugger and after the terrifying episode was over. When he saw Barbara, he was overwhelmed with intense feelings of warmth and relief.

An **emotion** is a positive or negative reaction to a perceived or remembered object, event, or circumstance; emotions are accompanied by subjective feelings (Damasio, 1999). Emotions not only help guide us to approach some things and withdraw from others, but they also provide visible cues that help other people know key aspects of our thoughts and desires.

1 What are the different emotions?

2 What causes emotion?

3 How does culture affect our emotional lives?

Types of Emotion: What Can You Feel?

Think of the emotions you have experienced in your life. Fear? Guilt? Guilt tinged with fear? Love? Love tinged with joy? The range of human emotions is huge. In the realm of emotion the brain apparently uses the trick of producing many gradations and types of experienced reactions by combining sets of simple signals. Just as all colors can be produced by mixtures of three primary colors, researchers have argued that all emotions, even the most complex, arise from combinations of a simple set we all possess, which, like primary colors on an artist's palette, lie ready for us to blend, experience, and present to the world.

Emotion: A positive or negative reaction to a perceived or remembered object, event, or circumstance, accompanied by a subjective feeling.

Basic Emotions

Charles Darwin (1872), for one, believed that many emotional behaviors—the outward acts that arise from our emotions—are inborn. He noticed that people of many races and cultures appear to have very similar facial expressions to signal similar emotional states. Moreover, blind people show those same expressions, even if they have never had the chance to observe the way others look when they have particular emotional reactions. Are we all born with a built-in set of emotions? If so, these emotions would be an essential part of what we call "human nature," constituting a defining characteristic of what it means to be human in every time and culture.

Ekman and Friesen (1971) described the results of experiments that were designed to investigate this possibility (see Figure 7.1 on page 242). They wanted to know whether people who had never seen Caucasian faces could nevertheless identify the emotions underlying their facial expressions. They visited a New Guinea tribe, the Fore, who had rarely if ever seen white people in person, in movies, or on television. Nonetheless, the Fore were able to identify expressions of happiness, anger, sadness, disgust, fear, and surprise. The one difficulty they had was in distinguishing the expression of fear from that of surprise, probably because the two are very similar emotions. Also, it is possible that in Fore culture the two often go together: Most surprises in the jungle, such as the unexpected wild boar, are life-threatening, fear-inducing ones. In an interesting twist on their original study, Ekman and Friesen also videotaped the faces of members of the Fore as they displayed these same six emotions and showed the tapes to American college students. The students, too, could identify which emotions were being displayed, even though they had never before seen the people displaying them.

Ekman (1984) concludes that surprise, happiness, anger, fear, disgust, and sadness are **basic emotions**, emotions that are innate and shared by all humans. Other theorists have proposed slightly different lists of basic emotions. Tomkins (1962) proposes surprise, interest, joy, rage, fear, disgust, shame, and anguish, for example. Some of the apparent disagreements may just be simply a matter of word choice; *joy* and *happiness,* for example, probably label the same emotion (LeDoux, 1996). Although the precise number of basic emotions is debated (LeDoux, 1996), there is widespread agreement that humans do have a set of built-in emotions that express the most basic types of reactions. Evidence about the way the brain gives rise to emotion also supports the existence of distinct basic emotions; for example, damage to the brain can selectively disrupt the ability to detect fear and sadness without disrupting the ability to discern other emotions (Adolphs et al., 1996).

But even when there is agreement that a particular emotion is "basic," that does not mean it is "simple." Basic emotions may be complex. For example, Rozin and colleagues (1994) distinguish among three types of disgust, each of which is signaled by a different facial expression. A nose-wrinkling expression of disgust is associated with bad smells (and, sometimes, bad tastes); an open mouth with the tongue hanging down is associated with foods perceived as disgusting (the "yech" reaction); and a raised upper lip accompanies feelings of disgust such as those associated with death and filth.

Separate But Equal Emotions

Have you ever watched a movie that was a certified four-star tear-jerker and found yourself racked with sobs *and* rolling with laughter? There is good evidence that positive and negative emotions are not really opposite sides of the same coin. Rather, positive and negative emotions can occur separately, in any combination (Bradburn, 1969; Cacioppo et al., 1997; Diener & Emmons, 1984; Goldstein & Strube, 1994). The notion that positive and negative emotions are independent is in part supported by what happens in the brain when people experience emotions. Davidson and his colleagues have provided several types of evidence that there are separate systems in the brain for two general types of human emotions:

Basic emotion: An innate emotion that is shared by all humans, such as surprise, happiness, anger, fear, disgust, and sadness.

Figure **7.1** **Recognition of Basic Emotions**

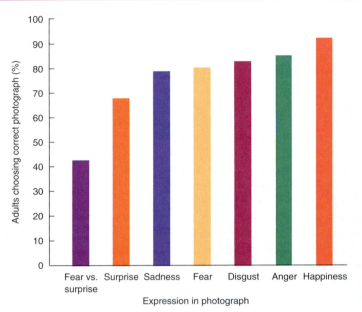

Note: Chance performance would be 33.3%.

The participants were asked to select the picture that matched a short description.

Participants could distinguish all of the emotions except fear and surprise.

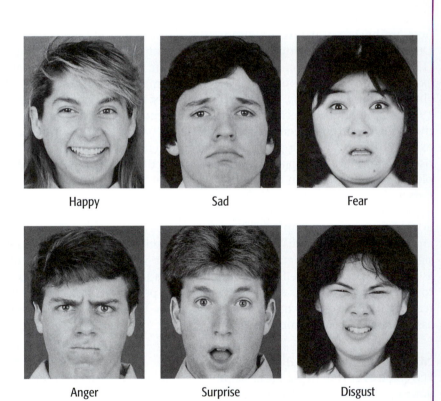

The six basic emotions that Ekman and others identified and studied. In the Ekman and Friesen study (1971), all the faces were Caucasian, however.

approach emotions (such as love and happiness) and *withdrawal* emotions (such as fear and disgust; Davidson, 1992a, 1992b, 1993, 1998; see also Lang, 1995; Solomon & Corbit, 1974a). In general, approach emotions are positive, and withdrawal emotions are negative. EEG recordings show that the left frontal lobe tends to be more active when people have approach emotions, whereas the right frontal lobe tends to be active when people have withdrawal emotions. Moreover, people who normally have more activation in the left frontal lobe tend to have a rosier outlook on life than people who have more activation in the right frontal lobe. Positron emission tomography (PET) scanning has also shown that clinically depressed patients have relatively diminished metabolic activity in the left frontal lobe (Davidson, 1993, 1994a, 1998; Davidson et al., 1999).

What Causes Emotions?

Distinguishing among and characterizing different emotions is interesting, but it doesn't tell us what emotion is for, or why particular emotions arise as they do, any more than a theory of how color arises can explain how Leonardo painted the *Mona Lisa*. Why did John feel fear *after* the mugger had left? What possible good would that do him? The major theories of emotion, and the ideas arising from them, provide the impetus for much of the research into these questions.

Theories of Emotion: Brain, Body, and World

It seems both obvious and logical that emotion would work like this: You are in a particular situation; that situation induces a specific emotion; that emotion leads you to behave in a certain way. John is mugged, becomes afraid, and runs. Over 100 years ago, William James (1884) argued that this intuitively plausible relation between emotion and behavior is exactly backward. James believed that you feel emotions *after* your body reacts (see Figure 7.2). For example, if you come across someone who begins acting like a mugger, James would say that you would first run and *then* feel afraid, not the other way round. The emotion of fear, according

Figure 7.2 Four Theories of Emotion

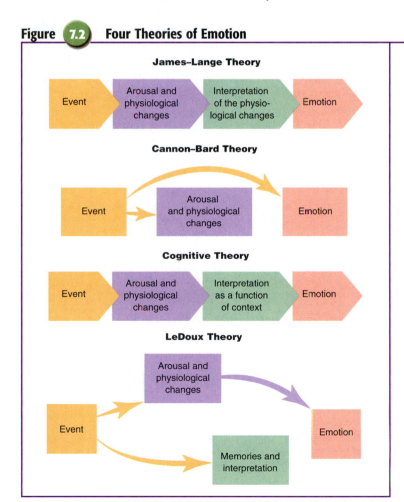

Theories of emotion differ in the relationship they assume between bodily events, interpretations of events, and distinct brain systems.

to James, arises because you sense your bodily state as you are fleeing. You are aroused, and you sense your heart speeding up, your breathing increasing, and the other signs of your sympathetic nervous system's activation (see Chapter 2). According to his theory, different emotions arise from different sets of bodily reactions, and that's why emotions feel different. Carl Lange (1887), a Danish physiologist, independently developed a similar theory, and thus the theory has come to be called the *James–Lange theory* (Lang, 1994).

Walter Cannon (1927) claimed that the James–Lange theory focused too much on noticing bodily signals, such as heart and breathing rates. He raised a telling criticism of the James–Lange theory—that it takes many seconds for the body to become aroused and yet emotions are usually present well before this happens. Instead, he claimed, the brain itself is all that matters. You perceive the potential mugger, and the results of that perception marshal the body's resources for fleeing or fighting *at the same time* that they generate an emotion. According to the *Cannon–Bard theory* (see Figure 7.2), formulated by Cannon and Philip Bard, another physiologist, physiological arousal and the experience of emotion arise in tandem.

A third theory, *cognitive theory,* holds that an emotion arises when you interpret the situation as a whole—your bodily state in the context of everything that surrounds it. According to this theory, unlike James–Lange, you don't react to a stimulus and then feel an emotion after the reaction; and unlike Cannon–Bard, you don't have separate bodily and emotional reactions. Rather, your reactions and the general situation are all of a piece. For example, the act of running and the accompanying arousal have equal chances of accompanying the emotions of joy (as you rush to embrace someone you love), fear (as you flee a pursuing mugger), or excitement (as you join the crowd on the field to celebrate a football victory). The difference is not in the bodily state, but in how you interpret it at the time it occurs. Richard Lazarus, Stanley Schachter, and Magda Arnold were pioneers in developing this view. In general, cognitive theories of emotion rest on the idea that, as Lazarus puts it, emotion "cannot be understood solely in terms of what happens in the person or in the brain, but grows out of ongoing transactions with the environment that are evaluated" (Lazarus, 1984, p. 124). This statement of course embodies our by-now familiar approach of looking at events at the levels of brain, person, and group.

Joseph LeDoux (1996) has modified the cognitive theory in an important way. He claims that there are different brain systems for different emotions. Some of these systems operate as reflex systems do, *independent* of thought or interpretation, whereas others *depend* on thought and interpretation. Fear, for example, is experienced through the activation of the amygdala, without need for cognitive interpretation. But other emotions, such as guilt, rely on cognitive interpretation and memories of previous similar situations. Thus, the emotions we feel at any moment arise from (1) a mixture of brain and body reactions and (2) interpretations and memories pertaining to the situation.

Which theory comes closest to the mark? To find out, let's take a closer look at the nature of emotion.

Physiological Profiles: Are Emotions Just Bodily Responses?

Suppose John had been so anxious about his anniversary date that he took a powerful tranquilizer beforehand. If this drug kept his heart from pounding and otherwise prevented his sympathetic nervous system from becoming fully activated, would he still have felt fear after the mugging? Yes, he probably would have. Let's see why.

Perhaps the strongest evidence against James's idea that emotions arise when people interpret their own bodily states is the finding that even people with spinal cord injuries so severe that they receive no sensations from their bodies still report having emotions (Bermond et al., 1991). However, it is possible that these patients experience emotions differently than do people with intact spinal cords. For example, one such patient described in this way what it felt like when a lit cigarette fell onto his bed: "I could have burned up right there, but the funny thing is, I didn't get all shook up about it. I just didn't feel afraid at all, like you would suppose." Speaking about another common emotion, he said, "Sometimes I act angry when I see some injustice. I yell and cuss and raise hell, because if you don't do it sometimes, I've learned people will take advantage of you, but it doesn't have the heat to it that it used to. It's a mental kind of anger" (Hohman, 1966, pp. 150–151). These quotations suggest that this man's emotions were largely rational evaluations, not reactions to events that were accompanied by feelings.

The James–Lange theory implies that we feel different emotions because each emotion corresponds to a different physiological state. John's heart was pounding and his palms began to sweat when he felt a sharp object jabbing into his ribs, and these bodily events may have played a key role in the emotions he felt. The lag in time for these bodily events to arise after the mugging could explain why John continued to feel fear after he had fled the alley. In contrast, the Cannon–Bard theory implies that our bodies are aroused similarly in different arousing situations. According to this view, arousal is arousal; it occurs not only if you are mugged but also if you win the lottery. But physiological evidence leads us to question the Cannon–Bard theory. Many emotions are accompanied by *distinct patterns* of heart rate, temperature, sweat, and other reactions. For example, when you feel anger, your heart rate increases and so does the temperature of your skin; and when you feel fear, your heart rate increases but your skin temperature actually decreases (Levenson et al., 1990). Even if some of these distinct bodily responses arise because of the different levels of effort required to respond to various emotion-causing situations (Boiten, 1998), distinguishing bodily events do accompany at least some different emotions.

It is possible that emotion also corresponds to another bodily state, one that is not defined in terms of autonomic reactions. There are 44 separate muscles in your face, only 4 of which are used for chewing—the rest are involved in forming facial expressions (Rinn, 1984). When you move these muscles, your brain receives feedback from them. According to the **facial feedback hypothesis,** you feel emotions in part because of the way your muscles are positioned in your face (Izard, 1971; Tomkins, 1962).

There is evidence that "putting on a happy face" is not just a good lyric; it can actually make you feel happier. Following up on other studies (Duclos et al., 1989; Laird, 1974, 1984), Ekman and colleagues (Ekman, 1992; Ekman et al., 1990) tested this idea by leading participants to shift parts of their faces until they held specific expressions—for example, lifting the corners of the mouth until a smile and other signs of happiness were formed. The participants maintained these configurations while they rated their mood. If their faces were posed in a positive expression, they tended to rate their mood more positively than if their faces were posed in a negative expression.

However, putting on a happy face does not lead our brains to be in exactly the same state as when we are genuinely happy (Ekman & Davidson, 1993). Thus, although facial feedback may affect emotions, smiles, frowns, and glowers are not the only causes of our emotional experiences.

Cognitive Interpretation

Bodily factors are not enough to explain the range of feelings we have. What's missing? Our own interpretation of objects and events, and the context in which they occur, both of which affect our feelings.

The classic experiment in this area was reported by Stanley Schacter and Jerome Singer in 1962; it is illustrated in Figure 7.3 on page 246. The participants, who believed that they would be taking part in a test of vision, received an injection of what they were told was a vitamin supplement. The injection was really a shot of epinephrine, which causes general arousal. Each participant then waited in a room

Stick a pencil sideways (not point first) in your mouth, so that as you bite down on it, the corners of your lips turn up. Simply making this motion will actually make you feel happier (Strack et al., 1988). For more dramatic results, try to make a big smile, raising your cheeks.

Facial feedback hypothesis: The idea that emotions arise partly as a result of the position of facial muscles.

Figure **7.3** **The Schacter–Singer Experiment**

Participants received an epinephrine injection.

Stooges acted very differently while the participants waited.

And the participants reacted very differently to the drug, depending on what the stooge was doing.

Misattribution of arousal: The failure to interpret signs of bodily arousal correctly, which leads to the experience of inappropriate emotions.

before beginning the "vision test." Also waiting in the room was a "stooge"—that is, someone posing as a participant who in fact cooperates with the investigators in establishing the conditions of the experiment. The experiment consisted of having the stooge act in different ways during the "waiting period" and recording the effects of his behavior on the participant. In one condition, the stooge was manic-like, playing with a hula hoop, tossing paper airplanes, and generally acting silly. In another condition, the stooge was sullen and irritable; he tried to make the participant angry, and eventually stormed out of the room. The participants who had waited with the manic stooge reported that they felt happy, whereas the participants who had waited with the angry stooge reported that they felt angry.

Although the participants had the same physiological arousal induced by the drug, they experienced this arousal very differently depending on the context in which it occurred; and this difference apparently led them to attribute different causes to the arousal. In contrast, when participants were told in advance about the drug and its effects, they did *not* feel differently in the different contexts; it was only when they interpreted the arousal as arising from the context that their feelings differed. In addition, participants in a control group, who did not receive an injection, experienced no effects of context. It is worth noting that this study took place more than 35 years ago; today, giving participants drugs without their knowledge is considered unethical and would not be done.

If you interpret signs of bodily arousal incorrectly, making a cognitive error called the **misattribution of arousal,** you may experience emotions that ordinarily would not arise in that situation. For example, in one study male participants were given false feedback about their own internal responses (Valins, 1966). They had been asked, while looking at slides of partially nude women, to listen to what they were told was their own heartbeat. The heartbeats they heard were in fact not their own; they were sometimes faster and sometimes slower than their actual heart rates. When the participants later were asked to rate the attractiveness of each woman, their ratings were based not just on what they saw but also on what they heard: If they had associated a rapid heartbeat with a picture, they rated the woman as more attractive. It is clear that our interpretation of bodily feedback depends on the situation—and how we interpret the situation depends at least in part on bodily feedback (Palace, 1999). Emotion is a complex mixture that arises from the "whispers and shouts" of the body as filtered through the expectations and interpretations of the mind.

Fear: The Amygdala and You

Because it is one of the emotions scientists understand best, fear has become a testing ground for theories of emotion. Fear causes changes in the brain, in the autonomic nervous system, in hormones, and in behavior. When people are afraid, they tend to freeze (to be "paralyzed by fear"), and they have an increased tendency to be startled (Davis, 1992; Lang, 1995; Vrana et al., 1988). As John walked down the alley, the noises he heard made him afraid, which made him even more susceptible to being startled, so that he was particularly thrown off balance when the mugger grabbed him.

Researchers have discovered four important facts about fear from studying the brain systems that produce it. First, after you have learned to fear an object, fear can well up later as a kind of "emotional reflex," with no thought or interpretation at all (LeDoux, 1996). The amygdala, a small structure located at the front inside part of the temporal lobes (see Chapter 2), plays a crucial role in producing the reactions you have when you are afraid. It sends signals to other brain areas, such as the hypothalamus, that cause your heart to speed up, your muscles to freeze (as John did when he was grabbed), and all the other autonomic reactions associated with fear. In fact, conscious awareness is not needed for a stimulus to trigger the amygdala into producing a fear response. For example, in an fMRI brain-scanning study, the amygdala responded when participants were briefly shown faces with fearful expressions—so briefly that they were not even aware of having seen the expressions (Whalen et al., 1998). Moreover, in this study the amygdala actually decreased activation when happy faces were presented, even when the participants were not aware of the expressions.

Second, there is evidence that once you learn to associate fear with an object or situation, you will always do so. To this day, whenever John sees that alley, his palms sweat and his heart beats a little faster. Even after he thought he was finally over the experience, he found himself avoiding that block. Fear is a classically conditioned response, and even after extinction, the sets of neurons that were created by an association still fire together (see Chapter 4). This is one reason why it is so easy to reinstate conditioned fear. Even though you are not aware of the association, it is never fully lost (LeDoux, 1996).

Third, in spite of its reflexive nature, fear interacts with mental processes. For example, if you merely visualize yourself in a scary situation, you become susceptible to being startled (Cook et al., 1991; Lang et al., 1990; Vrana & Lang, 1990). The parts of the brain involved in cognition play a key role in "setting you up" to be easily startled.

Finally, the amygdala plays a role in producing the emotional "feel" of fear. People with damaged amygdalas sound a lot like the patient described earlier, who knew he should be afraid when his lighted cigarette fell, and angry at injustice, but really couldn't get riled up about anything. In addition, people with damage to the amygdala (but with little other brain impairment) cannot recognize fear or anger in the tone of other people's voices (Scott et al., 1997); the emotional response produced by the amygdala apparently plays a role in the recognition of other people's emotions (Adolphs et al., 1996; Calder et al., 1996; Hamann et al., 1996; Young et al., 1996).

What does all this tell us about emotion in general? First, there are distinct events that underlie fear, a finding that is consistent with the James–Lange theory. However, these states are not just bodily reactions; they also involve specific brain systems. Second, the events underlying fear appear to produce both the experience and the bodily reaction at the same time, which fits the Cannon–Bard theory. However, the experience and reaction are not entirely separate; rather, your interpretation of the event can affect both. Third, although interpretation is not always necessary, it is clear that mental events do interact with emotion. Thus, aspects of cognitive theory are supported.

In short, the three oldest theories capture important aspects of fear; all contain a grain of truth. However, the sum total of the findings is most consistent with LeDoux's revision of cognitive theory, which includes roles for both brain-based, reflexive reactions and for the interpretation of bodily states in particular contexts.

Happiness: More Than a Feeling

Lest you think that psychologists have a morbid fascination with the dark side, we must note that much has also been learned about happiness (Diener, 2000;

Myers, 2000; Peterson, 2000; Ryan & Deci, 2000). What kinds of events make us happy? Self-reported measures of happiness depend on many variables, which affect events at the different levels of analysis. Many of these factors reflect events at the level of the group. Not surprisingly, a survey of happiness in 40 countries found that money *can* buy happiness, at least to some extent: People tend to be happier when they are living in better economic conditions (Schyns, 1998). But we must be cautious about generalizing from one culture to another. When asked about the sources of happiness, Chinese people focused on interpersonal interactions and external evaluation, whereas Westerners focused on the achievement of personal goals and internal evaluation (Lu & Shih, 1997a).

Researchers have also found that in 16 of 17 countries they examined (the exception was Northern Ireland), marriage is linked to greater happiness than is either being single or living with someone to whom you aren't married. This increase in happiness was comparable for both men and women (Ross, 1995; Stack & Eshleman, 1998; Weerasinghe & Tepperman, 1994). Apparently, most of the effects of marriage on happiness are indirect: increasing satisfaction with household finances and improving perceived health. However, this is not all there is to it; the simple fact of being married, all by itself, contributed to happiness.

It is also clear that events at the level of the person affect happiness. For example, at least in Western countries, assertive people tend to be happier than nonassertive people (Argyle & Lu, 1990). At the level of the brain, at least some of the factors that affect whether you are happy are biological. We have already noted that people with more activation in the left frontal lobe (not only during a particular task, but in general) tend to be happier than people with more activation in the right frontal lobe (Davidson, 1992a, 1992b, 1993, 1994a, 1998). Other specific brain areas, including the ventral medial frontal cortex, were activated when participants in a study watched or recalled films that induced happiness, but not other emotions (Lane et al., 1997a).

Expressing Emotions: Letting It All Hang Out?

Emotions occur in the social context of family, friends, and culture. As in John's story, many of our emotions arise from social interactions, both positive (the comforting dinner with Barbara) and negative (his fear during and in the wake of the mugging). Not only do social stimuli trigger emotions, but emotions in turn serve social roles; these roles range from communicating to providing connections among people.

Culture and Emotional Expression: Rules of the Mode

In many ways emotional experience is a private affair, inaccessible to others. But emotional expression is crucial for our daily interactions with other people. According to Ekman (1980), each of us learns a set of **display rules** for our culture that indicate when, to whom, and how strongly certain emotions can be shown. For example, he notes that in the United States people will find it suspicious if at a man's funeral his secretary seems more upset than his wife. In the display rules of U.S. culture, the closer the relation to the deceased, the more emotion may be displayed. Display rules are partly a function of habit (individuals do differ in their styles), but they largely reflect "the way things are done" in a particular region, class, or ethnic culture.

Ekman (1984) describes a fascinating test of his theory that all people share the same basic emotions but that emotional expression may be different because of different display rules. He challenged the stereotype that Asians are less emotional than Westerners. Americans in Berkeley and Japanese in Tokyo were shown the same films, one positive (scenery) and one negative (a surgical procedure). Par-

Display rule: A culture-specific rule that indicates when, to whom, and how strongly certain emotions can be shown.

ticipants viewed the films either alone or in the company of a white-coated scientist. Both national groups showed the same range of emotional expression when they viewed the films in individual screenings, one person at a time, but the Japanese participants were notably more restrained when they were in company. Ekman analyzed slow-motion videotapes of the participants as they watched. The tapes revealed that a Japanese participant watching alone reacted in the same way as the Americans. But a Japanese watching in company would begin showing an emotional reaction, then quickly squelch it. According to Ekman, the initial Japanese reaction reflected the basic, innate emotions; then display rules came to the fore, and the participants regulated their show of emotions accordingly.

Culture affects not only how willing you are to express emotion in specific situations, but also how sensitive you are to the emotional expressions of others (Stephan et al., 1996). It is almost as if when a culture makes emotions harder to detect, its members develop better abilities to detect them. For example, although China has more restrained display rules than Australia, Chinese children can detect basic emotions more accurately than Australian children (Markham & Wang, 1996).

Body Language: Broadcasting Feelings

Nonverbal communication isn't really language, but it is a form of communication that is particularly effective at conveying emotion. We are remarkably good at reading cues about emotion, acquiring information from even minimal cues. Men and women differ in their characteristic nonverbal behavior. Hall (1978) performed a meta-analysis of studies of nonverbal behavior and found that men tend to be more restless (for instance, they had more frequent leg movements) and expansive (such as by leaving their legs open) than women, but women tend to be more expressive, as evidenced by their gestures (Gallaher, 1992). These conclusions are consistent with the finding that women are more expressive than men when watching emotional films (Kring & Gordon, 1998). There are also gender differences in the ability to decode nonverbal cues. Apparently women can register nonverbal signs of happiness better than men, but men can register unspoken signs of anger better than women (Coats & Feldman, 1996).

As these differences may suggest, at least some of our nonverbal behaviors may result from innate factors. Although there has yet to be a good rigorous study of this, one anecdote is highly suggestive. In reviewing 30 studies of identical twins who were separated and raised apart, Faber (1981) wrote: "As with voice, the way the twins held themselves, walked, turned their heads, or flicked their wrists was more alike than any quantifiable trait the observers were able to measure. . . . If one twin had a limp, moist handshake, so did the other. If one had a spirited prance, so did the partner" (pp. 86–87). However, the ability to *read* nonverbal communications is at least partly determined by experience. For example, children who watch more television tend to be better at judging emotional expressions (Feldman et al., 1996).

Body language also plays a role in unwanted sexual encounters. This is important for students to recognize because college women experience sexual victimization three to four times more frequently than women in general (Cummings, 1992; Hanson & Gidycz, 1993). Researchers asked observers to view videotapes of ordinary people walking down the street and to rate how vulnerable they were to physical assault (Grayson & Stein, 1981). Those viewed as victims tended to move awkwardly and disjointedly, whereas "nonvictims" moved smoothly, in a coordinated, confident way. Murzynski and Degelman (1996) conducted an experiment to discover exactly which aspects of body language lead women to be perceived as vulnerable to sexual assault. They defined two victim profiles. In one, potential victims tend to walk with a long, exaggerated stride and lift their feet up rather than smoothly swinging them; in the other, they may walk with short, mincing steps. Both police officers and college students rated the women who walked in the manner of the victim profiles as more likely to be sexually assaulted than the women who walked in the style of the nonvictim profile.

Animals also express emotion with body language. If you see a gorilla sticking out its tongue, avoid getting too close—this signal means the animal is angry.

Lie Detection

John reported the mugging to the police but was frustrated when they failed to identify a suspect. And even if they did make an arrest, would they be able to prove anything? Lie detector tests may not be admissible evidence in court, but they are used in various investigations nonetheless. What do they really "detect"?

If different brain states and bodily states accompany different emotions, researchers have reasoned, then there might be distinct biological "footprints" of the feeling of guilt. This idea underlies a long history of attempts to detect deception objectively. One result has been machines called **polygraphs,** known misleadingly as lie detectors. These machines don't "detect lies" directly; they monitor the activity of the sympathetic and parasympathetic nervous systems—in particular, changes in skin conductance, breathing, and heart rate.

The most basic technique used with a polygraph is the *relevant/irrelevant technique* (*RIT*; Larson, 1932). Suppose you are trying to determine whether the suspect in a crime is telling the truth. When the RIT is used, the suspect is asked crime-related questions ("Did you break into Mr. Johnson's house last night?") and neutral questions ("Do you live at 43 Pleasant Street?"). The responses to the two types of questions are then compared. However, there is clearly a large difference in the emotional weight of the two types of questions. Thus, a greater physiological response to a crime-related question may reflect not guilt but simply the fact that the idea posed by the question is more arousing. To avoid this possibility, the *control question technique* (*CQT;* Reid, 1947) includes comparison questions that should have an emotional weight roughly equivalent to that of the crime-related questions. For example, in addition to the two questions above, the suspect might be asked, "Did you ever do anything you were ashamed of?"

A more recent technique is the *guilty knowledge test* (*GKT;* sometimes called the "concealed information test"), developed by Lykken (1959, 1960). In contrast to the RIT and CQT, the GKT does not rely on asking direct questions about the crime. Instead, this test uses indirect questions that presumably only the guilty person would be in a position to answer correctly. In addition, the GKT relies on multiple-choice questions. So the suspect might be asked, "Was the color of the walls in Mr. Johnson's bedroom white? yellow? blue?" Someone who has never been in the room should have comparable responses to each of the choices, whereas someone who has guilty knowledge should respond selectively to the actual color. A modification of this approach is the *guilty actions test* (Bradley & Warfield, 1984; Bradley et al., 1996), which observes responses when people are given statements about actions they may have committed.

Do these techniques work? Ben-Shakhar and Furedy (1990) report that in the laboratory the CQT on average correctly classifies 80% of the guilty and 63% of the innocent (p. 44). Thus, this technique unfortunately leads too often to the classification of honest responses as lies. The GKT has a better track record; the guilty were detected 84% of the time, and the innocent 94%. However, the range of accuracy in the reviewed studies was from 64% to 100% for detecting the guilty, and 81% to 100% for detecting the innocent. More recent techniques that measure electrical activity in the brain can sometimes be as high as 95% accurate, but there is still enough variability to cast doubt on the test's ability to classify individual answers or reports from individual people as untruthful (Allen & Iacono, 1997).

How can we best understand lie detection? The goal of lie detection is to assess a particular social interaction in which one person is misleading another person. However, the technique depends on interactions among events at the three levels of analysis. Perhaps the greatest problem with all the traditional techniques is that they are methods of detecting guilt (the level of the person). If the person being tested lies but does not *feel* guilty, the palms won't become sweaty, heart rate won't increase, and so forth; the brain will not produce the autonomic responses associated with guilt. And the interviewer will not have any basis

Polygraphs are used to detect changes in autonomic nervous system activity, which may signal that the person being interviewed is lying.

for detecting the lie, which in turn may alter how the person is being treated during the interview (a social interaction), and that treatment in turn affects the person's reactions to the questions. Thus, to understand lie detection, we need to consider all three levels of analysis: the activity in the brain that produces the autonomic results; the personality differences that could lead a person to feel guilty; and the rules of the society, together with the person's understanding of them, that would lead the person to feel guilty under certain circumstances.

CONSOLIDATE!

1 *What are the different emotions?* Ekman and his collaborators offer much evidence that six emotions are "basic"—happiness, anger, sadness, disgust, surprise, and fear—but the last two are more easily confused with each other than are any of the others. Each of these emotions can be categorized as "approach" or "withdrawal," and each can be further differentiated into subtypes (for example, Rozin and his collaborators have identified three different types of disgust).

2 *What causes emotion?* The James–Lange theory states that emotion follows bodily reactions; the Cannon–Bard theory holds that emotions and bodily reactions occur at the same time, not in the order claimed by James and Lange; cognitive theory holds that emotions arise when bodily states are interpreted in the context of the specific situation; and, most recently, LeDoux's revision of cognitive theory maintains that some emotions arise reflexively from specific brain activity whereas others rely on cognitive interpretation and memory. All the theories have captured a facet of how emotions work. As James–Lange predicts, emotions may be caused in part by differences in internal bodily state (such as heart rate and breathing rate) and in facial expression. As Cannon–Bard predicts, some emotions are reflexes that simultaneously produce both the experience and the bodily reaction. As cognitive theory predicts, how you interpret the causes of your bodily states influences which emotion you will feel. But as LeDoux predicts, some emotions (in some circumstances) rely more on cognitive interpretation than others. Environmental events also play a key role in emotion; a person's happiness, for example, depends in part on his or her economic and cultural context.

3 *How does culture affect our emotional lives?* Culture affects the display rules we use, which determine the circumstances in which emotions are shown. Culture also helps determine what conditions will make us happy. In addition, culture affects how well we read body language to discern other people's emotions (but the specific strengths are different for men and women).

Motivation and Reward: Feeling Good

John enjoyed his work so much that on the afternoon of his first anniversary celebration, he completely forgot his plans for dinner and thereafter—until he looked at the clock. When he saw the time, all thoughts of work flew from his head and he focused entirely on getting to the restaurant. Because of the pleasures that he believed lay in store for him—and because he didn't want to risk spoiling the evening by being late—John was highly *motivated* to get to the restaurant from the moment he left work, and even more so after the mugging. We often take a particular action because we expect to feel good afterward; in this sense, emotions motivate us. To motivate is to set in motion, and in psychology the term **motivation** is used to refer to the requirements and desires that lead animals (including humans) to behave in a particular way at a particular time and place.

 What are the sources of motivation?

 What is the difference between "needs" and "wants," and how does culture affect them?

Polygraph: A machine that monitors the activity of the sympathetic and parasympathetic nervous systems, particularly changes in skin conductance, breathing, and heart rate. These machines are used in attempts to detect lying.

Motivation: The requirements and desires that lead animals (including humans) to behave in a particular way at a particular time and place.

Getting Motivated: Sources and Theories of Motivation

There is no single, widely accepted, grand theory that can explain all of human motivation. There are motives based on biological needs (such as the need to keep warm) and motives based on learning (such as the desire for money); motives rooted in the internal state of a person (such as hunger) and motives sparked by the external world (such as exploration); motives based on a current situation and motives based on an expected future situation. Psychologists have analyzed, classified, and identified human motives in numerous ways, developing a variety of theories of motivation. Let's look at the key concepts in these theories and find out what each has to offer as an explanation of human behavior.

Instincts: My Genes Made Me Do It

Why do birds fly south for the winter and spiders make certain kinds of webs? Instinct. For many animals, instincts provide the main motivation for behaviors. An **instinct** is an inherited tendency to produce organized and unalterable responses to particular stimuli. For several decades at the beginning of the 20th century, some psychologists tried to explain human motivation in terms of instincts (for example, McDougall, 1908, 1960); their approach is termed *instinct theory*. Much of Freud's theory, for example, hinges on ideas about how we grapple with our sexual urges, which he considered to be instinctive (these ideas are discussed in Chapter 8). But unlike many other animals, we humans are remarkably flexible in the way we can respond to any stimulus, so it is difficult to assign an important role to instincts in human motivation.

Evolutionary psychology has offered an alternative to instinct theory. Instead of proposing that a behavior itself is "hard-wired," these theorists believe that goals that motivate us (such as finding attractive mates) and general cognitive strategies for achieving goals (such as deception) are inborn (Barkow et al., 1992; Buss, 1998; Cosmides & Tooby, 1996; Pinker, 1997; Plotkin, 1997). However, evolutionary theories of motivation are notoriously difficult to test because we can never know for sure what our ancestors were like and how they evolved. Nevertheless, evolutionary thinking can be a source of inspiration and can lead to novel hypotheses that can be tested in their own right (Pinker, 1997).

Drives and Homeostasis: Staying in Balance

Instinct theory and evolutionary theory focus on specifying particular innate behaviors or goals and strategies. In contrast, *drive theory* focuses on the mechanisms that underlie such tendencies, whether or not they are innate. A **drive** is an internal imbalance that pushes you to reach a particular goal, which in turn will reduce that imbalance. Drives differ in terms of the goals to which they direct you, but all are aimed at satisfying a requirement (decreasing an imbalance). For example, hunger is a drive that orients you toward food; thirst is a drive that impels you toward drink; being cold is a drive that nudges you toward a source of warmth. Some drive theories link drives and reinforcement: Something is reinforcing only if it reduces tension caused by an imbalance. According to this theory, if you are hungry, food is reinforcing because it reduces the tension experienced when you have the hunger drive; if you are not hungry, food is not reinforcing.

What is the nature of the imbalance that is quelled by reinforcement? In 1932 Walter B. Cannon published a groundbreaking book titled *The Wisdom of the Body*, in which he pointed out that for life to be sustained, certain characteristics and substances of the body must be kept within a certain range, neither rising too high nor falling too low. These characteristics and substances include body temperature and the amounts of oxygen, minerals, water, and food taken in. Bodily processes such as digestion and respiration work toward keeping the levels steady. The process of

Instinct: An inherited tendency to produce organized and unalterable responses to particular stimuli.

Drive: An internal imbalance that motivates an animal to reach a particular goal, which in turn will reduce that imbalance.

maintaining a steady state is called **homeostasis.** Homeostasis works not simply to keep the system in balance, but to keep it in balance in the range in which the body functions best. The usual analogy to homeostasis is a thermostat and furnace: the thermostat turns the furnace on when the temperature drops too low and turns it off when the temperature reaches the desired level. But Cannon pointed out that in living creatures, homeostasis often involves active behavior, not simply the passive registering of the state of the environment. To stay alive, you must nourish yourself by obtaining and taking in food and water, and you must maintain body temperature by finding shelter and wearing clothing. If the homeostatic balance goes awry, tension results—and behavior is initiated to correct the imbalance.

Arousal Theory: Avoiding Boredom, Avoiding Overload

People are also motivated to maintain another kind of balance, one that has nothing to do with physiological homeostasis: Simply put, we don't like stimuli that are either too boring or too arousing and instead seek to maintain an intermediate level of stimulation. Berlyne (1960, 1974) showed that people like random patterns, paintings, or music best when they are neither too simple nor too complex, but rather somewhere in the middle. What counts as "simple" or "complex" depends partly on the person as well as the nature of the stimulus. For example, children find patterns complex that adults find less so.

Figure 7.4   The Yerkes–Dodson Law

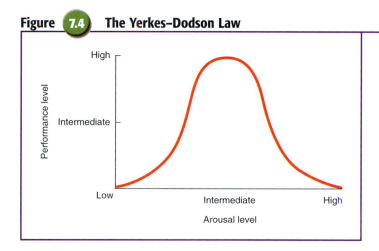

People perform best at intermediate levels of arousal.

These findings conform to the *Yerkes–Dodson law* (Figure 7.4), named after the researchers who first described it. This law states that we perform best when we are at an intermediate level of arousal. If we are underaroused, we are sluggish; if we are overaroused, we can't focus and sustain attention. Intermediate levels of arousal may occur when we are challenged not too much and not too little. For example, if you have to speak before a large group, you may become tongue-tied because of overarousal; if you are rehearsing the speech alone in your room, you may be understimulated and give a lackluster presentation. Indeed, people adapt to a constant set of stimuli, become bored, and then seek additional stimulation (Helson, 1964). We are apparently drawn to moderate stimulation. As intuitive as this idea may seem, not all studies have supported it (for example, Messinger, 1998), perhaps because it is difficult to define precisely levels of stimulation and how they vary.

Incentives and Reward: Happy Expectations

Homeostasis is a useful concept for understanding thirst, hunger, and certain other drives (such as those for salt, oxygen, and temperature control), and arousal theory helps explain why people select certain activities and situations and reject others. However, neither principle helps to explain other motivations, such as sex (Beach,

Homeostasis: The process of maintaining a steady state, a constant level of a bodily substance or condition.

What motivated medieval architects to design castles so that the staircases spiral upward in the clockwise direction? This design gave the defenders (if they were right-handed, and they usually were) an advantage over the invaders because it allowed more room for the defenders' fighting hand to move freely in the tight confines of the staircase. Thinking along the same lines, a Scottish clan of left-handers built their castles so that the stairs spiraled in the opposite direction. How can you understand the motivation for such designs in terms of incentives?

Incentive: A stimulus that draws a person toward a particular goal, in anticipation of a reward.

Intrinsic motivation: Motivation that leads a person to want to engage in an activity for its own sake.

Extrinsic motivation: Motivation that leads a person to want to engage in an activity for external reasons.

Need: A condition that arises from the lack of a requirement; needs give rise to drives.

Want: A condition that arises when an animal has an unmet goal that will not fill a requirement; wants turn goals into incentives.

Deprived reward: A reward that occurs when a biological need is filled.

1956). Your body doesn't actually need sex in the way you need food and oxygen; you can't die from celibacy. Moreover, sex is an example of seeking high arousal, not the intermediate levels we apparently prefer in other areas of stimulation. Like sex, much of what motivates us is best understood in terms of **incentives**, which are stimuli or events that draw us to achieve a particular goal in anticipation of a reward. Drives push, incentives pull. Sex is a good example of incentive-related motivation; so, too, is any money-making activity.

We can further distinguish between two types of incentives—those that are intrinsic to performing a task and those that are not. When an activity is inherently rewarding, it is said to provide **intrinsic motivation:** The activity is desirable for its own sake. An activity that is attractive for other reasons, such as a favorable response from other people or satisfactory payment, is said to provide **extrinsic motivation.** Some research has shown that rewarding children for activities they already enjoy can make them less likely to engage in the activity when they are no longer reinforced for doing so (Deci et al., 1999; Lepper et al., 1999).

Needs and Wants: The Stick and the Carrot

Different things motivate different people: A monk is not motivated to make money; an entrepreneur is not motivated to give away all earthly possessions and seek enlightenment on a mountaintop. Moreover, you are not motivated by the same forces day in and day out; rather, motivations may shift over the course of the day (or year, or life span). A particular motivation comes to the fore when you have a *need* or *want*. A **need** is a condition that arises from the lack of a requirement. Needs give rise to drives, which push you to reach a particular goal that will reduce the need. Lacking nutrients is a need; being hungry is a drive. In contrast, a **want** is a condition that arises when you have an unmet goal that will not fill a requirement. A want causes the goal to act as an incentive. You might *need* to eat, but you don't *need* a fancier wristwatch, although you might desperately *want* one—and the promise of a Rolex as a reward for getting good grades would be an incentive for you to work hard. You are not necessarily aware of your needs or wants. After the mugging John wasn't aware of his need to eat, but he was only too well aware of his wanting to be with Barbara.

Is There More Than One Type of Reward?

For all needs and wants, we think of the goal as reinforcing the behaviors that lead to it. But what makes the goal rewarding? What is "reward"? Even the strongest regulatory needs, creating drives such as hunger and thirst, arise from the brain—and those needs are satisfied not by what we do directly, but rather by the effects of our actions on the brain. To understand why something is rewarding, we must look more closely at the brain's response to events in the world. By looking at the brain mechanisms underlying reward, we find support for the distinction between needs and wants.

Olds and Milner (1954) found that rats who received electrical stimulation in certain brain areas acted as if they desired more of it. Later research showed that Olds and Milner had stumbled on a brain system that underlies reward when an animal has been deprived of the reinforcer. **Deprived reward** is reward that occurs when you have filled a biological need. Such reward arises from the brain pathway that runs from certain parts of the brain stem, through the (lateral) hypothalamus, on up to specific parts of the limbic system and the frontal lobes (Kalivas & Nakamura, 1999; Rolls & Cooper, 1974; Wise, 1996). Many of these neurons use the neurotransmitter *dopamine*. Drugs that block the action of dopamine also block the rewarding effect of brain stimulation (Nader et al., 1997) and of normal rein-forcers such as food or water. When given these dopamine-blockers, experimen-tal animals (usually rats) begin to respond normally, but then lose interest. Because the drugs are blocking the rewarding effect of the reinforcer, the animals' response undergoes extinction (Beninger, 1983, 1989; Geary & Smith, 1985; Schneider et al., 1990; Wise, 1982). At least in some situations, the dopamine may actually sig-nal that a reward is expected, not simply that a reward has been obtained (Garris et al., 1999; Hollerman & Schultz, 1998; Hollerman et al., 1998; Schultz, 1997; Schultz et al., 1997).

There is strong evidence that the brain has a second system, which operates for **nondeprived reward**, reward that occurs when you haven't actually required the rewarding stimulus or activity—in other words, when you had a want but not a need. John hadn't eaten since noon on the day of the mugging. After the fear and excitement of that experience, and the calming effect of Barbara's company, he realized how hungry he was. The pleasure he then found in eating was medi-ated by brain circuits used in deprived reward, which rely on dopamine. In con-trast, at the end of the meal, even though he was no longer hungry, he ordered a sinful ice-cream-drenched-in-hot-chocolate-sauce dessert simply for the pleasure of eating. In this case, he was nondeprived. Although dopamine plays a crucial role in producing the rewarding effects of a stimulus or activity that fills a depri-vation, it does not play a role when you are not deprived. The part of the brain involved in nondeprived reward is in the brainstem. Lesions in this area knock out the system that registers reward when an animal is not deprived, but leave intact the system for deprived reward (Bechara & Van der Kooy, 1992; Berridge, 1996; Nader et al., 1997).

The existence of two different brain systems for reward is grounds for draw-ing a psychological distinction between needs and wants, between motivation that arises when a requirement must be filled and motivation that arises when a goal that is not a requirement is desired. Figure 7.5 summarizes the relation between these different facets of motivation.

Figure 7.5   Needs and Wants

Needs and wants can be either intrinsic or extrinsic, and either con-scious or unconscious.

Types of Needs: No Shortage of Shortages

There are psychological as well as bodily needs. Researchers have proposed that these include a need to be competent, to be autonomous (Sheldon et al., 1996), to have social approval, to use cognition (Cacioppo et al., 1996), to be dominant or in control (Kim & Kim, 1997), to be affiliated with others, to be powerful (McClelland et al., 1989), to reach closure (Kruglanski & Webster, 1996; Taris, 2000), to understand, to maintain self-esteem, and even to find the world benev-olent (Stevens & Fiske, 1995). Most of the pertinent studies examine individual

Nondeprived reward: Reward that occurs even when a requirement is not being met.

differences in various needs. These individual differences probably arise from differences in personal inherited temperament (Kagan, 1994a) and differences in personal experiences, such as interactions with peers (Harris, 1998) and family (Sulloway, 1996).

A classic example of a psychological need is the **need for achievement** (*nAch;* McClelland & Atkinson, 1953), and there is a large body of research assessing the consequences of differences in this need (for example, Neel et al., 1986; Spangler, 1992). People who have a high need for achievement tend to assume that their successes are due to their personal characteristics, whereas their failures are due to environmental circumstances (Nathawat et al., 1997; Weiner & Kukla, 1970). In a meta-analysis, Spangler (1992) found that measures of "implicit" (that is, not conscious) need for achievement predict actual success better than "explicit" (or conscious) need, as measured by questionnaires filled in by participants.

Abraham Maslow (1970) created a hierarchy of physical and emotional needs, illustrated in Figure 7.6. Lower-level needs are considered more essential to life, and must be met before needs further up the hierarchy can be addressed and satisfied. Ascending the hierarchy, the needs are considered less basic because they arise less frequently and, if not met, do not seriously impair the quality of life. You can live without understanding the world, but not without air or food. According to Maslow's theory, once a need is met, it becomes less important, and unmet, higher-level needs become more important. During crises (such as loss of a home by fire), needs regress to a lower level and higher-level needs are put on hold.

Maslow's hierarchy of needs has had an enormous impact on how people think about motivation, particularly in the business world (Soper et al., 1995). But is it right? There are three major difficulties with Maslow's theory. First, research has produced mixed evidence, at best, for the idea that needs are organized into a hierarchy. Results of questionnaire studies generally show that the levels are not clearly distinct from one another, as revealed by factor analysis (Wahba & Bridwell, 1976). In addition, there is no clear-cut ordering of needs (Soper et al., 1995;

Figure 7.6 Maslow's Hierarchy of Needs

According to Maslow's theory, needs lower in the pyramid must be met before needs higher in the pyramid become the focus of concern.

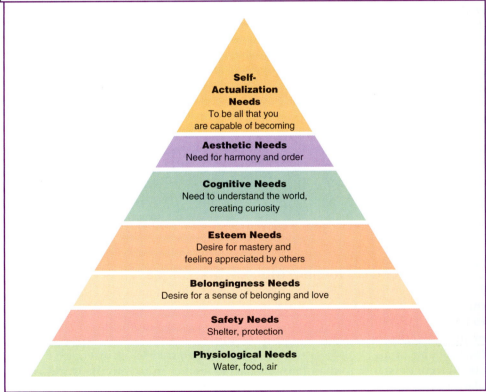

Self-Actualization Needs
To be all that you are capable of becoming

Aesthetic Needs
Need for harmony and order

Cognitive Needs
Need to understand the world, creating curiosity

Esteem Needs
Desire for mastery and feeling appreciated by others

Belongingness Needs
Desire for a sense of belonging and love

Safety Needs
Shelter, protection

Physiological Needs
Water, food, air

Wahba & Bridwell, 1976). Beer (1966), for example, found that female clerks reported strong social needs and a strong need for self-actualization but not a strong need for self-esteem. Second, there is no good evidence that unmet needs become more important and that met needs become less important. In fact, Hall and Nougaim (1968) found that the longer a need was satisfied, the more important it became. Third, it fails to explain various phenomena—for example, why people voluntarily go to war and put themselves in the line of fire (Fox, 1982).

Achievement in Individualist Versus Collectivist Cultures

Many of the goals that motivate us are provided by groups, and the structure of the society determines what sorts of activities will be reinforced. Cultures can be divided into two general types that affect achievement motivation differently. **Individualist cultures,** such as that of the United States, emphasize the rights and responsibilities of the individual over those of the group. **Collectivist cultures,** such as those of Asia, emphasize the rights and responsibilities of the group over those of the individual. Such cultural differences have been shown to affect achievement goals. For example, Anglo-Australians (from an individualist culture) have been found to be focused more on personal success than on family or groups, whereas Sri Lankans (from a collectivist culture) are oriented more toward their families and groups (Niles, 1998). Similarly, Sagie, Elizur, and Hirotsugu (1996) found that Americans had higher achievement motivation (as measured by scales that emphasize individual achievement) than Japanese or Hungarians, members of collectivist cultures.

Thus, growing up in one or the other type of culture influences a person's needs and wants. Some of these effects may occur because people have different ideas about their important characteristics; for example, Americans have been found to report higher feelings of self-competence than do Chinese. But the effects of their growing up in an individualist culture are not without a cost: Tafarodi and Swann (1996) found that Americans like themselves less than do Chinese. Why? Tafarodi and Swann believe that members of collectivist cultures are raised in a way that leads others to like them, in part by deemphasizing competition among individuals. This may lead to greater self-liking if we assume that our self-liking is increased if other people like us. In individualist cultures, on the other hand, members are raised to strive for freedom and independence, which tends to produce competition and conflict. In such cultures, there are more feelings of self-competence, but fewer of self-liking.

What sorts of needs do you suppose motivated President Franklin Delano Roosevelt? During all the days of FDR's presidency (1933–1945), he could not walk without the use of metal braces or crutches (he contracted polio in 1921 and was paralyzed thereafter). However, this did not stop him from getting around the White House on his own by using his hands to crawl from one room to another.

LOOKING AT LEVELS

Learned Helplessness

People not only can learn new strategies for coping with problems, but they also can learn to give up trying. Martin Seligman and his colleagues first described **learned helplessness,** which occurs when an animal has an aversive experience in which nothing it does can affect what happens to it, and so it simply gives up and stops trying to change the situation or to escape (Mikulincer, 1994). As shown in Figure 7.7 on page 258 (Overmeier & Seligman, 1967), when dogs were put in a cage in which they could not escape shocks, they eventually gave up responding and just huddled on the floor and endured—and they continued to do so even when they were moved to a new cage in which it was easy to escape the shocks. This condition can also afflict humans who experience a lack of control over negative events: If nothing you do seems to make an abusive spouse stop tormenting you, you may eventually just give up and stop trying. Learned helplessness can lead to depression and a range of stress-related problems.

It is clear that learned helplessness depends on events at the different levels of analysis. At the level of the group, others may create the situation from which you cannot escape. For example, a child trapped in an abusive family,

Figure **7.7** **The Classic Experiment of Overmeier and Seligman**

An animal is placed in a cage and shocked. Initially, the animal tries to escape, but it can do nothing to avoid or prevent the shocks.

The animal eventually gives up.

When the animal is moved into a new cage in which only a small barrier separates the side where shocks are delivered from the side where no shocks occur, it does not try to escape the shock, even when the shock is signaled by a tone.

who has no control over the situation, may eventually exhibit learned helplessness. Events at the level of the group can directly interact with an individual's experience, which then affects the tendency toward learned helplessness. This connection was clearly demonstrated when rats were given inescapable shocks either alone or in pairs. When in pairs, the rats fought with each other when they were being shocked. When tested individually 2 days later, the rats who were stressed in pairs displayed less learned helplessness than those stressed alone (Zhukov & Vinogradova, 1998). The fighting may simply have distracted them from the shocks, or this effect may reflect neural events that occurred when the rats fought, which in turn protected them against learned helplessness.

In addition, many studies have examined what happens in the brain when an animal has received uncontrollable shocks and descends into learned helplessness. The findings indicate that learned helplessness has a wide range of complex effects throughout the brain. For example, there is evidence that learned helplessness can lower the levels of the neurotransmitter serotonin, or decrease the numbers of receptors that are affected by it, in various parts of the brain (Amat et al., 1998; Papolos et al., 1996). Clearly, events at the different levels interact, and all must be taken into account if we are to understand when and why animals and humans come to behave as if they were helpless—even when they're not.

CONSOLIDATE!

1. **What are the sources of motivation?** Motivation arises for many reasons, including evolutionarily shaped instincts, drives, the maintenance of homeostasis, a desire to have an intermediate level of arousal, and incentives. Motivations can be intrinsic or extrinsic, and rewards may have different effects on the two types of motivation.

2. **What is the difference between "needs" and "wants," and how does culture affect them?** Needs arise when a requirement (physiological or psychological) is not met, which leads to a drive to fill the requirement (for example, a need for water

leads to a drive to drink). Needs may be related to a system in the brain that provides a reward when a deprivation is satisfied. In contrast, wants arise when an animal has an unmet goal that will not fulfill a requirement, which causes the goal to act as an incentive; wants may be related to a system in the brain that provides a reward when you achieve a desired goal but are not deprived. There are many types of needs and wants, and the importance of any given one depends partly on your culture—for example, on whether it is individualist versus collectivist.

Hunger and Eating: Not Just About Fueling the Body

When he sat down to dinner the evening of the mugging, John ate mechanically, paying little attention to what was in front of him. Food was now the last thing on John's mind, and he didn't have much of an appetite, even after joining Barbara in the safety and warmth of the restaurant. But after the first few bites, he realized that he was terrifically hungry and had no trouble polishing off a large dinner. He particularly liked Italian food, partly because it was one of his mother's specialties. Now, just smelling the richness and flavor of the homemade ravioli and fresh tomato sauce relaxed him and made his mouth water.

One of the drives that is best understood—and that motivates each of us every day—is hunger. Hunger is the classic drive that relies on the deprived reward system; by definition, to be hungry is to be deprived of food. However, not all eating occurs because we are hungry. Sometimes we eat because it's fun, in which case the pleasure ultimately relies on the operation of the nondeprived reward system. Hunger, and its satisfaction, affects many aspects of our lives, social and experiential as well as physiological.

1 What makes us hungry and leads us to eat particular foods at particular times?

2 How is our weight kept relatively constant? And why do some people become obese?

Eating Behavior: The Hungry Mind in the Hungry Body

Hunger arises from a particular state of the body, but eating is not always a result of hunger (Woods et al., 2000). What factors determine what and when we eat?

Is Being Hungry the Opposite of Being Full?

Although you might think of hunger as a continuum from starvation to satiety, hunger in fact arises from the action of two distinct brain systems. One system leads you to feel a need to eat; another leads you to feel satiated (Davis & Levine, 1977; Yeomans & Gray, 1997).

The feeling of a need to eat arises when your brain senses that the level of food molecules in your blood is too low. The brain registers the quantities of two major types of food molecules: *glucose* (a type of sugar) and *fatty acids* (Friedman, Tordoff, & Kare, 1991; Friedman, Tordoff, & Ramirez, 1986). In contrast, "feeling full" does not depend on the level of food molecules in the blood: You feel full well before food is digested and food molecules enter the bloodstream. If you suspect that feeling full has something to do with the state of your stomach, you're on the right track. If food is removed with a flexible tube from the stomach of a rat that has just eaten to satisfaction, the rat will eat just enough to replace the loss (Davis & Campell, 1973). But a full stomach is not enough to tell an animal to stop eating. Filling an animal's stomach with saltwater does not diminish appetite as much as filling it with milk, even if the fluids are placed directly into the stomach so that the animals cannot taste them (Deutsch et al., 1978). The stomach contains detectors that register the food value of its contents, and this information is transmitted to the brain. People know when to stop eating largely because of signals sent by sensory neurons in the stomach to the brain. Similar signals are also sent by other organs, including the upper part of the small intestine and the liver.

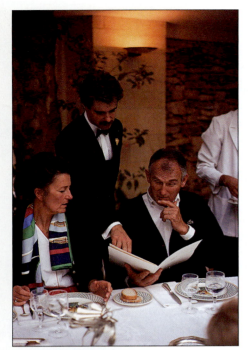

The brain system that regulates eating is surprisingly complex, as is revealed when it is disrupted by a stroke. For example, a person can develop what is known as gourmand syndrome, *a neurological disorder in which people become obsessed with fine food. Such people do not report being hungry all of the time, and may not overeat—but their entire lives become centered on food.*

What part of the brain detects these signals? Some 50 years ago researchers thought they had found "start" and "stop" eating centers in the brain. They had discovered that even small lesions (holes) in the lateral (side) part of the hypothalamus caused an animal to lose interest in food, even to the point of death by starvation. When this structure was electrically stimulated, the animal ate more and worked harder for food (Anand & Brobeck, 1952; Teitelbaum & Stellar, 1954). In contrast, the ventromedial (bottom, central) part of the hypothalamus was thought to be the center in the brain that told an animal it was full and should stop eating.

Other research, however, soon highlighted the difficulties in interpreting these findings. Lesions to the lateral hypothalamus suppressed the animals' interest not only in eating but also in drinking, sex, and even caring for their young; the result was often a general sluggishness. Researchers found that the lesions were disrupting not only the neurons in the lateral hypothalamus, but also connections between other areas. Similarly, when the ventromedial hypothalamus is damaged, animals don't just fail to stop eating, they become picky eaters (Ferguson & Keesey, 1975); indeed, they initially overeat carbohydrates (Sclafani & Aravich, 1983; Sclafani et al., 1983).

Improved methods allowed researchers to clear these muddy waters. When chemicals are used to destroy only the neurons in the lateral hypothalamus and none of the connections that pass through it, hunger *is* reduced more than most other drives (Dunnett et al., 1985; Stricker et al., 1978). The ventromedial hypothalamus appears to affect other brain regions that allow stored food molecules to be released; thus, when it is damaged, the animal has no choice but to keep eating (Weingarten et al., 1985). Rather than having centers in the hypothalamus that say "eat" or "don't eat," we, and other animals, have some neurons that signal when nutrient levels are low, and others that signal when stored food molecules should be released. These neurons act not so much like buttons or switches as like sensors that provide information that guides attention and behavior.

Appetite: A Moving Target

The early phases of eating depend on the taste of food. When you take the first bites of a meal or snack, you probably experience the *appetizer effect;* if those first bites taste good, your appetite is stimulated. This effect is driven in part by *opioids* in the brain; as you might suspect from their name, opioids are chemicals that behave like opium-derived drugs and cause you to experience pleasure. The opioids are released when you first eat food that tastes good (Yeomans & Gray, 1997).

As you continue to eat, your responses to food-related stimuli change. After eating some fresh-baked cookies, the smell of them doesn't seem quite as heavenly as it did before you ate them. If people have had their fill of a certain food, they rate its odor as less pleasant than they did before eating it (Duclaux et al., 1973). However, when the flavor, texture, color, or shape of a food is changed, people will eat more of the same food (Rolls, Rowe et al., 1981). After you've eaten a few chocolate chip cookies, you might find yourself not interested in more cookies, but happy to have some fresh-baked bread.

Not surprisingly, these changes in your appetite are linked to events in the hypothalamus. Neurons in the lateral hypothalamus initially fire to the sight or taste of a food, and then reduce their firing after an animal has eaten its fill of that food (Burton et al., 1976). These neurons are selective: After they stop responding to one food, they can still be stimulated by another (Rolls, Rowe et al., 1981; Critchley & Rolls, 1996, report similar findings in regions of the frontal lobe that are involved in emotional responses).

To understand why you eat the amount you do, you need to consider events at the different levels of analysis. Eating is not simply about events in the brain. The presence of other people influences how much you eat (De Castro, 1990). People report eating a greater amount when more people are present for a meal. Part of this effect may simply reflect the fact that when more people are present, the meal takes longer to complete. But this can't be all there is to it: When people eat in groups, they do not vary the size of their meals to reflect their degree of hunger—for example, by eating less for dinner if they had a late lunch—but they do make such adjustments when eating alone.

Anything that reminds you of good food you've eaten on a previous occasion—an event at the level of the person—can increase hunger. This effect occurs in part because your body responds not only to perceptions of food but also to thoughts of food by secreting **insulin**. Insulin is a hormone that stimulates the storage of food molecules in the form of fat. Thus, insulin reduces the level of food in the blood, which may increase hunger.

Tarantulas can go for 2 years without eating. Humans, on the other hand, can last for about a month without eating, provided that they can drink.

Why Does It Taste Good?

What about preferences for specific foods? Some of our tastes clearly are a consequence of beliefs that develop with experience. Some people develop disgust reactions to certain foods (Rozin & Fallon, 1986), and the very idea of that food then keeps them away from it. Such *cognitive taste aversion* is apparently long-lasting and can be formed without classical conditioning (for instance, without being nauseated after eating the food; Batsell & Brown, 1998). Rozin and his colleagues have shown that people apparently believe that "once in contact, always in contact." If a neutral food was in contact with an aversive food, the aversive properties seem to transfer. Suppose someone dunked a sterilized, dead cockroach briefly in your glass of water. Would you want to take a sip? The answer is probably a resounding no. Similarly, if a morsel of premium chocolate fudge were molded into the shape of feces, the shape alone would make it unappealing. Rozin and his colleagues have also shown that Americans harbor exaggerated beliefs about the harmful effects of some foods; in fact, many believe that salt and fat are harmful even at trace levels (Rozin et al., 1996).

Beliefs also play another role in determining what we want to eat: Perhaps unconsciously, people believe that "you are what you eat." Nemeroff and Rozin (1989) asked people to rate qualities of people who "ate boar" and those who "ate turtle." The boar eaters were believed to be more likely to have boarlike qualities, such as being bearded and heavy-set.

Culture plays a key role in shaping our tastes in food: Koreans find pickled snakes delicious; Filipinos enjoy unhatched chicks in the shell; the French would never give up their beloved snails or rabbit; the Germans savor stuffed pig intestines; and Chileans eat a kind of sea anemone whose looks would qualify it to star in a science-fiction movie. Cultures even differ in what they consider food: Every time you lick a stamp, you're consuming 1/10 of a calorie, so in Israel the glue on postage stamps has to be certified kosher.

Overeating: When Enough Is Not Enough

We humans like the taste of fatty foods, which is bad news because eating too much fat can lead to a variety of diseases, such as diabetes, cardiovascular disease, cancer, high blood pressure, and gallbladder disease (Schiffman et al., 1999). Diet books *and* cookbooks are best-sellers. Does this seem ironic to you? Do we want to lose weight so that we can eat more? Or does our love of eating make us need to diet? Our culture places a premium on being thin. Nonetheless, some of us overeat, and some of us are obese.

Set Point: Your Normal Weight

Animals, including humans, settle at a particular body weight that is easiest to maintain; this weight is called the **set point**. The set point is relatively constant, and homeostatic mechanisms keep it that way (Nisbett, 1972; Stunkard, 1982). Your life

Insulin: A hormone that stimulates the storage of food molecules in the form of fat.

Set point: The particular body weight that is easiest for an animal (including a human) to maintain.

is sustained by your body's **metabolism**, the sum of the chemical events in each of your cells, events that convert food molecules to the energy needed for the cells to function. Between meals, food molecules enter the bloodstream from fat cells and supply most of the energy your body needs to keep going. If your weight falls below the set point, fat cells become less likely to give up their stored fat. Receptors in your brain that are sensitive to low levels of fat then become active and make you hungry. Thus you end up gaining weight and getting back to your set point.

The set point is relatively constant, but it can be changed. If you overeat at a party, your body will still be able to keep your weight near its set point; the extra pound or two will come off easily within the week. But if you overeat for a prolonged time, the number of fat cells in your body increases, and your body has difficulty maintaining the set point weight. Thus, you gain weight. Moreover, the set point itself may change, becoming higher. In contrast, when you lose weight, each fat cell becomes thinner, but you don't lose fat cells. This may explain why the set point goes up as a result of chronic overeating—but then does not go down easily. Regular, moderately vigorous exercise can speed up your metabolism, leading your cells to need more energy even when you are not exercising. This is the best method of adjusting your set point.

Obesity

An obese person is defined as one who is more than 20% heavier than the medically ideal weight for that person's sex, height, and bone structure. By this standard, almost one-third of Americans are obese. Do these people have weak characters that make them slaves to food? No. The personality characteristics of obese and nonobese people are similar (Nilsson et al., 1998; Poston et al., 1999). Indeed, President William Howard Taft (1909–1913) was a grossly obese man, weighing over 300 pounds. He was so overweight that, after getting stuck in a White House bathtub, he had a new tub constructed that would hold four average-sized men. However, his size did not deter him from achieving the highest office in the land.

So why are some people obese? Some explanations have grown out of psychodynamic theory. According to one such theory, people become obese because they are threatened by their own sexuality. This *defense mechanism theory* holds that such people are afraid of being attractive and overeat to make themselves unattractive to others. However, as Bess (1997) points out, there is no scientific support for this theory. Another psychodynamically inspired theory maintains that obese people eat when they feel stress, again as a kind of defense. In this case, the evidence is mixed: Obese people do not always overeat when they feel stress and may instead tend to overeat when aroused, positively or negatively (Andrews & Jones, 1990; McKenna, 1972).

There is good reason to believe that at least some forms of obesity have a genetic basis. In fact, Bouchard, a researcher in this area, estimates that several dozen genes may affect weight in one way or another: "Some affect appetite, some affect satiety. Some affect metabolic rate" (quoted in Gladwell, 1998, p. 53). Thus, the genetics of obesity will not be a simple story, but the story is beginning to be told. First, the neurons involved in brain regions that register satiety appear to rely in part on the neurotransmitter serotonin (Blundell, 1977, 1984, 1986; Blundell & Halford, 1998), and mutant mice that lack specific receptors for this neurotransmitter will keep eating until they become obese (Tecott et al., 1995). The notion that humans may act the same way is supported by the finding that people gain weight if they take medication that happens to block these receptors (Fitton & Heel, 1990); in addition, people who take drugs that activate these receptors report being less hungry, and actually lose weight while on the medication (Sargent et al., 1997).

As we have seen, genes determine a reaction range, and the environment sets individuals within that range (Chapters 2 and 6). Some people have a propensity to become fat, but do so only in certain environments. Overeating is encouraged

Obese people have the same "will power" to resist eating junk food as nonobese people.

by many aspects of our environment: Food is relatively cheap, fast foods are high in fat, and portions have grown larger in the United States (but not in many parts of Europe). At the same time, people exercise less not only because most of us drive or ride to work, but also because our amusements, such as watching television and surfing the Web, are sedentary.

Some obese people are capable of losing large amounts of weight, and keeping the weight off (Tinker & Tucker, 1997). These people are able to adopt healthier eating and exercise habits. Note, however, that changes in the environment will be effective only if the reaction range for weight is relatively large (that is, if the genes define a wide range of possibilities). If the reaction range of certain genes that result in obesity is small, then people who have those genes may not have much choice in determining how heavy they are.

Genes can make a big difference. Researchers found that by altering a single gene, they could increase the production of substances that make a rat obese.

LOOKING AT LEVELS

The Starvation Diet

In our culture most of us are at some point concerned about our weight and thus may go on a diet. The most commonly recommended diet for obese people requires them to cut their normal food intake in half (Stallone & Stunkard, 1994). Keys and his colleagues (1950) studied the effects of such a diet on a group of 36 healthy young men. After 6 months, these men weighed on average 25% less than they had at the outset. In addition, they experienced many dramatic psychological changes, resulting from events at all three levels of analysis. At the level of the brain, their perceptual processes and sleep patterns changed. They slept less, became more sensitive to light and noise, had less tolerance for cold, and showed various other physical symptoms.

At the level of the person, the content of their thoughts changed. They became obsessed with food. Many began to hoard not only food, but also random junk. (This also happens with rats that are put on such diets [Fantino & Cabanac, 1980] and with people who have eating disorders and put themselves on similar diets [Crisp et al., 1980].) At the level of the group, they lost interest in sex and in interacting with other people. They also became irritable, anxious, depressed, and argumentative. Many of these symptoms persisted for months after the men began to eat normally again.

Of course, the effects at the three levels also interacted. Because the men were more irritable, others were less likely to seek their company and thus provide distraction from thoughts of food. Because their senses had become more acute, they were likely to avoid social situations. The most sobering point about this study is the realization that many people today voluntarily put themselves on stringent diets, without realizing the consequences.

CONSOLIDATE!

1 *What makes us hungry and leads us to eat particular foods at particular times?* Hunger occurs when the brain determines that the level of glucose and fatty acids in the bloodstream is too low. Hunger is not the opposite of being full; different mechanisms determine whether you are hungry or full. Being sated depends in large part on having nutrients in your stomach. At the beginning of a meal, taste plays an especially important role in determining whether you eat. As a meal progresses, changes in the type of food will keep your appetite up, and taste (as well as thoughts) that cause insulin to be released will increase hunger. Beliefs about the history of a food item (such as

whether it was ever in contact with something repulsive) and even associations linked to the shape of a food affect how appealing it is. You eat not only when you are hungry, but also when certain environmental and social cues are present.

2 *How is our weight kept relatively constant? And why do some people become obese?* The set point operates to keep your weight constant. However, chronic overeating can lead the set point of your body weight to move up, and once moved up, set points are difficult to move down again. At least some obese people are genetically predisposed to becoming obese.

Sex: Not Just About Having Babies

John had planned his anniversary dinner with Barbara carefully. He picked a restaurant that was a sentimental favorite of theirs, with fabulous food, soft lighting, and relaxing music. He suggested that they eat early so that there would be time for a romantic evening at his apartment. Unfortunately, after the mugging, he wasn't in the mood. But when they arrived at his apartment, he found that romantic thoughts returned and he enjoyed Barbara's company more than ever.

1 What is the nature of sexual response? What factors lead to it?

2 What determines whether we are attracted to the same sex or to the opposite sex?

3 What is "normal sexual behavior"? How does culture affect our standards of normality?

Sexual Behavior: A Many-Splendored Thing

People engage in sexual relations for two general reasons: to have babies (*reproductive sex*) and for pleasure (*recreational sex*). The vast majority of sexual acts, on the order of 98% (Linner, 1972), are for pleasure, as opposed to procreation. Sex leads to some of the most intense of all positive emotions, and hence it is valued highly by members of our species. The earliest known attempts at contraception were developed 4,000 years ago by the Egyptians; they thought dried crocodile dung would do the job.

Alfred Kinsey began the first systematic surveys about human sexual behavior in the late 1940s. He and his colleagues interviewed thousands of Americans about their sex lives. Kinsey found that people frequently reported sexual practices then considered rare or even abnormal. However, attempts to study sexual behavior ran into some unique problems. As Freud wrote (1910, p. 41), "People in general are not candid over sexual matters, they do not show their sexuality freely, but to conceal it wear a heavy overcoat of a tissue of lies, as though the weather were bad in the world of sexuality." Psychologists have had difficulty getting beyond this "tissue of lies," and even today there is debate about whether we have reliable information about many facets of human sexuality.

Most studies of sexual behavior rely on surveys. But would you volunteer to be in a study of sexual behavior? How about filling in a questionnaire about your most intimate moments? Researchers have found that not everybody is equally willing to participate in studies of sexual behavior, and thus the data are likely to come from a biased sample. Bogaert (1996), for example, found that the undergraduate males who volunteered for a study on human sexuality differed in many ways from those who volunteered for a study on personality: The former group had more sexual experience, were more interested in sexual variety, were more inclined to seek out sensation and excitement, and were less socially conforming and likely to follow rules (Trivedi & Sabini, 1998, report similar findings). In addition, people from different cultures may respond differently when asked about their sexual and reproductive behavior: Researchers found that Hispanic women reported less sexual activity when their interviewers were older, but African American women did not display this bias as strongly (Ford & Norris, 1997). The researchers suspected that this bias arose because the Hispanic culture has traditionally frowned on premarital sex for women, leading Hispanic women to under-report their sexual activity to older women who might disapprove.

In short, interview data about sex are suspect. Sampling bias as well as response bias can distort the results.

Sexual Responses: Step by Step

William Masters and Virginia Johnson (1966) were the first researchers to study systematically actual sexual behavior, not just reports of descriptions of it, with a large sample of participants. Their effort was the first that provided a look behind the "tissue of lies" about sex. Over the course of many years, Masters and Johnson brought thousands of men and women into their laboratory and devised ways to measure what the body does during sex. The outcome was a comprehensive description of the **sexual response cycle (SRC)**, the stages the body passes through during sexual activity. They discovered that both men and women pass through four such stages: (1) *excitement* (during the initial phases, when the person becomes aroused); (2) *plateau* (a full level of arousal); (3) *orgasm* (accompanied by muscle contractions, and ejaculation in men); and (4) *resolution* (the release of sexual tension). These stages meld into one another, with no sharp divisions separating them (Levin, 1980, 1994).

The mountain of research they conducted led Masters and Johnson to reach four general conclusions: (1) Men and women are similar in their bodily reactions to sex; (2) women tend to respond more slowly than men, but stay aroused longer; (3) many women can have multiple orgasms, whereas men typically have a *refractory period,* a period of time following orgasm when they cannot become aroused again; and (4) women reported that penis size is not related to sexual performance, unless the man is worried about it.

Others have built on Masters and Johnson's research, sometimes focusing on the very first stages of sexual activity, triggered by *sexual desire* (Kaplan, 1979). Our current understanding is that *sexual attraction* leads to *sexual desire, sexual excitement* (arousal), and possibly *sexual performance* (which involves becoming fully aroused, reaching orgasm, and then experiencing resolution).

The Role of Hormones: Do Chemicals Dictate Behavior?

In 1849, German scientist Arnold Berthold wondered why castrated roosters acted like hens. They stopped crowing, mating with hens, fighting, and engaging in other typical rooster behaviors. So he castrated roosters and then put the testes into their abdominal cavities. Shortly thereafter, the roosters started behaving like roosters again. Berthold reasoned that the testes produced their effects not because of nerves or other physical connections, but because they released something into the bloodstream. We now know that what the testes release is the male hormone *testosterone.*

Hormones are chemicals that are secreted into the bloodstream primarily by endocrine glands and that trigger receptors on neurons and other types of cells (see Chapter 2). Hormones are controlled in large part by the pituitary gland, the brain's "master gland." The pituitary gland in turn is controlled by the hypothalamus, which plays a major role in emotion and motivation and is affected by hormones produced in the body. When you are sexually aroused, hormones from the gonads (the testes and ovaries) act on the brain and genital tissue. **Androgens** are male hormones (such as testosterone), which cause many male characteristics such as beard growth and a low voice. **Estrogens,** female hormones, cause many female characteristics such as breast development and the bone structure of the female pelvis. The presence of the different hormones is not all-or-none between the sexes. Both types of hormones are present in both males and females, but to different degrees.

Sexual response cycle (SRC): The stages the body passes through during sexual activity, now characterized as including sexual attraction, desire, excitement, and performance (which includes plateau, orgasm, and resolution).

Androgens: Male hormones, which cause many male characteristics such as beard growth and a low voice.

Estrogens: Female hormones, which cause many female characteristics such as breast development and the bone structure of the female pelvis.

Unlike their direct effects on physical characteristics, hormones don't directly dictate behavior. Rather, they lead to a tendency to *want* to behave in certain ways in the presence of particular stimuli. That is, they modify motivation.

For example, changes in the level of sex hormones over the course of a woman's menstrual cycle affect the degree to which she is inclined to become sexually aroused. Slob and colleagues (1996) found that erotic videos increased the temperature of the female genital area more during the days just before ovulation than during the days following ovulation, and the women who were about to ovulate generally had increased sexual desire and sexual fantasies for the next 24 hours. In fact, researchers have found that women who were about to ovulate tended to classify very briefly presented pictures as sexual stimuli, both when the stimuli were in fact in this category (pictures of nude men) and when they were not (pictures of babies or objects related to body care; Krug et al., 1994). However, the effects of shifting hormone levels are only tendencies, affecting different people to different degrees (Regan, 1996). For example, Van Goozen and colleagues (1997) found that only those women who had premenstrual complaints had peak sexual interest during the ovulatory phase.

The relationship between hormones and motivation runs in both directions. In a famous study, a researcher who signed his paper only as "Anonymous" (1970) reported the effects of his building anticipation of female companionship after sustained periods of enforced celibacy. This man was a scientist who worked on a small island and only occasionally visited the mainland, where he would have brief periods of contact with the opposite sex. He apparently had time on his hands when he was alone, and decided to measure his beard growth every day by weighing his beard clippings after shaving. He found that his beard grew thicker as his visits to the mainland approached. Just thinking about the visit apparently caused increases in male hormones, which in turn caused increased beard growth.

But we are not simply creatures of our hormones. To study the role of testosterone on sexual behavior and mood, Schiavi and colleagues (1997) injected men who had difficulty having erections with the hormone twice a week for 6 weeks; this course was followed by injections of a placebo for 4 weeks (the change was not known to the participants). Although the participants did ejaculate more often when they were receiving the testosterone than when they were receiving the placebo, little else changed. Testosterone did not affect the amount of sexual satisfaction, the rigidity of the penis during sex, or mood. Clearly, sex is about much more than just hormones.

Figure 7.8 Motives for Having Sex

People engage in sex for many reasons, which Cooper and colleagues (1998) characterize as falling along two dimensions.

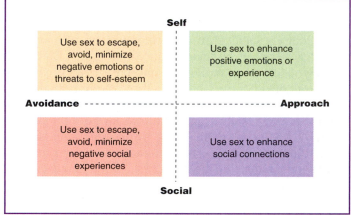

Chapter 7 Emotion and Motivation: Feeling and Striving   www.ablongman.com/kosslynbrief

Sexual Motivation

People use sex to satisfy different psychological needs. Cooper and colleagues (1998) showed that motivations for having sex can be thought of in terms of the two dimensions illustrated in Figure 7.8, which range from avoidance to approach (the horizontal dimension) and from social connection to independence (the vertical dimension). The importance of these dimensions is different for different people and in different contexts—for instance, for people in stable relationships, exclusive relationships, or relationships that are both stable and exclusive.

Certain genes that affect the brain receptors for the neurotransmitter dopamine influence the age at which people first have sexual intercourse (Miller et al., 1999).

Sexual Orientation: More Than a Choice

People who are sexually attracted to the opposite sex are termed **heterosexual;** people attracted to the same sex are termed **homosexual;** people attracted to both sexes are termed **bisexual.** Sexuality might best be regarded as a continuum, with most people being primarily heterosexual and somewhere between 4% and 10% of the U.S. population being primarily homosexual in their behavior (Fay et al., 1989). Studies of bisexual men have shown that many of them tend to become more homosexually oriented over time (Stokes et al., 1997). For many years, homosexuality was considered either a personal choice or the result of being raised a certain way (for instance, with a weak father and an overly strict mother). However, programs to train homosexuals to prefer the opposite sex have failed, even those that relied on extreme techniques such as electric shock to punish homosexual thoughts or behavior (Brown, 1989, offers a personal account).

There is now evidence that people do not simply choose to be homosexual or heterosexual, nor are homosexuals or heterosexuals created by the ways their parents treat them as young children. Rather, biological events appear to play a major role in determining sexual orientation. LeVay (1991) studied the brains of homosexual men and found that a small part of their hypothalami, about as large as an average-sized grain of sand, was approximately twice as small as in the brains of heterosexual men (Allen & Gorski, 1992, report related evidence). This is interesting in part because others had previously found that this same structure typically is smaller in women than in men. However, all of the brains LeVay studied came from men who had died of AIDS, and it is possible that the disease had something to do with the structural abnormality. When this same structure was surgically disrupted in monkeys, however, they displayed atypical sexual behavior (Slimp et al., 1978). These and similar data suggest that there is a biological predisposition for some people to become homosexual (for a review, see LeVay & Hamer, 1994).

Other differences between heterosexual and homosexual people point toward biological differences. Consider, for example, the sound that is emitted from the ears of some people in some circumstances (see the discussion in Chapter 3). In some cases the sound is a response to a heard click, and the ears of some people actually emit sound even without such a trigger event. It turns out that this response to a click is less frequent and weaker for homosexual and bisexual women than for heterosexual women—in fact, men in general have less frequent and weaker ear responses than heterosexual women (McFadden & Pasanen, 1999). Apparently, parts of the ear are different in these women. However, no such difference appears among heterosexual, bisexual, and homosexual men. Thus, these results not only show a biological difference for homosexual and bisexual women, but may also hint at different biological bases for male and female homosexuality.

Heterosexual: A person who is sexually attracted to members of the opposite sex.

Homosexual: A person who is sexually attracted to members of the same sex.

Bisexual: A person who is sexually attracted to members of both sexes.

The findings of biological differences between homosexual and heterosexual people do not indicate whether the causes are hereditary (that is, genetic), the result of experiences in the womb, or the result of experiences during early childhood. Hamer and his colleagues (1993) studied 114 families that included a homosexual man and found that inheritance of homosexuality seemed to be passed from the mother. This result led them to examine the X chromosome, which is the sex chromosome from the mother (females have two X chromosomes, one from the mother and one from the father; males have only one X chromosome, from the mother, and a Y chromosome from the father). And in fact a small portion of the X chromosome appears to be related to homosexual preference and behavior. Although Bailey and Pillard (1991) conducted a study with twins that supported the idea that homosexuality is at least partly inherited, a more recent study failed to find this effect (Rice et al., 1999). Thus, the evidence for the claim that homosexuality is determined in part by genes is mixed, and we must await further research before reaching strong conclusions.

To say that homosexuality has biological roots is not to rule out a role for the environment. Bem (1996, 1998) has argued that young boys who are not typical of their sex, in that they are not physically strong and have gentle temperaments, prefer to play with girls—and it is this socialization experience that later leads them to become homosexual. In Bem's view, "exotic becomes erotic": If young boys identify with girls and engage in girl-like behavior, it is boys who become "dissimilar, unfamiliar and exotic" and thus "erotic." For girls, the reverse would hold true, with "tomboy" girls choosing to associate with boys and engage in boy-like activities, and thus later finding girls exotic and hence erotic. According to this theory, biology would affect the body and temperament, and only indirectly affect sexual orientation. However, to explain why it has proved so difficult to alter sexual orientation in adulthood, we would need to assume that at a certain age sexual orientation is set and thereafter difficult to modify.

What's Normal?

For many years the manual of the American Psychiatric Association classified homosexuality as a psychological disorder, but (after conducting a poll of its members) in 1973 this classification was deleted. What is normal sexual behavior?

Cultural Variations: Experience Counts

Sexual behavior is partly instinctive, but like eating, it is also molded by personal tastes and by culture (see Figure 7.9). For example, among the people of the Grand Valley Dani in Indonesia the men apparently have extraordinarily little interest in sex (Heider, 1976). They reportedly do not have intercourse with their wives for 5 years after a child is born; nor do they seem to have other sexual outlets. Nonetheless, these people do not seem unhappy. At the opposite extreme, the Mangaians, who live on an island in the South Pacific, may have sex up to the time when a woman goes into labor and may resume sex within a few days after the birth of a child, although they typically wait a few months (Marshall, 1971).

Cultural variations occur over time, even within a single group. In the 20 years that followed the decade of the 1950s, attitudes about sex changed dramatically in the United States, in large part because of the development of effective birth control. "Free sex," a motto of the '60s generation, encouraged sexual liberation; people should be free, proponents said, to have sex when and where they choose (in those days, young women sometimes brought a condom and toothbrush with them on the first date). Today, with the spread of AIDS and the resurgence of fundamentalist and evangelical religions, sexual behavior may be changing again, becoming less casual. Culture clearly affects how, when, and where sexual behavior occurs.

Figure **7.9** **Major Factors That Affect Human Sexual Activity**

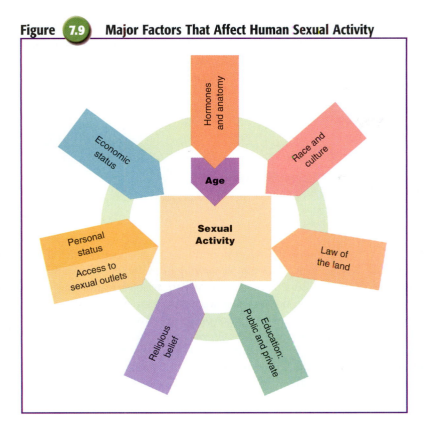

Sexual Dysfunction: When Good Things Go Wrong

Despite the many variations in human sexual behavior in different times and places, psychologists do consider some sexual behaviors to be dysfunctional. Categorizing a behavior as "dysfunctional" depends in part on the individual, in part on the relationship, and in part on the standards of the surrounding culture. *Sexual dysfunctions,* according to the fourth edition of the *Diagnostic and Statistical Manual of Mental Disorders* (American Psychiatric Association, 1994), "are characterized by disturbance in sexual desire and the psychophysiological changes that characterize the sexual response cycle and cause marked distress and interpersonal difficulty" (p. 493). Included in this description are disorders of sexual desire, arousal, orgasmic disorders, and sexual pain. Many, if not most, problems in the sexual response cycle have psychological causes; they are not caused by physical problems with the sex organs. An example is the inability to reach orgasm. In men, the disorder is called *male erectile dysfunction* (or *impotence*); in women, it is known as *female arousal dysfunction* (previously called *frigidity*). Masters and Johnson found that such sexual disorders often arise because of a preoccupation with personal problems, fears about the possible consequences of sexual activity, or anxiety about sexual performance.

However, at least some sexual dysfunction may have a biological cause. The drug Viagra caused quite a stir when it was first released in the late 1990s because it provided a safe and effective medical treatment for impotence. Viagra doesn't cause an erection. Rather, the drug operates only when a man is sexually excited, by increasing the flow of blood to the penis. Thus Viagra is not a cure but a treatment for impotence, and it is effective only if it continues to be taken. The user of this drug who would derive the most benefit would be a middle-aged man who has difficulty keeping an erection and wants to be sexually active. Some women also use this drug now that it has proved to have a similar effect on the clitoris. However, Viagra commonly has side effects, which range from headache and stomachache to changes in color vision (such as difficulty discriminating between green

The male praying mantis can copulate only after its head has been ripped off, a service readily provided by the receptive female. Some lions copulate over 50 times a day. Human sexual behavior is also shaped by our biologies, but it is much more variable than that of other animals.

and blue). Furthermore, in some cases impotence is an early warning sign of something more serious: the veins carrying blood to the penis can become narrowed by buildup of plaque in the blood vessels, which can also lead to heart attacks and stroke. Thus, purchasing Viagra over the Web without seeing a physician is not medically sound.

LOOKING AT LEVELS

Homophobia

To study one possible basis of strong negative views of homosexuals, Adams and colleagues (1996) asked two groups of male heterosexuals to watch videotapes that showed heterosexuals, lesbians, or gay men engaging in explicit sex acts. One group of men had scored high on a test of *homophobia,* which is a strong aversion to homosexuality; the other group scored low. While both groups watched the tapes, the researchers recorded changes in penile circumference as an indication of sexual arousal. All the participants became aroused when they saw the heterosexual and lesbian videos, but only the homophobic males were aroused by the homosexual male videos. The investigators note that psychoanalytic theory might explain these results by claiming that the homophobic men had repressed homosexual impulses. Alternatively, they note that another theory would explain the results in terms of anxiety (Barlow, 1986). In this view, the homosexual stimuli produce negative emotions, which in turn lead to anxiety, which in turn enhances arousal, which leads to erection.

Consider this result from the levels perspective. First, it is clear that visual stimuli can trigger the brain mechanisms that lead to arousal. Second, which stimuli are arousing depends on personal characteristics: Men who disliked homosexuals had stronger penile responses to the homosexual videos than did men who were not homophobic. Third, we are led to ask the question, Why did some men strongly dislike homosexuals? It is easy to speculate that they would not have felt this way in a different culture, such as that of ancient Greece, in which homosexuality was accepted. If the arousal was in fact sexual, these men may actually have been denying their own homosexual tendencies because cultural norms stigmatized such behavior. On the other hand, if the arousal was a consequence of a negative reaction to the films, this response too may have been mitigated had they grown up in a different culture. And of course, such a reaction affects how these people behave and think. For example, they may avoid certain bars or have negative reactions to gays or embrace socially restrictive policies regarding homosexuals.

CONSOLIDATE!

1. *What is the nature of sexual response? What factors lead to it?* According to the most accepted descriptions of sexual activity, people first experience sexual attraction, next desire, and then excitement (arousal), which may be followed by sexual performance; sexual performance involves becoming fully aroused (plateau), orgasm, and finally resolution (followed by a refractory period for men). Hormones play a role in sexual behavior by biasing people to behave in certain ways.

2. *What determines whether we are attracted to the same sex or the opposite sex?* Biological events, caused by either the genes or events in the womb or childhood, appear to play a key role in determining sexual orientation. It is possible that biological events may only indirectly affect sexual orientation, by leading the child to select environments and have experiences that in turn shape sexual orientation.

3. *What is "normal sexual behavior"? How does culture affect our standards of normality?* Sexual variations are considered disorders only if they "cause marked distress and interpersonal difficulty." Although some such variations may have biological roots, many disorders arise for psychological reasons. Standards of normality are established by culture and can vary over time.

Recap and Thought Questions

Emotion: I Feel, Therefore I Am

Ekman and his collaborators have identified six basic emotions: happiness, anger, sadness, disgust, surprise, and fear. Research results have shown that surprise and fear are more easily confused with each other than are any of the others. Emotions can be organized into two broad categories, approach and withdrawal, which rely on different parts of the brain.

Although theories of emotion are often considered alternative views, each in fact has captured a grain of the truth. The James–Lange theory holds that you feel emotion after your body reacts to a situation; the Cannon–Bard theory holds that emotions and bodily reactions occur at the same time; cognitive theory claims that emotions arise when you interpret your bodily reactions in the context of the specific situation; and LeDoux's revision of cognitive theory rests on the idea that some emotions arise from brain responses that do not involve interpretation whereas others arise from cognitive interpretation. As James–Lange predicts, emotions may be caused in part by differences in bodily reactions, such as heart rate, breathing rate, and facial expression. As Cannon–Bard predicts, some emotions, such as fear, are reflexes that produce the experience and the bodily reaction simultaneously. As cognitive theory predicts, how you interpret the causes of your bodily reactions does in fact influence which emotion you feel. Finally, as claimed by LeDoux, some emotions, such as fear, arise via brain mechanisms (particularly those involving the amygdala) that do not rely on interpretation, whereas others do rely on interpretation. Environmental events influence emotion; our happiness, for example, depends in part on our economic and cultural context. Emotions also arise in response to other people's emotional signals, which vary depending on their cultures. Culture affects the display rules we use, the rules that determine when and how we express emotion. In addition, culture affects how effectively we can read body language to determine another person's emotion.

Can basic emotions allow us to understand Barbara's emotional state during her dinner with John? Probably not. Emotions are communicated both verbally and nonverbally, and women are particularly good at such nonverbal communication. When John first arrived, Barbara no doubt perceived his emotional state and was probably alarmed, sympathetic, and supportive. None of these emotions is simple, but rather all are examples of the complex mixtures of emotion that nuance our lives.

Think It Through. Would the world necessarily be a better place if people could control their emotions perfectly? Do you think children have the same emotions as adults? If interpretation plays a key role, in what ways would this limit the emotions very young children feel? How might this change with increasing development?

What would be the advantages and disadvantages of a machine that always detected lies and never mistook the truth for lies? If your school offered a course in reading body language, would you take it? Why or why not?

Motivation and Reward: Feeling Good

Motivation arises for many reasons. Some of our motivations arise from evolutionarily shaped instincts, sex being an obvious example; others are drives, such as thirst; some drives are designed to maintain homeostasis, such as occurs when we are cold and seek warmth; other motivations center on a preference for an intermediate level of arousal, as happens when we withdraw from even a pleasurable sensation such as music when we've "had enough." We are often motivated by incentives, such as the potential rewards (including money) for engaging in a behavior. Intrinsic motivations propel us to do something for its own sake, and extrinsic motivations propel us to do something for external reasons, such as for a reward you may receive.

A need is a condition that arises when you lack a requirement, which in turn gives rise to a drive to acquire specific rewards to fulfill the requirement; a want is a condition that arises when you have an unmet goal that will not fulfill a requirement, which in turn causes the goal to act as an incentive. The distinction between needs and wants lines up with a distinction between two different brain systems involved in motivation. Needs may be related to a brain system that provides an internal reward when a deprivation is satisfied, such as by eating when you are hungry. In contrast, many wants may be related to a system that provides a reward when you achieve a desired goal but are not deprived. There are many types of needs; the importance of a given need depends partly on your culture, particularly on whether the culture is individualist or collectivist.

Which theory of emotion best explains John's reactions during the mugging? You could make a case for instinct theory, but this theory would not explain why John was particularly prone to being startled as he rushed down the alley. Probably the best account would stem from

LeDoux's revision of cognitive theory: John's cognitive interpretation of the situation "potentiated" the brain circuitry (which relies on the amygdala) that is responsible for startle and for freezing. After the mugging, his interpretation of his bodily state, in that context, probably produced his continued fear and left him emotionally unsettled. And when he finally met Barbara, the same mechanisms shifted him to a more positive emotional state.

> **Think It Through.** If you could design a school for young children, how would you organize it so that the children were motivated as strongly as possible? How can you find out what motivates a particular person?
>
> If wants can never be satisfied for very long, does it make sense to try to fulfill them at all? How could you tell if a motivation is a need or a want?
>
> Do you think it might be useful to develop a drug that blocks the deprived reward system? The nondeprived system? Why might such a drug be dangerous? beneficial?

Hunger and Eating: Not Just About Fueling the Body

We eat for many reasons: pleasure, nutrition, as a social activity. The brain senses when the quantity of nutrients in the blood is too low and causes us to feel hungry. We usually eat until signals from the stomach (and other digestive organs) indicate that we've consumed enough food. At the beginning of a meal, taste plays an especially important role in determining whether you want to eat. As you continue to eat, changes in the type of food will keep your appetite up, and tastes (as well as thoughts) that cause insulin to be released will increase hunger. Beliefs about the history of a food item (for example, whether it was ever in contact with something repulsive) and even associations with the shape of the food affect how appealing it is. Overeating can lead the set point of your body weight to move up, and once moved up, set points are difficult to move down again. Obese people do not have "weak characters" but rather often may be genetically predisposed to becoming obese.

During their anniversary dinner, could John and Barbara have been eating for different reasons? John was not hungry initially, and only after beginning to eat did he become hungry. In spite of her sympathy for John's plight, Barbara had not experienced the same hunger-dampening trauma and thus would probably have begun eating because she was sensitive to signals that her blood sugar level was low. Toward the end of the meal, John may have decided to "reward himself for surviving" and thus indulged in a large dessert, whereas Barbara may have had no such desire.

> **Think It Through.** In the 1930s, Coke bottles held 6.5 ounces; today, they hold a liter—more than five times the original amount. We tend to think of a bottle as a single serving or perhaps two servings. What effects do you think this sort of change has on consumption? Does it make a difference that a lot of Coke is consumed on social occasions with a lot of people? If so, how could such a difference be minimized?

Sex: Not Just About Having Babies

Sexual attraction leads to sexual desire, sexual excitement (arousal), and possibly sexual performance (which involves becoming fully aroused, reaching orgasm, and then experiencing resolution followed, for men, by a refractory period). Hormones play a key role in sexual development and modify motivation toward sexual behavior.

There is evidence that male homosexuals have differences in certain brain structures, and that female homosexuals have differences in the operation of certain neural systems (involved in hearing), from heterosexuals. Such biological differences are caused either by genes or by events in the womb or during childhood. There is evidence that at least some forms of homosexuality are genetic. Sexual behaviors differ in different cultures, and what constitutes normal sexual behaviors varies widely. Sexual variations are considered disorders only if they cause "marked distress and interpersonal difficulty."

Could John have been sexually aroused because of his traumatic experience? Sexual arousal depends partly on the context; when John was in fight-or-flight mode, he was not likely to be thinking of sex. However, in another context, he might misattribute the beating of his heart, heavy breathing, and so on as indicators of sexual arousal. In this case, he probably correctly attributed his emotional upheaval and during dinner may even have misattributed bodily signs of arousal as additional results of his mugging—leading him to be less sexually aroused than he would otherwise have been.

> **Think It Through.** Could someone feel sexual desire for a partner but have a hard time becoming sexually aroused? Why or why not? Would it be ethical to use a perfume or aftershave lotion that contained chemicals that made you sexually attractive when you were going out on a date?
>
> Do you think researchers should be trying to find a gene (or genes) for homosexuality? What positive uses could such knowledge have? What negative uses? Would it be ethical to try to alter such genes either before conception or in the womb?

REVIEW TEST

For each of the following items, choose the single correct or best answer. The correct answers appear at the end.

1 When people have approach emotions (e.g., love and happiness), the _____ tends to be active.
   a. left frontal lobe
   b. left temporal lobe
   c. right temporal lobe
   d. right frontal lobe

2 Schacter and Singer (1962) found that when physiologically aroused through the administration of a drug, research participants _____.
   a. became distraught and angry
   b. reacted differently, depending on the context
   c. reacted the same, regardless of the context
   d. became happy and compliant

3 Which of the following statements about fear is *not* true?
   a. Fear that has been associated with a particular object or situation is virtually impossible to extinguish completely.
   b. You cannot become fearful simply by imagining a scary situation.
   c. Complex cognitive processing is not necessary for a stimulus to elicit fear.
   d. People with damage to the amygdala cannot recognize fear or anger in the tone of other people's voices.

4 Thirst is a good example of a(n) _____, while sex is a good example of a(n) _____.
   a. drive; incentive
   b. drive; motive
   c. incentive; drive
   d. motive; drive

5 If you play the piano only because you get paid for doing so, you are _____ motivated to play.
   a. extrinsically
   b. intrinsically
   c. inherently
   d. expectantly

6 Lacking nutrients is an example of a(n) _____.
   a. need
   b. want
   c. incentive
   d. motive

7 The neurotransmitter underlying deprived reward is _____.
   a. adrenaline
   b. GABA
   c. dopamine
   d. serotonin

8 People in individualist cultures have a higher need for _____ than people in collectivist cultures.
   a. dominance
   b. achievement
   c. affiliation
   d. cognition

9 The two major types of food molecules registered by the brain are _____ and _____.
   a. endorphins; proteins
   b. proteins; fats
   c. glucose; protein
   d. fatty acids; glucose

10 If your weight falls below your body's set point, _____.
   a. fat cells give up more fat
   b. insulin is released
   c. fat cells give up less fat
   d. weight loss speeds up

11 In comparison to nonobese people, obese people are _____.
   a. lazier
   b. weaker
   c. smarter
   d. no different

12 People who significantly diet (cutting approximately half of their normal food intake) experience all of the following except _____.
   a. less tolerance for cold
   b. decreased interest in social interaction
   c. irritability, anxiety, and depression
   d. decreased sensitivity to light and noise

13 Hormones are controlled largely by the _____, the brain's "master gland."
   a. pituitary gland
   b. central gland
   c. hippocampus
   d. amygdala

14 In a study of men who had difficulty having erections, injections of testosterone _____.
   a. increased sexual satisfaction
   b. increased desire
   c. caused more ejaculations
   d. diminished desire

15 Homosexuality is probably the result of _____.
   a. extreme fear of the opposite sex
   b. a biological predisposition
   c. childhood sexual abuse
   d. inadequate parenting

ANSWERS: 1.a 2.b 3.b 4.a 5.a 6.a 7.c 8.b 9.d 10.a 11.d 12.d 13.a 14.c 15.b

8 Personality

VIVE LA DIFFERENCE!

Tina and Gabe met in their introductory psychology class. They were immediately attracted to each other and started studying together. After a few conversations they were pleased to discover they had similar values and political views. Predictably, they began going out together. On their fourth date, though, Tina began to realize that she and Gabe weren't as much alike as she had thought; she was surprised by this because their views on so many issues were so similar. Tina sometimes had trouble "reading" Gabe because he was shy and emotionally steady, without many highs or lows; his manner was "mellow." She wondered why he wasn't more enthusiastic when she proposed activities she thought would be fun to do together, such as in-line skating, bungee-jumping, or biking. "Well, opposites attract, I guess," she thought. And although Gabe enjoyed Tina's spirit, her outgoingness and emotional vibrancy, her interest in trying new things, now and then he asked her why she was so emotional and always in such a hurry. Tina began to worry that, even though they were strongly attracted to each other, a long-term relationship might reveal persistent problems between them that would be difficult to overcome.

Do these differences reveal something fundamental about Tina and Gabe as people? Do they reflect their personalities? And if so, are personalities set in stone?

This chapter explores the idea of personality, the ways that psychologists measure it, and the perspectives of a number of different theorists who have sought to describe and explain it. We'll consider issues such as the genetic influence on personality development; the relation of inner motives, thoughts, and feelings to personality; and the effects of the social environment on personality.

What Is Personality?

As Tina got to know Gabe, she began to make certain assumptions about him, about who he was as a person. He studied hard and did well on psychology exams and quizzes, so Tina figured he was smart, hard-working, and conscientious. (Tina did well on her psychology exams and quizzes, too, but she didn't study much. She considered herself smart, but not particularly hard-working.) So she was surprised to discover that Gabe's apartment was a disaster area—she had assumed he would be as orderly and neat in his personal space as he was in his approach to schoolwork, and so she wondered whether his "personality," as she thought of it, was altogether consistent. Tina also noticed that, on dates, Gabe preferred to get together for dinner and a movie, not for lunch or an afternoon break ("Too much studying," he said). If she suggested going to a party together, Gabe invariably declined; he didn't like parties. Tina attributed this reluctance to his shyness.

The concept of personality infuses daily life. When you describe a coworker as "intense," wonder how a friend will handle a piece of bad news, or think about the type of partner you would like to have in life, personality is exerting its influence. What exactly is this quality, which is part and parcel of each of us? **Personality** has been described as a consistent set of characteristics that people display over time and across situations, and that distinguish individuals from each other. Thus the very concept of personality implies that people have enduring, stable qualities such as, say, talkativeness or curiosity. These qualities are called **personality traits**, relatively consistent characteristics exhibited across a range of situations. But notice the "relatively" in the preceding sentence. Let's see just what that means.

1 Does such a thing as a consistent personality really exist, or do our behaviors, thoughts, and feelings depend primarily on the situation?

2 How do psychologists group personality traits into sets of personality types?

3 What methods do psychologists use to measure personality?

Personality: Traits or Situations?

Traits exist on a continuum (for example, from extremely quiet to extremely talkative). Gabe's shyness and Tina's adventurousness can be considered traits. Many trait theorists—personality psychologists who study traits and believe that personality is built on traits—assume that everyone has the same set of traits, but that for each person each trait falls at a different point on its continuum. Some trait theorists propose that our traits lead us to behave in certain ways; this view would suggest that Gabe avoided parties because of his trait of shyness. Not all trait theorists share the belief in this cause-and-effect relationship, however; some trait theorists regard traits simply as labels for collections of behaviors rather than as causes of them (Buss & Craik, 1984).

Traits by definition imply consistency. But are our personality traits always consistent? Bem and Allen (1974) found that people are not equally consistent on *all* traits. When they asked participants to rate how *consistently* friendly and conscientious they were, they found large variability in consistency; not all partici-

Personality: A consistent set of characteristics that people display over time and across situations, and that distinguish individuals from each other.

Personality trait: A relatively consistent characteristic exhibited in different situations.

Chapter 8 Personality: Vive la Difference!

pants felt that they were consistent on these traits. People who rated themselves as consistent on the trait of friendliness were more likely to have their behaviors reflect that trait than people who viewed themselves as inconsistent on the trait of friendliness. For instance, those consistent on the trait of friendliness were more likely to strike up a conversation with a sales clerk. Similar results were found for the trait of conscientiousness: People who rated themselves as consistent on this trait were more likely to exhibit relevant behaviors, such as carefully double-checking term papers for typing and spelling errors. Kenrick and Stringfield (1980) further refined Bem and Allen's research by showing that everyone is consistent on some traits, but that the particular traits on which people differ vary across individuals. Thus, everyone does not have some level of each trait; some traits are just irrelevant for some of us—they aren't important in our lives (Britt & Shepperd, 1999). For example, Gabe may be inconsistent on the general dimension of conscientiousness, which would explain the coexistence of his conscientious attention to schoolwork and his careless housekeeping at home. Whether or not traits are viewed as causing behavior, they certainly aren't always accurate in *predicting* behavior (witness Gabe's domestic messiness). The situations in which we find ourselves can exert powerful influences on behavior, thoughts, and feelings.

The names of Snow White's seven dwarves fit their personalities. Imagine the personalities of dwarves named Dirty, Hungry, Shifty, Flabby, Puffy, Crabby, Awful, and Doleful, all of which were on Disney Studios' list of possible names (Seuling, 1976). The final choices work so well because we view their personalities as consistent with their names; but what if Grumpy were, in fact, upbeat and easy-going!

Situationism: Different Traits for Different Contexts

Does the following paragraph represent an accurate description of your personality?

> You have a strong need for other people to like you and for them to admire you. You have a tendency to be critical of yourself. You have a great deal of unused capacity which you have not turned to your advantage. While you have some personality weaknesses, you are generally able to compensate for them. Your sexual adjustment has presented some problems for you. Disciplined and controlled on the outside, you tend to be worrisome and insecure inside. At times you have serious doubts as to whether you have made the right decision or done the right thing. You prefer a certain amount of change and variety and become dissatisfied when hemmed in by restrictions and limitations. You pride yourself as being an independent thinker and do not accept others' opinions without satisfactory proof. You have found it unwise to be too frank in revealing yourself to others. At times you are extroverted, affable, sociable, while at other times you are introverted, wary, and reserved. Some of your aspirations tend to be pretty unrealistic. (Ulrich et al., 1963, p. 832)

Does this sound like you? If you had taken a personality test and this paragraph was given to you as a summary of your test results, you probably would have agreed with it. That is exactly what happened in a study in which undergraduate participants were asked to take a personality test and then *all the participants* were given this same paragraph as a summary of their results, *regardless of their responses on the test*. The students rated the summary interpretation as good or excellent (Snyder & Larson, 1972; Ulrich et al., 1963). But how could "one size fit all"—how can we make sense of these results? Because most people experience some of the traits described in the summary *in some situations* and at *some points in their lives*. Hence, the statements were true—some of the time. Reread the paragraph, and note how many of the statements present descriptions of two opposing characteristics, such as being extroverted at times, introverted at other times. This kind of dual presentation is what makes horoscopes so often seem to be on the mark.

A larger question arises, then, about the consistency of personality traits: If much of our behavior depends on the situation in which we find ourselves, is there such a thing as a consistent personality trait at all? To investigate this question, Hartshorne and May (1928) gave grade-school children the opportunity for undetected deceit: to lie about how many push-ups they were able to do, to lie to their parents about how much work they did at home, to cheat on a school test, and to keep money they were given for other purposes. The researchers found that children who were dishonest in one situation were not necessarily dishonest in another; a child who cheated on a test would not necessarily lie to his or her parents. Although the children showed some consistency across situations, less than 10% of the variation of behaviors across situations could be explained by a single, common, underlying trait of honesty. Not surprisingly, though, the less similar the situations, the lower were the correlations of honesty between situations; lying and stealing were not highly correlated. Remember that a correlation (see Chapter 1) is an index of how closely related two sets of measured variables are—in this case, lying and stealing.

Similarly, Mischel and Peake (1982) observed college students and recorded 19 different behaviors reflecting conscientiousness, as defined by how regularly they attended class, how promptly they completed assignments, how neatly they made their beds, and how neatly they recorded class notes. They found that the students were likely to be consistent in similar situations, but not across different types of situations. The researchers did not find a single "conscientiousness trait" that governed behavior in all situations.

 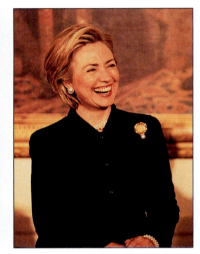

Most Americans do not view Hillary Rodham Clinton as having a light-hearted, fun-loving personality. Situationism would say that people have a certain view of her personality because we usually only see photos or video clips of her in a particular kind of situation (political), but don't see her in other types of situations (relaxed and having fun). If we did, her personality would not appear so consistent. This is what makes the photo on the right striking; it suggests a different personality than the one we usually see.

In later research, Mischel (1984) found that inconsistency across situations is pervasive; he found this not only with the traits of honesty and conscientiousness, but also with other traits, such as aggression and dependency. Furthermore, different measures of what should be the same trait often were only weakly correlated, or not related at all. Such findings led to the theory of **situationism**, which holds that a person's behavior is mostly a function of a given situation, not of internal traits. Situationism recognizes that, in part, we create our own situations, not necessarily by our actions but simply by who we are. In other words, characteristics such as age, sex, race, religion, ethnicity, and socioeconomic status can influence other people's behavior toward us, often in culturally determined ways, creating a different "situation," which can in turn lead to differences in people's behavior (see the discussion of microenvironments in Chapter 6). Nineteen-year-old Tina behaves very differently with Gabe—drinking from his cup, calling him after midnight—than with her 52-year-old female economics professor. In each case, Tina's age, sex, and status relative to the other person might be said to change her behavior. If you knew Tina only from economics lectures, you might be surprised by how different her "personality" seemed when she was with Gabe.

Interactionism: Who, Where, and When

Not surprisingly, situationism has had strong critics who point out that, over long periods of time and over many situations, people are fairly consistent, and that the more precisely a trait is defined, the more accurate it is in predicting behavior (Wiggins, 1992). Thus, saying that someone is sociable will not predict his or her behavior at a party nearly as well as saying the person appears at ease in interactions with new people. This is the tradeoff: The more narrowly a trait is defined, the better it is a predictor of behavior, but the fewer circumstances there are to which it can be applied.

Nevertheless, the power of the situation cannot be denied: People do behave differently in different contexts. Thus, a synthesis of the traditional trait view and situationism evolved, called **interactionism**, which suggests that traits, situations, and their interactions affect thoughts, feelings, and behavior. As proof, the interactionists point to studies such as the one by Endler and Hunt (1969), in which participants were asked to describe their reaction to various threats. Some of the threats involved a loss of self-esteem, such as might accompany failing an exam; others involved physical harm, such as being on a high ledge of a mountain; and still others involved an ambiguous threat, such as getting a summons from the police. The results showed that *both* individual differences in traits *and* differences in the situation affected people's reactions. Some people appeared to be generally more fearful than others (a trait), and some situations (such as being approached by cars racing abreast) were more fear-provoking than others (such as sitting in a favorite restaurant). Moreover, people differed with regard to which situations were particularly fear-provoking, and how they responded to those situations. Similarly, on personality tests, Asian Americans tend to show lower levels of assertiveness than do whites. However, Zane and colleagues (1991) found that this is true only when the people involved are strangers. Thus, the interactionists say, it isn't really accurate to describe Asian Americans as "low on the assertiveness trait" in general; a better characterization would be the more specific "unassertive when among strangers."

Thus, people's personalities can affect their situations in two major ways. First, people often can choose their situations—their jobs, their friends, their leisure activities. And, insofar as they are able, people tend to choose environments that fit their personalities. It's up to you, for instance, to decide whether to go bungee-jumping or sunbathing at the beach for the day. Second, people also find opportunities to create their environments. An aggressive person, for instance, will create a tense situation by words or deeds (A. Buss, 1995), and others will react accordingly.

Factors of Personality: The Big Five? Three? More?

How many personality traits are there? The answer depends on how specific you want to be about a given trait. You could be very specific, narrowing down behavior all the way to a "shy-so-only-goes-on-dates-to-dinner-and-a-movie-but-not-to-parties" trait. Narrowing traits to this level of precision, however, poses certain problems. Each trait explains only particular patterns of thoughts and behaviors in very specific instances. For example, you could consider sociability (which personality psychologists call "extraversion") a trait. Or you could say that extraversion is really a combination of the more specific traits of warmth, gregariousness, and assertiveness. In this case, you could say that sociability is a *personality dimension,* a set of related personality traits. Using the statistical technique of factor analysis (see Chapter 6), some researchers have sought to discover whether specific traits are in fact associated and, together, constitute a more general trait; such a personality dimension is sometimes called a *superfactor.*

Many factor analytic studies have revealed that traits can be reduced to five superfactors, which are listed along with their included traits in Table 8.1 (Digman,

TABLE 8.1 **The Big Five Superfactors and Their Traits**   Source: Adapted from Costa, McCrae, & Dye (1991).

SUPERFACTOR	TRAITS
Extraversion (also called *Sociability*)	Warmth, gregariousness, assertiveness, activity, excitement seeking, positive emotions.
Neuroticism (also called *Emotionality*)	Anxiety, hostility, depression, self-consciousness, impulsiveness, vulnerability.
Agreeableness	Trust, straightforwardness, altruism, compliance, modesty, tender-mindedness.
Conscientiousness (also called *Dependability*)	Competence, order, dutifulness, achievement striving, deliberation, self-discipline.
Openness	Fantasy, aesthetics, feelings, actions, ideas, values.

1990; McCrae & Costa, 1987). These superfactors are sometimes referred to as the Five Factor Model, or the **"Big Five"** (Goldberg, 1981): extraversion (also called *sociability*), neuroticism (also called *emotionality*), agreeableness, conscientiousness (also called *dependability*), and openness to experience (Costa et al., 1991). However, depending on the personality inventory used, different individual traits may make up each of the five superfactors, and hence some of the superfactors are given different names by different researchers. Some versions of extraversion and neuroticism, however, are found in almost all lists, perhaps reflecting how fundamental these two dimensions are to personality.

Psychologist Hans Eysenck identified not five but three superfactors or, as he labeled them, personality dimensions: extraversion, neuroticism, and psychoticism. While Eysenck's first two dimensions resemble the Big Five's superfactors of the same names, the third—psychoticism—was originally thought to measure a propensity toward becoming psychotic, that is, toward loss of touch with reality, as occurs in schizophrenia (Eysenck, 1992). It is true that people with schizophrenia score high on this dimension; however, psychoticism as defined by Eysenck also contains traits related to social deviance, such as criminality and substance addiction, and to a lack of conventional socialization, such as respect for rules and the feelings of others (Costa & McCrae, 1995). For this reason, Eysenck's psychoticism includes some of the traits listed under the Big Five's superfactors of agreeableness and conscientiousness (or lack thereof) (Draycott & Kline, 1995; Saggino, 2000).

Instead of using the term psychoticism, others have suggested using a broader term such as *nonconformity* or *social deviance* to highlight the traits of creativity and nonconformity that are also a part of this dimension. Artists, for example, tend to score higher on this personality dimension than people who are truly psychotic (Zuckerman et al., 1988). The Big Five's openness superfactor has no direct counterpart in Eysenck's model.

Although personality dimensions may be a useful way of conceptualizing personality, they are less predictive of behavior than the traits on which they are built (Paunonen, 1998). And although the identification and description of traits and personality dimensions were and continue to be important contributions to the process of understanding personality, this sort of cataloging work doesn't take the crucial next step: attempting to explain and thereby predict human behavior. For this exploration we must turn to theories of personality that focus on explaining and predicting behavior. An essential tool in all such theories is reliable measurement.

Measuring Personality: Is Grumpy Really Grumpy?

Let's assume for the moment, despite the view taken by situationism, that personality does exist. If so, psychologists, employers, teachers, and parents—indeed, all of us—might be able to understand and predict the behavior of others by discovering as much as possible about their personalitities. Various instruments for assessing personality attempt to do just that. Most personality assessments focus on measuring overt behaviors that psychologists believe to be manifestations of a given trait, inferring the strength of a trait from an individual's behavior. The use of behavior to infer personality traits is at the heart of all the methods of personality assessment discussed here.

Interviews

Interviews to assess personality are usually *structured;* that is, the interviewer asks all interviewees questions from predetermined sets, adding or omitting specific questions spontaneously based on the subjects' responses. The questions often focus on specific behaviors or beliefs and do not require the person being interviewed to reflect on his or her personality. An advantage of the structured inter-

"Big Five": The five superfactors of personality—extraversion, neuroticism, agreeableness, conscientiousness, and openness—determined by factor analysis.

view is that the interviewer comes away with a sense of knowing the interviewee and is able to infer different aspects of his or her personality.

The interview also has disadvantages: Unless the interviewee answers the questions honestly and accurately, the personality assessment is not valid. In addition, from a research perspective, it is difficult to generalize about personality characteristics beyond one interviewee. An interviewer might discover that Gabe has many conscientious behaviors and beliefs, yet he confesses to keeping a messy apartment. It does not follow that all people who have many conscientious behaviors and beliefs are terrible housekeepers.

Observation

Whether we are aware of it or not, we all use observation to learn about other people's personalities; that's what Tina did to get a sense of Gabe's personality. When psychologists use observation to assess personality, they assign observers, known as "judges," to rate participants' behaviors. Each participant's personality is then inferred from the ratings.

How accurate are observations? The better the judge knows the person about whom ratings are being made, the more accurate the ratings (Paulhus & Bruce, 1992; Wiggins & Pincus, 1992). But strangers can also provide accurate ratings as long as their judgments are based on observations of the appropriate behaviors related to the personality trait being assessed (Ozer & Reise, 1994). If you attempt to assess assertiveness by counting how often someone raises a hand in class, for example, your conclusion may not be very accurate: Reluctance to volunteer may reflect reading assignments that were never read!

Inventories: Check This

Perhaps the most common method of personality assessment is a **personality inventory,** a paper-and-pencil test that requires those being assessed to read statements and indicate whether each is true or false about themselves (only two choices) or how much they agree or disagree with each statement along a multipoint rating scale (three or more choices). Personality inventories usually assess many different traits and contain a great number of statements, often more than 300. This comprehensiveness, including statements on different aspects of each trait, ensures the validity of the inventory.

Rather than producing a single indicator of personality (such as "friendly" or "seeks excitement"), the results of a personality inventory provide information about a number of traits in the form of a *personality profile,* a summary of the different traits that constitute someone's personality (see Figure 8.1 on page 282). Personality inventories are used in a variety of settings and for a variety of purposes: by mental health professionals to assess psychopathology; by research psychologists to assess how personality traits are related to other variables; by employers to assess personality characteristics related to aspects of the job (Borman et al., 1997).

The advantage of personality inventories is that they are easy to administer; the drawback is that responses can be biased in several ways. Some people are more likely to check off "agree" than "disagree," regardless of the content of the statement. This response style, called *acquiescence,* can be reduced by wording half the items negatively. Thus an item such as "I often feel shy when meeting new people" would be reworded as "I don't usually feel shy when meeting new people." Another bias is **social desirability:** answering questions in a way that you think makes you look "good," even if the answer is not true. For instance, some people might not agree with the statement "It is better to be honest, even if others don't like you for it" but think that they should, and respond accordingly. To compensate for this bias, many personality inventories have a scale that assesses the respondent's propensity to answer in a socially desirable manner. This scale is then used to adjust or, in the language of testing, to "correct" the scores on the part of the inventory that measures traits. Some researchers have found relatively high correlations between personality

Personality inventory: A pencil-and-paper method for assessing personality that requires test-takers to read statements and indicate whether each is true or false about themselves.

Social desirability: A bias in responding to questions such that people try to make themselves "look good" even if it means giving untrue answers.

Figure **8.1**   **Personality Profiles and Employment**

Completed personality inventories provide personality profiles of different traits. According to Cattell's personality inventory (the 16PF for 16 personality factors), writers, creative artists, and airline pilots show different profiles.

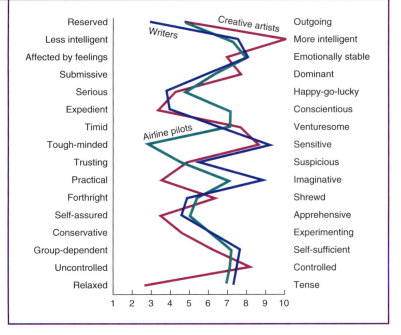

	1	2	3	4	5	6	7	8	9	10	
Reserved											Outgoing
Less intelligent											More intelligent
Affected by feelings											Emotionally stable
Submissive											Dominant
Serious											Happy-go-lucky
Expedient											Conscientious
Timid											Venturesome
Tough-minded											Sensitive
Trusting											Suspicious
Practical											Imaginative
Forthright											Shrewd
Self-assured											Apprehensive
Conservative											Experimenting
Group-dependent											Self-sufficient
Uncontrolled											Controlled
Relaxed											Tense

Minnesota Multiphasic Personality Inventory-2 (MMPI-2): A personality inventory primarily used to assess psychopathology.

Projective test: A method used to assess personality and psychopathology that involves asking the test-taker to make sense of an ambiguous stimulus.

Rorschach test: A projective test consisting of a set of inkblots that people are asked to "interpret."

assessment by inventory and judges' ratings of personality (J. A. Johnson, 2000; McCrae & Costa, 1989b), lending support for the idea that the easier-to-administer personality inventories yield information similar to personality assessment by judges. One personality inventory is Raymond Cattell's 16PF (Cattell et al., 1970; see Figure 8.1). Another, the **Minnesota Multiphasic Personality Inventory-2 (MMPI-2)**, is commonly used to assess psychopathology (Butcher & Rouse, 1996).

Projective Tests: Faces in the Clouds

A **projective test** presents the respondent with an ambiguous stimulus, such as a shapeless blot of ink or a drawing of people, and asks the respondent to make sense of the stimulus. The respondent is then asked to provide the story behind the stimulus: What does the inkblot look like? What are the people in the drawing doing? The theory behind projective tests is that people's personalities can be revealed by what they project onto an ambiguous stimulus as their minds impose structure on it. This is the reasoning behind the **Rorschach test** (see Figure 8.2).

Figure **8.2**   **The Rorschach Test**

This inkblot is similar to those used in the Rorschach test, which asks the viewer to decide what the inkblot resembles or represents, and tell why he or she thinks so.

Developed by Herman Rorschach (1884–1922), this commonly used projective technique has 10 cards, each with a different inkblot. The ambiguous shapes of the inkblots allow people to use their imaginations as they decide what the shapes might represent or resemble (for example, a bat or a butterfly) and what features of the inkblot made them think so.

The *Thematic Apperception Test (TAT)*, developed in the 1930s by Henry Murray, relies on the same concept as the Rorschach but uses detailed black-and-white drawings, often with people in them. The reliability and validity of the Rorschach test and the TAT have been the targets of criticism. One person taking the test on two occasions, for example, may give dramatically different answers each time, leading to different personality assessments (Anastasi, 1988; Entwisle, 1972).

People are shown a drawing like this one from the Thematic Apperception Test (TAT) and asked to explain what is happening in the picture, what led up to it, what will happen later, and what the characters are thinking and feeling.

LOOKING AT LEVELS

Genes and Personality Dimensions

As you have seen, psychologists have categorized personality traits by clustering them into personality dimensions, or superfactors. Is this the best way to categorize traits, or is there perhaps a better way? Cloninger and his colleagues (1993) suggest organizing personality traits so that they correspond to distinct biological systems. These researchers believe that people differ on four basic personality dimensions: novelty seeking (an "exhilaration or excitement in response to novel stimuli"); harm avoidance; dependence on rewards; and persistence. Cloninger further proposes that there are distinct biological systems that correspond to these four traits, each of which cuts across the Big Five. For example, novelty seeking corresponds to a combination of a high score on extraversion and a low score on conscientiousness in the Big Five (as cited in Benjamin et al., 1996). Cloninger and his colleagues hypothesized that the novelty-seeking dimension arises directly from the functioning brain systems that use dopamine. Earlier studies with animals had shown that dopamine is involved in exploratory behavior, and a lack of dopamine in people with Parkinson's disease leads to low novelty seeking (Cloninger et al., 1993). In normal people, according to Cloninger, differences in novelty seeking are caused by genetically determined differences in the effects of dopamine.

To test this hypothesis, Ebstein and colleagues (1996) examined people who have a particular gene that produces a type of dopamine receptor. They found that people who have this gene score higher on novelty seeking than do people without it. This result held true for men and women, for different age groups, and for different ethnic backgrounds. Although the effects of this gene were evident (in opposite ways) on extraversion and conscientiousness when the Big Five scales were used, these effects were captured more simply by the single trait of novelty seeking.

Consider in more detail what this novelty-seeking scale measures, and the implications of genetic influence. Ebstein and colleagues note that people who score higher than average on this measure are "impulsive, exploratory, fickle, excitable, quick-tempered and extravagant, whereas those who score lower than average tend to be reflective, rigid, loyal, stoic, slow-tempered, and frugal" (p. 78). Take loyalty, for example. This is a key aspect of most intimate human relationships. Is it possible that genes affect whether a person is likely to be loyal? If so, we would then have startling interactions among the levels of analysis, with genes affecting events in the brain, which affect personality, which in turn affects relationships and the social activities to which people are drawn. According to this theory, genes can produce consistent impulsive, extravagant behavior; what sort of person would be attracted to someone with that personality? If in this instance "opposites attract" and someone at the other end of the range becomes the partner, how are things likely to go for this couple in which one member is not particularly loyal and loves novelty and excitement?

It is important to emphasize, however, that although genes do bias people in certain ways, these influences are biases only and do not inevitably and unvaryingly lead to those behaviors (see Chapters 2 and 6). The average difference in novelty-seeking scores between people who did and did not have the dopamine receptor gene were about half a standard deviation (this is a difference similar to that between an IQ of 110 and an IQ of 118, which is not a huge difference). Nevertheless, it is clear that, to understand personality, we need to look at all three levels of analysis: events at the level of the brain (in this case dopamine), the person, and the group (including the situation and physical environment).

CONSOLIDATE!

1 *Does such a thing as a consistent personality really exist, or do our behaviors, thoughts, and feelings depend primarily on the situation?* Trait theorists argue that personality is composed of enduring traits that lead people to behave in specific ways. Situationist theorists argue that there are no enduring personality traits; rather, behavior depends on the situation. Theorists who posit interactionism propose that some enduring personality traits do exist, and the interaction of traits with the situation determines thoughts, feelings, and behavior.

2 *How do psychologists group personality traits into sets of personality types?* The Big Five superfactors refer to the Five Factor Model of personality, which was derived through the statistical technique of factor analysis of personality inventories. The five superfactors are extraversion, neuroticism, agreeableness, conscientiousness, and openness to experience. Each superfactor is composed of a number of specific traits. Eysenck proposes three rather than five personality dimensions (his term for superfactors): extraversion, neuroticism, and psychoticism. Cloninger proposes a different set of four dimensions, based on biological systems.

3 *What methods do psychologists use to measure personality?* There are four major ways to assess personality: interviews; observation; inventories, such as Cattell's 16PF, which yields a personality profile; and projective tests, such as the Rorschach test and the Thematic Apperception Test (TAT). Psychologists most commonly use inventories to assess personality.

The Brain:
The Personality Organ

As their relationship progressed, Tina began to notice a host of ways in which she and Gabe were different: She loved in-line skating, biking, dancing, and skiing; he liked to read outdoors (weather permitting), go on long walks, and watch movies. She liked to meet new people or hang out with her friends and generally didn't enjoy being alone; Gabe had a few close friends but was happy spending time by himself. Tina was fairly straightforward and, up to a point, flexible; Gabe seemed less direct and more rigid. Tina was spontaneous and a bit anxious; Gabe was not spontaneous and never seemed anxious, depressed, or worried. Tina could be impatient, sometimes even snappish; Gabe was always kind and gentle. When Tina was finally able to drag Gabe to a party (he kept forgetting he had agreed to go), she was surprised by his reaction: He stayed in a corner talking to one person for half an hour, then announced that he'd had enough and was ready to leave. Tina, on the other hand, felt like the party was just beginning. Taken together, the differences between them left Tina increasingly puzzled and wondering why they were attracted to each other.

As described in Cloninger's classification of personality, some aspects of personality are biologically based, so personalities are partly born, not made. Is Gabe shy and mellow because of his biology? Is Tina outgoing and a bit anxious because of her genes or hormones? And given that there is a biological factor to personality, are our personalities set in stone before we are even born, or does the environment play a role in forming our personalities? Let's explore the biological basis of personality.

 What are "introverts" and "extraverts"? How does Eysenck's theory explain the origin of personality?

2 What, exactly, is temperament?

3 What does the field of behavioral genetics say about the genes' effects on personality?

Eysenck's Theory

Hans Eysenck viewed each of his three personality dimensions—extraversion, neuroticism, and psychoticism—as the top point of a pyramid, built on a most basic level of associations between stimulus and response (see Figure 8.3), which form habit responses, which then form traits. However, Eysenck went beyond simply describing personality dimensions and attempted to discover the origins of their variations. Eysenck viewed these three dimensions and their associated traits as hereditary and universal among humans. From his own research and that of other investigators, he came to view personality differences as arising in large part from biological differences, not differences in environment or social surroundings. Eysenck argued that these biological differences affect everyday behaviors and thus personality (Eysenck, 1967). As you will see, there is support for Eysenck's idea of a biological basis of personality (Matthews & Gilliland, 1999).

Figure 8.3   Eysenck's Pyramid

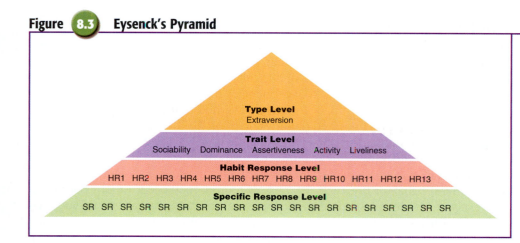

Eysenck proposed a hierarchy of personality in which the base of the pyramid consists of single stimulus–response associations. At the next level are habit responses such as shyness when meeting new people. Higher up are traits (which are composed of correlated habit responses), and at the top are extraversion, neuroticism, and psychoticism. This figure illustrates only extraversion.

The Extraverted Nervous System

Think about someone (a real or fictitious person) whom you'd describe as subdued, quiet, perhaps shy and solitary; now think of someone who enjoys people and social stimulation. The first person would probably score low on Eysenck's extraversion dimension and would be termed an *introvert;* the second, scoring high, would be an *extravert.* Researchers have identified differences at the level of the brain between introverts and extraverts. The nature of these differences seems at first surprising, but less so after a little thought.

In contrast to introverts, extraverts are less "arousable" (Haier et al., 1984); it takes more stimulation to arouse or overstimulate them (Eysenck & Eysenck, 1967). This at first seems an unlikely finding, but consider what it means: Because of this greater need, extraverts seek out activities that are more stimulating and arousing (recreational activities such as hang gliding, or occupations such as espionage). Introverts and extraverts also have different biological responses to caffeine, nicotine, and sedatives (Corr & Kumari, 1997; Corr et al., 1995; Stelmack, 1990).

The Neurotic Nervous System

Those who score high on the dimension of neuroticism are easily and intensely emotionally aroused and so are more likely to experience conditioned emotional

Research suggests that extraverts are more easily conditioned by rewards (such as winning money), whereas introverts are more easily conditioned by punishments (such as losing money). These differences may be related to differences in brain structure or function (Gray, 1987).

responses—that is, emotional responses elicited by previously neutral stimuli (see Chapter 4; Eysenck, 1979). Thus, someone high on this dimension who is stuck in an elevator is more likely to develop an elevator phobia than someone low on this dimension. Zuckerman (1991) hypothesizes that an increased sensitivity of the amygdala is responsible for this ease of emotional arousal (see Chapter 7).

Canli and colleagues (2001) used fMRI to monitor brain activity while women looked at positive pictures (such as puppies playing, a happy couple) and negative pictures (such as people crying, a cemetery). The investigators then looked at the relation between the women's extraversion and neuroticism scores and their brain activity in several regions. Extraversion scores were correlated with activation in one set of brain areas when the women looked at the positive pictures (compared with negative ones); in contrast, neuroticism scores were correlated with activation in another set of brain areas when the women looked at negative pictures (compared with positive ones). This result is convincing evidence that these dimensions are measuring different types of processing.

The High–Psychoticism Nervous System

Eysenck views those high on psychoticism as having less control over their emotions and therefore as more likely to be aggressive or impulsive. Zuckerman suggests that those high on psychoticism have difficulty learning not to engage in particular behaviors. Eysenck theorized that tendencies toward criminal behavior among males are genetically determined. In fact, he claimed that 50–60% of the variability in such tendencies is inherited (Eysenck, 1990b). This does not mean that some people are born crooks, but rather that some are born with autonomic and central nervous system underarousal that indirectly leads them to seek risks—and some of these risks, given exposure to certain environmental influences, may be associated with criminal behavior (Eysenck, 1977). Low arousal may occur in part because of low levels of activity of the neurotransmitter serotonin in the central nervous system, a condition that has been associated with impulsive behavior (Klinteberg et al., 1993; Linnoila et al., 1983). Indeed, Raine and colleagues (1990) showed that underarousal at age 15 (as assessed by three different measures of autonomic and central nervous system activity) predicted criminality at age 24 in 75% of cases.

Although showing an impressive link between biology and criminality, these findings do not prove that biology is destiny, in this or most other areas. By analogy, our biology leads us all to need to eat, but how, what, and when we eat are determined in large part by the way we are raised. Twin studies have found that environmental factors play a strong role in the development of criminality (Eysenck & Gudjonsson, 1989; Henry et al., 1996; McGuffin & Gottesman, 1985; Plomin et al., 1997).

Temperament: Waxing Hot or Cold

Psychologists use the term **temperament** to refer to innate inclinations to engage in a certain style of behavior. Arnold Buss (1995) views temperament as having more influence on behavior than personality traits or factors, affecting not just *what* people do, think, and feel, but *how* they act, think, and feel. Such inborn tendencies can appear at an early age and persist through adulthood. Longitudinal studies have found that children's temperaments at age 3 are correlated with their personalities, as assessed by a personality inventory, at age 18 (Caspi, 2000; Chess & Thomas, 1996). A study of 21-year-olds also linked temperament with health-

Temperament: Innate inclinations to engage in a certain style of behavior.

risk behaviors such as unsafe sex, alcohol dependence, violent crime, and dangerous driving (Caspi et al., 1997). One such temperament is *sensation seeking:* the pursuit of novelty, often in high-stimulation situations, such as sky diving, fast driving, or drug and alcohol use, or occupations, such as working in a hospital emergency room (Zuckerman, 1979). A study of personality predictors of driving accidents found that those drivers who had car accidents or traffic violations were more likely to be thrill seekers and risk takers compared with drivers who had neither (Trimpop & Kirkcaldy, 1997). Tina appears to have a sensation-seeking temperament, and Gabe, who actively shies away from adventurous activities, doesn't. Sensation seeking is associated with lower levels of the chemical monoamine oxidase (MAO) in the blood, at least in males (Shekim et al., 1989).

Buss and Plomin (1984; A. Buss, 1995) propose four dimensions of temperament: activity, sociability, emotionality, and impulsivity. **Activity** is the general expenditure of energy; it has two components: *vigor* (intensity of activity) and *tempo* (speed of activity). People can differ in the intensity of vigorous activity they prefer (for example, preferring skiing to bowling), and the pace of the activities (for instance, preferring fast-paced activities and performing activities more quickly). Tina seems to have a temperament that is vigorous *and* has a fast tempo, as evidenced by her enjoyment of in-line skating, biking, and skiing, and by the impression she gives of perpetually being in a hurry.

Other dimensions of temperament are **sociability**, the preference to be in the company of other people rather than alone, and **emotionality**, the inclination to become aroused in emotional situations, but only when the emotions of distress, fear, and anger are involved. Emotionality is similar to the Big Five superfactor of neuroticism, also known as "emotional instability." Studies of identical versus fraternal twins have shown that a person's degree of emotionality is partly inherited. In these studies, twins answered questionnaires about their own temperaments (Eaves et al., 1989; Saudino et al., 1999) and about their cotwins' temperaments (Heath, Neale, et al., 1992); parents were asked about the temperaments of their twin children (these questionnaires also included ratings of activity and sociability, with results that also indicated genetic influence) (Buss & Plomin, 1975; Plomin & Foch, 1980). Research on twins who are raised apart has also produced evidence that activity level and sociability are partly inherited (Loehlin et al., 1985; emotionality was not assessed).

The fourth dimension of temperament, **impulsivity**, is the propensity to respond to stimuli immediately, without reflection or concern for consequences. Impulsivity refers to the time lag from stimulus to response, as opposed to tempo, which refers to the rate of a response once it is initiated.

Genes and Personality

We pointed out earlier that the personality dimension of novelty seeking can be influenced by a single gene, which in turn influences your biology. Since biology can influence personality, the question arises, are all personality differences genetically determined? Behavioral geneticists seek to ascertain the influence of heredity on behavior, and in so doing investigate a wide range of psychological phenomena, including personality. One way these researchers try to tease apart the effects of heredity from those of the environment is to compare twins separated at birth and raised apart with twins raised together (see Chapter 6). Also compared are identical and fraternal twins who share an environment but have exactly the same genes (identical twins) or on average only half their genes in common (fraternal twins). If the identical twins are more similar than the fraternal twins, that difference is usually attributed to effects of the genes.

The largest study of twins reared apart, the Minnesota Study of Twins Reared Apart (MISTRA), was undertaken at the University of Minnesota. In this study, the researchers located 59 pairs of identical twins and 47 pairs of fraternal twins

Arctic explorer Matthew Henson, the first person to reach the North Pole, spent years patiently navigating the Arctic cold, wind, and ice. He endured months of minimal, if any, companionship, and physical hardships such as starvation, isolation, and freezing weather. Do polar explorers have to have a certain kind of temperament?

Activity: A temperament dimension characterized by the general expenditure of energy; activity has two components—vigor (intensity of the activities) and tempo (speed of the activities).

Sociability: A temperament dimension characterized by a preference to be in other people's company rather than alone.

Emotionality: A temperament dimension characterized by an inclination to become aroused in situations in which the predominant emotions are distress, fear, and anger.

Impulsivity: A temperament dimension characterized by the propensity to respond to stimuli immediately, without reflection or concern for consequences.

These identical twins were separated in infancy and adopted by different working-class families. In school, neither liked spelling, but both liked math; as adults, both worked as part-time deputy sheriffs, vacationed in Florida, had first wives named Linda, second wives named Betty, and gave their sons the same names (although with different spellings: James Alan and James Allan). They both drove Chevys, had dogs named Toy, liked carpentry (Holden, 1980), and built nearly identical benches around trees in their backyards (Rosen, 1987). Moreover, their medical histories were remarkably similar, including the onset of migraine headaches at age 18. However, they wore their hair differently and preferred different ways of expressing themselves: one preferred writing, the other talking (Holden, 1980). Are these similarities a result of coincidence, or of their shared genetics? How many similarities would any two random people have if they compared such detailed information?

adopted into different families at some point after birth (Bouchard, 1994). Once enrolled in the program, adult twins spent 6 days taking personality, intelligence, psychophysiological, and medical tests, and answering 15,000 written questions (Rosen, 1987; Segal, 1999). In addition, about 24,000 pairs of twins raised together were studied. The results indicate that both extraversion and neuroticism have substantial heritability—the fraction of observed variability of a characteristic that arises from inherited factors (see Chapter 6). Similar results have been found when twins rate themselves and when others rate them (Angleitner et al., 1995). However, longitudinal studies of adoptive families have not found such high correlations (Loehlin et al., 1981). In sum, although most twin research finds evidence of substantial heritability of some personality dimensions, not all nontwin research supports this finding. In addition, although personality traits may have some heritability, even in research among twins not all traits are equally heritable, as shown in Figure 8.4 (Heath & Martin, 1990; Loehlin, 1992; Pederson et al., 1988).

Despite these conflicting results, some researchers propose that very specific behaviors have a genetic origin (Bergeman et al., 1990; Kendler et al., 1992; Lyons et al., 1993), from the amount of time spent watching television (Prescott et al.,

Figure 8.4 Heritability of Personality

Heritability of the five superfactors and Eysenck's three dimensions of personality based on research with twins. (Data for Big Five superfactors from Loehlin, 1992. Data for Eysenck's three dimensions of personality—extraversion and neuroticism from Pederson et al., 1988; psychoticism from Heath & Martin, 1990.)

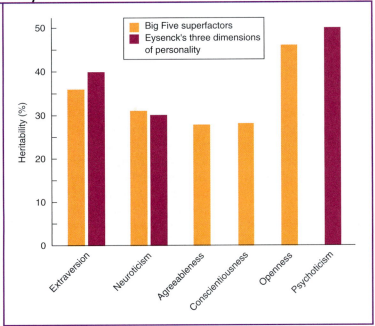

1991) and childhood accidents (Phillips & Matheny, 1995) to divorce (McGue & Lykken, 1992) and religious attitudes (Waller et al., 1990). Similarly, Lykken and colleagues (1993) found a heritability of 50% in work and leisure interests in a twin study and estimate that a subjective sense of well-being (what some might call happiness) has a heritability of between 44% and 80% (Lykken & Tellegen, 1996)!

Of course, nobody claims that the amount of time you spend watching television is explicitly coded in your genes. What some researchers do claim, however, is that certain aspects of temperament and personality dimensions, which may have a genetic component, will produce specific behaviors such as watching television. If, for instance, your activity level is both "low vigor" and "low tempo" and you tend to be shy, you are more likely to spend time alone in sedentary pursuits (such as watching television) than if you are a gregarious person who likes vigorous, fast-paced activity. It is also important to note that simply because some aspects of personality have a genetic component does not mean that personality is fixed from birth to death. All researchers agree that other factors, such as environment and experience, also shape personality. Even Eysenck (1993), who argues that much of behavior is biologically determined, concedes that the environment makes a difference in whether someone high in psychoticism will become a creative, productive researcher or an artist, or be disabled by schizophrenia.

Personality psychologists generally consider two aspects of the environment to play roles in forging personality. One is the individual's unique experiences, such as winning a spelling bee or single-handedly causing the team to lose the soccer finals. The other is the common family environment; the relatively small contribution of a common family environment to other personality traits may simply reflect the fact that many important aspects of the family environment are *not* shared. Parents do not treat each of their children in exactly the same way. Instead, children create their own microenvironments based on their own temperaments and personalities at birth, leading parents to develop different patterns of interaction with, and different expectations of, each child (Graziano et al., 1998; Plomin & Bergeman, 1991; Scarr & McCartney, 1983). Similarly, the same family event, such as a divorce, will be experienced differently by children of different ages and cognitive abilities (Hoffman, 1991). Moreover, it is possible that individual differences exist in susceptibility to environmental forces in personality development (Holden, 1980).

LOOKING AT LEVELS

The Wallflower Personality

Are you shy, or do you know someone who is? Have you ever wondered what causes one person to be shy and another outgoing? Is shyness innate? To understand the origins of shyness, it is necessary to look at shy people from the vantage points of events at all three levels—the brain, the person, and the group.

At the level of the brain, Kagan and his colleagues (1988) have found that some babies are more reactive, or sensitive, to environmental stimuli and thus are more fussy than other babies. These "high-reactive" infants are more likely than "low-reactive" babies to respond to a recording of a woman's voice or to a colored toy with crying, general distress, and increased motor activity. Such infants tend to have a reactive nervous system, as indicated by faster heart rates and higher levels of the stress hormone cortisol. Kagan and his colleagues have shown that babies with a fast heart rate in the womb are more likely later to become inhibited, fearful children who startle more easily;

in fact, the heart activity of even 2-week-old infants can predict later inhibition (Snidman et al., 1995). These children's sympathetic nervous systems are more easily aroused, leading to a preference for situations less likely to create high arousal. As these inhibited children get older, they are usually the ones who hide behind their parents in a room full of adults.

At the level of the person, shy people are extremely self-conscious, so much so that they may painfully and ruthlessly analyze their behavior after a social interaction, an unhappy process that leads them to avoid interaction with others in the future. They become preoccupied with their shyness and its effects ("I can't stop imagining what they're thinking about me"). These preoccupying thoughts can occur in response to autonomic nervous system reactions (a pounding heart), to behavior (what to do with the hands), and to thoughts ("No one wants to talk to me"). Fear and distress in social situations are common feelings for inhibited people.

But not all inhibited toddlers are still inhibited at age 7, and not all inhibited children become shy adults (Kagan, 1989a). Events at the level of the group can play a role either in diminishing the effects of shyness or in maintaining shyness into adulthood. Fox (cited in Azar, 1995) found that the home environment, specifically parents, can help inhibited children by recognizing and supporting the children's temperaments. As one previously inhibited 7-year-old explained, "My parents introduced me to new things slowly" (Azar, 1995).

Events at the three levels all interact: Having a reactive autonomic nervous system may produce a bias toward shyness, but the view taken by the environment of family and culture toward such behavior will determine how a person thinks and feels about him- or herself. American culture tends to favor outgoing people, a social bias that puts shy people at a disadvantage. Their self-image as social beings is more likely to be negative, and this negative self-concept increases the likelihood of an autonomic reaction in social situations, thereby perpetuating the cycle. Moreover, Kagan (1989a) has found that a larger proportion of inhibited children are later-borns, whereas a larger proportion of uninhibited children are firstborns. He hypothesizes that those with an inhibited temperament who have older siblings live in a more stressful environment, which exaggerates their autonomic responses. Those who are firstborn or only children grow up in a less stressful environment and are less likely to become shy children or adults.

CONSOLIDATE!

1 *What are "introverts" and "extraverts"? How does Eysenck's theory explain the origin of personality?* Eysenck proposed that personality varies along three dimensions, each with distinct physiological underpinnings: extraversion, neuroticism, and psychoticism. Extraverts are less "arousable" than introverts and are more sensitive to reward; introverts are more easily overstimulated and are more sensitive to punishment. Neuroticism, or emotionality, is hypothesized to be related to the functioning of the amygdala.

2 *What, exactly, is temperament?* Temperament refers to an innate style of behavior. Examples of temperament dimensions are shyness, activity (which has two components, vigor and tempo), sociability, emotionality, and impulsivity.

3 *What does the field of behavioral genetics say about the genes' effects on personality?* Based on twin studies, behavioral geneticists propose that personality is between 28% and 50% heritable, but this value depends in part on the trait or factor being assessed and whether the studies were conducted with twins or nonbiological family members. Despite this high percentage, environmental factors still play an important role in personality development.

The Person: Beliefs and Behaviors

Tina wanted to understand why Gabe was the way he was—or, put another way, why he had the personality he did. Lately when they studied together, he'd have a big bag of pistachio nuts and sit there cracking and eating nuts while they read. It was driving Tina, well, nuts. She couldn't understand how he could just sit there hour after hour, cracking and crunching nuts. She wanted to ask him about it—why didn't he just buy shelled nuts—but she didn't feel comfortable asking him. Why were they so different? How do our personalities develop, and why do they develop differently? Does experience build on the genetic and biological framework of our personalities, affecting our beliefs, motivations, and views of ourselves? Among the notable theories that attempt to answer these questions are the psychodynamic theory of Sigmund Freud, humanistic theory, and the cognitive view of personality.

1 What is the Freudian view of personality?

2 What is the main emphasis of humanistic theories?

3 What is the cognitive approach to personality theory?

Freud's Theory: The Dynamic Personality

Sigmund Freud viewed personality as a bubbling cauldron, rocked by unconscious, irrational forces at war with one another, competing for expression and preventing the individual's exercise of free will. He believed in **psychological determinism**, the view that all behavior, even something as mundane as forgetting someone's name or being late for an appointment, has an underlying psychological cause. Freud proposed that two major drives, sex and aggression, are the primary motivating forces of human behavior. Tension occurs when these drives are not given opportunity for expression.

The Structure of Personality

To understand Freud's view of the structure of personality, it is necessary first to understand his view of consciousness. Freud proposed that consciousness is not one thing, but rather can be thought of as divided into three layers (see Figure 8.5). The topmost layer is normal awareness, or the *conscious*, which includes thoughts, feelings, and motivations of which you are aware. The second layer, the *preconscious*, holds subjective material that can easily be brought into conscious awareness but of which you are not aware most of the time. For example, your telephone number is in your preconscious until someone asks you what it is, at which point it moves into your conscious awareness. The final layer is the *unconscious*, which houses the thoughts, feelings, and motivations that you cannot bring into consciousness but which nevertheless influence you. A much greater proportion of your thoughts, feelings, and motivations are in the unconscious than are in the conscious.

As part of the dynamic nature of personality, Freud proposed three personality structures—the id, superego, and ego (see Figure 8.5). These are not physical structures, but abstract mental entities. The **id**, which exists from birth, houses the sexual and aggressive drives, physical needs such as the need to sleep or eat, and simple psychological needs such as the need for comfort; these needs and drives constantly vie for expression. The id lives by the *pleasure principle,* wanting immediate gratification of its needs by a reduction in pain, discomfort, or tension, regardless of the consequences. Because of this insistent urge for immediate gratification, the id is sometimes compared with a demanding infant. Freud proposed that when the id's instincts threaten to erupt, anxiety can develop. When that anxiety reaches a sufficiently high level, abnormal behavior and mental illness can result.

A second structure, the **superego**, forms during early childhood; this entity houses the child's (and later the adult's) sense of right and wrong. The child learns morality by internalizing—that is, taking in—the values of the parents and of the immediate culture. The superego tries to prevent the expression of the id's sexual and aggressive impulses. The superego thus isn't a Jiminy Cricket whispering in your ear, but the internalized voice of society. The superego's morality, however, because it was internalized during early childhood, remains childlike in nature.

The superego is the home of the conscience, and depending on the parents' way of teaching right and wrong, it can be more or less punishing. If your superego is very harsh, you experience much anxiety and strive for perfection. The superego can cause feelings of *guilt,* an uncomfortable sensation of having done something wrong, which results in feelings of inadequacy. The superego's morality is responsible for the *ego ideal,* which provides the ultimate standard of what a person should be (Nye, 1992).

Psychological determinism: The view that all behavior, no matter how mundane or insignificant, has a psychological cause.

Id: A psychic structure, proposed by Freud, that exists at birth and houses sexual and aggressive drives and physical needs.

Superego: A psychic structure, proposed by Freud, that is formed during early childhood and houses the sense of right and wrong, based on the internalization of parental and cultural morality.

Figure 8.5 Freud's Drawing of Personality Structure

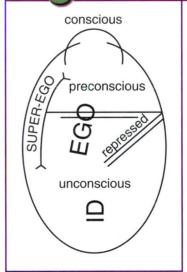

In Freud's view, only part of the mind is available for inspection and provides normal awareness (conscious); some of it is occasionally conscious (preconscious), and some is hidden, not available for observation (unconscious). Repressed thoughts, feelings, and wishes are hidden from awareness. Freud's drawing also illustrates the relationship among the id, ego, and superego.

A third structure, the **ego**, also develops in childhood, before the superego, and works very hard to balance the demands of the id and superego. The ego tries to give the id enough gratification to prevent it from making too much trouble, while at the same time making sure that no major moral lapses lead the superego to become too punishing. The ego must also make sure that the actions of the id and superego, as well as its own actions, don't create problems in the real world. The ego is guided by the *reality principle,* which leads it to assess what is realistically possible in the world. Although he believed that the ego develops out of the id, in his later life Freud (1937) wrote that the ego's characteristics may be determined by heredity (Nye, 1992). The ego is also responsible for cognitive functions such as problem solving and reasoning.

Personality Development: Avoiding Arrest

Freud viewed childhood as central in determining the formation of personality. He proposed five distinct phases, or stages, of development, each having an important task requiring successful resolution for healthy personality development. Four of Freud's five stages involve specific erogenous zones, areas of the body (mouth, anus, and genitals) that can provide satisfaction of instinctual drives. Freud believed that each zone demanded some form of sexual gratification, with a different zone prominent during each stage. For this reason, Freud's stages are called **psychosexual stages.**

If a child does not satisfy the needs of a given stage, he or she will develop a *fixation,* a state in which energy is still focused on an earlier stage of development even as the child moves on to the next stage. A fixation results from incomplete resolution of an earlier stage. In times of stress, Freud argued, the person will regress to the thoughts, feelings, and behaviors of the fixated stage. Such arrested development could create a **neurosis:** an abnormal behavior pattern relating to a conflict between the ego and either the id or the superego. According to Freud (1938), conflict between the ego and reality results in *psychosis,* a break with reality.

Oral Stage. The *oral stage* extends from birth until approximately age 1½. In this stage, the child's pleasures come from the mouth, primarily via sucking and biting; the developmental task in the oral stage is successful weaning from mother's breast or the bottle. If oral needs are frustrated at this stage, the child will develop a fixation, developing one of two kinds of personality. One is the *oral–receptive,* which is characterized by oral pleasure seeking, such as putting food or cigarettes into the mouth. According to Freud, people with oral–receptive personalities tend to become dependent on others and expect others to take care of them. The other personality style, the *oral–aggressive,* is characterized by a predilection for oral pleasures that emphasize biting, such as chewing ice or smoking pipes. Freudian theory proposes that oral–aggressive people are often verbally hostile in relationships. Would Freud have interpreted Gabe's preference for pistachio nuts as a sign of an oral–aggressive personality? Possibly, although Gabe doesn't exhibit other signs of the oral–aggressive personality; maybe he just likes pistachios.

Anal Stage. The developing child leaves the oral stage for the *anal stage,* which lasts from about age 1½ to age 3. The primary zone of pleasure shifts from the mouth to the anus. Retaining and expelling feces are the primary pleasures in this stage, and the developmental task is successful toilet training. Freud believed that parents who are rigid about toilet training, requiring their children to "go" on demand, can create a battle of wills, resulting in a fixation in adulthood. One type of fixation, the *anal–retentive,* can be thought of as producing a constipated personality that waits until the last moment to "go." Such people are more likely to delay gratification and, according to Freudian theory, are neat, methodical, miserly, and stubborn. In contrast, the *anal–expulsive* personality is characterized by cruelty, destructive acts, emotional outbursts, and a disregard for conventional rules. Although a Freudian might see in Gabe's personality some traits akin to the anal–retentive type (his methodical manner, his organized schoolwork, his fairly

Ego: A psychic structure, proposed by Freud and developed in childhood, that tries to balance the competing demands of the id, superego, and reality.

Psychosexual stages: Freud's developmental stages based on erogenous zones; the specific needs of each stage must be met for its successful resolution.

Neurosis: An abnormal behavior pattern relating to a conflict between the ego and either the id or the superego.

Chapter 8 Personality: Vive la Difference! www.ablongman.com/kosslynbrief

inflexible nature), he does not entirely fit the bill because he isn't neat in other aspects of his life and is not miserly, but in fact quite generous.

Phallic Stage. The third stage, the *phallic stage,* occurs from around 3 to 6 years old. The locus of pleasure is now the clitoris or penis, gratification occurring primarily through masturbation. The developmental task is successful identification with the same-sex parent. Freud proposed that children of this age are preoccupied with the discovery that girls don't have penises, a discovery that in girls creates jealousy of the male's penis, and in boys fear of castration. Freud took inspiration from the ancient Greek story of Oedipus, who unknowingly killed his father and married his mother. Freud believed that boys in this stage jealously love their mothers and view their fathers as competitors for their mothers' love, so they both fear and hate their fathers. Freud called this dynamic the *Oedipus complex.* A boy fears that, as punishment for loving his mother and hating his father, his father will cut off his penis, the primary zone of pleasure; this concern leads to the boy's **castration anxiety.** For successful resolution, a boy must renounce his passionate love for his mother and make peace with his father, choosing to identify with him and accept his position instead of viewing him as a competitor. In doing so, the boy "introjects," or internalizes, his father's morality as part of his superego. According to Freud, fixations at this stage can create either a Don Juan personality, obsessed with attaining sexual gratification, or, following poor identification with the father, a less masculine, more feminine personality, possibly although not necessarily homosexual.

Girls' personality development at this stage, according to Freud, is different from that of boys; girls' version of the Oedipus complex has been labeled the *Electra complex,* after a Greek myth about a girl who avenges her father's murder, committed by her mother and her mother's lover, by persuading her brother to kill their mother. Girls at this stage experience *penis envy,* a sense of being ineffectual owing to the lack of a penis and the ensuing desire to have a penis. Girls also struggle with feelings of anger and jealousy toward the mother: anger for neither providing a penis for her daughter nor having one herself, and jealousy because of the mother's relationship with the father. Girls ambivalently identify with their mothers. As a product of the Victorian era, Freud justified women's inferiority to men by explaining that they only partially resolved this stage. Because they do not experience castration anxiety, they are not motivated to resolve fully this ambivalent identification with their mothers. They remain fixated at this stage, and as a result have a less-well-developed superego, less ego strength, and less ability to negotiate reality and the id.

Latency Period. After the phallic stage, sexual impulses in both boys and girls become subdued for a time during the *latency period,* which lasts from approximately age 6 until puberty. In this stage sexual urges are repressed, and the developmental task is transforming these repressed urges into socially acceptable activities. Stimulation of an erogenous zone is not the focus of this stage; rather, sexual urges are transformed into more culturally acceptable, nonsexual behaviors. For example, competitive games with peers may take the place of the Oedipal drama for a boy fixated at the phallic stage.

Genital Stage. Freud's final psychosexual stage is the *genital stage,* which begins at puberty; the erogenous zones now are the vagina for girls and the penis for boys. Gratification occurs in sexual intimacy, and one of the two developmental tasks of this stage, the ability to form a sexual love relationship, marks the beginning of mature sexual relationships. The other task of this stage is to develop interests and talents related to productive work. Freud believed that individuals with fixations at earlier developmental stages would have problems in the genital stage. According to Freud, girls' erogenous zones now shift from the "immature" clitoris to the "mature" vagina, and the "vaginal orgasm" is evidence of successful resolution of this stage. There is no evidence, however, that women experience two different kinds of orgasm; rather, the female orgasm involves both clitoris and vagina, not "either/or" (Harris, 1976; Kaplan, 1981; Masters & Johnson, 1966).

Castration anxiety: A boy's anxiety-laden fear that, as punishment for loving mother and hating father, his father will cut off his penis (the primary zone of pleasure).

Defense Mechanisms: Protecting the Self

The ego's job of handling threatening material is made easier by the use of **defense mechanisms**, unconscious psychological means by which we try to prevent unacceptable thoughts or urges from reaching conscious awareness, thereby decreasing anxiety (see Table 8.2). Freud proposed a number of defense mechanisms; these were further developed by his daughter, Anna Freud (1895–1982), herself a noted psychoanalyst. The most important defense mechanism is **repression**, a process that occurs when the unconscious prevents threatening thoughts, impulses, and memories from entering consciousness. An example of repression might be "forgetting" to go to a dreaded dentist appointment. According to Freud, overreliance on particular defense mechanisms may lead to the development of neuroses.

TABLE 8.2 **Common Defense Mechanisms** *Source: Freud (1933/1965), p. 70.*

Note: Defense mechanisms are used by the ego to prevent threatening thoughts from entering awareness.

DENIAL
Threatening thoughts are denied outright. *Example:* You have a drinking problem but deny that it is a problem (and truly believe this).

INTELLECTUALIZATION
Threatening thoughts or emotions are kept at arm's length by thinking about them rationally and logically. *Example:* While watching a frightening part of a horror movie, you focus on the special effects, make-up, camera angles, and other emotionally nonthreatening details.

PROJECTION
Threatening thoughts are projected onto (attributed to) others. *Example:* You accuse your partner of wanting to have an affair rather than recognizing your own conscious or unconscious wish to have one yourself.

RATIONALIZATION
Creating explanations to justify threatening thoughts or actions. *Example:* In response to watching a football game instead of studying, and subsequently doing poorly on an exam, you say, "Oh, I can make up for it on the final and the research paper."

REACTION FORMATION
Unconsciously changing an unacceptable feeling into its opposite. *Example:* You harbor aggressive impulses toward your boss, but instead you experience warm, positive feelings toward him, transforming your anger about his obnoxious behavior into an appreciation of "his fairness as a manager."

REPRESSION
Anxiety-provoking thoughts, impulses, and memories are prevented from entering consciousness. *Example:* After failing an exam, you keep forgetting to tell your parents about it.

SUBLIMATION
Threatening impulses are directed into more socially acceptable activities. *Example:* You sublimate your unacceptable aggressive urges to engage in physical fights by playing ice hockey.

UNDOING
Your actions try to "undo" a threatening wish or thought. *Example:* After having the thought of eating several slices of chocolate cake, you go to the gym and work out for an hour.

Freud's Followers

Freud attracted many followers, a number of whom modified his theory of personality or added ideas of their own. Among those who expanded on Freud's work, termed *neo-Freudians*, were Carl Jung, Alfred Adler, and Karen Horney.

Carl Jung (1875–1961) was a Swiss psychiatrist whom Freud befriended but with whom he later severed communication over disagreements about theory. Jung agreed with Freud's concepts of the unconscious, ego, and id but diverged from Freud over his emphasis on the centrality of sexuality in personality development. Jung developed his own theory of personality that added to Freud's concepts of the unconscious, ego, and id an entity Jung termed the *collective unconscious*. According to Jung, the collective unconscious contains a rich storehouse of ideas and memories common to all humankind, which we all share on an unconscious level. The common themes in myths and stories around the world and throughout the ages, Jung claimed, spring forth from the collective uncon-

Defense mechanism: An unconscious psychological means by which a person tries to prevent unacceptable, id-based thoughts or urges from reaching conscious awareness.

Repression: A defense mechanism that occurs when the unconscious prevents threatening thoughts, impulses, and memories from entering consciousness.

Chapter 8 Personality: Vive la Difference!

scious in each generation. Stored in the collective unconscious are many **archetypes**, symbols that represent "aspects of the world that people have an inherited tendency to notice" (Carver & Scheier, 1996, p. 268). Among these archetypes are God, the shadow (that is, the dark side of personality), and Mother Earth.

Whereas Freud viewed sexual and aggressive impulses as integral to personality development, Alfred Adler (1870–1937) viewed feelings of inferiority and helplessness as important in forming personality (1956). Feelings of inferiority fuel a *striving for superiority,* which Adler viewed as the source of all motivation. When severe, such inferiority feelings can hamper strivings for superiority and lead to strong feelings of inferiority—an **inferiority complex**. This can arise from parents' neglect or hatred. Adler viewed the Oedipus complex not as universal, but as experienced only by children who are overindulged by the opposite-sex parent (Adler, 1964).

Karen Horney (1885–1952) agreed with Freud that anxiety-inducing childhood experiences are central to later psychological problems. She disagreed, however, about the role and primacy of sexual and aggressive drives. Horney emphasized the importance of parent–child interactions in early childhood. If parents do not provide their children with consistent and real interest, warmth, and respect, Horney claimed, the children are likely to grow up with *basic anxiety,* an "all-pervading feeling of being lonely and helpless in a hostile world" (Horney, 1937, p. 89). Horney offered an alternate explanation for penis envy, which she called *privilege envy.* Rather than wanting a penis per se, Horney theorized, girls desire the privileges that go along with having a penis. Even privilege envy, however, is not a cultural universal; in some cultures, Horney noted, men are envious of women's reproductive ability. Horney felt that Freud had disregarded the cultural and social factors that influence personality development.

Critiquing Freudian Theory: Is It Science?

Psychoanalytic theory remains fascinating a century after Freud first conceived it, and legions of people worldwide—psychologists, writers, filmmakers, and others—have seen truth in its insights into personality. But as fascinating as Freud's theory may be, is it grounded in good science? First, as you saw in Chapter 1, a scientific theory must be testable, but many aspects of Freud's theory are difficult to test. Some key concepts were not concretely defined, some changed over time, and often the interpretation of these concepts was left open. For example, as you also saw in Chapter 1, when Freud was asked about the meaning of his sucking on a cigar, he replied, "Sometimes a cigar is only a cigar." Maybe so, but a good theory would tell us when it is and when it isn't "only a cigar."

A second criticism of Freud's theory is that it is so complicated, it can explain, or explain away, almost anything. When there is an apparent contradiction within someone's personality, it is almost always possible to appeal to a defense mechanism to explain that contradiction. If Gabe had had a difficult time with toilet training, resulting in frequent constipation, we could predict that he would have an anal–retentive personality. But how do we then explain that he is often generous and, at home, downright sloppy? Psychodynamic theory could say that his generosity and sloppiness are an undoing of his desire to be selfish and orderly.

Third, Freud developed his theory by analyzing patients, mostly women, and by analyzing himself. And Freud's views of women, of proper parenting, and of appropriate development were all biased by his sensibilities and surroundings, as we are biased by ours. He and his patients were upper-middle-class or upper-class products of late 19th-century Vienna; their sensibility was not necessarily representative of other classes, times, or cultures. Applying a theory based on a particular group of people at a particular time to other people at another time raises issues of validity.

However, some aspects of Freud's theory have received support from contemporary research (see Westen, 1998, 1999). For example, the type of attachment we have to our parents predicts the type of attachment we will have to a partner and to our own children (see Shaver & Hazan, 1994, for a review). Although not supporting Freud's specific psychosexual stages, such findings support the general

Archetype: A Jungian concept of symbols that represent basic aspects of the world.

Inferiority complex: The experience that occurs when inferiority feelings are so strong that they hamper striving for superiority.

Self-actualization: An innate motivation to attain the highest possible emotional and intellectual potential.

Flow: The experience of complete absorption in and merging smoothly into an activity and losing track of time.

idea that relationships with parents can affect aspects of later development. Moreover, research on defensive styles has supported some aspects of Sigmund and Anna Freud's views on defense mechanisms (Bond et al., 1983; Mikulincer & Horesh, 1999; Newman, Duff et al., 1997; Silverman, 1976). More generally, research on conditioned emotional responses (see Chapter 4), implicit memory (see Chapter 5), and aspects of thinking (see Chapter 6) support the broad idea that some mental processes can be unconscious—that is, without awareness. Despite the difficulty in evaluating most of Freud's theory, many aspects of it remain with us because it offers a truly comprehensive, and sometimes insightful, view of people and of personality.

Humanistic Psychology

Partly as a reaction to Freud's theory, which in many ways draws a pessimistic picture of human nature and personality formation, the humanist psychologists focused on the positive aspects of the individual—on people's innate goodness, creativity, and free will. Rather than being driven by forces outside of their control, as the Freudians claimed, the humanists believe that people can create solutions to their problems. A cornerstone of their theories is that we all have a drive toward **self-actualization**, an innate motivation to attain our highest emotional and intellectual potential. The work of two psychologists, Abraham Maslow and Carl Rogers, represents the humanistic perspective on personality.

Maslow

The personality theory developed by Abraham Maslow (1908–1970) is really a theory of motivation based on a hierarchy of physical and emotional needs (see Chapter 7). Lower-level needs, said Maslow, must be met before needs farther up the hierarchy can be satisfied; the highest-level need is that for self-actualization. During crises, needs regress to a lower level, and higher-level needs are put on hold.

Maslow studied the lives and characteristics of historical figures he considered to be at the self-actualizing level, including Albert Einstein, Mahatma Gandhi, Abraham Lincoln, and Eleanor Roosevelt. His investigation led him to propose that people who are self-actualizing have these qualities: a true perception of reality, an acceptance of themselves and their environments, an appreciation of the ordinary, a focus on cultural rather than personal problems, few but deep personal relationships, and what Maslow called "oceanic feelings" (see Table 8.3). Maslow regarded oceanic feelings as *peak experiences,* moments of intense clarity of perception (Privette & Landsman, 1983), a suspended sense of time, and wonderment at the experience. Oceanic feelings are similar to the idea of **flow**, the feeling of complete absorption with and merging smoothly into an activity and losing track of time (Csikszentmihalyi & Csikszentmihalyi, 1988). You may have had such an experience, becoming totally engrossed in, say, sketching, listening to music, or playing a musical instrument. Various researchers have studied Maslow's theory, particularly as it relates to motivation on the job. In the end, many of Maslow's concepts are difficult to test, and the validity of his theory remains questionable (Fox, 1982; Soper et al., 1995; Wahba & Bridwell, 1976).

TABLE 8.3 Characteristics of Self-Actualizing People

Source: Maslow (1968).

• Perceive reality accurately and efficiently	• Try to solve cultural rather than personal problems
• Accept themselves, others, and nature	• Form deep relationships, but only with a few people
• Appreciate ordinary events	• Often experience "oceanic feelings" (a sense of oneness with nature that transcends time and space)

Rogers

Carl Rogers (1902–1987) is noted for his formulation of client-centered therapy and his notions of personality and its development. In **client-centered therapy**, the therapist provides not interpretation but an unconditionally supportive and positive environment for the client. Like Maslow, Rogers viewed humans as possessing a need for self-actualization. But rather than viewing the satisfaction of lower- to higher-order needs as the driving force behind personality, he believed that the *self-concept*—our sense of ourselves and of how others see us—is central to personality development. Rogers proposed that our feelings about ourselves are in part a function of how others see us. Thus we have a basic need for **unconditional positive regard**, acceptance without any conditions. Receiving unconditional positive regard, according to Rogers, is crucial for the development of a healthy self-concept. Of course, it is impossible to receive or provide unconditional positive regard all the time, and the socialization process praises children for behaving in accordance with societal rules. This praise for specific behaviors leads us to learn *conditions of worth,* or "what it takes" to be treated as worthwhile. According to Rogers, people whose lives revolve around meeting such conditions of worth will not achieve their full human potentials. To prevent such obstruction of potential, yet meet society's need for children to learn what it considers appropriate behavior, Rogers advised parents to make the distinction between a child's inappropriate *behavior* and his or her *worth* as a human being.

Humanistic theories appeal to many because of their emphasis on the uniqueness of each person and on free will. According to this view, how you live your life is determined not by unconscious forces but with your conscious awareness and the freedom to choose your experiences. Critics of humanistic theory point out that, as with psychodynamic theory, many of its concepts are difficult to test and have received little research support. Moreover, the uplifting, positive view of human nature has struck a discordant note for many in light of the amount of violence and evil in the world.

Good or bad child? Rogers argues that a child may at times behave unsuitably, but that does not mean he or she is a bad child. Labeling children as "bad" may affect their developing self-concepts.

The Cognitive View of Personality: You Are What You Expect

The cognitive approach to personality emphasizes that the development of personality is affected by people's thoughts: Thoughts influence feelings and behavior, and consistent thoughts (consistent at least in a given situation) create personality. One aspect of the cognitive view of personality development is the idea of **expectancies:** What you *expect* to happen has a powerful influence on your thoughts, feelings, and behavior, in turn personality. Expectancies about the outcomes of behavior, often based on past experiences, can explain why operant conditioning works. You learn that a certain stimulus signals a likely outcome if you behave in a certain way, so you come to expect certain outcomes from particular behaviors in certain situations. Perhaps Gabe doesn't like parties because, from his previous experience of them, he expects that he will have a miserable time and feel socially isolated (in the language of conditioning, this would be "punishment" for attending the party; see Chapter 4). Such expectancies have a powerful influence on behavior even without our awareness. Killen and his colleagues (1996) found that among ninth-grade nondrinkers, both male and female, those who had the expectancy that drinking would enhance social behavior (that is, the outcome of drinking would be more or better social behavior) were more likely to begin drinking within a year.

One type of personality difference related to expectancy focuses on **locus of control**, the source we perceive as exerting control over our life events (Rotter, 1966). People who have an internal locus of control, called *internals,* are more likely to see control over events as coming from within themselves when the situation is ambiguous; that is, they feel personally responsible for what happens to them. Gabe's

Client-centered therapy: Therapy developed by Rogers that focuses on the client's potential for growth and the therapist's role as provider of unconditional support.

Unconditional positive regard: Acceptance without any conditions.

Expectancies: Expectations that have a powerful influence on thoughts, feelings, behavior, and, in turn, personality.

Locus of control: The source perceived to be the center of control over life's events.

Our expectancies can shape our behavior in consistent ways. Is Peter Sellers's character, Inspector Clouseau (The Pink Panther movies), paranoid because he expects to be attacked when he walks into his apartment? No. He has been attacked often enough when entering his apartment that he expects to be attacked—his expectancies shape his thoughts, feelings, and behaviors: He is prepared.

Efficacy expectancy: The sense of being able to follow through and produce the behaviors one would like to perform.

Reciprocal determinism: The interactive relationship between the environment, cognitive/personal factors, and behavior.

responsible approach to studying would indicate that he has an internal locus of control. In contrast, *externals* are people with an external locus of control; these people are more likely to see control as coming from outside forces, and they feel less personal responsibility. Because Tina does well in her classes without studying much, she chalks up her good grades to easy tests. She feels less personally responsible for her success than does Gabe. In this way, she seems to have more of an external locus of control.

Internals and externals have different responses to success and failure. Internals are more likely to increase their expectancies in response to success and to lower their expectancies in response to failure. Externals are likely to do the opposite, lowering their expectancies after success and raising them after failure. Thus, what you believe about a situation depends on whether you attribute the consequences to your own behavior or to outside forces. As an internal, Gabe has lowered expectations about future parties because of what he sees as his failures at past ones. Tina, as an external, doesn't fully expect to maintain her high grades because she doesn't feel completely responsible for them in the first place.

People also differ with respect to **efficacy expectancy**, the sense that we have the ability to follow through and produce the behaviors we would like to perform (Bandura, 1977b). Efficacy expectancy is distinct from locus of control, which focuses on whether consequences arise from internal or external causes when the situation is unclear. Albert Bandura hypothesized that efficacy expectancy helps people believe in themselves and in their ability to change or perform behaviors previously viewed as difficult or impossible. Those with high efficacy expectancy persist more than others when working on difficult problems (Brown & Inouye, 1978). Both Gabe and Tina have high efficacy expectancies, a correspondence that partly accounts for the initial sense they had of being a lot alike.

Another aspect of the cognitive view of personality stems from the idea of self-reinforcement (Bandura, 1976, 1977a)—that is, the reinforcement we give ourselves for our behavior. Tina might reward herself for studying all day by going skating the next day. Self-reinforcement can occur by just thinking about your actions. When you like the way you behaved in a given situation, you praise yourself (providing reinforcement), and when you disapprove of your behavior, you blame yourself (providing punishment). Self-reinforcement is a powerful tool in determining behavior and feelings, which in turn contribute to personality.

Bandura (1978) regarded human behavior as part of an interactive process involving psychological and social forces: Thoughts, expectancies, feelings, and other personal factors influence both the environment (including the social world) and behavior; in turn, the environment and personal factors influence, and are influenced by, behavior (see Figure 8.6). Bandura called this interactive relationship **reciprocal determinism.** In essence, Bandura was calling attention to the interaction among events at different levels of analysis, as we do in our Looking at Levels sections, except that he did not include biologically based factors. Reciprocal determinism might explain Tina's desire for highly stimulating activities (such as bungee-jumping) by pointing out that because of certain aspects of her environment, such as moving a lot as a child, Tina came to *expect* a certain level of newness, excitement, even danger, from her experiences (cognitive/personal). These expectations influence her thrill-seeking behavior (bungee-jumping), but all the factors influence one another. Because Tina has a great time bungee-jumping, she expects to enjoy doing something similarly thrilling next time, and she seeks out such stimuli in her environment.

Figure 8.6   Reciprocal Determinism

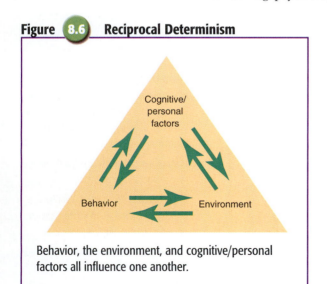

Behavior, the environment, and cognitive/personal factors all influence one another.

Rose-Colored Glasses Can Make a Rosy World

Expectancies do not operate only at the level of the person. That expectancies affect, and are in turn affected by, the other levels of the brain and the group is nicely illustrated by a study by Snyder and colleagues (1977). Participants were asked to talk on the telephone with a member of the opposite sex. Some of the men were led to believe that the woman to whom they were speaking was physically attractive; others were told that their telephone partner was not physically attractive. The women on the receiving end knew nothing of this manipulation. The two sides of the conversations were recorded separately, and tape recordings of the women's parts of the conversations were given to judges to rate how friendly, attractive, and sociable each seemed. Like the women themselves, the judges knew nothing about the manipulation; nevertheless, they could pick out those women who had been identified to the men as attractive simply from the women's style of conversation; these women spoke in a friendly, warm manner.

The men apparently behaved differently depending on their expectations, which in turn induced different behavior on the part of the women. When judges heard only the men's part of the conversations, they rated the men who thought they were talking to attractive women as more sociable, interesting, outgoing, and humorous than the others.

Here we see how beliefs (at the level of the person) can affect how we interpret and organize information (at the level of the brain), which can give rise to pleasure if, in this instance, a man thinks he is charming an attractive woman. This pleasure in turn makes the man more relaxed, sociable, and so on, which in turn makes the woman respond more positively, and thus fuels a social interaction (level of the group). It is clear that events at all three levels operate at the same time, and unless we appreciate how those events interact, we cannot fully understand what is happening in this situation.

CONSOLIDATE!

1 *What is the Freudian view of personality?* There are three different levels of consciousness (unconscious, preconscious, and conscious), and three structures of personality (id, ego, and superego) in a dynamic relationship with each other. Freud proposed five psychosexual stages (oral, anal, phallic, latency, and genital) and theorized that when resolution of a psychosexual stage is incomplete, a person's development is arrested, creating a neurosis. Moreover, sexual and aggressive impulses can create anxiety, prompting the use of defense mechanisms. Neo-Freudians—Carl Jung, Alfred Adler, and Karen Horney—added to or altered aspects of Freud's theory. Although a comprehensive and intriguing theory, many aspects of Freud's theory are difficult to test scientifically.

2 *What is the main emphasis of humanistic theories?* Humanistic theories (for example, those of Abraham Maslow and Carl Rogers) celebrate each person's uniqueness and stress positive qualities of human nature and free will. They also emphasize self-actualization. Although uplifting, many aspects of humanistic theories are difficult to test scientifically.

3 *What is the cognitive approach to personality theory?* The cognitive approach stresses the roles of expectancies on people's thoughts, feelings, and behaviors: What you expect to happen will influence personality development. Expectancies arise from people's locus of control, the source we perceive as exerting control over our life events, and are affected by efficacy expectancy, the sense that we have the ability to follow through and produce the behaviors we would like to perform. Albert Bandura proposed the notion of reciprocal determinism to explain the interactive influence of behavior, environment, and cognitive/personal factors on one another.

The World: Social Influences on Personality

Tina wondered whether some of the differences between Gabe and herself might reflect the different environments in which they had grown up. Gabe was an only child; Tina was the youngest of three, with two older brothers. Gabe grew up in a rural part of the United States and, before college, had lived in the same town his whole life. Tina, an Air Force "brat," had lived in half a dozen countries before she was 12.

Although some percentage of personality may have genetic or biological components, the environment also plays a role. Our family environments and the ways in which we are raised contribute substantially toward personality traits of social closeness and positive emotionality. Other environmental influences on personality that psychologists have investigated include birth order, peer relationships, gender differences, and culture.

1. To what extent does birth order shape personality?

2. Can friends affect the way personality develops?

3. Do social factors produce gender differences in personality?

4. Do different cultures produce different types of personalities?

Birth Order: Are You Number One?

Have you ever noticed that people who are firstborns seem more responsible and better organized, and that last-borns seem more agreeable and accommodating? If you have, you're not the first person to make a connection between personality and birth order. Alfred Adler (1964), himself a younger sibling raised in the shadow of a high-achieving brother, was one of the early personality theorists who proposed that birth order affects personality. In the past, research has not shown clear-cut evidence for the impact of birth order on personality development (see Ernst & Angst, 1983, for a review), but more recent reviews of birth order research, using meta-analytic procedures, have found consistent and interesting results.

Science historian Frank Sulloway (1997) used meta-analyses to support his proposal that at least one aspect of personality, openness to experience (one of the Big Five superfactors), is shaped by birth order. But, Sulloway was careful to point out, birth order acts along with other factors, such as the number of children in a family and the level of conflict between each child and his or her parents. Moreover, a person's sex (and that of his or her siblings), the number of years between siblings, temperament, social class, and loss of a parent can also affect this aspect of personality.

Sulloway developed his theory in an attempt to understand why, throughout history, some people have supported scientific and political revolutions whereas others have insisted on maintaining the status quo, and especially why such opposite views occur within the same family. From available information about the lives of historical figures, Sulloway proposed that, in general, firstborns, because of their place in the birth order, are more likely to support parental authority, see things as their parents do, and be less open to new ideas and experiences. Younger siblings, because they must find a different niche in the family and in the world around them, are more likely to be open to new ideas. In their personalities, "only" children are similar to firstborn children.

Although not all psychologists agree with his meta-analytic conclusions about birth order and personality development (Modell, 1996), and not all subsequent research has supported his theory (Freese et al., 1999), Sulloway (1999) has extended and replicated his results with over 5,000 adults; the results are summarized in Table 8.4. Salmon's work (1998, 1999; Salmon & Daly, 1998) has focused on middle-born children. She found that middle-borns were less close to their families than were their elder or younger siblings. For instance, when hearing political speeches, middle-borns responded most positively to the speeches when the speaker used the term *friend* than when the terms *brothers* and *sisters* were used. In contrast, first- and last-borns responded most positively to speeches in which family terms were

TABLE 8.4   The Effects of Birth Order on Personality

FIRSTBORNS AND ONLY CHILDREN	MIDDLE-BORNS	LATER-BORNS
• More responsible, ambitious, organized, academically successful, energetic, self-disciplined (*Conscientious*)	• Less closely identified with family	• More tender-minded, easy-going, trusting, accommodating, altruistic (*Agreeable*)
• More temperamental, more anxious about their status (*Neurotic*)	• Less likely to ask for parental help in an emergency	• More adventurous, prone to fantasy, attracted by novelty, untraditional (*Open to experience*)
• More assertive, dominant (*Extraverted*) (Sulloway, 1997)	• Less likely to report having been loved as child	• More sociable, affectionate, excitement seeking, fun-loving (*Extraverted*)
	• Compared with siblings, more likely to live farther from parents and less likely to visit parents (Salmon, 1999; Salmon & Daley, 1998)	• More self-conscious (*Neurotic*) (Sulloway, 1997)

used (Salmon, 1998). Further, when asked to define themselves, middle-borns were least likely to define themselves by their last names, that is, their family names (Salmon & Daly, 1998).

Peer Relationships: Personality Development by Peer Pressure

In 1995, Judith Harris wrote an article (and later a book, *The Nurture Assumption*) proposing that, beyond the genes they give their children, parents do not really affect their children's personality and social behavior. She claimed that it is children's peers, not their families, who shape how they behave and determine the nongenetic elements of their personalities. For example, she pointed out that immigrant children learn their new country's language fluently, even though they may speak their native language at home with their parents. She proposed that both contact with their peers and the desire to fit in lead children quickly to learn how to speak the new language without an accent.

According to Harris (1998), there are only two main ways that parents' behaviors can have enduring effects on their child's personality and social behavior. These are severe abuse and choice of where to live and where to send their children to school (and the latter is significant only because it gives parents some small control over their children's peer group). Beyond this, she theorizes, parents have little lasting influence on their children's personality and social behavior.

Harris's view of minimal parental influence on childhood development rests on the assumption that all children in the same family experience the same environment, but there are several flaws with this assumption. First, as we have noted, people create their own microenvironments based on their temperaments, past experiences, and appearances. Thus, there is no single "family environment" that is the same for each child, and any measure of an aspect of family environment, such as the number of books in the house, does not necessarily reflect the actual environment for a particular child. Second, if families had no effect on children's personalities, then birth order effects would not exist (Sulloway, 1998). The fact that firstborns have been shown to have consistently different personalities than their younger brothers and sisters speaks to the fact that interactions within the family—including the manner in which parents treat their children—*does* affect personality.

Third, the same event in a family has different meaning for each of its members, based on age and cognitive ability (Hoffman, 1991). This can be clearly seen in studies of the effects of parents' divorce on their children. Children who are 5 years old

Parents can influence how each of their children feels about him- or herself, which in turn affects the child's thoughts, feelings, and behaviors (in essence, personality). Parents can also influence their children's values, which ultimately affects their personalities.

when parents divorce respond in predictable ways that are *different* from the predictable ways that 11-year-olds respond. Five-year-olds assume the divorce is a result of something they did, whereas 11-year-olds can reason and understand that the divorce may be caused by other factors. Thus, siblings of different ages may have the same stimulus, in this case the divorce, but the effects on their personalities are very different (Hoffman, 1991).

Research designed to test elements of Harris's hypothesis directly has thus far provided mixed results at best (Loehlin, 1997; Vernon et al., 1997). For example, twins who have more friends in common have more similar personalities than do twins who have fewer friends in common; however, the statistics indicate this relationship is weak.

Gender Differences in Personality: Nature and Nurture

In general, personality differences between females and males are not very great, especially when compared with the large differences among people within each sex. For example, there are no notable sex differences in social anxiety, locus of control, impulsiveness, or reflectiveness (Feingold, 1994).

Nonetheless, some consistent differences have been found (Feingold, 1994). Women tend to score higher on traits reflecting *social connectedness*, which is a focus on the importance of relationships (Gilligan, 1982). In contrast, men tend to score higher on traits reflecting *individuality* and *autonomy*, with a focus on separateness from others, achievement, and self-sufficiency. Women tend to be more empathic than men (Lennon & Eisenberg, 1987) and report more nurturing tendencies (Feingold, 1994). In addition, as noted in Chapter 7, women do better on tasks assessing emotion in other people (Hall, 1978, 1987). For example, women are better than men at spotting when their partners are deceiving them (McCornack & Parks, 1990).

One cultural explanation for gender differences in personality is that as boys between the ages of 3 and 5 realize they are a different sex than their mothers, they lose their identification and connection with her, and come to see themselves as more autonomous than do girls (Choderow, 1978).

While some studies have found a sex difference in individuality, others have not (Archer & Waterman, 1988). The observed sex differences in individuality and social connectedness show themselves in part in the way males and females try to resolve moral dilemmas. Gilligan (1982) and others have argued that females think through moral dilemmas differently from, not less well than, males. Females are more likely to pay attention to the interpersonal context of a moral decision, to whether and how others will be hurt by the decision; males are more likely to make a moral decision based on laws or abstract principles. We will discuss this in more detail in Chapter 9.

Males and females also differ in their amounts of neuroticism, with men scoring lower (Lynn & Martin, 1997; Zuckerman et al., 1988). However, women generally score lower on anger and aggression (Shields, 1987) and on assertiveness (Feingold, 1994).

These findings are consistent with stereotypes about men and women, but the fact that a difference exists doesn't tell us *why* it exists—what might be the role of biological or cultural factors (sex differences caused by cultural factors are sometimes referred to as *gender differences*)? Biological explanations for sex differences include the effects of testosterone (see Chapters 2 and 7), as well as the premise that men and women have evolved differently because of differences in mate selection and parenting strategies (D. Buss, 1995). According to this view, women have a greater investment in their offspring because they cannot have as many children as can men. This greater investment, and their caretaker role, caused women to develop more of an attachment to their children, an attachment with an evolutionary advantage: These women were more likely to have children who survived into adulthood and had children themselves.

Several cultural and social theories attempt to explain personality differences between men and women. Social role theory proposes that boys and girls learn different skills and beliefs. For example, some computer games pitched to girls emphasize social interactions and a concern for others, and portray getting along as more important than winning. This emphasis is in contrast to the more typical genre, which involves killing the enemy, capturing others' territory, and defending against capture or death. These two types of computer games let the user cultivate different skills and lead to different moral lessons. Expectancy effects can also play a role in sex differences in personality; through direct interaction with their environments, boys and girls come to have different expectancies about likely responses when gender-role appropriate or inappropriate behavior is exhibited (Henley, 1977).

An additional cultural explanation for gender differences in assessing others' emotions is the difference in power between men and women. Traditionally, women have been less likely to hold positions of power. In such circumstances, being able to read the emotions of others provides some degree of safety by being able to make rapid assessments of a situation (Snodgrass, 1985; Tavris, 1991).

The importance of context, or situation, has raised the question of whether examining sex differences in personality is valid; after all, different situations can yield contradictory findings (Eagly, 1987, 1995; Lott, 1996). In addition, Moskowitz (1993) found differences between men and women when participants interacted with same-sex friends (males were more dominant, females were more friendly), but those differences disappeared when the interactions were between opposite-sex strangers. Thus, although differences between men's and women's personalities have been observed, they do not necessarily hold in all situations.

From what we know of Tina and Gabe, we cannot say with certainty that the personality differences between them are explained by sex or gender differences. Although he prefers to be alone more than she, he does have friends, and we can't say if their contrasting preferences reflect a gender difference, a difference in social connectedness and individuality, temperament, or their learning histories.

Culture and Personality: Are There National Personalities?

It is more difficult to compare personalities across cultures than you might think. Although it is possible to translate personality measures into other languages, some concepts don't translate very well, even if the words themselves can be rendered in different languages. For example, it is possible to translate the phrase *self-esteem* into French, but the concept of self-esteem as we understand it is not generally familiar in France, and so a simple translation of words from English to French doesn't convey the meaning of the idea.

Nevertheless, personality measures that have been carefully translated to compensate for such problems reveal the same Big Five personality factors in many, although not all, cultures (Katigbak et al., 1996; McCrae & Costa, 1997; McCrae et al., 1998; Paunonen & Ashton, 1998; Paunonen et al., 2000). Personality measures developed in the native language of a culture, rather than translated into it, may be more accurate for that culture. For example, Chinese college students were asked to rate other people on qualities described by Chinese adjectives (not English adjectives translated into Chinese); five factors were identified, but they were not the same as the Big Five found in English-language tests (Yang & Bond, 1990).

In general, personality differences have been found between collectivist and individualist cultures (see Chapter 7). Collectivist cultures often find the needs of the group more important than those of the individual: Chinese, African, Latin American, and Arab cultures tend to have this orientation (Buda & Elsayed-Elkhouly,

1998). In contrast, individualist countries such as the United States, Great Britain, Canada, and Australia emphasize the individual, even at the expense of others. Collectivist countries tend to value humility, honoring the family, and efforts to maintain the social order (Triandis et al., 1990), and are more likely to have a populace that cares about others, even strangers (Hui & Triandis, 1986). Individualist countries value personal freedom, equality, and enjoyment. This distinction between cultures has been used to explain differences in crime rates, which are higher in individualist cultures: Collectivist cultures exert more social control over the individual, and criminals' actions reflect not only on themselves but also on their families. And, in fact, as the global economy leads collectivist cultures to shift their work habits and values to those of individualist countries, crime rates and other social ills increase (Strom, 2000).

Consider that, using the five-factor approach, bilingual Hong Kong university students were given a personality inventory. Results showed that, compared with North American university students, Hong Kong students were low in extraversion in general, and in the particular traits of excitement seeking, competence, and altruism. Moreover, they were high in vulnerability, straightforwardness, and compliance (McCrae et al., 1998). As proof of the impact of culture on personality, after Chinese immigrants move to North America, their personality profiles begin to resemble those of native-born North Americans; the longer they have lived in North America, the more similar the profiles (McCrae et al., 1998).

Although the United States is an individualist country, individualism varies by region (Vandello & Cohen, 1999). The Deep South (perhaps because of its strong self-identification as a cultural region, its history of collective farming, and the prominence of religion) is the most collectivist. The states of the Southwest are also collectivist; these states have a distinct history and an influx of immigrants from Mexico, a collectivist country. In contrast, the Great Plains and western mountain states are particularly individualistic, in part because of the "vast distances, sparse population, and harsh, unpredictable weather" in this part of the country (Shortridge, 1993, p. 1011), as well as the frontier values of individuality. Thus, although people may live in a country that falls on a particular location on the collectivist–individualist continuum, there are regional, as well as individual, differences. So, to the extent that experience shapes personality, the very different experiences of Tina's and Gabe's childhood years may well have contributed to their different approaches to life.

People in collectivist cultures tend to define themselves as part of a group, are very attached to the group, and see their personal goals as secondary to the group's goals. People from individualist cultures define themselves as individuals, are less attached to the group, and see their personal goals as more important than the group's goals (Triandis et al., 1988).

LOOKING AT LEVELS

Two's Company

How can we explain cultural differences in personality? Perhaps people from different cultures have different genes, or the environment leads different genes to be expressed in certain cultures and not others. Let's look again at a study by Ekman (1980) described in Chapter 7. Japanese and Americans watched emotional films, either alone or with a white-coated investigator in the room. When alone, the Japanese and the Americans reacted to various events in the film in very similar ways. But in company, the Japanese tended to respond more politely and with a narrower range of emotions, whereas the Americans responded much as they did when alone. Thus, it isn't the case that the Japanese actually had different emotional responses than the Americans, that they had lower levels of emotionality. Rather, their learned behaviors (politeness and less expression of emotion) masked their true emotional responsiveness.

When in the company of authoritative strangers (such as the white-coated investigator), the Japanese do not display the same range of emotions that is permissible when alone. The collectivist Japanese culture leads to a change in behavior (changing facial expressions), and the Japanese have learned to make this change very well, extremely quickly, and apparently automatically. Both their initial response to the film and their subsequent learned responses can be considered elements of personality, although they are influenced by different factors.

The initial response may be influenced more by temperament (emotionality, at the level of the brain), whereas the subsequent response is influenced more by the social environment (in this case, culture). The cultural differences in personality between the Americans and the Japanese trace back to learning during childhood (level of the person)—learning that not only shapes the individual's personality, but also regulates the expression of biological responses.

CONSOLIDATE!

1 *To what extent does birth order shape personality?* From studying historical figures, Sulloway suggests that birth order, along with other moderating variables such as the number of children in a family and the level of conflict between parents and children, can influence openness to experience. Further research has found additional differences between first-, middle-, and later-borns. Specifically, first-borns are less open to new experiences and are more conscientious, middle-borns identify less closely with family, and later-borns are more agreeable and more open to new experiences.

2 *Can friends affect the way personality develops?* Research suggests that peer relationships *can* affect personality. However, findings are mixed at best that peer relationships are the main environmental element that influences personality development.

3 *Do social factors produce gender differences in personality?* Although men and women exhibit few broad personality differences, there are noteworthy differences in social connectedness (versus individuality) and in emotionality (high versus low). Social explanations for these differences range from social role theory, identification with the primary caretaker, and differences in power. Given the importance of context, gender may not be predictive of behavior in a given situation.

4 *Do different cultures produce different types of personalities?* There are cultural differences in personality: The native-born citizens of countries that emphasize the needs of the group tend to have personalities that reflect the collectivist orientation. In contrast, the native-born citizens of countries that emphasize individualism tend to have personalities that reflect the individualist orientation.

A DEEPER LEVEL

Recap and Thought Questions

What Is Personality?

Personality is a consistent set of characteristics that people display over time and across situations, and that distinguish individuals from each other. People do not behave in the same manner in all situations: The context, or situation, influences the way people behave, and people can influence the situation. Some researchers have found that personality traits can be statistically grouped under five superfactors (extraversion, neuroticism, agreeableness, conscientiousness, and openness) or, according to Eysenck, three personality dimensions (extraversion, neuroticism, and psychoticism). Personality can be measured by interviews, observation, inventories (such as Cattell's 16PF), and projective tests (such as the Rorschach test and the Thematic Apperception Test, or TAT), with inventories being the most common method.

Do the differences between Tina and Gabe reflect their different personalities? Some of the differences probably do reflect personality differences, but the situation also exerts its own influence, evidenced by Tina's different behavior when with her economics professor and with Gabe.

Think It Through. Suppose you are interested in dating someone and wanted to assess his or her personality before getting too involved. Why would you choose a particular type of assessment method? If you could assess a prospective employer's personality, why might you use the same method or a different one? Would you be able to predict your future employer's behavior if you knew his or her Big Five characteristics? Why or why not? Why might it change the accuracy of your predictions if you knew more about the scores on the specific traits that make up the five superfactors?

The Brain: The Personality Organ

Eysenck proposed that each of his three personality dimensions (extraversion, neuroticism, and psychoticism) has a corresponding biologically distinct system. Aspects of this theory have been supported by brain-scanning and other physiological research. Some psychologists and behavioral geneticists estimate that approximately 50% of the variations in personality is inherited, although some traits appear more heritable than others. These innate inclinations, often referred to as temperaments, include activity, sociability, emotionality, and impulsivity. Differences in biological characteristics, such as emotional arousability, can affect thoughts, feelings, motivation, and behavior, and can make people more or less prone to conditioned emotional responses and shyness.

Were Tina and Gabe born with their personalities? Based on behavioral genetics research, it is likely that Tina and Gabe were born with some elements of their personalities, particularly their temperaments. However, other elements have likely been forged by their cultural experiences, family events, and learning histories.

Think It Through. Imagine that you know a family in which both parents are highly extraverted, emotionally stable, not particularly creative, and very conscientious. Would you predict that their child would have the same personality features? Why or why not? If their child was very shy (one of Kagan's "inhibited" children), would that mean that the child will always be shy, or might he or she become like the parents? (Hint: Think about what you have learned about temperament.)

The Person: Behaviors and Beliefs

Questions of motives, thoughts, and feelings are at the heart of Freud's psychodynamic theory, which focuses on the three structures of personality (id, ego, and super-ego, and their dynamic relationships), three levels of awareness (unconscious, preconscious, and conscious), as well as sexual and aggressive drives, defense mechanisms, and psychosexual stages (oral, anal, phallic, latency, and genital). According to Freud, when resolution of a psychosexual stage is incomplete, a person's development is arrested, creating a neurosis. Moreover, sexual and aggressive impulses can create anxiety, causing the use of defense mechanisms. Neo-Freudians (such as Jung, Adler, and Horney) added to or altered aspects of Freud's theory. Maslow's and Rogers's humanistic theories also address motives, feelings, and the self, but celebrate each person's uniqueness, stress positive qualities of human nature and free will, and emphasize self-actualization. The cognitive view of personality focuses on the roles of expectancies on people's thoughts, feelings, and behaviors: What we expect to happen will influence our personality development. Personality differences in expectancies include locus of control, the source we perceive as exerting control over life events, and efficacy expectancy, the sense that we have the ability to follow through and produce the behaviors we would like to perform.

How might Tina's and Gabe's inner motives, thoughts, and feelings reflect their personalities? We don't know enough about Tina and Gabe or their childhood experiences to be able to understand how each one's personality reflects their motives, thoughts, and feelings. We could infer such attributes based on Freudian, humanistic, and cognitive theories of personality, but based on our limited knowledge of Tina and Gabe, these would be mere speculations.

Think It Through. If you used Freudian theory to understand a historical figure's personality and motivations, do you think you could be sure of your analysis? Why or why not? Could you use a humanist theory to understand this person? What would you need to know about him or her? Which aspects of this person's life would you need to know about to apply a cognitive theory of personality?

The World: Social Influences on Personality

Birth order, along with other moderating factors, such as the number of children in a family and the level of conflict between parents and children, can influence openness to experience and other aspects of personality. Moreover, although there are a few broad personality differences between women and men (social connectedness versus individuality, and high versus low emotionality), in general differences between the sexes tend to be small, and it is not clear whether they are due to biological or social factors. Social explanations for these differences range from social role theory, identification with the primary caretaker, and differences in power. Context may be more predictive of personality than sex. Personality differences have also been found between citizens of cultures that are collectivist as opposed to individualist, with people in each culture tending to have personality traits that are more valued in their culture.

Could Tina's and Gabe's different childhood environments have affected how their personalities developed? It is possible that aspects of Tina's and Gabe's different childhood environments could have influenced their personalities. Their differences could reflect their birth order positions (perhaps Gabe is conscientious because he is a firstborn), sex differences (perhaps Tina was raised to be more emotionally responsive because she is female), or cultural differences. Moreover, family events, such as divorce, would have affected their personalities.

Think It Through. What are two possible explanations for regional personality differences between "mellow" Californians and "fast-paced" northeasterners? (Hint: Genetic? Environmental?) How might you go about trying to determine whether your explanation is supported by research data? What type of study could you design, and what kinds of participants would you need? What is your hypothesis—that is, what kind of results would you expect to find?

REVIEW TEST

For each of the following items, choose the single correct or best answer. The correct answers appear at the end.

1 Researchers have found that most people are ____.
   a. consistent across some traits, but not across others
   b. consistent across positive traits, but inconsistent across negative ones
   c. inconsistent across all personality traits
   d. consistent across most personality traits

2 The more ____ a trait is defined, the ____ it is as a predictor of behavior.
   a. narrowly; worse   c. narrowly; better
   b. precisely; worse   d. broadly; better

3 Hans Eysenck identified three superfactors of personality: ____.
   a. extraversion, neuroticism, psychoticism
   b. neuroticism, psychoticism, conscientiousness
   c. extraversion, neuroticism, conscientiousness
   d. extraversion, psychoticism, agreeableness

4 The Rorschach test is a(n) ____.
   a. observational method for assessing personality
   b. structured interview for assessing psychopathology
   c. a paper-and-pencil test for assessing psychopathology
   d. projective test of personality

5 A person scoring high on a(n) ____ scale is very likely to develop a phobia after a car accident.
   a. extraversion   c. neuroticism
   b. psychoticism   d. introversion

6 The propensity to respond to stimuli immediately, without reflection or consideration for consequences, is called ____.
   a. impulsivity   c. emotionality
   b. psychoticism   d. neuroticism

7 Kagan has found that a large proportion of inhibited children are ____.
   a. firstborns   c. prone to dissociation
   b. only children   d. laterborns

8 Which of the following is *not* a personality structure relating to consciousness, according to Freud?
   a. preconscious   c. conscious
   b. subconscious   d. unconscious

9 A person's feelings of sexual attraction for his or her mother are in his or her ____.
   a. subconscious   c. preconscious
   b. unconscious   d. conscious

10 Freud proposed that the eruption of the id's instincts is responsible for feelings of ____.
   a. guilt   c. anxiety
   b. anger   d. depression

11 To be reverent, obedient, and honest is part of Jim's ____.
   a. conscience   c. ego ideal
   b. ego   d. conscious

12 A person who disregards conventional rules and who is cruel and destructive would be said to be ____, according to Freud.
   a. oral-expulsive   c. anal-retentive
   b. oral-retentive   d. anal-expulsive

13 Freud developed his theory through ____.
   a. analysis of his patients and himself
   b. extensive readings
   c. careful research in the laboratory
   d. animal studies

14 Which of the following statements would be most detrimental to a child's healthy personality development, according to Rogers?
   a. "You're just like your mother."
   b. "Good boys eat their peas."
   c. "I don't like your behavior."
   d. "You're just like your father."

15 In collectivist cultures, rates of ____ are lower.
   a. teen pregnancy   c. mental illness
   b. alcoholism   d. crime

ANSWERS: 1.a 2.c 3.a 4.d 5.c 6.a 7.d 8.b 9.b 10.c 11.c 12.d 13.a 14.b 15.d

9 Psychology

Over the Life Span

GROWING UP, GROWING OLDER, GROWING WISER

"**S**pielbug," some of his classmates called him. Girls thought he was nerdy and unattractive. His father, Arnold, a pioneer in the use of computers in engineering, was hardly ever around and, to make matters worse, frequently uprooted his family, moving from Ohio to New Jersey, to Arizona, and finally to Northern California. Steven was a perpetual new kid on the block. He was also, by all accounts, an unusual child, both in his appearance (he had a large head and protruding ears) and in his fearful and awkward behavior (McBride, 1999). Spielberg himself has said that he "felt like an alien" throughout his childhood. He desperately wanted to be accepted, but didn't fit in. So at age 12 he began making films, "little 8mm things. I did it to find something that, for me, could be permanent" (quoted in R. Sullivan, 1999, p. 66). Spielberg continued to make movies as a teenager, often casting his three sisters in roles. He discovered that making movies was one way to win his peers' acceptance, as well as some small measure of power—for he sometimes induced his worst enemies to appear in his films.

When he was 16, Spielberg's parents divorced, and Spielberg blamed his father's constant traveling for the breakup. His unhappiness only deepened when his father remarried, taking for his second wife a woman Spielberg couldn't stand. At the same time that he withdrew from his father, Spielberg continued to have a close relationship with his mother, Leah, a concert pianist and artist. The split with his father lasted some 15 years.

In many ways, Spielberg's films, like the rest of his life, are shaped by his childhood. Spielberg himself has said about *E.T., The Extra-Terrestrial,* "The whole movie is really about divorce. . . . Henry's [the main character's] ambition to find a father by bringing E.T. into his life to fill some black hole—that was my struggle to find somebody to replace the dad who I felt had abandoned me" (Sullivan, 1999, p. 68). Many of Spielberg's other films include children who are separated from their parents (such as the girl in *Poltergeist* and the boy in *Close Encounters of the Third Kind*). And *Back to the Future* might represent his longings to change the past, if only he could. Only when he turned 40 did he turn to adult contexts. As he matured, Spielberg's identification with oppressed people in general (not just oppressed children) led him to make movies such as *The Color Purple, Schindler's List,* and *Amistad.*

Steven Spielberg married and had a child, but eventually divorced his wife, actress Amy Irving. His own experiences made him extremely sensitive to the effect of the divorce on his son, and he made every attempt to ensure that his son, Max, did not feel abandoned. When he married again, he became deeply involved with his family (which includes seven children, some of them adopted). There was a happy development in the previous generation's father–son relationship as well: Arnold became a well-loved grandfather who is now a regular presence in the Spielberg household.

Spielberg's journey is one version of the universal story of human development: A skinny kid beset by fears and with few friends becomes one of the most powerful figures in the global entertainment industry; from a family with little family life develops a man's resolve to make the best possible life for his own family; across generations, a father and a son come to like each other, now as father and grandfather, after 15 years of estrangement. *Developmental psychologists* study exactly these sorts of events in our lives: the fascinating and varied process of human development over the life span. In this chapter, we begin by considering prenatal development and the newborn, and we see that even here genes and environment are intimately intertwined. We next turn to infancy and childhood and observe the interplay between maturation and experience in the shaping of the child's physical, mental, emotional, and social development. Then we consider adolescence, a crucial time in development. And finally, we discuss adulthood and aging, and gain insights that help us understand how Arnold could develop from a less-than-optimal father into a terrific grandfather.

In the Beginning: From Conception to Birth

Steven Spielberg has been celebrated as one of the most successful moviemakers of all time. He just seemed to have a natural bent for making movies (he never attended film school). Where did his talent come from? In this section we begin at the beginning and think about the foundations of our skills and abilities.

1 How does development progress in the womb?

2 What are the capabilities of newborns?

Prenatal Development: Nature and Nurture From the Start

For each of us, life began with the meeting of two cells, a sperm and an egg (or *ovum,* which in Latin means "egg"). These specialized cells are sex cells, or *gametes.*

The sperm penetrated the egg, and the genetic material of the sperm melded with that of the ovum. The ovum is not a passive partner in this dance of life; the sperm is drawn to the egg by chemical reactions on the surface of the egg. And when a sperm has been accepted within the egg, other reactions prevent additional sperm from penetrating. The ovum is a supercell, the largest in the human body. Even so, it is barely the size of a pin prick, and sperm are much smaller (about 1/500 of an inch). But despite their small sizes, within the ovum and sperm reside all the machinery necessary to create a new life. And, even at this earliest stage of development, *genes* (*nature*) and the *environment* (*nurture*) are intimately intertwined.

Getting a Start in Life

The genetic heritage of every normal human being is 23 pairs of chromosomes, one member of each pair coming from an egg and the other from a sperm. A *chromosome* is a strand of *DNA* (*deoxyribonucleic acid*) in the nucleus of the cell. A molecule of DNA is shaped like a twisted ladder—the famous "double helix"—in which the rungs are formed by the bonds between pairs of chemicals. Each *gene* on the chromosome is a series of particular "rungs" (see Chapter 2). All cells in the body except the *gametes* (eggs and sperm) contain all 23 pairs of chromosomes; each gamete contains only a single member of each chromosome pair. In an egg, one of these 23 is a chromosome known as *X;* in a sperm, the corresponding chromosome is either an *X* chromosome or a shorter version called a *Y* chromosome.

The fertilization of the egg by the sperm creates a cell called a **zygote**, in which the chromosomes from the egg and from the sperm pair up so that the zygote contains the full complement of 23 pairs. If the sperm contributes an *X* chromosome, the offspring will be female (*XX*); if *Y,* male (*XY*). The *Y* chromosome contains a gene that produces a chemical substance that ultimately causes the zygote to develop into a male; if this substance is not present, genes on the *X* chromosome will produce other substances that cause the baby to be female (Goodfellow & Lowell-Badge, 1993; Hawkins, 1994).

Much of early development is determined by **maturation**, the process that produces genetically programmed changes with age. But from the very start, genes and the environment interact. Although the genes of both the sperm that fertilizes the egg and the genes of the egg will have a major impact on what kind of person develops, the environment plays a crucial role in whether the sperm ever reaches the egg. Sperm actually "surf" on subtle muscle contractions in the uterus; these waves usually move in the correct direction in fertile women, but they either move in the wrong direction or are weak in infertile women (Kunz et al., 1997; Lyons & Levi, 1994). In addition, the fluid in the uterus must be the right consistency and have the right chemical composition for the sperm to complete their journey (Mori et al., 1998; Shibahara et al., 1995; Singh, 1995).

The members of each pair of chromosomes are similar—but they are not identical. For example, the gene for the shape of your earlobes is on the same spot on both chromosomes, but because of its particular chemical composition, the gene on one chromosome may code for an attached earlobe and the gene on the other for an unattached earlobe. The gametes are formed from specialized cells that, while themselves containing the full 23 pairs, in the course of division produce cells with half that number, with only one member of each pair. So, because the members of each pair are not identical, the genetic contents of the resulting gametes are not all the same. And there's another wrinkle, which further contributes to our wonderful human variety: In the course of cell division, the chromosomal decks of cards are shuffled so that pieces of the parent chromosomes in each pair are exchanged, as shown in Figure 9.1 on page 312, to form new combinations of genes.

Human development in the womb is divided into *trimesters*, three equal periods of 3 months each. The first trimester is divided into three stages: the zygote, the **embryo** (from the point where the major axis is present until all major structures are present—from about 2 to 8 weeks after conception), and the **fetus** (and the developing baby is called a fetus thereafter, until he or she is born). At the end

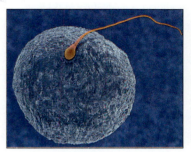

At the moment of conception, a sperm penetrates an ovum. The egg, however, is not a passive recipient; by changing its surface properties, it actively regulates the behavior of the sperm.

Zygote: A fertilized ovum (egg).

Maturation: The developmental process that produces genetically programmed changes with increased age.

Embryo: The period of development from the point where the major axis of the baby is present until all major structures are present, spanning from about 2 weeks to 8 weeks after conception.

Fetus: The final phase of development in the womb, from about age 8 weeks until birth.

Figure **9.1**   **The Long Road to a Zygote**

The chromosomes in eggs and sperm are not simply copies of those of the parent, but rather unique combinations of the material in the two chromosomes in each pair of the parent's chromosomes. The sperm and egg combine to form the basis of a unique individual (or individuals, in the case of identical twins).

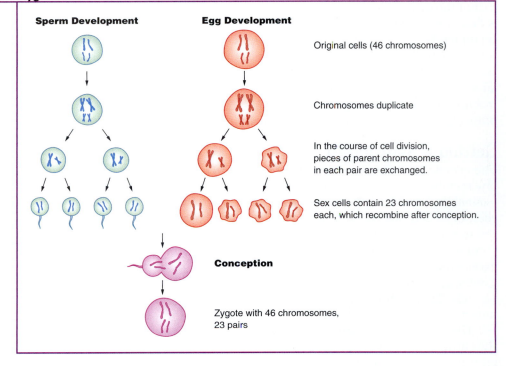

Sperm Development   **Egg Development**

Original cells (46 chromosomes)

Chromosomes duplicate

In the course of cell division, pieces of parent chromosomes in each pair are exchanged.

Sex cells contain 23 chromosomes each, which recombine after conception.

Conception

Zygote with 46 chromosomes, 23 pairs

of the second trimester, the great bulk of the neurons each individual possesses are in place (Nowakowski, 1987; Rakic, 1975; Rodier, 1980), but they are not completely fixed; researchers have found that new neurons can be produced in adult brains (Gould et al., 1999).

The path from zygote to birth is not always smooth. Perhaps surprisingly, about half of all fertilized eggs contain some kind of abnormality in their chromosomes. Most of these eggs are spontaneously aborted (in fact, about 30% of zygotes don't even make it to the embryo phase), but even so, about 1 in 250 babies is born with an abnormality that is obvious, and probably more have abnormalities that are not obvious (Plomin et al., 1997, p. 54; Sadler, 1995).

In the Womb

A popular—and misleading—image shows the fetus floating peacefully asleep in the womb. But in truth the fetus is active nearly from the start, at first with automatic movements, such as the heart beating, and then with large-scale coordinated behaviors. As the fetus develops, the heart rate slows down (but becomes more variable), the fetus moves less often but more vigorously when it does stir, and the heart rate and movement patterns become coordinated. Some researchers have even reported sex differences in behavior in the womb, with male fetuses more active than females (DiPietro et al., 1996). After 20 to 25 weeks of gestation, the fetus is sensitive to both sound and light (Nilsson & Hamberger, 1990; Pujol et al., 1990). How do we know this? Because if a fetus is examined, as is sometimes medically necessary, by a special light-emitting instrument called a *fetoscope*, it will actually move its hands to shield its eyes. As the fetus develops, its movements become increasingly coordinated, and by 28 weeks, it responds to external stimulation. A bit later its heart rate can change if the mother is startled (DiPietro et al., 1996; Kisilevsky & Low, 1998), and between 25 and 34 weeks, a fetus can detect human speech (Cheour-Luhtanen et al., 1996; Zimmer et al., 1993).

In addition, there is evidence that fetuses can learn. Sandman and colleagues (1997) measured the heart rate of fetuses between 30 and 32 weeks after conception while a buzzing vibrator was placed on the mother's belly, positioned right over the fetus's head. The fetus's heart would speed up when it first received a series of stimuli, but this response decreased as more stimuli were presented in the series. This is a classic case of habituation—that is, diminishing response with repeated exposure to the same stimulus. The researchers then presented a new stimulus, which differed in both frequency and intensity, and the fetus's heart speeded up again. This finding shows not only that a fetus can discriminate between the two stimuli, but also that the diminishing response was not the result of the fetus's becoming fatigued or failing to sense the stimuli. In a third round, a series of the original stimuli was presented again. This time the fetus consistently responded to these stimuli, not habituating as it had done previously. What does this mean? The different response to the second presentation of the original stimuli shows that the fetus learned their properties from the first time they were presented—if it hadn't, it would have responded to the second presentation the same way that it did originally.

This fetus may look primitive and passive, but looks can be deceiving. The fetus is, in fact, capable of a rich range of behaviors well before birth.

Teratogens: When the Environment Hurts

A **teratogen** is a chemical, virus, or type of radiation that can cause damage to the zygote, embryo, or fetus. Because of events at different stages in the course of development, different organs are vulnerable to teratogens at different times. Unfortunately, the central nervous system is vulnerable at virtually every phase. For example, the development of the brain can be disrupted if the mother catches a virus, such as chicken pox or rubella (3-day German measles); more than half the babies born to mothers who contract rubella will be mentally retarded if the developing child is in the embryonic period at the onset of the disease. In addition, a mother who is HIV-positive can pass the virus on to the baby during gestation or birth (but only about one-third of these babies contract the virus). The HIV virus causes brain damage, leading to problems in concentration, attention, memory, movement control, and the ability to reason (Clifford, 2000; Grant et al., 1999). Another potential teratogen is alcohol, which can damage the eggs before fertilization (Kaufman, 1997) as well as affect the developing baby throughout pregnancy, starting with the embryo phase. Using heroin or cocaine during pregnancy can cause a host of problems: physical defects, irritability, and sleep and attentional problems in the newborn (Fox, 1994; Miller et al., 1995; Vogel, 1997). Moreover, various environmental pollutants and ionizing radiation can have effects ranging from birth defects and cancer to behavioral difficulties, such as in paying attention. It is known that, in other animals at least, these effects can be passed on to the third generation, to the offspring of the offspring (Friedler, 1996). In fact, even the father's health habits can affect the fetus and subsequently the child. Certain drugs (both prescription and illegal, such as cocaine) can affect the sperm and thereby affect the growing fetus and child (Yazigi et al., 1991).

Major diseases and strong drugs are not the only threats to healthy prenatal development. Excessive amounts of caffeine (three cups of coffee a day, according to one study) can lead to miscarriage or low birth weight, irritability, and other symptoms (Eskenazi, 1993; Eskenazi et al., 1999). Another study found that children of mothers who drink four or more cups of coffee per day had increased risk of *sudden infant death syndrome* (*SIDS*) (Ford et al., 1998). Smoking during pregnancy affects both mother and fetus; it is correlated with higher rates of miscarriage, lower birth weights, stillbirth, and infant mortality, and can cause attentional difficulties in the infant (Floyd et al., 1993; Fried & Makin, 1987; Fried & Watkinson, 2000). A mother's poor diet can lead her infant to have fewer brain cells than normal (Morgane et al., 1993), and the lack of even a single important vitamin or mineral can have significant effects. For example, insufficient folic acid (vitamin B) can disrupt the early development of the nervous system (Nevid et al., 1998).

Stressors in the mother's life can also endanger the developing fetus, and when the stress is severe enough, infants may experience attentional difficulties, be

Teratogen: Any chemical, virus, or type of radiation that can cause damage to the zygote, embryo, or fetus.

unusually anxious, and exhibit unusual social behavior (Weinstock, 1997). In fact, fetuses of mothers of lower socioeconomic status, who are often more stressed than those of higher socioeconomic status, move less often and less vigorously, and show other differences from fetuses of better-off mothers (Pressman et al., 1998). There are several biological reasons for these effects. When the mother is stressed, more of her blood flows to parts of the body affected by the fight-or-flight response (such as the limbs and heart), and less to the uterus. She produces hormones such as cortisol, which slows down the operation of genes that guide prenatal development of the brain, suppressing brain growth (Brown, 1999). There is evidence that the babies of stressed mothers are born with smaller heads than those of unstressed mothers, which may be related to the poorer behavioral functioning scores seen for such babies (Lou et al., 1994).

Positive Environmental Events: The Earliest Head Start

The previous paragraphs might seem to suggest that our species would be better off if maturation alone controlled development. But environmental effects are not all bad, and some prenatal experiences help the fetus. Consider a study by Lafuente and colleagues (1997). Each of 172 pregnant women was assigned to an experimental or a control group. The participants in the experimental group were given a waistband with a tape recorder and small speakers, on which they played tapes of violin music for an average of 70 hours, starting at about 28 weeks after conception and continuing until the birth of the baby. The researchers then tracked the development of the babies during their first 6 months of life and found that the children of mothers in the experimental group were more advanced than those in the control group; for example, they had better motor control and better vocal abilities of the sort that precede language. Steven Spielberg's mother played piano frequently while she was pregnant; could these prenatal concerts have had long-term positive effects on him?

A particularly powerful example of interactions among events at different levels of analysis is the fact that interactions with friends and family can lead to healthier babies being born to stressed mothers (McLean et al., 1993). Social support presumably helps to reduce the mother's stress, which in turn keeps her from the fight-or-flight state and its accompanying unfortunate consequences for the developing baby.

The Newborn: A Work in Progress

In many ways, the human infant compares unfavorably with the infants of some other species. A baby kitten is much more competent, able to walk on its own and explore its environment at only 6 weeks, an age when the human infant has no hope of even crawling. The human brain is not fully developed at birth, perhaps because if it were, the baby's head would not fit through the birth canal. Much human brain development continues after birth.

Nevertheless, although the typical infant may seem thoroughly incompetent, capable of eating, sleeping, cooing, crying, drooling, and not much else, such an assessment would be off the mark. The baby is not a blank slate, waiting for learning or maturity to descend. On the contrary, babies come equipped with a surprising range of abilities and capacities.

Sensory Capacities

Even at the earliest phases of development, babies have the beginnings of sophisticated sensory capabilities. They are born sensitive to the range of frequencies of women's voices (see Hauser, 1996) and have a relatively sensitive sense of smell. Even babies who are fed by bottle prefer the odor of a woman who is breast-feeding another infant to that of a woman who is not breast-feeding (Porter et al., 1992).

Reflexes

Infants also come equipped with a wide range of reflexes, the most important of which are summarized in Table 9.1. A *reflex* is an automatic response to an event,

TABLE 9.1   Major Reflexes Present at Birth

REFLEX	STIMULUS	RESPONSE	DURATION (approx.)
Withdrawal	Sharp stimulus to sole of foot	Leg flexes	Weakens after 10 days of age
Stepping	Held upright over flat surface	Stepping movements	Until about 2 months of age
Sucking	Finger in mouth	Sucking	Until about 3 months of age
Rooting	Stroking cheek lightly	Turns head toward stimulus, starts trying to suck	Until about 3 or 4 months of age
Palmar grasp	Pressing the palm	Grasps object pressing the palm	Until about 4 months of age
Moro (startle)	Sudden loud sound	Throws apart arms and extends legs, then brings arms together, cries	Until 5 months of age
Swimming	Face-down in water	Kicks and paddles in water	Until about 6 months of age
Tonic neck	Head turned to one side	One arm straightens while other bends, and one knee bends (resembling a "fencing" position)	Until 7 months of age
Plantar	Pressing the ball of the foot	All toes curl under	Until about 1 year of age
Babinski	Stroking sole of the foot	Big toe flexes, other toes fan out	Until about 1 year of age
Eye blink	Bright light in eyes	Eyes close	Life

Stepping

Rooting

Moro (startle)

an action that does not require thought. Some of these reflexes have obvious survival value, such as sucking, and some may have had survival value for our ancestors, such as the Moro reflex, in which the startled baby throws its arms wide, as if to grab hold of someone. Other reflexes, such as the Babinski reflex, in which the baby's big toe flexes while the other toes fan out when the sole of his or her foot is stroked, are less obviously useful. Curiously, many of the reflexes that babies have at birth disappear after a while.

Temperament: Instant Personality

A friend describing the birth of his second son expressed amazement as he realized, when handed the child immediately after birth, that the infant was already *different* from his first son, calmer and steadier. Our friend should not have been surprised. From their earliest hours, babies show the makings of individual personalities. They demonstrate differences in *temperament,* in their innate inclinations to engage in a certain style of behavior (see Chapter 8). Some babies may be inclined toward "approach," others toward "withdrawal" (Thomas & Chess, 1996). Infants characterized by an approach response generally react positively to new situations or stimuli, such as a new food, toy, person, or place. Infants characterized by a withdrawal response typically react negatively to new situations or stimuli, either by crying, fussing, or otherwise indicating their discomfort (Chess & Thomas, 1987). Some babies are considered "easy" in that they do not cry often and are not demanding, whereas others are "difficult" in that they are fussy and demanding.

For temperament, like other characteristics, the story of development over the life span reveals themes of both stability and change. Some of the stability of temperament may arise not from inherited predispositions, but from early nurturing experiences. Probably the most compelling evidence of this comes from research with nonhuman animals. Michael Meaney and his colleagues (Anisman et al., 1998; Liu et al., 1997; Meaney et al., 1991; Zaharia et al., 1996) have shown that simply handling rat pups during the first 10 days after birth has enormous effects on the way the animals later respond to stressful events. As adults, these animals don't become as nervous as other rats when put in a large open field (as reflected by fewer feces, less "freezing" responses, and more exploration), and have lower cortisol responses (and thus are less vulnerable to the negative effects of prolonged exposure to cortisol, as discussed in Chapter 5). They are also less prone to learned helplessness (discussed in Chapter 7; Costela et al., 1995). The effects of handling occur naturally when the mother rat licks her pups and engages in nursing with an arched back (so the pups are directly under her); offspring of mothers that behaved this way later had lower amounts of the type of RNA that produces cortisol (Liu et al., 1997). We have good reason to believe that similar effects extend to humans: Touching infants not only can enhance growth and development, but also can reduce the right frontal lobe EEG activation that is associated with depression (even in 1-month-old infants!) and can boost immune function (Field, 1998; Field et al., 1986; Jones et al., 1998).

LOOKING AT LEVELS

Social Support for Premature Infants

Social support has been shown to help combat the effects of stress on a mother's developing fetus. Social support can also help babies who are born prematurely. These infants used to be kept in incubators and were rarely touched. However, work by Field and her colleagues (1986) changed that; she found that 15-minute sessions of touching (moving the babies' limbs, stroking their bodies), three times a day, made a difference in their development: A group of "touched" premature infants grew 50% faster, developed more quickly behaviorally, were more alert and active, and were discharged from the hospital sooner than those premature infants who were not touched three times a day. And the "touched" babies were still doing better months after release from the hospital.

Touching is clearly a social interaction, and the extent to which it occurs depends partly on beliefs: When nurses and caregivers felt that touching premature infants was unwarranted, they didn't do so—and now that they know its benefits, touching is routine. The reason these beliefs changed is that this social act affected the brains of the developing infants, triggering the release of hormones and probably enhancing neural development (see Chapter 2). And of course, by becoming more alert, the babies interacted more actively with the caregivers, which in turn resulted in additional stimulation from them. This happy feedback cycle is a good illustration of how events at the different levels interact.

CONSOLIDATE!

1. **How does development progress in the womb?** The genes and environment interact even in the womb. Your mother's and father's genes recombined when their gametes (eggs and sperm) were formed, leading you to have a unique combination of alleles. Development unfolds in an orderly progression through a series of stages, or trimesters, as the zygote becomes first an embryo, then a fetus. The developing fetus is active and becomes increasingly coordinated over time. Moreover, the fetus is capable of some forms of learning and can detect human speech, preferring the mother's

voice. These maturational processes can be disrupted by teratogens or enhanced by certain environmental events, such as those that reduce the level of stress experienced by the mother.

2. **What are the capabilities of newborns?** Newborns have a good sense of smell and are equipped with a host of inborn reflexes, such as sucking and the Moro reflex. These reflexes often disappear as the child grows and develops. However, in some infants aspects of temperament that are present at birth may persist for many years.

Infancy and Childhood: Taking Off

Spielberg has repeatedly noted that his ability to make movies that appeal to children and to "the child inside adults" stems from the fact that he's never grown up himself. But although he may retain many childlike characteristics, the filmmaker has indeed matured. That is, his motor, perceptual, cognitive, and even social abilities have long outstripped those of even a preadolescent child. In this section we will see how this development occurs.

1 How does the ability to control the body develop with age?

2 What perceptual, linguistic, and cognitive abilities emerge during the course of development?

3 How do social and emotional development occur?

Physical and Motor Development: Getting Control

Developmental psychologists have spent many years studying the precise ways in which babies' movements change as they grow. Two of the early pioneers, Arnold Gesell (Gesell & Thompson, 1938) and Myrtle McGraw (1943), described a series of milestones that all babies, from all races and cultures, pass in an orderly progression. In general, control progresses from the head down the trunk to the arms, and finally to the legs; at the same time, control extends out from the center of the body to the periphery (hands, fingers, toes). By the age of 2, the child has good control over all the limbs.

The early theorists believed that the consistent and universal order of motor development implied that it was entirely maturational. However, later studies of motor control showed that this view cannot be correct. Developing motor control also involves learning about the body and the world, such as the properties of gravity (Thelen, 1995). Some of us do this better than others; Steven Spielberg, for example, was notoriously clumsy and uncoordinated throughout his childhood.

Perceptual, Linguistic, and Cognitive Development: Extended Horizons

A parent probably would not tell as elaborate a story to a 3-year-old as to a 10-year-old. The reason is obvious: The younger child not only has a shorter attention span and understands fewer concepts about objects and events, but also can grasp only concepts of simple relations (such as that one object can physically cause another to move). Where do these concepts come from? In part from perception, the organization and identification of information received through our senses; in part from cognition, our mental processes; and in part from our social environment.

Perceptual Development: Opening Windows on the World

Along with the rest of the body, the sensory organs develop with age. Visual acuity, for example, increases in part because of developments in the eye, particularly in the lens and the retina (Banks & Bennett, 1988).

Babies are placed on the sheet of glass over a floor that appears to be directly under the glass. A short distance ahead, the floor drops down (although the glass remains level). If the baby can perceive depth, he or she will be reluctant to crawl on the glass that is over the "deep end." This is the famous "visual cliff" invented by Gibson and Walk (1960).

You obviously can't ask them, so how might you determine what babies are capable of seeing? Psychologists working in this area have developed a number of clever techniques. For example, to determine depth perception, infants are placed on a level sheet of glass that at first lies directly on the floor, but then extends over a part of the floor that has been stepped down. In this *visual cliff* experiment, researchers have found that even 6-month-old infants don't want to crawl over the "deep end"—even when coaxed by their mothers—thus demonstrating that they can perceive depth before they can talk (Gibson & Walk, 1960).

But the visual cliff task is of no use with babies who are not yet able to crawl, so it is possible that even younger babies can see depth. How can we tell? Other techniques for examining infants' visual perception measure the amount of time they look at stimuli. For example, the *habituation technique* (also sometimes called the *looking time technique*), illustrated in Figure 9.2, is based on the fact that animals *habituate* to a stimulus: if a baby looks at a particular shape long enough, he or she will no longer find it interesting—and thus will prefer to look at something new. This technique can be used to discover what babies can see, hear, or feel as "different." If you simply added a copy of the habituated stimulus, it would be no more interesting than the original. The infant has to perceive it as different to find it interesting. By varying how two stimuli differ (in shape, distance, color, pattern of movement, and so on), and seeing in what circumstances babies will prefer a new stimulus after habituating

Figure 9.2   The Habituation Technique

In the habituation task, the baby is first shown one stimulus and allowed to look at it until he or she is bored with it (has habituated to it).

After habituation, the baby is shown the original stimulus along with another stimulus. The baby prefers to look at something new. This technique can be used to determine what shape differences babies see and whether they see depth or other physical properties.

to a previous one, it is possible to discover what differences they can detect. Habituation techniques have shown that babies can detect depth at between 2 and 3 months of age.

Newborns aren't very attentive companions; they don't even look at your face when you talk. This state of affairs soon changes as visual perception develops during infancy and early childhood. At first, infants notice only isolated portions of objects, but within 2 or 3 months, they can perceive overall shapes (Spelke et al., 1993). As they get older, they become increasingly adept at making finer differentiations in what they see (Gibson, 1969), partly because of developments in the lens and retina of the eye (Banks & Bennett, 1988). This ability allows them to distinguish among increasingly similar objects (such as distinguishing among different toys, a prerequisite to having a single favorite toy). As they grow older, babies need less stimulus information to recognize patterns. It is tempting to speculate that their enjoyment of playing "peek-a-boo" may reflect this developing ability, in which they can use top-down processing (see Chapter 3), using their knowledge about objects to infer a whole from a part.

Compared with visual perception, auditory perception appears to be more fully developed at an earlier age. Even 6-month-old infants seem to hear well enough to detect different musical intervals. Schellenberg and Trehub (1996) showed that when infants hear pairs of tones, one after the other, they notice a change (as is evidenced by their turning their heads toward the appropriate audio speaker) from the first to the second only when the second is different according to a simple frequency ratio, such as a perfect fifth. In another study, researchers played to 4-month-old infants consonant or dissonant versions of two sequences of tones. When the sequence was consonant, the infants looked longer at the speakers than when it was dissonant. Not only did they look away when the stimulus was dissonant, but they were more physically active. The authors suggest that infants are innately tuned to find consonance more pleasing than dissonance (Zentner & Kagan, 1998). Apparently, to appreciate dissonant music, you must learn to overcome preferences that may be innate.

Perceptual development continues beyond the first year of life. When, for instance, toddlers (2- and 3-year-olds) are shown an array of objects and asked whether it includes a specific object, they look haphazardly from place to place (Vurpillot, 1968). But 6- to 9-year-olds will search the array systematically, left to right, then top to bottom, as if they were reading a page. In general, by about age 11, children have perceptual abilities that are similar to (although often slower than) those of adults (Lobaugh et al., 1998; Piaget, 1969; Semenov et al., 2000), but some aspects of perceptual processing (used in organizing complex patterns) probably continue to develop until late adolescence (Sireteanu, 2000).

Language Development: Out of the Mouths of Babes

All normal humans learn language without needing to be taught it explicitly, an accomplishment no computer has even come close to mastering. It is clear that we humans are innately gifted with the ability to acquire language. But this doesn't mean that we acquire language all at once; many genetically influenced characteristics do not appear full-blown at birth. Language ability develops in an orderly progression.

Foundations of Language: Organizing the Linguistic World. To help the child learn language, caregivers (typically, in Western culture, mothers) intuitively adjust their speech so that the baby receives clear messages. The language that caregivers use to talk to babies, once called "motherese" and now dubbed **child-directed speech (CDS)**, relies on short sentences with clear pauses between phrases, careful enunciation, and exaggerated intonation that is spoken in a high-pitched voice (Bornstein et al., 1992; Cooper et al., 1997; Fernald et al., 1989). A similar pattern has been observed in the sign language caregivers use to communicate with deaf infants: They make signs more slowly, often repeat a sign, and use exaggerated

Child-directed speech (CDS): Speech to babies that relies on short sentences with clear pauses, careful enunciation, exaggerated intonation, and a high-pitched voice; also known as *motherese*.

movements (Masataka, 1996); babies attend more closely to such signing than to the more rapid, fluent signing used between adults.

Infants are surprisingly sophisticated in their abilities to encode spoken sounds. Although adults have difficulty hearing distinctions in spoken sounds that are not used in their language (for instance, English speakers often have trouble distinguishing between the two slightly different "wah" sounds used in French), babies have no such difficulty (Jusczyk, 1995). Infants 2 to 3 months old can register in less than half a second that a syllable has been changed ("ga" to "ba"; Dehaene-Lambertz & Dehaene, 1994). However, after about 6 months of age, they start to ignore distinctions among sounds that are not used in the language spoken around them (Kuhl et al., 1992). Moreover, by 14 months, infants pay attention to different sound distinctions in different tasks: When they are required to distinguish between speech sounds, they are sensitive to differences in the sounds that they ignore when they are learning to pair words with particular objects (Stager & Werker, 1997).

The ability of infants to discriminate and organize sounds outstrips their ability to produce them. All babies, even deaf ones, begin by babbling at around 6 months of age (Stoel-Gammon & Otomo, 1986). Initial babbling includes the sounds made in all human languages. However, as the child is exposed to speaking adults, the range of sounds narrows; at about 1 year, the child's babbling begins to have adultlike intonation patterns (Levitt & Wang, 1991). Deaf children do not develop the more advanced types of babbling, but if they are exposed to sign language, their hand and arm motions develop in corresponding ways—beginning with a wide range of motions and eventually narrowing down to the ones used in the sign language they see around them (Petitto & Marentette, 1991). The first words children in all languages say grow directly out of their babbles, such as "mama" and "da-da."

The Young Linguist. Most children begin to speak when they are about a year old. Two-year-olds can learn words even when the object or action being named is not present (Akhtar & Tomasello, 1996). By the time they are 6 years old, children know approximately 10,000 words (Anglin, 1993). The rate of learning is different for boys and girls, however, as shown in Figure 9.3. Children begin by understanding words far in advance of their ability to say them. Indeed, they can understand about 50 words at about 13 months but cannot say this many words until about 18 months (Menyuk et al., 1995).

Even 3-year-olds can often learn words, or facts about objects, after hearing them only a single time (Carey, 1978; Markson & Bloom, 1997). Which words chil-

Figure 9.3 **The Number of New Words Understood During the First Two Years of Life**

Notice the difference in comprehension rates for boys and girls.

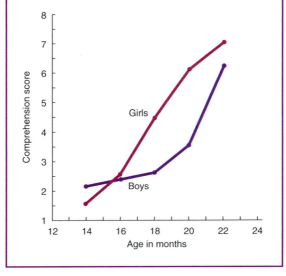

Chapter 9 Psychology Over the Life Span

www.ablongman.com/kosslynbrief

dren learn first depends partly on their cultures; in Vietnam, children learn the respectful pronouns used to refer to elders before learning the words for many objects (Nelson, 1981). However, rather than learning the entire meaning of words in one fell swoop, children sometimes make **overextensions,** using words over-broadly when referring to new objects or situations. They might call a dog a dog, and a cat a dog, and a horse a dog, and even a sawhorse a dog. This makes sense if their initial idea of "dog" is anything with four legs. With learning, they discover which features—in the case of a dog, more than just four-leggedness—restrict the appropriate use of the word (Clark, 1983, 1993). Overextensions may sometimes occur simply because the child has trouble recalling the appropriate word and uses the apparently next best one instead. Children also make up new uses for words, such as *cutter* for someone who is teaching them how to cut out shapes from paper; when they learn and can recall a conventional name, such as *teacher,* they abandon the invented one (Clark, 1995).

The heart of any language is its grammar, which by its rules allows words to be combined into an infinite number of sentences. By looking at the patterns of sounds to which babies became habituated, Marcus and colleagues (1999) showed that even 7-month-old babies can already abstract grammarlike rules. However, it is only at around 2 years of age that children start putting words together into the simplest sentences, two-word utterances such as "Go dog." These utterances are often called **telegraphic speech** because, like the telegrams of days gone by (and the text messages people send to cell phones today) they pack a lot of information into a few choice words. Within the next year, children who speak English start to use sentences that follow the sequence subject–verb–object ("Dog chase cat"). Words such as *the, a,* and *of* are left out. The particular order of the words depends on the language being learned, but in all cases the child at this stage makes sentences with words in the appropriate order (de Villiers & de Villiers, 1992).

Most verbs in a language are *regular,* following an easily derived rule for changes in tense—*play* becomes *played, work* becomes *worked.* But typically the most frequently used verbs in a language are *irregular*—for example, *eat* becomes *ate.* Children may start off using irregular verbs properly, but then begin to make mistakes such as *runned* instead of *ran.* These **overregularization errors,** mistakes caused by the misapplication of the rule for regular verb formation, occur because the child has now learned the rule and begins to apply it systematically, even when it is inappropriate (Pinker, 1999). The same thing happens with plurals; a child who could use *feet* correctly last week may suddenly start saying, "Mommy, my feets are tired."

Throughout history, there have been reports of children who grew up in the wild, never exposed to human language, who never learned proper language (Ball, 1971; Lane, 1976; Pinker, 1994). When such cases occur in real life, they provide a key test of the theory that language can be learned only during a narrow window of time called the **critical period.** Critical periods differ from **sensitive periods,** which define time windows when learning is easiest, but are not the only times when such learning can occur. Careful studies have shown that children who are not exposed to language before puberty never grasp the rules of grammar fully; there does seem to be a critical period for acquiring grammar (Grimshaw et al., 1998; Pinker, 1994).

Stages of Cognitive Development: Piaget's Theory

The great Swiss psychologist Jean Piaget (1896–1980) developed a far-reaching and comprehensive theory of cognitive development. Interest in Piaget's theory helped generate other lines of research that have focused on how changes in information processing, the maturation of the brain, and the social environment contribute to cognitive development.

Early in his career, Piaget worked in Paris with Alfred Binet's collaborator, Theodore Simon, helping to standardize Binet's newly developed intelligence tests for children (see Chapter 6). Piaget was curious about the types of reasoning mistakes children were likely to make. This new interest connected with his long-term

Overextension: An overly broad use of a word to refer to a new object or situation.

Telegraphic speech: Speech that packs much information into few words.

Overregularization error: A speaking error that occurs because the child applies a rule even to cases that are exceptions to the rule.

Critical period: A narrow window of time when certain types of learning are possible.

Sensitive period: A window of time when a particular type of learning is *easiest,* but not the only time it can occur.

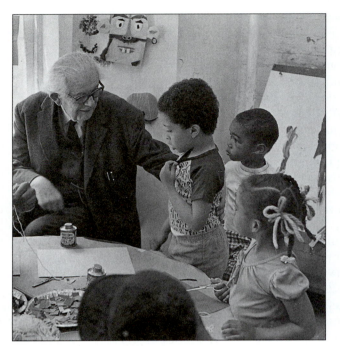

Piaget was an extraordinarily sensitive observer of children's behavior.

interests in biology and in the nature of the mind, and led him to a general investigation of the reasoning processes of children at various ages. Piaget believed that babies begin with very simple, innate **schemas**, mental structures that organize perceptual input and connect it to the appropriate responses. For the youngest infant, such schemas trigger grasping and sucking at the nipple when the infant is hungry and in the presence of a bottle or breast. According to Piaget, the process of **assimilation** allows the infant to use existing schemas to take in new stimuli and respond accordingly. For example, the schema for sucking a breast can also be used for sucking a bottle or thumb. In contrast, the process of **accommodation** results in schemas changing as necessary to cope with a broader range of situations. As the child develops, the schemas develop in two ways. First, they become more fully *articulated;* for example, more precise motions are used to locate the nipple and suck. Second, they become *differentiated;* an original schema may give rise to two separate schemas, one for bottles and one for thumbs, which in turn may give rise to schemas for drinking with a straw, drinking from a cup, and eating solid food.

Schema: A mental structure that organizes perceptual input and connects it with the appropriate responses.

Assimilation: In Piaget's theory, the process that allows use of existing schemas to take in new sets of stimuli and respond accordingly.

Accommodation: In Piaget's theory, the process that results in schemas changing as necessary to cope with a broader range of situations.

These two processes—assimilation and accommodation—together are the engine that powers cognitive development. Piaget's theory of development hinges on the results of assimilation and accommodation working in tandem, which he claimed produce a system of rules—in Piaget's terms, a "logic"—that guides the child's thought. Depending on the available schemas, different kinds of logical operations are possible. Thus, according to Piaget, the child's thinking changes systematically over time as new schemas develop.

Piaget described four major stages, or *periods,* of cognitive development, as shown in Table 9.2; each period is governed by a different type of logic and includes many substages, with key characteristics. The periods overlap slightly, and they may occur at different ages for different children; thus, the ages given in the table are only approximate.

Sensorimotor Period. The infant's experience begins in the *sensorimotor period,* which extends from approximately birth to 2 years of age. According to Piaget's theory, infants initially conceive of the world solely in terms of their perceptions

TABLE 9.2 Piaget's Periods of Cognitive Development

PERIOD	AGE	ESSENTIAL CHARACTERISTICS
Sensorimotor	0–2 years	The child acts on the world as perceived and is not capable of thinking about objects in their absence.
Preoperational	2–7 years	Words, images, and actions are used to represent information mentally. Language and symbolic play develop, but thought is still tied to perceived events.
Concrete Operations	7–11 years	Reasoning is based on a logic that is tied to what can be perceived. The child is capable of organizing information systematically into categories, and can reverse mental manipulations.
Formal Operations	11 years (at the earliest)	Reasoning is based on a logic that includes abstractions, which leads to systematic thinking about hypothetical events.

and actions. In this period infants lack the ability to form mental representations that can be used to think about an object in its absence. In the early stages of the sensorimotor period, the infant does not yet have the concept of **object permanence**, the understanding that objects (including people) continue to exist even when they cannot be immediately perceived. For example, a rattle dropped by an infant over the side of the high chair is quickly forgotten—and more than forgotten: Out of sight means not just out of mind but out of existence! Piaget claimed that by the end of the sensorimotor period, by about age 2, the toddler understands that objects exist even when they are no longer perceived. In addition, Piaget claimed that a second major achievement of the sensorimotor period is the ability to imitate.

Preoperational Period. Once out of the sensorimotor period, the toddler enters the *preoperational period,* from roughly age 2 until age 7. Armed with the ability to form mental representations, children in the preoperational period are able to think about objects and events that are not immediately present. As a result, they can imitate actions that occurred in the past. This newfound capacity for mental representation allows the child to engage in fantasy play. Whereas the infant might play with a bar of soap in the bath by squeezing it and watching it pop out, the preoperational child, performing the same actions, might think of the soap as a submerged submarine that is breaking the surface.

A cook asks two boys who have just ordered a large pizza, "How many slices do you want me to cut your pizza into, 8 or 12?" One boy immediately answers, "Please cut it into 12 pieces, because I'm very hungry!" This is a joke for older children and grown-ups, but not for preoperational children, whose thoughts are limited in part because they do not yet have a logic for manipulating, or *operating* on, mental representations. Therefore, they often reason on the basis of appearances. One important result is that they do not understand **conservation**, the principle that properties of an object, such as its amount or mass, remain the same even when the appearance changes, provided that nothing is added or removed. Many studies have documented that preoperational children do not conserve, and so they would not realize that cutting a pizza into 12 pieces instead of 8 does not increase the total amount of pizza. A classic example, illustrated in Figure 9.4 on page 324, is that preoperational children do not understand that pouring liquid from a short wide glass into a tall thin glass does not alter the amount of liquid. Similarly, they typically think that flattening a ball of clay decreases the amount of clay and that spreading the objects in a row farther apart changes the number of objects in the row.

Both sensorimotor and preoperational children show **egocentrism**, which does not mean "selfishness" in the ordinary sense of the word, but instead the inability to take another's point of view. For example, children in this period will hold a picture they've drawn up to the telephone, to "show" it to Grandma. They mistakenly assume that others see the same things they do.

Period of Concrete Operations. By the end of the preoperational period, about age 7, children develop the ability to take another person's perspective. This ability is linked to the fact that they can now perform **concrete operations**, manipulating mental representations in much the same way they could manipulate the corresponding objects. So the child is now able to begin to classify objects and their properties, to grasp concepts such as length, width, volume, and time, and to understand various mental operations such as those involved in simple arithmetic. This *period of concrete operations* is Piaget's third period of cognitive development, which takes place roughly between the ages of 7 and 11. Concrete operations allow the child to reason logically, partly because this mode of conceptualizing is *reversible;* that is, it can be used to make or undo a transformation. For example, having seen the liquid being poured into a tall thin glass, the child

Only after a baby has object permanence does he or she understand that objects continue to exist even after they are no longer being perceived.

Object permanence: The understanding that objects (including people) continue to exist even when they cannot be immediately perceived.

Conservation: The principle that certain properties of objects remain the same even when their appearance changes, provided that nothing is added or removed.

Egocentrism: In Piaget's theory, the inability to take another person's point of view.

Concrete operation: In Piaget's theory, a (reversible) manipulation of the mental representation of perceived events and actions that corresponds to the corresponding actual physical manipulation.

Figure **9.4** **Conservation of Liquids**

In the classic conservation of liquids test, the child is first shown two identical glasses with water at the same level.

The water is poured from one of the short, wide glasses into the tall, thin one.

When asked whether the two glasses have the same amount, or if one has more, the preoperational child replies that the tall, thin glass has more. This is a failure to conserve liquids.

can mentally reverse the process and imagine the liquid being poured back into the original container. Seeing that no liquid has been added or subtracted in the process, the child realizes that the amount in both glasses must be the same.

Period of Formal Operations. By definition, concrete operations cannot be used for reasoning about abstract concepts; children in the period of concrete operations cannot figure out, for example, that whenever 1 is added to an even number, the result will always be an odd number. To be able to reason abstractly, Piaget said, requires that the child be capable of **formal operations**, reversible mental acts that can be performed even with abstract concepts. This ability emerges roughly during the ages of 11 or 12, at the onset of what Piaget termed the *period of formal operations*. Rather than simply understanding the logic of "what is," as occurs with concrete operations, the emerging adolescent is now able to imagine the possibilities of "what could be." Formal operations allow children to engage in abstract thinking, to think about "what-would-happen-if" situations, and to think systematically about the possible outcomes of an act by being able to list alternatives in advance and consider each in turn. For example, formal operations would permit a child to think about how best to spend his or her money and to weigh the benefits and drawbacks of each possible budget decision.

The Child's Concepts: Beyond Piaget

Do children follow the stages Piaget described? When researchers use techniques different from Piaget's to see what children do or do not understand, they often come up with results that differ from his. Although Piaget conducted very clever tasks (such as those used to assess conservation), they typically assessed only easily observable aspects of behavior. When more subtle measurements are taken, evidence sometimes emerges that children can show competence well before they have reached the appropriate Piagetian stage.

Andrew Meltzoff and his colleagues (notably, Meltzoff & Moore, 1977) have found that 2- to 3-week-old infants can show true imitation, and others have found that even 2-day-old infants can imitate happy and sad facial expressions (Field et al., 1982). Other researchers have shown that babies as young as 3 months old know that previously seen objects continue to exist after they are removed from sight, thus refuting the idea that object permanence does not establish itself until the

Formal operation: In Piaget's theory, a mental act that can be performed (and reversed) even with abstract concepts.

child is a toddler (Baillargeon, 1993; Spelke et al., 1992). Indeed, even 3-month-old infants can remember faces after a 24-hour interval (Pascalis et al., 1998). Moreover, when appropriately tested, children as young as 3 years show that they understand the conservation of amount or mass (Gelman, 1972).

Piaget's theory seems to underestimate the sophistication of young children's conceptions of the world. Infants demonstrate an understanding of some physical laws even before they have developed the kinds of perceptual–motor schemas that Piaget claimed are the foundations of such knowledge. By applying looking time techniques, which take advantage of infants' preference for novel stimuli (see Figure 9.2), researchers have concluded that even young infants realize that objects need to be physically supported to remain stable (Figure 9.5), that objects can't move *through* other objects, and that objects don't flit from place to place but shift along connected paths (Spelke, 1991; Spelke et al., 1992).

Very young infants can imitate some facial expressions, as shown in these photos from Meltzoff and Moore's study.

Figure 9.5   Early Perception of Possible Events

Possible Event

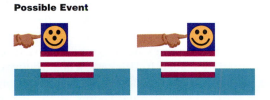

This panel shows a possible event: A box on top of another box is slid over to the edge, but it is still fully supported.

Impossible Event

This panel shows an impossible event: The top box is slid so far over that only 15% of it is supported, and yet it does not fall. Between 3 and 6½ months, babies realize that one box must rest on top of the other to be supported.

Piaget's ideas about egocentrism also have been revised. Current thinking suggests that children develop a **theory of mind**, a theory of other people's mental states—their beliefs, desires, and feelings. This theory allows them to predict what other people can understand and how they will react in a given situation (Flavell, 1999; Frye et al., 1998; S. Johnson, 2000; Lillard, 1999; Wellman, 1990). One way to assess children's theory of mind is to tell a story and see whether the children draw the proper inferences about the protagonist's mental state. In one story used for this purpose, a boy hides his candy in a drawer, but after he leaves the room, his mother moves the candy to a cupboard. Children are then told that the boy returns and is asked where he thinks his candy is hidden. By age 4 (which is before the age at which Piaget believed children rise above their egocentric outlook), children believe that the boy thinks the candy is still where he put it originally, but children under 4 do not—they often think that the boy believes the candy is in the cupboard.

The particular theory of mind a child develops depends in part on the surrounding culture. Among many African tribes, calamities such as AIDS or fires are believed to have supernatural causes (Lillard, 1999). Even within a culture, different subgroups can develop different types of theories. Lillard and colleagues (1998, as cited in Lillard, 1999) asked children to explain the behavior of a character in a story and found that children growing up in cities tended to use psychological explanations—for example, referring to the character's likes and dislikes—even at 7 years of age. In contrast, children growing up in the country rarely used such explanations (20% of the time, compared with 60% for children growing up in the city). Instead, rural children usually relied on aspects of the situation to explain behavior. It is not clear why this difference exists.

In short, the finding that many abilities are evident much earlier than Piaget expected challenges his idea that all of a given child's thought reflects a single

Theory of mind: A theory of other people's mental states (their beliefs, desires, and feelings) that allows prediction of what other people can understand and how they will react in a given situation.

underlying logic, a logic that changes with increasing age and development. Moreover, later research showed that many children do not enter the period of formal operations until high school, and some never enter it at all (Hooper et al., 1984; Lunzer, 1978). Nevertheless, Piaget has been proven correct in his seminal observation that there are qualitative shifts in children's performance as they age. He must also be credited with discovering many counterintuitive phenomena, such as a failure to conserve and egocentrism, that all theories of cognitive development must now be able to explain.

Information Processing and Neural Development

Efforts to explain the findings sparked by Piaget's theory have looked at specific changes in the way children process information and how their brains mature. The *information processing approach* is based on the idea that perception and cognition rely on a host of distinct processes, and not all necessarily develop at the same rate.

One common reason young children may perform more poorly than older children is that their *working memory*—their ability to use information held in an active state—does not stack up well against that of older children or adults (Case, 1985, 1992a). It has been shown that measures of working memory capacity increase with age throughout childhood (Case, 1977, 1978). When the child has enough working memory capacity, he or she can perform tasks that were previously beyond reach.

The finding that working memory increases with age allows us to explain many of the phenomena documented by Piaget. In this case, a *quantitative* change (simple increase in size) in capacity can lead to *qualitative* changes in performance (the transition to new stages; see Case, 1992b; Pascual-Leone, 1970). By analogy, if you have a relatively small amount of RAM memory in your computer, then only relatively simple programs will run (such as basic word processing or e-mail), but not more complicated ones (such as a spreadsheet). If you increase the amount of memory, you can run not only more complex programs, but also multiple programs at the same time. A quantitative change in the amount of memory underlies a qualitative change in performance.

What accounts for the child's improvements in working memory with age? The initial immaturity of the brain may be key. The brain undergoes rapid growth spurts (Epstein, 1980) around the times of transitions to new periods in Piaget's scheme. Some of the increase in brain weight with age may be due to myelinization (the laying down of myelin, a fatty substance that serves as an insulator, on the axons), which increases the speed and efficiency of neural transmission, and some to larger numbers of synapses and long-distance connections (Case, 1992c; Thatcher, 1994; Thompson et al., 2000). These changes might allow more information to be activated at the same time, which in turn would increase working memory capacity.

Vygotsky's Sociocultural Theory: Outside/Inside

Appreciating the importance of events at different levels of analysis leads us to look beyond any single source to explain psychological events. Thus, it isn't surprising that at least some aspects of cognitive development reflect not brain events, but social interactions. Russian psychologist Lev S. Vygotsky (1896–1934) emphasized the role of social interaction during development (Vygotsky, 1978, 1934/1986). Whereas Piaget believed that the child constructs representations of the world in the course of experiencing it firsthand, Vygotsky believed that the child constructs representations of the world by absorbing his or her culture, and the culture, as represented in the child's mind, then serves to guide behavior (Beilin, 1996; Kitchener, 1996). According to Vygotsky, adults promote cognitive development by guiding and explicitly instructing the child, and cultural creations, particularly language, play a crucial role in development (Cole & Wertsch, 1996; Karpov & Haywood, 1998).

One of Vygotsky's key ideas is that once children learn language, they begin to use "private speech" to direct themselves (Berk, 1994a; Smolucha, 1992; Vygotsky,

1962, 1988). **Private speech** (also sometimes called *inner speech*) is language used by the child in planning or prompting him- or herself to behave in specific ways. Children initially begin to use language in this way by actually speaking aloud to themselves, but then language becomes internalized and silent. As Vygotsky predicted, researchers have found that young children use private speech more when trying to solve a difficult task (such as folding paper in a particular way or arranging events into a story; Duncan & Pratt, 1997; see also Berk, 1992a, 1994b) than when working on an easy task. They also use private speech more after they have made an error (Berk, 1992a, 1994b). Preschoolers (ages 3 to 5) also use private speech more frequently when they have to decide what to do in a free play situation than when they are put in a highly structured play situation (Krafft & Berk, 1998).

Private speech: The use of language in planning or in prompting oneself to behave in specific ways.

Attachment: An emotional bond that leads us to want to be with someone and to miss him or her when we are separated.

Separation anxiety: The fear of being away from the primary caregiver.

Social and Emotional Development: The Child in the World

The psychological development of a child includes more than improvements in mental processing and the acquisition of knowledge and beliefs. Equally impressive development occurs in the child's social interactions, such as the ability to form relationships.

Attachment: More Than Dependency

In our closest relationships we develop deep attachments to other people. **Attachment** is an emotional bond that leads us to want to be with someone and to miss him or her when we are separated. The tendency to form such an emotional bond begins during infancy, when normal infants become attached to their primary caregivers.

What is the origin of the infant's attachment? Decades ago, a prominent theory—sometimes called the "cupboard theory" because it centered on food—held that infants become attached because their caregivers feed them and thus become associated with positive feelings (Sears et al., 1957). However, classic experiments by Harry Harlow and his collaborators disproved this and similar theories. These researchers found that baby monkeys became much more attached to a model "mother" that had a pleasing texture and a more realistic face than to one without these characteristics, even though it was the only one that fed them. The impulse to seek comfort from something warm and soft is an innate rather than a learned characteristic of mammals.

British psychoanalyst John Bowlby (1969) developed a theory of attachment that has become widely accepted among developmental psychologists. According to Bowlby, children go through phases during the development of attachment. Just as in Piaget's stages, the order of the phases is thought to be determined biologically, but the precise ages depend on experience. A major shift, usually occurring between 6 months and 2 years, is characterized by **separation anxiety**, which is fear of being away from the primary caregiver. This shift may arise on the heels of cognitive development, specifically because infants can now think about and remember objects (including the primary caregiver) when they are no longer present.

Baby monkeys were separated from their mothers shortly after birth and were raised with two substitute "moms." One was wire and held the baby bottle, and each young monkey needed to climb on this one to be fed. The other was covered with terry cloth and did not provide food. Baby monkeys preferred to cling to the fuzzy models, even though those models never provided food.

Not all babies become attached to their caregivers in the same way. Ainsworth and her colleagues (1978) developed a way to assess attachment using a scenario they called the *Strange Situation*. The setup involves a staged sequence of events designed to discover how a child reacts when left with a

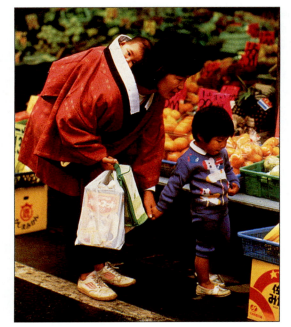

We know that at least some aspects of attachment are learned because infants in different cultures become attached differently. For example, American infants show less resistant attachment than do Japanese infants. In Japan, many more women are full-time mothers than in the United States, and their children are not used to being left with other adults (Takahashi, 1990).

Self-concept: The beliefs, desires, values, and attributes that define a person to himself or herself.

Knowledge of your appearance is part of your self-concept.

stranger or alone in an unfamiliar situation. If the child has developed strong attachment, he or she should show separation anxiety, becoming upset when the mother leaves, and should not be soothed equally well by a stranger or by the mother. Studies using the Strange Situation revealed four types of attachment:

Secure attachment (about 60–70% of American babies) is evident if babies venture away from the mother, are upset when she leaves and not well comforted by a stranger, but calm down quickly when the mother returns.

Avoidant attachment (about 15–20% of American babies) is evident if babies don't seem to care very much whether the mother is present or absent, and are equally comfortable with her and a stranger; when she returns, they do not immediately gravitate to her.

Resistant attachment (about 10–15% of American babies) is evident if babies do not use the mother as a base of operations but rather stay close to her and become angry when she leaves; some of these babies may go so far as to hit the mother when she returns and do not calm down easily thereafter.

Disorganized/disoriented attachment (5–10% of American babies) is evident if the babies become depressed and have periods of unresponsiveness along with spurts of sudden emotion at the end of the procedure.

The type of early attachment can have long-lasting effects. Infants with secure attachment who were later studied at age 11 were found to have closer friendships and better social skills than children who had not been securely attached as infants (Shulman et al., 1994). Moreover, secure attachment can lead the child to be more comfortable exploring, which leads to better learning and can lead to more intimate love relationships later in life (Sroufe & Fleeson, 1986; Weiss, 1986).

Self-Concept and Identity: The Growing Self

A critical aspect of social development is the emerging sense of who you are and how you stand relative to other people. Psychologists use the term **self-concept** to refer to the beliefs, desires, values, and attributes that define a person to him- or herself. A key aspect of Steven Spielberg's self-concept as a child was his many fears, both large and small; part of his gift for making movies today is his ability to engage other people in sharing his own fears and fantasies (McBride, 1999).

For young children, the self-concept is necessarily grounded in their level of cognitive development. Thus, preschoolers think of themselves concretely in terms of behaviors and physical appearance (Keller et al., 1978). At what age do children begin to conceive of themselves as having specific characteristics? To find out, a dab of red paint was placed on babies' noses without their knowledge, and the babies then looked in a mirror. Some babies of about 15 months of age notice the smudge and rub it off. By age 2, virtually all children have this response (Amsterdam, 1972; Lewis & Brooks-Gunn, 1979). However, this test may in fact assess understanding of temporary changes in appearance, not self-concept (Asendorpf et al., 1996). Other researchers have argued that the roots of the self-concept are present much earlier than toddler age. Even newborns distinguish between touching themselves and being touched by someone else, a distinction that may mark the beginning of a self-concept (Rochat & Hespos, 1997).

By 3 years of age, children begin to appreciate that they have distinct psychological characteristics, such as being happy in certain situations and not in others (Eder, 1989). Children of about 8 to 11 begin to describe themselves in terms of personality traits, perhaps as "energetic" or "musical." This ability to self-label depends on reasoning abilities of the sort that develop during the period of formal operations.

Gender Identity: Not Just Being Raised With Pink or Blue

A crucial aspect of the self-concept is **gender identity**, which is the belief that you are male or female. There is evidence that biological factors strongly predispose us to view ourselves as male or female. Consider the following case history (Colapinto, 2000): At 8 months of age, a boy's penis was accidentally sliced off as his split foreskin was being surgically repaired. The family and surgeons decided that it would be best to raise the boy as a girl, and so his testicles were removed and a vagina was surgically formed. The boy, previously known as "John," was now called "Joan," and her past was never discussed. Joan was treated in every way like a girl, and her friends and classmates had no reason to suspect that she was in any way extraordinary. When Joan was 9 years old, John Money (1975) wrote a famous paper in which he reported that Joan had a female gender identity, in sharp contrast to her identical twin brother, who had a strong male gender identity. This report, and others like it, led researchers to believe that gender identity was essentially neutral at birth and was formed by culture and upbringing.

However, Diamond and Sigmundson (1997) revisited John/Joan some 20 years later and recount a very different story. They found that as a young child she sometimes ripped off her dresses and tried to urinate standing up. At 14, she refused to have any more vaginal surgery or to live as a girl. She was not attracted to boys and considered suicide. Even though she had been treated as a girl and even received female hormones that caused breasts to develop, she was deeply unhappy and confused. Her father finally broke down and told her about the accident. Instead of being upset on learning that she had been born a boy, she was greatly relieved. She renounced her female identity, underwent surgery to remove her breasts and reconstruct a penis, and was determined to establish a relationship with a woman. Joan became John once again. He eventually married and adopted his wife's children from a previous marriage.

What was going on here? The crucial event probably was that John's brain had been exposed to high levels of male sex hormones in the womb, which let him "know" that he was male. This gender identity was not something that could be arbitrarily changed simply by treating him as a female. Indeed, certain disorders result in a fetus's being exposed to high levels of male hormones in the womb, even if the fetus is genetically female. Studies of such children have shown that the hormones can affect gender identity. These girls later preferred to play with boys' toys and participate in boys' games (Berenbaum, 1999; Berenbaum & Hines, 1992). Boys can also be affected by the hormonal environment; boys who receive relatively little male sex hormone in the womb engage in less rough-and-tumble play than do boys who are exposed to the usual amount (Hines & Kaufman, 1994).

Moral Development: The Right Stuff

A key aspect of social development is the emergence of more complex ideas of morality, which center on the ability to tell right from wrong. As children grow older, their developing cognitive abilities allow them to draw more subtle inferences. The young child may feel that a girl who knocks over a lamp and breaks it is equally to blame if she smashed it intentionally, bumped it by accident while horsing around, or fell against it accidentally when the dog jumped on her. The older child would make clear distinctions among the three cases, seeing decreasing blame for each in turn. Piaget was a pioneer in the study of moral as well as cognitive development. His studies often involved telling children stories in which he varied the intentions of the characters and the results of their actions, then asking the children to evaluate the characters' morality. Lawrence Kohlberg extended Piaget's approach and developed an influential theory of moral development. He presented boys with **moral dilemmas**, situations in which there are both moral pros and cons for each of a set of possible actions. Kohlberg asked participants to

Gender identity: A person's belief that he or she is male or is female.

Moral dilemmas: Situations in which there are moral pros and cons for each of a set of possible actions.

decide what the character should do, and why. This is the famous dilemma that confronted Heinz (Puka, 1994):

> In Europe, a woman was near death from a special kind of cancer. There was one drug that the doctors thought might save her. It was a form of radium that a druggist in the same town had recently discovered. The drug was expensive to make, but the druggist was charging 5 times what it cost him to make the drug. He paid $400 for the radium, and charged $2,000 for a small dose of the drug. The sick woman's husband, Heinz, went to everyone he knew to borrow the money, but he could only get together about $1,000, half of what it cost. He told the druggist that his wife was dying, and asked him to sell it cheaper or let him pay later. But the druggist said, "No, I discovered the drug and I'm going to make money from it, so I won't let you have it unless you give me $2,000 now." So Heinz got desperate and broke into the man's store to steal the drug for his wife.
>
> Should Heinz have done that? Why?

Kohlberg was not so much interested in what the children decided as in the way that they reached their decisions. What kinds of factors did they consider? Which conflicts did they identify (such as the conflict between the value of human life and the value of private property), and how did they try to resolve these conflicts? Kohlberg interviewed boys and men at length, and from their responses he identified three general levels of moral development (Kohlberg, 1969; Rest, 1979). The *preconventional level* rests on the idea that good behaviors are rewarded and bad ones are punished. Correct action is what an authority figure says it is. A preconventional response to the Heinz dilemma might be, "If you let your wife die, you will get in trouble" (this and the following examples are adapted from Kohlberg, 1969, and Rest, 1979).

The *conventional level* rests on the role of rules that maintain social order and allow people to get along. The focus is no longer simply on the personal consequences of a behavior. For example, the child wants to be viewed as a "good person" by friends and family and tries to follow the Golden Rule ("Do unto others as you would have them do unto you"). Morality is still closely tied to individual relationships ("If he lets his wife die, people would think he was some kind of heartless lizard").

The *postconventional level* (also called the *principled level*) rests on the development of abstract principles that govern the decision to accept or reject specific rules. In the most advanced stage of this level, principles are adopted that are believed to apply to everyone. The principles are abstract and are held above all specific rules and laws ("Human life is the highest principle, and everything else must be secondary. People have a duty to help one another to live").

Some researchers have questioned the generality of Kohlberg's stages. For example, Carol Gilligan (1982) argued that because the theory was based on studies of boys and men, it applies only to males. She believed that females tend to focus on an *ethic of care,* a concern and responsibility for the well-being of others. In contrast, Kohlberg's higher stages of moral development focus on abstract rights and justice, which Gilligan saw as a male-oriented perspective. However, later studies have shown that the differences between the moral reasoning of males and females do not reflect fundamental differences in the way their minds work. Although there is evidence that males and females do emphasize different principles in their moral reasoning (Wark & Krebs, 1996), this seems more a reflection of their daily activities (and the assumptions and general orientations that result from such activities) than an enduring gender difference. Men and women reason in the same ways (Clopton & Sorell, 1993). In addition, males and females score comparably on Kohlberg's tests, and both sexes reveal concerns with both caring and justice (Jadack et al., 1995; Walker, 1995).

Finally, moral development is not rapid; in fact, a majority of people move into the most advanced form (Kohlberg posits two stages within each of his levels) of the conventional level only at about age 32 (Colby et al., 1983), and very few people move into the postconventional level. Moreover, it is not clear that the stages are like traits, which characterize a person in all situations. Rather, people may use different types of moral reasoning, depending on the details of the dilemma (Trevethan & Walker, 1989). Thus, to the extent that we pass through stages, they may only define general tendencies to reason in a certain way, which can be affected by the situation.

Gender roles: The culturally determined appropriate behaviors of males versus females.

LOOKING AT LEVELS

Gender Role Development

Gender roles are the culturally determined appropriate behaviors of males versus females. It is one thing to identify yourself as male or female, but something else again to understand what behaviors are appropriate for your gender. Gender roles vary in different cultures, social classes, and time periods; for example, a proper woman in Victorian England (or, perhaps, 19th-century America) would probably be very surprised to learn that a woman can be a senator or the president of a major corporation today. Conceptions about gender roles develop early. President Theodore Roosevelt's wife, Ethel, was particularly good at sports—so good that her son Quentin commented, "I'll bet Mother was a boy when she was little" (Seuling, 1978, p. 49). Even preschool boys apparently believe that if they played with cross-gender toys (say, dishes instead of tools), their fathers would think that was "bad" (Raag & Rackliff, 1998). Indeed, by age 2 children have apparently learned about gender role differences (Caldera & Sciaraffa, 1998; Witt, 1997).

Freud argued that children identify with the same-sex parent, and that this is the main way in which gender roles develop (see Chapter 8). But Eleanor Maccoby believes that identification with the same-sex parent may be the *result* of sex-role development, not the cause. Her account rests on events at all three levels. At the level of the group, in Maccoby's view, peer-group interactions are key to learning gender roles. It is in the peer group, she argues, that boys first learn about how to gain and maintain status in the hierarchy, and that girls develop their styles of interaction (Maccoby, 1990, 1991). Maccoby and Jacklin (1987) found that by age 4 children spent about three times as much time playing with same-sex peers as with opposite-sex peers, and this ratio shot up to 11 times more when the children were 6 years old. According to Maccoby (1990, p. 514), "Gender segregation . . . is found in all the cultural settings in which children are in social groups large enough to permit choice."

Why does gender segregation occur? Maccoby (1988) suggests that part of the answer many harken back to biological, particularly hormonal, differences. Boys play more aggressively than do girls, and their orientation toward competition and dominance may be aversive to many girls. However, shifting to the level of the person, Maccoby (1990) also notes that girls may not like playing with boys because they believe that boys are too difficult to influence; the polite manner in which girls tend to make suggestions apparently doesn't carry much weight with boys. Girls find this response (or lack of response) frustrating and retreat to the company of other girls.

In short, even for something as clearly influenced by culture as gender role development, we must consider events at all three levels of analysis. As usual, these events interact: If not for hormonal differences between the sexes, girls probably would not come to believe that boys are difficult to influence, and if not for that belief, they would have different interactions with boys.

Boys and girls play in characteristic ways, partly because of biological differences.

CONSOLIDATE!

 How does the ability to control the body develop with age? In general, control progresses from the head down the trunk to the arms and, finally, to the legs; at the same time, control extends out from the center of the body to the periphery (hands, fingers, toes). Motor control involves not only attaining more control over muscles but also learning how muscles interact with one another and with properties of the world (such as gravity).

2 *What perceptual, linguistic, and cognitive abilities emerge during the course of development?* Perception develops so that the child can make finer discriminations, needs less stimulus information to recognize objects, and can search more systematically. In addition, very young children learn to ignore the distinctions in sounds that are not used in their language, and young children typically overextend words and overregularize rules of grammar. Research findings suggest that to master the grammar of a language, we must learn it during a critical period, prior to puberty. Piaget proposed that during cognitive development the child moves through a series of major periods, each subdivided into stages, but researchers have since found that children have at least the rudiments of many abilities far earlier than Piaget's theory would predict. Cognitive development arises in part from improved information processing, particularly

more efficient working memory, which to some degree probably reflects increased neural development. Finally, as Vygotsky pointed out, culture and instruction also play a role in cognitive development.

3 *How do social and emotional development occur?* Children become attached to their caregivers, going through a series of stages, but may end up being attached in different ways. The self-concept begins to develop during very early infancy, which in turn probably affects many social interactions, including gender roles. Gender identity is part of the self-concept, which is determined in part by biological factors present since conception; these biological factors may persist in spite of a child's being raised as a member of the opposite sex. People may move through a series of stages in the way they tend to reason about moral issues, and males and females may tend to reason slightly differently at the later stages—but this divergence is mostly a function of their different concerns in daily life, and is not intrinsic to their genders per se.

Adolescence: Between Two Worlds

Steven Spielberg's adolescence was different from that of many of his peers in many ways; nonetheless, the challenges he faced in those years—forming friendships, testing limits, coming to terms with a changing and unfamiliar body—are essentially universals. Because his family had moved so often, in high school none of his friends from early childhood were still with him; most of his classmates, on the other hand, were firmly established in cliques. Spielberg craved their acceptance and used his newfound love of moviemaking and storytelling as a way of gaining it. Nevertheless, his obsession with movies and his lack of interest in most of the usual teenage pursuits of dating, sports, and schoolwork continued to set him apart.

Not surprisingly, Spielberg's adolescence was not an easy time for him or, sometimes, for those around him. On one occasion he and some friends spent 3 hours throwing rocks through plateglass windows at a shopping mall, causing about $30,000 worth of damage (McBride, 1999, p. 88). He later said that *Poltergeist* was "all about the terrible things I did to my younger sisters" (McBride, 1999, p. 89). He fought his father's wishes for him to study math and science, declaring that someday he was going to be a famous movie director and didn't need to know those kinds of things (McBride, 1999). Extreme behavior, yes. Adolescent behavior, yes.

1 How does puberty affect the body?

2 How do thought processes change in adolescence?

3 Does adolescence always lead to emotional upheaval?

Physical Development: In Puberty's Wake

Adolescence begins with **puberty**, the time when hormones cause the sex organs to mature and secondary sexual characteristics begin to appear, such as breasts for women and facial hair for men. These changes typically begin between ages 8 and 14 for girls and between ages 9 and 15 for boys. **Adolescence** is the period between the appearance of these sexual characteristics and, roughly, the end of the teenage years. McClintock and Herdt (1996) have argued that puberty actually starts with hormonal changes that begin at age 6, and it is clear that crucial changes often occur at about age 8. For example, 8-year-old girls begin to store more fat on their bodies than do boys, a trend that continues through puberty. Although both sexes develop more muscle during puberty, this is especially the case for boys. Moreover, boys develop greater lung capacity and larger hearts than do girls, as well as more red blood cells, which allow more oxygen to be carried to the larger muscles (Katchadourian, 1977).

During infancy and childhood, the body grows from the trunk outward; the upper arms grow before the lower arms, which in turn grow before the hands. At puberty, the trend is reversed: Rapid growth of the hands, feet, and legs is followed by growth of the torso (Wheeler, 1991). Do you remember when you stopped needing larger shoes but still needed larger coats? That's why. The uneven growth during adolescence can lead to an awkward, gawky look, which doesn't do wonders for a teen's sense of self-confidence.

Once the sex hormones start operating in earnest, pubic hair develops, the shoulders of young boys grow large relative to their hips, and vice versa for girls. At age 11, girls typically are taller and heavier than boys because their major growth spurt starts about 2 years before that of boys. By age 14, however, boys' heights and weights have taken off, whereas girls have stopped growing or begun to grow more slowly. American girls typically stop growing at around age 13 (some may continue to grow until about age 16), but American boys usually continue to grow until about their 16th birthdays (some may continue growing until they are almost 18 years old; Malina & Bouchard, 1991; Tanner, 1990).

Girls tend to mature faster than boys.

Cognitive Development: Getting It All Together

The major cognitive development of adolescence, achieved by some but not all adolescents, is the ability to reason abstractly. Piaget's period of formal operations describes the adolescent's cognitive achievements. According to Piaget, formal operational thinking allows a person not only to think abstractly, but also to think systematically about abstract concepts and possible scenarios. In one of his experiments, now regarded as a classic, Piaget gave a child a set of weights, string that could be attached to the weights, and a bar to which the string could be attached, allowing the weight to swing like a pendulum. The child was asked to vary both the weight and the length of the string to discover what factors would make the weight swing most quickly. Adolescents in the formal operational period are not only able to figure out the possibly relevant factors (size of weight, length of string, how high the weight is raised before being dropped, force with which it is pushed),

Puberty: The time when hormones cause the sex organs to mature and secondary sexual characteristics begin to appear, such as breasts for women and facial hair for men.

Adolescence: The period between the onset of puberty and, roughly, the end of the teenage years.

but also to understand that to discover the role of each variable, they must alter only one thing at a time. These adolescents have grasped the very essence of scientific experimentation: holding everything else constant while systematically varying one factor at a time. In short, all the cognitive machinery necessary to think scientifically can be present by about 11 or 12 years of age. But not all adolescents develop these abilities this early, and some never do.

Most adolescents in Western societies are able to grasp the rules that underlie algebra and geometry. The ability to think systematically about abstractions also allows them to think about concepts such as justice and politics, as well as relationships and the causes of human behavior.

How does the ability to think abstractly and logically emerge? It might be tempting to conclude that it is a result of the final stages of brain maturation (and the brain does in fact continue to develop well into adolescence—see Sowell et al., 1999), but the assumption that events at any one level alone could account for such a sweeping change would be rash indeed. Cole (1990) has found that, in many traditional African societies, even the adults cannot use the kinds of abilities described by "formal operations," but there is no indication that their brains have failed to develop fully. Culture must play a role, perhaps shaping the developing child's thought, as Vygotsky theorized.

Social and Emotional Development: New Rules, New Roles

A bridge between childhood and adulthood, adolescence is a time of transition. This transition involves not only changing roles in the larger society, which requires obeying new sets of rules, but also learning to live with cognitive and biological changes that affect interactions with others in many ways.

"Storm and Stress": Raging Hormones?

The picture of adolescents as moody and troubled is nothing new. In the 18th century, German authors developed an entire genre of stories about passionate, troubled young people so immersed in anguish and heartache that they committed impetuous acts of self-destruction. This body of literature came to be called *Sturm und Drang,* which translates roughly as "storm and stress." G. Stanley Hall (1904) popularized this term among psychologists when he wrote his now-classic two-volume work on adolescence.

The notion that adolescents experience a period of "storm and stress" has waxed and waned in popularity. Anna Freud (1958) not only believed that adolescent "angst" was inevitable but also that "normal" behavior during adolescence was in itself evidence of deep *abnormalities* in the individual. A strong reaction to this view soon followed, and only a few years ago, many psychologists were dismissing the idea as another popular misconception. However, recent studies have shown that there is in fact a tendency for adolescents to have three sorts of problems.

First, adolescents tend to have conflicts with their parents (Laursen et al., 1998). The *frequency* of the conflicts is greatest in early adolescence, whereas the *intensity of the conflicts* is greatest in midadolescence (Laursen et al., 1998). Adolescent–parent conflicts occur most often between mothers and daughters on the brink of adolescence (Collins, 1990). These conflicts can be even worse if the parents are not getting along or become divorced. Steven Spielberg claims that *E.T.* is really about the trauma he suffered during the divorce of his parents (McBride, 1999, p. 72); he broke down sobbing at the end of its first screening (p. 333).

Second, adolescents experience extreme mood swings (Buchanan et al., 1992; Larson & Richards, 1994; Petersen et al., 1993), and by the middle of the teen years about one-third of adolescents are seriously depressed (Petersen et al., 1993). Adolescents also often report feeling lonely and nervous.

Third, adolescents are prone to taking risks. Anticipating Anna Freud's view, Hall (1904) went so far as to say that "a period of semicriminality is normal for all boys" (Vol. 1, p. 404, referring to adolescent boys). Steven Spielberg's rock-throwing episode at the shopping mall is a perfect example of what Hall had in mind. Adolescents are relatively likely to commit crimes, drive recklessly, and have high-risk sex (Arnett, 1992; Gottfredson & Hirschi, 1990; Johnston et al., 1994). Such behaviors tend to peak in late adolescence.

Not all adolescents have these problems; rather, as Arnett (1999) documents, these problems are simply more likely to occur during adolescence than at other times. But why do they occur at all? Many people assume that they are an unavoidable result of the hormonal changes that follow puberty. The notion that the emotional turmoil of adolescence is rooted in biology was neatly captured by Greek philosopher Aristotle's remark that adolescents "are heated by Nature as drunken men by wine."

In fact, the hormonal changes that follow puberty do make the adolescent prone to emotional swings (Brooks-Gunn et al., 1994; Buchanan et al., 1992). But hormones only predispose, they do not cause; environmental events trigger these emotional reactions. Moreover, the biological effects can be indirect. For example, such changes can lead adolescents to want to stay up late at night and sleep late in the morning (Carskadon et al., 1993). If they are forced to wake up early to go to school, their mood and general emotional tenor will no doubt be affected.

Anthropologist Margaret Mead (1901–1978) appeared to have solid evidence against the view that biology caused the "storm and stress" of adolescence when she returned from fieldwork on the tropical island of Samoa. In 1928 she reported that the adolescents in Samoan culture had a very smooth transition to adulthood. She attributed this to cultural variables such as relaxed attitudes toward sexuality and open social relationships. However, Freeman (1983) found a very different picture when he studied this same culture. It seems that bored Samoan teenagers had enjoyed pulling Mead's leg, filling her with stories of the way they *wished* things were rather than how they actually were. In fact, even in this far-off, seemingly idyllic isle, being an adolescent is not easy, and Samoans have reported experiences much like those of adolescents in Western society.

In sum, adolescents do tend to experience "storm and stress," which arises in part from the workings of hormones. However, this is only a tendency, and the degree to which an adolescent will experience such turmoil depends on personal and cultural circumstances.

Adolescent Egocentrism: It's All in Your Point of View

The enhanced cognitive abilities of adolescents allow them to take other points of view easily—in particular, to see themselves as they imagine others see them. Theorists have claimed that these new abilities can lead to two kinds of distortions in their conception of how others view them.

First, the *imaginary audience* is a belief sometimes held by adolescents, in which they view themselves as actors and everyone else as an audience (Elkind, 1967; Elkind & Bowen, 1979). This leads teenagers to be extremely self-conscious and easily embarrassed; a pimple feels like a beacon, not unlike Rudolph's nose. Second, some teenagers have a *personal fable*, which is a story in which they are the star, and as the star they have extraordinary abilities and privileges. Teenagers may have unprotected sex and drive recklessly because they believe that they are immune to the possible consequences (Lapsley, 1990; Lapsley et al., 1988). Adolescents often report

Who is the "imaginary audience"?

feeling that their experiences are so unique that no one could possibly understand what they are going through; this feeling too is part of the personal fable.

One possible consequence of the imaginary audience is that teenagers are especially vulnerable to peer pressure, particularly regarding their appearance (Brown, Clasen et al., 1986). Because they are so self-conscious, they are vulnerable to being made to feel different. This tendency can work in combination with a personal fable of invulnerability ("bad things happen to other people, not me") to lead teenagers into dangerous activities such as illegal drug use. In spite of these tendencies, adolescents are mostly influenced by peers in domains of social behavior, and remain influenced primarily by their families with regard to basic values and goals (Brown, Clasen et al., 1986).

LOOKING AT LEVELS

Sex and the Teenager

In 1990 approximately 1,040,000 American teenage girls became pregnant, and slightly over half delivered their babies (Alan Guttmacher Institute, 1994). In general, U.S. teenage girls engage in amounts of sexual activity comparable to those of girls in other industrialized societies, but U.S. teens do not use contraception as effectively. In fact, somewhere between one-third and one-half of sexually active U.S. teenagers do not use condoms regularly (or at all; Braverman & Strasburger, 1993). In 1995, 75% of the births to American teenagers were to unmarried mothers.

Which teenagers are likely to become pregnant? Those at greatest risk are poor students who do not have clear career plans. Maynard (1996) reports that a third of the teenagers who become pregnant drop out of school even before they become pregnant. Further, over half of teenage mothers were living in poverty when they had their children. For many of these young women, particularly African Americans, having a baby is part of "coming of age," and is in many ways equivalent to a career choice (Merrick, 1995).

Consider these events from the different levels of analysis. First, sex is a biological drive, but your brain is constructed so that you can regulate your urges. The frontal lobes allow us to inhibit impulses, if we so choose. Second, why would someone choose to forgo immediate pleasure?

Only if there were a good reason—so good that it overshadowed the passions of the moment. If you don't believe that staying in school will give you a future, and if you believe that having a child is the easiest way to create meaning in your life, why worry about becoming pregnant? Third, cultures create norms about when and in what circumstances—married, not married, financially secure, financially insecure—people should have babies. And of course, events at the different levels interact. Your belief structure leads you either to heed societal norms or to ignore them in favor of your own goals. Moreover, the specific consequences of having a child depend on your behavior and social group: If teenage mothers do not drop out of school, they are about as likely to graduate as other girls who did not give birth, and African Americans appear to suffer the fewest economic consequences of having given birth as a teenager. Apparently, African American girls tend to live at home, continue school, and benefit from the assistance of other members of their families (Rosenheim & Testa, 1992). The consequences of having a baby for changing the mother's brain via education are very different for members of different social groups. Events at the different levels of analysis clearly interact, even when we consider a decision as personal as whether to risk getting pregnant.

CONSOLIDATE!

1 *How does puberty affect the body?* Sex hormones affect muscle mass and lung and heart capacities as boys and girls develop. Hormones are also responsible for the fact that the extremities (arms and legs) grow rapidly, with the trunk lagging behind, a pattern that can produce a gawky appearance. During this period the body grows pubic hair and acquires other sex characteristics.

2 *How do thought processes change in adolescence?* Adolescents can become capable of rea-

soning logically. In addition, if the adolescent reaches the period of formal operations, he or she can reason about abstract concepts systematically—and thus becomes capable of scientific thought. The enhanced reasoning abilities that appear during adolescence affect all aspects of thinking, including conceptions of self and society.

3 *Does adolescence always lead to emotional upheaval?* The adolescent is prone to experiencing "storm and stress," but this turmoil is not inevitable. Although hormones do prime the adolescent to experience more conflicts with parents as well as to have major mood swings and be prone to taking risks, these tendencies are neither certain nor necessarily severe. Some of the changes during adolescence arise from enhanced cognitive capacity, which allows the teen to think about relationships in more sophisticated ways and can lead to the distorting formulations of an imaginary audience and a personal fable.

Adulthood and Aging: The Continuously Changing Self

Steven Spielberg was an unhappy teenager and—in some aspects of life—a spectacularly successful young adult. But being successful in his chosen career did not mean that he was successful in all aspects of life. His first marriage ended; his relationship with his father was strained; and he was concerned that he himself would not measure up as a father (several of his movies deal with difficult relationships between fathers and sons). When he had children of his own, he realized that he needed to be an adult for them; he, and his relationships, had to change, and they did.

Famous moviemaker or not, the grown-up Steven Spielberg is in a very different phase of life than his children; he is also in a very different phase of life than his father. This is the human condition, and we now turn to an exploration of the stages of adult development.

1 How do changes in the body affect us as we age?

2 How does aging affect perception, memory, and intelligence?

3 What is the course of social and emotional development during adulthood?

4 How do people cope with the knowledge of their own impending deaths, and with the deaths of friends and family members?

The Changing Body: What's Inevitable, What's Not

By your early 20s, it is unlikely that you will grow taller, and your weight has typically stabilized for many years to come. For the next several decades, changes in your body should be relatively minor. True, you may come to need bifocals, and your hair may begin to gray or to thin. But the basic systems continue to function well. However, after age 50 or so, noticeable changes in the body begin to occur (Lemme, 1995).

Aging has two aspects: changes that are programmed into the genes and changes that arise from environmental events (Busse, 1969; Rowe & Kahn, 1998). Many aspects of aging may in fact arise not from inevitable processes, but rather from lack of adequate nutrition (such as the hunched posture that results from osteoporosis-related calcium deficiency; Hendricks & Hendricks, 1986), lack of exercise (resulting in obesity in some elderly people and frailty in others), or lack of meaningful activities (which can lead to feelings of helplessness or apathy; Avorn & Langer, 1982; Langer & Rodin, 1976; Rodin & Langer, 1977; Rowe & Kahn, 1998).

A major challenge of aging is to accommodate to those changes that are inevitable and to forestall undesirable changes when you can. Many older people develop diseases or conditions that are uncomfortable or even painful, such as arthritis or collapsed vertebrae. However, in most cases, older people can cope with pain effectively, particularly if they adopt a "can-do" attitude (Melding, 1995;

If women do not get enough calcium, through diet or supplements, their bones are liable to become weak as they age. This condition can be avoided with proper nutrition at critical periods in the life span.

Rowe & Kahn, 1998). One of the inevitable age-related changes in women is *menopause,* the gradual ending of menstruation that typically occurs between the ages of 45 and 55; following menopause, eggs are no longer released and pregnancy is not possible (Wise et al., 1996). Hormone changes that accompany menopause can lead to various bodily sensations (such as "hot flashes"); the knowledge that childbearing is no longer possible, along with the decline in youthful appearance, can adversely affect a woman's self-concept and self-esteem. On the other hand, for many women the physical discomforts are slight, if present at all, and the idea of sexual intercourse without the threat of an unwanted pregnancy provides new pleasure. Some women discover "post-menopausal zest" and are reinvigorated by this change and the freedom it represents. Men have no known corresponding physiological event, but do experience declining vigor (strength and energy) with age that can affect sexual performance.

Why do all of us inevitably become less vigorous as we age? The combined effects of changes in the body have been likened to the effect of hitting a table with a hammer over and over (Birren, 1988). Eventually, the table will break, not because of the final blow, but because of the cumulative effects of all the blows. Some researchers believe that aging and death are programmed into the genes. An oft-cited piece of evidence for this idea was reported by Hayflick (1965), who found that human cells grown in the lab will divide on average only about 50 times, and then simply stop. However, all the findings that suggest programmed death can also be interpreted in other ways. Instead of accepting that the genes have been programmed for death, we might assume that over time errors accumulate, and finally there are so many errors that the genes no longer function properly. If you photocopy a drawing or page of text, and then copy the copy, and so on, you'll see how errors in reproduction multiply over repeated copying. In the case of the body, the damage may not be caused by the copying process itself, but rather by the repeated effects of bodily chemicals on each copy (Arking, 1991; Harman, 1956; Levine & Stadtman, 1992).

Perception and Cognition in Adulthood: Taking the Good With the Bad

Cognitive abilities remain relatively stable through most of adulthood, but by age 50 signs of decline begin to appear in some abilities. Is mental decline an inevitable result of aging? Yes and no. The bad news is that you are constantly losing brain cells even if you don't drink too much alcohol or take drugs, destructive behaviors that only hasten the process. The good news is that through most of adulthood these changes are not noticeable because your brain has built-in redundancy and apparently becomes more efficient at processing as you age. However, unlike pruning during infancy, which eliminates nonfunctional neurons and connections, this cell loss continues as you age (Matsumae et al., 1996). Aging most severely affects the white matter of the brain—connections among neurons (Guttmann et al., 1998). These changes in the brain will eventually catch up with you and lead you to perform more slowly and be more prone to making errors. Indeed, by age 60 people perform most cognitive tasks more slowly than do younger people (Birren et al., 1962; Cerella, 1990; Salthouse, 1991b). The harder the task, the larger the difference in time taken by young adults and the elderly.

Perception: Through a Glass Darkly?

During early and middle adulthood, worsening vision can usually be corrected with eyeglasses. Later in life, however, more severe visual difficulties emerge. Over half the population 65 and up has *cataracts,* a clouding of the lens of the eye, and in older people, the pupil, the opening of the eye through which light enters, becomes smaller. Surgery can remove cataracts and result in greatly improved vision. Until that point, even moderate optical difficulties cause older people to need greater contrast to see differences in light (Fozard, 1990). Contrasts between lit and unlit surfaces, such as shadows caused by steps, can define differences in depth, and if older people cannot perceive such definition, they are more likely to stumble over a step. Simply providing more light will not necessarily help older people to see well; because of the clouding of the lens, more light causes more glare. Thus, the best level of illumination is a compromise between what produces the best contrast and the least glare.

Hearing is also affected by age. After age 50 or so, people have increased difficulty hearing high-frequency sounds (Botwinick, 1984; Lemme, 1995). Because consonants (such as *k, c, p,* and *t*) are produced with higher-frequency sounds than are vowels, older people will have trouble distinguishing between words that differ by a single consonant, such as *kill* and *pill.* Older people also have more difficulty shutting out background noise, a problem that may actually be worsened by hearing aids, which boost the loudness of irrelevant background sounds as well as of relevant sounds.

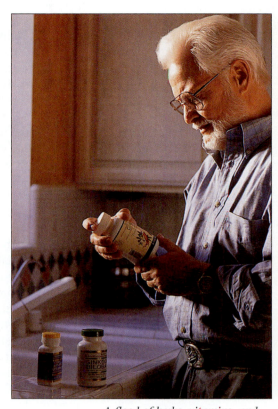

Memory: Difficulties in Digging It Out

Parts of the brain that produce the neurotransmitter acetylcholine become impaired with age (Albert & Moss, 1996); this neurotransmitter is crucial for the proper functioning of the hippocampus, which plays a key role in memory. The loss of efficient processing in this part of the brain is probably one reason why older people often have trouble with some kinds of memory (Schacter, 1996).

Even so, aging affects some aspects of memory more than others. *Semantic memory* (memory for facts, words, meanings, and other information that is not associated with a particular time and place) remains relatively intact into very old age (Light, 1991), and the storing of new *episodic memories* (memory for specific events) is often relatively intact. People in their 70s and 80s do relatively well if they are given a list of words and then asked to pick out these words from a longer list that also contains other words (Craik & McDowd, 1987). Moreover, they can recall the gist of a description and its implications at least as well as younger people (Radvansky, 1999).

However, the elderly have difficulty when they must actively recall specific episodic memories: For example, they do poorly if they are given a list of common words to remember and later asked to recall them (Craik & McDowd, 1987). Tasks that require the *recall* of specific information appear to rely on the frontal lobes to dig the information out of memory, and these processes are not as efficient in the elderly as they are in younger people. Frontal lobe impairment probably also is responsible for difficulties the elderly have with tasks involving working memory. Such deficits are particularly evident when the elderly must hold information in mind while doing something else at the same time (Craik et al., 1995). If strategies are needed to perform a task (such as figuring out the most efficient way to move through a store to collect different items), the frontal lobe impairments of the elderly can affect their performance (Gabrieli, 1996). As Salthouse (1985) suggests, slowed cognitive processes may also lead the elderly to use inefficient strategies, strategies composed of many steps, each relatively simple.

A flood of herbs, vitamins, and other medicinal remedies promise to reverse the negative cognitive effects of aging. For example, the herb Ginkgo biloba and the drug acetyl-L-carnitine have been reported to improve blood flow to the brain (Dean et al., 1993). However, much more research is necessary before we will know for sure whether such treatments work as advertised for everyone.

Intelligence: All Is Not Lost

It might seem likely that as you age, your accumulated life experience becomes increasingly important in determining your intelligence. But this is not so.

Researchers were surprised to discover that genetic influences on general intelligence actually *increase* with age (Finkel et al., 1995; Plomin et al., 1994). In addition, investigators have asked whether aging affects all types of intelligence in the same way. In particular, they have examined the effects of age on *fluid intelligence,* which involves flexibility in reasoning and the ability to figure out novel solutions, and *crystallized intelligence,* which involves using knowledge as a basis of reasoning (see Chapter 6). It might seem that crystallized intelligence, which by definition relies on effects of experience, would be less influenced by age than fluid intelligence would. How could we tell? These two types of intelligence have been assessed in **longitudinal studies**, which test the same group repeatedly, at different ages. These findings suggest that *both* types of intelligence are stable until somewhere between the mid-50s and early 70s, at which point both decline (Hertzog & Schaie, 1988). However, the very strength of longitudinal studies, the continuing use of the same group, also leads to a weakness: The participants become familiar with the type of testing, and this familiarity can influence their performance on later assessments. **Cross-sectional studies** involve testing different groups of people, with each group at a different age. The key here is to ensure that the groups are equated on all possible measures other than age (such as sex, educational level, and health status). Such studies have led most researchers to believe that fluid intelligence begins to decline as early as the late 20s (Salthouse, 1991a), whereas crystallized intelligence may actually grow with age and decline only at the very end of life (Baltes, 1987).

Crystallized intelligence, rooted in experience, may be thought of as underlying much of what we mean by "wisdom." The ability to draw on such intelligence may explain why researchers found that older adults were rated as telling more interesting, higher-quality, and more informative stories than younger adults (James et al., 1998). This should be cheering news for Steven Spielberg, who plans to keep telling stories as long as he can.

In general, only about 25% of the variation in cognitive abilities among people is related to their ages (Salthouse, 1991b). Furthermore, aging has varying effects on different people and on different cognitive abilities. In short, depending on genetics and personal experiences, some aspects of intelligence will be affected by aging more than others (Schaie & Willis, 1993).

Practice can improve some abilities in the elderly (Baltes, 1987; Salthouse & Somberg, 1982; Verhaeghen et al., 1992), such as the ability to perform calculations (Campbell & Charness, 1990). However, practice is not equally effective for all cognitive abilities. In contrast to the ability to do calculations, the ability of the elderly to use working memory was only slightly improved by practice (Campbell & Charness, 1990).

People can often compensate for declining abilities by using abilities that are still intact (Baltes, 1987; Baltes et al., 1984). Some typists can retain their speed as they age by looking farther ahead on the page, thus taking in more as they go (Salthouse, 1984). Similarly, tennis players may compensate for reduced speed and vigor by developing better strategies (Perlmutter, 1988; see Lemme, 1995).

Social and Emotional Development During Adulthood

The term "grown up" might seem to imply that psychological development is like height: After a certain age, you reach a plateau, and that's where you stay. Not so. At least in mentally healthy people, development continues through the life span. In discussing Steven Spielberg's 15-year split with his father, an expert on father–son relationships, James Levine, commented: "In such a split, you don't recognize that under the anger is sadness. There's denial: pretending it's not important to heal the rift. But a split in the father–child relationship always has an

Longitudinal study: A study in which the same people are tested repeatedly, at different ages.

Cross-sectional study: A study in which different groups of people are tested, with each group at a different age.

Chapter 9 Psychology Over the Life Span

www.ablongman.com/kosslynbrief

effect" (quoted in R. Sullivan, 1999, p. 67). Still, as in Spielberg's case, relationships change and evolve over time.

Theories of Psychosocial Stages in Adulthood

Some theorists, Freud included, believed that personality stops developing in childhood. But Erik Erikson (1921–1994) believed there are three stages of adult **psychosocial development**, or effects of maturation and learning on personality and relationships, in addition to five stages of psychosocial development through childhood and adolescence (see Table 9.3). The adult stages were defined by issues that adults are most likely to confront and need to resolve. The first, *intimacy versus isolation,* occurs in young adulthood. To navigate this phase successfully, the young adult must develop deep and intimate relations with others and avoid becoming socially isolated. Steven Spielberg had serious difficulty being intimate with people, which may be one reason why his first marriage dissolved (McBride, 1999, p. 295). The second stage, characterized by *generativity versus self-absorption,* occurs during the middle adult years. The challenge now is for men and women to think about the future and decide what their contributions will be for their children or for society at large. People in this stage who fail to accomplish these goals will be faced with a sense of meaninglessness in life. Steven Spielberg not only cares for his own children but also makes it a point to help young directors who are just starting out; such altruism is another type of generativity. The third stage, characterized by *integrity versus despair,* occurs during old age. The task here is to be able to reflect back on life and feel that it was worthwhile, thereby avoiding feelings of despair and fear of death.

After a 15-year split, Steven Spielberg developed a new relationship with his dad.

Many theorists have picked up where Erikson left off, modifying his theory or replacing it altogether (Gould, 1978; Havinghurst, 1953; Vaillant, 1977; Lemme, 1995, reviews this literature). Levinson (Levinson, 1977, 1978, 1986, 1990; Levinson et al., 1978), basing his work on interviews with 40 men, developed an influential theory of developmental transitions in men's lives. Perhaps the most important and interesting aspect of Levinson's theory is the *mid-life transition*

Psychosocial development: The effects of maturation and learning on personality and relationships.

TABLE 9.3 Erikson's (1950) Psychosocial Stages

ISSUE TO BE RESOLVED	AVERAGE AGE	SUMMARY
Basic trust vs. mistrust	0–1 year	Depending on how well they are treated by caregivers, infants either develop a basic trust that the world is good or fail to develop such a basic trust.
Autonomy vs. doubt	1–3 years	The child either is allowed to choose and make independent decisions or is made to feel ashamed and full of self-doubt for wanting to do so.
Initiative vs. guilt	3–6 years	The child either develops a sense of purpose and direction or is overly controlled by the parents and made to feel constrained or guilty.
Industry vs. inferiority	6–11 years	The child either develops a sense of competence and ability to work with others or becomes beset with feelings of incompetence and inferiority.
Identity vs. role confusion	Adolescence	The adolescent either successfully grapples with questions of identity and future roles as an adult or becomes confused about possible adult roles.
Intimacy vs. isolation	Young adulthood	The young adult either develops deep and intimate relations with others or is socially isolated.
Generativity vs. self-absorption	Middle adulthood	The adult in the "prime of life" must look to the future and determine what to leave behind for future generations; failing this task leads to a sense of meaninglessness in life.
Integrity vs. despair	Old age	In reflecting back on life, a person either feels that life was worthwhile as it was lived or feels despair and fears death.

Average age of the Rolling Stones in 1994: 50.6 years.

Average age of top GM executives in 1994: 49.8 years.

Many roles are open to us as we age, despite stereotypes to the contrary!

(between about age 40 and 45), which occurs when a man begins to shift from thinking of his life as being marked by the time that's passed since birth to thinking of his life as being marked by the time left until death. According to Levinson, many men have midlife crises, which can lead them to end old marriages and begin new marriages, change jobs, or make other major life changes.

Research by others (for example, McCrae & Costa, 1984) has cast doubt on whether most men in fact undergo a midlife crisis, and little evidence exists to support this view. In addition, Levinson's original study focused only on men; it was not long before others undertook similar studies involving women. Roberts and Newton (1987), for example, noted that women's lives were often "conflicted and unstable" throughout much of early adulthood and into middle age. Others who have studied women (such as Mercer, Nichols, & Doyle, 1989) report that women do not follow a regular stagelike progression through life.

The findings that do support the existence of stages in adulthood can be interpreted as evidence that our society poses different challenges to people of different ages or as evidence that personality develops with age. Research findings suggest that this second interpretation is probably incorrect. Costa and McCrae (1988) tested more than a thousand people, both men and women, using standardized measures (not interviews) of the Big Five personality dimensions: openness to experience, conscientiousness, extraversion, agreeableness, and neuroticism (see Chapter 8). The participants ranged in age from 21 to 96 years. In addition to asking the participants to complete the measures, they also asked 167 spouses to fill in the measures about the participants. Eighty-nine men and 78 women were tested twice, 6 years apart; thus, both cross-sectional and longitudinal data were collected. The results were clear: There were very few differences in any of the dimensions of personality over the years, and when such differences were found, they were very small. Moreover, Costa and McCrae found that personality was equally stable over time for men and women. They concluded that "aging itself has little effect on personality. This is true despite the fact that the normal course of aging includes disease, bereavement, divorce, unemployment, and many other significant events for substantial portions of the population" (p. 862). Thus, most apparent changes in personality over time probably reflect not so much changes in the person as changes in the life challenges being confronted at the time.

A later meta-analysis showed, however, that adult personality does continue to develop in one respect: Until around age 50, people become increasingly consistent in the degree to which they can be described by particular traits, and thereafter are stable (Roberts & DelVecchio, 2000). Consistency, in this sense, refers to the relative ordering of people according to a trait—with increasing age, your ranking relative to other people will become more stable. This stability could reflect, in part, your settling into a niche in life, and thus restricting the range and variety of situations you encounter.

Adult Relationships: Stable Changes

In general, as people age they interact with fewer people, but these interactions tend to be more intimate (Carstensen, 1991, 1992). Relationships earlier in life tend to include more friends than relatives, but with age the mix reverses, with more time spent with relatives than with friends. This pattern is even more pronounced among Latinos than Anglos (Levitt et al., 1993). In later life, a relationship long dormant can be picked up and reestablished with minimal effort (Carstensen, 1992); after young adulthood, temperament and personality variables are relatively stable, which makes it easy to "know" someone again even after a long lapse.

During young adulthood, people are concerned that their relationships with friends and relatives are equitable—that neither party gives more than he or she receives (Lemme, 1995; Walster et al., 1978). As people age, such concerns recede into the background. In successful marriages, the members of the couple think of themselves as a team, not separate people who are in constant negotiations (Keith & Schafer, 1991). Because they are in it for the long haul, people trust that the balance of favors and repayment will even out over time.

At one point, approximately 2,500 people well over 100 years old were reported to be living in countries comprising the former Soviet Union. One purportedly 168-year-old gentleman, who was still walking half a mile daily and gardening, attributed his longevity to the fact that he didn't marry until he was 65 (Seuling, 1986). Many elderly people, such as this Belgian couple—he's 98 and she's 74!—enter second marriages.

Death and Dying

We began this chapter with the very earliest phase of development, and we close it with the last of life's experiences. The psychology of death has two faces: The effects on the person who is dying and the effects on friends and family. Perhaps the most influential theorist of the psychology of death is Elisabeth Kübler-Ross (1969), who studied the psychological events that accompany the knowledge of impending death. After extensive interviews with people dying of cancer (usually in middle age), she developed a theory that there are five stages people pass through in dealing with their own impending deaths:

Stage 1: Shock, disbelief, and denial

Stage 2: Anger and a sense of injustice

Stage 3: Bargaining, with God and others, for continued life

Stage 4: Depression and withdrawal

Stage 5: Acceptance

However, these stages probably apply only to people who are dying at a relatively early age, and even then, not everyone follows the stages in order or experiences every stage (Retsinas, 1988). Kübler-Ross's theory also suffers from the usual problems of theories based on interviews (such as faulty recollection and a desire to avoid embarassment), and there is little empirical evidence to back it up.

Concern about our own deaths apparently does not increase with age: Death anxiety either stays the same over the course of life, or may actually decrease near the end (Lemme, 1995). Women report fearing death more than do men (Lonetto & Templer, 1986). However, this finding could simply mean that women are more honest or self-aware, or that men are consciously or unconsciously avoiding confronting the topic. In addition, because women tend to live longer than men, they may have had more opportunity to witness and become concerned about death than men.

Cultural differences clearly influence the ways people view death (Kalish & Reynolds, 1977; Platt & Persico, 1992). Researchers who studied the Mayan people of South America found that they did not try to fight death. Elderly people announce that their time has come and then retire to a mat or hammock and wait to die. They refuse food or water, ignore attempts by others to talk to them, and soon die. Their attitude toward death is fostered by their strong belief in an afterlife in paradise (Steele, 1992). In contrast, the Kaliai, a tribe in Papua New Guinea, almost never die of old age, instead meeting death in battle or as a result of an accident. Thus, they do not view death as a natural occurrence; they look for someone to blame, usually a sorcerer (Counts & Counts, 1992).

Grief is the emotion of distress that follows the loss of a loved one, and **bereavement** is the experience of missing a loved one and longing for his or her company. People in the United States tend to go through the grieving process in three phases (Lindemann, 1991). First, until about 3 weeks after the death, the bereaved person is in a state of shock. He or she feels empty, disoriented, and, sometimes, in a state of denial and disbelief; these feelings eventually settle into a state of deep sorrow. (This shock may be buffered by having to make funeral arrangements, deal with lawyers, and so on, but nevertheless apparently develops during this period.) Second, from 3 weeks to about a year following the death, the bereaved person experiences emotional upheavals, from anger to loneliness and guilt. During this time, people often review their relations with the deceased, wondering whether they should have done things differently, whether the death was inevitable. During this phase, people may think that they catch glimpses of the deceased in crowds or hear the person talk to them. Third, by the beginning of the second year, grief lessens. The bereaved person may largely stop thinking of the deceased and, in the case of a spouse's death, be ready to become committed to a new intimate relationship. However, bereavement may continue indefinitely, particularly when a person is reminded of the deceased by special places or events, such as anniversaries or birthdays.

The effects of the death of a friend or loved one depend in part on the age of the deceased. Most deaths in the United States and Canada tend to occur at a relatively old age; the average age of death in some Latin American countries is much younger. The grief for someone who has had a full life is different from the grief for someone who has been cut down in his or her prime.

LOOKING AT LEVELS

Keeping the Aging Brain Sharp

In old age, particularly the years just before death, many people do not function as well mentally as they did earlier in life, even if they are physically healthy (Small & Bäckman, 1999). Is this deterioration inevitable? As people age, the brain receives less blood, which means that it is sustained by fewer nutrients and oxygen (Ivy et al., 1992). The blood supply to the brain decreases with age because the vessels themselves become smaller. Why does this happen? One reason may be that the brain cells are not working as hard, so they need less blood—which in turn leads the vessels to adjust (Ivy et al., 1992). This is a catch-22: The neurons don't work as effectively because they receive fewer blood-borne nutrients and less oxygen, but the reason they don't receive as much is that they haven't been functioning as effectively as they did before. Thus, if your otherwise healthy grandparents are understimulated by their surroundings (as occurs in some nursing homes as well as in many home environments), this could affect their brains. The lack of mental challenge and engagement can lead to a change in their self-concepts and levels of self-esteem. These changes then may lead them to become lethargic and not to try to challenge themselves (including with other people), which could lead to even less effective neural functioning, and so on. Events at all three levels clearly interact.

Although the appropriate research has yet to be conducted, it is tempting to hypothesize that if you managed to engage your elderly parents, grandparents, or other family members in more challenging tasks, you could literally increase the blood supply to their brains and improve their thinking abilities. This result is plausible because "mental workouts" appear to enhance cognitive function in the elderly (Rowe & Kahn, 1998). Moreover, dendrites continue to grow normally even into old age (Coleman & Flood, 1986), and as neurons die, new connections may be formed to compensate for losses (Cotman, 1990). In one study, when elderly rats were moved from their standard cages into a rat playpen full of toys and other rats, they developed heavier brains with more extensive connections among neurons. Very likely the same would be true for humans who were moved to more stimulating environments (see Avorn & Langer, 1982; Langer & Rodin, 1976; Rodin & Langer, 1977; Rowe & Kahn, 1998).

However, it is unlikely that *all* the functions that are impaired with age can be helped simply by getting your grandparents to use their brains more. MRI scans of over 3,600 apparently normal elderly people (aged 65 to 97) revealed that slightly over one-third had brain lesions. These were often small and usually affected subcortical structures, but some of the lesions may have been large enough to affect a specific cognitive function (Bryan et al., 1997). Thus, possible effects of changing beliefs and social interactions must be considered within the context of the state of the brain. As always, events at the three levels interact.

CONSOLIDATE!

1 *How do changes in the body affect us as we age?* The adult body remains relatively stable until around age 50. At about this point, women experience menopause, and both men and women may become less vigorous. Many of the changes in the body can be treated, however, either by dietary supplements (such as calcium for bone weakness) or changes in activities (such as increased exercise).

2 *How does aging affect perception, memory, and intelligence?* With age the lens clouds and the pupils dilate less, leading to difficulty in seeing light–dark contrasts; the elderly also have difficulty hearing high-frequency sounds such as consonants. With advancing old age, working memory operates less effectively, and people sometimes have difficulty recalling information. Although intelligence declines with advanced age, fluid intelligence may be more affected than crystallized intelligence.

3 *What is the course of social and emotional development during adulthood?* Many theorists,

including Erik Erikson and Daniel Levinson, have proposed that people pass through psychosocial stages as they age. These stages may be a result of challenges posed by a particular culture; little evidence points to personality changing after age 30. Adult relationships focus on fewer people (often relatives) and tend to be stable over long periods of time.

4 *How do people cope with the knowledge of their own impending deaths and with the deaths of friends and family members?* People may go through a series of stages in coming to terms with their own impending deaths (at least if they are middle-aged). Grief for another's death may also pass through stages, which may extend over 2 years following the death; the sense of bereavement may never entirely disappear. Concern about our own deaths does not increase, and may in some cases decrease, with age.

A DEEPER LEVEL

Recap and Thought Questions

In the Beginning: From Conception to Birth

The development of both the brain and the body relies on the activation of specific genes, which are regulated in part by environmental events. If those events disrupt gene function, the brain and body may develop abnormally. The newborn comes into the world equipped with a variety of reflexes, many of which disappear in short order. In addition, a newborn has sophisticated sensory capacities, including those necessary to begin organizing sounds into words and recognizing objects. Individual newborns differ in their temperaments, and may retain their temperaments indefinitely.

Was Steven Spielberg born with his abilities to make movies? Probably not. Like all of us, his abilities developed over time and were affected by a combination of innate factors, effects of teratogens, nutrition, and appropriate stimulation (perhaps even the sounds of his mother's piano playing) during his prenatal development.

Infancy and Childhood: Taking Off

As they grow, children are increasingly able to control their bodies. They learn to coordinate muscles in the context of perception and knowledge of specific properties of the world. Perceptual development involves increasingly finer discriminations and the use of more and more complex sources of information. Language development relies in part on the child's learning which perceptual features to attend to and which to ignore, as well as learning the rules of grammar. As characterized by Jean Piaget, cognitive development involves a series of stages, which research has shown in part reflect brain growth, increased capacity of working memory, and the results of explicit instruction. However, these stages may not be fixed, and many abilities are evident at earlier ages than originally believed. Culture plays a role in cognitive development, if only because language is acquired through immersion in a culture.

Social and emotional development are reflected by changes in attachment, self-concept, gender identity, moral reasoning, and gender roles. Even young babies have the beginnings of a self-concept and develop social relationships from the start, including attachment (of one type or another) to a caregiver. Further, babies apparently are born with a biological bias to be male or female, a bias that probably results from the effects of hormones in the womb. Simply raising babies as boys or girls is not likely to make them comfortable or happy with that gender if their experiences in the womb inclined them toward the other gender.

According to Lawrence Kohlberg, moral reasoning also develops through a series of stages. However, it isn't clear whether all these stages actually exist, or whether they depend at least in part on culture and the tasks of daily life (which may include having to take care of children or elderly parents). Moral reasoning appears to depend on the cognitive capacity to engage in certain types of thinking.

Has Steven Spielberg exhibited full perceptual and cognitive development? His movies give every evidence of his having developed a sophisticated ability to reason, not only about physical events, but also about psychological and even moral dilemmas (as illustrated in *Amistad, The Color Purple,* and *Schindler's List*).

Adolescence: Between Two Worlds

The hormonal changes that herald the onset of puberty not only affect the body in dramatic ways, but also alter the child's emotional and social interactions. Adolescence is usually accompanied by cognitive changes that allow the adolescent to conceive of events in the world in more abstract and complex ways. Emotional, social, and cognitive changes can lead to a period of "storm and stress," although not every adolescent experiences such a period and those who do may experience it to different extents.

Was adolescence a particularly important period for Steven Spielberg? Apparently so, given the themes that recur in his films. Not only was his parents' divorce a key event in his life, but so was his striving to be accepted by his teenage peers.

Adulthood and Aging: The Continuously Changing Self

Some of the bodily effects of aging are programmed into the genes, but some are not. Proper diet and exercise can help the body function effectively well into old age. Although most perceptual abilities (such as vision and hearing) decline with advanced age, they need not impair the ability to get around or communicate with others. Similarly, although it may become more difficult to retrieve information from long-term memory in old age, many aspects of memory continue to function effectively. The brain functions well until close to death, and intelligence, particularly crystallized intelligence, may remain highly effective until shortly before death.

As people age, they face different social and emotional challenges. If these challenges are not resolved satisfactorily, they will be unhappy and not well adjusted to the realities of growing old. During middle age, people must learn to cope with the deaths of those they love, and at the end of life, they must come to terms with their own death.

Have Steven Spielberg's relationships changed as he has gotten older? Yes. Like most people, his relatives seem to have become more important. If he is like other people, the size of his circle of friends may shrink. Nevertheless, it will be easy for him to retain old friendships.

Think It Through. If you could choose several of your own abilities to protect from decaying with age, which would they be? Why? As you age, what factors do you think will influence whether you stay close to friends you made earlier in life?

REVIEW TEST

For each of the following items, choose the single correct or best answer. The correct answers appear at the end.

1. Each person begins as _____ pairs of chromosomes.
   a. 12   b. 21   c. 22   d. 23

2. The reflex in which a startled baby throws his or her arms wide, as if to grab someone, is called the _____ reflex.
   a. Moro   b. Babinski   c. flexation   d. tonic neck

3. Tiffany Field found that touching premature infants resulted in _____.
   a. higher levels of cortisol production
   b. increased physical and behavioral growth
   c. decreased immune functioning
   d. increased anxiety and depression

4. Which of the following does *not* describe child-directed speech?
   a. careful enunciation
   b. low pitch
   c. clear pauses between phrases
   d. exaggerated intonation

5. Jeremy called the man in the store "Daddy" since he was tall and had dark hair like his own "Daddy." Jeremy was using a(n) _____.
   a. morpheme
   b. synopheme
   c. overextension
   d. underextension

6. The visual cliff experiments have led researchers to understand that infants have _____.
   a. innate fear
   b. acute hearing
   c. color perception
   d. depth perception

7. As a child develops, schemas become _____, giving rise to different schemas for different situations.
   a. articulated
   b. assimilated
   c. accommodated
   d. differentiated

8. Vygotsky put forth the idea that children use _____ to direct themselves, especially when working on difficult tasks.
   a. private speech
   b. spoken thoughts
   c. theory of mind
   d. working memory

9. Babies who are as easily comforted by strangers as by their mothers in the *Strange Situation* would be classified as _____ attached.
   a. avoidantly
   b. resistantly
   c. disorganized
   d. securely

10. Gender identity is most strongly influenced by _____.
    a. exposure to levels of hormones prenatally
    b. cultural and societal expectations
    c. peer influences in preschool and early elementary years
    d. parental behaviors both before and after a baby is born

11. Eleanor Maccoby believes that _____ is (are) key to the development of gender roles.
    a. parents
    b. the peer group
    c. genetics
    d. teachers

12. The major cognitive development of adolescence is _____.
    a. the ability to conserve mass and volume
    b. the ability to reason abstractly
    c. the development of a theory of mind
    d. the self-directed use of private speech

13. Which of the following statements about teen pregnancy is *false*?
    a. Only a little over half of pregnant American teens deliver their babies.
    b. American teens engage in more sexual activity than teens in other industrialized countries.
    c. Most pregnant teens do not marry before the baby is born.
    d. American teens are less likely to use birth control than teens in other industrialized countries.

14. About _____ of the variation in cognitive abilities among people is related to age.
    a. 40%   b. 5%   c. 25%   d. 10%

15. According to Kübler-Ross, what is the second stage that people pass through in dealing with death?
    a. depression, withdrawal
    b. bargaining with God and others
    c. shock, disbelief, denial
    d. anger and sense of injustice

ANSWERS: 1. d   **2.** a   **3.** b   **4.** b   **5.** c   **6.** d   **7.** d   **8.** a   **9.** a   **10.** a   **11.** b   **12.** b   **13.** b   **14.** c   **15.** d

10

Stress, Health,

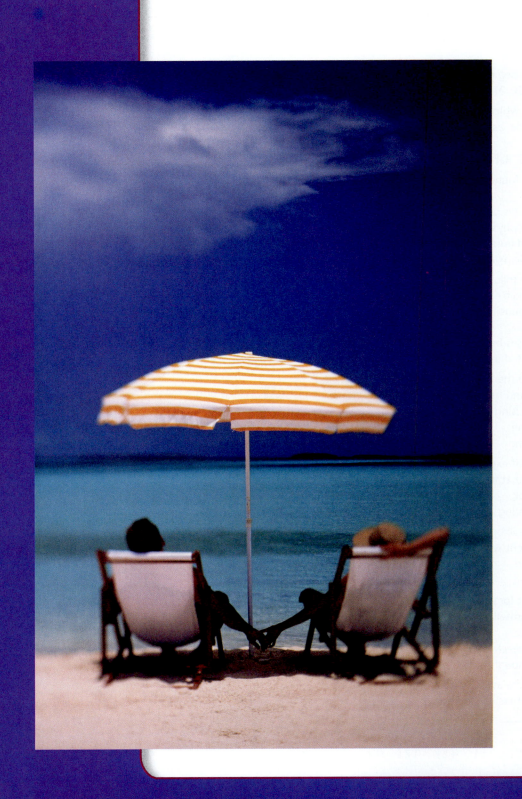

and Coping

Lisa, a college sophomore, was becoming worried about her father, Al. Only 54 years old, he always seemed exhausted, regardless of the time of day or the amount of work he'd been doing. Whenever Lisa asked him why he was so tired, he answered in generalities: "Oh, work's crazy and I'm not sleeping all that well. That's all, honey." He'd also been coughing a lot, and when Lisa asked about this, he'd reply, "I've been sick more than usual—it's just been a bad winter."

Lisa used to look forward to her visits home and her telephone conversations with her father, but now she dreaded talking to him because he always sounded so tired and dejected. Lisa suggested that he see his doctor, exercise, or maybe read about how to combat insomnia. Al finally told her the real reason he was so tense and tired: His company had laid off several of his colleagues, and he was afraid he'd be next. It also meant that now Al's department was responsible for more work with less staff, and the department had moved to smaller quarters. He had trouble concentrating, and he knew his work was suffering, which made him even more concerned that he'd be fired. There was a possibility of a job offer from another company, but at a substantially lower salary. Lisa, listening to his story, understood that he had tried to protect her by not telling her. If he was fired, or took the other job, he wouldn't be able to help with her college expenses, and she was already working 25 hours a week. If Al's fears materialized, she would probably have to leave school, at least for a while, or take out very large loans. He was worried himself, and worried about his daughter; Lisa understood the burden of those worries, which she now shared. She worried, too, about his persistent cough—was it just from lots of winter colds, or was it something more?

This situation produced stress in both father and daughter. Just what is "stress"? Can it affect our health? How can we deal with it?

What Is Stress?

Al began to hate going to work. Often as he worked at his desk, he felt as if he'd just finished a race—heart beating, palms sweating, breath coming hard—but without any accompanying sense of relief or accomplishment. He was simply exhausted all the time and felt as if his heart wasn't pumping his blood fast enough for his body's needs. He began to be seriously worried about his health, as well as his job.

But Maya, a colleague who so far had survived at the company, didn't seem disturbed by the changes happening around them. Maya had two children and, like Al, needed her job, but she seemed to be taking this difficult situation in stride. Al didn't understand how Maya was able to stay so calm—didn't she understand what was going on?

And what about Lisa's response to pressures? She had been managing the demands of college and job well; but after her father explained his situation at work and the possible repercussions for both of them, she noticed physical symptoms in herself—sweaty palms, racing heart—even while studying or taking class notes. Al and Lisa are responding to stress.

1. What exactly is stress?
2. What is the biology of stress?
3. What are common sources of stress?

Stress: The Big Picture

Today even third graders complain of feeling "stressed out," and adults take evening courses in "stress management." But what exactly *is* stress? **Stress** is the general term describing the psychological and bodily response to a stimulus that alters your equilibrium (Lazarus & Folkman, 1984). The stimulus that throws the body's equilibrium out of balance is called a **stressor;** a piece of glass that you step on while walking barefoot is a stressor. For Al, the threat of losing his job is a stressor, and the resulting combination of physical reactions (heart racing and so on) and psychological reactions (difficulty concentrating at work) is the stress. More specifically, the body's response to a stressor is the **stress response**, also called the *fight-or-flight* response, the bodily changes that occur to help you cope with the stressor. If you step on a piece of glass, your body may produce chemicals called endorphins and enkephalins, its own version of painkillers, and cause white blood cells to congregate at the site of the injury to fight off any infectious agents. These responses work to bring the body back to normal, to restore homeostasis.

The list of potential stressors is long, and categorized according to a number of criteria (Table 10.1). Stressors can be short-term (**acute stressor**) or long-term (**chronic stressor**); they can be physical, "psychological" (which affect events at the level of the person), or social (or, of course, some combination). Physical stressors,

Stress: The general term describing the psychological and bodily response to a stimulus that alters a person's state of equilibrium.

Stressor: A stimulus that throws the body's equilibrium out of balance.

Stress response: The physiological changes that occur to help people cope with a stressor; also called the *fight-or-flight response.*

Acute stressor: A stressor of short-term duration.

Chronic stressor: A stressor of long-term duration.

TABLE 10.1 **Examples of Types of Stressors**

TYPE OF STRESSOR	TYPE OF STRESSOR	
	Acute	Chronic
Physical	Being injured in a car crash	Being underfed; having cancer
Psychological	Working against a deadline	Chronically feeling pressured by work
Social	Getting fired	Chronic isolation; overcrowding

such as not eating for 2 days, generally apply to most people; psychological and social stressors, on the other hand, can be much more subjective. Going to a dance club for hours can be a party animal's idea of a great time or a shy person's nightmare. In general, it is our *perception* of a stimulus that determines whether it will elicit the stress response, not necessarily the objective nature of the stimulus itself.

The Biology of Stress: The General Adaptation Syndrome

Austrian-born researcher Hans Selye (1907–1982), who pioneered the study of stress, established that the body responds to stressors in generally predictable ways (Selye, 1976). He called the overall stress response the **general adaptation syndrome (GAS)** and suggested that it has three distinct phases: alarm, resistance, and exhaustion (Figure 10.1).

Figure 10.1 **Selye's Three-Stage Stress Response**

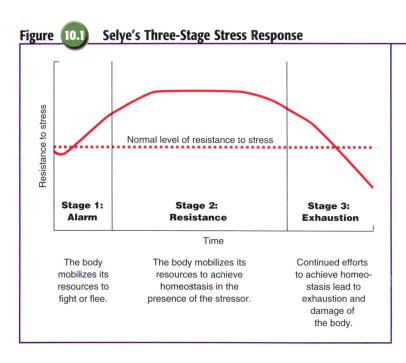

Hans Selye proposed that the body's response to prolonged stress comprises three stages: alarm, resistance, and exhaustion.

The Alarm Phase: Fight or Flight

Perception of a stressor triggers the **alarm phase**, which is characterized by the fight-or-flight response. In this response, the body mobilizes itself to fight or to flee from a threatening stimulus, which can be a physical threat, such as a knife at the throat, or a psychological one, such as an emotional rejection.

General adaptation syndrome (GAS): The technical name for the three phases of the body's response to stress.

Alarm phase: The first phase of the GAS, in which a stressor is perceived and a fight-or-flight response is activated.

When you perceive a threat, your brain responds to it by activating the sympathetic nervous system and inhibiting the parasympathetic nervous system (see Chapter 2 and Figure 2.8). Neurotransmitters and hormonal secretions such as epinephrine and norepinephrine cause breathing, heart rate, and blood pressure to increase. (Norepinephrine is considered a neurotransmitter when it is found in the brain, but a hormone when dispersed in other parts of the body.) This serves to bring more oxygen to the muscles as you prepare to "fight" or "flee." In addition, these sympathetic nervous system changes cause the pupils to dilate (allowing more light to enter for greater visual acuity) and the palms to sweat (for better gripping).

When the stress response is triggered, the hypothalamus secretes a substance that causes the release of **glucocorticoids**, another group of hormones. *Cortisol,* a glucocorticoid, not only increases the production of energy from glucose, but also has an anti-inflammatory effect, which makes it effective in helping restore the body's equilibrium after physical injury. In the short run, all these changes sharpen the senses, improve some qualities of memory (Sapolsky, 1997), and make it easier to fight or flee. Although this general stress response occurs with all stressors, the speed of action and amount of each hormone produced may differ, depending on the particular stressor (Henry, 1977; Romero & Sapolsky, 1996).

For most of us, however, the threats we experience do not require the kind of *physical* response required of our distant ancestors. Taking a final exam requires sitting in a chair, not running or climbing away from an enemy. Nonetheless, your body still reacts with the fight-or-flight response; it gets all revved up with nowhere to go.

Resistance and Exhaustion

Once your body is primed to fight or flee, you enter the **resistance phase** (also known as the *adaptation phase*), in which the body mobilizes its resources to achieve equilibrium despite the continued presence of the stressor. In other words, it *adapts* to the stressor.

Both the initial stress response and the resistance phase require energy, which comes from fat cells, muscles, and the liver. The increased blood flow (which results from increased heart and respiration rates) helps deliver the energy quickly and efficiently to the parts of the body that need it most. Digestion, growth, sex drive, and reproduction are slowed during times of stress. In women, menstruation may stop, or occur irregularly; in men, sperm and testosterone levels may decrease. As a matter of survival, why waste energy on these processes when it is needed elsewhere? In addition to these changes, no new energy is stored during stress; this means that with chronic stress, no reserve of energy is available to repair bodily damage, leaving a sense of fatigue.

During the resistance phase, cortisol serves to help the body return to a more normal state in the presence of continued stressors (McEwen & Schmeck, 1994). The more extreme the stressors, the more glucocorticoids are produced in an attempt to restore equilibrium, and this process decreases the functioning of the immune system. If the stressor continues, the **exhaustion phase** sets in; the continued stress response begins to damage the body, leading to a risk of stress-related diseases. In addition, cortisol can damage hippocampal cells (see Chapter 5), adversely affecting learning and memory (Newcomer et al., 1999; Sapolsky, 1992).

Sources of Stress

Is a new relationship stressful? Writing a term paper? Hearing a baby cry? Being stuck in a traffic jam? The answer to all these is maybe, maybe not. Many psychological, social, and even physical stimuli are stressors only if you *perceive* them as stressful. Some people are more likely to perceive many stimuli as stressful, and some situations are more likely than others to be perceived as stressful.

Glucocorticoids: A type of hormone that is released when the stress response is triggered. Glucocorticoids have anti-inflammatory properties.

Resistance phase: The second phase of the GAS, in which the body mobilizes its resources to attain equilibrium, despite the continued presence of the stressor; also called the *adaptation phase.*

Exhaustion phase: The final stage of the GAS, in which the continued stress response itself becomes damaging to the body.

Stressors in the Eyes of the Beholder

Maya is not bothered about the recent firings because she wants to spend more time with her children. Part of her wouldn't mind being out of work (and collecting unemployment) so that she could stay home for a while; between savings and her husband's paycheck, the family could get by for a few months. So for Maya, the threat of being fired is not a stressor. It is the *perception* of whether a stimulus is a stressor that is crucial for determining whether the stress response will occur (Lazarus & Folkman, 1984).

The importance of perceptions in determining whether something is a stressor was demonstrated in a classic study by Speisman and colleagues (1964). Participants were asked to watch a film of a primitive ritual involving a crude genital operation called "subincision." Participants in one group heard a "trauma" soundtrack for the film that emphasized the pain experienced by those undergoing the rite. Another group heard a "denial" soundtrack, which emphasized the positive aspects of the ritual and minimized the experience of pain. A third group heard an "intellectualization" soundtrack, which described the ceremony in a detached, clinical manner. Those in either the denial or the intellectualization group showed less of an autonomic response to the film and reported being less upset than those in the trauma group. This study demonstrated that the content of the narration about the ritual (the context, and therefore how the stimulus is perceived) affected the stress response of the participants in the study.

This process of appraising a stimulus occurs in two phases. First, the stimulus is assessed for the likelihood of danger; this is the *primary appraisal*. This assessment is followed by *secondary appraisal*, the determination of the resources available to deal with the stressor. In other words, the question "Am I in danger?" is followed by the question "What can I do about it?" (Bishop, 1994). After secondary appraisal comes **coping**; that is, the person experiencing stress takes some course of action regarding the stressor, its effects, or his or her reaction to it.

Even among college students, what is considered stressful differs for traditional students (who went to college straight from high school) and nontraditional students (who took some time off between high school and college, or have multiple roles such as student and parent or employee). Social activities have a larger impact on traditional students, whereas nontraditional students are more likely to enjoy doing homework and going to classes and worry less about how they are doing academically (Dill & Henley, 1998).

Perceived Control

It is clear that certain stimuli, such as illness or injury, are associated with physical stress; similar associations apply to certain types of psychological and social stressors. One such stimulus is the lack of a sense of control. Actual control is not important; what is important is whether you *perceive* a sense of control (Shapiro et al., 1996). The perception of control can affect your performance.

Not everyone is equally eager to feel in control; in fact, some people experience more stress when they perceive themselves as having more control, such as some cancer patients who find that taking responsibility for and control of their medical treatment is overwhelming and stressful. Such patients prefer not to learn about and weigh the statistics and other facts about their illness, and want their doctors to make all the decisions about chemotherapy, radiation, and other treatments. On the other hand, some people want very much to feel that they can control a situation but may, at least after a certain point, not have much real opportunity to do so. Once graduate school or job applications are written and interviews past, for example, there's not much you can do to get yourself accepted or hired; nothing is left but to wait for the answer. Thus, there can be a mismatch between perceived control and the preferred level of control (Shapiro et al., 1996).

Cultural factors also affect people's perception of control. Western, particularly U.S., culture emphasizes active control of yourself and mastery of your environment.

Coping: Taking a course of action regarding the stressor, its effects, or the person's reaction to it.

Some other cultures emphasize adaptation—accepting yourself and circumstances (Shapiro et al., 1996).

Even for those who prefer to have more control, perceiving a lack of control doesn't always produce stress. This apparent contradiction is resolved by another factor: Many things that are beyond our control are at least predictable. You have no control over whether you take math quizzes (at least, not if you want to pass the course), but announced quizzes are likely to be less stressful than surprise quizzes. If quizzes are announced, you can relax on the days none is scheduled, but the possibility of surprise quizzes means that the beginning of every class can be stressful as you wait to learn your fate. However, if the surprise quizzes are a frequent feature of the course, you would habituate to them and not view them to be as great a stressor—the quizzes, unpleasant as they might be, would no longer be so unpredictable.

Perceived lack of control in the face of a stressor can lead to the onset of *learned helplessness* (see Chapter 7). When animals cannot escape being shocked, they may respond with learned helplessness and depression. This is also true for humans who feel they have no control in an aversive situation. Another example of the importance of control and unpredictability is seen in the administration of pain medication. When postsurgery patients are allowed to determine when and how much pain medication they receive (through a pump connected to an IV by their beds), they give themselves less medication than when it is administered by a nurse they have called. Why is this? Because a patient who must ring for a nurse has little control of the situation *and* cannot predict what will happen—what the dosage will be, when the nurse will come, even if the nurse has heard the call. So the uncertainty and unpredictability of when the pain medication will come can heighten the experience of pain. When medication is self-regulated, predictability and control are restored, and the pain becomes more manageable (Chapman, 1989).

Although warning of an upcoming stressor can reduce the sensations of stress, vague information can make the stress worse. When Al heard that there were going to be unspecified changes at work, this vague information only served to increase his general level of stress response. This is the feeling Shakespeare's Macbeth had when, trying to unravel the three witches' mysterious prophecies, he remarked, "Present fears are less than horrible imaginings." But even specific warnings are not helpful if they come either too far in advance of or immediately before an event. When too far in advance, the information serves only to increase anticipation; when immediately before, there may be no time to put coping strategies to use (Sapolsky, 1997).

In general, perceived control is helpful only when you can see how much worse things could have been; then you can feel positive about what you have controlled. In the face of a catastrophic stressor, such as the diagnosis of a terminal illness, perceived control actually *increases* the stress: Things can't be much worse, and with perceived control the person diagnosed may feel responsible for the catastrophic stressor (Pitman et al., 1995; Sapolsky, 1997).

Researchers looking at the role of social class in the perception of control and health found that, not surprisingly, people with lower incomes perceived less control in their lives *and* were in poorer health. Those who did have a greater sense of control, regardless of income, had better health (Lachman & Weaver, 1998).

Internal Conflict

Stress can be caused by internal **conflict**, the emotional predicament people experience when they make difficult choices. The choices may involve competing goals, actions, impulses, or situations. Miller (1959) categorized three types of conflict. **Approach–approach conflict** results when competing alternatives are equally positive. Although this kind of conflict can be stressful, it is not necessarily experienced as unpleasant because both options are pleasing. For instance, if you have to choose between two very good job offers and want both jobs about equally, you would be

Conflict: The emotional predicament experienced when making difficult choices.

Approach–approach conflict: The internal predicament that occurs when competing alternatives are equally positive.

Chapter 10 Stress, Health, and Coping

facing an approach–approach conflict. The contrary case is **avoidance–avoidance conflict**, which results when competing alternatives are equally unpleasant. In such circumstances, making a choice can be very stressful. Faced with the choices of either taking a job you really don't want or being unemployed (and needing to pay back college loans), you would experience an avoidance–avoidance conflict. The third type, **approach–avoidance conflict**, occurs when a possible course of action has both positive and negative aspects and thus produces *both* approach *and* avoidance. When offered a job that you want, but that requires you to move to a city in which you don't want to live, you would experience approach–avoidance conflict.

Life's Hassles

In the 1960s, researchers began to explore the stressfulness of various life experiences. These investigations led to the idea that certain events, such as divorce or job loss, were stressful for almost everyone (Holmes & Rahe, 1967). What was perhaps more surprising was the finding that positive events, such as vacations and job promotions, could also be stressors. Subsequent research, however, has not shown these events, positive or negative, to be reliable predictors of stress-related illness. Because this line of research focused on the events themselves and not the *perception* of the events, it was not in fact a valid way to measure life's stressors. More recent work has focused on life's daily hassles, rather than major changes in life circumstances, as more predictive of distress and stress-related illnesses (Chamberlain & Zika, 1990; Tein et al., 2000).

All the daily hassles—the "little things" (which are sometimes not so little, but ongoing), such as concern about the health of someone in your family, having too many things to do, misplacing or losing things, trying to lose weight—add up to create stress. Those who report more daily hassles also report more psychological (Kanner et al., 1981) and physical symptoms (DeLongis et al., 1982) and are more likely to have suppressed immune systems (Bosch et al., 1998; Martin & Dobbin, 1988), as well as have higher cholesterol levels (Twisk et al., 1999). Consider this study: Participants were asked to solve a three-dimensional puzzle within 8 minutes; the participants did not know that a full solution was impossible. They were then asked to explain to another person how to solve the puzzle. To increase the stressful nature of the task, the explanations had to be verbal only; they could not demonstrate with the puzzle pieces themselves or use gestures. Those participants who had experienced a high number of daily hassles over the previous 2 months were more likely to have suppression of their immune systems after the puzzle task than those who did not report a high number of daily stressors (Brosschot et al., 1994). Thus, experiencing frequent daily stressors can cause an encounter with a mild stressor, as represented by the puzzle task, to be experienced as more distressful and more apt to provoke a change in the immune system. Think what this means for the stress levels of the many people caring for an ill relative or friend, as occurs in nearly a quarter of American households (National Alliance for Caregiving and American Association of Retired Persons, 1997). The stress of such daily, long-term caretaking creates a risk of illness for the caregiver.

Interruptions are another feature of daily life that can be a stressor. Think how you feel when you're trying to study or write a paper and are repeatedly interrupted by phone calls or visitors. If your reaction is to feel more "stressed out," you're not alone. Interruptions during a mentally challenging task can be stressful enough to cause large increases in cortisol levels (Earle et al., 1999; Suarez et al., 1998).

Hostility

Some people seem to experience stress more than others, regardless of their circumstances. Cardiologists Meyer Friedman and Ray Rosenman (1974) studied men who had coronary heart disease and discovered a common set of traits, including a sense of urgency, competitiveness, and interpersonal hostility. Friedman and

Avoidance–avoidance conflict: The internal predicament that occurs when competing alternatives are equally unpleasant.

Approach–avoidance conflict: The internal predicament that occurs when a course of action has both positive and negative aspects.

Hostility: The personality trait associated with heart disease, characterized by mistrust, an expectation of harm and provocation by others, and a cynical attitude.

Rosenman called this constellation of traits *Type A* personality. Subsequent research was unable to obtain the same clear-cut findings relating Type A personality and the incidence of coronary heart disease, but investigators were able to refine the concept of a stressed, heart disease–prone personality (Hecker et al., 1988). The most important component of the Type A personality in predicting heart disease was **hostility**, a trait characterized by mistrust, an expectation of harm and provocation by others, and a cynical attitude (Miller et al., 1996; Williams et al., 2000). For instance, Barefoot and his colleagues (1983) found that medical students who scored in the top 20% on a hostility scale were more than four times as likely to develop heart disease 25 years later than their low-hostility colleagues. Those same high-hostility doctors were seven times more likely to die of any cause by age 50 than their low-hostility colleagues. Further research (Barefoot et al., 1989) found that, among lawyers, increased mortality was associated with an untrusting and cynical view of people, repeated negative emotions in personal interactions, and recurrent expressions of overt anger and aggression in the face of difficulties or frustrations.

Men are generally more hostile than women (Miller, Dopp et al., 1999; Räikkönen et al., 1999), and researchers found that even at the same level of hostility, men's blood pressure is more affected by their hostility than women's (Räikkönen et al., 1999). When interrupted while concentrating on a task, highly hostile men had elevated heart rates, blood pressure, and cortisol production, as well as other bodily changes associated with a negative mood such as anger (Suarez et al., 1998). Regardless of sex, people high in hostility are more likely to have a higher heart rate and blood pressure throughout the day, no matter what their mood. In contrast, people low in hostility had cardiac changes only when they were in a negative mood (Davis et al., 2000; Räikkönen et al., 1999).

Hostility need not be a lifelong trait. Cognitive and behavioral programs designed to help reduce anger levels (see Chapter 12) can reduce not only the trait of hostility (Beck & Fernandez, 1998), but also anger-related arousal and blood pressure increases (Gidron et al., 1999); these changes were generally maintained 1 year after the end of a 5-week program (Deffenbacher et al., 1996).

As everyone knows, it is better, or healthier, to "vent" your anger so that it "drains away," right? Wrong. In fact, the opposite is true: Venting your anger is more likely to keep you angry and make your behavior toward others more aggressive. A study by Bushman and his colleagues (1999) illustrates how the expression of anger begets more anger. Participants were divided into two groups. One group, called the *procatharsis* group (*catharsis* comes from a Greek word that means "a cleansing") read about a study that found that venting anger *decreased* anger. The second group, the *anticatharsis* group, read about a study that showed the opposite, that venting anger *increased* anger. All participants were then asked to write a one-paragraph essay about abortion, taking whatever position they wanted, and were told that each essay would be read by another participant. Although the essays were not in fact read, the participants received written negative comments about their essays that were designed to make them angry.

Some participants in each group were then asked, among other things, to hit a punching bag while the others were asked just to sit for 2 minutes. Bushman and colleagues then asked participants to compete in pairs on a reaction time test, each participant trying to press a button as fast as possible after hearing a signal. The winning participants could select how loud and for how long an obnoxious noise would sound when their opponents lost.

Researchers found that those participants exposed to the message that venting anger is good were more likely to be

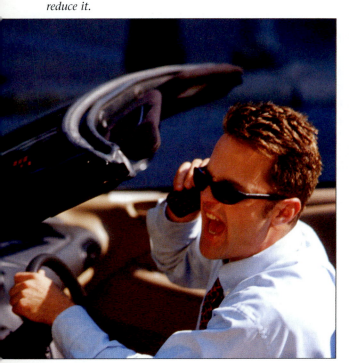

Road rage is a way of expressing anger and frustration. However, research shows that directly venting anger in this way may actually heighten people's anger, not reduce it.

aggressive toward another person, as measured by the loudness and duration of the obnoxious sound they imposed on their partners, compared with those who received either the anticatharsis message or no message (control group). Moreover, those who were in the group that hit a punching bag were more likely to be aggressive against their opponents in the reaction time test than those who simply sat still for 2 minutes. This part of the study demonstrated that venting anger leads to more anger and aggression. The study also showed the influence of culture: In an environment that encourages the venting of anger, people are more likely to be aggressive against others. But even if people believe that venting anger will lower their anger levels, that doesn't happen; the expression of anger makes them more likely to act aggressively and maintain their anger.

LOOKING AT LEVELS

The Hostile Heart

Hostile people, as measured in many studies by a self-report paper-and-pencil test or by a structured interview, are more likely than nonhostile people to experience stress in social situations—that is, they perceive stressors in situations in which those who are not hostile do not perceive stressors (level of the person). Hostile and nonhostile people do not have different levels of stress hormones or blood pressure when experiencing a nonsocial stressor such as figuring out a math problem (Sallis et al., 1987). Yet when they are asked to play a role that involves confrontation with another person, such as asking an acquaintance to repay a small loan (level of the group), those who were more hostile had a greater sympathetic nervous system response (level of the brain), as evidenced by higher levels of epinephrine and norepinephrine and higher blood pressure (Hardy & Smith, 1988). Similar results were found when participants were interrupted while trying to solve a puzzle (Suarez & Williams, 1989). Social stressors such as these did not elevate the stress response in nonhostile people.

The way life's little social stressors become large stressors for hostile people can be seen as an interaction of events at the levels of the group, person, and brain. Social stressors, which by definition are events at the level of the group, are influenced by hostility, a characteristic at the level of the person. Specifically, the way hostile people perceive of and think about other people affects their responses to social stimuli (level of the brain). Moreover, changing events at one level of analysis (decreasing behaviors associated with hostility—level of the person) can affect events at other levels. In this case, the changed behaviors result in a decreased risk of a subsequent heart attack (which in turn affects the functioning of the brain; Friedman, Thoresen, & Gill, 1986) and a different pattern of interaction with people (level of the group).

CONSOLIDATE!

1 *What exactly is stress?* Stress is the general term describing the psychological and bodily response to a stimulus that alters equilibrium. A stressor is a stimulus that throws the body's equilibrium out of balance. Stressors can be acute or chronic in duration, and physical, "psychological," or social in nature.

2 *What is the physiology of stress?* The stress response consists of changes in the activity of the sympathetic and parasympathetic nervous systems that prepare the body for physical effort and repair injury. These include changes in heart and respiration rates and the release of epinephrine, norepinephrine, and glucocorticoids. These changes occur during the alarm phase of the general adaptation syndrome. If the stressor continues, the body tries to return to homeostasis in the adaptation (resistance) phase. During the exhaustion phase, the stress response itself begins to cause damage, leading to stress-related diseases.

3 *What are common sources of stress?* The perception of whether a stimulus is a stressor is critical in determining if a given stimulus will lead to a stress response; this is often called primary appraisal. Certain factors likely to lead to a stress response include a lack of perceived control, unpredictability, internal conflict, and daily hassles. Some people are more stress-prone than others: Hostile people are more likely than others to view social situations as stressors.

B cell: A type of white blood cell that matures in the bone marrow.

T cell: A type of white blood cell that matures in the thymus.

Natural killer (NK) cell: A type of T cell that destroys damaged or altered cells, such as precancerous cells.

Stress, Disease, and Health

Al was clearly experiencing a great deal of stress, and his being sick so often just made matters worse. He'd had to miss work some days, which didn't help his sense of control in his difficult situation at work. Sometimes he'd cough so much he would have trouble sleeping, and then he'd lie awake worrying that he had lung cancer. He started having a few drinks in the evening to help him get to sleep, and he wasn't getting any exercise; he worried that if he started exercising, he'd bring on a heart attack. In short, Al wasn't doing very well, and he knew it.

The stress response is a good thing, very useful when the stressor is acute, such as the physical danger of a piece of glass in the foot; unfortunately, there can be too much of a good thing. Too strong a stress response for too long a time can lead to stress-related illnesses.

1 Can stress affect the immune system and make illness more likely?

2 Are stress and cancer related?

3 Can stress cause a heart attack or heart disease?

4 What is the relationship between stress and sleep?

The Immune System: Catching Cold

No question about it—stress can affect the immune system, which functions to defend the body against infection. Critical to the immune system are two classes of white blood cells: **B cells**, which mature in the bone marrow, and **T cells**, which mature in the thymus, an organ located in the chest. One type of T cell is the **natural killer (NK) cell**, which detects and destroys damaged or altered cells, such as precancerous cells, before they become tumors. Glucocorticoids, which are released when the stress response is triggered, hinder the formation of some white blood cells (including NK cells) or kill white blood cells (Cohen & Herbert, 1996; McEwen et al., 1997), making the body more vulnerable to infection and tumor growth. For this reason, many studies investigating the relationship between stress and the immune system look at the number of circulating white blood cells, such as NK cells. People who exhibit greater sympathetic nervous system responses to stress also show the most changes in immune system functioning (Bachen et al., 1995; Manuck et al., 1991), indicating that changes in the immune system are moderated by changes in the sympathetic nervous system.

Even day-to-day events and stresses, such as taking exams (Kiecolt-Glaser et al., 1986), can affect functioning of the immune system (Stone et al., 1994). A study looking at the relationship between stress and catching a cold found that the more stress a participant reported before exposure to a cold virus, the more likely he or she was to catch a cold (Cohen et al., 1991). The aspects of stress that best predicted whether participants would get a cold were how uncontrollable and unpredictable they rated their lives to be and how likely they were to experience negative feelings (such as guilt, anger, and being upset) (Cohen et al., 1993).

Because stress can impair the functioning of the white blood cells, it can play a role in the length of time it takes a wound to heal: The wounds of women who experienced a high level of stress by caring for a relative with Alzheimer's disease took 9 days longer to heal than those of women of similar age and economic status who were not engaged in such caretaking (Kiecolt-Glaser et al., 1995). In another study, dental student participants received slight mouth wounds on two different occasions (3 days before a major test and during summer vacation). The

The immune system's job is to fend off infectious agents such as viruses, tumors, and precancerous cells. The release of glucocorticoids (as occurs during stress) suppresses the functioning of the immune system, making it more difficult to fight the invader and leaving the body more vulnerable to infection. This photo shows two natural killer (NK) cells (yellow) attacking a leukemia cell (red). The NK cells have made contact and are beginning to engulf and destroy the leukemia cell.

wounds given before exams when, presumably, the students were experiencing more stressors, took 40% longer to heal (Marucha et al., 1998).

Major stressors such as natural disasters (devastating earthquakes and hurricanes) or victimization (being robbed or raped) can affect the immune system. Among people living in Florida neighborhoods damaged by Hurricane Andrew in 1992, the victims who perceived their losses to be most severe experienced the most changes in NK cells (Ironson et al., 1997). But not everyone who is exposed to trauma responds the same way. Some survivors later (sometimes considerably later) experience *posttraumatic stress disorder (PTSD)*, a psychological disorder characterized by an involuntary reexperiencing of the trauma through unwanted thoughts, sensations, and dreams, heightened arousal, and an avoidance of anything associated with the trauma. (A further discussion of PTSD appears in Chapter 11.)

In general, trauma survivors who had higher heart rates immediately after the trauma were more likely to develop posttraumatic stress disorder (Yehuda et al., 1998). Moreover, those who did develop posttraumatic stress disorder often had a hyperresponsivity or hyperarousal to stimuli similar to those present during the trauma (Casada et al., 1998; Keane et al., 1998). Thus, for example, survivors of Hurricane Andrew who have posttraumatic stress disorder are more likely to experience a large stress response on a windy day compared with people who have never experienced a severe hurricane. Even when not in the presence of such stimuli, those who go on to develop posttraumatic stress disorder are generally more autonomically reactive (Cohen, Kotler et al., 1998).

Traumatic events, such as experiencing the devastation of a hurricane, can affect the immune system, as well as produce psychological symptoms such as anxiety and depression.

Cancer

Although stress can't cause cancer, there is evidence that it can affect the growth of some cancerous tumors. How can this happen? First, if the immune system is suppressed, NK cells do not work as well to prevent the spread of tumor cells. Levy and her colleagues (Levy et al., 1985, 1987, 1988) found a relationship among the perception of inadequate social support, feelings of distress and fatigue with little joy, and lower NK cell activity levels. Such negative psychological experiences, by weakening the immune system, left people more vulnerable to the growth of cancerous tumors. Locke and colleagues (1984) found similar results.

A second way that stress can affect tumor growth is by facilitating the growth of capillaries feeding into the tumor. When stress has a distinct physical cause, our bodies produce more capillaries to supply blood to that area. If the stressor is an injury or infection (such as would be caused by glass in the foot), capillary growth is beneficial because the vessels carry more white blood cells to the part of the body that needs it. However, if a tumor is already present in the body, the stress response will cause more blood to be supplied to the tumor, literally feeding it and supporting its growth. Stress does not appear to *cause* a tumor to develop, only to assist in its growth.

The perception of control can also play a role in the progression of some types of cancer. Among cancer patients, those who did not perceive much control and felt helpless about their cancer were likely to have a recurrence sooner and die earlier from the cancer (Andersen et al., 1994; Watson et al., 1991).

Although psychological factors can affect the immune system, these findings should be interpreted with caution. The type of cancer, and biological factors related to cancer progression, can outweigh psychological factors in tumor growth (Compas et al., 1998; Grossarth-Maticek et al., 2000), especially in the final stages of the disease (Cohen & Herbert, 1996). Moreover, some people may be genetically endowed with an immune system more likely to ward off illness. Data on twins reared together and apart suggest that, on average, identical twins have more key antibodies in common (seven out of a possible nine) than fraternal twins (four out of a possible nine) (Kohler et al., 1985).

Heart Disease

The increased blood pressure created by stress, in combination with the hormonally induced narrowing of the arteries, promotes plaque buildup, or **atherosclerosis**, in the arteries (Figure 10.2). As plaque, or fatty deposits on the insides of the artery walls, accumulates, the arteries narrow so that the heart has to work even harder to meet the body's need for blood and oxygen. Working harder means pumping the blood with more power, creating more damage to the arteries, and a vicious cycle is created. This chronic wear and tear on the cardiovascular system can lead to heart damage, which can lead to sudden death from inadequate blood supply to the heart muscle or from irregular electrical firing of the muscle, preventing coordinated heartbeats. For someone who already has heart disease, even extremely positive states of stress, such as joy or orgasm, can precipitate these demands on the heart and cause sudden death.

Figure 10.2 **Stress on the Arteries**

Each time a stressor causes an increase in blood pressure, the branching points of arteries are at risk for damage. The hormones released during the fight-or-flight response also cause blood vessels to constrict, which has the net effect of making blood pressure increase even more. Thus, if someone experiences frequent stressors, his or her blood vessels take a pounding. With each stressed heartbeat, blood pounds against the same spot, wearing away some of the lining, creating a place for plaque to attach itself to the artery wall. Once this occurs, the artery gets narrower and narrower (as plaque builds and builds). This atherosclerosis makes the work of pumping blood through the body even harder for the heart.

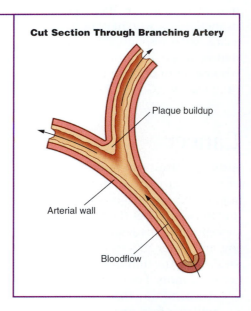

Cut Section Through Branching Artery

Plaque buildup

Arterial wall

Bloodflow

The course of heart disease can be affected by a change in lifestyle. A study of people with severe coronary heart disease found that intensive changes in diet, exercise, stress management (such as meditation), and social support made a difference not only in halting the narrowing of the arteries, but also in reversing the atherosclerosis, as well as in minimizing further damage to the heart (Ornish et al., 1998).

Depression appears to be a stressor that increases the likelihood of heart disease. People with depression have a faster heartbeat even when at rest (Moser et al., 1998) and tend to have high blood pressure (Carney et al., 1999). It isn't surprising, then, that those who have had an episode of depression have a higher risk of developing heart problems, and once having had a heart attack, those who are depressed are more likely to have further health problems (Frasure-Smith et al., 1999). When the depression is treated, however, these stress-related responses subside, and heart rate and blood pressure decrease (Kolata, 1997).

Atherosclerosis: A medical condition characterized by plaque buildup in the arteries.

Sleep

Al was having a difficult time sleeping. Could stress be affecting his sleep? In fact, stress and health problems can affect sleep; for instance, whether someone is able to fall asleep once in bed with the lights out or whether he or she feels rested in the morning. In addition, not getting enough sleep—sleep deprivation—can affect your health and ability to cope. To understand this reciprocal relationship, we need to know more about sleep.

Stages of Sleep: Working Through the Night

Some people think that sleep is like an electric light—either on (awake) or off (asleep). Until the invention of the electroencephalograph (EEG) (see Chapter 2) in 1928, that is what scientists used to think as well (Hobson, 1995). With the use of this new technology, they learned that **sleep**, a naturally recurrent experience during which normal consciousness is suspended, is not a single state. By using EEGs to record brain activity during sleep, researchers discovered several different types of sleep, which occur in five stages during the night. Everyone proceeds through these stages, but people differ in how much time they spend in each stage (Anch et al., 1988).

The initial sleep stage, lasting approximately five minutes and sometimes described as **hypnogogic sleep**, marks the transition from relaxed wakefulness to sleep. In Stage 1 sleep, your breathing becomes deeper and more regular, and the EEG registers brain waves that are less regular and of lower amplitude than those that mark the waking state (see Figure 10.3). You can be awakened relatively easily from Stage 1 sleep, and if you are, you do not feel as if you have been asleep at all. In this stage you may "see" flashing lights and geometric patterns, experience a gentle falling or floating sensation, or feel your body jerk suddenly and rather violently in a movement called a hypnic jerk.

In Stage 2, once you are clearly asleep, your EEG pattern begins to record *sleep spindles*, brief bursts of brain activity measuring 12 to 14 Hz, and single high-amplitude waves (this pattern, known as the *K-complex*, is shown in Figure 10.3).

Sleep: The naturally recurrent experience during which normal consciousness is suspended.

Hypnogogic sleep: Characterized by the experience of gentle falling or floating, or "seeing" flashing lights and geometric patterns; describes Stage 1 sleep.

Figure 10.3 Brain Waves During the Stages of Sleep

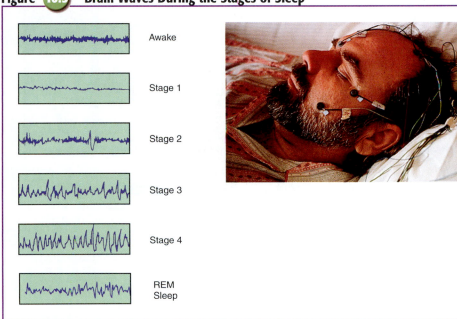

Awake

Stage 1

Stage 2

Stage 3

Stage 4

REM Sleep

Recordings show that brain waves differ by both amplitude (the height of the wave) and frequency (how often they occur). By examining individuals' EEG patterns when asleep, which differ from their EEG patterns when awake, researchers have identified five phases of sleep, each with its own unique EEG pattern.

You are now more relaxed and less responsive to your environment, although still relatively easy to awaken. But if you are awakened now, you will most likely report that you have been asleep. This phase lasts for approximately 20 minutes.

In Stages 3 and 4, your brain produces *delta waves*—slow, high-amplitude waves of 1 to 2 Hz on your EEG (see Figure 10.3). In Stage 3, 20% to 50% of EEG-recorded brain activity is in the form of delta waves; in Stage 4, the proportion is greater than 50%. In Stage 3, your heart rate and body temperature decrease, and you are no longer easily awakened. By the time you reach Stage 4, you are in a very deep sleep indeed, so deep that attempts by a friend (or an alarm clock) to wake you won't readily succeed. If you do wake up directly from this stage, you are likely to be briefly disoriented. During Stage 4 sleep, your heart rate, blood pressure, breathing, and body temperature slow down; all are now at their lowest ebb.

REM Sleep

About an hour after going to sleep, you begin to reverse the sleep cycle, coming back from Stage 4 through Stages 3 and 2. Instead of going all the way back to Stage 1, though, you now enter a state of *rapid eye movement (REM)* under the lids and, as shown in Figure 10.3, your EEG registers marked brain activity—even more activity than when you are awake. It is in this stage of sleep that you are likely to have dreams vivid enough to remember. During **REM sleep**, your breathing and heart rate are fast and irregular, and your genitals may show signs of arousal (men may have an erection; women may have increased genital blood flow and vaginal lubrication). These events occur in REM sleep regardless of the content of your dreams, unless a dream is particularly anxiety-provoking, in which case genitals may not be aroused (Karacan et al., 1966). During REM sleep, your muscles are relaxed and unresponsive; in fact, except for the muscles needed for the respiratory and vascular systems, your muscles are so paralyzed that you could not physically enact the behaviors in your dreams. Nevertheless, your brain remains more active than usual; for this reason, REM sleep is sometimes called **paradoxical sleep.**

After REM sleep, you descend again through at least some of the earlier stages, and then return, as shown in Figure 10.4. Each cycle takes about 90 minutes and

Figure 10.4 The March of Sleep Cycles

During the earlier part of the night, more time is spent in Stages 3 and 4, but later in the night, REM periods lengthen and Stages 3 and 4 shorten, eventually disappearing.

Figure **10.5** **Proportion of REM Sleep Over a Lifetime**

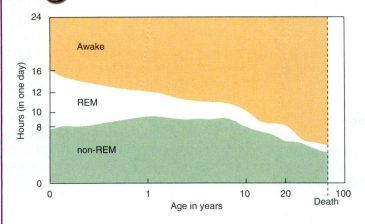

As we get older, we spend less time sleeping overall and less time in REM sleep.

occurs four or five times each night. However, the time you spend in each stage varies over the course of the night, and the course of a lifetime.

The phrase "I slept like a baby" turns out to have more truth to it than most of us realize. Infants sleep longer than adults (13 to 16 hours per night in the first year; see Figure 10.5) and have a higher percentage of REM sleep. They often enter REM immediately after falling asleep and change stages often. With age, this percentage changes so that when you enter your forties, the amount of time spent in deep, slow-wave sleep begins to decrease. With less slow-wave activity, your sleep is shallower and more fragmented, you wake more easily, and the sleep you do get is less satisfying (Hobson, 1995). Stage 4 sleep is even less frequent as you move from middle age to older adulthood. With increasing age, the decreased production of hormones involved in the sleep process make deep sleep difficult (Center for the Advancement of Health, 1998; Klinkenborg, 1997). As the quality of your sleep declines, so does its restorative effect on the cardiovascular and endocrine systems.

Why Do We Dream?

In addition to the biological changes that occur in sleep, there is a distinct change in consciousness—that of dreaming. It is *not* true that dreams take place only during REM sleep, but it *is* true that the dreams that take place during REM sleep are more memorable than those occurring during non-REM, or NREM, stages (Dement, 1974). If awakened during REM sleep, people recall dreams 78% of the time, compared with 14% recall during NREM sleep; moreover, NREM dreams are less vivid, less story-like, and less emotional (Farthing, 1992).

Dreams can offer us a pleasant respite from the daily grind, bring us terror in the form of a nightmare, or leave us puzzled about their confusing or curious content. In some societies, such as the Maya, telling dreams to others can provide a way to communicate feelings or solve problems (Degarrod, 1990; Tedlock, 1992).

Researchers and nonresearchers alike have long sought to know why we dream. The first modern dream theory was proposed by Sigmund Freud. Freud (1900), convinced that dream content originates in the unconscious—outside our conscious awareness—dubbed dreams the "royal road to the unconscious." Further, Freud believed that dreams allow us to fulfill unconscious desires. Such *wish fulfillment*

"WHEN I GROW UP I'D LIKE TO BE LIKE YOU, EXCEPT I DON'T KNOW IF I COULD SLEEP THAT MUCH."

Is this cartoon based on fact? How can we understand Dennis's comment if we know that children sleep more than adults, and much more than older adults?

Can someone interpret your dreams? Although dream interpretation can be interesting and fun, it is unclear that any meaning inferred from the content of dreams is accurate.

may not always be apparent from the **manifest content** of a dream, that is, its obvious, memorable content. We have to dig to find the **latent content** of the dream, its symbolic content and meaning, which, according to Freud, might reflect sexual or aggressive themes associated with an inner conflict. Although Freud's theory of the unconscious origin of the content of dreams has yet to be supported by solid, objective evidence, the idea of dream interpretation has both ancient appeal and present fascination—witness the large number of dream interpretation books and Web sites on the Internet.

Freudians find dreams brimming over with meaningful, albeit disguised, content. The opposite view is at the heart of the **activation-synthesis hypothesis**, which contends that dreams arise from random bursts of nerve cell activity. These bursts may affect brain cells involved in hearing and seeing, and the brain's response is to try to make sense of the hodgepodge of stimuli (Hobson & McCarley, 1977), but the dreams do not disguise meaning, as Freud suggested (Goode, 1999a). The brain synthesizes the burst and stored information to create the experience of a dream. This theory would explain why dreams sometimes seem so bizarre and unrelated: Stickgold and colleagues (1994) asked people to write down their dreams and then literally cut their reports in half. They asked other people to reassemble each dream, deciding which half came first. This proved a very difficult task, a result that is understandable if dreams are merely attempts to interpret random activity and have no cohesive story line.

As part of his effort to understand consciousness, Crick also investigated dreams, which he believes are used to edit out unnecessary or accidental brain connections formed during the day (Crick & Mitchison, 1983, 1986). Other theories of dreaming focus on the reverse notion: that dreams are used to *strengthen* such connections. This view is supported by a study by Karni and colleagues (1994). Participants learned to discriminate between two visual stimuli before falling asleep; those who slept normally improved their performance on the task when tested the following morning. But participants who were awakened when they entered REM sleep did not improve when tested in the morning. In contrast, participants who slept but were deprived of slow-wave, Stage 4 sleep did not show any learning impairment—which suggests that REM sleep is crucial for cementing in memory information gleaned during the day.

The largest and most systematic study of the neurological bases of dreaming was reported by Solms (1997), of the London Hospital Medical College. Solms interviewed more than 350 stroke patients about the changed nature of their dreams after their strokes. Consistent with the idea that consciousness arises from many parts of the brain, Solms found that dreaming was affected by damage to any number of areas. Perhaps Solms's most intriguing discovery was that dreaming stopped completely if a patient had damage that disconnected parts of the frontal cortex from the brainstem and the limbic system. These connections coordinate brain areas involved in curiosity, interest, and alert involvement with goals in the world (Pankseep, 1985, cited in Solms, 1997). This finding suggests that dreaming is not simply the brain giving itself a neurological tune-up, but is connected with our needs, goals, and desires. Solms speculates that dreaming may occur in response to any type of arousal that activates brain structures involved in motivation (Goode, 1999a). However, the inhibiting mechanisms of sleep pre-

Manifest content: The obvious, memorable content of a dream.

Latent content: The symbolic content and meaning of a dream.

Activation-synthesis hypothesis: The theory that dreams arise from random bursts of nerve cell activity, which may affect brain cells involved in hearing and seeing; the brain attempts to make sense of this hodgepodge of stimuli, resulting in the experience of dreams.

vent us from acting on these thoughts or desires, thus converting them into a symbolic hallucination.

So, although we cannot yet definitively answer *why* we dream, we do know something about *how* we dream. We know that dreaming is a neurological process, involving brain activity. We don't know whether dreams represent deep desires and conflicts, random bursts of nerve cell activity, the editing of unneeded neural connections, or the strengthening of neural connections. But it is interesting that all these theories, despite their differences, agree that in some way the day's events, or the neural connections they instigate, affect dreams.

The Chemistry of Sleep: Ups and Downs

We spend about one third of our lives asleep. During that time our brains and bodies are working away, responding to outside stimuli such as light and dark, and sending out fluctuating levels of neurotransmitters and hormones. These chemical changes are crucial to our daily functioning.

When you are awake, the cells in the system that release the neurotransmitter acetylcholine are inhibited; when you are in REM sleep, they are activated (Hobson et al., 2000; McCarley & Hobson, 1975). Your dreams of walking, flying, or falling may occur because of the increased acetylcholine during REM, which activates the motor and visual areas of your brain and may cause you to dream of a wild roller-coaster ride or other types of motion (Hobson, 1995). Perhaps it is because of motor system activation that dreams, according to sleep researcher Hobson, rarely portray sedentary activities such as computing, reading, or writing (Kelley, 1998). Moreover, the cells in parts of your brainstem that produce other neurotransmitters, specifically serotonin and norepinephrine, are most active when you are awake. Sleeping pills work in part by blocking production of these two "wake-up" neurotransmitters (Garcia-Arraras & Pappenheimer, 1983).

The hormone melatonin, which is secreted by the pineal gland, plays a role in promoting sleep. The body normally begins secreting melatonin around dusk, tapering off production at dawn. A person who takes melatonin in pill form soon feels drowsy and, if undisturbed, falls asleep within a half an hour. Unlike other sleep aids, melatonin appears to induce a natural sleep, with the appropriate amount and time of REM and NREM sleep (Zhdanova & Wurtman, 1996). Some have argued that taking melatonin at the right times can help a traveler overcome jet lag, but this effect has not yet been proven scientifically.

Circadian Rhythms

Our brain activity and internal chemistry dance in time to the daily rhythm of light and dark in a pattern called **circadian rhythms** (*circadian* means "about a day"). Daily fluctuations governed by circadian rhythms include blood pressure, pulse rate, body temperature, blood sugar level, hormone levels, and metabolism. Every one of us has an internal clock that coordinates these fluctuations; this clock is regulated by a small part of the hypothalamus just above the optic chiasm, called the **suprachiasmatic nucleus (SCN)**, which is illustrated in Figure 10.6 on page 366. The suprachiasmatic nucleus registers changes in light, which lead it to produce hormones that regulate various bodily functions. Researchers have found a gene in mice that is responsible for the regulation of their daily clocks; tissues in the eyes and the suprachiasmatic nucleus of the hypothalamus generate the signals that let the mice know, among other bodily functions, when to sleep and when to awaken (Antoch et al., 1997). The rudiments of circadian rhythms appear in human infants as early as one week after birth (McGraw et al., 1999).

What happens to the human sleep–wake cycle in the absence of external cues of dark and light (except for electric light, which can be turned on and off at will) and cultural cues such as clocks? Volunteers who have lived this way as part of a research project ended up living a 24.9-hour day. In a variant of this study, in which

Circadian rhythms: The body's daily fluctuations in response to the dark and light cycle, which affects blood pressure, pulse rate, body temperature, blood sugar level, hormone levels, and metabolism.

Suprachiasmatic nucleus (SCN): A small part of the hypothalamus just above the optic chiasm that registers changes in light, which lead to production of hormones that regulate various bodily functions.

Figure **10.6** **The Suprachiasmatic Nucleus and the Optic Chiasm**

This illustration of a human brain shows the proximity of the SCN to the optic chiasm. Given the SCN's role in regulating circadian rhythms, it is not surprising that it is so close to the optic chiasm, which relays visual input about light and dark to the brain.

only subdued lighting was provided, with no opportunity for stronger reading light, participants were more likely to have a 24.2-hour day (Czeisler et al., 1999).

But what about people who are completely blind and cannot detect light at all? They too show evidence of a 24.9-hour day, with 76% of the blind people studied reporting difficulty falling asleep at their usual bedtimes, based on a 24-hour day (Coren, 1996; Miles et al., 1977). Thus the 24-hour schedule, so ingrained in us by the daily rotation of the earth, is not necessarily "natural" but instead is maintained by exposure to light–dark cycles, whether natural or artificial, and by cues from mechanical instruments such as clocks and radios.

Even within a 24-hour day, however, not everyone prefers to wake up or go to sleep at the same time. As you have no doubt noticed, some people are energetic and alert early in the morning, whereas others do not perk up until late morning or afternoon. People differ in the timing of their circadian rhythms: Morning people, or "larks," experience peak body temperature, alertness, and efficiency in the morning; evening people, or "owls," peak at night (Luce, 1971). Normally you are not aware of your circadian rhythms until you try to function well at your nonpeak time. If you're a night owl, for example, how do you feel when faced with a 9:00 A.M. class? Flying across time zones is bound to make you aware of your own circadian rhythms, especially if it's a long trip. Regardless of the time of day that finds you most alert, however, most people have a late-afternoon dip in energy level. More industrial and traffic accidents occur between 1:00 and 4:00 P.M. than at any other time of day (Klinkenborg, 1997). Perhaps it is not a coincidence that many societies have a siesta or tea break during this period.

Are you grouchy on a Monday morning? If so, it might be more than simply "waking up on the wrong side of the bed." Boivin and colleagues (1997), who studied mood and circadian rhythms, found that bad moods occurred during times of day when the participants' circadian clocks said they should be asleep. These results suggest that even minor alterations in a sleep schedule, relative to individual circadian rhythms, can have a noticeable effect on mood after awakening. Thus, if you go to bed later and sleep later on weekends, you may be adversely altering your circadian rhythms. You are, in a sense, putting yourself in another time zone for the weekend, so when Monday morning rolls around, you are hit with jet lag. Even fifth-grade children are affected by having to wake up earlier to go to school. Regardless of how much sleep they had, those children who had to be in school by 7:10 A.M. reported more daytime fatigue and poorer attention and concentration at school than those whose school day started at 8:00 A.M. (Epstein et al., 1998).

What can you do if your schedule conflicts with your natural circadian tendencies? One remedy is to sleep on a disciplined schedule seven days a week. If, as in the case of jet lag, that isn't possible, try exposing yourself to plenty of light on Monday mornings; this may help reset your internal clock.

Sleep Deprivation: Is Less Just as Good?

Al wasn't sleeping well. He wondered if his sleep deprivation was affecting his performance at work—it certainly felt like it did. He rarely slept more than six hours each night.

In today's world of overscheduled lives and 10-hour workdays, can anyone claim to be getting a natural amount of sleep? A 1998 survey by the National Sleep Foundation found that two out of three people are not getting enough sleep (defined as approximately 8 hours), and one of those three gets less than 6 hours each night. Falling asleep in a dull class *may* signal sleep deprivation; "boredom doesn't cause sleepiness, it merely unmasks it" (Dement, as cited in Brody, 1998). What else happens when you don't get enough sleep, or miss a night's sleep entirely?

When you don't get enough REM sleep on a given night, a higher percentage of the next night's sleep will be REM sleep (Brunner et al., 1990); this phenomenon is called **REM rebound.** You can become REM deprived by not getting enough sleep at either end (going to bed late or waking up early) or by using depressants of the central nervous system such as alcohol or sleep medications, which suppress REM sleep. If these substances are used habitually and then discontinued, REM rebound dreams can be so vivid, bizarre, and generally unpleasant that people resume their use to fall asleep, and to suppress dreaming as well. Some people with posttraumatic stress disorder (victims of rape or assault, for example) cite disturbing dreams or nightmares (Inman et al., 1990) as a reason for using alcohol or drugs before sleep.

If you have ever stayed up late, say, studying or partying, and then awakened early the next morning, you have probably experienced sleep deprivation. In fact, you may be sleep deprived right now. If so, you have company: 37% of adults claim to be so sleepy during the day that daily activities are affected (National Sleep Foundation, 1998). What happens as a result of sleep deprivation? Young adults who volunteered for a sleep deprivation study were allowed to sleep for only five hours each night, for a total of seven nights. After three nights of restricted sleep, volunteers complained of cognitive, emotional, and physical difficulties. Moreover, their performance on a visual motor task declined after only two nights of restricted sleep. Visual motor tasks usually require participants to concentrate on detecting a change in a particular stimulus, and then to respond as quickly as they can after they perceive the change by pressing a button (Dinges et al., 1997). Thus, you may be able to perform short mental tasks normally when sleep deprived, but if a task requires sustained attention and a motor response, your performance will suffer; driving a car is an example of such a task. In a survey by the National Sleep Foundation (1998), 25% of the respondents reported that they had at some time fallen asleep at the wheel; sleepy drivers account for at least 100,000 car crashes each year.

Moods are also affected by sleep deprivation (Dinges et al., 1997; Monk et al., 1997). The loss of even one night's sleep can lead to increases in the next day's level of cortisol (Leproult, Copinschi et al., 1997). As mentioned earlier in this chapter, cortisol helps the body meet the increased demands imposed by stress. However, sleep deprivation can lead to a change in cortisol level that, in turn, alters other bodily functions, creating an increased risk for diabetes. As we have seen, chronically increased cortisol levels can cause memory deficits (Sapolsky, 1996) and decreased immune system functioning (Kiecolt-Glaser et al., 1995).

And what about a series of all-nighters, when you get no sleep at all, as might occur during finals period? Results from volunteers who have gone without sleep for long stretches (finally sleeping after staying awake anywhere from 4 to 11 days) show profound psychological changes, such as hallucinations, feelings of losing

REM rebound: The higher percentage of REM sleep following a night's sleep deprived of REM.

control or going crazy, anxiety, and paranoia (Coren, 1996). Moreover, going without sleep alters the normal circadian rhythms of changes in temperature, metabolism, and hormone secretions (Leproult, Van Reeth et al., 1997). These findings are also seen in adult rats who are forced to stay awake. Within two weeks, they show major negative bodily changes; despite eating two and a half times their usual amount, they begin to lose weight. Moreover, their temperature does not stay in the normal range, and they die within 21 days (Rechtschaffen et al., 1983). Even rats deprived only of REM sleep (they are awakened each time they enter the REM stage) experience temperature regulation changes, but these changes are less extreme (Shaw et al., 1998). Results of a PET study on sleep-deprived humans found a different pattern of brain activation when learning verbal material, compared to the pattern of activation when not sleep deprived, suggesting an attempt to compensate for the brain changes induced by sleep deprivation (Drummond et al., 2000).

Thus, sleep deprivation affects us in at least three important psychological areas: mood, attention, and performance.

Troubled Sleep

Al's tiredness during the day was starting to wear him down, and drinking before bed didn't seem to help him sleep soundly. He craved a good night's sleep. Feeling tired during the day, or having difficulty sleeping, may be caused by insomnia or sleep apnea.

Insomnia. Al probably had insomnia. The symptoms of **insomnia** include repeated difficulty falling asleep or staying asleep, or waking too early. If you suffer from this disorder, you are certainly not alone. Half the adults in the United States experience occasional insomnia. Temporary insomnia may be related to environmental factors such as stress, which can cause increased sympathetic nervous system activity and make sleep difficult. When sleep does not occur rapidly, the stressed person becomes frustrated. The frustration serves to increase arousal, compounding the problem.

For many Americans insomnia is a way of life. Chronic insomnia may stem from other disorders, such as anxiety and depression, as you will see in Chapter 11. Sleeping pills are the most common, but not necessarily the most effective, treatment for insomnia. They not only suppress needed REM sleep but also are addictive. Moreover, people develop tolerance to sleeping pills, requiring larger and larger dosages to get the same effect.

What can you do if you have trouble sleeping? The following nonmedical techniques may help (Hobson, 1995; Lacks & Morin, 1992; Maas, 1998):

Restrict your sleeping hours to the same nightly pattern. When they were the First Couple, both Martha and George Washington went to bed promptly at 9:00 P.M. each evening (Seuling, 1978). The Washingtons were on to something: Keep regular sleeping hours. Avoid sleeping late in the morning, napping longer than an hour, or going to bed earlier than usual, all of which will throw you off schedule, creating even more sleep difficulties later. And try to get up at the same time every day, even on weekends or days off.

Control bedtime stimuli so that things normally associated with sleep are associated only with sleep, not with the frustration of insomnia. Use your bed only for sleep or sex (don't read or watch TV in bed). If you can't fall asleep within 10 minutes, get out of bed and do something else.

Avoid ingesting substances with stimulant properties. Don't smoke cigarettes or drink beverages with alcohol or caffeine in the evening. Alcohol may cause initial drowsiness, but it has a "rebound effect" that leaves many people wide awake in the middle of the night. Don't drink water close to bedtime; getting up to use the bathroom can lead to poor sleep.

Insomnia: Repeated difficulty falling asleep, difficulty staying asleep, or waking up too early.

Consider meditation or progressive muscle relaxation. Either technique can be helpful (see Chapter 12). Regular aerobic exercise four times a week may be a long-term solution, but it can take up to 16 weeks for the effect on insomnia to kick in (King et al., 1997).

Sleep Apnea. Snoring can be a nuisance to those sharing a room with a snorer, but it can also be a sign of a more troublesome problem. **Sleep apnea** is a disorder characterized by a temporary cessation of breathing during sleep, usually preceded by a period of difficult breathing accompanied by loud snoring. Breathing may stop for up to 70 seconds, startling the sleeper into a lighter state of sleep. This ailment, which affects 1% to 4% of American adults, can produce many such events each hour, preventing restful sleep (Klinkenborg, 1997). Perhaps this explains the results of a research study of medical students who snore versus those who do not: 13% of nonsnorers failed their exams, compared with 42% of frequent snorers (Ficker et al., 1999). If the snorers had sleep apnea, they would not function as well because of their troubled sleep.

Sleep apnea results when muscles at the base of the throat relax and consequently block the airway. In obese patients, weight loss can help reduce the obstruction, although normal-weight people also can have sleep apnea. A device called Continuous Positive Airway Pressure (CPAP) can assist a person's breathing while asleep; alternatively, surgery is sometimes recommended. Those with undiagnosed sleep apnea may take barbiturates to get a good night's sleep—this is unfortunate because barbiturates seriously compound the problem by depressing the central nervous system, interfering with the normal reflex to begin breathing again.

LOOKING AT LEVELS

Breast Cancer Support Groups

Knowing that stress can affect the immune system and the progression of cancerous tumors, we can examine the results of a study of the effectiveness of breast cancer support groups from the different levels of analysis. Spiegel, Bloom and colleagues (1989) conducted a study of 86 women with breast cancer that had spread to other parts of their bodies. All the women received treatment for the cancer, and 50% were assigned to a yearlong weekly breast cancer support group. The goal of the group was to improve the women's quality of life—to help them live "as fully as possible," communicate better with others, control pain, and master concerns about death. They were taught self-hypnosis for pain management but were not encouraged to think that their participation in the group would make them live longer. An unanticipated finding was that women in the support group survived twice as long as those who were not in the support group. How can a support group make such a difference? Although the exact mechanisms are not yet known, we can understand this remarkable phenomenon by looking at events at the levels of brain, person, and group. At the level of the brain, social support lowers stress, which in turn boosts immune functioning, including NK cell activity levels. In fact, these women had higher NK cell activity than the women in the control group. At the level of the person, Spiegel and his colleagues propose that the skills learned in the support group, such as pain management, may have increased interest in eating and decreased pain-related depressive symptoms, thereby elevating the immune system. This, in turn, encouraged better self-care and helped to eliminate feelings of hopelessness and perceived lack of control. The support group also may have motivated the women to comply more rigorously with their treatments and provided a sense of community (level of the group), decreasing isolation.

More recent research on the role of the support group for breast cancer patients has found that women who were not in a support group (as compared with women who were) were more likely either to tolerate chemotherapy poorly or to refuse that treatment entirely. Moreover, those who were not in a support group had higher levels of cortisol 4 to 8 months after their surgery and were more depressed than those who were in a support group (Kass, 1999). Events at the three levels interact: The more the breast cancer patients could control their pain and side effects, alleviate their depression, and feel less isolated, the more likely their immune systems were to increase functioning. And the better they felt about the group, the more enthusiastically and faithfully they participated in it.

1 *Can stress affect the immune system and make illness more likely?* Yes. Stress increases the production of glucocorticoids, which can depress the immune system, including the formation and functioning of white blood cells such as natural killer (NK) cells. This makes the body more vulnerable to infection, tumor growth, and slowed healing.

2 *Are stress and cancer related?* Although stress does not cause tumors to develop, increased glucocorticoid production (part of the stress response) can depress the level of tumor-fighting cells, such as natural killer cells, and can increase capillary growth that provides a blood supply to nourish a tumor. Conversely, decreasing the stress response leads to an increase in natural killer cells' ability to fight tumors. However, not all cancers are equally responsive to psychological stressors or their absence.

3 *Can stress cause a heart attack or heart disease?* The stress response causes blood pressure to increase and the arteries to narrow. These two events can promote atherosclerosis, the buildup of plaque. This requires the heart to work even harder to supply blood to the body and can lead to coronary heart disease. The course of heart disease can be affected by psychological and social factors, such as stress management and social support.

4 *What is the relationship between sleep and stress?* Stress can affect the ability to get a good night's sleep by causing either temporary or chronic insomnia. Also, a lack of sleep—sleep deprivation—can create stress by impairing attention, concentration, performance, and mood.

Strategies for Coping

Once the realization that he was truly in bad shape sank in, Al finally recognized that he needed to take action. He worried that his drinking was getting out of control. He looked around the office to see how other people were doing, how they were handling the stress of the difficult situation at work. He paid particular attention to Maya, who didn't seem ruffled by the unsettled atmosphere and the layoffs. Al was puzzled by her reaction, or apparent lack thereof, and he talked with Lisa about it. Lisa suggested that perhaps Maya had particularly effective ways of dealing with stress. She pointed out that the perception of stress depends not only on your view of a situation, but also on the conscious actions you take in response to the stressors. *Coping* is the inclusive term for the multitude of techniques that people employ to handle stress. Some of these may "come naturally," resulting from temperament; others can be learned; and some strategies are more adaptive than others.

1 What are the different types of coping strategies?

2 How do relationships affect stress and health?

3 What are mind–body interventions?

4 Do gender and culture play a role in coping?

Coping Strategies: Approaches and Tactics

Different people tend to use different coping strategies, and the use of a particular strategy may also depend on the situation. People may be born with a propensity to use certain strategies, and they can learn to use others.

Problem-focused coping: Coping focused on changing the environment itself, or how the person interacts with the environment.

Problem-Focused and Emotion-Focused Coping

One way to classify coping strategies is by considering whether they address internal or external circumstances (Carver et al., 1989). **Problem-focused coping** strate-

TABLE Problem-Focused and Emotion-Focused Coping Strategies

Source: Adapted from Carver et al. (1989).

STRATEGY	DESCRIPTION
Problem-Focused Strategies	
Active coping	Actively tries to remove or work around stressor, or to ameliorate its effects.
Planning	Thinks about how to manage stressor.
Instrumental social support	Seeks advice, assistance, information.
Suppression of competing activities	Puts other activities on hold to cope with stressor.
Restraint coping	Waits to act until the appropriate time.
Emotion-Focused Strategies	
Emotional social support	Gets moral support, sympathy, understanding from others.
Venting emotions	Focuses on and talks about distressing feelings.
Positive reinterpretation/growth	Reinterprets the situation in a positive way.
Behavioral disengagement	Reduces efforts to deal with the stressor (as occurs with learned helplessness).
Mental disengagement	Turns to other activities to distract attention from the stressor.

gies alter either the environment itself or the way in which the person and the environment interact (see Table 10.2). This type of coping is more common when people believe that their actions can affect the stressor, and it tends to be used by people with a high score on the Big Five personality factor conscientiousness (see Chapter 8; Watson & Hubbard, 1996). In contrast, **emotion-focused coping** strategies change a person's emotional response to the stressor (see Table 10.2). This type of coping usually decreases arousal. People are more likely to adopt emotion-focused coping when they do not think their actions can affect the stressor itself and so they must alter their perception of, or response to, the stressor.

Typically, people use more than one strategy in response to a given stressor. Whether a particular strategy is effective depends in part on whether a person is correct in assessing whether the environment can in fact be changed. For example, suppose Lisa assumes that if she gets straight A's in the spring term, she can probably get a scholarship to cover next year's tuition. Here she is approaching the need to pay for her education with the problem-focused coping strategy of planning: She is coping with a stressor by thinking about how to manage it (see Table 10.2). She works hard all spring and carefully rations her social time. Lisa is using two problem-focused strategies: active coping and suppression of competing activities. What Lisa doesn't know, however, is that the financial aid office has already awarded all of next year's scholarships before the end of the spring term, so her efforts for top grades do not help her achieve her goal of a scholarship. As this example demonstrates, although it is adaptive to try to exert problem-focused coping in the face of stressors, such a strategy is effective only when applied to factors that are controllable. Accurate information and appraisal are important to determine if this is the case.

The coping strategies people use are affected by the level of stressors in their lives: The more stressors they face, the more people are likely to use avoidance coping strategies such as distraction, or behavioral or mental disengagement, which aim to decrease the focus on the stressor and increase the focus on other matters (Ingledew et al., 1997). In *behavioral disengagement,* people reduce their efforts to deal actively with the stressor (Table 10.2). In its extreme form, this disengagement can lead to a sense of helplessness. In *mental disengagement,* people turn to other activities to distract their attention from the stressor. So, the more

Emotion-focused coping: Coping focused on changing the person's emotional response to the stressor.

stressors Al and Lisa have, the less likely they are to cope actively with them. Studies (with male participants) have indicated that those perceiving less control over events are less likely to use problem-focused coping strategies involving direct action and more likely to use emotion-focused strategies such as distraction and emotional support (David & Suls, 1999). If Al doesn't think anything he does at work ultimately affects whether he gets laid off, he is less likely to use active coping strategies.

Another type of emotion-focused coping is *venting* (see Table 10.2)—that is, focusing on and talking about the stressor. As noted earlier, venting anger does not help. But what about venting other emotions? Pennebaker (1989) asked a group of college students to write for 20 minutes a day for 4 consecutive days; they were told their writing samples would remain confidential. He gave half of them, referred to as the "emotional expressiveness" group, the following instructions:

> *During each of the 4 writing days, I want you to write about the most traumatic and upsetting experiences of your whole life. You can write on different topics each day or on the same topic for all 4 days. The important thing is that you write about your deepest thoughts and feelings. Ideally, whatever you write about should deal with an event or experience that you have not talked about with others in detail.*

Another group, serving as a control, was asked to write each day about superficial topics. In this study and other variants of it, students who were asked to write about an emotional topic were more likely to report negative moods immediately after writing, although their overall moods were more positive by the end of the school year (Pennebaker et al., 1990). Perhaps paradoxically, those who wrote about traumatic events were less likely to get sick (as measured by visits to the student health center) in the months following the expressive writing. Other studies asking medical students and first-year college students to write either about traumatic experiences or about the transition from high school to college had similar results (Pennebaker & Francis, 1996; Pennebaker et al., 1990), with the additional finding of enhanced immune function (Petrie et al., 1995, 1998). Written emotional expression among university employees was associated with decreased absenteeism from work (Francis & Pennebaker, 1992). Studies using expressive writing with people with asthma and rheumatoid arthritis found comparable results: Four months after writing, patients underwent a positive change in their health, as compared with patients who wrote about superficial matters (Smyth et al., 1999). It appears, however, that writing only briefly, say just a 3-minute outline of a traumatic experience, isn't enough emotional expression to derive the benefits; the participants must actively process their experiences by writing about them in detail (Páez et al., 1999). These studies suggest that focusing on and "working through" feelings about a traumatic experience has positive effects, although it may take a while for these effects to appear. "Venting" in this sense does not mean that internal "pressure" is released, as Freud believed. Rather this process could simply help a person come to terms with an emotion—to make sense of and make peace with emotional events.

Thought Suppression

Purposefully trying not to think about something emotionally arousing or distressing is **thought suppression** (Wegner et al., 1987). Suppose Al and Lisa used thought suppression. They would try not to think about Al's work situation and all that depended on it. However, research has shown that trying *not* to think about something can have the paradoxical effect of causing that "suppressed" thought to pop into consciousness more than not trying to suppress it. This phenomenon is referred to as a *rebound effect*. Research on the application of thought suppression to health and illness has shown that the act of suppressing emotional thoughts actually magnifies both the intensity of the thoughts and the autonomic reactions to those thoughts (Clark et al., 1991; Wegner et al., 1987). Attempts at suppressing thoughts that are emotionally charged (either positive or negative)

Thought suppression: The coping strategy that involves purposefully trying not to think about something emotionally arousing or distressing.

have also been associated with changes in the sympathetic nervous system (Gross & Levenson, 1997).

Pennebaker and colleagues (Petrie et al., 1998) examined the effects of both emotional expressiveness and thought suppression. Their study began in the usual way by dividing the participants, in this case medical students, into two groups: an "emotional expressiveness" group and a control group. They asked the emotional expressiveness group to write about a stressful event and the control group to write about something superficial. However, after spending 15 minutes writing, half the students in each group were then asked to try to put what they had written out of their minds. The other half of each group was asked to focus exclusively on what they had written. The study found that thought suppression led to decreases in some aspects of immune functioning, regardless of the type of thoughts participants were trying to suppress (stressful or superficial). Moreover, those who had written about a stressful event viewed the study as having had more of a positive impact in their lives, and as more meaningful, than did the control group, regardless of whether they were asked to use thought suppression. These results, along with those of similar studies, point to the positive effects of emotional expression on the immune system and the negative effects of thought suppression (Futterman et al., 1992; Pennebaker, 1993).

Aggression: Coping Gone Awry

For good or ill, one way to cope with stressors is by **aggression,** which has been defined as "behavior directed toward the goal of harming another living being who is motivated to avoid such treatment" (Baron & Richardson, 1994, p. 5). Thus, couples who were more verbally and physically aggressive with each other were more likely to report a higher number of stressful events than couples who were not as abusive (Straus, 1980). However, this is of course only a correlation, and thus cause and effect are unclear: It is possible that stress leads to aggression, but it is also possible that people who are abusive *create* more stressful events in their lives by their aggressive manner (see Chapters 6 and 8 for detailed discussions of how people create their own microenvironments). However, using both correlational designs, which assess only whether two factors vary together, not whether one causes the other, and experimental ones, which can reveal causation, investigators have found a number of specific stressors that are associated with or lead to aggression.

External factors in the environment, such as noise and heat, can spark aggression in some people, and the target is usually innocent people who happen to be in the line of fire. Depression and pain are also associated with increased aggression (Berkowitz, 1998). These unpleasant experiences have in common the ability to predispose people to make a negative appraisal of a stimulus, particularly if the potential for threat is ambiguous. For instance, if Al has a headache, he may be more likely to assume that a colleague's comment ("Hey Al, quitting early?" on a day he's going to pick up Lisa for a weekend visit) has hostile intent than if he were pain-free. Rather than taking the remark as office kidding, he might worry that he was viewed as a slacker and thus a good candidate to be laid off next.

Although external stressors such as noise and pain can clearly lead to inaccurate and negative appraisals of a stimulus, some people are more likely than others to make a negative appraisal of an ambiguous, or even neutral, stimulus, even without the presence of such stressors. The propensity to misread the intentions of others, interpreting them negatively, is referred to as the **hostile attribution bias** (Dodge & Newman, 1981; Nasby et al., 1979). Because Al doesn't have a hostile attribution bias, he would not normally interpret his colleague's statement as a threat.

Frustration, which results when an obstacle is placed in the way of achieving expected gratification, has long been thought to be a precursor to aggression (Dollard et al., 1939). An implication of this view is the prediction that when unemployment is high, frustration will also be high, as will aggression. And in fact,

Aggression: Behavior directed toward harming another living being who is motivated to avoid such treatment.

Hostile attribution bias: The propensity to misread the intentions of others as negative.

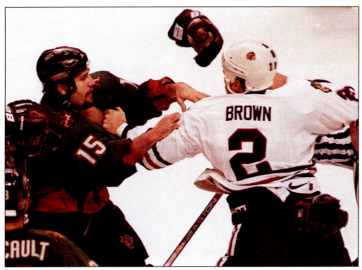

Some people are more aggressive than others. For example, the personality trait of aggressiveness (measured by a self-report paper-and-pencil test) predicts actual aggressive behavior. Hockey players who scored higher on aggressiveness before the hockey season spent more time in the penalty box for aggressive penalties, but not for nonaggressive penalties (Bushman & Wells, 1998).

researchers have found increased rates of homicide and domestic abuse when unemployment is high (Berkowitz, 1998).

Most stressors lead to an unpleasant internal state and increased negative mood, which in turn leads to the fight-or-flight response. Whether a person responds to this internal state with aggression is determined in part by the person's biology (including his or her genes, hormones, arousal levels, and central nervous system traumas or abnormalities); in part by his or her thoughts, beliefs, feelings, and expectations; in part by his or her history of reinforcement and observational learning; and in part by the culture's expectations of appropriate behavior. And all these factors interact (Berkowitz, 1998).

Clearly, however, not everyone responds to an unpleasant emotional state and negative mood with aggression. Some people, whose initial response to a threat is fear, will try to "flee" by escaping or avoiding whatever instigated the negative mood. Others will respond initially with irritation, annoyance, or anger (see Figure 10.7). Berkowitz proposes that this initial response is then tempered by further cognitive processing about the desired goals and expectations of punishment, reward, or harm, allowing people to make a final determination of a feeling of anger or fear, although some people fight or flee without further appraisal.

If aggression is defined by physical acts, then as children and adults, males are more aggressive than females. The results of a meta-analysis by Eagly and Steffen (1986) found that females are less likely to be aggressive if they think the aggres-

Figure 10.7 Factors Leading to Aggression

When do an unpleasant emotional state and negative mood lead to aggression? Various factors, at the level of the brain, person, and group, and their interactions, help determine whether aggression will be the end result. (Adapted from Berkowitz, 1998, p. 50.)

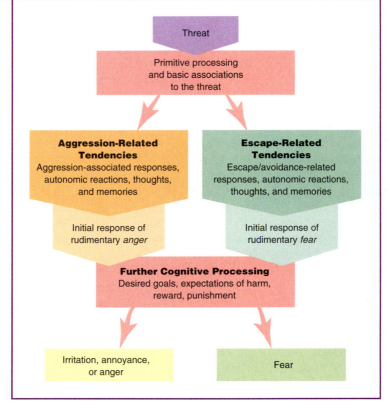

sion will physically harm another person, backfire on themselves, or cause them to feel considerable guilt or shame. However, when considering acts of aggression that do not cause physical harm, such as hurting other people's relationships (or threatening to do so), males are not necessarily more aggressive than females. Nonphysical aggression includes threatened or actual social exclusion of a friend, gossiping, or withdrawing acceptance of another person. Because of her gender (that is, the social expectations for someone of her sex), Lisa may be less likely to shove someone when she feels aggressive; however, she might gossip about someone, or slight that person in some way. *Relational aggression* is the term for nonphysical aggression that damages relationships or uses relationships to injure others psychologically, for example, by socially excluding them (Crick & Grotpeter, 1995); relational aggression is instigated more by females than by males.

Males and females differ with regard to the types of situations likely to elicit aggression, whether physical or verbal. Results from a meta-analytic study show that males are more likely to be aggressive in response to criticism of their intellectual ability, and females are less likely to respond aggressively (Bettencourt & Miller, 1996).

Not surprisingly, hostile people are more likely than others to behave aggressively (Anderson & Bushman, 1997). However, determining why some people use aggression as a coping strategy is more difficult than you may think. Conventional wisdom, at least in the United States, has been that aggression is more likely to be perpetrated by people who feel badly about themselves—that is, who have low self-esteem—and that their aggression toward others is a way of bolstering their view of themselves. Is conventional wisdom right? Recent lines of research indicate that the answer is a resounding no (Baumeister et al., 1996; Bushman, 1998). On the contrary, most aggressors are people who think exceedingly well of themselves (that is, have high self-esteem) and experience an insult as a threat to their positive self-view. Their aggression is a response to a perceived threat (Bushman, 1998). Not *all* people with high self-esteem are likely to be more aggressive; the aggressors in this group are a subset of people whose positive view of themselves may be either overinflated (that is, it doesn't correspond to reality) or unstable (Baumeister et al., 1996). This subset may view a threat to their positive self-image as likely to lead to a drop in self-esteem and thus defend against this drop with aggressive behavior.

This subcategory of aggressive people high in self-esteem has been referred to as *narcissists:* people who think well of themselves but whose feelings of high self-esteem are not firmly grounded in reality (Bushman, 1998). That is, they have an overinflated, unjustified positive view of themselves. Other people who are high in self-esteem may have a well-founded self-assessment. The concept of narcissism (or exaggerated self-love, as originally conceived by Freud) takes its name from the Greek myth of Narcissus, who fell in love with his own reflection in the water, pined away, and died from unrequited love of his own image. Just as men are more likely to be physically aggressive, men also score higher on scales of narcissism (Bushman, 1998); they also have higher self-esteem in general.

Imagine that you agreed to participate in a psychological study and, as part of the study, wrote an essay on some topic. You get the essay back with the comment, "This is the worst essay I've ever read." Later, you are competing with the person who wrote this comment on a reaction time test (like the one described in this chapter, pp. 356–357), in which the winner sets the loudness of a buzzer. How would you respond? How obnoxious would you let the sound be? Bushman (1998) hypothesized that people who score high on narcissism would be more likely to behave aggressively than those who score low, and indeed that is what he found. For high narcissists, a poor evaluation endangered their view of themselves, and was enough to elicit aggression toward the person doing the evaluating. Low narcissists were less likely to perceive negative evaluations of their essays as threats, and they were less aggressive. Not only was Bushman correct in his prediction, but he also found that high narcissists were more likely to be aggressive *even if their*

On April 20, 1999, Littleton, Colorado's Colombine High School students Dylan Klebold (left inset) and Eric Harris (right inset) killed 14 people (including themselves). It was reported that Eric Harris would get enraged at the smallest slight (Lowe, 1999), as would be predicted from the work on aggression and threats to self-esteem among narcissists. Before the rampage, Harris had received several rejections, including a rejection for entry into the Marine Corps 5 days before the killings.

essays were positively received; a negative evaluation simply increased their aggressive behavior. For narcissists, then, it appears that *any* evaluation is a stressor that threatens their view of themselves.

Thus, to someone whose high self-esteem is unwarranted or unstable, accurate feedback (such as justified criticism) is unwelcome. It will be perceived as a threat and will elicit an aggressive response (Baumeister et al., 1990, 1996). The aggression serves to punish the evaluator (and thus discourage a repetition) and may even cause the evaluator to "undo" the evaluation by saying it was in error. The aggression also allows the narcissist to feel superior by establishing dominance over the evaluator and thus restoring some measure of positive self-esteem. In reviewing the literature on rape and murder, Baumeister and his colleagues (1996) find evidence supporting the theory that these forms of aggression are related to a threat to shaky or unstable high self-esteem. This work on aggression also helps explain some triggers to violence in the workplace: Not getting an expected or hoped-for promotion or raise might be experienced as a threat by someone with unstable high self-esteem. Some have suggested that nationalism, the belief that one's own country is superior to others, is narcissism on a grand scale. Prejudice, oppression, and genocide may stem from the same root—threatened self-esteem—on a cultural level (Baumeister et al., 1996).

Other personality traits may lead people to seek out situations that are more likely to elicit aggression. People who are sensation seekers (see Chapter 8) may be more prone to be in situations that are likely to lead to violence (Gottesman et al., 1997). At least some of these personality variables have a moderate level of heritability (see Chapter 8).

We are all, at one time or another, confronted by stressors that can elicit aggression; Thornton Wilder has written, "We have all murdered, in thought." Why do only some of us act on our aggressive thoughts? Baumeister and Boden (1998) propose that the answer may lie in the difficulty aggressive people have in regulating, or controlling, themselves. In turn, the ability to control ourselves and our impulses toward aggression are related to a host of factors, including community standards, the likelihood of punishment, our ability to monitor our behavior, and a conscious decision *not* to control ourselves (as occurs when people, knowing the likely outcome will be physical aggression, still decide to drink or use drugs).

Drugs and Alcohol

Al started out drinking to help him get to sleep. Now, however, he drinks because he feels it helps him unwind from the day, from the stress and anxiety of work. Al's drinking illustrates how substances—drugs and alcohol—are used as coping strategies. Although the use of substances may change the perception of the stressor while someone is in an altered state of consciousness, substance use as a coping strategy does not change the stressor, nor does it provide any lasting change in how the stressor is viewed. At what point does such a coping strategy become problematic and maladaptive?

A woman drinks heavily, but only over the weekend, and she never misses work because of it. Is she an alcoholic? How about the man who smokes marijuana at the end of the day to feel relaxed, or the student who downs four cups of caffeinated coffee each evening while studying? Have these people crossed some biological or psychological line between use and abuse? The American Psychiatric Association (1994) has developed three main criteria for **substance abuse:** (1) a pattern of substance use that leads to significant distress or difficulty functioning in major areas of life (for instance, at home, work, or school or in relationships); (2) substance use that occurs in dangerous situations (for instance, while or before driving a car); and (3) substance use that leads to legal difficulties.

Substance dependence results from chronic abuse. It is characterized by seven symptoms (see Table 10.3), the two most important of which are tolerance and withdrawal (American Psychiatric Association, 1994). **Tolerance** is the condition, resulting from repeated use, in which the same amount of a substance produces a diminished effect (thus, more of the substance is required to achieve the same effect). Tolerance typically occurs with the use of alcohol, barbiturates, amphetamines, and opiates such as morphine and heroin. Withdrawal is the cessation of the use of a substance; **withdrawal symptoms** are the uncomfortable or life-threatening effects that may be experienced during withdrawal. Substance abuse presents costs to society as a whole as well as to the individual: In 1994 in New York City, for example, the cost of substance abuse and addiction was estimated to be over $20 billion, including treatment, prevention, the criminal justice and social service systems, and business-related costs (National Center on Addiction and Substance Abuse at Columbia University, 1994).

TABLE 10.3 The Seven Symptoms of Substance Dependence

Source: American Psychiatric Association (1994).

1. Tolerance.
2. Withdrawal.
3. Larger amounts of substance taken over a longer period of time than intended.
4. Unsuccessful efforts or a persistent desire to decrease or control the substance use.
5. A lot of time spent in obtaining the substance, using it, or recovering from its effects.
6. Important work, social, or recreational activities are given up as a result of the substance.
7. Despite knowledge of recurrent or ongoing physical or psychological problems caused or exacerbated by the substance, substance use continues.

Depressants: Focus on Alcohol. The **depressants,** also called *sedative-hypnotic drugs,* include barbiturates, alcohol, opiates, and antianxiety drugs such as Valium. Drugs in this category tend to slow a person down, decreasing the user's behavioral activity and level of awareness.

Approximately 9% of adults in the United States (14 million people) are considered to have either alcohol abuse or dependence (Leary, 1997), and more than 5% are considered to be heavy drinkers. The younger people are when they start

Substance abuse: Drug or alcohol use that leads to legal difficulties, causes distress or difficulty functioning in major areas of life, or occurs in dangerous situations.

Substance dependence: Chronic substance abuse that is characterized by seven symptoms, the two most important being tolerance and withdrawal.

Tolerance: The condition of requiring more of a substance to achieve the same effect (or the usual amount providing a diminished response).

Withdrawal symptoms: The onset of uncomfortable or life-threatening effects when the use of a substance is stopped.

Depressant: A class of substances, including barbiturates, alcohol, opiates, and antianxiety drugs, that depress the central nervous system, decreasing the user's behavioral activity and level of awareness; also called *sedative-hypnotic drugs.*

drinking, the more likely they are to develop an alcohol disorder (Grant & Dawson, 1997). Binge drinking, defined as four or more drinks per episode, occurs on some college campuses, in some states more than others. College students in California are less likely to be binge drinkers than their counterparts across the nation, perhaps because California students are older on average and more likely to be married (Wechsler et al., 1997), and thus presumably more mature. Men are more likely than women to be binge drinkers (Schulenberg et al., 1996); women at women's colleges tend to binge drink less than do their female counterparts at coeducational colleges (Dowdall et al., 1998). Binge drinking is likely to occur in contexts in which the objective is to get drunk (Schulenberg et al., 1996). People who engage in binge drinking are also at risk for other alcohol-related behaviors, such as driving while their functioning is impaired (Wechsler et al., 1998).

A blood alcohol content of 0.1% (well over the legal limit for driving in most states) is usually produced by having one drink for every 40 pounds of body weight in one hour (see Table 10.4); one drink is equivalent to 12 ounces of beer, 5 ounces of wine, or 1.5 ounces of 80 proof liquor (Grilly, 1994). The same amount of alcohol will have a slightly greater effect on a woman of the same size and weight as a man because men and women metabolize the drug differently (Frezza et al., 1990). Although the numbers in Table 10.4 are based on blood alcohol level, not everyone responds to the same dose of alcohol in the same way—some people have a more intense response than others. This response variability appears to be mediated in part by genes (Schuckit, 1999). People's expectations of what will happen to them as a result of drinking can also affect their behavior (see Kirsch & Lynn, 1999).

TABLE 10.4   Blood Alcohol Levels and Their Effects

Blood Alcohol Level*	Behavioral Effects
0.05	Lowered alertness, impaired judgment, release of inhibitions, feelings of well-being or sociability.
0.10	Slowed reaction time and impaired motor function, less caution.
0.15	Large, consistent increases in reaction time.
0.20	Marked depression in sensory and motor capability, decidedly intoxicated behavior.
0.25	Severe motor disturbance and impairment of sensory perceptions.
0.30	In a stupor but still conscious—no comprehension of events in the environment.
0.35	Surgical anesthesia; lethal dose for about 1% of adults.
0.40	Lethal dose for about 50% of adults.

*In milligrams of alcohol per 100 milliliters of blood.

Alcohol is classified as a depressant because it depresses the nervous system through its inhibiting effect on excitatory transmitters. Although the exact mechanisms are not yet known, alcohol changes the structure of the membrane of the neuron, altering neural transmission (Goldstein, 1994; Grilly, 1994). But depressants such as alcohol can also inhibit the action of inhibitory neurotransmitters, so some neurons fire that otherwise would be inhibited. Thus, in addition to depressing some neural activity, depressants activate neurons that otherwise would not fire. This phenomenon is called **disinhibition.**

Although it takes about an hour for alcohol to be fully absorbed into the blood, drinkers can feel an effect within a few minutes. The effects of alcohol depend on the dosage. At low doses, alcohol can cause a sense of decreased awareness and increased relaxation, and the drinker may become talkative or outgoing. At moderate doses, the drinker experiences slowed reaction time and impaired judgment (which is why drinking and driving don't mix). At higher doses, cognition, self-

Disinhibition: The inhibition of inhibitory neurons, which make other neurons (the ones that are usually inhibited) more likely to fire; usually occurs as a result of depressant use.

control, and self-restraint are impaired, and the drinker may become emotionally unstable or overly aggressive. "Barroom brawls" often occur because a drunk patron misconstrues a casual remark that otherwise might have passed unnoticed. As the effects of the alcohol take hold, the drinker's responses are more likely to be out of proportion to the situation. At very high doses, the drinker can have a diminished sense of cold, pain, and discomfort (which is why some people drink when in pain). At these high doses, the drinker may *feel* warmer. This sensation arises because alcohol causes dilation of the peripheral blood vessels, which increases the amount of blood circulating through the skin and makes the drinker both feel warmer and lose heat faster. Thus, heavy drinking in the cold increases the chance of hypothermia (that is, decreased body temperature) and frostbite. Such high doses can bring on respiratory arrest, coma, or death.

Steele and Southwick (1985) conducted a meta-analysis of the effects of alcohol on social behavior, specifically in "high-conflict" and "low-conflict" situations. The type of conflict considered here is within the person, between two opposing desires. Specifically, Steele and Southwick wanted to see whether the use of alcohol changes the way people behave when they experience such internal conflict. They found a pattern of what they called **inhibitory conflict:** If a person in a high-conflict situation was sober, his or her response was "both strongly instigated and inhibited"; that is, the person would both want to act and not want to act (an approach–avoidance conflict). A person might very much want to engage in a particular behavior, but the consequences (moral, legal, social, personal) were great enough to inhibit it. After drinking, however, the same person would not restrain his or her behavior. And the more alcohol consumed, the greater the likelihood of engaging in the act despite societal or other sanctions. When the conflict level was low, it was still possible to inhibit the behavior; only in high-conflict situations was inhibition overcome by alcohol. This finding explains how date rape can happen: When sober, a man might want to have sexual relations but be inhibited from using force. But under the influence of alcohol, he might be more likely to act—in a high-conflict, sexually charged situation, he might have difficulty attending to the consequences that would otherwise cause him to inhibit such aggressive behavior.

Steele and his colleagues also looked at the effect of alcohol on conflict in helping situations (Steele et al., 1985). After doing tedious and boring paperwork for 30 minutes, participants in the study were asked if they would agree to do more of the same, without additional pay, while waiting for the investigator to arrange for their payment. Some participants were given an alcoholic drink before the request for additional help, and some were given water. Some participants received more pressure to help (high-conflict), and some were asked simply if they would mind helping but were not pressured by personal appeal (low-conflict). In the low-conflict situation, alcohol had no effect, and participants were able to inhibit themselves from continuing the boring task. In the high-conflict situation, alcohol affected participants' ability to inhibit their response, and they were more likely to agree to help. This result is consistent with the earlier findings: Alcohol made it more difficult for participants to inhibit their responses in the high-conflict situation. This set of findings may explain why, after drinking some alcohol, people may have a harder time saying no to a sexual proposition in high-conflict circumstances, such as the conflict between the desire for sexual intimacy and the simultaneous wish (for either moral or personal reasons) to delay a sexual encounter. In general, when people experience a high-conflict situation as stressful, and drink before it to relieve the stress, their behavior will likely be different than if they had not been drinking. One solution is to abstain from alcohol if a high-conflict situation is likely to occur.

The results of many studies have shown that the use of alcohol facilitates aggressive behavior (Bushman & Cooper, 1990). You have already seen one path for increased aggression with alcohol use: Alcohol can make it difficult to inhibit behavior in a high-conflict situation. Aggression can also result from misreading a situation, as in the barroom brawl example. Alcohol impairs the ability to abstract

Inhibitory conflict: A response that is both strongly instigated and inhibited.

Alcohol myopia: The disproportionate influence of immediate experience on behavior and emotion, due to the effects of alcohol use.

and conceptualize information (Tarter et al., 1971) and to notice many situational cues (Washburne, 1956). This impairment results in **alcohol myopia**, "a state of shortsightedness in which superficially understood, immediate aspects of experience have a disproportionate influence on behavior and emotion" (Steele & Josephs, 1990, p. 923). Thus, stimuli that elicit aggression (such as someone's clenched fists or a date's refusal to have sexual intercourse) loom larger than stimuli that must be abstracted or require more thought (such as considerations that the aggressive behavior may be immoral, illegal, or unnecessary). Drinking also makes it more difficult to process ambiguous social situations, such as occasions when someone's words and body language are contradictory. For example, suppose friends have gone out drinking and all are now quite drunk. One of them might announce he is sick, but laugh about it. The others might not understand that their friend really *is* sick and needs medical care.

Given the fact that more than 50% of on-campus date rapes occur when men are under the influence of alcohol (Muehlenhard & Linton, 1987), some researchers (Johnson et al., 2000) set out to determine exactly how drinking might be involved. They asked male volunteers to drink different levels of alcohol, then watch one of two videos of a woman on a blind date. In one video, she exhibited friendly, cordial behavior; in the other, she was unresponsive. The men were then asked how acceptable it would be for a man to be sexually aggressive toward his date (see Figure 10.8). Among the men who viewed the video with the unresponsive woman, alcohol intake made no difference in the men's answers. However, alcohol intake did make a difference for the men who viewed the video of the friendly woman: Those men who had more to drink thought that sexual aggres-

Figure 10.8   Alcohol and Sexual Aggression

Male participants were assigned to one of four alcohol consumption groups: moderate alcohol intake, low alcohol intake, placebo alcohol intake (alcohol rubbed on the rim of glasses holding nonalcoholic drinks), and control group (drank ice water). The three alcohol groups did not know the strength of their drinks.

One group of men watched a video about a blind date in which the woman was very friendly; the other group watched a video about a blind date in which the woman was unresponsive and cold.

Regardless of alcohol intake, the participants who watched the unresponsive date were not very accepting of the idea of sexual aggression by the man and attributed any responsibility for aggression to *him.* In contrast, there was clear alcohol myopia in those who watched the friendly date: The more alcohol they drank, the more the men accepted the idea of sexual aggression toward the woman and the more they attributed any aggression by the man as being the *woman's* responsibility (Johnson et al., 2000).

sion toward a friendly date was acceptable. The alcohol impaired the men's ability to understand that the friendliness the woman showed did not mean that it was all right for a man to force her to have sex. This type of reasoning, which involves conceptualization and abstraction, was compromised.

Alcoholics come from all socioeconomic classes. Historically, more males than females have become alcoholics, and this pattern continues today, although the gap is narrowing (Nelson et al., 1998). Chronic alcohol abuse can cause severe memory deficits, even **blackouts**, periods of time for which the alcoholic has no memory of events that occurred while he or she was intoxicated. The chronic alcoholic often experiences difficulty with abstract reasoning, problem solving, and perceptual motor functions. It has been difficult for researchers to sort out to what degree these memory deficits are caused by the action of the alcohol itself or by the malnutrition that often accompanies alcoholism. Alcohol is highly caloric but contains very little in the way of nutrients; consequently, many heavy drinkers are inadequately nourished. Severe alcoholics may develop **Korsakoff's syndrome**, a disorder in which the brain's mammillary bodies are destroyed; these small structures receive input from the hippocampus that is critical for learning new information. Thus, these patients have profound learning and memory problems. They may be unable to learn the names of the nurses on the ward, and sometimes they cannot even remember why they are in the hospital; in general, they have grave difficulty learning new facts and the meanings of new words.

Barbiturates, including Amytal, Nembutal, and Seconal, mimic the effects of alcohol in that they depress the central nervous system. Usually prescribed to aid sleep or to reduce anxiety, they can be lethal when combined with alcohol. Users will develop both tolerance and withdrawal symptoms: Withdrawal may be accompanied by agitation and restlessness, hallucinations, and delirium tremens.

Stimulants: Focus on Cocaine. In contrast to depressants, **stimulants** excite the central nervous system, stimulating behavioral activity and heightened arousal. Low doses of amphetamines and cocaine can lead to a perception of increased physical and mental energy, diminished hunger, and a sense of invulnerability. Because "coming down" from this state is a disappointment, stimulant users often want to repeat the experience and so are at risk for continued drug use. Of all drugs, stimulants are the most likely to induce dependence.

In 1997 an estimated 1.5 million people in the United States used cocaine (Department of Health and Human Services, 1998). Cocaine is commonly inhaled in its powdered form, and it has a local anesthetic effect. The user has an enhanced sense of physical and mental capacity and a simultaneous loss of appetite. Chronic users develop paranoia, teeth grinding, and repetitive behaviors and may also experience disturbances in the visual field, such as seeing snow, or feel that insects ("cocaine bugs") are crawling on their skin. This latter sensation is actually the spontaneous firing of sensory neurons caused by the cocaine.

Cocaine exerts its effects by inhibiting the reuptake of dopamine and norepinephrine (Figure 10.9 on page 382). This increased presence of neurotransmitter in the synaptic cleft leads to a pleasurable, even euphoric, feeling. With continued use of cocaine, the drug becomes the main trigger for activation of the reward system, leading other sources of pleasure, such as food or sex, to have little or no effect (National Institute on Drug Abuse, 1998).

Cocaine in crystalline form, or **crack**, is usually smoked in a pipe ("free-basing") or rolled into a cigarette. Crack is faster acting and more intense in its effect than cocaine powder inhaled through the nostrils; however, because its effects last for only a few minutes, the user tends to take greater amounts of crack than of powdered cocaine. Crack cocaine has more potential for abuse and dependence (Cone, 1995). The user experiences a feeling of euphoria, perceived clarity of thought, and increased energy. Crack increases heart rate and blood pressure and constricts blood vessels—a potentially lethal combination. After the drug wears

Blackout: A period of time for which an alcoholic has no memory of events that transpired while intoxicated.

Korsakoff's syndrome: A disorder, related to alcoholism, in which the brain's mammillary bodies are destroyed, damaging learning and memory abilities.

Stimulant: A class of substances that excite the central nervous system, leading to increases in behavioral activity and heightened arousal.

Crack: Cocaine in crystalline form, usually smoked in a pipe (free-basing) or rolled into a cigarette.

Figure 10.9 **Action of Amphetamines on Neurotransmitters**

Cocaine and other amphetamines create their stimulant effects by blocking reuptake—preventing the normal reabsorption into the terminal button—of some norepinephrine and dopamine at the synaptic cleft. The net effect is more of these neurotransmitters in the synaptic cleft.

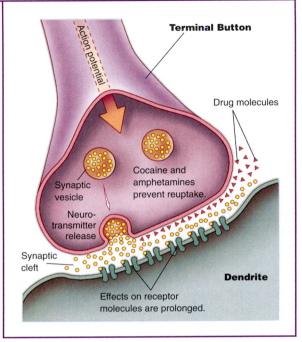

off, the user experiences a massive "crash," with an intense depression and intense craving for more crack. Both cocaine and crack can create strong dependence, particularly if injected or smoked. The user can develop tolerance; with crack, the development of tolerance is particularly swift. Sudden death can occur even in healthy people who use the drug occasionally.

Amphetamines are synthetic stimulants such as Benzedrine and dextroamphetamine (Dexedrine). They are usually taken in pill form or injected. With high doses, the user can suffer amphetamine psychosis, which is similar to paranoid schizophrenia (discussed in Chapter 11); symptoms include delusions, hallucinations, and paranoia. Chronic use of amphetamines stimulates violent behaviors (Leccese, 1991). MDMA (also known as ecstasy, or "e") is a neurotoxic amphetamine—it destroys certain neurons. Research on animals indicates that MDMA, used even once, can permanently damage neurons that produce serotonin, affecting memory, learning, sleep, and appetite (Fischer et al., 1995). Many of the side effects that occur with other stimulants also occur with MDMA.

Caffeine is present in coffee, tea, chocolate, and colas, among other foods. It causes increased alertness, raises the pulse and heart rate, and produces insomnia, restlessness, and ringing in the ears. There is some degree of tolerance, and chronic users will experience withdrawal headaches if they miss their customary morning coffee. *Nicotine,* present in cigarettes and tobacco in any form, can cause increased alertness and relaxation, as well as irritability, increased blood pressure, stomach pains, dizziness, emphysema, and heart disease. Nicotine works by triggering the release of several neurotransmitters that lead to a pleasurable sensation. Nicotine is addictive, causing some level of tolerance and withdrawal symptoms when its use is stopped.

Narcotic Analgesics: Focus on Heroin. Certain drugs, including heroin, morphine, codeine, Percodan, and Demerol, are called **narcotic analgesics** because they are strongly addictive drugs that dull the senses and provide analgesia; that is, they relieve pain. These drugs affect certain endorphin receptors (see Chapter 3). Generally, drugs of this type are prescribed to relieve pain, severe diarrhea, pro-

Amphetamines: Synthetic stimulants.

Narcotic analgesic: A class of strongly addictive drugs, such as heroin, that relieves pain.

tracted coughing, and troubled sleep. Heroin, an illegal drug, is one of the stronger narcotic analgesics. Like morphine, from which it is derived, heroin is an **opiate**, produced from the opium poppy.

Heroin can bring about a feeling of relaxation and euphoria, but these effects are very short-term and are followed by negative changes in mood and behavior. Like other opiates, heroin is a central nervous system depressant, causing a slowing of neural activity in brainstem areas responsible for respiration and coughing, as well as in other areas of the brain. When heroin is in the body, the user may experience pupil constriction, slower breathing, and lethargy. Tolerance and withdrawal symptoms occur, usually with periods of yawning, chills, hot flashes, restlessness, diarrhea, and goose bumps on the skin, followed by up to 12 hours of sleep.

As well as activating the dopamine-based reward pathway in the brain, heroin and other opiates work by binding to the brain's opiate receptors, where the body's own opiates such as endorphins usually bind. This creates a negative feedback loop, leading the body to decrease its production of endorphins and leaving the heroin user without natural means to relieve pain. Thus, more heroin is needed to achieve the analgesic effect. When the user tries to quit, endorphins do not kick in to alleviate the withdrawal symptoms, thus heightening the discomfort—and making it difficult to quit.

Hallucinogens: Focus on LSD. A **hallucinogen** is a substance that induces the perceptual experiences known as hallucinations. Hallucinogens include mescaline, peyote, psilocybin, lysergic acid diethylamide (LSD), phencyclidine (PCP), ketamine ("Special K"), and marijuana. In general, all but marijuana can cause visual hallucinations at moderate dosages; much higher dosages are needed before marijuana will do so.

LSD is a synthetic substance that produces perceptual alterations. Exactly how LSD works is not well understood, but it is known to alter the functioning of serotonin. Users commonly experience visual hallucinations, which often include geometric shapes, vivid colors, and violent movement. At higher doses, geometric shapes give way to quickly changing meaningful objects. Users may feel as if they are becoming part of whatever they observe. Auditory hallucinations include hearing invented foreign languages or symphonies. These symptoms may last several hours, and the user's expectations can shape the experience induced by LSD.

Although some people report that they feel more creative as a result of taking LSD, research does not support the subjective experience of increased creativity after use (Dusek & Girdano, 1980). On the contrary, LSD can produce frightening experiences ("bad trips"), which could be caused by a change in dose, mood, expectations, and environment. A user may panic during a bad trip and need to be "talked down," repeatedly reminded that the frightening experience is in fact a drug-induced state that will wear off. Occasionally, suicide or murder takes place in the course of a user's hallucination. Hallucinations can recur without use of the drug; these spontaneous, perhaps alarming **flashbacks**, a common side effect, can happen weeks, even years, afterward, and can be triggered by entering a dark environment (Abraham, 1983).

The most common hallucinogen in America is marijuana, whose active ingredient is tetrahydrocannabinol (THC). Although marijuana is less powerful than most other hallucinogens, every year approximately 100,000 Americans attend treatment centers in an effort to stop using it (Blakeslee, 1997). The effects of marijuana are dependent on the user's mood, expectations, and environment: If alone, the user may experience drowsiness and go to sleep; if with others, the user may feel euphoric. The effects of the drug can be subtle, including perceptual alterations in which sights and sounds seem more vivid. Distortions of space and time are also common, and perceptual motor skills may be impaired, making driving unsafe (Petersen, 1977, 1979; Sterling-Smith, 1976).

Opiate: A narcotic, such as morphine, derived from the opium poppy.

Hallucinogen: A substance that induces hallucinations.

Flashback: A hallucination that recurs without the use of a drug.

The substance ketamine, similar to phencyclidine, is legally used as an anesthetic for animals. Use by humans can induce hallucinations, anesthesia, and stimulation of the cardiovascular and respiratory systems. Ketamine use is also associated with violence, a loss of contact with reality, and impairment in thinking (White & Ryan, 1996). Users are likely to develop tolerance and dependence.

Coping and Social Support

Social support, the help and support gained through interacting with others, buffers the adverse effects of stress. Certain types of positive relationships, such as a good marriage, positive contact with friends and family, participation in group activities, and involvement in a religious organization, can lengthen life expectancy. Just having such connections can have as much influence on mortality as being a nonsmoker or being physically active (House et al., 1988). In a study of over 4,000 men and women in Alameda County, California, death rates for socially isolated people were twice those of people with strong social ties (Berkman & Syme, 1979). Deaths were due not only to coronary heart disease, but also to cancer, infectious disease, and other causes. The benefits of social support can also be gained simply by holding hands or making some other kind of physical contact (Sapolsky, 1997); for those undergoing a painful and frightening surgical procedure, just talking with their doctors the night before surgery can affect recovery (Egbert et al., 1964). In a study of people with severe coronary heart disease, half the group without social support died within 5 years, three times the rate of those who had a close friend or spouse (Williams et al., 1992). Social support may also provide a buffer against depression: Among college students experiencing high levels of stress, those reporting high levels of social support were less likely to be depressed than those reporting lower levels of social support (Pengilly & Dowd, 1997).

Social support is also related to immune system functioning (Seeman et al., 1994). For example, participants who reported more loneliness had lower immune functioning (Kiecolt-Glaser et al., 1984). Looking at the relation between social support and catching a cold, researchers found that participants who had a wide range of acquaintances (friends, neighbors, relatives, work colleagues, people from social or religious groups, and so forth) were half as likely to catch a cold as those who were socially isolated (Cohen et al., 1997). The key is not the total number of supportive relationships, rather their variety. Not just any relationship will do the trick: Bad marriages are associated with suppressed immune function, at least in men (Kiecolt-Glaser et al., 1988), and relationships filled with conflict and criticism can increase stress.

Perceived social support, the subjective sense that support is available should it be needed, is distinct from the actual size and variety of your social network, and from **enacted social support**, specific support that is provided to you, such as a friend bringing you a meal when he or she knows you aren't feeling well. Research has shown that it is perceived support, not enacted support, that provides the buffer against stress (Cohen & Wills, 1985). It has also been shown that the perception of

The person (dressed in yellow) in the photo is receiving enacted social support. However, she may not necessarily have the sense that support is available when she needs it (perceived social support) because these two aspects of social support are not necessarily correlated. Also, what constitutes support may differ from person to person.

support is unrelated to actual support (Lakey & Heller, 1988). In addition, people who perceive low support tend to view a given social interaction more negatively (Lakey & Dickenson, 1994); if Al is such a person, that would explain both his reluctance to tell his friends about what is happening to him at work and his feeling that his interactions with his colleagues during this crisis are more negative than positive.

Mind–Body Interventions

The focus of mind–body interventions is not on changing a stressful stimulus, but on adapting to the stimulus. Mind–body interventions often address changes in awareness and consciousness. Natural methods of altering consciousness, such as relaxation techniques, meditation, and hypnosis (Wickramasekera et al., 1996), all involve a mind–body interaction and can lead to alterations in heart and breathing rates, hormone secretion, and brain activation. Even sitting quietly with your eyes closed for a few minutes causes a decrease in pulse rate (Forbes & Pekala, 1993). Moderate physical exercise also helps buffer the effects of stress (Brown, 1991).

Many mind–body interventions for people who are physically ill provide specific cognitive and behavioral coping strategies, relaxation training (to decrease arousal and increase perceived control), social support (Andersen, 1997), disease-related information, and a supportive environment in which to address fears about the illness. These interventions can lead to improvement in mood and immune system functioning (Fawzy et al., 1990; Zakowski et al., 1992), pain control (NIH Technology Assessment Panel, 1996), and decreases in emotional distress and poor coping strategies (Timmerman et al., 1998).

The effectiveness of placebos also illustrates the link between mind and body. Simply believing that you are receiving a remedy (even if it has no medicinal effects) can affect your immune system's functioning. Certain properties of the placebo itself and the way it is dispensed can make it more effective. If the person dispensing the treatment is friendly, is sympathetic, and shows an interest in the patient's problems, the placebo is more likely to be effective (Shapiro & Morris, 1978). Even the practitioner's own view of a placebo's effectiveness can make a difference: If the treatment provider has high expectations for the treatment, it is more likely to be effective (Shapiro, 1964). To avoid this effect, research with placebos often has a double-blind design, in which the provider doesn't know whether he or she is dispensing a placebo or active medication. In a review of research that reported successful results from five treatments (for three diseases) that were later proved worthless, Roberts and colleagues (1993) found that when presented enthusiastically, placebos were 70% effective.

The effectiveness of placebo medications is an illustration of the power of the mind–body interaction. Research shows that certain properties of a placebo medication can make it more or less effective. For example, placebo injections can be more effective than oral medication, capsules are more effective than pills, and more (placebo) pills work better than fewer (placebo) pills. Finally, the color of the capsule can make a difference: Blue capsules work best as tranquilizers; yellow, pink, and red ones work best as stimulants (Buckalew & Ross, 1981).

Gender, Culture, and Coping

Do men and women experience the same amounts of stress? Do people in different cultures experience different amounts of stress? Do they cope with stress to different degrees of effectiveness? Psychologists have begun to pose questions such as these in an effort to learn if stressors affect different groups of people differently.

There is some evidence that women in Western cultures experience more stress than men. A survey of 2,500 Swedes found that women, particularly younger women, reported feeling more hassled, depressed, anxious, and hostile (Scott & Melin, 1998). As women have entered the workforce, a number of studies have focused on the effects of their multiple roles: employee, wife, mother, daughter.

The effects of having multiple roles can be both positive and negative; when women are also parents, they tend to have more to do than men, experience more conflict among their different roles, and be less able than men to unwind at home (Clay, 1995). Women generally report more stress with multiple roles than do men, and women employed outside the home generally do more work than men in their "second shift" at home: cooking, cleaning, and shopping (Hochschild, 1989; Phillips & Imhoff, 1997). However, these multiple roles can also confer advantages: increased feelings of self-esteem and control (Pietromonaco et al., 1986), financial gain, social support from colleagues (Brannon, 1996), and decreased psychological stress (Abrams & Jones, 1994). Thus, although employment outside the home can be more stressful (particularly if there are children), it is not necessarily more stressful for women than men. Having financial and familial resources and control over the job (Taylor et al., 1997; Tingey et al., 1996), as well as a sense of mastery at work (Christensen et al., 1998), can reduce the stress of multiple roles.

Culture can help determine what constitutes a stressor, as well as when and how to ask for assistance in coping with stressors. Moreover, culture plays a role in helping people experience a sense of control over stressors. Different cultures bring different understandings to various stressors, creating meaning and defining how much control a person believes he or she has over the stressor. For example, cultures that view certain kinds of illness as a result of sin or as caused by enemies require different types of actions and different coping strategies.

Crowding is an example of a culturally defined stressor. In different cultures, different levels of density produce the perception of crowding. Members of Asian cultures experience less stress than Westerners in high-density living conditions; Asians have also developed ways of creating a sense of privacy in the midst of density, thus providing a sense of control (Werner et al., 1997).

Culture also plays a role in defining the choices of coping strategies, as well as in the use of social support (Aranda & Knight, 1997; Patterson et al., 1998). For instance, although family caregivers of patients with Alzheimer's disease in San Diego, California, and Shanghai, China, all reported more physical health problems and depression compared with noncaregivers in those cities, the Chinese caregivers reported less access to social support (Patterson et al., 1998).

In examining the effects of culture on heart disease, Marmot and Syme (1976) studied more than 3,000 Japanese American men in the San Francisco area. Men whose upbringing was more traditionally Japanese and who still maintained strong ties with the Japanese culture had two and a half times less coronary heart disease than those Japanese American men whose upbringing was more assimilated. The difference held even when the researchers controlled for diet, smoking, and other risk factors. Those most closely tied to the Japanese culture were five times less likely to have heart disease than those least involved in Japanese culture. The researchers proposed that this difference arose because of the cultural and social cohesiveness found in Japanese culture, and that this cohesiveness protected against heart disease.

In the United States, people with lower socioeconomic status (SES) have consistently been found to have poorer health than those with higher SES. Those whose jobs have less status and who are paid less tend to live in poorer neighborhoods, which tend to have fewer shops, recreational facilities, health care facilities, and higher crime—all factors that make life more difficult and stressful. The residents have poorer health and higher mortality rates (Taylor et al., 1997). Familial and community environments can affect health in a variety of ways. Stressful living situations such as abuse or lack of emotional or financial resources can create a chronic stress response and inhibit the development of effective coping strategies. In addition, children tend to imitate the health behaviors of their family members and peers, so if those people have bad health habits, the children are more likely to acquire those habits by adulthood (Taylor et al., 1997).

Nocebo effect: A variation of the placebo effect in which the subject expects a negative outcome instead of a positive outcome.

Voodoo Death

In some cultures, it has been reported that when a shaman (religious leader) puts a curse on someone, death sometimes ensues; this phenomenon is known as voodoo death (Cannon, 1942). Although there is some debate as to whether voodoo death actually exists (see Hahn, 1997), research has shown that expectations of sickness can in fact cause sickness. This is the **nocebo effect**, a variation of the placebo effect, but with the expectation of a negative outcome rather than a positive outcome. (*Placebo* in Latin means "I will please"; *nocebo* means "I will harm.") Voodoo death represents an extreme example of the nocebo effect.

Among presurgery patients who consulted a psychiatrist before their surgeries about their fears of the procedure, expectations about the surgery affected its outcome. Weisman and Hackett (1961) report that all five patients who were convinced of their impending death did die during surgery, whereas most of those who were unusually apprehensive about the surgery, but not convinced of death, did not die. Moreover, research with people with asthma has found a powerful nocebo effect: One group of sufferers was asked to inhale what they were told was an irritant or allergen, but that was in fact a harmless saline solution. Almost half of this group experienced an asthmatic reaction. Another group of people with asthma received the same saline solution but without any such information and had no reaction (Luparello et al., 1968).

How can we understand the nocebo response? At the level of the brain, the expectation of a negative outcome appears to trigger a response consistent with the expected outcome. At the level of the person, the *expectation* of a negative outcome leads the person to be hypervigilant for any bodily changes and to attribute any changes to the nocebo instead of to some other stimulus. At the level of the group, the culture promotes certain ideas and expectations about sickness and health. Events at these levels interact: For the people with asthma who were told they were inhaling a noxious stimulus, their culture provided the context (level of the group), which led them to be hypervigilant (level of the person) to their physical response (level of the brain), which in turn led them to interpret the bodily changes in a particular way (level of the person).

CONSOLIDATE!

1 *What are the different types of coping strategies?* Coping strategies are the ways in which people handle stress. They can be classified into two general categories: problem-focused and emotion-focused. Problem-focused coping attempts to alter either the environment itself or the way in which the person and the environment interact, and is helpful when the person can affect the stressor. Emotion-focused coping attempts to change the emotional response to a stressor and can be particularly helpful when the stressor itself cannot be changed. Whether a given strategy will be effective depends on an accurate assessment of the possibility of changing the environment.

2 *How do relationships affect stress and health?* Positive relationships can provide social support, which can buffer the negative effects of stress and boost the immune system. There are different types of social support, including perceived support and enacted support. Perceived support is more effective in buffering stress, even though it can be unrelated to actual support provided by others.

3 *What are mind–body interventions?* Some coping strategies (such as relaxation, meditation, and hypnosis) take advantage of the mind–body interaction, using psychological tools to change psychological and bodily states.

4 *Do gender and culture play a role in coping?* Although a woman may experience more stress because of multiple roles (particularly if one of the roles is mother), these multiple roles can provide a buffer against stress and depression; the financial, self-esteem, and collegial benefits of the employee role can outweigh the increased daily stress. Culture helps determine what is perceived to be stressful and provides ways to increase a sense of control in the face of a stressor. Crowding is an example: The perception of crowding can vary from culture to culture as a function of density. In cultures with high density, such as parts of Japan, ways have been found to create a sense of privacy to help people feel some control over the stressor of crowding.

Recap and Thought Questions

What Is Stress?

Stress is the general term describing the psychological and bodily response to a stimulus that alters your equilibrium. The stress response of the autonomic nervous system increases heart rate and blood pressure and suppresses the immune system. Continued stressors lead to a shift within the general adaptation syndrome (GAS) from the alarm phase to the adaptation phase to the exhaustion phase. The *perception* of stress helps determine what constitutes a stressor. Common sources of stress include a sense of a lack of control and predictability, internal conflict, and the irritations of daily life.

How do we know that Al is experiencing stress? Al has many of the signs of the sympathetic nervous system's response to stressors, including a racing heart, sweaty palms, and fatigue. Moreover, his work situation is clearly perceived to be a stressor.

Think It Through. Suppose that you have several job offers upon graduation from college. All of them have advantages, and all of them have drawbacks. Would this be a stressful situation? Why or why not? What specific factors about the job offers would make you more likely to experience the choice as stressful? What factors would make the choice seem less stressful?

Stress, Disease, and Health

Frequent activation of the stress response can lead to changes in the immune system, such as increased vulnerability to contracting a cold or the growth of existing tumors, and cardiovascular changes and heart disease. Stress can also affect sleep; sleep deprivation itself can create stress through impaired performance, mood, and increased cortisol functioning.

Al has been sick and coughing a lot lately. Could stress be affecting his health? Stress could be affecting Al's health in a number of ways, direct and indirect. His immune system's functioning is affected by his general level of stress, which would explain his frequent illnesses. Al has also responded to stress and insomnia by overindulging in alcohol.

Think It Through. Suppose you were caught in a thunderstorm and were soaking wet by the time you got home. Would you now be more likely to catch a cold? Why or why not? What factors might make you more or less likely to catch a cold? What if you had been out very late, or if you had had a lot of sleep? Why might these factors matter, or would they not matter?

Strategies for Coping

A realistic appraisal of whether your actions can affect a stressor will help you to determine what coping strategies will be effective. Emotion-focused coping strategies are best when the situation can't be changed, and problem-focused strategies work best when it can. There are a variety of problem-focused and emotion-focused coping strategies. Substance use is not an effective long-term strategy because it does not change the stressor; it merely changes someone's perception of the stress while he or she is in an altered state of consciousness. Stress-management techniques—relaxation training, meditation, hypnosis—can decrease the physical effects of stress. Social support (particularly perceived social support) can be helpful in decreasing the experience of stress. And culture can affect both the appraisal of a stimulus as a stressor and the choice of coping strategies for managing the stressor.

Given Al's particular stressors, what are the best coping strategies for him? Al's stressors include a lack of perceived control and an uncertain future. It will be important for Al to assess carefully and realistically whether his actions can affect the stressors. This will help determine which coping strategies will be effective: emotion-focused coping when he can't change the situation, and problem-focused coping when he can. Right now, Al is employing such emotion-focused strategies as disengaging (by overindulging in alcohol) and thought suppression. Al might benefit from learning some stress-management techniques to decrease the physical effects of stress.

Think It Through. If your next-door neighbor plays music very loudly every night when you are trying to go to sleep, and you find this to be a stressor, what could you do to lower your stress response? What type of coping strategies would work best in this situation? If you were in a non-Western culture, would the nightly serenade be as stressful? Why or why not?

REVIEW TEST

For each of the following items, choose the single correct or best answer. The correct answers appear at the end.

1 Which of the following is not a phase of the general adaptation syndrome?
   a. exhaustion
   b. collapse
   c. resistance
   d. alarm

2 During the primary appraisal of a situation, _____.
   a. the GAS is activated
   b. the person asks, "What can I do about this?"
   c. cortisol is released
   d. the person asks, "Am I in danger?"

3 When are warnings about an upcoming stressor unlikely to be helpful?
   a. when they are immediately before the stressor
   b. when they are vague
   c. when they are too far in advance
   d. all of the above

4 Joey's mother tells him that he may either eat the broccoli or go to bed without dessert. Joey is experiencing an _____ conflict.
   a. approach-approach
   b. avoidance-avoidance
   c. approach-avoidance
   d. avoidance-approach

5 If you are angry at your roommate, the best thing to do is to _____.
   a. hit a punching bag
   b. give it a rest for a while
   c. yell at her
   d. yell at someone else

6 Glucocorticoids affect the immune system by _____.
   a. killing white blood cells or hindering their production
   b. killing red blood cells or hindering their production
   c. enhancing the production of white blood cells
   d. enhancing the production of red blood cells

7 The aspects of stress that diminish immune functioning are _____.
   a. the controllability/predictability of the stressor
   b. the experience of negative emotions
   c. both a and b
   d. neither a nor b, since stress doesn't actually affect immune functioning

8 According to the research by Avi Karni and colleagues (1994), the best way to strengthen brain connections made during the day is to _____.
   a. stay awake all night
   b. drink alcohol before going to bed

   c. go to sleep, but have a friend wake you up whenever you begin dreaming
   d. get a good night's sleep

9 Which of the following neurotransmitters are more active when we are awake than when we are asleep?
   a. serotonin and norepinephrine
   b. acetylcholine and melatonin
   c. acetylcholine and norepinephrine
   d. serotonin and melatonin

10 When you don't get enough REM sleep one night, the following night you are likely to _____.
   a. dream less
   b. be unable to sleep
   c. dream more
   d. experience no changes in dreaming

11 Problem-focused coping tends to be used by people who score high on the personality factor of _____.
   a. extraversion
   b. openness to experience
   c. neuroticism
   d. conscientiousness

12 Problem-focused coping is effective only when a stressor is _____.
   a. acute
   b. controllable
   c. man-made
   d. uncontrollable

13 Which of the following is *not* a criteria for substance abuse?
   a. use leads to legal difficulties
   b. significant distress or difficulty functioning in major areas of life
   c. tolerance
   d. use occurs in dangerous situations

14 Steele, Critchlow, and Liu (1985) found that in a high-conflict situation, individuals who had been drinking _____.
   a. acted out aggressively
   b. were overly demonstrative
   c. were unable to inhibit their responses
   d. passed out from the pressure

15 The most important stress-reducing factor in social support is _____.
   a. having more friends than family members
   b. the number of friends you have
   c. having more family members than friends
   d. the variety of supports you have

11 Psychological

Disorders

I

n 1998–1999, record numbers of people came to the National Gallery of Art in Washington, D.C., to see an exhibit of the works of Vincent van Gogh. Born in Holland in 1853, van Gogh created extraordinary art and took much joy in painting, but his life is a tale of misery. The son and grandson of Protestant ministers, van Gogh was the second of six children. A memoir by his sister-in-law records, "As a child he was of difficult temper, often troublesome and self-willed" (Roskill, 1963, p. 37). According to his parents, when punished, Vincent became more "difficult." As a child he showed no particular awareness of his great gifts; but on two occasions, when he modeled a clay elephant and drew a cat, he destroyed what he had made when he felt a "fuss" was being made about them (Roskill, 1963).

When he was 16, he worked as a clerk in an art gallery, but his long, moody silences and irritability isolated him from his coworkers. After 4 years, he was transferred to the gallery's London office, where he fell in love with his landlady's daughter, Ursula. They spent many months together until she revealed her engagement to a previous tenant and rejected van Gogh. Feeling utterly defeated, he found it difficult to concentrate at work. He frequently argued with his coworkers and was soon fired.

Van Gogh next decided on a career in the ministry but could not master the Greek and Latin necessary for the entrance exams. Instead, he became a lay pastor, preaching to miners in the Borinage, a coal-mining area in Belgium. He went without bathing and slept in a hut on bare planks as the miners did. But the miners feared this unkempt, wild-looking man, and the church elders dismissed him. Increasingly, van Gogh found comfort in painting and drawing.

His life continued to be marked by instability. After he left the Borinage, he lived in and out of his parents' home and wandered around the country. Whereas once his interest in religion had been intense, if not obsessional, he now turned his back on religion. He developed a relationship with a pregnant prostitute, Sien, but their liaison ended after about a year and a half. Van Gogh reported that he had "attacks" during which he would hear voices; at times he believed he was being poisoned.

When he was 35, van Gogh convinced fellow painter Paul Gauguin to share a house with him in Arles, France. As was true for all of van Gogh's relationships, he and Gauguin frequently quarreled. According to Gauguin, after one particularly violent argument in a tavern, van Gogh approached him threateningly with an open razor, but Gauguin stared him down. Van Gogh then ran to their house, where he cut off his earlobe, which he then sent to a local prostitute (not Sien). The next day he was found at home, bleeding and unconscious, and was taken to a hospital, where he remained for 2 weeks. His brother Theo spent time with him in the hospital and found Vincent in great spiritual anguish.

After his release from the hospital in January 1889, van Gogh's behavior became increasingly bizarre, so much so that within 2 months the residents of Arles petitioned for him to be confined, and he again stayed for a time in the hospital. In May, van Gogh moved to the asylum at Saint-Remy, not far from Arles, where he lived on and off for the next year and a half, and where he produced many paintings. Shortly after his last release, less than 2 years after the incident with Gauguin, he purposefully ended his anguish and his life by going out into a field with a gun and shooting himself in the stomach. Yet, a few weeks before his death, he could say, "I still love art and life very much indeed" (Roskill, 1963).

Questions of art aside, van Gogh's experiences focus our attention on psychological disorders: What defines a psychological disorder? Who establishes criteria for determining what is abnormal behavior? What are the symptoms and origins of some specific disorders?

Identifying Psychological Disorders: What's Abnormal?

What distinguishes unusual behaviors from behaviors that are symptoms of a psychological disorder? Before he rejected religion, van Gogh was tormented by religious ideas and believed in ghosts. Are these signs of psychological disturbance? What about his self-mutilation? What would you want to know about him before drawing any conclusions?

Mental health professionals face questions such as these every day. In this section you will see how formulations of and findings about psychological disorders suggest answers to those questions.

1 How is abnormality defined?

2 How are psychological disorders explained?

3 How are psychological disorders classified and diagnosed?

4 What are personality disorders?

Defining Abnormality

How are lines drawn between normal functioning and abnormal functioning—and who draws them? Let's take a look at some different levels of analysis.

We can begin by noting that abnormal biology, such as imbalances in particular neurotransmitters or hormones, or abnormalities in brain structure, can affect mental or emotional functioning. But what if those abnormalities are not accompanied by behavioral symptoms? An important aspect of a definition of psychological disorders rests on objective symptoms that are manifested in behavior. By this standard, people with psychological disorders exhibit objectively unusual behavior, such as spending an hour washing their hands or feeling too sad to get out of bed.

But sometimes people who neither exhibit unusual behavior nor have abnormal brain states nevertheless have the subjective experience of psychological distress or discomfort. They may feel they are not "normal," even though other people might not notice anything amiss. This sense, too, must be taken into account in defining abnormality. But if there are no behavioral or biological indicators of a disorder, could someone who feels this way be said to have a psychological disorder?

Context and culture also play a role in defining abnormality. Picture someone hopping on one leg, thumb in mouth, trying to sing the French national anthem during a hockey game. You would probably think this was abnormal; but what if the behavior was part of a fraternity initiation ritual, or a new kind of performance art? A behavior that is bizarre or inappropriate in one context may be entirely appropriate in another. Furthermore, a culture's definition of abnormality may shift over time. For example, in 1851, Dr. Samuel Cartwright of Louisiana wrote an essay in which he declared that slaves' running away was evidence of a serious mental disorder, which he called "drapetomania" (Eakin, 2000). More recently, homosexuality was officially considered a psychological disorder in the United States until 1973, when it was removed from the *Diagnostic and Statistical Manual of Mental Disorders,* the manual used by mental health clinicians to classify psychological disorders. And in the last decade, the determination of abnormality has taken a new turn in the United States; as health maintenance organizations (HMOs) and other types of managed care organizations try to keep costs down, they have developed their own criteria for the symptoms and disorders they will pay to have treated, as well as for the frequency and duration of the treatment.

Thus, when deciding what should be considered a psychological disorder, it can be helpful to be aware of all these factors: differences in biology, objective behaviors and subjective experiences, and the surrounding culture. The line between normal and abnormal behavior is perhaps easiest to draw in the case of **psychosis**, which is an obvious impairment in the ability to perceive and comprehend events accurately, combined with a gross disorganization of behavior. People with psychoses may have **hallucinations**, mental images so vivid that they seem real, or **delusions**, which are entrenched false beliefs (such as that their thoughts are being controlled by aliens). However, such beliefs, even if false (or at least not susceptible to rational proof), should not be considered abnormal if they are an accepted part of the culture. For instance, in some religious groups, such as Pentecostals, it is not considered abnormal to hear voices, especially the voice of God (Cox, 2000). Another example is *zar,* or spirit possession, experienced in some

Psychosis: An obvious impairment in the ability to perceive and comprehend events accurately, and a gross disorganization of behavior.

Hallucinations: Mental images so vivid that they seem real.

Delusions: Entrenched false beliefs that are often bizarre.

Van Gogh's painting of the church at Auvers is unusual because of its unconventional perspective, use of color, and brushstrokes. Do these differences reflect a psychological disorder, or just a different way of seeing or conveying the structure and its surroundings?

North African and Middle Eastern cultures. Those affected may shout, laugh, hit their heads against a wall, or exhibit other behavior that otherwise would be considered inappropriate; an experience of *zar* is not considered abnormal in the cultures in which it occurs (American Psychiatric Association, 1994). Because of such cultural differences, even psychosis can be difficult to identify.

It is difficult to give an exact definition of psychological disorders—also referred to as psychiatric disorders, mental disorders or, less systematically, mental illnesses—because they can encompass many aspects of behavioral, experiential, and biological functioning. However, a good working definition is that a **psychological disorder** is a constellation of cognitive, emotional, and behavioral symptoms that create significant distress, or impairment in work, school, family, relationships, or daily living. This definition takes into account three factors: distress, disability, and danger. People with psychological disorders may display or experience *distress,* perhaps repeatedly bursting into tears and expressing hopelessness about the future, for no apparent reason. People with psychological disorders may experience a *disability,* or inability to function in some aspect of life (examples might be a police officer subject to panic attacks on duty, or someone whose emotional outbursts drive others away). *Danger* can occur when symptoms of a psychological disorder cause an individual to put life (his or her own, or another's) at risk, either purposefully or accidentally. For instance, a visual hallucination may obscure the sight of an oncoming car, depression may lead to a suicide attempt, or extreme paranoia may provoke an attack on others.

Psychological disorders can be very debilitating, and worldwide they rank second among diseases that lead to death and disability, a higher ranking than cancer (Murray & Lopez, 1996). According to some estimates, up to 48% of Americans have experienced 1 of 30 common psychological disorders at some point in their lives (Kessler et al., 1994), and 20% of Americans have a diagnosable mental disorder in any given year (Regier et al., 1993; Satcher, 1999). Psychological disorders can affect people's relationships, their ability to care for themselves, and their functioning on the job. For every 100 workers, an average of 37 work days per month are lost either because of reduced workloads or absences necessitated by psychological disorders (Kessler & Frank, 1997).

Explaining Abnormality

Explanations for abnormal behavior have changed with the times and reflect the thinking of the culture. In ancient Greece, abnormal behaviors, as well as medical problems, were thought to arise from imbalances of the body's four fluids, or "humors": yellow bile, phlegm, blood, and black bile. Too much phlegm, for instance, made you sluggish and "phlegmatic"; too much black bile made you melancholic. In 17th century New England, abnormality was thought to be the work of the devil. In the middle of the 20th century, Sigmund Freud's work was influential, and psychodynamic theory was the instrument used to understand abnormality. Currently, to understand psychological disorders, many psychologists and others in the field have used the *biopsychosocial model*. This model focuses on factors at the levels of the brain, the person, and the group. In this discussion, we go one step further and show how events at those three levels are not discrete but affect one another in various interactions.

The Brain

Van Gogh's family history points to a possible cause of his psychological disorders. Van Gogh's brother Theo was often depressed and anxious, and he committed suicide within a year after Vincent's suicide; his sister Wilhelmina exhibited a long-standing psychosis; his youngest brother Cor is thought to have committed suicide. Does this history indicate that van Gogh inherited some vulnerability to a psychological disorder? Not necessarily, but researchers are finding increasing evidence that genetic factors frequently contribute to the development of some disorders.

Psychological disorder: A constellation of cognitive, emotional, and behavioral symptoms marked by an individual's significant distress, or impairment in work, school, family, relationships, or daily living.

Biological factors, including, for example, neurotransmitters (such as serotonin), hormones (such as adrenaline), and abnormalities in the structure of the brain, appear to play a role in the development of some psychological disorders. From this point of view, depression can be seen as a manifestation of an abnormal serotonin level. Similarly, the cause of an irrational fear of spiders could be the outcome of an overreactive amygdala. While these explanations may be valid, they are only a part of the picture. *Why* are someone's serotonin levels abnormal? *Why* is someone else's amygdala overreactive to the sight of a spider? As previously noted in many contexts, our own thoughts, feelings, and behaviors, as well as our interactions with others and our environment, can affect the workings of our brains.

Figure 11.1   The Diathesis–Stress Model

Most mental health researchers and professionals believe that both biological factors (diathesis) and environmental stressors (stress) together cause psychological disorders.

Thus, abnormality cannot be considered solely as a function of brain chemistry or structure. Many researchers and clinicians today believe that psychological disorders can best be explained by a **diathesis–stress model** (*diathesis* means a predisposition to a state or condition). This model, illustrated in Figure 11.1, states that "for a given disorder, there is both a predisposition to the disorder (a *diathesis*) and specific factors (*stress*) that combine with the diathesis to trigger the onset of the disorder" (Rende & Plomin, 1992, p. 177). According to the diathesis–stress model, because of certain biological factors (such as their genes, abnormality of brain structures, or neurotransmitters), some people may be more vulnerable to developing a particular disorder, but without certain environmental stressors, the disorder is not triggered. By the same token, when experiencing a stressor, people without a biological vulnerability for a disorder may not develop that disorder. From this perspective, neither factor alone can cause illness, and as noted in Chapter 10, not everyone perceives a particular event or stimulus to be a stressor. Whether because of learning or genetics, or an interaction of the two, some people are more likely to perceive more stimuli as stressors (and therefore to experience more stress) than others. For instance, although schizophrenia appears to have a genetic component, even if an identical twin has schizophrenia, the co-twin will not necessarily develop the disorder. The diathesis–stress model proposes that it is the *combination* of biological vulnerability and specific other factors, such as a trauma or the death of a loved one, that elicits the disorder.

The Person

Several factors at the level of the person also play a role in psychological disorders. One factor is classical conditioning, as in the case of Little Albert (Chapter 4),

Diathesis–stress model: A predisposition to a given disorder (diathesis) and specific factors (stress) that combine with the diathesis to trigger the onset of the disorder.

who developed a phobia of white furry things based on his classical conditioning experiences with a white rat and a loud noise. Operant conditioning and observational learning can also help explain some psychological disorders, as can the pattern of a person's thoughts. For instance, chronic negative thought patterns ("I'm incompetent; I can't do anything right") can lead to depressing feelings and contribute to the development or maintenance of depression. Learning, thoughts, and feelings may help explain why certain psychological disorders develop in some people.

The Group

For a period during the 1960s, a number of mental health professionals proposed the idea that mental illness is a myth, merely a label applied to culturally undesirable behavior (Szasz, 1961). In this view, the label determines how people are treated and, in a self-fulfilling prophecy, may even play a role in how the "mentally ill" person behaves, once labeled.

David Rosenhan (1973) tested an aspect of this idea. In his study, people without a psychological disorder gained admittance to psychiatric hospitals by claiming that they heard voices. Once in the hospital they behaved normally (see Figure 11.2). But because they were given a psychiatric diagnosis, their normal behavior was interpreted as pathological, and they were treated accordingly. For example, when these "pseudopatients" asked about eligibility for grounds privileges, the psychiatrists responded to such questions only 6% of the time; in 71% of the encounters, the doctors just moved on.

Rosenhan's experiment illustrates the power of labels. But does it tell us anything about the reality of mental disorders? The pseudopatients originally reported auditory hallucinations that were troubling enough to drive them to request admission to a mental hospital; people do not normally have such symptoms. How was the staff to know that the pseudopatients were lying when they described their "symptoms"? Kety (1974, p. 959) notes:

Figure 11.2   On Being Sane in Insane Places

David Rosenhan and six colleagues (pseudopatients) each went to the admissions office of a different hospital, complaining of hearing voices, although behaving normally. Each was admitted: six were diagnosed as *schizophrenic* and one as *manic depressive*.

Once hospitalized, the pseudopatients acted normally, and they said that they felt fine and that the voices had stopped. Even so, they were kept in the hospital for an average of 19 days. Not a single staff member questioned whether the diagnoses were correct, but some of the other patients did.

As soon as the pseudopatients were labeled schizophrenic, the doctors and nurses interpreted normal behaviors in a different way. For example, the pseudopatients kept notes on their experiences, and one of the nurses wrote in the case record "Patient engages in writing behavior."

If I were to drink a quart of blood and, concealing what I had done, came to the emergency room of any hospital vomiting blood, the behavior of the staff would be quite predictable. If they labeled and treated me as having a bleeding peptic ulcer, I doubt that I could argue convincingly that medical science does not know how to diagnose that condition.

Similarly, the fact that the staff in Rosenhan's experiment labeled and treated the pseudopatients as if their symptoms were genuine does not indicate that psychological disorders with these symptoms do not exist.

Certain disorders—schizophrenia being one—are recognized worldwide. But cultures differ in which behaviors they consider abnormal, and the symptoms, course, and prognosis of disorders may vary from culture to culture (Basic Behavioral Science Task Force, 1996), and even within a country such as the United States, cultural differences influence how people are diagnosed with and treated for psychological disorders. Moreover, diagnosing individuals involves making judgments that, like all judgments, are subject to error. A systematic type of error in diagnosis is called a *diagnostic bias* (Meehl, 1960), often with the result that some people receive certain diagnoses based on non-medical factors, such as race. For instance, studies of racial bias show that African American patients in the United States have an increased likelihood of being evaluated more negatively than white patients (Garb, 1997; Jenkins-Hall & Sacco, 1991; Strakowski et al., 1995) and are prescribed higher doses of medication (Strakowski et al., 1993).

Factors at the level of the group play a role in triggering psychological disorders, as well as in increasing the risk of a disorder's recurrence. For example, the "stress" part of posttraumatic stress disorder is usually caused by other people (such as a terrorist or a rapist) or the environment (natural disasters such as floods and earthquakes).

Events at all three levels and the interactions among them must be examined to understand the various psychological disorders discussed in this chapter. Biological factors; learning principles and thought patterns; familial, cultural, and environmental factors; and the relationships among them all play a role in explaining psychological disorders.

The film Girl, Interrupted *tells the disturbing true story of Susanna Kaysen, a troubled young woman who was institutionalized after an aspirin over-dose. After being labeled with a diagnosis during her hospitalization, she soon began to live up to the role it described. One underlying message of the film was that, during the late sixties, women were routinely institutionalized for socially unacceptable behavior.*

Categorizing Disorders: Is a Rose Still a Rose by Any Other Name?

Suppose a man comes to a clinical psychologist's office complaining that he feels he is going crazy and that he has a strong sense of impending doom. How would the clinical psychologist determine the nature of this man's difficulties and figure out how best to help him? What questions should the psychologist ask? One guide to help the psychologist and other mental health clinicians is the *Diagnostic and Statistical Manual of Mental Disorders*, known to its users simply as the *DSM*.

In 1952 the American Psychiatric Association published the inaugural edition of the *DSM*, the first manual of mental disorders designed primarily to help clinicians diagnose and treat patients. This edition was based on psychodynamic theory. In later editions of the manual, its developers tried to avoid relying on any one theory of the causes of disorders and to base the identification of disorders on a growing body of empirical research. The fourth edition, the *DSM-IV*, published in 1994, was an attempt to refine the diagnostic criteria and make the diagnostic categories more useful to mental health researchers and practitioners.

Since the third edition, the *DSM* has described five *axes*, or types of information, that should be considered in the assessment of a patient. Clinical disorders are noted on Axis I, and personality disorders and mental retardation on Axis II. Axis III notes any general medical conditions that might be relevant to a diagnosis on Axis I or II. Psychosocial and environmental problems are identified on Axis IV, and Axis V records the patient's highest level of functioning in major areas of life within the past year. An appendix to the manual outlines aspects of the patient's cultural context that clinicians should take into account when making a diagnosis. Most of the manual, however, is devoted to describing disorders. It defines 17 major categories of psychological problems. All told, almost 300 mental disorders are specified. A revision called *DSM-IV-TR* (*TR* stands for *Text Revision*) in 2000 included more up-to-date information on incidence rates and cultural factors, but did not change the diagnostic categories or the criteria.

The sheer number of disorders included in the *DSM-IV* has provoked criticism of the manual; the breadth of the major diagnostic categories is shown in Table 11.1. As the *DSM* has evolved, it has introduced categories that define medical problems as psychological disorders, leading to a pathologizing of people's mental health. For example, a new diagnosis in the *DSM-IV* is "Breathing-Related Sleep Disorder" (one cause of which is sleep apnea; see Chapter 10). Thus, the *DSM-IV* created a *psychological* or *psychiatric* disorder for a medical problem. Moreover, the *DSM-IV* does not provide a discrete boundary separating abnormality from nor-

TABLE 11.1 *DSM-IV's* 17 Major Categories of Disorders
Source: *Adapted from American Psychiatric Association (1994).*

MAJOR CATEGORY OF DISORDERS	EXPLANATION
Disorders usually first diagnosed in infancy, childhood, or adolescence	Although describing disorders usually first evident early in life, some adults are newly diagnosed with disorders in this category, such as attention-deficit/hyperactivity disorder.
Delirium, dementia, and amnestic and other cognitive disorders	Disorders of consciousness and cognition.
Mental disorders due to a general medical condition not elsewhere classified	Disorders in which mental and psychological symptoms are judged to be due to a medical condition (coded on Axis III).
Substance-related disorders	Disorders of substance dependence and abuse, as well as disorders induced by a substance, such as a substance-induced psychotic disorder.
Schizophrenia and other psychotic disorders	Disorders related to psychoses.
Mood disorders	Disorders of affect/feelings.
Anxiety disorders	Disorders of anxiety.
Somatoform disorders	Disorders in which physical/medical complaints have no known medical origin (or the symptoms are not proportional to a medical condition) and so are thought to be psychological in nature.
Factitious disorders	Disorders in which the person intentionally fabricates symptoms of a medical or psychological disorder, but not for external gain (such as disability claims).
Dissociative disorders	Disorders in which there is a disruption in the usually integrated functions of consciousness, memory, or identity.
Sexual and gender identity disorders	Disorders of sexual function, the object of sexual desire, and/or of gender identity.
Eating disorders	Disorders related to eating.
Sleep disorders	Disorders related to sleep.
Impulse-control disorders not elsewhere classified	Disorders related to the ability to contain impulses (such as kleptomania).
Adjustment disorders	Disorders related to the development of distressing emotional or behavioral symptoms in response to an identifiable stressor.
Personality disorders	Disorders related to personality traits that are inflexible and maladaptive, and that cause distress or difficulty with daily functioning.
Other conditions that may be a focus of clinical attention	A problem receiving treatment for which there is no psychological disorder, or the symptoms do not meet criteria for a disorder.

mality (Frances, 1998); a clinician's judgment determines whether an impairment is "clinically significant." Another criticism leveled at the *DSM-IV* is that some of the disorders are not clearly distinct from one another (Blais et al., 1997), although they are often presented as if they were (Tucker, 1998).

Despite these criticisms, the *DSM-IV* is the predominant means of categorizing psychological disorders in the United States. The discussion of disorders in this chapter uses the *DSM-IV* system of categorization.

Personality Disorders

As mentioned earlier, part of the multi-axial system of *DSM-IV* includes the possibility of a personality disorder on Axis II. Personality disorders may exist separately or in tandem with an Axis I disorder (Axis I disorders are discussed later in this chapter). A **personality disorder** refers to relatively stable personality traits (see Chapter 8 for a discussion about personality traits) that are inflexible and maladaptive, causing distress or difficulty with daily functioning in school, work, social life, or relationships (see Table 11.2). Whereas Axis I symptoms feel as if they are inflicted from the outside, the maladaptive traits of Axis II are often experienced as part of the person's personality. These maladapative traits can be subtle, and may not be evident during a brief encounter with the person. It is only after getting to know the person over time that a personality disorder

TABLE **Axis II Personality Disorders**   *Source: American Psychiatric Association (1994).*

Antisocial Personality Disorder
A pattern of disregard or violation of the rights of others.

Avoidant Personality Disorder
A pattern of social discomfort, feelings of inadequacy, and hypersensitivity to negative evaluation.

Borderline Personality Disorder
A pattern of instability in relationships, self-image, and feelings, and pronounced impulsivity (such as in spending, substance abuse, sex, reckless driving, or binge eating). Relationships are often characterized by rapid swings from idealizing another person to devaluing him or her. Recurrent suicidal gestures, threats, or self-mutilation, such as nonlethal cuts on the arm are common, as are chronic feelings of emptiness.

Dependent Personality Disorder
A pattern of clingy, submissive behavior due to an extreme need to be taken care of.

Histrionic Personality Disorder
A pattern of excessive attention seeking and expression of emotion.

Narcissistic Personality Disorder
A pattern of an exaggerated sense of self-importance, need for admiration, and lack of empathy.

Obsessive-Compulsive Personality Disorder
A pattern of preoccupation with perfectionism, orderliness, and control (but no obsessions or compulsions, as occur with obsessive-compulsive disorder).

Paranoid Personality Disorder
A pattern of suspiciousness and distrust of others to the extent that other people's motives are interpreted as ill-intentioned. However, unlike the paranoid subtype of schizophrenia, there are no delusions or hallucinations.

Schizoid Personality Disorder
A pattern of detachment from social relationships and a narrow range of displayed emotion.

Schizotypal Personality Disorder
A pattern of extreme discomfort in close relationships, odd or quirky behavior, and cognitive or perceptual distortions (such as sensing the presence of another person or spirit).

Personality disorder: Relatively stable personality traits that are inflexible and maladaptive, causing distress or difficulty with daily functioning.

Antisocial personality disorder: A long-standing pattern of disregard for others to the point of violating other people's rights.

may become evident. Consider the case of van Gogh, who might have initially appeared relatively normal in his early adult years. Only after getting to know him over time did he manifest some indications of a personality disorder. For example, his relationships were often unstable, where he would feel extremely positive about someone and then, after some period of time, think negatively of the same person. He could be quite impulsive, and expressed feelings of emptiness.

Some researchers argue that the combinations of traits now defined as personality disorders should not be called "disorders" at all. Doing so, they contend, either treats normal variations in personality as pathological or creates separate Axis II categories for conditions that could be part of an Axis I clinical disorder (Hyman, 1998; Livesley, 1998). For example, the clinging, submissive behavior that *DSM-IV* categorizes as Axis II "dependent personality disorder" might also characterize a personality that is within the normal range. And the symptoms of avoidant personality disorder overlap those of Axis I social phobia—only the greater severity of anxiety and depressive symptoms distinguishes avoidant personality disorder from social phobia (Johnson & Lydiard, 1995); the two disorders are quantitatively, not qualitatively, different.

Other researchers argue that each personality disorder is not a research-validated disorder distinct from all others (Atre-Vaidya & Hussain, 1999; Horowitz, 1998). Furthermore, the criteria for the various personality disorders do not all require the same level of dysfunction. Thus, a lesser—and in some cases quite mild—degree of impairment is required for a diagnosis of obsessive-compulsive, antisocial, and paranoid personality disorders (Funtowicz & Widiger, 1999).

From what is known about his life, it is not impossible that van Gogh had a personality disorder; but we have no way of knowing if he in fact met all of the criteria.

The most studied personality disorder is **antisocial personality disorder (ASPD)**, evidenced by a long-standing pattern of disregard for others to the point of violating their rights (American Psychiatric Association, 1994). People with this disorder have been called *psychopaths, sociopaths,* and *social deviants,* and they may engage in unlawful behavior. Symptoms include a superficial charm; egocentrism; impulsive, reckless, and deceitful behavior without regard for others' safety; a tendency to blame others for any adversity that comes their way; and a lack of conscience, empathy, and remorse. People with this disorder talk a good line and know how to manipulate others, but they don't have the capacity to know or care how another person feels.

John Wayne Gacy, a psychopathic serial killer, tortured and murdered 33 young men and boys and buried their bodies in the basement of his house.

Antisocial Personality Disorder From the Inside

A common feature among psychopaths is that they see *themselves* as the real victims. While discussing the murders he committed, John Wayne Gacy portrayed himself as the 34th victim:

> I was made an asshole and a scapegoat . . . when I look back, I see myself more as a victim than a perpetrator. . . . I was the victim; I was cheated out of my childhood. . . . [He wondered whether] there would be someone, somewhere who would understand how badly it had hurt to be John Wayne Gacy. (Hare, 1993, p. 43)

Antisocial personality disorder occurs three times more frequently in men than in women, and although only 1% to 2% of Americans are diagnosed with this disorder, 60% of male prisoners are estimated to have it (Moran, 1999). Cross-cultural studies have found a similar pattern of symptoms in both Western and non-Western cultures (Zoccolillo et al., 1999). Many people diagnosed with antisocial personality disorder also abuse alcohol and drugs (Nigg & Goldsmith, 1994).

Did Charles Whitman Have a Psychological Disorder?

If a person is violent, does this automatically mean that he or she has a psychological disorder? No; there is no simple, single criterion. Psychological disorders can most clearly be identified by looking at events at all three levels of analysis and their interactions. Consider the case of Charles Whitman. On August 1, 1966, long before anyone imagined today's far more common occasions of violence in schools and workplaces, Whitman, a 25-year-old student at the University of Texas in Austin, climbed to the top of a tower on the campus and opened fire on students casually walking below. After an hour and a half, 16 were dead and another 30 wounded. As Gary Lavergne, author of *A Sniper in the Tower: The Charles Whitman Murders* (1997) wrote, Whitman "introduced America to public mass murder" (p. xi). At the time, a local reporter described Whitman as "a good son, top Boy Scout, an excellent Marine, an honor student, a hard worker, a loving husband, a fine scout master, a handsome man, a wonderful friend to all who knew him—and an expert sniper" (p. xi).

What drove Whitman to murder? Was he unhappy at school? Yes; he was extremely frustrated by his heavy course load (an explanation at the level of the person). What about his relationship with his family? His parents were about to divorce, a circumstance that upset him greatly. He had a long history of bad blood with his abusive father. In fact, the night before his rampage, he killed his mother and his wife, and then wrote an angry letter about his father. In this same note, Whitman asked that his brain be examined after his death, to see if "there is any mental disorder."

Charles Whitman's hunch was correct—something *was* wrong with his brain. An autopsy uncovered a pecan-sized tumor near his hypothalamus, a part of the brain involved in emotion. Whitman had complained of massive headaches for weeks before the shooting and was seen regularly gobbling huge doses of aspirin.

Can we conclude that with the discovery of the tumor the case is closed—that Whitman had a medical disorder, not a psychological one? Probably not. It's unlikely that the brain tumor was the sole cause of his behavior. After all, most people with similar brain tumors don't become mass murderers. Perhaps the tumor intensified Whitman's violent feelings, but this still doesn't tell us how and why those feelings led to violent acts. Whitman was clearly deeply unhappy (level of the person), but again, this by itself was probably not enough to trigger his violent rampage.

Whitman's killing spree can best be understood by looking for interactions among events at all three levels. He may have interpreted the discomfort and feelings produced by the tumor in terms of his frustration over his school work and his unhappiness (level of the person), and his rage toward his parents and others (level of the group). Such thoughts may have caused severe stress, which amplified the headaches caused by the tumor (level of the brain), thereby ratcheting up his misery and rage. This in turn may have led him to finally revert to skills he acquired as a Marine and lash out at a world of innocent people on the ground below.

CONSOLIDATE!

1. **How is abnormality defined?** Abnormality, as distinct from insanity, can be defined by events at the levels of the brain, by biological abnormalities; of the person, by objective behaviors and subjective distress; and of the group, in which abnormality is defined by the culture and context of the behaviors.

2. **How are psychological disorders explained?** The diathesis–stress model explains psychological disorders, specifically that certain biological factors make some individuals more vulnerable to developing particular disorders, which are then triggered by stressors.

3. **How are psychological disorders classified and diagnosed?** Psychiatric disorders are classified in the *DSM-IV* along two axes: clinical and personality disorders. Three other axes address factors affecting the disorders, the nature of the problem, and the highest level of functioning attained. Impairment in functioning at work, in school, in relationships, or in daily living are necessary to merit a diagnosis of a disorder.

4. **What are personality disorders?** Personality disorders reflect relatively stable personality traits that have become inflexible and maladaptive, causing distress or difficulty with daily functioning in school, work, and other social spheres.

Anxiety disorder: A disorder whose hallmark is intense and pervasive anxiety and fear, or extreme attempts to avoid these feelings.

Panic disorder: A disorder whose hallmark is panic attacks.

Panic attack: An episode of intense fear or discomfort accompanied by physical and psychological symptoms such as palpitations, breathing difficulties, chest pain, fear of impending doom or doing something uncontrollable, and a sense of unreality.

Anxiety and Mood Disorders

We cannot diagnose from a distance, but we know enough about van Gogh's life and behavior to make some educated guesses about the nature of his moods and turmoil. We know, for example, that he had what he called "attacks." He frequently spoke of feeling sad; still, he clung to the commonality of human feeling, saying "I prefer feeling my sorrow to forgetting it or becoming indifferent" (Lubin, 1972, p. 22). Painting was the one thing that drove away his sadness, and sometimes he painted in a frenzy. He would have bouts of irritability, had difficulty concentrating, was often miserable, and frequently quarrelsome. People described him as odd, argumentative, very sensitive, nervous, and unpredictable. He described himself as an alcoholic. He had frequent thoughts of suicide, and in the end, at the age of 37, he died after he intentionally shot himself (Lubin, 1972).

Can we recognize a pattern in these symptoms? How would today's methods of identifying psychological disorders explain them? What might be their causes?

1 What are the main types of anxiety disorders? What are their symptoms and causes?

2 What are mood disorders? What causes them?

Anxiety Disorders

Many people are nervous when they have to speak in public. But suppose you become *so* nervous before an in-class presentation that your mouth is dry, you feel lightheaded, your heart begins to race, and you think you're having a heart attack and going crazy at the same time. These reactions are not normal "stage jitters." They are typical signs of an **anxiety disorder**, a state characterized by extreme fear (a response to an external stimulus, such as a snake) and extreme anxiety (a vague but persistent sense of foreboding or dread when not in the presence of the stimulus). Fear and anxiety are part of life, but people who have anxiety disorders experience *intense* or *pervasive* anxiety or fear, or *extreme* attempts to avoid these feelings. These experiences create exceptional distress that can interfere with the ability to function normally. Four major types of anxiety disorders are panic disorder, phobias, posttraumatic stress disorder, and obsessive-compulsive disorder.

Panic Disorder

The hallmark of **panic disorder** is the experience of **panic attacks**, episodes of intense fear or discomfort accompanied by symptoms such as palpitations, breathing difficulties, chest pain, nausea, sweating, dizziness, fear of going crazy or doing something uncontrollable, fear of impending doom, and a sense of unreality. Symptoms reach their peak within a few minutes of the beginning of an attack, which can last from minutes to hours. Often these attacks are not associated with a specific situation or object and may even seem to occur randomly. One study of college students found that 12% of the participants experienced spontaneous panic attacks in college or in the years leading up to college (Telch et al., 1989). Internationally, approximately 3% of all people will experience panic disorder during their lifetimes (Rouillon, 1997). Some people may have episodic outbreaks of panic disorder, with years of remission; others may have more persistent symptoms.

Panic attacks can interfere with everyday functioning. In the television series The Sopranos, *mob captain Tony Soprano seeks professional help to keep his panic attacks under control.*

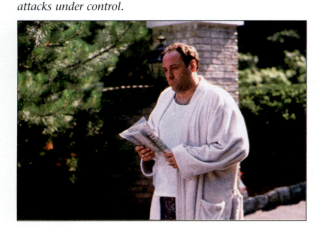

Panic Disorder From the Inside

Here is one person's description of a panic attack:

My breathing starts getting very shallow. I feel I'm going to stop breathing. The air feels like it gets thinner. I feel the air is not coming up through my nose. I take short rapid breaths. Then I see an image of myself gasping for air and remember what happened in the hospital. I think that I will start gasping. I get very dizzy and disoriented. I cannot sit or stand still. I start pacing. Then I start shaking and sweating. I feel I'm losing my mind and I will flip out and hurt myself or someone else. My heart starts beating fast and I start getting pains in my chest. My chest tightens up. I become very frightened. I get afraid that these feelings will not go away. Then I get really upset. I feel no one will be able to help me. I get very frightened I will die. I want to run to some place safe but I don't know where. (Beck et al., 1985, p. 107)

People with panic disorder worry constantly about having more attacks, and in their attempts to avoid or minimize panic attacks, they may change their behavior. Some people fear or avoid places that might be difficult to leave should a panic attack occur—for example, a plane or car. Such fear and avoidance can lead to **agoraphobia** (literally, "fear of the marketplace"), a condition in which the avoidance of places or activities restricts daily life. In severe cases, people with agoraphobia might not leave home at all, or do so only with a close friend or relative. In some cases, people have agoraphobia without panic attacks, avoiding many places because they fear either losing control of themselves in some way (such as losing bladder control) or they fear the occurrence of less severe but still distressing panic symptoms.

What causes panic attacks? A biological vulnerability for panic, an event at the level of the brain, is apparently inherited (Crowe et al., 1983; Torgersen, 1983). Evidence of one possible route to such a vulnerability comes from animal studies, which suggest that panic attacks may arise from a hypersensitivity involving the locus coeruleus, a small group of cells deep in the brainstem (Gorman et al., 1989). The locus coeruleus is the seat of an "alarm system" that triggers an increased heart rate, faster breathing, sweating, and other components of the fight-or-flight response (see Chapters 2, 7, and 10), and can lead to the experience of panic. People with panic disorder may be more biologically sensitive than others to changes in carbon dioxide inhalation (Beck et al., 1999; Papp et al., 1993, 1997), which can come about through hyperventilation. Changes in carbon dioxide levels can elicit panic, perhaps through a "suffocation alarm" in the brain (Klein, 1993).

How a person interprets and responds to these signals from the body—that is, events at the level of the person—may be critical to the development of panic disorder. For instance, people who have *anxiety sensitivity,* defined as the "belief that autonomic arousal can have harmful consequences" (Schmidt et al., 1997, p. 355), are at higher risk of experiencing spontaneous panic attacks (Schmidt et al., 1999). Those high in anxiety sensitivity believe that their experiences of shortness of breath necessarily indicate suffocation or that their heart palpitations must signal a heart attack.

The misinterpretation of the cause of biological events may itself increase sympathetic nervous system activity (Wilkinson et al., 1998) and lead to panic. For instance, changes in breathing can lead to changes in carbon dioxide levels, which are then misinterpreted and can lead to panic (Coplan et al., 1998). Thus, changes in the body act like an alarm (termed *false alarm;* Beck, 1976), and after several false alarms, the sensations associated with them become *learned alarms,* which themselves trigger panic (Barlow, 1988). People can also become hypervigilant for the signals that have led to panic in the past. Thus, in a vicious cycle, these people are more likely to experience anticipatory anxiety, which increases sympathetic nervous system activity (including increased heart rate and breathing changes), which in turn triggers panic.

Agoraphobia: A condition in which people fear or avoid places that might be difficult to leave should a panic attack occur.

At the level of the group, although 80% of people with panic disorder reported a stressful life event before the development of the panic disorder, the presence of such stress did not predict how severe the disorder would be, nor whether the symptoms would become chronic (Manfro et al., 1996; Rouillon, 1997).

Although van Gogh was anxious and irritable, we do not know enough about what happened during one of his so-called attacks to know whether these episodes were panic attacks or something else. In any event, panic disorder alone would not account for his symptoms of depression, irritability, impulsiveness, and bizarre behavior.

Phobias: Social and Specific

A **phobia** is an exaggerated fear of an object, class of objects, or situations, accompanied by avoidance that is extreme enough to interfere with everyday life. Phobias can be sorted into types, based on the object or situation that is feared. **Social phobia**, the fear of public embarrassment or humiliation and the ensuing avoidance of social situations likely to arouse this fear, is one of the most common psychiatric diagnoses (major depression is *the* most common; American Psychiatric Association, 2000). Estimates are that approximately 13% of Americans currently experience social phobia (Fones et al., 1998). People with social phobia fear what they perceive to be occasions of great embarrassment or public humiliation, and so avoid social situations in which they think this might occur (Kessler, Stein et al., 1998). They might try to avoid eating, speaking, or performing in public, or using public restrooms or dressing rooms. When unable to avoid these situations, they invariably experience anxiety or panic.

A **specific phobia** is focused on a specific object or situation. Most people with phobias about blood, for example, faint if they see blood and may, because of their phobia, avoid getting appropriate treatment for medical problems (Kleinknecht & Lenz, 1989). People may have specific phobias about flying or of heights, spiders, or dental work (see Table 11.3). The fear may occur in the presence of the stimulus or in anticipation of it, despite an intellectual recognition that the fear is excessive or unreasonable. By avoiding the object or situation, the sufferer avoids the fear, anxiety, or panic that it might elicit. In contrast, **generalized anxiety disorder** involves excessive anxiety and worry that is not linked to a specific object or situation. Approximately 5% of people have this disorder at any given point in time.

Studies with twins suggest that phobias have a genetic component that affects events at the level of the brain (Kendler et al., 1992). The genetic vulnerability may rest on hyperreactivity of the amygdala and other fear-related brain structures (see Chapter 7) in certain situations (LeDoux, 1996). However, not all identical co-twins are phobic if their twins are phobic, so nongenetic factors must play a role. Humans seem biologically *prepared* to develop phobias about certain stimuli and not others (see Chapter 7).

Phobia: A fear and avoidance of an object or situation extreme enough to interfere with everyday life.

Social phobia: A type of phobia involving fear of public humiliation or embarrassment and the ensuing avoidance of situations likely to arouse this fear.

Specific phobia: A type of phobia involving persistent and excessive or unreasonable fear triggered by a specific object or situation, along with attempts to avoid the feared stimulus.

Generalized anxiety disorder: A disorder whose hallmark is excessive anxiety and worry that is not triggered by a specific object or situation.

TABLE 11.3 **Five Subtypes of Specific Phobias** *Source: American Psychiatric Association (1994).*

PHOBIA SUBTYPE	EXAMPLES (Fear of . . .)
Animal fears	Snakes, rats, insects
Blood–injection–injury fears	Seeing blood or receiving an injection
Natural environment fears	Storms, heights, the ocean
Situation fears	Public transportation, tunnels, bridges, elevators, dental work, flying
Miscellaneous fears cued by stimuli not already mentioned	Choking, vomiting, contracting an illness, falling down

Learning may play a role in the development of a specific phobia. Classical and operant conditioning in particular could be involved in producing some phobias (Mowrer, 1939; see Chapter 4). If a stimulus such as a thunderstorm (the *conditioned stimulus*) is paired with a traumatic event (the *unconditioned stimulus*), anxiety and fear may become *conditioned responses* to thunderstorms. Furthermore, because fear and anxiety are lessened by avoiding the feared stimulus, the avoidant behavior is operantly reinforced. Observational learning from the behavior of other people who fear particular objects or situations can lead to the development of a phobia, by indicating what should be feared (Mineka et al., 1984). However, more recent work in this area questions the importance of classical conditioning because studies of people with phobias of spiders, heights, and water have not found evidence that such conditioning played the predicted role in the majority of cases (Jones & Menzies, 1995; Menzies & Clarke, 1993, 1995a, 1995b; Poulton et al., 1999). Nevertheless, operant conditioning principles are still involved in maintaining a phobia because avoidance of the feared stimuli decreases any fear and anxiety that would be experienced in the presence of the feared object or situation.

Posttraumatic Stress Disorder (PTSD)

An anxiety disorder can occur as a consequence of a traumatic event such as war, physical or sexual abuse, terrorism, or natural disasters. Victims of rape, for example, may be afraid to be alone, especially shortly after the attack. Women who have been raped may become afraid of and angry at all men, or they may experience more general feelings of anger, helplessness, guilt, pain, embarrassment, or anxiety. They may have sexual difficulties because the sexual act has been linked with such negative experiences and feelings. They may also develop physical symptoms of stress, such as stomachaches, headaches, back problems, inability to sleep, or diminished appetite. Depression may come and go over a long period. Long after the rape, they may remain afraid to trust anyone.

Some soldiers develop posttraumatic stress disorder.

Posttraumatic Stress Disorder From the Inside

Mr. E, age 65, complained that ever since World War II he experienced extreme nervousness that was somewhat alleviated by chewing tobacco. He also complained of amnestic periods lasting from seconds to minutes that he called blackout spells.... Mr. E stated that others would not tell him what happened during the blackout episodes, but family members reported that sometimes he would take his clothes off, pull at his hair, and scream. He was amnestic for a six-week period of his military service, during which he had been told that he was "crazy" and unfit for duty. After this wartime nervousness—consisting of subjective feelings of anxiety, itching, and shaking—developed [it got to the point where he experienced] eight such episodes in the month before he came to the hospital.

During the war Mr. E manned a landing craft that transported soldiers to the beaches. He was particularly distraught about an experience in which he felt something underfoot on a sandy beach and discovered that he was stepping on the face of a dead GI. He also described an incident in which his ship had been torpedoed and several crewmen killed. He experienced intense survivor guilt about this incident, and it was the precipitant for his six-week amnestic episode. (Hierholzer et al., 1992, p. 819)

The diagnosis of **posttraumatic stress disorder (PTSD)** is made when three conditions are met. First, the person experiences or witnesses an event that

Posttraumatic stress disorder (PTSD): A disorder experienced by some people after a traumatic event, whose symptoms include an unwanted reexperiencing of the trauma, avoidance of anything associated with the trauma, and heightened arousal.

Obsessive-compulsive disorder (OCD): A disorder marked by the presence of obsessions, and sometimes compulsions.

involves actual or threatened serious injury or death. Second, the traumatized person responds to the situation with fear and helplessness. Third, the traumatized individual then experiences three sets of symptoms. One set is the persistent reexperiencing of the traumatic event, which may take the form of intrusive, unwanted, and distressing recollections, dreams, or nightmares of the event, or may involve flashbacks that can include illusions, hallucinations, and a sense of reliving the experience. The second set of PTSD symptoms is a persistent avoidance of anything associated with the trauma and a general emotional numbing. The third set of symptoms is a heightened arousal, which can cause people with PTSD to startle easily (Shalev et al., 2000), have difficulty sleeping, or be in a constant state of hypervigilance. These symptoms do not always appear immediately after the traumatic event, and they can persist for months or even for years. The majority of people who experience trauma do not go on to experience PTSD (Breslau et al., 1998; Resnick et al., 1993; Shalev et al., 1998). Women are more likely to develop posttraumatic stress disorder when their traumas resulted from crimes rather than from natural disasters (Resnick et al., 1993).

Some people may be biologically at risk for developing symptoms of posttraumatic stress disorder, perhaps because of a genetic predisposition (Shalev et al., 1998; True et al., 1993). One possible way such a predisposition could manifest itself is in a hypersensitivity of the locus coeruleus, as occurs with panic disorder. In addition, the limbic system (including the amygdala) of people with this disorder appears to be more easily activated by mental imagery of traumatic events versus nontraumatic events (Rauch et al., 1996; Shin et al., 1997).

Factors at the level of the person include the traumatized person's psychological characteristics before, during, and after a trauma (Ehlers et al., 1998). A history of social withdrawal, depression, or a sense of not being able to control stressors all increase the risk of developing PTSD after a trauma (Joseph et al., 1995). The perception that your life is at risk during the traumatic event or that you have no control over it can also facilitate development of PTSD, regardless of the actual threat (Foa et al., 1989).

As in the case of phobias, classical and operant conditioning may help explain the avoidance symptoms of PTSD. Operant conditioning also helps us understand why people with PTSD are at a higher risk of developing drug abuse or dependence than those who experienced trauma that did not lead to PTSD (Chilcoat & Breslau, 1998). The substance abuse can be seen as leading to negative reinforcement: When the substances are taken, the symptoms of PTSD temporarily subside.

Whether trauma will lead to PTSD also depends, in part, on events at the level of the group. Support from friends, family, or counselors immediately after a trauma may help decrease the likelihood that PTSD will develop (Kaniasty & Norris, 1992; Kaniasty et al., 1990).

People with a handwashing compulsion may spend hours washing their hands until they are raw.

Obsessive-Compulsive Disorder (OCD)

Approximately 2% to 3% of Americans suffer from obsessive-compulsive disorder at some point in their lives (Robins & Regier, 1991), and although the same percentage of people experience this disorder in different countries, culture plays a role in the particular symptoms displayed (Weissman et al., 1994). **Obsessive-compulsive disorder (OCD)** is marked by the presence of *obsessions*, either alone or in combination with *compulsions*.

Obsessive-Compulsive Disorder From the Inside

One woman with OCD describes the ordeal of grocery shopping:

> Once I have attained control of the car, I have the burden of getting into it and getting it going. This can be a big project some days, locking and unlocking the doors, rolling up and down the power

windows, putting on and off the seat belts, sometimes countlessly.... Sometimes while driving I must do overtly good deeds, like letting cars out of streets in front of me, or stopping to let people cross. These are things everyone probably should do, but things I *must* do.... My trip in the car may take us to the grocery store. Inside I have certain rituals I must perform. I am relatively subtle about how I do them to avoid drawing attention to myself. Certain foods must have their packages read several times before I am allowed to purchase them. Some things need to be touched repetitively, certain tiles on the floor must be stepped on by myself and my family. I'll find myself having to go from one end of an aisle to the other and back again, just to make everything all right. I fear being accused of shoplifting sometimes because of the way I behave and the way I am always looking around to see if people have noticed my actions. (Steketee & White, 1990, pp. 12–13)

Obsessions are recurrent and persistent thoughts, impulses, or images that feel intrusive and inappropriate, and that are difficult to suppress or ignore. These are more than excessive worries about real problems, and may cause significant anxiety and distress. Common obsessions involve thoughts of contamination ("Will I become contaminated by shaking her hand?"), repeated doubts ("Did I lock the door? Did I turn off the stove?"), the need to have things in a certain order (a perfect alignment of cans of food in a cupboard), or aggressive or horrific impulses (such as the urge to shout an obscenity in church).

Compulsions are repetitive behaviors or mental acts that some individuals feel driven to perform in response to an obsession. Examples of compulsive behaviors are *washing* in response to thoughts of contamination (washing the hands repeatedly until they are raw), *checking* (checking again and again that the stove is turned off or the windows closed so that it can take hours to leave the house), *ordering* (putting objects in a certain order or in precise symmetry, a task that may take hours until perfection is attained), and *counting* (counting to 100 after each obsessive thought, such as thinking about hitting one's child or shouting an obscenity). Some people with OCD believe that a dreaded event will occur if they do not perform their ritual of checking, ordering, and so on, but these compulsions are not realistically connected to what they are trying to ward off, at least not in the frequency and duration with which the compulsion occurs.

OCD can be understood by looking at events at the three levels and their interactions. At the level of the brain, studies of families have produced evidence for a genetic contribution, although not a straightforward link: If one member of a family has OCD, others are more likely to have an anxiety disorder, but not necessarily OCD itself (Black et al., 1992; Torgersen, 1983). Brain structures and neurotransmitters have been implicated: Obsessions and compulsions have been related to a loop of neural activity that occurs in the caudate nucleus of the basal ganglia (Breiter et al., 1996; Jenike, 1984; Rauch et al., 1994). Obsessions may occur when the caudate nucleus does not do its normal job of "turning off" recurrent thoughts before they become obsessions about an object or circumstance; carrying out a compulsion may temporarily end the obsessional thoughts (Insel, 1992; Jenike, 1984; Modell et al., 1989). The neurotransmitter serotonin appears to play a role in the presence of OCD symptomatology; serotonin-based medications such as Prozac reduce symptoms, although the exact mechanism is unknown (Greenberg et al., 1997).

As with other anxiety disorders, operant conditioning may be involved. Because a compulsive behavior may momentarily relieve the anxiety created by the obsessions, the compulsion is reinforced and thus more likely to recur.

At the level of the group, people with more serious OCD tended to have families who were more rejecting of them and to have experienced more kinds of family stress (Calvocoressi et al., 1995). However, the direction of causation is unclear: Were families more rejecting because their OCD relatives were more symptomatic, and therefore more difficult to live with? Or did the strong rejection by the families produce stronger symptoms of OCD in the affected relatives? Perhaps future research will be able to say more about causation.

Obsession: A recurrent and persistent thought, impulse, or image that feels intrusive and inappropriate, and is difficult to suppress or ignore.

Compulsion: A repetitive behavior or mental act that an individual feels compelled to perform in response to an obsession.

Mood disorder: A condition marked by persistent or episodic disturbances in feeling states that interfere with normal functioning in at least one realm of life.

Major depressive disorder (MDD): A disorder characterized by at least 2 weeks of depressed mood or loss of interest in nearly all activities, along with sleep or eating disturbances, loss of energy, and feelings of hopelessness.

Mood Disorders

By some estimates, about half of those who have suffered from anxiety disorders will also suffer from depression (Kessler, Stang et al., 1998), which is a type of mood disorder. **Mood disorders** are conditions marked by persistent or episodic disturbances in feeling states that interfere with normal functioning in at least one realm of life. Among the most common mood disorders are major depressive disorder, dysthymia (a less intense but longer-lasting form of depression), and bipolar disorder (also known as manic-depressive disorder).

Major Depressive Disorder: Not Just Feeling Blue

When people are feeling sad or blue, they may say they are "depressed," but generally they do not mean they are suffering from a psychological disorder. **Major depressive disorder (MDD)** is characterized by at least 2 weeks of depressed mood or loss of interest in nearly all activities, along with at least four of the other symptoms of depression listed in Table 11.4 (American Psychiatric Association, 1994). Thus, major depression affects a person's "ABC's": affect (mood), behavior (actions), and cognition (thoughts). It is estimated that up to one in five people in the United States will experience this disorder in their lifetimes (APA, 2000; Ross, 1991), and that by the year 2020, depression will probably be the second most disabling disease in the nation, after heart disease (Schrof & Schultz, 1999). Some people with depression may experience only one episode; others experience recurrent episodes that may be frequent or separated by years; or the depression becomes more chronic (Judd et al., 1998). A recent 10-year study of over 300 people diagnosed with major depressive disorder found that more than one-third of the participants did not have a recurrence of depression (Solomon et al., 2000).

Artist Kate Monson, who experienced depression, describes her painting as a reflection of her depression.

Major Depressive Disorder From the Inside

The experience of depression is captured in words by Elizabeth Wurtzel, author of *Prozac Nation:*

In my case, I was not frightened in the least bit at the thought that I might live because I was certain, quite certain, that I was already dead. The actual dying part, the withering away of my physical body, was a mere formality. My spirit, my emotional being, whatever you want to call all that inner turmoil that has nothing to do with physical existence, were long gone, dead and gone, and only a mass of the most . . . god-awful excruciating pain . . . was left in its wake.

That's the thing I want to make clear about depression: It's got nothing at all to do with life. In the course of life, there is sadness and pain and sorrow, all of which, in their right time and season, are normal—unpleasant, but normal. Depression is in an altogether different zone because it involves a complete absence: absence of affect, absence of feeling, absence of response, absence of interest. The pain you feel in the course of a major clinical depression is an attempt on nature's part (nature, after all, abhors a vacuum) to fill up the empty space. But for all intents and purposes, the deeply depressed are just the walking, waking dead. (Wurtzel, 1995, p. 22)

Elizabeth Wurtzel's description of her depression captures the essence of the painful, extremely disturbing quality of many of the symptoms. In some cases, severely depressed people also have delusions or hallucinations. Often these psychotic symptoms feature themes of guilt, deserved punishment, and personal inadequacy, such as voices asserting the individual's worthlessness.

Major depressive disorder, the most common psychological disorder in the United States (Kessler et al., 1994), is found among all cultural and ethnic groups (Weissman et al., 1991), as well as across the economic spectrum. However, not

TABLE **11.4**   **Diagnostic Criteria for Major Depressive Disorder**

Source: American Psychiatric Association (1994).

During a period of at least 2 weeks, five or more of the following symptoms have occurred and represent a change in functioning.

- Depressed mood most of the day, almost daily (based on subjective report or observations of others).
- Markedly diminished interest or pleasure in nearly all daily activities (based on subjective or objective reports).
- Significant weight loss, not through dieting.
- Daily insomnia or hypersomnia (sleeping a lot).
- Daily psychomotor agitation (intense restlessness) or retardation (physical sluggishness).
- Daily fatigue, or loss of energy.
- Almost daily feelings of worthlessness, or inappropriate or excessive guilt.
- Almost daily diminished ability to think or concentrate, or indecisiveness (based on subjective or objective reports).
- Recurrent thoughts of death or suicide with or without a specific plan.

all cultures share exactly the same symptom list. In Latin and Mediterranean cultures, people with major depressive disorder tend to experience "nerves" or headaches, not necessarily sadness and guilt. In Asian cultures, people with major depression are likely to report weakness, tiredness, or a sense of "imbalance." In developing countries, rates are estimated to be about the same for men and for women (Culbertson, 1997), but American women are diagnosed with depression two to three times more frequently than American men (APA, 2000; Culbertson, 1997; Gater et al., 1998). Further, the overall rate of depression is increasing in the United States (Lewinsohn et al., 1993).

Many, if not most, suicide attempts seem to be motivated by the sense of hopelessness that is often a part of depression. Approximately 30% of people with depression attempt suicide, and half of those succeed. One estimate is that 19,200 depressed people in the United States commit suicide every year (American Foundation for Suicide Prevention, 1996). Suicide prevention programs try, in part, to treat depression and alcohol use, factors leading to suicide (Reifman & Windle, 1995). Several common misconceptions about suicide are listed in Table 11.5 on page 410. Test yourself to see if your views of suicide are accurate.

Some people—approximately 6% of the American population—experience a less intense but longer-lasting type of depression called **dysthymia** (American Psychiatric Association, 1994). When experiencing dysthymia, people have a depressed mood for most of the day for at least 2 years and experience two other symptoms of depression (see Table 11.4; APA, 1994) rather than the increased number and intensity of symptoms of major depression.

Bipolar Disorder: Going to Extremes

In contrast to depression, **bipolar disorder** is a mood disorder marked by a manic episode or the less intense hypomanic episode; some people with this disorder also experience depression. Approximately 1% of Americans have this disorder (Regier & Kaelber, 1995). A **manic episode** is a period of at least a week during which an abnormally elevated, expansive, or irritable mood persists. Being manic is not just having an "up" day. During a manic episode, the sufferer may be euphoric and enthusiastic about everything, starting conversations with strangers and making grandiose plans.

Dysthymia: A mood disorder similar to major depressive disorder, but less intense and longer lasting.

Bipolar disorder: A mood disorder marked by one or more episodes of either mania or hypomania.

Manic episode: A period of at least 1 week during which an abnormally elevated, expansive, or irritable mood persists.

TABLE 11.5 **Common Misconceptions of Suicide**

Source: Adapted from Suicide Awareness\Voices of Education (SA\VE), P.O. Box 24507, Minneapolis, MN 55424; Phone: (612) 946-7998; Internet: http://www.save.org; E-mail: save@winternet.com.

- *If you talk about suicide, you won't really do it.* (False: Most people who commit suicide gave some clue or warning. Threats or statements about suicide should not be ignored.)

- *People who attempt suicide are "crazy."* (False: Suicidal people are not "crazy"; they are likely to be depressed, upset, or feel hopeless.)

- *Someone determined to commit suicide can't be stopped.* (False: Almost all suicidal people have mixed feelings about living and dying up until the last moment. Moreover, most suicidal people don't want to die; they want their pain to stop. And the suicidal impulse often passes.)

- *People who commit suicide weren't willing to seek help.* (False: Studies have shown that more than half of suicide victims sought medical help within the 6 months before death.)

- *Talking about suicide could give someone the idea, so you shouldn't talk or ask about it.* (False. Discussing suicide openly can be helpful to someone who is suicidal.)

Bipolar Disorder From the Inside

Psychologist Kay Redfield Jamison describes her personal experience with mania:

> There is a particular kind of pain, elation, loneliness, and terror involved in this kind of madness. When you're high, it's tremendous. The ideas and feelings are fast and frequent like shooting stars, and you follow them until you find better and brighter ones. Shyness goes, the right words and gestures are suddenly there, the power to captivate others a felt certainty. There are interests found in uninteresting people. Sensuality is pervasive and the desire to seduce and be seduced irresistible. Feelings of ease, intensity, power, well-being, financial omnipotence, and euphoria pervade one's marrow. But, somewhere, this changes. The fast ideas are far too fast, and there are far too many; overwhelming confusion replaces clarity. Memory goes. Humor and absorption on friends' faces are replaced by fear and concerns. Everything previously moving with the grain is now against—you are irritable, angry, frightened, uncontrollable, and enmeshed totally in the blackest caves of the mind. You never knew those caves were there. It will never end, for madness carves its own reality. (Jamison, 1995, p. 67)

Psychologist Kay Redfield Jamison, like many people with bipolar disorder, had difficulty recognizing that she had a psychological disorder and resisted attempts at treatment for a number of years. People experiencing **hypomania** have less severe symptoms of mania, and their symptoms are less likely to interfere with social functioning. Manic or hypomanic episodes are often preceded or followed by episodes of depression, and the cycling of the mood usually takes place over a number of years, although some people may experience rapid cycling, with four or more mood shifts in a year. If left untreated, mood swings often become more frequent over time, leading to a poorer prognosis. The early phase of an episode, before the symptoms become acute, is termed the *prodromal phase* (a *prodrome* is a warning symptom). Some people with bipolar disorder report prodromal indicators of manic or depressive symptoms that signal that an episode will occur (Keitner et al., 1996).

Explaining Mood Disorders

Although bipolar and major depressive disorders are distinct disorders, recent research has characterized these disorders, as well as dysthymia, as lying along a spectrum of mood disorders that are related by biological and psychological factors (Akiskal, 1996; Angst, 1998). As with anxiety disorders, mood disorders can best be understood by considering events at three levels of analysis and their interactions: the brain, the person, and the group.

The Brain. Twin studies show that if one identical twin has a major depression, the co-twin is four times more likely to experience a depression than the co-twin

Hypomania: A mood state similar to mania, but less severe, with fewer and less intrusive symptoms.

of an affected fraternal twin (Bowman & Nurnberger, 1993; Kendler et al., 1999). This appears to be good evidence for genetic influence. However, adoption studies have not shown the same clear-cut evidence for a genetic role (Eley et al., 1998; Wender et al., 1986). More definitive support for biological factors comes from research with depressed people with relatives who also suffer from depression: The depressed people studied had unusually low activity in one area of the frontal lobe that has direct connections to many brain areas involved in emotion, such as the amygdala. This part of the frontal lobe also has connections to the systems that produce serotonin, norepinephrine, and dopamine (Kennedy et al., 1997). In contrast, there is evidence that the amygala is enlarged in people with bipolar disorder (Altshuler et al., 1998). These abnormalities in or affecting the amygdala in people with mood disorders are consistent with the role of the amygdala in regulating mood and accessing emotional memories (LeDoux, 1996; see Chapters 6 and 7). Recent brain-scanning studies of people with bipolar disorder have found shifts in temporal lobe activity during manic episodes that are not present during other mood states (Gyulai et al., 1997), which may be related to activity in parts of the limbic system that are located in this structure.

There is good evidence for an underlying genetic relationship between bipolar and depressive mood disorders. For example, if an identical twin has bipolar disorder, the co-twin has an 80% chance of developing some kind of mood disorder (such as depression), although not necessarily bipolar disorder (Karkowski & Kendler, 1997; Vehmanen et al., 1995).

Evidence that neurotransmitter or neuromodulator activity plays a role in depression was uncovered years ago. In fact, some researchers thought that the puzzle of depression was nearly solved with the discovery that medications that alter the serotonin or norepinephrine systems, discussed further in the next chapter, can diminish or remove symptoms of depression. Unfortunately, it is not yet clear which substances are most involved in depression; it is not even clear whether the problem is having too much or too little of those substances (Duman et al., 1997). What *is* clear, however, is that some change occurs in the activity of serotonin, norepinephrine, and possibly a more recently discovered neurotransmitter, *substance P* (Kramer et al., 1998), among people with depression.

Neurotransmitters are also implicated in bipolar disorder, although the exact mechanism is unknown. There is some support for the theory that bipolar disorder involves disturbances in the functioning of serotonin (Goodwin & Jamison, 1990). Moreover, it is known that lithium, the medication usually prescribed for bipolar disorder, lowers the activity level of norepinephrine in the brain (Bunney & Garland, 1983), but just how this happens is not yet known.

The Person. Events at the level of the person can be associated with a higher risk of depression. Compared with people who are not depressed, depressed people make more negative comments and less eye contact, are less responsive, and speak more softly and in shorter sentences (Gotlib & Robinson, 1982; Segrin & Abramson, 1994). Aaron Beck (1967) found evidence of a "negative triad of depression" in the thoughts of depressed people. This triad consists of (1) a negative view of the world, (2) a negative view of the self, and (3) a negative view of the future. Beck proposes that people with depression commit errors in their thinking, or "cognitive distortions," based on these three sets of beliefs, and that these errors in logic maintain an outlook on life that perpetuates depressing feelings and behaviors. These cognitive distortions may be based on early learning.

Of particular interest is evidence that people's views of themselves and the world can influence their risk of developing depression. A person's characteristic way of explaining life events—his or her **attributional style**—affects the risk of depression. For people who attribute blame to themselves (versus external factors), the risk of depression rises, especially after a stressful event (Monroe & Depue, 1991). Research on attributional styles and

Attributional style: A person's characteristic way of explaining life events.

Mothers with an internal attributional style during the second trimester of pregnancy were more likely to be depressed three months after childbirth (Peterson & Seligman, 1984).

depression find that those people who tend to attribute unfortunate events to internal causes (their own thoughts, abilities, behaviors, and the like), and who believe that these causes are stable, are more likely to become depressed. Thus, depressing thoughts (such as "I deserved to be fired . . . I wasn't as good at my job as some other people") are more likely to lead to depressing feelings. In contrast, patterns of attributing blame to external causes ("I was laid off because I didn't have enough seniority"), even if inaccurate, are less likely to lead to depression (Abramson et al., 1978).

The Group. Events at the level of the group have also been tied to depression. Life stresses that occur before the development of depression can influence the severity of the depression. Moreover, as would be expected according to the principles of operant conditioning (see Chapter 4), the less opportunity there is for social reinforcement because of decreased activity and contact with other people, the more likely it is that depressive symptoms will occur (MacPhillamy & Lewinsohn, 1974). Similarly, environments that not only lack positive reinforcements but also provide many "punishing" experiences (such as being regularly criticized) put people at risk for depression. Programs designed to help those with depression increase the frequency and quality of positive interactions with others (as well as decreasing the frequency and quality of punishing interactions) to minimize depressive symptoms (Teri & Lewinsohn, 1985).

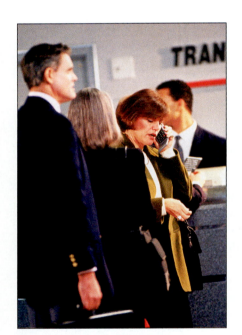

Events at the level of the group can affect the course of bipolar disorder. Events that disrupt social rhythms, such as moving to a new residence (Malkoff-Schwartz et al., 1998), and social stressors that affect biological rhythms or schedules, such as frequent plane travel or repeated changes in work schedules, can adversely affect the course of the disease (Johnson & Roberts, 1995; Post, 1992).

Although not necessarily associated with the *onset* of depression, the family environment can be influential in *recovery* from a depressive episode. Living with unsupportive and critical relatives can increase the risk of a relapse of depression (Hooley & Licht, 1997; Miller et al., 1992). First episodes of bipolar disorder are invariably preceded by significant stressors (Goodwin & Ghaemi, 1998). And, as with depression, people with bipolar disorder are more likely to relapse if they live with critical families (Honig et al., 1997; Miklowitz et al., 1988). Life stressors can also impede recovery after a hospitalization for bipolar disorder (Johnson & Miller, 1997). On a positive note, programs designed to reduce the critical behavior of families appear to be effective in reducing relapses (Honig et al., 1997).

Culture may also play a role in facilitating depression. Nolen-Hoeksema (1987) offered a cultural explanation for the finding that women in developed countries experience depression more often than men. She and others (Nolen-Hoeksema & Morrow, 1993; Vajk et al., 1997) have found that people in developed countries who ruminate about their depressed mood are more likely to have longer periods of depression. She proposes that as children, boys and girls are taught to respond differently to stressors, and they carry these response styles with them through adulthood. She contends that boys are encouraged to deemphasize feelings and to use distraction and action-oriented coping strategies, whereas girls are encouraged to be introspective and not to take action. A ruminative response is known to promote depression; action and distraction can serve as protection. And in fact, research has shown that depressed mood improves when college students learn to increase strategies of distraction and decrease their ruminations (Nolen-Hoeksema & Morrow, 1993). Other psychologists propose that the substantially higher rate of depression in women may also be due to biases in how the diagnosis is made and how depression is measured (Hartung & Widiger, 1998; Sprock & Yoder, 1997).

Events at the three levels are not independent but interact in a number of ways. In particular, James Coyne (1976; Coyne & Downey, 1991) has proposed an interactional theory of depression. He theorized that the depressed person, who may be biologically vulnerable to depression, alienates others who might provide support through his or her verbal and nonverbal actions (Nolan & Mineka, 1997). Such actions include negative attitudes, dependent behavior, and an inclination to ignore or be unable to use help or advice from others. These actions eventually lead other people to reject or criticize the depressed person, confirming the depressed person's negative view of him- or herself, and increasing the likelihood of negative future events.

We know that van Gogh suffered from bouts of depression, at times had poor hygiene, narrowed his activities severely, and took pleasure only in painting. MDD seems like a possible diagnosis. Van Gogh's attempted assault on Gauguin, as well as the self-mutilation of his ear might be explained by MDD with psychotic features. Perhaps the auditory hallucination that told him to kill Gauguin was caused by his depression. Although MDD could explain the majority of these symptoms, it is not the only possibility. Bipolar disorder is another potential diagnosis. Perhaps van Gogh's episodes of frenzied painting were manic episodes, although they could also have been an intense restlessness that can occur with depression. His attacks, which became more frequent over time, might have been episodes of mania that became psychotic; untreated episodes of mania do become more frequent.

LOOKING AT LEVELS

Depression Is as Depression Does

Have you ever noticed that it's no fun being with a depressed person? A depressed mood can be contagious, and family and friends of depressed people may find themselves being and acting somewhat depressed, further limiting their assistance to the depressed person (Coyne et al., 1987). Thomas Joiner (1994) found that people who spent time with depressed roommates over a period of 3 weeks themselves became more depressed. Indeed, anger, anxiety, depression, and sadness have also been found to be contagious (Coyne, 1976; Hsee et al., 1990; Joiner, 1994; Katz et al., 1999; Segrin & Dillard, 1992; Sullins, 1991).

One possible way that you "catch" emotions from others is by acting like them, which leads you to feel similarly. At the level of the brain, just as putting on a happy face can make you feel better, putting on a frown can make you feel worse (Ekman et al., 1990; see Chapter 7). This response could be unconscious. In fact, just seeing a happy or an angry face causes muscles in your own face to respond, and to respond very quickly—in less than a half a second (Dimberg & Thunberg, 1998). At the level of the person, when participants were asked to inhibit their facial movements when they watched happy films, they later reported enjoying the films less than when their facial muscles were allowed to move spontaneously as they watched; however, large differences were reported in the degree to which making an expression led to the experience of the corresponding emotion (Laird et al., 1994). Moreover, at the level of the group, someone's behavior may directly affect a close companion. For example, a depressed person is less responsive, which in and of itself may lead a companion to become depressed (Coyne, 1976). In addition, those who develop depression are more likely to behave in ways that create stress in their environments, which in turn can trigger the onset of depression in others (McGuffin et al., 1988; Rende & Plomin, 1992).

CONSOLIDATE!

1 *What are the main types of anxiety disorders? What are their symptoms and causes?* The anxiety disorders include panic disorder (with or without agoraphobia), specific and social phobias, PTSD, and OCD. Panic symptoms include nausea, dizziness, palpitations, and a fear of doing something crazy or uncontrollable. Phobias involve avoiding a feared object or situation that would cause anxiety or panic if encountered. PTSD occurs in response to traumatic events; it involves some symptoms of panic, as well as a reliving of the trauma. OCD involves obsessions and often compulsions. Anxiety disorders are caused by the interaction of events at the levels of the brain, the person, and the group.

2 *What are mood disorders? What causes them?* Mood disorders include major depressive disorder, dysthymia, and bipolar disorder (which may have psychotic features). Major depressive disorder is characterized by depressed mood, loss of pleasure, fatigue, weight loss, poor sleep, a sense of worthlessness or guilt, and poor attention and concentration. Dysthymia is a less intense but longer-lasting type of depression. Bipolar disorder involves the presence of manic or hypomanic episodes. Although all of these disorders appear to have a biological component, events at the levels of the person and group can play a role in onset or relapse.

Schizophrenia

In the last years of his life, van Gogh apparently had increasing difficulty distinguishing between his internal experiences and external reality. He would become disoriented and not know who he was. He had delusions of being poisoned and attacked. Gauguin claimed that van Gogh referred to himself as a ghost before cutting off part of his ear. During a period of mental clarity, when van Gogh was asked about the assault on Gauguin, he said that he was given to hearing voices, that he had heard voices telling him to kill Gauguin. Then he remembered the biblical injunction, "If thine own eye offend thee, pluck it out." His ear had offended him by "hearing" the voice that suggested he kill Gauguin, so he cut part of it off to do penance for his sin against Gauguin (Lubin, 1972).

These aspects of van Gogh's life and behavior suggest the possibility of schizophrenia. Books or movies sometimes portray schizophrenia as if it meant having a split personality, but schizophrenia is characterized by a split from reality, not a split from different aspects of oneself.

The word *schizophrenia* is derived from two Greek words, *schizo* meaning "to split" or "to cut," and *phren* meaning "mind" or "reason." **Schizophrenia** is a psychotic disorder that profoundly alters affect, behavior, and cognition, particularly the pattern or form of thought, and causes a deterioration of functioning.

1 What are the symptoms of schizophrenia?

2 What are the subtypes of schizophrenia?

3 Why do some people develop schizophrenia?

Symptoms: What Schizophrenia Looks Like

The term *schizophrenia* actually embraces a number of subtypes of this disorder, each with distinct symptoms and prognoses (prospects of recovery). Symptoms of schizophrenia are usually divided into two groups (see Table 11.6). **Positive symptoms** involve an excess or distortion of normal functions, such as hallucinations. They are called positive not because they indicate something desirable, but because

TABLE 11.6 Positive and Negative Symptoms of Schizophrenia

POSITIVE SYMPTOMS

Delusions of

- Persecution (beliefs that others are out to "get" you)
- Grandeur (beliefs that you are an important person)
- Reference (beliefs that normal events have special meaning directed toward you)
- Control (beliefs that your feelings, behaviors, or thoughts are controlled by others)

Hallucinations

- Disordered behavior
- Disorganized speech

NEGATIVE SYMPTOMS

- Flat affect
- Alogia (brief, slow, empty replies to questions)
- Avolition (inability to initiate goal-directed behavior)

Schizophrenia: A psychotic disorder in which the patient's affect, behavior, and the pattern or form of thoughts are profoundly altered and functioning deteriorates.

Positive symptom: An excess or distortion of normal functions, such as a hallucination.

they mark the *presence* of certain unusual behaviors. **Negative symptoms**, on the other hand, involve a *diminution* or *loss* of normal functions, such as a restriction in speech or movement.

Positive symptoms include *delusions* (distortions of thought) and *hallucinations*. Positive symptoms are usually more responsive than negative symptoms to antipsychotic medication (discussed in the next chapter). Delusions can be complex, centering on a particular theme, such as the belief that someone, or some people, are out to "get" you (see Table 11.6). Hallucinations in schizophrenia are typically auditory; hearing voices is a common symptom. *Disorganized behavior* can include inappropriate, childlike silliness or unpredictable agitation. People with disorganized behavior may have difficulty with everyday tasks such as organizing meals, maintaining hygiene, and selecting their clothes (they might wear two overcoats in the summer). Another positive symptom is *disorganized speech,* as in the following example: "I may be a 'Blue Baby' but 'Social Baby' not, but yet a blue heart baby could be in the Blue Book published before the war" (Maher, 1966, p. 413).

Negative symptoms include flat affect, alogia, and avolition (see Table 11.6). *Flat affect* is a general failure to express or respond to emotion. There may be occasional smiles or warmth of manner, but usually the facial expression is constant; eye contact is rare and body language minimal. *Alogia,* or "poverty of speech," is characterized by brief, slow, empty replies to questions. Alogia is not an unwillingness to speak; rather, the thoughts behind the words seem slowed down. Someone with alogia speaks less than others and doesn't use words as freely. *Avolition* is an inability to initiate or persist in goal-directed activities. Someone exhibiting avolition may sit for long periods without engaging in any behavior or social interaction.

Not all these symptoms are present in everyone affected with schizophrenia. According to the *DSM-IV,* a diagnosis of schizophrenia requires that two or more symptoms are displayed for at least a week and that other signs of socially inappropriate behavior are exhibited for at least 6 months. The average age of onset of schizophrenia is the 20s, although in some people (particularly women) onset does not come until later in life. Symptoms often occur gradually, with a prodromal phase characterized by slow deterioration in functioning, including withdrawal from other people, poor hygiene, and outbursts of anger. Eventually the symptoms reach an active phase, in which full-blown positive and negative symptoms arise.

Did van Gogh appear to exhibit symptoms of schizophrenia? We know that he had auditory hallucinations and that he exhibited inappropriate social behavior (including poor hygiene and outbursts of anger), but he does not appear to have had negative symptoms of schizophrenia (at least not between his attacks). Not enough is known about his behavior during his attacks to determine whether additional symptoms accompanied them.

Types of Schizophrenia

People with schizophrenia, as mentioned earlier, tend to suffer from only some of the full range of possible symptoms. The symptoms of schizophrenia tend to cluster into groupings, and from these groupings mental health professionals and researchers have identified subtypes of schizophrenia. The *DSM-IV* specifies four subtypes of schizophrenia (see Table 11.7 on page 416): paranoid, disorganized, catatonic, and undifferentiated.

Paranoid Schizophrenia From the Inside

Jeffrey DeMann describes his first hospitalization for schizophrenia at the age of 27:

> I recall vividly the delusion of believing my mother was to take my place in the shock treatments. Then I was to be quietly murdered and placed in an acid bath grave, which would dissolve any

Negative symptom: A diminution or loss of normal functions, such as a restriction in speech.

TABLE 11.7   Four Subtypes of Schizophrenia, According to *DSM-IV*

Source: American Psychiatric Association (1994).

Paranoid

Delusions of persecution are prominent; intellectual functioning and affect are relatively intact, but auditory hallucinations are common. People with this subtype have the best prognosis for recovery.

Disorganized

Disorganized speech and behavior and flat or inappropriate affect are prominent.

Catatonic

Catatonic (bizarre, immobile, or relentless) motor behaviors are prominent.

Undifferentiated

Symptoms do not clearly fall into any of the above three subtypes.

physical evidence of my existence. At this time, auditory hallucinations also were present. I could actually hear the slamming of my mother's body on the table while being administered the deadly shock. I truly believed my mother was now dead in my place. I also recall curling up on an old wooden bench and repeatedly chanting the words "Die quickly now." (DeMann, 1994, p. 580)

If van Gogh were in fact schizophrenic, the paranoid subtype diagnosis would seem to fit him best because his intellectual functioning and affect remained relatively intact between attacks. But he apparently did not have extended periods of paranoid delusions, and schizophrenia would not account for his lengthy bouts of depression.

Why Does This Happen to Some People, But Not Others?

With few exceptions, schizophrenia occurs at about the same rate worldwide, about 1 in 100 (Gottesman, 1991). However, industrialized countries have lower recovery rates than do developing nations (American Psychiatric Association, 1994). Explanations why some people and not others suffer from schizophrenia, and why recovery rates are different in different places and circumstances, involve the three levels of analysis and the interaction of events at these levels.

The Brain

Twin, family, and adoption studies point to the influence of genetic factors in the development of schizophrenia (Gottesman, 1991; Kendler & Diehl, 1993; Tiernari, 1991). Having relatives with schizophrenia increases the risk of developing schizophrenia; the closer the relative, the greater the risk. However, it is important to note that even for those who have a close relative with schizophrenia, the actual incidence is still quite low. More than 80% of people who have a parent or sibling diagnosed with schizophrenia do *not* have the disorder themselves (Gottesman & Moldin, 1998). Even in the case of the highest level of genetic resemblance, identical twins, the co-twin of a schizophrenic twin has only a 48% risk of developing schizophrenia. If the disease were entirely genetic, we would expect a 100% risk in this circumstance. And a fraternal co-twin has only a 17% likelihood of developing the disorder (Gottesman, 1991). Although genes may play a role in the etiology of schizophrenia, they are clearly not the only factor.

Evidence from autopsies and brain-scanning studies suggests that schizophrenia may involve abnormalities in brain structures. Someone with schizophrenia is more likely than others to have enlarged *ventricles,* cavities in the center of the brain filled with cerebrospinal fluid. Increased ventricle size means a reduction in the size of other brain areas, including the frontal cortex (Goldstein et al., 1999), which plays a central role in abstract thinking and planning.

Enlarged ventricles are also associated with decreases in the size of the temporal lobe (which, among other things, processes auditory information, some aspects of language, and visual recognition) and of the thalamus, which transmits sensory information to other parts of the brain (Andreasen et al., 1994). There is evidence that these abnormalities already exist at the time of a first episode of psychosis and thus are not the consequences of either the disorder or medications given to treat the disorder (Velakoulis et al., 1999).

Researchers looking at different ways in which these brain abnormalities might arise have found several possible causes. One focus has been on the fetus's developing brain, and how normal brain development may go awry during gestation, the 9 months the fetus is developing in the mother's uterus. Possibilities include maternal malnourishment during pregnancy (Brown, van Os, et al., 1999), maternal illness (Buka et al., 1999; Gilmore et al., 1997; Mednick et al., 1998), and prenatal or birth-related medical complications that lead to oxygen deprivation (Cannon, 1997; Geddes & Lawrie, 1995; McNeil et al., 2000; Zornberg et al., 2000). Because research has found a higher incidence of prenatal and birth complications in babies born to mothers with schizophrenia, some have further argued that fetuses with a genetic predisposition to schizophrenia have an increased likelihood of abnormal development, which in turn leads to the higher rate of prenatal and birth complications (Goodman, 1988). However, some researchers suggest that complications in and of themselves do not create a risk for schizophrenia in the absence of genetic vulnerability (Buka et al., 1999). Rather, it is the combination of the genetic vulnerability and the physical complications during gestation and birth that together heighten the risk for the alteration in brain development and later schizophrenia.

Similarly, children who are at risk for schizophrenia—those who show an extreme discomfort with close relationships and exhibit relatively high levels of quirky or odd behavior—are more reactive to stress and have higher baseline levels of the stress-related hormone cortisol (Walker et al., 1999; see Chapter 10). Some suggest that the increased biological changes and stressors of adolescence lead to higher levels of stress hormones, which in turn are thought to affect dopamine activity. Initial symptoms of schizophrenia often begin to emerge during adolescence.

Neurotransmitters, particularly dopamine, have been implicated in schizophrenia (Walker & Diforio, 1997). It was once thought that an overproduction of dopamine, or an increased number or sensitivity of dopamine receptors, was responsible for schizophrenia. This *dopamine hypothesis* received support from research showing that medications that decrease the amount of dopamine reduce the positive symptoms of schizophrenia. Moreover, when people who do not have schizophrenia are given drugs that increase dopamine activity, they experience schizophrenia-like symptoms (Syvalathi, 1994). Perhaps, it was thought, excess dopamine triggers a flood of unrelated thoughts, feelings, and perceptions, and the delusions are attempts to organize these disconnected events into a coherent, understandable experience (Gottesman, 1991). However, research soon indicated that the dopamine hypothesis is too simple. Although dopamine clearly plays a role in schizophrenia, other neurotransmitters and neural processes are also involved (Laruelle et al., 1993; Nestler, 1997; Syvalathi, 1994; Walker & Diforio, 1997; Weinberger & Lipska, 1995).

Using careful analyses of home movies taken during the childhoods of people who were later diagnosed with schizophrenia, Walker and colleagues (Grimes & Walker, 1994; Walker et al., 1993) found that those who went on to develop schizophrenia were different from their siblings. They found that from infancy through adolescence these people exhibited more involuntary movements, such

Well   Affected

28 year old males

Those with schizophrenia have larger ventricles, smaller amounts of frontal and temporal lobe cortex, and a smaller thalamus. This decreased cortical volume probably accounts for some of the cognitive deficits found in people with schizophrenia (Andreasen et al., 1986, 1992).

as writhing or excessive movements of the tongue, lip, or arm (Walker et al., 1994). The more severe the involuntary movements, the more severe the schizophrenic symptoms in adulthood (Neumann & Walker, 1996). Although the exact mechanisms responsible for this finding have not yet been discovered, these results are consistent with other findings of a biological vulnerability to schizophrenia that exists prior to adulthood.

Similar results were found in a group of Finnish people with schizophrenia. Looking back at their school performance, researchers found that the children who went on to develop schizophrenia did not do significantly worse academically than other children. But they did do significantly worse at sports and handicrafts, activities that require the frontal lobe processes involved in motor coordination (Cannon et al., 1999).

In sum, many researchers believe that prenatal and birth complications may play a role in the development of schizophrenia, and some individuals are genetically vulnerable to the disorder. These factors may create abnormalities in brain structure, particularly in the frontal lobe, and in the structure and function of neurotransmitter systems. The exact mechanism for the brain abnormalities in some people with schizophrenia, however, has yet to be found.

The Person

The home movies study mentioned above also found that those children who went on to develop schizophrenia exhibited fewer expressions of joy than their unaffected siblings (Walker et al., 1993). This emotional dampening may also cause other people to respond less positively (because of emotional contagion, as described earlier). In addition, for someone who has had episodes of schizophrenia, a stressful life event may act as a trigger, leading to a recurrence of symptoms (Gottesman, 1991; Ventura et al., 1989). And what counts as stressful, of course, depends on the person.

The Group

Almost two-thirds of people hospitalized with schizophrenia live with their families after leaving the hospital, and the way a family expresses emotion can affect the likelihood of a recurrence of acute symptoms, although it does not *cause* schizophrenia. Families that are critical, hostile, and overinvolved, termed **high expressed emotion** families, are more likely to include someone with schizophrenia who has had a recurrence; this higher rate is strongest for those with more chronic schizophrenia (Butzlaff & Hooley, 1998; Kavanagh, 1992; Vaughn & Leff, 1976). However, it is possible that high expressed emotion families may be responding to a relative with schizophrenia who is more bizarre or disruptive, and that low expressed emotion families include someone whose schizophrenic symptoms are less extreme. A longitudinal study of people with schizophrenia found that after their first psychotic episodes, those who had larger numbers of nonrelated people in their social support networks before their first episodes had the best recoveries 5 years later (Erikson et al., 1998).

A higher rate of schizophrenia is found in urban areas and in lower socioeconomic classes (Freeman, 1994; Mortensen et al., 1999). Why might this be? Two factors appear to play a role: *social selection* and *social causation* (Dauncey et al., 1993). **Social selection**, also called *social drift,* refers to the "drifting" to lower socioeconomic classes of those who have become mentally disabled. This often happens to those who are no longer able to work and who lack family support or care (Dohrenwend et al., 1992). **Social causation** refers to the chronic psychological and social stresses of life in an urban environment, particularly for the poor. The stress of these living conditions may trigger the disorder in persons who are biologically vulnerable (Freeman, 1994).

Events at the three levels interact: As suggested by the finding that 48% of identical co-twins develop schizophrenia if the twin has schizophrenia, biological

High expressed emotion: An emotional style in families that are critical, hostile, and overinvolved.

Social selection: The tendency of the mentally disabled to drift to the lower economic classes; also called *social drift.*

Social causation: The chronic psychological and social stresses of living in an urban environment that may lead to an increase in the rate of schizophrenia (especially among the poor).

factors play a role in the development of the illness, leading to a vulnerability theory of the disorder. Such a biological vulnerability, in combination with environmental and social factors, and with the individual's learning history, help determine whether the disorder will occur. Walker and Diforio (1997) propose a specific diathesis–stress model to explain how stress can worsen schizophrenic symptoms. They note that although people who develop schizophrenia do not experience more life stressors than people who do not develop the disorder, individuals with schizophrenia who experience more stressful events are likely to have more severe schizophrenic symptoms and experience more relapses (Hultman et al., 1997). And, in fact, people with schizophrenia have higher baseline levels of cortisol, an indicator of the stress response. This relationship goes even further, since not only people with schizophrenia but also those at risk for the disorder (because of family history or evidence of some symptoms of schizophrenia) are more likely to have higher levels of cortisol. And antipsychotic medications decrease cortisol levels in people with schizophrenia.

Walker and Diforio further propose that this heightened susceptibility to stress comes about because of cortisol's effect on dopamine activity, namely an overproduction of dopamine, which can worsen symptoms of schizophrenia. They propose that the negative symptoms of schizophrenia, such as social withdrawal, are attempts to reduce stress. Thus, genetic, prenatal, or birth factors increase a susceptibility to stress, and stress aggravates symptoms.

Van Gogh had a family history of schizophrenia, implicating a possible genetic factor, and some biographical material suggests that van Gogh's extremely strict father could be regarded as a high expressed emotion parent. And before becoming an artist, van Gogh repeatedly returned to live with his parents after leaving his various jobs. Moreover, after becoming an artist, he generally lived off monies sent by his brother Theo. He was so poor he often had to choose between spending Theo's gift of money on painting supplies or on food, and often chose the former (Auden, 1989).

LOOKING AT LEVELS

The Genain Quadruplets

All four of these identical quadruplets—from oldest to youngest, Nora, Iris, Myra, and Hester—went on to develop schizophrenia. Their symptoms and the onset and course of their illness differed. Nora and Myra were paired off by the parents as the smartest. Hester and Iris were paired off as the least able, and their illness was more disabling.

Now that you know more about schizophrenia and its causes, you can see how the factors at the different levels are involved, and how they interact. We can apply this knowledge to the Genain quadruplets, four girls born in the early 1930s in the Midwest into a family of limited financial means with an abusive, violent, alcoholic father and a strict mother. All four girls developed schizophrenia, although each presented different symptoms. Myra attained a substantially higher level of functioning than her sisters before the onset of the disorder and had fewer and briefer relapses than they did. The youngest and most sickly, Hester, fared the worst (Rosenthal, 1963).

The sisters' paternal grandmother had symptoms of paranoid schizophrenia, so they probably had a genetic vulnerability for the disorder (level of the brain). Still, from statistical probabilities, the odds of all four developing schizophrenia were one in a billion. However, the prenatal difficulties involved in carrying quadruplets, which may have led to impairment in brain development, would have increased the likelihood. CT scans of the quads when they were in their 50s showed similar brain abnormalities in all four sisters (Mirsky & Quinn, 1988). Although genetically identical quadruplets, they varied biologically: Nora and Hester showed more evidence of neurological difficulties and fared much worse when off medication.

At the level of the person, the quads, particularly Hester, exhibited odd behavior. Even as a child, Hester could not keep up mentally and physically with her sisters, and her bizarre behavior included putting on four new pairs of underwear over an old pair. In kindergarten, she appeared fearful and cried more than her sisters. The girls were forbidden to play with other children, had no outside social life, and were overprotected; they didn't mix well with other children at school and were teased. The sisters were seldom separated from one another and appeared unhappy to neighbors. Myra had the most social skills and social desire, even having a "boyfriend" at school, with whom she would exchange notes; she was not allowed to see him after school (Rosenthal, 1963). Nora and Myra made the most skilled pair, and Iris was often paired with Hester.

The Genain family would be considered a high expressed emotion family (level of the group). Psychologist David Rosenthal (1963) reported that the quads'

father was particularly critical, angry, and extremely controlling—he forbade his daughters to close any doors, even the one to the bathroom. Although Nora was less physically abused by him than her sisters were, her doctors and medical team thought that he may have sexually abused her. Nora was the closest to her father and was able to appease him. Myra was their mother's favorite. Hester, who was difficult to control, received the most physical punishment, including being whipped and having her head dunked in water. Other social stressors included a long history of financial problems.

On tests of attention taken when the quads were 20 years old, Myra was the only one to perform well enough to predict a possibility of a normal life; Iris's and Hester's attentional abilities indicated that they would not be able to live independently for long periods of time. In fact, their performance on these attentional tests fairly accurately predicted the course of their lives.

Events at the different levels interact: A family history of schizophrenia as well as prenatal and birth complications made the quads more vulnerable to developing schizophrenia. They were socially isolated, were teased by other children, and experienced physical and emotional abuse. Among the many familial stressors were high expressed emotion parents and financial hardship. Myra, the most socially motivated and skilled sister, was the one whose schizophrenia was least severe, and she was able to remain off medication and out of the hospital for long periods of time; she eventually married and had two sons (Mirsky & Quinn, 1988). Hester, the sickliest sister, was the one most physically abused and the most bizarre as a child. Had the quads grown up in a different home environment, with parents who treated them differently, it is possible that not all four would have developed schizophrenia, or if they had, they might have suffered fewer relapses.

CONSOLIDATE!

1 *What are the symptoms of schizophrenia?* Positive symptoms of schizophrenia include delusions, hallucinations, and disorders of behavior and speech. Negative symptoms include flat affect, alogia, and avolition.

2 *What are the subtypes of schizophrenia?* Subtypes of schizophrenia are paranoid, disorganized, catatonic, and undifferentiated.

3 *Why do some people develop schizophrenia?* A biological vulnerability to schizophrenia is a pre-

requisite. This vulnerability can be genetic, related to prenatal maternal illness, or derived from prenatal or birth complications; all these factors may lead to brain abnormalities. The biological, psychological, and interpersonal stressors of adolescence can play a role in the onset of schizophrenia, and environmental factors, such as living with high expressed emotion families or financial stressors, can increase the risk of relapse.

Other Axis I Disorders: Dissociative and Eating Disorders

Perhaps van Gogh, like many people, suffered from more than one psychological disorder. Consider that, at the age of 24, he spoke of an "evil self" that caused him to become a disgrace and bring misery to others. He sometimes had trouble with his memory. He wrote to Theo that his frail memory "also seems to me to prove that there is quite definitely something or other deranged in my brain, it is astounding to be afraid . . . , and to be unable to remember things" (Auden, 1989, p. 363).

At times van Gogh ate only breakfast and a dinner of coffee and bread. And while in the hospital during the last year of his life, he would eat only meager dinners of half-cooked chick-peas or alcohol or bread and a little soup (Auden, 1989). Not surprisingly, van Gogh had a history of stomach trouble, poor appetite, dizziness, and headaches.

1 What are dissociative disorders?

2 What are the symptoms and causes of eating disorders?

In addition to the disorders in the major diagnostic categories already discussed are several less common Axis I disorders; some unfortunately are becoming more common. Two such categories of disorders are dissociative and eating disorders.

Dissociative Disorders

The hallmark of **dissociative disorders** is a disruption in the usually integrated functions of consciousness, memory, or identity, often caused by a traumatic or very stressful event. The disruptions may be fleeting or chronic; they may come on suddenly or gradually. They can lead to several symptoms (Steinberg, 1994): *identity confusion,* a state of uncertainty about one's identity, or *identity alteration,* the adoption of a new identity; *derealization,* the sense that familiar objects have changed or seem "unreal"; *depersonalization,* the experience of observing oneself as if from the outside; and *amnesia,* the loss of memory. These symptoms are not necessarily signs of pathology; people often have dissociative experiences in the course of ordinary life. For example, it is common to experience derealization on returning home after a long absence: The ceiling may seem lower, the furniture smaller, and so on. Even identity alteration need not signify abnormality. In dissociative disorders, as defined by the *DSM-IV,* the dissociative experiences are severe enough to cause distress or to impair functioning. It is unclear how many people suffer from these disorders, although they are more frequently diagnosed now than in the past. In fact, some researchers and clinicians believe that several of these disorders are now overdiagnosed: One estimate is that 10% of Americans have been diagnosed with a dissociative disorder (Loewenstein, 1994).

One type of dissociative disorder is **dissociative amnesia**, marked by an inability to remember important personal information, usually about a traumatic or extremely stressful event; this inability to remember is often experienced as "gaps" in memory. A soldier who has seen several days of intense and brutal combat but then cannot remember much about the battlefield experience might be suffering from dissociative amnesia. If the soldier was dissociating during battle, he or she may not later have retrieval cues to access those memories. In time, some people are able to recall such terrible memories; others may never remember, developing instead a chronic form of amnesia.

Dissociative disorder: A disorder marked by a disruption in the usually integrated functions of consciousness, memory, or identity.

Dissociative amnesia: An inability to remember important personal information, often experienced as memory "gaps."

Renee Zellweger's character in the movie Nurse Betty *has some symptoms of a dissociative fugue: After witnessing the brutal death of her husband, she abruptly leaves her job and has some difficulty remembering aspects of her past.*

Dissociative fugue is another dissociative disorder, marked by unexpected disappearances from home or work, combined with an inability to remember some or all of the past. This disturbed state of consciousness may last hours, days, or months, and during it there are no obvious signs of a disorder, nor does the sufferer otherwise attract attention. People in a dissociative fugue may ultimately come to the attention of health care or law enforcement officials because of their loss of awareness of their identities. People suffering from this disorder do not usually create new identities for themselves. At any given point in time, only 0.2% of the American population experiences this disorder, but this rate may increase during times of war or large-scale natural disasters (American Psychiatric Association, 1994).

The most controversial dissociative disorder—because not everyone agrees that the disorder exists—estimated to affect 1% of the American population (Loewenstein, 1994) is **dissociative identity disorder (DID)**, a condition in which two or more distinct personalities take control of the individual's behavior. This disorder was formerly known as *multiple personality disorder* and attracted immense interest after it was portrayed in the movies *The Three Faces of Eve* (1958) and *Sybil* (1976). Each personality, or *alter,* may be experienced as if it had a distinct personal history, self-image, and identity, including a separate name, mannerisms, and way of talking. Not all alters know of the existence of the other alters, a circumstance that can lead to amnesia. The gaps in memory are substantial enough that they cannot be considered ordinary forgetfulness. People with dissociative identity disorder have been reported to have from 2 to 100 alters, although 10 or fewer are more commonly reported. Stress can trigger a transition to a different alter; this switch often occurs within seconds, although it can be more gradual.

Wendy illustrates her experience with her trauma and dissociative identity disorder through her artwork. The drawing on the left was done early in Wendy's therapy and shows the "mutant baby" inside her that she felt was bad and evil. The drawing on the right, made later in the course of treatment, symbolizes a memory of being raped and severely beaten by her mother.

Dissociative Identity Disorder From the Inside

Wendy's story captures the essence of DID:

As a child, Wendy lived with her violent and abusive mother in a small urban area; her father had left the household when Wendy's mother was pregnant with her.... [She] had been physically and sexually abused as far back as she could remember...and there were hospital records of severe physical abuse...that occurred before Wendy was 2 years old. Wendy's mother was extremely sadistic and had tortured her regularly with extreme and violent means. For example, without any provocation, Wendy's mother would burn and cut her on various parts of her body.... Wendy had learned to rely on her hypnotic abilities to psychologically distance herself from her distressing memories and emotions.... Since childhood, Wendy had developed more than 20 distinct personalities!... Even subtle cues or reminders of abuse incidents could trigger a dissociative episode in which Wendy would switch to a different personality; once she had returned to her usual state, Wendy could not recall what had occurred during the episode.... Each of Wendy's personalities had its own distinct pattern of behaviors (e.g., speech, posture, mannerisms), perceived ages, sex, and appearance. Each personality had a unique store of information, memories, and access to feelings...each of Wendy's personalities possessed different physical reactions or different physical abilities.... By dividing things up this way, Wendy was able to have parts of herself that could contain the feelings and knowledge about the tortures and abuse that were going on at home and thereby still be able to have other parts of herself that could handle going to . . . work. One personality handled being burned by her mother and was able to be insensitive to and tolerant of physical pain. Yet another personality was experienced as having no mouth, stemming from experiences where Wendy's mother burned her every time she screamed. (Brown & Barlow, 1997, pp. 102–108)

What might cause dissociative identity disorder? According to some researchers, most people who suffer this disorder share two characteristics: They experienced severe and usually repeated physical abuse as young children (Ross et al., 1991), and they have very high hypnotizability and capacity to dissociate (Bliss, 1984; Frischholz, 1985). These two factors are related: Children who experience extreme abuse later recount a sense of their minds temporarily leaving their bodies so that they might endure the abuse. In other words, because of the severity of the situation, they dissociate. With continued abuse, and continued use of dissociation, the dissociated state develops its own memories, feelings, and thoughts, and becomes an alter (Putnam, 1989). This view is supported by work by Perry and his colleagues (1995), who found that young children who have been severely traumatized have a tendency to dissociate or become hyperaroused in response to an aversive stimulus.

There are reports that different alters have different EEG patterns, visual acuity, pain tolerance, symptoms of asthma, sensitivity to allergens, and response to insulin (American Psychiatric Association, 1994). Some researchers and clinicians question whether dissociative identity disorder is a verifiably distinct diagnosis, since similar biological differences occur when researchers ask participants who do *not* have symptoms of the disorder to role-play the condition (Coons et al., 1982). Just as role play induces different bodily states, Sarbin (1995) proposes that DID is the product of the beliefs and expectations of the therapist, who, without realizing it, induces patients to behave in ways consistent with the condition known as dissociative identity disorder. However, researchers have found independent evidence of severe abuse histories in people diagnosed with DID (Lewis et al., 1997; Putnam, 1989; Swica et al., 1996). These same people had either amnesia or scant memories of the abuse (Lewis et al., 1997; Swica et al., 1996) and evidenced signs of dissociation in childhood (Lewis et al., 1997), as would be expected from the theory of how DID develops. Because symptoms of dissociative identity disorder overlap those of posttraumatic stress disorder, some researchers believe that dissociative identity disorder is a subtype of PTSD (Dell, 1998). Despite the debate about the existence of dissociative identity disorder, we do know that severe trauma can lead to disruptions in consciousness and to other dissociative disorders, and can have other adverse effects (Putnam, 1989; Putnam et al., 1995).

DID thus results from interacting events at the three levels: Severe trauma (level of the group) leads to changes in bodily reaction such as hyperarousal (level of the brain) and in knowledge and beliefs, which result from the increased use of dissociation (level of the person). These various types of changes are likely to become chronic responses to stressors. Repeated and lengthy dissociations become the building blocks for DID.

Could van Gogh's "attacks" have been episodes of dissociation? He once referred to his "evil self," but there is no evidence that he had any alters; and although he may have suffered some memory loss during his attacks, he could very well have been psychotic, not dissociative, at those times. Amnesia alone is not an indication of a dissociative disorder.

Eating Disorders: You Are How You Eat?

Do you have a friend who's on a diet? If you do, the chances are that friend is a woman. Is her mood determined by the numbers on the bathroom scale? Does she want to lose more weight, even if she stops menstruating and others tell her she is

Dissociative fugue: An abrupt, unexpected departure from home or work, combined with an inability to remember some or all of the past.

Dissociative identity disorder (DID): A disorder in which a person has two or more distinct personalities that take control of the individual's behavior.

too thin? If she eats more than she wants, does she feel that she must exercise, even if she's tired or sick? Is her view of herself dependent on whether she exercises today? Does she eat as little as possible during the day, and then find herself "losing control" with food in the afternoon or evening? A yes response, even to every question, does not necessarily indicate the presence of an eating disorder, but it does indicate a preoccupation with food, body image, and weight. These preoccupations are typical of people with **eating disorders**, disorders involving severe disturbances in eating behavior. And although more than 90% of those diagnosed with eating disorders are females, males are increasingly suffering from these disorders, too.

Anorexia Nervosa: You *Can* Be Too Thin

Anorexia nervosa is a potentially fatal disorder characterized by a refusal to maintain even a low normal weight. Someone with anorexia nervosa pursues thinness regardless of the physical consequences. Of those hospitalized with anorexia nervosa, 10% will eventually die of causes related to the disorder (American Psychiatric Association, 1994).

Anorexia Nervosa From the Inside

People with anorexia nervosa develop irrational and unhealthy beliefs about food, as recounted by one woman's experience:

> Yesterday . . . I had a grapefruit and black coffee for breakfast, and for dinner I had the . . . salad I eat every night. I always skip lunch. I had promised myself that I would only eat three-quarters of the salad since I've been feeling stuffed after it lately—but I think I ate more than the three-quarters. I know it was just lettuce and broccoli but I can't believe I did that. I was up all night worrying about getting fat. (Siegel et al., 1988, p. 17)

An anorexic woman writes in her journal as part of her counseling at Radar Institute in Culver City, California.

Included in the list of symptoms required for a diagnosis of anorexia nervosa are distortions of how people with this disorder see their bodies ("body image"), an intense fear of becoming fat, a refusal to maintain a healthy weight, and, among females, amenorrhea, or the cessation of menstruation. It is common for extremely anorexic women to "know" that they are underweight, yet when they look in the mirror, they "see" fat that is not there, or generally overestimate their body size (Smeets et al., 1997). They are often obsessed by thoughts of food, and these thoughts are usually based on irrational or illogical thinking (such as whether a food is "good" or "bad"). They often deny that their low weight is a problem, or even that they have a problem. Some symptoms of anorexia nervosa differ from culture to culture. For example, half of young Chinese women with this disorder do not have the fear of being fat common among North Americans, but explain their restricted diet in terms of a distaste for food or bodily discomfort when eating (Lee, 1996).

Some, but not all, people with anorexia nervosa periodically engage in *binge eating* (eating substantially more food within a certain time period than most people would eat in similar circumstances) or *purging* (getting rid of unwanted calories through vomiting or the misuse of laxatives, diuretics, or enemas), or both. Thus, there are two types of anorexia nervosa: the *binge-eating/purging type* and the classic *restricting type,* in which weight loss is achieved primarily by undereating, without purging.

Bulimia Nervosa

People with bulimia nervosa, like those with anorexia nervosa, are usually women, but they may be of normal weight or even overweight, and thus usually continue to menstruate. **Bulimia nervosa** is marked by recurrent episodes of binge eating, followed by an attempt to prevent weight gain. When that attempt is made through purging (by vomiting or with the use of laxatives), the diagnosis of bulimia nervosa is further specified as *purging type*. Attempts to restrict weight gain may also occur through other methods such as fasting or excessive exercise, and in this case the disorder is the *nonpurging type*.

Some people with bulimia purge even when their eating does not constitute a binge: "If I had *one* bite of bread, just one, I felt as though I blew it! I'd stop listening to whomever was talking to me at the table. I'd start thinking, *How can I get rid of this?* I'd worry about how fat I'd look, how I couldn't fit into my clothes. My head would be flooded with thoughts of what to do now. . . . I had to undo what I'd done. The night was blown. I was a mess" (Siegel et al., 1988, p. 18). Although most people with bulimia do not realize it, in the long run, purging does not usually eliminate all the calories ingested and is, in fact, a poor method of weight loss (Garner, 1997).

Explaining Eating Disorders

Why do people, most often women, develop eating disorders? There is evidence of a genetic predisposition for anorexia (level of the brain). In one study, 56% of identical co-twins were likely to have anorexia if their twins did, compared to 5% of co-twins of affected fraternal twins (Holland et al., 1988). Moreover, in a 1998 study, relatives of those with anorexia nervosa had a higher incidence of obsessive-compulsive symptoms than relatives of those with bulimia nervosa or control subjects. This finding suggests that obsessive personality traits in a family may increase the risk for anorexia nervosa (Lilenfeld et al., 1998). However, learning principles can also account for this finding: People with obsessional relatives may learn to be obsessional; those with eating disorders have focused the obsession on food and weight. The data for bulimia nervosa in twins shows a sharply different pattern: Twenty-three percent of identical co-twins were likely to have bulimia if their twins did, compared with 9% of co-twins of affected fraternal twins (Kendler et al., 1991). In bulimia, the environment, not genes, plays the larger role (Wade et al., 1998).

As was shown by the University of Minnesota starvation study (see Chapter 7), decreased caloric intake leads to pathological eating behaviors and other symptoms of eating disorders. The malnutrition and weight loss that occur with anorexia nervosa lead to changes in neurotransmitters, particularly serotonin. This neurotransmitter also plays a role in obsessive-compulsive disorder, and the obsessional thinking about food and pathological eating in anorexia is hypothesized to be related to alterations in serotonergic functioning (Kaye, 1995). Lower levels of serotonin have been implicated as a predisposing factor for bulimia nervosa (Pirke, 1995) since one effect of serotonin is to create a feeling of satiety (Halmi, 1996). The biological effects of dieting may also make women vulnerable to developing bulimia nervosa: Some, though not all, studies indicate that dieting preceded the onset of bulimia in some people (Garner, 1997). Although the research points to abnormalities or dysregulation of neurotransmitters, it is as yet unclear how the changes in different neurotransmitters are related; nor is it certain whether these changes *precede* the development of an eating disorder and thus may create a susceptibility to it, or whether they are a *consequence* of an eating disorder (Halmi, 1995).

Numerous personal characteristics have been linked with eating disorders. An increased risk of developing anorexia occurs among women who are perfectionists and have a negative evaluation of themselves (Fairburn et al., 1999). More generally, people with eating disorders often exhibit

Cultural pressure on women to be thin and attain an "ideal" body shape is influential in the development of eating disorders. It also explains why there is a higher incidence of eating disorders now than 50 years ago, as the ideal figure has changed from the generous proportions of Marilyn Monroe to the rail-thin profiles of actresses such as Calista Flockhart (Andersen & DiDomenico, 1992; Field et al., 1999; Nemeroff et al., 1994). Culture plays a role by simply promoting the idea that body shape can be changed and by determining the rationales that people offer for their symptoms (Becker & Hamburg, 1996).

irrational beliefs and inappropriate expectations about their bodies, jobs, relationships, and themselves (Garfinkel et al., 1992; Striegel-Moore, 1993). They tend to engage in dichotomous, black-or-white thinking: Fruit is "good"; pizza is "bad."

Perhaps people with these characteristics are especially likely to find rewards in the behaviors associated with eating disorders. Preoccupations with food can provide distractions from work, family conflicts, or social problems. By restricting their eating, people may gain a sense of increased control—over food and over life in general—although such feelings of mastery are often short-lived as the disease takes over (Garner, 1997). By purging, they may relieve the anxiety created by overeating.

The family and the larger culture also play important roles in the development of eating disorders (level of the group). They may contribute to these disorders by encouraging a preoccupation with weight and appearance. Children have an increased risk of developing eating disorders if their families are overly concerned about appearance and weight (Strober, 1995). Symptoms of eating disorders increase among immigrants from less weight-conscious cultures (such as the Chinese and the Egyptian) as they assimilate to American culture (Dolan, 1991; Lee & Lee, 1996). Eating disorders are increasing among men who regularly take part in appearance- or weight-conscious activities such as modeling and wrestling (Brownell & Rodin, 1992). Among U.S. women, the focus on appearance and weight may derive from their desire to meet the culture's ideal of femininity (Striegel-Moore, 1993).

Van Gogh had bizarre eating habits; could he have had an eating disorder? It is unlikely; although van Gogh often purposefully ate sparingly and peculiarly, he did not appear to be preoccupied with weight gain or body image, and no information suggests that he purged in any way.

LOOKING AT LEVELS

Binge Eating

You have learned what eating disorders are and explanations of why they might occur. Let's consider in detail a core aspect of bulimia nervosa—binge eating. Why do some people chronically binge eat? At the level of the brain, food restriction is a contributor to binge eating (Polivy & Herman, 1993). In their efforts to be "in control" of food, people with bulimia generally consume fewer calories at nonbinge meals than do nonbulimics, thus setting the stage for later binge eating because they are hungry and have food cravings (Walsh, 1993), and the bingeing becomes reinforced. A binge/purge episode may be followed by an endorphin rush (and the ensuing positive feelings that it creates), further reinforcing the binge/purge cycle. As one woman with bulimia reported, "I go to never-never land. Once I starting bingeing, it's like being in a stupor, like being drunk . . . I'm like a different person. It's very humiliating—but not then, not while I'm eating. While I'm eating, nothing else matters" (Siegel et al., 1988, p. 20).

The dichotomous thinking typical of people with eating disorders leads them to view themselves as either "good" (when dieting or restricting food intake), or "bad" (eating "forbidden foods" or feeling out of control while eating). This thinking (level of the person) sets the stage for bingeing if any small amount of forbidden food is eaten; a bite of a candy bar is followed by the thought, Well, I shouldn't have eaten *any* of the candy bar, but since I did, I might as well eat the whole thing, especially since I really shouldn't have a candy bar again. This line of reasoning is part of the *abstinence violation effect* (Polivy & Herman, 1993), the sense of letting go of self-restraint after transgressing a self-imposed rule about food: Once you violate the rule, why not go all the way? In addition, purging is negatively reinforcing (remember, negative reinforcement is reinforcement, not punishment; see Chapter 4): Eating too much, or eating forbidden foods, can cause anxiety, which is then relieved by purging. This reinforcement then increases the likelihood of purging in the future.

Bingeing and purging are usually done alone, increasing the affected person's sense of isolation and decreasing his or her social interactions; if social interactions are stressful, then bingeing and purging are reinforced by the isolation they provide (level of the group). Events at the levels interact: Cultural pressures to be thin, or to eat small meals, lead vulnerable individuals to try to curb their food intake. The hunger caused by this undereating may trigger a binge. The binge may also be triggered by stress, social interactions, or negative affect (Polivy & Herman, 1993); bingeing can create positive changes (such as decreased hunger, distraction from an uncomfortable feeling or thought, and removal from difficult social interactions). This immediate reinforcement often outweighs the negative consequences that are experienced later. Moreover, the social isolation may be positive and therefore reinforcing.

CONSOLIDATE!

1 *What are dissociative disorders?* Dissociative disorders are characterized by identity confusion or alteration, derealization, depersonalization, and amnesia. The diagnosis of dissociative identity order is marked by the presence of one or more alters.

2 *What are the symptoms and causes of eating disorders?* Symptoms of anorexia nervosa in American women include a fear of fat or weight gain, refusal to maintain a healthy weight, dis-

turbed body image, and amenorrhea. Symptoms of bulimia nervosa include recurrent binge eating, purging, and self-esteem linked to an idealized weight and shape. Eating disorders appear to be caused by an interaction of biological factors, rigid thinking about food and appearance, personal learning history, and family and cultural messages about weight.

A Cautionary Note About Diagnosis

The events of van Gogh's life present an opportunity to explore ways in which the human psyche can be troubled, and the ways in which the mental health field presently classifies disorders. But that is not the same as proposing a diagnosis of someone who, while in art is very close to us, is in his person very distant in time.

No mental health clinician can really know with certainty from what, if any, specific disorder van Gogh suffered. Major depressive disorder and schizophrenia are possibilities, as is bipolar disorder (Jamison, 1993). Alternatively, his attacks and hallucinations might have been due to *delirium tremens* (DTs), caused by withdrawal from alcohol (see Chapter 10); but such a diagnosis would not explain why van Gogh had attacks even during lengthy periods of sobriety (Lubin, 1972). Possibly he suffered from a form of epilepsy, and his "attacks" were seizures; before epileptic seizures, victims are sometimes overcome with religious feelings and delusions. The consideration of epilepsy, a neurological disorder but not a psychological one, in our speculations points to the importance of ensuring that the patient does not have a medical disorder that can cause psychological symptoms. Only after ruling out medical illnesses can the mental health clinician or researcher have confidence in a diagnosis of a psychological disorder.

A DEEPER LEVEL
Recap and Thought Questions

Identifying Psychological Disorders: What's Abnormal?

Significant impairment or distress interfering with work, school, relationships, or self-care is the hallmark of behaviors that constitute a psychological disorder, as compared with behaviors that are merely unusual in a given context. The catalog of psychiatric disorders in the *DSM-IV* distinguishes among disorders by the symptoms exhibited or reported, and by the history of the symptoms. The *DSM-IV* includes both clinical and personality disorders.

Did van Gogh have psychological problems? Given our definition of psychological disorders, it appears that van Gogh may have suffered from one or more psycho-

logical disorders: He had significant emotional distress, difficulty keeping a job or even painting without interruption by his so-called attacks, and his suicidal feelings and actions made him a danger to himself. Both van Gogh's own reports of his depression, attacks, and hallucinations, as well as reports by friends, family, and neighbors, suggest the strong possibility of a psychological disorder—but again, without the opportunity to examine him closely, we cannot know for sure.

Think It Through. If a classmate tells you in all seriousness that someone you both know is "weird" and a "basket case," how would you respond? What would you want to know about the behavior that led your friend to this conclusion? What other questions should you ask? Why?

Anxiety and Mood Disorders

Anxiety disorders include panic disorder, specific and social phobias, posttraumatic stress disorder, and obsessive-compulsive disorder. These disorders involve a biological vulnerability (possibly genetic) to the overactivity of certain brain areas or neurotransmitters. Classical and operant conditioning and social learning may be important in the evolution of these disorders.

Major depressive disorder is characterized by depressed mood, loss of pleasure, fatigue, weight loss, poor sleep, a sense of worthlessness or guilt, and poor attention and concentration. Bipolar disorder involves episodes of mania or hypomania, which may or may not alternate with depression. These disorders also involve a biological vulnerability (possibly genetic); further, neurotransmitters and neuromodulators play a role in both disorders, although the exact mechanisms are not yet understood. People's worldviews and attributional styles may also play a role in the development of major depressive disorder. Operant conditioning and the level of available reward or punishment in the environment also may be related to the development of depression.

Could extreme anxiety or profound disturbances in mood account for van Gogh's problems? Although van Gogh suffered from "attacks," we do not know enough about them to say if they were anxiety related, nor did he have the history or symptoms of someone with either PTSD or OCD. Van Gogh apparently suffered from depressive episodes, an indicator of some type of mood disorder. Although we have limited knowledge of the details of some of his symptoms, nothing we do know contradicts the possibility of MDD with psychotic features or bipolar disorder.

Think It Through. Suppose someone you know, someone whose sharp style of dress and confident manner you admire, starts looking unkempt and acting tired, nervous, and fidgety. Would this change suggest a psychological disorder? Why or why not? If so, what type of disorder do you have in mind and why? Would psychological impairment be the only explanation?

Schizophrenia

Schizophrenia involves a markedly restricted range of affect and odd or disorganized thoughts (delusions or hallucinations) and behaviors; it is characterized by positive and negative symptoms. The *DSM-IV* specifies four subtypes: paranoid, disorganized, catatonic, and undifferentiated. Research findings on schizophrenia point to genetic and biological abnormalities, as well as a heightened responsivity to stress as factors in the development of this disorder.

Would schizophrenia best explain van Gogh's symptoms? Van Gogh did not appear to have any prominent delusions when not experiencing a so-called attack, and if anything, his mood was apparently consistently depressed, not flat. When not having an attack, his behavior is not known to have been disorganized, but we do not know very much about his attacks. Paranoid schizophrenia might account for his hallucinations and, perhaps, his attacks; but this characterization leaves some symptoms unexplained, such as the predominance and lengthy history of his depressed mood.

Think It Through. Would someone who has exhibited positive and negative symptoms of schizophrenia be able to function relatively normally again? Does having a parent with schizophrenia guarantee the development of the disorder? Can the environment of someone with schizophrenia affect the symptoms? If so, in what way?

Other Axis 1 Disorders: Dissociative and Eating Disorders

Dissociative disorders are characterized by identity confusion, derealization, depersonalization, and amnesia. Trauma or severe stress influences the development of these disorders.

Eating disorders are characterized by preoccupations with weight and body image, as well as abnormal eating (restriction, binges, purges). Genetic factors are more influential in the development of anorexia than bulimia, and environmental factors, specifically the cultural emphasis on thinness, affect the development of both bulimia and anorexia. Biological factors related to food restriction and binge eating are also involved.

Could van Gogh have had a dissociative or eating disorder? Although van Gogh had some episodes that seem dissociative in nature, they did not appear to be beyond those normally experienced and so would not have been pathological. Despite the fact that he had bizarre eating habits and sometimes ate sparingly, an eating disorder is not indicated.

Think It Through. If a friend began eating less and lost weight, what else would you want to know before concluding that she might have an eating disorder? If she confessed to you that she sometimes didn't "feel like herself" anymore, that she wasn't sure who she "really was," might you suspect she had a dissociative disorder? Why or why not?

REVIEW TEST

For each of the following items, choose the single correct or best answer. The correct answers appear at the end.

1 False and persistent beliefs that have no basis in reality are called ____.
   a. hallucinations
   b. delusions
   c. psychoses
   d. insanity

2 Approximately ____% of Americans have experienced or will experience one of 30 common psychological disorders at some point during their lifetime.
   a. 10
   b. 75
   c. 25
   d. 50

3 In his classic study, David Rosenhan found that ____.
   a. people are treated as "ill" once given a psychiatric diagnosis
   b. dysfunctional parent–child relationships underlie many psychological disorders
   c. psychiatrists are notoriously bad at diagnosing illnesses
   d. neurotransmitter imbalances can create a psychological disorder

4 Studies of diagnostic bias have found that ____.
   a. black Americans are overlooked in studies of mental illness
   b. black Americans are prescribed higher doses of medication than white Americans
   c. white Americans are evaluated more negatively than black Americans
   d. white Americans have higher rates of mental illness than black Americans

5 Karen has just lost her job and her husband has asked her for a divorce. These events would be noted on Axis ____ of the *DSM-IV*.
   a. IV
   b. III
   c. II
   d. I

6 Which of the following is *not* a criticism of the *DSM-IV*?
   a. Disorders that overlap are presented as clearly distinct from one another.
   b. There is no discrete boundary between normal and abnormal.
   c. The criteria for mental disorders are vague.
   d. Some medical conditions are being called psychological disorders.

7 People with panic disorder report ____.
   a. more stressful events during childhood and adolescence
   b. more stressful events in the year before their disorder developed
   c. normal levels of stress throughout their lifespan
   d. work-related stressors but normal family relationships

8 Which of the following is *not* a symptom of post-traumatic stress disorder?
   a. avoidance of stimuli associated with the traumatic event
   b. reexperiencing the traumatic event
   c. panic attacks
   d. autonomic overarousal

9 Which of the following statements about suicide is true?
   a. People who attempt suicide are "crazy."
   b. Half of people who attempt suicide typically seek medical help in the six months preceding the attempt.
   c. People who talk about suicide don't actually attempt suicide.
   d. Talking about suicide to someone who is depressed will "put the ideas in their head."

10 Lithium, the medication prescribed for bipolar disorder, lowers ____ activity in the brain.
   a. serotonin
   b. norepinephrine
   c. substance P
   d. dopamine

11 People who attribute blame to ____ following a negative event are more likely to develop depression than people who do not.
   a. others
   b. fate
   c. themselves
   d. God

12 Which of the following is *not* a negative symptom of schizophrenia?
   a. flat affect
   b. disorganized behavior
   c. avolition
   d. alogia

13 Most people with dissociative identity disorder have ____ and ____.
   a. expressed emotion among family members; alcoholism
   b. a history of severe childhood abuse; alcoholism
   c. expressed emotion among family members; high hypnotizability
   d. a history of severe childhood abuse; high hypnotizability

14 Young Chinese women with anorexia explain their refusal to eat by stating that ____.
   a. they don't like the way the food tastes
   b. they think they are too fat
   c. they are afraid their friends will laugh at them
   d. they do not want to physically mature

15 Eating disorders have been linked to changes in ____ levels.
   a. dopamine
   b. norepinephrine
   c. serotonin
   d. acetylcholine

ANSWERS: 1.b 2.d 3.a 4.b 5.a 6.c 7.b 8.c 9.b 10.a 11.c 12.b 13.d 14.d 15.c

12 Treatment

At 2 A.M., Beth sat hunched over her textbook and notes, studying for her midterm. Concentration was difficult; she had to struggle to make sense of the words before her eyes. She'd read the same page four times and still couldn't remember what it said. She tried to give herself a pep talk ("Okay, Beth, read it one more time, and then you'll understand it"), but her upbeat words would be drowned out by a different, negative internal monologue (*Well, Beth, you've really screwed yourself, and there's no way out of it now. You're going to fail, get kicked out of school, never be employed, end up destitute, homeless, hopeless, talking to yourself on the street*).

Beth was 21 years old, a junior in college. She'd already had to walk out of two exams because she couldn't answer most of the questions, although she had understood the material in class. Her thoughts had been jumbled, and she'd had a hard time organizing her answers to the questions. She'd always been nervous before a test or class presentation, but this year her anxiety had spun out of control. Taking the first quiz of the semester, she simply drew a blank when she tried to answer the questions.

Since then, she'd become more anxious, and depressed as well. With each quiz she couldn't finish, with each paper that required more concentration than she could summon, she felt herself spiraling downward, helpless. She had no hope that the situation would change by itself, and no amount of good intentions or resolutions or even effort made a difference. She began cutting classes and spent much of her time in bed; she had no interest in doing anything with her friends because she felt she didn't deserve to have fun. She'd put off saying anything to her professors; at first she figured things would get better, and then she was too embarrassed to face them. But she knew that eventually she'd have to talk to them or else she'd definitely fail her courses.

She finally did talk to her professors. Several of them suggested that she seek treatment, or at least go to the campus counseling center, but she didn't want to do that. Taking that step, she felt, would be admitting to herself and to the world not only that something was wrong with her, but also that she was too weak to deal with it herself.

Beth was reluctant to seek help partly because when she was growing up, her mother had experienced bouts of depression severe enough that she had been hospitalized several times. Beth recognized that she, too, was becoming depressed, and she was afraid that if she went to see a therapist, she'd end up in the hospital.

Finally, Beth confided in a family friend, Nina, who had been the school nurse at Beth's elementary school. Nina told Beth that people with problems like hers often felt much better after psychotherapy and that her problems were not severe enough to warrant hospitalization. She also pointed out that there were many forms of therapy available to Beth that were not as readily available to her mother 20 years ago. Modern treatments, Nina said, ranged from psychologically based therapies such as insight-oriented, cognitive, and behavioral therapies to biologically based treatments such as medication. Beth agreed to see a therapist, but didn't know where to begin. The campus counseling center could be useful, Nina said, but Beth might also explore other possibilities, such as the Internet and referral organizations, in finding a therapist who would be right for her needs.

Let's make a similar exploration in this chapter, examining the different schools of therapy, how they work, and what research has to say about the effectiveness of the therapies.

Insight–Oriented Therapies

Beth didn't know much about psychotherapy, so she made an appointment with a psychotherapist whose name she had gotten from the counseling center. Beth didn't know it, but if the therapist she contacted was an insight-oriented therapist, chances are that the therapist would begin by asking Beth about her past, how she felt about her family and her relationships with the people in it, and about her feelings in general. This therapist might ask surprisingly little about Beth's current anxiety or her depression.

Therapies that aim to remove distressing symptoms by leading someone to understand their causes through deeply felt personal insights are called **insight-oriented therapies**. The key idea underlying this approach is that once someone truly understands the causes of distressing symptoms (which often arise from past relationships), the symptoms themselves will diminish. Psychoanalysis is the original insight-oriented therapy; client-centered therapy is also considered insight-oriented therapy because it rests on the belief that therapeutic change follows from the experience of insight.

1 What is the focus of treatment in psychodynamic therapy? What are its main techniques?

2 How would client-centered therapists approach treatment? What techniques would they use?

Insight-oriented therapy: Therapy that aims to remove distressing symptoms by leading people to understand the symptoms' causes through deeply felt personal insights.

Psychodynamic Therapy: Origins in Psychoanalysis

Developed by Sigmund Freud, **psychoanalysis** is a type of therapy directly connected to Freud's notion of personality, which holds that people's psychological difficulties are caused by conflicts among the three psychic structures of the mind: the id, ego, and superego. According to Freud, the id strives for immediate gratification of its needs, the superego tries to impose its version of morality, and the ego attempts to balance the demands of the id, superego, and external reality. These unconscious competing demands can create anxiety and other symptoms (see Chapter 8). The goal of psychoanalysis is to help patients understand the unconscious motivations that lead them to behave in specific ways; if the motivations and feelings remain unconscious, those forces are more likely to shape patients' behavior, without their awareness. According to this theory, only after true understanding—that is, insight—is attained can patients choose more adaptive, satisfying, and productive behaviors.

In psychoanalysis, patients talk about their problems, and the analyst tries to infer the root causes. Early on, this method was revolutionary because, before Freud, most European patients were treated medically for psychological problems. Freud started out using hypnosis but over time developed the method of **free association**, in which the patient says whatever comes into his or her mind. The resulting train of thought reveals the issues that concern the patient, as well as the way he or she is handling them. Because Freud (1900/1958) viewed dreams as the "royal road to the unconscious," another important feature of psychoanalysis is the use of **dream analysis**, the examination of the content of dreams to gain access to the unconscious. Freud did not believe that psychoanalysis was a cure, but rather that it could transform abject misery into ordinary unhappiness.

Psychoanalysis has declined in popularity over the last several decades, in part because of the cost and time required for the four to five sessions per week. The average patient engages in 835 sessions before completing psychoanalysis (Voth & Orth, 1973), which usually lasts at least 4 years. Some patients who begin psychoanalysis never complete it.

A less intensive form of psychoanalytically oriented treatment, and one that is more common today, is **psychodynamic therapy**. Although based on psychoanalytic theory, its techniques differ in some important ways, including less frequent sessions, a decreased emphasis on sexual and aggressive drives, and an increased emphasis on current life rather than past experiences. However, both psychoanalysis and psychodynamic therapy try to link the patient's current difficulties with past experiences, and both view the patient's relationship with the therapist as an integral part of treatment. Recent trends in psychodynamic therapy include the development of short-term versions of psychotherapy (Bloom, 1997; Malan, 1976; Sifneos, 1992), which might involve therapy lasting 12 to 20 sessions. At least one study found that psychiatrists referring patients for psychological treatment do not refer all prospective patients to psychodynamic therapy, only those who are healthier and who do not have a personality disorder (Svanborg et al., 1999). Such patients seeking help for relationship difficulties may find insight attained through short-term therapy useful in relieving symptoms (Kivlighan et al., 2000).

Theory

The goal of psychodynamic therapy, like that of psychoanalysis, is to bring unconscious impulses and conflicts into awareness. Doing so leads to both intellectual and emotional insights, which are supposed to give the patient more control over these impulses. With this control, the patient can actively and consciously *choose* behaviors instead of acting on unconscious impulses. More recent psychoanalytic theorists have placed greater emphasis on people's current relationships (as

Psychoanalysis: An intensive form of therapy, originally developed by Freud, based on the idea that people's psychological difficulties are caused by conflicts among the id, ego, and superego.

Free association: A technique used in psychoanalysis and psychodynamic therapies in which the patient says whatever comes to mind and the train of thought reveals the patient's issues and ways of dealing with them.

Dream analysis: A technique used in psychoanalysis and psychodynamic therapies in which the therapist examines the content of dreams to gain access to the unconscious.

Psychodynamic therapy: A less intensive form of psychoanalysis.

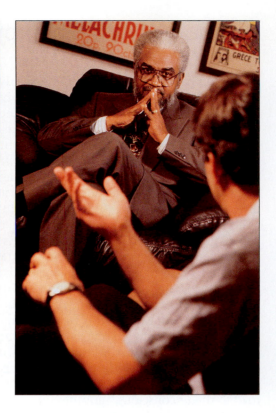

Psychoanalysis usually takes place 4 to 5 days a week for a number of years. Psychodynamic therapy can take place anywhere from several times a month to twice a week. The patient lies on a couch in psychoanalysis, and the analyst sits in a chair behind the couch, out of the patient's range of sight so that the patient can better free associate without having to see the analyst's reactions to his or her thoughts. In psychodynamic therapy, the client and therapist sit in chairs facing each other.

opposed to an almost exclusive emphasis on childhood relationships) and their possible role in the evolution of emotional distress (Greenberg & Mitchell, 1983; Kohut, 1977; Sullivan, 1953). Psychodynamic therapy uses the relationship between therapist and patient as an agent of change. Given the importance of relationships, the therapy relationship can provide a "corrective emotional experience"—that is, a new, positive experience of relationships, which can lead to changes in symptoms, behavior, and personality (Alexander & French, 1946).

From a psychodynamic perspective, Beth's anxiety and depression might reflect two competing desires. On the one hand, Beth wants to be different from her mother. Doing well in school and going on to graduate school represent a path different from that taken by her mother who, although she did well in college, elected not to pursue a graduate degree. Although her plan was not necessarily logically thought out, Beth hoped that by making different choices in her own life, she could avoid the intermittent depressions that had plagued her mother. On the other hand, Beth loves her mother, and the idea of academically passing a parent by, in essence, abandoning her, causes Beth to feel guilty about her accomplishments. Although Beth's anxiety and depression are upsetting and debilitating, part of her may feel relief that those symptoms prevent her from leaving her mother behind. Psychodynamic theory would say that, by gaining insight about these issues, Beth will not have to "act out" these ambivalent feelings unconsciously and will have more control over her anxiety and depression.

Techniques

Along with dream analysis and free association, psychodynamic therapists rely on **interpretation**, deciphering the patient's words and behaviors and assigning unconscious motivations to them. Through the therapist's interpretations, the patient becomes aware of his or her motives and potential conflicts within the unconscious. The patient's own interpretations are not considered as accurate as those of the therapist because they are biased by the patient's own conflicts. Slips

Interpretation: A technique used in psychoanalysis and psychodynamic therapies in which the therapist deciphers the patient's words and behaviors, assigning unconscious motivations to them.

of the tongue—"Freudian slips"—are interpreted as having unconscious meanings. For example, should Beth tell her therapist that her mother recommended that she come to therapy (instead of her mother's friend, which was the case, and what she meant to say), her therapist might interpret this as Beth's wish that her mother would take care of her by suggesting that she seek therapy.

Through interpretation, patients also become aware of their defense mechanisms, unconscious mechanisms used to handle conflictual and distressing thoughts and feelings (see Chapter 8). At some point in the course of psychodynamic therapy, patients are likely to experience **resistance**, a reluctance or refusal to cooperate with the therapist. Resistance can range from unconscious forgetting to outright refusal to comply with a therapist's request. Resistance can occur as the patient explores or remembers painful feelings or experiences in the past. Therapists may attribute resistance to a difficult phase of treatment, or to the patient's desire to avoid exploration of the topic. Thus, if Beth comes late to a therapy session, a psychodynamic therapist might interpret this behavior as resistance: Perhaps Beth does not want to work on the issues currently being explored or is concerned about something that she doesn't want to share with her therapist.

Over the course of therapy, patients may come to relate to their therapist as they did to someone who was important in their lives, perhaps a parent. This phenomenon is called **transference.** If Beth began asking how the therapist is feeling, or if she began to talk less about her own distressing feelings because she worried that the therapist might become upset, Beth would be "transferring" onto her therapist her usual style of relating to her mother, in which she views her mother as fragile and needing protection. The therapeutic value of transference is that patients can talk about what they are experiencing (which they may very well have been unable to do with the parent) to heighten understanding. Moreover, the therapist's acceptance of uncomfortable or shameful feelings helps patients accept those feelings in order to *choose* whether to act on them. An insight-oriented therapist would likely interpret Beth's questions about the therapist's well-being as transference. Beth and her therapist would then talk about what it was like for Beth to feel so protective and careful with her mother.

Humanistic Therapy: The Self in a Mirror

Like the humanistic approach to personality (see Chapter 8), humanistic therapy emphasizes free will, personal growth, self-esteem, and mastery. This approach is in contrast to psychodynamic therapy, which emphasizes the past, mental mechanisms, and the working through of conflictual impulses and feelings. One of the early proponents of humanistic psychology was Carl Rogers, who developed a therapeutic approach that came to be called **client-centered therapy**, which focuses on people's potential for growth and the importance of an empathic therapist. It is revealing that instead of using the term *patient,* a medical term that suggests illness, Rogers substituted the term *client.*

Rogers viewed people's distressing symptoms as caused by a blocked potential for personal growth. The goal of client-centered therapy is to dismantle that block so that people can reach their full potential. According to Rogers, problems arise because of a lack of a coherent, unified sense of self. An example is a mismatch, or **incongruence**, between the *real self* (who you actually are) and the *ideal self* (who you would like to be). By allowing people to become more like their ideal selves, client-centered therapy lessens the incongruence and the client feels better. According to client-centered therapy, Beth's problems may stem from incongruence between her real self (a self that has to work hard for good grades and feels shame and guilt about the imperfections that remind her of her mother's depressions) and her ideal self (a self that is without struggle—a good student who always does the "right thing" and who never experiences sadness, hopelessness, or anxiety). The tension between her real and ideal selves creates a fragmented

Resistance: A reluctance or refusal to cooperate with the therapist, which can range from unconscious forgetting to outright refusal to comply with a therapist's request.

Transference: The process by which patients may relate to their therapists as they did to some important person in their lives.

Client-centered therapy: A type of insight-oriented therapy that focuses on people's potential for growth and the importance of an empathic therapist.

Incongruence: According to client-centered therapy, a mismatch between a person's *real self* and his or her *ideal self.*

sense of self, which drains Beth's time and energy; these different parts of herself are in conflict with each other and prevent her from reaching her full potential.

The client-centered therapist should be warm, able to see the world as the client does, and able to empathize with the client. The therapist does not offer analyses to the client; instead the therapist reflects back the thrust of what the client has said. However, the therapist must not simply parrot the client's words or phrases but show *accurate* and *genuine* empathy. Such empathy lets the client know that he or she is really understood. If the therapist is inaccurate in reflecting what the client says, or if the empathy seems false, the intervention will fail. The therapist must also provide **unconditional positive regard**; that is, he or she must convey positive feelings for the client regardless of the client's thoughts, feelings, or actions. The therapist does this by continually showing the client that he or she is inherently worthy as a human being. Genuine empathy and unconditional positive regard allow the client to decrease the incongruence between the real and ideal selves. Although Beth was unable to take some of her exams (real self), a client-centered therapist's empathy and unconditional positive regard would allow Beth to see that she is still smart (ideal self) and that everyone sometimes has negative, uncomfortable feelings. This therapeutic approach could help Beth see her real and ideal selves in a different light and allow her to think of herself more positively.

Being rejected by a partner can leave a person feeling bad about him- or herself. Client-centered therapy would make a distinction between the person's actions in the relationship and the fact he or she is still a worthwhile, good person.

The client-centered therapist provides both genuine empathy and unconditional positive regard by making a distinction between the client as a person and the client's behaviors. The therapist could dislike a client's *behavior* but still view the client as a good person. If Beth were seeing a client-centered therapist, the topic of a therapy session might be what it was like for Beth during her mother's bouts of depression. A session might include this exchange:

BETH: I was so disappointed and ashamed when I'd come home from school and she'd still be in bed, wearing her bathrobe.

THERAPIST: Yes, it must have caused you to feel ashamed, anxious, and worried when you came home and found your mother still in bed.

BETH: And I felt that it was *my* fault, that I wasn't doing enough to make her feel better.

THERAPIST: Although you felt that it was your fault, you did all that you possibly could. You were concerned about her. You were, and still are, a good, worthwhile person.

BETH: And now I spend most of the day in bed and don't bother to get dressed . . . am I becoming like my mother?

THERAPIST: You and your mother are two separate individuals. Although you may have some things in common, and right now that may include depression, that doesn't mean that your path in life is identical to hers.

The therapist repeatedly emphasizes the worthiness of the client until the client comes to accept this valuation and is able to reach his or her potential, and make different, healthier choices and decisions. When successful, client-centered therapy can achieve its objective in a few months rather than years.

In sum, although there are differences between the insight-oriented therapies (Table 12.1), the clients most likely to benefit from these treatments are similar in

Unconditional positive regard: The stance taken by a client-centered therapist that conveys positive feelings for the client, regardless of the client's thoughts, feelings, or actions.

that they are relatively healthy, articulate individuals who are interested in knowing more about their own motivations.

TABLE (12.1) Differences Between Psychodynamic and Client-Centered Therapies

Although psychodynamic and client-centered therapies have in common their use of insight, the treatments differ in some important ways, including the focus of treatment, its goals, and techniques.

TYPE OF THERAPY	FOCUS	GOAL	TECHNIQUES
Psychodynamic therapy	Unconscious conflict and sexual/aggressive drives	To make unconscious conflict conscious	Free association, dream analysis, use of transference, interpretation
Client-centered therapy	Each person's unique experiences and potential for growth	To unblock the person's potential for growth by decreasing incongruence	Empathy, unconditional positive regard, genuineness toward the client

LOOKING AT LEVELS

The Importance of Expressing Emotions

In both types of insight-oriented therapy, clients spend time focusing on and talking about their feelings. Does the expression of emotion have a therapeutic effect? The answer appears to be yes. In studies where participants were asked to write about their feelings concerning a stressful event, participants in the writing group had fewer doctor visits, improved immune functioning, and a greater sense of well-being than those in the control group (these studies are discussed in greater detail in Chapter 10; see Esterling et al., 1999; Pennebaker et al., 1990). When participants were asked about their writing experiences, 76% described the benefits of writing as helping them attain insight: One said, "It made me think things out and really realize what my problem is" (Pennebaker et al., 1990). In fact, studies comparing the benefits of this particular form of expressive writing with the benefits of a few sessions of psychotherapy have found both interventions to have similarly positive effects in the long run (Murray et al., 1989), although those participants seeing a psychotherapist had more positive moods immediately after therapy sessions compared with those using expressive writing, who had more negative moods immediately after writing. It is as if the act of deliberately processing the emotional experience, whether in writing or with a therapist, transforms the experience into a less upsetting event and increases immune system functioning.

Both the psychotherapy sessions and writing exercise focused on feelings surrounding a traumatic event that occurred in the past, often an event about which the participants had not told anyone. Thus, the therapy and the writing provided an opportunity for participants to think about issues that they had not previously explored. It should be noted, however, that most studies on emotional expression through writing have used relatively healthy college undergraduates as participants. It remains to be seen whether the therapeutic results would be the same with participants who are diagnosed with psychological disorders.

Nonetheless, these results about the positive effects of expressing emotions and gaining insight support some of the basic tenets of psychodynamic therapy specifically and of insight-oriented therapy more generally. Moreover, the outcome can be understood from the levels approach. Expressing feelings by making what is unconscious conscious and deriving insight (level of the person) has an effect on the immune system (level of the brain). Further, participants in studies on emotional expressiveness who did express their feelings report feeling better in the long run and attribute this positive emotional state to the insights gained (level of the person). At the level of the group, those gaining insight through therapy had less negative moods immediately after sessions in which they expressed emotions than did those writing about their feelings, illustrating the importance of expressing the feelings *with another person*. In addition, cultural factors led the participants to have certain beliefs about what would occur in the therapy sessions and how they might feel about the sessions.

1 *What is the focus of treatment in psychody-namic therapy? What are its main techniques?*
Psychodynamic therapy seeks to help patients become aware of their unconscious motivations, which can cause psychological symptoms. Through insight, they can choose whether to respond to those impulses. At some point in the treatment, patients typically experience transference to the therapist and resistance. Techniques include dream analysis, free association, and interpretation.

2 *How would client-centered therapists approach treatment? What techniques would they use?*
Client-centered therapy focuses on helping clients experience congruence between their real and ideal selves, thereby reducing the clients' problems. The therapist should be warm, empathic, and genuine, and should show unconditional positive regard toward clients. These therapies are based on the idea that these elements are enough to bring about therapeutic change.

Behavior and Cognitive Therapy

A cognitive–behavior therapist would begin by asking Beth quite a different set of questions, questions that dealt with neither her family nor her feelings: What does she do before she sits down to study or take an exam? What does she think about when she starts to study or walks to a classroom to take an exam? What, in detail, does she do during the day? Has she ever tried any relaxation techniques? What does she believe about herself and her abilities? These are questions not about insight, but about thought patterns and behaviors.

1 What is the focus of behavior therapy? What are some of its techniques?

2 What are the goals of cognitive therapy? What techniques are used?

Behavior Therapy

Even after patients had developed an awareness of the origins of their problems through insight-oriented therapies, behavioral change did not necessarily follow. **Behavior therapy**, which focuses on observable, measurable behavior, developed out of frustration with this lack of change. Joseph Wolpe (1915–1997) profoundly changed the practice of psychotherapy in 1958 when he published *Psychotherapy by Reciprocal Inhibition*. He was a psychiatrist, but his emphasis on behavior rather than on unconscious motivation created a new form of treatment that particularly appealed to psychologists because of its emphasis on quantifiable results. Moreover, behavior therapy rested on well-researched principles of learning (see Chapter 4; Wolpe, 1997).

Theory

According to behavior therapy, distressing symptoms are seen as the result of learning, not of unconscious forces. Through the use of social learning—that is, modeling—as well as by classical and operant conditioning, clients can change unwanted behaviors by learning new ones; it is easiest to change a behavior by replacing it with a new, more adaptive one. The behavior therapist is interested in the ABCs of the behavior: its *antecedents* (what is the stimulus that triggers the behavior?), the *behavior* (what is the exact nature of the behavior?), and its *consequences* (what is reinforcing the behavior?). Behavior therapy's lack of interest or belief in an unconscious "root cause" was revolutionary. Behaviors and performance are emphasized,

Behavior therapy: A type of therapy, based on well-researched principles of learning, that focuses on observable, measurable behaviors.

the therapist takes a more active, directive role in treatment, and "homework"—between-session tasks on the part of the client—is an important component of the treatment. Therapists took a new look at treatment results: Did the client experience less frequent or less intense symptoms after therapy?

In Beth's case, a behavior therapist would be interested in the antecedent, or stimulus, of Beth's problematic behaviors. Consider her anxiety: The antecedent might be the act of sitting down to study for an exam, or waiting in class to receive her exam booklet. The behavior is the conditioned emotional response of fear and anxiety, evidenced by her sweating hands, racing heart rate, and other behaviors associated with anxiety (see Chapter 11). The consequences include negative reinforcement (the uncomfortable symptoms go away) when skipping an exam. Thus, related nonacademic avoidant behaviors such as sleeping through an exam are reinforced. In addition, her anxiety and subsequent social isolation led to a loss of pleasant activities and opportunities for social reinforcement, which in turn led to depression. Behavior therapy views depressive behaviors as leading to depressive thoughts (see Chapter 11; Emmelkamp, 1994).

Techniques

Behavioral techniques rest on classical conditioning, operant conditioning, and social learning principles. One classical conditioning technique is **systematic desensitization**, a procedure that teaches people to be relaxed in the presence of a feared object or situation. This technique, developed by Wolpe for treating phobias, grew out of the idea that someone cannot be fearful (and hence anxious) and relaxed at the same time. Systematic desensitization uses **progressive muscle relaxation**, a relaxation technique whereby the muscles are sequentially relaxed from one end of the body to the other, often from feet to head. Although progressive muscle relaxation is used in systematic desensitization, it is often used by itself to induce relaxation. You can try progressive muscle relaxation yourself by following the instructions below. Read them several times until you essentially know them and can say them to yourself with your eyes closed; or, have a friend read them to you; or tape record them for playback. The instructions should be recited slowly and clearly. If you're repeating the instructions to yourself from memory and you forget a group of muscles, the technique can still be effective. (If you have an injury in a particular part of your body, you may want to skip tensing the muscles in that area.) Like any new skill, relaxation induction becomes easier and more effective with practice.

> *Sit in a comfortable position, take a deep breath, and close your eyes. Curl your toes, and hold that position for a few seconds . . . not so tightly that it hurts, just enough so that you can notice what the tension in your foot muscles feels like (5–10 seconds). . . . Relax. . . . Notice the difference between the tension and the relaxation, the pleasantness of the relaxation. . . . Now point your toes up toward the ceiling, keeping your heels on the floor. . . . Feel the tension, the pull . . . keep breathing. . . . Relax. . . . As before, notice the difference between the tension and the relaxation. . . . Press your knees toward each other . . . not so much that it hurts, just enough to notice the tension in those muscles. . . . Relax. . . . Tense your thighs and buttocks, and notice your body lift slightly. . . . Notice the tension in the muscles, remember to breathe. . . . Relax. . . . Notice how pleasant the relaxation feels. . . . Tense your abdominal muscles as if you were a prize fighter. . . . Feel the tension, keep breathing. . . . Relax. . . . Take a deep breath and hold it while counting to 5, then slowly exhale. . . . Notice the way the muscles in your chest feel as you hold the breath and then exhale, and how your sense of relaxation is enhanced. . . . Raise your shoulders up toward your ears and hold it. . . . Notice what the tension feels like in those muscles, breathe. . . . Relax. . . . Now push your shoulders down toward the floor, focusing your awareness on how this new tension feels. . . . Relax. . . . Notice a sense of relaxation spreading over your body. . . . Purse your lips together and notice*

Systematic desensitization: A behavior therapy technique that teaches people to be relaxed in the presence of a feared object or situation.

Progressive muscle relaxation: A relaxation technique whereby the person relaxes muscles sequentially from one end of the body to the other.

the tension in the lower part of your face, your jaw, perhaps your neck. . . . Relax. . . . Notice the difference between the tension and the relaxation, and how much more pleasant relaxation is. . . . Close your eyes tightly, but not so tightly that it hurts. . . . Notice the tension. . . . Relax. . . . Notice the pleasantness of the relaxation. Take a moment and check your body for any residual tension; if you find any, tense and relax those muscles. . . . Enjoy the sensation of relaxation. In a few moments, open your eyes, and bring this sense of relaxation with you into the day. (Adapted from Jacobson, 1925)

Using systematic desensitization to overcome a phobia, the therapist and client construct a hierarchy of real or imagined activities related to the feared object or situation (such as a fear of elevators; see Figure 12.1). This hierarchy begins with the least fearful activity, such as pressing an elevator call button, progressing to the most fearful, being stuck in a stopped elevator. Over the course of a number of sessions, clients work on becoming relaxed when imagining increasingly anxiety-provoking activities. At the outset, the client is asked to relax. After becoming fully relaxed, the client is then asked to imagine the activity or object at the bottom of the hierarchy—that is, the least feared scenario. If anxiety intrudes (which the client indicates by some prearranged signal), the therapist asks the client to abandon imagining the fearful scene and use the relaxation technique until he or she is relaxed again. After successfully mastering this first scene—that is, thinking about it without feeling anxious—the client imagines the next most fearful scene in the hierarchy, again alternating imagining with relaxation when the anxiety is uncomfortable. The procedure continues in this fashion until the client can imagine being fully immersed in the actual feared situation without an anxious response. After these mental exercises, the client will experience the situation in reality, now better able to control any anxiety.

A behavioral therapist would have asked Beth about her "learning history": When did she start to feel anxious about tests? What external conditions made it worse? The therapist might teach Beth relaxation techniques and instruct her to practice them between sessions. Once Beth successfully learned to how to become relaxed, she and her therapist might begin systematic desensitization.

Another behavioral technique that relies on classical conditioning principles is **exposure with response prevention**, a planned, programmatic procedure that exposes the client to the anxiety-provoking object but prevents the usual maladaptive response. For instance, clients with an obsessive-compulsive disorder that compels them to wash their hands repeatedly would purposefully get their hands dirty during a therapy session and then be prevented from washing their hands immediately afterward. In this way, they would habituate to the anxiety. Exposure with response prevention has been found to be as effective as medication for OCD, and the behavioral treatment can have longer-lasting benefits (Marks, 1997). However, not all people who have OCD are willing to use this behavioral technique (Stanley & Turner, 1995). The technique is also used in treating bulimia nervosa: Clients would eat a food normally followed by forced vomiting, and then would not throw up (or would delay it as long as possible). Beforehand, client and therapist develop strategies that the client could use while trying *not* to engage in the maladaptive behavior. The technique of **stimulus control** involves controlling the exposure to a stimulus that elicits a conditioned response, so as to decrease or increase the frequency of the response. For example, if an alcoholic drank to excess only in a bar, limiting or eliminating the occasions of going to a bar would be using stimulus control.

Techniques based on operant conditioning make use of the principles of reinforcement, punishment, and extinction, with the goal of **behavior modification**— that is, changing the *behavior,* not focusing on thoughts or feelings. Setting the appropriate *response contingencies,* or behaviors that will earn reinforcement, is crucial. If Beth used behavior modification techniques, she would establish response contingencies for behaving in desired new ways: She might reward herself with a

Exposure with response prevention: A behavior therapy technique that, in a planned, programmatic way, exposes the client to an anxiety-provoking object and prevents the usual maladaptive response.

Stimulus control: A behavior therapy technique that involves controlling the exposure to a stimulus that elicits a conditioned response, so as to decrease or increase the frequency of the response.

Behavior modification: A category of therapeutic techniques for changing behavior based on operant conditioning principles.

Figure 12.1   Systematic Desensitization of an Elevator Phobia

With systematic desensitization, a man with an elevator phobia would list a hierarchy of activities related to using an elevator. Next, he would successfully learn to make himself relax, using techniques such as progressive muscle relaxation.

He then starts out imagining items at the low end of the hierarchy, such as pressing an elevator button. When he becomes anxious, he stops imagining that scene and uses relaxation techniques to become fully relaxed again.

When he can imagine the elevator-related situations on the lower end of the hierarchy without anxiety, he progresses to situations that make him more anxious, stopping to do the relaxation technique when he becomes anxious.

Systematic desensitization continues in this fashion until the man can imagine being fully immersed in the most feared situation (a stuck elevator) without anxiety. He would then follow the same procedure in a real elevator, although his anxiety may no longer be troublesome, making this final phase unnecessary.

movie or a dinner out after taking an exam, or allow herself an hour's conversation with a friend after working on a paper for 2 hours.

Extinction, eliminating a behavior by not reinforcing it, is another important tool of the behavioral therapist. **Self-monitoring techniques**, such as keeping a daily log of a problematic behavior, can help identify its antecedents (see Figure 12.2 on page 442). Daily logs are used for a variety of problems, including poor mood, anxiety, overeating, smoking, sleep problems, and compulsive gambling. Observational learning also plays a role in behavior therapy, particularly with children and in the treatment of some phobias, especially animal phobias (Goetestam & Berntzen, 1997).

Self-monitoring techniques: Behavioral techniques that help the client identify the antecedents, consequences, and patterns of a targeted behavior.

Figure 12.2   Daily Self-Monitoring Log

Name _____	Day _____	Date _____	

Time of Day	Problematic Behavior	Where the Behavior Occurred	What happened before the behavior occurred (thoughts/feelings, interactions with others, etc.)?

This daily self-monitoring log helps clients develop an awareness of the antecedents, or "triggers," to their problematic behaviors. The column for time of day helps determine whether there is a daily or weekly pattern. Noting where the behavior occurred helps establish whether certain environments play a role in the behavior, perhaps serving as conditioned stimuli. Writing down thoughts, feelings, interactions with others, or other factors (such as level of hunger) that preceded the problematic behavior helps identify irrational thought patterns, distressing feelings, states, or situations that lead to the behavior. With knowledge of the factors, the client and therapist can develop appropriate targets of change for the therapy.

Psychodynamic therapists predicted that some of clients' symptoms—that is, their maladaptive behaviors—might disappear with behavioral treatment, but that because the unresolved underlying conflicts remained, new symptoms would develop. The psychoanalysts termed this process *symptom substitution*. According to this view, should Beth's anxiety symptoms respond well to behavior therapy, her unconscious conflicts would reemerge through some other symptom—perhaps being unable to get up for classes in the morning or staying out partying every night. The new symptoms, just like the old ones, would impede Beth's academic success and, according to psychodynamic theory, new symptoms would continue to arise until her unconscious conflict was resolved. However, research has not supported the concept of symptom substitution (Nurnberger & Hingtgen, 1973). Other criticisms of behavior therapy focus on its exclusive emphasis on observable behaviors, which ignores thoughts, feelings, and motivation.

Cognitive Therapy: It's the Thought That Counts

The ripples of the cognitive revolution in psychology (see Chapter 1) were felt in therapy as well as in research. Therapists began to examine the mental processes that contribute to behavior, not simply physical stimuli. It was clear that people's thoughts ("cognitions"), not just their learning histories or "unconscious forces," influence their feelings and behavior, and do so in myriad ways. Just thinking about a past positive experience with love can put you in a good mood, and thinking about an unhappy love experience can have the opposite effect (Clark & Collins, 1993). A cognitive therapist would focus on Beth's thoughts and the way in which one thought leads to another, contributing to her emotional experience of anxiety and depression.

Theory

The way people perceive or interpret events can affect their well-being (Chapter 10). **Cognitive therapy** emphasizes the role of attempts to think rationally in the control of distressing feelings and behaviors. It is the perception of any experience that determines the response to that experience, and cognitive therapy highlights the importance of the way people perceive and think about events. Two particularly important contributors to cognitive therapy were Albert Ellis and Aaron Beck.

Albert Ellis (b. 1913) was a clinical psychologist who in the 1950s developed a treatment called *rational-emotive therapy (RET)* (now called *rational emotive behavior therapy,* or REBT). RET emphasizes rational, logical thinking and assumes that distressing feelings or symptoms are caused by faulty or illogical thoughts. People may develop illogical or irrational thoughts as a result of their experiences and never assess whether these thoughts are valid. They elevate irrational thoughts to "god-like absolutist musts, shoulds, demands, and commands" (Ellis, 1994a, p. 103). According to RET, Beth's thought that she needs to do well in school is a dysfunctional, irrational belief that to be a lovable, deserving human being, she must earn good grades; if she does not, she believes she will be unlovable and worthless.

RET thus focuses on creating more rational thoughts. In Beth's case, they might be, *I might be disappointed or disappoint others if I don't do well this semester, but they will still love and care about me.* This more rational thought should then cause the problematic behavior to diminish, allowing her to choose other thoughts and actions. Part of the goal of RET is educational, and clients should be able to use the techniques on their own once they have mastered them. Like behavior therapy, RET is oriented toward *solving* problems as opposed to psychologically exploring them.

Ellis (1994a) proposed three processes that interfere with healthy functioning: (1) *self-downing*—being critical of oneself for performing poorly or being rejected; (2) *hostility and rage*—being unkind to or critical of others for performing poorly; and (3) *low frustration tolerance*—blaming everyone and everything for "poor, dislikable conditions."

A rational-emotive therapist challenges the client but focuses on thoughts rather than feelings. The RET therapist challenges the client's assumptions, which are based on thoughts and beliefs, and helps the client develop more realistic, appropriate thoughts. The RET therapist strives to have the client feel accepted and encourages self-acceptance and a new way of thinking; self-blame is viewed as counterproductive because it involves faulty beliefs. Shortcomings or failures are viewed as simply part of life, not as crimes or signs of moral weakness.

Psychiatrist Aaron Beck (b. 1921) developed a form of cognitive therapy that, like RET, rests on the premise that irrational thoughts are the root cause of psychological problems, and that recognition of irrationality and adoption of more realistic, rational thoughts cause psychological problems to improve. Irrational thoughts that arise from a systematic bias, such as the belief that if you tell your friend you are mad at her she will reject you, are considered **cognitive distortions** of reality; several common distortions are presented in Table 12.2 on page 444. However, unlike RET, which relies on the therapist's attempts to persuade the client of the irrationality of his or her beliefs, Beck's version of cognitive therapy encourages the client to view beliefs as hypotheses to be tested. Thus, interactions with the world provide opportunities to perform "experiments" to ascertain the accuracy of the client's beliefs (Hollon & Beck, 1994). Beck and his colleagues have approached treatment empirically, developing measures to assess depression, anxiety, and other problems, and to evaluate the effectiveness of treatment.

Techniques

The RET therapist helps the client identify his or her irrational beliefs, relying on verbal persuasion (Hollon & Beck, 1994). The therapist works through a sequence of techniques with the client, which can be remembered by the alphabetical

Cognitive therapy: Therapy that focuses on the client's thoughts rather than his or her feelings or behaviors.

Cognitive distortion: Irrational thoughts that arise from a systematic bias in the way a person thinks about reality.

TABLE 12.2 **Five Common Cognitive Distortions** *Source: Adapted from Beck (1967).*

Dichotomous Thinking

Also known as black-and-white thinking, which allows for nothing in between the extremes; you are either perfect or a piece of garbage.

Example: Beth thinks that if she doesn't get an A on a test, she has failed in life.

The Mental Filter

Magnifying the negative aspects of something while filtering out the positive.

Example: Beth remembers only the things she did that were below her expectations but doesn't pay attention to (or remember) the things she did well.

Mind Reading

Thinking you know exactly what other people are thinking, particularly as it relates to you.

Example: Beth believes that she *knows* her professors think less of her because of what happened on the exams (when in fact they don't think less of her, but are concerned about her).

Catastrophic Exaggeration

Thinking that your worst nightmare will come true and that it will be intolerable.

Example: Beth's fear is that she'll be kicked out of school and end up homeless; a more likely reality is that she may have to take some courses over again.

Control Beliefs

Believing either that you are helpless and totally subject to forces beyond your control, or that you must tightly control your life for fear that, if you don't, you will never be able to regain control.

Example: Until talking to her family friend, Nina, Beth thought there was nothing she could do to change the downward spiral of events, and that she was either totally in control of her studying or else not in control at all.

---

sequence ABCDEF. Distressing feelings exist because an *activating event* (A) along with the person's *beliefs* (B) lead to a *highly charged emotional consequence* (C). It is not the event per se that created the problem, but rather the beliefs attached to the event that led to a problematic consequence. Thus, changing the beliefs will lead to a different consequence. This is done by helping the client *dispute* (D) the irrational beliefs and perceive their illogical and self-defeating nature. Such disputes lead to an *effect* (E; also called *effective new philosophies*), a new way of feeling and acting. Finally, clients may have to take *further action* (F) to solidify the change in beliefs. Each session is devoted to a specific aspect of the client's problem. Often at the outset of a session, client and therapist will determine what effect the client wants from the intervention.

Beth and a RET therapist might agree on what the effect should be when studying—namely, less anxiety—and would discuss the activating events (sitting down to study), beliefs (that if Beth does not do well on a test, she will be a failure as a person), and consequences (anxiety). The bulk of their work together would focus on disputing the beliefs: Beth is still a lovable person even if she doesn't do well on a test, and even if she gets a B or C, her grade is not a failure, nor is she. The end result of this process is that Beth should feel less anxiety.

When working on a dispute, a RET therapist helps the client distinguish between a thought that is a "must" and one that is a "prefer." Beth's thought *I must get an A* is irrational and creates unpleasant feelings. Its more realistic counterpart is *I prefer to get an A,* which makes it clearer that she has some choice about the grade she sets as a goal. The therapist sometimes argues with the client to help him or her confront (and dispute) the faulty cognitions that contribute to the client's distress. The RET therapist may also use role playing to help the client practice new ways of thinking and behaving (Ellis, 1994b). RET can be helpful with anxiety, unassertiveness (Haaga & Davison, 1989), and unrealistic expectations. Like insight-oriented treatment, RET is generally not successful with psychotic disorders.

Beck's cognitive therapy often makes use of a daily record of dysfunctional thoughts (see Figure 12.3). Clients are asked to identify the situation in which their

Figure **12.3** Daily Record of Dysfunctional Beliefs

Situation	Emotion(s)	Automatic Thought(s)	Rational Response	Outcome
Actual event or stream of thoughts	Rate (1–100%)	ATs that preceded emotion Rate belief in ATs (1–100%)	Write rational response to ATs Rate belief in rational response (1–100%)	Rerate AT (1–100%)
1. Sit down to study	Anxious 70%	I won't be able to do as well on the test as I would like. —100% (Dichotomous thinking)	I might not be able to do as well as I want, but that doesn't mean that I will necessarily fail. —50%	Anxious 50%
2. In bed in the morning	Sad 80%	There's no point in getting out of bed—the day will be awful. I fail at everything I try. —90% (Mental filter)	Although I may not "succeed" in the goals I set for myself, it is possible that my expectations are too high, that I have too many expectations, or that I only notice the goals I don't attain, and don't notice the ones I do. —70%	Sad 6%

Keeping a written daily record like Beth's, shown here, can help identify triggers to dysfunctional, automatic thoughts and make them more rational. (Format adapted from Beck et al., 1979.)

automatic thought (comparable to irrational beliefs) occurred, rate their emotional state (Emotions column), write down the automatic thought, their rational response to the automatic thought (comparable to the RET "dispute"), and then rerate their emotional state (Outcome column). Clients should rate their emotional state as lower after going through this process. Although this technique appears straightforward, it can be hard to do because the client is so used to believing the "truth" of the automatic thought that it doesn't seem to be distorted or irrational. The process of helping clients shift their thinking away from automatic, dysfunctional thoughts to more realistic ones is called **cognitive restructuring.** The therapist helps clients examine and assess the accuracy of the automatic thoughts, and search for alternative interpretations or solutions to their automatic thoughts and habitual ways of viewing themselves and the world. Cognitive therapy also makes use of **psychoeducation**—that is, educating clients about therapy and research findings pertaining to their disorder or problem. This knowledge is then used to help clients develop a more realistic, undistorted view of their problems.

In the last quarter of the 20th century, therapists began to use both cognitive and behavioral techniques within the same treatment. This merging of therapies grew out of the recognition that both cognitions and behaviors affect feelings and are a part of most psychological disorders. The two sets of techniques can work together to promote therapeutic change: Cognitive techniques change thoughts, which then affect feelings and behaviors; behavioral techniques change behaviors, which in turn lead to new experiences, feelings, ways of relating, and changes in how one thinks about oneself and the world. Treatment that combines both types of techniques is called cognitive-behavior therapy (CBT).

Despite differences between cognitive and behavioral therapies (see Table 12.3 on page 446), both approaches are appropriate for a wide range of clients and disorders. These treatments focus on clients' problems rather than on the client as a "whole" person, as insight-oriented treatments do. Cognitive therapy and behavior therapy provide the client with the opportunity to learn new coping strategies and master new tasks. These therapies are appropriate for any disorder.

Cognitive restructuring: The process of helping clients shift their thinking away from the focus on automatic, dysfunctional thoughts to more realistic ones.

Psychoeducation: The process of educating clients about therapy and research findings pertaining to their disorders or problems.

TABLE 12.3 **Differences Between Behavioral and Cognitive Therapies**

Although behavioral and cognitive therapies both address a client's symptoms more than insight-oriented therapies do, focus on symptom relief as a goal in and of itself, and employ between-session homework, they also have differences.

TYPE OF THERAPY	FOCUS	GOAL	TECHNIQUE
Behavioral therapy	Maladaptive behaviors	Change the behavior, its antecedents, or its consequences.	Relaxation techniques, systematic desensitization, exposure with response prevention, stimulus control, behavior modification, observational learning.
Cognitive therapy	Automatic, irrational thoughts	Change dysfunctional, unrealistic thoughts to more realistic ones. Recognize the relationship among thoughts, feelings, and behaviors.	Cognitive restructuring (or Ellis's ABCDEF technique), help the client develop more realistic thoughts, psychoeducation, role playing.

LOOKING AT LEVELS

Token Economies

As you have seen, behavioral techniques focus on changing maladaptive behaviors. They can also be used in inpatient psychiatric units. In these facilities, it is possible to change the response contingencies for an undesired behavior as well as for a desired behavior. Behavior modification can be used to change even severely maladaptive behaviors. Secondary reinforcers, those that are learned and don't inherently satisfy a biological need, are used in treatment programs not only with psychiatric patients but also with mentally retarded children and adults, and even in prisons. Patients and residents must earn "tokens" by behaving appropriately; these tokens then can be traded for small items such as cigarettes or candy at a "token store," or for privileges such as going out for a walk or watching a particular television show.

These **token economies**—treatment programs that use secondary reinforcers to change behavior—can be used to mold social behavior (level of the group) directly by modifying what patients say to one another and to nonpatients. For instance, using a token economy, hospitalized schizophrenics can learn to talk to others, answer questions, or eat more normally. The token economy itself is a social creation, and it is only within the confines of the values of the culture that certain behaviors come to be reinforced and others extinguished. Operant conditioning also modifies how patients perceive specific stimuli, such as interpreting a question as something that requires an answer (level of the person). At the level of the brain, operant conditioning can affect the dopamine-based reward system in the nucleus accumbens (see Chapter 4), increasing the likelihood of a reinforced behaviors occurring again. Thus, behavior modification as a treatment for severely disturbed behavior can best be understood by regarding events at the three levels: how conditioning changes the brain and how it changes the meaning of stimuli, which in turn changes behavioral interactions with objects. Moreover, such conditioning affects and is affected by social interactions. Although token economies can be effective, their use is declining because of ethical and moral questions about depriving patients and clients of secondary reinforcers (such as television, cigarettes, walks on the grounds) if they do not earn them through behavior change (Glynn, 1990).

CONSOLIDATE!

 What is the focus of behavior therapy? What are some of its techniques? Behavior therapy assumes that maladaptive behavior is based on previous learning and focuses on changing distressing or abnormal behavior via learning princi-

ples. Behavioral therapists use techniques such as systematic desensitization, exposure with response prevention, stimulus control, behavior modification programs, and observational learning.

What are the goals of cognitive therapy? What techniques are used? Cognitive therapy rests on the assumption that thoughts influence feelings and behaviors. According to this approach, someone experiencing distressing symptoms such as depression has irrational, automatic thoughts that affect feelings and behavior. The goal of cognitive therapy is to reduce these irrational cognitive distortions via cognitive restructuring, psychoeducation, and challenging irrational beliefs or, using Ellis's term, disputes.

Biomedical Therapies

During the course of her therapy, Beth talked about her vivid memories of her mother's episodes of depression, about the times when she would lie in bed most of the day. However, her mother had not had an episode of severe depression in the last 5 years. Thinking about her mother's depression led Beth to wonder whether medication might help her anxiety and depression, since medication seemed to help her mother. After her last hospitalization 5 years ago, Beth's mother had participated in a research study in the hospital, where she was treated successfully with antidepressant medication and cognitive–behavior therapy.

With recent advances in knowledge about the brain have come advances in biomedical treatments of many disorders.

 How are medications used to treat psychological disorders?

 What is electroconvulsive therapy?

 When is transcranial magnetic stimulation used as a treatment?

Psychopharmacology

The use of medication to treat psychological disorders and problems is known as **psychopharmacology.** In the last two decades, the number and types of medications for the treatment of psychological disorders have multiplied. As scientists learn more about the brain and neurotransmitter systems, researchers are able to develop new medications to target symptoms more effectively and with fewer side effects. Thus, for any given disorder, there are more medication options.

Schizophrenia and Other Psychotic Disorders

The most common type of medication for the treatment of schizophrenia and other psychotic disorders is **antipsychotic medication,** which generally reduces psychotic symptoms but does not cure the disorder. Antipsychotic drugs have long been known to have an effect on the positive symptoms of schizophrenia (see Chapter 11), such as hallucinations. Traditional antipsychotic medications include Thorazine and Haldol. However, long-term use of these medications can cause **tardive dyskinesia,** an irreversible movement disorder in which the affected person involuntarily smacks his or her lips, displays facial grimaces, and exhibits other symptoms. *Atypical antipsychotics* are a new group of antipsychotic drugs that affect the neurotransmitter dopamine (as does traditional antipsychotic medication) as well as other neurotransmitters. In addition to decreasing positive symptoms, such as hallucinations, these newer drugs also counteract negative symptoms such as apathy, lack of interest, and withdrawal, and are effective in improving cognitive functioning (Keefe et al., 1999), all of which allow psychological therapies to be more effective (Ballus, 1997). These drugs also appear to have fewer side effects than traditional antipsychotic medication. There are increasing amounts of data suggesting that pharmacological treatment administered soon after the first

Token economy: A treatment program that uses secondary reinforcers (tokens) to bring about behavior modification.

Psychopharmacology: The use of medication to treat psychological disorders and problems.

Antipsychotic medication: Medication that reduces psychotic symptoms.

Tardive dyskinesia: An irreversible movement disorder in which the person involuntarily smacks his or her lips, displays facial grimaces, and exhibits other symptoms, caused by traditional antipsychotic medication.

Studies so far show that the herbal remedy St. John's wort can be effective in treating mild to moderately severe depression. However, to date, no guidelines exist about the strength of each pill or the exact dosages for maximal effectiveness.

psychotic episode is associated with a better long-term prognosis, compared to treatment begun later (see Chapter 11; Wyatt et al., 1997).

Mood Disorders

Effective pharmacological treatment for depression began in earnest in the 1950s with the discovery of **tricyclic antidepressants (TCAs)**, named for the three rings in the chemical structure of these compounds. Elavil is an example of this class of drug. For decades, TCAs were the only effective antidepressant medication readily available, although common side effects include constipation, dry mouth, blurred vision, and low blood pressure. These medications affect serotonin levels, and they can take weeks to work. Although another type of medication, **monoamine oxidase inhibitors (MAOIs)**, was the first antidepressant medication discovered, it has never been as widely prescribed as TCAs, for two major reasons. First, MAOIs require users not to eat foods with tyramine (such as cheese and wine) because of potentially fatal changes in blood pressure. Second, they are particularly effective with atypical depression involving increased appetite and hypersomnia (increased need for sleep; Prien & Kocsis, 1995), and less effective with typical depressive episodes.

Then **selective serotonergic reuptake inhibitors (SSRIs)**, such as Prozac, Zoloft, and Paxil, were developed in the 1980s. Although they have fewer side effects (they only work on *selective* serotonin receptors), a common one is decreased sexual interest, and many people experience a "Prozac poop-out" after a while, no longer attaining the same benefit from what had previously been an effective dosage. A meta-analysis of the use of Prozac in treating depression found an effectiveness rate comparable to that of TCAs, but not greater (Agency for Health Care Policy and Research, 1999; Greenberg et al., 1997). Researchers continue to discover ways to alleviate symptoms of depression without as many side effects and to discover additional biological mechanisms so that those who do not respond to existing antidepressants can obtain relief from medication. Some newer antidepressants (such as Serzone, Effexor, and Remeron) don't fall into the existing categories; these drugs, which affect both the serotonin and norepinephrine systems, are sometimes referred to as **serotonergic/noradrenergic reuptake inhibitors (SNRIs)**. Antidepressant medications are also given to people experiencing dysthymia.

Studies of the effectiveness of an extract from the flowering plant **St. John's wort**, *Hypericum perforatum,* suggest that it may be effective as a short-term treatment of mild to moderately severe depression (Agency for Health Care Policy and Research, 1999; Gaster & Holroyd, 2000), although not without minor side effects. Further investigations about the exact dosages and long-term effects are under way. In addition, medications that block *substance P,* a neurotransmitter, show success in treating depression (Kramer et al., 1998), although further study will ultimately determine their effectiveness. Substance P–related medications do not operate by altering norepinephrine or serotonin, as do other antidepressants, but rather work by some other, as yet undetermined mechanism (Bender, 1998).

For bipolar disorder, mood stabilizers such as *lithium* can prevent a recurrence of both manic and depressive phases, although up to half of those with this disorder either will show no significant improvement or will be unable to tolerate the side effects. When this happens, a mood stabilizer such as Depakote or Tegretol is given to minimize the recurrence of manic episodes. During a manic episode, antipsychotic drugs or antianxiety drugs are often used. The usual medication regimen for schizophrenia and bipolar disorder may involve lifelong use of medication.

Anxiety Disorders

For most anxiety disorders, including panic disorder, the panic symptoms of specific phobias, and PTSD, **benzodiazepines** are often the medication prescribed. Xanax and Valium are types of benzodiazepines, which affect the target symptoms within 36 hours and do not need to be taken for 10 days or more to build up to an effective level, as is the case with antidepressants. However, they can cause drowsiness and are potentially lethal when taken with alcohol. In addition, a person using benzodiazepines can develop tolerance and dependence and can experience withdrawal reactions. For these reasons, drugs of this class are often prescribed only for short periods of time, such as during a particularly stressful period. Antidepressants (TCAs, SSRIs, or SNRIs) may be prescribed for long-term treatment of anxiety disorders, although the dosage may be lower than that used in the treatment of depression (Gorman & Kent, 1999). Social phobia may be treated with antianxiety or antidepressant medication. Obsessive-compulsive disorder can be treated effectively with SSRI antidepressants such as clomiprimine, although at a higher dose than that prescribed for depression or other anxiety disorders.

Electroconvulsive Therapy

Essentially a controlled brain seizure, **electroconvulsive therapy (ECT)** was developed in the 1930s as a treatment for schizophrenia. It was based on the idea that schizophrenia and epilepsy were incompatible, and thus that ECT-induced epilepsy would relieve the symptoms of schizophrenia. Although it did not cure schizophrenia, it is still a recommended treatment when medication does not work (Lehman & Steinwachs, 1998). ECT has been particularly helpful in treating certain mood disorders, specifically psychotic depression and manic episodes of bipolar disorder. In fact, 80% of those receiving ECT suffer from depression (Sackheim et al., 1995).

People with severe depression who have not received much benefit from psychotherapy or medication (Lam et al., 1999), or those for whom drugs are medically contraindicated, may receive ECT. Although the treatment can be effective, the reasons are not well understood. The patient is given a muscle relaxant before each ECT treatment and is under anesthesia during the procedure; because of the anesthesia, ECT is administered in a hospital and generally requires a hospital stay. Patients may experience temporary memory loss for events right before, during, or after each treatment. After a course of 6 to 12 sessions over several weeks, usually twice a week (Shapira et al., 1998; Vieweg & Shawcross, 1998), depression often lifts; relief may come sooner for the depressed elderly (Tew et al., 1999).

ECT was considered a major biomedical treatment in the 1940s and 1950s, but the ready availability of medications in subsequent decades led to a decline in its use. Another reason for its decreased use was that some patients seemed to experience significant cognitive impairments, including memory loss. And, as it became known that it was sometimes used in understaffed institutions to produce a docile patient population, ECT became politically unpopular. However, improvements in the way ECT is administered have significantly reduced the cognitive deficits and undesirable side effects, and since the 1980s, the use of ECT has increased. This trend reflects a new appreciation of its usefulness, and a recognition that not all people with depression, mania, or schizophrenia can either take medication or find it helpful. In recent years, ECT is more frequently administered to affluent patients than to those in publicly funded hospitals (Sackheim et al., 1995).

Transcranial Magnetic Stimulation

A new treatment currently being researched is **transcranial magnetic stimulation (TMS)**, a procedure in which an electromagnetic coil on the scalp transmits pulses of high-intensity magnetism to the brain in short bursts lasting 100 to 200 microseconds. Although it is not yet known exactly how this magnetic field changes brain neurophysiology and neurochemistry, TMS has varying effects, depending on the exact location of the coil on the head. Studies of TMS for people with psychological disorders have been experimental; early results suggest that it may provide a therapeutic benefit similar to that of ECT. Placebo studies of TMS (in which the

Electroconvulsive therapy (ECT): A controlled brain seizure, used to treat people with certain psychological disorders such as psychotic depression or those for whom medication has not been effective or recommended.

Transcranial magnetic stimulation (TMS): An experimental treatment for psychological disorders involving the use of electromagnetic stimulation.

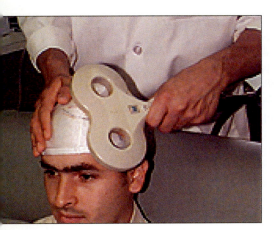

Unlike with ECT, the person receiving transcranial magnetic stimulation is awake and does not need anesthesia.

procedure of TMS is administered, but at an angle that does not affect the brain) have found actual TMS to be more effective than the placebo (George et al., 1999; Klein et al., 1999). Studies of people with depression who have not responded to medication have yielded positive results: Approximately half of those receiving TMS have not needed to go on to receive ECT (Epstein et al., 1998; Figiel et al., 1998; Klein et al., 1999). Preliminary results also suggest that TMS works as well or better with nonpsychotically depressed people, but that ECT is superior for those with psychotic depressions, indicating the possibility that the two procedures act through different mechanisms (George et al., 1999). Should additional studies confirm these early results, TMS offers a number of advantages over ECT, including easier administration (it requires neither anesthesia nor hospitalization) and minimal side effects. The most common short-term side effect, experienced by 5% to 20% of patients, is a slight headache.

TMS has been tried with people with depression, bipolar disorder (Grisaru, Chudakov et al., 1998), schizophrenia (see George et al., 1999, for a review), and PTSD (Grisaru, Amir et al., 1998). But more research is necessary before TMS can definitively be declared a treatment of choice rather than an experimental one. Information about the precise optimal location of the coil and the frequency and intensity of the stimulation is needed.

LOOKING AT LEVELS

Treating Obsessive-Compulsive Disorder

Medication can be effective in treating the symptoms of many disorders. Medication works by changing neurochemistry, which in turn affects thoughts, feelings, and behaviors. Does psychotherapy's beneficial effect work in a similar way? Until recently this question could not have been answered. But brain scanning has made it possible to begin to understand the positive effects of both medication and psychotherapy, at least in their effects on people with obsessive-compulsive disorder. We can understand their effects by looking at events at the three levels and their interactions.

Obsessive-compulsive disorder (OCD) is marked by intrusive, illogical thoughts and overpowering compulsions to repeat certain acts, such as hand washing (see Chapter 11). In some cases, OCD can be disabling. The brain functioning of nine people with OCD was examined by PET scanning before and after behavior therapy (Baxter et al., 1992), as were the brains of nine people with OCD before and after they received fluoxetine (Prozac), a medication that suppresses some of the symptoms of OCD. The scans revealed that behavior therapy and Prozac both change

the way a certain part of the brain works. In both cases, the activity in the right caudate (part of the basal ganglia involved in automatic behaviors) decreased following the intervention. (The drug also affected the anterior cingulate and thalamus, both of which are involved in attention.) The effects of behavior therapy on the brain were replicated by Schwartz, Stoessel and colleagues (1996).

At the level of the person, trying new behaviors (such as not washing dirty hands or not rechecking a locked door) and experiencing the success of not *having* to perform the compulsions gives the patient a sense of mastery and hope, which leads him or her to keep engaging in the new behaviors. At the level of the group, it was interactions with another person—the therapist—that changed the brain. In addition, personal relationships change. For example, some of the time and energy that was devoted to OCD rituals can now be spent on relationships. Thus, the three levels of analysis inform us about different aspects of the disorder and how events at the three levels interact.

CONSOLIDATE!

 How are medications used to treat psychological disorders? Antipsychotic medication can help people with schizophrenia and other psychotic disorders; antidepressants can help those with depression and anxiety; lithium can help people with bipolar disorder; and antianxiety drugs can help individuals with anxiety disorders.

Which Therapy Works Best?

After a number of sessions, and after her mother came in for one therapy session, Beth began to feel better. She was going to class more often, and felt better able to handle studying and preparing for tests. She wanted to know what it was about the therapy that was helping her, and why her therapist used specific techniques at certain times. Her treatment had not included medication, and she still wondered whether she would be feeling even better—or worse—if she had taken medication. She also wondered whether her therapy would be as effective for other people in her situation. If her best friend went to see Beth's therapist for anxiety and depression, would her friend fare as well as Beth, or perhaps even better?

1 What are other forms, or modalities, of therapy besides individual therapy?

2 What recent trends might affect the future of mental health care?

3 What key issues should be kept in mind when reading research studies of psychotherapy?

4 What are good ways to find a therapist?

Modalities: When Two or More Isn't a Crowd

Each therapy approach mentioned thus far can be implemented in a variety of **modalities**, or forms. **Individual therapy**—therapy in which one client is treated by one therapist—is a modality. Other modalities have one or more therapists working with a family, or with a group of people who share some commonality, such as the diagnosis of agoraphobia. Each theoretical orientation discussed earlier can be used in these various modalities: individual, family, or group.

Group Therapy

Clients with compatible needs who meet together with one or two therapists are engaging in **group therapy.** The course of treatment can range from a single occasion (usually an educational session) to ongoing treatment lasting for years. Some groups are specifically for members who have a particular problem or disorder, focusing on, for instance, recent divorce or posttraumatic stress disorder. These groups offer emotional support, psychoeducation, concrete strategies for managing the problem or disorder, or all these elements. Other groups have members who may not share such a specific problem or disorder, but rather want to learn more about maladaptive or inappropriate ways in which they are interacting with people; the therapy group provides an opportunity to change their patterns of behavior. Therapy groups can have theoretical orientations ranging from psychodynamic to client-centered, to CBT, or other orientations.

Modality: A form of therapy.

Individual therapy: A therapy modality in which one client is treated by one therapist.

Group therapy: A therapy modality in which a number of clients with similar needs meet together with one or two therapists.

Group therapy can help reduce shame and isolation and can provide social support and an opportunity to interact differently with other people.

In addition to offering information, support, and (if the group has a cognitive–behavioral orientation) between-session homework assignments, group therapy provides something that individual therapy cannot: interaction with other people who are experiencing similar difficulties. The group experience can decrease the sense of isolation and shame that clients sometimes feel. In revealing their own experiences and being moved by others', clients often come to see their own lives and difficulties in a new light. Also, because some clients' problems involve interpersonal interactions, the group provides a safe opportunity for clients to try out new behaviors.

Family Therapy

In **family therapy**, a family as a whole, or a subset of some of its members, such as a couple, are seen for treatment. "Family" is often defined as those who think of themselves or function as a family; thus, blended families created by marriage are seen in family therapy, as are other nontraditional families. The most common theoretical orientation among those providing family therapy is **systems therapy**, which starts from the premise that no client is an island: A client's symptoms occur in a larger context, or system (the family and subculture), and any change in one part of the system will affect the rest of the system. Thus, the client is referred to as the "identified patient," although the system (the couple, the family) is considered the "patient" that is to be treated. Systems therapy was originally used exclusively with families; in fact, some of the pioneers in systems therapy would refuse to see individuals without their families. For this reason, systems therapy is sometimes referred to as "family therapy," although this is a misnomer. Some therapists treat entire families, but not necessarily from a systems approach. They may use a psychodynamic or behavioral approach. Similarly, some systems therapists see individuals without their families, but the therapy makes use of systems theory. Systems therapy can also be the theoretical framework used to treat couples in therapy.

Systems therapy focuses on family communication, structure, and power relationships. The theory views the identified patient's symptoms as attempts to convey a message. Initially, a systems therapist takes a family history to discover which members of the family are close to one another or angry with one another, and to ascertain more generally how anger, sadness, and other feelings or issues are handled within the family. Systems therapists often illustrate these relationships graphically (see Figure 12.4). In some cases, one parent may be underinvolved and the other overinvolved; treatment would be directed to encourage the underinvolved parent to be more involved, and the overinvolved parent to be less involved. Or, the parents' relationship with each other may need strengthening, with consequences to others in the family, because conflict between parents affects their children's behavior (Kitz-

Family therapy: A therapy modality in which a family (or certain members of a family) is seen for treatment.

Systems therapy: Therapy that views a client's symptoms as occurring in a larger context, or system (the family and subculture), in which a change in one part of the system affects the rest of the system.

Figure 12.4 Systems Therapy: Family Interaction

This triangle graphically represents the following type of family interaction: The mother and father criticize each other and then reroute their conflict by both attacking their child. Systems therapy would focus on decreasing the conflict between the parents and strengthening their relationship. (From Minuchin, 1974, pp. 53, 61.)

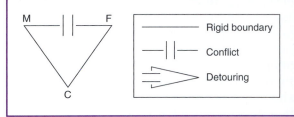

mann, 2000). For instance, in a family in which the parents fight a lot, an adolescent boy's rebelliousness may serve to unite his parents in their anger and frustration at him. The systems therapist might explain to the family that their son was purposefully being rebellious to keep his parents united, for fear of what would happen to the parents' relationship if he weren't causing them problems. The family therapist might praise the son for his efforts at keeping his parents together, and even urge him not to stop being rebellious yet, because his parents hadn't yet practiced how to relate to each other more effectively. This type of intervention is sometimes referred to as **paradoxical intention**, which encourages a behavior that seems contradictory to the desired goal (Stanton, 1981). This technique has also been called "prescribing the symptom" and is useful in treating families who appear resistant or unable to change, or aren't able to implement suggestions from the therapist. Other techniques include **reframing**, in which the therapist offers a new way of conceptualizing, or "framing," the problem, and **validation**, in which the therapist conveys his or her understanding of clients' feelings and wishes (Minuchin, 1974; Minuchin & Fishman, 1981).

A therapist with a systems orientation treating Beth might, after taking a family history, reframe the problem. The therapist might propose that Beth is sacrificing herself: Beth's difficulties allow her mother to be a "good mother" to Beth in ways she had not been when Beth was younger. Thus, Beth's illness serves the function of allowing her mother to feel good about herself as a mother. The therapist might even give Beth a paradoxical intention: Beth should not get better until her mother becomes a "nervous wreck" worrying about Beth. This paradoxical intention serves the purpose of indirectly pointing out how Beth's behavior may in fact have the opposite effect of the one she desires.

Self-Help Therapies

Self-help groups (sometimes referred to as *support groups*) can be used to supplement psychotherapy, or may be helpful on their own. Self-help groups are focused on a specific disorder or event. They do not usually have a clinically trained leader, although a mental health professional may be involved in some capacity (Shepherd et al., 1999). Alcoholics Anonymous (AA), the first self-help program, is based on 12 steps of recovery. Most 12-step programs view a belief in a Higher Power (for most people, God) as crucial to recovery, and meta-analytic results show that weekly attendance in group meetings is associated with drug or alcohol abstinence, whereas less than weekly attendance is not (Fiorentine, 1999). People who are not religious can also benefit from attendance at AA meetings (Winzelberg & Humphreys, 1999). A self-help group that does not use the 12-step approach is the National Depressive and Manic Depressive Association, which helps those suffering from bipolar disorder or depression, and their families and friends. Self-help groups are not only valuable sources of information and support, they can also make referrals to therapists who are knowledgeable about the particular disorder or problem. Relatives of those with a psychological disorder report that such groups are helpful in providing support and self-understanding (Citron et al., 1999). As is true in group therapy, self-help groups can be invaluable in decreasing feelings of isolation and shame.

The last decade has witnessed a proliferation of self-help books and tapes dealing with a wide range of problems; the use of such materials is sometimes referred to as **bibliotherapy**. Many of these materials incorporate philosophies and techniques of the therapies discussed in this chapter, and therapists often suggest that clients read particular books (Starker, 1988).

Innovations in Psychotherapy

Psychotherapy Integration: Mixing and Matching

In the last decade, many therapists have moved away from identifying their work as exclusively from one theoretical orientation, such as psychodynamic or behavioral. Surveys found more than two thirds of mental health professionals

Paradoxical intention: A systems therapy technique that encourages a behavior that seems contradictory to the desired goal.

Reframing: A therapy technique in which the therapist offers a new way of conceptualizing, or "framing," the problem.

Validation: A therapy technique in which the therapist conveys his or her understanding of the client's feelings and wishes.

Self-help group: A group whose members focus on a specific disorder or event and do not usually have a clinically trained leader; also called a *support group*.

Bibliotherapy: The use of self-help books and tapes for therapeutic purposes.

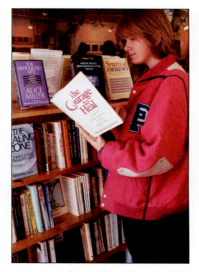

Meta-analyses of studies examining the effectiveness of self-help materials found that they helped primarily people with depression (Cuijpers, 1997), headache, sleep disturbances, and fears (Gould & Clum, 1993); anxiety is also lessened through the use of such materials (Finch et al., 2000; Scogin et al., 1990). At least for many people, the self-administered treatment programs available through books and audiotapes appear to be more effective than no treatment at all (Scogin et al., 1990).

identify themselves as eclectic in orientation (Jensen et al., 1990; Smith, 1982). A therapist using **psychotherapy integration** uses techniques from different theoretical orientations, with an overarching understanding of how the different techniques will achieve the goals of treatment. This integrative approach includes incorporating new techniques based on research findings and the clinical needs of a particular client at a specific point in the treatment (Stricker, 1993). Such an approach provides the aspects of therapy that are common to all theoretical orientations (such as offering hope, a caring listener, and a new way of thinking about problems) and employs specific techniques for a given disorder (Weinberger et al., 1995), such as exposure with response prevention for people with OCD. The therapist determines which techniques to use at any given point in treatment based on diagnosis, research findings, and consideration of the particular client; these create an individualized guide to treatment. Two clients with the same diagnosis may receive different integrative treatments from the same therapist, based on factors other than diagnosis—perhaps family issues, client preference for directive versus nondirective treatment, and other concerns.

Time and Therapy: Therapy Protocols and Brief Therapy

The last 20 years has seen a rise in the use of *therapy protocols,* detailed session-by-session manuals of how therapy should proceed for a specific disorder from a certain theoretical orientation (such as behavioral treatment for panic disorder, or cognitive therapy for depression). These manual-based treatments were created, in part, to ensure that when a research study was testing the effectiveness of a given therapy (for example, CBT), all CBT therapists were actually using the same techniques in the same way. This meant, of course, that the results of the study were in fact relevant to the effectiveness of the treatment because all therapies of the same orientation were comparable. The drawback of research studies using manual-based treatment is that they often exclude people whose symptoms do not meet the exact criteria for a disorder, or who may simultaneously have more than one diagnosis (such as depression *and* panic disorder).

Many of the protocols were developed for treatment lasting 15 to 20 sessions. Today, many managed care programs in different part of the United States will not pay for 20 sessions of treatment for many disorders, or at least not initially. Rather, they may approve 3 to 10 sessions, and the therapist must request additional sessions. Thus, although the course of treatment is becoming briefer, the total number of sessions cannot be used in a systematic way and may not fit into many of the existing protocols. Moreover, clients who have more than one problem may not reap the benefits of time-limited therapy. Research indicates that those with focused problems in one sphere of life (such as work) receive more benefit from brief psychotherapy than those who have difficulties in multiple spheres (Barkham & Shapiro, 1990; Klosko et al., 1990; Strupp & Binder, 1984).

In the future, computer technology may be commonly used to facilitate brief treatment. Research on the use of palmtop computers preprogrammed with cognitive–behavioral tasks found that 4 weeks of computer-assisted treatment (plus 8 weeks of practice with the palmtop) was, as determined at follow-up, as effective as 12 weeks of regular cognitive–behavior therapy (Newman, Kenardy et al., 1997).

High-tech gadgets such as this palmtop computer may be at the cutting edge of brief cognitive–behavioral treatments.

Issues in Psychotherapy Research

More than 400 types of psychotherapy are currently available (Garfield & Bergin, 1994), but many of them do not rest on well-constructed and replicated research. Research on psychotherapy is crucial for determining the effectiveness of a new or old therapy in treating a particular problem. It is easy to claim that a new therapy is a wonder cure, but harder to prove it. There are many issues to consider when evaluating findings about psychotherapy.

Psychotherapy integration: The use of techniques from different theoretical orientations with an overarching understanding of how the different techniques will be used to achieve the goals of treatment.

Researching Psychotherapy

Research that asks whether the client is feeling better, functioning better, living more independently, or has fewer symptoms after treatment is called **outcome research.** These questions are trickier to answer than it would seem because they depend on how you define "outcome"; in research lingo, the answers to the questions depend on what you designate as the therapy's dependent variable. For example, you could have clients rate their thoughts, feelings, or behaviors, which are not necessarily highly correlated and might yield different outcomes (Kazdin, 1994). You must also decide how long after the end of treatment to assess outcome: immediately afterward? a month later? a year later? Moreover, in their review of studies, Luborsky and colleagues (1999) noticed an "allegiance effect": Researchers of a particular orientation tend to find evidence supporting that orientation.

Initially, much outcome research focused on assessing the superiority of one treatment over another, not taking into account clients' diagnoses. Results revealed that therapy was more effective than no therapy. Most often, the no-therapy group was a wait-list control, people who were on a waiting list for therapy but had not yet received treatment (Lambert & Bergin, 1994). The findings also seemed to suggest that all therapies are equally effective, a position described as the *dodo bird verdict* of psychotherapy (Luborsky et al., 1975), named for the Dodo bird in *Alice's Adventures in Wonderland,* who declared, "Everyone has won, and all must have prizes."

Outcome research: Research that asks whether, after psychotherapy, the client is feeling better, functioning better, living more independently, or has fewer symptoms.

TABLE 12.4 Questions About Psychotherapy Research   *Source: Kazdin (1994).*

1. Are the participants randomly assigned?
2. Is a specific disorder being treated?
3. Are there exclusion criteria (must participants have only one diagnosis)?
4. Are the therapists' treatments representative of their stated approaches?
5. What types of outcome measures are selected, who is the evaluator, and how is success defined?
6. Are clients more likely to drop out of some types of therapy than others?
7. Is a follow-up assessment planned, and if so, at what interval of time after the end of treatment?

But is the dodo bird verdict all there is to it? Several questions, listed in Table 12.4, should be addressed when designing or evaluating studies of psychotherapy, and the answers to these questions determine what conclusions can be reached and how far those conclusions can generalize. Let's look at one well-known investigation in detail. Initiated in 1977, the National Institute of Mental Health sponsored a study called the Treatment of Depression Collaborative Research Program, or TDCRP, to assess the effectiveness of four different treatments for depression: cognitive–behavior therapy (CBT); interpersonal therapy (IPT); antidepressant medication with supportive visits with a psychiatrist; and a placebo medication with supportive visits with a psychiatrist. The medication group, which was taking the TCA imipramine (the study predated Prozac), was labeled IMI-CM (CM for "clinical management"), and the placebo group was labeled PLA-CM (see Figure 12.5).

Figure 12.5 The Four Groups in the Treatment of Depression Collaborative Research Program

Interpersonal therapy (IPT) focuses on the client's current relationships, issues that arise in those relationships, and attempts to link what happens in those relationships to mood. The goal of IPT is to help the client's relationships work better and become more satisfying. IPT rests on the assumption that if the relationships are functioning better, the depression will lessen. Therapeutic techniques include helping clients explore the consequences of their actions in their relationships and facilitating better personal communication, perhaps by encouraging clients to tell others how they feel. This type of therapy was developed in the late 1970s; most IPT treatments are based on IPT protocol manuals and can be considered insight-oriented. All treatments in all four TDCRP groups were brief, lasting 16 weeks.

Participants in the TDCRP were randomly assigned to one of the four treatment groups; the design of the study addressed Question 1 in Table 12.4. What would it mean if the assignments weren't random? Suppose those who were more depressed were put in the medication group, but the therapy groups were more effective; we couldn't then conclude that therapy was more effective than medication, because the participants in the medication group were in worse shape to begin with. Random assignment is crucial if we want to be able to infer anything about the effectiveness of one treatment over another.

In trying to determine whether certain types of treatment are more effective for certain disorders (Question 2), many studies exclude participants with more than one diagnosis (Question 3). Although this exclusion makes research findings more clear-cut, it limits their generalizability, because many clients going to a therapist's office have more than one type of diagnosis. For example, more than half of those diagnosed with an anxiety disorder have at least one additional disorder, and 30% to 40% of those with a diagnosis of depression also have a diagnosis of a personality disorder (Sleek, 1997). The TDCRP study restricted inclusion to those who met the exact criteria for major depressive disorder, without any other disorder.

One difficulty in assessing research on a particular therapeutic orientation is that therapists who by their own statements would seem to have different orientations may in fact be remarkably similar in the way they actually provide therapy (Lambert & Bergin, 1994). This makes comparisons among therapies difficult (Question 4). Suppose that in the TDCRP study, a self-defined CBT therapist focused on relationship issues, and a self-defined IPT therapist gave concrete suggestions, such as those given in assertiveness training or social skills training, for improving relationships. If there were no differences in outcome between the two therapy groups, it could be because therapists in the two groups were doing much the same thing! In an effort to address this problem, the TDCRP developed therapist manuals for each of the four treatments, providing in each case a detailed guide and techniques to be used with clients for each session. These standardized forms of treatment ensured that all therapists categorized as using one approach (for example, CBT) were actually providing similar therapy.

Question 5 addresses the difficult issue of how to measure outcome. Measures can focus on behaviors, thoughts, or feelings in relation to specific symptoms, or on more general patterns of functioning. Different types of therapy might be differentially effective with each of these possible outcome measures. In the TDCRP, medication might be more effective with some symptoms of depression (tiredness, poor appetite), but not help with relationships or negative thinking as much as psychological treatment (Segal et al., 1999). The type of outcome measures used can bias the results in favor of one form of therapy over another. To avoid this pitfall, the TDCRP study looked at multiple types of outcome measures, but surprisingly, it found comparable results for the different measures of outcome (Imber et al., 1991).

In addition, there is the problem that 50% or more of those who begin treatment in a research study may drop out (Kazdin, 1994). And if more participants drop out of one group than another, the conclusions you can draw about the treatment are limited (Question 6). The TDCRP results showed that *of those completing the study,* all four groups improved, but CBT and IPT treatment were about as effective as antidepressant medication in decreasing depressive symptoms (Antonuccio et al., 1995; Elkin et al., 1995). However, more participants dropped out of the medication group before the completion of the program because of unpleasant side effects. So, if you consider all those *starting* the TDCRP study rather than only those *completing* it, both CBT and IPT were *more* effective than medication-and-support or placebo-and-support groups (Elkin, 1994). Knowing the attrition rates can make a difference in understanding the results.

Finally, it is important to determine what happens after treatment ends, and if the outcome results change with the passage of time (Question 7). In the TDCRP study, CBT had a more sustained effect at an 18-month follow-up, with fewer relapses, particularly when compared with the group given imipramine (Elkin, 1994; Shea et al., 1992). This result is consistent with other findings (Antonuccio et al., 1995). However, further analyses showed that, across all four treatment groups, both medication and IPT were slightly more effective than CBT for severely depressed clients (Elkin et al., 1995). Moreover, the quality of the collaborative bond between client and therapist (as measured by independent raters who watched videotapes of the sessions) affected outcome; this influence was stronger than that of the type of treatment (Krupnick et al., 1996). In both CBT and IPT, clients reported feeling supported and reassured and indicated that the therapy had given them new ways of relating to others and had encouraged their independent opinions (Ablon & Jones, 1999). But not all therapies are equally useful for all disorders, as you will see in the following sections.

Psychotherapy Versus Medication

Is the TDCRP the only study to have found that psychotherapy can work as well as medication? And is depression the only disorder that can claim this general result? The answer to these questions is no (Gloaguen et al., 1998; Reynolds et al., 1999; Thase et al., 1997).

Medication does alleviate depression for many people; why, therefore, might someone choose psychotherapy over medication? According to research, the main drawback of medication becomes apparent when you look at how people fare over the long haul. When medication is discontinued, the relapse rate is high, a fact that has led some doctors to recommend continued use of medication for those at risk for additional depressive episodes (Hirschfeld, 1997). Cognitive–behavioral treatment appears to provide an equivalent benefit for many, without the side effects of drugs (Antonuccio et al., 1995). CBT may also be helpful in treating residual symptoms of depression following treatment with antidepressant medication. This supplemental use of CBT lowers the relapse rate when medication is discontinued (Fava et al., 1998a). At 6-year follow-up, those who had supplemental CBT were less likely to have had another episode of depression than those without CBT (Fava et al., 1998b). Similarly, a number of studies have found that medication and cognitive therapy combined may be more helpful than medication alone, even with severely depressed people (Macaskill & Macaskill, 1996; Thase et al., 1997), although not all studies have found an added benefit with combined treatment (Oei & Yeoh, 1999). Further research will help clarify the role of CBT in preventing relapse after medication is discontinued.

For anxiety disorders, research on the question of medication versus psychotherapy yields results similar to those of the research on depression: That is, particular types of psychotherapy (CBT, IPT) provide as much, if not more, long-term relief of symptoms than does medication (Gould et al., 1995). In the treatment of panic disorder, for instance, although medication and CBT may work about equally well, CBT does a better job of preventing symptom relapse (Chambless & Gillis, 1993; Otto et al., 1994). And as with OCD, behavior therapy is as helpful as medication. Early results of a large-scale study of OCD, similar in design to the TDCRP study, confirm that behavior therapy (in this case, exposure with response prevention) is as helpful as medication, and possibly more so over the long term. However, as with other manual-based treatments that exclude participants with more than one diagnosis, there are questions as to whether these findings generalize to behavior therapy with clients diagnosed with more than one disorder (Kozak et al., 2000).

Although medication can work in treating social phobias, such as a fear of public speaking, it is not necessarily superior to cognitive–behavior therapy because symptoms often return after medication is stopped. Cognitive–behavior therapy's benefits usually last after treatment ends.

In the treatment of social phobias, research shows that MAOIs and group CBT are equally helpful (Heimberg et al., 1998). However, research does not support the conclusion that medication is superior to therapy, particularly because of the high relapse rate after medication is discontinued. Meta-analytic studies of medication versus CBT with participants with bulimia nervosa have found CBT to be more effective (Whittal et al., 1999). However, for other disorders, such as schizophrenia and bipolar disorder, medication is clearly superior to psychotherapy. For people with these disorders, psychotherapy can play a role in helping them accept the need to take medication on a lifelong or long-term basis (Colom et al., 1998; Tohen & Grundy, 1999) and can provide an opportunity to learn new relationship skills after the medication has helped them to be more stable. Moreover, psychological treatment in conjunction with medication can be helpful in identifying triggers of psychotic, manic, or depressive episodes, and can help prevent relapses (Buchkremer et al., 1997; Goldstein, 1992).

However, like all research that has examined groups of people, the results do not necessarily apply to a particular individual. Thus, for any particular person, psychotherapy may be more effective than medication, and the opposite may be true for someone else with the exact same set of symptoms.

Which Therapy Works Best for Which Disorder?

For some disorders, the dodo bird verdict appears to be true, possibly because of common curative factors among all therapies; for other disorders, particular types of therapy are preferred. The results of thousands of research studies and meta-analyses show that some treatments are better than others for certain disorders: Cognitive therapy and interpersonal therapy provide relief from depression; exposure and response prevention provides long-term symptom relief for those with OCD; cognitive therapy is helpful for people with panic disorder (Clark et al., 1999; Wolfe & Maser, 1994) and agoraphobia (Hoffart, 1998); systematic desensitization works well for those with specific phobias (Seligman, 1995).

In contrast, psychodynamic therapy appears to work best with patients who are able to articulate their feelings and want to understand their unconscious (and who have the time and money for lengthy treatment). Some meta-analyses find short-term psychodynamic therapy to be as effective as other short-term treatments (Crits-Christoph, 1992), but other studies contradict this result (Svartberg & Stiles, 1991), particularly studies with a 1-year follow-up (Barkham et al., 1999).

There are several difficulties in evaluating the effectiveness of psychodynamic therapies. One is that there isn't much actual research to evaluate. Consider that for every research article on transference, there are 500 on theory. Moreover, although psychodynamic therapists may believe in the accuracy of their interpretations, they may not necessarily be therapeutic. For instance, research shows that interpretations of the transference relationship do not appear to be particularly helpful in psychodynamic treatment (Henry et al., 1994). Psychodynamic therapists have tended to view treatment failures as the patient's responsibility rather than the therapist's. It is possible that this view is correct—lack of behavioral change may result from insufficient insight—but insight is not objectively measurable, at least not yet.

Although Rogers did much to bring about the first real insight-oriented alternative to psychoanalysis and made the treatment amenable to research by tape recording therapy sessions, research has not been as supportive as he might have wished. Almost all forms of therapy agree with Rogers's view that the therapist's warmth, empathy, and positive regard for the client are fundamental for a working relationship between client and therapist (Lambert, 1983). However, not all agree that these factors are *enough* to bring about change. Moreover, although client-centered therapy was the first major school of therapy to focus on assessing the effectiveness of the treatment, it can be difficult to measure which clients have achieved their potentials.

And although cognitive, behavioral, and CBT treatments have been found to be helpful for specific disorders, these classifications may be too broad, and it seems that specific techniques from each approach are the appropriate units of comparison. For example, in the treatment of OCD, although exposure with response prevention (a behavioral technique) has been the most well-documented technique to produce long-term symptom relief, there is evidence that cognitive therapy may be as effective. In contrast, progressive muscle relaxation, another behavioral technique, was not as beneficial (Abramowitz, 1997). However, not all studies agree (van Balkom et al., 1994). Two distinct types of treatment, CBT without exposure and exposure therapy only, *both* worked well for social phobias (Feske & Chambless, 1995), although later research has found that the combination can be effective (Gould et al., 1997; Taylor, 1996). In the treatment of PTSD, both exposure with response prevention and cognitive restructuring worked equally well, and those two treatments combined were no more effective than each treatment by itself. However, all were superior to relaxation training (Marks et al., 1998). Similar results were found in a meta-analysis of various therapies for PTSD (Sherman, 1998).

As well as attempting to match disorders and therapy, research has also attempted to match clients and therapy, asking "Which type of therapy works best with what type of client?" This question has been addressed by the National Institute on Alcohol Abuse and Alcoholism (NIAAA). This organization sought to discover whether certain types of treatment for alcohol abuse are more effective with certain types of clients. Some client characteristics thought to be potentially relevant were the severity of the alcoholism, sex of the client, and presence of other psychiatric disorders. Treatment included CBT, a 12-step treatment program to prepare clients to join AA, and motivational enhancement therapy, which was directed toward increasing readiness to change drinking habits. Results found that all three treatments had good overall results, increasing the number of abstinent days from 20% before treatment to 80% after treatment, with only a slight dip after 1 year. However, none of the planned "matches" between client and assignment to a particular type of treatment enhanced treatment effectiveness (Project MATCH Research Group, 1997).

Research on matching a treatment to a given client has also looked at the possible effect of a patient's personality. For instance, among depressed clients in the TDCRP, those who also had an avoidant personality disorder (and thus didn't like to dwell on their experiences) were more likely to fare better with cognitive therapy, a result that was consistent with their externally oriented coping style. In contrast, depressed people who had an obsessive-compulsive personality did better in interpersonal therapy, consistent with their internally oriented coping style (Barber & Muenz, 1996). Similar results have been found for the superiority of CBT in helping depressed people who are externalizers versus internalizers (Beutler et al., 1991, 1993).

Treatment for an Ethnically Diverse Population

According to the 2000 census, at least 25% of the population of the United States are members of an ethnic minority, and this number continues to grow. As the composition of America changes, so too does the composition of those seeking mental health services. At least until the early 1990s, most psychotherapy research did not include information about race, education, or economic status. However, it has been shown that these factors may influence the effectiveness of a given treatment for a particular client (Francis & Aronson, 1990). Psychotherapists are now more aware of the need to consider a client's background, cultural values, and view of seeking psychological assistance (McGoldrick et al., 1996; Ramirez, 1999). A client's immigrant or refugee experience creates a stressor that can affect mental health. And members of minority groups who are born and raised in the United States may experience prejudice and other hardships that can affect mental health.

An example of the importance of understanding a symptom's cultural context can be found in *ataques de nervios* (Spanish for "attack of nerves"), which some Puerto Rican women experience. This condition is a physical expression of strong emotions and includes trembling, heart palpitations, numbness, difficulty breathing, loss of consciousness, and a hyperkinetic state (Rivera-Arzola & Ramos-Grenier, 1997). The context for this illness is a culture in which women are likely to

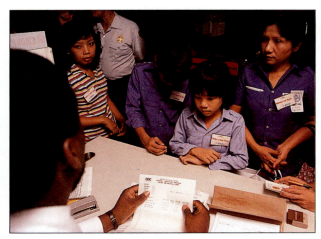

Therapists need to be aware of unique ethnic and cultural factors that can play a role in treatment, such as immigrant, cultural, or racial stressors.

endure great hardships, have little real power, and are actively discouraged from expressing anger. *Ataque de nervios* provides a culturally sanctioned way for them to express an inability to cope with a current situation, and the community responds (Rivera-Arzola & Ramos-Grenier, 1997). It is clear that the most effective therapist is one who is aware of both the cultural and familial contexts of a disorder.

It is part of a therapist's responsibility to be aware of cultural or racial issues that can affect all aspects of treatment—diagnosis, the process of the therapy, and its goals (Helms & Cook, 1999; Ramirez, 1999). The therapist should inquire about the client's understanding of the meaning of the problem, so that therapist and client can discuss and come to agreement on the nature of the problem, interventions to be used, and expected goals (Higgenbotham et al., 1988; Kleinman, 1978).

Although age, sex, and ethnicity do not appear to play a systematic role in therapy outcomes generally (Beutler et al., 1994), research suggests that some people (such as some Asian Americans) prefer a therapist from their ethnic group, and such matching leads to better outcomes for them (Sue et al., 1994). In general, however, there is no clear-cut evidence to date that matching by ethnicity for most ethnic groups results in better outcomes (Garfield, 1994). Some attempts have been made to develop particular therapies for different ethnic groups, with varying success; for example, *cuento therapy* (from the Spanish word for "fable"), which uses folktales or stories, has proved helpful with Latino American children (Sue et al., 1994).

How to Pick a Psychotherapist

Suppose you decide to seek psychotherapy. How do you pick a therapist? Keep several factors in mind when trying to find someone who could most effectively help you. If your problem is identifiable (such as depression or anxiety), it can be helpful to see someone who has experience in treating people with that problem. Many state and national referral agencies or professional associations are available, such as the American Psychological Association, the National Association of Social Workers, and the American Psychiatric Association. Regional organizations can also provide referrals for specific problems, such as the Massachusetts Eating Disorders Association or the Manic-Depressive and Depressive Association of Boston (MDDA-Boston). These organizations are members of national associations that can also supply the names of therapists with expertise in treating specific problems.

Try to get the names of more than one therapist because any one therapist may not have compatible office hours, location, and so on. You can also ask friends, family, teachers, and religious leaders for recommendations, as well as the counseling center at your college or university (Practice Directorate, 1998). Many insurance companies will reimburse or authorize psychotherapy only if the provider is on their list. If this is true for you, tell the therapists whom you are considering what insurance coverage you have and ask if their services are reimbursed by that company; if they don't know, call the company and check. Alternatively, call your insurance company and ask for referrals.

It is important that you feel comfortable with your therapist. If you don't, you may be less likely to talk about what's on your mind or share how you are really doing. And if you aren't able to talk about these things, the therapy can't be as helpful. It's also important to feel that the therapist is trustworthy—if the therapist doesn't have your trust, you will find it easy to discount what he or she says if it is something that you don't want to hear. If after one or two sessions, you realize you just don't feel comfortable, make an appointment with someone else and see whether the situation feels different.

How Do You Know Whether Psychotherapy Worked?

If you were designing a study to test the effectiveness of a particular therapy, how could you decide whether that treatment had been successful? The answer depends on what you measure, and the measures can be defined at each of the three levels of analysis. At the level of the group, you could ask members of the clients' families to report their impressions about their interactions with the client, or you could measure the frequency of certain social behaviors, such as the amount of time the client spends talking to other people. At the level of the person, you could have clients rate their thoughts, feelings, or behaviors, or fill in questionnaires about their psychological states. And at the level of the brain, you could take PET scans or other measures of brain activity, or you could obtain biochemical measures and examine the levels of key neuromodulators and neurotransmitters

(although not all new learning that occurs at the level of the brain can be assessed in this way). What would you think if some measures showed changes, but not others? Would you be willing to say that someone had improved if only the brain-based measures showed a change after therapy? What if only other people's reports of clients' social interactions, or only the clients' own subjective reports, showed a change? Sure, if he or she feels better, that may be good enough for the client—but unless changes actually occur in the brain and in behavior, what grounds are there for thinking of the improvement as enduring? The results of successful psychotherapy, whether they are having insight into problems, changing maladaptive behavior patterns, or replacing irrational thoughts with rational ones, create changes at all three levels of analysis.

CONSOLIDATE!

1 **What are other forms, or modalities, of therapy besides individual therapy?** As well as meeting with a therapist for individual therapy, a client and therapist can meet in a group (often a group of people with similar problems); the client can be a family (usually working with a therapist who has a systems approach) or a couple. Self-help groups and bibliotherapy may also be beneficial.

2 **What recent trends might affect the future of mental health care?** In integrative psychotherapy, the therapist systematically integrates two or more different theoretical approaches and their techniques into a treatment regimen based on research and clinical factors. With the increased trend toward less time-intensive therapies, in part due to constraints imposed by managed care, the use of protocol-based and brief treatments has increased and is the subject of ongoing research.

3 **What key issues should be kept in mind when reading research studies of psychotherapy?**

Overall, therapy is more beneficial than no treatment. However, methodological issues have a bearing on what conclusions we can draw from a psychotherapy study, such as what has been measured and when it was measured. Curative factors include (a) common factors that apply across all types of treatment and (b) specific factors that relate to a particular intervention of an approach. Studies should note the ethnic composition of the participants, and treatment should consider ethnic and cultural factors that may affect the treatment.

4 **What are good ways to find a therapist?** A therapist can be chosen by a referral from a counseling center, family and friends, self-help organizations, professional associations, and insurance companies. The therapist should be someone with whom the client feels comfortable; if trust is lacking, you should seek another therapist.

A DEEPER LEVEL

Recap and Thought Questions

Insight-Oriented Therapies

Insight-oriented therapies focus on helping people gain insight into their problems and propose that such insight will lead to changes in thoughts, feelings, and behavior. Psychodynamic and client-centered therapies are exam-

ples. These therapies rest on the belief that psychological problems are caused by emotional forces.

If Beth were seeing an insight-oriented therapist, what would be the focus of treatment? Beth's treatment would no doubt focus on her feelings (rather than her thoughts or behaviors) and on her relationships, with an emphasis on her relationships with people during her childhood, particularly her mother. This would be especially true if her therapist were psychodynamically oriented.

Think It Through. Imagine two people, one of whom is the ideal candidate for insight-oriented therapy and one of whom is the worst possible candidate. How would you describe these two people? If a friend tells you that he is in insight-oriented therapy, what can you assume about his therapy? What can't you assume?

Behavior and Cognitive Therapy

The foundation of behavior and cognitive therapies is the idea that psychological problems are a product of a client's learning histories or are caused by faulty perceptions or interpretations; they therefore seek to help the client develop more adaptive behaviors and realistic thoughts. Therapy is generally active, focuses on current problems, and often assigns between-session homework.

If Beth were in treatment with a cognitive–behavior therapist, what would be the likely focus of her treatment? Beth's treatment would focus on her thoughts and behavior. Specifically, a cognitive–behavior therapist would probably use cognitive techniques to modify Beth's automatic thoughts about tests and studying, as well as about her depression and fear of becoming like her mother. This therapist might also use behavioral techniques such as systematic desensitization for her anxiety about tests, daily logs to monitor her mood and anxiety and to identify their ABCs, and set up a schedule of pleasurable activities. Such a schedule would ensure that Beth has an opportunity to do enjoyable things: People who are depressed often restrict their social outings and become isolated, depriving themselves of positive social contact and opportunities to have a good time.

Think It Through. If you read about a study that claimed CBT treatment effectively reduces kleptomania (compulsive stealing done for pleasure, not for material need), what are some techniques that might be used, and how would those techniques decrease the symptoms of kleptomania? Why? Would CBT be effective if the client was not motivated or had a poor memory? Explain your answer.

Biomedical Therapies

Biologically based treatments include medications (such as antipsychotics, antidepressants, and antianxiety drugs)

and electroconvulsive therapy, which is used with severely depressed people when other treatments have failed. Still considered experimental is treatment by transcranial magnetic stimulation.

What biomedical therapies are available to Beth? Beth could take medication, and if her depression were severe enough and had not been relieved by other treatments, Beth might be a candidate for electroconvulsive therapy or the experimental transcranial magnetic stimulation.

Think It Through. Suppose your best friend's mother had bipolar disorder. What might be her likely treatment? Why? Suppose instead that your friend's father was schizophrenic; what treatment might he receive? Explain your answer. And if they were both depressed?

Which Therapy Works Best?

Psychological treatment exists in a variety of forms, including individual, family, and group therapy, and self-help resources. Psychotherapy protocols and integrative psychotherapy have been more widely practiced in recent years, partly because of the demands of managed care. Research on psychotherapy shows that, overall, those who receive psychotherapy fare better than those who don't receive treatment. This is generally true regardless of the therapeutic approach. However, research also shows that certain types of therapy are more effective with certain disorders than others; for example, exposure with response prevention is a particularly good treatment for OCD. It is also important to understand the ethnic and cultural factors related to a client's problems and goals.

How is Beth's therapy likely to turn out, based on research on the effectiveness of psychotherapy? As indicated by the dodo bird verdict, Beth's therapy may be effective, regardless of the orientation of the therapist. If the treatment is specifically designed for anxiety and depression, the likelihood of a positive treatment outcome would increase. However, it is difficult to apply group results to a specific individual.

Think It Through. Suppose you were designing a treatment program for depression for an ethnically diverse set of clients. What would you want to know about the clients? How would you use that information? How would you design a study to test the effectiveness of your new program? Why would you do it that way?

REVIEW TEST

For each of the following items, choose the single correct or best answer. The correct answers appear at the end.

1 The goal of psychoanalysis is ____.
  a. developing healthier interpersonal relationships
  b. understanding one's unconscious motivations
  c. changing the way one thinks about life's stressors
  d. changing one's reward structure in life

2 In client-centered therapy, ____ and ____ are important therapeutic techniques that allow clients to decrease incongruence.
  a. cognitive reinterpretation; behavior analysis
  b. free association; dream analysis
  c. corrective mirroring; parroting
  d. unconditional positive regard; genuine empathy

3 Studies have found that people have ____ moods immediately after psychotherapy and ____ moods immediately after expressive writing.
  a. positive; negative   c. negative; negative
  b. positive; positive   d. negative; positive

4 In behavior therapy, distressing symptoms are viewed as the result of ____.
  a. previous learning
  b. incongruence
  c. dysfunctional past relationships
  d. unconscious forces

5 When people with obsessive-compulsive disorder are made to get their hands dirty and then prevented from washing them, the technique of ____ has been used.
  a. stimulus control
  b. exposure with response prevention
  c. classical reconditioning
  d. systematic desensitization

6 The process of helping clients think more rationally using cognitive therapy is called ____.
  a. psychoeducation
  b. emotive understanding
  c. cognitive restructuring
  d. thought challenge

7 Token economies are not used as frequently as they used to be because ____.
  a. therapists are moving toward more cognitive and medical forms of treatment
  b. there are ethical issues in depriving patients of secondary reinforcers
  c. they are relatively ineffective
  d. there is less interest in institutional behavioral programs

8 Long-term use of antipsychotic medications can cause ____.
  a. increased sex drive   c. tardive dyskinesia
  b. increased appetite   d. depression

9 The tricyclics, MAOIs, and SSRIs are prescribed to treat ____.
  a. depression   c. mania
  b. bipolar disorder   d. schizophrenia

10 Electroconvulsive therapy (ECT) is ____.
  a. the first treatment of choice for depression
  b. only used in state-run hospitals
  c. no longer used to treat mental illness
  d. sometimes used to treat severe depression

11 Studies comparing the use of Prozac and behavior therapy in the treatment of obsessive-compulsive disorder revealed that, in the short term, ____.
  a. neither was effective in promoting change
  b. behavior therapy was more effective than Prozac
  c. both Prozac and behavior therapy caused changes in brain functioning
  d. Prozac was more effective than behavior therapy

12 The TDCRP study of the relative effectiveness of four different approaches to treating depression found that ____.
  a. considering everyone who started the study, medication and therapy were equally effective
  b. those receiving interpersonal therapy had a more sustained effect 18 months after completing the study
  c. both medication and interpersonal therapy were slightly more effective than cognitive-behavioral therapy for mildly depressed individuals
  d. the collaborative bond between the client and therapist was more important than the type of treatment received

13 In studies comparing the relative effectiveness of therapy and medication in the treatment of depression and anxiety, results have shown that ____.
  a. both therapy and medication are equally effective, but therapy has a higher rate of relapse after treatment ends
  b. both therapy and medication are equally effective, but medication has a higher rate of relapse after treatment ends
  c. therapy is clearly superior
  d. medication is clearly superior

14 Which type of treatment is most effective for specific phobias?
  a. interpersonal therapy   c. systematic desensitization
  b. response prevention   d. cognitive therapy

15 *Ataques de nervios* is a mental health condition experienced by ____.
  a. children from Guatemala   c. Mexican women
  b. Puerto Rican women   d. Cuban men

ANSWERS: 1.b 2.d 3.a 4.a 5.b 6.c 7.b 8.c 9.a 10.d 11.c 12.d 13.b 14.c 15.b

13

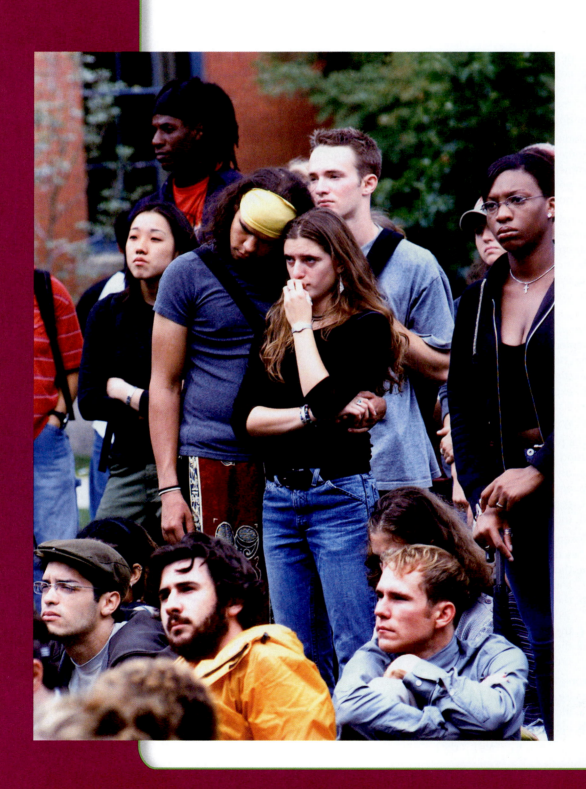

Psychology

MEETING OF THE MINDS

1n 1993 Sarah Delany, known as Sadie, and her younger sister Elizabeth, called Bessie, published their first book, *Having Our Say* (Delany, Delany, & Hearth, 1993). What's remarkable about these authors is that they were 104 and 102 at the time of publication. Their book recounts the story of their lives, their experiences as black children and then as black women during a century of American history. It was during their childhood that the South's Jim Crow laws came into effect, legalizing separate facilities—separate schools, separate water fountains, separate seats on the bus, separate toilets—for blacks and whites; it was during their adulthood that these laws were struck down.

Sadie and Bessie had eight brothers and sisters. Their father, Henry, had been born a slave but was freed by emancipation. He became vice principal of St. Augustine's School (now St. Augustine's College), a black college in Raleigh, North Carolina. Their mother, Nanny James, who had both black and white grandparents, was light-skinned. In addition to managing her ten children, she was the matron of the college, overseeing many of its daily functions. The Delany children were educated at "St. Aug's," where their father taught. All ten children became college-educated professional men and women—a remarkable feat for anyone of that era, regardless of race or sex. Sadie earned both a bachelor's and a master's degree from

Social psychology: The field of psychology pertaining to how people think about other people and interact in relationships and groups.

Columbia University and became a teacher. In 1926 she became the first black woman appointed to teach home economics at the high school level in New York City. Bessie went to dental school at Columbia in 1923, where she was the only black woman, and she was the second black woman licensed to practice dentistry in New York City.

The Delany family, well known in black society in North Carolina and in New York City's Harlem neighborhood, was considered to be part of an elite group of educated blacks. But the road was not easy for the sisters. People, black and white, developed attitudes toward and stereotypes about the sisters, and some discriminated against them—because they were black, because they were women, or simply because they were Delanys.

Like the Delanys, we are all targets of other people's attitudes and stereotypes, and we have attitudes and stereotypes of our own about other people. And like the Delanys, we all feel pressure from others to behave in certain ways and exert pressure on others to behave in certain ways. How we think about other people and interact in relationships and groups makes up the subfield of psychology called **social psychology.**

Many of the phenomena psychology seeks to understand—sensation, learning, and memory, to name just a few—take place primarily at the levels of the brain and the person, but are influenced, as shown in the Looking at Levels sections, by the environment and the social world. In this chapter, the central emphasis is the level of the group. By definition, social psychology is about our relationships with aspects of the world around us; it focuses on the way we think about other people and act toward them, individually and in groups. And these interactions affect our thoughts, feelings, behavior, even our brains. Are there psychological principles that underlie the ways we think about and behave toward other people? If so, what are they?

Social Cognition: Thinking About People

Sadie and Bessie's parents worked hard to protect their children as much as possible from prejudice, discrimination, and intimidation. They also tried to instill in their children a sense of dignity, self-respect, and respect for and support of others. They encouraged their children to think about the world and their places in it, in specific ways. For example, their parents called each other Mr. and Mrs. Delany in front of others, including their children. This was a conscious decision.

It was common for whites to call blacks by their first names in instances in which they would use surnames for whites; therefore, Mr. and Mrs. Delany deliberately chose to use formal titles to convey respect for each other and the expectation of respect from others.

Centenarians Bessie and Sadie Delany, like all of us, were influenced by social psychological phenomena.

1. What is the relationship between people's attitudes and their behaviors?

2. What are stereotypes? Why do people have them? What are the differences between stereotypes and prejudice?

3. How do we determine responsibility for positive and negative events, and what difference does it make?

In this chapter we focus largely on the ways people think about other people, in other words, on social cognition—*cognition* because it is about how we think, and *social* because the thoughts involve other people and the social world in general. **Social cognition** is concerned with the ways we attend to, store, remember, and use information about other people and the social world.

Attitudes and Behavior: Feeling and Doing

When you read or hear the news, your attitudes affect your interpretation of the events being reported. In a smaller arena, your attitudes about people from a particular ethnic group will determine how you feel about them. For instance, your attitude about African Americans will determine how you *feel* about African Americans, which will in turn affect how you feel when you read about the Delanys. And in your own circle, if your friend tells you she's had an abortion, your attitude toward abortion will help determine how you feel about your friend. An **attitude** is an overall evaluation—often considered a feeling—about some aspect of the world: people, issues, or objects (Petty & Wegener, 1998). Your beliefs and behavior can affect your attitudes, and your attitudes can affect your beliefs and behavior. The opportunity for the interplay of attitude and behavior can be seen in Sadie's father's comment to her: "Daughter, you are college material. You owe it to your nation, your race, and yourself to go. And if you don't go, then shame on you" (p. 91). His remarks reflected his attitude toward higher education for blacks: He was passionate about it (feeling); he had no doubt about the power of education to elevate the position of blacks in American society (belief); and this attitude was formed, in part, by his own experiences with education as well as those of his family (behavior).

Attitudes can be positive, such as being in favor of nuclear disarmament; negative, such as disliking speed limits on highways; or neutral, such as not being moved one way or the other by a political candidate. The same issue—for instance, whether American troops should intervene in a foreign war—can evoke equally strong negative (NO!) and positive (YES!) attitudes. These different evaluations are accompanied by different changes in facial muscles (Cacioppo, Petty, Losch et al., 1986) and brain activation (Davidson, 1992a). We can also have ambivalent attitudes, with simultaneous negative and positive attitudes being equally strong.

Attitudes and Cognitions

Attention can play an important role in how we process and remember perceptual information in the physical world (see Chapters 3 and 5). Similarly, attitudes play an important role in how we process information and remember events in our social world (Eagly & Chaiken, 1998). Particularly in ambiguous social situations, our attitudes help organize events and thus determine what information is attended to, processed, encoded, and remembered. This is one reason why people in the same social situation can come away with different versions of what occurred. In one study, Princeton and Dartmouth students watched a motion picture of a controversial Princeton–Dartmouth football game. Although all students saw the same motion picture of the game, students from the different schools described different events, such as which team started rough play (Hastorf & Cantril, 1954).

Our attitudes also affect the way we shape our goals and expectations, and how we interpret obstacles we encounter in trying to achieve our goals, perhaps therby inducing stress. (It is not an event itself, but how it is perceived that determines whether it induces stress; see Chapter 10.) Our attitudes guide us as we selectively evaluate information; generally, we find information that is contrary to our attitudes to be unconvincing, and we may even try to disprove it (Eagly &

Social cognition: The area of social psychology that focuses on how people attend to, store, remember, and use information about other people and the social world.

Attitude: An overall evaluation about some aspect of the world.

Chaiken, 1998). As an example, consider the effect of socioeconomic class in the workplace (Gerteis & Savage, 1998). If you think that someone from a lower socioeconomic class will make a bad colleague, you will look for any evidence of shoddy work. You may not notice your colleague's well-performed tasks, and if you do notice them, you make up reasons that discount or discredit your colleague's abilities—perhaps, you say, those are easy tasks.

Predicting Behavior

If you know someone's attitudes, can you predict their behavior? Consider the experience of psychologist Richard La Piere (1934), who traveled the country in the 1930s with a young Chinese couple. They stayed in 67 paid lodgings and ate in 184 restaurants and cafés. Six months after each visit, La Piere sent a questionnaire to those establishments inquiring whether they would accept Chinese people as customers. More than 90% of the lodgings and restaurants said no. Yet on their trip La Piere and his colleagues were refused only once. Attitudes influence behavior, but do not always lead to behavior consistent with attitudes.

Several factors determine how likely an attitude toward a behavior will lead to the behavior's occurrence. An attitude is more likely to affect behavior when it is (1) strong, (2) relatively stable, (3) directly relevant to the behavior, (4) important, or (5) easily accessed from memory (Eagly & Chaiken, 1998). For instance, suppose you strongly dislike eating Moroccan food—an attitude. Against your better judgment, you went to a Moroccan restaurant recently and only picked at the food. If a friend invites you today to a meal at a Moroccan restaurant, you are likely to suggest another place to go: Your attitude about Moroccan food is strong, stable, directly relevant to your behavior, and easily accessed from memory. But if you haven't eaten this type of food in years, don't feel that strongly about it now, and have almost forgotten why you ever disliked it, you would be less likely to object to your friend's choice of a Moroccan restaurant (Sanbonmatsu & Fazio, 1990). Attitudes based on indirect experience, such as hearsay, have less influence on behavior than those based on direct experience (Regan & Fazio, 1977).

Behavior Affects Attitudes

If a professor assigned an essay on a topic about which you didn't have very strong feelings (say, supporting curbside recycling versus recycling at a local center), do you think writing the essay would influence your subsequent views? Research has shown that it can: When people are asked repeatedly to assert an attitude on a given topic, thus priming that attitude and making it easier to access, they are more likely to behave in ways consistent with that attitude, compared with those who did not repeatedly express the attitude (Fazio et al., 1982; Powell & Fazio, 1984). In fact, repeatedly asserting an attitude can make the attitude more extreme (Downing et al., 1992). Many self-help or self-improvement programs capitalize on this finding, encouraging participants to express frequent "affirmations," positive statements about themselves, their intentions, and their abilities. Such repeated affirmations can strengthen people's positive attitudes about themselves.

Cognitive Dissonance

Attitudes and behavior don't always go hand in hand, as dramatically demonstrated by La Piere's study. But most people prefer that their attitudes and behavior be consistent (Snyder & Ickes, 1985). When an attitude and behavior—or two attitudes—are inconsistent, an uncomfortable state that psychologists refer to as **cognitive dissonance** arises. Cognitive dissonance is accompanied by heightened arousal (Losch & Cacioppo, 1990).

Festinger and Carlsmith's (1959) classic study on cognitive dissonance found that, counterintuitively, participants who were paid less to tell someone that a boring task was really enjoyable reported afterward that they enjoyed the task more than those who were paid a greater amount (Figure 13.1). How can we understand

Cognitive dissonance: The uncomfortable state that arises because of a discrepancy between an attitude and behavior or between two attitudes.

Figure 13.1   Cognitive Dissonance

In Festinger and Carlsmith's classic 1959 study, participants were asked to perform a very boring, repetitive task: putting spools on a tray, then dumping them out, and starting all over again.

Afterward, participants were given either $1 or $20 (a lot of money in those days). They were then asked to tell another person that the task was, in fact, quite interesting.

After telling the other person about the task, the participants were asked to rate how much they liked the task. Those who were paid $1 to tell the other person they liked the task reported actually liking the task more than those paid $20 to do so!

(From Festinger & Carlsmith, 1959.)

this? By the effects of cognitive dissonance reduction. The participants who were paid less, only $1, could not have justified performing a boring task for that amount. To reduce dissonance, they appear to have convinced themselves, unconsciously, that they really *did* enjoy the task, so much that they were willing to do it for little reimbursement. The participants who were paid more felt no such compulsion; the money they received, they felt, adequately compensated for the boredom, so there was no dissonance to be resolved. In general, research has shown that the less reason there is to engage in a behavior that is counter to our attitudes, the stronger the dissonance. Cognitive dissonance does not occur with every inconsistency; it is experienced only by people who believe that they have a choice and that they are responsible for the course of action, and thus for any negative consequences (Cooper, 1998; Goethals et al., 1979).

Because cognitive dissonance creates an uncomfortable state, we try to decrease it. How do we minimize cognitive dissonance once it has occurred? We can use indirect strategies, such as trying to feel good about ourselves in other areas of life, or direct strategies, which involve actually changing our attitudes or behavior. Direct strategies also include attempts to obtain additional information supporting our attitude or behavior. Or, we can trivialize an inconsistency between two conflicting attitudes (or between an attitude and a behavior) as being unimportant, and therefore less likely to cause cognitive dissonance (Simon et al., 1995). For example, suppose you really believe in, and talk about, a desire to help feed starving people. Then a friend points out that you talk about this desire repeatedly but don't do anything about it. This observation would probably induce cognitive dissonance in you. To lessen it, you could use an indirect strategy by telling yourself what a good person you are, or by finding information about how hard it is for one individual to do anything about world hunger, or simply by saying "Well, my heart's in the right place." Or, you could implement a direct strategy that has an impact on world hunger, such as volunteering to work in a food bank.

Some researchers have argued that it is not the inconsistency itself that leads to the dissonance, and thus to a change in an attitude or behavior, but rather the resulting threat to a person's self-image. A discrepancy between attitude and

Persuasion: Attempts to change people's attitudes.

behavior (or between two attitudes) makes the person who becomes aware of it look foolish, and so it is a threat to his or her integrity (Aronson et al., 1995). This threat explains why African Americans may discount the importance of their performance on standardized tests, and why women taking tests in math or science may do the same: They are concerned that their performance is seen as a reflection on their race or sex. The risk of seeming to conform to a negative stereotype in the eyes of others or oneself is termed *stereotype threat* (Steele & Aronson, 1995), which can cause people to perform poorly. Stereotype threat occurs not only in women and people of color: White athletes who derived their self-worth from their athletic performance showed stereotype threat and decreased performance when their performance was framed as an indication of their natural ability (Stone et al., 1999). Regardless of their performance on the tests, by discounting the importance of their test performance, the test-takers allow themselves to construct a positive self-identity from abilities in other domains (Steele, 1997).

Using cognitive dissonance to increase behaviors that promote health, Stone and his colleagues (1997) set up a situation in which participants were induced to feel that they were being hypocritical. Sexually active college students were asked to prepare and videotape a talk on AIDS prevention for high school students. Students who were asked to write speeches based on reasons they *personally* had not always used condoms were then more likely to purchase offered condoms than students who were asked to include in their speech reasons why *other* people might not use condoms.

Attitude Change: Persuasion

Walking to class, have you ever been approached by someone offering you a leaflet about an upcoming event, a political candidate, a new product? If so, someone (or some company) was trying to encourage you to do something: go to the event, vote for the candidate, buy the product. We are bombarded by attempts to change our attitudes about things, through advertisements, editorials, and conversations with friends. These efforts to change your attitudes are called **persuasion.**

Social psychologists have identified several factors that make attempts at persuasion more likely to be successful. You can probably guess some of them; others may surprise you. As you might expect, people are more likely to be persuaded by what they read, hear, or see when the person doing the persuading is an expert (Hovland & Weiss, 1951). If your doctor tells you to stop smoking, the instruction is more persuasive than when suggested by a friend. Similarly, an attractive persuader is more likely to change attitudes than an unattractive one; think about commercials and advertisements, and what the people in most of them look like (Kiesler & Kiesler, 1969). Fast speakers are generally more persuasive than slow speakers (Miller et al., 1976). And if the attempt at persuasion arouses strong emotions in you, particularly fear, it is more likely to work, especially if it includes specific advice about what you can do to bring about a more positive outcome (Leventhal et al., 1965). This technique is used in public service messages that try to scare people into behaving differently, such as ads that graphically describe how someone contracted AIDS by not using a condom and then strongly recommend condom use. Not surprisingly, people who are perceived as honest are more persuasive (Priester & Petty, 1995). People with low self-esteem are more susceptible to persuasion than people with high self-esteem (Janis, 1954).

Other methods of persuasion—and the audiences most easily persuaded—are less obvious. If you are not paying full attention to an attempt at persuasion, you are more likely to be persuaded, at least in part because you have less ability to develop a counterargument (Allyn & Festinger, 1961; Romero et al., 1996). So, if you are watching a television commercial while sorting the laundry, you are more likely to be persuaded by it than if you're focused on it. If you've ever heard a Repub-

In an effort to persuade smokers to quit, this ad uses persuasion techniques. Which techniques are at work here?

lican speaking to a group of Democrats (or vice versa), you may have noticed a persuasion technique used to convince people who hold the opposite view, whatever that view is: The would-be persuader uses a two-sided approach. The speaker presents both sides of an argument rather than only one side, as is common if the audience already agrees with the speaker. And when a message does not appear to be *trying* to persuade you to change your attitude, it is often more effective than one that is obviously trying to move you.

The ancient Egyptians recognized the power of some of these persuasion techniques. Their law courts met in the dark; the judges weren't able to see the accused, the accuser, or the witnesses, and were thus less likely to be persuaded by factors other than the merits of the case itself. Furthermore, the **mere exposure effect** can change attitudes: Simply becoming familiar with something can change your attitude toward it—generally, favorably.

Attempts at persuasion are often foiled by four common obstacles:

1. *Strong attitude.* If we, as listeners, already have a strong attitude about an issue, as opposed to a weak one, we are less likely to be persuaded to change our current attitude (Petty & Krosnick, 1996). Indeed, among identical twins reared apart (see Chapter 8), certain attitudes appear to be heritable, strong, and resistant to change. For instance, the attitude toward the death penalty has a high heritability; whatever is responsible for this attitude is, at least in part, affected by the genes (Tesser, 1993).

2. *Reactance.* Reactance is the development of a negative reaction to someone who is seen as trying too hard or too often to change our opinion. In this case, we may very well change our minds in the *opposite* direction from that intended by the persuader, even if we would not otherwise take that position; this response is called *negative attitude change* (Brehm, 1966).

3. *Forewarning.* If we know in advance that someone is going to try to persuade us of something, we are less likely to be persuaded (Cialdini & Petty, 1979; Petty & Cacioppo, 1981), although this is not always the case (Niemeyer et al., 1991; Romero et al., 1996).

4. *Selective avoidance.* We may simply bypass someone's attempt to persuade us by deliberate selective avoidance, such as changing the channel during television commercials.

Stereotypes: Seen One, Seen 'Em All

In the social world around us, we could easily be overwhelmed by the torrent of information conveyed by other people—their words, postures, gestures, facial expressions—to say nothing of what we can infer about their attitudes and goals, and even further, what other people have said about them. The world is full of information and stimuli, and if we had no way of organizing this input flying at us from all directions, assaulting our senses, we would live in chaos. In the physical realm, we categorize all this information by principles such as Gestalt groupings of visual stimuli (see Chapter 3). To avoid drowning in this sea of social information, we create *stereotypes,* a type of schema (see Chapter 6) that helps provide a cognitive shortcut for processing all this information about the social world (Gilbert & Hixon, 1991; Macrae et al., 1994). A **stereotype** is a belief (or set of beliefs) about people in a particular social category; the category can be defined by race, sex, social class, religion, hair color, sport, hobby, and myriad other characteristics. A stereotype may be positive, such as "women are nurturing"; neutral, such as "Mexicans eat spicy food"; or negative, such as "Australians drink too much." Stereotypes are caricatures, not reasoned formulations, and are to some extent outside conscious awareness; we may deny having them at all. Moreover, stereotypes are often incorrect. Not only can they affect how we feel about other people, but our expectations of others based on our stereotypes can lead *them* to behave in certain ways.

Mere exposure effect: The tendency to like previously perceived things better than unfamiliar ones.

Stereotype: A belief (or set of beliefs) about people in a particular social category.

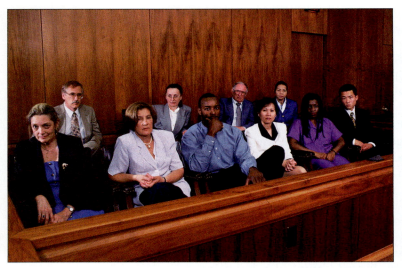

When lawyers select a jury, they try to have certain potential jurors excluded because of stereotypes about how people of a certain race, sex, age, or profession are likely to view the case. One study, however, found that lawyers' stereotype-based expectations of whether jurors would be likely to convict were often incorrect

The effect of errors we make when using stereotypes is anything but trivial. Perhaps because of our desire for cognitive efficiency, we prefer to read information consistent with our stereotypes, and we process such information more quickly (Smith, 1998). As with attitudes, we are less likely to attend to, and therefore encode or remember, information inconsistent with our stereotypes (Johnston & Macrae, 1994), and in fact we may deny the truth of such information (O'Sullivan & Durso, 1984). And once a stereotype is activated, we respond to a person's membership in a social category, not to the characteristics of the individual person. The stereotype thus lives on and may shape the rest of our thinking. One way this occurs is that additional information relevant to the stereotype is recalled faster than unrelated information (Dovidio et al., 1986). However, if we are motivated to be accurate, and do *not* assume that a stereotype applies to a particular individual, we can minimize the impact of stereotypes (Wyer et al., 2000).

Here's how this works. Suppose that you have a positive stereotype of New Englanders, believing them to be hard-working, thrifty, and honest. When you meet someone from Maine, your "New Englander" stereotype is activated. You will then be more likely to notice aspects of her behavior that are consistent with your stereotype, and in thinking about her, you will be more likely to remember those aspects. You may not notice when she comes in late, or you will come up with plausible excuses for her tardiness.

Sometimes the conflict between a stereotype and actual behavior is too great to be ignored—but rather than change a stereotype, we are more likely to create a new subtype within the stereotype (Anderson, 1983; Anderson et al., 1980). So in this case, when your New England acquaintance's chronic lateness and inefficiency are too great to ignore, you might create a subtype—"female New Englander on her first job." This allows you to preserve your stereotype of New Englanders as hard-working. Because of this psychological phenomenon—creating subtypes to preserve a stereotype—stereotypes can be extremely difficult to change or eliminate. However, under certain circumstances, stereotypes *can* change, when the exception is made to appear typical of its group and when we are encouraged to think that the person's behavior results from his or her characteristics, *not* the situation (Wilder et al., 1996).

Cognition and Prejudice

Stereotyping can lead to **prejudice**, which is an attitude, generally negative, toward members of a group. Prejudice includes not only beliefs and expectations about the group but also an emotional component: Simply thinking about members of a disliked group can produce strong feelings about them (Bodenhausen et al., 1994). As is the case with attitudes and stereotypes, information inconsistent with a prejudice is less likely to be attended to and remembered accurately than is information consistent with a prejudice, making prejudice self-perpetuating.

Prejudice may be conscious and intentional; it may also be conscious and unintentional, or even unconscious and unintentional (Carter & Rice, 1997; Fazio et al., 1995; Greenwald & Banaji, 1995). Conscious but unintentional prejudice occurs among people who are confused about their beliefs. They know their prejudice is unjustified but retain it and, at times, unintentionally display it. Other

Prejudice: An attitude (generally negative) toward members of a group.

people are unaware of their prejudice and even deny it, but it nonetheless manifests itself in actions or words.

Prejudice can stem from emotions in two ways. The presence of negative feelings may account for conscious prejudice, whether intentional or unintentional. But even if someone does not have negative feelings toward a group, prejudice can also arise from the *absence of positive feelings* (Pettigrew & Meertens, 1995), leading to unconscious prejudice. Thus, someone can be prejudiced against a group with whom he or she has no experience; for instance, someone from an Asian country might have a prejudice against people with red hair that is engendered by the absence of any positive feelings or experiences.

Some cognitive operations perpetuate unconscious prejudice. **Social categorization theory** proposes that people are driven to divide the world automatically into categories of "us" and "them." This sorting is done consciously as well as unconsciously. People usually think of their own group—the **ingroup**—favorably. The other group, the **outgroup,** is usually disliked, assumed to possess more undesirable traits, and generally believed to be more homogeneous (Brewer & Brown, 1998; Fiske, 1998; Judd et al., 1991; Lambert, 1995; Linville & Fischer, 1993; Rustemli et al., 2000; Vonk & van Knippenberg, 1995). When we identify with an ingroup, we are more inclined to like, trust, help, and cooperate with other ingroup members than we are to like, trust, help, and cooperate with outgroup members (Brewer & Brown, 1998). Our views of the ingroup and outgroup can lead to unconscious prejudice.

Another cognitive operation that can lead to unconscious prejudice is the *illusory correlation,* which is a tendency to overestimate the strength of a relationship between two things (Mullen & Johnson, 1990). This cognitive operation may explain why white people overestimate actual crime rates among African American men, and hence maintain their prejudice (Hamilton & Sherman, 1989). The *illusion of outgroup homogeneity* is an inclination to view an outgroup as more homogeneous (that is, it has members who are more similar to one another) than the ingroup. The corollary, *ingroup differentiation,* is the inclination to view members of an ingroup (that is, your own group) as more heterogeneous—members are more diverse than those of another group.

For example, a research study found that non-Hispanic Americans were less likely to distinguish among different types of Latinos (a perceived outgroup from the point of view of the non-Hispanics) than were Latinos themselves. However, Latinos only differentiated their own subgroup from all other Latino groups; thus, Mexican Americans were more likely to categorize themselves as a particular group—the ingroup—and lump Cuban Americans and Puerto Ricans together as Latinos—the outgroup (Huddy & Virtanen, 1995).

When Bessie Delany was in dental school, a white professor failed her on some work that she knew was good. A white girlfriend, also a dental student, offered to hand in Bessie's work as her own to see what grade the work would be given this time. Bessie's friend passed with the same work that had earned Bessie a failing grade.

Bessie's experience was one of discrimination; specifically, she suffered the effect of prejudiced behavior. Her professor's behavior was influenced by his prejudice against Bessie because of her race, her membership in a particular social category. As with stereotypes, people discriminate on the basis of just about anything that distinguishes groups: gender, race, social class, hair color, religion, college attended, height, and on and on. As with prejudice, discrimination may be subtle, and sometimes even unconscious.

Most Americans believe discrimination is wrong; and when their own discriminatory behavior is pointed out to them, they are uncomfortable (Devine & Monteith, 1993), and they may subsequently reduce their discriminatory behaviors (Monteith, 1996). This phenomenon provides another example of the way we act to reduce cognitive dissonance: Becoming aware of the discrepancy between

The illusion of outgroup homogeneity leads heterosexuals to view lesbians as similar to one another; a common stereotype is that they are all unattractive and don't care about their appearances. Like all stereotypes, this belief is a caricature and, as this photo shows, is not accurate.

Social categorization theory: The theory that people are driven to divide the world automatically into categories of "us" versus "them."

Ingroup: An individual's own group.

Outgroup: A group different than a person's own.

attitudes and behavior leads to the discomfort of cognitive dissonance, which can be reduced through changing future behaviors.

Why Does Prejudice Exist?

The effects of prejudice are limiting, damaging, and painful. Why then does prejudice exist? The *realistic conflict theory* (Bobo, 1983) suggests a reason: competition for scarce resources such as good housing, jobs, and schools. As groups compete for these resources, increasingly negative views of the other groups take form, eventually becoming prejudice.

A classic experiment, the Robber's Cave study, showed how easily prejudice can be created from competition (see Figure 13.2; Sherif et al., 1961). A set of 11-year-old boys was divided into two groups, Eagles and Rattlers, at a special overnight camp called the Robber's Cave. The two groups competed for valued prizes. Conflict between the two groups quickly escalated into prejudice and discrimination, with the groups calling each other names and destroying each other's property. However, such attitudes and behavior stopped when the two groups no longer competed for resources but cooperated for larger, mutually beneficial goals such as restoring the camp's water supply. Although the study has several limitations (it is unclear if the findings generalize to girls, nonwhite boys, or adults), it does illustrate how prejudice can both develop and dissipate (Sherif et al., 1961).

Figure 13.2   The Creation of Prejudice: The Robber's Cave Study

Eleven-year-old boys at a special overnight summer camp (called the Robber's Cave) were the participants in this study. In the initial phase of the study, the boys were randomly divided into two groups and separated from each other for a week. During this time, activities fostered a sense of cohesion in each group.

During the 2-week-long second phase, the two groups competed for highly desired prizes such as pocket knives and medals. Conflict between the two groups quickly escalated from name calling to direct acts (destroying the other group's personal property). Negative attitudes as well as negative behavior developed, with each group labeling the other with pejorative terms such as "coward."

In the third phase, the two groups were brought together to work on a number of superordinate goals such as restoring the camp's water supply. Tensions between the groups dissolved by the sixth day of this phase.

The Robber's Cave study supports the view of realistic conflict theory that competition between groups for scarce resources can produce prejudice. But are scarcity and competition necessary to produce prejudice, or can it arise without them? Social categorization theory provides one explanation for prejudice in the absence of scarcity or competition: In this view, the psychological forces leading to ingroup favoritism are so powerful that creating even an *arbitrary* "us" and "them" can lead to unconscious favoritism and discriminatory behavior (Feather, 1996; Perdue et al., 1990). This social categorization can lead to discrimination in two distinct ways: (1) The ingroup is actively favored; and (2) the outgroup is actively disfavored.

Although social categorization can perpetuate a skewed picture of other people, it is efficient because once we've made an "us" versus "them" distinction, we can then use our stereotypes about "us" and "them" to understand behavior, saving us the effort of paying close attention to other people and actively processing our observations of their behavior. Because we expect certain behaviors from outgroup members, just being in their presence can activate our stereotypes about them (Bargh et al., 1996). We may then behave in ways that elicit behavior from an outgroup member that is consistent with that stereotype, even if he or she wouldn't otherwise behave that way (Snyder, 1984, 1992). This process thus becomes a self-fulfilling prophecy: The elicited behavior confirms our stereotype, and we regard the outgroup member's behavior as "proof" of the validity of our prejudices (Fiske, 1998).

Once a prejudicial attitude is in place, *social learning theory* (see Chapter 4) explains how it can be spread and passed through generations as a learned stereotype. Parents, peers, television, movies, and other aspects of the culture provide models of prejudice (Pettigrew, 1969). When prejudice is translated into words and actions, it may be reinforced. Scarce resources, competition, natural cognitive mechanisms, and learning may all contribute to the development and maintenance of prejudice.

Changing Prejudice: Easier Said Than Done

Psychology has shown us how prejudice develops and deepens; equally important, can psychology show us how to arrest the development of prejudice? The answer is yes, but the task is not easily accomplished.

One method of decreasing prejudice is described by the *contact hypothesis,* which holds that increased contact between different groups will decrease prejudice between them (Pettigrew, 1981). Increased contact serves several purposes: (1) Both groups are more likely to become aware of similarities between the groups, which can enhance mutual attraction; (2) even though stereotypes resist change, when stereotypic views are met with enough inconsistent information or exceptions, those views *can* change (Kunda & Oleson, 1995); and (3) increased contact can shatter the illusion that the outgroup is homogeneous (Baron & Byrne, 1997).

Increased contact works best under certain conditions, such as when working toward a shared goal and when all participants are deemed to be equal (see Table 13.1). For example, politically influential members of Israeli and Palestinian groups met informally and unofficially for sessions of intensive interactive problem solving. The increased contact that occurred while working on the larger goal of resolving obstacles to peace talks was partly successful in lowering the barriers between the two sides. After the Oslo Peace Accord in 1993, many of those involved viewed these informal group meetings as directly and indirectly laying the foundation for

What are children in Bosnia being taught about Gavrilo Princip, the man who started World War I by assassinating Archduke Franz Ferdinand D'Este of Austria-Hungary in 1914? Textbooks in the Serb-controlled part of Bosnia call the act heroic; a Croatian textbook refers to Princip as an "assassin trained and instructed by the Serbs to commit this act of terrorism"; and a Muslim textbook refers to him as a nationalist and says the resulting anti-Serbian rioting "was only stopped by police from all three ethnic groups" (Hedges, 1997). Social learning theory explains how these different perspectives can lead to prejudice toward other ethnic groups.

TABLE 13.1 **Conditions in Which Intergroup Contact Decreases Prejudice**

Increased contact between two groups can decrease prejudice when

- The groups are cooperating toward a shared goal.
- The groups are similar in social, economic, or task-related status.
- Contact is informal and has the potential to create meaningful relationships.
- The interactions provide disconfirmation of each other's prejudicial views.
- Those in each group view members of the other as typical of their group.
- The setting assumes equality among participants.

Increased contact between two groups prejudiced against each other can decrease prejudice, but only if certain conditions are met (see Table 13.1). In what ways did the increased contact between the Israelis and Palestinians at the Oslo peace conference fail to fulfill all these conditions?

the beginning steps toward peace (Kelman, 1997). The meetings, although not designed to reduce prejudice, nonetheless fulfilled one of the steps in that direction: coming together to work toward a shared goal. Other conditions, however, were not met: The participants from the two sides were *not* equal (Brewer & Brown, 1998) nor did they view each other as typical of their respective populations. Although they were able to work together for this one overarching goal of beginning peace discussions, the larger task of hammering out an agreement and sticking to it did not progress as smoothly.

Another way to decrease prejudice is through **recategorization**—that is, shifting the categories of "us" and "them" so that the two groups are no longer distinct entities. Examples of recategorization are familiar in everyday life. An assembly-line worker who is promoted to management experiences recategorization: The identity of "us" and "them" changes. When distinctions between groups are minimized so that different groups can be thought of as a single entity, recategorization can decrease prejudice. Working together toward a common goal facilitates recategorization, such as occurred in the Robber's Cave study when, instead of being Eagles or Rattlers, all boys became simply campers who had no running water.

Attributions: Making Sense of Events

When you read about the Delany sisters' successes, how did you explain them? Did you say to yourself, *The sisters worked hard and persevered?* Or, *They were lucky?* Whatever your reaction, it reflects not only your attitudes, stereotypes, and prejudices, but the attributions you make. **Attributions** are our explanations for the causes of events or behaviors.

What Is the Cause?

Usually, events and actions have many possible causes. An unreturned telephone call to a friend might be an indication that your friend is very busy, is annoyed at you, or simply is out of town. If a politician you admire changes position on an issue, do you explain the behavior as a sincere change of heart, a cave-in to heavy campaign contributors, or a calculated attempt to appeal to new supporters?

The particular attributions people make are of two broad types: internal and external. **Internal attributions** (also called *dispositional attributions*) explain a person's behavior in terms of that person's preferences, beliefs, goals, or other characteristics. For instance, if a friend leaves a math lecture very confused, you could attribute his confusion to internal factors: "I guess he's not very good at math." **External attributions** (also called *situational attributions*) explain a person's behavior in terms of the situation (Kelley, 1972; Kelley & Michela, 1980). If you make an external attribution for your friend's confusion, you might say, "The professor gave a really bad lecture today."

The attributions you make about events affect both you and other people (see Table 13.2): Blaming yourself for negative events (internal attribution) can suppress your immune system (Segerstrom et al., 1996; see Chapter 10). Blaming yourself or others affects behavior: Mothers who view their children's misbehavior as the children's fault are likely to discipline their children more harshly than mothers who attribute such misbehavior to other causes, such as their mothering (Slep & O'Leary, 1998).

Recategorization: A means of reducing prejudice by shifting the categories of "us" and "them" so that the two groups are no longer distinct entities.

Attribution: An explanation for the cause of an event or behavior.

Internal attribution: An explanation of someone's behavior that focuses on the person's beliefs, goals, or other dispositions; also called *dispositional attribution.*

External attribution: An explanation of behavior that focuses on the situation; also called *situational attribution.*

TABLE 13.2 Types of Attributions

	INTERNAL ATTRIBUTIONS	EXTERNAL ATTRIBUTIONS
Attributions about oneself	*Positive:* I did a good job because I'm smart.	*Positive:* I did a good job because the task was easy.
	Negative: I did a bad job because I'm inept.	*Negative:* I did a bad job because the time allotted for the task was too short.
Attributions about others	*Positive:* She did a good job because she's smart.	*Postive:* She did a good job because the task was easy.
	Negative: She did a bad job because she's inept.	*Negative:* She did a bad job because the time allotted for the task was too short.

Taking Shortcuts: Attributional Biases

Like stereotypes, **attributional biases** are cognitive shortcuts for determining attributions that generally occur outside our awareness. They help lessen the cognitive load required to make sense of the world, but they can lead to errors. These errors have implications for social relationships, the legal system, and social policy. Suppose, for example, you are a member of a jury and hear that the defendant confessed to the crime. It turns out that the confession was extracted after many hours of tough, coercive questioning by police. The judge then throws out the confession, striking it from the record, and tells you, the jury, to ignore it. Would you? Could you? Researchers using mock juries found that jurors in this situation assume that the confession was heartfelt and vote guilty more often than jurors who do not hear about a confession (Kassin & Wrightsman, 1981). The "jurors" are demonstrating the **fundamental attribution error** (Ross et al., 1977), the strong tendency to interpret other people's behavior as caused by internal (dispositional) causes rather than external (situational) ones. In the courtroom example, jurors would thus be more likely to view the confession as evidence of guilt (an internal, dispositional attribute) than coercion (an external, situational attribute).

As its name suggests, the fundamental attribution error is one of the most common attributional biases and a frequent source of error. Like other aspects of social cognition, it is affected by mood. The fundamental attribution error is at work, for example, when the sight of a homeless man on a bench leads us to assume his plight is due to an internal trait such as laziness rather than external factors such as a run of bad luck, a high unemployment rate, and a lack of affordable housing. The fundamental attribution error helps perpetuate discrimination because fault is attributed to the person, not to the circumstances. Once you make the fundamental attribution error, you are likely to ignore the context of future behavior (that is, the surrounding situation), and thus the effect of the initial error is multiplied. Related to the fundamental attribution error is the **self-serving bias** (Brown & Rogers, 1991; Miller & Ross, 1975), the inclination to attribute your failures to external causes and your successes to internal ones and to attribute other people's failures to internal causes and their successes to external causes.

Not all cultures use these various biases to the same degree. Just as different cultures promote different personality traits (see Chapter 8), they also use attributional biases somewhat differently. For example, accounts of crimes in Chinese-language newspapers are more likely to give external explanations, whereas for the same offense, English-language newspapers are more likely to emphasize internal factors (Morris & Peng, 1994).

Attributions can also be distorted by a **belief in a just world** (Lerner, 1980), the assumption that people get what they deserve. Because most Americans are richer than most Egyptians, Colombians, or Bulgarians, they must, according to this bias, also be smarter or work harder. According to the belief in a just world, if you get what you deserve, you must have done something to deserve what you get—notice the circular reasoning here! The belief in a just world can shape reactions to violent crime (particularly rape; Karuza & Carey, 1984) and contributes to

Attributional bias: A cognitive shortcut for determining attribution that generally occurs outside our awareness.

Fundamental attribution error: The strong tendency to interpret other people's behavior as due to internal (dispositional) causes rather than external (situational) ones.

Self-serving bias: A person's inclination to attribute his or her own failures to external causes and successes to internal causes, but to attribute other people's failures to internal causes and their successes to external causes.

Belief in a just world: An attributional bias that assumes people get what they deserve.

the practice of *blaming the victim.* For example, those who strongly believe in a just world are more likely than others to view AIDS as a deserved punishment for homosexual behavior (Glennon & Joseph, 1993) and to view the plight of a disadvantaged group, such as immigrants, as deserved (Dalbert & Yamauchi, 1994). This belief maintains discriminatory behaviors (Lipkus & Siegler, 1993).

LOOKING AT LEVELS

Punishing Rapists

Think about how we can understand people's different beliefs about how severely rapists should be punished. The death penalty? At the level of the brain, we have seen that among identical twins reared apart, certain attitudes, such as the attitude toward the death penalty, are in part heritable; genetic factors indirectly affect this attitude, which can range from very much in favor to very much opposed. These attitudes will affect how we evaluate information about whether the death penalty is a successful deterrent in reducing crime. However, people's attitudes about the death penalty may not predict how they would vote on it unless their attitudes are strong, or based on direct experience with a capital crime.

At the level of the person, you have developed stereotypes about the kinds of people who are rapists or who are raped. Because of the nature of stereotypes, should you meet a convicted rapist who doesn't fit your stereotype, you are not likely to change your stereotype, but rather will create a separate subtype of rapist, leaving the larger category unchanged. If you like this person, you might attribute blame for the rape to the victim, not the rapist.

This analysis at the level of the person may conflict with analysis at the level of the group. If a member of your group, perhaps defined by class, race, or family, has been raped by someone not in your group, you may vilify all members of outgroups, particularly the ones to which the rapist belongs. Thus, events at the three levels need not be entirely consistent and will interact in complex ways. Depending on the precise situation, events at one level or another may win out; if so, the result may be cognitive dissonance, perhaps leading you to modify your behavior or attitudes.

CONSOLIDATE!

1 **What is the relationship between people's attitudes and their behaviors?** Attitudes affect how we process, encode, store, and retrieve information about the social world. Attitudes that are strong, stable, relevant, and salient are likely to affect behavior. Moreover, direct experience, mere exposure, and how we think we will be judged for the behavior all relate to an attitude's impact on behavior. Attitudes and future behavior can change as a result of cognitive dissonance and persuasion. A persuader is more likely to facilitate attitude change if he or she is an expert, is attractive, speaks quickly, or is perceived as honest.

2 **What are stereotypes? Why do people have them? What are the differences between stereotypes and prejudice?** Stereotypes are beliefs or sets of beliefs about people in a particular social category; these beliefs help us to organize efficiently, though perhaps incorrectly, the multitude of information presented by the social world. These cognitive shortcuts can be outside of our awareness and are resistant to change. Prejudice is an attitude that contains a generally negative view toward members of a group; prejudice can be either conscious or unconscious, intentional or unintentional. Prejudice can arise from negative feelings or from the absence of positive feelings. Social categorization theory, the illusory correlation, and other cognitive biases can account for the perpetuation of unconscious prejudice.

3 **How do we determine responsibility for positive and negative events, and what difference does it make?** Attributions are ways we explain the cause of events or behaviors. There are two types of attributions: internal (dispositional) and external (situational). The fundamental attribution error, the self-serving bias, and the belief in a just world can lead to incorrect attributions.

Social Behavior: Interacting With People

The Delanys had very definite ideas about how they were supposed to behave with people. Based on their ideas about marriage, both Sadie and Bessie decided early on not to marry. They both definitely wanted careers, and women of that era often had to choose between a career and marriage. Moreover, their father instilled in them a sense of self-reliance, as is evident by his advice to Sadie about going to Columbia University: He advised her not to take a scholarship because she might then feel indebted to the people who offered it. He encouraged her to pay for her own education.

The Delanys also had definite ideas about how other people should be treated. They were taught to help others, regardless of skin color; the family motto was "Your job is to help someone." The Delanys stuck by their beliefs, even when others did not agree. Bessie recounts a time she vacationed in Jamaica with a darker-skinned Jamaican-born friend. There, Bessie learned that there were two official classes of Jamaican Negroes: "white Negroes," who had more privileges in society, and "black Negroes," who were considered to be in a lower social class. The young women stayed with the family of Bessie's friend, who was a "black Negro." "White Negroes" extended invitations to Bessie (a lighter-skinned African American) and ignored her friend and hostess. Bessie refused all invitations until her friend was invited as well.

1. What psychological principles explain why we like certain people and not others?

2. Why do all groups have rules for social behavior and organization?

3. Why do we sometimes "go along" with or obey others even when we don't want to? What makes us able to refuse?

4. Does being part of a group change our behavior? How do groups make decisions?

5. Are some people more helpful than others? Why would we not help other people?

Relationships: Having a Date, Having a Partner

Sadie and Bessie's white maternal great-great-grandmother had a liaison with a slave while her husband was away fighting in the War of 1812. This relationship produced two daughters, half-sisters to the seven children she had already had with her husband. When her husband returned home, he adopted the two girls as his own. No one knew exactly what happened to her lover, although it was rumored that he ran away on the husband's return. The relationship between the Delanys' great-great-grandmother and biological great-great-grandfather would appear to have been based on more than a passing interest, given that the relationship spanned a number of years. Why were they attracted to each other? Why are we attracted to certain people? Why do we like particular people, and love others?

As the Delany children's ancestors undoubtedly experienced almost two centuries ago, and you may be experiencing now, relationships are strong stuff. They can lead to our most positive emotions and, as you saw in Chapter 10, can help us regulate our emotions in response to events outside the relationship (Berscheid & Reis, 1998). They can also be the source of negative emotions: When asked about the "last bad thing that happened to you," almost half the respondents reported conflict in a significant relationship (Cupach & Spitzberg, 1994).

Liking: To Like or Not to Like

Even though Sadie and Bessie decided not to marry, they still had boyfriends. Why were they attracted to certain men—why are you attracted to some people and not others? First impressions play an initial role, as does *repeated contact,* which usually leads to a more positive evaluation of someone (Moreland & Zajonc, 1982; Zajonc, 1968). The Delany sisters recounted that a lot of "racial mixing, especially after slavery days, was just attraction between people, plain and simple, just like happened in our family, on Mama's side. You know, when people live in close proximity, they can't help but get attracted to each other" (p. 76).

Similarity is a second factor in the development of liking; the more similar a stranger's attitudes are to your own, the more likely you are to be attracted (Tesser, 1993). In this case, the adage "Opposites attract" has *not* been borne out by research. Similarity of preferred activities (Lydon, Jamieson et al., 1988), even similar ways of communicating, can lead to increased attraction and liking. For instance, we are more likely to be attracted to someone whose nonverbal cues are the same as those used in our own culture (Dew & Ward, 1993). In general, the greater the similarity, the more probable it is that our liking for another person will endure (Byrne, 1971).

A third, and major, factor is *physical attraction* (Collins & Zebrowitz, 1995; Hatfield & Sprecher, 1986). In part, the role of physical attraction in liking may be influenced by our stereotypes about attractive people—such as that they are smarter and happier. Although the stereotype that people who are physically more attractive possess more desirable attributes is found in different cultures, what constitutes "more desirable" differs across cultures. For instance, in Korea (a collectivist country; see Chapters 7 and 8), attractive people are thought to have greater integrity and concern for others—qualities more valued in that collectivist culture than in individualist Western ones (Wheeler & Kim, 1997).

Recent research recognizes that physical distance itself may no longer be as important in defining "repeated contact." Internet chat rooms and interest groups, for example, make it possible for a couple to "meet" and have a relationship without any physical contact (Parks & Roberts, 1998).

Can all human beings agree on what makes someone attractive? Research that seeks to answer this question has generally focused on facial features. What makes a man attractive to women are large eyes, a large chin, prominent cheekbones, and a big smile (Cunningham et al., 1990); men prefer women with a small nose, prominent cheekbones, and a big smile (Cunningham, 1986). Findings of what constitutes attractiveness are consistent across cultures. For example, when shown photographs of faces of Hispanic, black, Asian, and white American women, ratings of attractiveness by recent Asian and Hispanic male immigrants were similar to those of American black and white men (Cunningham et al., 1995). There is some evidence that cultures rate as attractive faces that are "average" looking—that is, their proportions approximate the population average (Jones & Hill, 1993). One theory that explains this preference is that "average" faces are more likely to look familiar because they are more similar to the faces of the rest of the population, and familiarity, via the mere exposure effect, can lead to liking. We also prefer faces that are symmetrical (Grammer & Thornhill, 1994). Thus, one proposal is that people's preference for symmetry reflects a desire to choose a mate who "looks healthy" because facial asymmetries may reflect the presence of disease (Grammer & Thornhill, 1994; Thornhill & Gangestad, 1993). There is also evidence that people prefer men's and women's faces that are "feminized"—that is, faces that reflect higher levels of female hormones (Perrett et al., 1998; see Chapter 3).

Loving: How Do I Love Thee?

Despite all the poems and plays, novels and movies, that chronicle, celebrate, and analyze love, its mystery endures. Its variations, components, styles, and fate over time have all been examined by psychologists. Loving appears to be a qualitatively different feeling from liking, not simply very strong liking (Rubin, 1970). Moreover, attitudes about and experiences with love appear to be similar across cultures as diverse as Russia, Japan, and the United States (Sprecher, Aron, et al., 1994).

People talk about "loving" all sorts of things in all sorts of ways. You might say you love a pet, a friend, a parent, a mate, and pizza with anchovies; obviously you don't mean quite the same thing in each case. Sexual or **passionate love**—the intense, often sudden feeling of being "in love"—involves sexual attraction, a desire for mutual love and physical closeness, arousal, and a fear that the relationship will end. **Compassionate love** is marked by very close friendship, mutual caring, liking, respect, and attraction (Caspi & Herbener, 1990).

What do the various sorts of love have in common, and how can we understand their differences? Robert Sternberg has proposed a **triangular model of love** (1986a, 1988a). Love, he says, has three dimensions: (1) passion (including sexual desire); (2) intimacy (emotional closeness and sharing); and (3) commitment (the conscious decision to be in the relationship). Particular relationships reflect different proportions of each dimension, in amounts that are likely to vary over time (see Figure 13.3). According to Sternberg's theory, most types of love relationships involve two of the three components; only "consummate love" has passion, intimacy, *and* commitment.

Figure 13.3   Sternberg's Triangular Model of Love

According to Sternberg's triangular theory of love, passion, intimacy, and commitment form three points of a triangle. Any given relationship may have only one component (at a point), two components (one of the sides of the triangle), or all three components (the center of the triangle).

Attachment style is another way of thinking about different kinds of love relationships. The attachment style with a partner stems from the interaction pattern developed between parent and child (Waller & Shaver, 1994). For instance, adults who seek closeness and interdependence in relationships and are not worried about the possibility of the loss of the relationship, about 59% of an American sample, are said to have a *secure* style of attachment (Mickelson et al., 1997). Those who are uncomfortable with intimacy and closeness, about 25% of an American sample, have an *avoidant* style and structure their daily lives so as to avoid closeness (Tidwell et al., 1996). Those who want but simultaneously fear a relationship have an *anxious–ambivalent* style (Hazan & Shaver, 1990); about 11% of Americans have this style. Although by extrapolation from these studies, a majority of Americans have a secure style (Hazan & Shaver, 1987), an anxious–ambivalent style is more common in Japan and Israel, and an avoidant style more common in Germany (Shaver & Hazan, 1994).

As you may have experienced in your relationships, a sense of intimacy usually progresses in stages (Honeycutt et al., 1998), and how we feel in the relationship influences the relationship itself. A growing feeling of intimacy comes from three factors: (1) feeling understood by your partner; (2) feeling "validated," that

Passionate love: An intense feeling that involves sexual attraction, a desire for mutual love and physical closeness, arousal, and a fear that the relationship will end.

Compassionate love: A type of love marked by very close friendship, mutual caring, liking, respect, and attraction.

Triangular model of love: A theory of love marked by the dimensions of (1) passion (including sexual desire), (2) intimacy (closeness), and (3) commitment.

is, feeling that your emotions and point of view are respected; and (3) feeling that the other person cares for you (Reis & Shaver, 1988). As a relationship progresses, love seems to deepen over time (Sprecher, 1999). And just as mood can influence other aspects of our lives, such as memory and stereotyping, it influences us in this area as well: We are more likely to think our relationships are good when we're in a positive mood. Moreover, our attributions for serious conflicts in our relationships shift in response to our moods: In a bad mood, we are more likely to attribute relationship problems to vague, stable, internal factors; in a good mood, we are more likely to attribute the causes of conflict to specific, unstable, external factors (Forgas et al., 1994).

As noted, the way we think about people, things, and events can have a powerful effect on our feelings, behavior, and subsequent thoughts. This is also true of relationships. If you are asked to think about the external reasons and pressures to stay in a relationship (having something to do on Saturday nights, your parents' approval), you will view commitment to the relationship as less likely, and report less love for your partner, than if you think about the enjoyment you experience in the relationship and other intrinsic motivational factors (Seligman et al., 1980).

Mating Preferences: Your Cave or Mine?

Is love the reason why people settle down and have children? According to evolutionary theory, among our ancestors those couples more closely bonded to each other and to their children were more likely to have offspring who survived. Thus, evolutionary theorists propose, humans today are genetically predisposed not only to search for sex but also to fall in love and to tend to their children (Trivers, 1972).

Finding someone attractive and liking, or even loving, that person is different from choosing him or her as a mate; we may date people we wouldn't necessarily want to marry. Why do we view certain people as potential mates, and not others? Evolutionary theorists propose that men look for certain physical attributes that signal fertility and health, such as a well-proportioned body and symmetrical features (Thornhill & Gangestad, 1993). This view is supported by research with identical female twins; the twin whose face was more symmetrical was rated as more attractive (Mealey et al., 1999). In contrast, women find men attractive if they appear to be able to protect and nourish them and their children; in modern society, researchers translate this as having good earning potential (D. M. Buss, 1989, 1999; Sprecher, Sullivan, et al., 1994). Evolutionary psychologists have argued that characteristics associated with reproduction are particularly likely to have been shaped by natural selection. David Buss (1989) asked people in 37 countries to rank how important they believed 18 different characteristics are in ideal mates. In most respects, men and women valued the characteristics similarly; everybody agreed, for example, that kindness and intelligence are of paramount importance, and that emotional stability, dependability, and a good disposition are important (see also Cramer et al., 1996). Respondents also valued mutual attraction and love. However, men and women did not have identical desires: Men tended to focus on physical attractiveness, whereas women tended to focus on wealth and power. Basing his view on evolutionary theory (Trivers, 1972, 1985), Buss (1994) has argued that women seek characteristics in men that would direct resources to their children, whereas men seek characteristics in women that indicate high fertility.

However, Speed and Gangestad (1997) found slightly different results when they collected less subjective ratings. In their study, they asked members of a sorority and a fraternity house to nominate other members whom they felt scored high on specific qualities such as physi-

Evolutionary theorists propose that women are attracted to men who will be good providers and men are attracted to women who have physical attributes associated with fertility. However, not all research supports this view: As women gain more economic power, they become more interested in a man's attractiveness.

cal attractiveness and likelihood of financial success. The investigators then examined which of these characteristics predicted the frequency with which those nominated were asked out on dates. Perhaps the most interesting results concerned the men. As expected, romantically popular men were seen by their peers as confident, outgoing, and "trend-setting." However, they were not seen as likely to succeed financially or as the best leaders, both characteristics that would seem to reflect the qualities that evolution is supposed to favor in males.

Other studies have shown that as women come to have more economic power, their preference in mates becomes more similar to men's—that is, physical attractiveness becomes more important (Eagly & Wood, 1999; Gangestad, 1993). Women's preference for men who make good providers may reflect women's historic economic dependence on men rather than a true biological preference. In general, then, the sex differences are more pronounced in studies that use self-reports versus actual behavior (Feingold, 1990) and in situations in which women have less economic power.

However, evolution is more than natural selection (see Chapters 1 and 2); we have inherited some characteristics not because they are adaptive in themselves but rather because they are associated with other characteristics that are adaptive. Nor are the brain's circuits all dictated from birth: Learning rewires the brain, and development itself allows the environment to shape the way the brain works. Culture obviously plays an important role in shaping mate preferences: What is deemed an attractive body type changes with time (Wolf, 1991). Also, the characteristics that make a man a good provider depend in part on the culture; the properties that make a man a good rancher are not necessarily those of a good stockbroker. In short, it would be a serious error to assume that what people find attractive or unattractive can be entirely explained by analyses of what was useful for mating among our distant ancestors.

> **Group:** A social entity characterized by regular interaction among members, emotional connection, a common frame of reference, and interdependence.

What constitutes an "attractive" body type differs over time and across cultures. Women who today in America would be considered overweight or even obese have a body type that has been and continues to be attractive in some cultures.

Social Organization: Group Rules, Group Roles

The military tries to instill a sense of "groupness" in new recruits: The group's goal, such as a successful military action, is more important than an individual's goal, such as staying alive.

If you live with other people, in the same apartment or on the same dorm floor, you might agree that the people in your living unit constitute a group, even if you don't get along. But if you live in a building with a number of apartments, or a residence hall with many floors, would everyone living there be considered part of a larger group, even if they don't all know one another? What, exactly, constitutes a group? Social psychologists have long wrestled with such questions and have come up with a number of definitions. There are some commonalities, though, in the use of the term **group**: regular interaction among members, some type of emotional connection with one another, a common frame of reference, and some type of interdependence (Levine & Moreland, 1998). In a group, each of us may feel, think, and act less from the point of view of an individual and more from the point of view of a group member. Military training, such as boot camp, is a dramatic example of the shift from feeling like an individual to feeling like a group member: Loyalties and actions are no longer driven by individual goals but by group goals. In contrast, the use of the Internet for communication, although creating an opportunity to be part of a larger group in cyberspace, may not really promote a sense of interdependence, emotional connection, or "groupness." In one study, researchers examined the use of the Internet among people who did not previously have Internet access. Those who used the Internet more had decreased the size of their social circle from that of their pre-Internet days (and you know from Chapter 10 that social circles can provide a buffer against the harmful effects of stress), had less family communication, and experienced more loneliness and depression (Kraut et al., 1998).

At the other extreme of group experience is **deindividuation**, traditionally defined as the loss of sense of self that occurs when people in a group are literally *anonymous*—their identities are unknown to others in the group. This is often the situation in crowds. With deindividuation, attention is focused on external events, and a high level of arousal is experienced (Diener, 1977). When this occurs, the members of this temporary group respond to external cues and immediate feelings and act on them without monitoring the appropriateness of their behaviors. Violence by fans at European soccer matches has usually been explained by deindividuation. However, a meta-analytic study on deindividuation suggests that loss of self is not the precipitating cause of the behaviors attributed to deindividuation, as has traditionally been thought. Rather, the behaviors result from the sense, shared by members of the crowd, that in this limited circumstance certain behaviors are permissible that would not be acceptable otherwise (Postmes & Spears, 1998).

Recent research suggests that deindividuation may not be so much a loss of sense of self as situation-specific behaviors that are inconsistent with general expectations of appropriate behavior. At this European soccer match, disappointed fans behave violently, but they do not do so in other situations.

Norms

The Delany sisters recount that in their hometown of Raleigh, North Carolina, even strangers passing on the street would nod and say "good morning" or "good evening." But when Sadie and Bessie moved to New York City, they discovered that courteous behavior toward strangers did not always end in a pleasant exchange, and they had to learn new ways of behaving in their new social context. Perhaps you, like them on their arrival in New York, have at one time or another been the "new kid on the block"—in school or college, in a new neighborhood, in an already established group of people. Chances are you didn't know the "rules"—how people were supposed to behave toward one another, and especially how you, a new member, were supposed to behave. Once you figured things out by watching other people (Gilbert, 1995)—an obvious case of observational learning—you probably felt more comfortable in the group. And, in fact, groups create such rules and structures to help the group function.

The rules that implicitly or explicitly govern members of a group are called **norms.** They are, in essence, shared belief systems that are enforced through the group's use of sanctions, or penalties (Cialdini & Trost, 1998). Just as individuals have attitudes, groups have norms (Wellen et al., 1998). There are two kinds of

Deindividuation: The loss of sense of self that occurs when people are in a group but are anonymous.

Norm: A shared belief that is enforced through a group's use of penalties.

norms: *prescriptive norms,* which dictate which behaviors are acceptable (such as how much physical affection is allowed in a group), and *proscriptive norms,* which dictate what behaviors are not acceptable (such as passing gas while at a formal dinner). Some groups or cultures have "perverse" norms, norms that are formally agreed on but rarely enforced. On Boston's streets, for example, a traffic law for cars is that right turns may be made from the right lane only; however, it is not uncommon to see someone turn right from the left-hand lane in full view of police, who do not ticket for the offense. When perverse norms exist, those in authority maintain control by deciding when they are enforced (Dols, 1992, cited in M. Bond & Smith, 1996).

Although norms can endure over time, even if the members of the group change (Jacobs & Campbell, 1961), norms too can change. This is the case with the use of the title "Ms." When this form of address was introduced, it was seen as a title that would be used only by radical feminists. Now, however, Ms. is much more widely used and positively viewed (Crawford et al., 1998). Moreover, as adolescents in India watch Western television shows (and derive what they perceive of as Western norms), their attitudes about drugs, alcohol, and sex change, rejecting the social norms of Indian society and becoming more Western (Varma, 2000).

How we *perceive* norms is important. Even if those perceptions are not necessarily accurate, we still behave in accordance with them. For instance, some antidrug programs emphasize both *why* you should say no to drugs and *how* to say no. But it appears that training students *how* to say no leads them to think that offers of drugs, and drug use in general, are more common than they really are, thereby creating the impression of a pro–drug-use social norm and leading to an increase in drug use. This is particularly true for alcohol use among college students (see Table 13.3; Berkowitz, 1997). Programs that focus only on *why* you should say no appear to be more successful (Botvin, 1995; Cialdini & Trost; 1998; Donaldson, 1995; Hansen et al., 1988). Programs aimed at emphasizing a drug-abstinent norm or a moderate-drinking norm also appear to be effective (Barnett et al., 1996; Berkowitz, 1997).

This problem of falsely perceived norms may explain why eating disorder prevention programs that feature speakers who have recovered from an eating

Norms can affect all kinds of behavior, including a cold sufferer's willingness to wear a surgical mask when out in public. This Japanese woman is behaving according to one of her culture's proscriptive norms: It is frowned on for a cold sufferer to go outside without a mask and spread cold germs to others.

TABLE 13.3   Personal Attitudes and Perceived Norms

What college students *think* are the norms for alcohol use are not necessarily accurate. Most students in a 1986 study had a more conservative view of alcohol use than they thought their peers did, but their peers were similarly conservative. This table shows the percentage of students personally agreeing with each item, and the percentage of students who thought that an item was the "norm" on campus. As you can see, the only time students' personal attitudes were near the perceived norm was in the lack of enthusiasm for total abstinence.

Source: Adapted from Perkins & Berkowitz (1986).

ITEM	PERSONAL ATTITUDES (% OF STUDENTS AGREEING)	PERCEIVED NORM
Drinking is never a good thing to do.	1.4	0.1
Drinking is all right, but a student should never get "smashed."	12.7	0.8
An occasional "drunk" is okay as long as it doesn't interfere with grades or responsibilities.	66.0	35.4
An occasional "drunk" is okay even if it does occasionally interfere with grades or responsibilities.	9.3	33.2
A frequent "drunk" is okay if that's what the individual wants to do.	9.5	29.5

disorder may inadvertently lead students to develop eating disorder symptoms (Carter et al., 1997; Mann et al., 1997): Students inflate the perceived norm of eating disorders on campus after hearing and seeing the speaker and are thus led to change their behavior in the direction of the perceived norm.

Roles and Status

In contrast to norms, **roles** are the behaviors that members in different positions in a group are expected to perform. Groups often create different roles to fulfill different group functions. Sometimes roles are assigned officially, as when a group votes for a leader; sometimes roles are filled informally, without a specific election or appointment. Roles help a group delineate both responsibility *within* the group and responsibility *to* the group.

In a **status hierarchy**, different roles reflect the distribution of power in a group. The Delany sisters describe the status hierarchy of the South during and after Jim Crow laws: "White men were the most powerful, followed by white women. Colored people were absolutely below them and if you think it was hard for colored men, honey, colored women were on the bottom" (pp. 75–76). You can often tell who has a high-status position in a group from nonverbal cues: High-status members are more likely to maintain eye contact, be physically intrusive (somewhat "in your face"), and stand up straight (Leffler et al., 1982). You can also identify high-status members from what they say and how they say it: They are usually the ones who criticize or interrupt others or tell them what to do. In addition, other members direct their comments to the high-status member (Skvoretz, 1988). Perhaps because of the absence of nonverbal cues, social status differences have been found to be less prominent in groups communicating by email as opposed to face to face (Dubrovsky et al., 1991).

Yielding to Others: Going Along With the Group

In Raleigh when the Jim Crow laws were in effect, black customers in a white-owned shoe store were supposed to sit in the back of the store to try on shoes. On one occasion when Sadie shopped for shoes, she was asked by the white owner, Mr. Heller, to sit in the back. She asked, "Where, Mr. Heller?" And he gestured to the back saying, " 'Back there.' And I would say, 'Back *where?*' . . . Finally, he'd say, 'Just sit anywhere, Miss Delany.' And so I would sit myself down in the white section, and smile" (p. 84). What made Sadie able to resist Mr. Heller's request—or his order, backed by law? What made Mr. Heller give up his attempt to have Sadie comply with the law and social convention? What made him call her "Miss Delany" and not "Sadie"? What would you have done? In what circumstances do we go along with the group, do what someone asks of us, obey orders? When do we resist?

Conformity and Independence: Doing What's Expected

Social norms tell us how we ought to behave, and sometimes we change our beliefs or behavior so as to follow these norms. This change in beliefs or behavior because of pressure from others is known as **conformity.** For example, major league baseball players' wives live by an unwritten rule that they not go to the bars in hotels where the team is staying (Ortiz, 1997). The wife of a new player must decide whether to go along with this implicit norm. Similarly, immigrants must decide how much to conform to the norms of their new country and how much to retain the ways of their homeland (Lorenzo-Hernandez, 1998).

When and why do people conform? Suppose you are working in a study group that is trying to solve a complex engineering problem, or that you are part of a medical team trying to agree on a diagnosis of a particularly perplexing case. The majority agree on an answer that doesn't seem right to you. What would make

Role: The behaviors that a member in a given position in a group are expected to perform.

Status hierarchy: Roles that reflect who has power over whom.

Conformity: A change of beliefs or actions so as to follow a group's norms.

you more likely to go along with the majority view? Research indicates that *task difficulty* increases conformity: The harder the task, the more you are likely to conform—at least in part because you are less sure of yourself. *Social comparison* theory (Festinger, 1950) is consistent with this explanation: All people are driven to evaluate their abilities and opinions. When their abilities or views cannot be measured objectively, they seek out others, particularly people similar to themselves, to serve as a basis of comparison (Morris et al., 1976). Thus, even when we are initially certain, the disagreement of other members of our group can make us doubt (Orive, 1988). This process can explain why people succumb to the pressure to conform and why group members are ill tempered toward those who do not agree with the majority view (Levine, 1989).

Uncertainty in the face of a difficult task and social comparisons, however, cannot be the only explanations for conformity; people may also conform when tasks are easy, as demonstrated in pioneering research by Solomon Asch (1951, 1955). If you had been a participant in Asch's original study, you would have found yourself in a group with five to seven others asked to perform a task of visual perception. You are all shown a target line and asked to say which of three other lines matches the length of the target line. Each person gives an answer aloud; you are next to last. This sounds like an easy task, as you can see in Figure 13.4, but it soon becomes perplexing. For 12 of the 18 times you are shown the lines, everyone else gives the wrong answer! Will you agree with the answer everyone else is giving?

In fact, in Asch's experiment only one person in the group was the true participant; the others were accomplices playing a role. Seventy-six percent of participants

Figure 13.4   Asch's Conformity Study

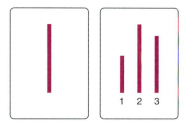

Participants in Asch's classic study on conformity were shown lines similar to these and asked the following type of question: Here are three lines of different lengths and a fourth target line. Which of the three lines matches the target line?

Only two people have yet to give their opinions, but everyone else appears to have given the same incorrect answer. Which would you say was the correct line if you were next in line? Asch (1951, 1955) created this situation with the use of accomplices, and the true participant was the next-to-last person. Although 76% of participants conformed to the incorrect group response at least once, over the entire experiment, approximately two thirds of responses were independent of the majority.

went along with the accomplices at least once, and overall approximately one-third of participants' responses conformed with the obviously wrong majority.

Why would these people conform with the norm established by the group? Variations on Asch's original experiment showed that characteristics of the situation are part of the answer. When participants *wrote* their answers instead of announcing them to the group, they gave the correct response 98% of the time, reflecting the fact that participants accurately perceived the lines. *Social support* also influences conformity. If a group member openly disagrees with the group consensus, conformity is less likely (Morris & Miller, 1975). When Asch had one accomplice disagree—that is, give the correct answer—91% of actual participants did not conform with the group answer. Furthermore, the more *cohesive* a group— the more attraction and commitment members have toward it—the more likely members are to conform, as are those who identify more strongly with its norms (Prapavessis & Carron, 1997; Terry & Hogg, 1996). And when a member of a less powerful group, such as a social or political minority, is in a group with more powerful members, the minority member may be more likely to conform (Roll et al., 1996). In general, despite the pressure to conform to group norms, not everyone is equally affected (Trafimow & Finlay, 1996).

One person not given to conformity for its own sake was Sadie and Bessie Delany's maternal grandfather, James Millam. A white man, he fell in love with a free woman, Martha Logan, who was one-quarter black; marriage between them was, at the time, illegal. In such situations, it was usual for the man to marry a white woman and establish the black woman as his mistress. Millam refused to conform to this convention; he lived openly with Martha Logan without benefit of marriage. Why would he not conform? Because to go along with the group, to conform, against one's beliefs or better judgment, leads to a loss of choice, of independence. The desire to retain a sense of individuality (Maslach et al., 1987) or control (Burger, 1992; Burger & Cooper, 1979) also provides reasons for not conforming. Thus, to understand someone's choice to conform, you need to look not only at the situation and the group but also at that person's characteristics—such as his or her commitment to the group or desire for individuality.

Were the people in Asch's study typical? All were men, but the results of later studies with women were similar (Eagly & Carli, 1981). However, Asch's original participants may have been influenced by their culture. His experiment has been repeated by many researchers in many countries, and studies in countries with a more collectivist orientation, such as China, found higher levels of conformity than did those in individualistic countries (R. Bond & Smith, 1996). Furthermore, the findings of conformity studies over the years suggest that conformity has decreased since Asch's original work (R. Bond & Smith, 1996). Thus, characteristics of the individual, his or her relationship to the group, characteristics of the group, and the larger culture can all affect conformity and independence.

Compliance: Doing What You're Asked

Even if you don't want to go along with a group's norms, you may be willing to comply with a direct request, as occurs when someone asks, "Could you please tell me how to get to the library?" **Compliance** is a change in behavior brought about through a direct request rather than by social norms. When the driver of the car in the next lane gestures to you, asking to be let into your lane in front of you, you will either comply or not.

Without realizing it, you are a target of multiple requests for compliance each day, from television commercials, in conversations with friends, or through questions on a survey form. Skill at getting people to comply is key to success in many occupations, from sales and advertising to lobbying, politics, and health prevention programs. Psychologist Robert Cialdini decided to find out from "compliance professionals"—people in jobs such as advertising, fundraising, and door-to-door

Compliance: A change in behavior prompted by a direct request rather than social norms.

sales—exactly what they know about the subject. He inferred that the essence of effective compliance techniques lies in six principles (Cialdini, 1994):

1. *Friendship/liking.* People are more likely to comply with a request from a friend than from a stranger.
2. *Commitment/consistency.* The likelihood of compliance increases when the request is consistent with a previous commitment.
3. *Scarcity.* People are more likely to comply with requests related to limited, short-term, rather than open-ended, opportunities.
4. *Reciprocity.* The likelihood of compliance rises when the request comes from someone who has provided a favor.
5. *Social validation.* The likelihood of compliance rises if people think that others similar to themselves would comply.
6. *Authority.* People tend to comply with a request if it comes from someone who appears to be in authority.

To see these principles at work, let's examine a few of the techniques most often used to win compliance. The commitment/consistency principle helps to explain why a classic compliance technique, the **foot-in-the-door technique**, works so often. In this method, first you make an insignificant request; if you meet with compliance, you follow up with a larger request. Consider the study by Freedman and Fraser (1966), who had a male experimenter phone housewives, asking what soap they used. Three days later, the same man telephoned and asked if five or six people could perform a 2-hour inventory of everything in the housewife's cupboards, drawers, and closets. Fifty-three percent of the housewives who had agreed to the simple first request agreed to this much larger second request. In contrast, when housewives did not receive the first request but were asked to allow the inventory, only 22% complied.

The foot-in-the-door technique appears to work, at least in part, because people want to seem consistent. If you agree to the first request, you are being a nice person; declining the second request would call this self-perception into question. The commitment/consistency principle also explains the success of an unethical sales technique, the **lowball technique**, which consists of first getting someone to make an agreement, and then increasing the cost of that agreement. Suppose you see an advertisement for some shoes you've been eyeing—for a very low price. You go the store and are told that the shoes are no longer available at that price, but you can get them for a somewhat higher (although still discounted) price. What do you do? Many people would comply with the request to buy the shoes at the higher price.

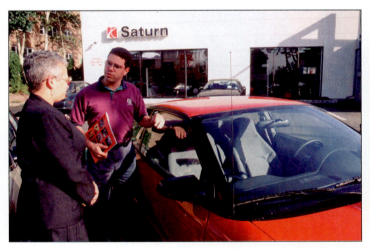

Turning the foot-in-the-door procedure backward also works; this is the **door-in-the-face technique.** You begin by making a very large request; when it is denied, as expected, you make a smaller request, for what you actually wanted in the first place. For instance, in one study (Cialdini et al., 1975), college students were stopped on campus and asked to serve as unpaid counselors to a group of juvenile delinquents for 2 hours a week for 2 years. Not surprisingly, no one agreed. Then the same students were asked to take the group on a 2-hour field trip. Fifty percent agreed. In contrast, when students were asked only to make the field trip without the larger, first request, only 17% agreed.

The door-in-the-face technique is a staple of diplomacy and labor–management negotiations. Why does it work? The reciprocity principle may hold the answer. If your first request is denied and you then make a smaller one, you appear to be making concessions, and the other party tries to reciprocate.

Car sales people are notorious for using the lowball technique. Some car makers, however, have changed their pricing policies so that there is less opportunity for the lowball technique.

Obedience: Doing as You're Told

If people can be so obliging in response to a polite request, what happens when they receive an order? Compliance with an order is called **obedience.** The nature of obedience attracted intense study in the United States after World War II, when the world heard about atrocities apparently committed in the name of obedience.

The most famous study of obedience was done by Stanley Milgram (1963). Milgram expected that Americans would not follow orders to inflict pain on innocent people. In testing this hypothesis, his challenge was to design a study that gave the appearance of inflicting pain without actually doing so. He hit on the following procedure: Suppose you volunteered to participate in a study of memory. You are asked to act the part of "teacher" (see Figure 13.5). You are paired with a "learner" (an accomplice), who, you are told, was asked to memorize a list of pairs of common words. You, the teacher, are to present one word from each pair and keep track of how well the learner does in correctly remembering the other word. If the learner makes a mistake, you are to administer a shock, increasing the voltage with each successive mistake. Although the shock generator is a phony and no shock at all is administered, you do not know this.

This is precisely what Milgram did; by prearrangement, at "120 volts" the learner shouted that the shocks were becoming too painful. At "150 volts" the learner asked to stop. At 180 he screamed that he couldn't stand the pain. At 300 volts he pounded on the wall and demanded to be set free. At 330 volts there was only silence—an "incorrect response" according to the directions of the experimenter, who stood beside the teacher.

Figure 13.5 The Milgram Obedience Study

Each participant was paired with another man, having drawn lots to decide who would be the "teacher" and the "learner." In fact, the participant was always the teacher. The learner was always the same 47-year-old accountant who was an accomplice in the study. The man who introduced himself as the experimenter was an actor. The learner was asked to memorize a list of pairs of common words; the teacher was to present the words, keep track of how well the learner did, and punish the learner for incorrect responses. The teacher watched as the learner was brought to a cubicle where the experimenter asked him to sit down and strapped him in a chair to "prevent excess movement." The experimenter attached shock electrodes to his wrist. Throughout the remainder of the study, the teacher could not see the learner, and all communication was via an intercom.

The teacher was seated in front of the shock generator. The generator had 30 switches labeled in 15-volt increments from 15 to 450 volts. A description below each switch ranged from "Slight Shock" to "Danger: Severe Shock." The labels under the last two switches were ominous: "XXX." At the outset the teacher was given a sample shock of 45 volts so that he could know what it felt like.

How far would you go in obeying the experimenter's instructions? If you were like the participants in Milgram's study, when the learner cried out in pain or refused to go on, you would turn to the experimenter for instructions, who would reply that the experiment had to proceed and that he would take full responsibility. Would you obey? When Milgram described the experiment to a group of psychiatrists, they predicted that only a "pathological fringe" of at most 2% of the population would go to the maximum shock level. In fact, much to Milgram's surprise, 65% of the participants went to the highest level. Some of the participants, but apparently not all, felt terrible about what they were doing. But they still continued to administer the shocks.

The willingness of so many of Milgram's participants to obey orders to hurt others disturbed many people. Was there something distinctive about Milgram's participants that could explain the results? In the original studies, the participants were men. Later studies, however, found similar results with women (Milgram, 1965, 1974), as well as with people in Jordan, Germany, and Australia, and with children (Kilham & Mann, 1974; Shanab & Yahya, 1977).

Why did so many participants obey orders to hurt someone else? Were there particular characteristics of the situation that fostered obedience? Compliance research suggests two ways in which the design increased the likelihood of obedience. First, Milgram's experiment applied something like the foot-in-the-door-technique: Participants were first asked to give a trivial amount of shock before going on to give apparently harmful ones. When the participants were allowed to set the punishment voltage themselves, none ever went past 45 volts. Second, additional research indicated that people become more likely to comply with a request if it comes from someone in authority; the same holds true for obedience (Bushman, 1984, 1988). In a variant of the study (Milgram, 1974), when a college student was the one who gave a fellow student the order to shock instead of an older, white-coated experimenter, compliance fell to only 20%. When the experimenters were two authority figures who disagreed with each other, no participants administered further shocks. It appears that the more authoritative the person who gives the order, the more likely it is to be obeyed.

Later variations of Milgram's original study point to other characteristics of the situation that have an important influence on obedience. *Proximity* to the learner is one. When teachers saw the learners while they were being shocked, and even held an electrode directly on the accomplice's skin (with a "special insulating glove"), 30% progressed to the maximum voltage, compared with 65% in the original design. Proximity to the experimenter also matters: When the experimenter telephoned his commands instead of giving face-to-face instructions, obedience dropped to 21%.

Disturbing as Milgram's results were, it is important to remember that not all participants obeyed the experimenter, and in some conditions the great majority did not obey; it is the specifics of the situation (such as proximity to the learner) that influences an individual's willingness to obey an order to hurt someone else (Blass, 1999; Gibson, 1991; Miller et al., 1995).

Performance in Groups: Working Together

When Sadie and Bessie went to New York City, they moved into their brother Hubert's apartment, along with another brother and sister. Now there were five Delanys living in a three-room apartment. In such tight quarters, it helped to be very organized and to have clear rules and clear roles. Even though the apartment was Hubert's, and they all participated in making decisions, Sadie would have the final say because she was the oldest. How do groups make decisions? What are the advantages and disadvantages of working as a group?

Decision Making in Groups: Paths to a Decision

After living in Hubert's apartment for a while, Sadie and Bessie got a place of their own in New York, and their mother came to live with them. However, at some point, their mother's health began to fade, and it was no longer safe for her to be home alone all day while her daughters were at work. The situation required that one of them leave her job to stay home with Mrs. Delany (it never occurred to them to hire someone to stay at home with their mother while they were out at work). How did they decide who would stay home? This question faces many families today, and the path to a solution often involves group decision making. Decision making also occurs in other contexts: Political parties, military planners, and athletic teams must decide on strategies; clinical groups must decide who receives what medical treatment and for how long; college admissions officers decide who is accepted and who is not. How are decisions made in groups?

In general, if a group is not initially unanimously in favor of a particular decision, it is likely that the view favored by the majority will prevail (Levine & Moreland, 1998). The larger the majority, the more likely it is that their choice will "win." This path is known as the *majority-win rule,* and it works well when the decision involves judgments or opinions. But there are times—you may have been present at some—when what began as the minority position eventually "wins." When there is an objectively correct answer, the *truth-win rule* works well because its inherent worthiness is recognized by the group (Kirchler & Davis, 1986). In general, groups reach a better decision when one solution can be shown to be correct (Hastie, 1986; Laughlin & Ellis, 1986). Consider the decision the Delany sisters made about caring for their mother: Bessie closed her dental practice and stayed home. Their reasoning was economic. Bessie was self-employed and had neither retirement benefits nor job stability. Sadie, as a teacher employed by a city, had both, as long as she worked until she was eligible for retirement. Thus, it was to the family's long-term financial advantage to have Bessie stay home, even though Sadie would have been more temperamentally suited for the task. In this case, the "truth"—the objectively advantageous long-term financial reality—won.

An interesting facet of group decision making is the way that a group "remembers" information to decide what to do. The memory of the group as a whole can in fact be better than the memory of any individual alone. Groups that learn new information together are more likely to remember the information accurately when together than those whose members learned the information individually, at least on some group tasks (Liang et al., 1995).

The variety of people in a group may also affect its decision-making process and performance. In general, as a group becomes more heterogeneous, it communicates less effectively (Maznevski, 1994; Zenger & Lawrence, 1989), and subgroups of similar members may form, causing nonsimilar members to feel alienated (Jackson et al., 1991). Some of the negative effects of heterogeneous groups can be minimized in the following ways: education about similarities and differences; recategorization by increasing a sense of the group as a team (creating an "us"); increasing social skills among members; and learning conflict resolution skills (Caudron, 1994). Paradoxically, although heterogeneity can create some group conflict, it can also have a positive effect on the group's performance (McLeod & Lobel, 1992) because of the increased innovation and flexibility that diversity brings to a group (Levine & Moreland, 1998).

Group decision making does not always lead to the best decision. The opinion of a powerful member can shift others' opinions by might rather than right. Group decisions can be marred by **group polarization**, the tendency of members of the group to take more extreme positions (in the same direction as their initial opinions) after discussion (Isenberg, 1986; Levine & Moreland, 1998). Thus, when debating the merits of impeaching President Clinton in 1998 in the House Judiciary Committee, Republicans who may have only moderately favored impeachment likely left the session more strongly in favor. As became clear during the

Group polarization: The tendency of group members' opinions to become more extreme (in the same direction as their initial opinions) after group discussion.

impeachment process, this polarization of attitude can last beyond the initial discussion (Liu & Latané, 1998).

One reason why group polarization develops is that some members of the group may give many very compelling reasons for their initial views. In listening to these reasons, members who are in general agreement may become more convinced of the correctness of that initial assessment and more extreme in their views (Burnstein, 1982). This route to group polarization is more likely to be a factor when an intellectual issue is at stake, or when the group's goal is to make a "correct" or task-oriented decision (Kaplan, 1987). Another reason behind group polarization is that, through discussion, members can figure out the group's "normative" position on the issue and may be tempted to increase their standing in the group (and improve their view of themselves) by taking a more extreme position in accordance with the group norm (Goethals & Zanna, 1979). Thus, seeing that most Republicans were in favor of *some* action against Clinton (the normative attitude), members of the committee began to outdo one another in presenting pro-impeachment arguments. This route to group polarization is likely when the issue requires judgments, and when the group is more focused on group harmony than on correctness (Kaplan, 1987).

Decisions can also go awry through **groupthink**—the tendency of people who try to solve problems together to accept one another's information and ideas without subjecting them to critical analysis. The phenomenon of groupthink impels every member to feel that the group's decision must be supported, and consensus becomes more important than the critical appraisal of different positions (Janis, 1982).

Groupthink: The tendency of people who try to solve problems together to accept one another's information and ideas without subjecting them to critical analysis.

Social loafing: The tendency to work less hard when responsibility for an outcome is spread over the group's members.

Social facilitation: The increase in performance that can occur simply by being part of a group or in the presence of other people.

Social Loafing

When responsibility for an outcome is spread among the members of the group, some members may be likely to let other members work harder (Latané et al., 1979), a phenomenon that has been called **social loafing.** One way to prevent social loafing is to instill a sense of importance and responsibility in each person's work, even if the work is boring or if the member's contribution is anonymous (Harkins & Petty, 1982). Making the task attractive also reduces social loafing, as does knowing that individual as well as group performance will be evaluated (Harkins & Szymanski, 1989; Hoeksema-van Orden et al., 1998; Karau & Williams, 1993). If you have lived with other people, you may have experienced the effects of social loafing: When dishes pile up in the sink or the bathroom goes uncleaned for weeks, each member of the household is doing a little social loafing, waiting for someone else to do the cleaning.

When a group as a whole is responsible for a task, some members may work less hard than they would if they were individually responsible for a task. This tendency toward social loafing can be countered by evaluating everyone's performance separately or by making the task attractive.

Although working in groups may lead some people to indulge in social loafing, it may lead others to engage in *social compensation,* working harder in a group than they do when they are alone. Social compensation usually occurs when some members of the group see the task to be done as important but don't expect that other members will pull their weight (Williams & Karau, 1991). Social compensation occurs when someone finally washes the dishes or cleans the bathroom: The mess bothers someone enough that he or she cleans it all up. But the one cleaning is doing more than his or her share.

Social Facilitation: Everybody Loves an Audience

Sometimes being part of a group, or just being in the presence of other people, can increase performance; this effect is called **social facilitation.** However, usually the presence of others enhances performance only on well-learned simple tasks; on complicated, less well-learned tasks, the presence of others can hinder our performance (Guerin, 1993). The presence of others appears to increase our arousal, which then facilitates our *dominant* response in that situation (Schmitt et al., 1986; Seta & Seta, 1992). Thus, well-learned responses are likely to come to the fore when we are aroused, and we will be less likely to execute complicated or recently learned behaviors. Hence, at a concert a musician may perform an old song better than a new one.

Helping Behavior: Helping Others

New York City's firefighters displayed their altruism both when they went into the burning World Trade Center towers in 2001 to rescue people inside, and when they searched through the burning rubble for survivors.

When Bessie Delany began her dentistry practice in 1923, both cleanings and extractions were $2 each, and a silver filling cost $5. When she retired in 1950, she charged the same rates and was proud of it. In fact, she treated people regardless of their ability to pay. The Delany family ethic was to help others. This quality is called **altruism**, the desire to increase the welfare of others without expecting anything in return. What made Bessie so willing to help others? Why do we help other people? What circumstances encourage altruism?

Prosocial Behavior

Acting to benefit others, called **prosocial behavior**, includes sharing, cooperating, comforting, and helping (Batson, 1998). Whether we help someone depends on factors about us and the person we could help. We are more likely to help others if we have certain personality traits, such as a high need for approval, or a predisposition to feeling personal and social responsibility, or an empathic concern for others (Batson et al., 1986; Eisenberg et al., 1989). People who tend to be helpers also have a sense of empathy, a belief in a just world, an internal locus of control, and less concern for their own welfare (Bierhoff et al., 1991). Bessie Delany seemed to feel a sense of personal and social responsibility toward others and could empathize with their plights. She also appeared to have less concern for her own welfare; when she was in dental school, a white girl born with syphilis came to the dental clinic—only Bessie volunteered to help her.

Some people in need of assistance are more likely to be helped than others. Who are they? First, we are more likely to help people we view as similar to ourselves. Consider an experiment in which Americans in three foreign cities asked for directions: Residents of those cities who were similar in age to the Americans requesting help were more likely to give directions (Rabinowitz et al., 1997). Second, we are more likely to help friends or people we like (remember, similarity facilitates liking). Third, we are more likely to help people we believe are not responsible for their predicaments, or people who give a socially acceptable justification for their plight (Weiner, 1980). In fact, the more justification the requester gives, the more likely he or she is to receive help (Bohm & Hendricks, 1997).

Sometimes we may be faced with a choice between acting in our own personal interest and acting for the common good. When we choose not to act on the group's behalf, our distressing feelings, often resulting from cognitive dissonance, may be assuaged in a number of ways. Some people perform a prosocial act *other than* the one facing them (McMillen & Austin, 1971); others minimize the impact they would have made had they chosen to cooperate—"I probably couldn't have made a difference anyway" (Kerr & Kaufman-Gilliland, 1997).

Group identity also plays a role in prosocial behavior. We are more likely to help and cooperate with other members of our group. Principles of learning (see Chapter 4) are also influential. Through our learning histories, we may have been reinforced for helping, or punished for not helping. Parents, teachers, and others were models for observational learning. Thus, in time, we come to reward ourselves for helping, feel good after helping, and punish ourselves or feel guilty when we don't (Batson, 1998).

Altruism: The desire to increase the welfare of others without expecting anything in return.

Prosocial behavior: Acting to benefit others.

Bystander Intervention

A great deal has been learned about a specific type of prosocial behavior—bystander intervention—as a result of research inspired by one dreadful incident. At about 3 A.M. on March 13, 1964, a 28-year-old woman named Catherine Genovese—known to her neighbors as Kitty—was brutally murdered in Queens, a borough of New York City, only minutes from her own apartment building. She was coming home from work as a manager of a bar. When her attacker first caught and stabbed her, she screamed for help. The lights came on in several apartments overlooking the scene of the crime, and a man yelled down to her attacker to leave her alone. Her attacker briefly stopped and walked away. The apartment lights went out. The attacker returned and stabbed her again; she screamed again, to no avail, although lights again came on in the surrounding apartments. The attacker left in a car, and Kitty Genovese dragged herself to the lobby of an apartment building near her own. The attacker returned again, and this time he kept stabbing her until she died. The gruesome ordeal took some 35 minutes and was viewed by at least 38 witnesses. Only one person called the police (Rosenthal, 1964).

Darley and Latané (1968) hypothesized that if only a few bystanders had witnessed the crime, those few would have been more likely to help Kitty Genovese. This relationship is known as the **bystander effect**: As the number of bystanders increases, offers of assistance decrease. To test this relationship, Darley and Latané, with the aid of accomplices, created the following situation. Imagine yourself as

Bystander effect: The decrease in offers of assistance that occurs as the number of bystanders increases.

Figure 13.6 Bystander Intervention

Participants thought they were involved in a study of campus life but instead were exposed to an "emergency" with a varying number of bystanders. Participants went into a private cubicle and were told that they could all hear one another, but only one student would be able to speak during any 2-minute period; when all had spoken, the cycle would start again. They were also told that the experimenter would not be listening. Participants were led to believe that either four, one, or no other students ("bystanders") were listening. In fact, there was only one true participant at a time; the rest of the voices on the intercom were prerecorded tapes.

The crisis came after one (prerecorded) voice confessed to having seizures in stressful situations. This person subsequently seemed to be having a seizure, and asked for help.

Would participants leave their cubicles to get help? Their responses depended greatly on the perceived number of bystanders. The great majority of participants went to get help when they thought they were the only ones aware of the problem, but they helped less often and were slower to get help the more bystanders they thought were aware of the problem.

Diffusion of responsibility: The diminished sense of responsibility to help that each person feels as the number of bystanders grows.

a participant in a study, taking part in a telephone conference about campus life with a number of others. Each participant speaks without interruption, and when everyone has spoken, the first person gets to speak again, and so on. Suppose another participant mentions that when stressed he gets seizures; then you hear that person stutter, start to choke, and ask for help. Would you go get help? If you were like most participants in Darley and Latané's study (1968) (see Figure 13.6), if you believed there were only two people in the telephone conference—you and the person with seizures—you would very likely seek help. But if you had been told there were three participants, you would be less likely to seek help, and even less likely with a total of six. In short, attempts to help rose as the number of apparent bystanders dropped. Thus, when participants thought that they were the only one aware of the "emergency," 85% of them left the cubicle and got the experimenter within the first minute. When they thought there was one other bystander, 65% helped within the first minute. When participants thought there were four other bystanders, only 25% helped within the first minute. At the end of 4 minutes, all in the smallest group helped, as did 85% of those in the mid-size group, but only 60% in the largest group.

From this and other studies, Darley and Latané (1970) described five steps, or "choice points," in bystander intervention.

Step 1. Is an emergency actually noticed by the bystander? If yes, proceed to Step 2. If no, no help is given.

Step 2. Is the bystander correctly perceiving the event as an emergency? If yes, proceed to Step 3. If no, no help is given.

Step 3. Does the bystander assume responsibility to intervene? If yes, proceed to Step 4. If no, no help is given.

Step 4. Does the bystander know what to do, how to be helpful? If yes, proceed to Step 5. If no, no help is given.

Step 5. Is the bystander motivated enough to help, despite possible negative consequences? If yes, then he or she intervenes.

At each step, various factors, such as the number of bystanders and characteristics of the bystanders, shape the likelihood that someone will help. For example, consider Step 2, perceiving the event. If a situation is ambiguous, leaving you uncertain about whether the emergency is real, you may hesitate to offer help. If other bystanders are present, your hesitancy may be increased by *evaluation apprehension*—a fear that you might be embarrassed or ridiculed if you try to intervene because there may be no emergency after all. The number of bystanders also influences Step 3, assuming responsibility. The more bystanders there are, the less each one feels responsible to help, creating a **diffusion of responsibility.** Interestingly, once people have learned about the bystander effect, they are subsequently more likely to intervene (Beaman et al., 1978).

LOOKING AT LEVELS

Cults

In 1997 members of the Heaven's Gate cult killed themselves in order to ascend to join an alien spaceship that they believed was hidden behind the Hale–Bopp Comet, which they believed would take them to the next level of existence. How is it that cults exert such a powerful influence on their members? We can best understand how cults function by looking at the phenomenon from the three levels of analysis and their interactions. At the level of the brain, the bodily functions of cult members, such as eating, sleeping, and sexual relations (in those cults that permit them), are carefully monitored. New recruits in many cults are often physically and mentally exhausted after listening to music, chanting, or other auditory stimuli for hours on end (Streiker, 1984), which can induce a meditative or hypnotic-like state that alters brain function as well as the sense of reality.

At the level of the person, many cults try to eliminate members' experience of themselves as individuals. In the Heaven's Gate group, each day was structured down to the minute so as to minimize the sense of self and individual choice. Moreover, members were forbidden to trust their own judgments or to have "inappropriate" curiosity (Bearak, 1997). Members, particularly new ones, were not allowed to be alone, even in the bathroom. These measures, as well as the altered state of consciousness and the exhaustion, can induce a sense of depersonalization (the experience of observing oneself as if from the outside) and derealization (the sense that familiar objects have changed or seem unreal), as well as deindividuation.

At the level of the group, the arousal and unpleasant effects of the derealization are calmed by listening to the group and by being cared for by others. This resulting dependency on the group increases the desire to remain part of the group. Performing actions at the behest of the group that would otherwise be refused, such as begging for money or having sexual relations (raising issues of compliance and obedience), can induce cognitive dissonance; only a change in attitude can then resolve the discomfort aroused. Moreover, members receive enormous amounts of attention and reinforcement, sometimes called "love-bombing," for behaving in desired ways—in other words, conforming to their expected role and to group norms. Group polarization and groupthink may affect the group's decision making. Perhaps these group processes led to the decision that group suicide was an effective way to join the alien spaceship.

Events at these levels of analysis interact: The unpleasant bodily and psychological states are relieved when desired behaviors are performed, in a process of negative reinforcement; this relief leads to a change in self-concept and a heightened importance of, and dependence on, the group.

CONSOLIDATE!

1 *What psychological principles explain why we like certain people and not others?* If our first impression of someone is positive, we are more apt to like that person with repeated contact, if the person is similar to us and is physically attractive to us. Liking is not the same as loving, which can be passionate or compassionate. According to Sternberg's triangular theory, love has three dimensions: passion, intimacy, and commitment. Relationships reflect different proportions of each dimension, and those proportions change over time. People's attachment styles—secure, avoidant, or anxious–ambivalent—also affect the pattern of relationships they will develop.

2 *Why do all groups have rules for social behavior and organization?* Social norms and roles help a group function, defining appropriate and inappropriate behavior for some or all members; they also help new members learn how to function in the group. The perception of a norm can affect members' behavior, even if that perception is inaccurate, as has been the case with some drug prevention programs. Within a group, a status hierarchy reflects the distribution of power assigned to each role.

3 *Why do we sometimes "go along" with or obey others even when we don't want to? What makes us able to refuse?* If we hold a minority position, we may come to doubt the correctness of our view; we tend to conform to the majority view when the task at hand is difficult. Furthermore, as Asch's studies showed, we are more likely to conform to the majority view when we are part of a cohesive group. In contrast, we are less likely to conform to the majority view if another member also does not conform to that position or if we have a strong desire to retain a sense of individuality. Compliance with a request can be maximized when the person making the request is a friend, someone who has provided a favor in the past, or someone in authority. We are also more likely to comply if we think people similar to ourselves would comply. A number of persuasion techniques make use of compliance principles, including the foot-in-the-door technique, the lowball technique, and the door-in-the-face technique. Obedience to a command with which we don't agree is more likely when compliance principles are used, as well as when the person issuing commands is nearby. However, not everyone obeys such orders, and the specifics of the situation help determine the level of obedience.

4 *Does being part of a group change our behavior? How do groups make decisions?* Groups can make decisions according to the majority-win or truth-win rule; the latter is more likely when one answer is objectively correct. Although more heterogeneous groups may communicate less effectively, they may also be more innovative and flexible because of their diversity. Examples of group decision making gone awry are found in group polarization and groupthink. Being part of a group can cause people to do less than their share (social loafing) or more than their share (social compensation). Moreover, just being in the presence of others can increase someone's performance of a well-learned task (social facilitation), but have the opposite effect on newly learned skills.

5 *Are some people more helpful than others? Why would we not help other people?* People with certain personality traits are more likely to help others. Those traits include a high need for approval and a feeling of social responsibility. We are more likely to help people who seem similar to ourselves, people we like, or people who have a socially justifiable reason for needing help. The more bystanders on hand (diffusion of responsibility) or the more ambiguous the situation, the less likely we are to help.

A Final Word: Ethics and Social Psychology

The researchers involved in many of the studies described in this chapter did not tell participants about the true nature of the experiments at the outset, and several used accomplices. As discussed in the section on ethics in Chapter 1, many of the classic social psychology studies were carried out before the discipline established rigorous ethical guidelines. In fact, many of the guidelines were formulated *because* these studies raised serious ethical concerns. Keep in mind several issues related to the use of deception in psychology. First, many of the pioneering researchers did not expect to cause psychological distress. For example, Milgram initially did not expect participants to be willing to shock learners at higher "voltage" levels, although he did continue to perform variants of his study after he knew the results of his first study. Second, some psychological phenomena are extremely difficult, if not impossible, to study if the participant knows the true nature of the experiment. For example, could you think of a way to design a study on conformity *without* using deception? Third, at present, to receive approval for a study that uses deception, researchers must show that the deception is absolutely necessary (that the information could not be ascertained without deception); that the information is valuable and the deception minimal; and that at the conclusion of the study, the investigators will fully explain to the participants the nature of the study and the reasons for deception. In short, today deception is permitted in research only if it is crystal clear that the participants will not be harmed and important knowledge will be gained.

A DEEPER LEVEL

Recap and Thought Questions

Social Cognition: Thinking About People

Attitudes and stereotypes help lessen the cognitive effort of understanding the social world. Our impressions, attitudes, stereotypes, and attributions affect how we encode, store, and retrieve information. Our attitudes can affect our behavior and are especially likely to do so when they are strong, stable, relevant, and salient. Conflict between attitudes and behavior (or between two attitudes) can lead to cognitive dissonance, which we are then driven to reduce. The human process of categorizing objects (including people) leads to stereotypes, and our stereotypes of others not only affect our behavior but can also affect the way others behave toward us and lead to prejudice and discrimination. Because stereotypes create biases in the way we process information, our stereotypes often seem more accurate than they really are and thus are difficult to change. Although we are driven to make attributions to understand events, our reasoning about the causes of these events may rely on the fundamental attribution error and other attributional biases, possibly leading us to understand people's behavior in inaccurate ways.

What does social cognition have to do with the Delanys? The Delanys, like all of us, tried to make sense of the social world around them. Rather than actively process every bit of information presented to them, they relied on cognitive shortcuts. Thus, the Delanys developed attitudes about other people (such as New Yorkers walking down the street or Mr. Heller), which influenced their behavior toward others. In addition, other people's stereotypes of blacks and women affected how they treated the Delanys; negative attitudes (prejudice) may have led to discriminatory behavior; prejudice toward the sisters may have been unconscious. All these cognitive processes influence the attributions people make to explain the Delany sisters' successes.

Think It Through. If you were to design an anti-smoking campaign based on your knowledge of persuasion and stereotypes, what strategies might you include? If you wanted to help people resist the pull of advertisements or political campaigns, what information would be particularly important to convey? Explain.

Social Behavior: Interacting With People

Psychological factors lead us to behave in certain ways when we are with others. In our intimate relationships, we are more likely to be attracted to, and to like, people we view as similar to ourselves. Love can be understood using Sternberg's triangular model or looking at different styles of attachment. All groups have norms and roles

and assign status to members; these factors are used to obtain conformity, compliance, and obedience from the members of the group. The style of a group's decision making depends on the group's goals and on the ways group members articulate their views on an issue before the group. Being in a group can help or harm a given individual's performance. Psychological principles are at work in determining when and whom we help.

How can psychological research results help us understand the Delany sisters' interactions with other people? The Delany sisters' interactions with others were governed by social psychological principles. For instance, their interactions with strangers on New York City streets were at first determined by their previous experience with the social norms and roles of Raleigh; when the social norms of New York proved different, their behavior changed accordingly. During and after Jim Crow, their behavior generally conformed to the norms (and laws), but not always, as Sadie's experience with Mr. Heller in the shoe store illustrates. Moreover, Bessie's altruism (performing dental work on the syphilitic girl) reflects a strong sense of empathy and social responsibility, traits that are more likely to lead to helping behavior.

Think It Through. Imagine that you have started a new job working in a large company. Based on what you have learned, what colleagues are you likely to be attracted to and why? What are you likely to know about the structure of your work group—its norms, roles, and the like—even before your first day? If your boss wants employees to do something "slightly illegal," what factors may make employees less likely to go along with this request (or order)? Will working as a group change the way the work is performed? Why or why not? If an employee is injured at work, what factors may make the employees who witness the incident more likely to help?

REVIEW TEST

For each of the following items, choose the single correct or best answer. The correct answers appear at the end.

 In the 1930s, psychologist La Piere found what relationship between behaviors and subsequently reported attitudes?
a. Positive attitudes predicted positive behaviors.
b. Negative attitudes predicted negative behaviors.
c. Positive attitudes predominated, but negative behaviors were present.
d. Negative attitudes predominated, but were not reflected in negative behaviors.

 Cognitive dissonance is likely to happen when ____.
a. people feel responsible for the course of action
b. people feel they have no choice
c. negative consequences occur
d. positive consequences occur

3 Stereotype threat is when ____.
a. we view others as conforming to negative stereotypes

b. we fear that our behavior will conform to a negative stereotype

c. we generalize behaviors as being consistent with a particular group

d. people make threatening comments toward another race or gender

4 Attempts at persuasion can be foiled if ____.
  a. the listener has no advance warning that someone is going to try to persuade him or her
  b. the persuader does not seem to be trying too hard to persuade the listener
  c. the listener deliberately bypasses attempts to be persuaded by ignoring the persuader
  d. the listener has an ambivalent attitude initially

5 The tendency to view members of one's own group as relatively heterogeneous is called ____.
  a. illusory correlation
  b. social categorization
  c. ingroup differentiation
  d. ingroup bias

6 Increased contact between groups works best to decrease prejudice when ____.
  a. the setting assumes equality among participants
  b. the groups are dissimilar in social class
  c. the groups are competing for the same goal
  d. contact is formal

7 Mothers who make internal attributions for their children's misbehavior are more likely to ____.
  a. punish their children harshly
  b. reward their children when they're being good
  c. blame themselves when their children misbehave
  d. try to reason with their children

8 We tend to attribute other people's failures to ____ causes and their successes to ____ causes.
  a. internal; internal
  b. external; internal
  c. internal; external
  d. external; external

9 According to Robert Sternberg, love has each of the following dimensions except ____.
  a. passion
  b. intimacy
  c. commitment
  d. physical attraction

10 The majority of people in Japan have a(n) ____ attachment style.
  a. avoidant
  b. secure
  c. resistant
  d. anxious-ambivalent

11 Even though the speed limit on the interstate is typically 65 mph, drivers frequently drive 70–75 mph and are rarely ticketed for doing so. Driving 70–75 mph, then, is a ____ norm.
  a. prescriptive
  b. proscriptive
  c. perverse
  d. permissible

12 Solomon Asch found an overall conformity rate of ____% in his original study.
  a. 20
  b. 10
  c. 33
  d. 50

13 Milgram found that participants in his obedience studies were least likely to obey his commands when ____.
  a. they could see the "learner"
  b. two authority figures gave conflicting orders
  c. a student gave the orders
  d. women instead of men were tested

14 Group polarization is more likely to occur when ____.
  a. there is no correct answer
  b. there is more focus on harmony than on correctness
  c. group members like each other
  d. the need to be correct is paramount

15 Which of the following is not a characteristic of people who help others?
  a. belief in a just world
  b. external locus of control
  c. high need for approval
  d. sense of empathy

ANSWERS: 1.d **2.**a **3.**b **4.**c **5.**c **6.**a **7.**a **8.**c **9.**d **10.**d **11.**a **12.**c **13.**b **14.**b **15.**b

Appendix A

STATISTICS

M ark Twain once said that there are three kinds of lies: "Lies, damn lies, and statistics." **Statistics** are numbers that summarize or indicate differences or patterns of differences in measurements. Twain's point was that statistics can be used to obscure the facts as easily as to illuminate them. For instance, although the divorce rate in the United States is about 50%, this does not necessarily mean that out of 10 couples only 5 will stay married. If 3 of those 10 couples divorce and remarry, and all 3 of those second marriages end in divorce, that makes 6 divorces out of 13 marriages; and if one of those ex-partners remarries a third time and divorces again, we now have 14 marriages and 7 divorces: a 50% divorce rate, even though 7 of the original 10 couples stayed married from the start. To understand and evaluate reports of psychological research, be they surveys in newspapers or television or formal research reports in scientific publications, you need to know a few basics about statistics.

There are two major types of statistics: One type describes or summarizes data, whereas the other indicates which differences or patterns in the data are worthy of attention. This is the distinction between descriptive statistics and inferential statistics. **Descriptive statistics** are concise ways of summarizing properties of sets of numbers. You're already familiar with such statistics: They are what you see plotted in bar graphs and pie charts, and presented in tables. Descriptive statistics include measures of *central tendency*, such as the familiar arithmetic average. But descriptive statistics are not limited to figures and tables. For example, in financial news, the Dow Jones Industrial Average is a descriptive statistic, as is the unemployment rate.

Inferential statistics, in contrast, are the results of tests that reveal whether differences or patterns in measurements reflect true differences in the population, or just chance variations. For instance, if you toss a coin 10 times and it lands heads up 7 times, instead of the 5 you would expect purely by chance, does this mean that it is a "trick coin," or an edge is worn away, or could this outcome also arise from just chance? Inferential statistics seek to address this question of whether patterns in a set of data are random, or if they reflect a true underlying phenomenon. A correlation (see Chapter 1) is an example of inferential statistics; if the correlation is high enough (we will discuss what "high enough" means later), it tells you that the scores on one variable do in fact vary systematically with the scores on another variable.

In this appendix we consider both types of statistics, starting with descriptive statistics and the nature of variables and data, then turning to an overview of key inferential statistics. We conclude by exploring how statistics can be used to deceive you, both in printed numbers and in graphs, and how you can use statistics in everyday life.

Descriptive Statistics

You already know a lot about descriptive statistics, but you may not be aware you know it—and you may not be familiar with the technical vocabulary scientists use to discuss such statistics. This section provides a review of the essential points of descriptive statistics.

Variables and Data

First, you need to learn about variables and data—what they are, how researchers obtain data, and how they use the data to answer the questions posed in their research.

In Chapter 1, a *variable* was defined as an aspect of a situation that is liable to change (or, in other words, that can *vary*). More precisely, a variable is a characteristic of a substance, quantity, or entity that is measurable. *Independent variables* are the characteristics manipulated, and *dependent variables* are those measured, whose values depend on the values of the independent variable. For example, in Chapter 1 you read about an experiment in which golfers were or were not asked to use "mental practice" between games (the independent variable), and their subsequent golfing performance (the dependent variable) was measured by their scores. *Data* are careful observations or numerical measurements of a phenomenon, such as golf scores. In other words, in an experiment, data are the measurements, the values of the dependent variable as it varies. Examples of dependent variables used in psychological research are response times (how fast it takes to press a button after perceiving a stimulus), scores on an intelligence test, and ratings of the severity of depression.

Values of variables can be described in two ways. For example, intelligence could be described numerically by a score (such as 104) or by the category in which a score falls (such as "average intelligence"). **Continuous variables** are those whose values can fall anywhere along the measurement scale, just as measures of length can fall anywhere along a ruler. Continuous variables allow you to perform math-

---

Statistics: Numbers that summarize or indicate differences or patterns of differences in measurements.

Descriptive statistics: A concise way of summarizing properties of sets of numbers.

Inferential statistics: Results of tests that reveal which differences or patterns in the measurements reflect actual differences in a population, as opposed to those that merely reflect random variations.

Continuous variables: Variables whose values can fall anywhere along the measurement scale.

ematical operations such as adding or subtracting two or more values. For example, suppose you developed a drug that you think boosts memory. If your drug works as promised, it would be in great demand—from language-learning schools to Wall Street firms. To test the effectiveness of your drug, you ask people to learn a set of words either after taking the drug or, on another day, after taking a placebo. You are interested in whether the participants can later recall more words if they've taken your drug than if they took the placebo; the condition, drug versus placebo, is the independent variable, and the number of words recalled is the dependent variable. Half the participants get the drug first and half get an identical-looking and -tasting placebo first. You've put the pills in coded envelopes so that your assistant doesn't know when she's giving the drug versus the placebo (nor do the participants, because you've used a *double-blind* procedure; see Chapter 1). The comparison, easily accomplished with values from a continuous scale, would be expressed as the number of words remembered following the drug minus the number following the placebo. Ten participants' scores in each condition are shown in Table A.1.

Some data cannot be expressed as continuous variables, such as sex (male versus female), city of residence (Toledo versus Austin), or stage of sleep (Stage 2, 3, 4, or REM). These are examples of **categorical variables**, which assign measurements to discrete classes. Such variables do not change gradually from one to the other, and you can't perform mathematical operations on them. Commonly used categorical variables are sex, race, location, and political party. However, note that continuous measurements can also be classified as categorical variables, such as assigning an IQ score to an "average" category.

TABLE A.1 Fictional Participant Data From Drug and Placebo Conditions

NUMBER OF WORDS REMEMBERED	
Placebo	Memory drug
15	27
12	34
18	21
21	17
22	31
38	47
28	31
15	23
14	40
17	19

Frequency Distributions

It can be useful to treat continuous measures as categorical if you want to get a sense of the way scores are distributed in a population (such as how many college students have above average IQ scores). **Frequency distributions** indicate the number of each type of case that was observed in a set of data. For example, the number of people who voted for a Democratic versus a Republican candidate can be considered for different ages. You could group the ages (making a continuous variable, age, into a categorical variable), perhaps starting with ages 18–30, and then considering each subsequent decade. For each category, you would indicate the number of people who voted Democrat versus Republican. If you were a political strategist trying to determine how best to spend your candidate's campaign money, such a distribution would be helpful: You could decide to target the age ranges that had previously voted your way, or—alternatively—you could figure that they are relatively secure and instead target age ranges that previously were *not* in your camp.

Measures of Central Tendency

When individual measurements are directly presented, they are considered *raw data*; Table A.1 presents raw data. Descriptive statistics are used to summarize characteristics of a set of such data. It is the transformation of raw data into statistical terms that makes the data useful, allowing you to illustrate the relationships among the values or scores. One important type of descriptive statistic is the **central tendency** of the data: the clustering of the most characteristic values, or scores, for a particular group or sample. Central tendency can be expressed three ways. The most common, and probably the one with which you are most familiar, is the arithmetic average, or **mean**, of the scores or values. You calculate a mean by adding up the values in the group or sample, then dividing that sum by the total number of entries you summed. As shown in Table A.2 on page A-4, the mean for

Categorical variables: Variables whose values are assigned to discrete classes.

Frequency distribution: A distribution that indicates the number of each type of case that was observed in a set of data.

Central tendency: A descriptive statistic that indicates the clustering of the most characteristic values, or scores, for a particular group or sample.

Mean: A measure of central tendency that is the arithmetic average of a set of scores or values.

TABLE A.2 Calculating the Mean

NUMBER OF WORDS REMEMBERED

Placebo condition	Total: 200	Memory drug condition	Total: 290

Mean = Total number of words remembered ÷ Number of participants

Mean: 200 ÷ 10 = 20	Mean: 290 ÷ 10 = 29

the placebo condition is 20 words remembered, and the mean for the drug condition is 29 words remembered.

A second way to specify central tendency is the **median**, which is the score that is the midpoint of the values for the group or sample; half the values fall above the median, and half fall below the median. It is easier to find the median if the data are arranged in order, as shown in Table A.3. The median in the placebo condition is 17.5, halfway between 17 and 18, the fifth and sixth ordered scores. In the memory drug condition, the median is 29.0, halfway between the fifth and sixth ordered scores of 27 and 31.

A third measure of central tendency is the **mode**, the value that appears most frequently in the group or sample. The mode can be any value, from the highest to the lowest. The mode in Table A.3 is 15 for the placebo condition and 31 for the memory drug condition. In addition, you can also use a mode for categorical scales, where the mode would be the most frequent category, such as "children" among all viewers of Sesame Street, or "Saturday night" as the evening most people go to bed the latest.

The mean is the measure of central tendency that is most sensitive to extreme values or scores; if you have a few values at the extreme end of the scale, the mean would change much more than the median (which often will not change at all). The mode does not generally change in response to an extreme score. If you changed the last score in Table A.3 in the placebo condition from 38 to 50, the mean would change from 20 to 21.2, but the median and mode would remain the same.

When a set of data has many scores near one extreme value and away from the center, it is said to have a **skewed distribution**. When a set of data has a skewed distribution, the median is often a more appropriate measure of central tendency than the mean (see Figure A.1).

TABLE A.3 Fictional Data From Drug and Placebo Conditions, Arranged in Order

NUMBER OF WORDS REMEMBERED

Placebo condition	Memory drug condition
12	17
14	19
15	21
15	23
17	27
- - - - Median 17.5	- - - - Median 29.0
18	31
21	31
22	34
28	40
38	47
Mode* = 15	Mode* = 31

Mode = Value that appears most frequently.

Median: A measure of central tendency that is the midpoint score of the values for the group or sample; half the values fall above the median, and half fall below the median.

Mode: A measure of central tendency that is the most frequently occurring value in a group or sample.

Skewed distribution: A set of data that has many scores near one extreme value and away from the center.

Figure A.1 Skewed Distributions

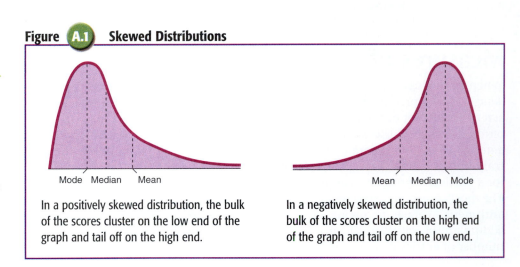

In a positively skewed distribution, the bulk of the scores cluster on the low end of the graph and tail off on the high end.

In a negatively skewed distribution, the bulk of the scores cluster on the high end of the graph and tail off on the low end.

Appendix A: Statistics

However, the three measures of central tendency generally yield similar results; this is especially likely as the number of observations (data points) becomes larger and if the data follow a normal distribution. As discussed in Chapter 6, the *normal distribution* is the familiar bell-shaped curve, in which most values fall in the midrange of the scale, and scores are increasingly less frequent as they taper off symmetrically toward the extremes (see Figure A.2). Normal curves occur many places in nature. For example, look at stone stairs in a very old building: You can usually see that they are worn more deeply in the center, and then less so as you move toward the sides. (If the building isn't old enough, you will see the beginnings of a normal curve, which over the generations will become deeper in the center until it resembles the shape of Figure A.2 upside down.) Or picture your classmates lined up according to height. Probably there are a few very tall or very short students on either end, with most clumping at an intermediate height. The same is true for many psychological qualities, such as scores on intelligence or personality tests.

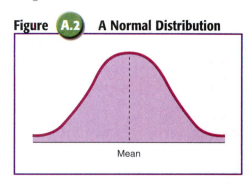

Figure A.2 A Normal Distribution

Mean

Measures of Variability

Whereas measures of central tendency convey information about the most common values or scores, measures of *variability* convey information about the spread of the scores. **Range**, the difference obtained when you subtract the smallest score from the largest, is the simplest measure of variability. For the data in Table A.3, for example, the range of scores in the placebo condition is 38 – 12, or 26. The range of scores for the drug condition is 47 – 17, or 30. But the range does not tell you how variable the scores are in general. Suppose you have developed two different drugs for improving memory, and participants who are given either one learn anywhere from 30 to 40 words; thus, both drugs have a range of 10. However, this measure of variability does not tell you that most participants who took drug A remember 37 or 38 words, whereas most of those who received drug B remember only 31 or 32 words. The range is the measure of variability most sensitive to extreme values.

Another method of assessing variability is the *standard deviation*, which is a kind of "average variability" in a set of measurements. In Chapter 6, you saw how important the standard deviation is for understanding IQ. Let's walk through how this important measure is computed:

Step 1: Calculate how much each score differs from the mean of the scores, as shown in Table A.4 on page A-6. Following this, it might be tempting to try to obtain an "average difference score" directly, by simply computing the average of the differences from the mean. But if you do this, you will get an average score of zero (each difference above the mean will be compensated by one below the mean; otherwise it wouldn't be the mean!). Instead, before taking the average of the deviations from the mean, you square them, which eliminates the plus or minus signs.

Step 2: Find the total of these squared values. This figure is often referred to as the *sum of squares*, or *SS*. As shown in Table A.4, the SS for the placebo condition data recorded in Table A.3 is 556.

Step 3: The sum of squares is then divided by the total number of deviation scores that contributed to this sum. The resulting value is the *variance*. The variance for the placebo condition is 55.6.

Step 4: Finally, because the difference scores were squared in the first step, the variance must be "unsquared" to get a number that conveys meaningful information about the average variability of the scores. The square root of the variance is the *standard deviation*. The *standard deviation* of the placebo condition is 7.46.

Range: The difference obtained by subtracting the smallest score from the largest; the simplest measure of variability.

TABLE A.4 **Computing the Standard Deviation From the Placebo Condition Data in Table A.3**

Step 1:

(Number of words remembered – Mean)^2 = Deviation score^2

$(12 - 20)^2 = -8^2 = 64$ $(18 - 20)^2 = -2^2 = 4$

$(14 - 20)^2 = -6^2 = 36$ $(21 - 20)^2 = 1^2 = 1$

$(15 - 20)^2 = -5^2 = 25$ $(22 - 20)^2 = 2^2 = 4$

$(15 - 20)^2 = -5^2 = 25$ $(28 - 20)^2 = 8^2 = 64$

$(17 - 20)^2 = -3^2 = 9$ $(38 - 20)^2 = 18^2 = 324$

Step 2: Sum of squares (SS) = Sum of squared deviation scores = 556

Step 3: Variance = SS ÷ Number of deviation scores = 556 ÷ 10 = 55.6

Step 4: Standard deviation = Square root of the variance = $\sqrt{55.6}$ = 7.46

Here is a simpler example. Say you want to know which of two Web search engines is likely to be consistently fastest. This means not just which engine has the fastest mean search time, or even the narrowest range of search times, but which has the tightest spread from the mean. The standard deviation is a measure of how consistently scores or values cluster near the mean, in this case how consistently fast a search engine can produce a list of hits for your query. The standard deviation is computed by taking each measured search time and subtracting it from the mean. Say, for simplicity's sake, that you measured the times for three searches of one search engine at 1, 3, and 5 seconds. The average (the mean) is 3 seconds. If you subtract each number from 3, you get –2, 0, and 2. Then, you square each of the differences from the mean (in this case, obtaining 4, 0, and 4), which gets rid of the plus and minus signs, and then sum these squared numbers and take their average (which gives you 8 divided by 3, or 2.67). If you then take the square root of this average (to undo the act of squaring), you have the standard deviation, a bit more than 1.6 seconds. You would do the same thing with the other search engine and compare the results. A smaller standard deviation would mean that the searches are, in general, closer to the average search time. To do this right, however, you would perform many more than three trials with each search engine.

For values that are normally distributed, the standard deviation will tell you the percentage of values that fall at different points on the distribution. For instance, as discussed more precisely in Chapter 6, about 68% of values fall between one standard deviation below the mean and one standard deviation above the mean. And about 95% of the values fall between two standard deviations below the mean and two standard deviations above the mean. Because 99.7% of values fall between three standard deviations below the mean and three standard deviations above the mean, you know that any value greater than three standard deviations is *really* different from the other values. The fact that standard deviations in a normal distribution always have these properties makes it easier to understand the relationship of standard deviations to the rest of the values in the data.

Let's go back to the earlier example of the placebo condition's standard deviation of 7.46 words (for simplicity's sake, we'll round this down to 7 words). What this means is that, with the placebo condition's mean of 20 words, roughly 68% of the participants in the placebo condition will remember somewhere between 13 and 27 words (20 – 7 to 20 + 7). At two standard deviations from the mean, roughly 95% of participants will remember between about 6 and 34 words.

Finally, it is well worth being familiar with the concept of a **confidence interval**, which specifies the range within which the mean of the actual population is likely to fall. The confidence interval is calculated like the standard deviation, but it is adjusted to reflect how the means of samples are distributed, not the individual data points (the details of this adjustment are not crucial here). You are proba-

Confidence interval: The range within which the mean of the population is likely to occur.

bly already familiar with this concept, having heard it referred to in news broadcasts as the "margin of error" that accompanies poll results. For example, you might hear that "Smith is preferred by 51% of the voters and Jones by 47%, with a margin of error of 4—which puts them in a dead heat." A margin of error of 4 is a way of saying "plus or minus 4." That is, Smith is preferred by somewhere between 47% and 55% of the voters—51% plus or minus 4%. The confidence intervals can be set more or less stringently. For example, the most common confidence interval, set at 95%, means that 95% of the time the mean of the population would fall within the range of the upper and lower ends of that confidence interval.

Relative Standing

Sometimes you want to know where a particular score stands relative to other scores. For example, college admissions officers want to know how an applicant's SAT scores stand relative to other applicants' scores. One way to convey this information is in terms of measures of variability. For example, you could specify how many standard deviations a score is from the mean. (This is the way IQ scores are set up, with 15 points on the WAIS indicating a standard deviation.) However, this isn't very useful if you are interested in the specific number or percentage of other cases that fall above or below a particular one. Another way of conveying information about a value relative to other values in a set of measurements is to use a **percentile rank:** the percentage of data that have values at or below a particular value. A value converted to a percentile rank of 50, for example, instantly tells you that 50% of the values in a sample fall at or below that particular score; the median is a percentile rank of 50. *Quartiles* are percentile ranks that divide the group into fourths (25th, 50th, 75th, and 100th percentiles); a score that is at the third quartile signifies that 75% of the group fall at or below that score. *Deciles* are percentile ranks that divide the group into tenths; a score at the sixth decile indicates that 60% of the scores fall at or below that value.

Inferential Statistics

S o far the discussion has focused on descriptive statistics. But you now have the tools to understand common inferential statistics.

Correlation: The Relationship Between Two Variables

Suppose you want to know not just about the central tendency and variability of a set of scores, but whether two variables are related to each other. Is a change in one variable accompanied by a change in another? You saw in Chapter 1 that *correlations* show only that two variables vary together, not that a change in one causes a change in the other. A positive relationship (in which increases in one variable are accompanied by increases in another) is indicated by a correlation value that falls between zero and 1.0; a negative relationship (in which increases in one variable are accompanied by decreases in another) is indicated by a correlation that is between zero and −1.0. Zero indicates no relationship between the two variables; they do not vary together. The closer the correlation is to 1.0 or −1.0, the stronger the relationship. So, for instance, you may read that people who exercise moderately don't get as severely depressed as people who don't exercise at all. If this information is based on a correlation, it would be a negative correlation: Increasing exercise is associated with less severe depression. However, concluding that exercise helps prevent severe depression (exercise *causes* less severe depression) based

Percentile rank: The percentage of data that have values at or below a particular value.

Tall people are as likely as short people to be aggressive or gentle, as is indicated by the zero correlation between the two variables.

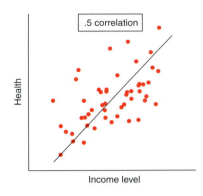

The more tightly the dots cluster around the line, the higher the correlation; the higher the correlation, the better the values on one dimension predict the values on the other. Here we see that knowing income level predicts health, but not very much.

We would expect smarter people to be better at solving problems, as reflected in this very high correlation. Although these are fictional data, why might you make these predictions?.

on that correlation would be a mistake. Perhaps people who are severely depressed don't have the energy to exercise. If that is true, the direction of causation would be in the other direction (more severe depression *causes* less exercise). With correlation, we know only that the two variables are related, either positively or negatively, not the direction of causality. It is possible that some third variable affects the other two variables. It could be that regularly getting out of the house or office and going to a gym (and therefore having a change of scenery and being around other people) affects the severity of depression, and so it is not the exercise per se but interacting with people that is related to less severe depression.

To think about how the correlation value is calculated, go back to the idea of a standard deviation. But now, instead of computing the deviations relative to the mean of all the numbers, imagine that you have a line fitting through the data (Figure A.3). The closer the data points hug the line, the higher the absolute value of correlation (that is, the higher the number—ignoring whether it is positive or negative). The *method of least squares* is a way to fit a line to a cloud of points. Again, squared numbers are used to eliminate the signs of the difference values. This method positions the line to minimize the square of the distance of each point from the line.

Correlations and other types of inferential statistics can be *significant* or *not significant*. What does "significant" mean? In statistics, it does not mean "important." Rather, it means that the measured relationship is not simply due to chance. If you correlate any two randomly selected sets of measurements, it is likely that the correlation will not be precisely zero. Say you correlated IQ with ear size and found a correlation of .12. Should you pay attention to this correlation, developing a grand theory to explain it? The size of a correlation needed for statistical significance, to be taken as more than just chance variation, depends on the number of pairs of values analyzed (each represented by a point in Figure A.3). As a general rule, the more observations considered when computing the correlation, the smaller the correlation value needs to be to achieve statistical significance. Why? Imagine that you were randomly throwing darts into a rectangular corkboard on the wall. It is possible that the first few on the left would be lower than those on the right. But as you tossed more and more darts, those initial quirks would be balanced out by quirks later in the process, so after 100 darts, there would no longer be any discernible pattern. The more observations you have, the less influence extreme values will have.

Statistical significance is expressed in terms of the probability (p) that a value (such as the size of a correlation) could be due to chance. For example, $p < .05$ means that the probability that the result was simply due to chance is less than 5 in 100; $p < .001$ means that the probability that it was due to chance is less than 1 in 1,000. By convention, any value with $p < .05$ or smaller is considered significant—not likely to be a result simply of chance variation in the data. You can look up a correlation value in a table to determine its significance, but most computer programs that compute correlation do this for you automatically.

Samples and Populations

Back to the memory-enhancing drug study. Did the drug work? If you had measured every person on the planet, all you would need to do is look at the descriptive statistics. Either the drug resulted in more learning than the placebo or it didn't. But such all-inclusive testing isn't practical. Virtually all research in psychology relies on studying data from a *sample*—a group drawn from the population at large—and the goal is to generalize from the findings with the sample to the larger population. Inferential statistics let you *infer* that the difference found between your samples does in fact reflect a difference in the corresponding populations.

Here's a simple example: Say you wanted to know whether seniors are generally friendlier than freshmen (you theorize that as they gain confidence and a sense of independence, students *do* become friendlier). To find out, you administer a questionnaire your professor has just designed and validated to measure friendliness. If you administered the questionnaire to five freshmen and five seniors, you would probably find a difference. But if you had ten from a single year and randomly assigned them to two groups of five, you would probably also find a difference between the groups! This difference would arise because of how you happened to assign students to groups. No matter how you did it, the groups would be likely to be different. Only if you had a large number of students would assigning them randomly to two groups be likely to result in groups that were very similar. When enough students from the same class have been tested, ones who score particularly high or low will be assigned equally often to each group, on average, and thus their disproportionate contributions will cancel out. When you compare freshmen and seniors, you can't know for sure whether you've got enough participants so that any difference between them is "real"—reflecting actual differences between the two classes in general—or is due to **sampling error**, differences that arise from the luck of the draw, not because two samples are in fact representative of different populations. In this example, if differences between freshmen and seniors are due to sampling error, the two classes of students are not different. There are tests that can indicate whether a difference between two groups is due to sampling error or reflects a real difference, although details about such tests are beyond the scope of this appendix.

Generalizing From the Results

Say that a research study found that exercise per se really does ward off severe depression. Does that mean that *you* should start exercising when you feel yourself getting depressed? Not necessarily. Generalizing from the results of a study should be done with caution. Consider the following questions before applying the results of this or any study to yourself or anyone else.

1. Are the results *valid*? If the study relied on an experimental design, were the participants randomly assigned? (See Chapter 1 for an explanation of why this is important.) If it used a correlational design, is the study implying that one variable causes another? If so, that conclusion isn't supported by the

Sampling error: A difference that arises by chance, not because the samples are representative of different populations.

data. Do you think the researchers were appropriately assessing the variables they claimed to be assessing? For instance, if they measured depression by simply comparing how slowly participants spoke at the end of the study with their speech speed at the beginning, would that be a valid assessment of depression?

2. If the study involved a new treatment or method of improving some aspect of life, was this method compared with a control group, perhaps a group given a placebo?

3. Did the researchers try to control for possible confounds?

4. Was the study performed with a wide cross-section of people or a small sample? For instance, if a positron emission tomography (PET) study found that people with attention-deficit/hyperactivity disorder (ADHD) had unusual activity levels in a particular part of the brain, you would want to ask the following questions before concluding that the findings generalize beyond the participants in the study: How many participants were involved? What was the gender of the participants? Are there other factors about the participants that make it difficult to generalize to you, to North Americans, or to all people? If the study was restricted to people of a certain geographic region, ethnic group, or those with a particular medical, psychological, or social history, it may not be appropriate to generalize the results, depending on the variable being assessed.

Lying With Statistics

Statistics can be used or misused. In a famous book entitled *How to Lie with Statistics,* Derrell Huff (1954) demonstrated many ways that people use statistics to distort the pattern of results. This book played a valuable role in inoculating many people against these deceptive techniques, and some of its high points are summarized here. Be on the look out for these manipulations whenever you see statistics.

Selective Reporting

Because different types of statistics convey different information, the same data can be manipulated to "say" different things. Look at Figure A.4 and Table A.5, which

Figure A.4 **Number of Symptoms After Therapy for Acrophobia**

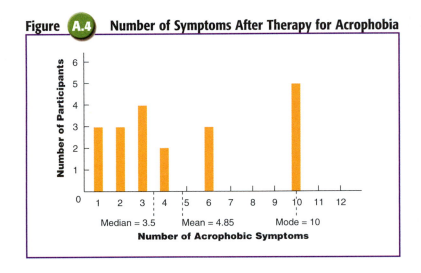

TABLE A.5 **Fictional Results of Therapy for Acrophobia**

Mean number of symptoms after therapy for acrophobia

= Total number of symptoms ÷ Total number of participants

= 1 + 1 + 1 + 2 + 2 + 2 + 3 + 3 + 3 + 3 + 4
  + 4 + 6 + 6 + 6 + 10 + 10 + 10 + 10 + 10

= 97 ÷ 20 = 4.85

Median = 3.5

Mode = 10

Appendix A: Statistics

present fictitious data for the results of a new type of therapy for people with acrophobia—a fear of heights. Before the therapy, participants reported 9 symptoms of acrophobia on average; that is, before treatment, the mean number of symptoms was 9. After the therapy, the mean number of symptoms was 4.85, the median was 3.5, and the mode was 10. Proponents of the new therapy make the following claims: On average, symptoms decreased by almost half (based on the mean), and more than 50% of participants had substantial symptom reduction (based on the median). Opponents, however, convey the data differently. A spokeswoman from the pharmaceutical company that manufactures a medication to treat acrophobia makes several counterclaims when she promotes the superiority of her company's medication: The number of symptoms most frequently reported was 10, which shows that the therapy actually made people *more* symptomatic (based on the mode). Also, the therapy achieved mixed results, as indicated by the fact that the number of symptoms after treatment ranged from 1 to 10.

As you can see, both supporters and detractors of the new treatment are correct. They are just presenting different aspects of the data. Thus, when hearing or reading about research or survey results, you should ask several questions before taking the results too seriously.

1. What is the distribution of the results? If they are normally distributed, the measures of central tendency will be similar to each other. If they are skewed, the measures of central tendency will convey different information, and the one presented will be the one that conveys the information the reporter wants you to know about. Do the other measures of central tendency paint a different picture of the results?

2. How variable are the data? What does it mean if the results vary a lot rather than a little?

Lying With Graphs

Many results are presented in graph form. Graphs work largely because of a single principle: *More is more* (Kosslyn, 1994a). Larger bars, higher lines, or bigger wedges all stand for greater amounts than smaller bars, lines, or wedges. Our tendency to see more on the page as standing for more of a substance can lead us astray if graphs are constructed to deceive. Be alert to the following tricks.

Shortening the Y (vertical) axis to exaggerate a difference. As you can see in Figure A.5, starting the Y axis at a high value and devoting the Y axis to a small part of

Figure A.5 Shortening the Y Axis Can Mislead

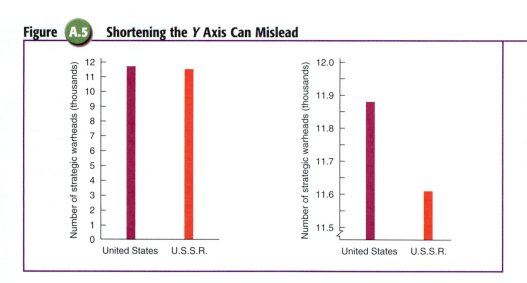

The left panel presents the actual numbers in a neutral way; the right panel exaggerates the difference. (From Kosslyn, 1994a, pp. 209 and 211. Data for illustration on left from Natural Resources Defense Council.)

Figure A.6 Lengthening the Y Axis Can Mislead

The left panel presents the actual numbers in a neutral way; the right panel minimizes the difference. (From Kosslyn, 1994a, pp. 209 and 211. Data for illustration on left from Natural Resources Defense Council.)

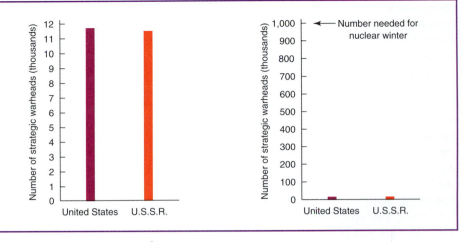

the scale, as in the right half of Figure A.6, make what is in fact a small difference look like a large one. If a difference is significant, it should look that way (and thus shortening the axis may be appropriate). But if it's not, then shortening the axis to exaggerate the difference is deception.

Using an inappropriately large range of values to minimize a difference. The flip side of the coin is illustrated in Figure A.6, in which a difference is made to appear smaller by using a large range in values on the Y axis.

Using three-dimensional graphics to exaggerate size. As shown in Figure A.7, a designer can take advantage of our tendency to impose size constancy (see Chapter 3), so that a bar that is farther away will be seen as *much* larger than a same-size one that is closer. And even if an actual difference exists, this technique can exaggerate its magnitude.

Figure A.7 Size Constancy Can Exaggerate 3-D Bar Size

Size constancy leads us to see the bars that are farther away as larger than they are, thereby exaggerating a difference. (From Kosslyn, 1994a, p. 227. Data from Hacker, 1992, p. 98, cited in *Newsweek*, 23 March 1992, p. 61.)

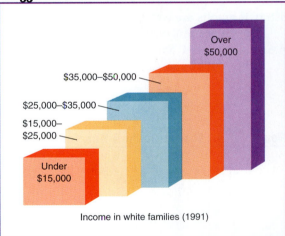

Transforming the data before plotting. Compare the two panels of Figure A.8. The first shows the size of the stock market in three countries over 3 years, the second the percentage increase over two 5-year periods. If you saw only the second, you wouldn't realize that the increases in the U.S. stock market were actually much greater than those in Japan. If the user is trying to sell Japanese stocks, you can bet which display will be preferred.

Appendix A: Statistics

The left panel shows the actual dollar figures, and the right shows the percentage change. Clearly, the message conveyed by the two displays is different. Which one is "more honest" depends on the purpose for which the graph is used. (From Kosslyn, 1994a, p. 219. Data from Morgan Stanley Capital International, cited in *The Economist World Atlas and Almanac,* 1989, p. 90.)

Changing width along with height. As shown in Figure A.9, our visual system does not register height and width separately, but rather we see them simultaneously, as specifying area. So changing the width along with the height gives a much larger impression of amount than is conveyed by changing height alone.

Figure **A.9** **Changing Width With Height Exaggerates Size**

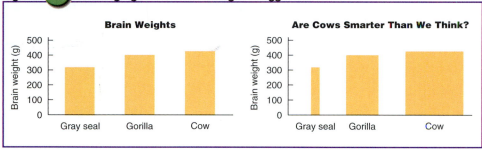

Expanding the bar width conveys the impression that more quantity is being presented than increasing the height alone signals. (From Kosslyn, 1994a, p. 225. Data from Weisberg, 1980, cited in Chambers et al., 1983, p. 371.)

Statistics in Daily Life

You can see that there is nothing magical or mysterious about statistics. Whenever you see a graph in the newspaper, you are seeing statistics; when you hear that a poll is accurate to "plus or minus 3 points," you know that you are being supplied with a confidence interval. The crucial ideas are that there are measures of central tendency (mean, median, and mode), measures of variability (range and standard deviation), and statistical tests that tell you the likelihood that a measured difference is due to chance alone.

What you've learned here is enough to enable you to read and understand many reports of original research in psychology. Appendix B focuses on other aspects of a research study and provides you with tools for analyzing what you read and for writing reports of your own.

Appendix B

HOW TO READ, CRITICALLY EVALUATE, AND WRITE RESEARCH PAPERS

Science is a community effort. Only through the cooperation (and competition) of many people does scientific knowledge inch forward. Both to get a sense of what's happening at the cutting edge of the science of psychology and to learn how to write better research papers yourself, you need to read articles published in psychology journals. These articles report new findings and theories and document the latest progress in the field. At first glance, a journal article may seem hopelessly dense and difficult to understand. One goal of this appendix, therefore, is to give you a brief guide to reading such articles, as well as to provide you with pointers on how to evaluate them. In addition, this appendix gives you background and resources that will help you write your own research papers.

Using the APA Format

Most articles published in psychology, and most of the papers you will be asked to write in psychology classes, are organized according to guidelines provided by the American Psychological Association (APA) in the *Publication Manual of the American Psychological Association* (5th ed., 2001; you can find more detailed information about these guidelines at http://www.apa.style.org). This standardized format not only ensures consistency across the scientific community but also helps authors to include all of the crucial information and allows readers to know what to expect. A paper that reports new research findings using the APA format follows this structure:

General Introduction

The General Introduction provides the context for the research. It consists of an overview of the topic being researched, describing previous studies on the topic, analyzing their flaws, pointing out gaps in what they examined, and noting contradictory findings. In this section, the authors introduce the general purpose of the study.

Study Introduction

Here, the study is introduced more narrowly, with background information supplied for the particular technique being used. If only one study is reported, this material is presented at the end of the General Introduction.

Method

The Method section explains, in detail, what was actually done. The type of method used, of the sort summarized in Chapter 1 (case study, quasi-experiment, and so on), and the specific details of how the study was conducted are provided. The goal is to describe the methodology in enough detail that someone else could repeat the study in precisely the same way. The Method section often has distinct subsections:

Participants (or *subjects*) describes the nature of the people or animals that took part in the study.

Materials describes the stimuli. For example, a questionnaire, words read aloud, pictures shown on a screen—all of these are typical materials in psychology studies.

Apparatus describes the physical props or instruments involved in the study (for example, the type of computer and monitor used to present stimuli, as well as the monitor settings). The apparatus is used to present the stimuli (described in *Materials*) and to record responses.

Procedure describes exactly how the study was conducted, step by step.

Results

The Results section reports what happened. This section includes descriptive statistics (such as means and standard deviations, as described in Appendix A) and inferential statistics (tests to determine which differences in and patterns of responses should be taken seriously; see Appendix A).

Discussion

Whereas the Results section provides just the bare facts, the Discussion section seeks to interpret them, often referring to previous studies or theories.

General Discussion

One journal article may report several studies. After a General Introduction, separate sections ranging from Study Introduction to Discussion—as described above—are included for each study. After the last study is reported, a General Discussion ties them all together. A General Discussion typically begins with a brief summary of all the results, provides an overarching interpretation of the results, speculates about the causes of unexpected results, and often ends with suggestions for additional research that would answer new questions raised by the results.

How to Organize and Evaluate What You Read and Write

Once you understand the structure of a journal article, you will find it useful to approach reading and writing such articles armed with what we call the **QALMRI** method. This method provides a means for critically evaluating a study in the literature, as well as for organizing your own study, and will help you see the connection between theory and data. That is, it will help you to be clear on what question is being asked, how to answer it, and whether the results really do support the preferred answer. In brief:

Q stands for the **question**. All research begins with a question, and the point of the research is to answer it. For example, we can ask whether a placebo is better than no action in curing depression. The first few paragraphs of the General Introduction should tell the reader what question the article is addressing. In addition, the context provided by the General Introduction's review of previous studies should explain why the question is important, why anybody should care about answering it. The General Introduction should provide the general context, providing the reasons why the question is worthy of consideration.

A stands for **alternatives**. A good report describes at least two possible answers to the question and explains why both are plausible. For example, the possibility that the placebo is better than doing nothing is plausible because beliefs arise from the brain, and brain activity can in turn affect the endocrine system—which could in turn affect mood. And the alternative possibility, that a placebo is no more effective than doing nothing in combating depression, is also plausible.

The General Introduction should also explain what alternatives are being considered. When reading or writing the General Introduction, identify the question and then the alternative answers that will be considered. If the alternatives in a study you read are not spelled out, try to figure out for yourself what they might be; if the study is simply seeking to confirm a theory's prediction, try to get a sense of whether other theories (or just common sense) would make the same prediction. If all the theories make the same prediction, it probably isn't worth testing. When writing your own reports, clearly describe the alternatives and why they are plausible.

L stands for the **logic** of the study. The goal of the study is to discriminate among the alternatives, and the logic is the general idea behind the study—the way the study will distinguish among the alternatives. The logic is typically explained toward the end of a study introduction and has the following structure: *If* alternative 1 (and not alternative 2) is correct, *then* when a particular variable is manipulated, the participant's behavior should change in a specific way. For example, the logic of a study of placebo effectiveness would rest on comparing a group receiving a placebo with a group receiving nothing. (In all other respects, the groups would be treated the same.) The logic would sound like this: *If* the placebo has a curative effect (and doing nothing doesn't), *then* the people receiving it should report fewer symptoms than the people receiving nothing. Notice that the logic depends crucially on the question and alternatives. For example, if we had asked a different question, such as whether a placebo is as effective as antidepressant medication, then the logic would require that we include a group receiving medication—but given the way we have formulated the question, this isn't necessary.

M stands for the **method**, found in the Method section. When reading an article, or writing your own, consider the following. With regard to *participants:* How were they selected? Are they a representative sample of the population in general? If the study involves more than one group, are they equivalent on important variables, such as age and education? For the placebo study, participants in both groups should be of identical age, education, and health status. It is crucial that they have the same level of depression prior to the study and the same prior experiences with medication. *Materials:* If questionnaires are used in the study, have they been shown to be valid (that is, do they measure what they are supposed to measure)?

Are they reliable (that is, do they produce consistent results)? Do the materials used in different parts of the study differ inappropriately in important ways? For the placebo study, one key would be the nature of the placebo itself: What did the pill look like? Did it resemble pills that the participants had already taken and knew to be effective? Did it taste like a sugar pill? *Apparatus:* Was a computer used? If so, exactly how did it present the stimuli? What other physical props were used? In the placebo study, were the pills dispensed using a special machine or just given in a bottle? *Procedure:* Try to visualize yourself in the study. Is it clear exactly what was done? How were the pills produced? provided to the participants? Were there proper control groups? Were participants given appropriate instructions (clear, but not leading them on)? For studies using a placebo group, as in all studies, it is crucial that the investigator treat the participants in the two groups exactly the same way; if the investigator is cheerful and friendly to the people in the placebo group but distant and cold to those in the control group, it could be this treatment—and not the presence or absence of placebo—that affects the participants' feelings of depression. Such nuts-and-bolts concerns can make or break a study; if they are not properly handled, the results are ambiguous at best.

R stands for the **results**, found in the Results section. What happened? First, look for (when reading) or report (when writing) measures of central tendency (means, medians, modes) and some measure of the sampling variability (commonly, standard deviations; see Appendix A). The actual results are descriptive. For example, the ratings of depression might be lower for the group receiving a placebo than for the group receiving nothing. Second, not all differences and patterns in the results should be taken seriously—some differences are simply quirks due to chance. Inferential statistics are performed to determine which patterns of variation are unlikely to have arisen due to chance.

For most studies in psychology, inferential statistics are used to assign a probability value to a comparison, noted as $p < .05$ (or $p > .1$, $p < .01$, and so on). As discussed in Appendix A, this number indicates the likelihood that the difference occurred merely due to chance; $p < .05$, for example, means that the probability that the difference occurred due to chance is less than 5 in 100. Usually, any p value of .05 or less means that the result is considered "statistically significant"—you can be reasonably certain that the difference found in the sample reflects an actual difference in the population as a whole. For example, if an inferential test showed that the difference between the placebo and the control group was "significant at $p < .001$," that would mean that the difference would occur by chance less than 1 time in 1,000 if the study were repeated over and over (see Appendix A).

Finally, **I** stands for the **inferences** that can be drawn about the question and alternatives, given the results. The Discussion section usually contains the inferences the authors want to draw from their results. If the study was well designed (the logic sound and the method rigorous), the results should allow you to eliminate at least one of the alternatives. For example, in the placebo study, the results might show that placebo really does help depression more than doing nothing. At this point, take a step back and think about potential *confounds* that could have led to the results. Were any alternative explanations *not* ruled out? And consider any loose ends. For example, perhaps the way the participants were treated when given the placebo is a major variable, and the effects of placebos can be enhanced or reduced by different social interactions with the caregivers.

Using Online Sources of Information

How do you find research or other relevant material about a topic when writing a paper? For that matter, how do you evaluate the references cited in journal articles? To take advantage of all that the research community has to offer, you should be seeking online as well as print sources of information. Much of this textbook was written using online sources. But as you probably know, the Web has at least as much misleading information as it has correct reporting. Nobody edits it, nobody monitors it, nobody certifies it. It's up to you to sort the wheat from the chaff.

How, then, can you find useful information on the Web, and how can you verify that it should be taken at face value? There are three general ways to use online sources.

Databases

First, if you already know of a likely source of information or a particular article, you can go directly to a specialized database, such as PsychInfo or Medline. Psych-Info is offered through many college libraries, and Medline's search is publicly available at http://www.nlm.nih.gov/medlineplus. At a database, you can usually retrieve abstracts of articles simply by entering key terms (including the author's name, if you know it). If you have access only to an abstract, beware: Abstracts sometimes aren't written by the authors themselves, and even when they are, they necessarily simplify the study and its findings. This simplification is sometimes so extreme that the results can be distorted. Thus, we urge you to use abstracts only as a "first pass," to narrow down likely sources. If the results seem important, get the actual paper.

Sometimes you can even obtain an entire paper online, often referred to as "Full-Text." The American Psychological Association offers a site where you can read complete versions of all papers published in APA journals since the late 1980s. The APA continues to enter earlier papers, so the database will have more older articles available over time. This site, however, is available only to members (including student members) of the APA and to schools or organizations that subscribe to the service.

Organizations' Web Sites

If you don't know which database to check, you can try the Web sites of relevant organizations, such as the American Psychological Association (www.apa.org). In this case, the challenge is to think of the most relevant organizations for your topic. In psychology, the two APAs (the American Psychological Association and the American Psychiatric Association) are good places to start. In fact, the American Psychological Association has a special online pamphlet for students—"Library Research in Psychology: Finding It Easily" (http://www.apa.org/science/lib.html)—and the American Psychiatric Association has links to many useful sources (http://www.psych.org/libr_publ/index.html). You can also search the Web sites of other psychological organizations, such as the Society for Research in Child Development (http://www.srcd.org) and the American Psychological Society (http://www.psychologicalscience.org/). Similarly, for many subfields in psychology, there are relevant national organizations with Web sites, such as the American Association for Mental Retardation (http://www.aamr.org) and the American Society for Clinical Hypnosis (www.asch.net). Links posted on such sites have more credibility than those found through a search engine, given the likelihood that they've been approved by the parent organization. However, the parent organization can't possibly ensure that all information on other sites is correct. So again, don't take what you find at face value. Look before you leap, and think before you quote.

Search Engines

Finally, what do you do if you're forced to cast your search more widely and browse the whole Web? You can simply use a search engine, such as Google (www.google.com) or Excite (www.altavista.com). We've found that the best searches have as many specific terms as possible; the more terms you include, the more irrelevant cites will be weeded out. It's instructive to look at a dozen or so of the sites that turn up following a search. You may be shocked to discover how much inconsistency there is; not only can the summaries of the research differ but so can the evaluations and conclusions that are based on it. And sometimes the authors of the secondary sources (which summarize or discuss an original article) just get it wrong—they either describe the study incorrectly or misinterpret the implications of the results.

As a first step in evaluating a site, see whether five or six other researchers reach consistent conclusions. Moreover, evaluate the source of each site. Does it have a reputable host? Are you reading an actual published paper, an unpublished paper, notes used in lectures, or notes used by someone else in writing a paper? In general, the more evaluation that a given paper receives (as happens with published papers, but not student notes), the better. Also consider whether the material is up-to-date. Check the date to make sure that the work reflects the most recent research. This isn't to say, however, that time-honored and well-replicated older studies are any less credible because of their age.

In Sum

Reading Research

When you read a study, remember to read it in terms of both the big picture outlined above and the details. Figure out exactly what question the authors wanted to answer and what alternative answers they've considered. Can you think of others? Always be on the lookout for potential confounds and alternative explanations, and look for features of the study that limit how well its results can be generalized; for example, can you assume that the results necessarily generalize to other ages, races, or cultures? Be sure to read the footnotes. The single most important advice we can give about reading a study is to be an active reader: Think about what the authors are claiming, and think about whether it makes sense.

Writing Your Own Papers

The same principles apply to writing your own research papers. Write the **Introduction** so that the reader clearly understands the question you are addressing, why it is important (in the context of the previously reported studies on the topic), the alternative possible answers you will consider (including, in most cases, your "favorite" one—often called simply the hypothesis), and the logic of the design (the basic idea underlying the study). In the **Method** section, be sure to include enough detail to allow another researcher to repeat, exactly, what you did. In the **Results** section, first present results that bear directly on the question and alternative answers. These results should be measures of central tendency and variability, which are often best presented in a graph. The results that address the question are most important—even if they are not as striking as some of the other findings. If your Introduction is clear, the reader is focused like a laser beam on the question and is waiting to find out which alternative answer is supported by the results. Don't keep the reader in suspense; present the results that speak to the question at the outset of the Results section. Finally, in the **Discussion,** return to the question and alternative answers, and discuss exactly what you can infer from your results. Have you shown that some of the alternatives must be discarded? Is only one viable? What should future research focus on to propel the field even further ahead?

When reading or writing a research report, always put yourself in the place of the intelligent reader. If a report has been written clearly, the reader will glide through it effortlessly, understanding what the author intended to convey, why the research was conducted in a particular way, what the discoveries were, and why the report is interesting and important.

References

Abel, T., Martin, K. C., Bartsch, D., & Kandel, E. R. (1998). Memory suppressor genes: Inhibitory constraints on the storage of long-term memory. *Science, 279,* 338–341.

Ablon, J. S., & Jones, E. E. (1999). Psychotherapy process in the National Institute of Mental Health Treatment of Depression Collaborative Research Program. *Journal of Consulting and Clinical Psychology, 67,* 64–75.

Abraham, H. D. (1983). Visual phenomenology of the LSD flashback. *Archives of General Psychiatry, 40,* 884–889.

Abramowitz, J. S. (1997). Effectiveness of psychological and pharmacological treatments for obsessive-compulsive disorder: A quantitative review. *Journal of Consulting and Clinical Psychology, 65,* 44–52.

Abrams, L. R., & Jones, R. W. (1994, August). *The contribution of social roles to psychological distress in businesswomen.* Paper presented at the 102nd annual convention of the American Psychological Association, Los Angeles, CA.

Abramson, L. Y., Seligman, M. E., & Teasedale, J. D. (1978). Learned helplessness in humans: Critique and reformulation. *Journal of Abnormal Psychology, 87,* 49–74.

Achter, J., Lubinski, D., & Benbow, C. P. (1996). Multipotentiality among the intellectually gifted: "It was never there and already it's vanishing." *Journal of Counseling Psychology, 43,* 65–76.

Adams, H. E., Wright, W. L., & Lohr, B. A. (1996). Is homophobia associated with homosexual arousal? *Journal of Abnormal Psychology, 105,* 440–445.

Adams, J. (1967). *Human memory.* New York: McGraw-Hill.

Ader, R. (1976). Conditioned adrenocortical steroid elevations in the rat. *Journal of Comparative and Physiological Psychology, 90,* 1156–1163.

Ader, R., & Cohen, N. (1975). Behaviorally conditioned immunosuppression. *Psychosomatic Medicine, 37,* 333–340.

Adler, A. (1964). *Social interest: A challenge to mankind.* New York: Capricorn Books. (Original work published 1933).

Adolphs, R., Damasio, H., Tranel, D., & Damasio, A. R. (1996). Cortical systems for the recognition of emotion in facial expressions. *Journal of Neuroscience, 16,* 7678–7687.

Agency for Health Care Policy and Research. (1999). Newer antidepressant drugs are equally as effective as older-generation drug treatments, research shows. AHCPR Pub. No. 99-E013. Rockville, MD.

Aguilar-Alonso, A. (1996). Personality and creativity. *Personality and Individual Differences, 21,* 959–969.

Ainsworth, M. D. S., Blehar, M. C., Waters, E., & Wahl, S. (1978). *Patterns of attachment: A psychological study of the Strange Situation.* Hillsdale, NJ: Erlbaum.

Akhtar, N., & Tomasello, M. (1996). Two-year-olds learn words for absent objects and actions. *British Journal of Developmental Psychology, 14,* 79–93.

Akiskal, H. S. (1996). The prevalent clinical spectrum of bipolar disorders: Beyond DSM–IV. *Journal of Clinical Psychopharmacology, 16* (Suppl. 1), 4S–14S.

Alan Guttmacher Institute. (1994). *Sex and America's teenagers.* New York.

Alba, J. W., & Hasher, L. (1983). Is memory schematic? *Psychological Bulletin, 93,* 203–231.

Albert, M. S., Duffy, F. H., & McAnulty, G. B. (1990). Electrophysiologic comparisons between two groups of patients with Alzheimer's disease. *Archives of Neurology, 47,* 857–863.

Albert, M. S., & Moss, M. B. (1996). Neuropsychology of aging: Findings in humans and monkeys. In E. L. Schneider, J. W. Rowe, T. E. Johnson, N. J. Holbrook, & J. H. Morrison, (Eds.), *Handbook of the biology of aging (4th ed.).* San Diego, CA: Academic Press.

Alcock, J. E. (1987). Parapsychology: Science of the anomalous of search for the soul? *Behavioral and Brain Sciences, 10,* 553–565.

Alexander, D. (1991). Keynote Address. In *President's Committee on Mental Retardation, Summit on the National Effort to Prevent Mental Retardation and Related Disabilities.*

Alexander, F., & French, T. (1946). *Psychoanalytic theory.* New York: Ronald.

Allen, J. J. B., & Iacono, W. G. (1997). A comparison of methods for the analysis of event-related potentials in deception detection. *Psychophysiology, 34,* 234–240.

Allen, L. S., & Gorski, R. A. (1992). Sexual orientation and the size of the anterior commissure in the human brain. *Proceedings of the National Academy of Sciences of the United States of America, 89,* 7199–7202.

Allyn, J., & Festinger, L. (1961). The effectiveness of unanticipated persuasive communications. *Journal of Abnormal and Social Psychology, 62,* 35–40.

Altshuler, L. L., Bartzokis, G., Grieder, T., Curran, J., & Mintz, J. (1998). Amygdala enlargement in bipolar disorder and hippocampal reduction in schizophrenia: An MRI study demonstrating neuroanatomic specificity. *Archives of General Psychiatry, 55,* 663–664.

Aluja-Fabregat, A., Colom, R., Abad, F., & Juan-Espinosa, M. (2000). Sex differences in general intelligence defined as *g* among young adolescents. *Personality & Individual Differences, 28,* 813–820.

Amabile, T. M. (1983). *The social psychology of creativity.* New York: Springer-Verlag.

Amabile, T. M. (1998, September–October). How to kill creativity. *Harvard Business Review,* pp. 76–87.

Amat, J., Matus-Amat, P., Watkins, L. R., & Maier, S. F. (1998). Escapable and inescapable stress differentially alter extracellular levels of 5-HT in the basolateral amygdala of the rat. *Brain Research, 812,* 113–120.

American Association for Mental Retardation. (1992). *Mental retardation: Definition, classification, and systems of supports* (9th ed.).

American Foundation for Suicide Prevention. (1996). *http://www. afsp.org/suicide/facts.html.*

American Psychiatric Association. (2000). *Diagnostic and statistical manual of mental disorders, 4th edition.* Washington, DC: American Psychiatric Association.

American Psychiatric Association. (2000). *Diagnostic and statistical manual of mental disorders: Text Revision, (4th ed., rev.).* Washington, DC: Author.

American Psychological Association (APA). (1992). *Ethical principles of psychologists & code of conduct* [www.document]. URL http:// www.apa.org/ethics/code.html.

Amsterdam, B. (1972). Mirror self-image reactions before age two. *Developmental Psychology, 5,* 297–305.

Anand, B. K., & Brobeck, J. R. (1952). Food intake and spontaneous activity of rats with lesions in the amygdaloid nuclei. *Journal of Neurophysiology, 15*, 421–430.

Anastasi, A. (1988). *Psychological testing* (6th ed.). New York: Macmillan.

Anch, A. M., Bowman, C. P., Mitler, M. M., & Walsh, J. K. (1988). *Sleep: A scientific perspective*. Englewood Cliffs, NJ: Prentice-Hall.

Andersen, A. E., & DiDomenico, L. (1992). Diet vs. shape content of popular male and female magazines: A dose response relationship to the incidence of eating disorders? *International Journal of Eating Disorders, 11*, 283–287.

Andersen, B. (1997, July). Psychological interventions for individuals with cancer. *Clinician's Research Digest* (Suppl. bulletin) *16*, 1–2.

Andersen, B. L., Kiecolt-Glaser, K. K., & Glaser, R. (1994). A biobehavioral model of cancer stress and disease course. *American Psychologist, 49*, 389–404.

Anderson, B. L., & Nakayama, K. (1994). Toward a general theory of stereopsis: Binocular matching, occluding contours, and fusion. *Psychological Review, 101*, 414–445.

Anderson, C. A. (1983). Abstract and concrete data in the perseverance of social theories: When weak data lead to unshakable beliefs. *Journal of Experimental Social Psychology, 19*, 930–1108.

Anderson, C. A., & Bushman, B. J. (1997). External validity of "trivial" experiments: The case of laboratory aggression. *Review of General Psychology, 1*, 19–41.

Anderson, C. A., Lepper, M. R., & Ross, L. (1980). Perseverance of social theories: This role of explanation in the persistence of discredited information. *Journal of Personality and Social Psychology, 39*, 1037–1049.

Anderson, J. R. (2000). *Cognitive psychology and its implications* (5th ed.). New York: Worth.

Anderson, N. B. (1998). Levels of analysis in health science: A framework for integrating sociobehavioral and biomedical research. In S. M. McCann, J. M. Lipton, et al. (Eds.), *Annals of the New York Academy of Sciences: Vol. 840, Neuroimmunomodulation: Molecular aspects, integrative systems, and clinical advances* (pp. 563–576). New York: New York Academy of Sciences.

Andreasen, N. C. (1987). Creativity and mental illness: Prevalence rates in writers and their first-degree relatives. *American Journal of Psychiatry, 144*, 1288–1292.

Andreasen, N. C., Nasrullah, H., Dunn, V., Olson, S., Grove, W., Erhardt, J., Coffman, J., & Crosett, J. (1986). Structural abnormalities in the fronal system in schizophrenia. *Archives of General Psychiatry, 43*, 136–144.

Andreasen, N. C., Rezai, K., Alliger, R., Swayze, V., Flaum, M., Kirchner, P., Cohen, G., & O'Leary, D. (1992). Hypofrontality in neuroleptic-naïve patients and in patients with chronic schizophrenia: Assessment with xenon-133 single proton emission computed tomography and the Tower of London. *Archives of General Psychiatry, 49*, 943–958.

Andreasen, N. C., Flashman, L., Flaum, M., Arndt, S., Swayze, V., O'Leary, D. S., Ehrhardt, J. C., & Yuh, W. T. (1994). Regional brain abnormalities in schizophrenia measured with magnetic resonance imaging. *Journal of the American Medical Association, 272*, 1763–1769.

Andrews, H. B., & Jones, S. (1990). Eating behaviour in obese women: A test of two hypotheses. *Australian Psychologist, 25*, 351–357.

Andrews, J. A., Hops, H., & Duncan, S. C. (1997). Adolescent modeling of parent substance use: The moderating effect of the relationship with the parent. *Journal of Family Psychology, 11*, 259–270.

Angier, N. (1999, September 7). Route to creativity: Following bliss or dots? *New York Times*, F3 (col. 1).

Angleitner, A., Riemann, R., & Strelau, J. (1995). A study of twins using the self-report and peer-report NEO-FFI scales. Paper presented at the seventh meeting of the International Society for the Study of Individual Differences, July 15–19, Warsaw, Poland.

Anglin, J. M. (1993). Vocabulary development: A morphological analysis. *Monographs of the Society for Research in Child Development, 58*(10, Serial No. 238).

Angst, J. (1998). The emerging epidemiology of hypomania and bipolar II disorder. *Journal of Affective Disorders, 50*, 143–151.

Anisman, H., Zaharia, M. D., Meaney, M. J., & Merali, Z. (1998). Do early-life events permanently alter behavioral and hormonal responses to stressors? *International Journal of Developmental Neuroscience, 16*, 149–164.

Anonymous. (1970). Effects of sexual activity on beard growth in man. *Nature, 226*, 867–870.

Antoch, M. P., Song, E. J., Chang, A. M., Vitaterna, M. H., Zhao, Y., Wilsbacher, L. D., Sangoram, A. M., King, D. P., Pinto, L. H., & Takahashi, J. S. (1997, May 16). Functional identification of the mouse circadian Clock gene by transgenic BAC rescue. *Cell, 89*(4), 655–667.

Antonuccio, D. O., Danton, W. G., & DeNelsky, G. Y. (1995). Psychotherapy versus medication for depression: Challenging the conventional wisdom with data. *Professional Psychology: Research & Practice, 26*, 574–585.

Aranda, M. P., & Knight, B. G. (1997). The influence of ethnicity and culture on the caregiver stress and coping process: A sociocultural review and analysis. *Gerontologist, 37*, 342–354.

Archer, S. L., & Waterman, A. S. (1988). Psychological indvidualism: Gender differences or gender neutrality? *Human Development, 31*, 65–81.

Arend, L. (1994). Surface colors, illumination and surface geometry: Intrinsic-image models of human color perception. In A. Gilchrist (Ed.), *Lightness, brightness, and transparency* (pp. 159–213). Hillsdale, NJ: Erlbaum.

Arguin, M., Cavanagh, P., & Joanette, Y. (1994). Visual feature integration with an attention deficit. *Brain and Cognition, 24*, 44–56.

Argyle, M. L., & Lu, L. (1990). Happiness and social skills. *Personality & Individual Differences, 11*, 1255–1261.

Arking, R. (1991). *Biology of aging: Observations and principles*. Englewood Cliffs, NJ: Prentice Hall.

Armstrong, S. L., Gleitman, L. R., & Gleitman, H. (1983). What some concepts might not be. *Cognition, 13*, 263–308.

Arnell, K. M., & Jolicoeur, P. (1999). The attentional blink across stimulus modalities: Evidence for central processing limitations. *Journal of Experimental Psychology: Human Perception and Performance, 25*, 630–648.

Arnett, J. (1992). Reckless behavior in adolescence: A developmental perspective. *Developmental Review, 12*, 339–373.

Arnett, J. J. (1999). Adolescent storm and stress, reconsidered. *American Psychologist, 54*, 317–326.

Aronson, J., Blanton, H., & Cooper, J. (1995). From dissonance to disidentification: Selectivity in the self-affirmation process. *Journal of Personality and Social Psychology, 68*, 986–996.

Asch, S. E. (1951). Effects of group pressure upon the modification and distortion of judgment. In H. Guetzkow (Ed.), *Groups, leadership, and men* (pp. 177–190). Pittsburgh: Carnegie.

Asch, S. E. (1955). Opinions and social pressure. *Scientific American, 193*, 31–35.

Asendorpf, J. B., Warkentin, V., & Baudonniere, P-M. (1996). Self-awareness and other-awareness: II. Mirror self-recognition, social contingency awareness, and synchronic imitation. *Developmental Psychology, 32*, 313–321.

Atre-Vaidya, N., & Hussain, S. M. (1999). Borderline personality disorder and bipolar mood disorder: Two distinct disorders or a continuum? *Journal of Mental and Nervous Disorders, 187*, 313–315.

Auden, W. H. (1989). *Van Gogh: A self-portrait*. New York: Marlowe.

Avorn, J., & Langer, E. (1982). Induced disability in nursing home patients: A controlled trial. *Journal of the American Geriatrics Society, 30*, 397–400.

Azar, B. (1995). Timidity can develop in the first days of life. *APA Monitor, 26* (11), 23

Azrin, N. H., Sisson, R. W., Meyers, R., & Godley, M. (1982). Alcoholism treatment by disulfiram and community reinforcement therapy. *Journal of Behavior Therapy and Experimental Psychiatry, 13*, 105–112.

Bachen, E. A., Manuck, S. B., Cohen, S., Muldoon, M. F., Raible, R., Herbert, T. B., & Rabin, B. S. (1995). Adrengergic blockage ameliorates cellular immune responses to mental stress in humans. *Psychosomatic Medicine, 57*, 366–372.

Baddeley, A. (1986). *Working Memory*. Oxford, England: Clarendon.

Baddeley, A. (1992). The magical number seven: Still magic after all these years? *Psychological Review, 101*, 353–356.

Baenninger, M., & Newcombe, N. (1989). The role of experience in spatial test performance: A meta-analysis. *Sex Roles, 20*, 327–344.

Bailey, J. M., & Pillard, R. C. (1991). A genetic study of male sexual orientation. *Archives of General Psychiatry, 48*, 1089–1096.

Baillargeon, R. (1993). The object concept revisited: New directions in the investigation of infants' physical knowledge. In C. E. Granrud

(Ed.), *Visual perception and cognition in infancy* (pp. 265–315). Hillsdale, NJ: Erlbaum.

Baily, C. H., & Chen, M. (1989). Time course of structural changes at identified sensory neuron synapses during long-term sensitization in Aplysia. *Journal of Neuroscience, 9,* 1774–1781.

Baker, R. R. (1980). Goal orientation by blindfolded humans after long-distance displacement: Possible involvement of a magnetic sense. *Science, 210,* 555–557.

Ball, D., Hill, L., Eley, T. C., Chorney, M. J., Chorney, K., Thompson, L. A., Detterman, D. K., Benbow, C., Lubinski, D., Owen, M., McGuffin, P., & Plomin, R. (1998). Dopamine markers and general cognitive ability. *NeuroReport, 9,* 347–349.

Ball, T. S. (1971). *Itard, Seguin, and Kephart: Sensory education—A learning interpretation.* Columbus, OH: Merrill.

Ballus, C. (1997). Effects of antipsychotics on the clinical and psychosocial behavior of patients with schizophrenia. *Schizophrenia Research, 28,* 247–255.

Baltes, P. B. (1987). Theoretical propositions of life-span developmental psychology: On the dynamics between growth and decline. *Developmental Psychology, 23,* 611–626.

Baltes, P. B., Dittmann-Kohli, F., & Dixon, R. A. (1984). New perspectives on the development of intelligence in adulthood: Toward a dual-process conception and a model of selective optimization with compensation. In P. B. Baltes & O. G. Brim, Jr. (Eds.), *Life-span development and behavior* (Vol. 6, pp. 33–76). San Diego, CA: Academic Press.

Bandura, A. (1976). Self-reinforcement: Theoretical and methodological considerations. *Behaviorism, 4,* 135–155.

Bandura, A. (1977a). *Social learning theory.* Englewood Cliffs, NJ: Prentice-Hall.

Bandura, A. (1977b). Self-efficacy: Toward a unifying theory of behavior change. *Psychological Review, 84,* 191–215.

Bandura, A. (1978). The self-system in reciprocal determinism. *American Psychologist, 33,* 344–358.

Bandura, A. (1986). *Social foundations of thought and action: A social-cognitive theory.* Englewood Cliffs, NJ: Prentice-Hall.

Bandura, A., Grusec, J. E., & Menlove, F. L. (1967). Vicarious extinction of avoidance behavior. *Journal of Personality & Social Psychology, 5,* 16–23.

Bandura, A., Ross, D., & Ross, S. A. (1961). Transmission of aggression through imitation of aggressive models. *Journal of Abnomal and Social Psychology, 63,* 575–582.

Bandura, A., Ross, D., & Ross, S. A. (1963). Imitation of film-mediated aggressive models. *Journal of Abnormal & Social Psychology, 66,* 3–11.

Banks, M. S., & Bennett, P. J. (1988). Optical and photoreceptor immaturities limit the spatial and chromatic vision of human neonates. *Journal of the Optical Society of America, 5,* 2059–2079.

Barber, J. (1997). Hypnosis and memory: A cautionary chapter. In G. A. Fraser (Ed.), *The dilemma of ritual abuse: Cautions and guides for therapists.* (pp. 17–29). Washington, DC: American Psychiatric Press.

Barber, J. P., & Muenz, L. R. (1996). The role of avoidance and obsessiveness in matching patients to cognitive and interpersonal psychotherapy: Empirical findings from the Treatment for Depression Collaborative Research Program. *Journal of Consulting and Clinical Psychology, 64,* 951–958.

Barefoot, J. C., Dahlstrom, W. G., & Williams, R. B. (1983). Hostility, CHD incidence, and total mortality: A 25-year follow-up study of 255 physicians. *Psychosomatic Medicine, 45,* 59–63.

Barefoot, J., Dodge, K., Peterson, B., Dahlstrom, W., & Williams, R. (1989). The Cook-Medley Hostility Scale: Item content and ability to predict survival. *Psychosomatic Medicine, 51,* 46–57.

Bargh, J. A., Chen, M., & Burrows, L. (1996). Automaticity of social behavior: Direct effects of trait construct and stereotype activation on action. *Journal of Personality and Social Psychology, 71,* 230–244.

Barkham, M., & Shapiro, D. A. (1990). Brief psychotherapeutic interventions for job-related distress: A pilot study of prescriptive and exploratory therapy. *Counseling Psychology Quarterly, 3,* 133–147.

Barkham, M., Shapiro, D. A., Hardy, G. E., & Rees, A. (1999). Psychotherapy in two-plus-one sessions: Outcomes of a randomized controlled trial of cognitive-behavioral and psychodynamic-interpersonal therapy for subsyndromal depression. *Journal of Consulting and Clinical Psychology, 67,* 201–211.

Barkow, J. H., Cosmides, L., & Tooby, J. (Eds.) (1992). *The adapted mind: Evolutionary psychology and the generation of culture.* New York: Oxford University Press.

Barlow, D. H. (1986). Causes of sexual dysfunction: The role of anxiety and cognitive interference. *Journal of Consulting and Clinical Psychology, 54,* 140–148.

Barlow, D. H. (1988). *Anxiety and its disorders.* New York: Guilford Press.

Barnett, L. A., Far, J. M., Mauss, A. L., & Miller, J. A. (1996). Changing perceptions of peer norms as a drinking reduction program for college students. *Journal of Alcohol & Drug Education, 41,* 39–62.

Baron, R., & Byrne, D. (1997). *Social Psychology* (8th ed.). Needham Heights, MA: Allyn & Bacon.

Baron, R. B., & Richardson, D. (1994). *Human aggression.* New York: Plenum.

Bartlett, F. C. (1932). *Remembering.* Cambridge, England: Cambridge University Press.

Bartoshuk, L. M., & Beauchamp, G. K. (1994). Chemical senses. *Annual Review of Psychology, 45,* 419–449.

Basic Behavioral Science Task Force of the National Advisory Mental Health Council. (1996). Basic behavioral science research for mental health, *American Psychologist, 51,* 722–731.

Batsell, W. R., Jr., & Brown, A. S. (1998). Human flavor-aversion learning: A comparison of traditional aversions and cognitive aversions. *Learning & Motivation, 29,* 383–396.

Batshaw, M., & Perret, Y. (1992). *Children with disabilities: A medical primer.* Baltimore: Brookes.

Batson, C. D. (1998). Altruism and prosocial behavior. In D. T. Gilbert, S. T. Fiske, & G. Lindzey (Eds.), *The handbook of social psychology* (4th ed., pp. 282–316). New York: McGraw Hill.

Batson, C. D., Bolen, M. H., Cross, J. A., & Neuringer-Benefiel, H. E. (1986). Where is the altruism in the altruistic personality? *Journal of Personality & Social Psychology, 50,* 212–220.

Baumeister, R. F., & Boden, J. M. (1998). Aggression and the self: High self-esteem, low self-control, and ego threat. In R. G. Geen and E. Donnerstein (Eds.), *Human aggression: Theories, research, and implications for social policy* (pp. 111–137). San Diego, CA: Academic Press.

Baumeister, R. F., Smart, L., & Boden, J. M. (1996). Relation of threatened egotism to violence and aggression: The dark side of high self-esteem. *Psychological Review, 103,* 5–33.

Baumeister, R. F., Stillwell, A., & Wotman, S. R. (1990). Victim and perpetrator accounts of interpersonal conflict: Autobiographical narratives about anger. *Journal of Personality and Social Psychology, 59,* 994–1003.

Baxter, L. R., Schwartz, J. M., Bergman, K. S., Szuba, M. P., Guze, B. H., Mazziota, J. C., Alazraki, A., Selin, C. E., Ferng, H. K., Munford, P., & Phelps, M. E. (1992). Caudate glucose metabolic rate changes with both drug and behavior therapy for obsessive-compulsive disorder. *Archives of General Psychiatry, 49,* 681–689.

Beach, F. A. (1956). Characteristics of masculine "sex drive." In M. Jones (Ed.), *Nebraska Symposium on Motivation* (pp. 1–32). Lincoln, NE: University of Nebraska Press.

Beaman, A., Barnes, P., Kletz, B., & McQuirk, B. (1978). Increasing helping rates through information dissemination: Teaching pays. *Personality and Social Psychology Bulletin, 4,* 406–411.

Bearak, B. (1997, March 29). Time of puzzles heartbreak binds relatives left behind. *New York Times,* 1.

Beatty, J. (1995). *Principles of behavioral neuroscience.* Dubuque, IA: Brown & Benchmark.

Bechara, A., Damasio, H., Tranel, D., & Damasio, A. R. (1997). Deciding advantageously before knowing the advantageous strategy. *Science, 275,* 1293–1294.

Bechara, A., & Van der Kooy, D. (1992). A single brain stem substrate mediates the motivational effects of both opiates and food in nondeprived rats but not in deprived rats. *Behavioral Neuroscience, 106,* 351–363.

Beck, A. T. (1967). *Depression: Causes and treatment.* Philadelphia: University of Pennsylvania Press.

Beck, A. T., Emery, G., & Greenberg, R. L. (1985). *Anxiety disorders and phobias: A cognitive perspective.* New York: Basic Books.

Beck, A. T., Rush, A. J., Shaw, B. F., & Emery, G. (1979). *Cognitive Therapy of depression: A treatment manual.* New York: Guilford Press.

Beck, H. (1976). Neuropsychological servosystems, consciousness, and the problem of embodiment. *Behavioral Sciences, 21,* 139–160.

Beck, J. G., Ohtake, P. J., & Shipherd, J. C. (1999). Exaggerated anxiety is not unique to CO_2 in panic disorder: A comparison of hypercapnic and hypoxic challenges. *Journal of Abnormal Psychology, 108,* 473–482.

Beck, R., & Fernandez, E. (1998). Cognitive-behavioral therapy in the treatment of anger: A meta-analysis. *Cognitive Therapy & Research, 22,* 63–74.

Becker, A., & Hamburg, P. (1996). Culture, the media, and eating disorders. *Cross-Cultural Psychiatry, 4,* 163–167.

Beer, M. (1966). *Leadership, employee needs, and motivation (Monograph No. 129).* Columbus, OH: Ohio State University, Bureau of Business Research, College of Commerce.

Beggs, J. M., Brown, T. H., Byrne, J. H., Crow, T., LeDoux, J. E., LeBar, K., & Thompson, R. F (1999). Learning and memory: Basic mechanisms. In M. J. Zigmond, F. E. Bloom, S. G. Landis, J. L. Roberts, & L. R. Squire (Eds.), *Fundamental neuroscience* (pp. 1411–1454). New York: Academic Press.

Behrmann, M. (2000). The mind's eye mapped onto the brain's matter. *Current Directions in Psychological Science, 9,* 50–54.

Beilin, H. (1996). Mind and meaning: Piaget and Vygotsky on causal explanation. *Human Development, 39,* 277–286.

Bell, A. E. (1977). Heritability in retrospect. *Journal of Heredity, 68,* 297–300.

Beller, M., & Gafni, N. (1996). The 1991 international assessment of educational progress in mathematics and sciences: The gender differences perspective. *Journal of Educational Psychology, 88,* 365–377.

Bem, D. J. (1996). Exotic becomes erotic: A developmental theory of sexual orientation. *Psychological Review, 103,* 320–335.

Bem, D. J. (1998). Is EBE theory supported by the evidence? Is it androcentric? A reply to Peplau et al. *Psychological Review, 108,* 395–398.

Bem, D. J., & Allen, A. (1974). On predicting some of the people some of the time: The search for cross-situational consistencies in behavior. *Psychological Review, 81,* 506–520.

Bem, D. J., & Honorton, C. (1994). Does psi exist? Replicable evidence for an anomalous process of information transfer. *Psychological Bulletin, 115,* 4–18.

Ben-Shakhar, G., & Furedy, J. J. (1990). *Theories and applications in the detection of deception: A psychophysiological and international perspective.* New York: Springer-Verlag.

Benbow, C. P., & Minor, L. L. (1990). Cognitive profiles of verbally and mathematically precocious students: Implications for identification of the gifted. *Gifted Child Quarterly, 34,* 21–26.

Bender, K. J. (1998). "Substance P" antagonist relieves depression. *Psychiatric Times, 15*(11).

Benedict, J. G., & Donaldson, D. W. (1996). Recovered memories threaten all. *Professional Psychology: Research & Practice, 27,* 427–428.

Beninger, R. J. (1983). The role of dopamine in locomotor activity and learning. *Brain Research Reviews, 6,* 173–196.

Beninger, R. J. (1989). Dissociating the effects of altered dopaminergic function on performance and learning. *Brain Research Bulletin, 23,* 365–371.

Beninger, R. J., Mason, S. T., Phillips, A. G., & Fibiger, H. C. (1980). The use of extinction to investigate the nature of neuroleptic-induced avoidance deficits. *Psychopharmacology, 69,* 11–18.

Benjafield, J. G. (1996). *The history of psychology.* Needham, MA: Allyn & Bacon.

Benjamin, J., Li, L., Patterson, C., Greenberg, B. D., Murphy, D. L., & Hamer, D. H. (1996). Population and familial association between the D4 dopamine receptor gene and measure of novelty seeking. *Nature Genetics, 12,* 81–84.

Berenbaum, S. A. (1999). Effects of early androgens on sex-typed activities and interests in adolescents with congenital adrenal hyperplasia. *Hormones & Behavior, 35,* 102–110.

Berenbaum, S. A., & Hines, M. (1992). Early androgens are related to childhood sex-typed toy preferences. *Psychological Science, 3,* 203–206.

Bergeman, C. S., Plomin, R., Pederson, N. L., McClearn, G. E., & Nesselraod, J. R. (1990). Genetic and environmental influences on social support: The Swedish Adoption/Twin Study of Aging (SATSA). *Journal of Gerontology: Psychological Sciences, 45,* P101–P106.

Berk, L. E. (1992a). Children's private speech: An overview of theory and the status of research. In R. M. Diaz & L. E. Berk (Eds.), *Private speech: From social interaction to self-regulation* (pp. 17–53). Hillsdale, NJ: Erlbaum.

Berk, L. E. (1994a). Vygotsky's theory: The importance of make-believe play. *Young Children, 50,* 30–39.

Berk, L. E. (1994b). Why children talk to themselves. *Scientific American, 271*(5), 78–83.

Berkman, L. F., & Syme, S. L. (1979). Social networks, host resistance, and mortality: A nine year follow-up study of Alameda Country residents. *American Journal of Epidemiology, 109,* 186–204.

Berkowitz, A. D. (1997). From reactive to proactive prevention: Promoting an ecology of health on campus. In P. C. Rivers & E. R. Shore (Eds.), *Substance abuse on campus: A handbook for college and university personnel.* Westport, CT: Greenwood Press.

Berkowitz, L. (1998). Affective aggression: The role of stress, pain, and negative affect. In R. G. Geen & E. Donnerstein (Eds.), *Human aggression: Theories, research, and implications for social policy* (pp. 49–72). San Diego, CA.: Academic Press.

Berlyne, D. E. (1960). *Conflict, arousal, and curiosity.* New York: Mcgraw-Hill.

Berlyne, D. E. (Ed.). (1974). *Studies in the new experimental aesthetics: Steps toward an objective psychology of aesthetic appreciation.* Washington, DC: Hemisphere.

Berman, S. M., & Noble, E. P. (1995). Reduced visuospatial performance in children with the D2 dopamine receptor A1 allele. *Behavior Genetics, 25,* 45–58.

Bermond, B. N., Fasotti, L., & Schuerman, J. (1991). Spinal cord lesions, peripheral feedback, and intensities of emotional feelings. *Cognition & Emotion, 5,* 201–220.

Berridge, K. C. (1996). Food reward: Brain substrates of wanting and liking. *Neuroscience and Biobehavioral Reviews, 20,* 1–20.

Berscheid, E., & Reis, H. T. (1998). Attraction and close relationships. In D. T. Gilbert, S. T. Fiske, & G. Lindzey (Eds.), *The handbook of social psychology* (4th ed., pp. 193–281). New York: McGraw Hill.

Bess, B. E. (1997). Human sexuality and obesity. *International Journal of Mental Health, 26,* 61–67.

Bettencourt, B. A., & Miller, N. (1996). Sex differences in aggression as a function of provacation: A meta-analysis. *Psycholoigical Bulletin, 119,* 422–447.

Beutler, L. E., Engle, D., Mohr, D., Daldrup, R. J., Bergan, J., Meredity, K., & Merry, W. (1991). Predictors of differential response to cognitive, experiential, and self-directed psychotherapeutic procedures. *Journal of Consulting & Clinical Psychology, 59,* 333–340.

Beutler, L. E., Machado, P. P., Engle, D., & Mohr, D. (1993). Differential patient X treatment maintenance among cognitive, experiential, and self-directed psychotherapies. *Journal of Psychotherapy Integration, 3,* 15–31.

Beutler, L. E., Machado, P. P., & Neufeldt, S. A. (1994). Therapist variables. In A. E. Bergin & S. L. Garfield (Eds.), *Handbook of psychotherapy and behavior change,* (4th ed., pp. 229–269). New York: Wiley.

Biederman, I. (1987). Recognition-by-components: A theory of human image understanding. *Psychological Review, 94,* 115–147.

Bierhoff, H. W., Klein, R., & Kramp, P. (1991). Evidence for the altruistic personality from data on accident research. *Journal of Personality, 59,* 263–280.

Bihrle, A. M., Brownell, H. H., Powelson, J. A., & Gardner, H. (1986). Comprehension of humorous and non-humorous materials by left and right brain-damaged patients. *Brain and Cognition, 5,* 399–411.

Birren, J. E. (1988). Behavior as a cause and a consequence of health and aging. In J. J. F. Schroots, J. E. Birren, & A. Svanborg (Eds.), *Health and aging* (pp. 25–41). New York: Springer.

Birren, J. E., Riegel, K. F., & Morrison, D. F. (1962). Age differences in response speed as a function of controlled variations of stimulus conditions: Evidence of a general speed factor. *Gerontologia, 6,* 1–18.

Bishop, G. D. (1994). *Health psychology: Integrating mind and body.* Boston, MA: Allyn & Bacon.

Black, D. W., Noyes, R., Goldstein, R. B., & Blum, N. (1992). A family study of obsessive-compulsive disorder. *Archives of General Psychiatry, 49,* 362–368.

Black, J. E., Jones, T. A., Nelson, C. A., & Greenough, W. T. (1998). Neuronal plasticity and the developing brain. In N. E. Alessi, J. T. Coyle, S. I. Harrison, & S. Eth (Eds.), *Handbook of child and adolescent psychiatry: Vol 6. Basic psychiatric science and treatment* (pp. 31–53). New York: Wiley.

Blais, M. A., Hilsenroth, M. J., & Castlebury, F. D. (1997). Psychometric characteristics of the Cluster B personality disorders under

DSM–III—R and DSM–IV. *Journal of Personality Disorders, 11,* 270–278.

Blakeslee, S. (1997). Brain studies tie marijuana to other drugs. *New York Times.* June 27:A16 (col. 4).

Blanton, H., Gibbons, F. X., Gerrard, M., Conger, K. J., & Smith, G. E. (1997). Role of family and peers in the development of prototypes associated with substance abuse. *Journal of Family Psychology, 11,* 271–288.

Blass, T. (1999). The Milgram Paradigm after 35 years: Some things we now know about obedience to authority. *Journal of Applied Social Psychology, 29,* 955–978.

Bliss, E. L. (1984). Spontaneous self-hypnosis in multiples personality disorder. *Psychiatric Clinics of North America, 7,* 135–148.

Block, J. (1995). A contrarian view of the five-factor approach to personality description. *Psychological Bulletin, 117,* 187–215.

Bloom, B. L. (1997). *Planned short-term psychotherapy: A clinical handbook* (2nd ed.). Boston, MA: Allyn & Bacon.

Blundell, J. E. (1977). Is there a role for 5-hydroxytryptamine in feeding? *International Journal of Obesity, 1,* 15–42.

Blundell, J. E. (1984). Serotonin and appetite. *Neuropharmacology, 23,* 1537–1551.

Blundell, J. E. (1986). Serotonin manipulations and the structure of feeding behaviour. *Appetite, 7,* 39–56.

Blundell, J. E., & Halford, J. C. G. (1998). Serotonin and appetite regulation: Implications for the pharmacological treatment of obesity. *CNS Drugs, 9,* 473–495.

Bly, B. M., & Kosslyn, S. M. (1997). Functional anatomy of object recognition in humans: Evidence from PET and fMRI. *Current Opinion in Neurology, 10,* 5–9.

Bobo, L. (1983). Whites' opposition to busing: Symbolic racism or realistic group conflict? *Journal of Personality and Social Psychology, 45,* 1196–1210.

Boden, M. A. (2000). State of the art: Computer models of creativity. *Psychologist, 13,* 72–76.

Bodenhausen, G. V. (1990). Stereotypes as judgmental heuristics: Evidence of circadian variations in discrimination. *Psychological Science, 1,* 319–322.

Bodenhausen, G. V., Kramer, G. P., & Susser, K. (1994). Happiness and stereotypic thinking in social judgment. *Journal of Personality and Social Psychology, 66,* 621–632.

Bogaert, A. F. (1996). Volunteer bias in human sexuality research: Evidence for both sexuality and personality differences in males. *Archives of Sexual Behavior, 25,* 125–140.

Bohm, J. K., & Hendricks, B. (1997). Effects of interpersonal touch, degree of justification, and sex of participant on compliance with a request. *Journal of Social Psychology, 137,* 460–469.

Boiten, F. A. (1998). The effects of emotional behavior on components of the respiratory cycle. *Biological Psychiatry, 49,* 29–51.

Boivin, D. B., Czeisler, C. A., Dijk, D., Duffy, J. F., Folkard, S., Minors, D. S., Totterdell, P., & Waterhouse, J. M. (1997). Complex interaction of the sleep-wake cycle and circadian phase modulates mood in healthy subjects. *Archives of General Psychiatry, 54,* 145–152.

Bond, M., & Gardiner, S. T., Christian, H., & Sigel, J. J. (1983). Empirical study of self-rated defense styles. *Archives of General Psychiatry, 40,* 333–338.

Bond, M. H., & Smith, P. B. (1996). Cross-cultural social and organizational psychology. *Annual Review of Psychology, 47,* 205–235.

Bond, R., & Smith, P. B. (1996). Culture and conformity: A meta-analysis of studies using Asch's (1952b, 1956) line judgment task. *Psychological Bulletin, 119,* 111–137.

Borg, E., & Counter, S. A. (1989). The middle ear muscles. *Scientific American, 261,* 74–80.

Boring, E. G. (1950). *A history of experimental psychology* (2nd ed.). New York: Appleton-Century-Crofts.

Borman, W. C., Hanson, M. A., & Hedge, J. W. (1997). Personnel selection. *Annual Review of Psychology, 48,* 299–337.

Bornstein, M. H., Tal, J., Rahn, C., Galperin, C. Z., et al. (1992). Functional analysis of the contents of maternal speech to infants of 5 and 13 months in four cultures: Argentina, France, Japan, and the United States. *Developmental Psychology, 28,* 593–603.

Bornstein, R. F. (1989). Exposure and affect: Overview and meta-analysis of research, 1968–1987. *Psychological Bulletin, 106,* 265–289.

Bornstein, R. F., & D'Agostino, P. R. (1994). The attribution and discounting of perceptual fluency: Preliminary tests of a perceptual fluency/attributional model of the mere exposure effect. *Social Cognition, 12,* 103–128.

Bornstein, R. F., Leone, D. R., & Galley, D. (1987). The generalizability of subliminal mere exposure effect: Influence on stimuli perceived without awareness on social behavior. *Journal of Personality and Social Psychology, 53,* 1070–1079.

Bosch, J. A., Brand, H. S., Ligtenberg, A. J. M., Bermond, B., Hoogstraten, J., & Nieuw Amgerongen, A. V. (1998). The response of salivary protein levels and S-IgA to an academic examination are associated with daily stress. *Journal of Psychophysiology, 12,* 384–391.

Bottini, G., Corcoran, R., Sterzi, R., Paulesu, E., Schenone, P., Scarpa, P., Frackowiak, R. S. J., & Frith, C. D. (1994). The role of the right hemisphere in the interpretation of figurative aspects of language: A positron emission tomography activation study. *Brain, 117,* 1241–1253.

Botvin, G. J. (1995). Drug abuse prevention in school settings. In G. J. Botvin, S. Schinke, & M. A. Orlandi (Eds.), *Drug abuse prevention with multiethnic youth* (pp. 169–192). Newbury Park, CA: Sage.

Botwinick, J. (1984). *Aging and behavior: A comprehensive integration of research findings.* New York: Springer.

Bouchard, T. J., & McGue, M. (1981). Familial studies of intelligence: A review. *Science, 212,* 1055–1059.

Bouchard, T. J., Jr. (1994). Genes, environment, and personality. *Science, 264,* 1700–1701.

Bouchard, T. J., Jr., Lykken, D. T., McGue, M., Segal, N. L., & Tellegen, A. (1990). Sources of human psychological differences: The Minnesota study of twins reared apart. *Science, 250,* 223–228.

Bouton, M. (1993). Context, time and memory retrieval in the interference paradigms of Pavlovian conditioning. *Psychological Bulletin, 114,* 80–99.

Bouton, M. (1994). Context, ambiguity and classical conditioning. *Current Directions in Psychological Science, 3,* 49–52.

Bower, G. H. (1972). Mental imagery and associative learning. In L. Gregg (Ed.), *Cognition and learning and memory* (pp. 51–88). New York: Wiley.

Bower, G. H. (1981). Mood and memory. *American Psychologist, 36,* 129–148.

Bower, G. H. (1992). How might emotions effect learning? In S.-Å. Christianson (Ed.), *The handbook of emotion and memory: Research and theory* (pp. 3–31). Hillsdale, NJ: Erlbaum.

Bowlby, J. (1969). *Attachment and loss: Vol. 1, Attachment.* New York: Basic Books.

Bowman, E. S., & Nurnberger, J. I. (1993). Genetics of psychiatry diagnosis and treatment. In D. L. Dunner (Ed.), *Current psychiatric therapy* (pp. 46–56). Philadelphia: Saunders.

Bradburn, N. M. (1969). *The structure of psychological well-being.* Chicago: Aldine.

Bradley, M. M., Greenwald, M. K., Petry, M. C., & Lang, P. J. (1992). Remembering pictures: Pleasure and arousal in memory. *Journal of Experimental Psychology: Learning, Memory, and Cognition, 18,* 379–390.

Bradley, M. T., MacLaren, V. V., & Carle, S. B. (1996). Deception and nondeception in Guilty Knowledge and Guilty Actions Polygraph Tests. *Journal of Applied Psychology, 81,* 153–160.

Bradley, M. T., & Warfield, J. F. (1984). Innocence, information, and the Guilty Knowledge Test in the detection of deception. *Psychophysiology, 21,* 683–689.

Bradshaw, G. L., & Anderson, J. R. (1982). Elaborative encoding as an explanation of levels of processing. *Journal of Verbal Learning & Verbal Behavior, 21,* 165–174.

Brannon, L. (1996). *Gender: Psychological perspectives.* Needham Heights, MA: Simon & Schuster.

Braverman, P. K., & Strasburger, V. C. (1993). Adolescent sexual activity. *Clinical Pediatrics, 32,* 658–668.

Bregman, A. S. (1990). *Auditory scene analysis: The perceptual organization of sound.* Cambridge, MA: MIT Press.

Bregman, A. S. (1993). Auditory scene analysis: Hearing in complex environments. In S. McAdams & E. Bigand (Eds.), *Thinking in sound: The cognitive psychology of human audition* (pp. 10–36). New York: Oxford University Press.

Bregman, E. O. (1934). An attempt to modify the emotional attitudes of infants by the conditioned response technique. *Journal of Genetic Psychology, 45,* 169–__.

Brehm, J. W. (1966). *A theory of psychological reactance.* New York: Academic Press.

Breiter, H. C., Rauch, S. L., Kwong, K. K., Baker, J. R., Weisskoff, R. M., Kennedy, D. N., Kendrick, A. D., Davis, T. L., Jiang, A., Cohen, M. S., Stern, C. E., Belliveau, J. W., Baer, L., O'Sullivan, R. L., Savage, C. R., Jenike, M. A., & Rosen, B. R. (1996). Functional magnetic resonance imaging of symptom provocation in obsessive-compulsive disorder. *Archives of General Psychiatry, 53,* 595–606.

Bremner, J. D., Stienberg, M., Southwick, S. M., Johnson, D. R., & Charney, D. S. (1993). Use of the structured clinical interview for DSM-IV dissociative disorders for systemic assessment of dissociative symptoms in posttraumatic stress disorder. *American Journal of Psychiatry, 150,* 1011–1014.

Breslau, N., Kessler, R. C., Chilcoat, H. D. Schultz, L. R., Davis, G. C., & Andreski, P. (1998). Trauma and posttraumatic stress disorder in the community: The 1996 Detroit Area Survey of Trauma. *Archives of General Psychiatry, 55,* 626–632.

Brewer, J. B., Zhao, Z., Desmod, J. E., Glover, G. H., & Gabrielli, J. D. E. (1998). Making memories: Brain activity that predicts how well visual experience will be remembered. *Science, 281,* 1185–1187.

Brewer, K. R., & Wann, D. L. (1998). Observational learning effectiveness as a function of model characteristics: Investigating the importance of social power. *Social Behavior & Personality, 26,* 1–10.

Brewer, M. B., & Brown, R. J. (1998). Intergroup relations. In D. T. Gilbert, S. T. Fiske, & G. Lindzey (Eds.), *The handbook of social psychology* (4th ed., pp. 554–594). New York: McGraw Hill.

Brewer, W. F. (1988). Qualitative analysis of the recalls of randomly sampled autobiographical events. In M. M. Gruneberg & P. E. Morris (Eds.), *Practical aspects of memory: Current research and issues, Vol. 1: Memory in everyday life.* (pp. 263–268). New York: John Wiley & Sons.

Britt, T. A., & Shepperd, J. A. (1999). Trait relevance and trait assessment. *Personality and Social Psychology Review, 3,* 108–122.

Broadbent, D. E. (1971). The magic number seven after fifteen years. In A. Kennedy & A. Wilkes (Eds.), *Studies in long-term memory* (pp. 2–18). New York: Wiley.

Brody, J. (1998, April 6). Dealing with sleep deprivation. *International Herald Tribune,* 9.

Brooks-Gunn, J., Graber, J. A., & Paikoff, R. L. (1994). Studying links between hormones and negative affect: Models and measures. *Journal of Research on Adolescence, 4,* 469–486.

Brosschot, J. F., Benschop, R. J., Godaert, G. L. R., Olff, M., de Smet, M., Heijnen, C. J., & Ballieux, R. E. (1994). Influence of life stress on immunological reactivity to mild psychological stress. *Psychosomatic Medicine, 56,* 216–224.

Brown, A. S., van Os, J., Driessens, C., Hoek, S. W., & Susser, E. S. (1999). Prenatal famine and the spectrum of psychosis. *Psychiatric Annals, 29,* 145–150.

Brown, B. (1999). Optimizing expression of the common human genome for child development. *Current Directions in Psychological Science, 8,* 37–41.

Brown, B. B., Clasen, D., & Eicher, S. (1986). Perceptions of peer pressure, peer conformity dispositions, and self-reported behavior among adolescents. *Developmental Psychology, 22,* 521–530.

Brown, D. E. (1991). *Human universals.* Philadelphia: Temple University Press.

Brown, I., Jr., & Inouye, D. K. (1978). Learned helplessness through modeling: The role of perceived similarity in competence. *Journal of Personality and Social Psychology, 36,* 900–908.

Brown, J. D. (1991). Staying fit and staying well: Physical fitness as a moderator of stress. *Journal of Personality and Social Psychology, 60,* 555–561.

Brown, J. D., & Rogers, R. J. (1991). Self-serving attributions: The role of physiological arousal. *Personality and Social Psychology Bulletin, 17,* 501–506.

Brown, P. L., & Jenkins, H. M. (1968). Auto-shaping of the pigeon's key peck. *Journal of the Experimental Analysis of Behavior, 68,* 503–507.

Brown, R. (1989). Roger Brown. In G. Lindzey (Ed.), *A history of psychology in autobiography,* Vol. 8 (pp. 37–60). Stanford, CA: Stanford University Press.

Brown, R., & Kulik, J. (1977). Flashbulb memories. *Cognition, 5,* 73–99.

Brown, T. A., & Barlow, D. H. (1997). *Casebook in abnormal psychology.* Pacific Grove, CA: Brooks/Cole.

Brownell, H. H., Potter, H. H., Michelow, D., & Gardner, H. (1984). Sensitivity to lexical denotation and connotation in brain-damaged patients: A double dissociation. *Brain and Language, 22,* 253–265.

Brownell, K. D., & Rodin, J. (1992). *Medical, metabolic, and psychological effects of weight cycling.* Unpublished manuscript, Yale University.

Brubaker, R. G., Prue, D. M., & Rycharik, R. G. (1987). Determinants of disulfiram acceptance among alcohol patients: A test of the theory of reasoned action. *Addictive Behaviors, 12,* 43–51.

Brugger, P., Landis, T., & Regard, M. (1990). A "sheep-goat effect" in repetition avoidance: Extrasensory perception as an effect of subjective probability? *British Journal of Psychology, 81,* 455–468.

Brunner, D. P., Dijk, D. J., Tobler, I., & Borbely, A. A. (1990). Effect of partial sleep deprivation on sleep stages and EEG power spectra: Evidence for non-REM and REM sleep homeostasis. *Electroencephalogr. Clin. Neurophysiol., 75,* 492–499.

Bryan, R. N., Wells, S. W., Miller, T. J., Elster, A. D., Jungreis, C. A., Poirier, V. C., Lind, B. K., & Manolio, T. A. (1997). Infarctlike lesions in the brain: Prevalence and anatomic characteristics at MR imaging of the elderly—data from the Cardiovascular Health Study. *Radiology, 202,* 47–54.

Bryant, R. A., & Barnier, A. J. (1999). Eliciting autobiographical pseudomemories: The relevance of hypnosis, hypnotizability, and attributions. *International Journal of Clinical & Experimental Hypnosis, 47,* 267–283.

Buchanan, C. M., Eccles, J., & Becker, J. (1992). Are adolescents the victims of raging hormones? Evidence for activational effects of hormones on moods and behavior at adolescence. *Psychological Bulletin, 111,* 62–107.

Buchkremer, G., Klingberg, S., Holle, R., Schulze-Moenking, H., & Hornung, W. P. (1997). Psychoeducational psychotherapy for schizophrenic patients and their key relatives or care-givers: Results of a 2-year follow-up. *Acta Psychiatrica Scandinavica, 96,* 483–491.

Buckalew, L. W., & Ross, S. (1981). Relationship of perceptual characteristics to efficacy of placebos. *Psychological Reports, 49,* 955–961,

Buckner, R. L., Kelley, W. M., & Petersen, S. E. (1999). Frontal cortex contributes to human memory formation. *Nature Neuroscience, 2,* 311–314.

Buda, R., & Elsayed-Elkhouly, S. M. (1998). Cultural differences between Arabs and Americans: Individualism-collectivism revisited. *Journal of Cross-Cultural Psychology, 29,* 487–492.

Buehler, R., Griffin, D., & Ross, M. (1994). Exploring the "planning fallacy": Why people underestimate their task completion times. *Journal of Personality & Social Psychology, 67,* 366–381.

Buka, S. L., Goldstein, J. M., Seidman, L. J., Zornberg, G. L., Donatelli, J. A., Denny, L. R., & Tsuang, M. T. (1999). Prenatal complications, genetic vulnerability, and schizophrenia: The New England Longitudinal Studies of Schizophrenia. *Psychiatric Annals, 29,* 151–156.

Bunce, S. C., Bernat, E., Wong, P. S., & Shevrin, H. (1999). Further evidence for unconscious learning: Preliminary support for the conditioning of facial EMG to subliminal stimuli. *Journal of Psychiatric Research, 33,* 341–347.

Bunney, W. E., & Garland, B. L. (1983). Possible receptor effects of chronic lithium administration. *Neuropharmacology, 22,* 367–372.

Burger, J. M. (1992). *Desire for control: Personality, social, and clinical perspectives.* New York: Plenum.

Burger, J. M., & Cooper, H. M. (1979). The desirability of control. *Motivation and Emotion, 3,* 381–393.

Burish, T. G., & Carey, M. P. (1986). Conditioned aversive responses in cancer chemotherapy patients: Theoretical and developmental analysis. *Journal of Counseling and Clinical Psychology, 54,* 593–600.

Burnstein, E. (1982). Persuasion as argument processing. In H. Brandstatter, J. H. Davis, & G. Stocker-Krechgauer (Eds.), *Group decision making* (pp. 103–124). London: Academic Press.

Burton, M. J., Rolls, E. T., & Mora, F. (1976). Effects of hunger on the responses of neurons in the lateral hypothalamus to the sight and taste of food. *Experimental Neurology, 51,* 668–677.

Bushman, B. J. (1984). Perceived symbols of authority and their influence on compliance. *Journal of Applied Social Psychology, 14,* 501–508.

Bushman, B. J. (1988). The effects of apparel on compliance: A field experiment with a female authority figure. *Personality and Social Psychology Bulletin, 14,* 459–467.

Bushman, B. J. (1998). Threatened egotism, narcissism, self-esteem, and direct and displaced aggression: Does self-love or self-hate lead to violence? *Journal of Personality and Social Psychology, 75,* 219–229.

Bushman, B. J., Baumeister, R. F., & Stack, A. D. (1999). Catharsis, aggression, and persuasive influence: Self-fulfilling or self-defeating prophesies? *Journal of Personality and Social Psychology, 76,* 367–376.

Bushman, B. J., & Cooper, H. M. (1990). Effects of alcohol on human aggression: An integrative research review. *Psychological Bulletin, 107*, 1–14.

Bushman, B. J., & Wells, G. L. (1998). Trait aggressiveness and hockey penalties: Predicting hot tempers on the ice. *Journal of Applied Psychology, 83*, 969–974.

Buss, A. H. (1995). *Personality: Temperament, social behavior, and the self.* Needham Heights, MA: Allyn & Bacon.

Buss, A. H., & Plomin, R. (1975). *A temperament theory of personality development.* New York: Wiley Interscience.

Buss, A. H., & Plomin, R. (1984). *Temperament: Early developing personality traits.* Hillsdale, NJ: Erlbaum.

Buss, D. M. (1989). Sex differences in human mate preferences: Evolutionary hypotheses tested in 37 cultures. *Behavioral and Brain Sciences, 12*, 1–49.

Buss, D. M. (1994). *The evolution of desire: Strategies of human mating.* New York: Basic Books.

Buss, D. M. (1995). Psychological sex differences: Origins through sexual selection. *American Psychologist, 50*, 164–168.

Buss, D. M. (1998). The psychology of human mate selection: Exploring the complexity of the strategic repertoire. In C. B. Crawford & D. L. Krebs (Eds.), *Handbook of evolutionary psychology: Ideas, issues, and applications* (pp. 405–429). Mahwah, NJ: Erlbaum.

Buss, D. M. (1999). *Evolutionary psychology: The new science of the mind.* Boston: Allyn & Bacon.

Buss, D. M., & Craik, K. H. (1984). Acts, dispositions, and personality. In B. A. Maher & W. A. Maher (Eds.), *Progress in experimental personality research* (Vol. 13). New York: Academic Press.

Busse, E. W. (1969). Theories of aging. In E. W. Busse & E. Pfeiffer (Eds.), *Behavior and adaptation in later life* (pp. 11–32). Boston: Little, Brown.

Butcher, J. N., & Rouse, S. V. (1996). Personality: Individual difference and clinical assessment. *Annual Review of Psychology, 47*, 87–111.

Butzlaff, R. L., & Hooley, J. M. (1998). Expressed emotion and psychiatric relapse: A meta-analysis. *Archives of General Psychiatry, 55*, 547–552.

Byrne, D. (1971). *The attraction paradigm.* New York: Academic Press.

Cabeza, R., & Nyberg, L. (1997). Imaging cognition: An empirical review of PET studies with normal subjects. *Journal of Cognitive Neuroscience, 9*, 1–26.

Cabeza, R., & Nyberg, L. (2000). Imaging cognition II: An empirical review of 275 PET and fMRI studies. *Journal of Cognitive Neuroscience, 12*, 1–47.

Cacioppo, J. T., Gardner, J. T., & Berntson, W. L. (1997). Beyond bipolar conceptualizations and measures: The case of attitudes and evaluative space. *Personality & Social Psychology Review, 1*, 3–25.

Cacioppo, J. T., Petty, R. E., Feinstein, J. A., & Jarvis, W. B. G. (1996). Disposition differences in cognition motivation: The life and times of individuals varying in need for cognition. *Psychological Bulletin, 119*, 197–253.

Cacioppo, J. T., Petty, R. E., Losch, M. E., & Kim, H. S. (1986). Electromyographic activity over facial muscle regions can differentiate the valence and intensity of affective reactions. *Journal of Personality and Social Psychology, 50*, 260–268.

Cahan, S., & Cohen, N. (1989). Age versus schooling effects on intelligence development. *Child Development, 60*, 1239–1249.

Cahill, L., Haier, R. J., Fallon, J., Alkire, M. T., Tang, C., Keator, D., Wu, J., & McGaugh, J. L. (1996). Amygdala activity at encoding correlated with long-term free recall of emotional information. *Proceedings of the National Academy of Sciences, USA, 93*, 8016–8021.

Cahill, L., Prins, B., Weber, M., & McGaugh, J. L. (1994). Adrenergic activation and memory for emotional events. *Nature, 371*, 702–704.

Cailliet, R. (1993). *Pain: Mechanisms and management.* Philadelphia: Davis.

Cain, W. S. (1973). Spatial discrimination of cutaneous warmth. *American Journal of Psychology, 86*, 169–181.

Cain, W. S. (1979). To know with the nose: Keys to odor identification. *Science, 203*, 467–470.

Cain, W. S. (1982). Odor identification by males and females: Predictions and performance. *Chemical Senses, 7*, 129–141.

Cain, W. S., & Gent, J. F. (1991). Olfactory sensitivity: Reliability, generality, and association with aging. *Journal of Experimental Psychology: Human Perception and Performance, 17*, 382–391.

Calder, A. J., Young, A. W., Rowland, D., Perrett, D. I., Hodges, J. R., & Etcoff, N. L. (1996). Face perception after bilateral amygdala damage: Differentially severe impairment of fear. *Cognitive Neuropsychology, 13*, 699–745.

Caldera, Y. M., & Sciaraffa, M. A. (1998). Parent-toddler play with feminine toys: Are all dolls the same? *Sex Roles, 39*, 657–668.

Calvocoressi, L., Lewis, B., Harris, M., Trufan, S. J., et al. (1995). Family accommodation in obsessive-compulsive disorder. *American Journal of Psychiatry, 152*, 441–443.

Campbell, J. I. D., & Charness, N. (1990). Age-related declines in working-memory skills: Evidence from a complex calculation task. *Developmental Psychology, 26*(6), 879–888.

Canli, T., Zhao, Z., Desmond, J. E., Kang, E., Gross, J., & Gabrieli, J. D. E. (2001). An fMRI study of personality influences on brain reactivity to emotional stimuli. *Behavioral Neuroscience.*

Cannon, M., Jones, P., Huttunen, M. O., Tanskanen, A., Huttunen, T., Rabe-Hesketh, S., & Murray, R. M. (1999). School performance in Finnish children and later development of schizophrenia: A population-based longitudinal study. *Archives of General Psychiatry, 56*, 457–463.

Cannon, T. D. (1997). On the nature and mechanisms of obstetric influences in schizophrenia: A review and synthesis of epidemiologic studies. *International Review of Psychiatry, 9*, 387–397.

Cannon, W. B. (1927). The James-Lange theory of emotions: A critical examination and an alternative theory. *American Journal of Psychology, 39*, 106–124.

Cannon, W. B. (1932). *The wisdom of the body.* New York: W. W. Norton.

Cannon, W. B. (1942). Voodoo death. *American Anthropologist, 44*, 169–181.

Canter, S. (1973). Personality traits in twins. In G. Claridge, S. Canter, & W. I. Hume (Eds.). *Personality differences and biological variations* (pp. 21–51). New York: Pergamon.

Carey, M. P., & Burish, T. G. (1988). Etiology and treatment of the psychological side effects associated with cancer chemotherapy: A critical review and discussion. *Psychological Bulletin, 104*, 307–325.

Carey, S. (1978). The child as word learner. In J. Bresnan, G. Miller, & M. Halle (Eds.), *Linguistic theory and psychological reality* (pp. 264–293). Cambridge, MA: MIT Press.

Carney, R. M., Freeland, K. E., Veith, R. C., Cryer, P. E., Skala, J. A., Lynch, T., & Jaffe, A. S. (1999). Major depression, heart rate, and plasma norepinephrine in patients with coronary heart disease. *Biological Psychiatry, 45*, 458–463.

Carraher, T. N., Carraher, D. W., & Schliemann, A. D. (1985). Mathematics in the streets and in schools. *British Journal of Developmental Psychology, 3*, 21–29.

Carroll, J. (1993). *Human cognitive abilities: A survey of factor-analytic studies.* New York: Cambridge University Press.

Carskadon, M., Vieria, C., & Acebo, C. (1993). Association between puberty and delayed phase preference. *Sleep, 16*, 258–262.

Carstensen, L. L. (1991). Socioemotional selectivity theory: Social activity in life-span context. In K. W. Schaie & M. P. Lawton (Eds.), *Annual review of gerontology and geriatrics* (Vol. 11, pp. 195–217). New York: Springer.

Carstensen, L. L. (1992). Social and emotion patterns in adulthood: Support for socioemotional selectivity theory. *Psychology and Aging, 7*, 331–338.

Carter, C., & Rice, C. L. (1997). Acquisition and manifestation of prejudice in children. *Journal of Multicultural Counseling and Development, 25*, 185–194.

Carter, J. C., Stewart, D. A., Dunn, V. J., & Fairburn, C. G. (1997). Primary prevention of eating disorders: Might it do more harm than good? *International Journal of Eating Disorders, 22*, 167–172.

Carver, C. S., & Scheier, M. F. (1996). *Perspectives on personality.* Boston: Allyn & Bacon.

Carver, C. S., Scheier, M. F., & Weintraub, J. K. (1989). Assessing coping strategies: A theoretically based approach. *Journal of Personality and Social Psychology, 56*, 267–83.

Casada, J. H., Amdur, R., Larsen, R., & Liberzon, I. (1998). Psychophysiologic responsivity in posttraumatic stress disorder: Generalized hyperresponsiveness versus trauma specificity. *Biological Psychiatry, 44*, 1037–1044.

Case, R. (1977). Responsiveness to conservation training as a function of induced subjective uncertainty, M-space, and cognitive style. *Canadian Journal of Behavioral Sciences, 9*, 12–25.

Case, R. (1978). Intellectual development from birth to adulthood: A neo-Piagetian approach. In R. S. Siegler (Ed.), *Children's thinking: What develops?* (pp. 37–71). Hillsdale, NJ: Erlbaum.

Case, R. (1985). *Intellectual development: A systematic reinterpretation*. New York: Academic Press.

Case, R. (1992a). The role of the frontal lobes in the regulation of cognitive development. *Brain & Cognition, 20,* 51–73.

Case, R. (1992b). *The mind's staircase*. Hillsdale, NJ: Erlbaum.

Case, R. (1992c). The role of the frontal lobes in the regulation of cognitive development. *Brain and Cognition, 20,* 51–73.

Caspi, A. (2000). The child is father of the man: Personality continuities from childhood to adulthood. *Journal of Personality and Social Psychology, 78,* 158–172.

Caspi, A., Begg, D., Dickson, N., Harrington, H., Langley, J., Moffitt, T. E., & Silva, P. A. (1997). Personality differences predict health-risk behaviors in young adulthood: Evidence from a longitudinal study. *Journal of Personality and Social Psychology, 73,* 1052–1063.

Caspi, A., & Herbener, E. S. (1990). Continuity and change: Assortative marriage and the consistency of personality in adulthood. *Journal of Personality and Social Psychology, 58,* 250–258.

Cattell, R. B. (1971). *Abilities: Their structure, growth, and action*. Boston: Houghton Mifflin.

Cattell, R. B., Eber, H. W., & Tatsuoka, M. M. (1970). *Handbook for the Sixteen Personality Factor Questionnaire (16PF)*. Champaign, IL: Institute for Personality and Ability Testing.

Caudron, S. (1994). Diversity ignites effective work teams. *Personnel Journal, 73,* 54–63.

Cave, C. B. (1997). Very long-lasting priming in picture naming. *American Psychological Society, 8,* 322–325.

Cave, C. B., & Kosslyn, S. M. (1993). The role of parts and spatial relations in object identification. *Perception, 22,* 229–248.

Ceci, S. J. (1991). How much does schooling influence general intelligence and its cognitive components? A reassessment of the evidence. *Developmental Psychology, 27,* 703–722.

Ceci, S. J., & Williams, W. M. (1997). Schooling, intelligence, and income. *American Psychologist, 52,* 1051–1058.

Center for the Advancement of Health (1998). Facts of life: An issue briefing for health reporters. 3(3), 2.

Cerella, J. (1990). Aging and information-processing rate. In J. E. Birren & K. W. Schaie (Eds.), *Handbook of the psychology of aging* (3rd ed., pp. 201–221). San Diego, CA: Academic Press.

Chamberlain, K., & Zika, S. (1990). The minor events approach to stress: Support for the use of daily hassles. *British Journal of Psychology, 81,* 469–481.

Chambers, J. M., Cleveland, W. S., Kleiner, B., & Turkey, P. A. (1983). *Graphical methods for data analysis*. Belmont, CA: Wadsworth.

Chambless, D. L., & Gillis, M. M. (1993). Cognitive therapy of anxiety disorders. *Journal of Consulting and Clinical Psychology, 61,* 248–260.

Chao, L. L., & Martin, A. (1999). Cortical regions associated with perceiving, naming, and knowing about colors. *Journal of Cognitive Neuroscience, 11,* 25–35.

Chapman, C. (1989). Giving the patient control of opioid analgesic administration. In C. Hill & W. Fields (Eds.). *Advances in Pain Research and Therapy*, Vol. 11. New York: Raven Press.

Chapman, C. R., & Nakamura, Y. (1999). A passion of the soul: An introduction to pain for consciousness researchers. *Consciousness and Cognition, 8,* 391–422.

Chase, W. G., & Ericsson, K. A. (1981). Skilled memory. In J. R. Anderson (Ed.), *Cognitive skills and their acquisition*. Hillsdale, NJ: Erlbaum.

Chen, W., Kato, T., Zhun, X.-H., Ogawa, S., Tank, D. W., & Uguibil, K. (1998). Human primary visual cortex and lateral geniculate nucleus activation during visual memory. *NeuroReport, 9,* 3669–3674.

Cheour-Luhtanen, M., Alho, K., Sainio, K., Rinne, T., & Reinikainen, K. (1996). The ontogenetically earliest discriminative response of the human brain. *Psychophysiology, 33,* 478–481.

Cherry, E. C. (1953). Some experiments on the recognition of speech with one and two ears. *Journal of the Acoustical Society of America, 25,* 975–979.

Chess, S., & Thomas, A. (1987). *Know your child*. New York: Basic Books.

Chess, S., & Thomas, A. (1996). *Temperament: Theory and practice*. New York: Brunner/Mazel.

Chilcoat, H. D., & Breslau, N. (1998). Posttraumatic Stress Disorder and Drug Disorders Testing Causal Pathways. *Arch Gen Psychiatry, 55,* 913–917.

Chipuer, H. M., Rovine, M. J., & Plomin, R. (1990). LISREL modeling: Genetic and environmental influences on IQ revisited. *Intelligence, 14,* 11–29.

Choderow, N. (1978). *The reproduction of mothering*. Berkeley: University of California Press.

Chomsky, N. (1957). *Syntactic Structures* . Mouton: The Hague.

Chomsky, N. (1972). *Language and mind*. New York: Harcourt Brace.

Chorney, M. K, Chorney, K., Seese, N., Owen, M. J., Daniels, J., McGufin, P., Thompson, L. A., Detterman, D. K., Benbow, C., Lubinski, D., Eley, T., & Plomin, R. (1998). A quantative trait locus associated with cognitive ability in children. *Psychological Science, 9,* 159–166.

Christensen, K. A., Stephens, M. A. P., & Townsend, A. L. (1998). Mastery in women's multiple roles and well-being: Adult daughters providing care to impaired parents. *Health Psychology, 17,* 163–171.

Chun, M. M. (1997). Types and tokens in visual processing: A double dissociation between the attentional blink and repetition blindness. *Journal of Experimental Psychology: Human Perception and Performance, 23,* 738–755.

Cialdini, R. B. (1994). Interpersonal influence. In N. S. Shavitt & T. C. Brock (Eds.), *Persuasion: Psychological insights and perspectives* (pp. 195–218). Boston: Allyn & Bacon.

Cialdini, R. B., & Petty, R. (1979). Anticipatory opinion effects. In B. Petty, T. Ostrom, & T. Brock (Eds.), *Cognitive responses in persuasion*. Hillsdale, NJ: Erlbaum.

Cialdini, R. B., & Trost, M. R. (1998). Social influence: Social norms, conformity, and compliance. In D. T. Gilbert, S. T. Fiske, & G. Lindzey (Eds.), *The Handbook of Social Psychology* (4th ed.). New York: McGraw Hill. 151–192.

Cialdini, R. B., Vincent, J. A., Lewis, S. K., Catalan, J., Wheeler, D., & Darby, B. L. (1975). Reciprocal concessions procedure for inducing compliance: The door-in-the-face technique. *Journal of Personality and Social Psychology, 31,* 206–215.

Citron, M., Solomon, P., & Draine, J. (1999). Self-help groups for families of persons with mental illness: Perceived benefits of helpfulness. *Community Mental Health Journal, 35,* 15–30.

Clancy, S. A., McNally, R. J., & Schacter, D. L. (1999). Effects of guided imagery on memory distortion in women reporting recovered memories of childhood sexual abuse. *Journal of Traumatic Stress, 12,* 559–569.

Clarey, J. C., Barone, P., & Imig, T. J. (1992). Physiology of thalmus and cortex. In A. N. Popper & R. R. Fay (Eds.), *The mammalian auditory pathway: Neurophysiology* (pp. 232–334). New York: Springer-Verlag.

Clark, D. M., Ball, S., & Pape, D. (1991). An experimental investigation of thought suppression. *Behaviour Research and Therapy, 29,* 253–257.

Clark, D. M., Salkovskis, P. M., Hackmann, A., Wells, A., Ludgate, J., & Gelder, M. (1999). Brief cognitive therapy for panic disorder: A randomized controlled trial. *Journal of Consulting and Clinical Psychology, 67,* 583–589.

Clark, E. V. (1983). Meanings and concepts. In P. H. Mussen (Ed.), *Handbook of child psychology: Vol. 3, Cognitive development* (pp. 787–840). New York: Wiley.

Clark, E. V. (1993). *The lexicon in acquisition*. Cambridge: Cambridge University Press.

Clark, E. V. (1995). The lexicon and syntax. In J. L. Miller & P. D. Eimas (Eds.), *Speech, language, and communication* (pp. 303–337). San Diego: Academic Press.

Clark, L. F., & Collins, J. E. (1993). Remembering old flames: How the past affects assessments of the present. *Personality & Social Psychology Bulletin, 19,* 399–408.

Clay, R. (1995). Working mothers: happy or haggard? *The APA Monitor, 26 (11),* 1, 37.

Clifford, D. B. (2000). Human immunodeficiency virus-associated dementia. *Archives of Neurology, 57,* 321–324.

Cloninger, R., Svarkic, D. M., & Prysbeck, T. R. (1993). Psychobiological model of temperament and character. *Archives of General Psychiatry, 50,* 975–990.

Clopton, N. A., & Sorell, G. T. (1993). Gender differences in moral reasoning: Stable or situational? *Psychology of Women Quarterly, 17,* 85–101.

Coats, E. J., & Feldman, R. S. (1996). Gender differences in nonverbal correlates of social status. *Personality & Social Psychology Bulletin, 22,* 1014–1022.

Cohen, H., Kotler, M., Matar, M. A., Kaplan, Z., Loewenthal, U., Miodownik, J., & Cassuto, Y. (1998). Analysis of heart rate variability in posttraumatic stress disorder patients in response to a trauma-related reminder. *Biological Psychiatry, 44,* 1054–1059.

Cohen, S., & Herbert, T. B. (1996). Health Psychology: psychological factors and physical disease from the perspective of human psychoneuroimmunology. *Annual Review of Psychology, 47,* 113–142.

Cohen, S., Tyrrell, D. A. J., & Smith, A. P. (1991). Psychological stress and susceptibility to the common cold. *New England Journal of Medicine, 325*, 606–612.

Cohen, S., Tyrrell, D. A. J., & Smith, A. P. (1993). Negative life events, perceived stress, negative affect, and susceptibility to the common cold. *Journal of Personality and Social Psychology, 64,* 131–140.

Cohen, S., Tyrrell, D. A. J., & Smith, A. P. (1997). Psychological stress in humans and susceptibility to the common cold. In T. W. Miller (Ed.), *Clinical disorders and stressful life events.* (pp. 217–235). Madison, CT: International Universities Press.

Cohen, S., & Wills, T. (1985). Stress, social support and the buffering hypothesis. *Psychological Bulletin, 98*, 310–357.

Colapinto, J. (2000). *As nature made him: The boy who was raised as a girl.* New York: HarperCollins.

Colby, A., Kohlberg, L., Gibbs, J. C., & Lieberman, M. (1983). A longitudinal study of moral judgment. *Monographs of the Society for Research in Child Development, 48* (1–2, Serial No. 200).

Cole, M. (1990). Cognitive development and formal schooling: The evidence from cross-cultural research. In L. C. Moll (Ed.), *Vygotsky and education* (pp. 89–110). New York: Cambridge University Press.

Cole, M., Gay, J., Glick, J. A., & Sharp, D. W. (1971). *The cultural context of learning and thinking.* New York: Basic Books.

Cole, M., & Wertsch, J. V. (1996). Beyond the individual-social antinomy in discussions of Piaget and Vygotsky. *Human Development, 39*, 250–256.

Coleman, P., & Flood, D. (1986). Dendritic proliferation in the aging brain as a compensatory repair mechanism. *Progress in Brain Research, 70*, 227–236.

Collier, B. A. C. (2000). *The library: Quotes.* Retrieved 19 July 2000 from the World Wide Web: http://www.uniblab.com/collie/Quotes/n.html.

Collins, M. A., & Zebrowitz, L. A. (1995). The contributions of appearance to occupational outcomes in civilian and military settings. *Journal of Applied Social Psychology, 25*, 129–163.

Collins, W. A. (1990). Parent-child relationships in the transition to adolescence: Continuity and change in interaction, affect, and cognition. In R. Montemayor, G. R. Adams, & T. P. Gullota (Eds.), *From childhood to adolescence: A transitional period?* (pp. 85–106). Newbury Park, CA: Sage.

Colom, F., Vieta, E., Martinez, A., Jorquera, A., & Gasto, C. (1998). What is the role of psychotherapy in the treatment of bipolar disorder? *Psychotherapy & Psychosomatics, 67*, 3–9.

Comery, T. A., Shah, R., & Greenough, W. T. (1995). Differential rearing alters spine density on medium-sized spiny neurons in the rat corpus striatum: Evidence for association of morphological plasticity with early response gene expression. *Neurobiology of Learning & Memory, 63*, 217–219.

Compas, B. E., Haaga, D. A. F., Keefe, F. J., Leitenberg, H., & Williams, D. A. (1998). Sampling of Empirically Supported Psychological Treatments From Health Psychology, *Journal of Consulting and Clinical Psychology, 66*, 89–112.

Cone, E. J. (1995). Pharmacokinetics and Pharmacodynamics of Cocaine. *Journal of Analytical Toxicology, 19*, 459–477.

Conway, M. A., & Rubin, D. C. (1993). The structure of autobiographical memory. In A. F. Collins, S. E. Gathercole, M. A. Conway, & P. E. Morris (Eds.), *Theories of memory* (pp. 103–137). Hillsdale, NJ: Erlbaum.

Cook, E. W., III, Hawk, L. W., Davis, T. L., & Stevenson, V. E. (1991). Affective individual differences and startle reflex modulation. *Journal of Abnormal Psychology, 100*, 5–13.

Coons, P. M., Milstein, V., & Marley, C. (1982). EEG studies of two multiple personalities and a control. *Archives of General Psychiatry, 39*, 823–825.

Cooper, J. (1998). Unlearning cognitive dissonance: Toward an understanding of the development of dissonance. *Journal of Experimental Social Psychology, 34*, 562–575.

Cooper, M. L., Shapiro, C. M., & Powers, A. M. (1998). Motivations for sex and risky sexual behavior among adolescents and young adults: A functional perspective. *Journal of Personality and Social Psychology, 75*, 1528–1558.

Cooper, R. P., Abraham, J., Berman, S., & Staska, M. (1997). The development of infants' preference for motherese. *Infant Behavior & Development, 20*, 477–488.

Coplan, J. D., Goetz, R., Klein, D. F., Papp, L. A., Fyer, A. J., Liebowitz, M. R., Davies, S. O., & Gorman, J. M. (1998). Plasma cortisol concentrations preceding lactate-induced panic: Psychological, biochemical, and physiological correlates. *Archives of General Psychiatry, 55*, 130–136.

Corbetta, M., Miezin, F. M., Dobmeyer, S., Shulman, G. L., & Petersen, S. E. (1990). Attentional modulation of neural processing of shape, color, and velocity in humans. *Science, 248*, 1556–1559.

Corbetta, M., Miezin, F. M., Dobmeyer, S., Shulman, G. L., & Petersen, S. E. (1991). Selective and divided attention during visual discriminations of shape, color, and speed: Functional anatomy by positron emission tomography. *Journal of Neuroscience, 11*, 2383–2402.

Corbetta, M., Miezen, F. M., Schulman, G. L., & Petersen, S. E. (1993). A PET study of visuospatial attention. *Journal of Neuroscience, 13*, 1202–1226.

Coren, S. (1996). *Sleep Thieves: An Eye-opening exporation into the science and mysteries of sleep*, New York: Free Press.

Corr, P. J., & Kumari, V. (1997). Sociability/impulsivity and attenuated-dopaminergic arousal: Critical flicker/fusion frequency and procedural learning. *Personality and Individual Differences, 22*, 805–815.

Corr, P. J., Pickering, A. D., & Gray, J. A. (1995). Sociability/impulsivity and caffeine-induced arousal: Critical flicker/fusion frequency and procedural learning. *Personality and Individual Differences, 18*, 713–730.

Cosmides, L., & Tooby, J. (1996). Are humans good intuitive statisticians after all? Rethinking some conclusions from the literature on judgment under uncertainty. *Cognition, 58*, 1–73.

Costa, P. T., & McCrae, R. R. (1988). Personality in adulthood: A six-year longitudinal study of self-reports and spouse ratings on the NEO personality inventory. *Journal of Personality and Social Psychology, 54*, 853–863.

Costa, P. T., & McCrae, R. R. (1995). Primary traits of Eysenck's P-E-N System: Three- and five-factor solutions. *Journal of Personality and Social Psychology, 69*, 308–317.

Costa, P. T., McCrae, R. R., & Dye, D. A. (1991). Facet scales for agreeableness and conscientiousness: A revision of the NEO Personality Inventory. *Personality and Individual Differences, 12*, 887–898.

Costela, C., Tejedor-Real, P., Mico, J. A., & Gilbert-Rahola, J. (1995). Effect of neonatal handling on learned helplessness model of depression. *Physiology and Behavior, 57*, 407–410.

Cotman, C. (1990). The brain: New plasticity/new possibility. In R. N. Butler, M. R. Oberlink, & M. Schechter (Eds.), *The promise of productive aging: From biology to social policy* (pp. 70–84). New York: Springer.

Counts, D. A., & Counts, D. R. (1992). "I'm not dead yet!" Aging and death: Process and experience in Kaliai. In L. A. Platt & V. R. Persico, Jr. (Eds.), *Grief in cross-cultural perspective: A casebook* (pp. 307–343). New York: Garland.

Cowan, N. (2001). The magical number 4 in short-term memory: A reconsideration of mental storage capacity. *Brain and Behavioral Sciences*.

Cowan, W. M., Fawcett, J. W., O'Leary, D. D. M., & Stanfield, B. B. (1984). Regressive events in neurogenesis. *Science, 225*, 1258–1265.

Cowey, A., & Stoerig, P. (1995). Blindsight in monkeys. *Nature, 373*, 247–249.

Cox, H. (2000). Personal communication.

Coyne, J. C. (1976). Toward an interactional description of depression. *Psychiatry, 39*, 28–40.

Coyne, J. C., & Downey, G. (1991). Social factors in psychopathology: Stress, social support, and coping processes. *Annual Review of Psychology, 42*, 401–425.

Coyne, J. C., Kessler, R. C., Tal, M., Turnbull, J., Wortman, C., & Greden, J. (1987). Living with a depressed person: Burden and psychological distress. *Journal of Clinical and Consulting Psychology, 55*, 347–352.

Craik, F. I., & McDowd, J. M. (1987). Age differences in recall and recognition. *Journal of Experimental Psychology: Learning, Memory, & Cognition, 13*, 474–479.

Craik, F. I. M., Anderson, N. D., Kerr, S. A., & Li, K. Z. H. (1995). Memory changes in normal aging. In A. D. Baddeley, B. A. Wilson, & F. N. Watts (Eds.). *Handbook of memory disorders* (pp. 211–241). New York: Wiley.

Craik, F. I. M., & Lockhart, R. S. (1972). Levels of Processing: A framework for memory research. *Journal of Verbal Learning and Verbal Behavior, 11*, 671–684.

Craik, F. I. M., & Tulving, E. (1975). Depth of processing and the retention of words in episodic memory. *Journal of Experimental Psychology: General, 104,* 268–294.

Cramer, R. E., Schaefer, J. T., & Reid, S. (1996). Identifying the ideal mate: More evidence for male–female convergence. *Current Psychology: Developmental, Learning, Personality, Social, 16,* 157–166.

Crawford, M., Stark, A. C., & Renner, C. H. (1998). The meaning of Ms.: Social assimilation of a gender concept. *Psychology of Women Quarterly, 22,* 197–208.

Crick, F., & Mitchison, F. (1983). The function of dream sleep. *Nature, 304,* 111–114.

Crick, F., & Mitchison, G. (1986). REM sleep and neural nets. *Journal of Mind and Behavior, 7,* 229–250.

Crick, N. R., & Grotpeter, J. K. (1995). Relational aggression, gender, and social-psychological adjustment. *Child Development, 66,* 710–722.

Crisp, A. H., Hsu, L. K., & Harding, B. (1980). The starving hoarder and voracious spender: Stealing in anorexia nervosa. *Journal of Psychosomatic Research, 24,* 225–231.

Critchley, H. D., & Rolls, E. T. (1996). Hunger and satiety modify the responses of olfactory and visual neurons in the primate orbitofrontal cortex. *Journal of Neurophysiology, 75,* 1673–1686.

Crits-Christoph, P. (1992). The efficacy of brief dynamic psychotherapy: A meta-analysis. *American Journal of Psychiatry, 149,* 151–158.

Croizet, J.-C., & Claire, T. (1998) Extending the concept of stereotype and threat to social class: The intellectual underperformance of students from low socioeconimic backgrounds. *Personality & Social Psychology Bulletin, 24,* 588–594.

Cronbach, L. J. (1990). *Essentials of psychological testing.* New York: Harper & Row.

Crowe, R., Noyes, R., Pauls, D., & Slyman, D. (1983). A family study of panic disorder. *Archives of General Psychiatry, 40,* 1065–1069.

Csikszentmihalyi, M., & Csikszentmihalyi, I. S. (Eds.). (1988). *Optimal Experience: Psychological studies of flow in consciousness.* New York: Cambridge University Press.

Cuijpers, P. (1997). Bibliotherapy in unipolar depression: A meta-analysis. *Journal of Behavior Therapy & Experimental Psychiatry, 28,* 139–147.

Culbertson, F. M. (1997). Depression and gender: An international review. *American Psychologist, 52,* 25–31.

Cummings, N. (1992). Self-defense training for college women. *Journal of American College Health, 40,* 183–188.

Cunningham, M. R. (1986). Measuring the physical in physical attractiveness: Quasi-experiments on the sociobiology of female facial beauty. *Journal of Personality and Social Psychology, 50,* 925–935.

Cunningham, M. R., Barbee, A. P., & Pike, C. L. (1990). What do women want? Facialmetric assessment of multiple motives in the perception of male facial physical attractiveness. *Journal of Personality and Social Psychology, 59,* 61–72.

Cunningham, M. R., Roberts, A. R., Barbee, A. P., Druen, P. B., & Wu, C. H. (1995). "Their ideas of beauty are, on the whole, the same as ours": Consistency and variability in the cross-cultural perception of female physical attractiveness. *Journal of Personality and Social Psychology, 68,* 261–279.

Cupach, W. P., & Spitzberg, B. H. (1994). *The dark side of interpersonal communication.* Hillsdale, NJ: Erlbaum.

Czeisler, C. A., Duffy, J. F., Shanahan, T. L., Brown, E. N., Mitchell, J. F., Rimmer, D. W., Ronda, J. M., Silva, E. J., Allan, J. S., Emens, J. S., Dijk, D. J., & Kronauer, R. E. (1999). Stability, precision, and near-24-hour period of the human circadian pacemaker. *Science, 284,* 2101–2103.

Dadds, M. R., Bovberg, D. H., Redd, W. H., & Cutmore, T. R. H. (1997). Imagery in human classical conditioning. *Psychological Bulletin, 122,* 89–103.

Dai, X. Y., & Lynn, R. (1994). Gender differences in intelligence among Chinese children. *The Journal of Social Psychology, 134,* 123–125.

Dalbert, C., & Yamauchi, L. (1994). Belief in a just world and attitudes toward immigrants and foreign workers: A cultural comparison between Hawaii and Germany. *Journal of Applied Social Psychology, 24,* 1612–1626.

Damasio, A. R. (1985). Disorders of complex visual processing: Agnosias, achromatopsia, Balint's syndrome, and related difficulties of orientation and construction. In M.-M. Mesulam (Ed.), *Principles of behavioral neurology* (pp. 259–288). Philadelphia: Davis.

Damasio, A. R. (1996). The somatic marker hypothesis and the possible functions of the prefrontal cortex. *Philosophical Transactions of the Royal Society London Series B, 351,* 1413–1420.

Damasio, H., Grabowski, T. J., Tranel, D., Hichwa, R. D., & Damasio, A. R. (1996). A neural basis for lexical retrieval. *Nature, 380,* 499–505.

Darley, J. M., & Latané, B. (1968). Bystander intervention in emergencies: Diffusion of responsibility. *Journal of Personality and Social Psychology, 10,* 202–214.

Darley, J. M., & Latané, B. (1970). Norms and normative behavior: Field studies of social interdependence. In J. Macauley and L. Berkowitz (Eds.), *Altruism and helping behavior.* (pp. 83–101). New York: Academic Press.

Darwin, C. (1872). *The expression of the emotions in man and animals.* Chicago: University of Chicago Press, 1965.

Dauncey, K., Giggs, J., Baker, K., & Harrison, K. (1993). Schizophrenia in Nottingham: Lifelong residential mobility of a cohort. *British Journal of Psychiatry, 163,* 613–619.

Davey, G. C. L. (1992). Classical condioting and the acquisition of human fears and phobias: A review of synthesis of the literature. *Advances in Behavior Research and Therapy, 14,* 29–66.

David, J. P., & Suls, J. (1999). Coping efforts in daily life: Role of Big Five traits and problem appraisals. *Journal of Personality, 67,* 265–294.

Davidson, R. J. (1992a). Emotion and affective style: Hemispheric substrates. *Psychological Science, 3,* 39–43.

Davidson, R. J. (1992b). A prolegomenon to the structure of emotion: Gleanings from neuropsychology. *Cognition and Emotion, 6,* 245–268.

Davidson, R. J. (1993). Parsing affective space: Perspectives from neuropsychology and psychophysiology. *Neuropsychology, 7,* 464–475.

Davidson, R. J. (1994a). Honoring biology in the study of affective style. In P. Ekman & R. J. Davidson (Eds.), *The nature of emotion: Fundamental questions* (pp. 321–328). New York: Oxford University Press.

Davidson, R. J. (1998). Affective style and affective disorders: Perspectives from affective neuroscience. *Cognition and Emotion, 12,* 307–330.

Davidson, R. J., Abercrombie, H., Nitschke, J. B., & Putnam, K. (1999). Regional brain function, emotion and disorders of emotion. *Current Opinion in Neurobiology, 9,* 228–234.

Davis, J. D., & Campbell, C. S. (1973). Peripheral control of meal size in the rat: Effects of sham feeding on meal size and drinking rate. *Journal of Comparative & Physiological Psychology, 83,* 379–387.

Davis, J. D., & Levine, M. W. (1977). A model for the control of ingestion. *Psychological Review, 84,* 379–412.

Davis, M. (1992). The role of the amygdala in conditioned fear. In J. P. Aggleton (Ed.), *The amygdala: Neurobiological aspects of emotion, memory, and mental dysfunction* (pp. 255– 306). New York: Wiley-Liss.

Davis, M. C., Matthews, K. A., & McGrath, C. E. (2000). Hostile attitudes predict elevated vascular resistance during interpersonal stress in men and women. *Psychosomatic Medicine, 62,* 17–25.

Dean, W., Morgenthaler, J., & Fowkes, S. W. (1993). *Smart drugs: II. The next generation: New drugs and nutrients to improve your memory and increase your intelligence (Smart Drug Series, Vol. 2).* Petaluma, CA: Smart Publications.

Deary, I. J., & Pagliari, C. (1991). The strength of *g* at different levels of ability: Have Detterman & Daniel rediscovered Spearman's "law of diminishing returns"? *Intelligence 15,* 247–250.

De Castro, J. M. (1990). Social facilitation of duration and size but not rate of the spontaneous meal intake of humans. *Physiology & Behavior, 47,* 1129–1135.

Deci, E. L., Koestner, R., & Ryan, R. M. (1999a). A meta-analytic review of experiments examining the effects of extrinsic rewards on intrinsic motivation. *Psychological Bulletin, 125,* 627–668.

Deese, J. (1959). On the prediction of occurrence of particular verbal intrusions in immediate recall. *Journal of Experimental Psychology, 58,* 17–22.

Deffenbacher, J. L., Oetting, E. R., Huff, M. E., Cornell, G. R., & Dalleger, C. J. (1996). Evaluation of two cognitive-behavioral approaches to general anger reduction. *Cognitive Therapy & Research, 20,* 551–573.

Degarrod, L. N. (1990). Coping with stress: Dream interpretation in the Mapuche family. *Psychiatric Journal of the University of Ottawa, 15,* 111–116.

Dehaene, S. (1997). *The number sense: How the mind creates mathematics.* New York: Oxford.

Dehaene-Lambertz, G., & Dehaene, S. (1994). Speed and cerebral correlates of syllable discrimination in infants. *Nature, 370,* 292–295.

Delany, S. L., Delany, A. E., & Hearth, A. H. (1993). *Having Our Say: The Delany Sisters' First 100 Years.* New York: Delta.

Delis, D. C., Robertson, L. C., & Efron, R. (1986). Hemispheric specialization of memory for visual hierarchical stimuli. *Neuropsychologia, 24*, 205–214.

Delk, J. L., & Fillenbaum, S. (1965). Difference in perceived color as a function of characteristic color. *American Journal of Psychology, 78*, 290–293.

Dell, P. F. (1998). Axis II pathology in outpatients with dissociative identity disorder. *Journal of Nervous & Mental Disease, 186*, 352–356.

DeLoache, J. S., Pierroutsakos, S. L., Uttal, D. H., Rosengren, K. S., & Gottlieb, A. (1998). Grasping the nature of pictures. *Psychological Science, 9*, 205–210.

DeLongis, A., Coyne, J. C., Dakof, G., Folkman, S., & Lazrus, R. S. (1982). Relationship of daily hassles, uplifts, and major life events to health status. *Health Psychology, 1*, 119–136.

DeMann, Jeffrey A. (1994). First person account: The evolution of a person with schizophrenia. *Schizophrenia Bulletin, 20*, 579–582.

De Marchi, N., & Mennella, R. (2000). Huntington's disease and its association with psychopathology. *Harvard Review of Psychiatry, 7*, 278–89.

Dement, W. C. (1974). *Some must watch while some must sleep.* San Francisco, CA: W. H. Freeman.

Denis, M., & Kosslyn, S. M. (1999). Scanning visual images: A window on the mind. *Current Psychology of Cognition, 18*, 409–465.

Dennis, W. (1966). Goodenough scores, art experience, and modernization. *Journal of Social Psychology, 68*, 211–228.

Department of Health and Human Services: Substance Abuse and Mental Health Services Administration. Preliminary Results from the 1997 National Household Survey on Drug Abuse. Rockville: SAHMSA, 1998.

DeQuardo, R. (1998). Pharmacologic treatment of first-episode schizophrenia: Early intervention is key to outcome. *Journal of Clinical Psychiatry, 59*, 9–17.

De Renzi, E., Liotti, M., & Nichelli, P. (1987). Semantic amnesia with preservation of autobiographic memory. A case report. *Cortex, 23*, 575–597.

D'Esposito, M., Detre, J. A., Alsop, D. C., Shin, R. K., Atlas, S., & Grossman, M. (1995). The neural basis of the central executive system of working memory. *Nature, 378*, 279–281.

Detterman, D. K., & Daniel, M. H. (1989). Correlates of mental tests with each other and with cognitive variables are highest for low IQ groups. *Intelligence, 13*, 349–359.

Deutsch, J. A., Young, W. G., & Kalogeris, T. J. (1978). The stomach signals satiety. *Science, 201*, 165–167.

De Valois, R. L., & De Valois, K. K. (1975). Neural coding of color. In E. C. Carterette & M. P. Friedman (Eds.), *Handbook of perception* (pp. 117–166). New York: Academic Press.

De Valois, R. L., & De Valois, K. K. (1993). A multi-stage color model. *Vision Research, 33*, 1053–1065.

de Villiers, P. A., & de Villiers, J. G. (1992). Language development. In M. H. Bornstein & M. E. Lamb (Eds.), *Developmental psychology: An advanced textbook* (3rd ed., pp. 337–418). Hillsdale, NJ: Erlbaum.

Devine, P. G., & Monteith, M. J. (1993). The role of discrepancy-associated affect in prejudice reduction. In D. M. Mackie & D. L. Hamilton (Eds.), et al. *Affect, cognition, and stereotyping: Interactive processes in group perception* (pp. 317–344). San Diego, CA: Academic Press.

Devlin, B., Daniels, M., & Roeder, K. (1997). The heritability of IQ. *Nature, 388*, 468–471.

deVries, M. W. (1984). Temperament and infant mortality among the Masai of East Africa. *American Journal of Psychiatry, 141*, 1189–1194.

De Wijk, R. A., & Cain, W. S. (1994). Odor identification by name and by edibility: Life-span development and safety. *Human Factors, 36*, 182–187.

De Wijk, R. A., Schab, F. R., & Cain, W. S. (1995). Odor identification. In F. R. Schab & R. G. Crowder (Eds.), *Memory for odors* (pp. 21–37). Mahwah, NJ: Erlbaum.

Dew, A. M., & Ward, C. (1993). The effects of ethnicity and culturally congruent and incongruent nonverbal behaviors on interpersonal attraction. *Journal of Applied Social Psychology, 23*, 1376–1389.

Dewhurst, S. A., & Conway, M. A. (1994). Pictures, images, and recollective experience. *Journal of Experimental Psychology: Learning, Memory, and Cognition, 20*, 1088–1098.

Diamond, M., & Sigmundson H. K. (1997). Sex reassignment at birth. Long-term review and clinical implications. *Archives of Pediatrics & Adolescent Medicine, 151*, 298–304.

Diamond, M. C., Rosenzweig, M. R., Bennett, E. L., Lindner, B., & Lyon, L. (1972). Effects of environmental enrichment and impoverishment on rat cerebral cortex. *Journal of Neural Biology, 3*, 47–64.

Diener, E. (1977).Deindividualtion: Causes and consequences. *Social Behavior and Personality, 5*, 143–155.

Diener, E. (2000). Subjective well-being: The science of happiness and a proposal for a national index. *American Psychologist, 55*, 34–43.

Diener, E., & Emmons, R. A. (1984). The independence of positive and negative affect. *Journal of Personality and Social Psychology, 47*, 1105–1117.

Dienstfrey, H. (1991). *Where The Mind Meets The Body.* New York: HarperCollins.

Digman, J. M. (1990). Personality structure: Emergence of the five-factor model. *Annual Review of Psychology, 41*, 417–440.

Dill, P. L., & Henley, T. B. (1998). Stressors of college: A comparison of traditional and nontraditional students. *Journal of Psychology, 132*, 25–32.

Dimberg, U., & Thunberg, M. (1998). Rapid facial reactions to emotion facial expressions. *Scandinavian Journal of Psychology, 39*, 39–46.

Dinges, D., Pack, F., Williams, K., Gillen, K., Powell, J., Ott, G., Aptowicz, C., & Pack, A. (1997). Cumulative sleepiness, mood disturbance, and psychomotor vigilance performance decrements during a week of sleep restricted to 4–5 hours per night. *Sleep, 20*, 267–277.

Dion, K., Berscheid, E., & Walster, E. (1972). What is beautiful is good. *Journal of Personality & Social Psychology, 24*, 285–290.

DiPietro, J. A., Hodgson, D. M., Costigan, K. A., Hilton, S. C., & Johnson, T. R. B. (1996). Fetal neurobehavioral development. *Child Development, 67*, 2553–2567.

Dobson, M., & Markham, R. (1993). Imagery ability and source monitoring: Implications for eyewitness memory. *British Journal of Psychology, 32*, 111–118.

Dodge, K. A., & Newman, J. P. (1981). Biased decision-making processes in aggressive boys. *Journal of Abnormal Psychology, 90*, 379.

Doheny, M. (1993). Effects of mental practice on performance of a psychomotor skill. *Journal of Mental Imagery, 17*(3–4), 111–118.

Dohrenwend, B. P., Levav, I., Shrout, P. E., Schwartz, S., Naveh, G., Link. B. G., Skodol, A. E., & Stueve, A. (1992). Socioeconomic status and psychiatric disorders: The causation-selection issue. *Science, 255*, 946–952.

Dohrmann, R. J., & Laskin, D. M. (1978). An evaluation of electromyographic biofeedback in the treatment of myofascial pain-dysfunction syndrome. *J Am Dent Assoc, 96*, 656–62.

Dolan, B. (1991). Cross-cultural aspects of anorexia nervosa and bulimia: A review. *International Journal of Eating Disorders, 10*, 67–79.

Dolan, R. J., & Fletcher, P. C. (1997). Dissociating prefrontal and hippocampal function in episodic memory encoding. *Nature, 388*, 582–585.

Dollard, J., Doob, L. W., Miller, N. E., Mowrer, O. H., Sears, R. R., Ford, C. S., Hovland, C. I., & Sollenberger, R. T. (1939). *Frustration and aggression.* New Haven: Yale Univ. Press.

Donaldson, S. O. (1995). Peer influence on adolescent drug use: A persepctive rom the trench of experimental evaulation research. *American Psychologist, 50*, 801–802.

Doty, R. L., Bartoshuk, L. M., & Snow, J. B., Jr. (1991). Causes of olfactory and gustatory disorders. In T. V. Getchell, R. L. Doty, L. M. Bartoshuk, & J. B. Snow, Jr. (Eds.), *Smell and taste in health and disease* (pp. 449–462). New York: Raven.

Dovidio, J. F., Evans, N., & Tyler, R. B. (1986). Racial stereotypes: The contents of their cognitive representations. *Journal of Experimental Social Psychology, 22*, 22–37.

Dowdall, G. W., Crawford, M., & Wechsler, H. (1998). Binge drinking among American college women: A comparison of single-sex and coeducational institutions. *Psychology of Women Quarterly, 22*, 705–715.

Dowling, J. E. (1992). *Neurons and networks: An introduction to neuroscience.* Cambridge, MA: Harvard University Press.

Downing, J. W., Judd, C. M., & Brauer, M. (1992). Effects of repeated expressions on attitude extremity. *Journal of Personality and Social Psychology, 63*, 17–29.

Draycott, S. G., & Kline, P. (1995). The Big Three or the Big Five—the EPQ—R vs the NEO-PI: A research note, replication and elaboration. *Personality & Individual Differences, 18*, 801–804.

Driskell, J., Copper, C., & Moran, A. (1994). Does mental practice enhance performance? *Journal of Applied Psychology, 79*(4), 481–492.

Druckman, D., & Swets, J. A. (Eds.), (1988). *Enhancing human performance: Issues, theories, and techniques.* Washington, D.C.: National Academy Press.

Drummond, S. P. A., Brown, G. G., Gillin, J. C., Stricker, J. L., Wong, E. C., & Buxton, R. B. (2000). *Nature, 403,* 655–657.

Dubrovsky, V. J., Kiesler, S., & Sethna, B. N. (1991). The equalization phenomenon: stauts effoects in computer-mediated and face-to-face decision-making groups. *Hum.-Comput. Interact., 6,* 119–146.

Duclaux, R., Feisthauer, J., & Cabanac, M. (1973). The effects of eating on the pleasantness of food and nonfood odors in man. *Physiology & Behavior, 10,* 1029–1033.

Duclos, S. E., Laird, J. D., Schneider, E., Sexter, M., Stern, L., & Van Lighten, O. (1989). Emotion-specific effects of facial expressions and postures on emotional experience. *Journal of Personality and Social Psychology, 57,* 100–108.

Duman, R. S., Heninger, G. R., & Nestler, E. J. (1997). A molecular and cellular theory of depression. *Archives of General Psychiatry, 54,* 597–606.

Duncan, H. F., Gourlay, N., & Hudson, W. (1973). *A study of pictorial perception among Bantu and White primary school children in South Africa.* Johannesburg, South Africa: Witwatersrand University Press.

Duncan, R. M., & Pratt, M. W. (1997). Microgenetic change in the quantity and quality of preschoolers' private speech. *International Journal of Behavioral Development, 20,* 367–383.

Duncker, K. (1945). On problem solving. *Psychological monographs, 58* (No. 270).

Dunnett, S. B., Lane, D. M., & Winn, P. (1985). Ibotenic acid lesions of the lateral hypothalamus: comparison with 6-hydroxydopamine-induced sensorimotor deficits. *Neuroscience, 14,* 509–518.

Dupuy, B., & Krashen, S. D. (1993). Incidental vocabulary acquisition in French as a foreign language. *Applied Language Learning, 4,* 55–63.

Dusek, D., & Girdano, D. A. (1980). *Drugs: A factual account.* Reading, MA: Addison Wesley.

Eagly, A. (1987). *Sex differences in social behavior: A social-role interpretation.* Hillsdale, NJ: Erlbaum.

Eagly, A. H. (1995). The science and politics of comparing women and men. *American Psychologist, 50* 145–158.

Eagly, A. H., & Carli, L. (1981). Sex of researchers and sex-typed communications as determinants of sex differences in influence-ability: A meta-analysis of social influence studies. *Psychological Bulletin, 90,* 1–20.

Eagly, A. H., & Chaiken, S. (1998). Attitude Structure and Function. In D. T. Gilbert, S. T. Fiske, & G. Lindzey (Eds.), The handbook of social psychology (4th ed.). New York: McGraw Hill. 269–322.

Eagly, A. H., & Steffen, V. J. (1986). Gender and aggressive behavior: A meta-analytic review of the social psychlogical literature. *Psychological Bulletin, 100,* 309–330.

Eagly, A. H., & Wood, W. (1999). The origins of sex differences in human behavior: Evolved dispositions versus social roles. *American Psychologist, 54,* 408–423.

Eakin, E. (2000, January 15). Bigotry as mental illness or just another norm. *New York Times,* p. A21.

Eals, M., & Silverman, I. (1994). The hunter-gatherer theory of spatial sex differences: Proximate factors mediating the female advantage on recall of object arrays. *Ethology and Sociobiology, 15,* 95–105.

Earle, T. L., Linden, W., & Weinberg, J. (1999). Differential effects of harassment on cardiovascular and salivary cortisol stress reactivity and recovery in women and men. *Journal of Psychosomatic Research, 46,* 125–141.

Eaves, L. J., Eysenck, H. J., & Martin, N. G. (1989). *Genes, culture and personality: An empirical approach.* London: Academic Press.

Ebbinghaus, H. (1885/1964). *Memory: A contribution to experimental psychology.* New York: Dover.

Ebstein, R. P., Novick, O., Umansky, R., Priel, B., Osher, Y., Blaine, D., Bennett, E. R., Nemanoc, L., Katz, M., & Belmaker, R. H. (1996). Dopamine D4 receptor (D4DR) exon III polymorphism associated with the human personality trait of Novelty Seeking. *Nature Genetics, 12,* 78–80.

The Economist World Atlas & Almanac (1989). New York: Prentice Hall.

Eder, R. A. (1989). The emergent personologist: The structure and content of 3-, 5-, and 7-year-olds' concepts of themselves and other persons. *Child Development, 60,* 1218–1228.

Egbert, L. D., Battit, G. E., Welch, C. E., & Barlett, M. K. (1964). Reduction of postoperative pain by encouragement and instruction of patients. *New England Journal of Medicine, 270,* 825–827.

Ehlers, A., Mayou, R. A., & Bryant, B. (1998). Psychological predictors of chronic posttraumatic stress disorder after motor vehicle accidents. *Journal of Abnormal Psychology, 107,* 508–519.

Eich, E. (1989). Theoretical issues in state dependent memory. In H. L. Roediger, III, & F. I. M. Craik (Eds.), *Varieties of memory and consciousness: Essays in honour of Endel Tulving* (pp. 331–354). Hillsdale, NJ: Erlbaum.

Eich, E. (1995). Searching for mood dependent memory. *Psychological Science, 6,* 67–75.

Eimas, P. D., & Corbit, J. D. (1973). Selective adaptation of linguistic feature detectors. *Cognitive Psychology, 4,* 99–109.

Eisenberg, N., Miller, P. A., Schaller, M., Fabes, R. A., Fultz, J., Shell, R., & Shea, C. L. (1989). The role of sympathy and altruistic personality traits in helping: A reexamination. *Journal of Personality, 57,* 41–67.

Ekman, P. (1980). Biological and cultural contributions to body and facial movement in the expression of emotion. In A. O. Rorty (Ed.), *Explaining emotions.* Berkeley, CA: University of California Press.

Ekman, P. (1984). Expression and the nature of emotion. In K. R. Scherer & P. Ekman (Eds.), *Approaches to emotion* (pp. 319–343). Hillsdale, NJ: Erlbaum.

Ekman, P. (1985). *Telling lies: Clues to deceit in the marketplace, marriage, and politics.* New York: Norton.

Ekman, P. (1992). Facial expressions of emotion: New findings, new questions. *Psychological Science, 3,* 34–38.

Ekman, P., & Davidson, R. J. (1993). Voluntary smiling changes regional brain activity. *Psychological Science, 4,* 342–345.

Ekman, P., & Friesen, W. (1971). Constants across cultures in the face and emotion. *Journal of Personality & Social Psychology, 17,* 124–129.

Ekman, P., Davidson, R. J., & Friesen, W. V. (1990). The Duchenne smile: Emotional expression and brain psychology II. *Journal of Personality & Social Psychology, 58,* 342–353.

Elber, T., Pantev, C., Wienbruch, C., Rockstroh, B., & Taub, E. (1995). Increased cortical representation of the fingers of the left hand in string players. *Science, 270,* 305–307.

Eley, T. C., Deater-Deckard, K., Fombone, E., Fulker, D. W., & Plomin, R. (1998). An adoption study of depressive symptoms in middle childhood. *Journal of Child Psychology & Psychiatry & Allied Disciplines, 39,* 337–345.

Elkin, I. (1994). The NIMH treatment of depression colarborative research program: Where we began and where we are. In A. E. Bergin & S. L. Garfield (Eds.), *Handbook of psychotherapy and behavior change, 4th edition* (pp. 114–142). New York: John Wiley & Sons.

Elkin, I., Gibbons, R., Shea, M. T., Sotsky, S. M., Watkins, J. T., Pilkonis, P. A., & Hedeker, D. (1995). Initial severity and differential treatment outcome in the National Institute of Mental Health Treatment of Depression Collaborative Research Program., 63 841–847.

Elkind, D. (1967). Egocentrism in adolescence. *Child Development, 38,* 1025–1034.

Elkind, D., & Bowen, R. (1979). Imaginary audience behavior in children and adolescence. *Developmental Psychology, 15,* 33–44.

Ellis, A. (1994a). The treatment of borderline personalities with rational emotive behaviour therapy. *Journal of Rational-Emotive & Cognitive Behavior Therapy, 12,* 101–119.

Ellis, A. (1994b). Rational emotive behavior therapy approaches to obsessive-compulsive disorder (OCD). *Journal of Rational-Emotive & Cognitive Behavior Therapy, 12,* 121–141.

Ellis, A. W., & Young, A. W. (1987). *Human cognitive neuropsychology.* Hillsdale, NJ: Lawrence Erlbaum.

Ellis, H. C. (1973). Stimulus encoding processes in human learning and memory. In G. H. Bower (Ed.), *The psychology of learning and motivation* (Vol. 7, pp. 124–182). New York: Academic Press.

Elman, J. L., Bates, E. A., Johnson, M. H., Karmiloff-Smith, A., et al. (1996). *Rethinking innateness: A connectionist perspective on development.* Cambridge: MIT Press.

Emmelkamp, P. M. G. (1994). Behavior therapy with adults. In A. E. Bergin & S. L. Garfield (Eds.), *Handbook of psychotherapy and behavior change, 4th edition* (pp. 379–427). New York: John Wiley & Sons.

Endler, N. S., & Hunt, J. McV. (1969). Generalizability of contributions from the sources of variance in the S-R inventories of anxiousness. *Journal of Personality, 37*, 1–24.

Entwisle, D. R. (1972). To dispel fantasies about fantasy-based measures of achievement motivation. *Psychological Bulletin, 77*, 377–391.

Epstein, C. M., Figiel, G. S., McDonald, W. M., Amazon-Leece, J., & Figiel, L. (1998). Rapid rate transcranial magnetic stimulation in young and middle-aged refractory depressed patients. *Psychiatric Annals, 28*, 36–39.

Epstein, H. T. (1980). EEG developmental stages. *Developmental Psychobiology, 13*, 629–631.

Erikson, D. H., Beiser, M., & Iacono, W. G. (1998). Social support predicts 5-year outcome in first-episode schizophrenia. *Journal of Abnormal Psychology, 107*, 681–685.

Erikson, E. H. (1950). *Childhood and society.* New York: Norton.

Ernst, C., & Angst, J. (1983). *Birth order: Its influence on personality.* Berlin: Springer-Verlag.

Eskenazi, B. (1993). Caffeine during pregnancy: Grounds for concern? *Journal of the American Medical Association, 270*, 2973–2974.

Eskenazi, B., Stapleton, A. L., Kharrazi, M., & Chee, W. Y. (1999). Associations between maternal decaffeinated and caffeinated coffee consumption and fetal growth and gestational duration. *Epidemiology, 10*, 242–249.

Esterling, B. A., L'Abate, L., Murray, E. J., & Pennebaker, J. W. (1999). Empirical foundations for writing in prevention and psychotherapy: Mental and phsycial health outcomes. *Clinical Psychology Review, 19*, 79–96.

Eyferth, K. (1961). Ein Vergleich der Beurteilung projektiver Tests durch verschiedene Berteiler [A comparison of judging projective tests by different judges]. *Zeitschrift fuer Experimentelle und Angewandte Psychologie, 8*, 329–338.

Eysenck, H. J. (1967). *The Biological Basis of Personality.* Springfield, IL: Charles C. Thomas, Publishers.

Eysenck, H. J. (1977). *Crime and Personality,* St. Albans, England: Paladin Frogmore.

Eysenck, H. J. (1979). The conditioning model of neurosis. *Behavioral and Brain Sciences, 2*, 155–199.

Eysenck, H. J. (1990b). Biological dimensions of personality. In L. A. Pervin (Ed.), *Handbook of personality: Theory and research* (pp. 244–276). New York: Guilford.

Eysenck, H. J. (1992). Four ways five factors are *not* basic. *Personality and Individual Differences, 13*, 667–673.

Eysenck, H. J. (1993). The structure of phenotypic personality traits: Comment. *American Psychologist, 48*, 1299–1300.

Eysenck, H. J. (1995). *Genius: The natural history of creativity.* Cambridge, England: Cambridge University Press.

Eysenck, H. J., & Gudjonsson, G. (1989). *The Causes and Cures of Criminality.* New York: Plenum Press.

Eysenck, S. B. G., & Eysenck, H. J. (1967). Salivary response to lemon juice as a measure of introversion. *Perceptional and motor skills, 24*, 1047–1053.

Faber, S. (1981). *Identical twins reared apart.* London: Blackwell.

Fairburn, C. G., Cooper, Z., Doll, H. A., & Welch, S. L. (1999). Risk factors for anorexia nervosa: Three integrated case-control comparisons. *Archives of General Psychiatry, 56*, 468–476.

Fantino, M., & Cabanac, M. (1980). Body weight regulation with a proportional hoarding response in the rat. *Physiology & Behavior, 24*, 939–942.

Farthing, G. (1992) *The psychology of consciousness.* Englewood Cliffs, NJ: Prentice-Hall.

Fatt, I., & Weissman, B. A. (1992). *Physiology of the eye: An introduction to the vegetative functions* (2nd ed.). Boston: Butterworth-Heinemann.

Fava, G. A. Rafanelli, C., Grandi, S., Conti, S., & Belluardo, P. (1998a). Prevention of Recurrent Depression With Cognitive Behavioral Therapy: Preliminary Findings. *Archives of General Psychiatry, 55*, 816–820.

Fava, G. A., Rafanelli, C., Grandi, S., Canestrari, R., & Morphy, M. A. (1998b). Six-year outcome for cognitive behavioral treatmetn of residual symptoms in major depression. *American Journal of Psychiatry, 155*, 1443–1445.

Fawzy, F. I., Kemeny, M. E., Fawzy, N. W., Elashoff, R., Morton, D., Cousins, N., Fahey, J. L. (1990). A structured psychiatric intervention for cancer patients: II. Changes over time in immunological measures. *Archives of General Psychiatry, 47*, 729–735.

Fay, R. E., Turner, C. F., Klassen, A. D., & Gagnon, J. H. (1989). Prevalence and patterns of same-gender sexual contact among men. *Science, 243*, 338–348.

Fazio, R. H., Chen, J., McDonel, E. C., & Sherman, S. J. (1982). Attitude accessibility and the strength of the object-evaluation association. *Journal of Experimental Psychology, 18*, 339–357.

Fazio, R. H., Jackson, J. R., Dunton, B. C., & Williams, C. J. (1995). Variability in automatic activation as an unobstrusive measure of racial attitudes: A bona fide pipeline? *Journal of Personality and Social Psychology, 69*, 1013–1027.

Feather, N. T. (1996). Social comparisons across nations: Variables relating to the subjective evaluation of national achievement and to personal and collective. *Australian Journal of Psychology, 48*, 53–63.

Feingold, A. (1990). Gender differences in effects of physical attractiveness on romantic attraction: A comparison across five research paradigms. *Journal of Personality and Social Psychology, 59*, 981–993.

Feingold, A. (1994). Gender differences in personality: A meta-analysis. *Psychological Bulletin, 116*, 429–456.

Feldman, D. H., & Goldsmith, L. T. (1991). *Nature's gambit: Child prodigies and the development of human potential.* New York: Teachers College Press.

Feldman, R. S., Coats, E. J., & Spielman, D. A. (1996). Television exposure and children's decoding of nonverbal behavior. *Journal of Applied Social Psychology, 26*, 1718–1733.

Felleman, D. J., & Van Essen, D. C. (1991). Distributed hierarchical processing in the primate cerebral cortex. *Cerebral Cortex, 1*, 1–47.

Ferguson, N. B., & Keesey, R. E. (1975). Effect of a quinine-adulterated diet upon body weight maintenance in male rats with ventromedial hypothalamic lesions. *Journal of Comparative & Physiological Psychology, 89*, 478–488.

Fernald, A., Taeschner, T., Dunn, J., Papousek, M., Boysson-Bardies, B., & Fukui, I. (1989). A cross-language study of prosodic modifications in mothers' and fathers' speech to infants. *Child Development, 64*, 637–656.

Ferveur, J.-F., Stoertkuhl, K. F., Stocker, R. F., & Greenspan, R. J. (1995). Genetic feminization of brain structures and changed sexual orientation in male Drosophila. *Science, 267*, 902–905.

Feske, U., & Chambless, D. L. (1995). Cognitive behavioral versus exposure only treatment for social phobia: A meta-analysis. *Behavior Therapy, 26*, 695–720.

Festinger, L. (1950). Informed social comjmunicano., *Psychological Review, 57*, 271–282.

Festinger, L., & Carlsmith, J. M. (1959). Cognitive consequences of forced compliance. *Journal of Abnormal and Social Psychology, 58*, 203–210.

Ficker, J. H. I., Wiest, G. H., Lehnert, G., Meyer, M., & Hahn, E. G. (1999). Are snoring medical students at risk of failing their exams? *Sleep, 22*, 205–209.

Field, A. E., Camargo, C. A., Jr., Taylor, B., Berkey, C. S., Colditz, G. A. (1999). Relation of peer and media influences to the development of purging behaviors among preadolescent and adolescent girls. *Archives of Pediatric Adolescent Medicine, 153*, 1184–1189.

Field, T., Schanberg, S., Scarfidi, F., Bauer, C., Vega-Lahr, N., Garcia, R., Nystrom, J., & Kuhn, C. (1986). Tactile/kinesthetic stimulation effects on preterm neonates. *Pediatrics, 77*, 654–658.

Field, T. M. (1998). Touch therapy effects on development. *International Journal of Behavioral Development, 22*, 779–797.

Field, T. M., Woodson, R., Greenberg, R., & Cohen, D. (1982). Discrimination and imitation of facial expressions by neonates. *Science, 218*, 179–181.

Figiel, G. S., Epstein, C., McDonald, W. M., Amazon-Leece, J., Figiel, L., Saldivia, A., & Glover, S. (1998). The use of rapid-rate transcranial magnetic stimulation (rTMS) in refractory depressed patients. *Journal of Neuropsychiatry & Clinical Neurosciences, 10*, 20–25.

Finch, A. E., Lambert, M. J., & Brown, G., (2000). Attacking anxiety: A naturalistic study of a multimedia self-help program. *Journal of Clinical Psychology, 56*, 11–21.

Finkel, D., Pedersen, N. L., McGue, M., & McClearn, G. E. (1995). Heritability of cognitive abilities in adult twins: Comparison of Minnesota and Swedish data. *Behavioral Genetics, 25*, 421–432.

Fiorentine, R. (1999). After drug treatment: Are 12-step programs effective in maintaining abstinence? *American Journal of Drug and Alcohol Abuse, 25*, 93–116.

Fischer, C., Hatzidimitriou, G., Wlos, J., Katz, J., & Ricaurte, G. (1995). Reorganization of ascending 5-HT axon projections in animals previously exposed to recreational drug 3,4-methelene-dioxymetham-phetamine (MDMA, "Ecstasy"). *Journal of Neuroscience, 15*, 5476–5485.

Fisher, P. J., Turic, D., Williams, N. M., McGuffin, P., Asherson, P., Ball, D., Craig, I., Eley, T., Hill, L., Chorney, K., Chorney, M. J., Benbow, C. P., Lubinski, D., Plomin, R., & Owen, M. J. (1999) DNA pooling identifies QTLs on Chromosome 4 for general cognitive ability in children. *Human Molecular Genetics, 8*, 915–922.

Fisher, R. P., & Craik, F. I. M. (1977). The interaction between encoding and retrieval operations in cued recall. *Journal of Experimental Psychology: Human learning and Perception, 3*, 153–171.

Fisher, R. P., & Geiselman, R. E. (1992). *Memory enhancing techniques for investigative interviewing: The cognitive interview.* Springfield: Charles C. Thomas.

Fisher, R. P., Geiselman, R. E., & Amador, M. (1989). Field test of the cognitive interview: Enhancing the recollection of actual victims and witnesses of crime. *Journal of Applied Psychology, 74*, 722–727.

Fiske, S. (1998). Stereotyping, prejudice, and discrimination. In D. T. Gilbert, S. T. Fiske, & G. Lindzey (Eds.), *The handbook of social psychology* (4th ed.). New York: McGraw Hill. 357–411.

Fitton, A., & Heel, R. C. (1990). Clozapine: A review of its pharacological properties and therapeutic use schizophrenia. *Drugs, 40*, 722–747.

Flavell, J. H. (1999). Cognitive development: Children's knowledge about the mind. *Annual Review of Psychology, 50*, 21–45.

Fletcher, A. C., Elder, G. H. Jr., & Mekos, D. (2000). Parental influences on adolescent involvement in community activities. *Journal of Research on Adolescence, 10*, 29–48.

Flexser, A., & Tulving, E. (1978) Retrieved independence in recognition and recall. *Psychological Review, 85*, 153–171.

Floyd, R. L., Rimer, B. K., Giovino, G. A., Mullen, P. D., & Sullivan, S. E. (1993). A review of smoking in pregnancy: Effects on pregnancy outcomes and cessation efforts. *Annual Review of Public Health, 14*, 379–411.

Flynn, J. R. (1984). The mean IQ of Americans: Massive gains 1932 to 1978. *Psychological Bulletin, 95*, 29–51.

Flynn, J. R. (1999a). Massive IQ gains in fourteen nations: What IQ tests really measure. *Psychological Bulletin, 101*, 171–191.

Flynn, J. R. (1999b). Searching for justice: The discovery of IQ gains over time. *American Psychologist, 54*, 5–20.

Flynn, J. R. (1999c). IQ trends over time: Intelligence, race and meritocracy. In S. Durlauf, K. Arrow, & S. Bowles (Eds.), *Meritocracy and inequality.* Princeton, NJ: Princeton University Press.

Foa, E. B., Steketee, G., & Olasov-Rothbaum, B. O. (1989). Behavioral/cognitive conceptualization of post-traumatic stress disorder. *Behavior Therapy, 20*, 155–176.

Fodor, J. A. (1968). *Psychological explanation: An introduction to the philosophy of psychology.* New York: Random House.

Fones, C. S. L., Manfro, G. G., & Pollack, M. H. (1998). Social phobia: An update. *Harvard Review of Psychiatry, 5*, 247–259.

Forbes, E. J., & Pekala, R. J. (1993). Psychophysiological effects of several stress management techniques. *Psychological Reports, 72*, 19–27.

Ford, C. S., & Beach, F. (1951). *Patterns of sexual behavior.* New York: Harper & Row.

Ford, K., & Norris, A. E. (1997). Effects of interviewer age on reporting of sexual and reproductive behavior of Hispanic and African American youth. *Hispanic Journal of Behavioral Sciences, 19*, 369–376.

Ford, R. P., Schluter, P. J., Mitchell, E. A., Taylor, B. J., Scragg, R., & Stewart, A. W. (1998). Heavy caffeine intake in pregnancy and sudden infant death syndrome. New Zealand Cot Death Study Group. *Archives of Disease in Childhood, 78*, 9–13.

Forgas, J. P., Levinger, G., & Moylan, S. (1994). Feeling good and feeling close: Mood effects on the perception of intimate relationships. *Personal Relationships, 2*, 165–184.

Fouts, R., & Mills, S. (1997). *Next of kin.* New York: William Morrow.

Fox, C. H. (1994). Cocaine use in pregnancy. *Journal of the American Board of Family Practice, 7*, 225–228.

Fox, S., & Spector, P. E. (2000). Relations of emotional intelligence, practical intelligence, general intelligence, and trait affectivity with interview outcomes: It's not all just 'G'. *Journal of Organizational Behavior, 21*, 203–220.

Fox, W. M. (1982). Why we should abandon Maslow's Need Hierarchy Theory. *Journal of Humanistic Education and Development, 21*, 29–32.

Fozard, J. (1990). Vision and hearing in aging. In J. E. Birren & K. W. Schaie (Eds.), *Handbook of the Psychology of aging* (3rd ed., pp. 150–170). San Diego: Academic Press.

Frances, A. (1998). Problems in defining clinical significance in epidemiological Studies. *Arch Gen Psychiatry, 55*, 119.

Francis, J. R., & Aronson, H. (1990). Communicative efficacy of psychotherapy research. *Journal of Consulting and Clinical Psychology, 58*, 368–370.

Francis, M. E., & Pennebaker, J. W. (1992). Putting stress into words: The impact of writing on physiological, absentee, and self-reported emotional well-being measures. *American Journal of Health Promotion, 6*, 280–286.

Frasure-Smith, N., Lesperance, F., Juneau, M., Talajic, M., & Bourassa, M. G. (1999). Gender, depression, and one-year prognosis after myocardial infarction. *Psychosomatic Medicine, 61*, 26–37.

Freedman, J. L., & Fraser, S. C. (1966). Compliance without pressure: The foot-in-the-door technique. *Journal of Personality and Social Psychology, 4*, 195–202.

Freedman, M. S., Lucas, R. J., Soni, B., von Schantz, M., Muñoz, M., David-Gray, Z., & Foster, R. (1999). Regulation of mammalian circadian behavior by non-rod, non-cone, ocular photoreceptors. *Science, 284*, 502–504.

Freeman, D. (1983). *Margaret Mead and Samoa: The making and unmaking of an anthropological myth.* Cambridge, MA: Harvard University Press.

Freeman, H. (1994). Schizophrenia and city residence. *British Journal of Psychiatry, 164* (Suppl. 23), 39–50.

Freeman, W. J. (1991). The psychology of perception. *Scientific American, 264*, 78–85.

Freese, J., Powell, B., & Steelman, L. C. (1999). Rebel without a cause or effect: Birth order and social attitudes. *American Sociological Review, 64*, 207–231.

Freud, A. (1958). Adolescence. *Psychoanalytic Study of the Child, 15*, 255–278.

Freud, S. (1900/1958). *The interpretation of dreams.* New York: Basic Books.

Freud, S. (1910). The origin & development of psychoanalysis. *American Journal of Psychology, 21*, 181–218.

Freud, S. (1927). *The ego and the id.* London: Hogarth Press.

Freud, S. (1933/1965). *New Introductory Lectures on Psychoanalysis.* New York: Norton.

Freud, S. (1937/1964). Analysis terminable and interminable. In J. Strachey (Ed. and Trans.), *The standard edition of the complete psychological works of Sigmund Freud* (Vol. 23, pp. 209–253).

Freud, S. (1938). *The basic writings of Sigmund Freud.* New York: Modern Library (Random House).

Frezza, M., di Padova, C., Pozzato, G., Terpin, M., Baraona, E., & Lieber, C. S. (1990). High blood alcohol levels in women: The role of decreased gastric alcohol dehydrogenase activity and first-pass metabolism. *New England Journal of Medicine, 322*, 95–99.

Fried, P. A., & Makin, J. E. (1987). Neonatal behavioral correlates of prenatal exposure to marijuana, cigarettes, and alcohol in a low risk population. *Neurobehavioral Toxicology and Teratology, 9*, 1–7.

Fried, P. A., & Watkinson, B. (2000). Visuoperceptual functioning differs in 9- to 12-year-olds prenatally exposed to cigarettes and marihuana. *Neurotoxicology & Teratology, 22*, 11–20.

Friedler, G. (1996). Paternal exposures: Impact on reproductive and developmental outcome: An overview. *Pharmacology, Biochemistry & Behavior, 55*, 691–700.

Friedman, M. I. (1991). Metabolic control of calorie intake. In M. T. Friedman, M. G. Tordoff, & M. R. Kare (Eds.), *Chemical senses.* New York: Marcel Dekker.

Friedman, M., & Rosenman, R. (1974). *Type A Behavior and Your Heart.* New York: Knopf.

Friedman, M., Thoresen, C., & Gill, J. (1986). Alteration of Type A behavior and its effect on cardiac recurrence in post-myocardial infarction patients: Summary results of the recurrent coronary prevention project. *American Heart Journal, 112*, 653–665.

Friedman, M. I., Tordoff, M. G., & Kare, M. R. (1991). *Chemical Senses, Volume 4: Appetite and Nutrition.* New York: Marcel Dekker.

Friedman, M. I., Tordoff, M. G., & Ramirez, I. (1986). Integrated metabolic control of food intake. *Brain Research Bulletin, 17*, 855–859.

Frischholz, E. J. (1985). The relationship among dissocation, hypnosis, and child abuse in the dvelopment of multiple personality. In R. P. Kluft (Ed.), *Childhood antecedents of multiples personality* (pp. 99–120). Washington, DC: American Psychiatric Press.

Frye, D., Zelazo, P. D., & Burack, J. A. (1998). Cognitive complexity and control: I. Theory of mind in typical and atypical development. *Current Directions in Psychological Science, 7*, 116–121.

Fryers, T. (1993). Epidemiological thinking in mental retardation: Issues in taxonomy and population frequency. In N. W. Bray (Ed.), *International review of research in mental retardation* (Vol. 19). Novato, Calif: Academic Therapy Publications.

Fuller, R. K., Branchey, L., Brightwell, D. R., Derman, R. M., Emrick, C. D., Iber, F. L., James, K. E., Lacoursiere, R. B., Lee, K. K., Lowenstaum, I., Maany, I., Neiderhiser, D., Nocks, J. J., & Shaw, S. (1986). Disulfiram treatment of alcoholism: A Veterans Administration cooperative study. *Journal of the American Medical Association 256*(11):1449–1455.

Funtowicz, M. N., & Widiger, T. A. (1999). Sex bias in the diagnosis of personality disorders: An evaluation of the *DSM–IV* criteria. *Journal of Abnormal Psychology, 108*, 195–201.

Fuster, J. M. (1997). Network memory. *Trends in Neuroscience, 20*, 451–459.

Futterman, A. D., Kemeny, M. E., Shapiro, D., Polonsky, W., & Fahey, J. L. (1992). Immunological variability associated with experimentally-induced positive and negative affective states. *Psychological Medicine, 22*, 231–238.

Gabrieli, J. D. E. (1996). Memory systems analyses of mnemonic disorders in aging and age-related diseases. *Proceedings of the National Academy of Sciences, USA, 93*, 13534–13540.

Gabrieli, J. D. E., Fleischman, D. A., Keane, M. M., Reminger, S. L., & Morrell, F. (1995). Double dissociation between memory systems underlying explicit and implicit memory in the human brain. *American Psychological Society, 6*, 76–82.

Gallaher, P. E. (1992). Individual differences in nonverbal behavior. Dimensions of style. *Journal of Personality and Social Psychology, 63*, 133–145.

Gangestad, S. W. (1993). Sexual selection and physical attraiveness: Implications fo rmating dynamics. *Human Nature, 4*, 205–235.

Garb, H. N. (1997). Race bias, social class bias, and gender bias in clinical judgment. *Clinical Psychology: Science & Practice, 4*, 99–120.

Garcia, J., & Koelling, R. (1966). Realtion of cue to consequence in avoidance learning. *Psychonomic Science, 4*, 123–124.

Garcia-Arraras, J. E., & Pappenheimer, J. R. (1983). Site of action of sleep-inducing muramyl peptide isolated from human urine: Microinjection studies in rabbit brains. *Journal of Neurophysiology, 49*, 528–533.

Gardner, H. (1975). *The shattered mind: The person after brain damage.* New York: Knopf.

Gardner, H. (1985). *The mind's new science: A history of the cognitive revolution.* New York: Basic Books.

Gardner, H. (1993b). *Frames of mind: The theory of multiple intelligences.* New York: Basic Books. (Original work published 1983.)

Gardner, H. (1995, November). Reflections on multiple intelligences: Myths and messages. *Phi Delta Kappan,* pp. 200–209.

Gardner, H. (1999). *Intelligence reframed: Multiple intelligences for the 21st century.* New York: Basic Books.

Gardner, H., Kornhaber, M. L., & Wake, W. K. (1996). *Intelligence: Multiple perspectives.* Ft. Worth, TX: Harcourt Brace.

Gardner, R. A., & Gardner, B. T. (1969). Teaching sign language to a chimpanzee. *Science, 165*, 664–672.

Garfield, S. L. (1994). Research on client variables in psychotherapy. In A. E. Bergin & S. L. Garfield (Eds.), *Handbook of psychotherapy and behavior change, 4th edition* (pp. 190–228). New York: John Wiley & Sons.

Garfield, S. L., & Bergin, A. E. (1994). Introduction and historical overview. In A. E. Bergin & S. L. Garfield (Eds.), *Handbook of psychotherapy and behavior change, 4th edition* (pp. 3–18). New York: John Wiley & Sons.

Garfinkel, P. E., Goldbloom, D., David, R., Olmsted, M. P., Garner, D. M., & Halmi, K. A. (1992). Body dissatisfaction in Bulimia Nervosa: Relationship to weight and shape concerns and psychological functioning. *International Journal of Eating Disorders, 11*, 151–161.

Garner, D. M. (1997). Psycho educational Principles in Treatment. In D. M. Garner & P. E. Garfinkel (Eds.), *Handbook of Treatment for Eating Disorders* (2nd edition). New York: Guilford Press.

Garris, P. A., Kilpatrick, M., Bunin, M. A., Michael, D., Walker, Q. D., & Wightman, R. M. (1999). Dissociation of dopamine release in the nucleus accumbens from intracranial self-stimulation. *Nature, 398*, 67–69.

Garry, M., & Polaschek, D. L. L. (2000). Imagination and memory. *Current Directions in Psychological Science, 9*, 6–10.

Gaster, B., & Holroyd, J. (2000). St. John's Wort for depression: A systematic review. *Archives of Internal Medicine, 160*, 152–156.

Gater, R., Tansella, M., Korten, A., Tiemens, B. G., Mavreas, V. G., & Olatawura, M. O. (1998). Report from the World Health Organization Collaborative Study on Psychological Problems in General Health Care. *Archives of General Psychiatry, 55*, 405–413.

Gauthier, I., Tarr, M. J., Anderson, A. W., Skudlarski, P., & Gore, J. C. (1997). Expertise training with novel objects can recruit the fusiform face area. *Society of Neuroscience Abstracts, 23*, 868.5.

Gazzaniga, M. S. (1995). Consciousness and the cerebral hemispheres. In M. S. Gazzaniga (Ed.), *The cognitive neurosciences* (pp. 1391–1400). Cambridge, MA: The MIT Press.

Gazzaniga, M. S., & LeDoux, J. E. (1978). *The integrated mind.* New York: Plenum.

Geary, D. C. (1996a). Sexual selection and sex differences in mathematical abilities. *Behavioral and Brain Sciences, 19*, 229–284.

Geary, N., & Smith, G. P. (1985). Pimozide decreases the positive reinforcing effects of sham fed sucrose in the rat. *Pharmacology, Biochemistry, & Behavior, 22*, 787–790.

Geddes, J. R., & Lawrie, S. M. (1995). Obstretric complications and shizophrenia: a meta-analysis. *British Journal of Psychiatry, 67*, 786–793.

Geiselman, R. E., Fisher, R. P., MacKinnon, D. P., & Holland, H. L. (1985). Eyewitness memory enhancement in the police interview. *Cognitive Journal of Applied Psychology, 70*, 401–412.

Gelfand, S. A. (1981). *Hearing.* New York: MarcelDekker.

Gelman, R. (1972). Logical capacity of very young children: Number invariance rules. *Child Development, 43*, 75–90.

George, M. S., Lisanby, S. H., & Sackheim, H. A. (1999). Transcranial Magnetic Stimuluation: Applications in neuropsychiatry. *Archives in General Psychiatry, 56*, 300–311.

Gerlai, R. (1996). Gene-targeting studies of mammalian behavior: Is it the mutation of the background genotype? *Trends in Neuroscience, 19*, 177–181.

Gershberg, F. B., & Shimamura, A. P. (1995). Impaired use of organizational strategies in free recall following frontal lobe damage. *Neuropsychologia, 33*, 1305–1333.

Gerteis, J., & Savage, M. (1998). The salience of class in Britain and America: A comparative analysis. *British Journal of Sociology, 49*, 252–274.

Gesell, A., & Thompson, H. (1938). *The psychology of early growth including norms of infant behavior and a method of genetic analysis.* New York: Macmillan.

Gibbons, F. X., & Gerrard, M. (1995). Predicting young adults' health-risk behavior. *Journal of Personality and Social Psychology, 69*, 505–517.

Gibson, E. J. (1969). Principles of perceptual learning and development. New York: Appleton-Century-Crofts.

Gibson, J. J. (1966). *The senses considered as perceptual systems.* Boston: Houghton Mifflin.

Gibson, J. J., & Walk, R. D. (1960). The "visual cliff." *Scientific American, 202*, 64–71.

Gibson, J. T. (1991). Training people to inflict pain: State terror and social learning. *Journal of Humanistic Psychology, 31*, 72–87.

Gick, M. L., & Holyoak, K. J. (1980). Analogical problem solving. *Cognitive Psychology, 12*, 306–355.

Gick, M. L., & Holyoak, K. J. (1983). Schema induction and analogical transfer. *Cognitive Psychology, 15*, 1–38.

Gidron, Y., Davidson, K., & Bata, I. (1999). The Short-Term Effects of a Hostility-Reduction Intervention on Male Coronary Heart Disease Patients. *Health Psychology, 18*, 416–420.

Gilbert, D. T. (1991). How mental systems believe. *American Psychologist, 46*, 107–119.

Gilbert, D. T. (1995). Attribution and interpersonal perception. In A. Tesser (Ed.), *Advanced Social Psychology* (pp. 99–147). New York: McGraw-Hill.

Gilbert, D. T., & Hixon, J. G. (1991). The trouble of thinking: Activation and application of stereotypic beliefs. *Journal of Personality and Social Psychology, 60*, 509–517.

Gilligan, C. (1982). *In a different voice.* Cambridge, MA: Harvard University Press.

Gilmore, J. H., Sikich, L., & Lieberman, J. A. (1997). Neuroimaging, neurodevelopment, and schizophrenia. *Child & Adolescent Psychiatric Clinics of North America, 6*(2), 325–341.

Gladwell, M. (1998, February 2). The pima paradox. *New Yorker,* pp. 44–57.

Glennon, F., & Joseph, S. (1993). Just world belief, self-esteem, and attitudes towards homosexuals with AIDS. *Psychological Reports, 72*, 584–586.

Gloaguen, V., Cottraux, J., Cucherat, M., & Blackburn, I. (1998). A meta-analysis of the effects of cognitive therapy in depressed patients. *Journal of Affective Disorders, 49,* 59–72.

Glynn, S. M. (1990). Token economy approaches for psychiatric patients: Progress and pitfalls over 25 years. *Behavior Modification, 14,* 383–407.

Godden, D. R., & Baddeley, A. D. (1975). Context-dependent memory in two natural environments: On land and underwater. *British Journal of Psychology, 66,* 325–331.

Goedde, H. W., & Agarwal, D. P. (1987). Aldehyde hydrogenase polymorphism: Molecular basis and phenotypic relationship to alcohol sensitivity. *Alcohol & Alcoholism* (Suppl. 1), 47–54.

Goetestam, K. G., & Berntzen, D. (1997). Use of the modelling effect in one-session exposure. *Scandinavian Journal of Behaviour Therapy, 26,* 97–101.

Goethals, G. R., Cooper, J., & Naficy, A. (1979). Role of foreseen, foreseeable, and unforeseeable behavioral consequences in the arousal of cognitive dissonance. *Journal of Personality and Social Psychology, 37,* 1179–1185.

Goethals, G. R., & Zanna, M. P. (1979). The role of social comparison in choice shifts. *Journal of Personality and Social Psychology, 37,* 1469–1185.

Goldberg, L. R. (1981). Language and individual differences: The search for universals in personality lexicons. In L. Wheeler (Ed.), *Review of personality and social psychology* (Vol. 2, pp. 141–165). Beverly Hills, CA: Sage.

Goldenberg, J., Mazursky, D., & Solomon, S. (1999). Essays on science and society: Creative sparks. *Science, 285,* 1495–1496.

Golding, J. M., Sanchez, R. P., & Sego, S. A. (1996). Do you believe in repressed memories? *Professional Psychology Research and Practice, 27,* 429–237.

Goldstein, A. (1994). *Addiction: From biology to drug policy.* New York: Freeman.

Goldstein, J. M., Goodman, J. M., Seidman, L. J., Kennedy, D. N., Makris, N., Lee, H., Tourville, J., Caviness, V. S., Jr., Faraone, S. V., & Tsuang, M. T. (1999). Cortical abnormalities in schizophrenia identified by structural magnetic resonance imaging. *Archives of General Psychiatry, 56,* 537–547.

Goldstein, M. D., & Strube, M. J. (1994). Independence revisited: The relation between positive and negative affect in a naturalistic setting. *Personality & Social Psychology Bulletin, 20,* 57–64.

Goldstein, M. J. (1992). Psychosocial strategies for maximizing the effects of psychotropic medications for schizophrenia and mood disorder. *Psychopharmacology Bulletin, 28,* 237–240.

Goleman, D. (1995). *Emotional intelligence.* New York: Bantam Books.

Gontkovsky, S. T. (1998). Huntington's disease: A neuropsychological overview. *Journal of Cognitive Rehabilitation, 16,* 6–9.

Goodale, M. A., & Milner, A. D. (1992). Separate visual pathways for perception and action. *Trends in Neurosciences, 15,* 20–25.

Goode, E. (1999a). *New Clues to Why We Dream.* Thursday, November 2, 1999, p. D1. New York Times.

Goodfellow, P. N., & Lovell-Badge, R. (1993). SRY and sex determination in mammals. *Annual Review of Genetics, 27,* 71–92.

Goodman, N. (1983). *Fact, fiction, and forecast* (4th edition). Cambridge: Harvard University Press.

Goodman, R. (1988). Are compicaitons of pregnancy and birth causes of schizphrenia? *Developmental Medical Child Neurology, 30,* 391–395.

Goodwin, F. K., & Ghaemi, S. N. (1998). Understanding manic–depressive illness. *Archives of General Psychiatry, 55,* 23–25.

Goodwin, F. K., & Jamison, K. R. (1990). *Manic-depressive illness.* New York: Oxford University Press.

Gorman, J. M., & Kent, J. M. (1999). SSRIs and SNRIs: Broad spectrum of efficacy beyond major depression. *Journal of Clinical Psychiatry, 60(Suppl. 4)* 33–39.

Gorman, J. M., Liebowitz, M. R., Fyer, A. J., & Stein, J. (1989). A neuroanatomical hypothesis for panic disorder. *American Journal of Psychiatry, 146,* 148–161.

Gotlib, I. H., & Robinson, L. A. (1982). Responses to depressed individuals: Discrepancies between self-report and observer rated behavior. *Journal of Abnormal Psychology, 91,* 231–240.

Gottesman, I. I. (1991). *Schizophrenia genesis: The origins of madness.* New York: Freeman.

Gottesman, I. I., Goldsmith, H. H., & Carey, G.. (1997). A developmental and a genetic perspective on aggression. In N. L. Segal, G. E. Weisfeld, C. C. Weisfield (Eds.), *Uniting psychology and biology: Integrative perspectives on human development.* (pp. 107–130). Washington, DC, USA: American Psychological Association.

Gottesman, I. I., & Moldin, S. O. (1998). Genotypes, Genes, Genesis, and pathogenesis in schizophrenia. In M. F. Lenzenweger & R. H. Dworkin (Eds.), *Origins and Development of Schizophrenia: Advances in Experimental Psychopathology.* Washington, DC: American Psychological Association. pp. 5–26.

Gottfredson, M. R., & Hirschi, T. (1990). *A general theory of crime.* Stanford, CA: Stanford University Press.

Gottlieb, G. (1998). Normally occurring environmental and behavioral influences on gene activity: From central dogma to probabilistic epigenesis. *Psychological Review, 105,* 792–802.

Gould, E., Tanapat, P., Hastings, N. B., & Shors, T. J. (1999). Neurogenesis in adulthood: A possible role in learning. *Trends in Cognitive Sciences, 3,* 186–192.

Gould, R. (1978). *Transformations.* New York: Simon & Schuster.

Gould, R. A., Buckminster, S., Pollack, M. H., Otto, M. W., & Yap, L. (1997). Cognitive-behavioral and pharmacological treatment for social phobia: A meta-analysis. *Clinical Psychology: Science & Practice, 4,* 291–306.

Gould, R. A., & Clum, G. A. (1993). A meta-analysis of self-help treatment approaches. *Clinical Psychology Review, 13,* 169–186.

Gould, R. A., Otto, M. W., & Pollack, M. H. (1995). A meta-analysis of treatment outcome for panic disorder. *Clinical Psychology Review, 15,* 819–844.

Gould, S. J., & Lewontin, R. C. (1979). The spandrels of San Marco and the Panglossian paradigm: A critique of the adaptationist programme. *Proceedings of the Royal Society of London, Series B, 205,* 581–598.

Grammer, K., & Thornhill, R. (1994). Human *(Homo sapiens)* facial attractiveness and sexual selecgtion: The role of symmetry and averageness. *Journal of Comparative Psychology, 108,* 233–242.

Grant, B. F., & Dawson, D. A. (1997). Age at onset of alcohol use and its association with DSM–IV alcohol abuse and dependence: Results from the National Longitudinal Alcohol Epidemiologic Survey. *Journal of Substance Abuse, 9,* 103–110.

Grant, I., Marcotle, T. D., Heaton, R. K., & HNRC Group, San Diego, CA, USA. (1999). Neurocognitive complications of HIV disease. *Psychological Science, 10,* 191–195.

Gray, J. A. (1987). Perspectives on anxiety and implusivesness: A commentary. *Journal of Research in Personality, 21,* 493–509.

Gray, J. R. (1999). A bias toward short-term thinking in threat-related negative emotional states. *Personality and Social Psychology Bulletin, 25,* 65–75.

Grayson, B., & Stein, M. I. (1981) Attracting assault: Victims' nonverbal cues. *Journal of Communication 31,* 68–75.

Graziano, W. G., Jensen-Campbell, L. A., & Sullivan-Logan, G. M. (1998). Temperament, Activity, and Expectations for Later Personality Development, *Journal of Persoanlity and Social Psychology, 74,* 1266–1277.

Green, D. M. (1976). *An introduction to hearing.* Hillsdale, NJ: Erlbaum.

Green, D. M., & Swets, J. A. (1966). *Signal detection theory and psychophysics.* New York: Wiley.

Green, J. P., Lynn, S. J., & Malinoski, P. (1998). Hypnotic pseudomemories, prehypnotic warnings, and malleability of suggested memories. *Applied Cognitive Psychology, 12,* 431–444.

Greenberg, B. D., Altemus, M., & Murphy, D. L. (1997). The role of neurotransmitters and neurohormones in obsessive-compulsive disorder. *International Review of Psychiatry, 9,* 31–44.

Greenberg, J. R., & Mitchell, S. A. (1983). *Object Relations in Psychoanalytic Theory.* Cambridge, MA: Harvard University Press.

Greenfield, P. M., & Savage-Rumbaugh, S. (1990). Grammatical combination in *Pan paniscus:* Processes of learning and invention in the evolution and development of language. In S. Parker & K. Gibson (Eds.), *"Language" and intelligence in monkeys and apes: Comparative developmental perspectives* (pp. 540–578). New York: Cambridge University Press.

Greenough, W. T., Black, J. E., & Wallace, C. S. (1987). Experience and brain development. *Child Development, 58,* 539–559.

Greenough, W. T., & Chang, F.-L. F. (1985). Synaptic structural correlates of information storage in mammalian nervous systems. In C. W. Cotman (Ed.), *Synaptic plasticity* (pp. 335–372). New York: Gilford.

Greenwald, A. G., & Banaji, M. R. (1995). Implicit social cognition: Attitudes, self-esteem, and stereotypes. *Psychological Review, 102,* 4–27.

Greenwald, A. G., Draine, S. C., & Abrams, R. L. (1996). Three cognitive markers of unconscious semantic activation. *Science, 273,* 1699–1702.

Greenwald, A. G., Spangenberg, E. R., Pratkanis, A. R., & Eskenazi, J. (1991). Double-blind tests of subliminal self-help audiotapes. *Psychological Science, 2,* 119–122.

Gregory, R. L. (1974). *Concepts and mechanisms of perception.* New York: Scribner.

Grice, H. P. (1975). Logic and conversation. In P. Cole & J. L. Morgan (Ed.), *Syntax and semantics: Vol. 3, Speech acts* (pp. 41–58). New York: Seminar Press.

Grill-Spector, K., Kushnir, T., Hendler, T., Edelman, S., Itzchak, Y., & Malach, R. (1998). A sequence of object-processing stages revealed by fMRI in the human occipital lobe. *Human Brain Mapping, 6,* 316–328.

Grilly, D. (1994). *Drugs and human behavior, 2nd edition.* Boston: Allyn and Bacon.

Grimes, K., & Walker, E. F. (1994). Childhood emotional expressions, educational attainments, and age at onset of illness in schizophrenia. *Journal of Abnormal Psychology, 103,* 784–790.

Grimshaw, G. M., Adelstein, A., Bryden, M. P., & MacKinnon, G. E. (1998). First-language acquisition in adolescence: Evidence for a critical period for verbal language development. *Brain & Language, 63,* 237–255.

Grisaru, N., Amir, M., Cohen, H., & Kaplan, Z. (1998). Effect of transcranial magnetic stimulation in posttraumatic stress disorder: A preliminary study. *Biological Psychiatry, 44,* 52–55.

Grisaru, N., Chudakov, B., Yaroslavsky, Y., & Belmaker, R. H. (1998). Transcranial magnetic stimulation in mania: A controlled study. *American Journal of Psychiatry, 155,* 1608–1610.

Grissmer, D. W., Kirby, S. N., Bevends, M., & Williamson, S. (1994). *Student achievement and the changing American family.* Santa Monica, CA: RAND.

Gross, J., & Levenson, R. W. (1997). Hiding feelings: The acute effects of inhibiting negative and positive emotion. *Journal of Abnormal Psychology, 106,* 95–103.

Grossarth-Maticek, R., Eysenck, H. J., Boyle, G. J., Heeb, J., Costa, C. D., & Diel, I. J. (2000). Interaction of psychosocial and physical risk factors in the causation of mammary cancer, and its prevention through psychological methods of treatment. *Journal of Clinical Psychology, 56,* 33–50.

Grossberg, S., Mingolla, E., & Ross, W. D. (1997). Visual brain and visual perception: How does the cortex do perceptual grouping? *Trends in Neuroscience, 20,* 106–111.

Grossman, R. P., & Till, B. D. (1998). The persistence of classically conditioned brand attitudes. *Journal of Advertising, 27,* 23–31.

Guerin, B. (1993). *Social faciliatation.* Paris: Cambridge University Press.

Guilford, J. P. (1967). *The nature of human intelligence.* New York: McGraw-Hill.

Guilford, J. P. (1979). Some incubated thoughts on incubation. *Journal of Creative Behavior, 13,* 1–8.

Gur, R. C., Turetsky, B. I., Matsui, M., Yan, M., Bilker, W., Hughett, P., & Gur, R. E. (1999). Sex differences in brain gray and white matter in healthy young adults: Correlations with cognitive performance. *Journal of Neuroscience, 19,* 4065–4072.

Guthrie, G. M., Guthrie, H. A., Fernandez, T. L., & Esterea, N. O. (1982). Cultural influences and reinforcement stratefies. *Behavior Therapy, 13,* 624–637.

Guttmann, C. R. G., Jolesz, F. A., Kikinis, R., Killiany, R. J., Moss, M. B., Sandor, T., & Albert, M. S. (1998). White matter changes with normal aging, *Neurology, 50,* 972–978.

Gyulai, L., Abass, A., Broich, K., & Reilley, J. (1997). I-123 lofetamine single-photon computer emission tomography in rapid cycling bipolar disorder: A clinical study. *Biological Psychiatry, 41,* 152–161.

Haaga, D. A., & Davison, G. C. (1989). Slow progress in rational-emotive therapy outcome research: Etiology and treatment. *Cognitive Therapy & Research, 13,* 493–450.

Hacker, A. (1992). *Two nations: Black and white, separate, hostile, unequal.* New York: Scribner's.

Hahn, R. A. (1997). The nocebo phenomenon: Scope and foundations. In A. Harrington (Ed.). *The Placebo Effect: An Interdisciplinary Exploration.* Cambridge, MA: Harvard University Press.

Haier, R. J., et al. (1984) Evoked potential augmenting-reducing and personality differences. *Personality & Indiv. Differences 5,* 293–301.

Hall, D. T., & Nougaim, K. E. (1968). An examination of Maslow's need hierarchy in an organizational setting. *Organizational Behavior and Human Performance, 3,* 12–35.

Hall, G. S. (1904). *Adolescence: Its psychology and its relation to physiology, anthropology, sociology, sex, crime, religion, and education* (Vols. I & II). Englewood Cliffs, NJ: Prentice-Hall.

Hall, J. A. (1978). Gender effects in decoding nonverbal cues. *Psychological Bulletin, 85,* 845–875.

Hall, J. A. (1987). On explaining gender differences: The case of nonverbal communication. In P. Shaver & C. Hendrick (Eds.). *Sex and gender.* Newbury Park, Calif.: Sage.

Hall, J. F. (1984). Backward conditioning in Pavlovian type studies: Reevaluation and present status. *Pavlovian Journal of Biological Science, 19,* 163–168.

Halle, M. (1990). Phonology. In D. N. Osherson, & H. Lasnik (Ed.), *An invitation to cognitive science: Vol. 1, Language* (pp. 43–68). Cambridge, MA: MIT Press.

Halmi, K. (1995). Basic Biological overview of eating disorders. IN F. E. Bloom & D. J. Kupfer (Eds.), *Psychopharmacology: The Fourth Generation of Progress.* New York; Raven Press, Ltd.

Halmi, K. (1996). The psychobiology of eating behavior in anorexia nervosa. *Psychiatry Research, 62,* 23–29.

Halpern, A. R. (1988). Mental scanning in auditory imagery for songs. *Journal of Experimental Psychology: Learning, Memory and Cognition, 14,* 434–443.

Halpern, A. R., & Zatorre, R. J. (1999). When that tune runs through your head: A PET investigation of auditory imagery for familiar melodies. *Cerebral Cortex, 9,* 697–704.

Halpern, D. F. (1992). *Sex differences in cognitive ability.* Hillsdale, NJ: Erlbaum.

Halpern, D. F. (1997). Sex differences in intelligence: Implications for education. *American Psychologist, 52,* 1091–1102.

Hamann, S. B., Stefanacci, L., Squire, L. R., Adolphs, R., Tranel, D., Damasio, H., & Damasio, A. (1996). Recognizing facial emotion. *Nature, 379,* 497.

Hamer, D. H., Hu, S., Magnuson, V. L., Hu, N., & Pattatucci, A. M. (1993). A linkage between DNA markers on the X chromosome and male sexual orientation. *Science, 261,* 321–327.

Hamilton, D. L., & Sherman, S. J. (1989). Illusory correlations: Implications for stereotype theory and research. In D. Bar-Tal, C. F. Graumann, A. W. Kruglanski, & W. Stroebe (Eds.), *Stereotyping and prejudice: Changing conceptions* (pp. 59–82). New York: Springer-Verlag.

Hamilton, M. E., Voris, J. C., Sebastian, P. S., Singha, A. K., Krejci, L. P., Elder, I. R., Allen, J. E., Beitz, J. E., Covington, K. R., Newton, A. E., Price, L. T., Tillman, E., & Hernandez, L. L. (1998). Money as a tool to extinguish conditioned responses to cocaine in addicts. *Journal of Clinical Psychology, 54,* 211–218.

Hampson, E. (1990). Estrogen-related variations in human spatial and articulatory motor skills. *Psychoneuroendocrinology, 15,* 97–111.

Hampson, E., & Kimura, D. (1988). Reciprocal effects of hormonal fluctuations on human motor and perceptual-spatial skills. *Behavioral Neuroscience, 102,* 456–459.

Hansen, W. B., Graham, J. W., Wolkenstein, B. H., Lundy, B. Z., Pearson, J., Flay, B. R., & Johnson, C. A. (1988). Differential impact of three alcohol prevetion curricula on hypothesized mediating variables. *Journal of Drug Educaiton, 18,* 143–153.

Hanson, K. A., & Gidycz, C. A. (1993). Evaluation of a sexual assault prevention program. *Journal of Consulting & Clinical Psychology, 61,* 1046–1052.

Hapidou, E. G., & De Catanzaro, D. (1988). Sensitivity to cold pressor pain in dysmenorrheic and non-dysmenorrheic women as a function of menstrual cycle phase. *Pain, 34,* 277–283.

Haraldsson, E., & Houtkooper, J. M. (1992). Effects of perceptual defensiveness, personality and belief on extrasensory perception tasks. *Personality and Individual Differences, 13,* 1085–1096.

Hardy, J. D., & Smith, T. W. (1988). Cynical hostility and vulnerability to disease: Social support, life stress, and physiological response to conflict. *Health Psychology, 7,* 447–459.

Hare, R. D. (1993). *Without conscience: The disturbing world of the psychopaths among us.* New York: Pocket Books.

Harkins, S., & Szymanski, K. (1989). Social loafing and group evaluation. *Journal of Personality and Social Psychology, 56,* 934–941.

Harkins, S. G., & Petty, R. E. (1982). Effects of task difficulty and task uniqueness on social loafing. *Journal of Personality & Social Psychology, 43,* 1214–1229.

Harman, D. (1956). Aging: A theory based on free radical and radiation chemistry. *Journal of Gerontology, 11*, 298–300.

Harris, H. (1976). The false controversy: Clitoral vs. vaginal orgasm. *Psychotherapy: Theory. Research, and Practice, 13*, 99–103.

Harris, J. R. (1995). Where is the child's environment? A group socialization theory of development. *Psychological Review, 102*, 458–489.

Harris, J. R. (1998). *The nurture assumption: Why children turn out the way they do.* New York: The Free Press.

Hart, J., Berndt, R. S., & Caramazza, A. (1985). Category-specific naming deficit following cerebral infarction. *Nature, 316*, 439–440.

Hartman, B. J. (1982). An exploratory study of the effects of disco music on the auditory and vestibular systems. *Journal of Auditory Research, 22*, 271–274.

Hartshorne, H., & May, M. A. (1928). *Studies in deceit.* New York: Macmillan.

Hartung, C. M., & Widiger, T. A. (1998). Gender differences in the diagnosis of mental disorders: Conclusions and controversies of the DSM–IV. *Psychological Bulletin, 123*, 260–278.

Hastie, R. (1986). Review essay: Experimental evidence on group accuracy. In B. Grofman & G. Owen (Eds.), *Information pooling and group decision making* (pp. 129–157). Greenwich, CT: JAI Press.

Hastorf, A. H., & Cantril, H. (1954). They saw a game; a case study. *Journal of Abnormal and Social Psychology, 49*, 129–134.

Hatfield, E., & Sprecher, S. (1986). Men's and women's preferences in marital partners in the United States, Russia, and Japan. *Journal of Cross-Cultural Psychology, 26*, 728–750.

Hauser, M. (1996). *The evolution of communication.* Cambridge, MA: MIT Press.

Havinghurst, R. (1953). *Human development and education.* New York: Longmans, Green.

Hawkins, J. R. (1994). Sex determination. *Human Molecular Genetics, 3*, 1463–1467.

Haxby, J. V., Grady, C. L., Horowitz, B., Ungerleider, L. G., Mischkin, M., Carson, R. E., Hercovitch, P., Schapiro, M. B., & Rapoport, S. I. (1991). Dissociation of object and spatial visual processing pathways in human extrastriate cortex. *Proceedings of the National Academy of Sciences, USA, 88*, 1621–1625.

Haxby, J. V., Horowitz, B., Ungerleider, L. G., Maisog, J. M., Pietrini, P., & Grady, C. L. (1994). The functional organization of human extrastriate cortex: A PET-rCBF study of selective attention to faces and locations. *Journal of Neuroscience, 14*, 6336–6353.

Hayflick, L. (1965). The limited in vitro lifetime of human diploid cell strains. *Experimental Cell Research, 37*, 614–636.

Hazan, C., & Shaver, P. R. (1987). Romantic love conceptualized as an attachment process. *Journal of Personality and Social Psychology, 52*, 511–524.

Hazan, C., & Shaver, P. R. (1990). Love and work: An attachment-theoretical perspective. *Journal of Personality and Social Psychology, 59*, 270–280.

Heath, A. C., & Martin, N. G. (1990) Psychoticism as a Dimension of Personality: A multivariate genetic test of Eysenck and Eysenck's Psychoticism construct. *Journal of Personality and Social Psychology, 58*, 11–121.

Heath, A. C., Neale, M. C., Kessler, R. C., Eaves, L. H., & Kendler, K. S. (1992). Evidence for genetic influences on personality from self-reports and informant ratings. *Journal of Personality and Social Psychology, 63*, 85–96.

Hecker, M., Chesney, M. N., Black, G., & Frautsch, N. (1988). Coronary-prone behaviors in the Western Collaborative Group Study. *Psychosomatic Medicine, 50*, 153–164.

Hedges, C. (1997, November 26). Bosnia's factions push their versions of war into the history books. *International Herald Tribune*, 5.

Heider, K. G. (1976). Dani sexuality: A low energy system. *Man, 11*, 188–201.

Heimberg, R. G., Liebowitz, M. R., Hope, D. A., Schneier, F. R., Holt, C. S., Welkowitz, L. A., Juster, H. R., Campeas, R., Bruch, M. A., Cloitre, M., Fallon, B., & Klein, D. F. (1998). Cognitive behavioral group therapy vs phenelzine therapy for social phobia: 12-week outcome. *Archives of General Psychiatry, 55*, 1133–1141.

Heit, G., Smith, M. E., & Halgren, E. (1988). Neural encoding of individual words and faces by the human hippocampus and amygdala. *Nature, 333*, 773–775.

Held, J. D., Alderton, D. L., Foley, P. P., & Segall, D. O. (1993). Arithmetic reasoning gender differences: Explanations found in the Armed Services Vocational Aptitude Battery. *Learning and Individual Differences, 5*, 171–186.

Hellige, J. B., & Michimata, C. (1989). Categorization versus distance: Hemispheric differences for processing spatial information. *Memory & Cognition, 17*, 770–776.

Helms, J. E., & Cook, D. A. (1999). *Using race and culture in counseling and psychotherapy: Theory and process.* Needham Heights, MA: Allyn & Bacon.

Helson, H. (1964). *Adaptation-level theory: An experimental and systematic approach to behavior.* New York: Harper & Row.

Hendricks, J., & Hendricks, C. D. (1986). *Aging in mass society: Myth and realities.* Boston: Little, Brown.

Henley, N. M. (1977). *Body politics: Power, sex, and non-verbal communication.* Englewood Cliffs, NJ: Prentice-Hall.

Henry, B., Caspi, A., Moffitt, T. E., & Silva, P. A. (1996). Temperamental and familial predictors of violent and nonviolent criminal convictions: Age 3 to Age 18. *Developmental Psychology, 32*, 614–623.

Henry, J. P. (1977). *Stress, health, and the environment.* New York: Springer-Verlag.

Henry, W. P., Strupp, H. H., Schacht, T. E., & Gaston, L. (1994). Psychodynamic approaches. In A. E. Bergin & S. L. Garfield (Eds.), *Handbook of psychotherapy and behavior change, 4th edition* (pp. 467–508). New York: John Wiley & Sons.

Hensel, H. (1982). *Thermal sensations and thermoreceptors in man.* Springfield, IL: Thomas.

Henslin, J. M. (1999). *Sociology: A down-to-Earth approach* (4th ed.). Needham Heights, MA: Allyn & Bacon.

Henson, R., Shallice, T., & Dolan, R. (2000). Neuroimaging evidence for dissociable forms of repetition priming. *Science, 287*, 1269–1272.

Hermann, J. A., deMontes, A. I., Dominguez, B., Montes, F., & Hopkins, B. L. (1973). Effects of bonuses for punctuality on the tardiness of industrial workers. *Journal of Applied Behavior Analysis, 4, 267–272.*

Herrnstein, R. J., & Murray, C. (1994). *The bell curve: Intelligence and class structure in American life.* New York: Free Press.

Hershman, D. J., & Lieb, J. (1988). *The key to genius/manic-depression and the creative life.* New York: Prometheus Books.

Hershman, D. J., & Lieb, J. (1998). *Manic depression and creativity.* New York: Prometheus Books.

Hertzog, C., & Schaie, K. W. (1988). Stability and change in adult intelligence: 2. Simultaneous analysis of longitudinal means and covariance structures. *Psychology and Aging, 3*, 122–130.

Hess, E. E. (1975). The role of pupil size in communication. *Scientific American, 233*, 110–119.

Heurta, P. T., Scearce, K. A., Farris, S. M., Empson, R. M., & Prusky, G. T. (1996). Preservation of spatial learning in fyn tryosine kinase knockout mice. *Neuroreport, 7*, 1685–1689.

Hierholzer, R., Munson, J., Peabody, C., & Rosenberg, J. (1992). Clinical presentation of PTSD in World War II combat veterans. *Hospital and Community Psychiatry, 43*, 816–820.

Higgenbotham, H. N., West, S., & Forsyth, D. (1988). *Psychotherapy and behavior change: Social, cultural and methodological perspectives.* New York: Pergamon.

Higgens, S. T., & Morris, E. K. (1984). Generality of free-operant avoidance conditioning to human behavior. *Psychological Bulletin, 96*, 247–272.

Hill, L., Craig, I. W., Asherson, P., Ball, D., Eley, T., Ninomiya, T., Fisher, P. J. Turic, D., McGuffin, P., Owen, M. J., Chorney, K., Chorney, M. J., Benbow, C. P., Lubinski, D., Thompson, L. A., & Plomin, R. (1999). DNA pooling and dense marker maps: A systematic search for genes for cognitive ability. *Neuroreport, 10*, 843–848.

Hines, M., & Kaufman, F. R. (1994). Androgen and the development of human sex-typical behavior: Rough-and-tumble play and sex of preferred playmates in children with congenital adrenal hyperplasia (CAH). *Child Development, 65*, 1042–1053.

Hirsch, J. (1971). Behavior-genetic analysis and its biosocial consequences. In R. Cancro (Ed.), *Intelligence: Genetic and environmental influences* (pp. 88–106). New York: Grune & Stratton.

Hirsch, J. (1997). The triumph of wishful thinking over genetic irrelevance. *Cahiers de Psychologie Cognitive/Current Psychology of Cognition, 16*, 711–720.

Hirschfeld, R. M. A. (1997). Long-term drug treatment of unipolar depression. *International Clinical Psychopharmacology, 11*, 211–217.

Hobson, J. A. (1995). *Sleep.* New York: Scientific American Library.

Hobson, J. A., & McCarley, R. W. (1977). The brain as a dream state generator: An activation-synthesis hypothesis of the dream process. *American Journal of Psychiatry, 134,* 1335–1348.

Hobson, J. A., Pace-Schott, E., & Stickgold, R. (2000). Dreaming and the Brain: Toward a Cognitive Neuroscience of Conscious States. *Behavioral and Brain Sciences,* 23, in press.

Hochschild, A. (1989). *The Second Shift: Working Parents and the Revolution at Home.* NewYork: Viking.

Hoeksema-van Orden, C. Y. D., Gaillard, A. W. K., & Buunk, B. P. (1998). Social loafing under fatigue. *Journal of Personality and Social Psychology, 75,* 1179–1190.

Hoffart, A. (1998). Cognitive and guided mastery therapy of agoraphobia: Long-term outcome and mechanisms of change. *Cognitive Therapy and Research, 22,* 195–207.

Hoffman, D. D., & Richards, W. A. (1984). Parts of recognition. *Cognition, 18,* 65–96.

Hoffman, L. W. (1991). The influence of the family environment on personality: Accounting for sibling differerences. *Psychological Bulletin, 110,* 187–203.

Hohlstein, L. A., Smith, G. T., & Atlas, J. G. (1998). An application of expectancy theory to eating disorders: Development and validation of measures of eating and dieting expectancies. *Psychological Assessment, 10,* 49–58.

Hohman, G. W. (1966). Some effects of spinal cord lesions on experienced emotional feelings. *Psychophysiology, 3,* 143–156.

Holden, C. (1980). Identical twins reared apart. *Science, 207,* 1323–1328.

Holland, A. J., Sicotte, N., & Treasure, J. (1988). Anorexia nervosa: Evidence for a genetic basis. *Journal of Psychosomatic Research, 32,* 561–571.

Hollerman, J. R., & Schultz, W. (1998). Dopamine neurons report an error in the temporal prediction of reward during learning. *Nature Neuroscience, 1,* 304–309.

Hollerman, J. R., Tremblay, L., & Schultz, W. (1998). Influence of reward expectation on behavior-related neuronal activity in primate striatum. *Journal of Neurophysiology, 80,* 947–963.

Hollis, K. L. (1997). Compenorary reserch on pavlovian conditioning: A 'new' functional analysis. *American Psychologist, 52,* 956–965.

Hollon, S. D., & Beck, A. T. (1994). Cognitive and cognitive-behavioral therapies. In A. E. Bergin & S. L. Garfield (Eds.), *Handbook of psychotherapy and behavior change, 4th edition* (pp. 428–466). New York: John Wiley & Sons.

Holmes, N. (1984). *Designer's guide to creating charts & diagrams.* New York: W. H. Freeman.

Holmes, T. H., & Rahe, R. H. (1967). The social readjustment rating scale. *Journal of Psychosomatic Research, 11,* 213–218.

Honeycutt, J. M., Cantrill, J. G., Kelly, P., & Lambkin, D. (1998). How do I love thee? Let me consider my options: Cognition, verbal strategies, and the escalation of intimacy. *Human Communication Research, 25,* 39–63.

Honig, A., Hofman, A., Rozendaal, N., & Dingemans, P. (1997). Psycho-education in bipolar disorder: Effect on expressed emotion. *Psychiatry Research, 72,* 17–22.

Honorton, C. (1997). The Ganzfeld novice: Four predictors of initial ESP performance. *Journal of Parapsychology, 61,* 143–158.

Hooley, J. M., & Licht, D. M. (1997). Expressed emotional and causal attributions in the spouses of depressed patients. *Journal of Abnormal Psychology, 106,* 298–306.

Hooper, F. H., Hooper, J. O., & Colbert, K. K. (1984) *Personality and memory correlates of intellectual functioning: Young adulthood to old age.* Basel, Switzerland: Karger.

Horn, J. (1985). Remodeling old models of intelligence. In B. B. Wolman (Ed.), *Handbook of intelligence* (pp. 267–300). New York: Wiley.

Horn, J. (1989). Models of intelligence. In R. L. Linn (Ed.), *Intelligence: Measurement, theory, and public policy* (pp. 29–73). Urbana, IL: University of Illinois Press.

Horn, J., & Cattell, R. B. (1966). Refinement and test of the theory of fluid and crystallized general intelligences. *Journal of Educational Psychology, 57,* 253–270.

Horn, J. L. (1986). Intellectual ability concepts. In R. J. Sternberg (Ed.), *Advances in the psychology of human intelligence,* Vol. 3 (pp. 35–77). Hillsdale, NJ: Erlbaum.

Horn, J. L. (1994). Theory of fluid and crystallized intelligence. In R. J. Sternberg (Ed.), *The encyclopedia of human intelligence,* Vol. 1 (pp. 443–451). New York: Macmillan.

Horn, J. L., & Noll, J. (1994). A system for understanding cognitive capabilities: A theory and the evidence on which it is based. In D. K. Detterman (Ed.). *Current topics in human intelligence, Volume 4: Theories of Intelligence.* Norwood, NJ: Ablex.

Horney, K. (1937). *Neurotic personality of our times.* New York: Norton.

Horowitz, M. J. (1998). Personality disorder diagnoses. *American Journal of Psychiatry, 155,* 1464.

House, J., Landis, K., & Umberson, D. (1988). Social relationships and health. *Science, 241,* 540–545.

Hovland, C. I., & Weiss, W. (1951). The influence of source credibility on communication effectiveness. *Public Opinion Quarterly, 15,* 635–650.

Hsee, C. K., Elaine, H., Carlson, J. G., & Chemtob, C. (1990). The effect of power on susceptibility to emotional contagion. *Cognition & Emotion, 4*(4), 327–340.

Huddy, L., & Virtanen, S. (1995). Subgroup differentiation and subgroup bias among Latinos as a function of familiarity and positive distinctiveness. *Journal of Personality and Social Psychology, 68,* 97–108.

Huff, D. (1954). *How to lie with statistics.* New York: Norton.

Hugdahl, K. (1995a). Classical conditioning and implicit learning: The right hemisphere hypothesis. In R. J. Davidson & K. Hugdahl (Eds.), *Brain asymmetry,* (pp. 235–267). Cambridge, MA: MIT Press.

Hui, C. H., & Triandis, H. C. (1986). Individualism-collectivism: A study of cross-cultural researchers. *Journal of Corss-cultural psychology, 17,* 225–248.

Hultman, C. M., Wieselgren, I., & Oehman, A. (1997). Relationships between social support, social coping and life events in the relapse of schizophrenic patients. *Scandinavian Journal of Psychology, 38,* 3–13.

Hummel, J. E., & Biederman, I. (1992). Dynamic binding in a neural network for shape recognition. *Psychological Review, 99,* 480–517.

Hummel, J. E., & Holyoak, K. J. (1997). Distributed representations of structure: A theory of analogical access and mapping. *Psychological Review, 104,* 427–466.

Humphreys, G. W., Riddoch, M. J., & Price, C. J. (1997). Top-down processes in object identification: Evidence from experimental psychology, neuropsychology and functional anatomy. *Philosophical Transactions of the Royal Society, London, 352,* 1275–1282.

Hunt, E. (1995). *Will we be smart enough? A cognitive analysis of the coming workforce.* New York: Russell Sage.

Hurvich, L. M., & Jameson, D. (1957). An opponent-process theory of color vision. *Psychological Review, 64,* 384–404.

Huttenlocher, P. (in press). *Neural plasticity.* Cambridge, MA: Harvard University Press.

Hyde, T. S., & Jenkins, J. J. (1973). Recall for words as a function of semantic, graphic, and syntactic orientation tasks. *Journal of Verbal Learning and Verbal Behavior, 12,* 471–480.

Hyman, A., Mentzer, T., & Calderone, L. (1979). The contribution of olfaction to taste discrimination. *Bulletin of Psychonomic Society, 13,* 359–362.

Hyman, I. E., & Billings, F. J. (1998). Individual differences and the creation of false childhood memories. *Memory, 6,* 1–20.

Hyman, I. E., & Pentland, J. (1996). The role of mental imagery in the creation of false childhood memories. *Journal of Memory and Language, 35,* 101–117.

Hyman, S. (1998). Personal communication.

Iansek, R., & Porter, R. C. (1980). The monkey globus pallidus: Neuronal discharge properties in relation to movement. *Journal of Physiology, 301,* 439–455.

Imber, S. D., Pilkonis, P. A., Sotsky, S. M., Elkin, I., Watkins, J. T., Collins, J. F., Shea, M. T., & Leber, S. R. (1991). Mode-specific effects among three treatments for depression. *Journal of Consulting and Clinical Psychology, 58,* 352–359.

Ingledew, D. K., Hardy, L., & Cooper, C. L. (1997). Do resources bolster coping and does coping buffer stress? An organizational study with longitudinal aspect and control for negative affectivity. *Journal of Occupational Health Psychology, 2,* 118–133.

Inman, D. J., Silver, S. M., & Doghramji, K. (1990). Sleep disturbance in Post-Traumatic Stress Disorder: A comparison with non-PTSD insomnia. *Journal of Traumatic Stress, 3,* 429–437.

Insel, T. R. (1992). Toward a neuroanatomy of obsessive-compulsive disorder. *Archives of General Psychiatry, 49,* 739–744.

Ironson, G., Wynings, C., Schneiderman, N., Baum, A., Rodriguez, M., Greenwood, D., Benight, C., Antoni, M., LaPerriere, A., Huang,

H., Klimas, N., & Fletcher, M. A. (1997). Posttraumatic stress symptoms, intrusive thoguhts, loss, and immune function after Hurricane Andrew. *Psychosomatic Medicine, 59,* 128–141.

Isenberg, D. J. (1986). Group polarization: A critical review and meta-analysis. *Journal of Personality & Social Psychology, 50,* 1141–115?.

Ivy, G., MacLeod, C., Petit, T., & Markus, E. (1992). A physiological framework for perceptual and cognitive changes in aging. In F. I. M. Craik & T. A. Salthouse (Eds.), *The handbook of aging and cognition* (pp. 273–314). Hillsdale, NJ: Erlbaum.

Izard, C. E. (1971). *The face of emotion.* New York: Appleton-Century-Crofts.

Jackson, N., & Butterfield, E. (1986). A conception of giftedness designed to promote research. In R. J. Sternberg & J. E. Davidson (Eds.), *Conceptions of giftedness* (pp. 151–181). New York: Cambridge University Press.

Jackson, S. E., Brett, J. F., Sessa, V. I., Cooper, D. M., Julin, J. A., & Peyronnin, K. (1991). Some differences make a difference: Indivdiual dissimilarity and group hetergeneity as correlates of recruitment, promotion, and turnover. *Journal of Applied Psychology, 76,* 675–689.

Jacobs, R. C., & Campbell, D. T. (1961). The perpetuation of an arbitrary tradition through several generations of a laboratory microculture. *Journal of Abnormal and Social Psychology, 62,* 649–648.

Jacobsen, A., & Gilchrist, A. (1988a). Hess and Pretori revisited: Resolution of some old contradictions. *Perception & Psychophysics, 43,* 7–14.

Jacobsen, A., & Gilchrist, A. (1988b). The ratio principle holds over a million-to-one range of illumination. *Perception & Psychophysics, 43,* 1–6.

Jacobson, E. (1925). Progressive Relaxation. *American Journal of Psychology, 36,* 73–87.

Jadack, R. A., Hyde, J. S., Moore, C. F., & Keller, M. L. (1995). Moral reasoning about sexually transmitted diseases. *Child Development, 66,* 167–177.

Jakobson, R., & Halle, M. (1956). *Fundamentals of language* . The Hague: Mouton.

James, L. E., Burke, D. M., Austin, A., & Hulme, E. (1998). Production and perception of "verbosity" in younger and older adults. *Psychology and Aging, 13,* 355–367.

James, W. (1884). What is emotion? *Mind, 9,* 188–205.

James, W. (1890/1950). *Principles of psychology.* New York: Dover.

Jamison, K. R. (1989). Mood disorders and patterns of creativity in British writers and artists. *Psychiatry, 52,* 125–134.

Jamison, K. R. (1993). *Touched With Fire: Manic-Depressive Illness and the Artistic Temperament.* New York: Free Press.

Jamison, K. R. (1995). *An Unquiet Mind: A Memoir of Moods and Madness.* New York: Vintage Books, p. 67.

Jamison, K. R., Gerner, R. H., Hammen, C., & Padesky, C. (1980). Clouds and silver linings: Positive experiences associated with primary affective disorders. *American Journal of Psychiatry, 137,* 198–202.

Jancke, L., & Steinmetz, H. (1994). Interhemispheric-transfer time and corpus callosum size. *NeuroReport, 5,* 2385–2388.

Janis, I. L. (1954). Personality correlates to susceptibility to persuasion. *Journal of Personality, 22,* 504–518.

Janis, I. L. (1982). *Victims of groupthink* (2nd ed.). Boston: Houghton Miffin.

Janowsky, J. S., Oviatt, S. K., & Orwoll, E. S. (1994). Testosterone influences spatial cognitin in older men. *Behavioral Neuroscience, 108,* 325–332.

Jeannerod, M. (1994). The representing brain: Neural correlates of motor intention and imagery. *Behavioral & Brain Sciences, 17,* 187–245.

Jeannerod, M. (1995). Mental imagery in the motor context. *Neuropsychologia, 33,* 1419–1432.

Jenike, M. (1984). Obsessive-comulsive disorder: A question of a neurologic lesion. *Compr. Psychiatry, 25,* 298–304.

Jenkins-Hall, K., & Sacco, W. P. (1991). Effects of client race and depression on evaluations by white therapists. *Journal of Social Clinical Psychology, 10,* 322–333.

Jensen, A. R. (1980). *Bias in mental testing.* New York: Free Press.

Jensen, A. R. (1998). *The g factor: The science of mental ability.* Westport, CT: Praeger.

Jensen, J. P., Bergin, A. E., & Greaves, D. W. (1990). The meaning of eclecticism: New survey and analysis of commponents. *Professional Psychology: Research and Practice, 21,* 124–130.

Johnson, J. A. (2000). Predicting observers' ratings of the Big Five from the CPI, HPI, and NEO-PI-R: A comparative validity study. *European Journal of Personality, 4,* 1–19.

Johnson, J. D., Noel, N. E., & Sutter, J. (2000). Alcohol and male sexual aggression: A cognitive disruption analysis. *Journal of Applied Social Psychology.*

Johnson, M. K., Hashtroudi, S., & Lindsy, D. S. (1993). Source monitoring. *Psychological Bulletin, 114,* 3–28.

Johnson, M. K., Nolde, S. F., Mather, M., Kounios, J., Schacter, D. L., & Curran, T. (1997). The similarity of brain activity associated with true and false recognition memory depends on test format. *Psychological Science, 8,* 250–257.

Johnson, M. K., & Raye, C. L. (1981). Reality monitoring. *Psychological Review, 88,* 67–85.

Johnson, M. R., & Lydiard, B. (1995). Personality disorders in social phobia. *Psychiatric Annals, 25,* 554–563.

Johnson, S. (2000). The recognition of mentalistic agents in infancy. *Trends in Cognitive Sciences, 4,* 22–28.

Johnson, S. L., & Miller, I. (1997). Negative life events and time to recovery from episodes of bipolar disorder. *Journal of Abnormal Psychology, 106,* 449–457.

Johnson, S. M., & Roberts, J. E. (1995). Life events and bipolar disorder: Implications from biological theories. *Psychological Bulletin, 117,* 434–449.

Johnston, L. C., & Macrae, C. N. (1994). Changing soical stereotypes: The case of the information seeker. *European Journal of Social Psychology, 24,* 581–592.

Johnston, L. D., O'Malley, P. M., & Bachman, J. G. (1994). *National survey results on drug use from the Monitoring the Future study, 1975–1993* (NIH Publication No. 94–3810). Washington, DC: U.S. Government Printing Office.

Johnstone, E. C. (1998). Predictive symptomatology, course, and outcome in first-episode schizophrenia. *International Clinical Psychopharmacology, 13,* S97–S99.

Joiner, T. E. (1994). Contagious depression: Existence, specificity to depressed symptoms, and the role of reassurance seeking. *Journal of Personality and Social Psychology, 67,* 287–296.

Jolicoeur, P. (1998). Modulation of the attentional blink by on-line response selection: Evidence from speeded and unspeeded Task 1 decisions. *Memory & Cognition, 26,* 1014–1032.

Jones, D., & Hill, K. (1993). Criteria of facial attractiveness in five populations. *Human Nature, 4,* 271–296.

Jones, M. K., & Menzies, R. G. (1995). The etiology of fear of spiders. *Anxiety, Stress & Coping: An International Journal, 8,* 227–234.

Jones, N. A., Field, T., & Davalos, M. (1998). Massage therapy attenuates right frontal EEG asymmetry in one-month-old infants of depressed mothers. *Infant Behavior & Development, 21,* 527–530.

Jones, T. A., & Greenough, W. T. (1996). Ultrastructural evidence for increased contact between astrocytes and synapses in rats reared in a complex environment. *Neurobiology of Learning and Memory, 65,* 48–56.

Joseph, S., Williams, R., & Yule, W. (1995). Psychosocial perspectives on post-traumatic stress disorder. *Clinical Psychology Review, 15,* 515–544.

Judd, C. M., Ryan, C. S., & Parke, B. (1991). Accuracy in the judgment of in-group and out-group variability. *Journal of Personality and Social Psychology, 61,* 366–379.

Judd, L. L., Akiskal, H. S., . Maser, J. D., Zeller, P. J., Endicott, J., Coryell, W., Paulus, M. P., Kunovac, J. L., Leon, A. C., Mueller, T. I., Rice, J. A., & Keller, M. B. (1998). A Prospective 12–Year Study of Subsyndromal and Syndromal Depressive: Symptoms in Unipolar Major Depressive Disorders. *Archives of General Psychiatry, 55,* 694–700.

Jusczyk, P. W. (1995). Language acquisition: Speech sounds and phonological development. In J. L. Miller & P. D. Eimas (Eds.), *Handbook of perception and cognition: Vol. 11. Speech, language, and communication* (pp. 263–301). Orlando, FL: Academic Press.

Kagan, J. (1989a). Temperamental contributions to social behavior. *American Psychologist, 44,* 668–674.

Kagan, J. (1994a). *Galen's prophecy.* New York: Basic Books.

Kagan, J., Reznick, J. S., & Snidman, N. (1988). Biological bases of childhood shyness. *Science, 240,* 167–171.

Kalish, R. A., & Reynolds, D. K. (1977). The role of age in death attitudes. *Death Education, 1,* 205–230.

Kalivas, P. W., & Nakamura, M. (1999). Neural systems for behavioral activation and reward. *Current Opinion in Neurobiology, 9,* 223–227.

Kamin, L. (1969). Predictability, surprise, attention and conditioning. In B. A. Camppbell and R. M. Church (Eds.), *Punishment and aversive behavior*. New York: Appleton-Century-Crofts.

Kaniasty, K., & Norris, F. H. (1992). Social support and victims of crime: Matching event, support, and outcome. *American Journal of Community Psychology, 20*, 211–241.

Kaniasty, K. Z., Norris, F. H., & Murrell, S. A. (1990). Received and perceived social support following natural disaster. *Journal of Applied Psychology, 20*, 85–114.

Kanner, A. D., Coyne, J. C., Schaefer, C., & Lazarus, R. S. (1981). Comparison of two modes of stress management: Daily hassles and uplifts versus major life events. *Journal of Behavioral Medicine, 4*, 1–39.

Kanwisher, N. (1991). Repetition blindness and illusory conjunctions: Errors in binding visual types with visual tokens. *Journal of Experimental Psychology: Human Perception and Performance, 17*, 404–421.

Kanwisher, N. G. (1987). Repetition blindness: Type recognition without token individuation. *Cognition, 27*, 117–143.

Kaplan, H. S. (1979). *Disorders of sexual desire*. New York: Brunner/Mazel.

Kaplan, H. S. (1981). *The New Sex Therapy: Active Treatment of Sexual Dysfunctions*. New York: Brunner/Mazel.

Kaplan, M. F. (1987). The influencing procedss in group decision making. In C. Hendrick (Ed.), *Review of Personality and Social Psychology* (Vol. 8, pp. 189–212). Newbury Park, CA: Sage.

Karacan, I., Goodenough, D. R., Shapiro, A., & Starker, S. (1966). Erection cycle during sleep in relatin to dream anxiety. *Archives of General Psychiatry, 15*, 183–189.

Karau, S. J., & Williams, K. D. (1993). Social loafing: A meta-analytic review and theoretical integration. *Journal of Personality and Social Psychology, 65*, 681–706.

Karkowski, L. M., & Kendler, K. S. (1997). An examination of the genetic relationship between bipolar and unipolar illness in an epidemiological sample. *Psychiatric Genetics, 7*, 159–163.

Karni, A., & Sagi, D. (1993). The time course of learning a visual skill. *Nature, 365*, 250–252.

Karni, A., Tanne, D., Rubenstein, B. S., Askenasi, J. J. M., & Sagi, D. (1994). Dependence on REM sleep of overnight improvement of a perceptual skill. *Science, 265*, 679–682.

Karpov, Y. V., & Haywood, H. C. (1998). Two ways to elaborate Vygotsky's concept of mediation. *American Psychologist, 53*, 27–36.

Karuza, J., & Carey, T. O. (1984). Relevance preference and adaptiveness of behavioral blame for observers of rape victims. *Journal of Personality, 52*, 249–262.

Kass, S. (1999). Breast cancer intervention group aids physical healing, research find. *APA Monitor*, October, p. 7.

Kassin, S. M., & Wrightsman, L. S. (1981). Coerced confessions, judicial instruction, and mock juror verdicts. *Journal of Applied Social Psychology, 11*, 489–506.

Katchadourian, H. (1977). *The biology of adolescence*. San Francisco: Freeman.

Katigbak, M. S., Church, A. T., & Akamine, T. X. (1996). Cross-Cultural generalizability of personality dimensions: Relating indigenous and imported dimensions in two cultures. *Journal of Personality and Social Psychology, 70*, 99–114.

Katz, J., Beach, S. R. H., & Joiner, T. E. (1999). Contagious depression in dating couples. *Journal of Social & Clinical Psychology, 18*(1), 1–13.

Kaufman, M. H. (1997). The teratogenic effects of alcohol following exposure during pregnancy, and its influence on the chromosome constitution of the pre-ovulatory egg. *Alcohol & Alcoholism, 32*, 113–128.

Kavanagh, D. J. (1992). Recent developments in expressed emoition in schizophrenia. *British Journal of Psychiatry, 148*, 601–620.

Kaye, W. H. (1995). Neurotransmitters and anorexia nervosa. In K. D. Brownell & C. G. Fairburn (Eds.), *Eating Disorders and Obesity: A Comprehensive Handbook* (pp. 255–260). New York: Guilford Press.

Kazdin, A. E. (1994). Methodology, design, and evaluation in psychotherapy research. In A. E. Bergin & S. L. Garfield (Eds.), *Handbook of psychotherapy and behavior change, 4th edition* (pp. 19–71). New York: John Wiley & Sons.

Keane, R. M., Kolb, L. C., Kaloupek, D. G., Orr, S. P., Blanchard, E. B., Thomas, R. G., Hsieh, F. Y., & Lavori, P. W. (1998). Utility of psychophysiology measurement in the diagnosis of posttraumatic stress disorder: Results from a department of Veteran's Affairs cooperative study. *Journal of Consulting and Clinical Psychology*, 914–923.

Keefe, R. S. E., Silva, S. G., Perkins, D. O., & Lieberman, J. A. (1999). The effects of atypical antipsychotic drugs on neurocognitive impairment in schizophrenia: A review and meta-analysis. *Schizophrenia Bulletin, 25*, 201–222.

Keith, P. M., & Schafer, R. B. (1991). *Relationships and well-being over the life stages*. New York: Praeger.

Keitner, G. I., Solomon, D. A., Ryan, C. E., Miller, I. W., & Mallinger, A. (1996). Prodromal and residual symptoms in bipolar I disorder. *Comprehensive Psychiatry, 37*, 362–367.

Keller, A., Ford, L. H., & Meacham, J. A. (1978). Dimensions of self-concept in preschool children. *Developmental Psychology, 14*, 483–489.

Kelley, H. H. (1972). Attribution in social interaction. In E. E. Jones, D. E. Kanouse, H. H. Kelley, R. E. Nisbett, S. Vahns, & B. Weiner (Eds.), *Attribution: Perceiving the causes of behavior*. Morristown, NJ: General Learning Press.

Kelley, H. H., & Michela, J. L. (1980). Attribution theory and research. *Annual Review of Psychology, 31*, 57–501.

Kelley, T. (1998, October 1). To surf, perchance to dream. *New York Times*, E1, E5.

Kelley, W. M., Miezin, F. M., McDermott, K. B., Buckner, R. L., Raichle, M. E., Cohen, N. J., Ollinger, J. M., Akbudak, E., Conturo, T. E., Znyder, A. Z., & Petersen, S. E. (1998). Hemispheric specialization in human dorsal frontal cortex and medial temporal lobe for verbal and nonverbal memory encoding. *Neuron, 20*, 927–936.

Kellogg, W. N., & Kellogg, L. A. (1933). *The ape and the child*. New York: McGraw-Hill.

Kelman, H. (1997). Group processes in the resolution of international conflicts. *American Psychologist, 52*, 212–220.

Kemp, D. T. (1978). Stimulated acoustic emissions from within the human auditory system. *Journal of the Acoustical Society of America, 64*, 1386–1391.

Kemp, D. T. (1979). Evidence of mechanical nonlinearity and frequency selective wave amplification in the cochlea. *Archives of Otology, Rhinology, and Laryngology, 224*, 37–45.

Kendler, K. S., & Diehl, S. R. (1993). The genetics of schizophrenia: A current genetic-epidemiologic perspective. *Schizophrenia Bulletin, 19*, 87–112.

Kendler, K. S., Gardner, C. O., & Prescott, C. A. (1999). Clinical Characterisics of Major Depression That Predict Risk of Depression in Relatives. *Archives of General Psychiatry, 56*, 322–327.

Kendler, K. S., MacLean, C., Neale, M., Kessler, R. C., Heath, A. C., & Eaves, L. J. (1991). The genetic epidemiology of bulimia nervosa. *American Journal of Psychiatry, 148*, 1627–1637.

Kendler, K. S., Neale, M., Kessler, R. C., Heath, A., & Eaves, L. (1992). The genetic epidemiology of phobias in women: The interrelationship of agoraphobia, social phobia, situational phobia and simple phobia. *Archives of General Psychiatry, 49*, 273–281.

Kennedy, S. H., Javanmard, M., Franco, J., & Vaccarino, F. J. (1997). A review of functional neuroimaging in mood disorders: Positron Emission Tomography and Depression. *Canadian Journal of Psychiatry, 42*, 467–475.

Kenrick, D. T., & Stringfeld, D. O. (1980). Personality traits and the eye of the beholder: Crossing some traditional philosophical boundaries in search for consistency in all the people. *Psychological Review, 87*, 88–104.

Kerr, N. L., & Kaufman-Gilliland, C. M. (1997). " . . . and besides, I probably couldn't have made a difference anyway": Justification of social dilemma defection via perceived self-inefficacy. *Journal of Experimental Social Psychology, 33*, 211–230.

Kessler, R. C., & Frank, R. G. (1997). The impact of psychiatric disorders on work loss days. *Psychological Medicine, 27*, 861–873.

Kessler, R. C., McGonagle, K. A., Zhao, S., Nelson, C. B., Hughes, M., Eshelman, S., Whittchen, H. N., & Dendler, K. S. (1994). Lifetime and 12-month prevalence of DSM–III—R psychiatric disorders in the United States: Results from the National Comorbidity Study. *Archives of General Psychiatry, 51*, 8–19.

Kessler, R. C., Stang, P. E., Wittchen, H., Ustun, T., Bedirhan, R., Burne, P. P., & Walters, E. E. (1998). Lifetime panic-depression comorbidity in the National Comorbidity Survey. *Archives of General Psychiatry, 55*, 801–808.

Kessler, R. C., Stein, M. B., & Berglund, P. (1998). Social phobia subtypes in the National Comorbidity Survey. *American Journal of Psychiatry, 155*, 613–619.

Kety, S. S. (1974). From rationalization to reason. *American Journal of Psychiatry, 131*, 957–963.

Keys, A., Brozek, J., Henschel, A., Mickelsen, O., & Taylor, H. L. (1950). *The biology of human starvation*. Minneapolis: University of Minnesota Press.

Kiecolt-Glaser, J., Garner, W., Speicher, C., Penn, G., & Glaser, R. (1984). Psychosocial modifiers of immuno-competence in medical students. *Psychosomatic Medicine, 46,* 7–14.

Kiecolt-Glaser, J., Glaser, R., Strain, E., Stout, J., Tarr, K., Holliday, J., & Speicher, C. (1986). Modulation of cellular immunity in medical students. *Journal of Behavioral Medicine, 9,* 5–?.

Kiecolt-Glaser, J. K., Kennedy, S., Malkoff, S., Fisher, L., Speicher, C., & Glaser, R. (1988). Marital discord and immunity in males. *Psychosomatic Medicine, 50,* 213–229.

Kiecolt-Glaser, J. K., Marucha, P. T., Malarky, W. B., Mercado, A. M., & Glaser, R. (1995). Slowing of wound healing by psychological stress. *The Lancet, 346,* 1194–1196.

Kiesler, C. A., & Kiesler, S. B. (1969). *Conformity.* Reading, MA: Addison-Wesley.

Kihlstrom, J. F. (1985). Hypnosis. *Annual Review of Psychology, 36,* 385–418.

Kilham, W., & Mann, L. (1974). Level of destructive obedience as a function of transmitter and executant roles in the Milgram obedience paradigm. *Journal of Personality and Social Psychology, 29,* 696–702.

Killen, J. D., Hayward, C., Wilson, D. M., Haydel, K. F., Robinson, T. N., Taylor, C. B., Hammer, L. D., & Varady, A. (1996). Predicting onset drinking in a community sample of adolescents: The role of expectancy and temperament. *Addictive Behaviors, 21,* 473–480.

Kim, J., Lim, J., & Bhargava, M. (1998). The role of affect in attitude formation: A classical conditioning. *Journal of the Academy of Marketing Science, 26,* 143–152.

Kim, K. H. S., Relkin, N. R., Lee, K., & Hirsch, J. (1997). Distinct cortical areas associated with native and second languages. *Nature, 388,* 171–174.

Kim, M., & Kim, H. (1997). Communication goals: Individual differences between Korean and American speakers. *Personality & Individual Differences, 23,* 509–517.

Kimble, G. A. (1981). *Biological and cogntive constraints of learning.* In L. T. Benjamin, Jr. (Ed.) *The G. Stanley Hall Lecture Series* (Vol. 1). Washington, DC: American Psychological Association.

Kimura, D. (1994). Body asymmetry and intellectual pattern. *Personality and Individual Differences, 17,* 53–60.

King, A. C., Oman, R. F., Brassington, G. S., Bliwise, D. L., & Haskell, W. L. (1997). Moderate-Intensity Exercise and Self-rated Quality of Sleep in Older Adults: A Randomized Controlled Trial. *Journal of the American Medical Association, 277,* 32–37

Kintsch, W. (1998). *Comprehension: A paradigm for cognition.* New York: Cambridge University Press.

Kirchler, E., & Davis, J. H. (1986). The influence of member status differences and task type on group consensus and member position change. *Journal of Personality and Social Psychology, 51,* 83–91.

Kirsch, I., & Lynn, S. J. (1999). Automaticity in Clinical Psychology. *American Psychologist, 54,* 504–515.

Kisilevsky, B. S., & Low, J. A. (1998). Human fetal behavior: 100 years of study. *Developmental Review, 18,* 1–29.

Kitchener, R. F. (1996). The nature of the social for Piaget and Vygotsky. *Human Development, 39,* 243–249.

Kitzmann, K. M. (2000). Effects of marital conflict on subsequent triadic family interactions and parenting. *Developmental Psychology, 36,* 3–13.

Kivlighan, D. M., Jr., Multon, K. D., & Patton, M. J. (2000). Insight and symptom reduction in time-limited psychoanalytic counseling. *Journal of Counseling Psychology, 47,* 50–58.

Klein, D. F. (1993). False suffocation alarms, spontaneous panics, and related conditions: An integrative hypothesis. *Archives of General Psychiatry, 50,* 306–317.

Klein, E., Kreinin, I., Chistyakov, A., Koren, D., Mecz, L., Marmur, S., Ben-Shachar, D., & Feinsod, M. (1999). Therapeutic Efficacy of Right Prefrontal Slow Repetitive Transcranial Magnetic Stimulation in Major Depression: A Double-blind Controlled Study. *Archives of General Psychiatry, 56,* 315–320.

Kleinknecht, R. A., & Lenz, J. (1989). Blood/injury fear, fainting and avoidance of medical treatment: A family correspondence study. *Behaviour Research and Therapy, 27,* 537–547.

Kleinman, A. (1978). Clinical relevance of anthropological and cross-cultural research: Concepts and strategies. *American Journal of Psychiatry, 135,* 427–431.

Klinkenborg, V. (1997, January 5). Awakening to sleep. *Sunday New York Times Magazine,* 26.

Klinteberg, B., Andersson, T., Magnusson, D., & Stattin, H. (1993). Hyperactive behavior in childhood as related to subsequent alcohol problems and violent offending: A longitudinal study of male subjects. *Personality and Individual Differences, 15,* 381–388.

Klosko, J. S., Barlow, D. H., Tassinari, R., & Cerny, J. A. (1990). A comparison of alprazolam and behavior therapy in treatment of panic disorder. *Journal of Consulting and Clinical Psychology, 58,* 77–84.

Knapp, S., & VandeCreek, L. (1996). Risk management for psychologists: Treating patients who recover lost memories of childhood abuse. *Professional Psychology Research and Practice, 27,* 452–459.

Koffka, K. (1935). *Principles of Gestalt psychology.* New York: Harcourt Brace.

Kohlberg, L. (1969). Stage and sequence: The cognitive-developmental approach to socialization. In D. S. Goslin (Ed.), *Handbook of socialization theory and research* (pp. 347–480). Chicago: Rand McNally.

Kohler, P. F., Rivera, V. J., Eckert, E. D., Bouchard, T. J., Jr., & Heston, L. L. (1985). Genetic regulation of immunoglobulin and specific antibody levels in twins reared apart. *Journal of Clinical Investigation, 75,* 883–888.

Kohler, S., Kapur, S., Moscovitch, M., Winocur, G., & Houle, S. (1995). Dissociation of pathways for object and spatial vision: A PET study in humans. *Neuroreport, 6,* 1865–1868.

Köhler,W. (1925/1956). *The mentality of apes.* New York: Vintage.

Kohn, M. L., & Schooler, C. (1973). Occupational experience and psychological functioning: An assessment of reciprocal effects. *American Sociological Review, 38,* 97–118.

Kohut, H. (1977). *The restoration of self.* New York: International Universities Press.

Kolata, G. (1997, January 14). Which comes first: Depression or heart disease? *New York Times,* C1.

Konishi, M. (1993). Listening with two ears. *Scientific American, 268,* 66–73.

Koob, G. F., & Bloom, F. E. (1988). Cellular and molecular mechanisms of drug dependence. *Science, 242,* 715–723.

Kosslyn, S. M. (1975). On retrieving information from visual images. In R. Schank & B. Nash-Webber (Eds.), *Theoretical issues in natural language processing.* Arlington, VA: Association for Computational Linguistics.

Kosslyn, S. M. (1976). Can imagery be distinguished from other forms of internal representation? Evidence from studies of information retrieval times. *Memory and Cognition, 4,* 291–297.

Kosslyn, S. M. (1978). Measuring the visual angle of the mind's eye. *Cognitive Psychology, 10,* 356–389.

Kosslyn, S. M. (1980). *Image and mind.* Cambridge, MA.: Harvard University Press.

Kosslyn, S. M. (1994a). *Elements of graph design.* New York: Freeman.

Kosslyn, S. M. (1994b). *Image and brain: The resolution of the imagery debate.* Cambridge, MA: MIT Press.

Kosslyn, S. M., & Koenig, O. (1995). *Wet mind: The new cognitive neuroscience.* New York: Free Press.

Kosslyn, S. M., Alpert, N. M., Thompson, W. L., Maljkovic, V., Weise, S. B., Chabris, C. F., Hamilton, S. E., & Buonano, F. S. (1993). Visual mental imagery activates topographically organized visual cortex: PET investigations. *Journal of Cognitive Neuroscience, 5,* 263–287.

Kosslyn, S. M., Digirolamo, G. J., Thompson, W. L., & Alpert, N. M. (1998). Mental rotation of objects versus hands: Neural mechanisms revealed by positron emission tomography. *Psychophysiology, 35,* 151–161.

Kosslyn, S. M., Koenig, O., Barrett, A., Cave, C. B., Tang, J., & Gabrieli, J. D. E. (1989). Evidence for two types of spatial representations: Hemispheric specialization for categorical and coordinate relations. *Journal of Experimental Psychology: Human Perception and Performance, 15,* 723–735.

Kosslyn, S. M., Pascual-Leone, A., Felician, O., Camposano, S., Keenan, J. P., Thompson, W. L., Ganis, G., Sukel, K. E., & Alpert, N. M. (1999). The role of area 17 in visual imagery: Convergent evidence from PET and rTMS. *Science, 284,* 167–170.

Kosslyn, S. M., Segar, C., Pani, J., & Hillger, L. A. (1990). When is imagery used in everyday life? A diary study. *Journal of Mental Imagery. 14,* 131–152.

Kosslyn, S. M., Thompson, W. L., & Alpert, N. M. (1997). Neural systems shared by visual imagery and visual perception: A positron emission tomography study. *NeuroImage, 6,* 320–334.

Kosslyn, S. M., Thompson, W. L., Kim, I. J., Rauch, S. L., & Alpert, N. M. (1996). Individual differences in cerebral blood flow in area 17 predict the time to evaluate visualized letters. *Journal of Cognitive Neuroscience, 8,* 78–82.

Koutstaal, W., & Schacter, D. L. (1997). Inaccuracy and inaccessibility in memory retrieval: Contributions from cognitive psychology and cognitive neuropsychology. In P. S. Appelbaum, L. Uyehara, & M. Elin (Eds.), *Trauma and memory: Clinical and legal controversies* (pp. 93–137). New York: Oxford University Press.

Kovacs, I. (1996). Gestalten of today: Early processing of visual contours and surfaces. *Behavioural Brain Research, 82,* 1–11.

Kovacs, I., & Julesz, B. (1993). A closed curve is much more than an incomplete one: Effect of closure in figure-ground segmentation. *Proceedings of the National Academy of Sciences, USA, 90,* 7495–7497.

Kozak, M. J., Liebowitz, M. R., & Foa, E. B. (2000). Cognitive behavior therapy and pharmacotherapy for obsessive-compulsive disorder: The NIMH-sponsored collaborative study. In W. K. Goodman, M. V. Rudorfer, & J. D. Masur (Eds.). *Obsessive-compulsive disorder: Contemporary issues in treatment* (pp. 501–530). Mahwah, NJ: Erlbaum.

Kraepelin, E. (1921). Ueber Entwurtzelung [Depression]. *Zietschrift fuer die Gasamte Neurologie und Psychiatrie, 63,* 1–8.

Krafft, K. C., & Berk, L. E. (1998). Private speech in two preschools: Significance of open-ended activities and make-believe play for verbal self-regulation. *Early Childhood Research Quarterly, 13,* 637–658.

Kramer, M. S., Cutler, N., Feighner, J., Shrivastava, R., Carman, J., Sramek, J. J., et al. (1998). Distinct mechanism for antidepressant activity by blockade of central substance P receptors. *Science, 281,* 1640–1645.

Kraut, R., Patterson, M., Lundmark, V., Kiesler, S., Mukophadhyay, T., & Scherlis, W. (1998). Internet paradox: A social technology that reduces social involvement and psychological well-being? *American Psychologist, 53,* 1017–1031.

Kring, A. M., & Gordon, A. H. (1998). Sex differences in emotion: Expression, experience, and physiology. *Journal of Personality & Social Psychology, 74,* 686–703.

Krug, R., Pietrowsky, R., Fehm, H. L., & Born, J. (1994). Selective influence of menstrual cycle on perception of stimuli with reproductive significance. *Psychosomatic Medicine, 56,* 410–417.

Kruglanski, A. W., & Webster, D. M. (1996). Motivated closing of the mind: "Seizing" and "freezing." *Psychological Review, 103,* 263–283.

Krupnick, J. L., Sotsky, S. M., Simmens, S., Moyer, J., Elkin, I., Watkins, J., & Paulinis, P. A. (1996). The role of the therapeutic alliance in psychotherapy and pharmacotherapy outcome: Findings in the National Institute of Mental Health Treatment of Depression Collaborative Research Program. *Journal of Consulting & Clinical Psychology, 64,* 532–539.

Kübler-Ross, E. (1969). *On death and dying.* New York: Macmillan.

Kuhl, P. K. (1989). On babies, birds, modules, and mechanisms: A comparative approach to the acquisition of vocal communication. In R. J. Dooling & S. H. Husle (Eds.), *The comparative psychology of audition: Perceiving complex sounds* (pp. 379–419). Hillsdale, NJ: Erlbaum.

Kuhl, P. K., Williams, K. A., Lacerda, F., Stevens, K. N., et al. (1992). Linguistic experience alters phonetic perception in infants by 6 months of age. *Science, 255,* 606–608.

Kunda, Z., & Oleson, K. C. (1995). Maintaining stereotypes in the face of disconfirmation: Constructing grounds for subtyping deviants. *Journal of Personality and Social Psychology, 68,* 565–579.

Kunz, G., Beil, D., Deiniger, H., Einspanier, A., Mall, G., & Leyendecker, G. (1997). The uterine peristaltic pump. Normal and impeded sperm transport within the female genital tract. *Advances in Experimental Medicine and Biology, 424,* 267–277.

Kvale, G., & Hugdahl, K. (1994). Cardiovascular conditioning and anticipatory nausea and vomiting in cancer patients. *Behavioral Medicine, 20,* 78–83.

Lachman, M. E., & Weaver, S. L. (1998). The sense of control as a moderator of social class differences in health and well-being. *Journal of Personality and Social Psychology, 74,* 763–773.

Lacks, P., & Morin, C. M. (1992). Recent advances in the assessment and treatment of insomnia. *Journal of Consulting & Clinical Psychology, 60,* 586–594.

Lafuente, M. J., Grifol, R., Segarra, J., Soriano, J., Gorba, M. A., & Montesinos, A. (1997). Effects of the Firstart method of prenatal stimulation on psychomotor development: The first six months. *Pre- & Peri-Natal Psychology Journal, 11,* 151–162.

Laird, J. D. (1974). Self-attribution of emotion: The effects of expressive behavior on the quality of emotional experience. *Journal of Personality & Social Psychology, 29,* 475–486.

Laird, J. D. (1984). The real role of facial response in the experience of emotion: A reply to Tourangeau and Ellsworth, and others. *Journal of Personality & Social Psychology, 47,* 909–917.

Laird, J. D., Alibozak, T., Davainis, D., Deignan, K., Fontanella, K., Hong, J., Levy, B., & Pacheco, C. (1994). Individual differences in the effects of spontaneous mimicry on emotional contagion. *Motivation and Emotion, 18,* 231–247.

Lakey, B., & Dickenson, L. G. (1994). Antecedents of perceived support: Is perceived family environment generalized to new social relationships? *Cognitive Therapy and Research, 18,* 39–53.

Lakey, B., & Heller, K. (1988). Social support form a friend, perceived support, and social problem solving. *American journal of Community Psychology, 16,* 811–824.

Lalumiere, M. L., & Quinsey, L. (1998). Pavlovian conditioning of sexual interests in human males. *Archives of Sexual Behavior, 27,* 241–252.

Lam, R. W., Bartley, S., Yatham, L. N., Tam, E. M., & Zis, A. P. (1999). Clinical predictors of short-term outcome in electroconvulsive therapy. *Canadian Journal of Psychiatry, 44,* 158–163.

Lambert, A. J. (1995). Stereotypes and social judgment: The consequences of group variability. *Journal of Personality and Social Psychology, 68,* 388–403.

Lambert, M. J. (1983). Introduction to assessment of psychotherapy outcome: Historical perspective and current issues. In M. J. Lambert, E. R. Christensen, & S. S. DeJulio (Eds.), *The assessment of psychotherapy outcome* (pp. 3–32). New York: Wiley-Interscience.

Lambert, M. J., & Bergin, A. E. (1994). The effectiveness of psychotherapy. In A. E. Bergin & S. L. Garfield (Eds.), *Handbook of psychotherapy and behavior change, 4th edition* (pp. 143–189). New York: John Wiley & Sons.

Land, E. H. (1959). Experiments in color vision. *Scientific American, 200,* 84–99.

Land, E. H. (1977). The retinex theory of color vision. *Scientific American, 237,* 108–128.

Land, E. H. (1983). Recent advances in retinex theory and some implications for cortical computations: Color vision and the natural image. *Proceedings of the National Academy of Sciences, USA, 80,* 5163–5169.

Lane, H. (1976). *The wild boy of Aveyron.* Cambridge, MA: Harvard University Press.

Lane, R. D., Reiman, E. M., Ahern, G. L., & Schwartz, G. E. (1997a). Neuroanatomical correlates of happiness, sadness, and disgust. *American Journal of Psychiatry, 154,* 926–933.

Lang, P. J. (1994). The varieties of emotional experience: A meditation on the James-Lange theory. *Psychological Review: Special Issue: The Centennial Issue of the Psychological Review, 101,* 211–221.

Lang, P. J. (1995). The emotion probe: Studies of motivation and attention. *American Psychologist, 50,* 372–385.

Lang, P. J., Bradley, M. M., & Cuthbert, B. N. (1990). Emotion, attention, and the startle reflex. *Psychological Review, 97,* 377–395.

Lange, C. (1887). *Uber gemuthsbewegungen.* Leipzig: Theodor Thomas.

Langer, E. J., & Rodin, J. (1976). The effects of choice and enhanced personal responsibility for the aged: A field experiment in an institutional setting. *Journal of Personality & Social Psychology, 34,* 191–198.

La Piere, R. T. (1934). Attitude and actions. *Social Forces, 13,* 230–237.

Lapsley, D. K. (1990). Egocentrism theory and the "new look" at the imaginary audience and personal fable in adolescence. In R. M. Lerner, A. C. Petersen, & J. Brooks-Gunn (Eds.), *The encyclopedia of adolescence* (pp. 281– 286). New York: Garland.

Lapsley, D. K., Jackson, S., Rice, K., & Shadid, G. (1988). Self-monitoring and the "new look" at the imaginary audience and personal fable: An ego-developmental analysis. *Journal of Adolescent Research, 3,* 17–31.

Larson, J. A. (1932). *Lying and its detection: A study of deception and deception tests.* Chicago, IL: University of Chicago Press.

Larson, R., & Richards, M. H. (1994). *Divergent realities: The emotional lives of mothers, fathers, and adolescents.* New York: Basic Books.

Laruelle, M., Ai-Dargham, A., Casanova, M., Toti, R., Weinberger, D., & Kleinman, J. (1993). Selective abnormalities of prefrontal serotonergic receptors in schizophrenia. *Archives of General Psychiatry, 50,* 810–818.

Latané, B., Williams, K., & Harkins, S. (1979). Many hands make light the work: The causes and consequences of social loafing. *Journal of Personality and Social Psychology, 37*, 822–832.

Laughlin, P. R., & Ellis, A. L. (1986). Demonstrability and social combination processes on mathematical intellective tasks. *Journal of Experimental Social Psycology, 22* 177–189.

Laursen, B., Coy, K. C., & Collins, W. A. (1998). Reconsidering changes in parent-child conflict across adolescence: A meta-analysis. *Child Development, 69*, 817–832.

Lavergne, G. M. (1997). *A sniper in the tower: The Charles Whitman murders.* Denton, TX: University of North Texas Press.

Lawless, H. T. (1984). Oral chemical irritation: Psychophysical properties. *Chemical Senses, 9*, 143–155.

Lazarus, R. S. (1984). On the primacy of cognition. *American Psychologist, 39*, 124–129.

Lazarus, R. S., & Folkman, S. (1984). *Stress, appraisal, and coping.* New York: Springer.

Lazev, A. B., Herzog, T. A., & Brandon, T. H. (1999). Classical conditioning of environmental cues to cigarette smoking. *Experimental and Clinical Psychopharmacology, 7*, 56–63.

Leary, W. (1997, December 18). Responses of alcoholics to therapists seem similar. *New York Times*, A17.

Leavitt, F. (1997). False attribution of suggestibility to explain recovered memory of childhood sexual abuse following extended amnesia. *Child Abuse & Neglect, 21*, 265–272.

LeBihan, D., Jezzard, P., Turner, R., Cuenod, C. A., Pannier, L., & Prinster, A. (1993). Practical problems and limitations in using z-maps for processing of brain function MR images. *Abstracts of the 12th Meeting of the Society of Magnetic Resonance in Medicine, 1*, 11.

Leccese, A. P. (1991). *Drugs and society: Behavioral medicines and abusable drugs.* Englewood Cliffs, NJ: Prentice-Hall, Inc.

LeDoux, J. E. (1995). Emotion: Clues from the brain. *Annual Review of Psychology, 46*, 209–235.

LeDoux, J. E. (1996). *The emotional brain: The mysterious underpinnings of emotional life.* New York: Simon & Schuster.

LeDoux, J. E., Wilson, D. H., & Gazzaniga, M. S. (1977). A divided mind: Observations on the conscious properties of the separated hemispheres. *Annals of Neurology, 2*, 417–421.

Lee, A. M., & Lee, S. (1996). Disordered eating and its psychosocial correlates among Chinese adolescent females in Hong Kong. *International Journal of Eating Disorders, 20*, 177–183.

Lee, E. S. (1951). Negro intelligence and selective migration: A Philadelphia test of the Klineberg hypothesis. *American Sociological Review, 16*, 227–233.

Lee, S. (1996). Clinical lessons from the cross-cultural study of anorexia nervosa. *Eating Disorders Review, 7*(3), 1.

Leffler, A., Gillespie, D. L., & Conaty, J. C. (1982). The effects of status differentiation on non-verbal behavior. *Social Psychology Quarterly, 45*, 153–151.

Lehman, A. F., & Steinwachs, D. M. (1998). Translating research into practice: The Schizophrenia Patients Outcome Research Team (PORT) Treatment Recommendations. *Schizophrenia Bulletin, 24*, 1–10.

Leibowitz, H. W. (1971). Sensory, learned and cognitive mechanisms of size perception. *Annals of the New York Academy of Sciences, 188*, 47–62.

Lemme, B. H. (1995). *Development in adulthood.* Needham Heights, MA: Allyn & Bacon.

Lennon, R., & Eisenberg, N. (1987). Gender and age differences in empathy and sympathy. In N. Eisenberg & J. Strayer (Eds.), *Empathy and its development* (pp. 195–217). New York: Cambridge University Press.

Lepper, M. R., Henderlong, J., & Gingras, I. (1999). Understanding the effects of extrinsic rewards on intrinsic motivation—Uses and abuses of meta-analysis: Comment on Deci, Koestner, and Ryan (1999). *Psychological Bulletin, 125*, 669–676.

Leproult, R., Copinschi, G., Buxton, O., & Van Cauter, E. (1997). Sleep loss results in an elevation of cortisol levels the next evening. *Sleep, 20*, 865–870.

Leproult, R., Van Reeth, O., Byrne, M. M., Sturis, J., & Van Cauter, E. (1997). Sleepiness, performance, and neuroendocrine function during sleep deprivation: Rffects of exposure to bright light or exercise. *Journal of Biological Rhythms, 12*, 245–258.

Lerner, M. J. (1980). *The belief in a just world: A fundamental illusion.* New York: Plenum Press.

LeVay, S. (1991). A difference in hypothalamic structure between heterosexual and homosexual men. *Science, 253*, 1034–1037.

LeVay, S., & Hamer, D. (1994). Evidence for a biological influence in male homosexuality. *Scientific American, 270*, 44–49.

Levenson, R. W, Ekman, P., & Friesen, W. V. (1990). Voluntary facial action generates emotion-specific autonomic nervous system activity. *Psychophysiology, 27*, 363–384.

Leventhal, G. S., Singer, R., & Jones, S. (1965). The effects of fear and specificity of recommendation upon attitudes and behavior. *Journal of Personality and Social Psychology, 2*, 20–29.

Levie, W. H., & Lentz, R. (1982). Effects of text illustrations: A review of research. *Educational Communication and Technology Journal, 30*, 195–232.

Levin, J. R., Anglin, G. J., & Carney, R. N. (1987). On empirically validating functions of pictures in prose. In D. M. Willows & H. A. Houghton (Eds.), *The psychology of illustration: I. Basic research* (pp. 51–85). New York: Springer-Verlag.

Levin, R. J. (1994). Human male sexuality: Appetite and arousal, desire and drive. In C. R. Legg & D. Booth (Eds.), *Appetite: Neural and behavioral bases.* (pp. 127–164). New York: Oxford University Press.

Levin, R. S. (1980). The physiology of sexual function in women. *Clinics in Obstetrics and Gynaecology, 7*, 213–252.

Levine, D. N. (1982). Visual agnosia in monkey and man. In D. J. Ingle, M. A. Goodale, & R. J. W. Mansfield (Eds.), *Analysis of Visual Behavior* (pp. 629–670). Cambridge: MIT Press.

Levine, J. M. (1989). Reaction to opinion deviance in small groups. In P. B. Paulus (Ed.), *Psychology of group influence* (2nd ed., pp. 187–231).

Levine, J. M., & Moreland, R. L. (1998). Small groups. In D. T. Gilbert, S. T. Fiske, & G. Lindzey (Eds.), The handbook of social psychology (4th ed., pp. 415–469). New York: McGraw Hill.

Levine, R. L., & Bluni, T. D. (1994). Magnetic field effects on spatial discrimination learning in mice. *Physiology and Behavior, 55*, 465–467.

Levine, R. L., & Stadtman, E. R. (1992). Oxidation of proteins during aging. *Generations, 16*(4), 39–42.

Levinson, D. J. (1977). The mid-life transition: A period in adult psychosocial development. *Psychiatry: Journal for the Study of Interpersonal Processes, 40*, 99–112.

Levinson, D. J. (1978). Eras: The anatomy of the life cycle. *Psychiatric Opinion, 15*, 10–11, 39–48.

Levinson, D. J. (1986). A conception of adult development. *American Psychologist, 41*, 3–13.

Levinson, D. J. (1990). A theory of life structure development in adulthood. In C. N. Alexander & E. J. Langer (Eds.), *Higher stages of human development: Perspectives on adult growth* (pp. 35– 53). New York: Oxford University Press.

Levinson, D., Darrow, C., Klein, E. Levinson, M., & Braxton, M. (1978). *The seasons of a man's life.* New York: Ballantine.

Levitt, A. G., & Wang, Q. (1991). Evidence for language-specific rhythmic influences in the reduplicative babbling of French- and English-learning infants. *Language and Speech, 34*, 235–249.

Levitt, M. J., Weber, R. A., & Guacci, N. (1993). Convoys of social support: An intergenerational analysis. *Psychology and Aging, 8*, 323–326.

Levy, S. M., Herberman, R. B., Lippman, M. N., & d'Angelo, T. (1987). Correlation of stress factors with sustained depression of natural killer cell activity and predicted prognosis in patients with breast cancer. *Journal of Clinical Oncology, 5*, 348–353.

Levy, S. M., Herberman, R. B., Maluish, A. M., Schlien, B., & Lippman, M. (1985). Prognostic risk assessment in primary breast cancer by behavioral and immunological parameters. *Health Psychology, 4*, 99–113.

Levy, S. M., Lee, J., Bagley, C., & Lippman, M. (1988). Survival hazards analysis in first year recurrent breast cancer patients: Seven-year follow-up. *Psychosomatic Medicine, 50*, 520–528.

Lewinsohn, P. M., Rohde, P., Seeley, J. R., & Fischer, S. A. (1993). Age-cohort changes in the lifetime occurrence of depression and other mental disorders. *Journal of Abnormal Psychology, 102*, 110–120.

Lewis, D. O., Yeager, C. A., Swica, Y., Pincus, J. H., & Lewis, M. (1997). Objective documentation of child abuse and dissociation in 12 murderers with dissociative identity disorder. *American Journal of Psychiatry, 154*, 1703–1710.

Lewis, M., & Brooks-Gunn, J. (1979). *Social cognition and the acquisition of self.* New York: Plenum.

Lewontin, R. C. (1976a). Further remarks on race and the genetics of intelligence. In N. J Block & G. Dworkin (Eds.), *The IQ controversy* (pp. 107–112). New York: Pantheon Books.

Lewontin, R. C. (1976b). Race and intelligence. In N. J. Block & G. Dworkin (Eds.), *The IQ controversy* (pp. 78–92). New York: Pantheon Books.

Liang, D. W., Moreland, R., & Argote, L. (1995). Group versus individual training and group performance: The mediating factor of transactive memory. *Personality & Social Psychology Bulletin, 21,* 384–393.

Liddell, C. (1997). Every picture tells a story—or does it? Young South African children interpreting pictures. *Journal of Cross-Cultural Psychology, 28,* 266–282.

Light, L. (1991). Memory and aging: Four hypotheses in search of data. *Annual Review of Psychology, 42,* 333–376.

Lilenfeld, L. R., Kaye, W. H., Greeno, C. G., Merikangas, K. R., Plotnicov, K., Pollice, C., Raol, R., Strober, M., Bulik, C. M., & Nagy, L. (1998). A controlled family study of anorexia nervosa and bulimia nervosa: Psychiatric disorders in first-degree relatives and effects of proband comorbidity. *Archives of General Psychiatry, 55,* 603–610.

Lillard, A. S. (1999). Developing a cultural theory of mind: The CIAO approach. *Current Directions in Psychological Science, 8,* 57–61.

Lindemann, E. (1991). The symptomatology and management of acute grief. *American Journal of Psychiatry, 144,* 141–148.

Lindsay, D. S., & Johnson, M. K. (1989). The eyewitness suggestibility effect and memory for source. *Memory & Cognition, 17,* 349–358.

Linner, B. (1972). *Sex and society in Sweden.* New York: Harper Colophon Books.

Linnoila, M., Virkkunen, M., Scheinin, M., Nuutila, A., Romin, R., & Goodwin, F. K. (1983). Low cerebrospinal fluid 5-hydroxindoleacetic acid concentration differentiates impulsive from non-impulsive violent behavior. *Life Sciences, 33,* 2609–2614.

Linville, P. W., & Fischer, G. W. (1993). Exemplar and abstraction models of perceived group variability and stereotypicality. *Social Cognition, 11,* 92–125.

Lipkus, I. M., & Siegler, I. C. (1993). The belief in a just world and perceptions of discrimination. *Journal of Psychology, 127,* 465–474.

Liu, D., Diorio, J., Tannenbaum, B., Caldji, C., Francis, D., Freedman, A., Sharma, S., Pearson, D., Plotsky, P. M., & Meaney, M. J. (1997). Maternal care, hippocampal glucocorticoid receptors, and hypothalamic-pituitary-adrenal responses to stress. *Science, 277,* 1659–1662.

Liu, J. H., & Latané, B. (1998). Extremitization of attitudes: Does thought- and discussion-induced polarization cumulate? *Basic & Applied Social Psychology, 20,* 103–110.

Livesley, W. J. (1998). Suggestions for a framework for an empirically based classification of personality disorder. *Canadian Journal of Psychiatry 43,* 137–147.

Livingstone, M. S., & Hubel, D. H. (1984). Anatomy and physiology of a color system in the primate visual cortex. *Journal of Neuroscience, 4,* 309–356.

Lobaugh, N. J., Cole, S., & Rovet, J. F. (1998). Visual search for features and conjunctions in development. *Canadian Journal of Experimental Psychology, 52,* 201–212.

Locke, S. E., Kraus, L., Leserman, J., Hurst, M. W., Heisel, J. S., & Williams, R. M. (1984). Life change stress, psychiatric symptoms, and natural killer-cell activity. *Psychosomatic Medicine, 46,* 441–453.

Loehlin, J. C. (1989). Partitioning environmental and genetic contributions to behavioral development. *American Psychologist, 44,* 1285–1292.

Loehlin, J. C. (1992). *Genes and environment in personality development.* Newbury Park, CA: Sage.

Loehlin, J. C. (1997). A test of J. R. Harris' theory of peer influences on personality. *Journal of Personality and Social Psychology, 72,* 1197–1201.

Loehlin, J. C., Horn, J. M., & Willerman, L. (1981). Personality resemblance in adoptive families. *Behavior Genetics, 11,* 309–330.

Loehlin, J. C., Willerman, L., & Horn, J. M. (1985). Personality resemblances in adoptive families when the children are late-adolescent or adult. *Journal of Personality and Social Psychology, 48,* 376–392.

Loewenstein, R. J. (1994). Diagnosis, epidemiology, clinical course, treatment, and cost effectiveness of treatment for dissociative disorders and MPD: Report submitted to the Clinton Administration Task Force on Health Care Financing Reform. *Dissociation: Progress in the Dissociative Disorders, 7,* 3–11.

Loftus, E. F. (1993). The reality of repressed memories. *American Psychologist, 48,* 518–537.

Loftus, E. F., & Pickrell, J. E. (1995). The formation of false memories. *Psychiatric Annals, 25,* 720–725.

Loftus, G. R. (1972). Eye fixations and recognition memory for pictures. *Cognitive Psychology, 3,* 525–551.

Logie, R. H., & Baddeley, A. D. (1990). Imagery and working memory. In P. J. Hampson & D. F. Marks (Eds.), *Imagery: Current developments.* (pp. 103–128). London: Routledge.

Logie, R. H., & Marchetti, C. (1991). Visuo-spatial working memory: Visual, spatial or central executive? In R. H. Logie & M. Denis, (Eds.), *Mental images in human cognition* (pp.105–115). Amsterdam: North-Holland.

Logie, R. H. (1986). Visuo-spatial processing in working memory. *Quarterly Journal of Experimental Psychology, 80,* 229–247.

Lonetto, R., & Templer, D. (1986). *Death anxiety.* New York: Hemisphere.

Looren de Jong, H. (1996). Levels: Reduction and elimination in cognitive neuroscience. In C. W. Tolman, F. Cherry, et al. (Eds.), *Problems of theoretical psychology* (pp. 165–172). North York, ON, Canada: Captus Press.

Lorenzo-Hernandez, J. (1998). How social categorization may inform the study of Hispanic immigration. *Hispanic Journal of Behavioral Sciences, 20,* 39–59.

Losch, M., & Cacioppo, J. (1990). Cognitive dissonance may enhance sympathetic tonis, but attitudes are changed to reduce negative effect rather than arousal. *Journal of Experimental Social Psychology, 26,* 289–304.

Lott, B. (1996) Politics or science? The question of gender sameness/difference. *American Psychologist, 51,* 153–154.

Lou, H. C., Hansen, D., Nordentoft, M., Pryds, O., et al. (1994). Prenatal stressors of human life affect fetal brain development. *Developmental Medicine & Child Neurology, 36,* 826–832.

Lowe, C. F. (1979). Determinants of human operant behaviour. In M. D. Zeiler and P. Harzem (Eds.), *Advances in analysis of behavior (Vol. 1). Reinforcement and the organization of behavior.* New York: Wiley.

Lowe, P. (1999, May 2). Alike and different. *Denver Post.*

Lu, L., & Shih, J. B. (1997a). Sources of happiness: A qualitative approach. *Journal of Social Psychology, 137,* 181–188.

Lubin, A. J. (1972). *Stranger on the Earth: Vincent van Gogh.* New York: Da Capo Press.

Luborsky, L., Diguer, L., Seligman, D. A., Rosenthal, R., Krause, E. D., Johnson, S., Halperin, G., Bishop, M., Berman, J. S., & Schweizer, E. (1999). The researcher's own therapy allegiances: A "wild card" in comparisons of treatment efficacy. *Clinical Psychology: Science & Practice 6,* 95–106.

Luborsky, L., Singer, B., & Luborsky, L. (1975). Comparative studies of psychotherapies: Is it true that "everyone has won and all must have prizes"? *Archives of General Psychiatry, 32,* 995–1008.

Lucas, R. J., Freedman, M. S., Muñoz, M., Garcia-Fernandez, J-M., & Foster, R. G. (1999). Regulation of the mammalian pineal by non-rod, non-cone, ocular photoreceptors. *Science, 284,* 505–507.

Luce, G. G. (1971). *Biological rhythms in human and animal physiology.* New York: Dover.

Luck, S. J., Vogel, E. K., & Shapiro, K. L. (1996). Word meanings can be accessed but not reported during the attentional blink. *Nature, 383,* 616–618.

Lunzer, E. A. (1978). Formal reasoning: A reappraisal. In B. Z. Presseisen, D. Goldstein, & M. H. Appel (Eds.), *Topics in cognitive development: Vol. 2. Language and operational thought* (pp. 47–76). New York: Plenum.

Luparello, T. J., Lyons, H. A., Bleecker, E. R., & McFadden, E. R. (1968). Influences of suggestion on airway reactivity in asthmatic subjects. *Psychosomatic Medicine, 30,* 819–825.

Lush, J. L. (1937). *Animal breeding plans.* Ames, IA: Collegiate Press.

Lydon, J. E., Jamieson, D. W., & Zanna, M. P. (1988). Interpersonal similarity and the social and intellectual dimensions of first impressions. *Social Cognition, 6,* 269–286.

Lykken, D., Bouchard, T. J., Jr., McGue, M., & Tellegen, A. (1993). Heritability of Interests: A twin study. *Journal of Applied Psychology, 78,* 649–661.

Lykken, D., & Tellegen, A. (1996). Happiness is a stochastic phenomenon. *Psychological Science, 7,* 186–189.

Lykken, D. T. (1959). The GSR in the detection of guilt. *Journal of Applied Psychology, 43,* 385–388.

Lykken, D. T. (1960). The validity of the guilty knowledge technique: The effects of faking. *Journal of Applied Psychology, 44,* 258–262.

Lynn, R. (1990). The role of nutrition in secular increases in intelligence. *Personality & Individual Differences, 11,* 273–285.

Lynn, R., & Martin, T. (1997). Gender differences in extraversion, neuroticism, and psychoticism in 37 nations. *Journal of Social Psychology, 137,* 369–373.

Lyons, E. A., & Levi, C. S. (1994). Sperm are not like salmon: Altered myometrial contractility is significant in unexplained infertility rates. *Radiology, 193[P],* 144.

Lyons, M. J., Goldberg, J., Eisen, S. A., True, W., Tsuang, M. T., Meyer, J. M., & Henderson, W. G. (1993). Do genes influence exposure to trauma: A twin study of combat. *American Journal of Medical Genetics (Neuropsychiatric Genetics), 48,* 22–27.

Lytton, H., & Romney, D. M. (1991). Parents' differential socialization of boys and girls: A meta-analysis. *Psychological Bulletin, 109,* 267–296.

Maas, J. B. (1998). *Power sleep.* New York: Harper Perennial.

Macaskill, N. D., & Macaskill, A. (1996). Rational-emotive therapy plus pharmacotherapy versus pharmacotherapy alone in the treatment of high cognitive dysfunction depression. *Cognitive Therapy & Research, 20,* 575–592.

Maccoby, E. E. (1988). Gender as a social category. *Developmental Psychology, 26,* 755–765.

Maccoby, E. E. (1990). Gender and relationships: A developmental account. *American Psychologist, 45,* 513–520.

Maccoby, E. E. (1991). Gender and relationships: A reprise. *American Psychologist, 46,* 538–539.

Maccoby, E. E., & Jacklin, C. N. (1987). Gender segregation in childhood. In H. W. Reese (Ed.), *Advances in child development and behavior* (Vol. 20, pp. 239–288). New York: Academic Press.

MacGregor, A. J., Griffiths, G. O., Baker, J., & Spector, T. D. (1997). Determinants of pressure pain threshold in adult twins: Evidence that shared environmental influences predominate. *Pain, 73,* 253–257.

Macmillan, M. (1992). Inhibition and the control of behavior: From Gall to Freud via Phineas Gage and the frontal lobes. *Brain & Cognition, 19,* 72–104.

Macmillan, M. B. (1986). A wonderful journey through skull and brains: The travels of Mr. Gage's tamping iron. *Brain & Cognition, 5,* 67–107.

MacPhillamy, D. J., & Lewinsohn, P. M. (1974). Depression as a function of levels of desired and obtained pleasure. *Journal of Abnormal Psychology, 83,* 651–657.

Macrae, C. N., Bodenhausen, G. V., Milne, A. B., & Jetten, J. (1994). Out of mind but back in sight: Stereotypes on the rebound. *Journal of Personality and Social Psychology, 67,* 808–817.

Maguire, E. A., Gadian, D. G., Johnsrude, I. S., Good, C. D., Ashburner, J., Frackowiak, R. S. J., & Frith, C. D. (2000). Navigation-related structural change in the hippocampi of taxi drivers. *Proceedings of the National Academy of Sciences, USA,* 10.1073/pnas.070039597.

Maher, B. A. (1966). *Principles of psychopathology: An experimental approach.* New York: McGraw-Hill.

Malan, D. H. (1976). *The frontier of brief psychotherapy: An example of the convergence of research and clinical practice.* New York: Plenum Medical Book Co.

Malina, R. M., & Bouchard, C. (1991). *Growth, maturation, and physical activity.* Champaign, IL: Human Kinetics Books.

Malkoff-Schwartz, S., Frank, E., Anderson, B., Sherrill, J. T., Siegel, L., Patterson, D., & Kupfer, D. J. (1998). Stressful Life Events and Social Rhythm Disruption in the Onset of Manic and Depressive Bipolar Episodes: A Preliminary Investigation. *Archives of General Psychiatry, 55,* 702–707.

Manabe, T., Noda, Y., Mamiya, T., Katagirl, H., Houtani, T., Nishi, M., Noda, T., Takahashi, T., Sugimoto, T., Nabeshima, T., & Takeshima, H. (1998). Facilitation of long-term potentiation and memory in mice lacking nociceptin receptors. *Nature, 394,* 577–581.

Mandler, G. (1967). Organization in memory. In K. W. Spence & J. T. Spence (Eds.), *The psychology of learning and motivation* (Vol. 1, pp. 327–372). San Diego: Academic Press.

Manfro, G. G., Otto, M. W., McArdle, E. T., Worthington, J. J., III, Rosenbaum, J. F., & Pollack, M. H. (1996). Relationship of antecedent stressful life events to childhood and family history of anxiety and the course of panic disorder. *Journal of Affective Disorders, 41,* 135–139.

Mann, T., Nolen-Hoeksema, S., Huang, K., Burgard, D., Wright, A., & Hanson, K. (1997). Are Are Two Interventions Worse than None? Joint Primary and Secondary Prevention of Eating Disorders in College Females. *Health Psychology, 16,* 3.

Mansour, C. S., Haier, R. J., & Buchsbaum, M. S. (1996). Gender comparisons of cerebral glucose metabolic rate in healthy adults during a cognitive task. *Personality and Individual Differences, 20,* 183–191.

Manuck, S. B., Cohen, S., Rabin, B. S., Muldoon, M. F., & Bachen, E. A. (1991). Individual differences in cellular immune response to stress. *Psychological. Science, 2,* 111–115.

Marcus, G. F., Vijayan, S., Rao, S. B., & Vishton, P. M. (1999). Rule learning by seven-month-old infants. *Science, 283,* 77–80.

Markham, R., & Wang, L. (1996). Recognition of emotion by Chinese and Australian children. *Journal of Cross-Cultural Psychology, 27,* 616–643.

Marks, I. (1997). Behaviour therapy for obsessive-compulsive disorder: A decade of progress. *Canadian Journal of Psychiatry, 42,* 1021–1027.

Marks, I., Lovell, K., Noshirvani, H., Livanou, M., & Sian, T. (1998). Treatment of Posttraumatic Stress Disorder by Exposure and/or Cognitive Restructuring: A Controlled Study. *Archives of General Psychiatry, 55,* 317–325.

Marks, I. M. (1969). *Fears and phobias.* New York: Academic Press.

Markson, L., & Bloom, P. (1997). Evidence against a dedicated system for word learning in children. *Nature, 385,* 813–815.

Marmot, M. G., & Syme, S. L. (1976). Acculturation and coronary heart disease in Japanese-Americans. *American Journal of Epidemiology, 104,* 225–247.

Marr, D. (1982). *Vision: A computational investigation into the human representation and processing of visual information.* New York: Freeman.

Marshall, D. S. (1971). Sexual behavior on Mangaia. In D. S. Marshall & R. C. Suggs (Eds.), *Human sexual behavior* (pp. 103–162). New York: Basic Books.

Martin, A., Wiggs, C. L., Ungerlieder, L. G., & Haxby, J. V. (1996). Neural correlates of category-specific knowledge. *Nature, 379,* 649–652.

Martin, R. A., & Dobbin, J. P. (1988). Sense of humor, hassles, and immunoglobulin A: Evidence for a stress-moderating effect of humor. *International Journal of Psychiatry in Medicine, 18,* 93–105.

Marucha, P. T., Kiecolt-Glaser, J. K., & Favagehi, M. (1998). Mucosal wound healing is impaired by examination stress. *Psychosomatic Medicine, 60,* 362–365.

Masataka, N. (1996). Perception of motherese in a signed language by 6-month-old deaf infants. *Developmental Psychology, 32,* 874–879.

Maslach, C., Santee, R. T., & Wade, C. (1987). Individuation, gender role, and dissent: Personality mediators of situational forces. *Journal of Personality and Social Psychology, 53,* 1088–1194.

Maslow, A. H. (1954). *Motivation and personality.* New York: Harper.

Maslow, A. H. (1968). *Toward a psychology of being* (2nd ed.). New York: Van Nostrand.

Maslow, A. H. (1970). *Motivation and personality* (2nd ed.). New York: Harper and Row.

Masters, W. H., & Johnson, V. E. (1966). *Human sexual response.* Boston: Little, Brown.

Matarazzo, J. D. (1972). *Wechsler's measurement and appraisal of adult intelligence.* Baltimore: Williams & Wilkins.

Mather, M., Henkel, L. A., & Johnson, M. K. (1997). Evaluating characteristics of false memories: Remember/know judgments and memory characteristics questionnaire compares. *Memory & Cognition, 25,* 826–837.

Matsumae, M., Kikinis, R., Mórocz, I. A., Lorenzo, A. V., Sándor, T., Albert, M. S., Black, P. M., & Jolesz, F. A. (1996). Age-related changes in intracranial compartment volumes in normal adults assessed by magnetic resonance imaging. *Journal of Neurosurgery, 84,* 982–992.

Matthews, B. A., Shimoff, E., Catania, A. C., & Sagvolden, T. (1977). Uninstructed human responding: Sensitivity to ratio and interval contingencies. *Journal of the Experimental Analysis of Behavior, 27,* 453–467.

Matthews, G., & Gilliland, K. (1999). The personality theories of H. J. Eysenck and J. A. Gray: A comparative review. *Personality and Individual Differences, 26,* 583–626.

Mayer, J. D., & Salovey, P. (1997). What is emotional intelligence? In P. Salovey & D. J. Sluyter (Eds.), *Emotional development and emotional intelligence.* New York: Basic Books.

Mayes, A. R., & Downes, J. J. (Eds.). (1997). *Theories of organic amnesia.* Hove, England: Psychology Press/Erlbaum (UK) Taylor & Francis.

Maynard, R. A. (Ed.). (1996). *Kids having kids: A Robin Hood Foundation special report on the costs of adolescent childbearing*. New York: Robin Hood Foundation.

Maznevski, M. L. (1994). Understanding our differences: Performance in decision—making groups with diverse members. *Human Relations, 47*, 531–552.

McBride, J. (1999). *Steven Spielberg: A biography*. New York: Da Capo.

McCarley, R. W., & Hobson, J. A. (1975). Neuronal excitability modulation over the sleep cycle: A structural and mathematical model. *Science, 189*, 58–60.

McCartney, K., Harris, M. J., & Bernieri, F. (1990). Growing up and growing apart: A developmental meta-analysis of twin studies. *Psychological Bulletin, 107*, 226–237.

McClelland, D. C., & Atkinson, J. W. (1953). *The achievement motive*. New York: Appleton-Century-Crofts.

McClelland, D. C., Koestner, R., & Weinbereger, J. (1989). How do self-attributed and implicit motives differ? *Psychological Review, 96*, 690–702.

McClintock, M. K., & Herdt, G. (1996). Rethinking puberty: The development of sexual attraction. *Current Directions in Psychological Science, 5*, 178–183.

McCornack, S. A., & Parks, M. R. (1990). What women know that men don't: Sex differences in determining the truth behind deceptive messages. *Journal of Social and Personal Relationships, 7*, 107–118.

McCrae, R. H., & Costa, P. T., Jr. (1987). Validation of the five-factor model of personality across instruments and observers. *Journal of Personality and Social Psychology, 52*, 81–90.

McCrae, R. H., & Costa, P. (1984). *Emerging lives, enduring dispositions: Personality in adulthood*. Boston: Little, Brown.

McCrae, R. H., & Costa, P. T., Jr. (1997). Personality trait structure as a human universal. *American Psychologist, 52*, 509–516.

McCrae, R. H., Costa, P. T., Jr., DelPilar, G. H. Rolland, J. P., & Parker, W. D. (1998). Cross-cultural assessment of the five-factor model: The Revised NEO Personality Inventory. *Journal of Cross-Cultural Psychology, 29*, 171–188.

McDaniel, M. A., & Einstein, G. O. (1986). Bizarre imagery as an effective memory aid: The importance of distinctiveness. *Journal of Experimental Psychology: Learning, Memory, & Cognition, 12*, 54–65.

McDaniel, M. A., Einstein, G. O., DeLosh, E. L., & May, C. P. (1995). The bizarreness effect: It's not surprising, it's complex. *Journal of Experimental Psychology: Learning, Memory, & Cognition, 21*, 422–435.

McDermott, K. B., & Roediger, H. L., III. (1998). Attempting to avoid illusory memories: Robust false recognition of associates persists under conditions of explicit warnings and immediate testing. *Journal of Memory and Language, 39*, 508–520.

McDougall, W. (1908/1960). *Introduction to social psychology*. New York: Barnes & Noble.

McEwen, B. S. (1997). Possible mechanisms for atrophy of the human hippocampus. *Molecular Psychiatry, 2*, 255–262.

McEwen, B. S., Biron, C. A., Brunson, K. W., Bulloch, K., Chambers, W. H., Dhabhar, F. S., Goldfarb, R. H., Kitson, R. P., Miller, A. H., Spencer, R. L., & Weiss, J. M. (1997). The role of adrenocorticoids as modulators of immune function in health and disease: Neural, endocrine and immune interactions. *Brain Research Review, 23*, 79–133.

McEwen, B. S., & Schmeck, H. M., Jr. (1994). *The Hostage Brain*. New York: Rockefeller University Press.

McFadden, D., & Pasanen, E. G. (1999). Spontaneous otoacoustic emissions in heterosexuals, homosexuals, and bisexuals. *Journal of the Acoustical Society of America, 105*, 2403–2413.

McGaugh, J. L., & Herz, M. J. (1972). *Memory Consolidation*. San Francisco, CA: Albion.

McGoldrick, M., Giordano, J., & Pearce, J. K. (Eds.) (1996). *Ethnicity and family therapy (2nd ed.)*. New York: Guilford Press.

McGraw, K., Hoffman, R. I., Harker, C., & Herman, J. H. (1999). The development of circadian rhythms in a human infant. *Sleep, 22*, 303–310.

McGraw, M. B. (1943). *The neuromuscular maturation of the human infant*. New York: Columbia University Press.

McGue, M., & Lykken, D. T. (1992). Genetic influence on the risk of divorce. *Psychological Science, 3*, 368–373.

McGue, M., Bouchard, T. J., Jr., Iacono, W. G., & Lykken, D. T. (1993). Behavioral genetics of cognitive ability: A life-span perspective. In R. Plomin & G. E. McClearn (Eds.). *Nature, nurture & psychology* (pp. 59–76). Washington, DC, USA: American Psychological Association.

McGuffin, P., & Gottesman, I. I. (1985). Genetic influences on normal and abnormal development. In M. Rutter & L. Hersov (Eds.), *Child and Adolescent Psychiatry: Modern Approaches*. (2nd edition, pp. 17–33). Oxford: Blackwell Scientific.

McGuffin, P., Katz, R., Aldrich, J., & Bebbington, P. (1988). The Camberwell Collaborative Depression Study. II. Investigation of family members. *British Journal of Psychiatry, 152*, 766–774.

McHugh, T. J., Blum, K. I., Tsien, J., Tonegawa, S., & Wilson, M. (1996). Impaired hippocampal representation of space in CA1-specific NMDAR1 knockout mice. *Cell, 87*, 1339–1349.

McKellar, P. (1965). The investigation of mental images. In S. A. Bartnet & A. McLaren (Eds.), *Penguin science survey B (biological sciences)* (pp. 79–94). New York: Penguin Books.

McKenna, R. J. (1972). Some effects of anxiety level and food cues on the eating behavior of obese and normal subjects: A comparison of the Schachterian and psychosomatic conceptions. *Journal of Personality and Social Psychology, 22*, 311–319.

McLaughlin, S., & Margolskee, R. F. (1994). The sense of taste. *American Scientist, 82*, 538–545.

McLean, D. F., Timajchy, K. H., Wingo, P. A., & Floyd, R. L. (1993). Psychosocial measurement: Implications of the study of preterm delivery in black women. *American Journal of Preventive Medicine, 9*, 39–81.

McLeod, P. L., & Lobel, S. A. (1992). The effects of ethinic diversity on idea generation in small groups. *Academy of Management Best Paper Proceedings, 22*, 227–231.

McMillen, D. L., & Austin, J. B. (1971). Effect of positivev feedback on complaince following transgression. *Psychonomic Science, 24*, 59–61.

McNeil, T. F., Cantor-Graae, E., & Weinberger, D. R. (2000). Relationship of obstetric complications and differences in size of brain structures in monozygotic twin pairs discordant for schizophrenia. *American Journal of Psychiatry, 157*, 203–212.

McNicol, D. (1972). *A primer of signal detection theory*. London: Allen & Unwin.

Mead, M. (1928). *Coming of age in Samoa*. New York: Morrow.

Mealey, L., Bridgestock, R., & Townsend, G. C. (1999). Symmetry and perceived facial attractiveness: A monozygotic co-twin comparison. *Journal of Personality and Social Psychology, 76*, 151–158.

Meaney, M. J., Mitchell, J. B., Aitken, D. H., Bhatnagar, S., Bodnoff, S. R., Iny, L. J., & Sarrieau, A. (1991). The effects of neonatal handling on the development of the adrenocortical response to stress: Implications for neuropathology and cognitive deficits in later life. *Psychoneuroendocrinology, 16*, 85–103.

Medin, D. L., Lynch, E. B., & Solomon, K. O. (2000). Are there kinds of concepts? In S. T. Fiske, D. L. Schacter, & C. Zahn-Waxler (Eds.), *Annual Review of Psychology, 51*, 121–147.

Medin, D. L., & Schaffer, M. M. (1978). A context theory of classification learning. *Psychological Review, 85*, 207–238.

Mednick, S. (1962). The associative basis of the creative process. *Psychological Review, 69*, 220–232.

Mednick, S. A., Watson, J. B., Huttunen, M., Cannon, T. D., Katila, H., Machon, R., Mednick, B., Hollister, M., Parnas, J., Schulsinger, F., Sajaniemi, N., Voldsgaard, P., Pyhala, R., Gutkind, D., & Wang, X. (1998). A two-hit workikng model of the etiology of schizophrenia. In M. F. Lenzenweger & R. H. Dworkin (Eds.), *Origins and Development of Schizophrenia: Advances in Experimental Psychopathology*. Washington, DC: American Psychological Association. pp. 27–66.

Meehl, P. (1960). The cognitive activity of the clinician. *American Psychologist, 15*, 19–27.

Melchert, T. P. (1996). Childhood memory and a history of different forms of abuse. *Professional Psychology Research and Practice, 27*, 438–446.

Melding, P. S. (1995). How do older people respond to chronic pain? A review of coping with pain and illness in elders. *Pain Review, 2*, 65–75.

Mellet, E., Petit, L., Mazoyer, B., Denis, M., & Tzourio, N. (1998). Reopening the mental imagery debate: Lessons from functional neuroanatomy. *NeuroImage, 8*, 129–139.

Mello, C. V., Vicario, D. S., & Clayton, D. F. (1992). Song presentation induces gene expression in the songbird forebrain. *Proceedings of the National Academy of Science, USA, 89*, 6818–6822.

Meltzoff, A. N., & Moore, M. K. (1977). Imitation of facial and manual gestures by human neonates. *Science, 198*, 75–78.

Melzack, R., & Wall, P. D. (1982). *The challenge of pain*. New York: Basic Books.

Menyuk, P., Liebergott, J. W., & Schultz, M. C. (1995). *Early language development in full-term and premature infants*. Hillsdale, NJ: Erlbaum.

Menzies, R. G., & Clarke, J. C. (1993). The etiology of childhood water phobia. *Behaviour Research & Therapy, 31,* 499–501.

Menzies, R. G., & Clarke, J. C. (1995a). The etiology of acrophobia and its relationship to severity and individual response patterns. *Behaviour Research & Therapy, 33,* 795–803.

Menzies R. G., & Clarke, J. C. (1995b). The etiology of phobias: A nonassociative account. *Clinical Psychology Review, 15,* 23–48.

Mercer, R. T., Nichols, E. G., & Doyle, G. C. (1989). *Transitions in a woman's life: Major life events in developmental context.* New York: Springer.

Merrick, E. N. (1995). Adolescent childbearing as career "choice": Perspective from an ecological context. *Journal of Counseling & Development, 73,* 288–295.

Merzenich, M. M., Kaas, J. H., Wall, J., Nelson, R. J., & Sur, M. (1983). Topographic reorganization of somatosensory cortical areas 3b and 1 in adult monkeys following restricted deafferentation. *Neuroscience, 8,* 33–55.

Messinger, S. M. (1998). Pleasure and complexity: Berlyne revisited. *Journal of Psychology, 132,* 558–560.

Mickelson, K. D., Kessler, R. C., & Shaver, P. R. (1997). Adult attachment in a nationally representative sample. *Journal of Personality & Social Psychology, 73,* 1092–1106.

Miklowitz, D. J., Goldstein, M. J., Nuechterlein, K. H., Snyder, K. S., & Mintz, J. (1988). Family factors and the course of bipolar affective disorder. *Archives of General Psychiatry, 45,* 225–231.

Mikulincer, M. (1994). *Human learned helplessness: A coping perspective.* New York: Plenum.

Mikulincer, M., & Horesh, N. (1999). Adult attachment style and the perception of others: The role of projective mechanisms. *Journal of Personality and Social Psychology, 76,* 1022–1034.

Miles, L. E. M., Raynal, D. M., & Wilson, M. A. (1977). Blind man living in normal society has circadian rhythms of 24.9 hours. *Science, 198,* 421–423.

Milgram, S. (1963). Behavioral study of obedience. *Journal of Abnormal and Social Psychology, 67,* 371–378.

Milgram, S. (1965). Some conditions of obediencce and disobedience to authority. *Human Relations, 18,* 57–76.

Milgram, S. (1974). *Obedience to authority: An experimental view.* New York: Harper & Row.

Miller, A. G., Collins, B. E., & Brief, D. E. (1995). Perspectives on obedience to authority: The legacy of the Milgram experiments. *Journal of Social Issues, 51,* 1–19.

Miller, G. A. (1956). The magical number seven, plus or minus two: Some limits on our capacity for processing information. *Psychological Review, 63,* 81–97.

Miller, G. E., Dopp, J. M., Stevens, S. Y., & Fahey, J. L. (1999). Psychosocial predictors of natural killer cell mobilzation during marital conflict. *Health Psychology, 18,* 262–271.

Miller, I. W., Keitner, G. E., Whisman, M. A., Ryan, C. E., Epstein, N. B., & Bishop, D. S. (1992). Depressed patients with dysfunctional families: Description and course of illness. *Journal of Abnormal Psychology, 101,* 637–646.

Miller, J. G. (1997). A cultural-psychology perspective on intelligence. In R. J. Sternberg & E. Grigorenko (Eds.), *Intelligence, heredity, and environment* (pp. 269–302). New York: Cambridge University Press.

Miller, J. M., Boudreaux, M. C., & Regan, F. A. (1995). A case-control study of cocaine use in pregnancy. *American Journal of Obstetrics and Gynecology, 172,* 180–185.

Miller, M. G., & Ross, M. (1975). Self-serving biases in attribution of causality: Fact or fiction? *Psychological Bulletin, 82,* 313–325.

Miller, N., Maruayama, G., Beaber, R. J., & Valone, K. (1976). Speed of speech and persuasion. *Journal of Personality and Social Psychology, 34,* 615–624.

Miller, N. E. (1959). Liberalization of basic S-R concepts: Extensions to conflict behavior, motivation, and social learning. In S. Koch (Ed.), *Psychology: A study of scicence: Vol. 2.* New York: McGraw–Hill.

Miller, T. Q., Smith, T. W., Turner, C. W., Guijarro, M. L., & Hallet, A. J. (1996). A meta-analytic review of research on hostility and physical health. *Psychological Bulletin, 119,* 322–348.

Milner, A. D., & Goodale, M. A. (1995). *The visual brain in action.* Oxford University Press.

Milner, B., Corkin, S., & Teuber, H. L. (1968). Further analysis of the hippocampal amnesic syndrome: 14-year followup study of H. M. *Neuropsychologia, 6,* 215–234.

Milton, J., & Weisman, R. (1999a). Does psi exist? Lack of replication of an anomalous process of information transfer. *Psychological Bulletin, 125,* 387–391.

Milton, J., & Weisman, R. (1999b). A meta-analysis of mass-media tests of extrasensory perception. *British Journal of Psychology, 90,* 235–240.

Mineka, S., Davison, M., Cook, M., & Keir, R. (1984). Observational conditioning of snake fear in Rhesus monkeys. *Journal of Abnormal Psychology, 93,* 355–372.

Minuchin, S. (1974). *Families and Family Therapy.* Cambridge, MA: Harvard University Press.

Minuchin, S., & Fishman, H. C. (1981). *Family Therapy Techniques.* Cambridge, MA: Harvard University Press.

Mirsky, A. F., & Quinn, O. W. (1988). The Genain quadruplets. *Schizophrenia Bulletin, 14,* 595–612.

Mischel, W. (1984). Convergences and challenges in the search for consistency. *American Psychologist, 39,* 351–364.

Mischel, W., & Peake, P. K. (1982). Beyond déjà vu in the search for cross-situational consistency. *Psychological Review, 90,* 394–402.

Mischel, W., Shoda, Y., & Rodriguez, M. L. (1989). Delay of gratification in children. *Science, 244,* 933–938.

Mishkin, M. (1982). A memory system in the monkey. *Philosophical Transactions of the Royal Society of London Series B, 298,* 85–95.

Mishkin, M., & Appenzeller, T. (1987). The anatomy of memory. *Scientific American, 256,* 80–89.

Modell, J. (1996). Family niche and intellectual bent. [Review of *Born to Rebel* by Frank J. Sulloway]. *Science, 275,* 624.

Modell, J., Mountz, J., Curtis, G., & Greden, J. (1989). Neurophysiologic dysfunction in basal ganglia/limbic striatal and thalamocortical circuits as a pathogenetic mechanisms of obsessive-compulsive disorder. *Journal of Neuropsychiatry, 1,* 27–36.

Money, J. (1975). Ablatio penis: normal male infant sex-reassigned as a girl. *Archives of Sexual Behavior, 4,* 65–71.

Monk, T. H., Buysse, D. J., Reynolds, C. F., Berga, S. L., Jarrett, D. B., Begley, A. E., & Kupfer, D. J. (1997). Circadian rhythms in human performance and mood under constant conditions. *Journal of Sleep Research, 6,* 9–18.

Monroe, S. M., & Depue, R. A. (1991). Life stress and depression. In J. Becker & A. Kleinman (Eds.), *Psychosocial aspects of depression* (pp. 101–130). Hillsdale, NJ: Erlbaum.

Monteith, M. J. (1996). Affective reactions to prejudice-related discrepant responses: The impact of standard salience. *Personality and Social Psychology Bulletin, 22,* 48–59.

Montgomery, G. H., & Bovbjerg, D. H. (1997). The development of aniticpatory nausea in patients receiving adjuvant chemotherapy for breast cancer. *Physiology & Behavior, 5,* 737–741.

Moody, D. B., Stebbins, W. C., & May, B. J. (1990). Auditory perception of communication signals by Japanese monkeys. In W. C. Stebbins & M. A. Berkley (Eds.), *Comparative perception: Complex signals* (pp. 311–343). New York: Wiley.

Moran, P. (1999). The epidemiology of antisocial personality disorder. *Social Psychiatry & Psychiatric Epidemiology, 34,* 231–242.

Moreland, R. L., & Zajonc, R. B. (1982). Exposure effects in person perception: Familiarity, similarity, and attraction. *Journal of Experimental Social Psychology, 18,* 395–415.

Morgan, J. L., & Demuth, K. D. (1996). *Signal to syntax: Bootstrapping from speech to grammar in early acquisition.* Hillsdale, NJ: Erlbaum.

Morgane, P. J., Austin-LaFrance, R., Bronzino, J., Tonkiss, J., Diaz-Cintra, S., Cintra, L., Kemper, T., & Galler, J. R. (1993). Prenatal malnutrition and development of the brain. *Neuroscience and Biobehavioral Reviews, 17,* 91–128.

Mori, H., Kamada, M., Maegawa, M., Yamamoto, S., Aono, T., Futaki, S., Yano, M., Kido, H., & Koide, S. S. (1998). Enzymatic activation of immunoglobulin binding factor in female reproductive tract. *Biochemical and Biophysical Research Communications, 246,* 409–413.

Morris, C. D., Bransford, J. D., & Franks, J. J. (1977). Levels of processing versus transfer-appropriate processing. *Journal of Verbal Learning and Verbal Behavior, 16,* 519–533.

Morris, M. W., & Peng, K. (1994). Culture and cause: American and Chinese attributions for social and physical events. *Journal of Personality and Social Psychology, 67,* 949–971.

Morris, R. (1984). Developments of a water-maze procedure for studying spatial learning in the rat. *Journal of Neuroscience Methods, 11,* 47–60.

Morris, S. (1979) *The Book of Strange Facts and Useless Information.* Garden City, NY: Doubleday.

Morris, W., & Miller, R. (1975). The effects of consensus-breaking and consensus preempting partner onreduction in conformity. *Journal of Experimental Social Psychology, 11,* 215–23.

Morris, W. N., Worchel, S., Bois, J. L., Pearson, J. A., Rountree, C. A., Samaha, G. M., Wachtler, J., & Wright, S. I. (1976). Collective coping with stress: Group reactions to fear, anxiety, and ambiguity. *Journal of Personality and Social Psychology, 33,* 674–679.

Mortensen, P. B., Pedersen, C. B., Westergaard, T., Wohlfahrt, J., Ewald, H., Mors, O., Andersen, P. K., & Melbye, M. (1999). Effects of family history and place and season of birth on the risk of schizophrenia. *New England Journal of Medicine, 340,* 603–608.

Moscovitch, M., & Craik, F. I. M. (1976). Depth of processing, retrieval cues, and uniqueness of encoding as factors in recall. *Journal of Verbal Learning and Verbal Behavior, 15,* 447–458.

Moskowitz, D. S. (1993). Dominance and friendliness: On the interaction of gender and situation. *Journal of Personality, 61,* 387–409.

Mowrer, O. H. (1939). A stimulus-response analysis of anxiety and its role as a reinforcing agent. *Psychological Review, 46,* 553–565.

Muehlenhard, C. L., & Linton, M. A. (1987). Date rape and sexual aggression in dating situations: Incidence and risk factors. *Journal of Counseling Psychology, 34,* 186–196.

Mullen, B., & Johnson, C. (1990). Distinctiveness-based illusory correlations and stereotyping: A meta-analytic integration. *British Journal of Social Psychology, 29,* 11–28.

Murphy, C. (1986). Taste and smell in the elderly. In H. L. Meiselman & R. S. Rivlin (Eds.), *Clinical measurement of taste and smell* (pp. 343–371). New York: Macmillan.

Murray, C. J. L., & Lopez, A. D. (Eds.). (1996). *The global burden of disease. A comprehensive assessment of mortality and disability from diseases, injuries, and risk factors in 1990 and projected to 2020.* Cambridge, MA: Harvard School of Public Health.

Murray, E. J., Lamnin, A., & Carver, C. (1989). Emotional expression in written essays and psychotherapy. *Journal of Social and Clinical Psychology, 8,* 414–429.

Murzynski, J. & Degelman, D. (1996). Body language of women and judgments of vulnerability to sexual assault. *Journal of Applied Social Psychology, 26,* 1617–1626.

Myers, D. G. (2000). The funds, friends, and faith of happy people. *American Psychologist, 55,* 56–67.

Nadel, L., & Moscovitch, M. (1997). Memory consolidation, retrograde amnesia and the hippocampal complex. *Current Opinion in Neurobiology, 7,* 217–227.

Nader, K., Bechara, A., & van der Kooy, D. (1997). Neurobiological constraints on behavioral models of motivation. *Annual Review of Psychology, 48,* 85–114.

Nagel, E. (1979). *The structure of science: Problems in the logic of scientific explanation* (2nd ed.). Indianapolis: Hackett.

Nakayama, K., He, Z. J., & Shimojo, S. (1995). Visual surface representation: A critical link between lower-level and higher-level vision. In S. M. Kosslyn & D. N. Osherson (Eds.), *Visual cognition: An invitation to cognitive science, Vol. 2* (2nd ed) (pp. 1–70). Cambridge, MA: MIT Press.

Nakayama, K., & Mackeben, M. (1989). Sustained and transient components of focal visual attention. *Vision Research, 29,* 1631–1647.

Nasby, W., Hayden, B., & DePaulo, B. M. (1979). Attributional bias among aggressive boys to interpret unambiguous social stimuli as displays of hostility. *Journal of Abnormal Psychology 89,* 459–468.

Nathawat, S. S., Singh, R., & Singh, B. (1997). The effect of need for achievement on attributional style. *Journal of Social Psychology, 137,* 55–62.

National Alliance for Caregiving, and the American Association of Retired Persons. (1997). *Family Caregiving in the U.S.: Findings from a National Study.*

National Center on Addiction and Substance Abuse at Columbia University. (1994). *Cost of substance abuse to America's health care system; Report 2: Medicare Hospital Costs.*

National Institute on Drug Abuse (1998). Slide Teaching Packet I, For Health Practitioners, Teachers and Neuroscientists. Section III: Introduction to Drugs of Abuse: Cocaine, Opiates (Heroin) and Marijuana (THC).

National Opinion Research Center. (1994). *General social surveys, 1972–1994: Cumulative codebook.* Chicago: Author, pp. 881–889.

National Sleep Foundation. (1998). *Omnibus sleep in America poll.* www.sleepfoundation.org/publications/1998poll.html.

Neel, R. G., Tzeng, O. C., & Baysal, C. (1986). Need achievement in a cross-cultural contact study. *International Review of Applied Psychology, 35,* 225–229.

Neeper, S. A., Gómez-Pinilla, F., Choi, J., & Cotman C. (1995). Exercise and brain neurotropins. *Nature, 373,* 109.

Neeper, S. A., Gómez-Pinilla, F., Choi, J., & Cotman C. W. (1996). Physical activity increases mRNA for brain-derived neurotrophic factor and nerve growth factor in rat brain. *Brain Research, 726,* 49–56.

Neimeyer, G. J., MacNair, R., Metzler, A. E., & Courchaine, K. (1991). Changing personal beliefs: Effects of forewarning, argument quality, prior bias, and personal exploration. *Journal of Social & Clinical Psychology, 10,* 1–20.

Neisser, U. (1967). *Cognitive psychology.* New York: Appleton-Century-Crofts.

Neisser, U. (1982). *Memory observed: Remembering in natural contexts.* San Francisco: Freeman.

Neisser, U., Boodoo, G., Bouchard, T. J., Jr., Boykin, A. W., Brody, N., Ceci, S. J., Halpern, D. F., Loehlin, J. C., Perloff, R., Sternberg, R. J., & Urbina, S. (1996). Intelligence: Knowns and unknowns. *American Psychologist, 51,* 77–101.

Neisser, U., & Harsch, N. (1992). Phantom flashbulbs: False recollections of hearing news about *Challenger.* In E. Winograd & U. Neisser (Eds.), *Affect and accuracy in recall: Studies of "flashbulb memories"* (pp. 9–31). Cambridge, UK: Cambridge University Press.

Neitz, J., Neitz, M., & Jacobs, G. H. (1993). More than three different cone pigments among people with normal color vision. *Vision Research, 33,* 117–122.

Neitz, J., Neitz, M., & Kainz, P. M. (1996). Visual pigment gene structure and the severity of color vision defects. *Science, 274,* 801–804.

Nelson, C. A. (1999). Human plasticity and human development. *Current Directions in Psychological Science, 8,* 42–45.

Nelson, C. B., Heath, A. C., & Kessler, R. C. (1998). Temporal progression of alcohol dependence symptoms in the U.S. household population: results from the National Comorbidity Survey. *Journal of Consulting & Clinical Psychology, 66,3,* 474–483.

Nelson, K. (1981). Individual differences in language development: Implications for development and language. *Developmental Psychology, 17,* 170–187.

Nemeroff, C., & Rozin, P. (1989). "You are what you eat": Applying the demand-free "impressions" technique to an unacknowledged belief. *Ethos, 17,* 50–69.

Nemeroff, C. J., Stein, R., Diehl, N. S., & Smilach, K. M. (1994). From the Cleavers to the Clintons, Role choices and body orientation as reflected in magazine article content. *International Journal of Eating Disorders, 16,* 167–176.

Nestler, E. J. (1997). Schizophrenia: An emerging pathophysiology. *Nature, 385,* 578–579.

Neumann, C., & Walker, E. F. (1996). Childhood neuromotor soft signs, behavior problems, and adult psychopathoology. In: T. Ollendick & R. Prinz (Eds.), *Advances in Clinical Child Psychology.* New York: Plenum Press.

Nevid, J., Rathus, S., & Rubenstein, H. (1998). *Health in the new millennium.* New York: Worth.

Newcombe, N. S., Drummey, A. B., Fox, N. A., Lie, E., & Ottinger-Alberts, W. (2000). Remembering early childhood: How much, how, and why (or why not). *Current Directions in Psychological Science, 9,* 55–58.

Newcomer, J. W., Selke, G., Melson, A. K., Hershey, T., Craft, S., Richards, K., & Alderson, A. L. (1999). Decreased Memory performance in healthy humans induced by stress-level cortisol treatment. *Archives of General Psychiatry, 56,* 527–533.

Newman, E. A., & Zahs, K. R. (1998). Modulation of neuronal activity by glial cells in the retina. *Journal of Neuroscience, 18,* 4022–4028.

Newman, L. S., Duff, K. J., & Baumeister, R. F. (1997). A New Look at Defensive Projection: Thought Suppression, Accessibility, and Biased Person Perception. *Journal of Personality and Social Psychology, 72,* 980–1001.

Newman, M. G., Kenardy, J., Herman, S., & Taylor, C. B. (1997). Comparison of Palmtop-Computer-Assisted Brief Cognitive-Behavioral Treatment to Cognitive-Behavioral Treatment for Panic Disorder. *Journal of Consulting and Clinical Psychology, 65,* 178–183.

Nichols, R. C. (1978). Twin studies of ability, personality, and interests. *Homo, 29*, 158–173.

Nickerson, R. S., & Adams, M. J. (1979). Long-term memory for a common object. *Cognitive Psychology, 11*, 287–307.

Nigg, J. T., & Goldsmith, H. H. (1994). Genetics of personality disorders: Perspectives from personality and psychopathology research. *Psychological Bulletin, 115*, 346–380.

Niles, S. (1998). Achievement goals and means: A cultural comparison. *Journal of Cross-Cultural Psychology, 29*, 656–667.

Nilsson, L., & Hamberger, L. (1990). *A child is born*. New York: Delacorte.

Nilsson, T., Ericsson, M., Poston, W. S. C., Linder, J., Goodrick, G. K., & Foreyt, J. P. (1998). Is the assessment of coping capacity useful in the treatment of obesity? *Eating Disorders: The Journal of Treatment & Prevention, 6*, 241–251.

Nisbett, R. E. (1972). Hunger, obesity, and the ventromedial hypothalamus. *Psychological Review, 79*, 433–453.

Nisbett, R. E. (1996). *Race, genetics, and IQ*. In C. Jencks & M. Phillips (Eds.), *The black-white test score gap* (pp. 86–102). Washington, DC: Brookings Institution.

Nolan, S. A., & Mineka, S. (1997, November). Verbal, nonverbal, and gender-related factors in the interpersonal consequences of depression and anxiety. Presented at the annual meeting of the Association for the Advancement of Behavior Therapy, Miami Beach, FL.

Nolen-Hoeksema, S. (1987). Sex differences in unipolar depression: Evidence and theory. *Psychological Bulletin, 101*, 259–282.

Nolen-Hoeksema, S., & Morrow, J. (1993). Effects of rumination and distraction on naturally occurring depressed mood. *Cognition & Emotion, 7*, 561–570.

Norman, K. A., & Schacter, D. L. (1997). False recognition in younger and older adults: Exploring the characteristics of illusory memories. *Memory & Cognition, 25*, 838–848.

Nowakowski, R. S. (1987). Basic concepts of CNS development. *Child Development, 58*, 568–595.

Nurnberger, J. I., & Hingtgen, J. N. (1973). Is symptom substitution an important issue in behavior therapy? *Biological Psychiatry, 7*, 221–236.

Nyberg, L., Cabeza, R., & Tulving, E. (1996). PET studies of encoding and retrieval: The HERA model. *Psychonomic Bulletin & Review, 3*, 134–148.

Nyberg, L., McIntosh, A. R., Houle, S., Nilsson, L. G., & Tulving, E. (1996). Activation of medial temporal structures during episodic memory retrieval. *Nature, 380*, 715–717.

Nye, R. D. (1992). *Three Psychologies: Perspectives from Freud, Skinner, and Rogers*. California: Brooks-Cole.

Oei, T. P. S., & Yeoh, A. E. O. (1999). Pre-existing antidepressant medication and the outcome of group cognitive-behavioural therapy. *Australian & New Zealand Journal of Psychiatry, 33*, 70–76.

Ohman, A., Fredrikson, M., Hugdahl, K., & Rimmo, P.-A. (1976). The premise of equipotentiality in human classical conditioning: Conditioned electrodermal responses to potentially phobic stimuli. *Journal of Experimental Psychology: General, 105*, 313–337.

Ohzawa, I., DeAngelis, G. C., & Freeman, R. D. (1990). Stereoscopic depth discrimination in the visual cortex: Neurons ideally suited as disparity detectors. *Science, 249*, 1037–1041.

Ojemann, G. A. (1983). Brain organization for language from the perspective of electrical stimulation mapping. *Behavioral and Brain Sciences, 6*, 189–230.

Ojemann, G. A., Ojemann, J., Lettich, E., & Berger, M. (1989). Cortical language localization in left, dominant hemisphere. *Journal of Neurosurgery, 71*, 316–326.

Olczak, P. V., Kaplan, M. F., & Penrod, S. (1991). Attorneys' lay psychology and its effectiveness in selecting jurors: Three empirical studies. *Journal of Social Behavior and Personality, 6*, 431–452.

Olds, J., & Milner, P. (1954). Positive reinforcement produced by electrical stimulation of septal area and other regions of rat brain. *Journal of Comparative & Physiological Psychology, 47*, 419–427.

Olton, R. M. (1979). Experimental studies of incubation: Searching for the elusive. *Journal of Creative Behavior, 13*, 9–22.

O'Regan, J. K. (1992). Solving the "real" mysteries of visual perception: The world as an outside memory. *Canadian Journal of Psychology, 46*, 461–488.

Orive, R. (1988). Social projection and social comparison of opinions. *Journal of Personality and Social Psychology, 54*, 953–964.

Ornish, D., Scherwitz, L. W., Billings, J. H., Gould, K. L., Merritt, T. A., Sparler, S., Armstrong, W. T., Ports, T. A., Kirkeeide, R. L., Hogeboom, C., & Brand, R. J. (1998). Intensive lifestyle changes for reversal of coronary heart disease. *Journal of the American Medical Association, 280*, 2001–2007.

Ortiz, S. M. (1997). Traveling with the ball club: A code of conduct for wives only. *Symbolic Interaction, 20*, 225–249.

O'Sullivan, C. S., & Durso, F. T. (1984). Effects of schema-incongruent information on memory for stereotypical attributes. *Journal of Personality and Social Psychology, 47*, 55–70.

Otto, M. W., Gould, R. A., & Pollack, M. H. (1994). Cognitive-behavioral treatment of panic disorder: Considerations for the treatment of patients over the long term. *Psychiatric Annals, 24*, 307–315.

Overmeier, J. B., & Seligman, M. E. P. (1967). Effects of inescapable shock upon subsequent escape and avoidance responding. *Journal of Comparative and Physiological Psychology, 63*, 28–33.

Ozer, D. J., & Reise, S. P. (1994). Personality Assessment. *Annual Review of Psychology, 45*, 357–88.

Páez, D., Velasco, C., & González, J. L. (1999). Expressive writing and the role of alexythimia as a dispositional deficit in self-disclosure and psychological health. *Journal of Personality and Social Psychology, 77*, 630–641.

Paivio, A. (1971). *Imagery and verbal processes*. New York: Holt, Rinehart & Winston.

Palace, E. M. (1999). Response expectancy and sexual dysfunction. In I. Kirsch (Ed.), *How expectancies shape experience* (pp. 173–196). Washington, DC: American Psychological Association.

Palmer, S. E. (1992a). Modern theories of Gestalt perception. In G. W. Humphreys (Ed.), *Understanding vision: An interdisciplinary perspective* (pp. 39–70). Oxford: Blackwell.

Palmer, S. E. (1992b). Common region: A new principle of perceptual grouping. *Cognitive Psychology, 24*, 436–447.

Papolos, D. F., Yu, Y-M., Rosenbaum, E., & Lachman, H. M. (1996). Modulation of learned helplessness by 5-hydroxytrptamine-2A receptor antisense oligodeoxynucleotides. *Psychiatry Research, 63*, 197–203.

Papp, L. A., Klein, D. F., & Gorman, J. M. (1993). Carbon dioxide hypersensitivity, hyperventilation, and panic disorder. *American Journal of Psychiatry, 150*, 1149–1157.

Papp, L. A., Martinez, J. M., Klein, D. F., Coplan, J. D., Norman, R. G., Cole, R., de Jesus, M. J., Ross, D., Goetz, R., & Gorman, J. M. (1997). Respiratory psychophysiology of panic disorder: Three respiratory challenges in 98 subjects. *American Journal of Psychiatry, 154*, 1557–1565.

Parker, A., & Gellatly, A. (1997). Movable cues: A practical method for reducing context-dependent forgetting. *Applied Cognitive Psychology, 11*, 163–173.

Parkin, A. J. (1987). *Memory and amnesia: An introduction*. Oxford, England: Basil Blackwell.

Parks, M. R., & Roberts, L. D. (1998). "Making MOOsic": The development of personal relationships on line and a comparison to their off-line counterparts. *Journal of Social & Personal Relationships, 15*, 517–537.

Parsons, L. M. (1987). Imagined spatial transformation of one's body. *Journal of Experimental Psychology: General, 116*, 172–191.

Parsons, L. M. (1994). Temporal and kinematic properties of motor behavior reflected in mentally simulated action. *Journal of Experimental Psychology: Human Perception & Performance, 20*, 709–730.

Parsons, L. M., & Fox, P. T. (1998). The neural basis of implicit movements used in recognising hand shape. *Cognitive Neuropsychology, 15*, 583–615.

Pascalis, O., de Haan, M., Nelson, C. A., & de Schonen, S. (1998). Long-term recognition memory for faces assessed by visual paired comparison in 3- and 6-month-old infants. *Journal of Experimental Psychology: Learning, Memory, & Cognition, 24*, 249–260.

Pascual-Leone, A., Grafman, J., Cohen, L. G., Roth, B. J., & Hallett, M. (1997). Transcranial magnetic stimulation. A new tool for the study of higher cognitive functions in humans. In J. Grafman & F. Boller (Eds.), *Handbook of neuropsychology* (Vol. 11). Amsterdam: Elsevier B.V.

Pascual-Leone, A., Tormos, J. M., Keenan, J., Tarazona, F., Cañete, C., & Catalá, M. D. (1998). Study and modulation of human cortical excitability with transcranial magnetic stimulation. *Journal of Clinical Neurophysiology, 15*, 333–343.

Pascual-Leone, J. (1970). A mathematical model for the transition rule in Piaget's developmental stages. *Acta Psychologia, 32,* 301–345.

Patterson, R., & Martin, W. L. (1992). Human stereopsis. *Human Factors, 34,* 669–692.

Patterson, T. L., Semple, S. J., Shaw, W. S., Yu, E., He, Y., Zhang, M. Y., Wu, W., & Grant, I. (1998). The cultural context of caregiving: A comparison of Alzheimer's caregivers in Shanghai, China and San Diego, California. *Psychological Medicine, 28,* 1071–1084.

Paulhus, D. L., & Bruce, M. N. (1992). The effect of acquaintanceship on the validity of personality impressions: a longitudinal study. *Journal of Personality and Social Psychology, 63,* 816–824.

Paunonen, S. V. (1998). Hierarchical Organization of Personality and Prediction of Behavior. *Journal of Personality and Social Psychology, 74,* 538–556.

Paunonen, S. V., & Ashton, M. C. (1998). The structured assessment of personality across cultures. *Journal of Cross-Cultural Psychology, 29,* 150–170.

Paunonen, S. V., Zeidner, M., Engvik, H. A., Oosterveld, P., & Maliphant, R. (2000). The nonverbal assessment of personality in five cultures. *Journal of Cross-Cultural Psychology, 31,* 220–239.

Pavlov, I. P. (1927). *Condtioned reflexes* (G. V. Anrep, Trans.). London: Oxford University Press.

Pederson, N. L., Plomin, R., McClearn, G. E., & Friberg, L. (1988) Neuroticism, extraversion and related traits in adult twins reared apart and reared together. *Journal of Personality and Social Psychology, 55,* 950–957.

Peeck, J. (1987). The role of illustrations in processing and remembering illustrated text. In H. A. Houghton & D. M. Willows (Eds.), *The psychology of illustration,* Vol. 2 (pp. 115–152). New York: Springer-Verlag.

Penfield, W. (1955). The permanent record of the stream of consciousness. *Acta Psychologica, 11,* 47–69.

Penfield, W., & Perot, P. (1963). The brain's record of auditory and visual experience. *Brain, 86,* 595–696.

Penfield, W., & Rasmussen, T. (1950). *The cerebral cortex of man: A clinical study of localization of function.* New York: Macmillan.

Pengilly, J. W., & Dowd, E. T. (1997). Hardiness and social support as moderator of stress in college students. Paper presented at the 1997 annual convention of the Association for the Advancement of Behavior Therapy, Miami Beach, FL.

Pennebaker, J. W. (1993). Social mechanisms of constraint. In D. M. Wegner & J. W. Pennebaker (Eds.), *Handbook of mental control* (pp. 200–219). Englewood Cliffs, NJ: Prentice Hall.

Pennebaker, J. W., Colder, M., & Sharp, L. K. (1990). Accelerating the coping process. *Journal of Personality and Social Psychology, 58,* 528–537.

Pennebaker, J. W., & Francis, M. E. (1996). Cognitive, emotional, and language processes in disclosure. *Cognition & Emotion, 10,* 601–626.

Perdue, C. W., Dovidio, J. F., Gurtman, M. B., & Tyler, R. B. (1990). Us and them: Social categorization and the process of intergroup bias. *Journal of Personality and Social Psychology, 59,* 475–486.

Perkins, H. W., & Berkowitz, A. D. (1986). Perceiving the community norms of alchol use among students.: Some research implications for campus alcohol education programming. *International Journal of the Addictions, 21,* 961–976.

Perlmutter, M. (1988). Cognitive potential throughout life. In J. E. Birren & V. L. Bengtson (Eds.), *Emergent theories of aging* (pp. 247–267). New York: Springer.

Perrett, D. I., Lee, K. J, Penton-Voak, I., Rowland, D., Yoshikawa, S., Burt, D. M., Henzi, S. P., Castles, D. L., & Akamatsu, S. (1998). Effects of sexual dimorphism on facial attractiveness. *Nature, 394,* 884–887.

Perry, B. D., Pollard, R. A., Blakley, T. L., Baker, W. L., & Vigilante, D. (1995). Childhood trauma, the neurobiology of adaptation, and "use-dependent" development of the brain: How "states" become "traits." *Infant Mental Health Journal, 16,* 271–291.

Petersen, A. C., Compas, B. E., Brooks-Gunn, J., Stemmler, M., Ey, S., & Grant, K. E. (1993). Depression in adolescence. *American Psychologist, 48,* 155–168.

Petersen, R. C. (1977). Marihuana research findings: 1976: Summary. *NIDA Research Monograph, Jul (14),* 1–37.

Petersen, R. C. (1979). Importance of inhalation patterns in determining effects of marihuana use. *Lancet, 31,* 727–728.

Peterson, C. (2000). The future of optimism. *American Psychologist, 55,* 44–55.

Peterson, C., & Seligman, M. E. (1984). Causal explanations as a risk factor for depression: Theory and evidence. *Psychological Review, 91,* 347–374.

Petitto, L. A., & Marentette, P. F. (1991). Babbling in the manual mode: Evidence for the ontogeny of language. *Science, 251,* 1493–1496.

Petrie, K. J., Booth, R. J., & Pennebaker, J. W. (1998). The immunological effects of thought suppression. *Journal of Personality and Social Psychology, 75,* 1264–1272.

Petrie, K. J., Booth, R. J., Pennebaker, J. W., Davison, K. P., & Thomas, M. G. (1995). Disclosure of Trauma and Immune Response to a Hepatitis B Vaccination Program. *Journal of Consulting and Clinical Psychology, 63,* 787–792.

Petrill, S. A., Plomin, R., McClearn, G. E., Smith, D. L., Vignetti, S., Chorney, M. J., Chorney, K., Thompson, L. A., Detterman, D. K., Benbow, C., Lubinski, D., Daniels, J., Owen, M., & McGuffin, P. (1997a). No association between general cognitive ability and the A1 allele of the D2 dopamine receptor gene. *Behavior Genetics, 27,* 29–31.

Petrill, S. A., Plomin, R., McClearn, G. E., Smith, D. L., Vignetti, S., Chorney, M. J., Chorney, K., Thompson, L. A., Detterman, D. K., Benbow, C., Lubinski, D., Daniels, J., Owen, M., & McGuffin, P. (1997b). No association between general cognitive ability and the A1 allele of the D2 dopamine receptor gene. *Behavior Genetics, 27,* 29–31.

Pettigrew, T. F. (1969). Racially separate or together? *Journal of Social Issues, 24,* 43–69.

Pettigrew, T. F. (1981). Extending the stereotype concept. In D. L. Hamilton (Ed.), *Cognitive processes in stereotyping and intergroup behavior* (pp. 303– 331). Hillsdale, NJ: Erlbaum.

Pettigrew, T. F., & Meertens, R. W. (1995). Subtle and blatant prejudice in western Europe. *European Journal of Social Psychology, 25,* 57–75.

Petty, R. E., & Cacioppo, J. T. (1981). *Attitudes and persuasion: Classic and contemporary approaches.* Dubuque, IA: Wm. C. Brown.

Petty, R. E., & Krosnick, J. A. (1996). *Attitude strength: Anetecdents and consequences.* Hillsdale, NJ: Erlbaum.

Petty, R. E., & Wegener, D. T. (1998). Attitude Change: multiple roles for persuasion variables. In D. T. Gilbert, S. T. Fiske, & G. Lindzey (Eds.), *The handbook of social psychology* (4th ed.). New York: McGraw Hill. 323–390.

Pezdek, K., Finger, K., & Hodge, D. (1997). Planting false childhood memories: The role of event plausibility. *Psychological Science, 8,* 437–441.

Pfaffmann, C. (1978). The vertebrate phylogeny, neural code, and integrative processes of taste. In E. C. Carterette & M. P. Friedman (Eds.), *Handbook of perception* (pp. 51–123). New York: Academic Press.

Phelps, J. A., Davis, J. O., & Schartz, K. M. (1997). Nature, nurture, and twin research strategies. *Current Directions in Psychological Science, 6,* 117–121.

Phillips, D. P., & Smith, D. G. (1990). Postponement of death until symbolically meaningful occasions. *Journal of the American Medical Association, 263,* 1947–1951.

Phillips, D. P., Van Voorhees, C. A., & Ruth, T. E. (1992). The birthday: Lifeline or deadline. *Psychosomatic Medicine, 54,* 532–542.

Phillips, K., & Matheny, A. P., Jr. (1995). Quantitative genetic analysis of injury liability in infants and toddlers. *American Journal of Medical Genetics (Neuropsychiatric Genetics), 60,* 64–71.

Phillips, S. D., & Imhoff, A. R. (1997). Women and career development: A decade of research. *Annual Review of Psychology, 48,* 31–59.

Piaget, J. (1962). *Play, dreams, and imitation in childhood.* New York: W. W. Norton.

Piaget, J. (1969). *The mechanisms of perception.* (G. N. Seagrim, Trans.). New York: Basic Books.

Piazza, C. C., Hanley, G. P., Fisher, W. W., Ruyter, J. M., & Gulotta, C. S. (1998). On the establishing and reinforcing effects of termination of demands for destructive behavior maintained by positive and negative reinforcement. *Research in Developmental Disabilities, 19,* 395–407.

Pickles, J. O. (1988). *An introduction to the physiology of hearing* (2nd ed.). London: Academic Press.

Pietromonaco, P. R., Manis, J., & Frohardt-Lane, K. (1986). Psychological consequences of multiple social roles. *Psychology of Women Quarterly, 10,* 373–381.

Pinel, J. P. J. (1993). *Biopsychology (2nd ed.).* Boston: Allyn & Bacon.

Pinker, S. (1994). *The language instinct: How the mind creates language.* New York: Morrow.

Pinker, S. (1997). *How the mind works*. New York: Norton.

Pinker, S. (1999). *Words and rules: The ingredients of language*. New York: Basic Books.

Pirke, K. M. (1995). Physiology of bulimia nervosa. In K. D. Brownell & C. G. Fairburn (Eds.), *Eating Disorders and Obesity: A Comprehensive Handbook*. New York: Guilford Press, 261–265.

Pitman, D. L., Natelson, B. H., Ottenmiller, J. E., McCarty, R., Pritzel, T., & Tapp, W. N. (1995). Effects of exposure to stressors of varying predictability on adrenal function in rats. *Behavioral Neuroscience, 109*, 767–776.

Platt, L. A., & Persico, V. R., Jr. (Eds.) (1992). *Grief in cross-cultural perspective: A casebook*. New York: Garland.

Plomin, R. (1988). The nature and nurture of cognitive abilities. In R. J. Sternberg (Ed.), *Advances in the psychology of human intelligence*, Vol. 4 (pp. 1–33). Hillsdale, NJ: Erlbaum.

Plomin, R. (1990). *Nature and nurture : An introduction to human behavioral genetics*. Pacific Grove, CA: Brooks/Cole.

Plomin, R. (1995). Genetics and children's experiences in the family. *Journal of Child Psychology and Psychiatry, 36*, 33–68.

Plomin, R., & Bergeman, C. S. (1991). The nature of nurture: Genetic influences on "environmental" measures. *Behavioral and Brain Sciences, 14*, 373–427.

Plomin, R., & DeFries, J. C. (1998). The genetics of cognitive abilities and disabilities: Investigations of specific cognitive skills can help clarify how genes shape the components of intellect. *Scientific American, 278*, 40–47.

Plomin, R., DeFries, J. C., McClearn, G. E., & Rutter, M. (1997). *Behavioral genetics* (3rd ed.). New York: Freeman.

Plomin, R., & Foch, T. T. (1980). A twin study of objectrively assessed personality in childhood. *Journal of Personality and Social Psychology, 39*, 680–688.

Plomin, R., Pedersen, N. L., Lichtenstein, P., & McClearn, G. E. (1994). Variability and stability in cognitive abilities are largely genetic later in life. *Behavior Genetics, 24*(3), 207–215.

Plotkin, H. (1994). *The nature of knowledge: Concerning adaptations, instinct and the evolution of intelligence*. New York: Allen Lane/Viking Penguin.

Plotkin, H. (1997). *Evolution in mind: An introduction to evolutionary psychology*. Cambridge, MA: Harvard University Press.

Plutchik, R., & Kellerman, H. (1980). *Emotions: A psychoevolutionary synthesis*. New York: Harper Row.

Polivy, J., & Herman, C. P. (1993). Etiology of binge eating: Psychological mechanisms. In *Binge Eating: Nature, Assessment, and Treatment*. In C. G. Fairburn & G. T. Wilson (Eds.), New York: Guilford Press. 173–205.

Pope, K. S. (1996). Memory, abuse, and science: Questioning claims about the false memory syndrome epidemic. *American Psychologist, 51*, 957–974.

Porter, R. H. (1991). Human reproduction and the mother-infant relationship: The role of odors. In T. V. Getchell, R. L. Doty, L. M. Bartoshuk, & J. B. Snow, Jr. (Eds.), *Smell and taste in health and disease* (pp. 429–442). New York: Raven.

Porter, R. H., Cernoch, J. M., & Balogh, R. D. (1985). Odor signatures and kin recognition. *Physiology & Behavior, 24*, 445–448.

Porter, R. H., Makin, J. W., Davis, L. B., & Christensen, K. M. (1992). An assessment of the salient olfactory environment of formula-fed infants. *Physiology & Behavior, 50*, 907–911.

Posner, M. I., & Raichle, M. (1994). *Images of mind*. New York: Freeman.

Post, R. M. (1992). Transdirection of psychosocial stress into the neurobiology of recurrent affective disorder. *American Journal of Psychiatry, 149*, 999–1010.

Postmes, T., & Spears, R. (1998). Deindividuation and antinormative behavior: A meta-analysis. *Psychological Bulletin, 123*, 238–259.

Poston, W. S. C., Ericsson, M., Linder, J., Nilsson, T., Goodrick, G. K., & Foreyt, J. P. (1999). Personality and the prediction of weight loss and relapse in the treatment of obesity. *International Journal of Eating Disorders, 25*, 301–309.

Poulton, R., Menzies, R. G., Craske, M. G., Langley, J. D., & Silva, P. A. (1999). Water trauma and swimming experiences up to age 9 and fear of water at age 18: A longitudinal study. *Behaviour Research & Therapy, 37*, 39–48.

Powell, M. C., & Fazio, R. H. (1984). Attitude accedssibility as a function of repeatred attitudinal expression. *Personality and Social Psychology Bulletin, 10*, 139–148.

Practice Directorate. (1998). *How to find help through psychotherapy*. Washington DC: American Psychological Association.

Prapavessis, H., & Carron, A. V. (1997). Sacrifice, cohesion, and conformity to norms in sport teams. *Group Dynamics: Theory, Research, and Practice, 1*, 231–240.

Prasada, S. (2000). Acquiring generic knowledge. *Trends in Cognitive Science, 4*, 66–72.

Prescott, C. A., Johnson, R. C., & McArdle, J. J. (1991). Genetic contributions to television viewing. *Psychological Science, 2*, 430–431.

Pressley, M., Brown, R. El-Dinary, P. B., & Allferbach, P. (1995). The comprehension instruction that students need: Instruction fostering constructively responsive reading. *Learning Disabilities Research & Practice, 10*, 215–224.

Pressman, E. K., DiPietro, J. A., Costigan, K. A., Shupe, A. K., & Johnson, T. R. B. (1998). Fetal neurobehavioral development: Associations with socioeconomic class and fetal sex. *Developmental Psychobiology, 33*, 79–91.

Prien, R. F., & Kocsis, J. H. (1995). Long term treatment of mood disorders. In F. E. Bloom & D. J. Kupfer (Eds.), *Psychopharmacology: The Fourth Generation of Progress*. (pp. 1067–1080). New York: Raven Press.

Priester, J. R., & Petty, R. E. (1995). Source attributions and persuaion: Perceived honesty as a determinant of message scrutiny. *Personality and Social Psychology Bulletin, 21*, 637–654.

Privette, G., & Landsman, T. (1983). Factor analysis of peak performance: The full use of potential. *Journal of Personality and Social Psychology, 44*, 195–200.

Proctor, R. W., & Van Zandt, T. (1994). *Human Factors In Simple And Complex Systems*. Boston: Allyn & Bacon.

Project MATCH Research Group National Institute on Alcohol Abuse and Alcoholism Bethesda, MD (1997). Project MATCH secondary a priori hypotheses. *Addiction, 92*, 1671–169.

Pujol, R., Lavigne-Rebillard, M., & Uziel, A. (1990). Physiological correlates of development of the human cochlea. *Seminars in Perinatology, 14*, 275–280.

Puka, B. (Ed.) (1994). *Kohlberg's original study of moral development*. New York: Garland.

Putnam, F. W. (1989). *Diagnosis and treatment of Multiple Personality Disorder*. New York: Guilford Press.

Putnam, F. W., Helmers, K., Horowitz, L. A., & Trickett, P. K. (1995). Hypnotizability and dissociativity in sexually abused girls. *Child Abuse and Neglect, 19*, 645–655.

Putnam, H. (1973). Reductionism and the nature of psychology. *Cognition, 2*, 131–146.

Quinn, J. G. (1991). Encoding and maintenance of information in visual working memory. In R. H. Logie & M. Denis (Eds.), *Mental images in human cognition*. (pp. 95–104). Amsterdam: North-Holland.

Raag, T., & Rackliff, C. L. (1998). Preschoolers' awareness of social expectations of gender: Relationships to toy choices. *Sex Roles, 38*, 685–700.

Rabin, M. D., & Cain, W. S. (1986). Determinants of measured olfactory sensitivity. *Perception & Psychophysics, 39*, 281–286.

Rabinowitz, F. E., Sutton, L., Schutter, T., Brow, A., Krizo, C., Larsen, J., Styn, J., Welander, A., Wilson, D., & Wright, S. (1997). Helpfulness to lost tourists. *Journal of Social Psychology, 137*, 502–509.

Radvansky, G. A. (1999). Aging, memory, and comprehension. *Current Directions in Psychological Science, 8*, 49–53.

Räikkönen, K., Matthews, K. A., Flory, J. D., & Owens, J. F. (1999). Effects of Hostility on Ambulatory Blood Pressure and Mood During Daily Living in Healthy Adults. *Health Psychology, 18*, 44–53.

Raine, A., Venables, P. H., & Williams, M. (1990). Relationships between central and autonomic measures of arousal at age 15 years and criminality at age 24 years. *Archives of General Psychiatry, 47*, 1003–1007.

Rainville, P., Duncan, G. H., Price, D. D, Carrier, B., & Bushnell, M. C. (1997). Pain affect encoded in human anterior cingulate but not somatosensory cortex. *Science, 277*, 968–971.

Rakic, P. (1975). Timing of major ontogenetic events in the visual cortex of the rhesus monkey. In N. Buchwald & M. Brazier (Eds.), *Brain mechanisms in mental retardation* (pp. 3–40). New York: Academic Press.

Ramachandran, V. S. (1993). Behavioral and magnetoencephalographic correlates of plasticity in the adult human brain. *Proceedings of the National Academy of Sciences, 90*, 10413–10420.

Ramachandran, V. S., Rogers-Ramachandran, D., & Stewart, M. (1992). Perceptual correlates of massive cortical reorganization. *Science, 258*, 1159–1160.

Ramirez, M., III. (1999). *Mulitcultural Psychotherapy: An approach to invidividual and cultural differences (2nd edition)*. Needham Heights, MA: Allyn & Bacon.

Rao, S. C., Rainer, G., & Miller, E. K. (1997). Integration of what and where in the primate prefrontal cortex. *Science, 276,* 821–834.

Rauch, S. L., Jenike, M. A., Alpert, N. M., Baer, L., Breiter, H. C. R., Savage, C. R., & Fischman, A. J. (1994). Regional cerebral blood flow measured during symptom provocation in obsessive-compulsive disorder using oxygen 15-labeled carbon dioxide and poitron emission tomography. *Archives of General Psychiatry, 51,* 62–70.

Rauch, S. L., van der Kolk, B. A., Risler, R. E., Alpert, N. M., Orr, S. P., Savage, C. R., Fischman, A. J., Jenike, M. A., & Pitman, R. K. (1996). A symptom provocation study of posttraumatic stress disorder using positron emission tomography and script-driven imagery. *Archives of General Psychiatry, 53,* 380–387.

Raymond, J. E., Shapiro, K. L., & Arnell, K. M. (1992). Temporary suppression of visual processing in an RSVP task: An attentional blink? *Journal of Experimental Psychology: Human Perception and Performance, 18,* 849–860.

Razran, G. H. S. (1940). Conditioned response changes in rating and appraising sociopolitical solutions. *Psychological Bulletin, 37,* 481.

Rechtschaffen, A., Gilliland, M. A., Bergmann, B. M., & Winter, J. B. (1983). Physiological correlates of prolonged sleep deprivation in rats. *Science, 221:* 182–4.

Redd, W. H., Dadds, M. R., Futterman, A. D., Taylor, K. L., & Bovbjerg, D. J. (1993). Nausea induced by mental images of chemotherapy. *Cancer, 72,* 629–636.

Regan, D. T., & Fazio, R. H. (1977). On the consistency between attitudes and behavior: Look to the method of attitude formation. *Journal of Experimental Psychology, 13,* 38–45.

Regan, P. C. (1996). Rhythms of desire: The association between menstrual cycle phases and female sexual desire. *Canadian Journal of Human Sexuality, 5,* 145–156.

Regier D. A., & Kaelber, C. T. (1995). The Epidemiologic Catchment Area (ECA) program: studying the prevalence and incidence of psychopathology. In: M. T. Tsuang, M. Tohen, G. E. P. Zahner (Eds.), *Textbook in Psychiatric Epidemiology* (pp. 133–157). New York: John Wiley & Sons Inc.

Regier, D. A., Narrow, W. E., Rae, D. S., Manderscheid, R. W., Locke, B. Z., & Goodwin, F. K. (1993). The de facto US mental and addictive disorders service system. Epidemiologic Catchment Area prospective 1-year prevalence rates of disorders and services. *Archives of General Psychiatry, 50,* 85–94.

Reid, J. E. (1947). A revised questioning technique in lie-detection tests. *Journal of Criminal Law & Criminology, 37,* 542–547.

Reid, R. C. (1999). Vision. In M. J. Zigmond, F. E. Bloom, S. C. Landis, J. L. Roberts, & L. R. Squire (Eds.), *Fundamental neuroscience* (pp. 821–851). New York: Academic Press.

Reifman, A., & Windle, M. (1995). Adolescent suicidal behaviors as a function of depression, hopelessness, alcohol use, and social support: A longitudinal investigation. *American Journal of Community Psychology, 23,* 329–354.

Reinisch, J. M., & Sanders, S. A. (1992). Prenatal hormonal contributions to sex differences in human cognitive and personality development. In A. A. Gerall, H. Moltz, & I. I. Ward (Eds.), *Sexual differentiation: Vol. II. Handbook of behavioral neurobiology* (pp. 221–243). New York: Plenum.

Reis, H. T., & Shaver, P. (1988). Intimacy as an interpersonal process. In S. W. Duck (Ed.), *Handbook of basic principles* (pp. 367–389). Chichester, England: Wiley.

Rende, R., & Plomin, R. (1992). Diathesis-stress models of psychopathology: A quantitative genetic perspective. *Applied & Preventative Psychology, 1,* 177–182.

Rensink, R. A., O'Regan, J. K., & Clark, J. J. (1997). To see or not to see: The need for attention to perceive changes in scenes. *Psychological Science, 8,* 368–373.

Rescorla, R. A. (1967). Pavlovian conditioning and its proper control procedures. *Psychological Review, 74,* 71–80.

Resnick, H. S., Kilpatrick, D. G., Dansky, B. S., Saunders, B., & Best, C. L. (1993). Prevalence of civilian trauma and posttraumatic stress disorder in a representative national sample of women. *Journal of Consulting and Clinical Psychology, 61,* 984–991.

Rest, J. R. (1979). *Development in judging moral issues*. Minneapolis: University of Minnesota Press.

Retsinas, J. (1988). A theoretical reassessment of the applicability of Kübler-Ross's stages of dying. *Death Studies, 12,* 207–216.

Reynolds, C. F., III., Frank, E., Perel, J. M., Imber, S. D., Cornes, C., Miller, M. D., Mazumdar, S., Houck, P. R., Dew, M. A., Stack, J. A., Pollock, B. G., & Kupfer, D. J. (1999). Nortriptyline and interpersonal psychotherapy as maintenance therapies for recurrent major depression: A randomized controlled trial in patients older than 59 years. *Journal of the American Medical Association, 281,* 39–45.

Rice, G., Anderson, C., Risch, N., & Ebers, G. (1999). Male homosexuality: Absence of linkage to microsatellite markers at Xq28. *Science, 284,* 665–667.

Rice, M. E., & Grusec, J. E. (1975). Saying and doing: Effects on observer performance. *Journal of Personality and Social Psychology, 32,* 584–593.

Richert, E. S. (1997). Excellence with equity in identification and programming. In N. Colangelo & G. A. Davis (Eds.), *Handbook of gifted education* (2nd ed.), (pp. 75–88). Boston: Allyn & Bacon.

Rinn, W. E. (1984). The neuropsychology of facial expression: A review of the neurological and psychological mechanisms for producing facial expressions. *Psychological Bulletin, 95,* 52–77.

Rips, L. J., Shoben, E. J., & Smith, E. E. (1973). Semantic distance and the verification of semantic relations. *Journal of Verbal Learning and Verbal Behavior, 12,* 1–20.

Rivera-Arzola, M., & Ramos-Grenier, J. (1997). Anger, ataques de nervios, and la mujer puertorriquena: Sociocultural considerations and treatment implications. In J. G. Garcia & M. C. Zea (Eds.), *Psychological interventions and research with Latino populations.* Boston, MA: Allyn & Bacon, Inc.

Robbins, T. W., & Everitt, B. J. (1998). Motivation and reward. In M. J. Zigmond, F. E. Bloom, S. C. Landis, J. L. Roberts, & L. R. Squire (Eds.), *Fundamental neuroscience.* New York: Academic Press, pp. 1245–1260.

Roberts, A. H., Kewman, D. G., Mercier, L., & Hovell, M. (1993). The power of nonspecific effects in healing: implications for psychosocial and biological treatments. *Clinical Psychology Review, 13,* 375–391.

Roberts, B. W., & DelVecchio, W. F. (2000). The rank-order consistency of personality traits from childhood to old age: A quantitative review of longitudinal studies. *Psychological Bulletin, 126,* 3–25.

Roberts, P., & Newton, P. M. (1987). Levinsonian studies of women's adult development. *Psychology and Aging, 2,* 154–163.

Robertson, L. C., & Delis, D. C. (1986). "Part-whole" processing in unilateral brain damaged patients: Dysfunction of hierarchical organization. *Neuropsychologia, 24,* 363–370.

Robertson, L. C., Lamb, M. R., & Knight, R. T. (1988). Effects of lesions of temporal-parietal junction on perceptual and attentional processing in humans. *Journal of Neuroscience, 8(10),* 3757–3769.

Robins, L. N., & Regier, D. A. (1991). *Psychiatric disorder s in America: The epidemiological catchment area study.* New York: The Free Press.

Robinson, N. M., Abbott, R. D., Berninger, V. W., & Busse, J. (1996). The structure of abilities in math-precocious young children: Gender similarities and differences. *Journal of Educational Psychology, 88,* 341–352.

Rochat, P., & Hespos, S. J. (1997). Differential rooting response by neonates: Evidence for an early sense of self. *Early Development & Parenting, 6,* 105–112.

Rodier, P. (1980). Chronology of neuron development. *Developmental Medicine and Child Neurology, 22,* 525–545.

Rodin, J., & Langer, E. J. (1977). Long-term effects of a control-relevant intervention with the institutionalized aged. *Journal of Personality & Social Psychology, 35,* 897–902.

Roediger, H. L., & Thorpe, L. A. (1978). The role of recall time in producing hypermnesia. *Memory & Cognition, 6,* 296–305.

Roediger, H. L., III. (1980). Memory metaphors in cognitive psychology. *Memory & Cognition, 8,* 231–246.

Roediger, H. L., III, & McDermott, K. B. (1993). Implicit memory in normal human subjects. In F. Bohler & J. Grafman (Eds.), *Handbook of Neuropsychology* (Vol. 8, pp. 63–131). Amsterdam: Elsevier.

Roediger, H. L., III, & McDermott, K. B. (1995). Creating false memories: Remembering words not presented in lists. *Journal of Experimental Psychology: Learning, Memory, and Cognition, 21,* 803–814.

Roll, S., McClelland, G., Abel, T. (1996). Differences in susceptibility to influence in Mexican American and Anglo females. *Hispanic Journal of Behavioral Sciences, 18,* 13–20.

Rollman, G. B. (1991). Pain responsiveness. In M. A. Heller & W. Schiff (Eds.), *The psychology of touch* (pp. 91–114). Hillsdale, NJ: Erlbaum.

Rollman, G. B., & Harris, G. (1987). The detectability, discriminability, and perceived magnitude of painful electrical shock. *Perception & Psychophysics, 42,* 257–268.

Rolls, B. J., Rowe, E. A., Rolls, E. T., Kingston, B., Megson, A., & Gunary, R. (1981). Variety in a meal enhances food intake in man. *Physiology & Behavior, 26,* 215–221.

Rolls, E. T., & Cooper, S. J. (1974). Connection between the prefrontal cortex and pontine brain-stimulation reward sites in the rat. *Experimental Neurology, 42,* 687–699.

Romani, G. L., Williamson, S. J., & Kaufman, L. (1982). Tonotopic organization of the human auditory cortex. *Science, 216,* 1339–1340.

Romero, A. A., Agnew, C. R., & Insko, C. A. (1996). The cognitive mediation hypothesis revisited: An empirical response to methodological and theoretical criticism. *Personality & Social Psychology Bulletin, 22,* 651–665.

Romero, L., & Sapolsky, R. (1996). Patterns of ACTH secretagog secretion in response to psychological stimuli. *Journal of Neuroendocrinology, 8,* 243–258.

Rosch, E. (1973). Natural categories. *Cognitive Psychology, 4,* 328–350.

Rosch, E. (1975). The nature of mental codes for color categories. *Journal of Experimental Psychology: Human Perception and Performance, 1,* 303–322.

Rosch, E. (1978). Principles of categorization. In E. Rosch, & B. B. Lloyd (Ed.), *Cognition and categorization* (pp. 27–48). Hillsdale, NJ: Erlbaum.

Rosen C. M. (1987). The eerie world of reunited twins. *Discover, 8,* 36–46.

Rosenhan, D. L. (1973). On being sane in insane places. *Science, 179,* 250–258.

Rosenheim, M. K., & Testa, M. F. (Eds.) (1992). *Early parenthood and coming of age in the 1990s.* New Brunswick, NJ: Rutgers University Press.

Rosenthal, A. M. (1964). *Thiry-eight witnesses.* New York: McGraw-Hill.

Rosenthal, D. (1963). *The Genain Quadruplets.* New York: Basic Books.

Rosenthal, R. (1976). *Experimenter effects in behavioral research.* New York: Irvington.

Rosenthal, R. (1991). *Meta-analytic procedures for social research.* Beverly Hills, CA: Sage.

Roskill, M. (1963). *The letters of Vincent van Gogh.* London: William Collins.

Ross, C. A. (1991). Epidemiology of multiple personality disorder and dissociation. *Psychiatric Clinics of North America, 14,* 503–517.

Ross, C. A., Miller, S. D., Bjornson, L., Reagor, P., & Fraser, G. A. (1991). Abuse histories in 102 cases of multiple personality disorder. *Canadian Journal of Psychiatry, 36,* 97–101.

Ross, C. E. (1995). Reconceptualizing marital status as a continuum of social attachment. *Journal of Marriage & the Family, 57,* 129–140.

Ross, L., Greene, D., & House, P. (1977). The false consensus effect: An egocentric bias in social perception and attribution processes. *Journal of Experimental Social Psychology, 13,* 279–301.

Rotter, J. B. (1966). Generalized expectancies for internal versus extrnal control of reinforcement. *Psychological Monographs, 80* (1, Whole No. 609).

Rouillon, F. (1997). Epidemiology of panic disorder. *Human Psychopharmacology Clinical & Experimental, 12*(Suppl. 1), S7–S12.

Rowe, J. W., & Kahn, R. L. (1998). *Successful aging.* New York: Pantheon.

Rozin, P. (1982). "Taste-smell confusions" and the duality of the olfactory sense. *Perception and Psychophysics, 31,* 397–401.

Rozin, P., & Fallon, A. (1986). The acquisition of likes and dislikes for foods. In National Research Council et al., *What is America eating?: Proceedings of a symposium.* Washington, DC: National Academy Press.

Rozin, P., & Jonides, J. (1977). Mass reaction time: Measurement of the speed of the nerve impulse and the duration of mental processes in class. *Teaching of Psychology, 4,* 91–94.

Rozin, P., Ashmore, M., & Markwith, M. (1996). Lay American conceptions of nutrition: Dose insensitivity, categorical thinking, contagion, and the monotonic mind. *Health Psychology, 15,* 438–447.

Rozin, P., Lowery, L., & Ebert, R. (1994). Varieties of disgust faces and the structure of disgust. *Journal of Personality & Social Psychology, 66,* 870–881.

Rubin, L. J. (1996). Childhood sexual abuse: False accusations of "False memory"? *Professional Psychology Research and Practice, 27,* 447–451.

Rubin, Z. (1970). Measurement of romantic love. *Journal of Personality and Social Psychology, 16,* 265–273.

Rumelhart, D. E. (1975). Notes on schema for stories. In D. G. Bobrow & A. M. Collins (Eds.), *Representations and understanding: Studies in cognitive science* (pp. 211–236). New York: Academic Press.

Runco, M. A., & Albert, R. S. (1986). The threshold theory regarding creativity and intelligence: An empirical test with gifted and nongifted children. *Creative Child & Adult Quarterly, 11,* 212–218.

Rushton, J. P. (1975). Generosity in children: Immediate and long-term effects of modeling, preaching, and moral judgement. *Journal of Personality and Social Psychology, 31,* 459–466.

Rushton, J. P. (1995). *Race, evolution and behavior: A life-history perspective.* New Brunswick, NJ: Transaction.

Rustemli, A., Mertan, B., & Ciftci, O. (2000). In-group favoritism among native and immigrant Turkish cypriots: Trait evaluations of in-group and out-group targets. *Journal of Social Psychology, 140,* 26–34.

Ryan, R. M., & Deci, E. L. (2000). Self-determination theory and the facilitation of intrinsic motivation, social development, and well-being. *American Psychologist, 55,* 68–78.

Ryner, L. C., Goodwin, S. F., Castrillon, D. H., Anand, A., Villella, A., Baker, B. S., Hall, J. C., Taylor, B. J., & Wasserman, S. A. (1996). Control of male sexual behavior and sexual orientation in Drosophila by the fruitless gene. *Cell, 87,* 1079–1089.

Sackheim, H. A., Devanand, D. P., & Nobler, M. S. (1995). Electroconvulsive therapy. In F. E. Bloom & D. J. Kupfer (Eds.), *Psychopharmacology: The Fourth Generation of Progress.* New York: Raven Press. pp. 1123–1141.

Sacks, O. (1995). *An anthropologist on Mars: Seven paradoxical tales.* New York: Knopf.

Sadler, T. W. (1995). *Langman's medical embryology* (7th ed.). Baltimore: Williams & Wilkins.

Saggino, A. (2000). The Big Three or the Big Five? A replication study. *Personality & Individual Differences, 28,* 879–886.

Sagie, A., Elizur, S., & Hirotsugu, Y. (1996). The structure and strength of achievement motivation: A cross-cultural comparison. *Journal of Organization Behavior, 17,* 431–444.

Saldana, H. N., & Rosenblum, L. D. (1993). Visual influences on auditory pluck and bow judgments. *Perception & Psychophysics, 54,* 406–416.

Sallis, J., Johnson, C., Treverow, T., Kaplan, R., & Hovell, M. (1987). The relationship between cynical hostility and blood pressure reactivity. *Journal of Psychosomatic Research, 31,* 111–116.

Salmon, C. A. (1998). The Evocative Nature of Kin Terminology in Political Rhetoric. *Politics and the Life Sciences 17,* 51–57.

Salmon, C. A. (1999). On the impact of sex and birth order on contact with kin. *Human Nature, 10,* 183–197.

Salmon, C. A., & Daly, M. (1998). Birth order and familial sentiment: middleborns are different. *Evolution and Behavior, 19,* 299–312.

Salovey, P., & Mayer, J. D. (1990). Emotional intelligence. *Imagination, Cognition, and Personality, 9,* 185–211.

Salthouse, T. A. (1984). Effects of age and skill in typing. *Journal of Experimental Psychology: General, 113,* 345–371.

Salthouse, T. A. (1985). Speed of behavior and its implications for cognition. In J. E. Birren & K. W. Schaie (Eds.), *Handbook of the psychology of aging* (2nd ed., pp. 400–426). New York: Van Nostrand Reinhold.

Salthouse, T. A. (1991a). Cognitive facets of aging well. *Generations, 15*(1), 35–38.

Salthouse, T. A. (1991b). *Theoretical perspectives on cognitive aging.* Hillsdale, NJ: Erlbaum.

Salthouse, T. A. (1996). The processing-speed theory of adult age differences in cognition. *Psychological Review, 103,* 403–428.

Salthouse, T. A., & Somberg, B. L. (1982). Skilled performance: Effects of adult age and experience on elementary processes. *Journal of Experimental Psychology: General, 111,* 176–207.

Samoluk, S. B., & Stewart, S. H. (1998). Anxiety sensitivity and situation-specific drinking. *Journal of Anxiety Disorders, 12,* 407–419.

Sanbonmatsu, D. M., & Fazio, R. H. (1990). The Role of Attitudes in Memory-Based Decision Making. *Journal of Personality and Social Psychology, 59,* 614–622.

Sandman, C. A., Wadhwa, P., Hetrick, W., Porto, M., & Peeke, H. V. S. (1997). Human fetal heart rate dishabituation between thirty and thirty-two weeks gestation. *Child Development, 68,* 1031–1040.

Sapolsky, R. M. (1992). *Stress, the aging brain, and the mechanisms of neuron death.* Cambridge, MA: MIT Press.

Sapolsky, R. M. (1996). Why stress is bad for your brain. *Science, 273,* 749–750.

Sapolsky, R. M. (1997). *Why Zebras Don't Get Ulcers.* New York: Freeman.

Sarbin, T. R. (1995). On the belief that one body may be host to two or more personalities. *International Journal of Clinical & Experimental Hypnosis, 43,* 163–183.

Sargent, P. A., Sharpley, A. L., Williams, C., Goodall, E. M., & Cowen, P. J. (1997). 5-HT-sub(2C) receptor activation decreases appetite and body weight in obese subjects. *Psychopharmacology, 133,* 309–312.

Satcher, D. (1999). *Mental health: A report of the Surgeon General.* Washington, DC: Department of Health and Human Services.

Saudino, K. J., Gagne, J. R., Grant, J., Ibatoulina, A., Marytuina, T., Ravich-Scherbo, I., & Whitfield, K. (1999). Genetic and environmental influences on personality in adult Russian twins. *International Journal of Behavioral Development, 23,* 375–389.

Savage-Rumbaugh, S., McDonald, K., Sevcik, R. A., Hopkins, W. D., & Rubert, E. (1986). Spontaneous symbol acquisition and communicative use by pygmy chimpanzees (*Pan paniscus*). *Journal of Experimental Psychology: General, 112,* 211–235.

Scarr, S., & McCartney, K. (1983). How people make their own environments: A theory of genotype-environment effects. *Child Development, 54,* 424–435.

Scarr, S., & Weinberg, R. A. (1983). The Minnesota Adoption Studies: Genetic differences and malleability. *Child Development, 54,* 260–267.

Schacter, D. (1987). Implicit memory: History and current status. *Journal of Experimental Psychology: Learning, Memory, and Cognition, 13,* 501–518.

Schacter, D. L. (1996). *Searching for memory: The brain, the mind, and the past.* New York: Basic Books.

Schacter, D. L., Reiman, E., Curran, T., Yun, L. S., Bandy, D., McDermott, K. B., & Roediger, H. L., III (1996). Neuroanatomical correlates of veridical and illusory recognition memory: Evidence from positron emission tomography. *Neuron, 2,* 267–274.

Schacter, D. L., & Wagner, A. D. (1999). Medial temporal lobe activations in fMRI and PET studies of episodic encoding and retrieval. *Hippocampus, 9,* 7–24.

Schacter, S., & Singer, J. (1962). Cognitive, social and physiological determinants of emotional state. *Psychological Review, 69,* 379–399.

Schaffner, K. F. (1967). Approaches to reduction. *Philosophy of Science, 34,* 137–147.

Schaie, K. W., & Willis, S. L. (1993). Age difference patterns of psychometric intelligence in adulthood: Generalizability within and across ability domains. *Psychology and Aging, 8,* 44–55.

Schank, R. C., & Abelson, R. P. (1977). *Scripts, plans, goals, and understanding.* Hillsdale, NJ: Erlbaum.

Scheflin, A., & Brown, D. (1996). Repressed memory or dissociative amnesia: What science says. *Journal of Psychiatry and Law, 24,* 143–188.

Schellenberg, E. G., & Trehub, S. E. (1996). Natural musical intervals: Evidence from infant listeners. *Psychological Science, 7,* 272–277.

Schiavi, R. C., White, D., Mandeli, J., & Levine, A. C.(1997). Effect of testosterone administration on sexual behavior and mood in men with erectile dysfunction. *Archives of Sexual Behavior, 26,* 231–241

Schiffman, S. S., Graham, B. G., Sattely-Miller, E. A., & Warwick, Z. S. (1999). Orosensory perception of dietary fat. *Current Directions in Psychological Science, 7,* 137–143.

Schlaug, G., Jancke, L., Huang, Y., & Steinmetz, H. (1995). In vivo evidence of structural brain asymmetry in musicians. *Science, 267,* 699–701.

Schmidt, N. B., Lerew, D. R., & Jackson, R. J. (1997). The Role of Anxiety Sensitivity in the Pathogenesis of Panic: Prospective Evaluation of Spontaneous Panic Attacks During Acute Stress. *Journal of Abnormal Psychology, 106,* 355–364.

Schmidt, N. B., Lerew, D. R., & Jackson, R. J. (1999). Prospective evaluation of anxiety sensitivity in the pathogenesis of panic: Replication and extension. *Journal of Abnormal Psychology, 108,* 532–537.

Schmitt, B. H., Gilovich, T., Goore, N., & Joseph, L. (1986). Mere presence and social facilitation: One more time. *Journal of Experimental Social Psychology, 22,* 242–248.

Schmolck, H., Buffalo, E. A., & Squire, L. R. (2000). Memory distortions develop over time: Recollections from the O. J. Simpson trial verdict after 15 and 32 months. *Psychological Science, 11,* 39–45.

Schneider, L. H., Davis, J. D., Watson, C. A., & Smith, G. P. (1990). Similar effect of raclopride and reduced sucrose concentration on the microstructure of sucrose sham feeding. *European Journal of Pharmacology, 186,* 61–70.

Schrof, J. M., & Schultz, S. (1999). Melencholy Nation. *U.S. News and World Report. March 8, 126(9),* p. 56–63.

Schuckit, M. A. (1999). New Findings in the Genetics of Alcoholism. *Journal of the American Medical Association, 281,* 1875–1876.

Schul, R., Slotnick, B. M., & Dudai, Y. (1996). Flavor and the frontal cortex. *Behavioral Neuroscience, 110,* 760–765.

Schulenberg, J., Wadsworth, K. N., O'Malley, P. M., Bachman, J. G., & Johnston, L. D. (1996). Adolescent risk factors for binge drinking during the transition to young adulthood: Variable- and pattern-centered approaches to change. *Developmental Psychology, 32,* 659–674.

Schultz, W. (1997). Dopamine neurons and their role in reward mechanisms. *Current Opinion in Neurobiology, 7,* 191–197.

Schultz, W., Dayan, P., & Montague, P. R. (1997). A neural substrate of prediction and reward. *Science, 275,* 1593–1599.

Schwartz, J. M., Stoessel, P. W., Baxter, L. R., Martin, K. M., & Phelps, M. E. (1996). Systematic changes in cerebral glucose metabolic rate after successful behavior modification treatment of obsessive-compulsive disorder. *Archives of General Psychiatry, 53,* 109–113.

Schwartz, T. (1999, January 10). The test under stress. *New York Times Magazine,* pp. 30–63.

Schyns, P. (1998). Crossnational differences in happiness: Economic and cultural factors explored. *Social Indicators Research, 43,* 3–26.

Sclafani, A., & Aravich, P. F. (1983). Macronutrient self-selection in three forms of hypothalamic obesity. *American Journal of Physiology, 244,* R686–R694.

Sclafani, A., Aravich, P. F., & Xenakis, S. (1983). Macronutrient preferences in hypothalamic hyperphagic rats. *Nutrition & Behavior, 1,* 233–251.

Scogin, F., Bynum, J., Stephens, G., & Calhoon, S. (1990). Efficacy of self-administered treatment programs: Meta-analytic review. *Professional Psychology: Research & Practice, 21,* 42–47.

Scott, B., & Melin, L. (1998). Psychometric properties and standardised data for questionnaires measuring negative affect, dispositional style and daily hassles: A nation-wide sample. *Scandinavian Journal of Psychology, 39,* 301–307.

Scott, S. K., Young, A. W., Calder, A. J., Hellawell, D. J., Aggleton, J. P., & Johnson, M. (1997). Impaired auditory recognition of fear and anger following bilateral amygdala lesions. *Nature, 385,* 254–257.

Scott, T. R., & Plata-Salaman, C. R. (1991). Coding of taste quality. In T. V. Getchell, R. L. Doty, L. M. Bartoshuk, & J. B. Snow, Jr. (Eds.), *Smell and taste in health and disease* (pp. 345–368). New York: Raven.

Sears, R., Maccoby, E., & Levin, H. (1957). *Patterns of child rearing.* New York: Harper & Row.

Seeman, R. E., Berkman, L. F., Blazer, D., & Rowe, J. W. (1994). Social ties and support and neuroendocrine function: The MacArthur studies of successful aging. *Annals of Behavioral Medicine, 16,* 95–106.

Segal, N. L. (1999). *Entwined lives: Twins and what they tell us about human behavior.* New York: Dutton/Penguin Books.

Segal, Z. V., Gemar, M., & Williams, S. (1999). Differential cognitive response to a mood challenge following successful cognitive therapy or pharmacotherapy for unipolar depression. *Journal of Abnormal Psychology, 108,* 3–10.

Segerstrom, S. C., Taylor, S. E., Kemeny, M. E., Reed, G. M., & Visscher, B. R. (1996). Causal attributions predict rate of immune decline in HIV-seropositive gay men. *Health Psychology, 15,* 485–493.

Segrin, C., & Abramson, L. Y. (1994). Negative reactions to depressive behaviors: A communication theory analysis. *Journal of Abnormal Psychology, 103,* 655–668.

Segrin, C., & Dillard, J. P. (1992). The interactional theory of depression: A meta-analysis of the research literature. *Journal of Social & Clinical Psychology, 11(1),* 43–70.

Seligman, C., Fazio, R. H., & Zanna, M. P. (1980). Effects of salience of extrinsic rewards on liking and loving. *Journal of Personality and Social Psychology, 38,* 453–460.

Seligman, M. E. P. (1971). Phobias and preparedness. *Behavior Therapy, 2,* 307–320.

Seligman, M. E. P. (1995). The effectiveness of psychotherapy: The Consumer Reports study. *American Psychologist, 50,* 965–974.

Selye, H. (1976). *The Stress of Life.* New York: McGraw Hill.

Semenov, L. A., Chernova, N. D., & Bondarko, V. M. (2000). Measurement of visual acuity and crowding effect in 3–9-year-old children. *Human Physiology, 26,* 16–20.

Sereny, G., Sharma, V., Holt. J., & Gordis, E. (1986). Mandatory supervised Antabuse therapy in an outpatient alcoholism program: A pilot study. Alcoholism (NY) 10:290–292.

Serpell, R. (1979). How specific are perceptual skills? A cross-cultural study of pattern reproduction. *British Journal of Psychology, 70,* 365–380.

Seta, J. J., & Seta, C. E. (1992). Increments and decrements in mean arterial pressure as a function of audience composition: An averaging and summation analysis. *Personality and Social Psychology Bulletin, 18,* 173–181.

Seuling, B. (1976). *The loudest screen kiss and other little-known facts about the movies.* New York: Doubleday.

Seuling, B. (1978). *The last cow on the White House lawn and other little-known facts about the Presidency.* New York: Doubleday.

Seuling, B. (1986). *You can't sneeze with your eyes open and other freaky facts about the human body.* New York: Ballantine Books.

Shalev, A. Y., Peri, T., Brandes, D., Freedman, S., Orr, S. P., & Pitman, R. K. (2000). Auditory startle response in trauma survivors with posttraumatic stress disorder: A prospective study. *American Journal of Psychiatry, 157,* 255–261.

Shalev, A. Y., Sahar, T., Freedman, S., Peri, T., Glick, N., Brandes, D., Orr, S. P., & Pitman, R. K. (1998). A Prospective Study of Heart Rate Response Following Trauma and the Subsequent Development of Posttraumatic Stress Disorder. *Archives of General Psychiatry, 55,* 553–559.

Shallenberger, R. S. (1993). *Taste chemistry.* New York: Blackie Academic.

Shallice, T., Fletcher, P., Frith, C. D., Grasby, P., Frackowiak, R. S. J., & Dolan, R. J. (1994). Brain regions associated with acquisition and retrieval of verbal episodic memory. *Nature, 368,* 633–635.

Shallice, T., & Warrington, E. K. (1980). Single and multiple component central dyslexic syndromes. In M. Coltheart, K. E. Patterson, & J. C. Marshall (Eds.), *Deep dyslexia* (pp. 119–145). London: Routledge.

Shanab, M. E., & Yahya, K. A. (1977). A behavioral study of obedience in children. *Journal of Personality and Social Psychology, 35,* 530–536.

Shapira, B., Tubi, N., Drexler, H., Lidsky, D., Calev, A., & Lerer, B. (1998). Cost and benefit in the choice of ECT schedule: Twice versus three times weekly ECT. *British Journal of Psychiatry, 172,* 44–48.

Shapiro, A. K. (1964). Factors contributing to the placebo effect: Their significance for psychotherapy. *American Journal of Psychotherapy, 18,* 73–88.

Shapiro, A. K., & Morris, L. A. (1978). The placebo effect in medical and psychological therapies. In S. L. Garfield & A. E. Bergin (eds.), *Handbook of Psychotherapy and Behavior Change: An empirical analysis* (2nd ed.). New York: Wiley.

Shapiro, D. H. Jr., Schwartz, C. E., & Astin, J. A. (1996). Controlling ourselves, controlling our world: Psychology's role in understandinf positive and negative consequences of seeking and gaining control. *American Psychologist, 51,* 1213–1230.

Shaver, P. R., & Hazan, C. (1994). Attachment. In *Perspectives on Close Relationships.* A. L. Weber & J. H. Harvey (Eds.). Boston: Allyn & Bacon.

Shaw, P. J., Bergmann, B. M., & Rechtschaffen, A. (1998). Effects of paradoxical sleep deprivation on thermoregulation in the rat. *Sleep, 21,* p. 7–17.

Shaywitz, B. A., Shaywitz, S. E., Pugh, K. R., Constable, R. T., Skudlarski, P., Fulbright, R. K., Bronen, R. A., Fletcher, J. M., Shankweller, D. P., Katz, L., & Gore, J. C. (1995). Sex differences in the functional organization of the brain for language. *Nature, 373,* 607–611.

Shea, M. T., Elkin, I., Imber, S. D., Sotsky, S. M., Watkins, J. T., Collins, J. F., Pilkonis, P. A., Beckham, E., Glass, D. R., Dolan, R. T., & Parloff, M. B. (1992). Course of depressive symptoms over follow-up: Findings from the National Institute of Mental Health Treatment of Depression Collaborative Research Program. *Archives of General Psychiatry, 49,* 782–787.

Sheehan, P. W. (1988). Memory distortion in hypnosis. *International Journal of Clinical Experimental Hypnosis, 36,* 296–311.

Shekim, W. O., Bylund, D. B., Frankel, F., Alexson, J., Jones S. B., Blue, L. D., Kirby, J., & Corchoran, C. (1989). Platelet MAO activity and personality variations in normals. *Psychiatry Research, 27,* 81–88.

Sheldon, K. M., Ryan, R., & Reis, H. T. (1996). What makes for a good day? Competence and autonomy in the day and in the person. *Personality & Social Psychology Bulletin, 22,* 1270–1279.

Shepard, R. N. (1967). Recognition memory for words, sentences and pictures. *Journal of Verbal learning and Verbal Behavior, 6,* 156–163.

Shepherd, G. M. (1999). Information processing in dendrites. In M. J. Zigmond, F. E. Bloom, S. C. Landis, J. L. Roberts, & L. R. Squire (Eds.), *Fundamental neuroscience* (pp. 363–388). New York: Academic Press.

Sherif, M., Harvey, O. J., White, B. J., Hood, W. R., & Sherif, C. W. (1961). *Intergroup conflict and cooperation: The robber's cave experiment.* Norman, OK: The University Book Exchange.

Sherman, J. J. (1998). Effects of psychotherapeutic treatments for PTSD: A meta-analysis of controlled clinical trials. *Journal of Traumatic Stress, 11,* 413–435.

Shibahara, H., Shigeta, M., Toji, H., & Koyama, K. (1995). Sperm immobilizing antibodies interfere with sperm migration from the uterine cavity through the fallopian tubes. *American Journal of Reproductive Immunology, 34,* 120–124.

Shields, S. A. (1987). Women, men, and the dilemma of emotion. In P. Shaver & C. Hendrick (Eds.), *Sex and gender* (pp. 229–250). Newbury Park, Calif.: Sage.

Shin, L. M., Kosslyn, S. M., McNally, R. J., Alpert, N. M., Thompson, W. L., Raush, S. L., Macklin, M. L., & Pitman, R. K. (1997). Visual imagery and perception in posttraumatic stress disorder: A positron emission tomographic investigation. *Archives of General Psychiatry, 54,* 233–241.

Shortridge, J. R. (1993). The Great Plains. In M. K. Cayton, E. J. Gorn, & P. W. Williams (Eds.), *Encyclopedia of American Social History* (Vol. 2, pp. 1001–1015). New York: Scribner.

Shulman, S., Elicker, J., & Sroufe, L. A. (1994). Stages of friendship growth in preadolescence as related to attachment history. *Journal of Social & Personal Relationships, 11,* 341–361.

Siegel, J. L., & Longo, D. L. (1981). The control of chemotherapy induced emesis. *Annals of Internal Medicine, 95,* 352–359.

Siegel, M., Brisman, J., & Weinshel, M. (1988). *Surviving an Eating Disorder: Strategies for Family and Friends.* New York: Harper and Row.

Siegel, S. (1988). State dependent learning and morphine tolerance. *Behavioral Neuroscience, 102,* 228–232.

Sifneos, P. E. (1992). *Short-term anxiety-provoking psychotherapy: A treatment manual.* New York: Basicbooks, Inc.

Silverman, L. (1976). Psychoanalytic theory: The reports of my death are greatly exaggerated. *American Psychologist, 31,* 621–637.

Silverman, L. K. (1993a). Counseling families. In L. K. Silverman (Ed.), *Counseling the gifted and talented* (pp. 43–89). Denver: Love.

Silverman, L. K. (1993b). A developmental model for counseling the gifted. In L. K. Silverman (Ed.), *Counseling the gifted and talented* (pp. 51–78). Denver: Love.

Simmons, J. A., & Chen, L. (1989). The acoustic basis for target discrimination by FM echolocating bats. *Journal of the Acoustical Society of America, 86,* 1333–1350.

Simon, L., Greenberg, J., & Brehm, J. (1995). Trivialization: The forgotten mode of dissonance reduction. *Journal of Personality and Social Psychology, 68,* 247–260.

Simons, D. J. (1999). Current approaches to change blindness. *Visual Cognition, 7,* 1–15.

Simons, D. J., & Levin, D. T. (1997). Change blindness. *Trends in Cognitive Sciences, 1,* 261–267.

Simonton, D. K. (1984). *Genius, creativity, and leadership: Historiometric inquiries.* Cambridge, MA: Harvard University Press.

Simonton, D. K. (1988). Creativity, leadership, and chance. In R. J. Sternberg (Ed.), *The nature of creativity* (pp. 386–436). New York: Cambridge University Press.

Simonton, D. K. (1990). Political pathology and societal creativity. *Creativity Research Journal, 3,* 85–99.

Simonton, D. K. (1994). *Greatness: Who makes history and why.* New York: Guilford.

Simonton, D. K. (1997). Creative productivity: A predictive and explanatory model of career trajectories and landmarks. *Psychological Review, 104,* 66–89.

Singh, V. N. (1995). Human uterine amylase in relation to infertility. *Hormone and Metabolic Research, 27,* 35–36.

Sireteanu, R. (2000). Texture segmentation, "pop-out," and feature binding in infants and children. In C. Rovee-Collier & L. P. Lipsitt (Eds.), *Progress in infancy research, Vol. 1* (pp. 183–249). Mahwah, NJ: Erlbaum.

Skinner, B. F. (1938). *The behavior of organisms: An experimental analysis.* New York: Appleton-Century.

Skinner, B. F. (1953). *Science and human behavior.* New York: MacMillan.

Skinner, B. F. (1956). A case history in scientific method. *American Psychologist, 11,* 221–233.

Skuder, P., Plomin, R., McClearn, G. E., Smith, D. L., Vignetti, S., Chorney, M. J., Chorney, K., Kasarda, S., Thompson, L. A., Detterman,

D., Petrill, S. A., Daniels, J., Owen, M. J., & McGuffin, P. (1995). A polymorphism in mitochondrial DNA associated with IQ? *Intelligence, 21,* 1–11.

Skvoretz, J. (1988). Models of participation in status-differentiated groups. *Social Psychology Quarterly, 51,* 43–57.

Sleek, S. (1997, November). Online therapy services raise ethical questions. *APA Monitor,* p. 1, 38.

Slep, A. M. S., & O'Leary, S. G. (1998). The effects of maternal attributions on parenting: An experimental analysis. *Journal of Family Psychology, 12,* 234–243.

Slimp, J. C., Hart, B. L., & Goy, R. W. (1978). Heterosexual, autosexual and social behavior of adult male rhesus monkeys with medial preoptic-anterior hypothalamic lesions. *Brain Research, 142,* 105–122.

Slob, A. K., Bax, C. M., Hop, W. C. J., Rowland, D. L., & van der Werff ten Bosch, J. J. (1996). Sexual arousability and the menstrual cycle. *Psychoneuroendocrinology, 21,* 545–558.

Small, B. J., & Bäckman, L. (1999). Time to death and cognitive performance. *Current Directions in Psychological Science, 6,* 168–172.

Smeets, M. A. M., Smit, F., Panhuysen, G. E. M., & Ingleby, J. D. (1997). The influence of methodological differences on outcome of body size estimation studies in anorexia nervosa. *British Journal of Clinical Psychology, 36,* 263–277.

Smith, D. (1982). Trends in counseling and psychotherapy. *American Psychologist, 37,* 802–809.

Smith, D. V., & Frank, M. E. (1993). Sensory coding by peripheral taste fibers. In S. A. Simon & S. D. Roper (Eds.), *Mechanisms of taste transduction* (pp. 295–338). Boca Raton, FL: CRC Press.

Smith, E. E. (1988). Concepts and thought. In R. J. Sternberg & E. E. Smith (Eds.), *The psychology of human thought* (pp. 19–49). New York: Cambridge University Press.

Smith, E. E. (2000). Neural bases of human working memory. *Current Directions in Psychological Science, 9,* 45–49.

Smith, E. E., & Jonides, J. (1999). Storage and executive processes in the frontal lobes. *Science, 283,* 1657–1661.

Smith, E. E., & Medin, D. L. (1981). *Categories and concepts* . Cambridge, MA: Harvard University Press.

Smith, E. E., Patalano, A. L., & Jonides, J. (1998). Alternative strategies of categorization. *Cognition, 65,* 167–196.

Smith, E. R. (1998). Mental Representation and memory. In D. T. Gilbert, S. T. Fiske, & G. Lindzey (Eds.), *The handbook of social psychology* (4th ed.). New York: McGraw Hill. Vol. 1, pp. 391–445.

Smith, S. M., & Blankenship, S. E. (1989). Incubation effects. *Bulletin of the Psychonomic Society, 27,* 311–314.

Smith, S. M., & Blankenship, S. E. (1991). Incubation and the persistence of fixation in problem solving. *American Journal of Psychology, 104,* 61–87.

Smolucha, F. C. (1992). A reconstruction of Vygotsky's theory of creativity. *Creativity Research Journal, 5,* 49–67.

Smyth, J. M., Stone, A. A., Hurewitz, A., & Kaell, A. (1999). Effects of writing about stressful experiences on symptom reduction in patients with asthma or rheumatoid arthritis. *Journal of the American Medical Association, 281,* 1304–1329.

Snidman, N., Kagan, J, Riordan, L., & Shannon, D. C. (1995). Cardiac function and behavioral reactivity during infancy. *Psychophysiology, 32,* 199–207.

Snodgrass, S. E. (1985). Women's intuition: The effect of subordinate roel on interpersonal sensitivity. *Journal of Personality and Social Psychology, 49,* 146–155.

Snow, C. E. (1991). The language of the mother–child relationship. In M. Woodhead & R. Carr (Eds.), *Becoming a person* (pp. 195–210). London: Routledge.

Snow, C. E. (1999). Social perspectives on the emergence of language. In B. MacWhinney (Ed.), *The emergence of language* (pp. 257–276). Mahwah, NJ: Erlbaum.

Snow, C. E. (in press). Second language learners' contributions to our understanding of languages of the brain. In A. M. Galaburda, S. M. Kosslyn, & Y. Christen (Eds.), *Languages of the brain.* Cambridge, MA: Harvard University Press.

Snyder, C. R., & Larson, G. R. (1972). A further look at student acceptance of general personality interpretations. *Journal of Consulting and Clinical Psychology, 38,* 384–388.

Snyder, M. (1984). When belief creates reality. In L. Berkowitz (Ed.), *Advances in experimental social psychology* (Vol. 25, pp. 67–114). San Diego, CA: Academic Press.

Snyder, M. (1992). Motivational foundations of behavioral confirmation. In M. P. Zanna (Ed.), *Advances in experimental social psychology* (Vol. 18, pp. 248–306). New York: Academic Press.

Snyder, M., & Ickes, W. (1985). Personality and social behavior. In G. Lindzey & E. Aronson (Eds.), *Handbook of social psychology* (3rd ed.) (Vol. 2, pp. 883–947). New York: Random House.

Snyder, M., Tanke, E. D., & Berscheid, E. (1977). Social perception and interpersonal behavior: On the self-fulfilling nature of social stereotypes. *Journal of Personality and Social Psychology, 35,* 656–666.

Snyderman, M., & Herrnstein, R. J. (1983). Intelligence tests and the Immigration Act of 1924. *American Psychologist, 38,* 986–995.

Solms, M. (1997). *The neuropsychology of dreams: A clinico-anatomical study.* Mahwah, NJ: Erlbaum.

Solomon, D. A., Keller, M. B., Leon, A. C., Mueller, T. I., Lavori, P. W., Shea, M. T., Coryell, W., Warshaw, M., Turvey, C., Maser, J. D., & Endicott, J. (2000). Multiple recurrences of major depressive disorder. *American Journal of Psychiatry, 157,* 229–233.

Solomon, R. L., & Corbit, J. D. (1974a). An opponent-process theory of motivation: I. Temporal dynamics of affect. *Psychological Review, 78,* 3–43.

Soper, B., Milford, G. E., & Rosenthal, G. T. (1995). Belief when evidence does not support the theory. *Psychology & Marketing, 12,* 415–422.

Sowell, E. R., Thompson, P. M., Holmes, C. J., Jernigan, T. L., & Toga, A. W. (1999). In vivo evidence for post-adolescent brain maturation in frontal and striatal regions. *Nature Neuroscience, 2,* 859–61.

Spangler, W. D. (1992). Validity of questionnaire and TAT measures of need for achievement: Two meta-analyses. *Psychological Bulletin, 112,* 140–154.

Spearman, C. (1927). *The abilities of man.* New York: Macmillan.

Speed, A., & Gangestad, S. (1997). Romantic popularity and mate preferences: A peer-nomination study. *Personality & Social Psychology Bulletin, 23,* 928–935.

Speisman, J. C., Lazarus, R. S., Mordkoff, A., & Davison, L. (1964). Experimental reduction of stress based on ego-defense theory. *Journal of Abnormal and Social Psychology, 68,* 367–380.

Spelke, E. S. (1991). Physical knowledge in infancy: Reflections on Piaget's theory. In S. Carey & R. Gelman (Eds.), *The epigenesis of mind: Essays on biology and cognition* (pp. 133–169). Hillsdale, NJ: Erlbaum.

Spelke, E. S., Breinlinger, K., Jacobson, K., & Phillips, A. (1993). Gestalt relations and object perception: A developmental study. *Perception, 22,* 1483–1501.

Spelke, E. S., Breinlinger, K., Macomber, J., & Jacobson, K. (1992). Origins of knowledge. *Psychological Review, 99,* 605–632.

Sperling, G. (1960). The information available in brief visual presentations. *Psychological Monographs, 74,* 1–29.

Spiegel, D (1994). *Living beyond limits: new hope and help for facing life-threatening illness.* New York: Ballantine/Fawcett.

Spiegel, D. (1997). Psychosocial aspects of breast cancer treatment. *Seminars in Oncology, 24,* S1-36–S1-47.

Spiegel, D., Bloom, J., & Kraemer, H. (1989). Effect of psychosocial treatment on survival of patients with metastatic breast cancer. *The Lancet, 2,* 888–891.

Spiegel, D., Sephton, S., Terr, A., & Stites, D. (1998). Effects of psychosocial treatment in prolonging cancer survival may be mediated by neuroimmune pathways. In S. McCann, J. Lipton, E. Sternberg, et al. (Eds.), *Neuroimmunomodulation: Molecular aspects, integrative systems, and clinical advances* (pp. 674–683). New York: New York Academy of Sciences.

Spitzer, H., Desimone, R., & Moran, J. (1988). Increased attention enhances both behavioral and neuronal performance. *Science, 240,* 338– 340.

Sprecher, S. (1999). "I Love You More Today Than Yesterday": Romantic Partners' Perceptions of Changes in Love and Related Affect Over Time. *Journal of Personality and Social Psychology,76,* 46–53.

Sprecher, S., Aron, A., Hatfield, E., Cortese, A., Potapova, E., & Levitskaya, A. (1994). Love: American style, Russian style and Japanese style. *Personal Relationships, 1,* 349–369.

Sprecher, S., Sullivan, Q., & Hatfield, E. (1994). Mate selection preferences: Gender differences examined in a national sample. *Journal of Personality and Social Psychology, 66,* 1074–1080.

Springer, S. P., & Deutsch, G. (1998). *Left brain, right brain: Perspectives from cognitive neuroscience (5th ed.).* New York: W. H. Freeman.

Sprock, J., & Yoder, C. Y. (1997). Women and depression: An update on the report of the APA Task Force. *Sex Roles, 36,* 269–303.

Spyraki, C., Fibiger, H. C., & Phillips, A. G. (1982). Dopaminergic substrates of amphetamine-induced place preference conditioning. *Brain Research, 253* (1-sup-2), 185–193.

Squire, L. R. (1987). *Memory and the brain.* New York: Oxford University Press.

Squire, L. R. (1992). Memory and the hippocampus: A synthesis from findings with rats, monkeys, and humans. *Psychological Review, 99,* 195–231.

Squire, L. R., Ojemann, J. G., Miezin, F. M., Petersen, S. E., Videen, T. O., & Raichle, M. E. (1992). Activation of the hippocampus in normal humans: A functional anatomical study of memory. *Proceedings of the National Academy of Sciences, USA, 89,* 1837–1841.

Sroufe, L. A., & Fleeson, J. (1986). Attachment and the construction of relationships. In W. W. Hartup and Z. Rubin (Eds.), *Relationships and development* (pp. 51–71). Hillsdale, NJ: Erlbaum.

Stack, S., & Eshleman, J. R. (1998). Marital status and happiness. *Journal of Marriage and the Family, 60,* 527–536.

Stager, C. L., & Werker, J. F. (1997). Infants listen for more phonetic detail in speech perception than in word-learning tasks. *Nature, 388,* 381–382.

Stallone, D. D., & Stunkard, A. J. (1994). Obesity. In A. Frazer & P. B. Molinoff (Eds.), *Biological bases of brain function and disease* (pp. 385–403). New York: Raven Press.

Stanley, M. A., & Turner, S. M. (1995). Current status of pharmacological and behavioral treatment of obsessive-compulsive disorder. *Behavior Therapy, 25,* 153–186.

Stanton, M. D. (1981). Strategic approaches to family therapy. In A. S. Gurman & D. P. Kniskern (Eds.), *Handbook of Family Therapy* (pp. 361–402). New York: Brunner/Mazel.

Starker, S. (1988). Psychologists and self-help books: Attitudes and prescriptive practices of clinicians. *American Journal of Psychotherapy, 42,* 448–455.

Steele, C., & Aronson, J. (1995). Stereotype threat and the intellectual test performance of African Americans. *Journal of Personality and Social Psychology, 69,* 797–812.

Steele, C., & Josephs, R. A. (1990). Alcohol Myopia: Its prized and dangerous effects. *American Psychologist, 45,* 921–933.

Steele, C. M. (1997). A threat in the air: How stereotypes shape intellectual identity and performance. *American Psychologist, 52,* 613–629.

Steele, C. M., Critchlow, B., & Liu, T. J. (1985). Alcohol and Social Behavior II: The Helpful Drunkard. *Journal of Personality and Social Psychology, 48,* 35–46.

Steele, C. M., & Southwick, L. (1985). Alcohol and Social Behavior I: The Psychology of Drunken Excess. *Journal of Personality and Social Psychology, 48,* 18–34.

Steele, R. L. (1992). Dying, death, and bereavement among the Maya Indians of Mesoamerica: A study in antropological psychology. In L. A. Platt & V. R. Persico, Jr. (Eds.), *Grief in cross-cultural perspective: A casebook* (pp. 399–424). New York: Garland.

Steinberg, M. (1994). Systematizing dissociation: Symptomatology and diagnostic assessment. In D. Spiegel (Ed.), *Dissociation: Culture, mind, and body* (pp. 59–90). Washington, DC: American Psychiatric Press.

Steketee, G., & White, K. (1990). When Once Is Not Enough: Help for Obsessive-Compulsives. Oakland, CA: New Harbinger Publications, Inc.

Stelmack, R. M. (1990). Biological bases of extraversion: Psychophysiological evidence. *Journal of Personality, 58,* 293–311.

Stephan, W. G., Stephan, C. W., & de Vargas, M. C. (1996). Emotional expression in Costa Rica and the United States. *Journal of Cross-Cultural Psychology, 27,* 147–160.

Sterling-Smith, R. S. (1976). A special study of drivers most responsible in fatal accidents. Summary for Management Report, Contract DOT HS 310-3-595. Washington, DC: Department of Transportation.

Sternbach, R. A. (1978). Psychological dimensions and perceptual analyses, including pathologies of pain. In E. C. Carterette & M. P. Friedman (Eds.), *Handbook of perception* (pp. 231–261). New York: Academic Press.

Sternberg, R. J. (1985). *Beyond IQ: A triarchic theory of human intelligence.* Cambridge: Cambridge University Press.

Sternberg, R. J. (1986a). A triangular theory of love. *Psychological Review, 93,* 119–135.

Sternberg, R. J. (1986b). *What is intelligence?* Norwood, NJ: Ablex.

Sternberg, R. J. (1988a). *The triangle of love.* New York: Basic Books.

Sternberg, R. J. (1988b). *The triarchic mind: A new theory of human intelligence.* New York: Viking.

Sternberg, R. J. (1990). *Metaphors of mind: Conceptions of the nature of intelligence.* New York: Cambridge University Press.

Sternberg, R. J. (1997). Educating intelligence: Infusing the triarchic theory into school instruction. In R. J. Sternberg & E. L. Grigorenko (Eds.), *Intelligence, heredity, and environment* (pp. 343–362). New York: Cambridge University Press.

Sternberg, R. J., & Detterman, D. K. (Eds.). (1986). *What is intelligence? Contemporary viewpoints on its nature and definition.* Norwood, NJ: Ablex.

Sternberg, R. J., & Wagner, R. K. (1993). The g-ocentric view of intelligence and job performance is wrong. *Current Directions in Psychological Science, 2,* 1–5.

Sternberg, R. J., Wagner, R. K., & Okagaki, L. (1993). Practical intelligence: The nature and role of tacit knowledge in work. In J. M. Puckett, H. W. Reese, et al. (Eds.), *Mechanisms of everyday cognition.* Hillsdale, NJ: Erlbaum.

Stevens, L. E., & Fiske, S. T. (1995). Motivation and cognition in social life: A social survival perspective. *Social Cognition, 13,* 189–214.

Stickgold, R., Rittenhouse, C. D., & Hobson, J. A. (1994). Dream splicing: A new technique for assessing thematic coherence in subjective reports of mental activity. *Consciousness & Cognition: An International Journal, 3,* 114–128.

Stoel-Gammon, C., & Otomo, K. (1986). Babbling development of hearing-impaired and normally hearing subjects. *Journal of Speech and Hearing Disorders, 51,* 33–41.

Stokes, J. P., Damon, W., & McKirnan, D. J. (1997). Predictors of movement toward homosexuality: A longitudinal study of bisexual men. *Journal of Sex Research, 34,* 304–312.

Stone, A. A., Nele, J. M., Cox, D. S., Napoli, A., Valdimarsdottir, H., & Kennedy-Morre, E. (1994). Daily events are associated with a secretory immune response to an oral antigen in men. *Health Psychology, 13,* 440–446.

Stone, J., Cooper, J., Wiegand, A. W., & Aronson, E. (1997). When Exemplification Fails: Hypocrisy and the Motive for Self-Integrity. *Journal of Personality and Social Psychology, 72,* 54–65.

Stone, J., Lynch, C. I., Sjomeling, M., & Darley, J. M. (1999). Stereotype threat effects on black and white athletic performance. *Journal of Personality and Social Psychology, 77,* 1213–1227.

Stoolmiller, M. (1999). Implications of the restricted range of family environments for estimates of heritability and nonshared environment in behavior-genetic adoption studies. *Psychological Bulletin, 125,* 392–409.

Strack, F., Martin, L. L., & Stepper, S. (1988). Inhibiting and facilitating conditions of the human smile: A nonobtrusive test of the facial feedback hypothesis. *Journal of Personality & Social Psychology, 54,* 768–777.

Strakowski, S. M., Lonczak, H. S., Sax, K. W., West, S. A., Crist, R. M., & Thienhaus, O. J. (1995). The effects of race on diagbosis and disposition from a psychiatric emergency service. *Journal of Clinical Psychiatry, 56,* 101–107.

Strakowski, S. M., Shelton, R. C., & Kolbrener, M. L. (1993). The effects of race and comorbidity on clinical diagnosis in patients with psychosis. *Journal of Clinical Psychiatry, 54,* 96–102.

Straus, M. A. (1980). Social stress and marital violence in a national sample of American families. *Annals of the New York Academy of Sciences, 347,* 229–250.

Straus, M. A., & Gelles, R. J. (1980). *Behind closed dorrs: Violence in the American family.* New York: Anchor/Doubleday.

Straus, M. A., & McCord, J. (1998). Do physically punished children become violent adults? In S. Nolen-Hoeksema (Ed.). *Clashing views on abnormal psychology: A Taking Sides custom reader.* (pp. 130–155). Guilford, CT: Dushkin/Mcgraw-Hill (1998) xi, 272 pp.

Streiker, L. D. (1984). Mind-Bending: Brainwashing, Cults, and Deprogramming in the '80s. Garden City, New York: Doubleday.

Streissguth, A. P., Barr, H. M., Bookstein, F. L., Sampson, P. D., & Olson, H. C. (1999). The long-term neurocognitive consequences of prenatal alcohol exposure: A 14-year study. *Psychological Science, 10,* 186–190.

Streissguth, A. P., Barr, H. M., Sampson, P. D., Darby, B. L., & Martin, D. C. (1989). IQ at age 4 in relation to maternal alcohol use and smoking during pregnancy. *Developmental Psychology, 25,* 3–11.

Stricker, E. M., Swerdloff, A. F., & Zigmond, M. J. (1978). Intrahypothalamic injections of kainic acid produce feeding and drinking deficits in rats. *Brain Research, 158,* 470–473.

Stricker, G. (1993). The current status of psychotherapy integration. In *Comprehensive Handbook of Psychotherapy Integration.* pp. 533–545. G. Stricker & J. R. Gold (Eds.), New York: Plenum Press.

Striegel-Moore, R. H. (1993). Etiology of binge eating: A developmental perspective. In *Binge Eating: Nature, Assessment, and Treatment.* In C. G. Fairburn & G. T. Wilson (Eds.), New York: Guilford Press. 144–172.

Strober, M. (1995). Family-genetic perspective on anorexia nervosa and bulimia nervosa. In C. G. Fairburn & K. Brownell (eds.), *Comprehensive textbook of eating disorders and obesity* (pp. 212–218). New York: Guilford Press.

Strom, S. (2000, January 4). Tradition of equality fading in new Japan. *New York Times.*

Stromswold, K., Caplan, D., Alpert, N., & Rauch, S. (1996). Localization of syntactic comprehension by positron emission tomography. *Brain and Language, 52,* 452–473.

Stroop, J. R. (1935). Studies of interference in serial verbal reactions. *Journal of Experimental Psychology, 28,* 643–662.

Strupp, J. J., & Binder, J. L. (1984). *Psychotherapy in a new key: A guide to time-limited dynamic psychotherapy.* New York: Basic Books.

Stunkard, A. J. (1982). Anorectic agents lower a body weight set point. *Life Science, 30,* 2043–2055.

Stuss, D. T., Alexander, M. P., Palumbo, C. L., Buckle, L., et al. (1994). Organizational strategies with unilateral or bilateral frontal lobe injury in word learning tasks. *Neuropsychology, 8,* 355–373.

Suarez, E., & Williams, R. (1989). Situational determinants of cardiovascular and emotional reactivity in high and low hostile men. *Psychosomatic Medicine, 51,* 404–?.

Suarez, E. C., Kuhn, C. M., Schanberg, S. M., Williams, R. B., Jr., & Zimmermann, E. A. (1998). Neuroendocrine, cardiovascular, and emotional responses of hostile men: The role of interpersonal challenge. *Psychosomatic Medicine, 60,* 78–88.

Subrahmanyam, K., & Greenfield, P. M. (1994). Effect of video game practice on spatial skills in girls and boys [Special issue]. *Journal of Applied Developmental Psychology, 15,* 13–32.

Sue, S., Zane, N., & Young, K. (1994). Research on psychotherapy with culturally diverse populations. In A. E. Bergin & S. L. Garfield (Eds.), *Handbook of psychotherapy and behavior change, 4th edition* (pp. 783–820). New York: John Wiley & Sons.

Suga, N. (1990). Biosonar and neural computation in bats. *Scientific American, 262,* 60–68.

Sullins, E. S. (1991). Emotional contagion revisited: Effects of social comparison and expressive style on mood convergence. *Personality & Social Psychology Bulletin, 17*(2), 166–174.

Sullivan, H. S. (1953). *The interpersonal theory of psychiatry.* New York: Norton.

Sullivan, L. (1999). Looking at vision: Reflections on the role of religious vision in the project of visual truth. In M. Zyniewicz (Ed.), *The papers of the Henry Luce III fellows in theology, Vol. 3* (pp. 115–140). Atlanta: Scholars Press.

Sullivan, R. (1999, June). Dad again. *Life,* pp. 66–68.

Sulloway, F. J. (1996). *Born to rebel: Birth order, family dynamics, and creative lives.* New York, NY: Pantheon Books.

Sulloway, F. J. (1997). *Born to Rebel: Birth Order, Family Dynamics, and Creative Lives.* New York: Vintage.

Sulloway, F. J. (1998). Sensationalism as scientific radicalism: A reply to Judith Harris. *www.edge.org*

Suzuki, L. A., & Valencia, R. R. (1997). Race-ethnicity and measured intelligence: Educational implications. *American Psychologist, 52,* 1103–1114.

Svanborg, P., Gustavsson, J. P., & Weinryb, R. M. (1999). What patient characteristics make therapists recommend psychodynamic psychotherapy or other treatment forms? *Acta Psychiatrica Scandinavica, 99,* 87–94.

Svartberg, M., & Stiles, T. C. (1991). Comparative effects of short-term psychodynamic psychotherapy: A meta-analysis. *Journal of Consulting & Clinical Psychology, 59,* 704–714.

Swica, Y., Lewis, D. O., & Lewis, M. (1996). Child Abuse and Dissociative Identity Disorder/Multiple Personality Disorder: The Documentation of Childhood Maltreatment and the Corroboration of Symptoms. *Child & Adolescent Psychiatric Clinics of North America, 5,* 431–447.

Syvalathi, E. K. G. (1994). Biological factors in schizophrenia: Structural and functional aspects. *British Journal of Psychiatry, 164* (Suppl. 23), 9–14.

Szasz, T. S. (1961). *The myth of mental illness: Foundations of a theory of personal conduct.* New York: Hoeber-Harper.

Tafarodi, R. W., & Swann, W. B., Jr. (1996). Individualism-collectivism and global self-esteem: Evidence for a cultural trade-off. *Journal of Cross-Cultural Psychology, 27,* 651–672.

Takahashi, Y. (1990). Is multiple personality disorder really rare in Japan? *Dissociation, 3,* 57–59.

Tang, Y.-P., Shimizu, E., Dube, G. R., Rampon, C., Kerchner, G. A., Zhuo, M., Liu, G., & Tsien, J. Z. (1999). Genetic enhancement of learning and memory in mice. *Nature, 401,* 63–69.

Tanner, J. M. (1990). *Foetus into man* (2nd ed.). Cambridge, MA: Harvard University Press.

Taris, T. W. (2000). Dispositional need for cognitive closure and self-enhancing beliefs. *Journal of Social Psychology, 140,* 35–50.

Tarter, R. E., Jones, B. M., Simpson, C. D., & Vega, A. (1971). Effects of task complexity and practice on performance during acute alcohol intoxication. *Perceptual & Motor Skills, 33,* 307–318.

Tavris, C. (1991). The mismeasure of woman: Paradoxes and perspective in the study of gender. In J. D. Goodchilds (Ed.), *Psychological perspectives on human diversity in America* (pp. 89–136). Washington, DC: American Psychological Association.

Taylor, S. (1996). Meta-analysis of cognitive-behavioral treatment for social phobia. *Journal of Behavior Therapy & Experimental Psychiatry, 27,* 1–9.

Taylor, S. W., Repetti, R. L., & Seeman, T. (1997). Health psychology: What is an unhealthy environment and how does it get under the skin? *Annual Review of Psychology, 48,* 411–447.

Tecott, L. H., Sun, L. M., Akana, S. F., Strack, A. M., Lowenstein, D. H., Dallman, M. F., & Julius, D. (1995). Eating disorder and epilepsy in mice lacking 5-HT2C serotonin receptors. *Nature, 374,* 542–546.

Tedlock, B. (1992). The role of dreams and visionary narratives in Mayan cultural survival. *Ethos, 20,* 453–476.

Tein, J. Y., Sandler, I. N., & Zautra, A. J. (2000). Stressful life events, psychological distress, coping, and parenting of divorced mothers: A longitudinal study. *Journal of Family Psychology, 14,* 27–41.

Teitelbaum, P., & Stellar, E. (1954). Recovery from the failure to eat produced by hypothalamic lesions. *Science, 120,* 894–895.

Telch, M. J., Lucas, J. A., & Nelson, P. (1989). Nonclinical panic in college students: An investigation of prevalence and symptomatology. *Journal of Abnormal Psychology, 98,* 300–306.

Teri, L., & Lewinsohn, P. M. (1985). Group intervention for unipolar depression. *Behavior Therapist, 8,* 109–111, 123.

Terrace, H. S. (1979, November). How Nim Chimpsky changed my mind. *Psychology Today,* 23–28.

Terrace, H. S., Pettito, L. A., & Bever, T. G. (1976). *Project Nim, progress report I.* New York: Columbia University Press.

Terry, D. J., & Hogg, M. A. (1996). Group norms and the attitude-behavior relationship: A role for group identification. *Personality & Social Psychology Bulletin, 22,* 776–793.

Tesser, A. (1993). The importance of heritability of psychological research: the case of attitudes. *Psychological Review, 100,* 129–142.

Tew, J. D., Jr., Mulsant, B. H., Haskett, R. F., Prudic, J., Thase, M. E., Crowe, R. R., Dolata, D., Begley, A. E., Reynolds, C. F., III, & Sackheim, H. A. (1999). Acute efficacy of ECT in the treatment of major depression in the old-old. *American Journal of Psychiatry, 156,* 1865–1870.

Thase, M. E., Greenhouse, J. B., Frank, E., Reynolds, C. F., III, Pilkonis, P. A., Hurley, K., Grochocinski, V., & Kupfer, D. J. (1997). Treatment of major depression with psychotherapy or psychotherapy-pharmacotherapy combinations. *Archives of General Psychiatry, 54,* 1009–1015.

Thatcher, R. W. (1994). Cyclic cortical reorganization: Origins of human cognitive development. In G. Dawson & K. W. Fischer (Eds.), *Human behavior and the developing brain* (pp. 232–266). New York: Guilford.

Thelen, E. (1995). Motor development: A new synthesis. *American Psychologist, 50,* 79–95.

Thelen, E., & Ulrich, B. D. (1991). Hidden skills: A dynamic systems analysis of treadmill stepping during the first year. *Monographs of the Society for Research in Child Development, 56 (1, Serial No. 223).*

Thomas, A., & Chess, S. (1996). *Temperament: Theory and practice*. New York: Brunner/Mazel.

Thompson, P. M., Giedd, J. N., Woods, R. P., MacDonald, D., Evans, A. C., & Toga, A. W. (2000). Growth patterns in the developing brain detected by using continuum mechanical tensor maps. *Nature, 404*, 190–193.

Thompson, R. F. (1993). *The brain, a neuroscience primer* (2nd ed.). New York: Freeman.

Thompson, R. F., & Krupa, D. J. (1994). Organization of memory traces in the mammalian brain. *Annual Review of Neuroscience, 17*, 519–549.

Thompson, W. L., & Kosslyn, S. M. (2000). Neural systems activated during visual mental imagery: A review and meta-analyses. In A. W. Toga & J. C. Mazziotta (Eds.), *Brain mapping: The systems*. San Diego, CA: Academic Press.

Thorn, B. L., & Gilbert, L. A. (1998). Antecedents of work and family role expectations of college men. *Journal of Family Psychology, 12*, 259–267.

Thorndike, E. L. (1927). The law of effect. *American Journal of Psychology, 39*, 212–222.

Thorndike, E. L. (1933). A proof of the law of effect. *Science, 77*, 173–175.

Thorndike, E. L. (1949). The law of effect. in E. L. Thorndike, *Selected writings from a connectionist's psychology* (pp. 13–26). New York: Appleton-Century-Crofts. (Original work published 1933).

Thorndike, R. L., Hagen, E. P., & Sattler, J. M. (1986). *Stanford-Binet Intelligence Scale* (4th ed.). Itasca, IL: Riverside.

Thornhill, R., & Gangestad, S. W. (1993). Human facial beauty: Averageness, symmetry, and parasite resistance. *Human Nature, 4*, 237–269.

Thurstone, L. L. (1938). *Primary mental abilities*. Chicago: University of Chicago Press.

Thurstone, L. L., & Thurstone, T. G. (1941). *Factorial studies of intelligence*. Chicago: University of Chicago Press.

Tidwell, M. O., Reis, H. T., & Shaver, P. R. (1996). Attachment, attractiveness, and social interaction: A diary study. *Journal of Personality & Social Psychology, 71*, 729–745.

Tiernari, P. (1991). Interaction between genetic vulnerability and family environment: The Finnish adoptive family study of schizophrenia. *Acta Psychiatrica Scandinavica, 84*, 460–465.

Till, B. D., & Priluck, R. L. (2000). Stimulus generalization in classical conditioning: An initial investigation and extension. *Psychology & Marketing, 17*, 55–72.

Timmerman, I. G. H., Emmelkamp, P. M. G., & Sanderman, R. (1998). The effects of a stress-management training program in individuals at risk in the community at large. *Behaviour Research & Therapy, 36*, 863–875.

Tingey, H., Kiger, G., & Riley, P. J. (1996). Juggling multiple roles: Perceptions of working mothers. *Social Science Journal, 33*, 183–191.

Tinker, J. E., & Tucker, J. A. (1997). Motivations for weight loss and behavior change strategies associated with natural recovery from obesity. *Psychology of Addictive Behaviors, 11*, 98–106.

Tohen, M., & Grundy, S. (1999). Management of acute mania. *Journal of Clinical Psychology, 60*(Supplement 5), 31–34.

Tolman, E. C., & Honzik, C. H. (1930b). Degrees of hunger, reward and non-reward, and maze learning in rats. *University of California Publications in Psychology, 4*, 241–256.

Tolman, E. C., & Honzik, C. H. (1930c). Introduction and removal of reward, and maze performance in rats. *Univeristy of California Publications in Psychology, 4*, 257–275.

Tomkins, S. S. (1962). *Affect, imagery, consciousness, Vol I. The positive affects*. New York: Springer-Verlag.

Tootell, R. B. H., Mendola, J. D., Hadjikhani, N. K., Ledden, P. J., Liu, A. K., Reppas, J. B., Serano, M. I., & Dale, A. M. (1997). Functional analysis of V3A and related areas in human visual cortex. *The Journal of Neuroscience, 17*, 7060–7078.

Tootell, R. B. H., Silverman, M. S., Switkes, E., & DeValois, R. L. (1982). Deoxyglucose analysis of retinotopic organization in primate striate cortex. *Science, 218*, 902–904.

Torgersen, S. G. (1983). Genetic factors in anxiety disorders. *Archives of General Psychiatry, 40*, 1085–1089.

Torrance, E. P. (1980). Creativity and style of learning and thinking characteristics of adaptors and innovators. *Creative Child and Adult Quarterly, 5*, 80–85.

Trafimow, D., & Finlay, K. (1996). The importance of subjective norms for a minority of people: Between-subjects and with-subjects analyses. *Personality and Social Psychology Bulletin, 22*, 820–828.

Treisman, A. M. (1964a). Monitoring and storage of irrelevant messages in selective attention. *Journal of Verbal Learning and Verbal Behavior, 3*, 449–459.

Treisman, A. M. (1964b). Selective attention in man. *British Medical Bulletin, 20*, 12–16.

Treisman, A. M., & Gormican, S. (1988). Feature analysis in early vision: Evidence from search asymmetries. *Psychological Review, 95*, 15–48.

Treisman, A. M., & Schmidt, H. (1982). Illusory conjunctions in the perception of objects. *Cognitive Psychology, 14*, 107–141.

Treisman, A. M., & Souther, J. (1985). Search asymmetry: A diagnostic for preattentive processing of separable features. *Journal of Experimental Psychology: General, 114*, 285–310.

Trevethan, S. D., & Walker, L. J. (1989). Hypothetical versus real-life moral reasoning among psychopathic and delinquent youth. *Development and Psychopathology, 1*, 91–103.

Triandis, H. C., Bontempo, R. Villareal, M. J., Asai, M., & Lucca, N. (1988). Individualism and collectivism: Cross-cultural perspectives on self-ingroup relationships. *Journal of Prsonality and Social Psychology, 54*, 323–338.

Triandis, H. C., McCusker, C., & Hui, C. H. (1990). Multimethod probes of individualism and collectivism. *Journal of Personality and Social Psychology, 59*, 1006–1020.

Trimpop, R., & Kirkcaldy, B. (1997). Personality predictors of driving accidents. *Personality & Individual Differences, 23*, 147–152.

Trivedi, N., & Sabini, J. (1998). Volunteer bias, sexuality, and personality. *Archives of Sexual Behavior, 27*, 181–195.

Trivers, R. (1972). Parental investment and sexual selection. In B. Campbell (Ed.), *Sexual selection and the descent of man, 1871–1971* (pp. 136–179). Chicago: Aldine.

Trivers, R. (1985). *Social evolution*. Menlo Park, CA: Benjamin/Cummings.

True, W. R., Rice, J., Eisen, S. A., Heath, A. C., Phil, D., Goldberg, J., Lyons, M., & Nowak, J. (1993). A twin study of genetic and environmental contributions to liability for posttraumatic stress symptoms. *Archives of General Psychiatry, 50*, 257–264.

Tsien, J. Z., Chen, D. F., Gerber, D., Tom, C., Mercer, E. H., Anderson, D. J., Mayford, M., Kandel, E. R., & Tonegawa, S. (1996). Subregion- and cell type-restricted gene knockout in mouse brain. *Cell, 87*, 1317–1326.

Tucker, G. J. (1998). Putting DSM–IV in Perspective. *Am J Psychiatry 155*:2, February 1998, pp. 159–161.

Turkheimer, E., & Waldron, M. (2000). Nonshared environment: A theoretical, methodological, and quantitative review. *Psychological Bulletin, 126*, 78–108.

Turner, A. M., & Greenough, W. T. (1985). Differential rearing effects on rat visual cortex synapses. I. Synaptic and neuronal density and synapses per neuron. *Brain Research, 329*, 195–203.

Turvey, M. T. (1990). Coordination. *American Psychologist, 4*, 938–953.

Tversky, A., & Kahneman, D. (1974). Judgment under uncertainty: Heuristics and biases. *Science, 185*, 1124–1131.

Twisk, J. W. R., Snel, J., Kemper, H. C. G., & van Mechelen, W. (1999). Changes in daily hassles and life events and the relationship with coronary heart disease risk factors: A 2-year longitudinal study in 27–29-yr-old males and females. *Journal of Psychosomatic Research, 46*, 229–240.

Ubell, E. (1995). New devices can help you hear. *Parade Magazine*, Jan. 15, pp. 14–15.

Ullman, S. (1996). *High-level vision*. Cambridge: MIT Press.

Ulrich, R. E., Stachnik, T. J., & Stainton, N. R. (1963). Student acceptance of generalized personality interpretations. *Psychological Reports, 13*, 831–834.

Ungerleider, L. G. (1995). Functional brain imaging studies of cortical mechanisms for memory. *Science, 270*, 769–775.

Ungerleider, L. G., & Haxby, J. V. (1994). "What" and "where" in the human brain. *Current Opinion in Neurology, 4*, 157–165.

Ungerleider, L. G., & Mishkin, M. (1982). Two cortical visual systems. In D. J. Ingle, M. A. Goodale, & R. J. W. Mansfield (Eds.), *Analysis of visual behavior* (pp. 549–586). Cambridge, MA: MIT Press.

Vaillant, G. (1977). *Adaptation to life*. Boston: Little, Brown.

Vajk, F. C., Craighead, W. E., Craighead, L. W., & Holley, C. (1997). Risk of major depression as a function of response styles to depressed mood. Poster presented at the annual meeting of the Association for the Advancement of Behavior Therapy, November, Miami Beach, FL.

Valins, S. (1966). Cognitive effects of false heart-rate feedback. *Journal of Personality & Social Psychology, 4,* 400–408.

van Balkom, A. J. L. M., van Oppen, P., Vermeulen, A. W. A., Nauta, N. C. E., Vorst, H. C. M., & van Dyck, R. (1994). A meta-analysis on the treatment of obsessive-compulsive disorder: A comparison of antidepressants, behaviour and cognitive therapy. *Clinical Psychology Review, 14,* 359–381.

Van Goozen, S. H. M., Cohen-Kettenis, P. T., Gooren, J. J. G., Frijda, N. H., & Van De Poll, N. E. (1995). Gender differences in behaviour: Activating effects of cross-sex hormones. *Psychoneuroendocrinology, 20,* 343–363.

Van Goozen, S. H., Wiegant, V. M., Endert, E., Helmond, F. A., & Van de Poll, N. E. (1997). Psychoendocrinological assessment of the menstrual cycle: The relationship between hormones, sexuality, and mood. *Archives of Sexual Behavior, 26,* 359–382.

Vandello, J. A., & Cohen, D. (1999). Patterns of individualism and collectivism across the United States. *Journal of Personality and Social Psychology, 77,* 279–292.

Varma, A. (2000). Impact of watching international television programs on adolescents in India. *Journal of Comparative Family Studies, 31,* 117–126.

Vasterling, J., Jenkins, R. A., Tope, D. M., & Burish, T. G. (1993). Cognitive distraction and relaxation training for the control of side effects due to cancer chemotherapy. *Journal of Behavioral Medicine, 16,* 65–80.

Vaughn, C., & Leff, J. (1976). The measurement of expressed emotion in the families of psychiatric patients. *British Journal of Social and Clinical Psychology, 15,* 1069–1177.

Vehmanen, L., Kaprio, J., & Loennqvist, J. (1995). Twin studies on concordance for bipolar disorder. *Psychiatria Fennica, 26,* 107–116.

Velakoulis, D., Pantelis, C., McGorry, P. D., Dudgeon, P., Brewer, W., Cook, M., Desmond, P., Bridle, N., Tierney, P., Murrie, V., Singh, B., & Copolov, D. (1999). Hippocampal Volume in First-Episode Psychoses and Chronic Schizophrenia: A High-Resolution Magnetic Resonance Imaging Study. *Archives of General Psychiatry, 56,* 133–140.

Ventura, J., Nuechterlein, K. H., Lukoff, D., & Hardesty, J. P. (1989). A prospective study of stressful life events and schizophrenic relapse. *Journal of Abnormal Psychology, 98,* 407–411.

Verhaeghen, P., Marcoen, A., & Goosens, L. (1992). Improving memory performance in the aged through mnemonic training: A meta-analytic study. *Psychology and Aging, 7,* 242–251.

Vernon, P. A., Jang, K. L., Harris, J. A., & McCarthy, J. M. (1997). Environmental Predictors of Personality Differences: A Twin and Sibling Study. *Journal of Personality and Social Psychology, 72,* 177–183.

Vieweg, R., & Shawcross, C. R. (1998). A trial to determine any difference between two and three times a week ECT in the rate of recovery from depression. *Journal of Mental Health (UK), 7,* 403–409.

Vincent, K. R. (1991). Black/White IQ differences: Does age make the difference? *Journal of Clinical Psychology, 47,* 266–270.

Viney, W. (1993). *A history of psychology: Ideas and context.* Needham Heights, MA: Allyn & Bacon.

Vogel, G. (1996). School achievement: Asia and Europe top in the world, but reasons are hard to find. *Science, 274,* 1296.

Vogel, G. (1997). Cocaine wreaks subtle damage on developing brains. *Science, 278,* 38–39.

von der Heydt, R., & Peterhans, E. (1989). Mechanisms of contour perception in monkey visual cortex. I. Lines of pattern discontinuity. *Journal of Neuroscience, 9,* 1731–1748.

von der Heydt, R., Peterhans, E., & Baumgartner, G. (1984). Illusory contours and cortical neuron responses. *Science, 224,* 1260–1262.

Vonk, R., & van Knippenberg, A. (1995). Processing attitude statements from in-group and out-group members: Effects of within-group and within-person inconsistencies on reading times. *Journal of Personality and Social Psychology, 68,* 215–227.

Voth, H. M., & Orth, M. H. (1973). *Psychotherapy and the role of the environment.* New York: Behavioral Press.

Voudouris, N. J., Peck, C. L., & Coleman, G. (1985). Conditioned Placebo Responses. *Journal of Personality and Social Psychology, 48,* 47–53.

Vrana, S. R., & Lang, P. J. (1990). Fear imagery and the startle-probe reflex. *Journal of Abnormal Psychology, 99,* 181–189.

Vrana, S. R., Spence, E. L., & Lang, P. J. (1988). The startle probe response: A new measure of emotion? *Journal of Abnormal Psychology, 97,* 487–491.

Vurpillot, E. (1968). The development of scanning strategies and their relation to visual differentiation. *Journal of Experimental Child Psychology, 6,* 632–650.

Vygotsky, L. S. (1962). On inner speech. In E. Hanfman & G. Vakar (Eds. and Trans.), *Thought and language* (pp. 130–138). Cambridge, MA: MIT Press.

Vygotsky, L. S. (1978). *Mind in society: The development of higher mental processes.* Cambridge, MA: Harvard University Press. (Original works published 1930, 1933, and 1935).

Vygotsky, L. S. (1986). (A. Kozulin, Trans.). *Thought and language.* Cambridge, MA: MIT Press (originally published 1934).

Vygotsky, L. S. (1988). On inner speech. In M. B. Franklin & S. S. Barten (Eds.), *Child language: A reader* (pp. 181–187). New York: Oxford University Press.

Wade, T., Martin, N. G., & Tiggemann, M. (1998). Genetic and environmental risk factors for the weight and shape concerns characteristic of bulimia nervosa. *Psychological Medicine, 28,* 761–771.

Wagner, A. D., Schacter, D. L., Rotte, M., Koutstaal, W., Maril, A., Dale, A. M., Rose, B. R., & Buckner, R. L. (1998). Building memories: Remembering and forgetting of verbal experiences as predicted by brain activity. *Science, 281,* 1188–1191.

Wagner, R. K. (1997). Intelligence, training, and employment. *American Psychologist, 52,* 1059–1069.

Wahba, M. A., & Bridwell, L. G. (1976). Maslow reconsidered: A review of research on the need hierarchy theory. *Organizational Behavior & Human Decision Processes, 15,* 212–240.

Wahba, M. A., & Bridwell, L. G. (1976). Maslow reconsidered: A review of research on the need hierarchy theory. *Organizational Behavior and Human Performance, 15,* 212–240.

Walker, E. F., & Diforio, D. (1997). Schizophrenia: A neural diathesis-stress model. *Psychological Review, 104,* 667–685.

Walker, E. F., Grimes, K. E., Davis, D., & Smith, A. (1993). Childhood precursors of schizophrenia: Facial expressions of emotion. *American Journal of Psychiatry, 150,* 1654–1660.

Walker, E. F., Logan, C. B., & Walder, D. (1999). Inidcators of neurodevelopmental abnormality in schizotypcal personality disorder. *Psychiatric Annals, 29,* 132–136.

Walker, E. F., Savoie, T., & Davis, D. (1994). Neuromotor precursors of schizophrenia. *Schizophrenia Bulletin, 148,* 661–666.

Walker, L. J. (1995). Sexism in Kohlberg's moral psychology? In W. M. Kurtines & J. L. Gewirtz (Eds.), *Moral development: An introduction* (pp. 83–107). Boston: Allyn & Bacon.

Waller, N. G., Kojetin, B. A., Bouchard, T. J., Jr, Lykken, D. T., & Tellegen, A. (1990). Genetic and environmental influences on religious interests, attitudes, and values: A study of twins reared apart and together. *Psychological Science, 1,* 138–142.

Waller, N. G., & Shaver, P. R. (1994). The importance of non-genetic influences on romantic love styles: A twin family study. *Psychological Science, 5,* 268–274.

Walsh, B. T. (1993). Binge eating in bulimia nervosa. In *Binge Eating: Nature, Assessment, and Treatment.* In C. G. Fairburn & G. T. Wilson (Eds.), New York: Guilford Press. 37–49.

Walster, E., Walster, G. W., & Berscheid, E. (1978). *Equity: Theory and research.* Needham Heights, MA: Allyn & Bacon.

Walters, J., & Gardner, H. (1985). The development and education of intelligences. In F. Link (Ed.), *Essays on the intellect* (pp. 1–21). Washington, DC: Curriculum Development Association/Association for Supervision and Curriculum Development.

Wark, G. R., & Krebs, D. L. (1996). Gender and dilemma differences in real-life moral judgment. *Developmental Psychology, 32,* 220–230.

Warren, R. M., & Warren, R. P. (1970). Auditory illusions and confusions. *Scientific American, 223,* 30–36.

Warrington, E. K., & McCarthy, R. (1987). Categories of knowledge: Further fractionation and an attempted integration. *Brain, 110,* 1273–1296.

Warrington, E. K., & McCarthy, R. A. (1988). The fractionation of retrograde amnesia. *Brain and Cognition, 7,* 184–200.

Warrington, E. K., & Shallice, T. (1984). Category-specific semantic impairments. *Brain, 107,* 829–854.

Washburne, C. (1956). Alcohol, self and the group. *Quarterly Journal of Studies on Alcohol, 17,* 108–123.

Wason, P. C., & Johnson-Laird, P. N. (1972). *Psychology of Reasoning: Structure and content.* Cambridge, MA: Harvard University Press.

Watson, D., & Hubbard, B. (1996). Adaptation style and dispositional structure: Coping in the context of the five-factor model. *Journal of Personality, 64,* 737–774.

Watson, J., & Raynor, R. (1920). Conditioned emotional reactions. *Journal of Experimental Psychology, 3,* 1–14.

Watson, J. B. (1913). Psychology as a behaviorist views it. *Psychological Review, 20,* 158–177.

Watson, M., Greer, S., Rowden, L., Gorman, C., Robertson, B., Bliss, J. M., & Tunmore, R. (1991). Relationships between emotional control, adjustment to cancer, and depression and anxiety in breast cancer patients. *Psychological Medicine, 21,* 51–57.

Watt, C. A, & Morris, R. L. (1995). The relationship among performance on a prototype indicator of perceptual defence/vigilance, personality, and extrasensory perception. *Personality and Individual Differences, 19,* 635–648.

Wechsler, D. (1958). *The measurement and appraisal of adult intelligence* (5th ed.). Baltimore: Williams & Wilkins.

Wechsler, H., Dowdall, G. W., Maenner, G., Gledhill-Hoyt, J., & Lee, H. (1998). Changes in binge drinking and related problems among American college students between 1993 and 1997. *Journal of American College Health, 47,* 57–68.

Wechsler, H., Fulop, M., Padilla, A., Lee, H., & Patrick, K. (1997). Binge drinking among college students: A comparison of California with other states. *Journal of American College Health, 45,* 273–277.

Weerasinghe, J., & Tepperman, L. (1994). Suicide and happiness: Seven tests of the connection. *Social Indicators Research, 32,* 199–233.

Wegner, D. M., Schneider, D. J., Carter, S. R., & White, T. L. (1987). Paradoxical effects of thought suppression. *Journal of Personality & Social Psychology, 53,* 5–13.

Weinberg, R. A. (1989). Intelligence and IQ: Landmark issues and great debates. *American Psychologist, 44,* 98–104.

Weinberger, D. R., & Lipska, B. K. (1995). Cortical maldevelopment, anti-psychotic drugs, and schizophrenia: a search for common ground. *Schizophrenia Research, 16,* 87–110.

Weiner, B. (1980). A cognitive (attribution) emotion-action model of motivated behavior: An analysis of judgments of help-giving. *Journal of Personality and Social Psychology, 39,* 186–200.

Weiner, B., & Kukla, A. (1970). An attributional analysis of achievement motivation. *Journal of Personality & Social Psychology, 15,* 1–20.

Weingarten, H. P., Chang, P., & McDonald, T. J. (1985). Comparison of the metabolic and behavioral disturbances following paraventricular- and ventromedial-hypothalamic lesions. *Brain Research Bulletin, 14,* 551–559.

Weinstein, S. (1968). Intensive and extensive aspects of tactile sensitivity as a function of body part, sex, and laterality. In D. R. Kenshalo (Ed.), *The skin senses* (pp. 195–218). Springfield, IL: Thomas.

Weinstock, M. (1997). Does prenatal stress impair coping and regulation of hypothalamic-pituitary-adrenal axis? *Neuroscience & Biobehavioral Reviews, 21,* 1–10.

Weiskrantz, L. (1986). *Blindsight: A case study and implications.* New York: Oxford University Press.

Weisman, A. D., & Hackett, T. P. (1961). Predilection to death: Death and dying as a psychiatric problem. *Psychosomatic Medicine, 23,* 232–256.

Weiss, R. L., & Heyman, R. E. (1990). Observation of marital interaction. In F. D. Fincham & T. N. Bradbury (Eds.), *The psychology of marriage: Basic issues and applications* (pp. 87–117). New York: Guilford.

Weiss, R. S. (1986). Continuities and transformations in social relationships from childhood to adulthood. In W. W. Hartup and Z. Rubin (Eds.), *Relationships and development* (pp. 95–110). Hillsdale, NJ: Erlbaum.

Weissman, M. M., Bland, R. C., Canino, G. J., Greenwald, S., Hwu, H., Lee, C. K., Newman, S., Oakley-Brown, M. A., Rubio-Stipec, M.,

Wickramartne, P., Wittchen, H. U., & Yeh, E. K. (1994). The cross national epidemiology of obsessive compulsive disorder: The Cross National Collaborative Group. *Journal of Clinical Psychiatry, 55*(3, Suppl.), 5–10.

Weissman, M. M., Bruce, M. L., Leaf, P. J., Florio, L., & Holzer, C. (1991). Affective disorders. In L. N. Robins & D. A. Regier (Eds.), *Psychiatric disorders in America* (pp. 53–80). New York: The Free Press.

Wellen, J. M., Hogg, M. A., & Terry, D. J. (1998). Group norms and attitude-behavior consistency: The role of group salience and mood. *Group Dynamics: Theory, Research, and Practice, 2,* 48–56.

Wellman, H. M. (1990). *The child's theory of mind.* Cambridge, MA: Bradford/MIT Press.

Wender, P. H., Kety, S. S., Rosenthal, D., Schulsinger, F., Ortmann, J., & Luhde, I. (1986). Psychiatric disorders in the biological and adoptive families of adopted individuals with affective disorders. *Archives of General Psychiatry, 43,* 923–929.

Werner, C., Brown, B., & Altman, I. (1997). Environmental Psychology. In J. W. Berry, M. H. Segall, & C. Kagitçibasi (Eds.), Cross-Cultural Psychology, Volume 3: Social Behavior and Applications. 255–290

Wertheimer, M. (1923). Untersuchungen zur Lehre von der Gestalt, II. (Translated as Laws of organization in perceptual forms.). In W. D. Ellis (Ed.), *A source book of Gestalt psychology* (pp. 71–88). London: Routledge & Kegan Paul.

Westen, D. (1998). The scientific legacy of Sigmund Freud. Toward a psychodynamically informed psychological science. *Psychological Bulletin, 124,* 333–371.

Westen, D. (1999). The scientific status of unconscious processes: Is Freud really dead? *Journal of the American Psychoanalytic Association, 47,* Supplement, 1–45.

Whalen, P. J., Rauch, S. L., Etcoff, N. L., McInerney, S. C., Lee, M. B., & Jenike, M. A. (1998). Masked presentations of emotional facial expressions modulate amygdala activity without explicit knowledge. *Journal of Neuroscience, 18,* 411–418.

Wheeler, L., & Kim, Y. (1997). What is beautiful is culturally good: The physical attractiveness stereotype has different content in collectivistic cultures. *Personality and Social Psychology Bulletin, 23,* 795–800.

Wheeler, M. D. (1991). Physical changes of puberty. *Endocrinology and Metabolism Clinics of North America, 20,* 1–14.

White, A., & Hardy, L. (1995). Use of different imagery perspectives on the learning and performance of different motor skills. *British Journal of Psychology, 86*(2), 169–180.

White, J. M., & Ryan, C. F. (1996). Pharmacological properties of ketamine. *Drug & Alcohol Review, 15,* 145–155.

Whittal, M. L., Agras, W. S., & Gould, R. A. (1999). Bulimia nervosa: A meta-analysis of psychosocial and pharmacological treatments. *Behavior Therapy, 30,* 117–135.

Whorf, B. (1956). *Language, thought, and reality.* Cambridge, MA: MIT Press.

Wickramasekera, I., Davies, T. E., & Davies, S. M. (1996). Applied psychophysiology: A bridge between the biomedical model and the biopsychosocial model in family medicine. *Professional Psychology: Research & Practice, 27,* 221–233.

Wiggins, J. S. (1992). Have model, will travel. *Journal of Personality, 60,* 527–532.

Wiggins, J. S., & Pincus, A. L. (1992). Conceptions of personality disorders and dimensions of personality. *Psychological Assessment: Journal of Consulting and Clinical Psychology, 1,* 305–316.

Wilder, D. A., Simon, A. F., & Faith, M. (1996). Enhancing the impact of counterstereotypic information: Dispositional attributions for deviance. *Journal of Personality and Social Psychology, 71* 276–287.

Wilkinson, D. J. C., Thompson, J. M., Lambert, G. W., Jennings, G. L., Schwarz, R. G., Jefferys, D., Turner, A. G., & Esler, M. D. (1998). Sympathetic Activity in Patients With Panic Disorder at Rest, Under Laboratory Mental Stress, and During Panic Attacks. *Archives of General Psychiatry, 55,* 511–520.

Willer, J. C., Le, B. D., & De, B. T. (1990). Diffuse noxious inhibitory controls in man: Involvement of an opioidergic link. *European Journal of Pharmacology, 182,* 347–355.

Williams, J. E., Paton, C. C., I. C., Eigenbrodt, M. L., Nieto, F. J., & Tyroler, H. A. (2000). Anger proneness predicts coronary heart disease risk: Prospective analysis from the atherosclerosis risk in communities (ARIC) study. *Circulation, 101,* 2034–2039.

Williams, L. M. (1994). Recall of childhood trauma: A prospective study of women's memories of child sexual abuse. *Journal of Consulting and Clinical Psychology, 62*, 1167–1176.

Williams, R., Barefoot, J., Califf, R., Haney, T., Saunders, E., Pryor, D., Hlatky, M., Siefler, I., & Mark, D. (1992). Prognostic importance of social and economic resources among patients with angiographically documented coronary artery disease. *Journal of the American Medical Association, 267*, 520–?.

Williams, W. (1998). Are we raising smarter kids today? School-and-home-related influences on IQ. In U. Neisser (Ed.), *The rising curve: Long-terms gains in IQ and related measures* (pp. 125–154). Washington, DC: American Psychological Association.

Winer, G. A., & Cottrell, J. E. (1996). Does anything leave the eye when we see? Extramission beliefs of children and adults. *Current Directions in Psychological Science, 5*, 137–142.

Winer, G. A., Cottrell, J. E., Karefilaki, K. D., & Gregg, V. R. (1996). Images, words and questions: Variables that influence beliefs about vision in children and adults. *Journal of Experimental Child Psychology, 63*, 499–525.

Winner, E. (1996). *Gifted children: Myths and realities.* New York: Basic Books.

Winner, E. (1997). Exceptionally high intelligence and schooling. *American Psychologist, 52*, 1070–1081.

Winner, E. (2000). The origins and ends of giftedness. *American Psychologist, 55*, 159–169.

Winzelberg, A., & Humphreys, K. (1999). Should patients' religiosity influence clinicians' referral to 12-step self-help groups? Evidence from a study of 3,018 male substance abuse patients. *Journal of Consulting and Clinical Psychology, 67*, 790–794.

Wise, P. M., Krajnak, K. M., & Kashon, M. L. (1996). Menopause: The aging of multiple pacemakers. *Science, 273*, 67–70.

Wise, R. A. (1982). Neuroleptics and operant behavior: The anhedonia hypothesis. *Behavioral & Brain Sciences, 5*, 39–87.

Wise, R. A. (1996). Addictive drugs and brain stimulation reward. *Annual Review of Neuroscience, 19*, 319–340.

Witelson, S. F., Kigar, D. L., & Harvey, T. (1999). The exceptional brain of Albert Einstein. *Lancet, 353*, 2149–2153.

Witt, S. D. (1997). Parental influence on children's socialization to gender roles. *Adolescence, 32*, 253–259.

Wixted, J. T., & Ebbesen, E. B. (1991). On the form of forgetting. *Psychological Science, 2*, 409–415.

Wixted, J. T., & Ebbesen, E. B. (1997). Genuine power curves in forgetting: A quantitative analysis of individual subject forgetting functions. *Memory & Cognition, 25*, 731–739.

Wojciulik, E., Kanwisher, N., & Driver, J. (1998). Covert visual attention modulates face-specific activity in the human fusiform gyrus: An fMRI study. *Journal of Neurophysiology, 79*, 1574–1578.

Wolf, N. (1991). *The Beauty Myth.* New York: Anchor Books, Doubleday.

Wolfe, B. E., & Maser, J. D. (Eds.). (1994). *Treatment of panic disorder: A consensus development conference.* Washington, DC: American Psychiatric Press, Inc.

Wolpe, J. (1958). *Psychotherapy by reciprocal inhibition.* Stanford: Stanford University Press.

Woods, S. C., Schwartz, M. W., Baskin, D. G., & Seeley, R. J. (2000). Food intake and the regulation of body weight. *Annual Review of Psychology, 51*, 255–277.

Worthington, T. S. (1979). The use in court of hypnotically enhanced testimony. *International Journal of Clinical & Experimental Hypnosis, 27*, 402–416.

Wurtzel, E. (1995). *Prozac Nation: A Memoir.* New York: Riverhead Books.

Wyatt, R. J., Damiani, L. M., & Henter, I. D. (1998). First-episode schizophrenia: Early intervention and medication discontinuation in the context of course and treatment. *British Journal of Psychiatry, 172*, 77–83.

Wyatt, R. J., Green, M. F., & Tuma, A. H. (1997). Long-term morbidity associated with delayed treatment of first admission schizophrenic patients: A re-analysis of the Camarillo state hospital data. *Psychological Medicine, 27*, 261–268.

Wyer, N. A., Sherman, J. W., & Stroessner, S. J. (2000). The roles of motivation and ability in controlling the consequences of stereotype suppression. *Personality & Social Psychology Bulletin, 26*, 13–25.

Xerri, C., Merzenich, M. M., Jenkins, W., & Santucci, S. (1999). Representational plasticity in cortical area 3b paralleling tactual motor skill acquisition in adult monkeys. *Cerebral Cortex, 9*, 264–276.

Yagueez, L., Nagel, D., Hoffman, H., Canavan, A., Wist, E., & Hoemberg, V. (1998). A mental route to motor learning: Improving trajectoral kinematics through imagery training. *Behavioral and Brain Research, 90*, 95–106.

Yang, K., & Bond, M. H. (1990). Exploring implicit personliaty theories with indigenous or imported constructs: The Chinese case. *Journal of Personality and Social Psychology, 58*, 1087–1095.

Yazigi, R. A., Odem, R. R., & Polakoski, K. L. (1991). Demonstration of specific binding of cocaine to human spermatozoa. *Journal of the American Medical Association, 266*, 1956–1959.

Yehuda, R., McFarlane, A. C., & Shalev, A. Y. (1998). Predicting the development of posttraumatic stress disorder from the acute response to a traumatic event. *Biological Psychiatry, 44*, 1305–1313.

Yeomans, M. R., & Gray, R. W. (1997). Effects of naltrexone on food intake and changes in subjective appetite during eating: evidence for opioid involvement in the appetizer effect. *Physiology & Behavior, 62*, 15–21.

Yeshurun, Y., & Carrasco, M. (1998). Attention improves or impairs visual performance by enhancing spatial resolution. *Nature, 396*, 72–75.

Yeshurun, Y., & Carrasco, M. (1999). Spatial attention improves performance in spatial resolution tasks. *Vision Research, 39*, 293–306.

Yost, W. A., & Dye, R. H. (1991). Properties of sound localization by humans. In R. A. Altschuler, R. P. Bobbin, B. M. Clopton, & D. W. Hoffman (Eds.), *Neurobiology of hearing: The central auditory system* (pp. 389–410). New York: Raven.

Young, A. W., Hellawell, D. J., Van De Wal, C., & Johnson, M. (1996). Facial expression processing after amygdalotomy. *Neuropsychologia, 34*, 31–39.

Zaharia, M. D., Kulczycki, J., Shanks, N., Meaney, M. J., & Anisman, H. (1996). The effects of early postnatal stimulation on Morris water-maze acquisition in adult mice: Genetic and maternal factors. *Psychopharmacology, 128*, 227–239.

Zajonc, R. (1970). Brainwash: Familiarity breeds comfort. *Psychology Today, 3*, 32–35, 60–64.

Zajonc, R. B. (1968). Attitudinal effects of mere exposure. *Journal of Personality & Social Psychology, 9(2, Pt. 2)*, 1–27.

Zakowski, S., Hall, M. H., & Baum, A. (1992). Stress, stress management, and the immune system. *Applied and Preventative Psychology, 1*, 1–13.

Zane, N. W. S., Sue, S., Hu, L., & Kwon, J. H. (1991). Asian-American assertion: A social learning anyalysis of cultural differences. *Journal of Counseling Psychology, 38*, 63–70.

Zatorre, R. J., & Halpern, A. R. (1993). Effect of unilateral temporal-lobe excision on perception and imagery of songs. *Neuropsychologia, 31*, 221–232.

Zeki, S. M. (1978). Functional specialisation in the visual cortex of the rhesus monkey. *Nature, 274*, 423–428.

Zeki, S. M. (1993). *Vision of the brain.* London: Blackwell.

Zenger, T. R., & Lawrence, B. S. (1989). Organizational demography: The differential effect of age and tenure distributions on technical communication. *Academy of Management Journal, 32*, 353–376.

Zentner, M. R., & Kagan, J. (1998). Infants' perception of consonance and dissonance in music. *Infant Behavior & Development, 21*, 483–492.

Zhdanova, I., & Wurtman, R. (June, 1996). "How does Melatonin affect sleep?" Harvard Mental Health Newsletter, p. 8

Zhukov, D. A., & Vinogradova, E. P. (1998). Agonistic behavior during stress prevents the development of learned helplessness in rats. *Neuroscience & Behavioral Physiology, 28*, 206–210.

Zihl, J., von Cramon, D., & Mai, N. (1983). Selective disturbance of movement vision after bilateral brain damage. *Brain, 106*, 313–340.

Zimmer, E. Z., Fifter, W. P., Young-Ihl, K., Rey, H. R., Chao, C. R., & Myers, M. M. (1993). Response of the premature fetus to stimulation by speech sounds. *Early Human Development, 33*, 207–215.

Zoccolillo, M., Price, R., Ji, T., & Hwu, H. (1999). Antisocial personality disorder: Comparisons of prevalence, symptoms, and correlates in four countries. In P. Cohen, C. Slomkowski et al. (Eds.). *Historical and geographical influences on psychopathology.* (pp. 249–277). Mahwah, NJ: Erlbaum.

Zola-Morgan, S., Squire, L. R., & Amaral, D. G. (1986). Human amnesia and the medial temporal region: Enduring memory impairment following a bilateral lesion limited to field CA1 of the hippocampus. *Journal of Neuroscience, 6,* 2950–2967.

Zornberg, G. L., Buka, S. L., & Tsuang, M. T. (2000). Hypoxic-ischemia-related fetal/neonatal complications and risk of schizophrenia and other nonaffective psychoses: A 19-year longitudinal study. *American Journal of Psychiatry 157,* 196–202.

Zuckerman, M. (1979). *Sensation seeking: Beyond the optimal level of arousal.* Hillsdale, NJ: Erlbaum.

Zuckerman, M. (1991). *Psychobiology of Personality.* Cambridge: Cambridge University Press.

Zuckerman, M. (1995). Good and bad humors: Biochemical bases of personality and its disorders. *Psychological Science, 6,* 325–332.

Zuckerman, M., Kuhlman, D. M., & Camac, C. (1988). What lies beyond E and N? Factor analyses of scales believed to measure basic dimensions of personaity. *Journal of Personality and Social Psychology, 54,* 96–107.

Zurek, P. M. (1981). Spontaneous narrowband acoustic signal emitted by human ears. *Journal of Acoustical Society of America, 69,* 514–523.

Zurek, P. M. (1985). Acoustic emissions from the ear: A summary of results from humans and animals. *Journal of the Acoustical Society of America, 78,* 340–344.

Zwicker, E., & Schloth, E. (1984). Interrelation of different oto-acoustic emissions. *Journal of Acoustical Society of America, 75,* 1148–1154.

Glossary

Absolute threshold: The smallest amount of a stimulus needed to detect that the stimulus is present.

Academic psychologist: The type of psychologist who focuses on conducting research and teaching.

Accommodation: In Piaget's theory, the process that results in schemas changing as necessary to cope with a broader range of situations. The automatic adjustment of the eye that occurs when muscles change the shape of the lens so that it focuses light on the retina from objects at different distances.

Acquisition: The technical name given to the initial learning of the conditioned response (CR).

Action potential: A shifting change in charge that moves down the axon to the end, causing the terminal buttons to release a chemical signal.

Activation-synthesis hypothesis: The theory that dreams arise from random bursts of nerve cell activity, which may affect brain cells involved in hearing and seeing; the brain attempts to make sense of this hodgepodge of stimuli, resulting in the experience of dreams.

Active interaction: Occurs when people choose, partly based on genetic tendencies, to put themselves in specific situations and to avoid others.

Activity: A temperament dimension characterized by the general expenditure of energy; activity has two components—vigor (intensity of the activities) and tempo (speed of the activities).

Acute stressor: A stressor of short-term duration.

Adaptation: A characteristic that increases "fitness" for an environment.

Adolescence: The period between the onset of puberty and, roughly, the end of the teenage years.

Adoption study: A study of related or unrelated children who were separated at or near birth and raised in the same versus different households.

Affirming the consequent: A reasoning error that occurs because of the assumption that if a result is present, a specific cause must also be present.

Afterimage: The image left behind by a previous perception.

Aggression: Behavior directed toward harming another living being who is motivated to avoid such treatment.

Agonist: A chemical that mimics the effects of a neurotransmitter (sometimes by preventing reuptake).

Agoraphobia: A condition in which people fear or avoid places that might be difficult to leave should a panic attack occur.

Alarm phase: The first phase of the GAS, in which a stressor is perceived and a fight-or-flight response is activated.

Alcohol myopia: The disproportionate influence of immediate experience on behavior and emotions, due to the effects of alcohol use.

Algorithm: A set of steps that, if followed methodically, will guarantee the solution to a problem.

All-or-none law: States that if the neuron is sufficiently stimulated, it fires, sending the action potential all the way down the axon and releasing chemicals from the terminal buttons; either the action potential occurs or it doesn't.

Altruism: The desire to increase the welfare of others without expecting anything in return.

Amnesia: A loss of memory over an entire time span resulting from brain damage from an accident, infection, or stroke.

Amphetamines: Synthetic stimulants.

Amplitude: The height of the peaks in a light wave.

Amygdala: A subcortical structure that plays a special role in fear and is involved in other sorts of emotions, such as anger.

Androgens: Male hormones, which cause many male characteristics such as beard growth and a low voice.

Anorexia nervosa: An eating disorder characterized by the refusal to maintain even a low normal weight and an intense fear of gaining weight.

Antagonist: A chemical that blocks the effect of a neurotransmitter (sometimes by blocking a receptor or enhancing the reuptake mechanism).

Anterograde amnesia: Amnesia that leaves consolidated memories intact but prevents new learning.

Antipsychotic medication: Medication that reduces psychotic symptoms.

Antisocial personality disorder: A long-standing pattern of disregard for others to the point of violating other people's rights.

Anxiety disorder: A disorder whose hallmark is intense and pervasive anxiety and fear, or extreme attempts to avoid these feelings.

Applied psychologist: The type of psychologist who studies how to improve products and procedures and conducts research to help solve specific practical problems.

Approach–approach conflict: The internal predicament that occurs when competing alternatives are equally positive.

Approach–avoidance conflict: The internal predicament that occurs when a course of action has both positive and negative aspects.

Archetype: A Jungian concept of symbols that represent basic aspects of the world.

Assimilation: In Piaget's theory, the process that allows use of existing schemas to take in new sets of stimuli and respond accordingly.

Associative priming: Priming that makes related information more easily accessed in the future.

Atherosclerosis: A medical condition characterized by plaque buildup in the arteries.

Attachment: An emotional bond that leads us to want to be with someone and to miss him or her when we are separated.

Attention: The act of focusing on particular information, which allows it to be processed more fully than what is not attended to.

Attentional blink: A rebound period in which a person cannot pay attention to one thing after having just paid attention to another.

Attitude: An overall evaluation about some aspect of the world.

Attribution: An explanation for the cause of an event or behavior.

Attributional bias: A cognitive shortcut for determining attribution that generally occurs outside our awareness.

Attributional style: A person's characteristic way of explaining life events.

Autonomic nervous system (ANS): Controls the smooth muscles in the body, some glandular functions, and many of the body's "self-regulating" activities such as digestion and circulation.

Availability heuristic: The heuristic that the easier events or objects are to bring to mind, the more likely, common, or frequent they are judged to be.

Avoidance–avoidance conflict: The internal predicament that occurs when competing alternatives are equally unpleasant.

Avoidance learning: In classical conditioning, learning that occurs when a CS is paired with an unpleasant UCS that leads the organism to try to avoid the CS. In operant conditioning, the process by which an organism learns to avoid an unpleasant consequence by emitting a particular response.

Axon: The sending end of the neuron, or the long cable extending from the cell body, which affects other neurons.

Basal ganglia: Subcortical structures that play a role in planning and producing movement.

Base-rate rule: The rule stating that if something is sampled at random, the chances of obtaining a particular type are directly proportional to its percentage in the set from which the sample is taken.

Basic emotion: An innate emotion that is shared by all humans, such as surprise, happiness, anger, fear, disgust, and sadness.

Basic level: A level of specificity, which is usually the most likely to be applied to an object.

B cell: A type of white blood cell that matures in the bone marrow.

Behavior: The outwardly observable acts of an individual, alone or in a group.

Behavioral genetics: The field in which researchers attempt to determine how much of the differences among people are due to their genes and how much to the environment.

Behaviorism: The school of psychology that focuses on how a specific stimulus (object, person, or event) evokes a specific response (behavior in reaction to the stimulus).

Behavior modification: A category of therapeutic techniques for changing behavior based on operant conditioning principles. A technique that brings about therapeutic change in behavior through the use of secondary reinforcers.

Behavior therapy: A type of therapy, based on well-researched principles of learning, that focuses on observable, measurable behaviors.

Benzodiazepine: A type of antianxiety medication that affects the target symptoms within 36 hours and does not need to be taken for more than a week to be effective.

Bereavement: The experience of missing a loved one and longing for his or her company.

Bias: In signal detection theory, a person's willingness to report noticing a stimulus. Occurs when previous beliefs, expectations, or habits alter the participants' responses or affect the design or conduct of a study.

Bibliotherapy: The use of self-help books and tapes for therapeutic purposes.

"Big Five": The five superfactors of personality—extraversion, neuroticism, agreeableness, conscientiousness, and openness—determined by factor analysis.

Binocular cues: Cues to the distance of an object that arise from both eyes working together.

Biological preparedness: A built-in readiness for certain conditioned stimuli to elicit certain conditioned responses so that less learning is necessary to produce conditioning.

Bipolar disorder: A mood disorder marked by one or more episodes of either mania or hypomania.

Bisexual: A person who is sexually attracted to members of both sexes.

Blackout: A period of time for which an alcoholic has no memory of events that transpired while intoxicated.

Bottom-up processing: Processing that is initiated by stimulus input.

Brain circuit: A set of neurons that affect one another.

Brainstem: The set of neural structures at the base of the brain, including the medulla and pons.

Breadth of processing: Processing that organizes and integrates information into previously stored information, often by making associations.

Brightness and color constancy: Seeing objects as having the same lightness, brightness, or color in different viewing situations.

Bulimia nervosa: An eating disorder characterized by recurrent episodes of binge eating, followed by some attempt to prevent weight gain.

Bystander effect: The decrease in offers of assistance that occurs as the number of bystanders increases.

Case study: A scientific study that examines a single instance of a situation in detail.

Castration anxiety: A boy's anxiety-laden fear that, as punishment for loving mother and hating father, his father will cut off his penis (the primary zone of pleasure).

Categorical perception: Identifying sounds as belonging to distinct categories that correspond to the basic units of speech.

Categorical variables: Variables whose values are assigned to discrete classes.

Cell body: The middle part of a cell, which contains the nucleus.

Cell membrane: The skin of a cell.

Central executive: The set of processes that operates on information in one or another STM; part of working memory.

Central nervous system (CNS): The spinal cord and the brain.

Central tendency: A descriptive statistic that indicates the clustering of the most characteristic values, or scores, for a particular group or sample.

Cerebellum: A large structure at the base of the brain that is concerned in part with physical coordination, estimating time, and paying attention.

Cerebral cortex: The convoluted pinkish-gray surface of the brain, where most mental processes take place.

Cerebral hemisphere: A left or right half-brain, roughly half a sphere.

Channel: A small hole in the skin of cells that can open and close.

Chemical senses: Taste and smell, which rely on sensing the presence of specific chemicals.

Child-directed speech (CDS): Speech to babies that relies on short sentences with clear pauses, careful enunciation, exaggerated intonation, and a high-pitched voice; also known as *motherese*.

Chronic stressor: A stressor of long-term duration.

Chunk: A unit of information, such as a digit, letter, or word.

Circadian rhythms: The body's daily fluctuations in response to the dark and light cycle, which affects blood pressure, pulse rate, body temperature, blood sugar level, hormone levels, and metabolism.

Classical conditioning: A type of learning that occurs when a neutral stimulus becomes paired (associated) with a stimulus that causes a reflexive behavior and, in time, is sufficient to produce that behavior.

Client-centered therapy: A type of insight-oriented therapy that focuses on people's potential for growth and the importance of an empathic therapist. Therapy developed by Rogers that focuses on the client's potential for growth and the therapist's role as provider of unconditional support.

Clinical psychologist: The type of psychologist who provides psychotherapy and is trained to administer and interpret psychological tests.

Cocktail party phenomenon: The effect of not being aware of other people's conversations until your name is mentioned, and then suddenly hearing it.

Code: A mental representation; an internal "re-presentation" of a stimulus or event.

Cognitive dissonance: The uncomfortable state that arises because of a discrepancy between an attitude and behavior or between two attitudes.

Cognitive distortion: Irrational thoughts that arise from a systematic bias in the way a person thinks about reality.

Cognitive learning: The acquisition of information that often is not immediately acted on but is stored for later use.

Cognitive neuroscience: A blending of cognitive psychology and neuroscience (the study of the brain) that aims to specify how the brain stores and processes information.

Cognitive psychology: The approach in psychology that attempts to characterize how information is stored and operated on internally.

Cognitive restructuring: The process of helping clients shift their thinking away from the focus on automatic, dysfunctional thoughts to more realistic ones.

Cognitive therapy: Therapy that focuses on the client's thoughts rather than his or her feelings or behaviors.

Collectivist culture: A culture that emphasizes the rights and responsibilities of the group over those of the individual.

Color blindness: An inability, either acquired (by brain damage) or inherited, to perceive hue.

Compassionate love: A type of love marked by very close friendship, mutual caring, liking, respect, and attraction.

Complex inheritance: The transmission of characteristics that depends on joint actions of genes working together; in general, when a characteristic varies continuously, it reflects complex inheritance.

Compliance: A change in behavior prompted by a direct request rather than social norms.

Compulsion: A repetitive behavior or mental act that an individual feels compelled to perform in response to an obsession.

Computer-assisted tomography (CT, formerly CAT): A neuroimaging technique that produces a three-dimensional image of brain structure using X rays.

Concept: An unambiguous, sometimes abstract, internal representation that defines a grouping of a set of objects (including living things) or events (including relationships).

Concrete operation: In Piaget's theory, a (reversible) manipulation of the mental representation of perceived events and actions that corresponds to the corresponding actual physical manipulation.

Conditioned emotional response (CER): An emotional response elicited by a previously neutral stimulus.

Conditioned response (CR): A response that depends, or is conditional, on pairings of the conditioned stimulus with an unconditioned stimulus; the conditioned response occurs in response to the CS alone.

Conditioned stimulus (CS): An originally neutral stimulus that acquires significance through the "conditioning" of repeated pairings with an unconditioned stimulus (UCS).

Conduction deafness: A type of deafness caused by a physical impairment of the external or middle ear.

Cones: Retinal cells that respond most strongly to one of three wavelengths and that play a key role in producing color vision.

Confidence interval: The range within which the mean of the population is likely to occur.

Confirmation bias: A tendency to seek information that will confirm a rule, and not to seek information that is inconsistent with the rule.

Conflict: The emotional predicament experienced when making difficult choices.

Conformity: A change of beliefs or actions so as to follow a group's norms.

Confound (or confounding variable): An independent variable that varies along with the one of interest and could affect what is measured.

Conservation: The principle that certain properties of objects remain the same even when their appearance changes, provided that nothing is added or removed.

Consolidation: The process of converting information stored dynamically in long-term memory into a structural change in the brain.

Continuous reinforcement: Reinforcement given for each desired response.

Continuous variables: Variables whose values can fall anywhere along the measurement scale.

Contrapreparedness: A built-in disinclination (or even an inability) for certain conditioned stimuli to elicit particular conditioned responses.

Control condition: Like a control group, but administered to the same participants who receive the experimental condition.

Control group: A group that is treated exactly the same way as the experimental group, except for the one aspect of the situation under study—the independent variable—and so holds constant, or controls, all of the other variables.

Coping: Taking a course of action regarding the stressor, its effects, or the person's reaction to it.

Cornea: The transparent covering over the eye, which serves partly to focus the light onto the back of the eye.

Corpus callosum: The huge band of nerve fibers that connects the two halves of the brain.

Correlation: An index of how closely interrelated two measured variables are; the higher the correlation, the better the values of one variable predict the values of the other.

Cortisol: A hormone produced by the outer layer of the adrenal glands that helps the body cope with the extra energy demands of stress by breaking down and converting protein and fat to sugar.

Counseling psychologist: The type of psychologist who is trained to help people with issues that naturally arise during the course of life.

Crack: Cocaine in crystalline form, usually smoked in a pipe (free-basing) or rolled into a cigarette.

Creativity: The ability to produce something original of high quality or to devise effective new ways of solving a problem.

Critical period: A narrow window of time when certain types of learning are possible.

Cross-sectional study: A study in which different groups of people are tested, with each group at a different age.

Crystallized intelligence: According to Cattell and Horn, the kind of intelligence that relies on knowing facts and having the ability to use and combine them.

Cues: Stimuli that trigger or enhance remembering; reminders.

Dark adaptation: The process whereby exposure to darkness causes the eyes to become more sensitive, allowing for better vision in the dark.

Data: Careful observations or numerical measurements.

Debriefing: An interview after a study to ensure that the participant has no negative reactions as a result of participation and understands why the study was conducted.

Decay: The fading away of memories with time because the relevant connections between neurons are lost.

Deductive reasoning: Reasoning that applies the rules of logic to a set of assumptions (stated as premises) to discover whether certain conclusions follow from those assumptions; deduction goes from the general to the particular.

Defense mechanism: An unconscious psychological means by which a person tries to prevent unacceptable, id-based thoughts or urges from reaching conscious awareness.

Deindividuation: The loss of sense of self that occurs when people are in a group but are anonymous.

Delayed reinforcement: Reinforcement given some period of time after the desired behavior is exhibited.

Delusions: Entrenched false beliefs that are often bizarre.

Dendrite: A twiggy part of a neuron that receives messages from the axons of other neurons.

Deoxyribonucleic acid (DNA): The molecule that contains genes.

Dependent variable: The aspect of the experimental situation that is measured as an independent variable is changed; the value of the dependent variable *depends on* the value of the independent variable.

Depressant: Class of substances, including barbiturates, alcohol, opiates, and antianxiety drugs, that depress the central nervous system, decreasing the user's behavioral activity and level of awareness; also called *sedative-hypnotic drugs*.

Deprived reward: A reward that occurs when a biological need is filled.

Depth of processing: The number and complexity of the operations involved in processing information, expressed in a continuum from shallow to deep.

Descriptive statistics: A concise way of summarizing properties of sets of numbers.

Diathesis–stress model: A predisposition to a given disorder (diathesis) and specific factors (stress) that combine with the diathesis to trigger the onset of the disorder.

Difference threshold: The difference needed to notice a stimulus change half the time.

Diffusion of responsibility: The diminished sense of responsibility to help that each person feels as the number of bystanders grows.

Discrimination: The ability to distinguish between the desired response and a similar but undesirable one.

Discriminative stimulus: The cue that tells the organism whether a specific response will lead to the expected reinforcement.

Disinhibition: The inhibition of inhibitory neurons, which make other neurons (the ones that are usually inhibited) more likely to fire; usually occurs as a result of depressant use.

Display rule: A culture-specific rule that indicates when, to whom, and how strongly certain emotions can be shown.

Dissociative amnesia: An inability to remember important personal information, often experienced as memory "gaps."

Dissociative disorder: A disorder marked by a disruption in the usually integrated functions of consciousness, memory, or identity.

Dissociative fugue: An abrupt, unexpected departure from home or work, combined with an inability to remember some or all of the past.

Dissociative identity disorder (DID): A disorder in which a person has two or more distinct personalities that take control of the individual's behavior.

Dizygotic: From different eggs and sharing only as many genes as any pair of brothers or sisters—on average, half.

Door-in-the-face technique: A compliance technique in which someone makes a very large request; when it is denied, as expected, a second, smaller request (the desired one) is made.

Double blind design: An experimental procedure in which the participant is "blind" to (unaware of) the predictions of the study (and so cannot try, consciously or unconsciously, to produce the predicted results), and the experimenter is "blind" to the condition assigned to the participant (and so cannot induce the predicted results).

Double pain: The sensation that occurs when an injury first causes a sharp pain, and later a dull pain; the two kinds of pain arise from different fibers sending their messages at different speeds.

Down syndrome: A type of retardation that results from the creation of an extra chromosome during conception; it is genetic but not inherited.

Dream analysis: A technique used in psychoanalysis and psychodynamic therapies in which the therapist examines the content of dreams to gain access to the unconscious.

Drive: An internal imbalance that motivates an animal to reach a particular goal, which in turn will reduce that imbalance.

Dysthymia: A mood disorder similar to major depressive disorder, but less intense and longer lasting.

Eating disorder: A disorder involving a severe disturbance in eating behavior.

Effect: The difference in the dependent variable that is due to changes in the independent variable.

Efficacy expectancy: The sense of being able to follow through and produce the behaviors one would like to perform.

Ego: A Freudian psychic structure, developed in childhood, that tries to balance the competing demands of the id, superego, and reality.

Egocentrism: In Piaget's theory, the inability to take another person's point of view.

Elaborative encoding: Encoding that involves breadth of processing.

Electroconvulsive therapy (ECT): A controlled brain seizure, used to treat people with certain psychological disorders such as psychotic depression or those for whom medication has not been effective or recommended.

Electroencephalogram: A recording from the scalp of electrical activity over time, which produces a tracing of pulses at different frequencies.

Electroencephalograph (EEG): A machine that records electrical current produced by the brain.

Embryo: The period of development from the point where the major axis of the baby is present until all major structures are present, spanning from about 2 weeks to 8 weeks after conception.

Emotion: A positive or negative reaction to a perceived or remembered object, event, or circumstance, accompanied by a subjective feeling.

Emotional intelligence (EI): The ability to understand and regulate emotions effectively.

Emotionality: A temperament dimension characterized by an inclination to become aroused in situations in which the predominant emotions are distress, fear, and anger.

Emotion-focused coping: Coping focused on changing the person's emotional response to the stressor.

Empiricism (approach to language): The approach that views language as entirely the result of learning.

Enacted social support: The specific supportive behaviors provided by others.

Encoding: The process of organizing and transforming incoming information so that it can be entered into memory, to be either stored or compared to previously stored information.

Endorphins: Painkilling chemicals produced naturally in the brain.

Episodic memories: The memories of events that are associated with a particular context—a time, place, and circumstance.

Estrogens: Female hormones, which cause many female characteristics, such as breast development and the bone structure of the female pelvis, and are involved in the menstrual cycle.

Evocative (or reactive) interaction: Occurs when genetically influenced characteristics draw out behaviors from other people.

Evolution: Gene-based changes in the characteristics of members of a species over successive generations.

Evolutionary psychology: The approach in psychology that assumes that certain cognitive strategies and goals are so important that natural selection has built them into our brains.

Exhaustion phase: The final stage of the GAS, in which the continued stress response itself becomes damaging to the body.

Expectancies: Expectations that have a powerful influence on thoughts, feelings, behavior, and, in turn, personality.

Experimenter expectancy effects: Occur when an investigator's expectations lead him or her (consciously or unconsciously) to treat participants in a way that induces the expected results.

Explicit (or declarative) memories: The memories that can be retrieved at will and represented in STM; verbal and visual memories are explicit if the words or images can be called to mind.

Exposure with response prevention: A behavior therapy technique that, in a planned, programmatic way, exposes the client to an anxiety-provoking object and prevents the usual maladaptive response.

External attribution: An explanation of behavior that focuses on the situation; also called *situational attribution*.

Extinction: In classical conditioning, the process by which a CR comes to be eliminated through repeated presentations of the CS without the presence of the UCS. In operant conditioning, the fading out of a response following an initial burst of a behavior after the withdrawal of reinforcement.

Extrasensory perception (ESP): The ability to perceive and know things without using the ordinary senses.

Extrinsic motivation: Motivation that leads a person to want to engage in an activity for external reasons.

Facial feedback hypothesis: The idea that emotions arise partly as a result of the position of facial muscles.

Factor analysis: A statistical method that uncovers the particular attributes (factors) that make scores more or less similar; the more similar the scores, the more attributes they should have in common.

False memory: Memory for an event that did not actually occur.

Family therapy: A therapy modality in which a family (or certain members of a family) is seen for treatment.

Fetal alcohol syndrome: A type of retardation caused by excessive drinking of alcohol by the mother during pregnancy.

Fetus: The final phase of development in the womb, from about age 8 weeks until birth.

Figure: In perception, a set of characteristics (such as shape, color, texture) that corresponds to an object.

Fixed interval schedule: Reinforcement schedule in which reinforcement is given for a response emitted after a fixed interval of time.

Fixed ratio schedule: Reinforcement schedule in which reinforcement is given after a fixed ratio of responses.

Flashback: A hallucination that recurs without the use of a drug.

Flashbulb memory: An unusually vivid and accurate memory of a dramatic event.

Flow: The experience of complete absorption in and merging smoothly into an activity and losing track of time.

Fluid intelligence: According to Cattell and Horn, the kind of intelligence that underlies the creation of novel solutions to problems.

Food aversion (taste aversion): A classically conditioned avoidance of a certain food or taste.

Foot-in-the-door technique: A technique that achieves compliance by beginning with an insignificant request, which is then followed by a larger request.

Forebrain: The cortex, thalamus, limbic system, and basal ganglia.

Forgetting curve: A graphic representation of the rate at which information is forgotten over time: Recent events are recalled better than more distant ones, but most forgetting occurs soon after learning.

Formal operation: In Piaget's theory, a mental act that can be performed (and reversed) even with abstract concepts.

Fovea: The small, central region of the retina with the highest density of cones and the highest resolution.

Free association: A technique used in psychoanalysis and psychodynamic therapies in which the patient says whatever comes to mind and the train of thought reveals the patient's issues and ways of dealing with them.

Frequency: The rate at which light waves move past a given point.

Frequency distribution: A distribution that indicates the number of each type of case that was observed in a set of data.

Frequency theory: The theory that higher frequencies produce higher rates of neural firing.

Frontal lobe: The brain lobe located behind the forehead; the seat of planning, memory search, motor control, and reasoning, as well as numerous other functions.

Functional fixedness: When solving a problem, getting stuck on one interpretation of an object or one part of the situation.

Functionalism: The school of psychology that sought to understand the ways that the mind helps individuals *function,* or adapt to the world.

Functional magnetic resonance imaging (fMRI): A type of MRI that usually detects the amount of oxygen being brought to a particular place in the brain.

Fundamental attribution error: The strong tendency to interpret other people's behavior as due to internal (dispositional) causes rather than external (situational) ones.

g: "General factor," a single intelligence that underlies the positive correlations among different tests of intelligence.

Gate control of pain: The top-down inhibition of interneurons that regulate the input of pain signals to the brain.

Gender identity: A person's belief that he or she is male or is female.

Gender roles: The culturally determined appropriate behaviors of males versus females.

Gene: A stretch of DNA that produces a specific protein, which in turn forms the building blocks of our bodies (including our brains) or drives the processes that allow us to live.

General adaptation syndrome (GAS): The technical name for the three phases of the body's response to stress.

Generalization: The ability to generalize both to similar stimuli and from the desired response to a similar response.

Generalized anxiety disorder: A disorder whose hallmark is excessive anxiety and worry that is not triggered by a specific object or situation.

Gestalt laws of organization: A set of rules describing the circumstances under which marks will be grouped into perceptual units, such as proximity, continuity, similarity, closure, and good form.

Gestalt psychology: An approach to understanding mental processes that focuses on the idea that the whole is more than the sum of its parts.

Gifted: People who have IQs of at least 135, but more commonly between 150 and 180.

Glial cell: A cell that fills the gaps between neurons, influences the communication among them, and generally helps in the care and feeding of neurons.

Glove anesthesia: Hypnotically induced anesthesia of the hand.

Glucocorticoids: A type of hormone that is released when the stress response is triggered. Glucocorticoids have anti-inflammatory properties.

Grammar: The rules that determine how words that belong to different parts of speech can be organized into acceptable sentences.

Grief: The emotion of distress that follows the loss of a loved one.

Ground: In perception, the background, which must be distinguished to pick out figures.

Group: A social entity characterized by regular interaction among members, emotional connection, a common frame of reference, and interdependence.

Group polarization: The tendency of group members' opinions to become more extreme (in the same direction as their initial opinions) after group discussion.

Group therapy: A therapy modality in which a number of clients with similar needs meet together with one or two therapists.

Groupthink: The tendency of people who try to solve problems together to accept one another's information and ideas without subjecting them to critical analysis.

Gyrus: A bulge between sulci in the cerebral cortex that forms a crease.

Habit: A well-learned response that is carried out automatically (without conscious thought) when the appropriate stimulus is present.

Hair cells: The cells with stiff hairs along the basilar membrane of the inner ear that, when moved, produce nerve impulses that are sent to the brain; these cells are the auditory equivalent of rods and cones.

Hallucinations: Mental images so vivid that they seem real.

Hallucinogen: A substance that induces hallucinations.

Heritability: The degree to which variability in a characteristic is due to genetics.

Heterosexual: A person who is sexually attracted to members of the opposite sex.

Heuristic: A rule of thumb that does not guarantee the correct answer to a problem but offers a likely shortcut to it.

High expressed emotion: An emotional style in families that are critical, hostile, and overinvolved.

Hindbrain: The medulla, pons, and cerebellum.

Hippocampus: A subcortical structure that plays a key role in allowing new information to be stored in the brain's memory banks.

Homeostasis: The process of maintaining a steady state, a constant level of a bodily substance or condition.

Homosexual: A person who is sexually attracted to members of the same sex.

Hormone: A chemical produced by glands that can act as a neuromodulator.

Hostile attribution bias: The propensity to misread the intentions of others as negative.

Hostility: The personality trait associated with heart disease, characterized by mistrust, an expectation of harm and provocation by others, and a cynical attitude.

Humanistic psychology: The school of psychology that assumes people have positive values, free will, and deep inner creativity, the combination of which leads them to choose life-fulfilling paths to personal growth.

Hypnogogic sleep: Characterized by the experience of gentle falling or floating, or "seeing" flashing lights and geometric patterns; describes Stage 1 sleep.

Hypomania: A mood state similar to mania, but less severe, with fewer and less intrusive symptoms.

Hypothalamus: A brain structure that sits under the thalamus and plays a central role in controlling eating and drinking, and in regulating the body's temperature, blood pressure, and heart rate.

Hypothesis: A tentative idea that might explain a set of observations.

Id: A psychic structure, proposed by Freud, that exists at birth and houses sexual and aggressive drives and physical needs.

Immediate reinforcement: Reinforcement given immediately after the desired behavior is exhibited.

Immune system: The system that protects the body from disease by developing chemicals and specific types of cells to fight against foreign organisms.

Implicit memories: Memories that cannot be voluntarily called to mind, but nevertheless influence behavior or thinking in certain ways.

Impulsivity: A temperament dimension characterized by the propensity to respond to stimuli immediately, without reflection or concern for consequences.

Incentive: A stimulus that draws a person toward a particular goal, in anticipation of a reward.

Incidental learning: Learning that occurs without intention.

Incongruence: According to client-centered therapy, a mismatch between a person's *real self* and his or her *ideal self.*

Independent variable: The aspect of the experimental situation that is intentionally varied.

Individualist culture: A culture that emphasizes the rights and responsibilities of the individual over those of the group.

Individual therapy: A therapy modality in which one client is treated by one therapist.

Inductive reasoning: Reasoning that uses examples to figure out a rule; induction goes from the particular (examples) to the general (a rule).

Inferential statistics: Results of tests that reveal which differences or patterns in the measurements reflect actual differences in a population, as opposed to those that merely reflect random variations.

Inferiority complex: The experience that occurs when inferiority feelings are so strong that they hamper striving for superiority.

Informed consent: The requirement that a potential participant in a study be told what he or she will be asked to do and possible risks and benefits of the study before agreeing to take part.

Ingroup: An individual's own group.

Inhibitory conflict: A response that is both strongly instigated and inhibited.

Insight: A new way to look at a problem that implies the solution.

Insight learning: Learning that occurs when a person or animal suddenly grasps what something means and incorporates that new knowledge into old knowledge.

Insight-oriented therapy: Therapy that aims to remove distressing symptoms by leading people to understand the symptoms' causes through deeply felt personal insights.

Insomnia: Repeated difficulty falling asleep, difficulty staying asleep, or waking up too early.

Instinct: An inherited tendency to produce organized and unalterable responses to particular stimuli.

Insulin: A hormone that stimulates the storage of food molecules in the form of fat.

Intelligence: The ability to solve problems well and to understand and learn complex material.

Intelligence quotient (IQ): A score on an intelligence test, originally based on comparing mental age to chronological age but later based on norms.

Intentional learning: Learning that occurs as a result of trying to learn.

Interactionism: A view of personality in which both traits and situations are believed to affect behavior, thoughts, and feelings.

Interference: The disruption of the ability to remember one piece of information by the presence of other information.

Internal attribution: An explanation of someone's behavior that focuses on the person's beliefs, goals, or other dispositions; also called *dispositional attribution.*

Interneuron: A neuron that is connected to other neurons, not to sense organs or muscles.

Interpretation: A technique used in psychoanalysis and psychodynamic therapies in which the therapist deciphers the patient's words and behaviors, assigning unconscious motivations to them.

Interval schedule: Partial reinforcement schedule based on time.

Intrinsic motivation: Motivation that leads a person to want to engage in an activity for its own sake.

Introspection: The process of "looking within."

Ion: An atom that has a positive or negative charge.

Iris: The circular muscle that adjusts the size of the pupil.

Just-noticeable difference (JND): The size of the difference in a stimulus property needed for the observer to notice that a change has occurred.

Kinesthetic sense: The sense that registers the movement and position of the limbs.

Korsakoff's syndrome: A disorder, related to alcoholism, in which the brain's mammillary bodies are destroyed, damaging learning and memory abilities.

Language acquisition device (LAD): An innate mechanism, hypothesized by Chomsky, that contains the grammatical rules common to all languages and allows language acquisition.

Language comprehension: The ability to understand language.

Language production: The ability to speak or otherwise use language to send information.

Latent content: The symbolic content and meaning of a dream.

Latent learning: Learning that occurs without behavioral signs.

Law of Effect: Actions that subsequently lead to a "satisfying state of affairs" are more likely to be repeated.

Learned helplessness: The condition that occurs after an animal has an aversive experience in which nothing it does can affect what happens to it, and so it simply gives up and stops trying to change the situation or to escape.

Learning: A relatively permanent change in behavior that results from experience.

Lens: The flexible disk under the cornea that focuses light onto the back of the eye.

Lesion: A region of impaired tissue.

Level of the brain: Events that involve the structure and properties of the organ itself—brain cells and their connections, the chemical soup in which they exist, and the genes.

Level of the group: Events that involve relationships between people (e.g., love, competition, cooperation), relationships among groups, and culture. Events at the level of the group are one aspect of the environment; the other aspect is the physical environment itself (the time, temperature, and other physical stimuli).

Level of the person: Events that involve the nature of beliefs, desires, and feelings—the *content* of the mind, not just its internal mechanics.

Limbic system: A set of brain areas, including the hippocampus, amygdala, and other areas, that has long been thought of as being involved in fighting, fleeing, feeding, and sex.

Linguistic relativity hypothesis: The idea that perceptions and thoughts are shaped by language, and thus people who speak different languages think differently.

Lobes: The four major parts of each cerebral hemisphere—occipital, temporal, parietal, and frontal.

Locus of control: The source perceived to be the center of control over life's events.

Logic: The process of applying the principles of correct reasoning to reach a decision or evaluate the truth of a claim.

Longitudinal study: A study in which the same people are tested repeatedly, at different ages.

Long-term memory (LTM): A memory store that holds a huge amount of information for a long time (from hours to years).

Lowball technique: A compliance technique that consists of getting someone to make an agreement and then increasing the cost of that agreement.

Magnetic resonance imaging (MRI): A technique that uses magnetic properties of atoms to take sharp pictures of the structure of the brain.

Major depressive disorder (MDD): A disorder characterized by at least 2 weeks of depressed mood or loss of interest in nearly all activities, along with sleep or eating disturbances, loss of energy, and feelings of hopelessness.

Manic episode: A period of at least 1 week during which an abnormally elevated, expansive, or irritable mood persists.

Manifest content: The obvious, memorable content of a dream.

Maturation: The developmental process that produces genetically programmed changes with increased age.

Mean: A measure of central tendency that is the arithmetic average of a set of scores or values.

Median: A measure of central tendency that is the midpoint score of the values for the group or sample; half the values fall above the median, and half fall below the median.

Medulla: The lowest part of the lower brainstem, which plays a central role in automatic control of breathing, swallowing, and blood circulation.

Memory store: A set of neurons that serves to retain information over time.

Mendelian inheritance: The transmission of characteristics by individual dominant and recessive elements acting separately.

Meninges: The covering of the brain.

Mental images: Internal representations like those that arise during perception, but based on stored information rather than immediate sensory input.

Mentally retarded: People who have an IQ of 70 or less and significant limitations in at least two aspects of everyday life since childhood.

Mental processes: What the brain does when a person stores, recalls, or uses information, or has specific feelings.

Mere exposure effect: The tendency to like previously perceived things better than unfamiliar ones.

Meta-analysis: A technique that combines the results from different studies to discover patterns in the data.

Metabolism: The sum of the chemical events in each of the body's cells, events that convert food molecules to the energy needed for the cells to function.

Microelectrode: A tiny probe inserted into the brain to record electrical activity.

Microenvironment: The environment created by a person's own presence, which depends partly on appearance and behavior.

Midbrain: Brainstem structures that connect the forebrain and hindbrain, including the reticular formation.

Minnesota Multiphasic Personality Inventory-2 (MMPI-2): A personality inventory primarily used to assess psychopathology.

Misattribution of arousal: The failure to interpret signs of bodily arousal correctly, which leads to the experience of inappropriate emotions.

Mnemonic devices: Strategies that improve memory, typically by using effective organization and integration.

Modality: A form of therapy.

Modality-specific memory stores: The memories that retain input from a single sense, such as vision or audition, or from a specific processing system, such as language.

Mode: A measure of central tendency that is the most frequently occurring value in a group or sample.

Monoamine oxidase inhibitor (MAOI): A type of antidepressant medication that requires strict adherence to a diet free of tyramine-based foods.

Monocular static cues: Information that specifies the distance of an object that can be picked up with one eye without movement of the object or eye.

Monozygotic: From the same egg and having identical genes.

Mood disorder: A condition marked by persistent or episodic disturbances in feeling states that interfere with normal functioning in at least one realm of life.

Moral dilemmas: Situations in which there are moral pros and cons for each of a set of possible actions.

Morpheme: The smallest unit of meaning in a language.

Motion cues: Information that specifies the distance of an object on the basis of its movement.

Motivation: The requirements and desires that lead animals (including humans) to behave in a particular way at a particular time and place.

Motor neuron: A neuron that sends signals to muscles to control movement.

Motor strip: The gyrus, located immediately in front of the central sulcus, that controls fine movements and is organized by body part; also called the *primary motor cortex*.

Myelin: A fatty substance that helps impulses travel down the axon more efficiently.

Narcotic analgesic: A class of strongly addictive drugs, such as heroin, that relieve pain.

Nativism (approach to language): The approach that views crucial aspects of language as innate.

Natural killer (NK) cell: A type of T-cell that destroys damaged or altered cells, such as precancerous cells.

Natural selection: Changes in the frequency of genes in a population that arise because genes allow an organism to have more offspring that survive.

Need: A condition that arises from the lack of a requirement; needs give rise to drives.

Need for achievement: The need to reach goals that require skilled performance or competence to be accomplished.

Negative reinforcement: Occurs when an unpleasant event or circumstance is removed following a desired behavior, thereby increasing the probability of the behavior's occurring again.

Negative symptom: A diminution or loss of normal functions, such as a restriction in speech.

Nerve deafness: A type of deafness that typically occurs when the hair cells are destroyed by loud sounds.

Neuroendocrine system: The system regulated by the CNS, that makes hormones that affect many bodily functions; also provides the CNS with information.

Neuroimaging: Brain scanning techniques that produce a picture of the structure or functioning of neurons.

Neuromodulator: A chemical that alters the effects of neurotransmitters.

Neuron: A cell that receives signals from other neurons or sense organs, processes these signals, and sends the signals to other neurons, muscles, or bodily organs; the basic unit of the nervous system.

Neurosis: An abnormal behavior pattern relating to a conflict between the ego and either the id or the superego.

Neurotransmitter: A chemical that sends signals from the terminal buttons on one neuron to the dendrites or cell body of another.

Nocebo effect: A variation of the placebo effect in which the subject expects a negative outcome instead of a positive outcome.

Nondeprived reward: Reward that occurs even when a requirement is not being met.

Norm: A shared belief that is enforced through a group's use of penalties.

Normal curve: A particular distribution of scores, in which most fall in the middle, and symmetrically fewer toward the extremes; also known as a *bell curve.*

Norming: The process of setting the mean score and standard deviation of a test, based on results from a standardized sample.

Obedience: Compliance with an order.

Object permanence: The understanding that objects (including people) continue to exist even when they cannot be immediately perceived.

Observational learning: Learning that occurs through watching others, not through reinforcement.

Obsession: A recurrent and persistent thought, impulse, or image that feels intrusive and inappropriate, and is difficult to suppress or ignore.

Obsessive-compulsive disorder (OCD): A disorder marked by the presence of obsessions, and sometimes compulsions.

Occipital lobe: The brain lobe at the back of the head; concerned entirely with different aspects of vision.

Operant conditioning: The process by which a behavior becomes associated with its consequences.

Opiate: A narcotic, such as morphine, derived from the opium poppy.

Opponent cells: Cells that pit the colors in a pair, notably blue/yellow or red/green, against each other.

Opponent process theory of color vision: The theory that if a color is present, it causes cells that register it to inhibit the perception of the complementary color (such as red versus green).

Optic nerve: The large bundle of nerve fibers carrying impulses from the retina into the brain.

Outcome research: Research that asks whether, after psychotherapy, the client is feeling better, functioning better, living more independently, or has fewer symptoms.

Outgroup: A group different than a person's own.

Overextension: An overly broad use of a word to refer to a new object or situation.

Overregularization error: A speaking error that occurs because the child applies a rule even to cases that are exceptions to the rule.

Panic attack: An episode of intense fear or discomfort accompanied by physical and psychological symptoms such as palpitations, breathing difficulties, chest pain, fear of impending doom or doing something uncontrollable, and a sense of unreality.

Panic disorder: A disorder whose hallmark is panic attacks.

Paradoxical cold: A phenomenon that occurs when stimulation of nerves by something hot produces the sensation of cold.

Paradoxical intention: A systems therapy technique that encourages a behavior that seems contradictory to the desired goal.

Paradoxical sleep: Another name for REM sleep, used to emphasize the marked brain activity.

Parasympathetic nervous system: Part of the ANS that is "next to" the sympathetic system and that tends to counteract its effects.

Parietal lobe: The brain lobe at the top, center/rear of the head, involved in registering spatial location, attention, and motor control.

Partial reinforcement: Reinforcement given only intermittently.

Passionate love: An intense feeling that involves sexual attraction, a desire for mutual love and physical closeness, arousal, and a fear that the relationship will end.

Passive interaction: Occurs when the parents' or sibling's genetically shaped tendencies produce an environment that is passively received by the child.

Perceived social support: The subjective sense that support is available should it be needed.

Percentile rank: The percentage of data that have values at or below a particular value.

Perception: The act of organizing and interpreting sensory input as signaling a particular object or event.

Perceptual constancy: The perception of characteristics that occurs when an object or quality (such as shape or color) looks the same even though the sensory information striking the eyes changes.

Peripheral nervous system (PNS): The autonomic nervous system and the skeletal system.

Personality: A consistent set of characteristics that people display over time and across situations, and that distinguish individuals from each other.

Personality disorder: Relatively stable personality traits that are inflexible and maladaptive, causing distress or difficulty with daily functioning.

Personality inventory: A pencil-and-paper method for assessing personality that requires test-takers to read statements and indicate whether each is true or false about themselves.

Personality trait: A relatively consistent characteristic exhibited in different situations.

Persuasion: Attempts to change people's attitudes.

Phobia: A fear and avoidance of an object or situation extreme enough to interfere with everyday life. An irrational fear of a specific object or situation.

Phoneme: The basic building block of speech sounds.

Phonology: The structure of the sounds that can be used to produce words in a language.

Pitch: How high or low a sound seems; higher frequencies of pressure waves produce the experience of higher pitches.

Pituitary gland: The "master gland" that regulates other glands but is itself controlled by the brain, primarily via connections from the hypothalamus.

Placebo: A medically inert substance that nevertheless seems to have medicinal effects.

Place theory: The theory that different frequencies activate different places along the basilar membrane.

Polygraph: A machine that monitors the activity of the sympathetic and parasympathetic nervous systems, particularly changes in skin conductance, breathing, and heart rate. These machines are used in attempts to detect lying.

Pons: A bridge between the brainstem and the cerebellum that plays a role in functions ranging from sleep to control of facial muscles.

Pop-out: A phenomenon that occurs when a stimulus is sufficiently different from the ones around it that it is immediately evident.

Population: A group of people who share certain characteristics, such as age, sex, or other relevant variables. The entire set of relevant people or animals.

Positive reinforcement: Occurs when a desired reinforcer is presented after a response, thereby increasing the likelihood of a recurrence of that response.

Positive symptom: An excess or distortion of normal functions, such as a hallucination.

Positron emission tomography (PET): A neuroimaging technique that uses small amounts of radiation to track blood or energy consumption in the brain.

Posttraumatic stress disorder (PTSD): A disorder experienced by some people after a traumatic event, whose symptoms include an unwanted reexperiencing of the trauma, avoidance of anything associated with the trauma, and heightened arousal.

Pragmatics: The way that language conveys meaning indirectly, by implying rather than asserting.

Prediction: An expectation about specific events that should occur in particular circumstances if a theory or hypothesis is correct.

Prejudice: An attitude (generally negative) toward members of a group.

Primacy effect: Increased memory for the first few stimuli in a set.

Primary mental abilities: According to Thurstone, seven fundamental abilities that are not outgrowths of other abilities.

Primary reinforcer: An event or object that is inherently reinforcing, such as food, water, or relief from pain.

Priming: The result of having just performed a task that facilitates repeating the same or an associated task.

Private speech: The use of language in planning or in prompting oneself to behave in specific ways.

Proactive interference: Interference that occurs when previous knowledge makes it difficult to learn something new.

Problem: An obstacle that must be overcome to reach a goal.

Problem-focused coping: Coping focused on changing the environment itself, or how the person interacts with the environment.

Prodigies: People who early in life demonstrate immense talent in a particular domain, such as music or mathematics, but who are normal in other domains.

Progressive muscle relaxation: A relaxation technique whereby the person relaxes muscles sequentially from one end of the body to the other.

Projective test: A method used to assess personality and psychopathology that involves asking the test-taker to make sense of an ambiguous stimulus.

Prosocial behavior: Acting to benefit others.

Prototype: A representation of the most typical example of a category.

Pruning: A process whereby certain connections among neurons are eliminated.

Pseudopsychology: Theories or statements that look like psychology but are in fact superstition or unsupported opinion pretending to be science.

Psychiatric nurse: A nurse who holds a master's degree in nursing as well as a certificate of clinical specialization in psychiatric nursing (M.S.N., C.S.), and who provides psychotherapy and works with medical doctors to monitor and administer medications.

Psychiatrist: A physician who focuses on mental disorders; unlike psychologists, psychiatrists can prescribe drugs, but they are not trained to administer and interpret psychological tests, nor are they trained to interpret and understand psychological research.

Psychoanalysis: An intensive form of therapy, originally developed by Freud, based on the idea that people's psychological difficulties are caused by conflicts among the id, ego, and superego.

Psychodynamic theory: A theory of how thoughts and feelings affect behavior; refers to the continual push-and-pull interaction among various conscious and unconscious forces.

Psychodynamic therapy: A less intensive form of psychoanalysis.

Psychoeducation: The process of educating clients about therapy and research findings pertaining to their disorders or problems.

Psychological determinism: The view that all behavior, no matter how mundane or insignificant, has a psychological cause.

Psychological disorder: A constellation of cognitive, emotional, and behavioral symptoms marked by an individual's significant distress, or impairment in work, school, family, relationships, or daily living.

Psychology: The science of mental processes and behavior.

Psychopharmacology: The use of medication to treat psychological disorders and problems.

Psychophysics: The study of the relation between physical events and the corresponding experience of those events.

Psychosexual stages: Freud's developmental stages based on erogenous zones; the specific needs of each stage must be met for its successful resolution.

Psychosis: An obvious impairment in the ability to perceive and comprehend events accurately and a gross disorganization of behavior.

Psychosocial development: The effects of maturation and learning on personality and relationships.

Psychotherapy: Talking and listening to patients about their problems and helping them to see the causes and—more important—to find solutions.

Psychotherapy integration: The use of techniques from different theoretical orientations with an overarching understanding of how the different techniques will be used to achieve the goals of treatment.

Puberty: The time when hormones cause the sex organs to mature and secondary sexual characteristics begin to appear, such as breasts for women and facial hair for men.

Punishment: An unpleasant event that occurs as a consequence of a behavior, thereby decreasing the probability of the recurrence of the behavior.

Pupil: The opening in the eye through which light passes.

Range: The difference obtained by subtracting the smallest score from the largest; the simplest measure of variability.

Ratio schedule: Partial reinforcement schedule based on a specified number of emitted responses.

Reality monitoring: An ongoing awareness of perceptual and other properties that distinguish real from imagined stimuli.

Recall: The act of intentionally bringing explicit information to awareness, which requires transferring the information from LTM to STM.

Recategorization: A means of reducing prejudice by shifting the categories of "us" and "them" so that the two groups are no longer distinct entities.

Recency effect: Increased memory for the last few stimuli in a set.

Receptor: A site on the dendrite or cell body where a messenger molecule attaches itself; like a lock that is opened by one key, a receptor receives only one type of neurotransmitter or neuromodulator.

Reciprocal determinism: The interactive relationship between the environment, cognitive/personal factors, and behavior.

Recognition: The act of encoding an input and matching it to a stored representation. Your awareness when you perceive an object and simply know that it is familiar.

Reflex: An automatic response to an event.

Reframing: A therapy technique in which the therapist offers a new way of conceptualizing, or "framing," the problem.

Rehearsal: The process of repeating information over and over to retain it in STM.

Reinforcement: The process by which consequences lead to an increase in the likelihood that the response will occur again.

Reinforcer: Any object or event that follows the desired response and changes the likelihood of the recurrence of that response.

Reliability: A study is reliable if it yields the same results when repeated.

REM rebound: The higher percentage of REM sleep following a night's sleep deprived of REM.

REM sleep: Stage of sleep characterized by rapid eye movements and marked brain activity.

Repetition blindness: The inability to see the second occurrence of a stimulus that appears twice in succession.

Repetition priming: Priming that makes the same information more easily accessed in the future.

Replicate: To repeat a study and obtain the same results as were found previously.

Representation problem: The challenge of how best to formulate the nature of a problem.

Representativeness heuristic: The heuristic that the more similar something is to a prototype stored in memory, the more likely it is to belong to the prototype's category.

Repressed memories: Real memories that have been pushed out of consciousness because they are emotionally threatening.

Repression: A defense mechanism that occurs when the unconscious prevents threatening thoughts, impulses, and memories from entering consciousness.

Resistance: A reluctance or refusal to cooperate with the therapist, which can range from unconscious forgetting to outright refusal to comply with a therapist's request.

Resistance phase: The second phase of the GAS, in which the body mobilizes its resources to attain equilibrium, despite the continued presence of the stressor; also called the *adaptation phase.*

Response bias: A tendency to respond in a particular way regardless of knowledge or beliefs relevant to performing the task correctly.

Response contingency: The relationship that occurs when a consequence is dependent on the organism's emitting the desired behavior.

Reticular formation: A two-part structure in the brainstem; the "ascending" part plays a key role in keeping a person awake and alert; the "descending" part is important in producing autonomic nervous system reactions.

Retina: A sheet of tissue at the back of the eye containing cells that convert light to neural impulses.

Retinal disparity: The difference between the images striking the retinas of the two eyes; also called binocular disparity.

Retrograde amnesia: Amnesia that disrupts previous memories.

Reuptake: The process by which surplus neurotransmitter is reabsorbed back into the sending neuron so that the neuron can effectively fire again.

Rods: Retinal cells that are very sensitive to light but register only shades of gray.

Role: The behaviors that a member in a given position in a group is expected to perform.

Rorschach test: A projective test consisting of a set of inkblots that people are asked to "interpret."

s: "Specific factors," or aspects of performance that are particular to a given kind of processing—and distinct from *g.*

Sample: The group from which a researcher obtains measures or observations.

Sampling bias: Occurs when the participants or items are not chosen at random, so that an attribute is over- or underrepresented.

Sampling error: A difference that arises by chance, not because the samples are representative of different populations.

Schema: A collection of concepts that specify necessary and optional aspects of a particular situation. A mental structure that organizes perceptual input and connects it with the appropriate responses.

Schizophrenia: A psychotic disorder in which the patient's affect, behavior, and the pattern or form of thoughts are profoundly altered and functioning deteriorates.

Scientific method: A method that involves specifying a problem; systematically observing events; forming a hypothesis of the relation between variables; collecting new observations to test the hypothesis; using such evidence to formulate and support a theory; and, finally, testing the theory.

Secondary reinforcer: An event or object that is reinforcing but that does not inherently satisfy a physical need, such as attention, praise, money, good grades, or a promotion.

Selective attention: The process of picking out a particular quality, object, or event for relatively detailed analysis.

Selective serotonergic reuptake inhibitor (SSRI): A type of antidepressant medication that affects only *selective* serotonin receptors, with fewer side effects.

Selective serotonin-reuptake inhibitor (SSRI): A chemical that blocks the reuptake of the neurotransmitter serotonin.

Self-actualization: An innate motivation to attain the highest possible emotional and intellectual potential.

Self-concept: The beliefs, desires, values, and attributes that define a person to himself or herself.

Self-help group: A group whose members focus on a specific disorder or event and do not usually have a clinically trained leader; also called a *support group.*

Self-monitoring techniques: Behavioral techniques that help the client identify the antecedents, consequences, and patterns of a targeted behavior.

Self-serving bias: A person's inclination to attribute his or her own failures to external causes and successes to internal causes, but to attribute other people's failures to internal causes and their successes to external causes.

Semantic memories: The memories of the meanings of words, concepts, and general facts about the world.

Semantics: The meaning of a word or sentence.

Sensation: The immediate experience of basic properties of an object or event that occurs when a receptor is stimulated.

Sensitive period: A window of time when a particular type of learning is *easiest,* but not the only time it can occur.

Sensitivity: In signal detection theory, the threshold level for distinguishing between a stimulus and noise; the lower the threshold, the greater the sensitivity.

Sensory memory (SM): The "lowest" level of memory, which holds a large amount of perceptual input for a very brief time, typically less than one second.

Sensory neuron: A neuron that responds to input from sense organs.

Separation anxiety: The fear of being away from the primary caregiver.

Serotonergic/noradrenergic reuptake inhibitor (SNRI): A newer antidepressant that affects both serotonin and noradrenergic neurotransmitter systems.

Set point: The particular body weight that is easiest for an animal (including a human) to maintain.

Sexual response cycle (SRC): The stages the body passes through during sexual activity, now characterized as including sexual attraction, desire, excitement, and performance (which includes plateau, orgasm, and resolution).

Shape constancy: Seeing objects as having the same shape even when the image on the retina changes.

Shaping: The gradual process of reinforcing an organism for behavior that gets closer to the desired behavior.

Short-term memory (STM): A memory store that holds relatively little information (typically 5 to 9 items) for a few seconds (but perhaps as long as 30 seconds); people are conscious only of the current contents of STM.

Signal detection theory: A theory explaining why people detect signals, which are always embedded in noise, in some situations but not in others.

Situationism: A view of personality that regards behavior as mostly a function of the situation, not of internal traits.

Size constancy: Seeing an object as being the same size when viewed at different distances and visual angles.

Skeletal system: Consists of nerves that are attached to striated muscles and bones.

Skewed distribution: A set of data that has many scores near one extreme value and away from the center.

Sleep: The naturally recurrent experience during which normal consciousness is suspended.

Sleep apnea: Difficulty breathing accompanied by loud snoring during sleep.

Sociability: A temperament dimension characterized by a preference to be in other people's company rather than alone.

Social categorization theory: The theory that people are driven to divide the world automatically into categories of "us" versus "them."

Social causation: The chronic psychological and social stresses of living in an urban environment that may lead to an increase in the rate of schizophrenia (especially among the poor).

Social cognition: The area of social psychology that focuses on how people attend to, store, remember, and use information about other people and the social world.

Social desirability: A bias in responding to questions such that people try to make themselves "look good" even if it means giving untrue answers.

Social exchange theory: A theory that proposes that individuals act to maximize the gains and minimize the losses in their relationships.

Social facilitation: The increase in performance that can occur simply by being part of a group or in the presence of other people.

Social loafing: The tendency to work less hard when responsibility for an outcome is spread over the group's members.

Social phobia: A type of phobia involving fear of public humiliation or embarrassment and the ensuing avoidance of situations likely to arouse this fear.

Social psychology: The field of psychology pertaining to how people think about other people and interact in relationships and groups.

Social selection: The tendency of the mentally disabled to drift to the lower economic classes; also called *social drift*.

Social support: The help and support gained through interacting with others.

Social worker: A mental health professional who helps families (and individuals) with psychotherapy and helps clients use the social service systems in their communities.

Somasthetic senses: Senses that have to do with perceiving the body and its position in space—specifically, kinesthetic sense, vestibular sense, touch, temperature sensitivity, pain sense, and possibly magnetic sense.

Somatosensory strip: The gyrus, located immediately behind the central sulcus, that registers sensation on the body and is organized by body part.

Source amnesia: A failure to remember the source of information.

Specific phobia: A type of phobia involving persistent and excessive or unreasonable fear triggered by a specific object or situation, along with attempts to avoid the feared stimulus.

Speech segmentation problem: The problem of organizing a continuous stream of speech into separate parts that correspond to individual words.

Spinal cord: The flexible rope of nerves that runs inside the backbone, or spinal column.

Split-brain patient: A person whose corpus callosum has been severed for medical reasons, so that neuronal impulses no longer pass from one hemisphere to the other.

Spontaneous recovery: In classical conditioning, the process by which the CS will again elicit the CR after extinction has occurred. In operant conditioning, the process by which an old response reappears if there is a break after extinction.

St. John's wort: An herbal remedy for mild to moderate depression.

Standard deviation: A measure of the degree to which individual scores deviate from the mean.

Standardized sample: A random selection of people, drawn from a carefully defined population.

State-dependent retrieval: Recall that is better if it occurs in the same psychological state as when the information was first encoded.

Statistics: Numbers that summarize or indicate differences or patterns of differences in measurements.

Status hierarchy: Roles that reflect who has power over whom.

Stereopsis: The process that registers depth on the basis of retinal disparity.

Stereotype: A belief (or set of beliefs) about people in a particular social category.

Stimulant: A class of substances that excite the central nervous system, leading to increases in behavioral activity and heightened arousal.

Stimulus control: A behavior therapy technique that involves controlling the exposure to a stimulus that elicits a conditioned response, so as to decrease or increase the frequency of the response.

Stimulus discrimination: The ability to distinguish among similar conditioned stimuli and to respond only to actual conditioned stimuli.

Stimulus generalization: A tendency for the CR to be elicited by neutral stimuli that are like, but not identical to, the CS; in other words, the response *generalizes* to similar stimuli.

Strategy: An approach to solving a problem, determined by the type of representation used and the processing steps to be tried.

Stress: The general term describing the psychological and bodily response to a stimulus that alters a person's state of equilibrium.

Stressor: A stimulus that throws the body's equilibrium out of balance.

Stress response: The physiological changes that occur to help people cope with a stressor; also called the *fight-or-flight response*.

Stroke: A result of the failure of blood (with its life-giving nutrients and oxygen) to reach part of the brain, causing neurons in that area to die.

Structuralism: The school of psychology that sought to identify the basic elements of experience and to describe the rules and circumstances under which these elements combine to form mental *structures*.

Substance abuse: Drug or alcohol use that leads to legal difficulties, causes distress or difficulty functioning in major areas of life, or occurs in dangerous situations.

Substance dependence: Chronic substance abuse that is characterized by seven symptoms, the two most important being tolerance and withdrawal.

Successive approximations: The series of smaller behaviors involved in shaping a complex behavior.

Sulcus: A fold in the cerebral cortex.

Superego: A psychic structure, proposed by Freud, that is formed during early childhood and houses the sense of right and wrong, based on the internalization of parental and cultural morality.

Suprachiasmatic nucleus (SCN): A small part of the hypothalamus just above the optic chiasm that registers changes in light, which lead to production of hormones that regulate various bodily functions.

Survey: A set of questions, typically about beliefs, attitudes, preferences, or activities.

Sympathetic nervous system: Part of the ANS that readies an animal to fight or to flee by speeding up the heart, increasing breathing rate to deliver more oxygen, dilating the pupils, producing sweat, increasing salivation, inhibiting activity in the stomach, and relaxing the bladder.

Synapse: The place where an axon of one neuron meets the membrane (on a dendrite or cell body) of another neuron.

Synaptic cleft: The gap between the axon of one neuron and the membrane of another, across which communication occurs.

Syntax: The internal grammatical structure of a sentence, determined by how words that belong to different parts of speech are organized into acceptable arrangements.

Systematic desensitization: A behavior therapy technique that teaches people to be relaxed in the presence of a feared object or situation.

Systems therapy: Therapy that views a client's symptoms as occurring in a larger context, or system (the family and subculture), in which a change in one part of the system affects the rest of the system.

Tardive dyskinesia: An irreversible movement disorder in which the person involuntarily smacks his or her lips, displays facial grimaces, and exhibits other symptoms, caused by traditional antipsychotic medication.

Taste buds: Microscopic structures on the bumps on the tongue surface, at the back of the throat, and inside the cheeks; the four types of taste buds are sensitive to sweet, sour, salty, and bitter tastes.

T cell: A type of white blood cell that matures in the thymus.

Telegraphic speech: Speech that packs much information into few words.

Temperament: Innate inclinations to engage in a certain style of behavior.

Temporal lobe: The brain lobe under the temples, in front of the ears, where sideburns begin to grow down; among its many functions are visual memory and hearing.

Teratogen: Any chemical, virus, or type of radiation that can cause damage to the zygote, embryo, or fetus.

Terminal button: A structure at the end of axons that, when the neuron is triggered, releases chemicals into the space between neurons.

Test bias: Test design features that lead a particular group to perform well or poorly and that thus invalidate the test.

Testosterone: The hormone that causes males to develop facial hair and other sex characteristics and to build up muscle volume.

Texture gradients: Progressive changes in texture that signal distance.

Thalamus: A subcortical region that receives inputs from sensory and motor systems and plays a crucial role in attention; often thought of as a switching center.

Theory: A statement of a set of underlying principles that are supposed to explain a set of observations.

Theory of causal attribution: Rules for deciding whether to attribute a given behavior to a person's enduring traits or to the situation.

Theory of mind: A theory of other people's mental states (their beliefs, desires, and feelings) that allows prediction of what other people can understand and how they will react in a given situation.

Theory of multiple intelligences: Gardner's theory of eight distinct types of intelligence, which can vary separately for a given individual.

Thought suppression: The coping strategy that involves purposefully trying not to think about something emotionally arousing or distressing.

Threshold: The point at which stimulation is strong enough to be noticed.

Token economy: A treatment program that uses secondary reinforcers (tokens) to bring about behavior modification.

Tonotopic organization: The use of distance along a strip of cortex to represent differences in pitch.

Top-down processing: Processing that is initiated by knowledge, expectation, or belief.

Transcranial magnetic stimulation (TMS): An experimental treatment for psychological disorders involving the use of electromagnetic stimulation. A procedure that involves stimulation of the brain from the outside, by putting a wire coil on a person's head and delivering a magnetic pulse. The magnetic fields are so strong that they make neurons under the coil fire.

Transduction: The process whereby physical energy is converted by a sensory neuron into neural impulses.

Transfer appropriate processing: Processing that transfers to a task that requires similar processing.

Transference: The process by which patients may relate to their therapists as they did to some important person in their lives.

Triangular model of love: A theory of love marked by the dimensions of (1) passion (including sexual desire), (2) intimacy (closeness), and (3) commitment.

Trichromatic theory of color vision: The theory that color vision arises from the combinations of neural impulses from three different kinds of sensors, each of which responds maximally to a different wavelength.

Tricyclic antidepressant (TCA): A common set of antidepressant medications named for the three rings in the chemical compound.

Twin study: A study that compares identical and fraternal twins to determine the relative contribution of genes to variability in a behavior or characteristic.

Typicality: The degree to which an entity is representative of its category.

Unconditional positive regard: Acceptance without any conditions. The stance taken by a client-centered therapist that conveys positive feelings for the client, regardless of the client's thoughts, feelings, or actions.

Unconditioned response (UCR): The reflexive response elicited by a particular stimulus.

Unconditioned stimulus (UCS): A stimulus that elicits an automatic response (UCR), without requiring prior learning.

Unconscious: Outside conscious awareness and not able to be brought to consciousness at will.

Validation: A therapy technique in which the therapist conveys his or her understanding of the client's feelings and wishes.

Validity: A measure is valid if it does in fact measure what it is supposed to measure.

Variable: An aspect of a situation that can vary, or change.

Variable interval schedule: Reinforcement schedule in which reinforcement is given for a response emitted after a variable interval of time.

Variable ratio schedule: Reinforcement schedule in which reinforcement is given after a variable ratio of responses.

Vestibular sense: The sense that provides information about the body's orientation relative to gravity.

Volume: The strength of a sound; pressure waves with greater amplitude produce the experience of louder sound.

Want: A condition that arises when an animal has an unmet goal that will not fill a requirement; wants turn goals into incentives.

Wavelength: The time between the arrival of peaks of a light wave; shorter wavelengths correspond to higher frequencies.

Weber's law: The rule that a constant percentage of a magnitude change is necessary to detect a difference.

Wechsler Adult Intelligence Scale (WAIS): The most widely used intelligence test; consists of both verbal and performance subtests.

Working memory (WM): The system that includes specialized STMs and the "central executive" processes that operate on them.

Zygote: A fertilized ovum (egg).

Name Index

Note: Page numbers followed by *f* indicate figures; page numbers followed by *t* indicate tables.

Patterson, D., 412
Patterson, M., 484
Patterson, R., 98
Patterson, T. L., 386
Patton, M. J., 434
Paulesu, E., 195
Paulhus, D. L., 281
Paulinis, P. A., 457
Pauls, D., 403
Paulus, M. P., 408
Paunonen, S. V., 280, 303
Pavlov, I. P., 123–125
Peabody, C., 405
Peake, P. K., 277–278
Pearce, J. K., 459
Pearson, D., 316
Pearson, J., 485, 487
Peck, C. L., 134
Pedersen, C. B., 418
Pederson, N. L., 288, 289f, 340
Peeck, J., 100
Peeke, H. V. S., 312
Pekala, R. J., 385
Penfield, W., 69, 179
Peng, K., 477
Pengilly, J. W., 384
Penn, G., 384
Pennebaker, J. W., 372, 373, 437
Penrod, S., 472
Pentland, J., 177
Penton-Voak, I., 104, 480
Perdue, C. W., 474
Perel, J. M., 457
Peri, T., 406
Perkins, D. O., 447
Perkins, H. W., 485t
Perlmutter, M., 340
Perloff, R., 224, 226, 227, 229
Perot, P., 69
Perret, Y., 230
Perrett, D. I., 104, 247, 480
Perry, B. D., 423
Persico, V. R., Jr., 344
Peterhans, E., 97
Petersen, A. C., 334
Petersen, R. C., 383
Petersen, S. E., 89, 164, 165, 169
Peterson, B., 356
Peterson, C., 248, 411
Petit, L., 163, 201
Petit, T., 344
Petitto, L. A., 320
Petrie, K. J., 372, 373
Petrill, S. A., 222
Petry, M. C., 171
Pettigrew, T. F., 473, 475
Pettito, L. A., 196
Petty, R. E., 255, 467, 470, 471, 493
Peyronnin, K., 492
Pezdek, K., 177
Pfaffmann, C., 112
Phelps, J. A., 225
Phelps, M. E., 450
Phil, D., 406
Phillips, A., 318
Phillips, A. G., 145
Phillips, D. P., 66
Phillips, K., 289
Phillips, S. D., 386
Piaget, J., 149, 319, 321–324, 325, 326, 333
Piazza, C. C., 138
Pickering, A. D., 285
Pickles, J. O., 106
Pickrell, J. E., 177

Pietrini, P., 101
Pietromonaco, P. R., 386
Pietrowsky, R., 266
Pike, C. L., 480
Pilkonis, P. A., 456, 457
Pillard, R. C., 268
Pincus, A. L., 281
Pincus, J. H., 423
Pinel, J. P. J., 114
Pinker, S., 18, 98, 192, 196, 202, 252, 321
Pinto, L. H., 365
Pirke, K. M., 425
Pitman, D. L., 354
Pitman, R. K., 406
Plata-Salaman, C. R., 113
Plato, 84, 91, 199
Platt, L. A., 344
Plomin, R., 74, 76, 222, 223, 225, 226, 286, 287, 288, 289, 289f, 312, 340, 395, 411, 413
Plotkin, H., 18, 252
Plotnicov, K., 425
Plotsky, P. M., 316
Poirier, V. C., 345
Polakoski, K. L., 313
Polaschek, D. L. L., 177
Polivy, J., 426
Pollack, M. H., 404, 457, 459
Pollard, R. A., 423
Pollice, C., 425
Pollock, B. G., 457
Polonsky, W., 373
Pope, K. S., 181
Porter, R. C., 63
Porter, R. H., 116, 314
Porto, M., 312
Ports, T. A., 360
Posner, M. I., 69, 70
Post, R. M., 412
Postmes, T., 484
Poston, W. S. C., 262
Potapova, E., 481
Potter, H. H., 61
Poulton, R., 405
Powell, B., 300
Powell, J., 367
Powell, M. C., 468
Powelson, J. A., 61
Powers, A. M., 267f
Pozzato, G., 378
Practice Directorate, 460
Prapavessis, H., 488
Prasada, S., 209
Pratkanis, A. R., 110
Pratt, M. W., 327
Prescott, C. A., 288, 411
Pressley, M., 170
Pressman, E. K., 314
Price, C. J., 85, 101
Price, D. D., 115
Price, L. T., 130
Price, R., 400
Priel, B., 283
Prien, R. F., 448
Priester, J. R., 470
Priluck, R. L., 131
Prins, B., 171
Prinster, A., 201
Pritzel, T., 354
Privette, G., 296
Proctor, R. W., 144
Project MATCH Research Group National Institute on Alcohol Abuse and Alcoholism Bethesda, 459

Prudic, J., 449
Prue, D. M., 133
Prusky, G. T., 166
Pryds, O., 314
Pryor, D., 384
Prysbeck, T. R., 283
Pugh, K. R., 193, 229
Pujol, R., 312
Puka, B., 330
Putnam, F. W., 423
Putnam, H., 9
Putnam, K., 243
Pyhala, R., 417

Quinn, J. G., 162
Quinn, O. W., 419, 420
Quinsey, L., 130

Raag, T., 331
Rabe-Hesketh, S., 418
Rabin, B. S., 358
Rabin, M. D., 111
Rabinowitz, F. E., 494
Rackliff, C. L., 331
Radvansky, G. A., 339
Rae, D. S., 394
Rafanelli, C., 457
Rahe, R. H., 355
Rahn, C., 319
Raible, R., 358
Raichle, M., 69, 70
Raichle, M. E., 164, 165, 169
Räikkönen, K., 356
Raine, A., 286
Rainer, G., 101
Rainville, P., 115
Rakic, P., 311
Ramachandran, V. S., 73
Ramirez, I., 259
Ramirez, M., III, 459, 460
Ramos-Grenier, J., 459, 460
Rampon, C., 166
Rao, S. B., 321
Rao, S. C., 101
Raol, R., 425
Rapoport, S. I., 101
Rasmussen, T., 68
Rathus, S., 313
Rauch, S. L., 194, 201, 247, 406, 407
Ravich-Scherbo, I., 287
Raye, C. L., 177
Raymond, J. E., 104
Raynal, D. M., 366
Raynor, R., 125–126, 127, 128
Razran, G. H. S., 131
Reagor, P., 422
Rechtschaffen, A., 368
Redd, W. H., 129, 134
Reed, G. M., 476
Rees, A., 458
Regan, D. T., 468
Regan, F. A., 313
Regan, P. C., 266
Regard, M., 116
Regier, D. A., 394, 406, 409
Reid, J. E., 250
Reid, R. C., 94, 95, 96
Reid, S., 482
Reifman, A., 409
Reilly, J., 411
Reiman, E. M., 177, 248
Reinikainen, K., 312
Reinisch, J. M., 229
Reis, H. T., 255, 479, 482
Reise, S. P., 281

Relkin, N. R., 196
Reminger, S. L., 165
Rende, R., 395, 413
Renner, C. H., 485
Rensink, R. A., 103
Repetti, R. L., 386
Reppas, J. B., 99
Rescorla, R. A., 128
Resnick, H. S., 406
Rest, J. R., 330
Retsinas, J., 343
Rey, H. R., 312
Reynolds, C. E., III, 367, 449, 457
Reynolds, D. K., 344
Rezai, K., 417
Reznick, J. S., 289
Ricaurte, G., 382
Rice, C. L., 472
Rice, G., 268
Rice, J., 406, 408
Rice, K., 335
Rice, M. E., 152
Richards, K., 352
Richards, N. J., 334
Richards, W. A., 101
Richardson, D., 373
Richert, E. S., 231
Riddoch, M. J., 85, 101
Riegel, K. F., 338
Riemann, R., 288
Riley, P. J., 386
Rimer, B. K., 313
Rimmer, D. W., 366
Rimmo, P. -A., 126
Rinn, W. E., 245
Rinne, T., 312
Riordan, L., 289
Rips, L. J., 202
Risch, N., 268
Risler, R. E., 406
Rittenhouse, C. D., 364
Rivera, V. J., 360
Rivera-Arzola, M., 459, 460
Robbins, T. W., 146
Roberts, A. H., 385
Roberts, A., 480
Roberts, B. W., 342
Roberts, J. E., 412
Roberts, L. D., 480
Roberts, P., 342
Robertson, B., 359
Robertson, L. C., 61
Robins, L. N., 406
Robinson, L. A., 411
Robinson, N. M., 229
Robinson, T. N., 297
Rochat, P., 328
Rockstroh, B., 70
Rodier, P., 312
Rodin, J., 337, 345, 426
Rodriguez, M., 359
Rodriguez, M. L., 141
Roeder, K., 225
Roediger, H. L., III, 164, 176, 177, 178, 184, 185
Rogers, C., 16–17, 297, 435, 458
Rogers, R. J., 477
Rogers-Ramachandran, D., 73
Rohde, P., 409
Roll, S., 488
Rolland, J. P., 303, 304
Rollman, G. B., 115
Rolls, B. J., 260
Rolls, E. T., 254, 260
Romani, G. L., 108
Romero, A. A., 470, 471

Werker, J. F., 320
Werner, C., 386
Wertheimer, M., 14, 19t, 97
Wertsch, J. V., 326
West, S., 460
West, S. A., 397
Westen, D., 295
Westergaard, T., 418
Whalen, P. J., 247
Wheeler, D., 489
Wheeler, L., 480
Wheeler, M. D., 333
Whisman, M. A., 412
White, A., 25
White, B. J., 474
White, D., 266
White, J. M., 384
White, K., 407
White, T. L., 372
Whitfield, K., 287
Whittal, M. L., 458
Whittchen, H. N., 394, 409
Whorf, B., 198
Wickramartne, P., 406
Wickramasekera, I., 385
Widiger, T. A., 400, 412
Wiegand, A. W., 470
Wiegant, V. M., 266
Wienbruch, C., 70
Wieselgren, I., 419
Wiest, G. H., 369
Wiggins, J. S., 278, 281
Wiggs, C. L., 204
Wightman, R. M., 255
Wilder, D. A., 472
Wilder, T., 376
Wilkinson, D. J. C., 403
Willer, J. C., 115
Willerman, L., 287, 288
Williams, C., 262
Williams, C. J., 472
Williams, D. A., 360
Williams, J. E., 356
Williams, K., 367, 493
Williams, K. A., 320
Williams, K. D., 493
Williams, L. M., 181

Williams, M., 286
Williams, N. M., 222
Williams, R., 356, 357, 384, 406
Williams, R. B., Jr., 355, 356
Williams, R. M., 359
Williams, S., 456
Williams, W., 229
Williams, W. M., 224
Williamson, S., 228
Williamson, S. J., 108
Willis, S. L., 340
Wills, T., 384
Wilsbacher, L. D., 365
Wilson, D., 494
Wilson, D. H., 60
Wilson, D. M., 297
Wilson, M., 166
Wilson, M. A., 366
Windle, M., 409
Winer, G. A., 84
Wingo, P. A., 314
Winn, P., 260
Winner, E., 231
Winocur, G., 101
Winter, J. B., 368
Winzelberg, A., 453
Wise, P. M., 338
Wise, R. A., 254, 255
Wist, E., 25
Witelson, S. F., 222
Witt, S. D., 331
Wittchen, H. U., 406, 408
Wixted, J. T., 178
Wlos, J., 382
Wohlfahrt, J., 418
Wojciulik, E., 89
Wolf, N., 483
Wolfe, B. E., 458
Wolkenstein, B. H., 485
Wolpe, J., 438
Wong, E. C., 368
Wong, P. S., 130
Wood, W., 483
Woods, R. P., 326
Woods, S. C., 259
Woodson, R., 324

Worchel, S., 487
Worthington, J. J., III, 404
Worthington, T. S., 186
Wortman, C., 413
Wotman, S. R., 376
Wright, A., 486
Wright, S., 494
Wright, S. I., 487
Wright, W. L., 270
Wrightsman, L. S., 477
Wu, C. H., 480
Wu, J., 171
Wu, W., 386
Wundt, W., 13, 19t
Wurtman, R., 365
Wurtzel, E., 408
Wyatt, R. J., 37, 448
Wyer, N. A., 472
Wynings, C., 359

Xenakis, S., 260
Xerri, C., 73

Yagueez, L., 25
Yahya, K. A., 491
Yamamoto, S., 311
Yamauchi, L., 478
Yan, M., 229
Yang, K., 303
Yano, M., 311
Yap, L., 459
Yaroslavsky, T., 450
Yatham, L. N., 449
Yazigi, R. A., 313
Yeager, C. A., 423
Yeh, E. K., 406
Yehuda, R., 359
Yeoh, A. E. O., 457
Yeomans, M. R., 259, 260
Yeshurun, Y., 88
Yoder, C. Y., 412
Yoshikawa, S., 104, 480
Yost, W. A., 109
Young, A. W., 61, 247
Young, K., 460
Young, T., 94
Young, W. G., 259

Young-Ihl, K., 312
Yu, E., 386
Yu, Y. M., 258
Yuh, W. T., 417
Yule, W., 406
Yun, L. S., 177

Zaharia, M. D., 316
Zahs, K. R., 49
Zajonc, R. B., 23, 480
Zakowski, S., 385
Zane, N., 460
Zane, N. W. S., 279
Zanna, M. P., 469, 480, 482, 493
Zapotoczky, H., 360
Zatorre, R. J., 110, 163
Zautra, A. J., 355
Zebrowitz, L. A., 480
Zeidner, M., 303
Zeki, S. M., 95, 99, 103
Zelazo, P. D., 325
Zeller, P. J., 408
Zenger, T. R., 492
Zentner, M. R., 319
Zhang, M. Y., 386
Zhao, S., 394, 409
Zhao, Y., 365
Zhao, Z., 165, 169, 286
Zhdanova, I., 365
Zhu, X. -H., 201
Zhukov, D. A., 258
Zhuo, M., 166
Zigmond, M. J., 260
Zihl, J., 99
Zika, S., 355
Zimmer, E. Z., 312
Zimmermann, E. A., 355, 356
Zis, A. P., 449
Znyder, A. Z., 169
Zoccolillo, M., 400
Zola-Morgan, S., 180
Zornberg, G. L., 417
Zuckerman, M., 29, 280, 286, 287, 302
Zurek, P. M., 106
Zwicker, E., 106

Subject Index

Note: Page numbers followed by *f* indicate figures; those followed by *t* indicate tables; **boldface** type indicates key terms and the pages where they are defined.

Attentional blink, 103, 103–104
Attitude, 467, 467–471
  behavior and, 468–470
  cognitions and, 467–468
  cognitive dissonance, 468–470, 469f, 473–474, 478
  about death penalty, 478
  persuasion to change, 470–471
  strong, 471
Attractiveness, physical, 104–105, 480, 482–483
Attributional biases, 477, 477–478
Attributional style, 411, 411–412
Attributions, 476, 476–478, 477t
Atypical antipsychotics, 447
Audition. See Hearing
Auditory imagery, 110
Auditory scene analysis, 109
Autobiographical memories, 163
Autonomic nervous system (ANS), 53, 53–55
Autonomy, 302
Autonomy versus doubt, 341t
Availability heuristic, 210, 210–211
Avoidance, selective, 471
Avoidance-avoidance conflict, 355
Avoidance coping strategies, 371–372
Avoidance learning, 125, 139
Avoidant attachment, 328, 481
Avoidant personality disorder, 399t
Avolition, 415
Awareness
  attention as gateway to, 88
  hearing without, 110
  vision without, 102–104
Axon, 46, 46f

Babbling, 320
Babinski reflex, 315t
Balance, sense of, 114
Bandura, Albert, 150–151
Barbiturates, 381
Basal ganglia, 63, 63–64
Base-rate rule, 210
Basic anxiety, 295
Basic emotions, 241, 242f
Basic level, 203, 204f
Basic trust versus mistrust, 341t
Basilar membrane, 107, 108, 108f
B cells, 358
BDNF (brain-derived neurotrophic factor), 74
Beauty, physical, 104–105. See also Physical attractiveness
Bechterev, Vladimir, 125
Beck, Aaron, 443, 444–445
Beethoven, Ludwig, 110
Behavior, 9
  attitudes and, 468–470
  eating, 259–261
  predicting, 468
  social. See Social behavior
Behavioral disengagement, 371
Behavioral genetics, 74, 74–75
Behaviorism, 15–16, 16, 19t
Behavior modification, 140, 140–141, 440, 440–441, 446
Behavior therapy, 438, 438–442, 446t

Belief in a just world, 477, 477–478
Beliefs, tastes in food and, 261
Benzodiazepines, 448, 448–449
Bereavement, 344
Bias, 33, 88
  attributional, 477–478
  confirmation, 209–210
  diagnostic, 397
  hostile attribution, 373
  in personality inventories, 281–282
  response, 33
  sampling, 33
  self-serving, 477
  toward shyness, 290
  test, 227
Bibliotherapy, 453
Big Five, 279t, 280, 283
Bilingualism, 196
Binet, Alfred, 212
Binge drinking, 378
Binge eating, 424, 426
Binocular cues, 98, 100f
Binocular disparity, 98
Biological preparedness, 126, 126–127
Biomedical therapies, 447–450
Biopsychosocial model, 394
Bipolar disorder, 409, 409–410, 411, 412, 413, 448
Birth order, 300–301, 301t
Bisexuality, 267, 267–268
Blackouts, 381
Blaming the victim, 478
Blindness
  color, 95–96
  repetition, 103, 104
Blindsight, 103
Blind spot, 92–93, 93f
Blood alcohol level, 378–379, 378t
Bodily-kinesthetic intelligence, 218
Body language, 249
Body odor, 116
Borderline personality disorder, 399t
Boredom, avoiding, 253
Bottom-up processing, 85, 101, 110
Brain, 42–81. See also Nervous system
  aging and, 338–340, 344–345
  classical conditioning and, 129–130
  concepts in, 204
  cranial nerves in, 52
  damaged, 66, 67–68
  dreams and, 364–365
  emotions and, 247
  evolution and, 75–78
  genetics and, 71–75, 72f
  hemispheres of, 58–61
  hunger and, 260
  immune system and, 65–66
  language areas of, 61, 194f, 196
  learned helplessness and, 258
  learning and, 145–147
  level of the, 9, 10, 12
  lobes of, 55, 56f, 56–58
  long-term memories and, 162–165, 166
  mechanisms underlying reward, 254–255
  mood disorders and, 410–411
  neuroendocrine system and, 64–65
  neuroimaging of, 69–70

  neurons in, 44–48, 45f, 46f
  neurotransmitters and neuromodulators in, 48–51
  panic attacks and, 403
  personality and, 284–290
  primary auditory cortex, 108
  probing, 67–71
  psychological disorders and abnormality of, 394–395
  recording activity in, 68
  schizophrenia and, 416–418
  sex differences in, 229
  size of brain areas, 70–71
  split-brain research, 59–60
  stimulation of, 68–69
  subcortical, 61–64, 62f
  visual area 4 (V4), 95
  visual imaging in, 201–202
Brain circuits, 45. See also Neurons
Brain damage, 57f, 66, 67–68
Brain-derived neurotrophic factor (BDNF), 74
Brainstem, 62f, 64
Brain waves during sleep stages, 361f, 361–362
Breadth of processing, 170, 170–171
Breast cancer support groups, 369
Brief therapy, 454
Brightness, 95
Brightness and color constancy, 100
Broca's area, 194f, 196
Brooks, Mel, 174
Bulimia nervosa, 19, 424, 424–425, 426
Bystander effect, 495, 495–496, 496f

CA (chronological age), 212, 213
Caffeine, 313, 382
Camouflage, 96
Cancer, stress and, 359–360, 369
Cannon-Bard theory of emotion, 243f, 244, 245, 247
Case study, 29, 29–30, 31t
Castration anxiety, 293
Cataracts, 339
Catastrophic exaggeration, 444t
Catatonic schizophrenia, 416t
Categorical perception, 109
Causation, social, 418
CBT (cognitive-behavior therapy), 445, 454, 457, 458
Cell body, 46, 46f
Cell membrane, 46, 46f
Central executive, 162
Central nervous system (CNS), 52, 52–53
CER (conditioned emotional response), 125–127
Cerebellum, 62f, 64
Cerebral cortex, 55, 55–58
Cerebral hemisphere, 55
Challenger disaster, 172
Channels, 46
Chemotherapy, anticipatory nausea before, 134
Child abuse, 181, 422–23
Child-directed speech, 29, 319
Childhood amnesia, 180
Childhood development. See Infancy and childhood

Chimpanzees, language in, 196–197
Chomsky, Noam, 17
Chromosomes, 268, 311, 312f
Chronic stressor, 350
Chronological age (CA), 212, 213
Chunk, 160
Circadian rhythms, 93, 211, **365,** 365–367
Clairvoyance, 115
Classical conditioning, 122, **123,** 123–135, 395–396
　application of, 130–134
　avoidance symptoms of posttraumatic stress disorder and, 406
　of fear, 126, 129f, 129–130, 247
　of immune system, 133–134
　operant conditioning versus, 146, 146t
　Pavlov's experiments, 123f, 123–125, 124f
　phases of, 124f
　phobias and, 405
　process of, 125–130
　punishment and, 140
Client-centered therapy, 16–17, **297, 435,** 435–437, 437t
Clinical neuropsychologists, 20
Clinical practice, ethics in, 36
Clinical psychologist, 19, 22t
Clinton, Bill, 492–493
Clinton, Hillary Rodham, 278
Closure, Gestalt law of, 97
CNS (central nervous system), 52–53
Cobain, Kurt, 232
Cocaine, 381–382
Cocktail party phenomenon, 110
Code, 168
Cognition
　attitudes and, 467–468
　cerebral hemispheres and, 58–61
　conditioned stimulus and, 128–129
　prejudice and, 472–474
　social. See Social cognition
Cognitive-behavior therapy (CBT), 445, 454, 457, 458
Cognitive development
　in adolescence, 333–334
　in adulthood, 339–340
　in infancy and childhood, stages of, 321–327, 322t
　Piaget's theory of, 321–324, 322t
Cognitive dissonance, 468, 468–470, 469f, 473–474, 478
Cognitive distortions, 443, 444t
Cognitive illusion, 210
Cognitive learning, 122, **148,** 148–149, 164
Cognitive neuroscience, 17, 19t
Cognitive psychologist, 21
Cognitive psychology, 17, 19t
Cognitive restructuring, 445
Cognitive revolution, 17
Cognitive taste aversion, 261
Cognitive theory of emotion, 243f, 244, 245–246
Cognitive therapy, 442–446, **443,** 446t
Cognitive view of personality, 297–299
Cohesiveness, conformity and, 488
Collective unconscious, 294–295

Collectivist cultures, 256, 257, 303–304, 305
Colombine High School massacre (1999), 376
Color blindness, 95, 95–96
Color vision, 94–96
Communication
　by chimpanzees, 196–197
　nonverbal, 249, 486
　sign language, 196, 320
　verbal. See Language
Compassionate love, 481
Complex inheritance, 222
Compliance, 488, 488–489
Compulsions, 407
Computer, cognitive revolution and, 17
Computer-assisted cognitive-behavioral treatment, 454
Computer-assisted tomography (CT), 69, **70**
Concealed information test, 250
Concepts, 202, 202–204
　children's, 324–326, 325f
Concrete operations, 322t, **323,** 323–324
Conditioned emotional response (CER), 125, 125–127
Conditioned response (CR), 124f, **125,** 127, 131, 132, 405
Conditioned stimulus (CS), 124f, **125,** 127, 128–129, 131, 132, 405
Conditioning. See **Classical conditioning; Operant conditioning**
Conditions of worth, 297
Conduction deafness, 108
Cones, 92, 93, 93f, 94–96
Confirmation bias, 209, 209–210
Conflict, 354, 354–355
　inhibitory, 379
　realistic conflict theory, 474–475
Conformity, 486, 486–488, 487f
Confounds (confounding variables), 27
Conscientiousness, 279t, 280
Conscious, 291
Consciousness, natural methods of altering, 385
Conservation, 323
Consolidation, 169
Constancies, perceptual, 99–100
Contact hypothesis, 475–476, 475t
Continuity, Gestalt law of, 97
Continuous Positive Airway Pressure (CPAP), 369
Continuous reinforcement, 143
Contraception, 264, 336
Contrapreparedness, 127
Control
　locus of, 297–298
　perception of, 353–354, 359
　stimulus, 440
Control beliefs, 444t
Control condition, 27
Control group, 27
Control question technique (CQT), 250
Control sequence, 166
Conventional level of moral development, 330
Convergent thinking, 231

Cooke, Alistair, 185–186
Coping, 353, 370–386
　aggression for, 373–376
　culture and, 386
　emotion-focused, 371–372, 371t
　gender and, 385–386
　mind-body interventions, 385
　problem-focused, 370–372, 371t
　social support and, 384–385
Cornea, 91, 92f
Corpus callosum, 55, 59–60
Correlation, 28, 28f, 28–29, 473
Correlational research, 28–29, 31t
Cortisol, 65, 166–167, 289, 352, 367, 369
Counseling psychologist, 20, 22t
Counter-irritant, 115
CQT (control question technique), 250
Crack, 381, 381–382
Cranial nerves, 52
CR (conditioned response), 124f, 125, 127, 131, 132, 405
Creative intelligence, 219
Creativity, 230, 231–233
Critical period, 321
Cross-sectional studies, 340
Crowding, as culturally defined stressor, 386
Crystallized intelligence, 216, 340
CS (conditioned stimulus), 124f, 125, 127, 128–129, 131, 132, 405
CT (computer-assisted tomography), 69, 70
Cuento therapy, 460
Cues, 174, 174–175
　binocular, 98, 100f
　of body language, 249
　depth, 99, 99f, 100f
　monocular static, 99
　motion, 98–99
Cults, 496–497
Culture, 11
　attributional biases, 477
　coping and, 386
　death and dying and, 344
　eating disorders and, 425, 426
　emotional expressions and, 248–249
　facilitating depression and, 412
　gender role development and, 331
　individualist versus collectivist, 256, 257, 303–304, 305
　interpretation of smell and, 116
　memory and, 175
　perception of control and, 353–354
　personality and, 303–305
　physical attractiveness and, 480
　sexual behavior and, 268–269
　tastes in food and, 261
　teenage pregnancy and, 336
　theory of mind and, 325
　treatment for ethnically diverse population, 459–460

Daily logs, 441, 442f
Dark adaptation, 92, 93
Darwin, Charles, 14, 18, 241
Data, 24
Date rape, 380–381

Deafness, 108, 110, 320
Death, voodoo, 387
Death and dying, 338, 343–344
Death penalty, attitudes about, 478
Debriefing, 35
Decay, 179
Decision making in groups, 492–493
Declarative memory, 163–165, 165f
Deductive reasoning, 209
Defense mechanisms, 294, 294t, 435
   theory of obesity, 262–263
Deindividuation, 484
Delany, Sadie and Bessie, 465–466, 473,
      479, 480, 484, 486, 488, 491, 492,
      494
Delayed reinforcement, 141
Delta waves, 362
Delusions, 393, 393–394
   of schizophrenia, 414t, 415
Dendrites, 46, 46f
Denial, 294t
Deoxyribonucleic acid (DNA), 72, 72f,
      311
Dependent personality disorder, 399t
Dependent variable, 26, 26f, 26–27
Depersonalization, 421, 497
Depressants, 377, 377–381
Depression
   as contagious, 413
   heart disease and, 360
   interactional theory of, 412–413
   major depressive disorder, 408–409,
      408t, 410–411, 413
   negative triad of, 411
   treatment for, 448, 449, 450, 457
Deprived reward, 254, 254–255
Depth cues, 99, 99f, 100f
Depth of processing, 169, 169–170
Derealization, 421, 497
Desensitization, systematic, 130, 439–440,
      441f
D'Este, Franz Ferdinand, 475
Developmental psychologist, 22, 22t, 310
Developmental psychology, 21
Development over life span, 308–347. *See*
      also Cognitive development; Moral
      development; Physical and motor
      development; Social and emotional
      development
   adolescence, 332–337
   adulthood and aging, 337–345
   infancy and childhood, 317–331
   newborn, 314–316
   prenatal, 310–314
Dewey, Thomas, 33
Diagnostic and Statistical Manual of Mental
      Disorders (DSM), 269, 393, 397–399,
      398t
Diagnostic bias, 397
Diana, Princess, 172
Diathesis-stress model, 395, 395f, 419
Dichotomous thinking, 444t
Dickens, Charles, 232
DID (dissociative identity disorder),
      422–423
Diet, starvation, 263
Difference threshold, 86
Diffusion of responsibility, 496

Discrimination, 141, 141–142, 473–474
   among choices, 173, 173f
   stimulus, 128
Discriminative stimulus, 141, 141–142
Disease, stress and, 358–360. *See also*
      Health
Disinhibition, 378
Disorganized behavior, 415
Disorganized/disoriented attachment, 328
Disorganized schizophrenia, 416t
Disorganized speech, 415
Display rules, 248, 248–249
Dispositional attributions, 476
Dissociative amnesia, 421
Dissociative disorders, 421, 421–423
Dissociative fugue, 422
Dissociative identity disorder (DID),
      422, 422–423
Dissonance, cognitive, 468–470, 469f,
      473–474, 478
Divergent thinking, 231
Divorce, 66, 301–302
Dizygotic twins, 75
DNA (deoxyribonucleic acid), 72, 72f, 311
Dodo bird verdict of psychotherapy, 455
Door-in-the-face technique, 489
Dopamine, 50, 63, 145, 254–255, 267, 381
Dopamine agonist, 145
Dopamine blockers, 254–255
Dopamine hypothesis of schizophrenia,
      417
Double blind design, 33, 33–34
Double pain, 115
Down syndrome, 230, 230–231
"Drapetomania," 393
Dream analysis, 433
Dreams, 363–654
Drive(s), 252, 252–253
   hunger, 259–263
   sex, 264–270
Drought among the Maasai, 11–12
Drugs. *See also* Alcohol; *specific types of*
      drugs
   classical conditioning and overdose of,
      130
   coping by using, 377–384
   modeling parents' use of, 152–153
   as teratogen, 313
DSM (*Diagnostic and Statistical Manual of*
      Mental Disorders), 269, 393, 397–399,
      398t
Dual codes, 168
Dynamic memory, 169
Dynamic personality, Freud's theory of,
      291–296
Dysthymia, 409

Ear, 107f, 107–108, 114
Early processing, 85
Eating behavior, 259–261
Eating disorders, 423–426, 424
Ebbinghaus, Hermann, 161, 178
Echoic memory, 160
ECT (electroconvulsive therapy), 449, 450
Educational psychologist, 22, 22t
EEG (electroencephalograph), 68, 69f
Effect, 27
Efficacy expectancy, 298

Ego, 292, 433
Egocentrism, 323, 324f
   adolescent, 335–336
Ego ideal, 291
EI (emotional intelligence), 220
Einstein, Albert, 222, 296
Elaborative encoding, 170, 170–171
Electra complex, 293
Electroconvulsive therapy (ECT), 449,
      450
Electroencephalogram, 68, 69f
Electroencephalograph (EEG), 68, 69f
Electromagnetic radiation, range of, 91f
Ellis, Albert, 443
Embryo, 311
Emotion, 240, 240–251. *See also specific*
      emotions
   amygdala and, 63
   basic, 241, 242f
   causes of, 243–248
   cognitive interpretation of, 245–246
   expression of, 248–251, 437
   high expressed, 418
   physiological profiles of, 244–245
   theories of, 243f, 243–244, 245, 247
   types of, 240–243
Emotional expressiveness, coping using,
      372, 373
Emotional intelligence (EI), 220
Emotionality, 287
Emotionally charged memory, 171–172
Emotional response, conditioned,
      125–127
Emotion-focused coping, 371, 371–372,
      371t
Empathy, 436, 494
Empiricism, 194
Enacted social support, 384
Encoding, 168, 168–172
Endocrine glands, 65, 65f
Endorphins, 115
Environment(s)
   genes and, 73–74, 78
   intelligence and, 224–226
   obesity and, 262–263
   perceived versus objective, 225
   personality and, 288–289, 299–305
   physical, 11
   prenatal development and, 313–314
   race differences in IQ and, 227–228
   sexual orientation and, 268
   social, 10–11
Episodic memories, 163, 339
Erikson, Erik, 341
ESP (extrasensory perception), 34,
      115–116
Estrogens, 265
Ethic of care, 330
Ethics, 34–37, 37t, 498
Ethnically diverse population, treatment
      for, 459–460
Evaluation apprehension, 496
Events, 24–25
Evocative (or reactive) interaction, 74
Evolution, 76
   brain and, 75–78
   mating preferences and, 482–83
Evolutionary psychology, 18, 19t, 252

Personal fable, 335–336
Personality, 274–307, **276**
  in adulthood, 342–343
  birth order and, 300–301, 301t
  brain and, 284–290
  cognitive view of, 297–299
  culture and, 303–305
  development of, 292–293, 301–302
  Eysenck's theory of, 285f, 285–286
  factors of, 279–280, 279t
  Freud's theory of, 291f, 291–296
  gender differences in, 302–303
  genes and, 283–284, 287–289, 289f
  humanistic view of, 296–297
  measuring, 280–284
  of newborn, 315–316
  peer relationships and, 301–302
  shyness and, 289–290
  social influences on, 299–305
  structure of, 291f, 291–292
  temperament and, 286–287
  traits versus situations and, 222,
    276–279, 279t
  type A, 356
Personality dimensions, 279–280, 279t,
  283–284
Personality disorders, 399, 399–401, 399t
Personality inventory, 281, 281–282,
  282f
Personality profile, 281, 282f
Personality psychologist, 21, 22, 22t
Personality traits, 222, **276,** 276–279,
  279t
Persuasion, 470, 470–471
PET (positron emission tomography), 70
Phallic stage, 293
Phantom limb, 61
Phobia, 126, 126f, **404,** 404–405, 404t
  social, 404, 458, 459
  systematic desensitization of, 130, 440,
    441f
Phonemes, 193
Phonemic restoration effect, 110
Phonology, 193
Physical and motor development
  in adolescence, 333
  changes in adulthood, 337–338
  in infancy and childhood, 317
Physical attraction, liking and, 480
Physical attractiveness, 104–105, 480,
  482–483
Physical environment, 11
Physical punishment, 139
Physiological profiles of emotions,
  244–245
Physiological psychologist, 22, 22t
Piaget, Jean, 321–324, 322t, 325
Pitch, 106
Pituitary gland, 65, 265
PK (psychokinesis), 115, 116
Placebo, 133, 133–134, 385
Place theory, 107, 107–108, 108f
Plantar reflex, 315t
Plateau phase of sexual response cycle,
  265
Plato, 84, 91, 199
Pleasure principle, 291
Polygraphs, 250–251, **251**

Pons, 62f, **64**
Pop-out, 88, 88f
Population, 31, 214
Positive correlation, 28–29
Positive reinforcement, 138, 139t, 140
Positive symptoms, 414, 414–415, 414t
Positron emission tomography (PET), 70
Postconventional level of moral
  development, 330
Posttraumatic stress disorder (PTSD),
  359, 367, 397, **405,** 405–406, 459
Power, gender differences in personality
  and, 303
Practical intelligence, 219
Pragmatics, 195
Precognition, 115
Preconscious, 291
Preconventional level of moral
  development, 330
Predictions, 25
Pregnancy, 311–314, 336
Prejudice, 472, 472–476
  changing, 475–476, 475t
  cognition and, 472–474
  creation of, 474f, 474–475
Premature infants, social support for, 316
Prenatal development, 310–314
  schizophrenia and, 417, 418
Preoperational period, 322t, 323
Prescriptive norms, 485
Primacy effect, 161
Primary appraisal, 353
Primary auditory cortex, 108
Primary mental abilities, 216
Primary motor cortex, 58
Primary reinforcers, 140
Priming, 165
Princip, Gavrilo, 475
Principled level of moral development,
  330
Private speech, 327
Privilege envy, 295
Proactive interference, 179
Problem, 205
  representation, 205–206
Problem-focused coping, 370, 370–372,
  371t
Problem solving, 204–208
Prodigies, 230, 231
Prodromal phase, 410
Profile of intelligences, 219
Progressive muscle relaxation, 439,
  439–440
Projection, 294t
Projective test, 282, 282–283
Proscriptive norms, 485
Prosocial behavior, 494, 494–496
Prototypes, 202, 202–203, 207–208
Proximity, 97, 491
Pruning, 73
Pseudopatients, 396f, 396–397
Pseudopsychology, 34
Psychiatric nurse, 20, 22t
Psychiatrist, 20, 22t
Psychoanalysis, 433, 433–434
Psychodynamic theory, 15, 19t
Psychodynamic therapy, 433, 433–435,
  437t, 458

Psychoeducation, 445
Psychokinesis (PK), 115, 116
Psychological determinism, 291
Psychological disorders, 390–429, **394**
  anxiety disorders, 402–407
  categorizing, 397–399, 398t
  defining, 393–394
  diagnosis, cautions about, 427
  dissociative disorders, 421–423
  eating disorders, 423–426
  explaining, 394–397
  mood disorders, 408–413
  personality disorders, 399–401, 399t
  schizophrenia, 414–420
  treatment of. *See* Treatment
Psychologists, types of, 19–22, 22t
Psychology, 8
  defining, 8–9
  evolution of, 13–18
  levels of analysis in, 9–12, 10f
Psychoneuroimmunology, 65–66
Psychopharmacology, 447, 447–449
  psychotherapy versus, 457–458
Psychophysics, 86, 86–88
Psychosexual stages, 292, 292–293
Psychosis, 292, 393, 393–394
  amphetamine, 382
  treating, 447–448
Psychosocial development, 341,
  341–343, 341t
Psychotherapist, picking, 460
Psychotherapy, 20, 22t
  innovations in, 453–454
  medication versus, 457–458
Psychotherapy by Reciprocal Inhibition
  (Wolpe), 438
Psychotherapy integration, 453–454,
  454
Psychotherapy research, issues in,
  454–460, 455t
Psychotic disorders. *See* **Psychosis;**
  Schizophrenia
Psychoticism, 280, 286
PTSD (posttraumatic stress disorder), 359,
  367, 397, 405–406, 459
Puberty, 64, 333. *See also* **Adolescence**
Punishment, 138, 138–140, 139t
Pupil, 91, 92f
  attention and size of, 89
Purging, 424, 425, 426

Quasi-experimental design, 27–28, 31t

Race differences in intelligence, 227–228
Rage, 443
Random-access memory (RAM), 160
Rape, 380–381, 405
  punishing rapists, 478
Rapid eye movement (REM), 362–365
RAS (reticular activating system), 64
Rational-emotive therapy (RET), 443–444,
  445
Rationalization, 294t
Ratio schedules, 143
Reactance, 471
Reaction formation, 294t
Reactive interaction, 74
Realistic conflict theory, 474–475

Reality monitoring, 177, 177–178
Reality principle, 292
Real self, 435–436
Reasoning, 209–210, 211
Rebound effect, 372
Recall, 173, 173–174, 185, 339
Recategorization, 476
Recency effect, 161
Receptors, 49
Reciprocal determinism, 298, 298f
Recognition, 173, 173–174
Recreational sex, 264
Reflexes, 53, 314, 315t
Refractory period, 265
Reframing, 453
Rehearsal, 160
Reinforcement, 16, 137, 138, 139t
   immediate versus delayed, 141
   punishment in combination with, 140
   self-reinforcement, 298
Reinforcement schedules, 142–145, 144f
Reinforcer, 137, 137–138
   primary and secondary, 140–141
Relational aggression, 375
Relationships, 479–483
   adult, 343
   liking, 480
   loving, 480–482
   mating preferences, 482–483
Relaxation techniques, 439–440
Relevant/irrelevant technique (RIT), 250
Reliability, 31, 214
Remembering, act of, 172–175
REM rebound, 367
REM sleep, 362, 362–365, 363f
Repeated contact, liking and, 480
Repetition blindness, 103, 104
Repetition priming, 165
Replication, 24
Representation problem, 205, 205–206
Representativeness heuristic, 210
Repressed memories, 181
Repression, 294, 294t
Reproductive sex, 264
Research
   with animals, 36
   ethics in, 35–36, 498
   genetic, 75. *See also* **Adoption studies;
      Twin studies**
   with people, 35
   psychotherapy, issues in, 454–460, 455t
   scientific, techniques of, 26–31, 31t
   split-brain, 59–60
Resistance, 435
Resistance phase, 351f, 352
Resistant attachment, 328
Resolution phase of sexual response cycle,
   265
Response
   conditioned (CR), 124f, 125
   sexual, 265
   stress, 350
   unconditioned (UCR), 124, 124f,
      124–125, 131, 132
Response bias, 33
Response contingency, 137, 440, 446
Restricting type of anorexia nervosa, 424
Reticular activating system (RAS), 64

Reticular formation, 62f, **64**
Retina, 92, 92f
Retinal disparity, 98
RET (rational-emotive therapy), 443–444,
   445
Retroactive interference, 179
Retrograde amnesia, 180
Reuptake, 49
Rewards, 253–255
Rhodopsin, 92
Rhyming words (mnemonic device), 184
RIT (relevant/irrelevant technique), 250
Road rage, 356
Robber's Cave study, 474f, 474–475, 476
Rods, 92, 93, 93f
Rogers, Carl, 16–17, 297, 435
Roles, 486
   gender, 331
Roosevelt, Eleanor, 296
Roosevelt, Ethel, 331
Roosevelt, Franklin Delano, 257
Roosevelt, Theodore, 331
Rooting reflex, 315t
Rorschach, Herman, 283
Rorschach test, 282, 282f, 282–283

s, 215, 216
St. John's wort (*Hypericum perforatum*),
   448
Sample, 31
   standardized, 214
Sampling bias, 33
Saturation, 95
Schemas, 204, 322
Schizoid personality disorder, 399t
Schizophrenia, 37, 395, **414,** 414–420
   electroconvulsive therapy for, 449
   explaining, 416–419
   in Genain quadruplets, 419–420
   medication for, 447–448
   symptoms of, 414–415, 414t
   types of, 415–416, 416t
Schizotypal personality disorder, 399t
School psychologist, 22, 22t
Science, 8
Scientific method, 24, 24–26
Scientific research, techniques of, 26–31,
   31t
SCN (suprachiasmatic nucleus),
   365, 366f
Scopolamine, 145
Secondary appraisal, 353
Secondary reinforcers, 140, 140–141
Secure attachment, 328, 481
Sedative-hypnotic drugs, 377–381
Selective attention, 88
Selective avoidance, 471
**Selective serotonin-reuptake inhibitors
   (SSRIs), 50,** 448
Self, real versus ideal, 435–436
Self-actualization, 17, 296, 296t
Self-concept, 297, 328, 329
Self-downing, 443
Self-esteem, aggression and, 375–376
Self-help groups, 453
Self-monitoring techniques, 441, 442f
Self-reinforcement, 298
Self-serving bias, 477

Sellers, Peter, 298
Semantic memories, 163, 339
Semantics, 194, 194–195
Semicircular canal, 114
Sensation, 84–86, 85
   perception without, 199–202
   psychophysics and, 86–88
Sensation seeking, 287
Sense(s), 90–116
   hearing, 105–111
   of newborn, 314
   other, 115–116
   smell, 111–112, 112f, 113, 116
   somasthetic, 113–115
   taste, 112–113, 261
   vision, 90–105
Sensitive period, 321
Sensitivity, 87, 87–88
Sensorimotor period, 322–323, 322t
Sensory memory (SM), 159, 159–160
Sensory neurons, 44
Separation anxiety, 327
**Serotonergic/noradrenergic reuptake
   inhibitors (SNRIs), 448**
Serotonin, 286, 365, 407
Set point, 261, 261–262
Sex chromosomes, 268
Sex differences. *See* Gender differences
Sex hormones, 265–266, 329, 333
Sexual abuse, repressed memory of
   childhood, 181
Sexual assault, body language and
   vulnerability to, 249
Sexual behavior, 264–270
   alcohol and sexual aggression, 380f,
      380–381
   cultural variations, 268–269
   hormones and, 265–266
   motivation and, 267f
   sexual dysfunction, 269–270
   sexual orientation and, 267–268
   sexual responses, 265
   teenagers and, 336
Sexual dysfunction, 269–270
Sexual orientation, 266–268
Sexual response cycle (SRC), 265
Shape constancy, 100
Shaping, 142, 143f, 147
Short-term memory (STM), 160, 161,
   162, 163, 168, 169, 173
Shyness, 289–290
Sickle-cell anemia, 77
SIDS (sudden infant death syndrome),
   313
Signal detection theory, 87, 87–88
Sign language, 196, 320
Similarity, 97, 480
Simon, Herbert A., 17
Simon, Theodore, 212, 321
Simonides, 183
Single-cell recording, 68
Situational attributions, 476
Situationism, 277–278, 278
Size constancy, 100
Skeletal system, 53
Skin, sense of touch and, 114
Skinner, B. F., 16, 136–137
Skinner box, 136–137, 137f

Therapy protocols, 454
Thinking. *See* Thought
Thorndike, Edward Lee, 16, 136
Thought, 197–208
  concepts and, 202–204
  divergent versus convergent, 231
  mental imagery and, 199–202, 200f
  problem solving, 204–208
  words and, 198–199
Thought suppression, 372, 372–373
Threshold, 86, 86–87
  signal detection theory and, 87–88
Titchener, Edward, 13
TMS (transcranial magnetic stimulation),
  68–69, 449–450
Token economies, 445, 446, **447**
Tolerance, 377
Tonic neck reflex, 315t
Tonotopic organization, 108
Top-down processing, 85, 85–86, 101,
  109
Touch, sense of, 114
Traits, 222, 279–276, 279t
**Transcranial magnetic stimulation
  (TMS),** 68–69, **449,** 449–450
Transduction, 91
Transfer appropriate processing, 170
Transference, 435
Trauma, posttraumatic stress disorder and,
  359, 367, 397, 405–406, 459
Treatment, 430–463. *See also*
    Psychotherapy
  behavior therapy, 438–442, 446t
  biomedical therapies, 447–450
  cognitive therapy, 442–446, 446t
  effectiveness of, 451–461
  electroconvulsive therapy, 449, 450
  for ethnically diverse population,
    459–460
  humanistic therapy, 435–437
  insight-oriented therapies, 432–438
  modalities of, 451–453
  psychodynamic therapy, 433–435,
    437t, 458
  psychopharmacology, 447–449,
    457–458
  transcranial magnetic stimulation,
    68–69, 449–450
Treatment of Depression Collaborative
  Research Program (TDCRP), 455–457,
  456f, 459
Trial-and-error learning, 136
Triangular model of love, 481, 481f
**Trichromatic theory of color vision,
  94**
Tricyclic antidepressants (TCAs), 448
Trimesters of pregnancy, 311
Truman, Harry, 33
Truth-win rule, 492

Twin studies, 75
  of eating disorders, 425
  effect of environment in, 224–225
  of mood disorders, 410–411
  of personality, 287–288
  of schizophrenia, 416
Tympanic membrane, 107
Type A personality, 356
Typicality, 202

Unconditional positive regard, 297, 436
Unconditioned response (UCR), 124,
  124f, 124–125, 131, 132
Unconditioned stimulus (UCS), 124,
  124f, 125, 127, 131, 132, 405
Unconscious, 15, 291
  collective, 294–295
Undifferentiated schizophrenia, 416t
Undoing, 294t
University of Minnesota starvation study,
  425

Validation, 453
Validity, 32, 32–33
  of IQ test, 214–215
van Gogh, Vincent, 391–392, 393, 394,
  399–400, 404, 413, 414, 415, 416,
  419, 421, 423, 426, 427
Variable(s), 25
  confounding, 27
  dependent, 26f, 26–27
  independent, 26f, 26–27
Variable interval schedules, 143,
  143–144, 144f
Variable ratio schedules, 144, 144f,
  144–145
Venting, 356–357, 372
Ventricles (brain), enlarged, 416–417
Vestibular sense, 114
Viagra, 269–270
Victim profiles, body language and,
  249
Vigilance, 88
Vigor of activity, 287
Violence
  psychological disorder and, 401
  television, 152
  in workplace, 376
Vision, 90–105
  in adulthood, 338–339
  without awareness, 102–104
  cerebral hemispheres and, 59f, 59–60
  color, 94–96
  distance and, 98–99, 99f, 100f
  early, 90, 91–96
  eye and, 91–93, 92f, 93f
  in infancy and childhood, 318
  intermediate, 90, 96–100
  late, 90, 101–104

  light and, 91, 91f
  perceptual constancies, 99–100
  perceptual organization, 96–97
  recognition and identification, 101–104
Visual cliff experiment, 318
Visual illusions, 87f
Visual images, 201–202
Visuospatial sketchpad, 162
Volume, 106
Voodoo death, 387
Vygotsky, L. S., 326–327

Wallace, Alfred Russel, 76
Want, 254, 254–255, 257
Washington, Martha, 215
Watson, John B., 16
Wavelength, 91
Weber, Ernst, 86
Weber's law, 86
**Wechsler Adult Intelligence Scale
  (WAIS), 212,** 213t, 214f
Wechsler Intelligence Scale for Children
  (WISC), 212
Wernicke's area, 194f, 196
Wertheimer, Max, 14
White blood cells, stress and, 358–359
Whitman, Charles, 401
Wisdom of the Body, The (Cannon), 252
Wish fulfillment, dreams and, 363–364
Withdrawal emotions, 242–243
Withdrawal reflex, 315t
Withdrawal symptoms, 377
Within-group versus between-group
  differences, 226–227
Wolpe, Joseph, 438
Women
  intelligence in, 228–229
  menopause in, 338
  personality differences between men
    and, 302–303
  stress and coping by, 385–386
Woods, Tiger, 7–8, 9, 10, 11, 13, 14, 15,
  16, 17, 21, 24, 26
Words, thought and, 198–199. *See also*
    Language
Working memory (WM), 161–162, **162,**
  162f, 326
Workplace, violence in, 376
Wundt, Wilhelm, 13

X chromosome, 268, 311

Y chromosome, 311
Yerkes-Dodson law, 253, 253f
Young, Cy, 232
Young, Thomas, 94

Zar (spirit possession), 393–394
Zygote, 311, 312f

Credits

Text and Illustrations

Figure 1, p. 3: From *Elements of Graphic Design* by Stephen M. Kosslyn. © 1994 by W.H. Freeman and Company. Used with permission.

Figure 2, p. 4: Based on a chart by Nigel Holmes from *Designer's Guide to Creating Charts and Diagrams,* 1984. Reprinted with permission.

Figure 1.3, p. 28: From *Introduction to the Practice of Statistics,* Second Edition, by David S. Moore and George P. McCabe. © 1993 by W.H. Freeman and Company. Used with permission.

Table 1.5, p. 37: Abridgment and adaptation of Code of Ethics, American Psychological Association, www.apa.org/ethics/cod.html. Copyright by the American Psychological Association. Reprinted with permission.

Figure 2.1, p. 45: Figure from Dowling, J. E. (1992). *Neurons and Networks: An Introduction to Neuroscience.* Reprinted by permission of Cajal Institute, CSIC, Madrid, Spain.

Figure 2.13, p. 60: From Gazzaniga, M. S., and LeDoux, J. E. *The Integrated Mind.* New York: Plenum Press, 1978. Reprinted by permission.

Figure 3.1, p. 86: From *Psychology,* Third Edition, by Peter Gray. © 1991, 1994, and 1999 by Worth Publishers. Used with permission.

Figure 3.6, p. 93: From Dowling, J. E., & Boycott, B. B. (1966). *Proceedings of the Royal Society* (London), B166, 80–111, Figure 7. Reprinted by permission.

Figure 4.4, p. 127: From Brooks, D. C., & Bouton, M. E., "A retrieval cue for extinction attenuates spontaneous recovery," *Journal of Experimental Psychology: Animal Behavior Processes, 19,* 77–89. Copyright © 1993 by the American Psychological Association. Adapted with permission.

Figure 4.5, p. 129: Illustration by Roberto Osti from J. E. LeDoux, "Emotion, memory and the brain," *Scientific American,* June 1994, Vol. 270, p. 56. Reprinted by permission of Roberto Osti.

Figure 4.12, p. 144: Figure from "Teaching machines" by B. F. Skinner, *Scientific American,* 1961. Reprinted by permission of the Estate of Mary E. and Dan Todd.

Figure 4.13, p. 149: From Tolman, E. C., & Honzik, C. H., *Introduction and Removal of Reward and Maze Performance in Rats.* Copyright © 1930 The Regents of the University of California.

Figure 5.2, p. 161: Figure adapted from Glanzer, M., & Cunitz, A. R., "Two storage mechanisms in free recall," *Journal of Verbal Learning and Verbal Behavior, 5,* 351–360, 1996. Reprinted by permission of the author.

Figure 5.3, p. 162: From Baddeley, Alan (1986), *Working Memory.* Oxford: Clarendon Press. Reprinted by permission of Oxford University Press.

Figure 5.4, p. 165: Reprinted with permission from Squire, L. R., & Zola-Morgan, S., 1991, "The medical temporal lobe memory system" *Science, 253:* 1380–1386. Copyright © 1991 American Association for the Advancement of Science.

Figure 6.2, p. 200 (top left and bottom left): From Kosslyn, S. M., Ball, T. M., & Reiser, B. J., "Visual images preserved metric spatial information: Evidence from studies of image scanning," *Journal of Experimental Psychology: Human Perception and Performance, 4,* 47–60. Copyright © 1978 by the American Psychological Association. Reprinted with permission.

Figure 6.9, p. 223: From *Behavior Genetics* by R. Plomin, J. C. DeFries, G. E. McClearn, and M. Rutter. © 1997 by W.H. Freeman and Company. Used with permission.

Figure 7.2, p. 242: From Lefton, Lester A., *Psychology,* Seventh Edition. Copyright © 2000 by Allyn & Bacon. Reprinted by permission.

Figure 7.8, p. 266: Figure from Cooper, M. L., Shapiro, C. M., & Powers, A. M., "Motivations for sex and risky sexual behavior among adolescents and young adults: A functional perspective," *Journal of Personality and Social Psychology, 75,* 1528–1558. Copyright © 1998 by the American Psychological Association. Reprinted with permission.

Figure 7.9, p. 269: From Levin, R. J. (1994), "Human male sexuality: Appetite and arousal, desire and drive," *Appetite: Neural and Behavioral Bases* edited by Charles R. Legg and David Booth, pp. 127–164. © European Brain and Behavior Society, 1994. Reprinted by permission of Oxford University Press.

Figure 8.1, p. 282: Adapted from Cattell, Eber, & Tatsuoka. Copyright © 1970 by the Institute for Personality and Ability Testing Inc. Reproduced by permission. "16PF" is a trademark belonging to IPAT, Inc.

Figure 8.3, p. 285: From H. J. Eysenck, *The Biological Basis of Personality,* 1967. Courtesy of Charles C. Thomas, Publisher, Ltd., Springfield, Illinois.

Figure 8.5, p. 291: From *New Introductory Lectures on Psycho-Analysis* by Sigmund Freud, translated by James Strachey. Copyright © 1965, 1964 by James Strachey. Used by permission of W. W. Norton & Company Inc. Sigmund Freud © Copyrights, The Institute of Psycho-Analysis and The Hogarth Press for permission to quote from *The Standard Edition of the Complete Psychological Works of Sigmund Freud,* translated and edited by James Strachey.

Figure 9.3, p. 320: Figure from Reznick, J. S., & Goldfield, B. A., "Rapid change in lexical development in comprehension and production," *Developmental Psychology, 28,* 406–413. Copyright © 1992 by the American Psychological Association. Reprinted with permission.

Figure 9.5, p. 325: Figure from Baillargeon, Renee (1994) "How do infants learn about the physical world?" *Current Directions in Psychological Science, 3*(5), 133–140. Reprinted by permission of Blackwell Publishers.

Figure 10.1, p. 351: From Selye, Hans (1978). *The Stress of Life,* Second Edition. Copyright 1976. Reprinted with permission of The McGraw-Hill Companies.

Figure 10.4, p. 362: From *Sleep* by J. Allan Hobson © 1989 by Scientific American Library. Used with the permission of W.H. Freeman.

Figure 10.5, p. 363: Reprinted with permission from Roffwarg, H. P., Muzio, J. N., & Dement, W. C., "Ontogenetic development of human sleep-dream cycle," *Science, 152,* 604–619. Copyright 1996 American Association for the Advancement of Science.

Table 11.5, p. 410: Excerpt adapted from "Common Misconceptions About Suicide" from www.save.org. Reprinted by permission.

Figure 13.3, p. 481: Sternberg's Triangular Theory of Love. Reprinted by permission of Robert Sternberg.

Photos